Mastering
AutoCAD® 2011
and AutoCAD LT® 2011

Mastering

AutoCAD® 2011
and AutoCAD LT® 2011

Autodesk®
Official Training Guide

George Omura

Wiley Publishing, Inc.

Senior Acquisitions Editor: Willem Knibbe
Development Editor: Denise Santoro Lincoln
Technical Editor: Jon McFarland
Production Editor: Rachel McConlogue
Copy Editor: Judy Flynn
Editorial Manager: Pete Gaughan
Production Manager: Tim Tate
Vice President and Executive Group Publisher: Richard Swadley
Vice President and Publisher: Neil Edde
Media Associate Project Manager: Jenny Swisher
Media Associate Producer: Doug Kuhn
Media Quality Assurance: Josh Frank
Book Designers: Maureen Forys and Judy Fung
Compositor: Craig Woods, Happenstance Type-O-Rama
Proofreader: Publication Services, Inc.
Indexer: Ted Laux
Project Coordinator, Cover: Lynsey Stanford
Cover Designer: Ryan Sneed
Cover Image: © Ashley Jouhar/Cultura/Getty Images

Library of Congress Cataloging-in-Publication Data
Omura, George.
  Mastering AutoCAD 2011 and AutoCAD LT 2011 / George Omura. — 1st ed.
    p. cm.
    ISBN-13: 978-0-470-62197-4 (pbk.)
    ISBN-10: 0-470-62197-4 (pbk.)
    ISBN: 978-0-470-89098-1 (ebk)
    ISBN: 978-0-470-89099-8 (ebk)
    ISBN: 978-0-470-89091-2 (ebk)
  1. Computer graphics. 2. AutoCAD. I. Title.
  T385.O482754 2010
  620'.00420285536—dc22
                        2010013500

Dear Reader,

Thank you for choosing *Mastering AutoCAD 2011 and AutoCAD LT 2011*. This book is part of a family of premium-quality Sybex books, all of which are written by outstanding authors who combine practical experience with a gift for teaching.

Sybex was founded in 1976. More than 30 years later, we're still committed to producing consistently exceptional books. With each of our titles, we're working hard to set a new standard for the industry. From the paper we print on to the authors we work with, our goal is to bring you the best books available.

I hope you see all that reflected in these pages. I'd be very interested to hear your comments and get your feedback on how we're doing. Feel free to let me know what you think about this or any other Sybex book by sending me an email at nedde@wiley.com. If you think you've found a technical error in this book, please visit http://sybex.custhelp.com. Customer feedback is critical to our efforts at Sybex.

Best regards,

Neil Edde
Vice President and Publisher
Sybex, an Imprint of Wiley

Acknowledgments

Many talented and hardworking folks gave their best effort to produce *Mastering AutoCAD 2011 and AutoCAD LT 2011*. I offer my sincerest gratitude to those people who helped bring this book to you.

Heartfelt thanks go to the editorial and production teams at Sybex for their efforts. Willem Knibbe, as always, made sure things got off to a great start and was always there for support. Denise Santoro Lincoln kept a watchful eye on the progress of the book. Jon McFarland did an excellent job of ensuring that I didn't make any glaring mistakes and offered suggestions based on his own writing experience. On the production side, Rachel McConlogue kept the workflow going and answered my dumb questions during the review process, and Judy Flynn made sure I wasn't trying out new uses of the English language.

At Autodesk, special thanks go to Diane Li for taking the time from her busy schedule to write the foreword. Thanks for the kind words. Thanks also go to Denis Cadu, who has always given his steadfast support of my efforts over many projects. Jim Quanci always gives his generous and thoughtful assistance to us author types—I'd be lost without your help, Jim. Thanks to Barbara Vezos and J.C. Malitzke for the thorough and quick review. Finally, as always, a big thanks to Shaan Hurley, Lisa Crounse and the Autodesk beta team for generously allowing us to have a look at the prerelease software.

And, a great big thank you to my family and friends, who have been there for me through thick and thin.

About the Author

George Omura is a licensed architect, Autodesk Authorized Author, and CAD specialist with more than 20 years of experience in AutoCAD and over 30 years of experience in architecture. He has worked on design projects ranging from resort hotels to metropolitan transit systems. George has written numerous other AutoCAD books for Sybex, including *Introducing AutoCAD 2010, Mastering AutoCAD 2010 and AutoCAD LT 2010,* and *Introducing AutoCAD 2009.*

Contents at a Glance

Contents

Foreword

Congratulations!

Welcome to AutoCAD 2011 and to the excellent resource you now have in your hands with *Mastering AutoCAD*. In my time at Autodesk, I have been focused on delivering innovative solutions to help architects and engineers more easily create and collaborate on designs. During this time, I have come to truly appreciate the community of AutoCAD experts who go out of their way to help other users become more productive in their daily work. This comprehensive guide to AutoCAD is an indispensible resource that will help you do just that—and to go further by expanding what you can design and document with AutoCAD.

Mastering AutoCAD will allow you to uncover the power of the design and documentation tools in AutoCAD 2011, whether you are an experienced AutoCAD user or a newer member of the community. You can use it as a reference the next time you need to learn how to use a new feature or enhancement in AutoCAD, or to learn new ways of working that make you more proficient with AutoCAD. Either way, you'll find this book a useful resource for learning about and taking advantage of the tools and improvements available in AutoCAD 2011.

I am personally very impressed with the wealth of information included in this book, the range of topics covered, and the clear organization of the detailed information. Everything from the AutoCAD basics to new ways of modeling in 3D to installation and customization are clearly and comprehensively documented in this guide. In addition, you have access to real-world AutoCAD drawings so you can follow along step-by-step with exercises in each chapter of the book.

So, go ahead and get started in your journey to learning more about AutoCAD. Find out how to use the powerful new productivity enhancements and surface modeling tools for conceptual design that are available in AutoCAD 2011. Learn more about the tools you use frequently and discover new ways of working with them. Or, pick a new topic each week to learn more about. Begin with mastering a few new tools and grow your expertise from there.

Whether you're just getting started with AutoCAD or building on many years of expertise, you will find this book an invaluable resource. On behalf of the entire AutoCAD team, happy learning and we look forward to keeping in touch with you in the AutoCAD community.

—*Diane Li*
AutoCAD Senior Product Manager

Introduction

Welcome to *Mastering AutoCAD 2011 and AutoCAD LT 2011*. As many readers have already discovered, this book is a unique blend of tutorial and reference that includes everything you need to get started and stay ahead with AutoCAD. With this edition, you get coverage of the latest features of both AutoCAD 2011 and AutoCAD LT 2011, plus the latest information on new features.

How to Use This Book

Rather than just showing you how each command works, this book shows you AutoCAD 2011 in the context of a meaningful activity. You'll learn how to use commands while working on an actual project and progressing toward a goal. This book also provides a foundation on which you can build your own methods for using AutoCAD and become an AutoCAD expert. For this reason, I haven't covered every single command or every permutation of a command response. You should think of this book as a way to get a detailed look at AutoCAD as it's used on a real project. As you follow the exercises, I encourage you to also explore AutoCAD on your own, applying the techniques you learn to your own work.

Both experienced and beginning AutoCAD users will find this book useful. If you aren't an experienced user, the way to get the most out of this book is to approach it as a tutorial—chapter by chapter, at least for the first two parts of the book. You'll find that each chapter builds on the skills and information you learned in the previous one. To help you navigate, the exercises are shown in numbered steps. To address the needs of all readers worldwide, the exercises provide both U.S. (feet/inches) and metric measurements.

After you've mastered the material in Parts 1 and 2, you can follow your interests and explore other parts of the book in whatever order you choose. Part 3 takes you to a more advanced skill level. There you'll learn more about storing and sharing drawing data and how to create more complex drawings. If you're interested in 3D, check out Part 4. If you want to start customizing right away, go to Part 5. You can check out Chapters 29 and 30 at any time because they give you general information about sharing AutoCAD files with your coworkers and consultants. Chapter 30 focuses on AutoCAD's Sheet Set Manager, which offers a way to organize your multi-sheet projects.

You can also use this book as a ready reference for your day-to-day problems and questions about commands. Optional exercises at the end of each chapter will help you review and look at different ways to apply the information you've learned. Experienced users will also find this book a handy reference tool.

Finally, if you run into problems using AutoCAD, see the section "When Things Go Wrong" in Appendix C. You'll find a list of the most common issues that users face when first learning AutoCAD.

AutoCAD 2011 and AutoCAD LT 2011

Autodesk has released both AutoCAD 2011 and AutoCAD LT 2011 simultaneously. Not surprisingly, they're nearly identical in the way they look and work. You can share files between the two programs with complete confidence that you won't lose data or corrupt files. The main differences are that LT doesn't support all the 3D functions of AutoCAD 2011, nor does it support the customization tools of AutoLISP or the .NET Framework. But LT still has plenty to offer in both the productivity and customization areas. Because they're so similar, I can present material for both programs with only minor adjustments.

When a feature is discussed that is available only in AutoCAD 2011, you'll see the AutoCAD Only icon.

You'll also see warning messages when tutorials vary between AutoCAD 2011 and LT. If only minor differences occur, you'll see either a warning message or directions embedded in the tutorial indicating the differences between the two programs.

In the few instances in which LT has a feature that isn't available in AutoCAD 2011, you'll see the LT Only icon.

I've also provided work-around instructions wherever possible when LT doesn't offer a feature found in AutoCAD 2011.

Getting Information Fast

In each chapter, you'll find extensive tips and discussions in the form of sidebars set off from the main text. These provide a wealth of information I have gathered over years of using AutoCAD on a variety of projects in different office environments. You may want to browse through the book and read these boxes just to get an idea of how they might be useful to you.

Another quick reference you'll find yourself using often is Appendix D. It contains descriptions of all the dimension settings with comments on their uses. If you experience any problems, you can consult the section "When Things Go Wrong" in Appendix C.

The Mastering Series

The Mastering series from Sybex provides outstanding instruction for readers with intermediate and advanced skills, in the form of top-notch training and development for those already working in their field and clear, serious education for those aspiring to become pros. Every Mastering book includes the following:

◆ Real-World Scenarios, ranging from case studies to practical information you can use now, that show how the tool, technique, or knowledge presented is applied in actual practice

◆ Skill-based instruction, with chapters organized around real tasks rather than abstract concepts or subjects

◆ Self-review test questions, so you can be certain you're equipped to do the job right

What to Expect

Mastering AutoCAD 2011 and AutoCAD LT 2011 is divided into five parts, each representing a milestone in your progress toward becoming an expert AutoCAD user. Here is a description of those parts and what they will show you.

Part 1: The Basics

As with any major endeavor, you must begin by tackling small, manageable tasks. In this first part, you'll become familiar with the way AutoCAD looks and feels.

Chapter 1, "Exploring the AutoCAD and AutoCAD LT Interface," shows you how to get around in AutoCAD.

Chapter 2, "Creating Your First Drawing," details how to start and exit the program and how to respond to AutoCAD commands.

Chapter 3, "Setting Up and Using AutoCAD's Drafting Tools," tells you how to set up a work area, edit objects, and lay out a drawing.

Chapter 4, "Organizing Objects with Blocks and Groups," explores some tools unique to CAD: symbols, blocks, and layers. As you're introduced to AutoCAD, you'll also get a chance to make some drawings that you can use later in the book and perhaps even in future projects of your own.

Chapter 5, "Keeping Track of Layers and Blocks," shows you how to use layers to keep similar information together and object properties such as linetypes to organize things visually.

Part 2: Mastering Intermediate Skills

After you have the basics down, you'll begin to explore some of AutoCAD's more subtle qualities.

Chapter 6, "Editing and Reusing Data to Work Efficiently," tells you how to reuse drawing setup information and parts of an existing drawing.

Chapter 7, "Mastering Viewing Tools, Hatches, and External References," details how to use viewing tools and hatches and how to assemble and edit a large drawing file.

Chapter 8, "Introducing Printing, Plotting, and Layouts," shows you how to get your drawing onto hard copy.

Chapter 9, "Understanding Plot Styles," discusses methods for controlling line weights and shading in your printer output.

Chapter 10, "Adding Text to Drawings," tells you how to annotate your drawing and edit your notes.

Chapter 11, "Using Fields and Tables," shows you how to add spreadsheet functionality to your drawings.

Chapter 12, "Using Dimensions," gives you practice in using automatic dimensioning (another unique CAD capability).

Part 3: Mastering Advanced Skills

At this point, you'll be on the verge of becoming a real AutoCAD expert. Part 3 is designed to help you polish your existing skills and give you a few new ones.

Chapter 13, "Using Attributes," tells you how to attach information to drawing objects and how to export that information to database and spreadsheet files.

Chapter 14, "Copying Existing Drawings into AutoCAD," details techniques for transferring paper drawings to AutoCAD.

Chapter 15, "Advanced Editing and Organizing," is where you'll complete the apartment building tutorial. During this process you'll learn how to integrate what you've learned so far and gain some tips on working in groups.

Chapter 16, "Laying Out Your Printer Output," shows you the tools that let you display your drawing in an organized fashion.

Chapter 17, "Making 'Smart' Drawings with Parametric Tools," introduces you to parametric drawing. This feature lets you quickly modify a drawing by changing a few parameters.

Chapter 18, "Using Dynamic Blocks," shows you how you can create blocks that can be edited with grips without having to redefine them.

Chapter 19, "Drawing Curves," gives you an in-depth look at some special drawing objects, such as splines and fitted curves.

Chapter 20, "Getting and Exchanging Data from Drawings," is where you'll practice getting information about a drawing and learn how AutoCAD can interact with other applications, such as spreadsheets and page-layout programs. You'll also learn how to copy and paste data.

Part 4: 3D Modeling and Imaging

Although 2D drafting is AutoCAD's workhorse application, AutoCAD's 3D capabilities give you a chance to expand your ideas and look at them in a new light.

Chapter 21, "Creating 3D Drawings," covers AutoCAD's basic features for creating three-dimensional drawings.

Chapter 22, "Using Advanced 3D Features," introduces you to some of the program's more powerful 3D capabilities.

Chapter 23, "Rendering 3D Drawings," shows how you can use AutoCAD to produce lifelike views of your 3D drawings.

Chapter 24, "Editing and Visualizing 3D Solids," takes a closer look at 3D solids and how they can be created, edited, and displayed in AutoCAD 2011.

Chapter 25, "Exploring 3D Mesh and Surface Modeling," introduces you to free-form 3D modeling using mesh and surface objects. With this latest addition to AutoCAD, there isn't anything you can't model in 3D.

Part 5: Customization and Integration

One of AutoCAD's greatest strengths is its openness to customization, which you'll explore in this section.

Chapter 26, "Using the Express Tools," gives you a gentle introduction to the world of AutoCAD customization. You'll learn how to load and use existing Express tools that expand AutoCAD's functionality, and you'll be introduced to AutoLISP as a tool to create macros.

Chapter 27, "Exploring AutoLISP," is a primer to AutoCAD's popular macro language. You'll learn how you can create custom commands built on existing ones and how you can retrieve and store locations and other data.

Chapter 28, "Customizing Toolbars, Menus, Linetypes, and Hatch Patterns," shows you how to use workspaces, customize the user interface, and create custom linetypes and hatch patterns. You'll also be introduced to the Diesel macro language.

Chapter 29, "Managing and Sharing Your Drawings," shows you how to adapt AutoCAD to your own work style. You'll learn about the tools that help you exchange drawings with others and how to secure your drawings to prevent tampering.

Chapter 30, "Keeping a Project Organized with Sheet Sets," shows you how to use the new Sheet Set Manager to simplify your file management. By using the Sheet Set Manager, you can automate some of the more tedious drawing coordination tasks.

The Appendices

Finally, this book has several appendices.

Appendix A, "The Bottom Line," contains the solutions to the book's Master It review questions.

Appendix B, "Installing and Setting Up AutoCAD," contains an installation and configuration tutorial. If AutoCAD isn't already installed on your system, follow the steps in this tutorial before starting Chapter 1.

Appendix C, "Hardware and Software Tips," provides information about hardware related to AutoCAD. It also provides tips on improving AutoCAD's performance and troubleshooting and provides more detailed information on setting up AutoCAD's plotting feature.

Appendix D, "System Variables and Dimension Styles," provides a reference to dimension style settings.

Appendix E, "About the Companion DVD," provides information about the content on the DVD and how to troubleshoot any problems.

Appendix F, "The AutoCAD 2011 Certification Exams," shows you where in the book the learning objectives are covered for the Certified Associate and Certified Professional Exam. If you want to get certified, this information will be very useful.

What's on the DVD

The included companion DVD contains the sample drawing files from all the exercises in this book. You can pick up an exercise anywhere you like without having to work through the book from front to back. You can also use these sample files to repeat exercises or to just explore how files are organized and put together. In addition, you'll find the following:

◆ A searchable PDF version of the book

◆ Video tutorials that complement the instructions in Part 1 of the book

◆ Video demos of the new features in AutoCAD 2011

◆ A trial version of AutoCAD 2011

◆ Trial software of companion products to AutoCAD 2011

THE AUTOCAD FREE TRIAL

If you don't have AutoCAD, you can install a trial version from the companion DVD found in this book. Be aware that the trial is good for only 30 days—don't start to use it until you're certain you'll have plenty of free time to practice using AutoCAD.

The Minimum System Requirements

This book assumes you have an IBM-compatible computer with at least a Pentium IV or equivalent CPU. Your computer should have at least one CD drive and a hard disk with 2 GB or more of free space for the AutoCAD program files and about 120 MB of additional space for sample files and the workspace. In addition to these requirements, you should have enough free disk space to allow for a Windows virtual memory page file that is about 1.5 times the amount of installed RAM. Consult your Windows manual or Appendix C of this book for more on virtual memory.

AutoCAD 2011 runs best on systems with at least 2 GB or more of RAM, although you can get by with 1 GB. Your computer should also have a high-resolution monitor and an up-to-date display card. An SVGA display with a resolution of 1024 × 768 or greater will work fine with AutoCAD, but if you want to take full advantage of AutoCAD's new 3D features, you should have a 128 MB or greater, OpenGL-capable, workstation-class graphics card. If you intend to use a digitizer tablet, you'll need one free USB, or serial, port available. I also assume you're using a mouse and have the use of a printer or a plotter. A DVD reader is needed to install AutoCAD and the software from this book. Finally, you'll need an Internet connection to take full advantage of the support offerings from Autodesk.

If you want a more detailed explanation of hardware options with AutoCAD, see Appendix C. You'll find a general description of the available hardware options and their significance to AutoCAD.

Doing Things in Style

Much care has been taken to see that the stylistic conventions in this book—the use of uppercase or lowercase letters, italic or boldface type, and so on—are the ones most likely to help you learn AutoCAD. On the whole, their effect should be subliminal. However, you may find it useful to be conscious of the following rules:

◆ Menu selections are shown by a series of options separated by the ➤ symbol (for example, choose File ➤ New). These are typically used to show selections from a shortcut menu or the Application menu, which you will learn about in Chapter 1.

◆ Keyboard entries are shown in boldface (for example, enter **Rotate.↵**).

◆ Command-line prompts are shown in a monospaced font (for example, `Select objects:`).

For most functions, this book describes how to select options from Ribbon panels and the Application menu, which are two new interface features. In addition, where applicable, I include related keyboard shortcuts and command names in parentheses. These command names provide continuity for readers accustomed to working at the Command prompt.

New Features of AutoCAD 2011

AutoCAD 2011 has refined its interface by adding some new elements like animated tool tips and a new Web-based help system. A new Welcome screen offers short videos to help you learn basic functions. Dig a little deeper and you'll find that some new features have been added to simplify your work so you don't have to keep track of so many details. Here are some of the new features I cover in this book:

◆ Advanced surface modeling with procedural and NURBS surface tools give you a new level of control in 3D modeling.

◆ Streamlined materials and rendering tools make it easier to produce presentation-quality renderings from diagrammatic sketches to photo-real presentations.

◆ Powerful new hatch pattern interface greatly simplifies fill patterns.

◆ Expanded transparency control adds transparency to any pattern or object.

◆ Multifunction grips give you expanded control over 2D and 3D objects.

◆ New selection features enable you to isolate and select similar objects quickly and easily.

Contact the Author

I hope that *Mastering AutoCAD 2011 and AutoCAD LT 2011* will be of benefit to you and that, after you've completed the tutorials, you'll continue to use the book as a reference. If you have comments, criticism, or ideas about how the book can be improved, you can e-mail me at `george.omura@gmail.com`.

If you find errors, please let my publisher know. Visit the book's web page, `www.sybex.com/go/masteringautocad2011`, and click the Errata link to find a form on which you can identify the problem.

And thanks for choosing Mastering AutoCAD 2011 and AutoCAD LT 2011.

Part 1

The Basics

Chapter 1

Exploring the AutoCAD and AutoCAD LT Interface

Before you can start to use AutoCAD 2011's new capabilities, you'll need to become familiar with the basics. If you're completely new to AutoCAD, you'll want to read this first chapter carefully. It introduces you to many of AutoCAD's basic operations, such as opening and closing files, getting a close-up look at part of a drawing, and changing a drawing. If you're familiar with earlier versions of AutoCAD, you should review this chapter anyway to get acquainted with the features you haven't already used.

Autodesk releases new versions of AutoCAD every year. Part of this strategy is to introduce improvements that focus on a particular category of features. This latest version, AutoCAD 2011, includes several new features that are related to curves in both 2D drafting and 3D Modeling. There are also a number of enhancements that allow you to easily select similar objects in a drawing. The ability to make objects appear transparent has also been improved.

Autodesk has discovered that the number of 3D users is on the upswing, so with this version, you'll see some new 3D features that will give you more freedom to create 3D shapes. These features include some new ways to create surface forms and the editing tools that enable you to easily manipulate 3D solids and surfaces. The Materials feature has also been improved to make it easier to create realistic 3D renderings.

You'll get a chance to explore these new features and many more as you work through this book. Before you begin the exercise later in this chapter, make sure that you have loaded the sample files from this book's companion DVD. See the introduction for details.

In this chapter, you'll learn about the following topics:

◆ Use the AutoCAD window

◆ Get a closer look with the Zoom command

◆ Save a file as you work

◆ Make changes and open multiple files

Taking a Guided Tour

In this section, you'll get a chance to familiarize yourself with the AutoCAD screen and how you communicate with AutoCAD. As you do the exercises in this chapter, you'll also get a feel for how to work with this book. Don't worry about understanding or remembering everything you see in this chapter. You'll get plenty of opportunities to probe the finer details of the program as you work through the later chapters. To help you remember the material, you'll find a brief set of questions at the end of each chapter. For now, just enjoy your first excursion into AutoCAD.

GET ADDITIONAL HELP ON THE DVD

On the DVD accompanying this book, you'll find a set of video tutorials that you can complete to practice the concepts presented in this chapter. Four tutorials give you an overview of the main topics of this chapter. The video entitled "The AutoCAD Window" covers the highlights of the material in "Taking a Guided Tour." The video entitled "Getting Started and a Closer Look" touches on some of the material in "Working with AutoCAD." "Saving a File as you Work" covers the material from the section with the same name in this chapter. Finally, "Opening Multiple Files" covers the material in "Working with Multiple Files."

While they don't follow the exercise in this chapter word for word, these videos show you how AutoCAD behaves in real time, thereby giving you a more direct experience of the program.

AUTOCAD REFERENCES IN THIS BOOK

In this chapter, and throughout the rest of the book, when I say AutoCAD, I mean both AutoCAD and AutoCAD LT. Some topics apply only to AutoCAD. In those situations, you'll see an icon indicating that the topic applies only to AutoCAD and not to AutoCAD LT. If you're using AutoCAD LT 2011, these icons can help you focus on the topics that are more relevant to your work.

AutoCAD 2011 is designed to run on Windows XP and Windows Vista. This book was written using AutoCAD 2011 running on Windows XP Professional.

Launching AutoCAD

If you already installed AutoCAD (see Appendix B) and are ready to jump in and take a look, proceed with the following steps to launch the program:

1. Choose Start ➤ All Programs ➤ Autodesk ➤ AutoCAD 2011 ➤ AutoCAD 2011. You can also double-click the AutoCAD 2011 icon on your Windows Desktop. LT users will use AutoCAD LT 2011 in place of AutoCAD 2011.

2. Next, you see the Welcome screen, which offers a set of tutorials and videos showing you the new features of AutoCAD 2011. Close the Welcome screen by clicking the X at the far right side of the title bar. You can always get back to these tutorials through the Welcome screen option in the Help menu.

3. The AutoCAD window displays a blank default document named Drawing1.dwg. AutoCAD users may see the Sheet Set Manager palette to the left of the AutoCAD window. LT users may see the Info palette to the left of the AutoCAD window.

If you're using the trial version, you'll see the Product License Activation window before step 2 in the preceding steps. This window shows you the number of days you have left in the trial version. It also enables you to activate the product if you purchase a license. Click the Try button to continue to the Welcome screen described in step 2.

Now let's look at the AutoCAD window in detail. Don't worry if it seems like a lot of information. You don't have to memorize it, but by looking at all the parts, you'll be aware of what is available in a general way.

CUSTOMIZATION BASED ON YOUR INDUSTRY

Before we move on, you may want to know about the Initial Setup dialog box. This dialog box lets you select the industry that is closest to the work you do. AutoCAD will then set up a workspace with the tools that will fit the needs of your industry. When you're more comfortable with AutoCAD, you can go ahead and run the initial setup for your type of work. You can always open the Initial Setup dialog box from the User Preferences tab of the Options dialog box. See Appendix B for more on the Options dialog box.

The AutoCAD Window

The AutoCAD program window is divided into eight parts:

- Application menu
- Quick Access toolbar
- InfoCenter
- Ribbon
- Drawing area
- UCS icon (User Coordinate System icon)
- Command window
- Status bar

Figure 1.1 shows a typical layout of the AutoCAD program window. You can organize the AutoCAD window into any arrangement you want and save it as a *workspace*. You can save and recall a workspace at any time using the Workspace Switching tool in the Quick Access toolbar (you'll learn more about this tool in the next chapter). The default workspace in Figure 1.1 is called the 2D Drafting & Annotation workspace, which is one of several workspaces built into AutoCAD.

Figure 1.2 shows AutoCAD's 3D Modeling workspace, which has a different set of screen elements. Figure 1.2 also shows a standard AutoCAD drawing file with a few setting changes to give it a 3D appearance. Beneath these external changes, the underlying program is the same.

You'll learn more about workspaces later in this chapter and in Chapter 28.

In the upper-left corner of the AutoCAD program window, the red AutoCAD icon features the Application menu, which offers a set of options not directly related to drawing; I'll elaborate on this menu in the next section. The Quick Access toolbar at the top of the drawing area (shown in Figure 1.3) includes the basic file-handling functions that you find in nearly all Windows programs. The InfoCenter is AutoCAD's online help facility; you'll learn more about it in Chapter 2. The Ribbon provides nearly all the commands you'll need using icon tools; you'll learn more about the Ribbon in the section "Using the Ribbon" later in this chapter.

FIGURE 1.1
A typical arrangement of the elements in the AutoCAD window. The Sheet Set Manager palette (or Info palette for LT) is closed for clarity.

Quick Access Toolbar

Application Menu

Ribbon

Drawing Area

ViewCube

Navigation Bar

UCS

Command Window

Status Bar

InfoCenter

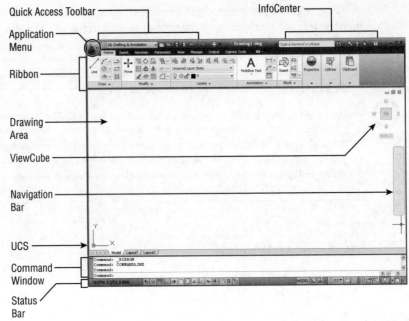

FIGURE 1.2
The 3D Modeling workspace offers an alternative arrangement of the elements in the AutoCAD window.

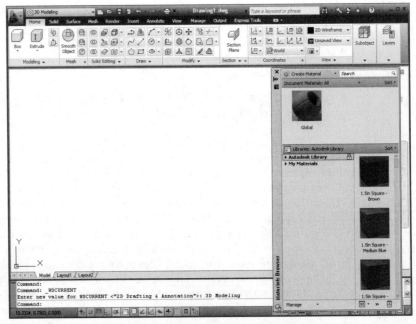

FIGURE 1.3
The Quick Access toolbar, featuring basic Windows file-handling functions, appears above the Ribbon.

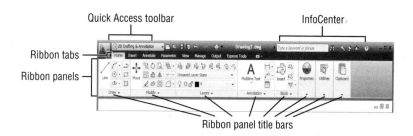

Quick Access toolbar

InfoCenter

Ribbon tabs

Ribbon panels

Ribbon panel title bars

The drawing area occupies most of the screen. Everything you draw appears in this area. As you move your mouse around, crosshairs appear to move within the drawing area. This is the drawing cursor that lets you point to locations in the drawing area. You'll get your first chance to work with the drawing area later in the section "Picking Points in the Drawing Area."

Within the drawing area, you see three items in the lower-left and upper-right corners. The UCS icon appears in the lower-left corner. You'll learn more about the UCS icon in a moment (see the section "Using the UCS Icon"). In the upper-right corner, you see the ViewCube. The ViewCube is primarily for 3D modeling, and you'll learn more about it in Chapter 21. You'll also see a navigation bar along the right edge of the AutoCAD window. This bar offers tools you can use to get around in your drawing. Basic tools like Zoom and Pan can be found here as well as some advanced tools for viewing 3D models.

Just below the drawing area in the lower-left corner are the Model and Layout tabs. These tabs enable you to quickly switch between different types of views called the *model* and *layout* views. You'll get to see firsthand how these work in a section called "Working with AutoCAD" later in this chapter.

The Command window, located just below the drawing area, gives you feedback about AutoCAD's commands as you use them. You can move and resize this window just as you move and resize other display components. By default, the Command window is in its docked position, as shown in Figure 1.4. I'll elaborate on the Command window in the section "Working in the Command Window" later in this chapter.

FIGURE 1.4
The Command window and the status bar

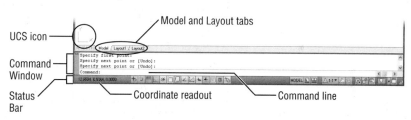

UCS icon

Model and Layout tabs

Command Window

Status Bar

Coordinate readout

Command line

Below the Command window is the status bar (also shown in Figure 1.4). The status bar gives you information at a glance about the state of the drawing. For example, the coordinate readout at the far left of the status bar tells you the location of your cursor. The tools in the status bar offer aids to the drafting process.

Using the Application Menu

The Application menu offers tools to help you manage your AutoCAD files. It is basically the File pull-down menu from previous versions of AutoCAD. Try it out to see how it works firsthand:

1. Click the Application menu icon. A list of options appears.

2. Move the highlight cursor slowly down the list of options in the left column. As you highlight the options, additional options appear in a column to the right.

3. Highlight the Export option to see the different formats available for export (see Figure 1.5).

FIGURE 1.5
The Export option
in the Application
menu showing
the list of export
options

The Application menu also gives you a convenient way to find recently used files or to get to a file you already have open. If you move your cursor away from the list of options to the left in the Application menu, you'll see Recent Documents in the upper-left portion of the menu. You'll also see two icon tools named Open Documents and Recent Documents (see Figure 1.6).

The Open Documents option lets you quickly change from one open file to another when you are viewing your files full-screen. The Recent Documents option displays a list of documents you've recently worked on.

You can use the View tool in the upper-right portion of the Application menu to select the way the list of files is displayed in a manner similar to the way you would use the Windows Explorer View option. You can click this icon and select Small Images to have the list display the files with thumbnail images of their content. Hover over a filename and you will see a tool tip that displays a larger thumbnail of the drawing.

FIGURE 1.6
The Open Documents and Recent Documents tools

Open Documents

Recent Documents

List of Recent Documents

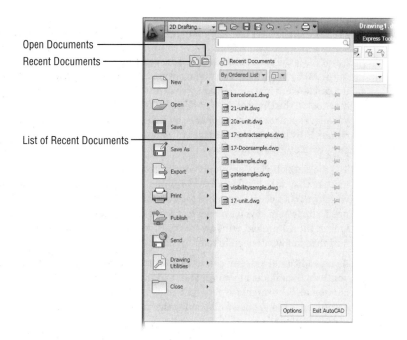

Using the Ribbon

The most prominent feature in the AutoCAD window, besides the drawing area, is the Ribbon (see Figure 1.7). This is where you'll be selecting tools to draw, edit, or perform other functions. The Ribbon contains a set of panels representing groups of tools and features. The name of each Ribbon panel is found in its title bar at the bottom of the panel. Ribbon panels are further organized by the tabs that appear above them. All of the tools in the Ribbon offer *tool tips* and *cue cards* that provide a short description to help you understand what each tool icon represents.

FIGURE 1.7
A typical cue card from a Ribbon panel tool

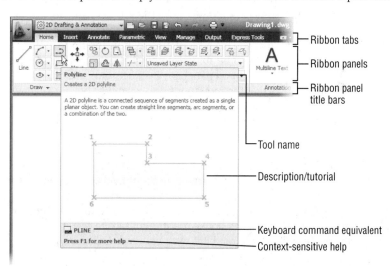

Ribbon tabs

Ribbon panels

Ribbon panel title bars

Tool name

Description/tutorial

Keyboard command equivalent

Context-sensitive help

COMMUNICATING WITH THE COMMAND WINDOW AND DYNAMIC INPUT DISPLAY

AutoCAD is the perfect servant: It does everything you tell it to and no more. You communicate with AutoCAD by using tools and menu options. These devices invoke AutoCAD commands. A *command* is a single-word instruction you give to AutoCAD telling it to do something, such as draw a line (the Line tool in the Draw Ribbon panel) or erase an object (the Erase tool in the Modify Ribbon panel). Whenever you invoke a command, by either typing it or selecting a menu option or tool, AutoCAD responds by presenting messages to you in the Command window and the Dynamic Input display or by displaying a dialog box.

The messages in the Command window, or in the Dynamic Input display, often tell you what to do next, or they may display a list of options. A single command often presents a series of messages, which you answer to complete the command. These messages serve as an aid to new users who need a little help. If you ever get lost while using a command or forget what you're supposed to do, look at the Command window for clues. As you become more comfortable with AutoCAD, you'll find that you won't need to refer to these messages as frequently.

As an additional aid, you can right-click to display a context-sensitive shortcut menu. That is, if you're in the middle of a command, this menu displays a list of options specifically related to that command. For example, if you right-click your mouse before picking the first point for the Rectangle command, a menu opens, displaying the same options that are listed in the Command prompt plus some additional options.

Finally, the Dynamic Input display allows you to enter dimensional data of objects as you draw them. Besides echoing the command-line messages, the Dynamic Input display shows temporary dimensions, coordinates, and angles of objects you're drawing and editing. As you enter coordinate or angle values through the keyboard, they appear in the Dynamic Input display. You can easily turn the Dynamic Input display on or off by clicking the Dynamic Input tool in the status bar. When the Dynamic Input display is turned off, your keyboard input appears only in the Command window.

If you see only the Ribbon tabs, click the arrowhead in the Ribbon Control tool. If you don't even see the tabs, press the Esc key twice and type **Ribbon**↵.

Move the arrow cursor onto one of the Ribbon panel tools and leave it there for a moment; you'll see a tool tip appear just below the cursor. Hold the cursor there a bit longer and the tool tip changes to give you even more information about the tool.

In most cases, you'll be able to guess what each tool does by looking at its icon. The icon with an arc in the Draw Ribbon panel, for instance, indicates that the tool draws arcs; the one with the circle shows that the tool draws circles; and so on. For further clarification, the tool tip gives you the name of the tool.

As a new user, you'll find these tool tips helpful because they show you the name of the tool and a brief description of how to use it. Typically, when I ask you to select a tool, I'll use the name shown in the tool tip to help you identify the tool. In the case of a tool with flyouts, the tool name changes under different conditions. For those tools, I'll use a general description to identify the tool. You'll learn more about flyouts a bit later in this chapter (see the section "Understanding Flyouts").

As you work through this book, I will ask you to select tools from the Ribbon panels. You'll often be asked to switch between different tabs to select tools from other sets of panels. To make the process simpler to read, I'll use a somewhat abbreviated description of a tools location. For example, for the Line tool, I'll say, "Click the Line tool from the Home tab's Draw panel." For the Move tool, I'll say, "Click the Move tool in the Home tab's Modify panel."

EXPANDING PANELS

In addition to the visible tools, a few tools are hidden from view. You can expand many of the Ribbon panels to select more tools. If you see an arrowhead to the right of a panel's title bar, you can click the title bar to expand the panel (see Figure 1.8). The set of tools expands to reveal some additional tools. If you move the cursor to the drawing area, the expanded panel shrinks to its original size. As an alternative, you can click the pushpin icon in the expanded panel title bar to lock the panel in its open position.

FIGURE 1.8
The arrowhead in the panel title bar tells you that additional tools are available.

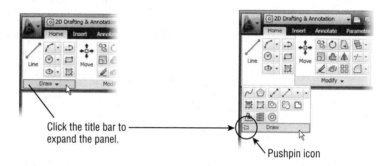

Click the title bar to expand the panel.

Pushpin icon

From now on, I'll refer to the location of additional tools as the "expanded panel." For example, I'll say, "Click the Ray tool in the expanded Draw panel" when I want you to select the Ray tool.

If you are working on a smaller screen with low resolution, some of the Ribbon panels to the far right may look different from what you are shown in this book. On a low-resolution screen, AutoCAD will automatically reduce the size of the panels to the right so they show only their title (Figure 1.9).

FIGURE 1.9
The Properties, Utilities, and Clipboard panels are reduced to single icons with a smaller AutoCAD window.

To see the tools, hover over the panel (Figure 1.10).

FIGURE 1.10
Hover over the panel to see the tools.

UNDERSTANDING FLYOUTS

One more feature you'll want to know about are the *flyouts*. Flyouts are similar to the expanded panels because you can click an arrowhead to gain access to additional tools. Unlike a whole panel, however, flyouts give you access to different methods for using a particular tool. For example, AutoCAD lets you draw circles in several different ways, so it offers a flyout for the Circle tool in the Home tab's Draw panel. If you click the arrowhead next to the circle icon in the Draw panel, you'll see additional tools for drawing circles (see Figure 1.11).

FIGURE 1.11
Flyouts

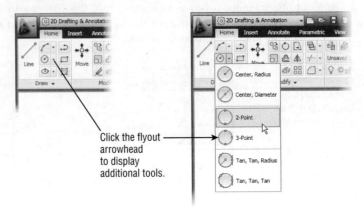

Click the flyout arrowhead to display additional tools.

If you select a tool option from a flyout, that option becomes the default tool for the icon you chose. For example, if you hover your cursor over the circle icon in the Draw panel, you'll see that the tool tip shows "Center, Radius" for the tool's name. If you click the arrowhead next to the Center, Radius tool and select 2-Point, then 2-Point becomes the default tool and you'll see "2-Point" for the name of the tool in the tool tip (see Figure 1.12).

FIGURE 1.12
The tool with a flyout will change to the last tool used.

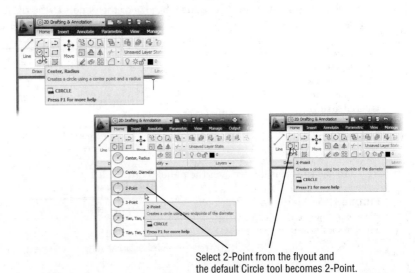

Select 2-Point from the flyout and the default Circle tool becomes 2-Point.

GENERAL TOOL NAMES VS. TOOL TIP NAMES

Since the tool tip names of tools with flyouts can change, describing them by name can be a bit problematic. The name may have changed based on the last tool you used from a flyout. For this reason, if a tool has a flyout, I'll refer to it by a general name that is related to the set of tools in a flyout rather than by the tool tip name. For example, I'll call the circle icon tool the Circle tool rather than the Center, Radius tool. Likewise, I'll refer to the magnifying glass icon in the View tab's Navigate panel as the Zoom tool instead of the Extents tool.

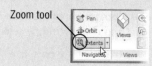

TOOLS VS. THE KEYBOARD

Throughout this book, you'll be told to select tools from the Ribbon panels to invoke commands. For new and experienced users alike, the Ribbon panels offer an easy-to-remember method for accessing commands. If you're an experienced AutoCAD user, you can type commands directly from the keyboard. Most of the keyboard commands you know and love still work as they did before.

Many tools and commands have *aliases*. Aliases are one-, two-, or three-letter abbreviations of a command name. As you become more proficient with AutoCAD, you may find these aliases helpful. As you work through this book, the shortcuts will be identified for your reference.

Finally, if you're feeling adventurous, you can create your own aliases and keyboard shortcuts for executing commands by adding them to the AutoCAD support files. Chapter 28 discusses how to customize menus, Ribbon panels, toolbars, and keyboard shortcuts.

Picking Points in the Drawing Area

Now that you've seen the general layout of AutoCAD, take a look at the coordinate readout and the drawing cursor to get a sense of how the parts of the AutoCAD screen work together:

1. Move the cursor around in the drawing area. As you move it, notice how the coordinate readout changes to tell you the cursor's location. It shows the coordinates in an X, Y, Z format.

2. Place the cursor in the middle of the drawing area and click the left mouse button. Move the cursor and a rectangle follows. This is a *window selection*; you'll learn more about this window in Chapter 2. You also see a coordinate readout following the cursor and the message `Specify opposite corner:`. This display at the cursor is called the *dynamic input display*. You'll learn more about it a little later in this chapter (Figure 1.13).

FIGURE 1.13
The Dynamic Input
Display cursor

If you don't see the Dynamic Input display, click the Dynamic Input tool in the status bar to turn it on.

3. Move the cursor a bit in any direction; then, click the left mouse button again. Notice that the window selection disappears, as does the Dynamic Input display.

4. Try picking several more points in the drawing area. Notice that as you click the mouse, you alternately start and end a window selection.

If you happen to click the right mouse button, a shortcut menu appears. A right-click frequently opens a menu containing options that are *context sensitive*. This means the contents of the shortcut menu depend on the location where you right-click as well as the command that is active at the time. If there are no appropriate options at the time of the right-click, AutoCAD treats the right-click as an ↵. You'll learn more about these options as you progress through the book. For now, if you happen to open this menu by accident, press the Esc key to close it.

Using the UCS Icon

In the lower-left corner of the drawing area, you see an L-shaped line. This is the *User Coordinate System (UCS)* icon, which tells you your orientation in the drawing. This icon becomes helpful as you start to work with complex 2D drawings and 3D models. The X and Y indicate the X- and Y-axes of your drawing. Chapter 22 discusses this icon in detail. For now, you can use it as a reference to tell you the direction of the axes.

IF YOU CAN'T FIND THE UCS ICON

The UCS icon can be turned on and off, so if you're on someone else's system and you don't see the icon, don't panic. If you don't see the icon or it doesn't look as it does in this chapter, see Chapter 22 for more information.

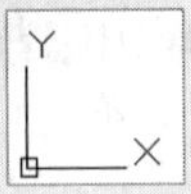

Working in the Command Window

As mentioned, at the bottom of the screen, just above the status bar, is a small horizontal window called the *Command window*. Here, AutoCAD displays responses to your input. By default, it shows four lines of text. The bottom line shows the current messages, and the top lines show messages that have scrolled by or, in some cases, components of the current message that don't fit in a single line. Right now, the bottom line displays the message Command (see Figure 1.4, earlier in this chapter). This *prompt* tells you that AutoCAD is waiting for your instructions. When you click a point in the drawing area, you see the message Specify opposite corner:. At the same time, the cursor starts to draw a window selection that disappears when you click another point. The same message appears in the Dynamic Input display at the cursor.

As a new user, pay special attention to messages displayed in the Command window and the Dynamic Input display because this is how AutoCAD communicates with you. Besides giving you messages, the Command window records your activity within AutoCAD. You can use the scroll bar to the right of the Command window to review previous messages. You can also enlarge the window for a better view. (Chapter 2 discusses these components in more detail.)

Now, let's look at AutoCAD's window components in detail.

THE COMMAND WINDOW AND DYNAMIC INPUT DISPLAY

The Command window and the Dynamic Input display allow AutoCAD to provide text feedback on your actions. You can think of these features as a chat window to AutoCAD—as you enter commands, AutoCAD responds with messages. As you become more familiar with AutoCAD, you may find you don't need to rely on the Command window and Dynamic Input display as much. For new and casual users, however, the Command window and Dynamic Input display can be helpful in understanding what steps to take as you work.

Working with AutoCAD

Now that you've been introduced to the AutoCAD window, you're ready to try using a few AutoCAD commands. First you'll open a sample file and make a few modifications to it. In the process, you'll become familiar with some common methods of operation in AutoCAD.

Opening an Existing File

In this exercise, you'll get a chance to see and use a typical Select File dialog box.

Before you start, make sure you have installed the sample files for this book from the DVD. See the introduction for instructions on how to find the sample files.

To start, you'll open an existing file:

1. Click the close icon in the upper-right corner of the drawing area. It looks like an *X*.

   A message appears, asking whether you want to save the changes you've made to the current drawing. Click No.

2. Click the Open tool in the Quick Access toolbar to open the Select File dialog box. This is a typical Windows file dialog box, with an added twist: In the large Preview box on the right, you can preview a drawing before you open it, thereby saving time while searching for files. To the left is a panel known as the Places list in which you can find frequently used locations on your computer or the Internet (see Figure 1.14).

If you don't see a Preview box in the Select File dialog box, click the word *Views* in the upper-right corner and select Preview from the list that appears.

FIGURE 1.14

The Select File
dialog box

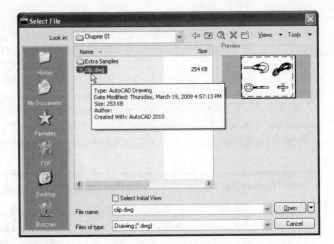

3. In the Select File dialog box, open the Look In drop-down list and locate the Chapter 01 folder of the Mastering AutoCAD 2011 sample files. (You may need to explore the list to find it.)

4. Move the arrow cursor to the clip.dwg file and click it. Notice that the clip.dwg filename now appears in the File Name input box below the file list. The Preview box also now shows a thumbnail image of the file. Be aware that a thumbnail may not show for files from older versions of AutoCAD.

5. Click the Open button at the bottom of the Select File dialog box. AutoCAD opens the clip.dwg file, as shown in Figure 1.15.

The clip.dwg file opens to display a *layout* view of the drawing. A layout is a type of view in which you lay out different views of your drawing in preparation for printing. You can tell you are in a layout view by the white area over the gray background. This white area represents your drawing on a printed page. This view is like a print preview.

FIGURE 1.15

The Layout1
view of the
clip.dwg file

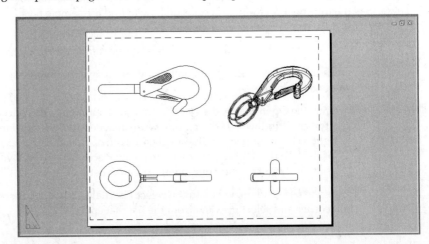

Also note that the AutoCAD window's title bar displays the name of the drawing. This offers easy identification of the file.

This particular file contains both 2D drawings and a 3D model of a typical locking clip. The layout view shows a top, front, and right-side view as well as an isometric view.

Getting a Closer Look

One of the most frequently used commands is Zoom, which gives you a closer look at part of your drawing. This command offers a variety of ways to control your view. In this section, you'll enlarge a portion of the clip drawing to get a more detailed look. To tell AutoCAD which area you want to enlarge, you use what is called a *zoom window*.

You'll start by switching to a Model Space view of the drawing. The Model Space view places you in a workspace where you do most of your drawing creation and editing. Follow these steps:

1. Click the Model tab below the drawing area, or if you don't see the tab, click the Model tool in the status bar (Figure 1.16).

Your view changes to show the full 3D model with the 2D representations of the model (see Figure 1.17).

2. Type **PLAN⏎W⏎**. Your display changes to a two-dimensional view looking down on the drawing, as shown in Figure 1.18.

FIGURE 1.16
Click the Model tab (left) or the Model tool in the status bar (right).

FIGURE 1.17
3D model with 2D representations of the model

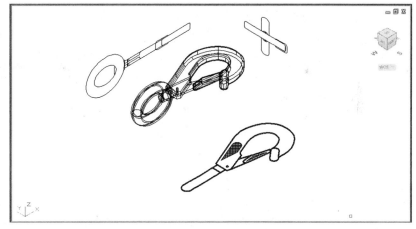

FIGURE 1.18
Placing the zoom
window around
the clip

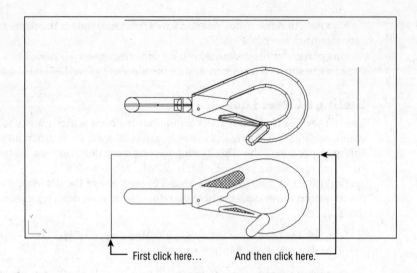

First click here…   And then click here.

3. Click the Zoom Window tool from the Zoom flyout in the navigation bar (Figure 1.19). Remember that to open the flyout, you need to click the arrowhead next to or below the tool.

FIGURE 1.19
The Zoom Window
tool from the Zoom
flyout in the navi-
gation bar.

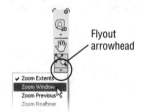

Flyout
arrowhead

You can also click the Window tool from the Zoom flyout in the View tab's Navigate panel (Figure 1.20) or type the command **Z**↵.

FIGURE 1.20
The Zoom flyout
and Window tool
in the View tab's
Navigate panel.

Click the flyout
arrowhead.

Select Window.

4. The Dynamic Input display shows the Specify corner of window: prompt with some options. Look at the image in Figure 1.18. Move the crosshair cursor to a location similar to the one shown in the figure; then, left-click the mouse. Move the cursor and the rectangle appears with one corner fixed on the point you just picked; the other corner follows the cursor.

5. The Dynamic Input display now shows the `Specify first corner:` and `Specify opposite corner:` prompts. Position the other corner of the zoom window so it encloses the lower image of the clip, as shown in Figure 1.18, and left-click the mouse again. The clip enlarges to fill the screen.

In this exercise, you used the Window option of the Zoom command to define an area to enlarge for your close-up view. You saw how AutoCAD prompts you to indicate first one corner of the window selection and then the other. These messages are helpful for first-time users of AutoCAD. You'll use the Window option frequently—not just to define views but also to select objects for editing.

Getting a close-up view of your drawing is crucial to working accurately, but you'll often want to return to a previous view to get the overall picture. To do so, choose Previous from the Zoom flyout in the View tab's Navigate panel (Figure 1.21).

FIGURE 1.21
The Zoom
Previous option

Do this now and the previous view—the one showing the entire clip—returns to the screen. You can also find the Zoom Previous option in the navigation bar's Zoom flyout.

You can quickly enlarge or reduce your view by using the Zoom Realtime option of the Zoom command. Follow these steps to change your view with Zoom Realtime:

1. Click the Zoom Realtime tool from the navigation bar's Zoom flyout. You can also right-click in the drawing area and select Zoom from the shortcut menu or select Zoom Realtime from Zoom flyout on the View tab's Navigate panel.

2. Place the Zoom Realtime cursor slightly above the center of the drawing area, and then click and drag downward. Your view zooms out to show more of the drawing.

3. While still holding the left mouse button, move the cursor upward. Your view zooms in and enlarges. When you have a view similar to the one shown in Figure 1.22, release the mouse button. (Don't worry if you don't get *exactly* the same view as the figure. This is just for practice.)

4. You're still in Zoom Realtime mode. Click and drag the mouse again to see how you can further adjust your view. To exit, you can select another command besides a Zoom or Pan, press the Esc key, or right-click your mouse and choose Exit from the shortcut menu.

5. Right-click now and choose Exit from the shortcut menu to exit the Zoom Realtime command.

FIGURE 1.22
The final view
you want to
achieve in step 3
of the exercise

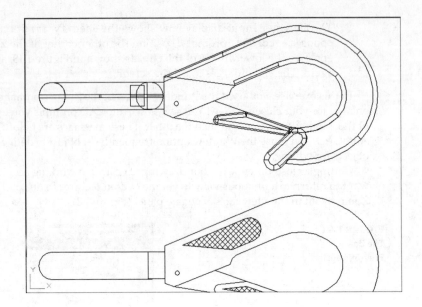

If you prefer, you can use the wheel on your mouse to zoom and pan over your view. Roll the wheel to zoom in and out or click and drag the wheel to pan. Be aware that Zoom Realtime offers finer control over the amount of magnification compared to the mouse wheel.

As you can see from this exercise, you have a wide range of options for viewing your drawings, just by using a few tools. These tools are all you need to control the display of 2D drawings.

Saving a File as You Work

It's a good idea to save your file periodically as you work on it. As with any Windows program, you can save it under its original name (click the Save tool on the Quick Access toolbar) or under a different name (choose Save As from the Application menu), thereby creating a new file.

By default, AutoCAD automatically saves your work at 10-minute intervals under a name that is a combination of the current filename plus a number and that ends with the .sv$ filename extension; this is known as the *Automatic Save* feature. Using settings in the Options dialog box or system variables, you can change the name of the autosaved file and control the time between autosaves. See "The Open and Save Tab" in Appendix B for details.

Making Changes

You'll frequently make changes to your drawings. One of AutoCAD's primary advantages is the ease with which you can make changes. The following exercise shows you a typical sequence of operations involved in changing a drawing:

1. Use the Save As option in the Application menu to save the current clip.dwg file under the name MyFirst. For convenience, you can save your files in the My Documents folder.

2. From the Home tab's Modify panel, click the Erase tool (the one with a pencil eraser touching paper). This activates the Erase command.

Notice that the cursor has turned into a small square. This square is called the *pickbox*. You also see `Select objects:` in the Command window and the Dynamic Input display. This message helps remind new users what to do.

3. Move the pickbox over the drawing, placing it on various parts of the clip. Don't click anything yet. Notice that as you hover your cursor over objects with the pickbox, they're highlighted. This helps you see the objects that the pickbox is likely to select should you click the left mouse button.

4. Place the pickbox on the crosshatch pattern of the clip (see Figure 1.23), and click. The crosshatch changes in appearance from a dark highlight to a light highlight. The pickbox and the `Select objects:` prompt remain, indicating that you can continue to select objects.

5. Press ↵. The crosshatch disappears. You've just erased a part of the drawing.

FIGURE 1.23
Erasing a portion of the clip

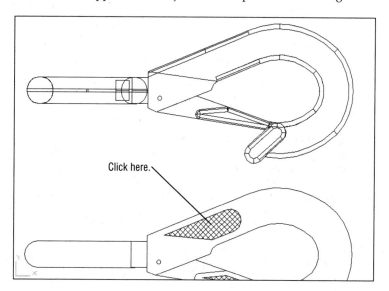

Click here.

 Real World Scenario

"I CAN'T FIND MY AUTOMATIC SAVES!"

As an IT manager at ELS Architecture and Urban Planning, one of the most common questions I get is "Where does AutoCAD put the Automatic Save files?" By default, in Windows XP, the Automatic Save file is stored in `C:\Documents and Settings\`*User Name*`\Local Settings\Temp\`. You can find the exact location for your system by typing **Savefilepath**↵ at the Command prompt. This file location is often set as a hidden folder, so you may need to set up Windows Explorer to display hidden folders before you can get to the Automatic Save file. You can also specify a different location for the Automatic Save files. See Appendix B for information on how to locate hidden files and specify a location for your files.

In this exercise, first you issued the Erase command, and then you selected an object by using a pickbox to click it. The pickbox tells you that you must select items on the screen, and it shows you what you're about to select by highlighting objects as you hover the cursor over them. Once you've clicked an object or a set of objects, press ↵ to move on to the next step. This sequence of steps is common to many of the commands you'll work with in AutoCAD.

You can also click an object or a set of objects and then press the Delete key.

Working with Multiple Files

You can have multiple documents open at the same time in AutoCAD. This can be especially helpful if you want to exchange parts of drawings between files or if you want another file open for reference. Try the following exercise to see how multiple documents work in AutoCAD:

1. Click the New tool on the Quick Access toolbar to open the Select Template dialog box.

   If you see the Create New Drawing dialog box, click the Start From Scratch button and select Imperial; then click OK and AutoCAD will display a default document. You'll learn more about the Create New Drawing dialog box in Chapter 2.

2. Make sure acad.dwt is selected, and then click Open.

3. In the View tab's Windows panel, click Tile Vertically to get a view of both drawing files.

When you create a new file in AutoCAD, you're actually opening a copy of a *template file*, as you saw in step 1. A template file is a blank file that is set up for specific drawing types. The acad.dwt file is a generic template set up for Imperial measurements. Another template file, called acadiso.dwt, is a generic template useful for metric measurements. Other templates are set up for specific drawing-sheet sizes and measurement systems. You'll learn more about templates in Chapter 6.

Next, let's try drawing a rectangle to see how AutoCAD behaves while drawing objects:

1. Click the Rectangle tool in the Home tab's Draw panel, as shown in Figure 1.24.

FIGURE 1.24
Click the Rectangle tool in the Draw panel.

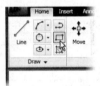

Notice that the Command window now shows the following prompt:

```
Specify first corner point or [Chamfer/Elevation/Fillet/Thickness/Width]:
```

AutoCAD is asking you to select the first corner for the rectangle and, in brackets, it's offering a few options that you can take advantage of at this point in the command. Don't worry about those options right now. You'll have an opportunity to learn about command options in Chapter 2. You also see the same prompt, minus the bracketed options, in the Dynamic Input display at the cursor. You can view the command options at the cursor by pressing the down arrow key on your keyboard.

WORKING WITH AUTOCAD | **23**

2. Click a point roughly in the lower-left corner of the drawing area, as shown in Figure 1.25. Now, as you move your mouse, a rectangle follows the cursor, with one corner fixed at the position you just selected. You also see the following prompt in the Command window, with a similar prompt in the Dynamic Input display:

```
Specify other corner point or [Area/Dimensions/Rotation]:
```

FIGURE 1.25
Selecting the first point of a rectangle

Click here to start the rectangle.

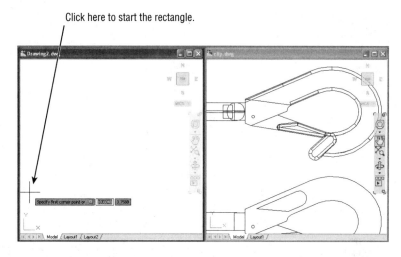

3. Click another point anywhere in the upper-right region of the drawing area. A rectangle appears (see Figure 1.26). You'll learn more about the different cursor shapes and what they mean in Chapter 2.

4. Let's try copying objects between these two files. Click in the window with the clip drawing to make it active.

FIGURE 1.26
After you've selected the first point of the rectangle, you'll see a rectangle follow the motion of your mouse.

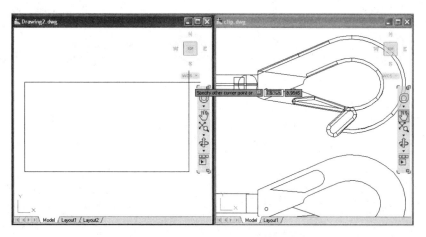

5. Click All from the Zoom flyout in the View tab's Navigate panel to get an overall view of the drawing (see Figure 1.27). You can also click the Zoom All tool from the navigation bar's Zoom flyout.

FIGURE 1.27
The Zoom All option gives you an overall view of your drawing.

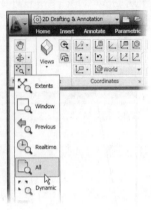

6. Click the 2D version of the clip at the bottom of the drawing to select it. A series of squares and arrows appears on the drawing. These are called *grips,* and you'll learn more about them in the next chapter (see Figure 1.28).

FIGURE 1.28
Grips shown in the 2D drawing

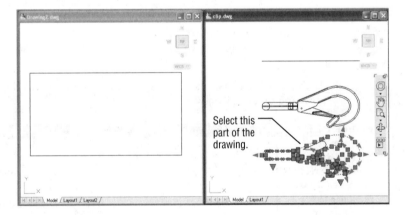

7. Right-click and select Clipboard and then Copy.

8. Click inside the other drawing window to make it active.

9. Right-click and select Clipboard and then Paste. The clip appears at the cursor in the new drawing.

10. Position the clip in the middle of the rectangle you drew earlier and left-click the mouse. The clip is copied into the second drawing.

11. This ends the exercises for this chapter. Save the new file as My Clip and then exit AutoCAD. You don't have to save the `clip.dwg` file.

Note that you've had two files open at once. You can have as many files open as you want as long as your computer has adequate memory to accommodate them. You can control the individual document windows as you would any window, using the window control buttons in the upper-right corner of the document window.

Adding a Predrawn Symbol with the Tool Palettes

In the preceding exercise, you saw how you can easily copy an object from one file to another by using the standard Windows Cut and Paste feature. AutoCAD offers several tool palettes that enable you to click and drag predrawn objects into your drawing.

You can open the tool palettes by clicking the Tool Palettes tool in the View tab's Palettes panel, as shown in Figure 1.29.

FIGURE 1.29
The Tool Palettes tool opens a set of tool palettes.

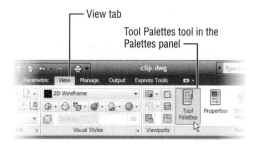

Once the tool palettes are open, you can select a tab in the tool palettes containing the predrawn objects you want to use and then click the specific object you want to add. The object appears at the cursor, ready for you to select a location (see Figure 1.30).

In addition to predrawn objects, the tool palettes offer a way to add hatch patterns and other components quickly to your drawing. They're great tools to help you manage your library of custom, predrawn symbols. Chapter 29 shows you how to use and customize the tool palettes.

The Bottom Line

Use the AutoCAD window.   AutoCAD is a typical Windows graphics program that makes use of menus, toolbars, Ribbon panels, and palettes. If you've used other graphics programs, you'll see at least a few familiar tools.

Master It   Name the components of the AutoCAD window you can use to select a function.

FIGURE 1.30

The tool palettes offer predrawn symbols that you can easily place in your drawings.

Select a tab containing predrawn symbols you want to use.

Click on a symbol.

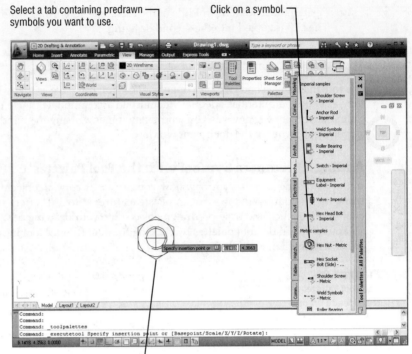

The symbol appears at the cursor ready to be placed in the drawing.

Get a closer look with the Zoom command.   One of the first things you'll want to learn is how to manipulate your views. The Zoom command is a common tool in graphics programs.

   Master It   Name at least two ways of zooming into a view.

Save a file as you work.   Nothing is more frustrating than having a power failure cause you to lose hours of work. It's a good idea to save your work frequently. AutoCAD offers an Automatic Save feature that can be a lifesaver if you happen to forget to save your files.

   Master It   How often does the AutoCAD Automatic Save feature save your drawing?

Make changes and open multiple files.   As with other Windows programs, you can have multiple files open and exchange data between them.

   Master It   With two drawings open, how can you copy parts of one drawing into the other?

Chapter 2

Creating Your First Drawing

This chapter examines some of AutoCAD's basic functions. You'll get a chance to practice with the drawing editor by building a simple drawing to use in later exercises. You'll learn how to give input to AutoCAD, interpret prompts, and get help when you need it. This chapter also covers the use of coordinate systems to give AutoCAD exact measurements for objects. You'll see how to select objects you've drawn and how to specify base points for moving and copying.

If you're not a beginning AutoCAD user, you may want to move on to the more complex material in Chapter 3. You can use the files supplied on the companion DVD to continue the tutorials at that point.

In this chapter, you'll learn to do the following:

- ◆ Specify distances with coordinates
- ◆ Interpret the cursor modes and understand prompts
- ◆ Select objects and edit with grips
- ◆ Use dynamic input
- ◆ Get help
- ◆ Display data in a text window
- ◆ Display the properties of an object

GET ADDITIONAL HELP ON THE DVD

The companion DVD offers four video tutorials that give you an overview of the main topics of this chapter. The video entitled "Commands and Methods" covers some general features of AutoCAD that you'll need to know as a beginner. The video entitled "Entering Coordinates" touches on some of the material in "Specifying Distances with Coordinates." "Selecting Objects" covers the material from the "Selecting Objects" section. Finally, "Editing with Grips" covers the material in the section with the same name.

Getting to Know the Home Tab's Draw and Modify Panels

Your first task in learning how to draw in AutoCAD is simply to draw a line. Since AutoCAD is designed as a precision drawing tool, you'll be introduced to methods that allow you to input exact distances. But before you begin drawing, take a moment to familiarize yourself with the features you'll be using more than any other to create objects with AutoCAD: the Draw and Modify panels. Try these steps:

1. Start AutoCAD just as you did in Chapter 1, by choosing Start ➢ All Programs ➢ Autodesk ➢ AutoCAD 2011 ➢ AutoCAD 2011.

2. If you see the Create New Drawing dialog box, click the Start From Scratch icon and then click OK to go directly to the default Drawing1 document. The Start From Scratch icon looks like a blank page.

3. If the default Drawing1.dwg file shows a gray 3D workspace, click the New tool in the Quick Access toolbar, select acad.dwt from the Select Template dialog box, and click Open (see Figure 2.1).

FIGURE 2.1
The Select Template dialog box

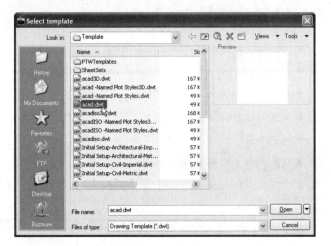

4. Make sure you are in the 2D Drafting & Annotation workspace by clicking the Workspace Switching tool in the status bar or in the Quick Access toolbar. If you use the status bar, you should see a checkmark next to 2D Drafting & Annotation. If not, click 2D Drafting & Annotation in the list.

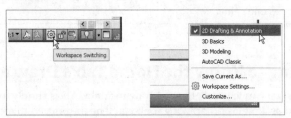

5. Move the arrow cursor to the Line tool in the Home tab's Draw panel at the far upper-left portion of the AutoCAD window, and rest it there so that the tool tip appears. As you hold the cursor over the tool, first one tool tip appears and then another (see Figure 2.2).

FIGURE 2.2

The Draw panel

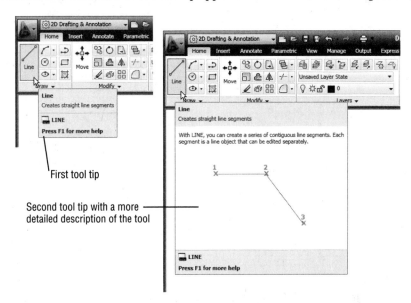

First tool tip

Second tool tip with a more detailed description of the tool

6. Slowly move the arrow cursor to the right over the other tools in the Home tab's Draw panel, and read each tool tip.

In most cases, you'll be able to guess what each tool does by looking at its icon. The icon with an arc, for instance, indicates that the tool draws arcs; the one with the ellipse signifies that the tool draws ellipses; and so on. If you hover over the tool, you'll see the tool tip name and the keyboard command associated with the tool. Hold the cursor for a bit longer and a tool tip that gives a brief explanation of how to use the tool appears.

DON'T GET STUCK ON THE PROMPTS

In many of the exercises in this book, I'll mention the Command prompt that appears in the Command window. They are shown for your reference, but don't let yourself get too bogged down by them. For example, I'll say, "At the Specify lower left corner or [ON/OFF] <0.0000,0.0000>: prompt, press ↵." The important part is to "press ↵." You can skim over the prompt. Just keep in mind that the prompts can offer some direction and show the options for the current command. They can also serve as helpful reminders later when you're working on your own.

You see three rows of tools in the Home tab's Draw and Modify panels. In Chapter 1, you saw that if you click the arrow in a panel's title bar, the panel expands to reveal more tools (see Figure 2.3). Once you've selected a tool from the expanded Draw or Modify panel, the expanded panel closes. If you want to keep the expanded panel open, click the pushpin icon at the left end of the expanded panel's title bar.

FIGURE 2.3
The Home tab's
Draw and Modify
panel tools

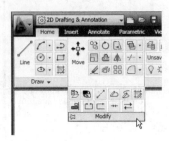

Starting Your First Drawing

In Chapter 1, you looked at a pre-existing sample drawing. This time, you'll begin to draw your own drawing by creating a door that will be used in later exercises. First, though, you must learn how to tell AutoCAD what you want, and even more important, you must understand what AutoCAD wants from you.

> **IMPERIAL AND METRIC**
>
> In this chapter, you'll start to see instructions for both Imperial and metric measurements. In general, you'll see the instructions for Imperial measurement first, followed by the metric instructions. You won't be dealing with inches or centimeters yet, however. You're just getting to know the AutoCAD system.

You'll start by opening a new drawing and setting the size of the work area, known as the drawing *limits*. These limits aren't fixed in any way, and you aren't forced to stay within the bounds of the drawing limits unless the limits ON/OFF option is turned on. But limits can help to establish a starting area from which you can expand your drawing:

1. Click the Close icon in the upper-right corner of the drawing area to close the current file. In the Save Changes dialog box, click No. Notice that the Ribbon disappears and the AutoCAD drawing window appears blank when no drawings are open.

2. Click the New icon in the Quick Access toolbar to open the Select Template dialog box.

3. Select the `acad.dwt` template, and click Open.

You have a new blank file, but it's a little difficult to tell how big your drawing area is. Next, you'll set up the work area so you have a better idea of the space you're working with:

1. Enter **Limits**⏎.

2. At the `Specify lower left corner or [ON/OFF] <0.0000,0.0000>:` prompt, press ⏎.

3. At the `Specify upper right corner <12.0000,9.0000>:` prompt, metric users should enter **40,30**⏎. If you use Imperial units (feet and inches), then press ⏎ to accept the default of 12.0000,9.0000.

4. Type **Z**⏎ **A**⏎ to "Zoom All". You can also select All from the Zoom flyout on the View tab's Navigate panel or Zoom All from the navigation bar.

In the last step, the All option of the Zoom command uses the limits you set up in steps 2 and 3 to determine the display area. In a drawing that contains objects, the Zoom tool's All option displays the limits plus the area occupied by the objects in the drawing if they happen to fall outside the limits. Now give your file a unique name:

1. Choose Save As from the Application menu or type **Saveas**⏎ to open the Save Drawing As dialog box.

2. Type **Door**. As you type, the name appears in the File Name text box.

3. Save your file in the `My Documents` folder, or if you prefer, save it in another folder of your choosing. Just remember where you put it because you'll use it later.

4. Click Save. You now have a file called `Door.dwg`, located in the `My Documents` folder. Of course, your drawing doesn't contain anything yet. You'll take care of that next.

UNDERSTANDING THE DRAWING AREA

The new file shows a drawing area roughly 12 inches wide by 9 inches high. Metric users have a file that shows an area roughly 40 mm wide by 30 mm high. This is just the area you're given to start with, but you're not limited to it in any way. No visual clues indicate the size of the area. To check the area size for yourself, move the crosshair cursor to the upper-right corner of the drawing area and observe the value in the coordinate readout in the lower-left corner. The coordinate readout won't show exactly 12 × 9 inches, or 40 × 30 mm for metric, because the proportions of your drawing area aren't likely to be exactly 12 × 9 or 40 × 30. AutoCAD does try to optimize the display for the drawing area when you choose the All option of the Zoom command.

You're almost ready to do some drawing. Before you begin, turn off the Dynamic Input display. The Dynamic Input display is a great tool, but while you're learning how to enter coordinates, it can be a distraction:

1. Locate the Dynamic Input tool in the status bar.

2. Click the Dynamic Input tool to turn it off. You can tell it is off when it turns a light gray color.

You'll get a chance to work with the Dynamic Input display a bit later in this chapter. Now you can begin to explore the drawing process. To begin a drawing, follow these steps:

1. Click the Line tool on the Home tab's Draw panel, or type **L**↵.

You've just issued the Line command. AutoCAD responds in two ways. First, you see the message

```
Specify first point:
```

in the Command prompt, asking you to select a point to begin your line. Also, the cursor changes its appearance; it no longer has a square in the crosshairs. This is a clue telling you to pick a point to start a line.

2. Using the left mouse button, select a point on the screen near the center. After you select the point, AutoCAD changes the prompt to this:

```
Specify next point or [Undo]:
```

Now, as you move the mouse around, notice the line with one end fixed on the point you just selected and the other end following the cursor in a *rubber-banding* motion (see the first image in Figure 2.4).

3. Move the cursor to a location directly to the left or right of the point you clicked and you'll see a dotted horizontal line appear along with a message at the cursor. This action also occurs when you point directly up or down. Your cursor seems to jump to a horizontal or vertical position.

This feature is called *Polar Tracking*. Like a T square or triangle, it helps to restrict your line to an exact horizontal or vertical direction. You can turn Polar Tracking on or off by clicking the Polar Tracking tool in the status bar. You'll learn more about Polar Tracking in Chapter 3.

4. Continue with the Line command. Move the cursor to a point below and to the right of the first point you selected, and click again. You've just drawn a line segment, and a second rubber-banding line appears (see the second image in Figure 2.4).

FIGURE 2.4
A rubber-
banding line

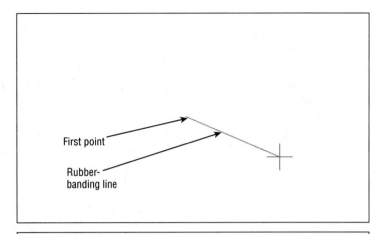

First point

Rubber-
banding line

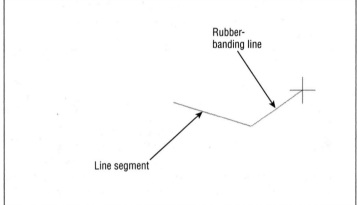

Rubber-
banding line

Line segment

5. If the line you drew isn't the exact length you want, you can back up during the Line command and change it. To do this, type U↵. The line you drew previously rubber-bands as if you hadn't selected the second point to fix its length.

6. Right-click and select Enter. This terminates the Line command.

The Undo and Redo tools in the Quick Access toolbar offer Undo and Redo drop-down lists from which you can select the exact command you want to undo or redo. See the sidebar "Getting Out of Trouble" in this chapter for more information.

You've just drawn, and then undrawn, a line of an arbitrary length. The Line command is still active. Two onscreen clues tell you that you're in the middle of a command. If you don't see the word Command in the bottom line of the Command window, a command is still active. Also, the cursor is the plain crosshair without the box at its intersection.

From now on, I'll refer to the crosshair cursor without the small box as the Point Selection mode of the cursor. If you look ahead to Figure 2.10, you'll see all the modes of the drawing cursor.

Real World Scenario

WHY USE THE KEYBOARD COMMANDS?

For many years, Autodesk has been encouraging users to move away from the command line and keyboard method of command entry, but it seems that AutoCAD users will have none of that. Although I would expect the "gristled veteran" users to stick with the keyboard entry method, I've been surprised to find that the young "fresh out of school" apprentice architects also prefer the keyboard over the newer palettes and toolbars in AutoCAD.

I mentioned this to one of the designers of AutoCAD at a recent Autodesk function. Without hesitation, he answered that "keyboard entry is much faster." In my own experience, it isn't just faster. Entering commands via the keyboard gives you a more "connected" feeling with AutoCAD. Work seems to flow much smoother. If you learn the keyboard commands, you'll also find that customizing AutoCAD is much easier. So for these reasons, I encourage you to try both the keyboard and the tools to see which you prefer. You'll find that, wherever possible, I'll give the keyboard command equivalent to a tool selection in the exercises of this book. Remember that a tool's tool tip will also show its keyboard command.

Specifying Exact Distances with Coordinates

Next, you'll continue with the Line command to draw a plan view (an overhead view) of a door, to no particular scale. This will give you some practice in drawing objects to exact distances. Later, you'll resize the drawing to use in future exercises. The door will be 3.0 units long and 0.15 units thick. For metric users, the door will be 9 units long and 0.5 units thick. To specify these exact distances in AutoCAD, you can use either relative polar coordinates or Cartesian coordinates.

GETTING OUT OF TROUBLE

Beginners and experts alike are bound to make a few mistakes. Before you get too far into the tutorial, here are some powerful but easy-to-use tools to help you recover from accidents:

Backspace If you make a typing error, press the Backspace key to back up to your error, and then retype your command or response. The Backspace key is in the upper-right corner of the main keyboard area.

Escape (Esc) This is perhaps the single most important key on your keyboard. When you need to exit a command or a dialog box quickly without making changes, press the Esc key in the upper-left corner of your keyboard. In most cases, you need to press Esc only once, although it won't hurt to press it twice. (Press Esc before editing with grips or issuing commands through the keyboard.)

U If you accidentally change something in the drawing and want to reverse that change, click the Undo tool in the Quick Access toolbar (the left-pointing curved arrow). You can also type **U**↵ at the Command prompt. Each time you do this, AutoCAD undoes one operation at a time, in reverse order. The last command performed is undone first, then the next-to-last command, and so on. The prompt displays the name of the command being undone, and the drawing reverts to its state prior to that command. If you need to, you can undo everything back to the beginning of an editing session. You can also select the exact command to back up to by using the Undo drop-down list in the Quick Access toolbar.

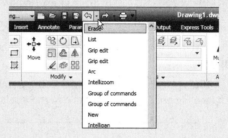

You can open the Undo drop-down list by clicking the downward-pointing arrow found to the right of the Undo tool.

Undo If you want more control over the way Undo works, you can use the Undo command, which allows you to "bookmark" places in your editing session that you can "undo" to. Type **Undo**↵ and you'll see the Enter the number of operations to undo or [Auto/ Control/BEgin/End/Mark/Back] <1>: prompt. You can enter a number indicating the number of steps you want to "undo." Use the Mark option to "bookmark" a location; then use Back to undo your work to that "bookmark." You can use Begin and End to mark the beginning and end of a set of operations that will be undone all at once. Control offers options to control the behavior of the Undo command. Auto is an option that is on by default and causes AutoCAD to undo the action of the whole command rather than the individual actions within a command.

Redo If you accidentally undo one too many commands, you can redo the last undone command by clicking the Redo tool (the right-pointing curved arrow) in the Quick Access toolbar. Or, type **Redo**↵. You can redo several operations that you may have undone with the Undo command. You can also select the exact command to redo to by using the Redo drop-down list in the Quick Access toolbar.

The Imperial and metric distances aren't equivalent in the exercises in this chapter. For example, 3 units in the Imperial-based drawing aren't equal to 9 metric units. These distances are arbitrary and based on how they appear in the figures in this chapter.

Specifying Polar Coordinates

To enter the exact distance of 3 (or 9 metric) units to the right of the last point you selected, do the following:

1. Click the Line tool on the Home tab's Draw panel, or type **L**↵.

2. Click a point slightly to the left of the center of the drawing area to select the start point.

3. Type **@3<0**. Metric users should type **@9<0**. As you type, the letters appear at the Command prompt.

4. Press ↵. A line appears, starting from the first point you picked and ending 3 units to the right of it (see Figure 2.5). You've just entered a relative polar coordinate.

FIGURE 2.5
Notice that the rubber-banding line now starts from the last point selected. This indicates that you can continue to add more line segments.

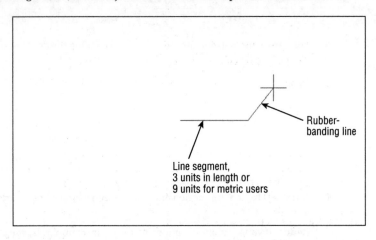

Rubber-banding line

Line segment, 3 units in length or 9 units for metric users

The "at" sign (@) you entered tells AutoCAD that the coordinate you're specifying is from the last point you selected. The 3 (or 9 metric) is the distance, and the less-than symbol (<) tells AutoCAD that you're designating the angle at which the line is to be drawn. The last part is the value for the angle, which in this case is 0 for 0°. This is how to use polar coordinates to communicate distances and directions to AutoCAD.

If you're accustomed to a different method for describing directions, you can set AutoCAD to use a vertical direction or downward direction as 0°. See Chapter 3 for details.

Angles are given based on the system shown in Figure 2.6, in which 0° is a horizontal direction from left to right, 90° is straight up, 180° is horizontal from right to left, and so on. You can specify degrees, minutes, and seconds of arc if you want to be that exact. I'll discuss angle formats in more detail in Chapter 3.

FIGURE 2.6

AutoCAD's default system for specifying angles

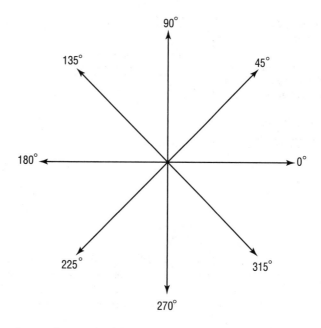

Specifying Relative Cartesian Coordinates

For the next line segment, let's try another method for specifying exact distances:

1. Enter **@0,0.15**↵. Metric users should enter **@0,0.5**↵. A short line appears above the endpoint of the last line. Once again, @ tells AutoCAD that the coordinate you specify is from the last point picked. But in this example, you give the distance in X and Y values. The X distance, 0, is given first, followed by a comma, and then the Y distance, 0.15. This is how to specify distances in relative Cartesian coordinates.

COMMAS AND PERIODS

Step 1 indicates that metric users should enter **@0,0.5**↵ for the distance. Instead, you could enter **@0,.5** (zero comma point five). The leading zero is included for clarity. European metric users should be aware that the comma is used as a separator between the X and Y components of the coordinate. In AutoCAD, commas aren't used for decimal points; you must use a period to denote a decimal point.

---

2. Enter **@-3,0**↵. Metric users should enter **@-9,0**↵. This distance is also in X,Y values, but here you use a negative value to specify the X distance. The result is a drawing that looks like Figure 2.7.

FIGURE 2.7
These three sides
of the door were
drawn by using the
Line tool. Points
are specified by
using either rela-
tive Cartesian or
polar coordinates.

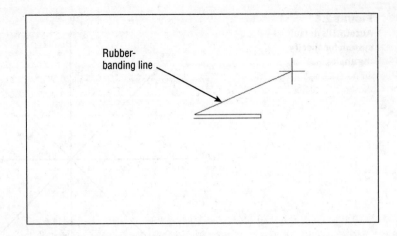

Positive values in the Cartesian coordinate system are from left to right and from bottom to top (see Figure 2.8). (You may remember this from your high school geometry class!) If you want to draw a line from right to left, you must designate a negative value. It's also helpful to know where the origin of the drawing lies. In a new drawing, the origin—or coordinate 0,0—is in the lower-left corner of the drawing.

3. Type **C⏎**. This C stands for the Close option. It closes a sequence of line segments. A line connecting the first and last points of a sequence of lines is drawn (see Figure 2.9), and the Line command terminates. The rubber-banding line also disappears, telling you that AutoCAD has finished drawing line segments. You can also use the rubber-banding line to indicate direction while simultaneously entering the distance through the keyboard. See the sidebar "Other Ways to Enter Distances."

To finish drawing a series of lines without closing them, you can press Esc, ⏎, or the spacebar.

FIGURE 2.8
Positive and nega-
tive Cartesian coor-
dinate directions

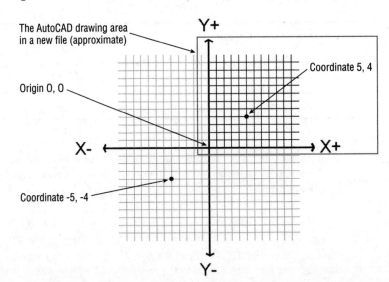

FIGURE 2.9

Distance and direction input for the door. Distances for metric users are shown in brackets.

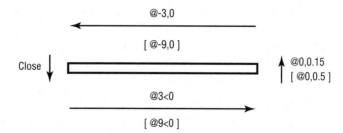

Interpreting the Cursor Modes and Understanding Prompts

The key to working with AutoCAD successfully is understanding the way it interacts with you. This section will help you become familiar with some of the ways AutoCAD prompts you for input. Understanding the format of the messages in the Command window and recognizing other events on the screen will help you learn the program more easily.

Understanding Cursor Modes

As the Command window aids you with messages, the cursor gives you clues about what to do. Figure 2.10 illustrates the various modes of the cursor and gives a brief description of the role of each mode. Take a moment to study this figure.

FIGURE 2.10

The drawing cursor's modes

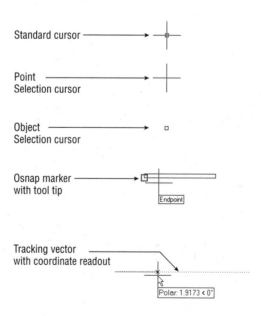

The Standard cursor tells you that AutoCAD is waiting for instructions. You can also edit objects by using grips when you see this cursor. *Grips* are squares, rectangles, or arrowheads that appear at endpoints and at the midpoint of objects when they're selected. (You might know them as *workpoints* from other graphics programs.)

OTHER WAYS TO ENTER DISTANCES

A third method for entering distances is to point in a direction with a rubber-banding line and then enter the distance through the keyboard. For example, to draw a line 3 units long from left to right, click the Line tool on the Home tab's Draw panel, click a start point, and then move the cursor so the rubber-banding line points to the right at some arbitrary distance. With the cursor pointing in the direction you want, type **3**↵. The rubber-banding line becomes a fixed line 3 units long. Using this method, called the Direct Distance method, along with the Ortho mode or Polar Tracking described in Chapter 3, can be a fast way to draw orthogonal lines of specific lengths.

If you turn on the Dynamic Input tool, you can also specify an exact angle along with the distance. For example, start the line command and then pick the first point. Type **3** for the length but don't press ↵. Press the Tab key instead. The line segment will become fixed at 3 units, and as you move the cursor, the segment will rotate freely around the first point. Next type an angle in degrees, **30**↵ for example, and the line will be drawn at 30 degrees. Or, instead of typing in an angle, just adjust the angle of the line visually until you see the angle you want on the Dynamic Input temporary angle dimension, and then click the mouse.

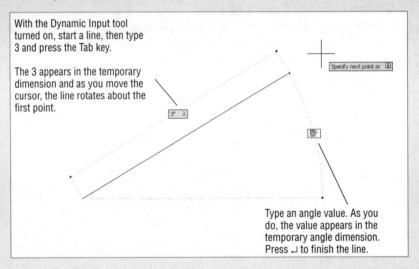

With the Dynamic Input tool turned on, start a line, then type 3 and press the Tab key.

The 3 appears in the temporary dimension and as you move the cursor, the line rotates about the first point.

Specify next point or

Type an angle value. As you do, the value appears in the temporary angle dimension. Press ↵ to finish the line.

If you watch the temporary dimensions as you press the Tab key, you'll see that the Tab key lets you move from the length dimension to the angle dimension and back again. You can press the Tab key at any time to shift back and forth between dimensions. A lock appears next to a dimension that you have entered, telling you that the dimension is "locked" until you tab to it again.

You'll learn more about how to enter values with the Dynamic Input's temporary dimensions later in this chapter.

The Point Selection cursor appears whenever AutoCAD expects point input. It can also appear in conjunction with a rubber-banding line. You can either click a point or enter a coordinate through the keyboard.

The Pickbox cursor tells you that you must select objects—either by clicking them or by using any of the object-selection options available.

The Osnap (object snap) marker appears along with the Point Selection cursor when you invoke an osnap. Osnaps let you accurately select specific points on an object, such as endpoints or midpoints.

The tracking vector appears when you use the Polar Tracking or Object Snap Tracking feature. Polar Tracking aids you in drawing orthogonal lines, and Object Snap Tracking helps you align a point in space relative to the geometry of existing objects. Object Snap Tracking works in conjunction with osnaps. You'll learn more about the tracking vector in Chapters 3 and 4.

If you're an experienced AutoCAD user, you may prefer to use the old-style crosshair cursor that crosses the entire screen. Choose Options from the bottom of the Application menu to open the Options dialog box, and then click the Display tab. Set the Crosshair Size option near the bottom right of the dialog box to 100. The cursor then appears as it did in previous versions of AutoCAD. As the option name implies, you can set the crosshair size to any percentage of the screen you want. The default is 5 percent.

Choosing Command Options

Many commands in AutoCAD offer several options, which are often presented to you in the Command window in the form of a prompt. This section uses the Arc command to illustrate the format of AutoCAD's prompts.

Usually, in a floor-plan drawing in the United States, an arc is drawn to indicate the direction of a door swing. Figure 2.11 shows a drawing that includes other standard symbols used in architectural-style drawings.

Here, you'll draw the arc for the door you started in the previous exercise:

1. Click the Arc tool in the Home tab's Draw panel. The `Specify start point of arc or [Center]:` prompt appears, and the cursor changes to Point Selection mode.

Examine the `Specify start point of arc or [Center]:` prompt. The start point contains two options. The default option is the one stated in the main part of the prompt. In this case, the default option is to specify the start point of the arc. If other options are available, they appear within square brackets. In the Arc command, you see the word `Center` within brackets telling you that, if you prefer, you can also start your arc by selecting a center point instead of a start point. If multiple options are available, they appear within the brackets and are separated by slashes (/). The default is the option AutoCAD assumes you intend to use unless you tell it otherwise.

2. Type **C↵** to select the Center option. The `Specify center point of arc:` prompt appears. Notice that you had to type only the C and not the entire word *Center*.

When you see a set of options in the Command window, note their capitalization. If you choose to respond to prompts by using the keyboard, these capitalized letters are all you need to enter to select the option. In some cases, the first two letters are capitalized to differentiate two options that begin with the same letter, such as `LAyer` and `LType`.

FIGURE 2.11
Samples of standard symbols used in architectural drawings

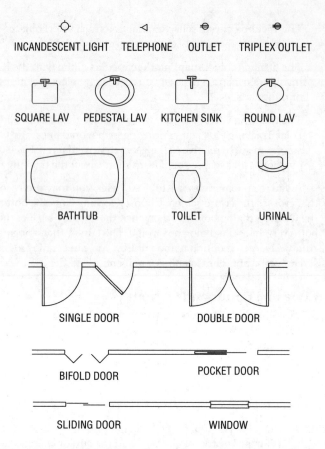

INCANDESCENT LIGHT   TELEPHONE   OUTLET   TRIPLEX OUTLET

SQUARE LAV   PEDESTAL LAV   KITCHEN SINK   ROUND LAV

BATHTUB   TOILET   URINAL

SINGLE DOOR   DOUBLE DOOR

BIFOLD DOOR   POCKET DOOR

SLIDING DOOR   WINDOW

3. Pick a point representing the center of the arc near the upper-left corner of the door (see Figure 2.12). The Specify start point of arc: prompt appears.

4. Type @3<0↵. Metric users should type @9<0↵. The **Specify end point of arc or [Angle/chord Length]:** prompt appears.

5. Move the mouse and a temporary arc appears, originating from a point 3 units to the right of the center point you selected and rotating about that center, as in Figure 2.12. (Metric users will see the temporary arc originating 9 units to the right of the center point.)

As the prompt indicates, you now have three options. You can enter an angle, a chord length, or the endpoint of the arc. The prompt default, to specify the endpoint of the arc, picks the arc's endpoint. Again, the cursor is in Point Selection mode, telling you it's waiting for point input. To select this default option, you only need to pick a point on the screen indicating where you want the endpoint.

6. Move the cursor so that it points in a vertical direction from the center of the arc. You'll see the Polar Tracking vector snap to a vertical position.

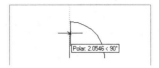

Polar: 2.0546 < 90°

7. Click any location with the Polar Tracking vector in the vertical position. The arc is now fixed in place, as in Figure 2.12.

FIGURE 2.12
Using the Arc command

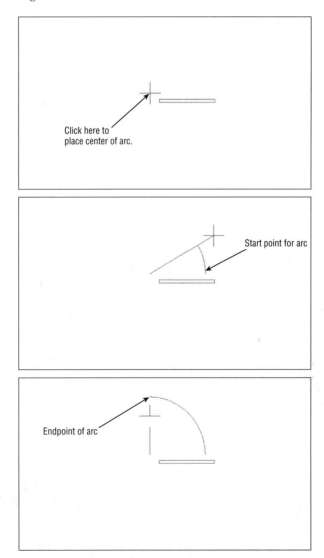

Click here to place center of arc.

Start point for arc

Endpoint of arc

This exercise has given you some practice working with AutoCAD's Command window prompts and entering keyboard commands—skills you'll need when you start to use some of the more advanced AutoCAD functions.

As you can see, AutoCAD has a distinct structure in its prompt messages. You first issue a command, which in turn offers options in the form of a prompt. Depending on the option you select, you get another set of options or you're prompted to take some action, such as picking a point, selecting objects, or entering a value.

As you work through the exercises, you'll become intimately familiar with this routine. After you understand the workings of the Ribbon panels, the Command window prompts, and the dialog boxes, you can almost teach yourself the rest of the program!

SELECTING OPTIONS FROM A SHORTCUT MENU

Now you know that you can select command options by typing them. You can also right-click at any time during a command to open a shortcut menu containing those same options. For example, in step 2 in the previous exercise, you typed **C**↵ to tell AutoCAD that you wanted to select the center of the arc. Instead of typing, you can also right-click the mouse to open a menu of options applicable to the Arc command at that time.

Notice that in addition to the options shown in the Command prompt, the shortcut menu shows you a few more: Enter, Cancel, Pan, and Zoom. The Enter option is the same as pressing ↵. Cancel cancels the current command. Pan and Zoom let you adjust your view as you're working through the current command.

The shortcut menu is context sensitive, so you see only those options that pertain to the command or activity that is currently in progress. Also, when AutoCAD is expecting a point, an object selection, or a numeric value, right-clicking doesn't display a shortcut menu. Instead, AutoCAD treats a right-click as ↵.

The location of your cursor when you right-click determines the contents of the shortcut list. A right-click in the Command window displays a list of operations you can apply to the command line, such as repeating one of the last several commands you've used or copying the most recent history of command activity to the Clipboard.

A right-click in the drawing area when no command is active displays a set of basic options for editing your file such as the command most recently used, Pan, and Zoom, to name a few (see Figure 2.13). The Cut, Paste, Undo, and Repeat commands can be found under the Clipboard option. .

FIGURE 2.13
A set of basic
list options

If you're ever in doubt about what to do in AutoCAD, you can right-click to see a list of options. You'll learn more about these options later in this book. For now, let's move on to the topic of selecting objects.

Selecting Objects

In AutoCAD, you can select objects in many ways. This section has two parts: The first part covers object-selection methods unique to AutoCAD, and the second part covers the more common selection method used in most popular graphic programs, the Noun/Verb method. Because these two methods play a major role in working with AutoCAD, it's a good idea to familiarize yourself with them early on.

If you need to select objects by their characteristics rather than by their location, see Chapter 15, which describes the Quick Select and Object Selection Filters tools. These tools let you easily select a set of objects based on their properties, including object type, color, layer assignment, and so on.

Selecting Objects in AutoCAD

With many AutoCAD commands, you'll see the Select objects:.prompt. Along with this prompt, the cursor changes from crosshairs to a small square (look back at Figure 2.10). Whenever you see the Select objects: prompt and the square Pickbox cursor, you have several options while making your selection. Often, as you select objects on the screen, you'll change your mind about a selection or accidentally select an object you don't want. Let's look at most of the selection options available in AutoCAD and learn what to do when you make the wrong selection.

Before you continue, you'll turn off two features that, although extremely useful, can be confusing to new users. These features are called Running Osnaps and Osnap Tracking. You'll get a chance to explore these features in depth later in this book, but for now follow these steps to turn them off:

1. Check to see if either Object Snap or Object Snap Tracking is turned on in the status bar. If they're turned on, they will be a light blue. Also make sure that Quick Properties is off.

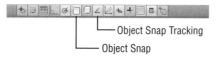

2. To turn off Object Snap or Object Snap Tracking, click the tool in the status bar. When turned off, they turn gray.

Now, let's see how to select an object in AutoCAD:

1. Choose Move from the Home tab's Modify panel, or type **M**↵.

2. At the Select objects: prompt, click each of the two horizontal lines that constitute the door. As you know, whenever AutoCAD wants you to select objects, the cursor turns into the small square Pickbox. This tells you that you're in Object Selection mode. As you place the cursor over an object, it appears thicker to give you a better idea of what you're about to select. As you click an object, it's highlighted, as shown in Figure 2.14.

If objects don't become "thicker" as you roll over them with your selection cursor, the Selection preview system variable may be turned off. You can turn it back on by entering **selectionpreview**⏎ **3**⏎. This setting can also be found in the Selection tab of the Options dialog box. See Appendix B for more on the Options dialog box and Appendix D for more on system variables.

3. After making your selections, you may decide to deselect some items. Enter **U**⏎ from the keyboard. Notice that one line is no longer highlighted. When you type **U**⏎, objects are deselected, one at a time, in reverse order of selection.

4. You can deselect objects in another way. Hold down the Shift key and click the remaining highlighted line. It reverts to a solid line, showing you that it's no longer selected for editing.

FIGURE 2.14
Selecting the lines of the door and seeing them highlighted

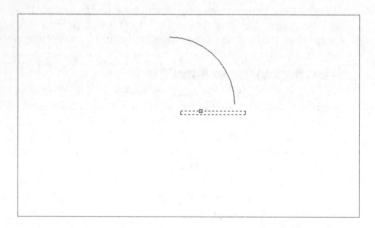

5. By now, you've deselected both lines. Let's try another method for selecting groups of objects. To select objects with a window selection, type **W**⏎. The cursor changes to a Point Selection cursor, and the prompt changes to

   `Specify first corner:`

6. Click a point below and to the left of the rectangle representing the door. As you move your cursor across the screen, a selection window appears and stretches across the drawing area. Also notice that the window has a blue tint.

7. After the selection window completely encloses the door but not the arc, click this location to highlight the entire door. This window selects only objects that are completely enclosed by the window, as shown in Figure 2.15.

Don't confuse the selection window you're creating here with the zoom window you used in Chapter 1, which defines an area of the drawing you want to enlarge. Remember that the Window option works differently under the Zoom command than it does for other editing commands.

FIGURE 2.15
Selecting the
door in a selection
window

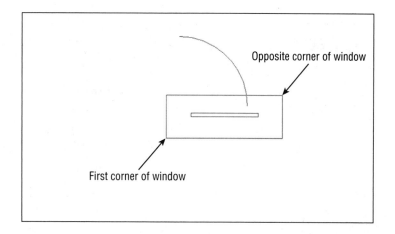

Opposite corner of window

First corner of window

8. Press ↵. This tells AutoCAD that you've finished selecting objects. It's important to remember to press ↵ as soon as you finish selecting the objects you want to edit. A new prompt, Specify base point or [Displacement] <Displacement>:, appears. The cursor changes to its Point Selection mode.

Now you've seen how the selection process works in AutoCAD—but you're in the middle of the Move command. The next section discusses the prompt that's on your screen and describes how to enter base points and displacement distances.

PROVIDING BASE POINTS

When you move or copy objects, AutoCAD prompts you for a base point, which is a difficult concept to grasp. AutoCAD must be told specifically *from* where and *to* where the move occurs. The *base point* is the exact location from which you determine the distance and direction of the move. After the base point is determined, you can tell AutoCAD where to move the object in relation to that point.

Follow these steps to practice using base points:

1. To select a base point, press Shift+right-click. A menu appears, displaying the Object Snap options (see Figure 2.16).

When you right-click the mouse, make sure the cursor is within the AutoCAD drawing area; otherwise, you won't get the results described in this book.

2. Choose Intersection from the Object Snap menu. The Object Snap menu closes.

3. Move the cursor to the lower-right corner of the door. Notice that as you approach the corner, a small x-shaped graphic appears on the corner. This is called an *Osnap marker*.

4. After the x-shaped marker appears, hold the mouse motionless for a second or two. A tool tip appears, telling you the current osnap point AutoCAD has selected.

5. Click the left mouse button to select the intersection indicated by the Osnap marker. Whenever you see the osnap marker at the point you want to select, you don't have to point exactly at the location with your cursor. Just left-click the mouse to select the exact osnap point (see Figure 2.17). In this case, you selected the exact intersection of two lines.

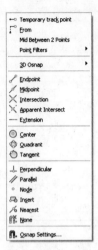

FIGURE 2.17
Using the Point
Selection cursor
and Osnap marker

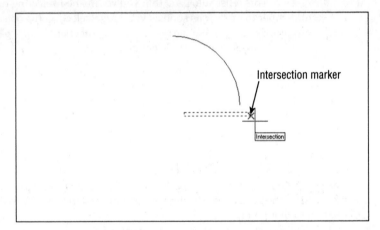

6. At the Specify second point or <use first point as displacement>: prompt, hold down the Shift key and right-click again to open the Object Snap menu.

7. This time you'll use the Endpoint osnap, but instead of clicking the option with the mouse, type **E**.

8. Pick the lower-right end of the arc you drew earlier. (Remember that you need to move your cursor close to the endpoint just until the Osnap marker appears.) The door moves so that the corner connects exactly with the endpoint of the arc (see Figure 2.18).

As you can see, the osnap options let you select specific points on an object. You used Endpoint and Intersection in this exercise, but other options are available. Chapter 3 discusses some of the other osnap options. You may have also noticed that the Osnap marker is different for each of the options you used. You'll learn more about osnaps in Chapter 3. Now, let's continue with our look at point selection.

FIGURE 2.18
Moving the rectangle to its new position using the Endpoint osnap

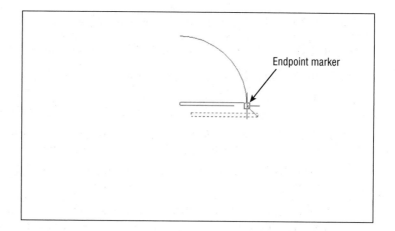

Endpoint marker

CONTROLLING THE STATUS BAR DISPLAY

To the far right of the status bar, you'll see a downward-pointing arrow. This arrow opens a menu that controls the display of the status bar. You use this menu to turn the items in the status bar on or off. A checkmark by an item indicates that it's currently on. If for some reason you don't see all the buttons mentioned in the previous exercise, check this menu to make sure all the status-bar options are turned on. Note that AutoCAD LT doesn't have an Otrack option in the status bar.

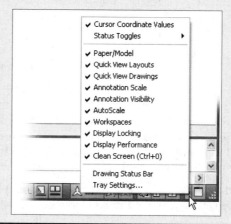

You may have noticed the statement Use first point as displacement in the prompt in step 6. This means that if you press ↵ instead of clicking a point, the object will move a distance based on the coordinates of the point you selected as a base point. If, for example, the point you click for the base point is at coordinate 2,4, the object will move 2 units in the X axis and 4 units in the Y axis.

If you want to specify an exact distance and direction by typing a value, select any point on the screen as a base point. As an alternative, you can type @ followed by ↵ at the base point prompt; then, enter the second point's location in relative coordinates. Remember that @ means the last point selected. In the next exercise, you'll try moving the entire door an exact distance of 1 unit at a 45° angle. Metric users will move the door 3 units at a 45° angle. Here are the steps:

1. Click the Move tool on the Home tab's Modify panel.

2. Type **P**↵. The set of objects you selected in the previous exercise is highlighted. P is a selection option that selects the previously selected set of objects.

3. You're still in Object Selection mode, so click the arc to include it in the set of selected objects. The entire door, including the arc, is highlighted.

4. Press ↵ to tell AutoCAD that you've finished your selection. The cursor changes to Point Selection mode.

5. At the `Specify base point or [Displacement] <Displacement>:` prompt, choose a point on the screen between the door and the left side of the screen (see Figure 2.19).

FIGURE 2.19
The highlighted door and the base point just to the left of the door. Note that the base point doesn't need to be on the object that you're moving.

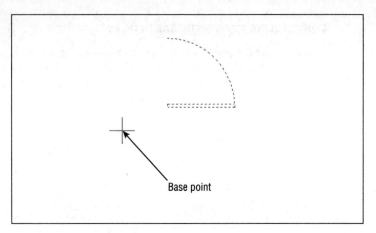

Base point

6. Move the cursor around slowly and notice that the door moves as if the base point you selected were attached to it. The door moves with the cursor, at a fixed distance from it. This demonstrates how the base point relates to the objects you select.

7. Type **@1<45**↵. (Metric users should type **@3<45**↵.) The door moves to a new location on the screen at a distance of 1 unit (3 for metric users) from its previous location and at an angle of 45°.

If AutoCAD is waiting for a command, you can repeat the last command used by pressing the spacebar or pressing ↵. You can also right-click in the drawing area and select the option at the top of the list. If you right-click the Command window, a shortcut menu offers the most recent commands.

This exercise illustrates that the base point doesn't have to be on the object you're manipulating; it can be virtually anywhere on your drawing. You also saw how to reselect a group of objects that were selected previously without having to duplicate the selection process.

Using Noun/Verb Selection

Nearly all graphics programs today allow the Noun/Verb method for selecting objects. This method requires you to select objects before you issue a command to edit them—that is, you identify the "noun" (the object you want to work on) before the "verb" (the action you want to perform on it). The following exercises show you how to use the Noun/Verb method in AutoCAD.

You've seen that when AutoCAD is waiting for a command, it displays the crosshair cursor with the small square. As mentioned, this square is a pickbox superimposed on the cursor. It indicates that you can select objects even while the Command prompt appears at the bottom of the screen and no command is currently active. The square momentarily disappears when you're in a command that asks you to select points.

OTHER SELECTION OPTIONS

There are several other selection options you haven't tried yet. You'll see how these options work in exercises later in this book. Or, if you're adventurous, try them now on your own. To use these options, type their keyboard abbreviations (shown in brackets in the following list) at any Select objects: prompt.

Add [add↵]   Switches from Remove mode to the Add mode. See the description for Remove later in this sidebar.

All [all↵]   Selects all the objects in a drawing except those in frozen or locked layers. (See Chapter 5 for information on layers.)

Box [b↵]   Forces the standard selection window so a left-to-right selection uses a standard window and a right-to-left selection uses a crossing window.

Crossing [c↵]   Similar to the Window selection option (described later in this sidebar) but selects anything that is entirely within or crosses through the window that you define.

Crossing Polygon [cp↵]   Acts exactly like Window Polygon (see later in this sidebar), but like the Crossing selection option, selects anything that crosses through a polygon boundary.

Fence [f↵]   Selects objects that are crossed by a temporary line called a *fence*. This operation is like using a line to cross out the objects you want to select. After you invoke this option, you can then pick points, as when you're drawing a series of line segments. After you finish drawing the fence, press ↵, and then go on to select other objects or press ↵ again to finish your selection.

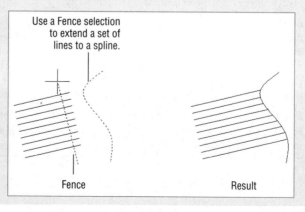

Use a Fence selection to extend a set of lines to a spline.

Fence

Result

Group [g↵]   Allows you to select a group by name.

Last [l↵]   Selects the last object you created.

Multiple [m↵]   Lets you select several objects first, before AutoCAD highlights them. In a large file, selecting objects individually can cause AutoCAD to pause after each selection while it locates and highlights each object. The Multiple option can speed things up by letting you first select all the objects quickly and then highlight them all by pressing ↵. This has no menu equivalent.

Previous [p↵]   Selects the last object or set of objects that was edited or changed.

Remove [r↵]   Switches to a selection mode whereby the objects you click are removed from the selection set.

Window [w↵]   Forces a standard window selection. This option is useful when your drawing area is too crowded to use the Autoselect feature to place a window around a set of objects. (See the Auto entry later in this sidebar.) It prevents you from accidentally selecting an object with a single pick when you're placing your window.

Window Polygon [wp↵]   Lets you select objects by enclosing them in an irregularly shaped polygon boundary. When you use this option, you see the First polygon point: prompt. You then pick points to define the polygon boundary. As you pick points, the Specify endpoint of line or [Undo]: prompt appears. Select as many points as you need to define the boundary. You can undo boundary line segments as you go by pressing U↵. With the boundary defined, press ↵. The bounded objects are highlighted and the Select objects: prompt returns, allowing you to use more selection options.

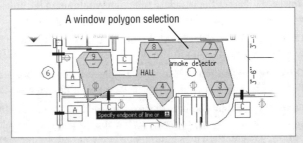

A window polygon selection

The following two selection options are also available but are seldom used. They're intended for use in creating custom menu options or custom tools:

Auto [au↵]   Forces the standard automatic window or crossing window when a point is picked and no object is found. (See the section "Using Autoselect" later in this chapter.) A standard window is produced when the two window corners are picked from left to right. A crossing window is produced when the two corners are picked from right to left. After this option is selected, it remains active for the duration of the current command. Auto is intended for use on systems on which the Autoselect feature has been turned off.

Single [si↵]   Forces the current command to select only a single object. If you use this option, you can pick a single object and the current command acts on that object as if you had pressed ↵ immediately after selecting it. This has no menu equivalent.

In addition to Noun/Verb selection, AutoCAD offers selection options that let you use familiar GUI techniques. See Appendix B to learn how you can control object-selection methods. This appendix also describes how to change the size of the Standard cursor.

Try moving objects by first selecting them and then using the Move command:

1. Press the Esc key twice to make sure AutoCAD isn't in the middle of a command you might have accidentally issued. Then click the arc. The arc is highlighted, and you may also see squares and arrowheads appear at various points on the arc. As stated earlier, these squares and arrowheads are called *grips*. You'll get a chance to work with them later.

2. Choose Move from the Home tab's Modify panel. The cursor changes to Point Selection mode. Notice that the grips on the arc disappear but the arc is still selected.

3. At the `Specify base point or [Displacement] <Displacement>:` prompt, pick any point on the screen. The following prompt appears:

   ```
   Specify second point or
   <use first point as displacement>:
   ```

4. Type **@1<0↵**. Metric users should type **@3<0↵**. The arc moves to a new location 1 unit (3 units for metric users) to the right.

If this exercise doesn't work as described here, chances are the Noun/Verb setting has been turned off on your copy of AutoCAD. To turn on the Noun/Verb setting, choose Options from the Application menu to open the Options dialog box and then click the Selection tab. In the Selection Modes group, place a checkmark in the check box next to the Noun/Verb Selection option and click OK.

In this exercise, you picked the arc *before* issuing the Move command. Then, when you clicked the Move tool, you didn't see the `Select objects:` prompt. Instead, AutoCAD assumed you wanted to move the arc that you selected and went directly to the `Specify base point or [Displacement] <Displacement>:` prompt.

USING AUTOSELECT

Next you'll move the rest of the door in the same direction by using the Autoselect feature:

1. Pick a point just above and to the left of the rectangle representing the door. Be sure not to pick the door itself. A selection window appears that you can drag across the screen as you move the cursor. If you move the cursor to the left of the last point selected, the window outline appears dotted with a green tint inside the window (see the first image in Figure 2.20). If you move the cursor to the right of that point, the outline appears solid with a blue tint inside (see the second image in Figure 2.20).

2. Pick a point below and to the right of the door so that the door is completely enclosed by the window but not the arc, as shown in the bottom image in Figure 2.20. The door is highlighted (and again, you may see grips appear at the lines' endpoints and midpoints).

3. Click the Move tool again. Just as in the preceding exercise, the `Specify base point or [Displacement] <Displacement>:` prompt appears.

4. Pick any point on the screen; then enter **@1<0↵**. Metric users should enter **@3<0↵**. The door joins with the arc.

The two selection windows you've just seen—the blue solid one and the dotted green one—represent a standard window and a crossing window. If you use a *standard window,* anything completely within the window is selected. If you use a *crossing window,* anything that crosses through the window is selected. These two types of windows start automatically when you click any blank portion of the drawing area with a Standard cursor or a Point Selection cursor, hence the name *Autoselect.*

FIGURE 2.20
The dotted window (first image) indicates a crossing selection; the solid window (second image) indicates a standard selection window.

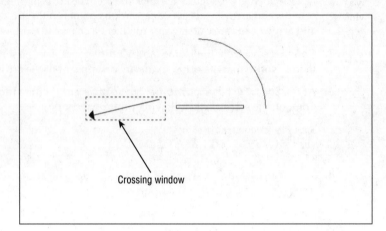

Crossing window

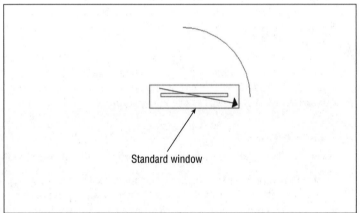

Standard window

Next, you'll select objects with an automatic crossing window:

1. Pick a point below and to the right of the door. As you move the cursor left, the crossing (dotted) window appears.

2. Select the next point so that the window encloses the door and part of the arc (see Figure 2.21). The entire door, including the arc, is highlighted.

3. Click the Move tool.

4. Pick any point on the screen; then enter **@1<180**↵. Metric users should type **@3<180**↵. The door moves back to its original location.

You'll find that, in most cases, the Autoselect standard and crossing windows are all you need when selecting objects. They really save you time, so you'll want to become familiar with these features.

FIGURE 2.21
The door enclosed by a crossing window

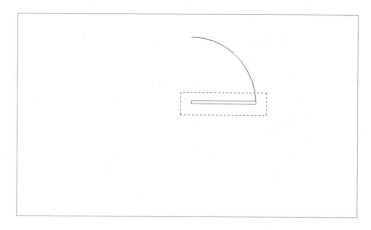

Before continuing, click the Save tool in the Quick Access toolbar to save the Door.dwg file. You won't want to save the changes you make in the next section, so saving now stores the current condition of the file on your hard disk for safekeeping.

RESTRICTIONS ON NOUN/VERB OBJECT SELECTION

For many of the modifying or construction-oriented commands, the Noun/Verb selection method is inappropriate because for those commands, you must select more than one set of objects. You'll know whether a command accepts the Noun/Verb selection method right away. Commands that don't accept the Noun/Verb selection method clear the selection and then ask you to select an object or set of objects.

If you'd like to take a break, now is a good time to do so. If you want, exit AutoCAD, and return to this point in the tutorial later. When you return, start AutoCAD and open the Door.dwg file.

Editing with Grips

Earlier, when you selected the door, grips appeared at the endpoints, center points, and midpoints of the lines and arcs. You can use grips to make direct changes to the shape of objects or to move and copy them quickly.

If you didn't see grips on the door in the previous exercise, your version of AutoCAD may have the Grips feature turned off. To turn them on, refer to the information on grips in Appendix B.

So far, you've seen how operations in AutoCAD have a discrete beginning and ending. For example, to draw an arc, you first issue the Arc command and then go through a series of operations, including answering prompts and picking points. When you're finished, you have an arc and AutoCAD is ready for the next command.

The Grips feature, on the other hand, plays by a different set of rules. Grips offer a small yet powerful set of editing functions that don't conform to the lockstep command/prompt/input routine you've seen so far. As you work through the following exercises, it's helpful to think of grips as a subset of the standard method of operation in AutoCAD.

To practice using the Grips feature, you'll make some temporary modifications to the door drawing.

Stretching Lines by Using Grips

In this exercise, you'll stretch one corner of the door by grabbing the grip points of two lines:

1. Press the Esc key to make sure you're not in the middle of a command. Click a point below and to the left of the door to start a selection window.

2. Use the Zoom Realtime tool from the Zoom tool in the View tab's Navigate panel to adjust your view so the size of the door is similar to what is shown in Figure 2.22.

3. Click above and to the right of the rectangular part of the door and then place the selection window around the door and click to select it.

4. Place the cursor on the lower-left corner grip of the rectangle, *but don't press the mouse button yet*. Notice that the cursor jumps to the grip point and that the grip changes color.

5. Move the cursor to another grip point. Notice again how the cursor jumps to it. When placed on a grip, the cursor moves to the exact center of the grip point. This means, for example, that if the cursor is placed on an endpoint grip, it's on the exact endpoint of the object.

6. Move the cursor to the upper-left corner grip of the rectangle and click. The grip becomes a solid color and is now a *hot grip*. The prompt displays the following message:

```
**STRETCH**
Specify stretch point or [Base point/Copy/Undo/eXit]:
```

This prompt tells you that Stretch mode is active. Notice the options in the prompt. As you move the cursor, the corner follows, and the lines of the rectangle stretch (see Figure 2.22).

You can control the size and color of grips by using the Selection tab in the Options dialog box; see Appendix B for details.

7. Move the cursor upward toward the top end of the arc and click that point. The rectangle deforms, with the corner placed at your pick point (see Figure 2.22).

Here you saw that a command called Stretch is issued by clicking a grip point. As you'll see in these next steps, a handful of other hot-grip commands are also available:

1. Notice that the grips are still active. Click the grip point that you moved before to make it a hot grip again.

2. Right-click the mouse to open a shortcut menu that contains a list of grip edit options (see Figure 2.23).

When you click the joining grip point of two contiguous line segments, AutoCAD selects the overlapping grips of two lines. When you stretch the corner away from its original location, the endpoints of both lines follow.

3. Choose Base Point from the list, and then click a point to the right of the hot grip. Now as you move the cursor, the hot grip moves relative to the cursor.

FIGURE 2.22
Stretching lines by using hot grips. The first image shows the rectangle's corner being stretched upward. The next image shows the new location of the corner at the top of the arc.

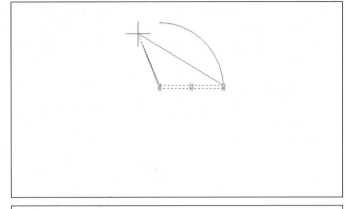

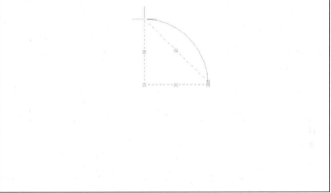

FIGURE 2.23
A list of grip edit options

4. Right-click again, choose Copy from the shortcut menu, and enter @1<-30↵. (Metric users should enter @3<-30↵.) Instead of the hot grip moving and the lines changing, copies of the two lines are made with their endpoints 1 unit (or 3 units for metric users) below and to the right of the first set of endpoints.

5. Pick another point just below the last. More copies are made.

6. Press ↵ or enter **X**↵ to exit Stretch mode. You can also right-click again and choose Exit from the shortcut menu.

In this exercise, you saw that you can select a base point other than the hot grip. You also saw how you can specify relative coordinates to move or copy a hot grip. Finally, you saw that with grips selected on an object, right-clicking the mouse opens a shortcut menu that contains grip edit options.

Moving and Rotating with Grips

As you've just seen, the Grips feature is an alternative method for editing your drawings. You've already seen how you can stretch endpoints, but you can do much more with grips. The next exercise demonstrates some other options. You'll start by undoing the modifications you made in the preceding exercise:

1. Type **U⏎**. The copies of the stretched lines disappear.

2. Press ⏎ again. The deformed door snaps back to its original form.

Pressing ⏎ at the Command prompt causes AutoCAD to repeat the last command entered—in this case, U.

3. You are going to select the entire door. First click a blank area below and to the right of the door.

4. Move the cursor to a location above and to the left of the rectangular portion of the door and click. Because you went from right to left, you created a crossing window. Recall that the crossing window selects anything enclosed and crossing through the window.

5. Click the lower-left grip of the rectangle to turn it into a hot grip. Just as before, as you move your cursor, the corner stretches.

6. Right-click and choose Move from the shortcut menu. The Command window displays the following:

   ```
   **MOVE**
   Specify move point or [Base point/Copy/Undo/eXit]
   ```

Now as you move the cursor, the entire door moves with it.

7. Position the door near the center of the screen and click. The door moves to the center of the screen. Notice that the Command prompt returns but the door remains highlighted, indicating that it's still selected for the next operation.

8. Click the lower-left grip again, right-click, and choose Rotate from the shortcut menu. The Command window displays the following:

   ```
   **ROTATE**
   Specify rotation angle or [Base point/Copy/Undo/Reference/eXit]:
   ```

As you move the cursor, the door rotates about the grip point.

9. Position the cursor so that the door rotates approximately 180° (see Figure 2.24). Then Ctrl+click the mouse (hold down the Ctrl key and press the left mouse button). A copy of the door appears in the new rotated position, leaving the original door in place.

FIGURE 2.24
Rotating and copying the door by using a hot grip. Notice that more than one object is affected by the grip edit, even though only one grip is hot.

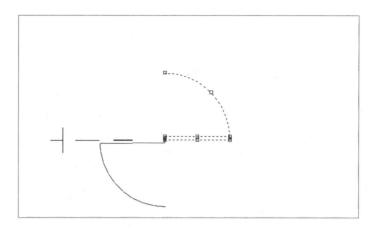

10. Press ↵ to exit Grip Edit mode.

You've seen how the Move command is duplicated in a modified way as a hot-grip command. Other hot-grip commands (Stretch, Rotate, Scale, and Mirror) have similar counterparts in the standard set of AutoCAD commands. You'll see how those work in Chapters 12 and 14.

After you complete any operation by using grips, the objects are still highlighted with their grips active. To clear the grip selection, press the Esc key.

In this exercise, you saw how hot-grip options appear in a shortcut menu. Several other options are available in that menu, including Exit, Base Point, Copy, and Undo..

You can access many of these grip edit options by pressing the spacebar or ↵ while a grip is selected. With each press, the next option becomes active. The options then repeat if you continue to press ↵. The Ctrl key acts as a shortcut to the Copy option. You have to use it only once; then, each time you click a point, a copy is made.

SCALING WITH GRIPS

Grips can be used to scale an object graphically to fit between two other objects. For example, a door can be scaled to fit within a door frame. Place the door so its hinge side is at the door frame and the door is oriented properly for the frame. With the door selected, click the grip at the hinge side. Right-click and select Scale. Type **R**↵, and then click the grip at the hinge again. Click the grip at the end of the arc representing the door swing. Finally, click the opposite side of the door frame.

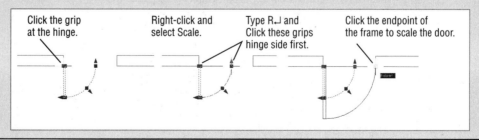

A QUICK SUMMARY OF THE GRIPS FEATURE

The exercises in this chapter include only a few of the grips options. You'll get a chance to use other hot-grip options in later chapters. Meanwhile, here is a summary of the Grips feature:

◆ Clicking endpoint grips stretches those endpoints.

◆ Clicking the midpoint grip of a line moves the entire line.

◆ If two objects meet end to end and you click their overlapping grips, both grips are selected simultaneously.

◆ You can select multiple grips by holding down the Shift key and clicking the desired grips.

◆ When a hot grip is selected, the Stretch, Move, Rotate, Scale, and Mirror options are available to you; right-click the mouse.

◆ You can cycle through the Stretch, Move, Rotate, Scale, and Mirror options by pressing ↵ while a hot grip is selected.

◆ All the hot-grip options let you make copies of the selected objects by either using the Copy option or holding down the Ctrl key while selecting points.

◆ All the hot-grip options let you select a base point other than the originally selected hot grip.

Using Dynamic Input

Earlier in this chapter, you turned off the Dynamic Input display so you could get an uncluttered view of what was going on in AutoCAD's display. In this section, you'll get a chance to explore the Dynamic Input display through grip editing.

You'll start by going back to the original version of the Door.dwg drawing that you saved earlier:

1. Click the Close icon in the upper-right corner of the drawing area.

2. When you're asked if you want to save changes, click No.

3. Click Open from the Quick Access toolbar, and then locate and select the Door.dwg file you saved earlier. You can also open the doorsample.dwg file from the sample files you installed from this book's companion DVD.

4. The door appears in the condition you left it when you last saved the file.

5. Click the Dynamic Input tool in the status bar to turn it on. It should be a light blue color.

6. Click the arc to expose its grips.

7. Place the cursor on the outward-pointing arrow grip at the middle of the arc, but don't click it. (This is called *hovering* over a grip.) You see the dimensions of the arc appear. This feature is useful when you need to check the size of objects you've drawn (see Figure 2.25).

FIGURE 2.25
Hovering over
a grip

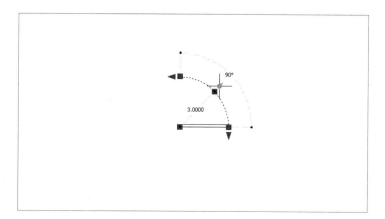

8. Click the arrow you're hovering over. The Command prompt appears at the cursor, and the radius dimension changes to a text box.

9. Move the cursor toward the upper-right corner of the drawing area. The radius dimension changes as you move the cursor.

10. Enter 4↵. Metric users enter 130↵. As you type, the new value appears in the radius dimension. When you press ↵, the arc changes to the new radius.

11. Click the Undo button to revert to the original arc size.

Here you saw the basic methods for using the Dynamic Input display. You can hover over an object's grip to display its dimensions. Click the grip and, if available, those dimensions can be edited directly through the keyboard. In this example, you were able to change the radius of the arc to an exact value. Depending on the grip you click, you can change a dimension through direct keyboard input. For example, if you want to change the degrees the arc covers instead of its radius, you can click the arrow grip at either end of the arc.

Next, try Dynamic Input display on a line:

1. Click the bottommost line of the door, as shown in Figure 2.26; hover over the rightmost grip on the selected line. Just as with the arc, you can see the dimensions of the line, including its length and directional angle.

2. Click the grip you're hovering over, and then move the cursor upward and to the right. You see two dimensions: One indicates the overall length and the other shows the change in length of the line. You also see the Command prompt at the cursor. Notice that the dimension indicating the change in length is highlighted (see Figure 2.27).

FIGURE 2.26
Selecting a line on
the door

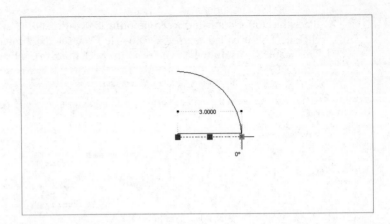

FIGURE 2.27
The overall length
dimension and the
change in length
dimension

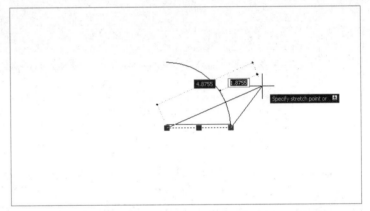

3. Enter **1** and press the Tab key to increase the length of the line by 1 unit. Metric users should enter **30** and press the Tab key. Now as you move the cursor, the line is locked at a new length that is 1 or 30 units longer than its original length. Also notice that the overall dimension is highlighted. You also see a lock icon on the length dimension (see Figure 2.28).

FIGURE 2.28
The line locked at a
new length

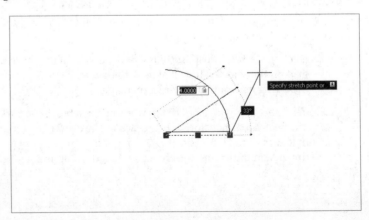

4. Press the Tab key again. The angle value is highlighted.

5. Enter **45** and press the Tab key to lock the angle of the line at 45°.

6. Make sure the cursor isn't too close to the locked endpoint of the line and then click the left mouse button. The line is now in its new orientation with a length of 4 (130 for metric users) and an angle of 45°, as shown in Figure 2.29.

FIGURE 2.29
The line's new length and orientation

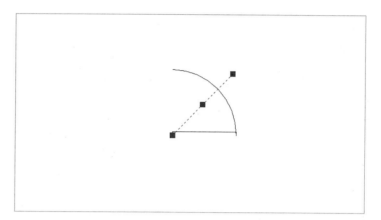

You can see that the Dynamic Input display lets you enter specific dimensions for the selected object, making possible precise changes in an object's size.

You can also use the Dynamic Input display while using other grip-editing features. Try the following exercise to see how the Dynamic Input display works while moving objects:

1. Click above and to the right of the door drawing to start a crossing selection window.

2. Click below and to the left to select the entire door drawing.

3. Click the middle grip of the arc.

4. Right-click and choose Move. You see the Command prompt at the cursor with the distance value highlighted. As you move the cursor, you can see the distance and angle values in the Dynamic Input display change (see Figure 2.30).

FIGURE 2.30
The Dynamic Input display

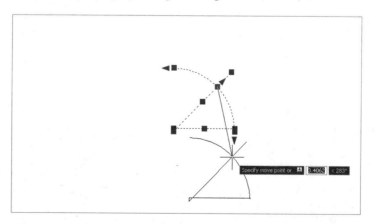

5. Enter **4**, and then press the Tab key. As you move the cursor, the distance from the original location of the arc's midpoint is locked at 4 units. The angle value is now highlighted and available for editing.

6. Enter **225**, and then press the Tab key to lock the angle at 225°.

7. Click a location away from the door drawing. The door moves to its new location, exactly 4 units from its original location.

As you can see from these exercises, the Dynamic Input display adds some helpful methods for editing objects. To summarize, here is a rundown of the basic Dynamic Input display features:

♦ You can easily turn the Dynamic Input display on or off by clicking the Dynamic Input tool in the status bar.

♦ You can quickly check the dimensions of an object by selecting it and then hovering over a grip.

♦ You can alter an object's dimensions by entering values into the highlighted dimensions of the Dynamic Input display.

♦ To highlight a different dimension, press the Tab key.

♦ To accept any changes you've made using Dynamic Input display, click the mouse at a location away from the grip you're editing. You can also press ⏎ or the spacebar.

Not all grips offer dimensions that can be edited. If you click the midpoint grip on the line, for example, you won't see the dimensions of the line, although you'll see the Command prompt and you'll be able to enter a new coordinate for the midpoint.

As you've seen in the arc and line examples, each object offers a different set of dimensions. If you like the way the Dynamic Input display works, you can experiment on other types of objects. AutoCAD offers a number of settings that let you control the behavior of the Dynamic Input display. You'll learn about those settings later in Appendix B.

TYPING COORDINATES WITH DYNAMIC INPUT

When entering coordinates through the keyboard while Dynamic Input is on, you have to use a slightly different notation for relative and absolute coordinates. If you're entering relative coordinates, you can leave off the @ sign, so instead of typing **@12,9**⏎, you can simply type **12,9**⏎. If you are entering absolute coordinates, you need to precede your coordinate list with a # sign. So instead of entering **1,1**⏎ to specify a point at coordinate 1,1, you would need to enter **#1,1**⏎.

Getting Help

Eventually, you'll find yourself somewhere without documentation and you'll have a question about an AutoCAD feature. AutoCAD provides an online help facility that gives you information on nearly any topic related to AutoCAD. Here's how to find help:

1. Click the Help tool from the InfoCenter to open the AutoCAD 2011 Help website.

2. Take a moment to see what is offered on this website. On the left is a column of topics that act like tabs. The User Guide is at the top followed by Command Reference, Customization Guide and so on.

3. Click Command Reference. The middle of the page changes to show the Commands, System Variables, and Miscellaneous headings along with an alphabetical list that acts like an index.

4. Click *M* under the Commands heading and you see a list of command names that start with *M*.

You also have the Home and Index options in the upper left of the page as well as a search box in the upper right.

FIGURE 2.31
The AutoCAD 2011
Help website

Using the InfoCenter

If you want to find information about a topic based on a keyword, you can use the InfoCenter in the upper-right corner of the AutoCAD window. Follow these steps:

1. Type **change** in the InfoCenter text box at the top right of the AutoCAD window, and then click the Search tool to the right of the input box (see Figure 2.32).

2. The InfoCenter expands to display a list of resources for the word *change*.

This list is a bit overwhelming. You can use Boolean AND, OR, NEAR, and NOT in conjunction with other keywords to help filter your searches, just as in a typical search engine that you might use in your web browser. After you've found a topic you want, select it from the Select Topic list, and then click the Display button to display information related to the topic in the panel on the right.

FIGURE 2.32
The InfoCenter
displays a list of
resources

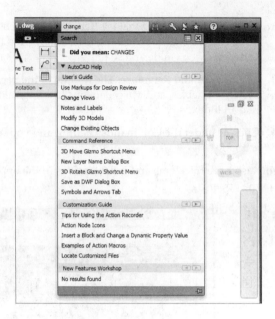

Besides using a keyword for searches, you can use phrases or questions. Try the following steps to see how you can use a question:

1. In the InfoCenter text box, type **How do I zoom into my view**⏎. The list below the text box changes to show several items that relate to adjusting views in AutoCAD.

2. Click Pan Or Zoom A View from the list. The AutoCAD 2011 Help web-site opens to display a description of how the Pan or Zoom command works (see Figure 2.33).

FIGURE 2.33
The AutoCAD
2011 Help web-site
opens to the Pan or
Zoom a View topic

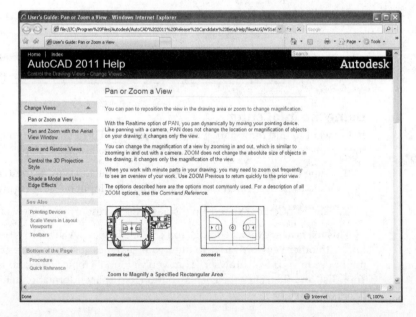

Using Context-Sensitive Help

AutoCAD also provides *context-sensitive help* to give you information related to the command you're currently using. To see how this works, try the following:

1. Close or minimize the Help window, and return to the AutoCAD window.

2. Click the Move tool in the Home tab's Modify panel to start the Move command.

3. Press the F1 function key or click the Help tool in the InfoCenter to open the Help window. A description of the Move command appears in the AutoCAD 2011 Help web-site.

4. Press the Esc key to exit the Move command.

Finding Additional Sources of Help

The InfoCenter is the main online source for reference material, but you can also find answers to your questions through the other options in the InfoCenter's Help flyout menu. You can open this menu by clicking the arrowhead next to the InfoCenter Help tool. Here is a brief description of them:

Help   Opens the AutoCAD 2011 Help web-site.

Welcome screen   In a new installation of AutoCAD, you will see a welcome screen that offers information on how to use AutoCAD. If you're totally new to AutoCAD, the welcome screen offers some basic tutorials on how to draw. You'll also find information on other learning resources.

New Features Workshop   The New Features Workshop option offers descriptions and tutorials focused on the new features in AutoCAD 2011. You can update this unique support tool through the Autodesk website.

Additional Resources   Here you'll find several options to choose from.

Support Knowledge Base takes you to Autodesk's knowledge base site, which offers answers to your technical support questions. You can often find answers to problems here.

Online Training Resources takes you to the Autodesk Training site, where you'll find further information on where to get training and tutorial information.

If you're a developer, you'll be interested in the Online Developer Center. This option takes you to the Autodesk Developer Center website, where you can find more information about getting started with your own AutoCAD-related application.

If you're already customizing AutoCAD, the Developer Help option takes you to the Developer Help section of the AutoCAD Help window. Here you'll find specific information about how to use the customization tools built into AutoCAD.

Finally, if you would like to join an established community of AutoCAD users, the Autodesk User Group International option takes you to the AUGI website. AUGI offers a wide range of resources for users of Autodesk products. You can join a forum to discuss issues with other AutoCAD users. AUGI also offers its own knowledge base.

Send Feedback   Autodesk offers the product feedback web page, which enables you to send comments to Autodesk. The Send Feedback option takes you directly to this page.

Customer Involvement Program   The Customer Involvement Program is really a way for Autodesk to monitor the condition of AutoCAD by allowing its customers to send comments about program errors or crashes. This voluntary program lets you participate anonymously, or you can provide contact information for follow-up contacts.

About   This option provides information about the version of AutoCAD you're using.

Staying Informed with the Communication Center

Another feature that can help you stay informed about the latest news on AutoCAD is the Communication Center. To the far right of InfoCenter, you'll see the Communication Center icon. Click the Communication Center icon to open the Communication Center list (see Figure 2.34).

FIGURE 2.34

AutoCAD 2011 Communication Center icon

The Communication Center offers a way to stay informed about the latest software updates and support issues for AutoCAD. Click the InfoCenter Settings tool at the top of the Communication Center list to open the InfoCenter Settings dialog box (see Figure 2.35).

FIGURE 2.35

AutoCAD 2011 InfoCenter Settings dialog box

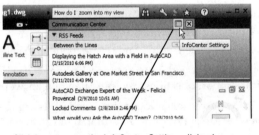

Click here to open the InfoCenter Settings dialog box

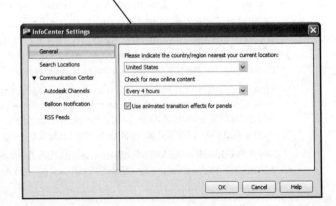

You may need to minimize the size of some of the panels to get to the Settings button. Here you can select your country from the Country/Region drop-down list to ensure that the information is correct for your country. The Check For New Online Content option lets you select the frequency at which the Communication Center checks for new information; you can choose 1 hour, 4 hours, daily, weekly, monthly, or never. If you want to turn off the balloon message, you can check the Balloon Notification settings, which let you control the conditions for balloon notifications.

The Communication Center works best if you use an "always on" Internet connection such as DSL or high-speed cable. If you don't have such a connection, you can set the Check For New Content option to Never. You can then check for updates when you connect to the Internet.

Displaying Data in a Text Window

You may have noticed that as you work in AutoCAD, the activity displayed in the Command window scrolls up. Sometimes, it's helpful to view information that has scrolled past the view shown in the Command window. For example, you can review the command activity from your session to check input values or to recall other data-entry information. Try the following exercise to see how the Text Window works:

1. From the Home tab's Properties panel, click the List tool.

2. At the `Select objects:` prompt, click the arc and press ↵. Information about the arc is displayed in the AutoCAD Text Window (see Figure 2.36). Toward the bottom is the list of the arc's properties. Don't worry if the meaning of some listed properties isn't obvious yet; as you work through this book, you'll learn what the properties of an object mean.

FIGURE 2.36
The AutoCAD Text Window showing the data displayed by the List tool

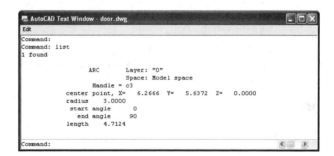

3. Press F2 to close the AutoCAD Text Window. Pressing F2 is a quick way to switch between the drawing editor and the AutoCAD Text Window.

The scroll bar to the right of the AutoCAD Text Window lets you scroll to earlier events. You can even set the number of lines that AutoCAD retains by using the Options dialog box, or you can have AutoCAD record the AutoCAD Text Window information in a text file.

When you have more than one document open, the AutoCAD Text Window displays a listing for the drawing that is currently active.

Displaying the Properties of an Object

While we're on the subject of displaying information, you'll want to know about the Properties palette. In the preceding exercise, you saw how the List command showed some information regarding the properties of an object, such as the location of an arc's center and endpoints. You can also double-click an object to display a Properties palette that shows similar information. (You might accidentally display the Properties palette from time to time! Since the Properties palette is so useful, you may want to consider leaving it open all the time.)

To see what this palette is for, try the following exercise:

1. Select the arc in the drawing, right-click it, and select Properties to open the Properties palette, which displays a list of the arc's properties. Don't worry if many of the items in this palette are undecipherable; you'll learn more about this palette as you work through the early chapters of this book. For now, just be aware that you can get to this palette with a right-click and that it displays the object's properties. You can also use it to modify many of the properties listed (see Figure 2.37).

FIGURE 2.37
Object Properties palette

2. Click the small Auto-hide box at the top of the Properties palette. It's the icon that looks like a double arrow. The icon changes to a single arrow. The Auto-hide option in the Properties palette lets you keep the palette open without having it take up too much of the drawing area. This can be useful when you need to edit the properties of many objects.

3. Move the cursor away from the Properties palette. The Properties palette collapses so that only the title bar remains.

4. Hover the cursor on the Properties palette title bar. The Properties palette opens to display all the options again.

5. Click the Auto-hide box again to restore the "always open" mode of the palette.

6. Close the Properties palette by clicking the X in its upper corner. (The X appears in the upper-left or upper-right corner, depending on the placement of the palette in the AutoCAD window.) You can also right-click the title bar on the side of the Properties palette and then choose Close from the shortcut menu.

7. You're finished with the door drawing, so choose Close from the Application menu.

8. In the Save Changes dialog box, click the No button. (You've already saved this file just as you want it, so you don't need to save it again.)

In many cases, you can open the Properties palette by double-clicking an object. Some objects, however, display a dialog box to allow you to edit them.

Another feature related to the Properties palette is the Quick Properties tool and palette. If you turn on Quick Properties by clicking the Quick Properties tool in the status bar, you'll see the Quick Properties palette whenever you select an object or set of objects (Figure 2.38).

FIGURE 2.38
The Quick Properties palette

The Quick Properties palette lets you control just a few properties of an object (color, layer, and line type). When turned on, it pops up every time you select an object, so you may want to limit its use to those times when you are adjusting the color, layer, and line type of objects in your drawing.

USING ROTATE REFERENCE TO ALIGN OBJECTS

You can use the Rotate command's Reference option to graphically align a set of objects to another object. For example, suppose you want to rotate a set of circles inside a hexagon to align with the corner of the hexagon.

To do this, you can use the Reference option as follows:

1. Start the Rotate command, and select the circles.

2. At the `Specify base point:` prompt, use the Center osnap to select the center of the hexagon as represented by the central circle. Once you do this, the objects rotate around the selected point as you move your cursor.

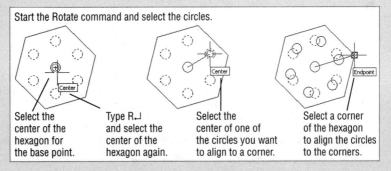

3. At the `Specify rotation angle or [Copy/Reference]:` prompt, enter **R**↵.

4. At the Specify the reference angle <0>: prompt, use the Center osnap to select the center of the hexagon again. You can also enter **@**↵ since the last point you selected was the center.

5. At the Specify second point: prompt, use the Center osnap to select the center of one of the circles you want to align with the hexagon. Now as you move the cursor, the circle whose center you selected is aligned with the cursor angle.

6. At the Specify the new angle or [Points]: prompt, use the Endpoint osnap to select one of the corners of the hexagon. The circles align with the corners.

You can also use grips to align objects. Here's how: Select the object or set of objects and then click a grip. The grip you select becomes the rotation point so select this first grip carefully. Right-click and select Rotate. Type **R**↵ and select the grip you just selected and another point to determine the reference angle. Finally, select the new angle for the object or set of objects. If you want to rotate about a point other than the first grip, use the grip Base right-click option.

The Bottom Line

Specify distances with coordinates.   One of the most basic skills you need to learn is how to indicate exact distances through the keyboard. AutoCAD uses a simple annotation system to indicate distance and direction.

Master It   What would you type to indicate a relative distance of 14 units at a 45 ° angle?

Interpret the cursor modes and understand prompts.   AutoCAD's cursor changes its shape depending on the command that is currently active. These different cursor modes can give you a clue regarding what you should be doing.

Master It   Describe the Point Selection cursor and the Pickbox cursor.

Select objects and edit with grips.   Grips are small squares or arrowheads that appear at key points on the object when they're selected. They offer a powerful way to edit objects.

Master It   How do you select multiple grips?

Use Dynamic Input.   Besides grips, objects display their dimensional properties when selected. These dimensional properties can be edited to change an object's shape.

Master It   How do you turn on Dynamic Input? And once it's on, what key lets you shift between the different dimensions of an object?

Get help.   AutoCAD's Help window is thorough in its coverage of AutoCAD's features. New and experienced users alike can often find answers to their questions thorough the Help window, so it pays to become familiar with it.

Master It   What keyboard key do you press for context-sensitive help?

Display data in a text window.   AutoCAD offers the AutoCAD Text Window, which keeps a running account of the commands you use. This can be helpful in retrieving input that you've entered when constructing your drawing.

Master It   Name a command that displays its results in the AutoCAD Text Window.

Display the properties of an object.   The Properties palette is one of the most useful sources for drawing information. Not only does it list the properties of an object, it lets you change the shape, color, and other properties of objects.

Master It   How do you open the Properties palette for a particular object?

Chapter 3

Setting Up and Using AutoCAD's Drafting Tools

Chapters 1 and 2 covered the basic information you need to understand the workings of AutoCAD. Now you'll put this knowledge to work. In this architectural tutorial, which begins now and continues through Chapter 15, you'll draw an apartment building composed of studios. The tutorial illustrates how to use AutoCAD commands and gives you a solid understanding of the basic AutoCAD package. With these fundamentals, you can use AutoCAD to its fullest potential regardless of the kinds of drawings you intend to create or the enhancement products you may use in the future.

In this chapter, you'll start drawing an apartment's bathroom fixtures. In the process, you'll learn how to use AutoCAD's basic tools. You'll also be introduced to the concept of drawing scale and how the size of what you draw is translated into a paper sheet size.

In this chapter, you'll learn to do the following:

◆ Set up a work area

◆ Explore the drawing process

◆ Plan and lay out a drawing

◆ Use the AutoCAD modes as drafting tools

GET ADDITIONAL HELP ON THE DVD

The companion DVD offers four video tutorials that give you an overview of the main topics of this chapter. The video entitled "Object Snaps" covers the discussion of the Object Snaps found in the later part of this chapter. The video entitled "Setting Up a Drawing" touches on some of the material in "Setting Up a Work Area." "Exploring the Drawing Process" covers the material in the section of the same name. And finally, "Object Snap Tracking" covers the material in "Aligning Objects by Using Object Snap Tracking."

Setting Up a Work Area

Before beginning most drawings, you should set up your work area. To do this, determine the *measurement system*, the *drawing sheet size*, and the *scale* you want to use. The default work area is roughly 16″ × 9″ at full scale, given a decimal measurement system in which 1 unit equals 1 inch.

Metric users will find that the default area is roughly 550 mm × 300 mm, in which 1 unit equals 1 mm. If these are appropriate settings for your drawing, you don't have to do any setting up. It's more likely, however, that you'll make drawings of various sizes and scales. For example, you might want to create a drawing in a measurement system in which you can specify feet, inches, and fractions of inches at 1″ = 1′ scale and print the drawing on an 8½″-×-11″ sheet of paper.

In this section, you'll learn how to set up a drawing exactly the way you want.

Specifying Units

You'll start by creating a new file called Bath. Then you'll set up the unit style.

Use these steps to create the file:

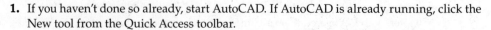

1. If you haven't done so already, start AutoCAD. If AutoCAD is already running, click the New tool from the Quick Access toolbar.

2. In the Select Template dialog box, select acad.dwt and click Open. Metric users should select acadiso.dwt and then click Open.

3. Type Z↵ A↵ or click Zoom All from the Zoom flyout in the navigation bar.

4. Choose Save As from the Application menu.

5. In the Save Drawing As dialog box, enter **Bath** for the filename.

6. Check to make sure you're saving the drawing in the My Documents folder or in the folder where you've chosen to store your exercise files, and then click Save.

USING THE IMPERIAL AND METRIC EXAMPLES

Many of the exercises in this chapter are shown in both the metric and Imperial measurement systems. Be sure that if you start with the Imperial system, you continue with it throughout this book.

The metric settings described in this book are only approximations of their Imperial equivalents. For example, the drawing scale for the metric example is 1:10, which is close to the 1″ = 1′-0″ scale used in the Imperial example. In the grid example, you're asked to use a 30-unit grid, which is close to the 1′ grid of the Imperial example. Dimensions of objects are similar, but not exact. For example, the Imperial version of the tub measures 2′-8″×5′-0″ and the metric version of the tub is 81 cm × 152 cm. The actual metric equivalent of 2′-8″×5′-0″ is 81.28 cm × 152.4 cm. Measurements in the tub example are rounded to the nearest centimeter.

Metric users should also be aware that AutoCAD uses a period as a decimal point instead of the comma used in most European nations, South Africa, and elsewhere. Commas are used in AutoCAD to separate the X, Y, and Z components of a coordinate.

The next thing you want to tell AutoCAD is the *unit style* you intend to use. So far, you've been using the default, which is a generic decimal unit. This unit can be interpreted as inches, centimeters, feet, kilometers or light years. When it comes time to print your drawing, you can tell AutoCAD how to convert these units into a meaningful scale.

If you are a U.S. user, decimal units typically represent inches. If you want to be able to enter distances in feet, you must change the unit style to a style that accepts feet as input. You'll do this through the Drawing Units dialog box shown in Figure 3.1.

If you're a civil engineer, you should know that the Engineering unit style lets you enter feet and decimal feet for distances. For example, the equivalent of 12'-6" is 12.5'. If you use the Engineering unit style, you'll ensure that your drawings conform to the scale of drawings created by your architectural colleagues.

FIGURE 3.1

The Drawing Units dialog box

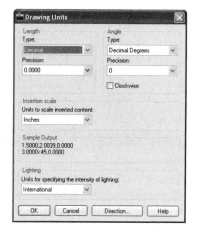

Follow these steps to set a unit style:

1. Click Drawing Utilities ➢ Units from the Application menu or type **Un**⏎ to open the Drawing Units dialog box.

2. Let's look at a few of the options available. Click the Type drop-down list in the Length group. Notice the unit styles in the list.

3. Click Architectural. The Sample Output section of the dialog box shows you what the Architectural style looks like in AutoCAD. Metric users should keep this setting as Decimal.

SHORTCUT TO SETTING UNITS

You can also control the Drawing Units settings by using several system variables. To set the unit style, you can type **'lunits.**⏎ at the Command prompt. (The apostrophe lets you enter this command while in the middle of other commands.) At the **Enter new value for LUNITS <2>:** prompt, enter **4** for Architectural. See Appendix D for other settings.

---

4. Click the Precision drop-down list just below the Type list. Notice the options available. You can set the smallest unit AutoCAD will display in this drawing. For now, leave this setting at its default value of 0'-0 1/16". Metric users will keep the setting at 0.0000.

5. Press the Esc key to close the drop-down list, and then click the Direction button at the bottom of the Drawing Units dialog box to open the Direction Control dialog box. The Direction Control dialog box lets you set the direction for the 0° angle. For now, don't change these settings—you'll read more about them in a moment.

6. Click the Cancel button.

7. Click the drop-down list in the Insertion Scale group. The list shows various units of measure.

8. Click Inches; if you're a metric user, choose Centimeters. This option lets you control how AutoCAD translates drawing scales when you import drawings from outside the current drawing. You'll learn more about this feature in Chapter 29.

9. Click OK in the Drawing Units dialog box to return to the drawing.

If you use the Imperial system of measurement, you selected Architectural measurement units for this tutorial, but your work may require a different unit style. You saw the unit styles available in the Drawing Units dialog box. Table 3.1 shows examples of how the distance 15.5 is entered in each of these styles.

TABLE 3.1:   Measurement systems available in AutoCAD

MEASUREMENT SYSTEM	AUTOCAD'S DISPLAY OF MEASUREMENT
Scientific	1.55E+01 (inches or metric)
Decimal	15.5000 (inches or metric)
Engineering	1'-3.5" (input as 1'3.5")
Architectural	1'-3½" (input as 1'3-½")
Fractional	15½" (input as 15-½")

In the previous exercise, you needed to change only two settings. Let's look at the other Drawing Units settings in more detail. As you read, you may want to refer to Figure 3.1.

Fine-Tuning the Measurement System

Most of the time, you'll be concerned only with the units and angles settings of the Drawing Units dialog box. But as you saw in the preceding exercise, you can control many other settings related to the input and display of units.

TAKING MEASUREMENTS

To measure the distance between two points, click Distance from the Measure flyout on the Home tab's Utilities panel, or type **Di**↵, and then click the two points. (*Di* is the shortcut for entering **Dist**↵.) If this command doesn't give you an accurate distance measurement, examine the Precision option in the Drawing Units dialog box. If it's set too high, the value returned by the Dist command may be rounded to a value greater than your tolerances allow even though the distance is drawn accurately.

The Precision drop-down list in the Length group lets you specify the smallest unit value that you want AutoCAD to display in the status bar and in the prompts. If you choose a measurement system that uses fractions, the Precision list includes fractional units. You can also control this setting with the Luprec system variable.

The Angle group lets you set the style for displaying angles. You have a choice of five angle styles: Decimal Degrees, Degrees/Minutes/Seconds, Grads, Radians, and Surveyor's Units. In the Angle group's Precision drop-down list, you can specify the degree of accuracy you want AutoCAD to display for angles. You can also control these settings with the Aunits and Auprec system variables.

You can find out more about system variables on the AutoCAD 2011 Help website. Select the Command Reference option in the left column of the page, and then select the first letter of a system variable name from the System Variable listing.

You can tell AutoCAD which direction is positive, either clockwise or counterclockwise. The default, which is counterclockwise, is used in this book. The Direction Control dialog box lets you set the direction of the 0 base angle. The default base angle (and the one used throughout this book) is a direction from left to right. However, at times you may want to designate another direction as the 0 base angle. You can also control these settings with the Angbase and Angdir system variables.

The Insertion Scale setting in the Drawing Units dialog box lets you control how blocks from the tool palettes or DesignCenter are scaled as they're imported into your current drawing. A *block* is a collection of drawing objects that form a single object. Blocks are frequently used to create standard symbols. You'll learn more about blocks in Chapter 4. The Insertion Scale setting lets you compensate for drawings of different scales by offering an automatic scale translation when importing blocks from an external file. The Insunits system variable also controls the Insertion Scale setting. You'll learn more about this setting in Chapter 29.

If you're new to AutoCAD, don't worry about the Insertion Scale setting right now. Make a mental note of it. It may come in handy in your work in the future.

Setting Up the Drawing Limits

One of the big advantages of using AutoCAD is that you can draw at full scale; you aren't limited to the edges of a piece of paper the way you are in manual drawing. But you may find it difficult to start drawing without knowing the drawing boundaries. You can set up some arbitrary boundaries using the Limits feature. You got a taste of the Limits feature in Chapter 1. You'll use it again here to set up a work area for your next drawing.

THINGS TO WATCH FOR WHEN ENTERING DISTANCES

When you're using Architectural units, you should be aware of two points:

◆ Use hyphens only to distinguish fractions from whole inches.

◆ You can't use spaces while specifying a dimension. For example, you can specify eight feet, four and one-half inches as 8′4-½″ or 8′4.5, but not as 8′-4 ½″.

These idiosyncrasies are a source of confusion to many architects and engineers new to AutoCAD because the program often displays architectural dimensions in the standard architectural format but doesn't allow you to enter dimensions that way.

Here are some tips for entering distances and angles in unusual situations:

◆ When entering distances in inches and feet, you can omit the inch (″) sign. If you're using the Engineering unit style, you can enter decimal feet and forgo the inch sign entirely.

◆ You can enter fractional distances and angles in any format you like, regardless of the current unit style. For example, you can enter a distance as **@½<1.5708r**, even if your current unit system is set for decimal units and decimal degrees (1.5708r is the radian equivalent of 90°).

◆ If you have your angle units set to degrees, grads, or radians, you don't need to specify g, r, or d after the angle. You do have to specify g, r, or d, however, if you want to use these units when they aren't the current default angle system.

◆ If your current base angle is set to something other than horizontal from left to right, you can use a double less-than symbol (<<) in place of the single less-than symbol (<) to override the current base angle . The << assumes the base angle of 0° to be a direction from left to right and the positive direction to be counterclockwise.

◆ If your current angle system uses a different base angle and direction and you want to specify an angle in the standard base direction, you can use a triple less-than symbol (<<<) to indicate angles. Note that this works only if Dynamic Input is turned off.

◆ You can specify a denominator of any size when specifying fractions. However, be aware that the value you've set for the maximum number of digits to the right of decimal points (under the Precision setting in the Length group of the Drawing Units dialog box) restricts the fractional value AutoCAD reports. For example, if your units are set for a maximum of two digits of decimals and you give a fractional value of 5/32, AutoCAD rounds this value to 3/16. Note that this doesn't affect the accuracy of the actual drawing dimensions.

◆ You can enter decimal feet for distances in the Architectural unit style. For example, you can enter 6′-6″ as **6.5′**.

You'll be drawing a bathroom that is roughly 8′ × 5′ (230 cm × 150 cm for metric users). You'll want to give yourself some extra room around the bathroom, so your drawing limits should be a bit larger than that actual bathroom size. You'll use an area of 11′ × 8′-6″ for the limits of your drawing. Metric users will use an area 297 cm × 210 cm. These sizes will accommodate your bathroom with some room to spare.

Now that you know the area you need, you can use the Limits command to set up the area:

1. Type **Limits**↵.

2. At the `Specify lower left corner or [ON/OFF] <0´-0˝,0´-0˝>:` prompt, specify the lower-left corner of your work area. Press ↵ to accept the default.

3. At the `Specify upper right corner <1´-0˝,0´-9˝>:` prompt, specify the upper-right corner of your work area. (The default is shown in brackets.) Enter **132,102**. Or if you prefer, you can enter **11´,8´6** because you've set up your drawing for architectural units. Metric users should enter **297,210**.

4. Click Zoom All from the Zoom flyout in the navigation bar, or type **Z↵A↵**. Although it appears that nothing has changed, your drawing area is now set to a size that will enable you to draw your bathroom at full scale.

5. Move the cursor to the upper-right corner of the drawing area and watch the coordinate readout. Notice that now the upper-right corner has a Y coordinate of approximately 8´-6˝, or 210 for metric users. The X coordinate depends on the proportion of your AutoCAD window. The coordinate readout also displays distances in feet and inches.

6. Click the Grid Display tool in the status bar to turn off the grid.

In step 5, the coordinate readout shows you that your drawing area is larger than before. The background grid can help you visualize the area you're working with. You can control the grid using the Grid Display tool in the status bar, which you'll learn about toward the end of this chapter. Grid Display shows a background grid that helps you visualize distances and can also show you the limits of your drawing. It can also be a bit distracting for a new user, so I've asked you to turn it off for now.

Looking at an Alternative to Limits

As an alternative to setting up the drawing limits, you can draw a rectangle that outlines the same area used to define the drawing limits. For example, in the previous exercise, you could use the Rectangle tool to draw a rectangle that has its lower-left corner at coordinate 0,0 and its upper-right corner at 132,102 (297,210 for metric users). You can set up the rectangle to be visible without printing using the Layer feature. You'll learn more about layers in Chapter 5.

COORDINATING WITH PAPER SIZES

At this point, you may have questions about how your full-scale drawing will fit onto standard paper sizes. AutoCAD offers several features that give you precise control over the scale of your drawing. These features offer industry-standard scales to match your drawing with any paper size you need. You'll learn more about these features as you work through the chapters of this book. However, if you're anxious to find out about them, look at the sections on layouts in Chapters 8 and 16 and also check out the Annotation Scale feature in Chapter 10.

Understanding Scale Factors

When you draft manually, you work on the final drawing directly with pen and ink or pencil. With a CAD program, you're a few steps removed from the finished product. Because of this, you need a deeper understanding of your drawing scale and how it's derived. In particular, you need to understand *scale factors*. For example, one of the more common uses of scale factors is translating the size of a graphic symbol, such as a section symbol in an architectural drawing, to the final plotted text size. When you draw manually, you draw your symbol at the size you want. In a CAD drawing, you need to translate the desired final symbol size to the drawing scale.

When you start adding graphic symbols to your drawing (see Chapter 4), you have to specify a symbol height. The scale factor helps you determine the appropriate symbol height for a particular drawing scale. For example, you may want your symbol to appear ½" high in your final plot. But if you draw your symbol to ½" in your drawing, it appears as a dot when plotted. The symbol has to be scaled up to a size that, when scaled back down at plot time, appears ½" high. For a ¼" scale drawing, you multiply the ½" text height by a scale factor of 48 to get 24". Your symbol should be 24" high in the CAD drawing in order to appear ½" high in the final plot. Where did the number 48 come from?

The scale factor for fractional inch scales is derived by multiplying the denominator of the scale by 12 and then dividing by the numerator. For example, the scale factor for ¼" = 1'-0" is (4 × 12) / 1, or 48/1. For 3/16" = 1'-0" scale, the operation is (16 × 12) / 3, or 64. For whole-foot scales such as 1" = 10', multiply the feet side of the equation by 12. Metric scales require simple decimal conversions.

You can also use scale factors to determine your drawing limits. For example, if you have a sheet size of 11" × 17" and you want to know the equivalent full-scale size for a ¼" scale drawing, you multiply the sheet measurements by 48. In this way, 11" becomes 528" (48 × 11"), and 17" becomes 816" (48 × 17"). Your work area must be 528" × 816" if you intend to have a final output of 11" × 17" at ¼" = 1'. You can divide these inch measurements by 12" to get 44' × 68'.

Table 3.2 shows scale factors as they relate to standard drawing scales. These scale factors are the values by which you multiply the desired final printout size to get the equivalent full-scale size. If you're using the metric system, you can use the drawing scale directly as the scale factor. For example, a drawing scale of 1:10 has a scale factor of 10, a drawing scale of 1:50 has a scale factor of 50, and so on. Metric users need to take special care regarding the base unit. Centimeters are used as a base unit in the examples in this book, which means that if you enter a distance as 1, you can assume the distance to be 1 cm.

TABLE 3.2:   Scale conversion factors

SCALE FACTORS FOR ENGINEERING DRAWING SCALES	DRAWING SCALE							
$n = 1''$	10'	20'	30'	40'	50'	60'	100'	200'
Scale factor	120	240	360	480	600	720	1200	2400

TABLE 3.2:   Scale conversion factors *(CONTINUED)*

SCALE FACTORS FOR ARCHITECTURAL DRAWING SCALES	DRAWING SCALE							
$n = 1'-0''$	1/16″	1/8″	1/4″	1/2″	1/4″	1″	1½″	3″
Scale factor	192	96	48	24	16	12	8	4

In older drawings, scale factors were used to determine text height and dimension settings. Chances are you will eventually have to work with drawings created by older AutoCAD versions, so understanding scale factors will pay off later. Plotting to a particular scale is also easier with an understanding of scale factors.

Using Polar Tracking

In this section, you'll draw the first item in the bathroom: the toilet. It's composed of a rectangle representing the tank and a truncated ellipse representing the seat. To construct the toilet, you'll use Polar Tracking, which is one of the more versatile drafting tools. Polar Tracking helps you align your cursor to exact horizontal and vertical angles, much like a T-square and triangle.

In this exercise, you'll use Polar Tracking to draw a rectangular box:

1. Start a line at the coordinate 5′-7″, 6′-3″ by entering **L↵ 5′7″,6′3″↵**. Metric users should enter **L↵ 171,189↵** as the starting coordinate. This starting point is somewhat arbitrary, but by entering a specific starting location, you're coordinated with the figures and instructions in this book. You can also use the Line tool in the Draw panel to start the line.

2. Make sure Polar Tracking is on (the Polar Tracking tool in the status bar should be blue), and then point the cursor directly to the right of the last point. The Polar Tracking cursor appears along with the Polar Tracking readout.

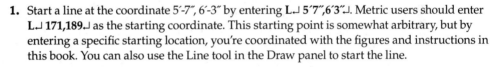

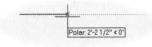

3. With the cursor pointing directly to the right, enter **1′-10″↵**. Metric users should enter **56↵**. You can use the spacebar in place of the ↵ key when entering distances in this way.

4. Point the cursor downward, enter **9↵** for 9″, and click this point. Metric users should enter **23↵**.

5. Continue drawing the other two sides of the rectangle by using Polar Tracking. After you've completed the rectangle, press ↵ or the Esc key to exit the Line tool. You should have a drawing that looks like Figure 3.2.

FIGURE 3.2
A plan view of
the toilet tank

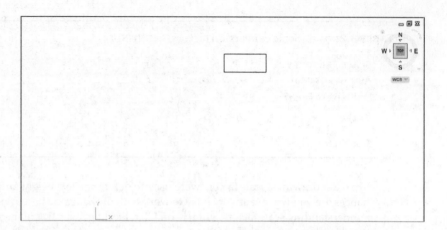

As you can see from the exercise, you can use Polar Tracking to restrain your cursor to horizontal and vertical positions, just as you would use a T-square and triangle. Later, you'll learn how you can set up Polar Tracking to set the angle to any value you want in a way similar to an adjustable triangle.

In some situations, you may find that you don't want Polar Tracking on. You can turn it off by clicking the Polar Tracking tool in the status bar. You can also press the F10 function key to turn Polar Tracking on or off.

Although this exercise tells you to use the Line tool to draw the tank, you can also use the Rectangle tool. The Rectangle tool creates what is known as a *polyline*, which is a set of line or arc segments that act like a single object. You'll learn more about polylines in Chapter 19.

By using the Snap modes in conjunction with the coordinate readout and Polar Tracking, you can locate coordinates and measure distances as you draw lines. This is similar to the way you draw when using a scale. The smallest distance registered by the coordinate readout and Polar Tracking readout depends on the area you've displayed on your screen. For example, if you're displaying an area the size of a football field, the smallest distance you can indicate with your cursor may be 6″, or 15 cm. On the other hand, if your view is enlarged to show an area of only one square inch or centimeter, you can indicate distances as small as 1/1000 of an inch or centimeter by using your cursor.

Setting the Polar Tracking Angle

You've seen how Polar Tracking lets you draw exact vertical and horizontal lines. You can also set Polar Tracking to draw lines at other angles, such as 30° or 45°. To change the angle Polar Tracking uses, you use the Polar Tracking tab in the Drafting Settings dialog box (see Figure 3.3).

Right-click the Polar Tracking tool in the status bar, and then choose Settings from the shortcut menu to open the Drafting Settings dialog box. As an alternative, you can type **DS↵** and then click the Polar Tracking tab.

To change the Polar Tracking angle, enter an angle in the Increment Angle text box or select a predefined angle from the drop-down list. You can do this while drawing a series of line segments, for example, so that you can set angles on the fly.

FIGURE 3.3
The Polar Tracking
tab in the Drafting
Settings dialog box

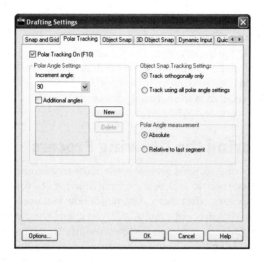

ORTHO MODE

Besides using Polar Tracking mode, you can restrain the cursor to a vertical or horizontal direction by using Ortho mode. To use Ortho mode, hold down the Shift key while drawing. You can also press F8 or click Ortho Mode in the status bar to keep Ortho mode on while you draw. When you move the cursor around while drawing objects, the rubber-banding line moves only vertically or horizontally. With Ortho mode turned on, Polar Tracking is automatically turned off.

Numerous other settings are available in the Polar Tracking tab. Here is a listing of their functions for your reference:

Additional Angles   This setting lets you enter a specific angle for Polar Tracking. For example, if you want Polar Tracking to snap to 12 degrees, click the New button next to the Additional Angles list box and enter 12. The value you enter appears in the list box, and when the Additional Angles check box is selected, Polar Tracking snaps to 12°. To delete a value from the list box, highlight it and click the Delete button.

The Additional Angles option differs from the Increment Angle setting in that the latter causes Polar Tracking to snap to every increment of its setting, whereas Additional Angles snaps only to the angle specified. You can enter as many angles as you want in the Additional Angles list box. As a shortcut, you can use the Polarang system variable (Polarang↵) to set the incremental angle without using the dialog box.

Object Snap Tracking Settings   These settings let you control whether Object Snap Tracking uses strictly orthogonal directions (0°, 90°, 180°, and 270°) or the angles set in the Polar Angle Settings group in this dialog box. (See the section "Aligning Objects by Using Object Snap Tracking" later in this chapter.)

Polar Angle Measurement   These radio buttons let you determine the zero angle on which Polar Tracking bases its incremental angles. The Absolute option uses the current AutoCAD setting for the 0° angle. The Relative To Last Segment option uses the last drawn object as the 0° angle. For example, if you draw a line at a 10° angle and the Relative To Last Segment option is selected with Increment Angle set to 90°, Polar Tracking snaps to 10°, 100°, 190°, and 280°, relative to the actual 0° direction.

Exploring the Drawing Process

The following sections present some of the more common AutoCAD commands and show you how to use them to complete a simple drawing. As you draw, watch the prompts and notice how your responses affect them. Also notice how you use existing drawing elements as reference points.

While drawing with AutoCAD, you create simple geometric forms to determine the basic shapes of objects, and you can then modify the shapes to fill in detail.

AutoCAD offers a number of basic 2D drawing object types; lines, arcs, circles, text, dimensions, traces, polylines, points, ellipses, elliptical arcs, spline curves, regions, hatches, and multiline text are the most common. All drawings are built on at least some of these objects. In addition, there are several 3D solids and meshes, which are three-dimensional shapes. You're familiar with lines and arcs; these, along with circles, are the most commonly used objects. As you progress through the book, you'll learn about the other objects and how they're used. You'll also learn about 3D objects in the section on AutoCAD 3D.

Locating an Object in Reference to Others

To define the toilet seat, you'll use an ellipse. Follow these steps:

1. Click the Center Ellipse tool in the Home tab's Draw panel, or type **El**↵.

2. At the Specify axis endpoint of ellipse or [Arc/Center]: prompt, pick the midpoint of the bottom horizontal line of the rectangle. To do this, Shift+right-click to open the Object Snap shortcut menu and select Midpoint; then move the cursor toward the bottom line. (Remember, Shift+click the right mouse button to open the Object Snap menu.) When you see the Midpoint Osnap marker on the line, click the left mouse button.

3. At the Specify other endpoint of axis: prompt, point the cursor downward and enter **1'-10"**↵. Metric users should enter **55**↵.

4. At the Specify distance to other axis or [Rotation]: prompt, point the cursor horizontally from the center of the ellipse and enter **8"**↵. Metric users should enter **20**↵. Your drawing should look like Figure 3.4.

FIGURE 3.4
The ellipse added
to the tank

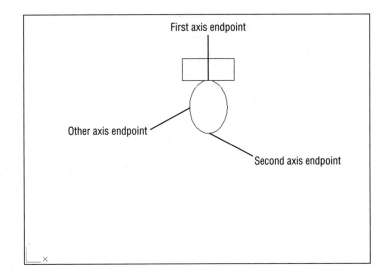

Getting a Closer Look

During the drawing process, you'll often want to enlarge areas of a drawing to edit its objects. In Chapter 1, you saw how to use the Zoom capability for this purpose. Follow these steps to enlarge the view of the toilet:

1. Click Zoom Window from the Zoom flyout in the navigation bar, or type **Z↵ W↵**.

2. At the `Specify first corner:` prompt, pick a point below and to the left of your drawing, at or near coordinate 5′-0″,3′-6″. Metric users should use the coordinate 150.0000,102.0000.

3. At the `Specify opposite corner:` prompt, pick a point above and to the right of the drawing, at or near coordinate 8′-3″,6′-8″ (246.0000,195.0000 for metric users). The toilet should be completely enclosed by the zoom window. You can also use the Zoom Realtime tool in conjunction with the Pan Realtime tool. The toilet enlarges to fill more of the screen. Your view should look similar to Figure 3.5 in the following section.

If you have a mouse with a scroll wheel, you can avoid using the Zoom command altogether. Just place the cursor on the toilet and turn the wheel to zoom into the image.

Modifying an Object

Now let's see how editing commands are used to construct an object. To define the back edge of the seat, let's put a copy of the line defining the front of the toilet tank 3″ (7 cm for metric users) toward the center of the ellipse:

1. Click the Copy tool in the Home tab's Modify panel, or type **co↵**.

2. At the `Select objects:` prompt, pick the horizontal line that touches the top of the ellipse. The line is highlighted. Press ↵ to complete your selection.

3. At the `Specify base point or [Displacement/mOde] <Displacement>:` prompt, pick a base point near the line. Then point the cursor down and enter 3"↵, or 7↵ if you're a metric user.

4. Press ↵ to exit the Copy command. Your drawing should look like Figure 3.5.

FIGURE 3.5
The line
copied down

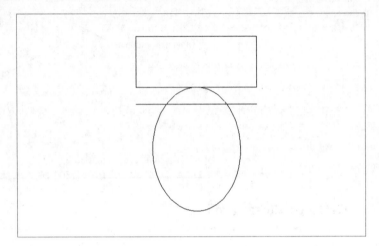

Notice that the Copy command acts exactly like the Move command you used in Chapter 2 except that Copy doesn't alter the position of the objects you select and you must press ↵ to exit Copy.

TRIMMING AN OBJECT

Now you must delete the part of the ellipse that isn't needed. You'll use the Trim command to trim off part of the ellipse:

1. Click the Trim tool in the Home tab's Modify panel. If you don't see the Trim tool, click the Trim/Extend flyout and select Trim. You'll see this prompt:

```
Current settings: Projection=UCS Edge=None
Select cutting edges ...
Select objects or <select all>:
```

2. Click the line you just created—the one that crosses through the ellipse—and press ↵ to finish your selection.

3. At the `Select object to trim or shift-select to extend or [Fence/Crossing/Project/Edge/eRase/Undo]:` prompt, pick the topmost portion of the ellipse above the line. This trims the ellipse back to the line.

4. Press ↵ to exit the Trim command.

In step 1 of the preceding exercise, the Trim command produces two messages in the prompt. The first message, `Select cutting edges...`, tells you that you must first select objects to define *the edge to which you want to trim an object.* In step 3, you're again prompted to select objects, this time to select the *object to trim.* Trim is one of a handful of AutoCAD commands that asks you to select two sets of objects: The first set defines a boundary, and the second is the set of objects you want to edit. The two sets of objects aren't mutually exclusive. You can, for example, select the cutting-edge objects as objects to trim. The next exercise shows how this works.

First, you'll undo the trim you just did. Then, you'll use the Trim command again in a slightly different way to finish the toilet:

1. Click the Undo button in the Quick Access toolbar, or enter **U**↵ at the Command prompt. The top of the ellipse reappears.

2. Start the Trim tool again by clicking it in the Modify panel.

3. At the `Select objects or <select all>:` prompt, click the ellipse and the line crossing the ellipse. (See the first image in Figure 3.6.)

4. Press ↵ to finish your selection.

5. At the `Select object to trim or [Fence/Crossing/Project/Edge/eRase/Undo]:` prompt, click the top portion of the ellipse, as you did in the previous exercise. The ellipse trims back.

6. Click a point near the left end of the trim line, outside the ellipse. The line trims back to the ellipse.

7. Click the other end of the line. The right side of the line trims back to meet the ellipse. Your drawing should look like the second image in Figure 3.6.

8. Press ↵ to exit the Trim command.

9. Click Save on the Quick Access toolbar to save the file in its current state, but don't exit the file. You may want to get in the habit of doing this every 20 minutes.

Here you saw how the ellipse and the line are both used as trim objects as well as the objects to be trimmed. The Trim options you've seen so far—Fence, Crossing, Project, Edge, eRase, and Undo—are described in the next section in this chapter. Also note that by holding down the Shift key in step 4, you can change from trimming an object to extending an object.

Exploring the Trim Options

AutoCAD offers six options for the Trim command: Fence, Crossing, Project, Edge, eRase, and Undo. As described in the following list, these options give you a higher degree of control over how objects are trimmed:

Fence/Crossing [F or C]   Lets you use a fence or crossing window to select objects.

Project [P]   Useful when you're working on 3D drawings. It controls how AutoCAD trims objects that aren't coplanar. Project offers three options: None, UCS, and View. The None option causes Trim to ignore objects that are on different planes so that only coplanar objects are trimmed. If you choose UCS, the Trim command trims objects based on a plan view of the current UCS and then disregards whether the objects are coplanar. (See the middle of Figure 3.7.) View is similar to UCS but uses the current view's "line of sight" to determine how non-coplanar objects are trimmed. (See the bottom of Figure 3.7.)

FIGURE 3.6

Trimming the
ellipse and the line

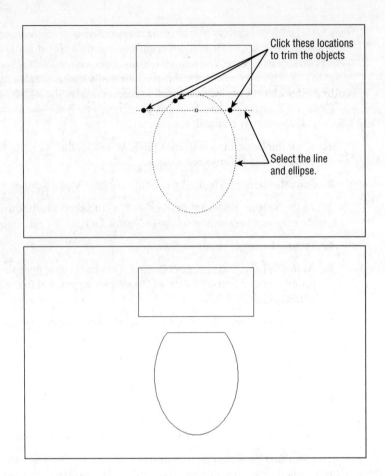

Click these locations
to trim the objects

Select the line
and ellipse.

Edge [E] Lets you trim an object to an apparent intersection, even if the cutting-edge object doesn't intersect the object to be trimmed (see the top of Figure 3.7). Edge offers two options: Extend and No Extend. You can also set these options by using the Edgemode system variable.

eRase [R] Allows you to erase an object while remaining in the Trim command.

Undo [U] Causes the last trimmed object to revert to its original length.

You've just seen one way to construct the toilet. However, you can construct objects in many ways. For example, you can trim only the top of the ellipse, as you did in the first trim exercise, and then use the Grips feature to move the endpoints of the line to meet the endpoints of the ellipse. As you become familiar with AutoCAD, you'll start to develop your own ways of working, using the tools best suited to your style.

If you'd like to take a break, now is a good time. You can exit AutoCAD and then come back to the Bath drawing file when you're ready to proceed.

FIGURE 3.7
The Trim command's options

Imagined extension of line

Actual extent of line

Result

With the Extend option, objects will trim even if the trimmed object doesn't actually intersect with the object to be trimmed.

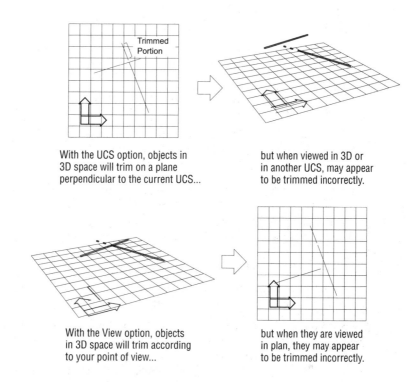

Trimmed Portion

With the UCS option, objects in 3D space will trim on a plane perpendicular to the current UCS...

but when viewed in 3D or in another UCS, may appear to be trimmed incorrectly.

With the View option, objects in 3D space will trim according to your point of view...

but when they are viewed in plan, they may appear to be trimmed incorrectly.

Planning and Laying Out a Drawing

For the next object, the bathtub, you'll use some new commands to lay out parts of the drawing. This will help you get a feel for the kind of planning you must do to use AutoCAD effectively. You'll begin the bathtub by using the Line command to draw a rectangle 2′-8″ × 5′-0″ (81 cm × 152 cm for metric users) on the left side of the drawing area. For a change this time, you'll use a couple of shortcut methods built into AutoCAD: the Line command's keyboard shortcut and the Direct Distance method for specifying distance and direction.

First though, you'll go back to the previous view of your drawing and arrange some more room to work. Follow these steps:

1. Return to your previous view, shown in Figure 3.8. A quick way to do this is to type **Z**↵ **P**↵. Your view returns to the one you had before the last Zoom command.

FIGURE 3.8
The view of the finished toilet after using the Zoom Previous tool. You can also obtain this view by using the Zoom All tool from the Zoom flyout.

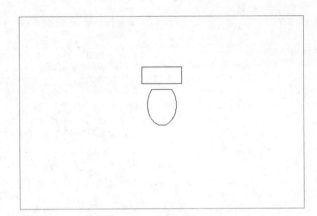

2. Type **L↵**, and then enter **9,10↵** to start the line at the 0′-9″,0′-10″ coordinate. Metric users should enter **24,27↵** for the coordinate 24.0000,27.0000.

3. Place your cursor to the right of the last point selected, so that the rubber-banding line is pointing directly to the right, and type **2′8″**. Then press ↵ for the first side of the tub. Metric users should enter **81↵**.

4. Point the rubber-banding line upward toward the top of the screen and type **5′**. Then press ↵ for the next side. Metric users should enter **152↵**.

5. Point the rubber-banding line directly to the left of the last point and type **2′8″** (81 for metric users). Then press ↵ for the next side.

6. Type **C↵** to close the rectangle and exit the Line command.

Instead of pressing ↵ during the Direct Distance method, you can press the spacebar, or you can right-click and choose Enter from the shortcut menu.

Now you have the outline of the tub. Notice that you don't have to enter the at sign (@) or angle specification. Instead, you use the Direct Distance method to specify direction and distance. You can use this method for drawing lines or moving and copying objects at right angles. The Direct Distance method is less effective if you want to specify exact angles other than right angles.

BE CAREFUL WITH HYPHENS

When you enter feet and inches in the command window, you must avoid hyphens or spaces. Thus, 2 feet 8 inches is typed as **2′8″**. But be aware that hyphens are allowed when using the Direct Distance method.

The keyboard shortcuts for some of the tools or commands you've used in this chapter are CO (Copy), E (Erase), EL (Ellipse), F (Fillet), M (Move), O (Offset), and TR (Trim). Remember that you can enter keyboard shortcuts, such as keyboard commands, only when the Command prompt is visible in the Command window.

Making a Preliminary Sketch

In this section, you'll see how planning ahead will make your use of AutoCAD more efficient. When drawing a complex object, you'll often have to do some layout before you do the actual drawing. This is similar to drawing an accurate pencil sketch using construction lines that you later trace over to produce a finished drawing. The advantage of doing this in AutoCAD is that your drawing doesn't lose any accuracy between the sketch and the final product. Also, AutoCAD enables you to use the geometry of your sketch to aid in drawing. While you're planning your drawing, think about what you want to draw, and then decide which drawing elements will help you create that object.

You'll use the Offset command to establish reference lines to help you draw the inside of the tub. This is where the Osnap overrides are useful. (See the sidebar "The Osnap Options" later in this chapter.)

You can use the Offset tool on the Home tab's Modify panel to make parallel copies of a set of objects, such as the lines forming the outside of your tub. Offset is different from the Copy command; while Offset allows only one object to be copied at a time, it can remember the distance you specify. The Offset option doesn't work with all types of objects. Only lines, arcs, circles, ellipses, splines, and 2D polylines can be offset.

Standard lines are best suited for the layout of the bathtub in this situation. In Chapter 6, you'll learn about two other objects, construction lines and rays, which are specifically designed to help you lay out a drawing. In this exercise, you'll use standard lines:

1. Click the Offset tool in the Home tab's Modify panel, or type **O**↵.

2. At the Specify offset distance or [Through/Erase/Layer] <Through>: prompt, enter **3**↵. This specifies the distance of 3″ as the offset distance. Metric users should enter **7** for 7 cm, which is roughly equivalent to 3 inches.

3. At the Select object to offset or [Exit/Undo] <Exit>: prompt, click the bottom line of the rectangle you just drew.

4. At the Specify point on side to offset or [Exit/Multiple/Undo]: prompt, pick a point inside the rectangle. A copy of the line appears. You don't have to be exact about where you pick the side to offset; AutoCAD only wants to know on which side of the line you want to make the offset copy.

5. The prompt Select object to offset or [Exit/Undo] <Exit>: appears again. Click another side to offset. Then click again on a point inside the rectangle.

6. Continue to offset the other two sides. Then offset these four new lines inside the rectangle toward the center. You'll have a drawing that looks like Figure 3.9.

7. When you're done, exit the Offset command by pressing ↵.

Using the Layout

Now you'll begin to draw the inside of the tub, starting with the narrow end. You'll use your offset lines as references to construct the arcs that make up the tub. Also in this exercise, you'll set up some of the osnap options to be available automatically whenever AutoCAD expects a point selection. Here are the steps:

1. Right-click the Object Snap tool in the status bar and select Settings from the shortcut menu. You can also type **Os**↵.

2. Click the Clear All button to turn off any options that may be selected.

FIGURE 3.9
The completed layout

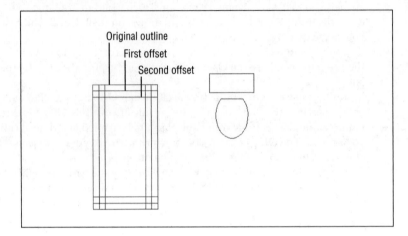

Look at the graphic symbols next to each of the osnap options in the Object Snap tab. These are the Osnap markers that appear in your drawing as you select osnap points. Each osnap option has its own marker symbol. As you use the osnaps, you'll become more familiar with how they work.

3. Click the Endpoint, Midpoint, and Intersection check boxes so that a checkmark appears in each box, and make sure the Object Snap On option is selected. Click OK (see Figure 3.10).

FIGURE 3.10
The Object Snap tab in the Drafting Settings dialog box

You've just set up the Endpoint, Midpoint, and Intersection osnaps to be on by default. This is called a *Running Osnap*; AutoCAD automatically selects the nearest osnap point without your intervention. Now let's see how a Running Osnap works:

1. First, turn off Dynamic Input mode in the status bar. This will help you see the osnap markers more easily.

2. Click the 3-Point Arc tool in the Home tab's Draw panel or type **a.↵**. See Figure 3.11 for other Arc options available from the Draw panel's Arc flyout.

FIGURE 3.11
The Arc flyout on the Draw panel offers several ways to draw an arc.

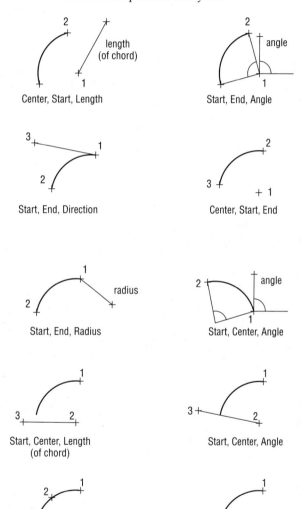

3. For the first point of the arc, move the cursor toward the intersection of the two lines as indicated in the top image in Figure 3.12. Notice that the Intersection Osnap marker appears on the intersection.

4. With the Intersection Osnap marker on the desired intersection, click the left mouse button.

FIGURE 3.12
Drawing the top, left side, and bottom of the tub

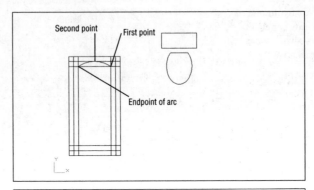

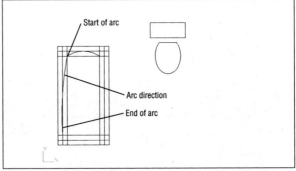

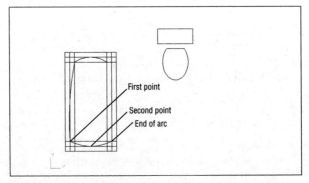

5. Move the cursor to the midpoint of the second horizontal line near the top. When the Midpoint Osnap marker appears at the midpoint of the line, click the left mouse button.

6. Use the Intersection Osnap marker to locate and select the intersection of the two lines at the upper-left side of the bathtub.

The top image in Figure 3.12 shows the sequence I just described.

If you have several Running Osnap modes on (Endpoint, Midpoint, and Intersection, for example), pressing the Tab key cycles through those osnap points on the object. This feature can be especially useful in a crowded area of a drawing.

ADJUSTING THE AUTOSNAP FEATURE

When you click the Options button in the Object Snap tab of the Drafting dialog box, you'll see the Drafting Settings tab of the Options dialog box. This tab offers a set of options pertaining to the AutoSnap feature. AutoSnap looks at the location of your cursor during osnap selections and locates the osnap point nearest your cursor. AutoSnap then displays a graphic called a *marker* showing you the osnap point it has found. If it's the one you want, left-click your mouse to select it.

The AutoSnap settings enable you to control various features:

Marker   Turns the graphic marker on or off.

Magnet   Causes the Osnap cursor to jump to inferred osnap points.

Display AutoSnap Tooltip   Turns the Osnap tool tip on or off.

Display AutoSnap Aperture Box   Turns the old-style Osnap cursor box on or off.

Colors   Controls the color of the AutoSnap marker. This option opens the Drawing Window Colors dialog box, which lets you select a color.

AutoSnap Marker Size   Controls the size of the graphic marker.

Next, you'll draw an arc for the left side of the tub:

1. Click the Arc tool in the Draw panel again.

2. Type @↵ to select the last point you picked as the start of the next arc.

It's easy for new users to select points inadvertently. If you accidentally select additional points after the last exercise and prior to step 1, you may not get the results described here. If this happens, issue the Arc command again; then, use the Endpoint osnap and select the endpoint of the last arc.

3. Type **E↵** to tell AutoCAD that you want to specify the other end of the arc instead of the next point. As another option, you can right-click anywhere in the drawing area and choose End from the shortcut menu.

4. At the `Specify end point of arc:` prompt, use the Intersection osnap to pick the intersection of the two lines in the lower-left corner of the tub. See the middle image in Figure 3.12 for the location of this point.

5. Type **D↵** to select the Direction option. You can also right-click anywhere in the drawing area and then choose Direction from the shortcut menu. The arc drags as you move the cursor, along with a rubber-banding line from the starting point of the arc.

6. Move the cursor to the left of the dragging arc until it touches the middle line on the left side of the tub. Pick that line, as shown in the middle image in Figure 3.12. You may need to turn off osnaps temporarily to do this.

In step 5 of the preceding exercise, the rubber-banding line indicates the direction of the arc. Be sure Ortho mode is off because Ortho mode forces the rubber-banding line and the arc in a direction you don't want. Check the status bar; if the Ortho tool is blue (on), press F8 or click the Ortho tool to turn off Ortho mode.

Now, you'll draw the bottom of the tub:

1. Click the Arc tool in the Draw panel again. You can also press ↵ to replay the last command.

2. Using the Endpoint Osnap marker, pick the endpoint of the bottom of the arc just drawn.

3. Using the Midpoint Osnap marker, pick the middle horizontal line at the bottom of the tub.

4. Pick the intersection of the two lines in the lower-right corner of the tub. (See the image at the bottom in Figure 3.12.)

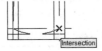

Next, create the right side of the tub by mirroring the left side:

1. Click the Mirror tool on the Home tab's Modify panel. You can also enter **mi↵** at the Command prompt.

2. At the `Select objects:` prompt, pick the long arc on the left side of the tub to highlight the arc. Press ↵ to indicate that you've finished your selection.

3. At the `Specify first point of mirror line:` prompt, pick the midpoint of the top horizontal line. By now, you should know how to use the automatic osnap modes you set up earlier.

4. At the `Specify second point of mirror line:` prompt, use Polar Tracking mode to pick a point directly below the last point selected.

5. At the `Erase source objects? [Yes/No] <N>:` prompt, press ↵ to accept the Mirror command's default `Erase source objects` option (No) and exit the Mirror command. A mirror image of the arc you picked appears on the right side of the tub. Your drawing should look like Figure 3.13.

FIGURE 3.13
The inside of the tub completed with the layout lines still in place

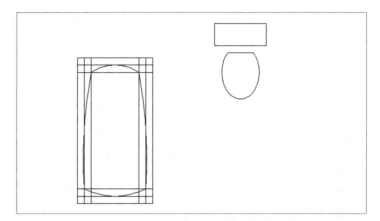

In this exercise, you were able to use osnaps in a Running Osnap mode. You'll find that you'll use osnaps constantly as you create your drawings. For this reason, you may want Running Osnaps on all the time. Even so, at times Running Osnaps can get in the way. For example, they may be a nuisance in a crowded drawing when you want to use a zoom window. The osnaps can cause you to select an inappropriate window area by automatically selecting osnap points.

Fortunately, you can toggle Running Osnaps on and off easily by clicking the Object Snap tool in the status bar. If you don't have any Running Osnaps set, clicking the Object Snap tool opens the Object Snap settings in the Drafting Settings dialog box, enabling you to select your osnaps. Or you can right-click the Object Snap tool and select Settings from the shortcut menu that appears.

Erasing the Layout Lines

Next, you'll erase the layout lines you created using the Offset command. But this time, you'll try selecting the lines *before* issuing the Erase command.

Follow these steps:

1. Click each internal layout line individually.

   If you have problems selecting just the lines, try using a selection window to select single lines. (Remember, a window selects only objects that are completely within it.)

2. After all the layout lines are highlighted, enter E⏎ to use the keyboard shortcut for the Erase command, or right-click and choose Erase from the shortcut menu. Your drawing will look like Figure 3.14.

FIGURE 3.14
The drawing after erasing the layout lines

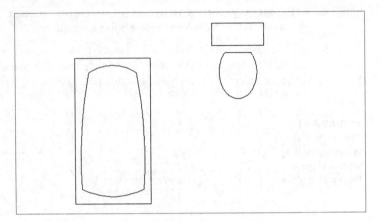

If you right-clicked to use the shortcut menu in step 2, you'll notice that you have several options besides Erase. You can move, copy, scale, and rotate the objects you selected. These options are similar to the tools on the Home tab's Modify panel in the way they act. But be aware that they act somewhat differently from the hot-grip options described in Chapter 2.

THE OSNAP OPTIONS

Earlier, you made several of the osnap settings automatic so they're available without having to select them from the Osnap shortcut menu. Another way to invoke the osnap options is to type their keyboard equivalents while selecting points or to Shift+right-click and type the capital letter shown in the Osnap shortcut menu for the option you want to use.

The following is a summary (in alphabetic order) of all the available osnap options, including their keyboard shortcuts. You've already used many of these options in this chapter and in the previous chapter. Pay special attention to those options you haven't yet used in the exercises but may find useful to your style of work. The full name of each option is followed by its keyboard shortcut name in brackets. To use these options, you can enter either the full name or the abbreviation at any point prompt. You can also select these options from the pop-up menu obtained by Shift+clicking the right mouse button.

Apparent Intersection [app] Selects the apparent intersection of two objects. This is useful when you want to select the intersection of two objects that don't actually intersect. You'll be prompted to select the two objects.

Center [cen] Selects the center of an arc or a circle. You must click the arc or circle itself, not its apparent center.

Endpoint [endp or end] Selects the endpoints of lines, polylines, arcs, curves, and 3D Face vertices.

Extension [ext]   Selects a point that is aligned with an imagined extension of a line. For example, you can pick a point in space that is aligned with an existing line but isn't on that line. To use that point, type **ext**⏎ during point selection or select Extension from the Osnap pop-up menu. Then move the cursor to the line whose extension you want to use and hold it there until you see a small, cross-shaped marker on the line. The cursor also displays a tool tip with the word *extension,* letting you know that the Extension osnap is active.

From [fro]   Selects a point relative to a picked point. For example, you can select a point that is 2 units to the left and 4 units above a circle's center. This option is usually used in conjunction with another osnap option, such as From Endpoint or From Midpoint.

Insert [ins]   Selects the insertion point of text, blocks, Xrefs, and overlays.

Intersection [int]   Selects the intersection of objects.

Mid Between 2 Points [m2p]   Selects a point that is midway between two other points.

Midpoint [mid]   Selects the midpoint of a line or an arc. In the case of a polyline, it selects the midpoint of the polyline segment.

Nearest [nea]   Selects a point on an object nearest the pick point.

Node [nod]   Selects a point object.

None [non]   Temporarily turns off Running Osnaps for a single point selection.

Parallel [par]   Lets you draw a line segment that is parallel to another existing line segment. To use this option, type **par**⏎ during point selection, or select Parallel from the Osnap pop-up menu. Then move the cursor to the line you want to be parallel to and hold it there until you see a small, cross-shaped marker on the line. The cursor also displays a tool tip with the word *parallel,* letting you know that the Parallel osnap is active.

Perpendicular [per]   Selects a position on an object that is perpendicular to the last point selected.

Point filters   Not really object snaps, but point-selection options that let you filter X, Y, or Z coordinate values from a selected point. (See Chapter 21 for more on point filters.)

Quadrant [qua]   Selects the nearest cardinal (north, south, east, or west) point on an arc or a circle.

Tangent [tan]   Selects a point on an arc or a circle that represents the tangent from the last point selected.

Temporary Track Point   Provides an alternate method for using the Object Snap Tracking feature described later in this chapter. (See Chapter 15 for more on Temporary Track Point.)

3D Osnaps   Offers additional osnaps for 3D modeling. With these osnap options, you can select a vector that is perpendicular to a surface or find the midpoint of an edge of a 3D object.

Sometimes you'll want one or more of these osnap options available as the default selection. Remember that you can set Running Osnaps to be on at all times. Type DS⏎, and then click the Object Snap tab. You can also right-click the Object Snap tool in the status bar and choose Settings from the shortcut menu to open the Drafting Settings dialog box, or just select osnap options directly from the shortcut menu.

If you need more control over the selection of objects, you'll find the Add/Remove Selection Mode setting useful. This setting lets you deselect a set of objects within a set of objects you've already selected. While in Object Selection mode, enter **R**↵, then proceed to use a window or other selection tool to remove objects from the selection set. Enter **A**↵ to continue to add options to the selection set. Or, if you need to deselect only a single object, Shift+click it.

Putting On the Finishing Touches

The inside of the tub still has some sharp corners. To round out these corners, you can use the versatile Fillet tool on the Home tab's Modify panel. Fillet enables you to join lines and arcs end to end, and it can add a radius where they join so there is a smooth transition from arc to arc or line to line. Fillet can join two lines that don't intersect, and it can trim two crossing lines back to their point of intersection.

Another tool, called Chamfer, performs a similar function, but instead of joining lines with an arc, Chamfer joins lines with another line segment. Since they perform similar functions, Fillet and Chamfer occupy the same location on the Modify panel. If you don't see the Fillet tool, click the Chamfer flyout and select Fillet.

Continue with your tutorial by following these steps:

1. Click the Fillet tool on the Home tab's Modify panel, or type **f**↵.

2. At the prompt

   ```
   Current settings: Mode = TRIM, Radius = 0´-0 1/2˝
   Select first object or [Undo/Polyline/Radius/Trim/Multiple]:
   ```

   enter **R**↵, or right-click and choose Radius from the shortcut menu.

3. At the Specify fillet radius <0´-0˝>: prompt, enter **4**↵. This tells AutoCAD that you want a 4˝ radius for your fillet. Metric users should enter **10**↵.

4. Pick two adjacent arcs. The fillet arc joins the two larger arcs.

5. Press ↵ again, and fillet another corner. Repeat until all four corners are filleted. Your drawing should look like Figure 3.15.

Aligning Objects by Using Object Snap Tracking

You saw how to use lines to construct an object such as the bathtub. In many situations, using these *construction lines* is the most efficient way to draw, but they can also be a bit cumbersome. AutoCAD offers another tool that helps you align locations in your drawing to existing objects without having to draw intermediate construction lines. The tool is called *Object Snap Tracking*, or *Osnap Tracking*.

FIGURE 3.15
A view of the finished toilet and tub with the tub corners filleted

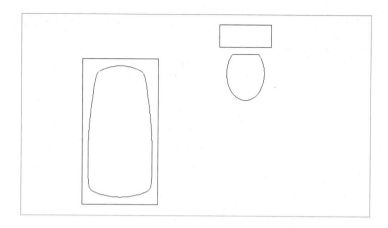

Osnap Tracking is like an extension of object snaps that enables you to *align* a point to the geometry of an object instead of just selecting a point on an object. For example, with Osnap Tracking, you can select a point that is exactly at the center of a rectangle.

In the following exercises, you'll draw a plan view of a bathroom sink as an introduction to the Osnap Tracking feature. This drawing will be used as a symbol in later chapters.

GETTING SET UP

First, as a review, you'll open a new file by using the Create New Drawing Wizard. Because this drawing will be used as a symbol for insertion in other CAD drawings, don't worry about setting it up to conform to a sheet size. Chances are you won't be printing individual symbols. Here are the steps:

1. Enter **Startup**↵ **1**↵. This turns on the Create New Drawing Wizard for new drawings.

2. Click the New tool from the Quick Access toolbar to create a new drawing for your bathroom sink.

3. Click the Use A Wizard button in the Create New Drawing dialog box.

4. Select Quick Setup from the list that appears below the buttons, and then click OK (see Figure 3.16).

5. In the Units screen, choose Architectural and then click Next. Metric users can use the Decimal option. This option performs the same operation as the Drawing Units dialog box you saw earlier in this chapter.

FIGURE 3.16

The Create New
Drawing dialog box

6. In the Area screen, enter **48** for the width and **36** for the length. Metric users should enter **122** for the width and **92** for the length. Click Finish. This option performs the same operation as the Limits command you used earlier.

7. Type **Z↵ A↵** to display the overall area of the drawing set by the limits.

8. Choose Save As from the Application menu to save the file under the name Sink.

9. Enter **Startup↵ 0↵** to turn off the Create New Drawing Wizard option. You can leave it turned on if you wish, but be aware that later exercises assume that it is turned off.

As you saw in steps 5 and 6, the Create New Drawing Wizard simplifies the drawing setup process by limiting the options with which you need to work.

If you find that you use the same drawing setup over and over, you can create template files that are already set up to your own, customized way of working. Templates are discussed in Chapter 6.

DRAWING THE SINK

You're ready to draw the sink. First, you'll draw the sink countertop. Then, you'll make sure Running Osnaps and Osnap Tracking are turned on. Finally, you'll draw the bowl of the sink.

Here are the steps for drawing the outline of the sink countertop:

1. If the grid is on, click the Grid tool in the status bar to turn it off.

2. Click the Rectangle tool in the Draw panel, or type **rec↵**.

3. At the prompt

   `Specify first corner point or [Chamfer/Elevation/Fillet/Thickness/Width]:`

   enter **0,0↵**. This places one corner of the rectangle in the origin of the drawing.

4. At the `Specify other corner point or [Area/Dimensions/Rotation]:` prompt, enter **@2´4,1´6↵** to place the other corner of the rectangle. Metric users should enter **@71,46↵**. This makes the rectangle 2´-4˝ wide and 1´-6˝ deep, or 71 cm wide and 46 cm deep for metric users. The rectangle appears in the lower half of the drawing area.

5. Click Zoom Extents from the Zoom flyout on the navigation bar or type **Z↵ E↵**. This enlarges the view of the sink outline so it fits in the drawing area.

6. Use the Zoom Realtime tool in the Zoom flyout to adjust your view so it looks similar to the one shown in Figure 3.17. You can also enter **Z**↵↵ to start the realtime zoom feature or just use your scroll wheel.

When you draw the bowl of the sink, the bowl will be represented by an ellipse. You want to place the center of the ellipse at the center of the rectangle you've just drawn. To do this, you'll use the midpoint of two adjoining sides of the rectangle as alignment locations. This is where the Osnap Tracking tool will be useful.

You need to make sure the Object Snap tool is turned on and that the Midpoint Object Snap option is also turned on. Then you'll make sure Osnap Tracking is turned on. Use these steps:

1. Right-click the Object Snap Tracking tool in the status bar and choose Settings from the shortcut menu to open the Drafting Settings dialog box at the Object Snap tab (see Figure 3.18).

2. Make sure the Midpoint check box in the Object Snap Modes group is selected.

3. Also make sure Object Snap On and Object Snap Tracking On are both selected. Click OK. You'll notice that the Object Snap and Object Snap Tracking buttons in the status bar are now in the on position.

FIGURE 3.18
The Object Snap
tab in the Drafting
Settings dialog box

Finally, you're ready to draw the ellipse:

1. Click the Center Ellipse tool in the Draw panel, or enter **El**⏎.

2. Move your cursor to the top, horizontal edge of the rectangle until you see the Midpoint tool tip.

3. Move the cursor directly over the Midpoint Osnap marker. Without clicking the mouse, hold the cursor there for a second until you see a small cross appear. Look carefully, because the cross is small. This is the Object Snap Tracking marker (see Figure 3.19).

FIGURE 3.19
The Object Snap
Tracking marker

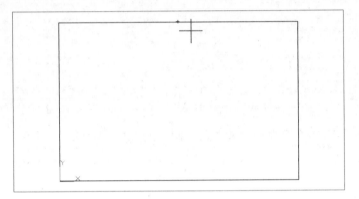

You can alternately insert and remove the Object Snap Tracking marker by passing the cursor over the Osnap marker.

4. As you move the cursor downward, a dotted line appears, emanating from the midpoint of the horizontal line. The cursor also shows a small X following the dotted line as you move it (see Figure 3.20).

FIGURE 3.20
A vertical dotted
line appears.

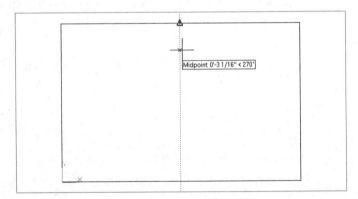

5. Move the cursor to the midpoint of the left vertical side of the rectangle. Don't click, but hold it there for a second until you see the small cross. Now as you move the cursor away, a horizontal dotted line appears with an X following the cursor (see Figure 3.21).

FIGURE 3.21
A horizontal dotted line appears.

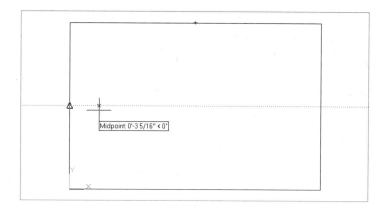

6. Move the cursor to the center of the rectangle. The two dotted lines appear simultaneously and a small *X* appears at their intersection (see Figure 3.22).

FIGURE 3.22
The vertical and horizontal dotted lines appear simultaneously.

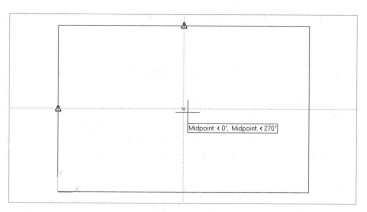

7. With the two dotted lines crossing and the *X* at their intersection, click the left mouse button to select the exact center of the rectangle.

8. Point the cursor to the right, and enter **8**↵ to make the width of the bowl 16″. Metric users should enter **20**↵ for a bowl 40 cm wide.

9. Point the cursor downward, and enter **6**↵ to make the length of the bowl 12″. Metric users should enter **15**↵ for a bowl with a length of 30 cm. The basic symbol for the sink is complete (see Figure 3.23).

10. Click Save in the Quick Access toolbar and close the current file. You can also save and close the Bath file and exit AutoCAD.

In this exercise, you saw how Object Snap Tracking enables you to align two locations to select a point in space. Although you used only the Midpoint osnap setting in this exercise, you aren't limited to one osnap setting. You can use as many as you need to select the appropriate geometry. You can also use as many alignment points as you need, although in this exercise you used only two. If you like, erase the ellipse and repeat this exercise until you get the hang of using the Object Snap Tracking feature.

FIGURE 3.23
The completed bathroom sink

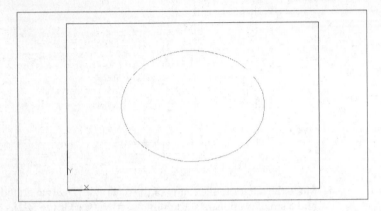

As with all the other tools in the status bar, you can turn Object Snap Tracking on or off by clicking the Object Snap Tracking tool.

Using the AutoCAD Modes as Drafting Tools

Before you finish this chapter, you'll want to know about a few of the other drafting tools that are common to drawing programs. These tools may be compared to a background grid (*Grid mode*) and the ability to "snap" to grid points (*Snap mode*). These drawing modes can be indispensable tools under certain conditions. Their use is fairly straightforward. You can experiment with them on your own using the information in the following sections.

Using Grid Mode as a Background Grid

Using Grid mode is like having a grid under your drawing to help you with layout, as shown in Figure 3.24. In this figure, the grids are set to a 1′ spacing with major grid lines at 5′. The grid also shows, in darker lines, the X and Y axis that start at the origin of the drawing.

FIGURE 3.24
A sample drawing showing the grids turned on

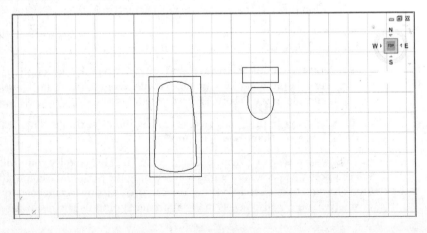

Grids will not print in your final output. They are a visual aid to help you gauge distances. In AutoCAD, Grid mode can also let you see the limits of your drawing because the grid can be set to display only within the limits setting of your drawing. Grid mode can help you visually determine the distances with which you're working in any given view. In this section, you'll learn how to control the grid's appearance. The F7 key toggles Grid mode on and off. You can also click the Grid Display tool in the status bar.

USING OBJECT SNAP TRACKING AND POLAR TRACKING TOGETHER

In addition to selecting as many tracking points as you need, you can use different angles besides the basic orthogonal angles of 0°, 90°, 180°, and 270°. For example, you can have AutoCAD locate a point that is aligned vertically to the top edge of the sink and at a 45° angle from a corner.

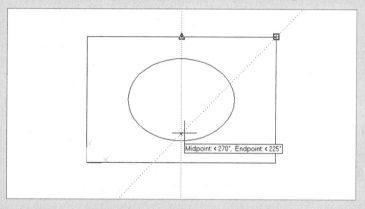

Midpoint < 270°, Endpoint < 225°

This can be accomplished by using the settings in the Polar Tracking tab of the Drafting Settings dialog box. (See the section "Setting the Polar Tracking Angle" earlier in this chapter.) If you set the increment angle to 45° and turn on the Track Using All Polar Angle Settings option, you'll be able to use 45° in addition to the orthogonal directions. You'll see firsthand how this works in Chapter 6.

To set up the grid spacing, follow these steps:

1. Right-click the Grid Display tool in the status bar and select Settings (or type **Ds.⏎**) to open the Drafting Settings dialog box, showing all the mode settings.

2. Click the Snap And Grid tab if it isn't already selected. You see six groups: Snap Spacing, Grid Style, Grid Spacing, Polar Spacing, Grid Behavior, and Snap Type. Notice that the Grid X Spacing text box contains a value of 1/2″. Metric users see a value of 10 (see Figure 3.25).

3. Enter the grid spacing you want in the Grid X Spacing and Grid Y Spacing input boxes.

4. Click the Grid On check box to make the grid visible. Notice the F7 in parentheses: This tells you that the F7 function key also controls the Grid On/Off function. Click OK to dismiss the Drafting Settings dialog box and save your settings.

FIGURE 3.25

The Snap And Grid
tab of the Drafting
Settings dialog box

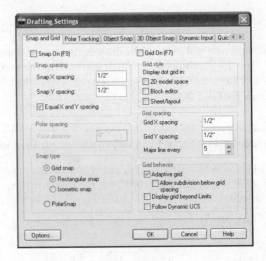

If you prefer, you can use the Gridunit system variable to set the grid spacing. Enter Gridunit↵, and at the `Enter new value for GRIDUNIT <0′-0 ″,0′-0 ″>:` prompt, enter a grid spacing in X,Y coordinates. You must enter the Gridunit value as an X,Y coordinate.

There are several other grid options in the Drafting Settings dialog box. The Grid Style group lets you display the grid as a series of dots instead of the graph-paper-style lines. Place a check by the view name where you want to display dots instead of grid lines.

In the Grid Behavior group, the Display Grid Beyond Limits check box lets you determine whether the grid displays outside the limits of the drawing.

The Adaptive Grid option adjusts the grid spacing depending on how much of the view is displayed. If you zoom out to a point where the grid becomes too dense to view the drawing, the grid automatically increases its interval. The Major Line Every option lets you control how frequently the major grid lines (lines that appear darker than the others) appear.

Once you've set up your grid, you can press F7 or click Grid in the status bar to turn the grid on and off. (You can also hold down the Ctrl key and press G.)

Using the Snap Modes

The *Snap mode* forces the cursor to move in steps of a specific distance. Snap mode is useful when you want to select points on the screen at a fixed interval. Two snap modes are available in AutoCAD: *Grid Snap* and *Polar Snap*. The F9 key toggles Grid Snap mode on and off, or you can click the Snap tool in the status bar. Follow these steps to access the Snap mode:

1. Right-click the Grid Display tool in the status bar and select Settings (or type **Ds**↵) to open the Drafting Settings dialog box.

2. In the Snap Spacing group of the dialog box, double-click the Snap X Spacing text box and enter a value for your snap spacing. Then press the Tab key to move to the next option. AutoCAD assumes you want the X and Y snap spacing to be the same unless you specifically ask for a different Y setting.

3. You can click the Snap On check box to turn on Snap mode from this dialog box.

4. Click OK to save your settings and close the dialog box.

CONTROLLING THE COLOR OF GRID LINES

If you find that the colors of the grid lines are too strong and they obscure your drawing, you can set them so they blend into the background. To do this, you use the Options dialog box (see Appendix B for more on the Options dialog box):

1. Right-click and select Options or type **Options⏎**.

2. Select the Display tab.

3. Click the Colors button in the Window Elements group.

4. Make sure 2D Model Space is selected in the Context window, and then select Grid Minor Lines from the Interface Element list.

5. Select a color for your grid line from the Color drop-down list.

6. Select Grid Major Lines from the Interface Element group and select a color from the Color drop-down list.

7. Click Apply & Close, and then select OK at the Options dialog box.

In step 5, you can select from the list of colors or choose the Select Color option at the bottom of the list to select a custom color.

With Snap mode on, the cursor seems to move in steps rather than in a smooth motion. The Snap Mode tool in the status bar appears blue, indicating that Snap mode is on. Press F9 or click Snap Mode in the status bar (you can also hold down the Ctrl key and press B) to turn Snap mode on or off.

Note that you can use the Snapunit system variable to set the snap spacing. Enter **Snapunit⏎**. Then, at the `Enter new value for SNAPUNIT <0′0″,0′0″>:` prompt, enter a snap distance value as an X,Y coordinate.

Take a moment to look at the Drafting Settings dialog box in Figure 3.25. The other option in the Snap Spacing group enables you to force the X and Y spacing to be equal (Equal X And Y Spacing).

In the Snap Type group, you can change the snap and grid configuration to aid in creating 2D isometric drawings by clicking the Isometric Snap radio button. The PolarSnap option enables you to set a snap distance for the Polar Snap feature. When you click the PolarSnap radio button, the Polar Distance option at the middle left of the dialog box changes from gray to black and white to allow you to enter a Polar Snap distance.

You can also set up the grid to follow the snap spacing automatically. To do this, set Grid X Spacing and Grid Y Spacing to 0.

The Bottom Line

Set up a work area. A blank AutoCAD drawing offers few clues about the size of the area you're working with, but you can get a rough idea of the area shown in the AutoCAD window.

Master It Name two ways to set up the area of your work.

Explore the drawing process. To use AutoCAD effectively, you'll want to know how the different tools work together to achieve an effect. The drawing process often involves many cycles of adding objects and then editing them.

Master It Name the tool that causes the cursor to point in an exact horizontal or vertical direction.

Plan and lay out a drawing. If you've ever had to draw a precise sketch with just a pencil and pad, you've probably used a set of lightly drawn guidelines to lay out your drawing first. You do the same thing in AutoCAD, but instead of lightly drawn guidelines, you can use any object you want. In AutoCAD, objects are easily modified or deleted, so you don't have to be as careful when adding guidelines.

Master It What is the name of the feature that lets you select exact locations on objects?

Use the AutoCAD modes as drafting tools. The main reason for using AutoCAD is to produce precision technical drawings. AutoCAD offers many tools to help you produce a drawing with the precision you need.

Master It What dialog box lets you set both the grid and snap spacing?

Chapter 4

Organizing Objects with Blocks and Groups

Drawing the tub, toilet, and sink in Chapter 3 may have taken what seemed to you an inordinate amount of time. As you continue to use AutoCAD, however, you'll learn to draw objects more quickly. You'll also need to draw fewer of them because you can save drawings as symbols and then use those symbols like rubber stamps, duplicating drawings instantaneously wherever they're needed. This saves a lot of time when you're composing drawings.

To make effective use of AutoCAD, begin a *symbol library* of drawings you use frequently. A mechanical designer might have a library of symbols for fasteners, cams, valves, or other parts used in their application. An electrical engineer might have a symbol library of capacitors, resistors, switches, and the like. A circuit designer will have yet another unique set of frequently used symbols.

In Chapter 3, you drew three objects—a bathtub, a toilet, and a sink—that architects often use. In this chapter, you'll see how to create symbols from those drawings.

In this chapter, you'll learn to do the following:

◆ Create and insert a symbol

◆ Modify a block

◆ Understand the annotation scale

◆ Group objects

GET ADDITIONAL HELP ON THE DVD

The companion DVD offers three video tutorials that give you an overview of the main topics of this chapter. The video entitled "Organizing with Blocks" covers the some general features described in "Creating a Symbol." The video entitled "Annotation Scale" touches on some of the material in "Understanding the Annotation Scale." "Grouping Objects" covers the material in section with the same name.

Creating a Symbol

To save a drawing as a symbol, you use the tools in the Home or Insert tab's Block panel. In word processors, the term *block* refers to a group of words or sentences selected for moving, saving, or deleting. You can copy a block of text elsewhere within the same file, to other files, or to a separate location on a server or USB storage device for future use. AutoCAD uses blocks in a similar fashion. In a file, you can turn parts of your drawing into blocks that can be saved and recalled at any time. You can also use entire existing files as blocks.

You'll start by opening the file you worked on in the previous chapter and selecting the objects that will become a block:

1. Start AutoCAD, and open the existing Bath file. Use the one you created in Chapter 3, or open the 04-bath.dwg sample file from this book's companion DVD. Metric users can use the 04-bath-metric.dwg file. The drawing appears just as you left it in the last session.

2. In the Block Ribbon panel, click the Create tool or type **B↵**, the keyboard shortcut for the Create tool. This opens the Block Definition dialog box (see Figure 4.1).

FIGURE 4.1
The Block Definition dialog box

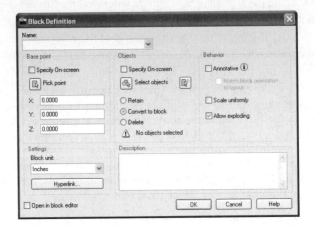

3. In the Name text box, type **Toilet**.

4. In the Base Point group, click the Pick Point button. This option enables you to select a base point for the block by using your cursor. (The *insertion base point* of a block is a point of reference on the block that is used like a grip.) When you've selected this option, the Block Definition dialog box temporarily closes.

   Notice that the Block Definition dialog box gives you the option to specify the X, Y, and Z coordinates for the base point instead of selecting a point.

5. Using the Midpoint osnap, pick the midpoint of the back of the toilet as the base point. Remember that you learned how to set up Running Osnaps in Chapter 3; all you need to do is point to the midpoint of a line to display the Midpoint Osnap marker and then left-click your mouse.

After you've selected a point, the Block Definition dialog box reappears. Notice that the X, Y, and Z values in the Base Point group now display the coordinates of the point you picked. For two-dimensional drawings, the Z coordinate should remain at 0.

Next, you need to select the objects you want as part of the block.

6. Click the Select Objects button in the Objects group. Once again, the dialog box momentarily closes. You now see the familiar Select objects: prompt in the Command window, and the cursor becomes a Pickbox cursor. Click a point below and to the left of the toilet. Then use a selection window to select the entire toilet. The toilet is now highlighted.

   Make sure you use the Select Objects option in the Block Definition dialog box to select the objects you want to turn into a block. AutoCAD lets you create a block that contains no objects. If you try to proceed without selecting objects, you'll get a warning message. This can cause confusion and frustration, even for an experienced user.

7. Press ↵ to confirm your selection. The Block Definition dialog box opens again.

8. Select Inches from the Block Unit drop-down list. Metric users should select Centimeters.

9. Click the Description list box, and enter **Standard Toilet**.

10. Make sure the Retain radio button in the Objects group is selected, and then click OK. The toilet drawing is now a block with the name Toilet.

11. Repeat the blocking process for the tub, but this time use the upper-left corner of the tub as the insertion base point and give the block the name Tub. Enter **Standard Tub** for the description.

    You can press ↵ or right-click the mouse and choose Repeat BLOCK from the shortcut menu to start the Create Block tool.

When you turn an object into a block, it's stored in the drawing file, ready to be recalled at any time. The block remains part of the drawing file even when you end the editing session. When you open the file again, the block is available for your use. In addition, you can access blocks from other drawings by using the AutoCAD DesignCenter and the Tool palettes. You'll learn more about the DesignCenter and the Tool palettes in Chapter 29.

A block acts like a single object, even though it's really made up of several objects. One unique characteristic of a block is that when you modify it, all instances of it are updated to reflect the modifications. For example, if you insert several copies of the toilet into a drawing and then later decide the toilet needs to be a different shape, you can edit the Toilet block and all the other copies of the toilet are updated automatically.

You can modify a block in a number of ways after it has been created. In this chapter, you'll learn how to make simple changes to individual blocks by modifying the block's properties. For more detailed changes, you'll learn how to redefine a block after it has been created. Later, in Chapter 18, you'll learn how to use the Block Editor to make changes to blocks.

Understanding the Block Definition Dialog Box

The Block Definition dialog box offers several options that can help make using blocks easier. If you're interested in these options, take a moment to review the Block Definition dialog box as you read the descriptions. If you prefer, you can continue with the tutorial and come back to this section later.

You've already seen how the Name option lets you enter a name for your block. AutoCAD doesn't let you complete the block creation until you enter a name.

You've also seen how to select a base point for your block. The base point is like the grip of the block: It's the reference point you use when you insert the block back into the drawing. In the exercise, you used the Pick Point option to indicate a base point, but you also have the option to enter X, Y, and Z coordinates just below the Pick Point option. In most cases, however, you'll want to use the Pick Point option to indicate a base point that is on or near the set of objects you're converting to a block.

The Objects group of the Block Definition dialog box lets you select the objects that make up the block. You use the Select Objects button to visually select the objects you want to include in the block you're creating. The Quick Select button to the right of the Select Objects button lets you filter out objects based on their properties. You'll learn more about Quick Select in Chapter 15. Once you select a set of objects for your block, you'll see a thumbnail preview of the block's contents near the top center of the Block Definition dialog box.

Other options in the Objects group and Settings group let you specify what to do with the objects you're selecting for your block. Table 4.1 shows a list of those other options and what they mean.

TABLE 4.1:   The Block Definition dialog box options

OPTION	PURPOSE
Base Point group	
Specify On-Screen	Lets you select the base point for the block after you click OK.
Pick Point	Lets you select the base point for the block before you click OK to dismiss the dialog box.
X, Y, and Z input boxes	Enable you to enter exact coordinates for the block's base point.
Objects group	
Specify On-Screen	Lets you select the objects for the block after you click OK.
Select Objects/Quick Select	Lets you select the objects for the block before you click OK to dismiss the dialog box.
Retain	Keeps the objects you select for your block as they are, or unchanged.
Convert To Block	Converts the objects you select into the block you're defining. The block then acts like a single object after you've completed the Block command.
Delete	Deletes the objects you selected for your block. You may also notice that a warning message appears at the bottom of the Objects group. This warning appears if you haven't selected objects for the block. After you've selected objects, the warning changes to tell you how many objects you've selected.

CREATING A SYMBOL | 115

TABLE 4.1:   The Block Definition dialog box options *(CONTINUED)*

OPTION	PURPOSE
Behavior group	
Annotative	Turns on the Annotative scale feature for blocks. This feature lets you use a single block for different scale views of a drawing. With this feature turned on, AutoCAD can be set to adjust the size of the block to the appropriate scale for the drawing.
Match Block Orientation To Layout	With the Annotative option turned on, this option is available. This option causes a block to appear always in its normal orientation regardless of the orientation of the layout view.
Scale Uniformly	By default, blocks can have a different X, Y, or Z scale. This means they can be stretched in any of the axes. You can lock the X, Y, and Z scale of the block by selecting this option. That way, the block will always be scaled uniformly and can't be stretched in one axis.
Allow Exploding	By default, blocks can be exploded or reduced to their component objects. You can lock a block so that it can't be exploded by turning off this option. You can always turn on this option later through the Properties palette if you decide that you need to explode a block.
Settings group	
Block Unit	Lets you determine how the object is to be scaled when it's inserted into the drawing using the DesignCenter feature discussed in Chapter 29. By default, this value is the same as the current drawing's insert value.
Hyperlink	Lets you assign a hyperlink to a block. This option opens the Insert Hyperlink dialog box, where you can select a location or file for the hyperlink.
Description and Open In Block Editor	
Description	Lets you include a brief description or keyword for the block. This option is helpful when you need to find a specific block in a set of drawings. You'll learn more about searching for blocks later in this chapter and in Chapter 29.
Open In Block Editor	If you turn on this option, the block is created and then opened in the Block Editor described in Chapter 18.

Inserting a Symbol

You can recall the Tub and Toilet blocks at any time, as many times as you want. In this section, you'll draw the interior walls of the bathroom first, and then you'll insert the tub and toilet. Follow these steps to draw the walls:

1. Delete the original tub and toilet drawings. Click the Erase tool in the Modify Ribbon panel, and then enter **All↵↵** to erase the entire visible contents of the drawing. (Doing so has no effect on the blocks you created previously.)

2. Draw a rectangle 7′-6″ × 5′. Metric users should draw a 228 cm × 152 cm rectangle. Orient the rectangle so the long sides go from left to right and the lower-left corner is at coordinate 1′-10″,1′-10″ (or coordinate 56.0000,56.0000 for metric users).

If you use the Rectangle tool to draw the rectangle, make sure you explode it by using the Explode command. This is important for later exercises. (See the section "Unblocking and Redefining a Block" later in this chapter if you aren't familiar with the Explode command.) Your drawing should look like Figure 4.2.

FIGURE 4.2
The interior walls
of the bathroom

Now you're ready to place your blocks. Start by placing the tub in the drawing:

1. In the Block Ribbon panel, click the Insert tool, or type **I↵** to open the Insert dialog box (see Figure 4.3).

FIGURE 4.3
The Insert
dialog box

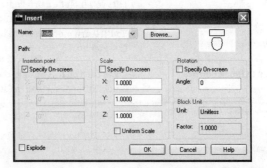

2. Click the Name drop-down list to display a list of the available blocks in the current drawing.

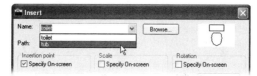

3. Click the block name Tub.

4. In the Insertion Point group and Rotation group, turn on the Specify On-Screen options. With this option turned on in the Insertion Point group, you're asked to specify an insertion point using your cursor. The Specify On-Screen option in the Rotation group lets you specify the rotation angle of the block graphically as you insert it.

5. Click OK and you will see a preview image of the tub attached to the cursor. The upper-left corner you picked for the tub's base point is now on the cursor intersection.

6. At the `Specify insertion point or [Basepoint/Scale/X/Y/Z/Rotate]:` prompt, pick the upper-left intersection of the room as your insertion point.

7. At the `Specify rotation angle <0>:` prompt, notice that you can rotate the block. This lets you visually specify a rotation angle for the block. You won't use this feature at this time, so press ↵ to accept the default of 0. The tub should look like the one in Figure 4.4.

You've got the tub in place. Now place the Toilet block in the drawing:

1. Open the Insert dialog box again, but this time select Toilet in the Name drop-down list.

2. Clear the Specify On-Screen check box in the Rotation group.

3. Place the toilet at the midpoint of the line along the top of the rectangle representing the bathroom wall as shown in the bottom image in Figure 4.4. Notice that after you select the insertion point, the toilet appears in the drawing; you aren't prompted for a rotation angle for the block.

Scaling and Rotating Blocks

When you insert the tub, you can see it rotate as you move the cursor. You can pick a point to fix the block in place, or you can enter a rotation value. This is the result of selecting the Specify On-Screen option in the Insert dialog box. You may find that you want the Rotation group's Specify On-Screen option turned on most of the time to enable you to adjust the rotation angle of the block while you're placing it in the drawing.

The options in the Insert dialog box that you didn't use are the Scale group options. These options let you scale the block to a different size. You can scale the block uniformly, or you can distort the block by individually changing its X, Y, or Z scale factor. With the Specify On-Screen option unchecked, you can enter specific values in the X, Y, and Z text boxes to stretch the block in any direction. If you turn on the Specify On-Screen option, you can visually adjust the X, Y, and Z scale factors in real time. Although these options aren't used often, they can be useful in special situations when a block needs to be stretched one way or another to fit in a drawing.

FIGURE 4.4

The bathroom, first with the tub and then with the toilet inserted

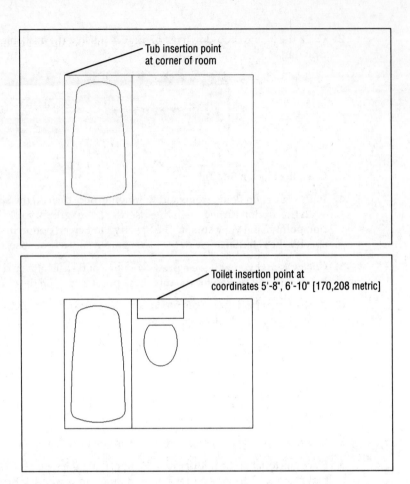

Tub insertion point at corner of room

Toilet insertion point at coordinates 5'-8", 6'-10" [170,208 metric]

You aren't limited to scaling or rotating a block when it's being inserted into a drawing. You can always use the Scale or Rotate tool or modify an inserted block's properties to stretch it in one direction or another. This exercise shows you how this is done:

1. Click the Toilet block to select it.

2. Right-click, and choose Properties from the shortcut menu to open the Properties palette. Take a moment to study the Properties palette. Toward the bottom, under the Geometry heading, you see a set of labels that show *Position* and *Scale*. These labels may appear as *Pos* and *Sca* if the width of the palette has been adjusted to be too narrow to show the entire label. Remember that you can click and drag the left or right edge of the palette to change its width. You can also click and drag the border between the columns in the palette.

3. If the first item label under the Geometry heading isn't visible, place the cursor on the label. A tool tip displays the full wording of the item, which is Position X.

4. Move the cursor down one line to display the tool tip for Position Y. This shows how you can view the label even if it isn't fully visible.

5. Continue to move the cursor down to the Scale X label. The tool tip displays the full title.

6. Let's try making some changes to the toilet properties. Click the Scale X value in the column just to the right of the Scale X label.

7. Enter **1.5↵**. Notice that the toilet changes in width as you do this.

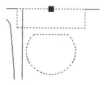

8. You don't really want to change the width of the toilet, so click the Undo tool in the Quick Access toolbar or enter **U↵**.

9. Close the Properties palette by clicking the X at the top of the Properties palette title bar.

If a block is created with the Scale Uniformly option turned on in the Block Definition dialog box, you can't scale the block in just one axis as shown in the previous exercise. You can only scale the block uniformly in all axes.

SYMBOLS FOR PROJECTS LARGE AND SMALL

A symbol library was a crucial part of the production of the San Francisco Main Library construction documents. Shown here is a portion of an AutoCAD floor plan of the library in which some typical symbols were used.

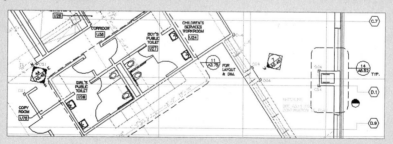

Notice the familiar door symbols, such as the door you created in Chapter 2. And yes, there are even toilets in the lower half of the plan in the public restrooms. Symbol use isn't restricted to building components. Room number labels, diamond-shaped interior elevation reference symbols, and the hexagonal column grid symbols are all common to an architectural drawing, regardless of the project's size. As you work through this chapter, keep in mind that all the symbols used in the library drawing were created using the tools presented here.

You've just seen how you can modify the properties of a block by using the Properties palette. In the exercise, you changed the X scale of the Toilet block, but you could have just as easily changed the Y value. You may have noticed other properties available in the Properties palette. You'll learn more about those properties as you work through this chapter.

You've seen how you can turn a drawing into a symbol, known as a block in AutoCAD. Now let's see how you can use an existing drawing file as a symbol.

Using an Existing Drawing as a Symbol

You need a door into the bathroom. Because you've already drawn a door and saved it as a file, you can bring the door into this drawing file and use it as a block:

1. In the Block Ribbon panel, click the Insert tool, or type I↵.

2. In the Insert dialog box, click the Browse button to open the Select Drawing File dialog box.

3. This is a standard Windows file browser dialog box. Locate the Door file and double-click it. If you didn't create a door file, you can use the door file from the Chapter 04 project files on this book's companion DVD.

   You can also browse your hard disk by looking at thumbnail views of the drawing files in a folder.

4. When you return to the Insert dialog box, make sure the Specify On-Screen options for the Insertion Point, Scale, and Rotation groups are checked, and then click OK. As you move the cursor around, notice that the door appears above and to the right of the cursor intersection, as in Figure 4.5.

FIGURE 4.5
The door drawing being inserted in the Bath file

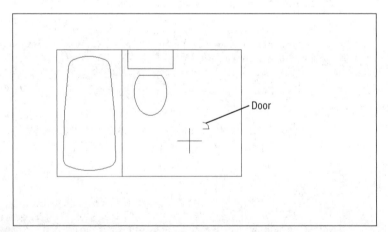

5. At this point, the door looks too small for this bathroom. This is because you drew it 3 units long, which translates to 3″. Metric users drew the door 9 cm long. Pick a point near coordinates 7′-2″,2′-4″ so that the door is placed in the lower-right corner of the room. Metric users should use the coordinate 210,70.

6. If you take the default setting for the X scale of the inserted block, the door will remain 3″ long, or 9 cm long for metric users. However, as mentioned earlier, you can specify a smaller or larger size for an inserted object. In this case, you want a 3′ door. Metric users want a 90 cm door. To get that from a 3″ door, you need an X scale factor of 12, or 10 for metric users. (You may want to review "Understanding Scale Factors" in Chapter 3 to see how this is determined.) At the `Enter X scale factor, specify opposite corner, or [Corner/XYZ] <1>:` prompt, enter **12**⏎. Metric users should enter **10**⏎.

7. Press ⏎ twice to accept the default Y = X and the rotation angle of 0°.

The Command prompt appears, but nothing seems to happen to the drawing. This is because when you enlarged the door, you also enlarged the distance between the base point and the object. This brings up another issue to be aware of when you're considering using drawings as symbols: All drawings have base points. The default base point is the absolute coordinate 0,0, otherwise known as the *origin*, which is located in the lower-left corner of any new drawing. When you drew the door in Chapter 2, you didn't specify the base point. When you try to bring the door into this drawing, AutoCAD uses the origin of the door drawing as its base point (see Figure 4.6).

FIGURE 4.6
By default, a drawing's origin is also its insertion point. You can change a drawing's insertion point by using the Base command.

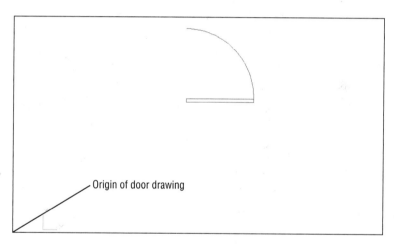

Origin of door drawing

Because the door appears outside the bathroom, you must first choose All from the Zoom flyout on the View tab's Navigate panel to show more of the drawing and then use the Move command on the Modify panel to move the door to the right-side wall of the bathroom. Let's do this now:

1. Click All from the Zoom flyout on the View tab's Navigate panel to display the area set by the limits of your drawing plus any other objects that are outside those limits. You can also use the Zoom flyout on the navigation bar. The view of the room shrinks and the door is displayed. Notice that it's now the proper size for your drawing (see Figure 4.7).

2. Choose the Move tool from the Modify Ribbon panel, or type **M**⏎.

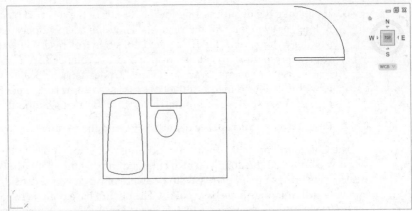

3. To pick the door you just inserted, at the `Select objects:` prompt, click a point anywhere on the door, and press ↵. Notice that now the entire door is highlighted. This is because a block is treated like a single object, even though it may be made up of several lines, arcs, and so on.

4. At the `Specify base point or [Displacement] <Displacement>:` prompt, turn on Running Osnaps, and pick the lower-left corner of the door. Remember that pressing the F3 key or clicking Object Snap in the status bar toggles Running Osnaps on or off.

5. At the `Specify second point or <use first point as displacement>:` prompt, use the Nearest Osnap override, and position the door so that your drawing looks like Figure 4.8.

Because the door is an object that you'll use often, it should be a common size so you don't have to specify an odd value every time you insert it. It would also be helpful if the door's insertion base point were in a more convenient location; that is, a location that would let you place the door accurately within a wall opening. Next you'll modify the Door block to better suit your needs.

FIGURE 4.8
The door on the right-side wall of the bathroom

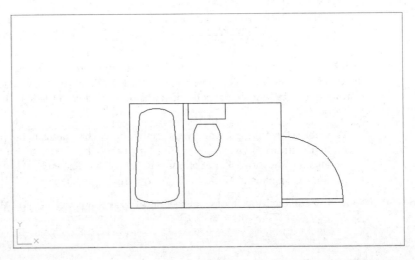

Modifying a Block

You can modify a block in three ways. One way is to completely redefine it. In earlier versions of AutoCAD, this was the only way to make changes to a block. A second way is to use the Block Editor. A third way is to use the Edit Reference tool on the Insert tab's Reference panel. The Edit Reference tool is also known as the Refedit command.

In the following sections, you'll learn how to redefine a block by making changes to the door symbol. Later, in Chapter 18, you'll see how the Block Editor lets you add adjustability to blocks, and in Chapter 7 you'll learn about the Edit Reference panel.

Double-clicking most objects displays the Properties palette. Double-clicking a block opens the Edit Block Definition dialog box, which gives you another way to edit blocks. You'll learn more about the Edit Block Definition dialog box in Chapter 18.

Unblocking and Redefining a Block

One way to modify a block is to break it down into its components, edit them, and then turn them back into a block. This is called *redefining* a block. If you redefine a block that has been inserted in a drawing, each occurrence of that block in the current file changes to reflect the new block definition. You can use this block-redefinition feature to make rapid changes to a design.

To separate a block into its components, use the Explode command:

1. Click Explode from the Home tab's Modify panel. You can also type **X.⏎** to start the Explode command.

2. Click the door, and press ⏎ to confirm your selection.

You can simultaneously insert and explode a block by clicking the Explode check box in the lower-left corner of the Insert dialog box.

Now you can edit the individual objects that make up the door, if you desire. In this case, you want to change only the door's insertion point because you've already made it a more convenient size. You'll turn the door back into a block, this time using the door's lower-left corner for its insertion base point:

1. In the Block Ribbon panel, select Create, or type **B.⏎**.

2. In the Block Definition dialog box, select Door from the Name drop-down list.

3. Click the Pick Point button, and pick the lower-left corner of the door.

4. Click the Select Objects button, and select the components of the door. Press ⏎ when you've finished making your selection.

5. Select the Convert To Block option in the Objects group to automatically convert the selected objects in the drawing into a block.

6. Select Inches (or cm for metric users) from the Block Unit drop-down list, and then enter **Standard door** in the Description box.

7. Click OK. You see a warning message that reads, "The block definition has changed. Do you want to redefine it?" You don't want to redefine an existing block accidentally. In this case, you know you want to redefine the door, so click the Redefine button to proceed.

The Select Objects and Pick Point buttons appear in other dialog boxes. Make note of their appearance, and remember that when you select them, the dialog box temporarily closes to let you select points or objects and otherwise perform operations that require a clear view of the drawing area.

In step 7, you received a warning message that you were about to redefine the existing Door block. But originally you inserted the door as a file, not as a block. Whenever you insert a drawing file by using the Insert Block tool, the inserted drawing automatically becomes a block in the current drawing. When you redefine a block, however, you don't affect the drawing file you imported. AutoCAD changes only the block in the current file.

You've just redefined the door block. Now place the door in the wall of the room:

1. Choose Erase from the Modify Ribbon panel, and then click the door. Notice that the entire door is one object instead of individual lines and an arc. Had you not selected the Convert To Block option in step 5 of the previous exercise, the components of the block would have remained individual objects.

2. Press ↵ to erase the door.

3. Insert the Door block again by using the Insert tool on the Home tab's Block panel. This time, use the Nearest Osnap override, and pick a point on the right-side wall of the bathroom, near coordinate 9′-4″,2′-1″. Metric users should insert the door near 284,63.4.

4. Use the Grips feature to mirror the door, using the wall as the mirror axis so that the door is inside the room. To mirror an object using grips, select the objects to mirror, click a grip, and right-click. Select Mirror from the shortcut menu; then, indicate a mirror axis with the cursor.

Your drawing will look like Figure 4.9.

FIGURE 4.9
The bathroom floor
plan thus far

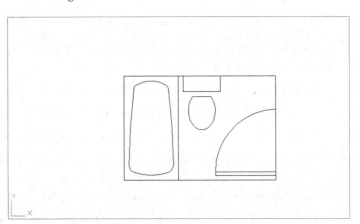

Next you'll see how you can update an external file with a redefined block.

Saving a Block as a Drawing File

You've seen that, with little effort, you can create a symbol and place it anywhere in a file. Suppose you want to use this symbol in other files. When you create a block by using the Block command, the block exists in the current file only until you specifically instruct AutoCAD to save it as a drawing file on disk. When you have an existing drawing that has been brought in and modified, such as the door, the drawing file on disk associated with that door isn't automatically updated. To update the Door file, you must take an extra step and use the Export option on the Application menu. Let's see how this works.

Start by turning the Tub and Toilet blocks into individual files on disk:

1. Press the escape key to make sure nothing is selected and no command is active.

2. From the Application menu, choose Export ➤ Other Formats to open the Export Data dialog box, which is a simple file dialog box.

3. Open the Files Of Type drop-down list, and select Block (*.dwg).

   If you prefer, you can skip step 2 and instead, in step 3, enter the full filename including the .dwg extension, as in Tub.dwg.

4. Double-click the File Name text box and enter **Tub**.

5. Click the Save button to close the Export Data dialog box.

6. At the [= (block=output file)/* (whole drawing)] <define new drawing>: prompt, enter the name of the block you want to save to disk as the tub file—in this case, **Tub** ↵.

   The Tub block is now saved as a file.

7. Repeat steps 1 through 6 for the Toilet block. Give the file the same name as the block.

OPTIONS FOR SAVING BLOCKS

AutoCAD gives you the option to save a block's file under the same name as the original block or save it with a different name. Usually, you'll want to use the same name, which you can do by entering an equal sign (=) after the prompt.

Normally, AutoCAD saves a preview image with a file. This enables you to preview a drawing file before opening it.

Replacing Existing Files with Blocks

The Wblock command does the same thing as choosing Export ➤ Other Formats, but output is limited to AutoCAD DWG files. Let's try using the Wblock command this time to save the Door block you modified:

1. Issue the Wblock command by typing **Wblock**↵, or use the keyboard shortcut by typing **w**↵. This opens the Write Block dialog box (see Figure 4.10).

2. In the Source group, click the Block radio button.

3. Select Door from the drop-down list. You can keep the old name or enter a different name if you prefer.

FIGURE 4.10
The Write Block
dialog box

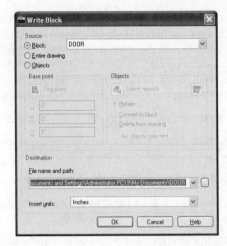

4. In this case, you want to update the door you drew in Chapter 2. Click the Browse button in the Destination group.

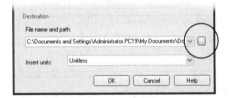

5. Locate and select the original Door.dwg file that you inserted earlier. Click Save to close the dialog box.

6. Click OK. A warning message tells you that the Door.dwg file already exists. Go ahead and click the "Replace the existing…." option to confirm that you want to overwrite the old door drawing with the new door definition.

In this exercise, you typed the Wblock command at the Command prompt instead of choosing Export ➤ Other Formats. The results are the same regardless of which method you use. If you're in a hurry, the Export ➤ Other Formats command is a quick way to save part of your drawing as a file. The Wblock option might be easier for new users because it offers options in a dialog box.

UNDERSTANDING THE WRITE BLOCK DIALOG BOX OPTIONS

The Write Block dialog box offers a way to save parts of your current drawing as a file. As you can see from the dialog box shown in the previous exercise, you have several options.

In that exercise, you used the Block option of the Source group to select an existing block as the source object to be exported. You can also export a set of objects by choosing the Objects option. If you choose this option, the Base Point and Objects groups become available. These options work the same way as their counterparts in the Block Definition dialog box, which you saw earlier when you created the Tub and Toilet blocks.

The other option in the Source group, Entire Drawing, lets you export the whole drawing to its own file. This may seem to duplicate the Save As option in the Application menu, but saving the entire drawing from the Write Block dialog box performs some additional operations, such as stripping out unused blocks or other unused components. This has the effect of reducing file size. You'll learn more about this feature later in this chapter.

Other Uses for Blocks

So far you've used the Block tool to create symbols, and you've used the Export and Wblock commands to save those symbols to disk. As you can see, you can create symbols and save them at any time while you're drawing. You've made the tub and toilet symbols into drawing files that you can see when you check the contents of your current folder.

However, creating symbols isn't the only use for the Block, Export, and Wblock commands. You can use them in any situation that requires grouping objects (though you may prefer to use the more flexible Object Grouping dialog box discussed later in this chapter). You can also use blocks to stretch a set of objects along one axis by using the Properties palette. Export and Wblock also enable you to save a part of a drawing to disk. You'll see instances of these other uses of the Block, Export, and Wblock commands throughout the book.

Block, Export, and Wblock are extremely versatile commands, and if used judiciously, they can boost your productivity and simplify your work. If you aren't careful, however, you can get carried away and create more blocks than you can track. Planning your drawings helps you determine which elements will work best as blocks and recognize situations in which other methods of organization are more suitable.

Another way of using symbols is to use AutoCAD's external reference capabilities. External reference files, known as *Xrefs*, are files inserted into a drawing in a way similar to how blocks are inserted. The difference is that Xrefs don't become part of the drawing's database. Instead, they're loaded along with the current file at startup time. It's as if AutoCAD opens several drawings at once: the main file you specify when you start AutoCAD and the Xrefs associated with the main file.

By keeping the Xrefs independent from the current file, you make sure that any changes made to the Xrefs automatically appear in the current file. You don't have to update each inserted copy of an Xref. For example, if you use the Attach tool on the Insert tab's Reference panel (discussed in Chapter 7) to insert the tub drawing and later you make changes to the tub, the next time you open the Bath file, you'll see the new version of the tub. Or if you have both the tub and the referencing drawing open and you change the tub, AutoCAD will notify you that a change has been made to an external reference. You can then update the tub Xref using the External Reference palette.

Xrefs are especially useful in workgroup environments, where several people are working on the same project. One person might be updating several files that have been inserted into a variety of other files. Before Xrefs were available, everyone in the workgroup had to be notified of the changes and had to update all the affected blocks in all the drawings that contained them. With Xrefs, the updating is automatic. Many other features are unique to these files. They're discussed in more detail in Chapters 7 and 15.

Understanding the Annotation Scale

One common use for AutoCAD's block feature is creating *reference symbols*. These are symbols that refer the viewer to other drawings or views in a set of drawings. An example would be a building-section symbol on a floor plan that directs the viewer to look at a location on another sheet to see a cross-section view of a building. Such a symbol is typically a circle with two numbers: one is the drawing sheet number and the other is the view number on the sheet (examples appear a little later, in Figure 4.15).

In the past, AutoCAD users had to insert a reference symbol block multiple times to accommodate different scales of the same view. For example, the same floor plan might be used for a ¼″ = 1′-0″ scale view and a 1/8″ = 1′-0″ view. An elevation symbol block that works for the ¼″ = 1′-0″ scale view would be too small for the 1/8″ = 1′-0″ view, so two copies of the same block were inserted, one for each scale. The user then had to place the two blocks on different layers to control their visibility. In addition, if sheet numbers changed, the user had to make sure every copy of the elevation symbol block was updated to reflect the change.

The annotation scale feature does away with this need for redundancy. You can now use a single instance of a block even if it must be displayed in different scale views. To do this, you must take some additional steps when creating and inserting the block. Here's how you do it:

1. Draw your symbol at the size it should appear when plotted. For example, if the symbol is supposed to be a ¼″ circle on a printed sheet, draw the symbol as a ¼″ circle.

2. Open the Block Definition dialog box by choosing the Create tool from the Block Ribbon panel.

3. Turn on the Annotative option in the Behavior section of the Block Definition dialog box. You can also turn on the Match Block Orientation To Layout option if you want the symbol to appear always in a vertical orientation (see Figure 4.11).

FIGURE 4.11
The Block Definition dialog box with the Annotative option turned on

4. Select the objects that make up the block, and indicate an insertion point as usual.

5. Give the block a name and then click OK.

After you've followed these steps, you need to apply an annotation scale to the newly created block:

1. Click the new block to select it.

2. Right-click and choose Annotative Object Scale ➢ Add/Delete Scales. The Annotation Object Scale dialog box appears (see Figure 4.12).

3. Click the Add button. The Add Scales To Object dialog box appears (see Figure 4.13).

FIGURE 4.12
The Annotation
Object Scale
dialog box

FIGURE 4.13
The Add Scales To
Object dialog box

4. Select from the list the scale you'll be using with this block. You can Ctrl+click to select multiple scales. When you're finished selecting scales, click OK. The selected scales appear in the Annotation Object Scale dialog box.

5. Click OK to close the Annotation Object Scale dialog box.

At this point, the block is ready to be used in multiple scale views. You need only to select a scale from the Model view's Annotation Scale drop-down list or the Layout view's Viewport Scale drop-down list, which are both in the lower-right corner of the AutoCAD window (see Figure 4.14).

The Annotation Scale drop-down list appears in Model view, and the Viewport Scale drop-down list appears in Layout view and when a viewport is selected. (See Chapter 16 for more about layouts and viewports.) In Layout view, you can set the Viewport Scale value for each individual viewport so the same block can appear at the appropriate size for different scale viewports (see Figure 4.15).

Note that if you want to use several copies of a block that is using multiple annotation scales, you should insert the block and assign the additional annotation scales and then make copies of the block. If you insert a new instance of the block, the block acquires only the annotation scale that is current for the drawing. You'll have to assign additional annotation scales to each new insertion of the block.

FIGURE 4.14
The Annotation
Scale and the
Layout view's
Viewport Scale
drop-down lists

FIGURE 4.15

A single block is used to create building section symbols of different sizes in these Layout views. Both views show the same floor plan displayed at different scales.

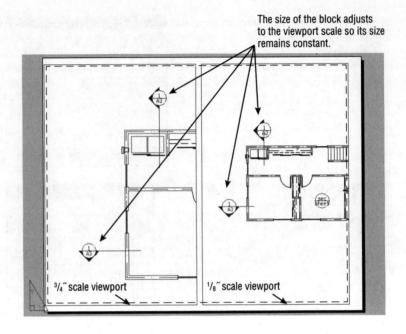

The size of the block adjusts to the viewport scale so its size remains constant.

If you're uncertain whether an annotation scale has been assigned to a block, you can click the block and you'll see the different scale versions of the block as ghosted images. Also, if you hover over a block, triangular symbols appear next to the cursor for blocks that have been assigned annotation scales.

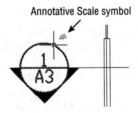

Annotative Scale symbol

If you need to change the position of a block for a particular layout viewport scale, go to Model view, select the appropriate scale from the Annotation Scale drop-down list, and then adjust the position of the block.

Grouping Objects

Blocks are extremely useful tools, but for some situations, they're too restrictive. At times, you'll want to group objects so they're connected but can still be edited individually.

For example, consider a space planner who has to place workstations on a floor plan. Although each workstation is basically the same, some slight variations in each station could make the use of blocks unwieldy. For instance, one workstation might need a different configuration to accommodate special equipment, and another workstation might need to be slightly larger than the standard size. You would need to create a block for one workstation and then, for each variation, explode the block, edit it, and create a new block. A better way is to draw a prototype workstation and turn it into a group. You can copy the group into position and then edit it for each individual situation without losing its identity as a group. AutoCAD LT offers a different method for grouping objects. If you're using LT, skip this exercise and continue with the following section, "Grouping Objects for LT Users."

The following exercise demonstrates how grouping works:

1. Save the Bath file, and then open the drawing Office1.dwg from the sample files from this book's companion DVD. Metric users should open Office1-metric.dwg.

2. Use the Zoom command to enlarge just the view of the workstation, as shown in the first image in Figure 4.16.

3. Type **G.⏎** or **Group.⏎** to open the Object Grouping dialog box (see Figure 4.17).

4. Type **Station1**. As you type, your entry appears in the Group Name text box.

FIGURE 4.16
A workstation in an office plan

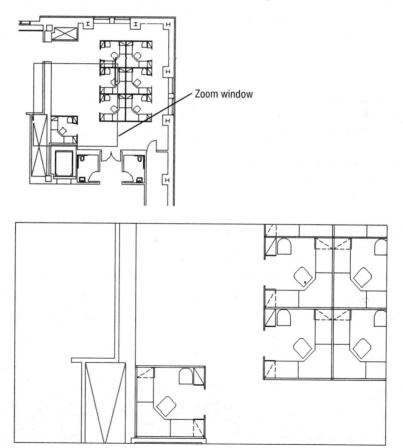

FIGURE 4.17
Object Grouping
dialog box

5. Click New < in the Create Group group, about midway in the dialog box. The Object Grouping dialog box temporarily closes to let you select objects for your new group.

6. At the Select objects: prompt, window the entire workstation in the lower-left corner of the plan, and press ↵ to display the Object Grouping dialog box. Notice that the name Station1 appears in the Group Name box at the top of the dialog box.

7. Click OK. You've just created a group.

Now whenever you want to select the workstation, you can click any part of it to select the entire group. At the same time, you can still modify individual parts of the group—the desk, partition, and so on—without losing the grouping of objects (see "Modifying Members of a Group" later in this chapter).

Grouping Objects for LT Users

LT users have to use a slightly different method to create a group. If you're using AutoCAD LT 2011, do the following:

1. Open Office1.dwg from the sample files on the DVD. Metric users should open Office1-metric.dwg.

2. Use the Zoom command to enlarge just the view of the workstation, as shown in the first image in Figure 4.16.

3. Type G↵ or Group↵ to open the Group Manager dialog box.

4. Move the dialog box so that you have a clear view of the workstation; then, use a selection window to select all the objects of the workstation. You can also click the individual objects of the workstation to make the selection.

5. In the Group Manager dialog box, click the Create Group button. A new listing appears in the Group Manager list box.

6. Type **Station1**↵ in the text box that appears in the group list.

7. Close the Group Manager dialog box.

Now whenever you want to select the workstation, you can click any part of it to select the entire group. At the same time, you can still modify individual parts of the group—the desk, partition, and so on—without losing the grouping of objects.

Modifying Members of a Group

Next you'll make copies of the original group and modify the copies. Figure 4.18 is a sketch of the proposed layout that uses the new workstations. Look carefully and you'll see that some of the workstations in the sketch are missing a few of the standard components that exist in the Station1 group. One pair of stations has a partition removed; another station has one less chair.

FIGURE 4.18
A sketch of the new office layout

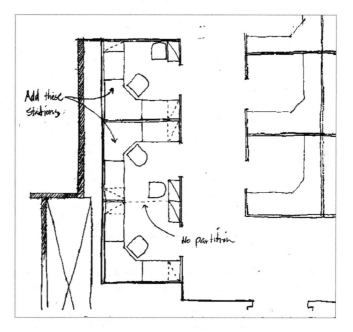

The exercises in this section show you how to complete your drawing to reflect the design requirements of the sketch.

Start by making a copy of the workstation:

1. Click Copy on the Modify Ribbon panel, or type **Co**↵, and click the Station1 group you just created. Notice that you can click any part of the station to select the entire station. If only a single object is selected, press Shift+Ctrl+A and try clicking another part of the group.

2. Press ↵ to finish your selection.

3. At the `Specify base point or [Displacement/mOde] <Displacement>:` prompt, enter **@**↵. Then enter **@8′2″<90** to copy the workstation 8′-2″ vertically. Metric users should enter **@249<90**. Press ↵ to exit the Copy command.

You can also use the Direct Distance method by typing @↵ and then pointing the rubber-banding line 90° and typing 8´2˝↵. Metric users should type 249↵.

4. Issue the Copy command again, but this time click the copy of the workstation you just created. Notice that it too is a group.

5. Copy this workstation 8´-2˝ (249 cm for the metric users) vertically, just as you did the original workstation. Press ↵ to exit the Copy command.

Next you'll use grips to mirror the first workstation copy:

1. Click the middle workstation to highlight it, and notice that grips appear for all the entities in the group.

2. Click the grip in the middle-left side, as shown in Figure 4.19.

FIGURE 4.19
Mirroring the
new group by
using grips

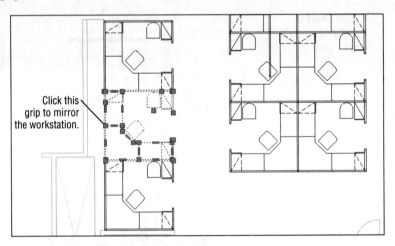

Click this grip to mirror the workstation.

3. Right-click the mouse, and choose Mirror from the shortcut menu. Notice that a temporary mirror image of the workstation follows the movement of your cursor.

4. Turn on Ortho mode, and pick a point directly to the right of the hot grip you picked in step 2. The workstation is mirrored to a new orientation.

5. Press the Esc key twice to clear the grip selection. Also, turn off Ortho mode.

Now that you've got the workstations laid out, you need to remove some of the partitions between the new workstations. If you had used blocks for the workstations, you would first need to explode the workstations that have partitions you want to edit. Groups, however, let you make changes without undoing their grouping.

Use these steps to remove the partitions:

1. At the Command prompt, press Shift+Ctrl+A. You should see the `<Group off>` message in the command line. If you see the `<Group on>` message instead, press Shift+Ctrl+A until you see `<Group off>`. This turns off groupings so you can select and edit individual objects within a group.

2. Erase the short partition that divides the two copies of the workstations, as shown in Figure 4.20. Since you made a mirror copy of the original workstation, you'll need to erase two partitions, the original and the copy.

FIGURE 4.20
Remove the partitions between the two workstations.

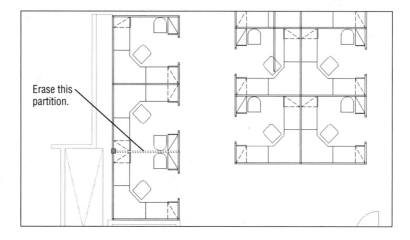

Erase this partition.

3. Press Shift+Ctrl+A again to turn groupings back on.

4. To check your workstations, click one of them to see whether all its components are highlighted together.

5. Close the file when you're finished. You don't need to save your changes.

Pickstyle is a system variable that controls how groups are selected. See Appendix B for more information about Pickstyle and other system variables.

Working with the Object Grouping Dialog Box

ACAD only

Each group has a unique name, and you can also attach a brief description of a group in the Object Grouping dialog box. When you copy a group, AutoCAD assigns an arbitrary name to the newly created group. Copies of groups are considered unnamed, but you can still list them in the Object Grouping dialog box by clicking the Include Unnamed check box. You can click the Rename button in the Object Grouping dialog box to name unnamed groups appropriately (see Figure 4.21).

FIGURE 4.21
The Object Grouping dialog box

Objects in a group aren't bound solely to that group. One object can be a member of several groups, and you can have nested groups (groups with groups).

AutoCAD LT users have a different set of options. See the next section, "Working with the LT Group Manager."

Table 4.2 gives a rundown of the options available in the Object Grouping dialog box.

TABLE 4.2:   Object Grouping dialog box options

OPTION	PURPOSE
Group Identification	Use these options to identify your groups with unique elements that let you remember what each group is for.
Group Name	This text box lets you create a new group by naming it first.
Description	This text box lets you include a brief description of the group.
Find Name <	Click this button to find the name of a group. The Object Grouping dialog box temporarily closes so you can click a group.
Highlight <	Click this button to highlight a group that has been selected from the Group Name list. This helps you locate a group in a crowded drawing.
Include Unnamed	This check box determines whether unnamed groups are included in the Group Name list. Check this box to display the names of copies of groups for processing by this dialog box.
Create Group	Here's where you control how a group is created.
New <	Click this button to create a new group. The Object Grouping dialog box closes temporarily so that you can select objects for grouping. To use this button, you must have either entered a group name or selected the Unnamed check box.
Selectable	This check box lets you control whether the group you create is selectable. See the description of the Selectable button in the Change Group group later in this table.
Unnamed	This check box lets you create a new group without naming it.
Change Group	These buttons are available only when a group name is highlighted in the Group Name list at the top of the dialog box.
Remove <	Click this button to remove objects from a group.
Add <	Click this button to add objects to a group. While you're using this option, grouping is temporarily turned off to allow you to select objects from other groups.
Rename	Click this button to rename a group.
Re-Order	Click this button to change the order of objects in a group. The order refers to the order in which you selected the objects to include in the group. You can change this selection order for special purposes such as tool-path machining.

TABLE 4.2:   Object Grouping dialog box options   *(CONTINUED)*

OPTION	PURPOSE
Description	Click this button to modify the description of a group.
Explode	Click this button to separate a group into its individual components.
Selectable	Click this button to turn individual groupings on and off. When a group is selectable, it can be selected only as a group. When a group isn't selectable, the individual objects in a group can be selected, but not the group.

If a group is selected, you can remove individual items from the selection with a Shift+click. In this way, you can isolate objects within a group for editing or removal without having to turn off groups temporarily.

Working with the LT Group Manager

LT only

If you're using AutoCAD LT, you use the Group Manager to manage groups. Table 4.3 offers a rundown of the tools that are available in the Group Manager.

TABLE 4.3:   AutoCAD LT 2011 Group Manager options

OPTION	PURPOSE
Create Group	Lets you convert a set of objects into a group. Select a set of objects, and then click Create Group.
Ungroup	Removes the grouping of an existing group. Select the group name from the list, and then select Ungroup.
Add To Group	Lets you add an object to a group. At least one group and one additional object must be selected before this option is available.
Remove From Group	Lets you remove one or more objects from a group. To isolate individual objects in a group, first select the group, and then Shift+click to remove individual objects from the selection set. After you isolate the object you want to remove, click Remove From Group.
Details	Lists detailed information about the group, such as the number of objects in the group and whether it's in Model Space or a layout. Select the group name from the group list, and then click Details.
Select Group	Lets you select a group by name. Highlight the group name in the group list, and then click Select Group.
Deselect Group	Removes a group from the current selection set. Highlight the group name in the group list, and then click Deselect Group.
Help	Opens the AutoCAD LT Help website and displays information about the Group Manager.

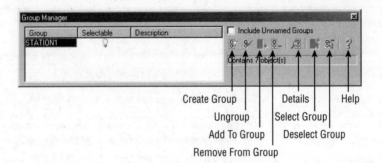

You've seen how you can use groups to create an office layout. You can also use groups to help you keep sets of objects temporarily together in a complex drawing. Groups can be especially useful in 3D modeling when you want to organize complex assemblies together for easy selection.

The Bottom Line

Create and insert a symbol. If you have a symbol that you use often in a drawing, you can draw it once and then turn it into an AutoCAD block. A block can be placed in a drawing multiple times in any location, like a rubber stamp. A block is stored in a drawing as a block definition, which can be called up at any time.

   Master It   Name the dialog box used to create a block from objects in a drawing, and also name the tool to open this dialog box.

Modify a block. Once you've created a block, it isn't set in stone. One of the features of a block is that you can change the block definition and all the copies of the block are updated to the new definition.

   Master It   What is the name of the tool used to "unblock" a block?

Understand the annotation scale. In some cases, you'll want to create a block that is dependent on the drawing scale. You can create a block that adjusts itself to the scale of your drawing through the annotation scale feature. When the annotation scale feature is turned on for a block, the block can be set to appear at the correct size depending on the scale of your drawing.

   Master It   What setting in the Block Definition dialog box turns on the annotation scale feature, and how do you set the annotation scale of a block?

Group objects. Blocks can be used as a tool to group objects together, but blocks can be too rigid for some grouping applications. AutoCAD offers groups, which are collections of objects that are similar to blocks but aren't as rigidly defined.

   Master It   How are groups different from blocks?

Chapter 5

Keeping Track of Layers and Blocks

Imagine a filing system that has only one category into which you put all your records. For only a handful of documents, such a filing system might work. However, as soon as you start to accumulate more documents, you would want to start separating them into meaningful categories, perhaps alphabetically or by their use, so you could find them more easily.

The same is true for drawings. If you have a simple drawing with only a few objects, you can get by without using layers. But as soon as your drawing gets the least bit complicated, you'll want to start sorting your objects into layers to keep track of what's what. Layers don't restrict you when you're editing objects such as blocks or groups, and you can set up layers so that you can easily identify which object belongs to which layer.

In this chapter, you'll learn how to create and use layers to keep your drawings organized. You'll learn how color can play an important role while you're working with layers, and you'll also learn how to include linetypes such as dashes and center lines through the use of layers.

In this chapter, you'll learn to do the following:

◆ Organize information with layers

◆ Control layer visibility

◆ Keep track of blocks and layers

GET ADDITIONAL HELP ON THE DVD

The companion DVD offers two video tutorials that give you an overview of the main topics of this chapter. The video entitled "Working with Layers" gives you an introduction to Layers. The video entitled "Using Linetypes and Lineweights" covers the material from the section entitled "Assigning Linetypes to Layers."

Organizing Information with Layers

You can think of layers as overlays on which you keep various types of information (see Figure 5.1). In a floor plan of a building, for example, you want to keep the walls, ceiling, plumbing fixtures, wiring, and furniture separate so that you can display or plot them individually or combine them in different ways. It's also a good idea to keep notes and reference symbols, as well as the drawing's dimensions, on their own layers. As your drawing becomes more complex, you can turn the various layers on and off to allow easier display and modification.

For example, one of your consultants might need a plot of just the dimensions and walls, without all the other information; another consultant might need only a furniture layout. Using manual drafting, you would have to redraw your plan for each consultant or use overlay drafting techniques, which can be cumbersome. With AutoCAD, you can turn off the layers you don't need and plot a drawing containing only the required information. A carefully planned layering scheme helps you produce a document that combines the types of information needed in each case.

FIGURE 5.1

Placing drawing elements on separate layers

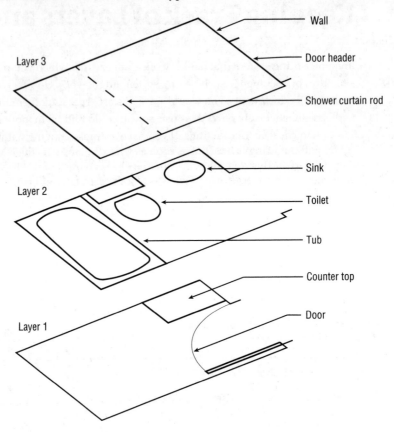

Layer 3

Layer 2

Layer 1

Wall

Door header

Shower curtain rod

Sink

Toilet

Tub

Counter top

Door

Using layers also lets you modify your drawings more easily. For example, suppose you have an architectural drawing with separate layers for the walls, the ceiling plan, and the floor plan. If any change occurs in the wall locations, you can turn on the ceiling plan layer to see where the new wall locations will affect the ceiling and then make the proper adjustments.

AutoCAD allows an unlimited number of layers, and you can name each layer anything you want using any characters with the exception of these: < > / \ " : ; ? * | , = '.

Creating and Assigning Layers

You'll start your exploration of layers by using a palette to create a new layer, giving it a name, and assigning it a color. Then you'll look at alternate ways of creating a layer through the command line. Next you'll assign the new layer to the objects in your drawing. Start by getting familiar with the Layer Properties Manager:

1. Open the Bath file you created in Chapter 4. (If you didn't create one, use either 04b-bath.dwg or 04b-bath-metric.dwg.)

2. To display the Layer Properties Manager, click the Layer Properties tool in the Home tab's Layers panel, or type **LA.** ↵ to use the keyboard shortcut.

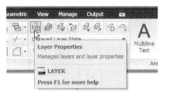

The Layer Properties Manager shows you at a glance the status of your layers. Right now, you have only one layer, but as your work expands, so will the number of layers. You'll then find this palette indispensable.

3. Click the New Layer button at the top of the palette. The button has an icon that looks like a star next to a sheet.

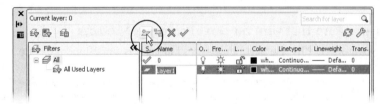

A new layer named Layer1 appears in the list box. Notice that the name is highlighted. This tells you that by typing, you can change the default name to something better suited to your needs.

4. Type **Wall**. As you type, your entry replaces the Layer1 name in the list box.

5. With the Wall layer name highlighted, click the Color icon in the Wall layer listing to display a dialog box in which you can assign a color to the Wall layer. The Color icon can be found under the Color column and currently shows White as its value. The icon is just to the left of the word *white*.

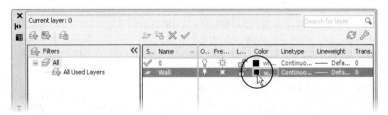

The Select Color dialog box opens (see Figure 5.2).

FIGURE 5.2
The Select Color
dialog box

6. In the row of standard colors next to the ByLayer button, click the green square, and then click OK. Notice that the color swatch in the Wall layer listing is now green.

7. Click the X at the top of the Layer Properties Manager's title bar to close it.

From this point on, any object assigned to the Wall layer will appear green unless the object is specifically assigned a different color.

USING AUTO-HIDE WITH THE LAYER PROPERTIES MANAGER

In AutoCAD 2011, the Layer Properties Manager is a non-modal palette, which means that any change you make within the palette will take effect immediately in the drawing. It also means that the palette can stay open even while you perform other, non-layer-related operations. Throughout this chapter, I'll ask you to open or close the Layer Properties Manager, but if you prefer, you can keep it open all the time. If you decide to keep it open, you may want to use the palette's Auto-Hide feature. Click the Auto-Hide icon toward the top of the palette's title bar so that it changes to a single-sided arrowhead.

With Auto-Hide on, the palette will minimize to display only its title bar. To open the palette, click the title bar. To minimize it, point the cursor anywhere outside the palette for a moment. You can also force the palette to the left or right margin of the AutoCAD window. To do this, right-click the palette title bar and select Anchor Left or Anchor Right.

USING TRUE OR PANTONE COLORS

In the preceding exercise, you chose a color from the Index Color tab of the Select Color dialog box. Most of the time, you'll find that the Index Color tab includes enough colors to suit your needs.

But if you're creating a presentation drawing in which color selection is important, you can choose colors from either the True Color or the Color Books tab of the Select Color dialog box.

The True Color tab offers a full range of colors through a color palette similar to the one found in Adobe Photoshop and other image-editing programs (see Figure 5.3).

FIGURE 5.3
The True Color tab

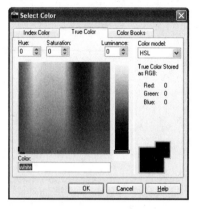

You have the choice of using hue, saturation, and luminance, which is the HSL color model, or you can use the RGB (red, green, blue) color model. You can select HSL or RGB from the Color Model drop-down list in the upper-right corner of the dialog box (see Figure 5.4).

FIGURE 5.4
The Color Model
drop-down list

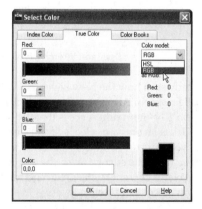

You can also select from PANTONE, RAL, and DIC *color books* by using the Color Books tab (see Figure 5.5).

Let's continue with our look at layers in AutoCAD.

UNDERSTANDING THE LAYER PROPERTIES MANAGER PALETTE

The Layer Properties Manager conforms to the Windows interface standard. The most prominent feature of this palette is the layer list box, as you saw in the preceding exercise. Notice that the bar at the top of the list of layers offers several buttons for the various layer properties. Just as you can in Windows Explorer, you can adjust the width of each column in the list of layers by clicking and dragging either side of the column head buttons. You can also sort the layer list based on a property by clicking the property name at the top of the list. And just as with other Windows list boxes, you can also Shift+click names to select a block of layer names, or you can Ctrl+click individual names to select multiple layers that don't appear together. These features will become helpful as your list of layers grows.

FIGURE 5.5
The Color
Books tab

Above the layer list, you can see four tool buttons.

You've already seen how the New Layer tool works. The tool next to the New Layer tool, the New Layer VP Frozen In All Viewports tool, looks similar to the New Layer tool and performs a similar function. The main difference is that the New Layer VP Frozen tool freezes the newly created layer. To delete layers, you select a layer or group of layers and then click the Delete Layer tool. Be aware that you can't delete layer 0, locked layers, or layers that contain objects. The Set Current tool enables you to set the current layer, the one on which you want to work. You can also see at a glance which layer is current by the green checkmark in the Status column of the layer list.

Another way to create or delete layers is to select a layer or set of layers from the list box and then right-click. A menu appears, offering the same functions as the tools above the layer list.

You'll also notice another set of three tools farther to the left of the Layer Properties Manager. Those tools offer features to organize your layers in a meaningful way. You'll get a closer look at them a little later in this chapter.

CONTROLLING LAYERS THROUGH THE LAYER COMMAND

You've seen how the Layer Properties Manager makes it easy to view and edit layer information and how you can easily select layer colors from the Select Color dialog box. But you can also control layers through the Command prompt.

You won't see the Pstyle option in the layer prompt or the Truecolor /COlor Books options in the color option prompt unless you're using named plot styles. See Chapter 9 for more on plot styles.

Use these steps to control layers through the Command prompt:

1. Press the Esc key to make sure any current command is canceled.

2. At the Command prompt, enter **–Layer.**⏎. Make sure you include the minus sign in front of the word *Layer*. The following prompt appears:

```
Enter an option
[?/Make/Set/New/Rename/ON/OFF/Color/Ltype/LWeight/TRansparency/MATerial/
Plot/Freeze/Thaw/LOck/Unlock/stAte/
Description/rEconcile]:
```

You'll learn about many of the options in this prompt as you work through this chapter.

3. Enter **N**⏎ to select the New option.

4. At the Enter name list for new layer(s): prompt, enter **Wall2**⏎. The [?/Make/Set/ New/Rename/ON/OFF/Color/Ltype/LWeight/TRansparency/MATerial/Plot/Freeze/ Thaw/LOck/Unlock/stAte/rEconcile]: prompt appears again.

5. Enter **C**⏎.

6. At the New color [Truecolor/COlorbook]: prompt, enter **Yellow**⏎. Or, you can enter **2**⏎, the numeric equivalent of the color yellow in AutoCAD.

7. At the Enter name list of layer(s) for color 2 (yellow) <0>: prompt, enter **Wall2**⏎. The [?/Make/Set/New/ Rename/ON/OFF/Color/Ltype/LWeight/ TRansparency/MATerial/Plot/Freeze/Thaw/LOck/Unlock/stAte/rEconcile]: prompt appears again.

8. Press ⏎ to exit the Layer command.

Each method of controlling layers has its own advantages. The Layer Properties Manager offers more information about your layers at a glance. On the other hand, the Layer command offers a quick way to control and create layers if you're in a hurry. Also, if you intend to write custom macros, you'll want to know how to use the Layer command as opposed to using the Layer Properties Manager because palettes can't be controlled through custom toolbar buttons or scripts.

ASSIGNING LAYERS TO OBJECTS

When you create an object, that object is assigned to the current layer. Until now, only one layer has existed—layer 0—and it contains all the objects you've drawn so far. Now that you've created some new layers, you can reassign objects to them by using the Properties palette:

1. Select the four lines that represent the bathroom walls. If you have trouble singling out the wall to the left, use a window to select the wall line.

2. With the cursor in the drawing area, right-click and choose Properties from the shortcut menu to open the Properties palette. This palette lets you modify the properties of an object or a set of objects. (See the upcoming sidebar "Understanding Object Properties.")

3. Click the Layer option on the list in the Properties palette. Notice that an arrow appears in the layer name to the right of the Layer option.

4. Click the downward-pointing arrow to the far right of the Layer option to display a list of all the available layers.

5. Select the Wall layer from the list. Notice that the wall lines you selected change to a green color. This tells you that the objects have been assigned to the Wall layer. (Remember that you assigned a green color to the Wall layer.)

6. Close the Properties palette by clicking the X at the top of its title bar.

The bathroom walls are now on the new layer called Wall, and the walls are changed to green. Layers are more easily distinguished from one another when you use colors to set them apart.

USING THE QUICK PROPERTIES PANEL

This chapter focuses on the tools in the Ribbon and the Properties palette to set the properties of an object. You can also use the Quick Properties panel to change the color, layer, and linetype of objects. When the Quick Properties panel is turned on, it appears automatically when you select an object. You can turn it on or off by clicking the Quick Properties tool in the status bar.

Next, you'll practice the commands you learned in this section and try some new ones by creating new layers and changing the layer assignments of the rest of the objects in your bathroom:

1. Click the Layer Properties tool in the Home tab's Layers panel to open the Layer Properties Manager. Create a new layer called Fixture, and give it the color blue.

    You can change the name of a layer in the Layer Properties Manager. Select the layer name that you want to change and click it again so that the name is highlighted, or press the F2 function key. You can then rename the layer. This works in the same way as renaming a file or folder in Windows.

2. Click the Tub and Toilet blocks, and then right-click and choose Properties from the shortcut menu to open the Properties palette.

3. Click Layer in the list of properties, and then select Fixture from the drop-down list to the right of the layer listing.

4. Click the X at the top of the title bar of the Properties palette to dismiss it, and then press the Esc key to clear your selection.

5. Create a new layer for the door, name the layer Door, and make it red. In a block, you can change the color assignment and linetype of only those objects that are on layer 0. See the sidebar "Controlling Colors and Linetypes of Blocked Objects" later in this chapter.

6. Just as you've done with the walls and fixtures, use the Properties palette to assign the door to the Door layer.

7. Use the Layer Properties Manager to create three more layers, one for the ceiling, one for the door jambs, and one for the floor. Create these layers, and set their colors as indicated (remember that you can open the Select Color dialog box by clicking the color swatch of the layer listing):

Ceiling	Magenta (6)
Jamb	Green (3)
Floor	Cyan (4)

UNDERSTANDING OBJECT PROPERTIES

It helps to think of the components of an AutoCAD drawing as having properties. For example, a line has geometric properties, such as its length and the coordinates that define its endpoints. An arc has a radius, a center, and beginning and ending coordinates. Even though a layer isn't an object you can grasp and manipulate, it can have properties such as color, linetypes, and lineweights.

By default, objects take on the color, linetype, and lineweight of the layer to which they're assigned, but you can also assign these properties directly to individual objects. These general properties can be manipulated through both the Properties palette and the Home tab's Properties panel.

Although many of the options in the Properties palette may seem cryptic, don't worry about them at this point. As you work with AutoCAD, these properties will become more familiar. You'll find that you won't be too concerned with the geometric properties because you'll be manipulating them with the standard editing tools in the Modify toolbar. The other properties will be explained in the rest of this chapter and in other chapters.

In step 3 of the previous exercise, you used the Properties palette, which offered several options for modifying the block. The options displayed in the Properties palette depend on the objects you've selected. With only one object selected, AutoCAD displays options that apply specifically to that object. With several objects selected, you'll see a more limited set of options because AutoCAD can change only those properties that are common to all the objects selected.

Working on Layers

So far, you've created layers and then assigned objects to those layers. In this section, you'll learn how to use the layer drop-down list in the Properties panel to assign layers to objects. In the process, you'll make some additions to the drawing.

CONTROLLING COLORS AND LINETYPES OF BLOCKED OBJECTS

Layer 0 has special importance to blocks. When objects assigned to layer 0 are used as parts of a block and that block is inserted on another layer, those objects take on the characteristics of their new layer. On the other hand, if those objects are on a layer other than layer 0, they maintain their original layer characteristics even if you insert or change that block to another layer. For example, suppose the tub is drawn on the Door layer instead of on layer 0. If you turn the tub into a block and insert it on the Fixture layer, the objects the tub is composed of will maintain their assignment to the Door layer even though the Tub block is assigned to the Fixture layer.

It may help to think of the block function as a clear plastic bag that holds together the objects that make up the tub. The objects inside the bag maintain their assignment to the Door layer even while the bag itself is assigned to the Fixture layer. This may be a bit confusing at first, but it should become clearer after you use blocks for a while.

AutoCAD also enables you to have more than one color or linetype on an object. For example, you can use the Color and Linetype drop-down list in the Properties palette to alter the color or linetype of an object on layer 0. That object then maintains its assigned color and linetype—no matter what its layer assignment. Likewise, objects specifically assigned a color or linetype aren't affected by their inclusion in blocks.

The current layer is still layer 0, and unless you change the current layer, every new object you draw will be on layer 0. Here's how to change the current layer:

1. First press the Esc key to clear any selections, and then click the Layer list box on the Home tab's Layers panel.

A drop-down list opens, showing you all the layers available in the drawing. Notice the icons that appear next to the layer names; they control the status of the layer. You'll learn how to work with these icons later in this chapter. Also notice the box directly to the left of each layer name. This shows you the color of the corresponding layer.

Momentarily placing the cursor on an icon in the layer drop-down list displays a tool tip that describes the icon's purpose.

2. Click the Jamb layer name. The drop-down list closes and the name *Jamb* appears in the panel's layer name box. Jamb is now the current layer.

You can also use the Layer command to reset the current layer. To do this here, enter **–Layer↵ S↵** and then enter **Jamb↵↵**.

3. Zoom in on the door, and draw a 5″ line; start at the lower-right corner of the door and draw toward the right. Metric users should draw a 13 cm line.

4. Draw a similar line from the top-right end of the arc. Your drawing should look like Figure 5.6.

FIGURE 5.6
Door at wall
with door
jambs added

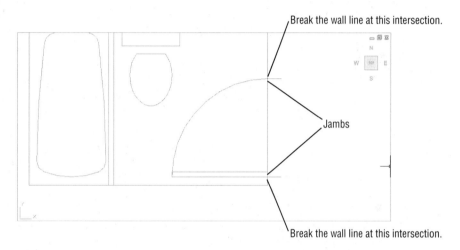

Break the wall line at this intersection.

Jambs

Break the wall line at this intersection.

Because you assigned the color green to the Jamb layer, the two lines you just drew to represent the door jambs are green. This gives you immediate feedback about which layer you're on as you draw.

Now you'll use the part of the wall between the jambs as a line representing the door header (the part of the wall above the door). To do this, you'll have to cut the line into three line segments and then change the layer assignment of the segment between the jambs:

1. Click the Break At Point tool in the Home tab's expanded Modify panel.

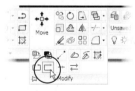

2. At the `Select object:` prompt, click the wall between the two jambs.

3. At the `Specify first break point:` prompt, use the Endpoint osnap override to pick the endpoint of the door's arc that is touching the wall, as shown previously in Figure 5.6.

4. Click Break At Point on the expanded Modify panel again and then repeat steps 2 and 3, this time using the jamb near the door hinge location to locate the break point (see Figure 5.6).

Although it may not be obvious, you've just broken the right-side wall line into three line segments: one at the door opening and two more on either side of the jambs. You can also use the Break tool (below the Break At Point tool) to produce a gap in a line segment.

The Break At Point tool won't work on a circle. You can, however, use the Break tool to place a small gap in the circle. If you create a small enough gap, the circle will still look like a full circle.

Next you'll change the Layer property of the line between the two jambs to the Ceiling layer. But instead of using the Properties palette as you've done in earlier exercises, you'll use a short-cut method:

1. Click the line between the door jambs to highlight it. Notice that the layer listing in the Layers panel changes to Wall. Whenever you select an object to expose its grips, the Color, Linetype, Lineweight, and Plot Style listings in the Properties panel change to reflect those properties of the selected object.

2. Click the layer name in the Layers panel to open the layer drop-down list.

3. Click the Ceiling layer. The list closes and the line you selected changes to the magenta color, showing you that it's now on the Ceiling layer. Also notice that the Object Color list in the Properties panel changes to reflect the new color for the line.

4. Press the Esc key twice to clear the grip selection. Notice that the layer returns to Jamb, the current layer.

5. Click the Zoom Previous tool from the Zoom flyout in the navigation bar. You can also enter **Z↵ P↵**.

In this exercise, you saw that when you select an object with no command active, the object's properties are immediately displayed in the Properties palette under Object Color, Linetype, and Lineweight. Using this method, you can also change an object's color, linetype, and line-weight independent of its layer. Just as with the Properties palette, you can select multiple objects and change their layers through the layer drop-down list. These options in the Home tab's Properties panel offer a quick way to edit some of the properties of objects.

Now, you'll finish the bathroom by adding a sink to a layer named Casework:

1. Open the Layer Properties Manager, and create a new layer called Casework.

2. With the Casework layer selected in the layer list, click the Set Current button at the top of the palette.

3. Click the color swatch for the Casework layer listing, and then select Blue from the Select Color dialog box. Click OK to exit the dialog box.

4. Click X in the Layer Properties Manager palette. Notice that the Layer drop-down list in the Layers panel indicates that the current layer is Casework.

Next you'll add the sink. As you draw, the objects will appear in blue, the color of the Casework layer.

5. Choose All from the Zoom flyout on the View tab's Navigate panel, or type **Z**⏎ **A**⏎.

6. Click the Insert tool on the Home tab's Block panel, and then click the Browse button in the Insert dialog box to open the Select Drawing File dialog box.

7. Locate the `sink.dwg` file, and double-click it.

8. In the Insert dialog box, make sure the Specify On-Screen options in both the Scale and Rotation groups aren't selected; then, click OK.

9. Place the sink roughly in the upper-right corner of the bathroom plan, and then use the Move command to place it accurately in the corner, as shown in Figure 5.7.

FIGURE 5.7
The bathroom with sink and counter-top added

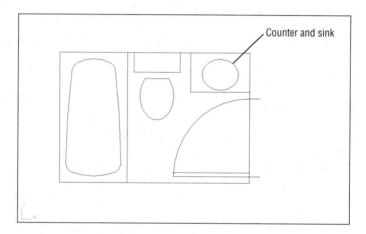

Counter and sink

Controlling Layer Visibility

I mentioned earlier that you'll sometimes want to display only certain layers to work with in a drawing. In this bathroom is a door header that would normally appear only in a reflected ceiling plan. To turn off a layer so that it becomes invisible, you click the Off button in the Layer Properties Manager, as shown in these steps:

1. Open the Layer Properties Manager by clicking the Layer Properties tool in the Layers panel.

2. Click the Ceiling layer in the layer list.

3. Click the lightbulb icon in the layer list, next to the Ceiling layer name. The lightbulb icon changes from yellow to gray to indicate that the layer is off.

4. Click the X at the top of the Layer Properties Manager's title bar to close it. The door header (the line across the door opening) disappears because you've made it invisible by turning off its layer.

GETTING MULTIPLE USES FROM A DRAWING USING LAYERS

Layering lets you use a single AutoCAD drawing for multiple purposes. A single drawing can show both the general layout of the plan and more detailed information such as equipment layout or floor-paving layout.

The following two images are reproductions of the San Francisco Main Library's lower level and show how one floor plan file was used for two purposes. The first view shows the layout of furnishings, and the second view shows a paving layout. In each case, the same floor plan file was used, but in the first panel, the paving information is on a layer that is turned off. Layers also facilitate the use of differing scales in the same drawing. Frequently, a small-scale drawing of an overall plan will contain the same data for an enlarged view of other portions of the plan, such as a stairwell or an elevator core. The detailed information, such as notes and dimensions, might be on a layer that is turned off for the overall plan.

You can also control layer visibility by using the Layer drop-down list on the Layers panel:

1. On the Home tab's Layers panel, click the Layer drop-down list.

2. Find the Ceiling layer, and notice that its lightbulb icon is gray. This tells you that the layer is off and not visible.

3. Click the lightbulb icon to make it yellow.

4. Click the drawing area to close the Layer drop-down list; the door header reappears.

Figure 5.8 explains the roles of the other icons in the Layer drop-down list.

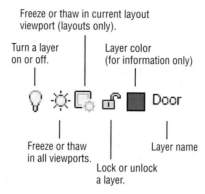

FIGURE 5.8

The Layer drop-down list icons

Freeze or thaw in current layout viewport (layouts only).

Turn a layer on or off.

Layer color (for information only)

Door

Freeze or thaw in all viewports.

Lock or unlock a layer.

Layer name

When you start to work with layouts in Chapters 8 and 16, you'll learn about *viewports*. A viewport is like a custom view of your drawing. You can have multiple viewports in a layout, each showing a different part of your drawing. Layer properties can be controlled for each viewport independently, so you can set up different linetypes, colors, and layer visibility for each viewport.

Finding the Layers You Want

With only a handful of layers, it's fairly easy to find the layer you want to turn off. It becomes much more difficult, however, when the number of layers exceeds 20 or 30. The Layer Properties Manager offers some useful tools to help you find the layers you want quickly.

Suppose you have several layers whose names begin with C, such as C-lights, C-header, and C-pattern, and you want to find those layers quickly. You can click the Name button at the top of the layer list to sort the layer names in alphabetic order. (You can click the Name button again to reverse the order.) To select those layers for processing, click the first layer name that starts with C, and then scroll down the list until you find the last layer of the group and Shift+click it. All the layers between those layers are selected. If you want to deselect some of those layers, hold down the Ctrl key while clicking the layer names you don't want to include in your selection. Another option is to Ctrl+click the names of other layers you want selected.

The Color and Linetype buttons at the top of the list let you sort the list by virtue of the color or linetype assignments of the layers. Other buttons sort the list by virtue of status: On/Off, Freeze/Thaw, Lock/Unlock, and so forth. (See the sidebar "Freeze, Lock, Transparency, and Other Layer Options" later in this chapter.)

Now try changing the layer settings again by turning off all the layers except Wall and Ceiling, leaving just a simple rectangle. In this exercise, you'll get a chance to experiment with the On/Off options of the Layer Properties Manager:

1. Click the Layer Properties tool in the Layers panel.

2. Click the top layer name in the list box; then Shift+click the last layer name. All the layer names are highlighted.

Another way to select all the layers at once in the Layer Properties Manager is to right-click the layer list and then choose the Select All option from the shortcut menu. If you want to clear your selections, right-click the layer list and choose Clear All.

3. Ctrl+click the Wall and Ceiling layers to deselect them and thus exempt them from your next action.

4. Click the lightbulb icon of any of the highlighted layers.

5. A message appears, asking if you want the current layer on or off. Select "Keep the current layer on" in the message box. The lightbulb icons turn gray to show that the selected layers have been turned off.

6. Close or minimize the Layer Properties Manager. The drawing now appears with only the Wall and Ceiling layers displayed. It looks like a simple rectangle of the room outline.

7. Open the Layer Properties Manager again, select all the layers as you did in step 2, and then click any of the gray lightbulbs to turn on all the layers at once.

8. Click the X at the top of the Layer Properties Manager's title bar to close it.

In this exercise, you turned off a set of layers by clicking a lightbulb icon. You can freeze/thaw, lock/unlock, or change the color of a group of layers in a similar manner by clicking the appropriate layer property. For example, clicking a color swatch of one of the selected layers opens the Select Color dialog box, in which you can set the color for all the selected layers.

Taming an Unwieldy List of Layers

Chances are you'll eventually end up with a fairly long list of layers. Managing such a list can become a nightmare, but AutoCAD provides some tools to help you organize layers so you can keep track of them more easily.

On the left side of the Layer Properties Manager is a set of tools and a list box designed to help you with your layer-management tasks (see Figure 5.9).

In the upper-left corner of the palette is a toolbar with three tools:

The New Property Filter tool lets you filter your list of layers to display only layers with certain properties, such as specific colors or names.

The New Group Filter tool lets you create named groups of layers that can be quickly recalled at any time. This tool is helpful if you often work with specific sets of layers. For example, you might have a set of layers in an architectural drawing that pertains to the electrical layout. You could create a group filter called Electrical that filters out all layers except those pertaining to the electrical layout. The filters don't affect the layers in any way; they just limit which layers are displayed in the main layer list.

The Layer States Manager tool lets you create sets of layer states. For example, if you want to save the layer settings that have only the wall and door layer turned on, you can do so by using this tool.

FIGURE 5.9

Tools in the Layer Properties Manager to help with your layer-management tasks

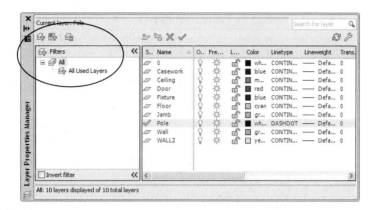

FREEZE, LOCK, TRANSPARENCY, AND OTHER LAYER OPTIONS

You may have noticed the Freeze and Thaw icons in the Layer Properties Manager. These options are similar to On and Off icons. However, Freeze not only makes layers invisible, it also tells AutoCAD to ignore the contents of those layers when you use the All response to the Select objects: prompt. Freezing layers can save time when you issue a command that regenerates a complex drawing. This is because AutoCAD ignores objects on frozen layers during regen. You'll get firsthand experience with Freeze and Thaw in Chapter 7.

Another pair of Layer Properties Manager options, Lock and Unlock, offer functionality similar to Freeze and Thaw. If you lock a layer, you can view and snap to objects on that layer, but you can't edit those objects. This feature is useful when you're working on a crowded drawing and you don't want to accidentally edit portions of it. You can lock all the layers except those you intend to edit and then proceed to work without fear of making accidental changes. The expanded Layers Ribbon panel offers a Locked Layer Fading slider that allows you to distinguish locked layers more easily by fading them. The slider does not affect plotter output because it is only a visual aid to use when you are editing your drawings.

Three more options—Lineweight, Plot Style, and Plot—offer control over the appearance of printer or plotter output. Lineweight lets you control the width of lines in a layer. Plot Style lets you assign plotter configurations to specific layers. (You'll learn more about plot styles in Chapter 9.) Plot lets you determine whether a layer gets printed in hard-copy output. This can be useful for setting up layers you may use for layout purposes only. The Linetype option lets you control line patterns, such as dashed or center lines.

Transparency is a new option in AutoCAD 2011, and as the name suggests, it enables you to make a layer transparent. You can enter a value from 0, which is completely opaque, to 90, which is the maximum transparency allowed. After setting the transparency value, you may need to enter **Re.↵** to see the transparency of the layer.

Finally, you can save layer settings for later recall by using the Layer States Manager tool in the upper-left corner of the Layer Properties Manager. This feature is extremely useful when you want to save different layer combinations. Chapter 15 shows you how to use this feature. This option is also accessible from the State option in the command-line version of the Layer command.

FILTERING LAYERS BY THEIR PROPERTIES

Below the New Property Filter, New Group Filter, and Layer States Manager tools is a filter list, which is a hierarchical list displaying the different sets of layer properties and group filters. Right now, you don't have any filters in place, so you see only All and All Used Layers.

In this section, you'll learn how the tools and the filter list box work. You'll start with a look at the New Property Filter tool:

1. Open the Layer Properties Manager by clicking the Layer Properties tool in the Layers panel.

2. Click the New Property Filter tool in the upper-left corner of the Layer Properties Manager to open the Layer Filter Properties dialog box. You see two list boxes. The Filter Definition list box at the top is where you enter your filter criteria. The Filter Preview list box below is a preview of your layer list based on the filter options. Right now, there are no filter options, so the Filter Preview list shows all the layers.

3. In the Filter Definition list box, click the blank box just below the Color label. A button appears in the box (see Figure 5.10).

FIGURE 5.10
The Layer
Filter Properties
dialog box

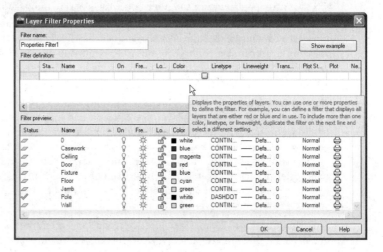

4. Click in the blank box again; then enter **red**↵. The Filter Preview changes to show only layers that are red. In the current drawing, only one layer has been assigned the color red.

5. Click twice in the blank box below the one you just edited. Again, a button appears.

6. This time, enter **green**↵. The layers that are green appear in the Filter Preview list.

   You can also select a color from the Select Color dialog box by clicking the button that appears in the box.

7. In the Filter Definition list, click in the Name column in the third row down. A cursor appears, followed by an asterisk.

8. Enter **F**↵. Two new layers that have names beginning with *F* are added to the Filter Preview list.

9. In the Filter Name text box at the upper-left corner of the dialog box, change the name Properties Filter 1 to **My List**, and then click OK.

Now you see the My List filter in the list box on the left side of the Layer Properties Manager.

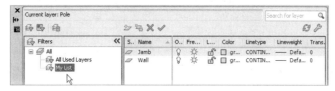

The layer list shows only the layers that have properties conforming to those you selected in the Layer Filter Properties dialog box. Notice that My List is highlighted in the filter list to the left. This tells you that My List is the current layer property filter being applied to the layer list to the right.

You can change the layer list display by selecting different options in the filter list. Try these steps:

1. Click the All option in the filter list at the left side of the dialog box. The layer list to the right changes to display all the layers in the drawing. Also note that a brief description of the current layer filter is displayed at the bottom of the dialog box.

2. Click the All Used Layers option in the filter list. Now all of the layers are displayed.

3. Click My List. The layer list changes back to the limited set of layers from your filter list.

4. Double-click My List. The Layer Filter Properties dialog box opens and displays the list of layer properties you set up earlier for My List. You can edit the criteria for your filter by making modifications in this dialog box.

5. Click Cancel to exit the Layer Filter Properties dialog box.

CREATING LAYER GROUPS

The preceding exercise shows how you can filter out layer names based on the properties you specify in the Layer Filter Properties dialog box. But suppose you want to create a layer filter list by graphically selecting objects on the screen. You can use the New Group Filter tool to do just that:

1. Click the New Group Filter tool in the upper-left corner of the Layer Properties Manager, and then press ↵ to accept the default name for the group. You see a new listing appear called Group Filter1.

2. Right-click the Group Filter1 listing panel to the left, and then choose Select Layers ➤ Add from the shortcut menu. Notice that your cursor is now a Pickbox cursor.

3. Click a line representing a wall of the bathroom; then click the door. Press ↵ when you're finished with your selection. The layers of the two objects you selected are displayed in the layer list. Also note that Group Filter1 is highlighted in the filter list to the left.

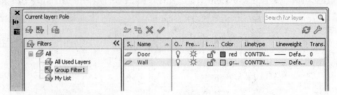

You may have noticed the Select Layers ➢ Replace option in the shortcut menu in step 2. This option lets you completely replace an existing group filter with a new selection set. It works just like the Select Layers ➢ Add option. You can also click and drag layers from the All layer list to the group filter list name in the left column.

Earlier you saw how you can double-click a properties filter to edit a properties filter list. But group filters work in a slightly different way. If you want to add layers to your group filter, you can click and drag them from the layer list to the group filter name. Here's how it's done:

1. In the Layer Properties Manager, select All from the filter list to the left.

2. Click the Fixture layer in the layer list; then Ctrl+click the Jamb layer in the list. These are the layers you'll add to the Group Filter1 layer group.

3. Click and drag the Fixture layer to the Group Filter1 listing in the filter list.

4. To check the addition to Group Filter1, click it in the filter list. The Fixture and Jamb layers have been added to the Group Filter1 list.

If you want to delete a layer from a group filter, you can use the shortcut menu, as shown in these steps:

1. With the Group Filter1 list selected, select the Jamb layer from the layer list, and then right-click it.

2. Select Remove From Group Filter in the shortcut menu. (Make sure you don't select Delete Layer.) Jamb is removed from the Group Filter1 list.

You can also convert a layer property filter into a group filter. Select the layer property filter from the filter list, right-click, and then select Convert To Group Filter. The icon for the layer property filter changes to a group filter icon, indicating that it's now a group filter.

You've seen how you can add property and group filters to the Layer Properties Manager by using the tools on the left side of the palette. One tool you haven't explored yet is the Layer States Manager. To understand how this tool works, you'll need to learn a little more about AutoCAD; look for a discussion of the Layer States Manager in Chapter 15.

Before you move on, you'll want to know about a few other options that appear in the Layer Properties Manager (see Figure 5.11):

The Invert Filter check box at the bottom of the Filters list changes the list of layers to show all layers *excluding* those in the selected filter. For example, if the My List filter contains layers that are red and you select Invert Filter, the layer list will display all layers *except* those that are red.

The Refresh tool in the upper-right corner updates the layer information in the Layer Properties Manager.

The Settings button in the upper-right corner opens the Layer Settings dialog box. This dialog box controls the way you're notified when new layers are added to a drawing (see Figure 5.12).

In the next section, you'll find some tips for how to use layer names so that you can use text filters more effectively.

FIGURE 5.11
Invert Filter, Refresh tool, and Settings button in the Layer Properties Manager

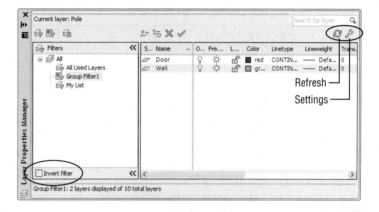

FIGURE 5.12
The Layer Settings dialog box

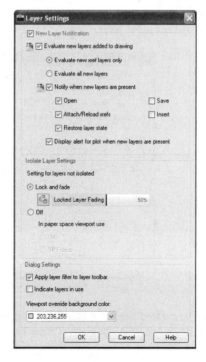

NAMING LAYERS TO STAY ORGANIZED

In the previous section, you saw how to create a layer property filter by using the name of a layer. If you name layers carefully, you can use them as a powerful layer-management tool. For example, suppose you have a drawing whose layer names are set up to help you easily identify floor-plan data versus ceiling-plan data, as in the following list:

- A-FP-WALL-JAMB

- A-FP-WIND-JAMB

- A-CP-WIND-HEAD

- A-CP-DOOR-HEAD

- L-FP-CURB

- C-FP-ELEV

The first character in the layer name designates the discipline related to that layer: *A* for architectural, *L* for landscape, *C* for civil, and so on. In this example, layers with names containing the two characters *FP* signify floor-plan layers. *CP* designates ceiling-plan information.

These layer examples are loosely based on a layer-naming convention devised by the American Institute of Architects (AIA). As you can see from this example, careful naming of layers can help you manage them.

If you want to isolate only those layers that have to do with floor plans, regardless of their discipline, enter **??FP*** in the Name column of the Layer Filter Properties dialog box. You can then give this layer property filter the name Floor Plan by entering **Floor Plan** in the Filter Name text box (see Figure 5.13).

FIGURE 5.13
Enter ??FP* in the Name column and Floor Plan in the Filter Name box as shown.

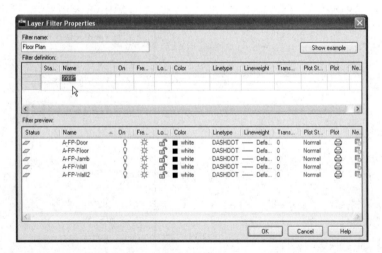

After you've created the Floor Plan layer properties list, you can pick Floor Plan from the filter list on the right side of the Layer Properties Manager and only those layers with names containing the letters *FP* as their third and fourth characters will appear in the list of layers.

You can turn off all these layers, change their color assignment, or change other settings quickly without having to wade through layers you don't want to touch. You can create other filter properties to isolate other groups of layers. AutoCAD keeps these filter lists for future use until you delete them by using the Delete option in the shortcut menu. (Right-click the name of the properties filter, and choose Delete.)

In the ??FP* example, the question marks (??) tell AutoCAD that the first two characters in the layer name can be anything. The *FP* tells AutoCAD that the layer name must contain *F* and *P* in these two places of the name. The asterisk (*) at the end tells AutoCAD that the remaining characters can be anything. The question marks and asterisk are known as *wildcard characters*. They're commonly used filtering tools for the Unix, Linux, and Windows operating systems.

As the number of layers in a drawing grows, you'll find layer filters an indispensable tool. But bear in mind that the successful use of layer filters can depend on a careful layer-naming convention. If you're producing architectural plans, you may want to consider the AIA layer naming guidelines.

Assigning Linetypes to Layers

You'll often want to use different linetypes to show hidden lines, center lines, fence lines, or other noncontinuous lines. You can assign a color and a linetype to a layer. You then see International Organization for Standardization (ISO) and complex linetypes, including lines that can be used to illustrate gas and water lines in civil work or batt insulation in a wall cavity.

AutoCAD comes with several linetypes, as shown in Figure 5.14. ISO linetypes are designed to be used with specific plotted line widths and linetype scales. For example, if you're using a pen width of 0.5 mm, set the linetype scale of the drawing to 0.5 as well. (See Chapter 16 for more information on plotting and linetype scale.) You can also create your own linetypes (see Chapter 28).

FIGURE 5.14
Standard, ISO, and complex AutoCAD linetypes

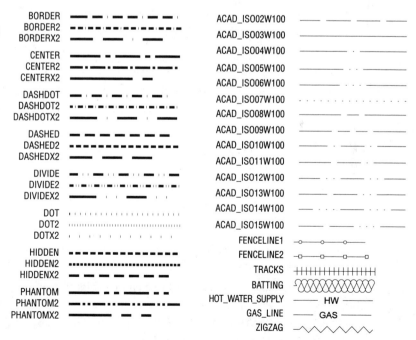

Linetypes that contain text, such as the gas line sample at the bottom of Figure 5.14, use the current text height and font to determine the size and appearance of the text displayed in the line. A text height of zero displays the text properly in most cases. See Chapter 10 for more on text styles.

AutoCAD stores linetype descriptions in an external file named Acad.lin, or Acadiso.lin for metric users. You can edit this file in a text editor like Notepad to create new linetypes or to modify existing ones. You'll see how this is done in Chapter 28.

Adding a Linetype to a Drawing

To see how linetypes work, you'll add a DASHDOT line in the bathroom plan to indicate a shower curtain rod:

1. Open the Layers Properties Manager, and select All from the filter list.

2. Click New, and then type **Pole** to create a new layer called Pole.

   If you're in a hurry, you can simultaneously load a linetype and assign it to a layer by using the Layer command. In this exercise, you enter **−Layer**⏎ at the Command prompt. Then enter **L**⏎, **DASHDOT**⏎, and **pole**⏎ and press ⏎ to exit the Layer command.

3. In the Pole layer listing, under the Linetype column, click the word *Continuous* to open the Select Linetype dialog box. To find the Linetype column, you may need to scroll the list to the right by using the scroll bar at the bottom of the list (see Figure 5.15).

FIGURE 5.15
The Select Line-
type dialog box

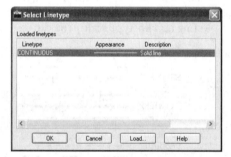

The word *Continuous* truncates to *Contin* when the Linetype column is at its default width and the Continuous option is selected.

4. The Select Linetype dialog box offers a list of linetypes to choose from. In a new file such as the Bath file, only one linetype is available by default. You must load any additional linetypes you want to use. Click the Load button at the bottom of the dialog box to open the Load Or Reload Linetypes dialog box. Notice that the list of linetype names is similar to the layer drop-down list. You can sort the names alphabetically or by description by clicking the Linetype or Description heading at the top of the list (see Figure 5.16).

5. In the Available Linetypes list, scroll down to locate the DASHDOT linetype, click it, and then click OK.

6. Notice that the DASHDOT linetype is added to the linetypes available in the Select Linetype dialog box.

FIGURE 5.16

The Load Or
Reload Linetypes
dialog box

Load or Reload Linetypes

File... [acad.lin]

Available Linetypes

Linetype	Description
ACAD_ISO02W100	ISO dash _ _ _ _ _ _ _ _ _ _ _ _ _ _
ACAD_ISO03W100	ISO dash space _ _ _ _ _ _
ACAD_ISO04W100	ISO long-dash dot ___ . ___ . ___ . ___ .
ACAD_ISO05W100	ISO long-dash double-dot ___ .. ___ .. ___ .
ACAD_ISO06W100	ISO long-dash triple-dot ___ ... ___ ... ___
ACAD_ISO07W100	ISO dot . . . .
ACAD_ISO08W100	ISO long-dash short-dash ___ _ ___ _ ___ _
ACAD_ISO09W100	ISO long-dash double-short-dash ___ _ _ ___ _
ACAD_ISO10W100	ISO dash dot _ . _ . _ . _ . _ . _ .
ACAD_ISO11W100	ISO double-dash dot . . _ _ . _ _ .

OK   Cancel   Help

7. Click DASHDOT to highlight it; then click OK. DASHDOT appears in the Pole layer listing under Linetype.

8. With the Pole layer still highlighted, click the Set Current button to make the Pole layer current.

9. Click X to exit the Layer Properties Manager.

10. Turn off Object Snap mode; then draw a line across the opening of the tub area, from coordinate 4′-4″,1′-10″ to coordinate 4′-4″,6′-10″. Metric users should draw a line from coordinate 133,56 to 133,208.

11. Press ↵ to finish the line.

CONTROLLING LINETYPE SCALE

Although you've designated this as a DASHDOT line, it appears solid. Zoom in to a small part of the line and you'll see that the line is indeed as you specified.

Because your current drawing is at a scale of 1″ = 1′, you must adjust the scale of your linetypes accordingly. This too is accomplished in the Linetype Manager dialog box. Here are the steps:

1. Click the Linetype drop-down list in the Home tab's Properties panel and select Other.

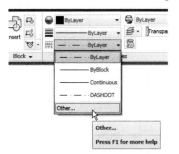

2. The Linetype Manager dialog box opens. Click the Show Details button in the upper-right corner of the dialog box. Some additional options appear at the bottom (see Figure 5.17).

FIGURE 5.17
The Linetype Man-
ager dialog box

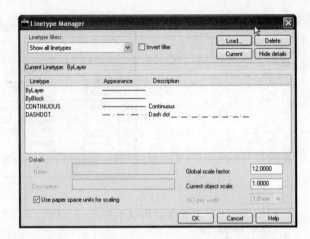

The Linetype Manager dialog box offers Load and Delete buttons that let you load or delete a linetype directly without having to go through a particular layer's linetype setting.

3. Double-click the Global Scale Factor text box, and then type **12** (metric users type **30**). This is the scale conversion factor for a 1″ = 1′ scale (see the section "Understanding Scale Factors" in Chapter 3).

4. Click OK. The drawing regenerates, and the shower curtain rod is displayed in the linetype and at the scale you designated.

5. Click the Zoom Previous tool from the navigation bar or from the View tab's Navigate panel so your drawing looks like Figure 5.18.

FIGURE 5.18
The completed
bathroom

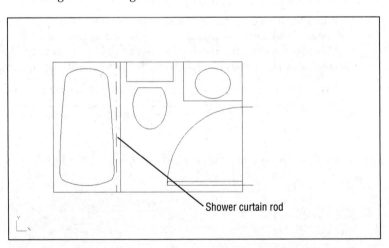

Shower curtain rod

You can also use the Ltscale system variable to set the linetype scale. Type **Ltscale↵**, and at the Enter new linetype scale factor <1.0000>: prompt, enter **12↵**.

LINETYPES TROUBLESHOOTING

If you change the linetype of a layer or an object but the object remains a continuous line, check the Ltscale system variable. It should be set to your drawing scale factor. If this doesn't work, set the Viewres system variable to a higher value (see Appendix B). (Viewres can also be set by the Arc And Circle Smoothness option in the Display tab of the Options dialog box.) The behavior of linetype scales depends on whether you're in Model Space or in a drawing layout. If your efforts to control linetype scale have no effect on your linetype's visibility, you may be in a drawing layout. See Chapter 16 for more on Model Space and layouts.

Remember that if you assign a linetype to a layer, everything you draw on that layer will be of that linetype. This includes arcs, polylines, circles, and traces. As explained in the sidebar "Assigning Colors, Linetypes, and Linetype Scales to Individual Objects" later in this chapter, you can also assign different colors and linetypes to individual objects rather than relying on their layer assignment to define color and linetype. However, you may want to avoid assigning colors and linetypes directly to objects until you have some experience with AutoCAD and a good grasp of your drawing's organization.

In the previous exercise, you changed the global linetype scale setting. This affects all non-continuous linetypes within the current drawing. You can also set the default linetype scale for all new objects with the Current Object Scale option in the Linetype Manager dialog box.

When individual objects are assigned a linetype scale, they're still affected by the global linetype scale set by the Ltscale system variable. For example, say you assign a linetype scale of 2 to the curtain rod in the previous example. This scale is then multiplied by the global linetype scale of 12, for a final linetype scale of 24.

You can also set the default linetype scale for individual objects by using the Celtscale system variable. After it's set, only newly created objects are affected. You must use the Properties palette to change the linetype scale of individual existing objects.

If the objects you draw appear in a different linetype from that of the layer they're on, check the default linetype by selecting Other from the Linetype drop-down list on the Home tab's Properties panel. Then, in the Linetype Manager dialog box, highlight ByLayer in the Linetype list and click the Current button. In addition, check the linetype scale of the object itself by using the Properties palette. A different linetype scale can make a line appear to have an assigned linetype that might not be what you expect. (See the sidebar "Assigning Colors, Linetypes, and Linetype Scales to Individual Objects.")

LINETYPES IN LAYOUTS

A system variable called Psltscale affects how layout viewports display linetypes. When the Psltscale system variable is set to 1, layout viewports display linetypes at the Ltscale setting, which is usually incorrect for the 1-to-1 scale of the layout. When Psltscale is set to 0, linetypes appear in layout viewports in the same way they appear in the Model tab.

ADDING THE FINAL DETAIL

If you're working through the tutorial, your final task is to set up an insertion point for the current drawing to facilitate its insertion into other drawings in the future. Follow these steps:

1. Type **Base**↵.

2. At the Enter base point <0´-0˝,0´-0˝,0´-0˝>: prompt, use the Endpoint object snap to pick the upper-left corner of the bathroom. The bathroom drawing is complete.

3. Click the Save tool in the Quick Access toolbar to record your work up to now.

Controlling Lineweights

You may have noticed a Lineweight column in the Layer Properties Manager. If you click this option for a given layer, the Lineweight dialog box opens, which enables you to control the plotted thickness of your lines. Plotted lineweights can also be set through direct object property assignment. You can view lineweights as they will appear in your final plot by making setting changes in the Lineweights Settings dialog box, which you'll learn about in Chapter 16.

With the Lineweight option and Lineweight Settings dialog box, you have greater control over the look of your drawings. This can save time because you don't have to print your drawing just to check for lineweights. You'll be able to see how thick or thin your lines are as you edit your drawing. You'll get a chance to delve into lineweights in Chapter 16.

Keeping Track of Blocks and Layers

The Insert dialog box and the Layer Properties Manager let you view the blocks and layers available in your drawing by listing them in a window. The Layer Properties Manager also includes information about the status of layers. However, you may forget the layer on which an object resides. You've seen how the Properties option on the shortcut menu shows you the properties of an object. The List tool in the Properties panel also enables you to get information about individual objects.

Use these steps to see an alternate way to view the properties of a block:

1. Click the List tool from the Home tab's Properties panel.

If you just want to quickly check which layer an object is on, click it. Its layer will appear in the Layer drop-down list of the Layers panel.

2. At the Select objects: prompt, click the Tub block, and then press ↵ to open the AutoCAD Text Window.

3. In the AutoCAD Text Window, a listing appears that shows not only the layer the tub is on, but also its space, insertion point, name, rotation angle, and scale.

The information in the Text Window, except the handle listing, is duplicated in the Properties palette you see when you right-click and choose Properties. But having the data in the AutoCAD Text Window gives you the flexibility to record it in a text file in case you need to store data about parts of your drawing. You can also use the AutoCAD Text Window to access and store other types of data regarding your drawings.

The Space property listed for the Tub block designates whether the object resides in Model Space or Paper Space. You'll learn more about these spaces in Chapters 8 and 16.

Getting a Text File List of Layers or Blocks

With complex drawings, it can be helpful to get a text file that lists the layers or blocks in your drawing. You can do this by using the log-file feature in AutoCAD. At the Command prompt, enter **Logfilemode**↵, and then enter **1**↵. Type **–La**↵**?**↵↵ (don't forget the minus sign at the beginning of the La command). If your list of layers is extensive, you may be asked to press ↵ to continue. Do so. Your list of layers appears in the Command window. For a list of blocks, enter **–Insert**↵**?**↵↵. When you've obtained your list, close the log-file feature by typing **Logfilemode**↵ **0**↵.

ASSIGNING COLORS, LINETYPES, AND LINETYPE SCALES TO INDIVIDUAL OBJECTS

If you prefer, you can set up AutoCAD to assign specific colors and linetypes to objects instead of having objects take on the color and linetype settings of the layer on which they reside. Normally, objects are given a default color and linetype called ByLayer, which means each object takes on the color or linetype of its assigned layer. (You've probably noticed the word *ByLayer* in the Properties panel and in various dialog boxes and tool palettes.)

Use the Properties panel to change the color or linetype of existing objects. This panel lets you set the properties of individual objects. For new objects, use the Object Color drop-down list on the Properties panel to set the current default color to red (for example) instead of ByLayer. Then everything you draw will be red, regardless of the current layer color. The Object Color drop-down list also offers a Select Colors option that opens the Select Color dialog box you saw earlier in this chapter.

For linetypes, you can use the Linetype drop-down list in the Properties panel to select a default linetype for all new objects. The list shows only linetypes that have already been loaded into the drawing, so you must first load a linetype before you can select it.

Another possible color and linetype assignment is ByBlock, which you also set with the Properties panel. ByBlock makes everything you draw white until you turn your drawing into a block and then insert the block on a layer with an assigned color. The objects then take on the color of that layer. This behavior is similar to that of objects drawn on layer 0. The ByBlock linetype works similarly to the ByBlock color.

Finally, if you want to set the linetype scale for each individual object instead of relying on the global linetype scale (the Ltscale system variable), you can use the Properties palette to modify the linetype scale of individual objects. In place of using the Properties palette, you can set the Celtscale system variable to the linetype scale you want for new objects.

As mentioned earlier, stay away from assigning colors and linetypes to individual objects until you're comfortable with AutoCAD; even then, use color and linetype assignments carefully. Other users who work on your drawing may have difficulty understanding your drawing's organization if you assign color and linetype properties indiscriminately.

Once the log-file feature is closed, you can use Windows Notepad to open the AutoCAD log file located in the C:\Documents and Settings*YourName*\Local Settings\Application Data\Autodesk\AutoCAD 2011\R18.1\enu\ folder. The name of the log file will start with the name of the current drawing, followed by a series of numbers and the .log filename extension, as in 04c-bath-metric_1_1_6500.log.

If you have difficulty finding the log file, enter **(getvar "logfilepath")** at the AutoCAD Command prompt to get a listing of the log-file location. The log file may also be in a hidden folder, so you may have to turn off the hidden folder setting in Windows Explorer. See Appendix B for instructions on how to do this.

With the log-file feature, you can record virtually anything that appears at the Command prompt. You can even record an entire AutoCAD session. The log file can also be helpful in constructing script files to automate tasks. (See Chapter 27 for more information on scripts.) If you want a hard copy of the log file, print it from an application such as Windows Notepad or your favorite word processor.

The Bottom Line

Organize information with layers.   Layers are perhaps the most powerful feature in AutoCAD. They help to keep drawings well organized and they give you control over the visibility of objects. They also let you control the appearance of your drawing by setting colors, lineweights, and linetypes.

Master It   Describe the process of creating a layer.

Control layer visibility.   When a drawing becomes dense with information, it can be difficult to edit. If you've organized your drawing using layers, you can reduce its complexity by turning off layers that aren't important to your current session.

Master It   Describe two methods for hiding a layer.

Keep track of blocks and layers.   At times, you may want a record of the layers or blocks in your drawing. You can create a list of layers using the log-file feature in AutoCAD.

Master It   Where do you go to turn on the log-file feature?

Part 2

Mastering Intermediate Skills

Chapter 6

Editing and Reusing Data to Work Efficiently

At least 5 AutoCAD commands are devoted to duplicating objects—10 if you include the grips options. Why so many? If you're an experienced drafter, you know that you frequently have to draw the same item several times in many drawings. AutoCAD offers a variety of ways to reuse existing geometry, thereby automating much of the repetitive work usually associated with manual drafting.

In this chapter, as you finish drawing the studio apartment unit, you'll explore some of the ways to exploit existing files and objects while constructing your drawing. For example, you'll use existing files as prototypes for new files, eliminating the need to set up layers, scales, and sheet sizes for similar drawings. With AutoCAD, you can also duplicate objects in multiple arrays. In Chapter 3, you saw how to use the Object Snap (Osnap) overrides on objects to locate points for drawing complex forms. This chapter describes other ways of using lines to aid your drawing.

Because you'll begin to use the Zoom command more in the exercises in this chapter, you'll review this command as you go along. You'll also discover the Pan command—another tool to help you get around in your drawing.

You're already familiar with many of the commands you'll use to draw the apartment unit. So, rather than going through every step of the drawing process, the exercises will sometimes ask you to copy the drawing from a figure and, using notes and dimensions as guides, put objects on the indicated layers. If you have trouble remembering a command you've already learned, go back and review the appropriate section of the book.

In this chapter, you'll learn to do the following:

- ◆ Create and use templates
- ◆ Copy an object multiple times
- ◆ Develop your drawing
- ◆ Find an exact distance along a curve
- ◆ Change the length of objects
- ◆ Create a new drawing by using parts from another drawing

Creating and Using Templates

Most programs today include what are called templates. A *template* is a file that is already set up for a specific application. For example, in your word processor, you might want to set up a document with a logo, a return address, and a date so you don't have to add these elements each time you create a letter. You might also want to format invoices in a slightly different way. You can set up a template for the needs of each type of document. That way, you don't have to spend time reformatting each new document you create.

Similarly, AutoCAD offers templates, which are drawing files that contain custom settings designed for a particular function. Out of the box, AutoCAD has templates for ISO, ANSI, DIN, GB, and JIS standard drawing formats that include generic title blocks. But you aren't limited to these "canned" templates. You can create your own templates for your particular style and method of drawing.

If you find that you use a particular drawing setup frequently, you can turn one or more of your typical drawings into a template. For example, you might want to create a set of drawings with the same scale and sheet size as an existing drawing. By turning a frequently used drawing into a template, you can save a lot of setup time for subsequent drawings.

Creating a Template

The following exercise guides you through creating and using a template drawing for your studio's kitchenette. Because the kitchenette will use the same layers, settings, scale, and sheet size as the bathroom drawing, you can use the Bath file as a prototype. Follow these steps:

1. Start AutoCAD in the usual way.

2. Choose Open from the Quick Access toolbar to open the Select File dialog box.

3. Locate the Bath file you created in the last chapter. You can also use the file 06-bath.dwg.

4. Click the Erase button on the Home tab's Modify panel, or enter e↵; then type all↵↵. This erases all the objects that make up the bathroom, but other elements, such as layers, linetypes, and stored blocks, remain in the drawing.

5. Choose Save As from the Application menu to open the Save Drawing As dialog box. Open the File Of Type drop-down list, and select AutoCAD Drawing Template (*.dwt). The file list window changes to display the current template files in the \Template\ folder.

6. In the File Name text box, enter the name **Arch8x11h**. If you're a metric user, enter the name **A4plan**.

7. Click Save to open the Template Options dialog box (see Figure 6.1).

LOCATING THE Template **FOLDER**

When you choose the AutoCAD Drawing Template option in the Save Drawing As dialog box, AutoCAD automatically opens the folder containing the template files. The standard AutoCAD installation creates the folder named Template to contain the template files. If you want to place your templates in a different folder, you can change the default template location by using the Options dialog box (choose Options from the bottom of the Application menu). Click the Files tab, double-click to expand Template Settings, and then double-click Drawing Template File Location in the list. Double-click the folder name that appears just below Drawing Template File Location; then select a new location from the Browse For Folder dialog box that appears.

8. Enter the following description: **Architectural one inch scale drawing on 8½ by 11 inch media**. Metric users should enter the description **Architectural 1:10 scale drawing on A4 media**.

9. Select English or Metric from the Measurement drop-down list, depending on the unit system you're using.

10. Click the Save All Layers As Reconciled option.

11. Click OK to save your new file and create a template. The template file you saved becomes the current file. (As with other Windows programs, choosing File ➤ Save As makes the saved file current.) This exercise shows that you can edit template files just as you would regular drawing files.

12. Close the template file.

Using a Template

Now let's see how a template is used. You'll use the template you just created as the basis for a new drawing you'll work on in this chapter:

1. Click the New tool from the Quick Access toolbar to open the Select Template dialog box. This is a typical file dialog box that you should be familiar with by now.

2. In the Select Template list box, click the filename Arch8x11h.dwt. Metric users should click the filename A4plan.dwt. Because this file is blank, you won't see anything in the preview window.

3. Click Open. It may not be obvious, but your new file is set up with the same architectural units and drawing limits as the bathroom drawing. It also contains the Door, Sink, Toilet, and Tub blocks.

4. You need to give your new file a name. Choose Save As from the Application menu to open the Save Drawing As dialog box. (Make sure you choose Save As or you won't get the Save Drawing As dialog box.) Enter **Kitchen** for the filename, and select the folder in which to save your new kitchen file. For example, you can save your file in the My Documents folder by clicking the My Documents shortcut in the left column.

5. Click Save to create the Kitchen file and close the dialog box.

You've created and used your own template file. Later, when you've established a comfortable working relationship with AutoCAD, you can create a set of templates that are custom-made to your particular needs.

However, if you're in a hurry, you don't need to create a template every time you want to reuse settings from another file. You can use an existing file as the basis or prototype for a new file without creating a template. Open the prototype file, and choose Save As from the Application menu to create a new version of the file under a new name. You can then edit the new version without affecting the original prototype file.

Copying an Object Multiple Times

Let's explore the tools that let you quickly duplicate objects. In this section, you'll begin to draw parts of a small kitchen. The first exercise introduces the Array command, which you can use to draw the gas burners of a range top.

As you'll see, an array can be either in a circular pattern, called a *polar array*, or a matrix of columns and rows, called a *rectangular array*.

Making Circular Copies

To start the range top, first set the layer on which you want to draw, and then draw a circle representing the edge of one burner:

1. Set the current layer to Fixture by selecting Fixture from the Layer drop-down list in the Home tab's Layers panel.

   Because you used the Bath file as a template, Running Osnaps for Endpoint, Midpoint, and Intersection are already turned on and available in this new file.

2. Click the Center, Radius Circle tool on the Home tab's Draw panel, or type **C**↵.

3. At the Specify center point for circle or [3P/2P/Ttr (tan tan radius)]: prompt, pick a point at coordinate 4´,4´. Metric users should pick a point at coordinate 120,120.

4. At the Specify radius of circle or [Diameter]: prompt, enter **3**↵. Metric users should enter **7.6**↵. The circle appears.

Now you're ready to use the Array command to draw the burner grill. You'll first draw one line representing part of the grill and then use the Array command to create the copies:

1. Zoom into the circle you just drew and then make sure the Snap mode is off by checking the Snap Mode tool in the status bar.

2. Draw a 4˝ line starting from the coordinate 4´-1˝,4´-0˝ and ending to the right of that point. Metric users should draw a 9 cm line starting at coordinate 122,120 and ending to the right of that point.

3. Adjust your view so it looks similar to Figure 6.2.

FIGURE 6.2
A close-up of the
circle and line

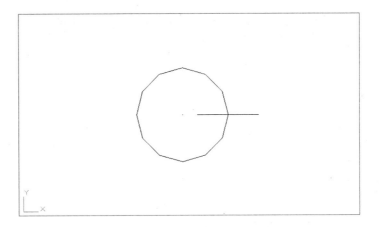

You've got the basic parts needed to create the burner grill. You're ready to make multiple copies of the line. For this part, you'll use the Array dialog box:

1. Click Array on the Modify panel, or type **AR**↵ to open the Array dialog box (see Figure 6.3).

FIGURE 6.3
The Array
dialog box

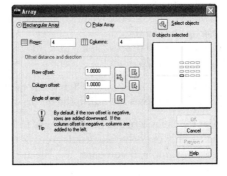

2. Click the Select Objects button. The dialog box temporarily closes, enabling you to select objects.

3. Type **L**↵ to select the last object drawn, or click the object you want to array.

4. Press ↵ to confirm your selection. The Array dialog reopens.

5. Click the Polar Array radio button at the top of the dialog box to tell AutoCAD you want a circular array. The Array dialog box displays the Polar Array options (see Figure 6.4).

6. Click the Pick Center Point button to temporarily close the Array dialog box.

FIGURE 6.4

The Polar Array options

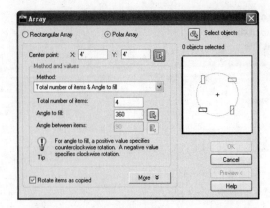

7. Shift+right-click and select Center, and then place the cursor on the circle. When you see the circular Osnap marker at the center of the circle, click the mouse. This selects the circle's exact center for the center of the polar array. After you've clicked, the Array dialog box returns.

Remember that to access osnaps other than those set up as Running Osnaps, you Shift+right-click the mouse and then select the osnap you want to use from the resulting menu.

At this point, you've selected an object to array, and you've indicated the center location of the array. If you've selected the wrong object or the wrong center point, you can go back and specify these options again.

Now to complete the process, tell AutoCAD the number of copies in the array and the extent of the array through the circle:

1. In the Array dialog box, enter **8** in the Total Number Of Items text box. This tells AutoCAD to make eight copies including the original.

2. Accept the default of 360 for the Angle To Fill text box. This tells AutoCAD to spread the copies evenly over the full 360 degrees of the circle. Of course, you can enter other values here. For example, if you enter 180, the array will fill half the circle.

   You can click the Pick Angle To Fill button to the right of the Angle To Fill text box to graphically select an angle in the drawing.

3. Make sure the Rotate Items As Copied check box in the lower-left corner of the dialog box is selected. This ensures that the arrayed object is rotated about the array center. If you clear this option, the copies will all be oriented in the same direction as the original object.

4. Click the Preview button. AutoCAD shows you the results of your array settings.

5. Right-click to accept the array. The circular array appears in the drawing, as shown in Figure 6.5.

In step 5, you could click to return to the Array dialog box and change settings before committing to a final array pattern. You could also press Esc. The Array dialog box gives you a lot of leeway in creating your array copies.

If you're a veteran AutoCAD user and you prefer the command-line version of the Array command, you can type **-Array**↵ or **-Ar**↵ at the Command prompt and then answer the prompts as you would in earlier versions of AutoCAD.

FIGURE 6.5
The completed
gas burner

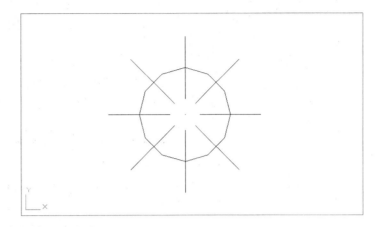

Making Row and Column Copies

Now you'll draw the other three burners of the gas range by creating a rectangular array from the burner you just drew. You'll first zoom back a bit to get a view of a larger area. Then you'll proceed with the Array command.

Follow these steps to zoom back:

1. Click Scale from the Zoom tool's flyout in the View tab's Navigate panel or the navigation bar. You can also type **Z↵ S↵**.

2. Enter **0.5x↵**. Your drawing will look like Figure 6.6.

If you're not too fussy about the amount you want to zoom out, you can click Out from the Zoom flyout on the View tab's Navigate panel to reduce your view quickly.

Entering 0.5x for the Zoom Scale factor tells AutoCAD you want a view that reduces the width of the current view to fill half the display area, enabling you to see more of the work area. If you specify a scale value greater than 1 (5, for example), you'll magnify your current view. If you leave off the x, your new view will be in relation to the drawing limits rather than the current view.

FIGURE 6.6
The preceding
view reduced by
a factor of 0.5

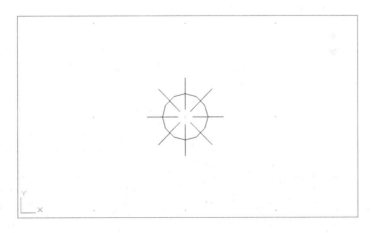

Next you'll finish the range top. You'll get a chance to use the Rectangular Array option to create three additional burners:

1. Click the Array tool on the Modify panel again, or type **AR↵**, to open the Array dialog box.

2. Click the Select Objects button to close the Array dialog box temporarily.

3. Select the entire burner, including the lines and the circle, and then press ↵ to confirm your selection.

4. In the Array dialog box, click the Rectangular Array radio button.

5. Change both the Rows and Columns text boxes to **2**.

6. Change the Row Offset text box value to **1′-2″** (**35.5** for metric users) and the Column Offset text box value to **1′-4″** (**40.6** for metric users). See Figure 6.7.

FIGURE 6.7
Changes to the
Row Offset text
box value and the
Column Offset text
box value

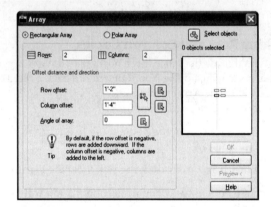

7. Click OK. Your screen will look like Figure 6.8.

AutoCAD usually draws a rectangular array from bottom to top and from left to right. You can reverse the direction of the array by giving negative values for the distance between columns and rows.

FIGURE 6.8
The burners
arrayed

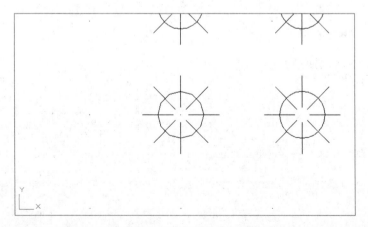

At times, you may want to create a rectangular array at an angle. To accomplish this, enter the desired angle in the Angle Of Array text box in the Array dialog box. You can also select the angle graphically by clicking the Pick Angle Of Array button just to the right of the Angle Of Array text box.

If you need to indicate an array cell graphically, you can do so by using options in the Offset Distance And Direction group of the Array dialog box (see the bottom image in Figure 6.9). An *array cell* is a rectangle defining the distance between rows and columns (see the top image in Figure 6.9). You may want to use this option when objects are available to use as references from which to determine column and row distances. For example, you might draw a crosshatch pattern, as on a calendar, within which you want to array an object. You use the intersections of the hatch lines as references to define the array cell, which is one square in the hatch pattern.

FIGURE 6.9
An array cell and the Array dialog box tool that let you graphically indicate array cells

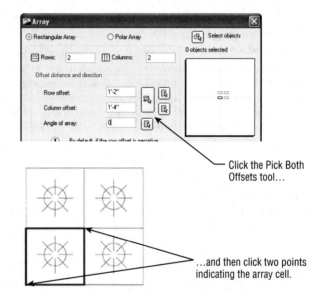

Click the Pick Both Offsets tool…

…and then click two points indicating the array cell.

In the Offset Distance And Direction group, the Pick Both Offsets tool lets you indicate the row and column distance by placing an array cell graphically in the drawing, as shown in the bottom image in Figure 6.9. You can also indicate a row or column distance graphically by using the Pick Row Offset button or the Pick Column Offset button to the right of the Pick Both Offsets button.

Fine-Tuning Your View

Back in Figure 6.8, you may have noticed that parts of the burners don't appear on the display. To move the view over so you can see all the burners, use the Pan command. Pan is similar to Zoom in that it changes your view of the drawing. However, Pan doesn't alter the magnification of the view the way Zoom does. Rather, Pan maintains the current magnification while moving your view across the drawing, just as you would pan a camera across a landscape.

QUICK ARRAY COPIES WITH GRIPS

Sometimes the Array tool can be overkill if you only need to make a few evenly spaced copies. Fortunately, grip editing offers a feature that lets you quickly make evenly spaced copies. Here's how it's done:

1. Press the Esc key to make sure you aren't in the middle of a command; then select the objects you want to copy.

2. Click a grip point as your base point.

3. Right-click your mouse, and select Move.

4. Ctrl+click a location to place a copy of the selected object. This first copy will determine the interval distance for additional copies.

5. Continue to hold down the Ctrl key and select additional points to make copies at regularly spaced intervals.

The copies snap to the distance you indicate with the first Ctrl+click point (in step 4). You can use osnaps to select a distance based on the position of another object. Once you've made the first copy with the Ctrl+click, you can release the Ctrl key to make multiple copies at random intervals. Another option is to use Polar Snap while making grip edit copies. With Polar Snap, you can enter a specific distance for the intervals. See Chapter 3 for more on Polar Snap.

To activate the Pan command, follow these steps:

1. Click the Pan tool on the View tab's Navigate panel or from the navigation Bar, or type **P↵**. You can also right-click and choose Pan from the shortcut menu. A small hand-shaped cursor appears in place of the AutoCAD cursor.

2. Place the hand cursor in the center of the drawing area, and then click and drag it downward and to the left. The view follows the motion of your mouse.

3. Continue to drag the view until it looks similar to Figure 6.10; then release the mouse button.

4. To finish the kitchen, you want a view that shows more of the drawing area. Right-click to open the Zoom/Pan shortcut menu, and then choose Zoom. The cursor changes to the Zoom Realtime cursor. The Zoom/Pan shortcut menu also appears when you right-click during the Zoom Realtime command.

5. Place the cursor close to the top of the screen, and click and drag the cursor downward to zoom out until your view looks like the top panel of Figure 6.11. You may need to click and drag the Zoom Realtime cursor a second time to achieve this view.

6. Right-click the mouse again, and choose Exit from the shortcut menu. You're now ready to add more information to the kitchen drawing.

You can also exit the Pan or Zoom Realtime command without opening the shortcut menu; just press the Esc key.

FIGURE 6.10
The panned view
of the range top

FIGURE 6.10
The panned view
of the range top

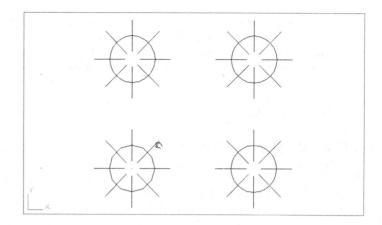

This exercise showed how you can fine-tune your view by easily switching between Pan and Zoom Realtime. After you get the hang of these two tools working together, you'll be able to access the best view for your needs quickly. The other options in the shortcut menu—Zoom Window, Zoom Original, and Zoom Extents—perform the same functions as the options in the Zoom flyout on the View tab's Navigate panel or in the navigation bar.

The Zoom Window option in the Zoom/Pan shortcut menu functions in a slightly different way from the standard Zoom Window option. Instead of clicking two points, you click and drag a window across your view.

FIGURE 6.11
The final view
of the range
top burners (top
image) and the
finished kitchen
(bottom image).
Metric dimensions
are shown in
brackets.

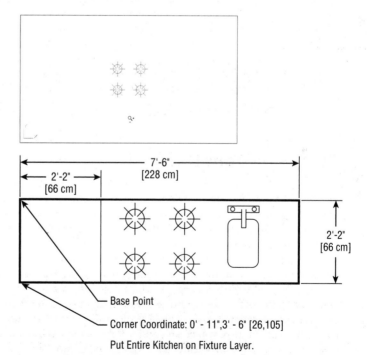

While we're on the subject of display tools, AutoCAD offers scroll bars to the right and bottom of the AutoCAD drawing area. They work like any other Windows scroll bars, offering a simple way to move up, down, left, or right in your current view. They also come in handy for quickly panning your view in one direction or another.

By default, the scroll bars are turned off. If you prefer to turn them on, open the Options dialog box (choose Options from the Application menu), click the Display tab, and make sure that the Display Scroll Bars In Drawing Window option is selected. Clear the box to turn them off.

Finishing the Kitchenette

Before you save and close the Kitchen file, you need to do one more thing. You'll be using this drawing as a symbol and inserting it into the overall plan of the studio apartment unit. To facilitate accurate placement of the kitchen, you'll change the location of the base point of this drawing to the upper-left corner of the kitchen. This will then be the drawing's *grip*:

1. Complete the kitchenette as indicated in the bottom panel of Figure 6.11, shown earlier in this chapter. As the figure indicates, make sure you put the kitchenette on the Fixture layer. This will help you control the visibility of the kitchenette in future edits of this file. Draw the sink roughly as shown in the figure.

2. Click the Set Base Point tool in the Home tab's expanded Block panel.

3. At the Enter base point: prompt, pick the upper-left corner of the kitchen, as indicated in the bottom image of Figure 6.11. The kitchen drawing is complete.

4. Click Save from the Quick Access toolbar, and exit the file.

Developing Your Drawing

As mentioned briefly in Chapter 3, when you're using AutoCAD, you first create the basic geometric forms used in your drawing, and then you refine them. In this section, you'll create two drawings—the studio apartment unit and the lobby—that demonstrate this process in more detail.

First, you'll construct a typical studio apartment unit by using the drawings you've created thus far. In the process, you'll explore the use of lines as reference objects.

You'll also further examine how to use existing files as blocks. In Chapter 4, you inserted a file into another file. The number of files you can insert is limitless, and you can insert files of any size. As you may already have guessed, you can also *nest* files and blocks; that is, you can insert blocks or files in other blocks or files. Nesting can help reduce your drawing time by enabling you to build one block out of smaller blocks. For example, you can insert your door drawing into the bathroom plan. In turn, you can insert the bathroom plan into the studio unit plan, which also contains doors. Finally, you can insert the unit plan into the overall floor plan for the studio apartment building.

Importing Settings

In this exercise, you'll use the Bath file as a prototype for the studio unit plan. However, you must make a few changes to it first. After the changes are made, you'll import the bathroom and thereby import the layers and blocks contained in the bathroom file.

As you go through this exercise, observe how the drawings begin to evolve from simple forms to complex, assembled forms.

Use these steps to modify the Bath file:

1. Open the Bath file. If you skipped drawing the Bath file in Chapter 5, use the file 05c-bath.dwg (or 05c-bath-metric.dwg).

2. Click the Set Base Point tool in the Home tab's expanded Block panel, and select the upper-left corner of the bathroom as the new base point for this drawing so you can position the Bath file more accurately.

3. Save the Bath file. If you use the online file, choose Save As from the Application menu and save it as Bath.

4. Click the Close icon in the upper-right corner of the drawing area or choose Close from the Application menu to close the bath drawing.

Next you'll create a new file. But this time, instead of using the Start From Scratch or Use A Template option in the Create New Drawing dialog box, you'll try the Use A Wizard option:

1. Click New from the Quick Access toolbar to open the Select Template dialog box.

2. Locate and select the acad.dwt template file. Metric users should locate the acadiso.dwt template file.

3. Click Open to open the new file.

4. If you're using Imperial measurements, choose Drawing Utilities ➢ Units from the Application menu; then in the Drawing Units dialog box, select Architectural from the Length group's Type drop-down list and click OK. Metric users, use the default decimal length type.

5. Type **Limits**↵. At the Specify lower left corner or [ON/OFF] <0'-0",0'-0">: prompt, press ↵ to accept the default drawing origin for the lower-left corner.

6. If you're using Imperial measurements, enter **528,408**↵ at the next prompt. These are the appropriate dimensions for an 8½″ × 11″ drawing at 1/4″ = 1'-0 ″ scale. Metric users should enter **1485,1050**. This is the work area for a 1:50 scale drawing on an A4 sheet.

7. Click All from the Zoom flyout on the View tab's Navigate panel or click Zoom All from the navigation bar.

Let's continue by laying out a typical studio unit. You'll discover how importing a file also imports a variety of drawing items such as layers and linetypes. Follow these steps:

1. Begin the unit by drawing two rectangles, one 14' long by 24' wide and the other 14' long by 4' wide. Metric users should make the rectangles 426 cm wide by 731 cm long and 426 cm wide by 122 cm long. Place them as shown in Figure 6.12. The large rectangle represents the interior of the apartment unit, and the small rectangle represents the balcony. The size and location of the rectangles are indicated in the figure.

FIGURE 6.12
The apartment unit interior and balcony. Metric locations and dimensions are shown in brackets.

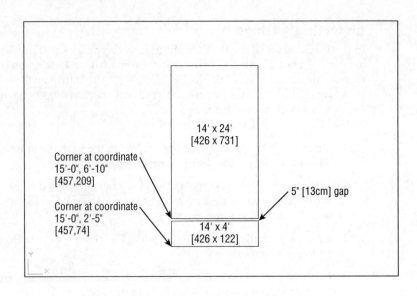

14' x 24'
[426 x 731]

Corner at coordinate
15'-0", 6'-10"
[457,209]

5" [13cm] gap

Corner at coordinate
15'-0", 2'-5"
[457,74]

14' x 4'
[426 x 122]

IF YOU USED THE RECTANGLE TOOL TO DRAW THE INTERIOR AND BALCONY...

...of the apartment unit, make sure you use the Explode tool on the Modify panel to explode the rectangles. The Rectangle tool draws a polyline rectangle instead of simple line segments, so you need to explode the rectangle to reduce it to its component lines. You'll learn more about polylines in Chapter 19.

---

2. Click the Insert tool on the Home tab's Block panel to open the Insert dialog box.

3. Click the Browse button, and locate and select the bathroom drawing by using the Select Drawing File dialog box. Then click Open. If you haven't saved a bathroom drawing from earlier exercises, you can use 05c-bath.dwg.

4. If you're using the 05c-bath.dwg file, do the following: After selecting 05c-bath.dwg in step 3, change the name that appears in the Name text box to Bath instead of 05c-bath before you click OK in step 5. This gives the inserted file a block name of Bath, even though its originating filename is 05c-bath.

5. Click OK in the Insert dialog box, and then click the upper-left corner of the unit's interior as the insertion point (see Figure 6.13). You can use the Endpoint osnap to place the bathroom accurately. Use a scale factor of 1.0 and a rotation angle of 0°.

6. If Running Osnaps haven't been set up in this file, you need to use the Osnap shortcut menu (Shift+right-click) to access the Endpoint osnap. You can set up Running Osnaps to take advantage of AutoCAD's AutoSnap functions by right-clicking the Osnap button in the status bar. Set the Running Osnaps as described in Chapter 3.

FIGURE 6.13
The unit after
the bathroom is
inserted

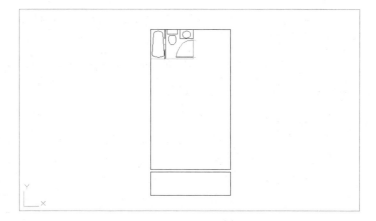

7. Assign the two rectangles that you drew earlier to the Wall layer. To do this, select the two rectangles so they're highlighted, and then open the Layer drop-down list in the Layers panel and select Wall. Press the Esc key twice to clear the selection.

By inserting the bathroom, you imported the layers and blocks contained in the Bath file. You were then able to move previously drawn objects to the imported layers. If you're in a hurry, this can be a quick way to duplicate layers that you know exist in another drawing. This method is similar to using an existing drawing as a template, but it lets you start work on a drawing before deciding which template to use.

Using Osnap Tracking to Place Objects

You'll draw lines in the majority of your work, so it's important to know how to manipulate lines to your best advantage. In the following sections, you'll look at some of the more common ways to use and edit these fundamental drawing objects. The following exercises show you the process of drawing lines rather than just how individual commands work. While you're building walls and adding doors, you'll get a chance to become more familiar with Polar Tracking and Osnap Tracking.

ROUGHING IN THE LINE WORK

The bathroom you inserted in the preceding section has only one side of its interior walls drawn. (Walls are usually shown by double lines.) In this next exercise, you'll draw the other side. Rather than trying to draw the wall perfectly the first time, you'll sketch in the line work and then clean it up in the next section, in a way similar to manual drafting.

Use these steps to rough in the wall lines:

1. Zoom in to the bathroom so that the entire bathroom and part of the area around it are displayed, as in Figure 6.14.

2. Select Wall from the Layer drop-down list in the Layers panel to make Wall the current layer.

3. Make sure that the Object Snap Tracking and Object Snap tools on the status bar are turned on.

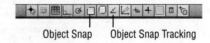

Object Snap   Object Snap Tracking

FIGURE 6.14
The enlarged view
of the bathroom

FIGURE 6.14
The enlarged view
of the bathroom

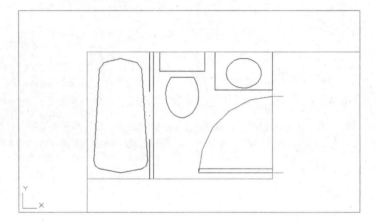

4. Click Line from the Draw panel, or type **L**↵.

5. At the `Specify first point:` prompt, hover your cursor over the lower-right corner of the bathroom so that the Endpoint Osnap marker appears, but don't click it.

6. Now move the cursor downward, and as you do, the tracking vector appears. (If the tracking vector doesn't appear at first, hover your cursor over the corner again until it does appear.)

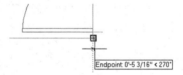

Endpoint 0'-5 3/16" < 270°

Remember that a little cross appears at the osnap location, telling you that Osnap Tracking has "locked on" to that location.

7. With the tracking vector visible, point the cursor directly downward from the corner, and then type **5**↵. Metric users should type **13**↵. A line starts 5″ (or 13 cm) below the lower-right corner of the bathroom.

8. Continue the line horizontally to the left, to cross the left wall of the apartment unit slightly, as illustrated in the top image in Figure 6.15. Press ↵.

FIGURE 6.15
The first wall line
and the wall line by
the door

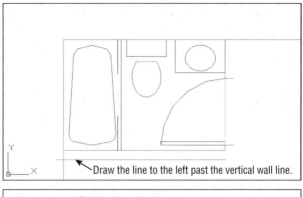

Draw the line to the left past the vertical wall line.

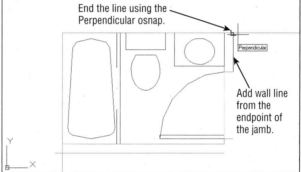

End the line using the Perpendicular osnap.

Perpendicular

Add wall line from the endpoint of the jamb.

9. Draw another line upward from the endpoint of the top door jamb to meet the top wall of the unit (see the bottom image in Figure 6.15). Use the Perpendicular osnap to pick the top wall of the unit. This causes the line to end precisely on the wall line in perpendicular position, as in the bottom image in Figure 6.15.

   You can also use the Perpendicular osnap override to draw a line perpendicular to a non-orthogonal line—one at a 45° angle, for instance.

SMOOTHING THE ARC

You may notice that some of the arcs in your bathroom drawing aren't smooth. Don't be alarmed; this is how AutoCAD displays arcs and circles in enlarged views. The arcs will be smooth when they're plotted. If you want to see them now as they're stored in the file, you can regenerate the drawing by typing **Regen.**↵ at the Command prompt. Chapter 7 discusses regeneration in more detail.

---

10. Draw a line connecting the two door jambs. Then assign that line to the Ceiling layer. (See the top panel in Figure 6.16.)

11. Draw a line 6″ downward from the endpoint of the door jamb nearest the corner. (See the top panel in Figure 6.16.)

FIGURE 6.16
The corner of the bathroom wall and the filleted wall around the bathroom

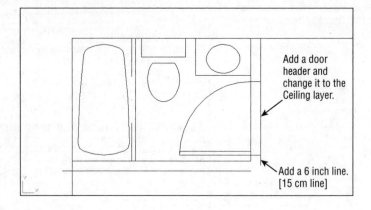

Add a door header and change it to the Ceiling layer.

Add a 6 inch line. [15 cm line]

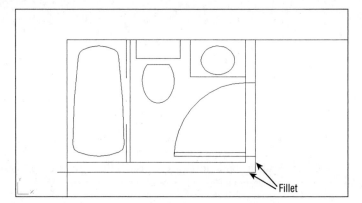

Fillet

In the previous exercise, Osnap Tracking mode enabled you to specify a starting point of a line at an exact distance from the corner of the bathroom. In step 7, you used the Direct Distance method for specifying distance and direction.

SELECTING POINTS FROM A KNOWN LOCATION

Instead of using a tracking vector in step 6 of the previous exercise, you can choose From on the Osnap shortcut menu and then open the shortcut menu again and select Endpoint. Select the corner and enter a polar coordinate such as **@5<-90** to accomplish the same task as this exercise.

CLEANING UP THE LINE WORK

You've drawn some of the wall lines, approximating their endpoint locations. Next you'll use the Fillet command to join lines exactly end to end and then import the kitchen drawing.

UNDERSTANDING THE OSNAP TRACKING VECTOR

The Osnap Tracking vector comes into play only after you've placed an Osnap marker on a location—in this case, the corner of the bathroom. It won't appear at any other time. If you have both Running Osnaps and Osnap Tracking turned on, you'll get the tracking vector every time the cursor lands on an osnap location. This can be confusing to novice users, so you may want to use Osnap Tracking sparingly until you become more comfortable with it.

Because Polar Tracking also uses a tracking vector, you may get the two confused. Remember that Polar Tracking lets you point the cursor in a specific direction while selecting points. If you're an experienced AutoCAD user, you can think of it as a more intelligent Ortho mode. On the other hand, Osnap Tracking lets you align points to osnap locations. Experienced AutoCAD users can think of Osnap Tracking as a more intelligent XYZ filter option.

Follow these steps to join the lines:

1. Click the Fillet tool on the Modify panel, or type **F↵**.

   The Chamfer and Fillet tools share the same location in the Modify toolbar, so the tool tip may say Chamfer instead of Fillet. If it does say Chamfer, then click the flyout arrowhead next to the tool and select Fillet.

2. Type **R↵0↵** to make sure the fillet radius is set to 0.

CHAMFER VS. FILLET

The Chamfer command performs a similar function to the Fillet command, but unlike Fillet, it enables you to join two lines with an intermediate beveled line rather than with an arc. Chamfer can be set to join two lines at a corner in exactly the same manner as Fillet.

3. Fillet the two lines by picking the vertical and horizontal lines, as indicated in the bottom panel in Figure 6.16 shown earlier in this chapter. Notice that these points lie on the portion of the line you want to keep. Your drawing will look like the bottom panel in Figure 6.16.

4. Fillet the bottom wall of the bathroom with the left wall of the unit, as shown in Figure 6.17. Make sure the points you pick on the wall lines are on the side of the line you want to keep, not on the side you want trimmed.

5. Fillet the top wall of the unit with the right-side wall of the bathroom, as shown in Figure 6.17.

You can select two lines at once for the fillet operation by using a crossing window; to do so, type **C↵** at the Select first object or ...: prompt. The two endpoints closest to the fillet location are trimmed.

FIGURE 6.17
The cleaned-up
wall intersections

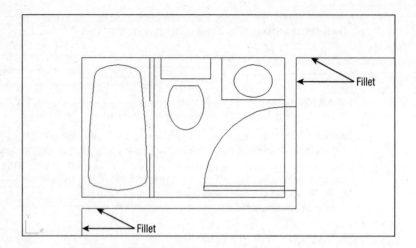

Where you select the lines affects how the lines are joined. As you select objects to fillet, the side of the line where you click is the side that remains when the lines are joined. Figure 6.18 illustrates how the Fillet command works and shows what the Fillet options do.

If you select two parallel lines during the Fillet command, the two lines are joined with an arc. Now import the kitchen plan you drew earlier in this chapter:

1. Click Insert on the Block panel, and then, in the Insert dialog box, click the Browse button to locate the kitchen drawing you created earlier in this chapter. Make sure you leave the Specify On-Screen check box unselected under the Scale and Rotation groups of the Insert dialog box.

2. Place the kitchen drawing at the wall intersection below the bathtub. (See the top image in Figure 6.19.)

If you didn't complete the kitchen earlier in this chapter, you can insert the 06a-kitchen.dwg file. Metric users can insert 06 kitchen-metric.dwg.

3. Adjust your view with Pan and Zoom so that the upper portion of the apartment unit is centered in the drawing area, as illustrated in the top image in Figure 6.19.

PLACING THE DOOR ACCURATELY

The next step is to add the entry door shown in the bottom image in Figure 6.19. In doing that, you'll use a number of new tools together to streamline the drawing process.

In this exercise, you'll practice using the Osnap Tracking feature and the From Osnap option to place the entry door at an exact distance from the upper corner of the floor plan:

1. Right-click in the Command window, and choose Recent Commands ➢ Insert from the shortcut menu to open the Insert dialog box.

2. Select Door from the Name drop-down list.

3. Make sure the Specify On-Screen option is checked in the Rotation group but not in the Scale group, and then click OK. You'll see the door follow the cursor in the drawing window.

FIGURE 6.18

Where you click the object to select it determines which part of an object gets filleted.

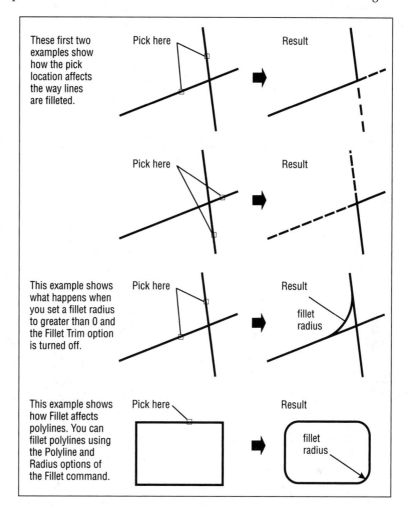

These first two examples show how the pick location affects the way lines are filleted.

This example shows what happens when you set a fillet radius to greater than 0 and the Fillet Trim option is turned off.

This example shows how Fillet affects polylines. You can fillet polylines using the Polyline and Radius options of the Fillet command.

4. Shift+right-click the mouse to open the Osnap shortcut menu, and then choose From.

5. Make sure the Object Snap and Object Snap Tracking buttons on the status bar are on; then use the Endpoint Running Osnap to pick the corner where the upper horizontal wall line meets the bathroom wall.

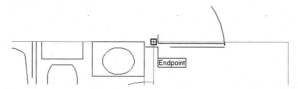

FIGURE 6.19
The view after
using Pan and
Zoom, with the
door inserted
and the jamb and
header added

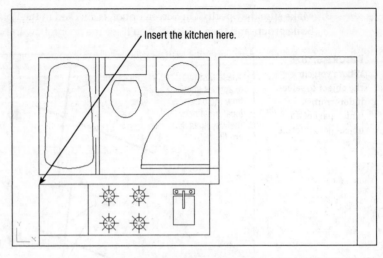

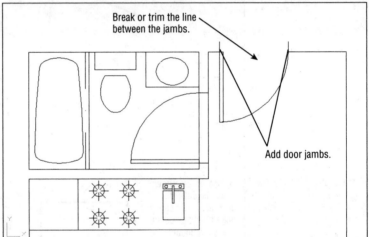

6. Move the cursor over the Osnap marker so that the Osnap Tracking vector appears from the corner. Now move the cursor to the right, and you'll see the Osnap Tracking vector extend from the corner.

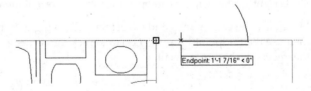

7. Continue to move the cursor to the right so that the tracking vector readout shows roughly 6˝, or 15 cm for metric users.

8. With the cursor in this position, enter **5**↵. Metric users should enter **13**↵. The door is placed exactly 5 (or 13) units to the right of the corner.

9. At the `Specify rotation angle <0>:` prompt, enter **270**↵. Or, if you prefer, turn on Polar Tracking to orient the door so that it's swinging *into* the studio. You've now accurately placed the entry door in the studio apartment.

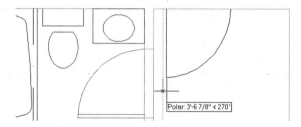

10. Make sure the door is on the Door layer.

For a shortcut to setting an object's layer, you can select the object or objects and then select a layer from the Layer drop-down list in the Layers panel.

Next, add the finishing touches to the entry door:

1. Add 5˝ (13 cm for metric users) door jambs as shown in the bottom image in Figure 6.19, and change their Layer property to the Jamb layer.

2. Choose the Break tool in the expanded Modify panel, and then select the header over the entry door. (See the bottom image in Figure 6.19.)

3. Type **F**↵ to use the first-point option; then select the endpoint of one of the door jambs.

4. At the `Specify second break point:` prompt, select the endpoint of the other jamb, as shown in the bottom image in Figure 6.19.

5. Draw the door header on the Ceiling layer, as shown in Figure 6.20.

6. Click Offset on the Modify panel, and offset the top wall lines of the unit and the door header up 5˝ (13 cm for metric users) so they connect with the top end of the door jamb, as shown in Figure 6.20. Don't forget to include the short wall line from the door to the bathroom wall.

7. Choose Save As from the Application menu to save your file as `Unit`.

USING POLAR AND OSNAP TRACKING AS CONSTRUCTION LINE TOOLS

So far, you've been using existing geometry to place objects in the plan accurately. In this section, you'll use the Polar and Osnap Tracking tools to extend the upper wall line 5˝ (13 cm for metric users) beyond the right-side interior wall of the unit. You'll also learn how to use the Construction Line tool to locate door jambs accurately near the balcony.

OTHER METHODS FOR USING THE BREAK COMMAND

In the exercise for finishing the unit plan, you used the Break command to place a gap in a line accurately over the entry door. In Chapter 5, you broke a line at a single point to create multiple, contiguous line segments.

In this chapter, you used the Break command's F option, which allows you to specify the first point of a break. You can also break a line without the F option, but with a little less accuracy. When you don't use the F option, the point at which you select the object is used as the first break point. If you're in a hurry, you can dispense with the F option and place a gap in an approximate location. You can then later use other tools to adjust the gap.

In addition, you can use locations on other objects to select the first and second points of a break. For example, you might want to align an opening with another opening some distance away. After you've selected the line to break, you can then use the F option and select two points on the existing opening to define the first and second break points. The break points will align in an orthogonal direction to the selected points.

FIGURE 6.20
The other side of the wall

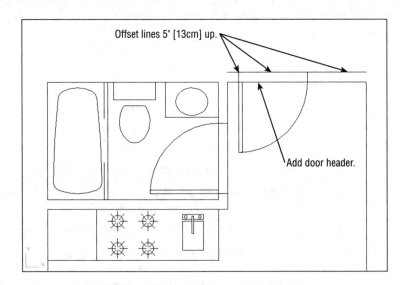

Offset lines 5" [13cm] up.

Add door header.

Start by changing the Polar Tracking setting to include a 45° angle:

1. Right-click the Polar Tracking button in the status bar at the bottom of the AutoCAD window, and choose Settings to open the Drafting Settings dialog box at the Polar Tracking tab (see Figure 6.21).

2. Select 45 from the Increment Angle drop-down list in the upper-left corner of the dialog box.

3. In the Object Snap Tracking Settings button group, make sure that the Track Using All Polar Angle Settings option is selected and click OK.

FIGURE 6.21
The Polar Tracking tab in the Drafting Settings dialog box

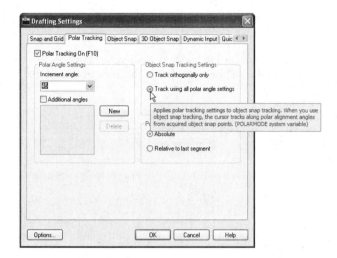

You're ready to extend the wall line. For this operation, you'll use grip editing:

1. Click the wall line at the top of the plan and to the right of the door to select the line and expose its grips.

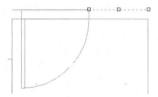

2. Click the Ortho Mode button in the status bar to turn on Ortho mode. This keeps the wall line straight as you edit it.

3. Click the rightmost grip of the line to make it hot.

4. Place the cursor on the upper-right corner of the plan until you see the Endpoint Osnap marker; then move the cursor away from the corner at a 45° angle. The Osnap Tracking vector appears at a 45° angle. Notice the small X that appears at the intersection of the Osnap Tracking vector and the line (see Figure 6.22).

FIGURE 6.22
The Osnap Track-ing vector

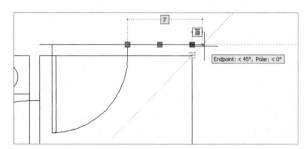

With the Osnap Tracking vector and the line intersecting, click the mouse button. The line changes to extend exactly 5 units beyond the vertical interior wall of the plan.

5. Press the Esc key twice to clear your selection. Then repeat steps 1 through 4 for the horizontal wall line to the left of the door to extend that line to the left corner (Figure 6.23).

FIGURE 6.23
Extend the wall line using the Osnap Tracking vector.

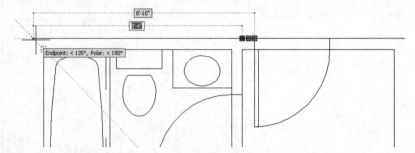

6. Click Zoom All from the Zoom flyout on the navigation bar, or type **Z↵ A↵** to view the entire drawing. It looks like Figure 6.24.

With Polar Tracking set to 45° and Osnap Tracking turned on in a crowded drawing, you may find that you're selecting points you don't really want to select. Just remember that if a drawing becomes too crowded, you can turn off these options temporarily by clicking the Object Snap Tracking or Polar Tracking button in the status bar.

In this exercise, you used Polar Tracking and Ortho mode to position the two lines used for the exterior walls of the studio unit accurately. This shows how you can take advantage of existing geometry with a combination of tools in the status bar.

FIGURE 6.24
The studio unit so far

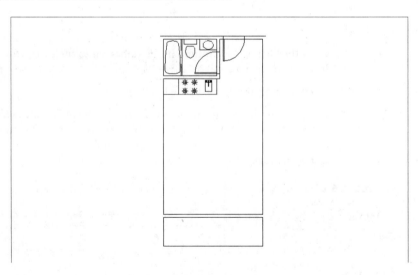

Now you'll finish the balcony by adding a sliding-glass door and a rail. This time, you'll use lines for construction as well as for parts of the drawing. First, you'll add the door jamb by drawing a construction line. A *construction line* is a line that has an infinite length, but unlike a ray, it extends in both directions. After drawing the construction line, you'll use it to position the door jambs quickly.

Follow these steps:

1. Zoom in to the balcony area, which is the smaller rectangle at the bottom of the drawing.

    Click the Construction Line tool on the expanded Draw panel. You can also type **XL**↵. You'll see this prompt:

    ```
    Specify a point or [Hor/Ver/Ang/Bisect/Offset]:
    ```

2. Type **O**↵ to select Offset.

3. At the `Specify offset distance or [Through] <0´-5″>:` prompt, type **4**↵. Metric users should type **122**↵.

4. At the `Select a line object:` prompt, click the wall line at the right of the unit.

5. At the `Specify side to offset:` prompt, click a point to the left of the wall to display the construction line. (See the top image of Figure 6.25.)

6. At the `Select a line object:` prompt, click the left wall line and then click to the right of the selected wall to create another construction line. Your drawing should look like the top image in Figure 6.25.

    Next you'll edit the construction lines to form the jambs.

7. Click Trim on the Modify panel, or type **Tr**↵.

8. Select the construction lines and the two horizontal lines representing the wall between the unit and the balcony, and press ↵. You can either use a crossing window or select each line individually. You've just selected the objects to trim to.

    You can also use the Fence selection option to select the lines to be trimmed.

9. Click the horizontal lines at any point between the two construction lines. Then click the construction lines above and below the horizontal lines to trim them. Your drawing looks like the bottom image in Figure 6.25.

10. Assign the trimmed construction lines to the Jamb layer.

11. Add lines on the Ceiling layer to represent the door header.

12. Draw lines between the two jambs (on the Door layer) to indicate a sliding-glass door (see Figure 6.25).

The wall facing the balcony is now complete. To finish the unit, you need to show a handrail and the corners of the balcony wall:

1. Offset the bottom line of the balcony 3″ toward the top of the drawing. Metric users should offset the line 7.6 units.

FIGURE 6.25
Drawing the
door opening

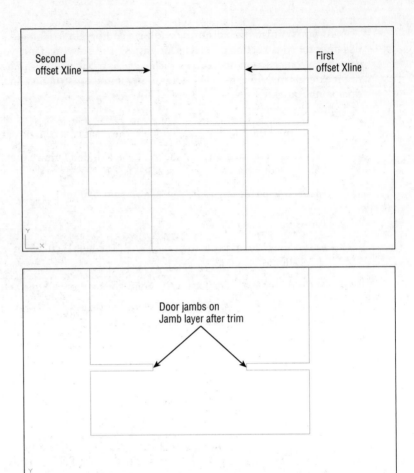

2. Create a new layer called F-rail, and assign this offset line to it.

3. Add a 5″ (13 cm for metric users) horizontal line to the lower corners of the balcony, as shown in Figure 6.26.

4. Click the Set Base Point tool from the Home tab's expanded Block panel to set the base point at the lower-left corner of the balcony, at the location shown in Figure 6.26.

5. Zoom back to the previous view. Your drawing should now look like Figure 6.27.

6. Click Save from the Quick Access toolbar to save the drawing, and then close the file.

Your studio apartment unit plan is now complete. The exercises you've just completed demonstrate a typical set of operations you'll perform while building your drawings. In fact, nearly 80 percent of what you'll do in AutoCAD is represented here.

Now, to review the drawing process and to create a drawing you'll use later, you'll draw the apartment building's lobby. As you follow the steps, refer to Figure 6.28.

FIGURE 6.26
Finishing the
sliding-glass door
and the railing

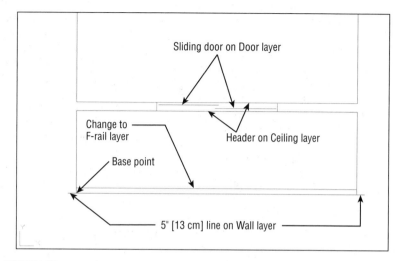

FIGURE 6.27
The completed
studio apart-
ment unit

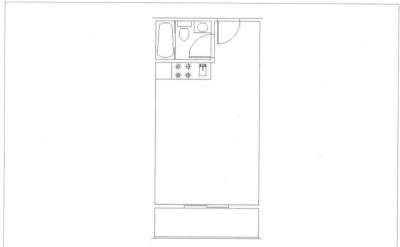

THE CONSTRUCTION LINE OPTIONS

There is more to the Construction Line command than you've seen in the exercises in this chapter. Here is a list of the Construction Line options and their uses:

Hor   Draws horizontal construction lines as you click points

Ver   Draws vertical construction lines as you click points

Ang   Draws construction lines at a specified angle as you pick points

Bisect   Draws construction lines bisecting an angle or a location between two points

Offset   Draws construction lines offset at a specified distance from an existing line

FIGURE 6.28
Drawing the
lobby plan. Metric
dimensions are
shown in brackets.

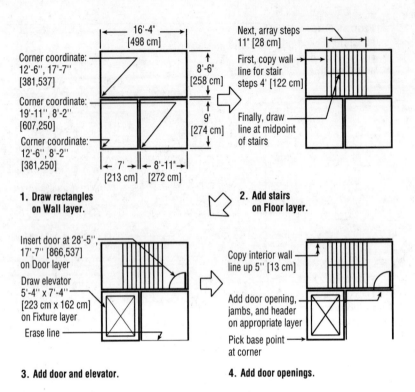

1. **Draw rectangles on Wall layer.**

2. **Add stairs on Floor layer.**

3. **Add door and elevator.**

4. **Add door openings.**

As is usual in floor plans, the elevator shaft is indicated by the box with the large X through it, and the stair shaft is indicated by the box with the row of vertical lines through it. If you're in a hurry, use the finished version of this file, called Lobby.dwg (Lobby-metric.dwg for metric users). To draw the apartment building lobby, follow these steps:

1. Create a new file called Lobby, using the Unit file as a prototype. (Open the Unit file, choose Save As from the Application menu, and enter **Lobby** for the new filename.)

2. Erase the entire unit (click the Erase tool from the Modify panel, and then type **All↵**).

3. Draw the three main rectangles that represent the outlines of the stair shaft, the elevator shaft, and the lobby.

4. To draw the stairs, copy or offset the stair shaft's left wall to the right a distance of 4′ (122 cm). This creates the first line representing the steps.

5. Array this line in one row of 10 columns, using 11″ (28 cm) column offset.

6. Draw the center line dividing the two flights of stairs.

7. Draw the elevator, insert the door, and assign the door to the Door layer. Practice using construction lines here.

8. Draw the door jambs. Edit the door openings to add the door jambs and headers.

9. Use the Base command to set the base point of the drawing. Your plan should resemble the one in Figure 6.28, step 4.

10. Save the Lobby file and close it.

USING RAYS

If you like the construction line tool but you would like to have one endpoint, you can use a ray (click Ray in the expanded Draw panel). A *ray* is like a line that starts from a point you select and continues off to an infinite distance. You specify the start point and angle of the ray. You can place a ray at the corner at a 45° angle and then fillet the ray to the horizontal wall line to shorten or lengthen the line to the appropriate length.

Finding an Exact Distance along a Curve

To find an exact distance along a curve or to mark off specific distance increments along a curve, do the following:

1. Click the Point Style tool in the Home tab's Utilities panel, or enter **ddpstyle**↵ to open the Point Style dialog box (Figure 6.29).

FIGURE 6.29
The Point Style dialog box

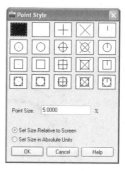

2. Click the X icon in the top row. Also be sure the Set Size Relative To Screen radio button is selected. Then click OK.

    You can also set the point style by setting the Pdmode system variable to 3.

3. Click Measure from the Point flyout on the expanded Draw panel, or type **me**↵ (see Figure 6.30).

THE DIFFERENCE BETWEEN DIVIDE AND MEASURE

The Divide tool (Divide from the Point flyout on the expanded Draw panel) marks off a line, an arc, or a curve into equal divisions, as opposed to divisions of a length you specify. You might use Divide to divide an object into 12 equal segments, for example. Aside from this difference in function, Divide works exactly the same way as Measure.

FIGURE 6.30
The Point flyout on the expanded Draw panel

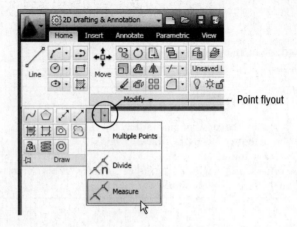

4. At the `Select object to measure:` prompt, click the end of the curve that you want to use as the starting point for your distance measurement.

5. At the `Specify length of segment or [Block]:` prompt, enter the distance you want. A series of Xs appears on the curve, marking off the specified distance along the curve. You can select the exact location of the Xs by using the Node Osnap override (see Figure 6.31).

FIGURE 6.31
Finding an exact distance along a spline curve by using points and the Measure command

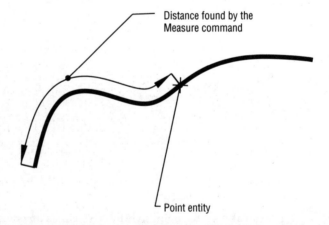

USING BLOCKS INSTEAD OF POINTS

The Block option of the Measure command enables you to specify a block to be inserted at the specified segment length in place of the Xs on the arc. You can align the block with the arc as it's inserted. (This is similar to the polar array's Rotate Objects As They Are Copied option.)

The Measure command also works on most objects, including arcs and polylines. You'll get a more detailed look at the Measure command in Chapter 19.

As you work with AutoCAD, you'll find that constructing temporary geometry such as the circle and points in the two previous examples will help you solve problems in new ways. Don't hesitate to experiment! Remember, you've always got the Save and Undo commands to help you recover from mistakes.

DIVIDE AND MEASURE AS AUTOLISP CUSTOMIZATION TOOLS

Divide and Measure are great tools for gathering information about objects in a drawing. A colleague of mine found it to be an excellent way to find the length of a complex object while working on an Autolisp macro. In Autolisp, you have to write some elaborate code just to find the length of a complex polyline. After struggling with his program code, he realized that he could use the Measure command to mark off known distances along a polyline and then count the points to find the overall length of the polyline.

Changing the Length of Objects

Suppose that, after finding the length of an arc, you realize you need to lengthen the arc by a specific amount. The Lengthen tool in the expanded Modify panel lets you lengthen or shorten arcs, lines, polylines, splines, and elliptical arcs. As an example, here's how to lengthen an arc:

1. Click Lengthen from the expanded Modify panel, or type **len**↵.

2. At the `Select an object or [DElta/Percent/Total/DYnamic]:` prompt, type **T**↵.

3. At the `Specify total length or [Angle] <1.0000)>:` prompt, enter the length you want for the arc.

4. At the `Select an object to change or [Undo]:` prompt, click the arc you want to change. Be sure to click at a point nearest the end you want to lengthen. The arc increases in length to the size you specified.

The Lengthen command also shortens an object if it's currently longer than the value you enter.

In this short example, you've learned how to change an object to a specific length. You can use other criteria to change an object's length, using these options available for the Lengthen command:

DElta   Lengthens or shortens an object by a specific length. To specify an angle rather than a length, use the Angle suboption.

Percent   Increases or decreases the length of an object by a percentage of its current length.

Total   Specifies the total length or angle of an object.

DYnamic   Lets you graphically change the length of an object using your cursor.

Creating a New Drawing by Using Parts from Another Drawing

This section explains how to use the Export command. Export can be used to turn parts of a drawing into a separate file in a way similar to the Wblock command described in Chapter 4. Here you'll use the Export command to create a separate staircase drawing by using the staircase you've already drawn for the lobby.

Follow these steps:

1. If you closed the Lobby file, open it now. If you didn't create the lobby drawing, open the Lobby.dwg (or Lobby-metric.dwg) file.

2. Chose Export ➢ Other Formats from the Application menu, or type **export**↵, to open the Export Data dialog box.

3. Enter **stair.dwg** in the File Name text box, and click Save. By including the .dwg file-name extension, you let AutoCAD know that you want to export to a drawing file and not a file in some other file format, such as DXF or WMF.

4. At the Enter name of existing block or [= (block=output file)/* (whole drawing)] <define new drawing>: prompt, press ↵. When you export to a DWG for-mat, AutoCAD assumes you want to export a block. Bypassing this prompt by pressing ↵ tells AutoCAD that you want to create a file from part of the drawing rather than from a block.

5. At the Specify insertion base point: prompt, pick the lower-right corner of the stair shaft. This tells AutoCAD the base point for the new drawing.

6. At the Select objects: prompt, use a window to select the stair shaft, as shown in Figure 6.32.

FIGURE 6.32
A selection win-
dow enclosing the
stair shaft

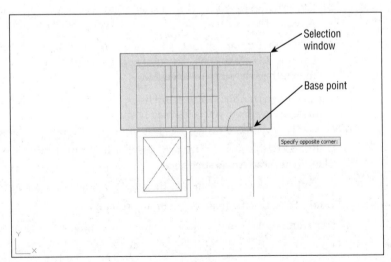

7. When the stair shaft, including the door, is highlighted, press ↵ to confirm your selection. The stairs disappear.

8. Because you want the stairs to remain in the lobby drawing, click the Undo button to bring them back. Undo doesn't affect any files you might export by choosing Export ➢ Other Formats from the Application menu, by using Wblock, or by using the Block tool.

Eliminating Unused Blocks, Layers, Linetypes, Shapes, Styles, and More

A template can contain blocks and layers you don't need in your new file. For example, the lobby you just completed contains the bathroom block because you used the Unit file as a prototype. Even though you erased this block, it remains in the drawing file's database. It's considered unused because it doesn't appear as part of the drawing. Such extra blocks can slow you down by increasing the amount of time needed to open the file. They also increase the size of your file unnecessarily. You can eliminate unused elements from a drawing by using the Purge command.

SELECTIVELY REMOVING UNUSED ELEMENTS

You use the Purge command to remove unused individual blocks, layers, linetypes, shapes, text styles, and other drawing elements from a drawing file. To help keep the file size small and to make layer maintenance easier, you should purge your drawing of unused elements. Bear in mind, however, that the Purge command doesn't delete certain primary drawing elements—namely, layer 0, the Continuous linetype, and the Standard text style.

Use these steps to practice using the Purge command:

1. Click Open from the Quick Access toolbar, and open the Lobby.dwg sample file.

2. Choose Drawing Utilities ➢ Purge from the Application menu to open the Purge dialog box (see Figure 6.33). You'll see a listing of drawing components that can be purged. If the drawing contains any of the types of components listed, a plus sign appears to the left of the component name.

3. Click the plus sign of the component you want to purge. In this exercise, click the plus sign next to the Blocks listing. The list expands to show the names of the items under the component category.

4. Select the name BATH from the expanded list. If you want to select more than one item, you can Ctrl+click individual names or Shift+click to select a group of names.

5. After the components are selected, click the Purge button in the lower-left corner of the dialog box. You then see a message box asking you to confirm that you want to purge the block.

REMOVING ALL UNUSED ELEMENTS

In the preceding exercise, you selected a single block for removal from the Lobby file. If you want to clear all the unused elements from a file at once, you can click the Purge All button at the bottom of the Purge dialog box (see Figure 6.33).

FIGURE 6.33
The Purge
dialog box

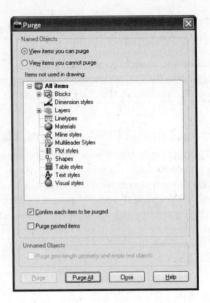

Here are the steps:

1. Choose Drawing Utilities ➢ Purge from the Application menu to open the Purge dialog box again.

2. Click the Purge Nested Items check box to turn on this option.

3. Click Purge All to open the Confirm Purge dialog box, which asks whether you want to purge a block.

4. Click Yes. The Confirm Purge dialog box displays the name of another block, asking you to confirm the purge. You can continue to click Yes and AutoCAD will display the Confirm Purge dialog box for each unused element still in the drawing.

5. Click the Purge All option to purge everything at once. The Confirm Purge dialog box closes.

6. In the Purge dialog box, click Close.

7. Close and save the Lobby file, and exit AutoCAD.

The Lobby file is now trimmed down to the essential data it needs and nothing else. You may have noticed that when you returned to the Purge dialog box in step 6, the items in the list box no longer showed plus signs. This indicates that there are no longer any unused items in the drawing.

In this last exercise, you used the Purge Nested Items option at the bottom of the dialog box. The Purge Nested Items option automatically purges unused blocks, including those nested within other blocks. If this option isn't checked, you might have to repeat the Purge operation to remove all unused elements in a drawing.

PURGING ZERO-LENGTH GEOMETRY AND BLANK TEXT

At the very bottom of the Purge dialog box, you'll see an option to "purge zero-length geometry and empty text objects." This has long been on the wish list of AutoCAD users, and it does just what it says: It purges objects that have no length as well as text objects that do not contain any text.

The Bottom Line

Create and use templates.   If you find that you're using the same settings when you create a new drawing file, you can set up an existing file the way you like and save it as a template. You can then use your saved template for any new drawings you create.

Master It   Describe the method for saving a file as a template.

Copy an object multiple times.   Many tools in AutoCAD allow you to create multiple copies. The Array command offers a way to create circular copies or row and column copies.

Master It   What names are given to the two types of arrays in the Array dialog box?

Develop your drawing.   When laying down simple line work, you'll use a few tools frequently. The exercises in the early part of this book showed you some of these commonly used tools.

Master It   What tool can you use to join two lines end to end?

Find an exact distance along a curve.   AutoCAD offers some tools that allow you to find an exact distance along a curve.

Master It   Name the two tools you can use to mark off exact distances along a curve.

Change the length of objects.   You can accurately adjust the length of a line or arc in AutoCAD using a single command.

Master It   What is the keyboard alias for the command that changes the length of objects?

Create a new drawing by using parts from another drawing.   You can save a lot of time by reusing parts of drawings. The Export command can help.

Master It   True or false: The Export command saves only blocks as drawing files.

Chapter 7

Mastering Viewing Tools, Hatches, and External References

Now that you've created drawings of a typical apartment unit and the apartment building's lobby and stairs, you can assemble them to complete the first floor of the apartment building. In this chapter, you'll take full advantage of AutoCAD's features to enhance your drawing skills as well as to reduce the time it takes to create accurate drawings.

As your drawing becomes larger, you'll find that you need to use the Zoom and Pan commands more often. Larger drawings also require some special editing techniques. You'll learn how to assemble and view drawings in ways that will save you time and effort as your design progresses. Along the way, you'll see how you can enhance the appearance of your drawings by adding hatch patterns.

In this chapter, you'll learn to do the following:

◆ Assemble the parts

◆ Take control of the AutoCAD display

◆ Use hatch patterns in your drawings

◆ Understand the boundary hatch options

◆ Use external references

Assembling the Parts

One of the best timesaving features of AutoCAD is its ability to duplicate repetitive elements quickly in a drawing. In this section, you'll assemble the drawings you've been working on into the complete floor plan of a fictitious apartment project. This will demonstrate how you can quickly and accurately copy your existing drawings in a variety of ways.

DON'T SEE THE NAVIGATION BAR?

In this chapter, you'll be asked to use the Zoom and Pan tools on the navigation bar frequently. If you don't see it in the AutoCAD window, then go to the View tab's Window panel, click the User Interface tool and turn on the Navigation Bar option. Or if you prefer, you can also find the Zoom and Pan tools in the View tab's Navigate panel.

Start by creating a new file for the first floor:

1. Create a new file named P1an to contain the drawing of the apartment building's first floor. This is the file you'll use to assemble the unit plans into an apartment building. If you want to use a template file, use acad.dwt. Metric users can use the acadiso.dwt template file. (These are AutoCAD template files that appear in the Select Template dialog box when you choose New from the Quick Access toolbar.)

2. Set the Units style to Architectural (choose Drawing Utilities ➤ Units from the Application menu). Metric users can leave the unit as decimal but change the Insertion scale to centimeters.

3. Set up the drawing for a 1/8″ = 1′-0″ scale on a 24″-×-18″ drawing area (you can use the Limits command for this.). Such a drawing requires an area 2,304 units wide by 1,728 units deep. Metric users should set up a drawing at 1:100 scale on an A2 sheet size. Your drawing area should be 5940 cm × 4200 cm.

4. Create a layer called Plan1, and make it the current layer.

5. Right-click the Snap Mode tool in the status bar and select Settings.

6. Set Snap Spacing to 1.

7. Choose Zoom All from the Navigation bar or type **Z↵A↵** to get an overall view of the drawing area.

Now you're ready to start building a floor plan of the first floor from the unit plan you created in the previous chapter. You'll start by creating a mirrored copy of the apartment plan:

1. Make sure the Object Snap tool is turned off, and then insert the 07a-unit.dwg drawing at coordinate 31′-5″,43′-8″. Metric users should insert the 07a-unit-metric.dwg drawing at coordinate 957,1330. Accept the Insert defaults. 07a-unit and 07a-unit-metric are the same drawings as the Unit.dwg file you were asked to create in earlier chapters.

    If you prefer, you can specify the insertion point in the Insert dialog box by removing the check mark from the Specify On-Screen check box. The Input options in the dialog box then become available to receive your input.

2. Zoom in to the apartment unit plan.

3. Click Mirror on the Home tab's Modify panel, select the Unit plan, and press ↵.

4. At the Specify first point of the mirror line: prompt, Shift+right-click the mouse, and choose From.

5. Shift+right-click again, and choose Endpoint.

6. Select the endpoint of the upper-right corner of the apartment unit, as shown in Figure 7.1.

7. Enter **@2.5<0↵**. Metric users should enter **@6.5<0↵**. A rubber-banding line appears, indicating the mirror axis.

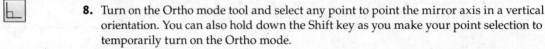

8. Turn on the Ortho mode tool and select any point to point the mirror axis in a vertical orientation. You can also hold down the Shift key as you make your point selection to temporarily turn on the Ortho mode.

9. At the `Erase Source Objects? [Yes/No] <N>:` prompt, press ↵. You'll get a 5″ wall thickness between two studio units. Your drawing should be similar to Figure 7.1.

FIGURE 7.1
The unit plan
mirrored

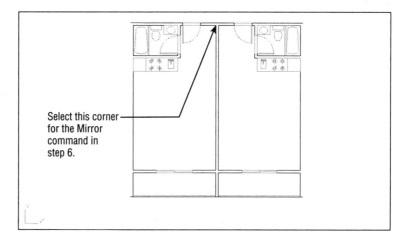

Select this corner
for the Mirror
command in
step 6.

You now have a mirror-image copy of the original plan in the exact location required for the overall plan. Next, make some additional copies for the opposite side of the building:

1. Press ↵ to reissue the Mirror command and select both units.

2. Use the From osnap option again, and using the Endpoint osnap, select the same corner you selected in step 6 of the preceding set of steps.

3. Enter **@24<90** to start a mirror axis 24″ directly above the selected point. Metric users should enter **@61<90**.

4. With Ortho mode on, select a point so that the mirror axis is exactly horizontal.

5. At the `Erase source objects? [Yes/No] <N>:` prompt, press ↵ to keep the two unit plans you selected in step 1 and complete the mirror operation.

With the tools you've learned about so far, you've quickly and accurately set up a fairly good portion of the floor plan. Continue with the next few steps to "rough in" the main components of the floor:

1. Click Zoom Extents from the Zoom flyout on the navigation bar, or type **Z**↵**E**↵, to get a view of the four plans. The Extents option forces the entire drawing to fill the screen at the center of the display area. Your drawing will look like Figure 7.2.

   If you happen to insert a block in the wrong coordinate location, you can use the Properties palette to change the insertion point for the block.

2. Copy the four units to the right at a distance of 28′-10″ (878 cm for metric users), which is the width of two units from center line to center line of the walls.

3. Insert the lobby at coordinate 89′-1″,76′-1″ (2713,2318 for metric users).

FIGURE 7.2
The unit plan,
duplicated
four times

FIGURE 7.2
The unit plan,
duplicated
four times

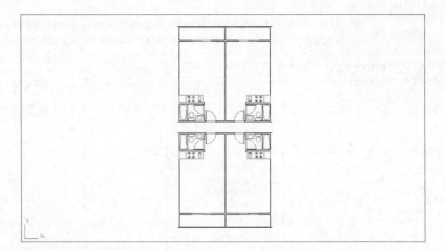

4. Copy all the unit plans to the right 74´-5″ (2267 cm for metric users), the width of four units plus the width of the lobby.

5. Click Zoom All from the Zoom flyout on the navigation bar, or type **Z↵A↵** to view the entire drawing, which should look like Figure 7.3.

FIGURE 7.3
The Plan drawing

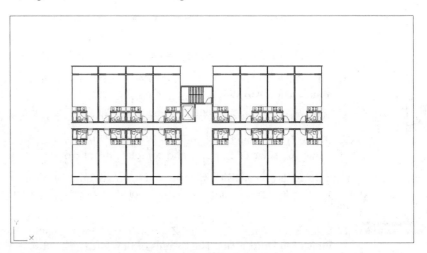

6. Click Save on the Quick Access toolbar to save this Plan.dwg file to disk.

Taking Control of the AutoCAD Display

By now, you should be familiar with the Pan and Zoom functions in AutoCAD. Many other tools can also help you get around in your drawing. In the following sections, you'll get a closer look at the ways you can view your drawing.

Understanding Regeneration and Redrawing

AutoCAD uses two commands for refreshing your drawing display: Regen (drawing regeneration) and Redraw. Each command serves a particular purpose, although it may not be clear to a new user.

To better understand the difference between Regen and Redraw, it helps to know that AutoCAD stores drawing data in two ways:

♦ In a database of highly accurate coordinate information that is part of the properties of objects in your drawing

♦ In a simplified database used just for the display of the objects in your drawing

As you draw, AutoCAD starts to build an accurate, core database of objects and their properties. At the same time, it creates a simpler database that it uses just to display the drawing quickly. AutoCAD uses this second database to allow quick manipulation of the display of your drawing. For the purposes of this discussion, I'll call this simplified database the *virtual display* because it's like a computer model of the overall display of your drawing. This virtual display is in turn used as the basis for what is shown in the drawing area. When you issue a Redraw command, you're telling AutoCAD to reread this virtual display data and display that information in the drawing area. A Regen command, on the other hand, tells AutoCAD to rebuild the virtual display based on information from the core drawing database.

You may notice that the Pan Realtime and Zoom Realtime commands don't work beyond a certain area in the display. When you reach a point where these commands seem to stop working, you've come to the limits of the virtual display data. To go beyond these limits, AutoCAD must rebuild the virtual display data from the core data; in other words, it must regenerate the drawing. You can usually do this by zooming out to the extents of the drawing.

Sometimes, when you zoom in to a drawing, arcs and circles may appear to be faceted instead of smooth curves. This faceting is the result of AutoCAD's virtual display simplifying curves to conserve memory. You can force AutoCAD to display smoother curves by typing **RE**↵, which is the shortcut for the Regen command.

CONTROLLING DISPLAY SMOOTHNESS

As you work in AutoCAD, you may notice that linetypes sometimes appear continuous even when they're supposed to be dotted or dashed. You may also notice that arcs and circles occasionally appear to be segmented lines although they're always plotted as smooth curves. A command called Viewres controls how smoothly linetypes, arcs, and circles are displayed in an enlarged view. The lower the Viewres value, the fewer the segments and the faster the redraw and regeneration. However, a low Viewres value causes noncontinuous linetypes, such as dashes or center lines, to appear as though they're continuous, especially in drawings that cover very large areas (for example, civil site plans).

Finding a Viewres value that best suits the type of work you do will take some experimentation. The default Viewres setting is 1000. You can try increasing the value to improve the smoothness of arcs and see if a higher value works for you. Enter **Viewres**↵↵ at the Command prompt to change the value. If you work with complex drawings, you may want to keep the value at 1000; then when you zoom in close to a view, use the Regen command to display smooth arcs and complete linetypes.

CREATING MULTIPLE VIEWS

So far, you've looked at ways to help you get around in your drawing while using a single view window. You can also set up multiple views of your drawing, called *viewports*. With viewports, you can display more than one view of your drawing at one time in the AutoCAD drawing area. For example, one viewport can display a close-up of the bathroom, another viewport can display the overall plan view, and yet another can display the unit plan.

When viewports are combined with AutoCAD's Paper Space feature, you can plot multiple views of your drawing. Paper Space is a display mode that lets you paste up multiple views of a drawing, much like a page-layout program. To find out more about viewports and Paper Space, see Chapters 16 and 24.

SAVING VIEWS

Another way to control your views is by saving them. You might think of saving views as a way of creating a bookmark or a placeholder in your drawing.

For example, a few walls in the Plan drawing aren't complete. To add the lines, you'll need to zoom in to the areas that need work, but these areas are spread out over the drawing. AutoCAD lets you save views of the areas you want to work on and then jump from saved view to saved view. This technique is especially helpful when you know you'll often want to return to a specific area of your drawing.

You'll see how to save and recall views in the following set of exercises. Here's the first one:

1. Click Zoom All from the Zoom flyout on the navigation bar, or type **Z↵A↵** to get an overall view of the plan.

2. Choose Named Views from the View tab's Views panel or type **V↵** to open the View Manager dialog box (Figure 7.4).

FIGURE 7.4
The View Manager
dialog box

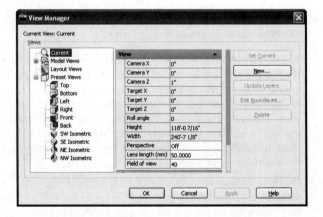

MANAGING SAVED VIEWS

In the View Manager dialog box, you can call up an existing view (Set Current), create a new view (New), or get detailed information about a view. You can also select from a set of predefined views that include orthographic and isometric views of 3D objects. You'll learn more about these options in Chapter 21.

3. Make sure the Current option is selected in the list to the left, and then click the New button to open the New View / Shot Properties dialog box (Figure 7.5). You'll notice some options related to the User Coordinate System (UCS) plus an option called View Category. You'll get a chance to look at the UCS in Chapters 21 and 22. The View Category option relates to the Sheet Set feature described in Chapter 30. Other options, including Visual Style, Background, and Boundary, give you control over the appearance of the background and layout of a saved view. For now, you'll concentrate on creating a new view.

FIGURE 7.5

The New View /Shot Properties dialog box

4. Click the Define Window radio button. The dialog boxes momentarily disappear, and the Dynamic input display turns on.

5. At the Specify first corner: prompt, click two points to place a selection window around the area around the elevator lobby, as shown in Figure 7.6. Notice that the display changes so that the non-shaded area shows the area you selected. If you aren't satisfied with the selection area, you can place another window in the view.

FIGURE 7.6
Select this area for
your saved view.

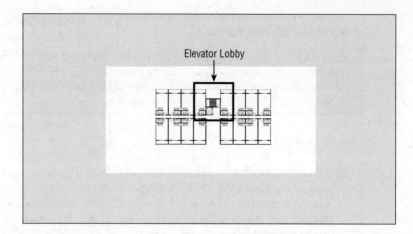

Elevator Lobby

6. When you're satisfied with your selection, press ↵ or right-click. The dialog boxes reappear.

7. Click the View Name input box, and type **Elevator Lobby** for the name of the view you just defined.

8. Click the OK button. The New View / Shot Properties dialog box closes, and you see Elevator Lobby in the Views list.

9. Click OK to close the View Manager dialog box.

10. Let's see how to recall the view that you've saved. From the View tab's Views panel, click the Views drop-down list, and select Elevator Lobby.

Your view changes to a close-up of the area you selected in step 5. You can also open the View Manager dialog box (enter **V↵**), select Elevator Lobby from the view list, click Set Current, and click OK.

If you need to make adjustments to a view after you've created it, you can do so by following these steps: Right-click the view name in the View Manager dialog box, select Edit Boundaries, and then select a window as you did in steps 5 and 6.

REPEAT THE LAST COMMAND

Remember that when no command is active, you can right-click the Command window and then select Recent Commands to repeat a recently issued command. You can also right-click the drawing area when AutoCAD is idle and repeat the last command.

If you prefer, you can use the keyboard to invoke the View command and thus avoid all the dialog boxes:

1. Click Extents from the Zoom flyout on the View tab's Navigate panel, or type **Z↵E↵** .

2. Enter **–View↵S↵** at the Command prompt, or use the **–V↵S↵** shortcut. (Don't forget the minus sign in front of *View* or *V*.)

3. At the `Enter view name to save:` prompt, enter **Overall↵**.

4. Save the Plan file to disk.

As you can see, this is a quick way to save a view. With the name Overall assigned to this view, you can easily recall it at any time. (Choosing the Zoom All flyout option from the navigation bar gives you an overall view too, but it may zoom out too far for some purposes, or it may not show what you consider an overall view.)

OPENING A FILE TO A PARTICULAR VIEW

The Select File dialog box contains a Select Initial View check box. If you open a drawing with this option selected, you're greeted with a Select Initial View dialog box just before the opened file appears on the screen. This dialog box lists any views saved in the file. You can then go directly to a view by double-clicking the view name. If you've saved views and you know the name of the view you want, using Select Initial View saves time when you're opening large files.

Understanding the Frozen Layer Option

As mentioned earlier, you may want to turn off certain layers to plot a drawing containing only selected layers. But even when layers are turned off, AutoCAD still takes the time to redraw and regenerate them. The Layer Properties Manager offers the Freeze option; this acts like the Off option, except that Freeze causes AutoCAD to ignore frozen layers when redrawing and regenerating a drawing. By freezing layers that aren't needed for reference or editing, you can reduce the time AutoCAD takes to perform regens. This can be helpful in large, multi-megabyte files.

Be aware, however, that the Freeze option affects blocks in an unusual way. Try the following exercise to see firsthand how the Freeze option makes entire blocks disappear:

1. Close the Plan file, and open the 07b-plan.dwg file from the sample files. Metric users should open 07b-plan-metric.dwg. This file is similar to the Plan file you created but with a few additional walls and stairs added to finish off the exterior. Also note that the individual units are blocks named 07a-unit-metric. This will be important in a later exercise.

2. Open the Layer Properties Manager dialog box, and then set the current layer to 0.

3. Click the yellow lightbulb icon in the Plan1 layer listing to turn off that layer. Nothing changes in your drawing. Even though you turned off the Plan1 layer, the layer on which the unit blocks were inserted, the unit blocks remain visible.

4. Right-click in the layer list, choose Select All from the shortcut menu, and then click a lightbulb icon (not the one you clicked in step 3). You see a message warning you that

the current layer will be turned off. Click Turn The Current Layer Off. Now everything is turned off, including objects contained in the unit blocks.

5. Right-click in the layer list, choose Select All from the shortcut menu, and then click a lightbulb icon to turn all of the layers back on.

6. Click the Plan1layer's Freeze/Thaw icon. (You can't freeze the current layer.) The yellow sun icon changes to a gray snowflake, indicating that the layer is now frozen (Figure 7.7). Only the unit blocks disappear.

FIGURE 7.7
Freezing the
Plan1 layer

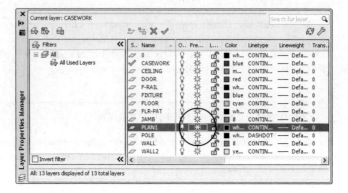

Even though none of the objects in the unit blocks were drawn on the Plan1 layer, the entire contents of the blocks assigned to the Plan1 layer are frozen when Plan1 is frozen. Another way to freeze and thaw individual layers is by clicking the Freeze/Thaw icon (which looks like a sun) in the Layer drop-down list in the Home tab's Layers panel.

You don't really need the Plan1 layer frozen. You froze it to see the effects of Freeze on blocks. Do the following to turn Plan1 back on:

1. Thaw layer Plan1 by going back to the Layer Properties Manager and clicking the snow-flake icon in the Plan1 layer listing.

2. Turn off the Ceiling layer. Exit the dialog box by clicking the X in the Layer Properties Manager's title bar.

The previous exercise showed the effect of freezing on blocks. When a block's layer is frozen, the entire block is made invisible regardless of the layer assignments of the objects contained in the block.

Keep in mind that when blocks are on layers that aren't frozen, the individual objects that are part of the block are still affected by the status of the layer to which they're assigned. This means that if some objects in a block are on a layer called Wall and the Wall layer is turned off or frozen, then those objects become invisible. Objects within the block that aren't on the layer that is off or frozen remain visible.

Using Hatch Patterns in Your Drawings

To help communicate your ideas to others, you'll want to add graphic elements that represent types of materials, special regions, or textures. AutoCAD provides hatch patterns for quickly placing a texture over an area of your drawing. In the following sections, you'll add a hatch pattern to the floor of the studio apartment unit, thereby instantly enhancing the appearance of one drawing. In the process, you'll learn how to update all the units in the overall floor plan quickly to reflect the changes in the unit.

Placing a Hatch Pattern in a Specific Area

It's always a good idea to provide a separate layer for hatch patterns. By doing so, you can turn them off if you need to. For example, the floor paving pattern might be displayed in one drawing but turned off in another so it won't distract from other information.

In the following exercises, you'll set up a layer for a hatch pattern representing floor tile and then add that pattern to your drawing. This will give you the opportunity to learn the different methods of creating and controlling hatch patterns.

Follow these steps to set up the layer:

1. Open the 07a-unit.dwg file. Metric users should open 07a-unit-metric.dwg. These files are similar to the Unit drawing you created in earlier chapters and are used to create the overall plan in the 07b-plan and 07b-plan-metric files. Remember that you also still have the 07b-plan or 07b-plan-metric file open.

2. Zoom in to the bathroom and kitchen area.

3. Create a new layer called Flr-pat.

4. Make Flr-pat the current layer.

Now that you've set up the layer for the hatch pattern, you can place the pattern in the drawing:

1. Click the Hatch tool on the Home tab's Draw panel, or type **H↵**. The Hatch Creation Ribbon tab appears (Figure 7.8).

FIGURE 7.8
The Hatch Creation Ribbon tab

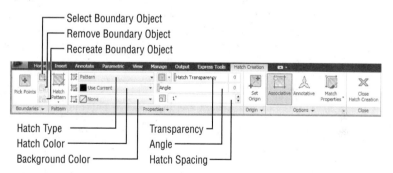

— Select Boundary Object
— Remove Boundary Object
— Recreate Boundary Object

Hatch Type ——
Hatch Color ——
Background Color ——
Transparency ——
Angle ——
Hatch Spacing ——

2. In the Hatch Type drop-down list box of the Properties panel (see Figure 7.8), select User Defined. The User Defined option lets you define a simple crosshatch pattern by specifying the line spacing of the hatch and whether it's a single- or double-hatch pattern.

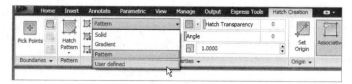

3. Double-click the Hatch Spacing text box in the lower right of the Properties panel (see Figure 7.8), and enter **6** (metric users should enter **15**). This tells AutoCAD you want the hatch's line spacing to be 6 inches, or 15 cm. Leave the Angle value at 0 because you want the pattern to be aligned with the bathroom.

4. Expand the Properties panel and click the Double button. This tells AutoCAD that you want the hatch pattern to run both vertically and horizontally.

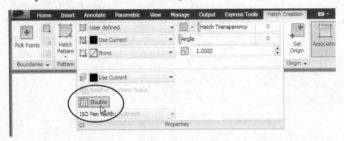

5. Hover the cursor over different parts of the bathroom layout but don't click anything. You will see a preview of your hatch pattern appear in each area that you hover over.

6. Click inside the area representing the bathroom floor. The hatch pattern is placed in the floor area. Notice that the area inside the door swing is not hatched. This is because the door swing area is not a contiguous part of the floor.

HATCHING AROUND TEXT

If you have text in the hatch boundary, AutoCAD will avoid hatching over it unless the Ignore option is selected in the Island Display Style options of the Advanced Hatch settings. See the section "Using Additional Hatch Features" later in this chapter for more on the Ignore setting.

7. Click inside the door swing to place the hatch pattern.

8. Right-click and select Enter or press the Enter key to exit the Hatch command.

As you saw from the exercise, AutoCAD gives you a preview of your hatch pattern before you place it in the drawing. In the previous steps, you set up the hatch pattern first by selecting the User Defined option, but you can reverse the order if you like. You can click in the areas you want to hatch first and then select a pattern and adjust the scale and apply other hatch options.

INHERITING PATTERNS

Say you want to add a hatch pattern that you've previously inserted in another part of the drawing. With the Match Properties tool in the Options panel of the Hatch Creation tab, you can select a previously inserted hatch pattern as a prototype for the current hatch pattern. However, this feature doesn't work with exploded hatch patterns.

Adding Predefined Hatch Patterns

In the previous exercise, you used the User Defined option to create a simple crosshatch pattern. You also have a number of other predefined hatch patterns to choose from. You can also find other hatch patterns on the Internet, and if you can't find the pattern you want, you can create your own (see Chapter 28).

Try the following exercise to see how you can add one of the predefined patterns available in AutoCAD:

1. Pan your view so that you can see the area below the kitchenette. Using the Rectangle tool in the Draw panel, draw the 3′-0″-×-8′-0″ outline of the floor tile area, as shown in Figure 7.9. Metric users should create a rectangle that is 91 cm × 228 cm. You can also use a closed polyline.

FIGURE 7.9
The area below the kitchen, showing the outline of the floor tile area

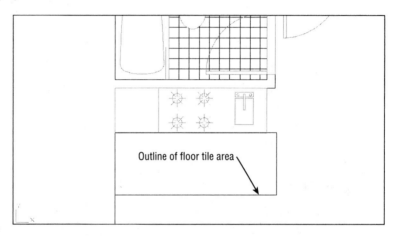

2. Click the Hatch tool in the Draw panel.

3. In the Properties panel of the Hatch Creation Ribbon tab, select the Pattern option in the Hatch Type drop-down list.

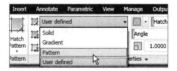

4. Click the Hatch Pattern tool in the Pattern panel. (If you don't see the Hatch Pattern tool, skip to step 6.) A flyout appears that displays a selection of hatch patterns (Figure 7.10). This list has a scroll bar to the right that lets you view additional patterns.

5. Scroll down the flyout and locate and select AR-PARQ1 (Figure 7.10).

6. If you didn't see the Hatch Pattern tool in step 4, scroll through the patterns in the Pattern panel using the down arrow to the right of the panel to locate and select the AR-PARQ1 pattern. You can also expand the panel by clicking the arrowhead below the scroll arrows (Figure 7.10).

FIGURE 7.10

The Hatch Pattern flyout (left) and the Hatch Pattern panel in a full-screen AutoCAD window (right).

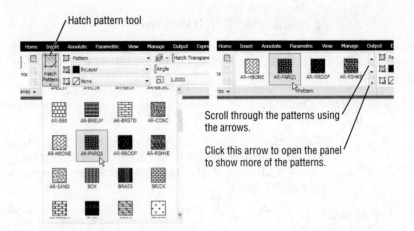

Hatch pattern tool

Scroll through the patterns using the arrows.

Click this arrow to open the panel to show more of the patterns.

7. Click inside the rectangle you just drew.

8. Right-click and select Enter or press the Enter key.

The predefined patterns with the *AR* prefix are architectural patterns that are drawn to full scale. In general, you should leave their Scale settings at 1. You can adjust the scale after you place the hatch pattern by using the Properties palette, as described later in this chapter.

ADDING SOLID FILLS

You can use the Solid option from the Hatch Type drop-down list in the Hatch Creation tab's Properties panel to create solid fills. The Hatch Color drop-down list lets you set the color of your solid fill. And don't forget that you can drag and drop solid fills and hatch patterns from the tool palettes you saw in Chapter 1.

Positioning Hatch Patterns Accurately

In the previous hatch pattern exercise, you may have noticed that the hatch pattern fit neatly into the 8'-×-3' rectangle. The AR-PARQ1 pattern is made up of 1' squares so they will fit exactly in an area that is of even 1' increments. In addition, AutoCAD places the origin of the pattern in the bottom-left corner of the area being filled by default.

You won't always have a hatch pattern fit so easily in an area. If you've ever laid tile in a bathroom, for example, you know that you have to carefully select the starting point for your tiles in order to get them to fit in an area with pleasing results. If you need to fine-tune the position of a hatch pattern within an enclosed area, you can do so by using the options in the Origin panel of the Hatch Creation tab.

Set Origin

The main tool in the panel, Set Origin, lets you select an origin point for your hatch pattern. You can also use the HPORIGIN system variable to accomplish this. You can also expand the Origin panel for a set of predefined origin locations. These locations are Bottom Left, Bottom Right, Top Left, Top Right, Center, and Use Current Origin. The Use Current Origin option refers to the X,Y origin of the drawing.

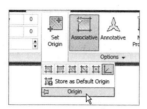

If you are hatching an irregular shape, these origin locations are applied to the *boundary extents* of the shape. An imaginary rectangle represents the outermost boundary, or the boundary extents of the shape, as shown in Figure 7.11.

FIGURE 7.11
The origin options shown in relation to the boundary extents of an irregular shape

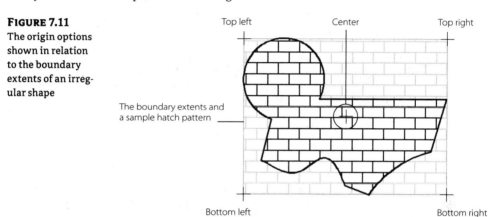

The Store As Default Origin option lets you save your selected origin as the default origin for future hatch patterns in the current drawing.

Now that you've learned how to add a hatch pattern, let's continue with a look at how your newly edited plan can be used. In the next exercise, you'll use this updated 07a-unit file to update all the units in the Plan file.

Updating a Block from an External File

As you progress through a design project, you make countless revisions. With traditional drafting methods, revising a drawing such as the studio apartment floor plan takes a good deal of time. If you change the bathroom layout, for example, you have to erase every occurrence of the bathroom and redraw it 16 times. With AutoCAD, on the other hand, revising this drawing can be a quick operation. You can update the studio unit you just modified throughout the overall plan drawing by replacing the current Unit block with the updated Unit file. AutoCAD can update all occurrences of the Unit block. The following exercise shows how this is accomplished.

For this exercise, remember that the blocks representing the units in the 07b-plan and 07b-plan-metric files are named 07a-unit and 07a-unit-metric:

1. Make sure you've saved the 07a-unit (07a-unit-metric for metric users) file with the changes, and then return to the 07b-plan file that is still open. Click the Open

Documents tool from the Application menu and then select 07b-plan.dwg. Metric users should use 07b-plan-metric.dwg.

YOU CAN'T UPDATE EXPLODED BLOCKS

Exploded blocks won't be updated when you update blocks from an external file. If you plan to use this method to update parts of a drawing, don't explode the blocks you plan to update. See Chapter 4.

---

2. Click the Insert tool on the Home tab's Block panel.

3. Click the Browse button. In the Select Drawing File dialog box, double-click the 07a-unit filename (07a-unit-metric for metric users).

4. Click OK in the Insert dialog box. A warning message tells you that a block already exists with the same name as the file. You can cancel the operation or redefine the block in the current drawing.

5. Click Redefine Block. The drawing regenerates.

6. At the Specify insertion point or [Basepoint/Scale/X/Y/Z/Rotate]: prompt, press the Esc key. You do this because you don't want to insert the Unit file into your drawing; you're just using the Insert feature to update an existing block.

7. Zoom in to one of the units. The floor tile appears in all the units as you drew it in the Unit file (see Figure 7.12).

Nested blocks must be updated independently of the parent block. For example, if you modified the Toilet block while editing the 07a-unit file and then updated the 07a-unit drawing in the 07b-plan file, the old Toilet block wouldn't be updated. Even though the toilet is part of the 07a-unit file, it's still a unique, independent block in the Plan file, and AutoCAD won't modify it unless specifically instructed to do so. In this situation, you must edit the original Toilet block and then update it in both the Plan and Unit files.

REPLACING BLOCKS

If you want to replace one block with another in the current file, type **–Insert**↵. (Don't forget the minus sign in front of *Insert*.) At the Block name: prompt, enter the block name followed by an equal sign (=), and then enter the name of the new block or the filename. Don't include spaces between the name and the equal sign.

FIGURE 7.12
The Plan drawing with the tile pattern

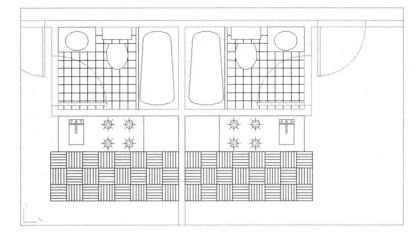

Also, block references and layer settings of the current file take priority over those of the imported file. For example, if a file to be imported has layers of the same name as the layers in the current file but those layers have color and linetype assignments that are different from the current file's, the current file's layer color and linetype assignments determine those of the imported file. This doesn't mean, however, that the imported file on disk is changed; only the inserted drawing is affected.

SUBSTITUTING BLOCKS

In the preceding example, you updated a block in your Plan file by using the Browse option in the Insert dialog box. In that exercise, the block name and the filename were the same. You can also replace a block with another block or a file of a different name. Here's how to do this:

1. Open the Insert dialog box.

2. Click the Browse button next to the Name input box, locate and select the file you want to use as a substitute, and then click Open to return to the Insert dialog box.

3. Change the name in the Name input box to the name of the block you want replaced.

4. Click OK. A warning message appears, telling you that a block with this name already exists. Click OK to proceed with the block substitution.

You can use this method of replacing blocks if you want to see how changing one element of your project can change your design. You might, for example, draw three different apartment unit plans and give each plan a unique name. You could then generate and plot three apartment building designs in a fraction of the time it would take you to do so by hand.

Block substitution can also reduce a drawing's complexity and accelerate regenerations. To substitute blocks, you temporarily replace large, complex blocks with schematic versions. For example, you might replace the Unit block in the Plan drawing with another drawing that contains just a single-line representation of the walls and bathroom fixtures. You would still have the wall lines for reference when inserting other symbols or adding mechanical or electrical information, but the drawing would regenerate much faster. When you did the final plot, you would reinsert the original Unit block showing every detail.

Changing the Hatch Area

You may have noticed the Associative option in the Hatch And Gradient dialog box. When this radio button is selected, AutoCAD creates an associative hatch pattern. *Associative* hatches adjust their shapes to any changes in their associated boundary, hence the name. The following exercise demonstrates how this works.

Suppose you want to enlarge the tiled area of the kitchen by one tile. Here's how it's done:

1. Click the Quick View Drawings tool in the status bar and select the Unit file from the preview panels. Click inside the drawing area when the Unit drawing appears (Figure 7.13).

FIGURE 7.13
The Quick View
Drawings view

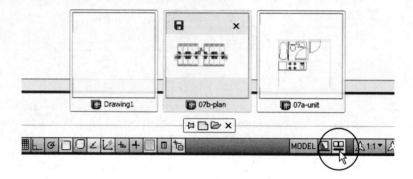

2. Click the outline border of the hatch pattern you created earlier. Notice the grips that appear around the hatch-pattern area.

3. Shift+click the grip in the lower-left corner of the hatch area.

SELECTING HATCH GRIPS

If the boundary of the hatch pattern consists of line segments, you can use a crossing window or polygon-crossing window to select the corner grips of the hatch pattern.

---

4. With the lower-left grip highlighted, Shift+click the lower-right grip.

5. Click the lower-right grip again, but don't Shift+click this time.

6. Enter @12<–90↲↲ (@30<–90 for metric users) to widen the hatch pattern by 1′, or 30 cm for metric users. The hatch pattern adjusts to the new size of the hatch boundary.

7. Press the Esc key twice to clear any grip selections.

8. Choose Save from the Quick Access toolbar to save the Unit file.

9. Return to the Plan file using the Quick View Drawings tool in the status bar, and repeat the steps in the section "Updating a Block from an External File" earlier in this chapter to update the units again.

The Associative feature of hatch patterns can save time when you need to modify your drawing, but you need to be aware of its limitations. A hatch pattern can lose its associativity when you do any of the following:

◆ Erase or explode a hatch boundary

◆ Erase or explode a block that forms part of the boundary

◆ Move a hatch pattern away from its boundary

These situations frequently arise when you edit an unfamiliar drawing. Often, boundary objects are placed on a layer that is off or frozen, so the boundary objects aren't visible. Also, the hatch pattern might be on a layer that is turned off and you proceed to edit the file not knowing that a hatch pattern exists. When you encounter such a file, take a moment to check for hatch boundaries so you can deal with them properly.

Modifying a Hatch Pattern

Like everything else in a project, a hatch pattern may eventually need to be changed in some way. Hatch patterns are like blocks in that they act like single objects. You can explode a hatch pattern to edit its individual lines. The Properties palette contains most of the settings you'll need to make changes to your hatch patterns. But the most direct way to edit a hatch pattern is to use the Hatch Edit dialog box.

EDITING HATCH PATTERNS FROM THE HATCH EDITOR TAB

Follow these steps to modify a hatch pattern by using the Hatch Edit dialog box:

1. Return to the Unit drawing using the Quick View Drawings tool in the status bar.

2. Press the Esc key to clear any grip selections that may be active from earlier exercises.

3. Click the hatch pattern in the kitchen to open the Hatch Editor Ribbon tab. It's the same as the Hatch Creation Ribbon tab.

A DOUBLE-CLICK OPENS THE PROPERTIES PALETTE

Clicking on a hatch pattern opens a Ribbon tab in which you can edit the pattern using the same tools you used to create it. If you prefer, you can access the Properties palette by double-clicking the pattern.

---

4. In the Pattern panel, locate and double-click the pattern named AR-BRSTD. It's the pattern that looks like a brick wall.

5. Press the Esc key to clear your selection of the hatch pattern. The AR-BRSTD pattern appears in place of the original parquet pattern.

6. Exit and save your file.

In this exercise, you were able to change the hatch just by clicking it. Although you changed only the pattern type, other options are available. You can, for example, modify a predefined pattern to a user-defined one by selecting User Defined from the Hatch Type drop-down list in the Properties panel of the Hatch Editor tab.

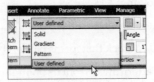

You can then enter angle and scale values for your hatch pattern in the options provided in the Properties panel of the Hatch Editor tab.

The other items in the Hatch Editor Ribbon tab are duplicates of the options in the Hatch Creation tab. They let you modify the individual properties of the selected hatch pattern. The upcoming section, "Understanding the Boundary Hatch Options," describes these other properties in detail.

EDITING HATCH PATTERNS FROM THE PROPERTIES PALETTE

If you prefer, you can use the older method to edit a hatch pattern. To open the Properties palette, double-click the hatch pattern you want to edit. The Properties palette displays a Pattern category, which offers a Pattern Name option (Figure 7.14).

FIGURE 7.14
The Pattern category in the Properties palette

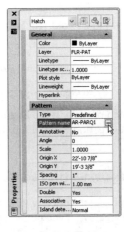

When you click this option, an ellipsis button appears, enabling you to open the Hatch Pattern Palette dialog box (Figure 7.15). You can then select a new pattern from the dialog box. The Type option in the Properties palette lets you change the type of hatch pattern from Predefined to User Defined or Custom.

TAKE A BREAK

If you're working through the tutorial in this chapter, this would be a good place to take a break or stop. You can pick up the next exercise in the section "Attaching a Drawing as an External Reference" at another time.

FIGURE 7.15
The Hatch Pattern
Palette dialog box

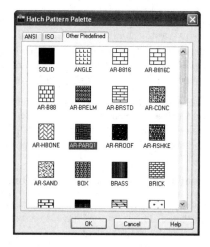

Understanding the Boundary Hatch Options

The Hatch Creation and Hatch Editor Ribbon panels offer many other options that you didn't explore in the previous exercises. For example, instead of clicking in the area to be hatched, you can select the objects that bound the area you want to hatch by clicking the Select Boundary Objects tool in the Boundaries panel. You can use the Select Boundary Objects tool to add boundaries to existing hatch patterns as well.

Controlling Boundaries with the Boundaries Panel

The previous exercises in this chapter have just touched on the tools in the Boundaries panel. Other options in the Boundaries panel are Pick Points, Select Boundary Objects, Remove Boundary Objects, Recreate Boundary.

Select Boundary Objects Lets you select objects to define a hatch boundary.

Remove Boundary Objects Lets you remove a bounded area, or *island*, in the area to be hatched. An example is the toilet seat in the bathroom. This option is available only when you select a hatch area by using the Add: Pick Points option and an island has been detected.

Recreate Boundary Draws a region or polyline around the current hatch pattern. You're then prompted to choose between a region or a polyline and to specify whether to reassociate the pattern with the re-created boundary. (See the Associative option discussed in a moment.)

Fine-Tuning the Boundary Behavior

The Boundary Hatch feature is view dependent; that is, it locates boundaries based on what is visible in the current view. If the current view contains a lot of graphic data, AutoCAD can have difficulty finding a boundary or can be slow in finding a boundary. If you run into this problem, or if you want to single out a specific object for a point selection boundary, you can further limit the area that AutoCAD uses to locate hatch boundaries by using the Boundary Set options:

Display Boundary Objects This highlights the objects that have been selected as the hatch boundary by AutoCAD.

Retain Boundary Objects   This retains outlines used to create the hatch pattern. This can be helpful if you want to duplicate the shape of the boundary for other purposes. Typically this is set to Don't Retain Boundaries, but you can use two other settings: Retain Boundaries – Polyline and Retain Boundaries – Region. The Retain Boundaries – Polyline option retains the boundaries as polylines. The Retain Boundaries – Regions option retains the boundaries as regions.

Select New Boundary Set   This lets you select the objects you want AutoCAD to use to determine the hatch boundary instead of searching the entire view. The screen clears and lets you select objects. This option discards previous boundary sets. It's useful for hatching areas in a drawing that contains many objects that you don't want to include in the hatch boundary.

Use Current Viewport   This uses the current viewport extents to define the boundary set.

The Boundary Set options are designed to give you more control over the way a point selection boundary is created. These options have no effect when you use the Select Objects button to select specific objects for the hatch boundary.

BOUNDARY RETENTION

The Hatch command can also create an outline of the hatch area by using one of two objects: 2D regions, which are like 2D planes, or polyline outlines. Hatch creates such a polyline boundary temporarily to establish the hatch area. These boundaries are automatically removed after the hatch pattern is inserted. If you want to retain the boundaries in the drawing, make sure the Retain Boundaries – Polyline option is selected. Retaining the boundary can be useful if you know you'll be hatching the area more than once or if you're hatching a fairly complex area.

Retaining a hatch boundary is useful if you want to know the hatched area's dimensions in square inches or feet because you can find the area of a closed polyline by using the List command. See Chapter 2 for more on the List command.

Controlling Hatch Behavior with the Options Panel

The Options panel offers a set of tools that control some additional features of the Hatch command. These features affect the way a hatch pattern fills a boundary area as well as how it behaves when the drawing is edited. Note that the Gap Tolerance, Separate Hatches, Normal Island Detection and Send Behind Boundary options are on the expanded Options panel. The following gives you a brief description of each of the Options panel's options:

Associative   Allows the hatch pattern to adjust to changes in its boundary. With this option turned on, any changes to the associated boundary of a hatch pattern cause the hatch pattern to flow with the changes in the boundary.

Annotative   Allows the hatch pattern to adjust to different scale views of your drawing. With this option turned on, a hatch pattern's size or spacing adjusts to the annotation scale of a viewport Layout or Model Space view. See Chapter 4 for more on the annotation scale.

Match Properties This group allows you to use an existing hatch pattern when inserting additional hatch patterns into a drawing. Select Use Current Origin when you want to use the current default hatch origin. Select Use Source Hatch Origin when you want to use the origin from the existing hatch pattern.

Gap Tolerance This option lets you hatch an area that isn't completely enclosed. The Gap Tolerance value sets the maximum gap size in an area you want to hatch. You can use a value from 0 to 5000.

Create Separate Hatches Creates separate and distinct hatches if you select several enclosed areas while selecting hatch areas. With this option off, separate hatch areas behave as a single hatch pattern.

Normal Island Detection (island detection options) Controls how islands within a hatch area are treated. Islands are enclosed areas that are completely inside a hatch boundary. There are four options in this list:

> **No Island Detection** This turns off island detection.

> **Normal Island Detection** This causes the hatch pattern to alternate between nested boundaries. The outer boundary is hatched; if there is a closed object within the boundary, it isn't hatched. If *another* closed object is inside the first closed object, *that* object is hatched. This is the default setting.

> **Outer Island Detection** This applies the hatch pattern to an area defined by the outermost boundary and a closed object within that boundary. Any boundaries nested in that closed object are ignored.

> **Ignore Island Detection** This supplies the hatch pattern to the entire area within the outermost boundary, ignoring any nested boundaries.

Send Behind Boundary (Draw Order) Allows you to specify whether the hatch pattern appears on top of or underneath its boundary. This is useful when the boundary is of a different color or shade and must read clearly or when the hatch pattern must cover the boundary. The options in this list are self-explanatory and are Do Not Assign, Send To Back, Bring To Front, Send Behind Boundary, and Bring In Front Of Boundary. See "Overlapping Objects with Draw Order" later in this chapter.

ANNOTATIVE HATCH PATTERNS

In Chapter 4, you learned about a feature in AutoCAD 2011 called the *annotation scale*. With this feature, you can assign several scales to certain types of objects and AutoCAD displays the object to the proper scale of the drawing. You can take advantage of this feature to allow hatch patterns to adjust their spacing or pattern size to the scale of your drawing. The Annotative option in the Options panel of the Hatch Creation Ribbon tab turns on the annotation scale feature for hatch patterns. Once this feature is turned on for a hatch pattern, you can set up the drawing scales that you want to apply to the hatch pattern using the same methods described for blocks in Chapter 4.

Using Additional Hatch Features

AutoCAD's Hatch command has a fair amount of "intelligence." As you saw in an earlier exercise, it was able to detect not only the outline of the floor area, but also the outline of the toilet seat that represents an island in the pattern area. If you prefer, you can control how AutoCAD treats these island conditions and other situations by selecting options available in the Hatch Creation and Hatch Editor Ribbon tab. You also have the option to create and edit hatch patterns using the Hatch And Gradient dialog box (Figure 7.16). If you have used AutoCAD before, this dialog box should be familiar to you.

To open the Hatch And Gradient dialog box, start the Hatch command by clicking the Hatch tool in the Home tab's Draw panel, then click the Hatch Settings tool in the right side of the Options panel title bar. This opens the Hatch And Gradient dialog box (Figure 7.16). Click the More Options button in the lower-right corner of the Hatch And Gradient dialog box.

This button expands the dialog box to show additional hatch options (Figure 7.16).

FIGURE 7.16
The Hatch And Gradient dialog box.

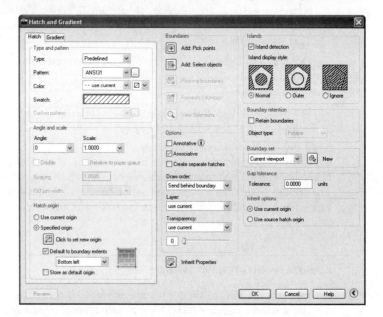

Nearly all of the settings and tools in the Hatch And Gradient dialog box are repeated in the Hatch Creation and Hatch Editor Ribbon tabs. They are just presented in a different way.

HATCH BOUNDARIES WITHOUT THE HATCH PATTERN

The Boundary command creates a polyline outline or region in a selected area. It works much like the Retain Boundary – Polyline option but doesn't add a hatch pattern.

Using Gradient Shading

You may have noticed Solid and Gradient options in the Hatch Type drop-down list. The solid hatch pattern lets you apply a solid color instead of a pattern to a bounded area. AutoCAD also offers a set of gradient patterns that let you apply a color gradient to an area.

You can apply a gradient to an area by using the same method you used to apply a hatch pattern, but when you select the Gradient option, you'll see a slight change in the Hatch Creation tab panels. The Scale input box in the Properties panel changes to a tint slider and the Pattern tab changes to show a set of different gradient patterns. The Origin panel also changes to show Centered as the only option (Figure 7.17).

FIGURE 7.17
The Gradient
Shading feature

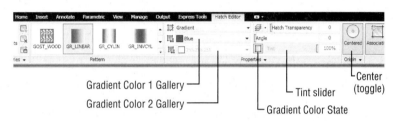

Gradient Color 1 Gallery ⎯

Gradient Color 2 Gallery ⎯

⎯ Tint slider

⎯ Gradient Color State

⎯ Center (toggle)

ACAD only

The Gradient Shading feature isn't available in AutoCAD LT.

CHOOSING A GRADIENT COLOR

Instead of offering hatch patterns, the Pattern panel offers a variety of gradient patterns. If you don't see the gradient patterns, you can click the Hatch Pattern tool to open a flyout of the gradient patterns. The Properties panel lets you control the color of the gradient. You can select the colors from the two color drop-down lists in the Properties panel.

If you don't see a color you want, you can click the Select Colors option at the bottom of the list to open the Select Color dialog box. This dialog box lets you choose from Index, True Color, or Color Book colors (Figure 7.18).

The Gradient Tint And Shade slider just to the right of the color drop-down lists lets you control the shade of the single-color gradient.

CHOOSING BETWEEN A SINGLE COLOR OR TWO COLORS

You can choose a gradient that transitions between shades of a single color by clicking the Gradient Tint And Shade tool in the Properties panel just to the left of the Gradient Tint And Shade slider. This turns on the Gradient Tint And Shade slider and disables the Color 2 drop-down list. When you turn off the Gradient Tint And Shade button, the Gradient Tint And Shade slider is disabled and the Color 2 drop-down list is enabled.

FIGURE 7.18
The True Color options in the Select Color dialog box

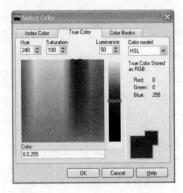

SELECTING GRADIENT PATTERNS

As mentioned earlier, you can choose from a set of gradient patterns from the Pattern panel. The Angle slider gives you further control over the gradient pattern by allowing you to rotate the angle of the pattern. The Centered option in the Origin panel places the center of the gradient at the center of the area selected for the pattern. This option is a toggle that is either on or off.

To place a gradient pattern, select a set of objects or a point in a bounded area, just as you would for a hatch pattern.

Tips for Using Hatch

Here are a few tips on using the Hatch feature:

◆ Watch out for boundary areas that are part of a large block. AutoCAD examines the entire block when defining boundaries. This can take time if the block is large. Use the Specify Boundary Set option to focus in on the set of objects you want AutoCAD to use for your hatch boundary.

◆ The Hatch feature is view dependent; that is, it locates boundaries based on what is visible in the current view. To ensure that AutoCAD finds every detail, zoom in to the area to be hatched.

◆ If the area to be hatched is large yet requires fine detail, first outline the hatch area by using a polyline. (See Chapter 19 for more on polylines.) Then use the Select Boundary Objects option in the Hatch Creation tab's Boundaries panel to select the polyline boundary manually instead of depending on Hatch to find the boundary for you.

◆ Consider turning off layers that might interfere with AutoCAD's ability to find a boundary.

◆ Hatch works on nested blocks as long as the nested block entities are parallel to the current UCS.

Space Planning and Hatch Patterns

Suppose you're working on a plan in which you're constantly repositioning equipment and furniture or you're in the process of designing the floor covering. You might be a little hesitant to place a hatch pattern on the floor because you don't want to have to rehatch the area each time you move a piece of equipment or change the flooring. You have two options in this situation: You can use Hatch's associative capabilities to include the furnishings in the boundary set, or you can use the Display Order feature.

USING ASSOCIATIVE HATCH

Associative Hatch is the most straightforward method. Make sure the Associative option is selected in the Hatch Creation tab's Options panel, and include your equipment or furniture in the boundary set. You can do this by using the Select option in the Boundaries panel.

   After the pattern is in place, the hatch pattern automatically adjusts to its new location when you move the furnishings in your drawing. One drawback, however, is that AutoCAD attempts to hatch the interior of your furnishings if they cross the outer boundary of the hatch pattern. Also, if any boundary objects are erased or exploded, the hatch pattern no longer follows the location of your furnishings. To avoid these problems, you can use the method described in the next section.

OVERLAPPING OBJECTS WITH DRAW ORDER

The Draw Order feature lets you determine how objects overlap. In the space-planning example, you can create furniture by using a solid hatch to indicate horizontal surfaces (see Figure 7.19).

FIGURE 7.19

Using Draw Order to create an overlapping effect over a hatch pattern

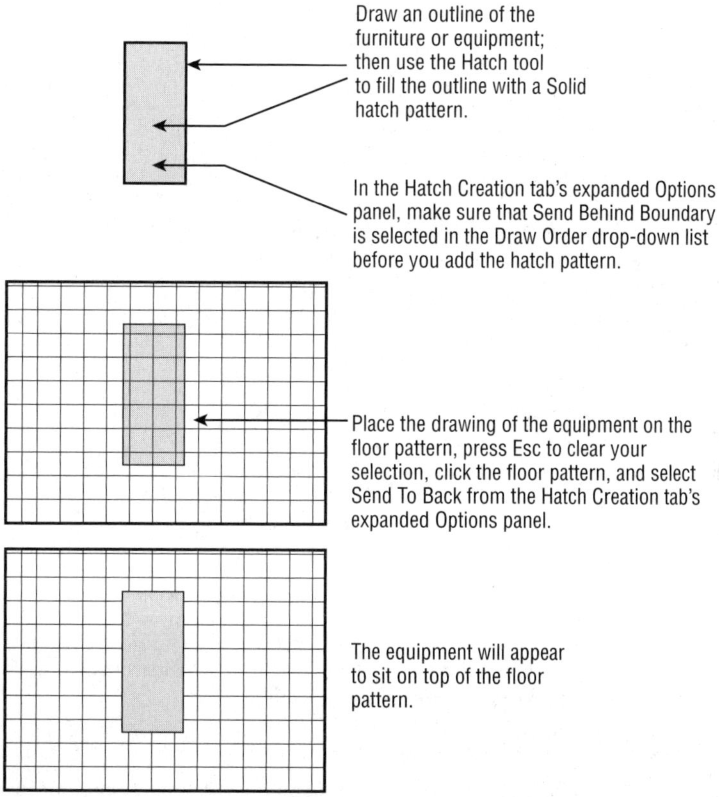

Draw an outline of the furniture or equipment; then use the Hatch tool to fill the outline with a Solid hatch pattern.

In the Hatch Creation tab's expanded Options panel, make sure that Send Behind Boundary is selected in the Draw Order drop-down list before you add the hatch pattern.

Place the drawing of the equipment on the floor pattern, press Esc to clear your selection, click the floor pattern, and select Send To Back from the Hatch Creation tab's expanded Options panel.

The equipment will appear to sit on top of the floor pattern.

HOW TO MATCH A HATCH PATTERN AND OTHER PROPERTIES QUICKLY

Another tool to help you edit hatch patterns is Match Properties, which is similar to Format Painter in the Microsoft Office system. This tool lets you change an existing hatch pattern to match another existing hatch pattern. Here's how to use it:

1. Choose Match Properties from the Home tab's Clipboard panel or type **Matchprop**.↵

2. Click the source hatch pattern you want to copy.

3. Click the target hatch pattern you want to change. The target pattern changes to match the source pattern.

The Match Properties tool transfers other properties as well, such as layer, color, and linetype settings. You can select the properties that are transferred by opening the Property Settings dialog box.

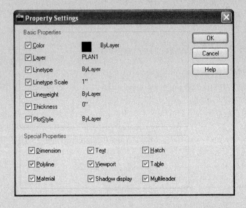

To open this dialog box, type **S**.↵ after selecting the object in step 2, or right-click and choose Settings from the shortcut menu. You can then select the properties you want to transfer from the options shown. All the properties are selected by default. You can also transfer text and dimension style settings. You'll learn more about text and dimension styles in Chapters 10 and 12.

You can then place the furniture on top of a floor-covering pattern and the pattern will be covered and hidden by the furniture. Here's how to do that. (These steps aren't part of the regular exercises of this chapter. They're shown here as general guidelines when you need to use the Draw Order feature.)

1. Draw the equipment outline, and make sure the outline is a closed polygon.

2. Start the Hatch tool described earlier in this chapter and place a solid hatch pattern inside the equipment outline.

3. In the Hatch Creation tab's expanded Options panel, make sure Send To Back is selected in the Draw Order drop-down list.

4. Turn the outline and solid hatch into a block, or use the Group command to group them.

5. Move your equipment drawing into place over the floor pattern.

6. Click on the floor hatch pattern, and then in the Hatch Editor tab's expanded Options panel, select Send To Back from the Draworder drop-down list. (see the bottom panel in Figure 7.19).

After you take these steps, the equipment will appear to rest on top of the pattern. You can also change the display order of objects relative to other objects in the drawing using the Draworder flyout in the Home tab's Modify panel.

The Draworder options are all part of the Draworder command. As an alternative to the Ribbon, you can type **Draworder⏎** at the Command prompt, select an object, and then enter an option at the prompt:

```
Enter object ordering option
[Above objects/Under objects/Front/Back] <Back>:
```

For example, the equivalent of choosing the Send To Back tool from the Draworder flyout is entering **Draworder⏎ B⏎**. You can also select the object you want to edit, right-click, and then choose Draw Order from the shortcut menu.

You've had a detailed look at hatch patterns and fills in this section. Remember that you can also use the tool palettes to help organize and simplify access to your favorite hatch patterns, or you can use the patterns already available in the tool palettes. The patterns in the tool palettes can be edited and manipulated in the same way as described in this chapter. If you want to know how to make full use of the Tool palettes, check out the discussion on the AutoCAD DesignCenter in Chapter 29.

Using External References

AutoCAD allows you to import drawings in a way that keeps the imported drawing independent from the current one. A drawing imported in this way is called an *external reference (Xref)*. Unlike drawings that have been imported as blocks, Xref files don't become part of the drawing's database. Instead, they're loaded along with the current file at startup time. It's as if AutoCAD were opening several drawings at once: the currently active file you specify when you start AutoCAD and any file inserted as an Xref.

If you keep Xref files independent from the current file, any changes you make to the Xref automatically appear in the current file. You don't have to update the Xref file manually as you do blocks. For example, if you use Xref to insert the Unit file into the Plan file and you later make changes to the Unit file, you will see the new version of the Unit file in place of the old the next time you open the Plan file. If the Plan file was still open while edits were made, AutoCAD will notify you that a change had been made to an Xref.

BLOCKS AND XREFS CAN'T HAVE THE SAME NAME

You can't Xref a file if the file has the same name as a block in the current drawing. If this situation occurs but you still need to use the file as an Xref, you can rename the block of the same name by using the Rename command. You can also use Rename to change the name of various objects and named elements.

Another advantage of Xref files is that because they don't become part of a drawing's database, drawing size is kept to a minimum. This results in more efficient use of your hard disk space.

Xref files, like blocks, can be edited only by using special tools. You can, however, use osnaps to snap to a location in an Xref file, or you can freeze or turn off the Xref file's insertion layer to make it invisible.

Attaching a Drawing as an External Reference

The next exercise shows how to use an Xref in place of an inserted block to construct the studio apartment building. You'll first create a new unit file by copying the old one. Then you'll bring a new feature, the External References palette, to the screen. Follow these steps to create the new file:

1. Use the Quick View Drawings tool in the status bar to return to the 07a-unit file.

2. Choose Save As from the Application menu to save it under the name unitxref.dwg, and then close the unitxref.dwg file. This will make a copy of the 07a-unit.dwg file for the following steps. Or, if you prefer, you can use the unitxref.dwg file for the following steps.

3. Return to the 07b-plan file, choose Save As, and save the file under the name Planxref. The current file is now Planxref.dwg.

4. Erase all the Unit plans (enter E↵All↵). In the next step, you'll purge the Unit plans from the file. (By completing steps 2 through 4, you save yourself from having to set up a new file.)

5. Choose Drawing Utilities ➢ Purge from the Application menu to open the Purge dialog box, and then click the Purge All button to open the Confirm Purge dialog box. This purges blocks that aren't in use in the drawing.

6. Click Purge All Items and close the Purge dialog box.

Now you're ready to use the External References palette:

1. Click the External References tool in the Insert tab's Reference panel title bar or type **XR**↵ to open the External References palette (see Figure 7.20).

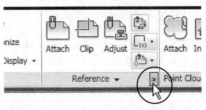

2. Click the Attach DWG button in the upper-left corner of the palette to open the Select Reference File dialog box. This is a typical AutoCAD file dialog box complete with a preview window.

FIGURE 7.20
The External
References palette

3. Locate and select the `unitxref.dwg` file, and then click Open to open the Attach External Reference dialog box (see Figure 7.21). Notice that this dialog box looks similar to the Insert dialog box. It offers the same options for insertion point, scale, and rotation.

FIGURE 7.21
The Attach
External Reference
dialog box

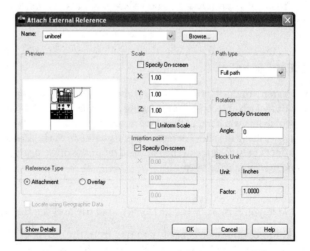

4. You'll see a description of the options presented in this dialog box. For now, click OK.

5. Enter **31′-5″,43′-8″⏎** (metric users enter **957,1330**) for the insertion point.

6. The inserted plan may appear faded. If it does, Click the Xref Fading tool in the Insert tab's expanded Reference panel to turn off the Xref Fading feature. This will give the plan a more solid appearance.

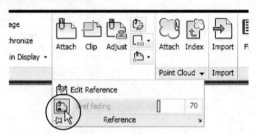

7. After the `unitxref.dwg` file is inserted, re-create the same layout of the floor plan you created in the first section of this chapter by copying and mirroring the `Unitxref.dwg` external reference.

8. Save the `Planxref` file.

You now have a drawing that looks like the `07b-plan.dwg` file you worked with earlier in this chapter, but instead of blocks that are detached from their source file, you have a drawing composed of Xrefs. These Xrefs are the actual `unitxref.dwg` file, and they're loaded into AutoCAD at the same time that you open the `Planxref.dwg` file. An icon in the lower-right corner of the AutoCAD window tells you that the current drawing contains Xrefs.

 This icon not only alerts you to Xrefs but also enables you to open the External References palette, as you'll see in the next exercise.

FADING XREFS

In step 6 of the previous exercise, you saw the Xref Fading tool. This tool is an aid to help you visualize which objects in your drawing are Xrefs. To the right of the Xref tool is the Xref Fading slider, which lets you control the amount of fading that is applied to the Xrefs in your drawing. You can either move the slider or enter a fading value in the input box to the far right. The Xref Fading tool affects only the appearance of the Xref in the drawing. It does not cause the Xref to fade in your printed or plotted output.

Next, you'll modify the `unitxref.dwg` file and see the results in the `Planxref.dwg` file:

1. To open the `Unitxref.dwg` file, from the current `Planxref` file, select and then right-click a unit and choose Open Xref from the shortcut menu. You can also enter **Xopen⏎** at the Command prompt and then select the unit plan Xref.

2. Erase the hatch pattern and kitchen outline for the floors, and save the unitxref.dwg file.

3. Use the Quick View Drawings tool in the status bar to return to the Planxref.dwg file. You see a message balloon pointing to the Manage Xrefs icon in the lower-right corner of the AutoCAD window. The balloon warns you that an Xref has changed. Right-click the Manage Xrefs icon in the lower-right corner of the AutoCAD window, and then choose External References from the pop-up menu to open the External References palette.

4. Right-click the unitxref name in the list box and then click Reload. Notice that the units in the Planxref drawing have been updated to include the changes you made to the Unitxref file.

You may have noticed that there is a Reload DWG Xrefs option in the Manage Xrefs icon shortcut menu. This will reload all xrefs in the current drawing without requiring you to select the individual file to reload in the External References palette.

Also, you may have noticed the Open option in step 4 when you used the right-click menu in the External References palette. This performs the same function as the Xopen command, which opens the selected Xref for editing.

Be aware that when an Xref has been modified, the Manage Xrefs icon at the lower right in the AutoCAD window changes to show an exclamation point. This alerts you to changes in an Xref in the current drawing.

Click the Manage Xrefs icon to open the External References palette. The Xref that has been changed is indicated by a warning icon in the Status column of the list box along with the "Needs reloading" message.

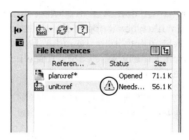

You can then select the Xref that needs to be updated, right-click, and choose the Reload option from the shortcut menu to reload the selected Xref. You can also select multiple Xrefs if more than one needs updating. Another option is to select Reload All References from the Refresh flyout at the top of the External References palette.

Here you saw how an Xref file is updated in a different way than a block. Because Xrefs are loaded along with the drawing file that contains them, the containing file, which in this case was the `Planxref` file, automatically displays any changes made to the Xref when it's opened. Also, you avoid having to update nested blocks because AutoCAD updates nested Xrefs as well as non-nested Xrefs. When an Xref is modified while you're editing a file, you're alerted to the change through the Xref icon located in the lower-right corner of the AutoCAD window. You can click the balloon message that appears from that icon to update any modified Xrefs.

Other Differences between External References and Blocks

Here are a few other differences between Xrefs and inserted blocks that you'll want to keep in mind:

◆ Any new layers, text styles, or linetypes brought in with Xref files don't become part of the current file. If you want to import any of these items, you can use the Xbind command (described in Chapter 15).

◆ If you make changes to the layers of an Xref file, those changes aren't retained when the file is saved unless you checked the Retain Changes To Xref Layers option in the Open And Save tab of the Options dialog box. This option, found in the External References (Xrefs) group, instructs AutoCAD to remember any layer color or visibility settings from one editing session to the next. In the standard AutoCAD settings, this option is on by default.

◆ Another way to ensure that layer settings for Xrefs are retained is to enter **Visretain**↵ at the Command prompt. At the `New value for VISRETAIN <0>:` prompt, enter **1**.

◆ To segregate layers in Xref files from layers in the current drawing, AutoCAD prefixes the names of the Xref file's layers with their file's name. A vertical bar separates the filename prefix and the layer name when you view a list of layers in the Layer drop-down list or the Layer Properties Manager dialog box (as in unitxref | wall).

◆ You can't explode Xrefs. You can, however, convert an Xref into a block and then explode it. To do this, select the Xref in the External References palette, then right-click and choose Bind to open another dialog box that offers two ways of converting an Xref into a block. See the section "Other External Reference Options" later in this chapter for more information.

◆ If an Xref is renamed or moved to another location on your hard disk, AutoCAD won't be able to find that file when it opens other files to which the Xref is attached. If this happens, you must select the path in the Found At field at the bottom of the External References palette and then click the Browse button (the ellipsis) to tell AutoCAD where to find the cross-referenced file.

◆ Take care when retargeting an Xref file with the Browse button. The Browse button can assign a file of a different name to an existing Xref as a substitution.

◆ Xref files are especially useful in workgroup environments in which several people are working on the same project. For example, one person might be updating several files that are inserted into a variety of other files. If blocks are used, everyone in the workgroup would have to be notified of the changes and would have to update all the affected blocks in all the drawings that contained them. With Xref files, however, the updating is automatic; you avoid confusion about which files need their blocks updated.

IMPORTING BLOCKS, LAYERS, AND OTHER NAMED ELEMENTS FROM EXTERNAL FILES

You can use the Xbind command to import blocks and other named elements from another file. First, use the External References palette to cross-reference a file; type **Xbind** at the Command prompt. In the Xbind dialog box, click the plus sign next to the Xref filename, and then select Block. Locate the name of the block you want to import, click the Add button, and click OK. Finally, open the External References palette, select the Xref filename from the list, right-click, and select Detach to remove the Xref file. The imported block remains as part of the current file. (See Chapter 15 for details on importing named elements.) You can also use the AutoCAD DesignCenter to import named elements from external files. DesignCenter is described in Chapter 29.

The tool palettes window gives you access to frequently used blocks and hatch patterns that reside in other drawings. You can open the tool palettes by clicking the Tool Palettes tool in the View tab's Palettes panel.

Tool
Palettes

In the standard AutoCAD installations, the tool palettes window is configured with sample 3D commands (not in LT), blocks, and hatch patterns that you can drag and drop into your current drawing. Select a tab for the Tool palette that contains the block or pattern you want, and then click and drag the item into your drawing. In the case of hatch patterns, click and drag the pattern into an area that is bounded on all sides by objects. When you're ready to customize the Tool Palettes window, you do so by clicking and dragging objects or tools into a new or existing palette. See Chapter 28 for more on customizing tool palettes.

Other External Reference Options

Many other features are unique to external reference files. Let's briefly look at some of the other options in the External References palette.

OPTIONS IN THE EXTERNAL REFERENCES PALETTE

Several options are available when you right-click an external reference name listed in the External References palette, shown in Figure 7.20 earlier in this chapter. You saw the Reload option in an earlier exercise. The following other options are available:

Attach Opens the Attach External Reference dialog box, in which you can select a file to attach and set the parameters for the attachment.

Detach Detaches an Xref from the current file. The file is then completely disassociated from the current file.

Reload Restores an unloaded Xref.

Unload Similar to Detach, but maintains a link to the Xref file so that it can be quickly reattached. This has an effect similar to freezing a layer and can reduce redraw, regeneration, and file-loading times.

Bind Converts an Xref into a block. Bind offers two options: Bind and Insert. Bind's Bind option maintains the Xref's named elements (layers, linetypes, and text and dimension styles) by creating new layers in the current file with the Xref's filename prefix (discussed again in Chapter 15). The Insert option doesn't attempt to maintain the Xref's named elements but merges them with named elements of the same name in the current file. For example, if both the Xref and the current file have layers of the same name, the objects in the Xref are placed in the layers of the same name in the current file.

Open Lets you open an Xref. Select the Xref from the list, and then click Open. The Xref opens in a new window when you close the External References palette. This option isn't available in AutoCAD LT.

Details A panel at the bottom of the External References palette. It's similar to the Properties palette in that it displays the properties of a selected external reference and also allows you to modify some of those properties. For example, the Reference Name option in the Details panel lets you give the external reference a name that is different from the Xref filename. Table 7.1 gives you a rundown of the options in the Details panel.

TABLE 7.1: The Details panel of the External References palette

OPTION	FUNCTION
Reference Name	Lets you give the Xref a name that is different from the Xref's filename. This can be helpful if you want to use multiple external references of the same file.
Status	Tells you whether the Xref is loaded, unloaded, or not found (read only).
Size	Gives you the file size information (read only).
Type	Lets you choose between the Attach and Overlay attachment methods for the Xref file. Xrefs attached as overlays don't include nested Xrefs.
Date	Gives you the date and time the file was attached (read only).
Saved Path	Tells you where AutoCAD expects to find the Xref file (read only).
Found At	Lets you select the location of the Xref file. When you click the text box for this option, a Browse button appears to the right. You can click this button to locate a lost Xref or use a different file from the original attached Xref.

THE ATTACH EXTERNAL REFERENCE DIALOG BOX

The Attach External Reference dialog box, shown in Figure 7.21 earlier in this chapter, offers these options:

Browse Opens the Select Reference File dialog box to enable you to change the file you're importing as an Xref.

Attachment Tells AutoCAD to include other Xref attachments that are nested in the selected file.

Overlay Tells AutoCAD to ignore other Xref attachments that are nested in the selected file. This avoids multiple attachments of other files and eliminates the possibility of circular references (referencing the current file into itself through another file).

Path Type Offers options for locating Xrefs. Xref files can be located anywhere on your system, including network servers. For this reason, you can easily lose links to Xrefs either by moving them or by rearranging file locations. To help you manage Xrefs, the Path Type option offers three options: Full Path, Relative Path, and No Path. Full Path retains the current full path. Relative Path maintains paths in relation to the current drawing. The current drawing must be saved before using the Relative Path option. The No Path option is for drawings in which Xrefs are located in the same folder as the current drawing or in the path specified in Support File Search Path in the Files tab of the Options dialog box (choose Options from the Application menu).

Specify On-Screen Appears in three places. It gives you the option to enter insertion point, scale factors, and rotation angles in the dialog box or in the Command window, in a way similar to inserting blocks. If you clear this option for any of the corresponding parameters, the parameters change to allow input. If they're selected, you're prompted for those parameters after you click OK to close the dialog box. With all three Specify On-Screen check boxes cleared, the Xref is inserted in the drawing using the settings indicated in the dialog box.

Show Details/Hide Details Displays or hides the path information for the selected Xref file.

Clipping Xref Views and Improving Performance

Xrefs are frequently used to import large drawings for reference or backgrounds. Multiple Xrefs, such as a floor plan, column grid layout, and site-plan drawing, might be combined into one file. One drawback to multiple Xrefs in earlier versions of AutoCAD was that the entire Xref was loaded into memory even if only a small portion of it was used for the final plotted output. For computers with limited resources, multiple Xrefs could slow the system to a crawl.

AutoCAD 2011 offers two tools that help make display and memory use more efficient when using Xrefs: the Xclip command and the Demand Load option in the Options dialog box.

CLIPPING VIEWS

The Clip command lets you clip the display of an Xref or a block to any shape you want, as shown in Figure 7.22. For example, you might want to display only an L-shaped portion of a floor plan to be part of your current drawing. Clip lets you define such a view. To access the command, choose Clip from the Insert tab's Reference panel.

You can clip blocks and multiple Xrefs as well. You can also specify a front and back clipping distance so that the visibility of objects in 3D space can be controlled. You can define a clip area by using polylines or spline curves, although curve-fitted polylines revert to decurved polylines. (See Chapter 19 for more on polylines and spline curves.)

CONTROLLING XREF SETTINGS IN THE OPTIONS DIALOG BOX

The External References (Xrefs) group in the Open And Save tab of the Options dialog box offers some tools to help you manage memory use and other features related to Xrefs. If you're working on large projects with others in a workgroup, you should be aware of these settings and what they do.

The Demand Load Xrefs drop-down list offers three settings: Disabled, Enabled, and Enabled With Copy. Demand Load is set to Enabled With Copy by default in the standard AutoCAD setup. In addition to reducing the amount of memory an Xref consumes, Demand

Load prevents other users from editing the Xref while it's being viewed as part of your current drawing. This helps aid drawing version control and drawing management. The Enabled With Copy option creates a copy of the source Xref file and then uses the copy, thereby enabling other AutoCAD users to edit the source Xref file.

Demand loading improves performance by loading only the parts of the referenced drawing that are needed to regenerate the current drawing. You can set the location for the Xref copy in the Files tab of the Options dialog box under Temporary External Reference File Location.

FIGURE 7.22
The first panel shows a polyline outline of the area to be isolated with Xclip. The second panel shows how the Xref appears after Xclip is applied. The last panel shows a view of the plan with the polyline's layer turned off.

a.

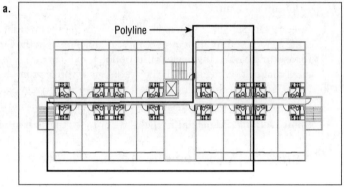

b.

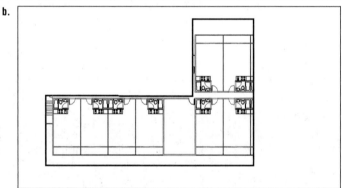

c.

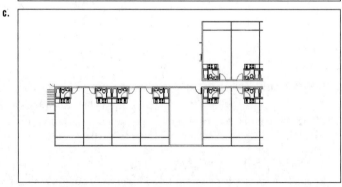

EXTERNAL REFERENCES IN THE SAN FRANCISCO MAIN LIBRARY PROJECT

Although the exercises in this chapter demonstrate how Xrefs work, you aren't limited to using them in the way shown here. Perhaps one of the more common ways of using Xrefs is to combine a single floor plan with different title block drawings, each with its own layer settings and title block information. In this way, single-drawing files can be reused in several drawing sheets of a final construction document set. This helps keep data consistent across drawings and reduces the number of overall drawings needed.

This is exactly how Xrefs were used in the San Francisco Main Library drawings. One floor-plan file contained most of the main information for that floor. The floor plan was then used as an Xref in another file that contained the title block as well as additional information such as furnishings or floor finish reference symbols. Layer visibility was controlled in each title block drawing so only the data related to that drawing appeared.

Multiple Xref files were also used by segregating the structural column grid layout drawings from the floor-plan files. In other cases, portions of plans from different floors were combined into a single drawing by using Xrefs, as shown here.

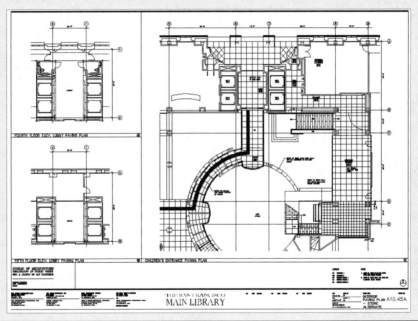

Two other options are also available in the Options dialog box:

Retain Changes To Xref Layers   Instructs AutoCAD to remember any layer color or visibility settings of Xrefs from one editing session to the next. In the standard AutoCAD settings, this option is on by default.

Allow Other Users To Refedit Current Drawing   Lets others edit the current drawing by choosing Edit Reference from the Insert tab's expanded Reference panel (Refedit). You'll learn about this command in the next section.

Editing Xrefs in Place

You've seen different methods for editing blocks and Xrefs as external files. There is a way to edit a block or an Xref directly in a file, without having to edit an external file: You can use the Xref And Block In-Place Editing option in the Tools drop-down menu. This option issues the Refedit command.

The following exercise demonstrates how Refedit works:

1. Open the 07-planxref.dwg file. This file is set up like the Planxref.dwg file you created in the previous exercises. 07-planxref uses a file called 07-unitxref.dwg instead of the unitxref.dwg file for the Xref units.

2. Zoom in to the unit plan in the lower-left corner of the drawing so you see a view similar to Figure 7.23.

FIGURE 7.23
The enlarged view of the unitxref in the Planxref file

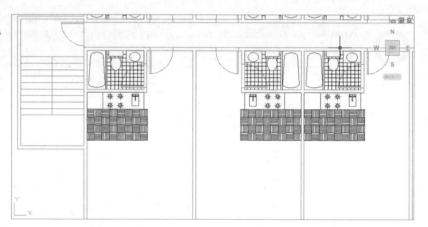

3. Click the corner unit to select it. Notice that the External Reference tab appears, offering several options that allow you to edit the Xref. You'll learn more about these options later.

4. Double-click the wall of the corner unit. The Reference Edit dialog box appears (Figure 7.24).

FIGURE 7.24
The Reference Edit dialog box

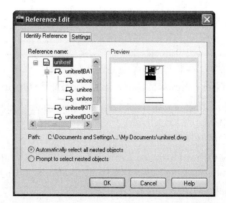

5. The Reference Edit dialog box contains two panels. The right panel shows a thumbnail view of the item that you're editing. The left panel shows a listing of the specific item you selected in the Xref. Notice that the listing shows the hierarchical relationship of the kitchenette block in relation to the 07-unitxref Xref.

   In the left panel, click the 07-unitxref|KITCHEN listing and then click OK. The Edit Reference panel appears in the current Ribbon tab.

6. Use a selection window to select the entire lower-left corner unit. Notice that only the grips in the kitchenette appear, indicating that the objects in the kitchenette are selected. Although the rest of the unit appears to be selected, it appears lighter in color. This shows you that only the kitchen is available for editing.

7. Press the Esc key to clear your selection.

SPECIAL SAVE AS OPTIONS THAT AFFECT DEMAND LOADING

AutoCAD offers a few additional settings that boost the performance of the Demand Load feature. When you choose Save As from the Application menu to save a file in the standard DWG format, you see the Tools button in the upper-right corner of the Save Drawing As dialog box. Choosing Tools ➢ Options opens the Saveas Options dialog box. Using the options in the Index Type drop-down list in the DWG Options tab can help improve the speed of demand loading. The index options are as follows:

None No index is created.

Layer AutoCAD loads only layers that are both turned on and thawed.

Spatial AutoCAD loads only portions of an Xref or raster image within a clipped boundary.

Layer & Spatial This option turns on both the Layer and Spatial options.

In step 5 of the previous exercise, the Refedit command isolates the objects you select for editing. You can't edit anything else in the Xref until you exit the Refedit command and start over. At this point, you can edit a block in an Xref. Now let's continue editing the kitchenette:

1. Zoom in on the kitchenette, and move the four burners to the right 8″ (20 cm for metric users).

2. Erase the sink.

3. Click the Save Changes tool on the Edit Reference panel. If your screen resolution is fairly low, you may have to expand the Edit Reference panel to see the Save Changes tool.

4. A warning message appears, telling you that the changes you've made to the Xref will be saved. Click OK.

5. Zoom back to your previous view. Notice that the other units reflect the changes you made to the 07-unitxref Xref (see Figure 7.25).

6. Open the 07-unitxref.dwg file, which can be found in the Chapter 7 sample file folder. The kitchen reflects the changes you made to the Xref of the unit in the 07-planxref file. This shows you that by choosing to save the reference edit in step 3, you save the changes back to the Xref's source file.

FIGURE 7.25
The Xrefs after
being edited

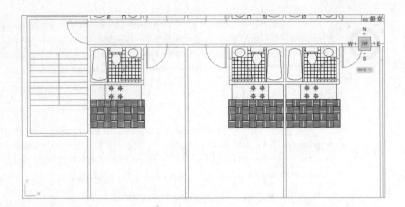

As you saw from these two exercises, it's possible to edit a specific block in an Xref, but to do that you must select the block name in the Reference Edit dialog box.

In these exercises, you edited a block contained in an Xref, but you could have just as easily edited a block in the current drawing. You can also edit nested blocks by using the Refedit command. Changes in blocks in the current file don't affect other files because blocks aren't linked to external files. The changes to blocks remain in the current file until you explicitly export the changed block to a file, as you saw in earlier exercises.

Using the External Reference Tab

Earlier, you saw that when you click an Xref, the External Reference tab appears. This tab offers several tools divided into three panels: Edit, Clipping, and Options. See Table 7.2 for a complete description of these tools.

TABLE 7.2: The External Reference tab options

TOOL NAME	FUNCTION
Edit Reference In-Place	Starts the Refedit command, which allows you to edit an Xref within the current drawing.
Open Reference	Opens the selected Xref.
Create Clipping Boundary	Starts the Xclip command, which allows you to hide portions of an Xref. This feature is similar to the image clipping command described in Chapter 14.
Removing Clipping	Removes a clipping boundary.
External References	Opens or closes the External References palette.

Adding and Removing Objects from Blocks and Xrefs

In the previous exercises, you removed objects from the Kitchen block by using the Erase command. You can also move objects from a block or an Xref into the current drawing without erasing them. To do this, choose Remove From Working Set from the Insert tab's expanded Edit Reference panel while in the Refedit command. This removes the objects from the block or Xref without erasing them. Likewise, you can add new objects to the block or Xref by choosing Add To Working Set from the Insert tab's expanded Edit Reference panel. Both menu options invoke the Refset command, with different options applied.

To see how Refset works, try the following exercise:

1. Close the `07-unitxref.dwg` file.

2. In the `07-planxref` file, zoom in to the kitchenette to get a view similar to the top panel of Figure 7.26.

3. Double-click the unit plan drawing. You can also choose Edit Reference from the Insert tab's expanded Reference panel and then click the unit plan.

4. Click the 07-unitxref|KITCHEN listing in the Reference Edit dialog box, and then click OK.

5. Use the Move tool to move the two burners on the right just to the right of the kitchenette, as shown in Figure 7.26.

6. Click the Remove From Working Set tool in the expanded Edit Reference panel.

7. Select the two burners you just moved, and then press ↵.

FIGURE 7.26
Moving the burners out of the Kitchen block and adding the rectangle

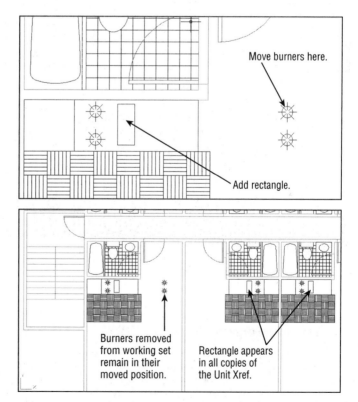

Notice that the burners become grayer to show that they're removed from the working set. They remain as part of the Planxref drawing, but they're no longer part of the Kitchen block. Now add a rectangle to the Kitchen block in place of the burners:

1. Draw a 7″-×-16″ (18 cm-×-40 cm) rectangle in place of the moved burners, as shown in the top panel of Figure 7.26. Anything you add to the drawing automatically becomes part of the working set.

2. Click Save Changes from the Edit Reference panel. You'll see a warning message stating that all reference edits will be saved. Click OK.

3. Zoom out enough to see the other units in the drawing (see Figure 7.27).

You can see that the burners have been replaced by the rectangle in all the other Xref units. The burners you moved are still there in the lower-left corner unit, but they have been removed from all the Xrefs. It's as if you extracted them from the block and placed them in the Plan drawing.

While you were using the Refedit command, any new objects you created were added to the working set automatically. When you drew the rectangle in step 1, for example, it was automatically included in the *working set*, which is the set of objects included in the block or Xref you're currently working on. You didn't have to specifically add it to the working set.

FIGURE 7.27
The Planxref drawing with the changes made to the 07-unitxref Xref

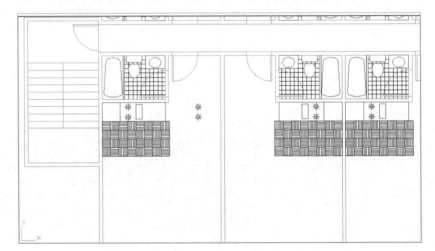

If you want to include existing objects in the working set, choose the Add To Working Set tool from the Edit Reference panel.

You've completed the exercises in this chapter, so you can exit AutoCAD without saving these changes.

Understanding the Reference Edit Dialog Box Options

The Reference Edit dialog box offers you the option to isolate specific blocks in the Xref by selecting them from the hierarchy list. You may have noticed the two radio button options: Automatically Select All Nested Objects and Prompt To Select Nested Objects. The default option, Automatically Select All Nested Objects, lets you select any object contained in the selected object in the hierarchy listing. If you select the Prompt To Select Nested Objects option, you're prompted to select objects on the screen before the Edit Reference panel appears.

In addition to the options you used in the exercises, the Reference Edit dialog box also includes the Settings tab with some options (Figure 7.28).

FIGURE 7.28

The Settings tab of the Reference Edit dialog box

CREATE UNIQUE LAYER, STYLE, AND BLOCK NAMES

When you use the Refedit command with the Automatically Select All Nested Objects option turned on, you can import nested blocks into the current drawing. For example, if you selected the Bath block in the hierarchy list in the previous exercise, you would have access to the Tub and Toilet blocks in the Bath block. You could then copy either of those blocks into the current file.

When you make a copy of a block from an Xref, AutoCAD needs to assign that block a name. The Create Unique Layer, Style, And Block Names option tells AutoCAD to use the original block name and append a $#$ prefix to the name (# is a numeric value starting with zero). If you were to import the Bath block, for example, it would become 0bath in the current drawing. This ensures that the block maintains a unique name when it's imported even if there is a block with the same name in the current drawing. If you turn off the Create Unique Layer, Style, And Block Names option, the original name is maintained. If the current drawing contains a block of the same name, the imported block uses the current file's definition of that block.

DISPLAY ATTRIBUTE DEFINITIONS FOR EDITING

If your drawing contains attributes (see Chapter 13 for more on attributes), this option is offered. If you turn on this option, you can then edit attribute definitions by using the Refedit command. If you select a block that contains an attribute definition while you're using the Refedit command, the attribute definition is exposed, enabling you to make changes. Changes to attribute definitions affect only new attribute insertions. Except for the attribute of the edited block, existing attributes aren't affected. If you want to update existing attributes to a newly edited definition, use the Sync option of the Block Attribute Manager (choose Manage Attributes from the Home tab's expanded Block panel).

LOCK OBJECTS NOT IN WORKING SET

In the Refedit exercises, you saw that objects that aren't selected in the Reference Edit dialog box are grayed out and aren't selectable. The Lock Objects Not In Working Set option controls this feature and is turned on by default.

The Bottom Line

Assemble the parts.   Technical drawings are often made up of repetitive parts that are drawn over and over. AutoCAD makes quick work of repetitive elements in a drawing, as shown in the first part of this chapter.

Master It   What is the object used as the basic building block for the unit plan drawing in the beginning of this chapter?

Take control of the AutoCAD display.   Understanding the way the AutoCAD display works can save you time, especially in a complex drawing.

Master It   Name the dialog box used to save views in AutoCAD. Describe how to recall a saved view.

Use hatch patterns in your drawings.   Patterns can convey a lot of information at a glance. You can show the material of an object, or you can indicate a type of view, like a cross section, by applying hatch patterns.

Master It   How do you open the Hatch And Gradient dialog box?

Understand the hatch options.   The hatch options give you control over the way hatch patterns fill an enclosed area.

Master It   Describe an island as it relates to boundary hatch patterns.

Use external references.   External references are drawing files that you've attached to the current drawing to include as part of the drawing. Because external references aren't part of the current file, they can be worked on at the same time as the referencing file.

Master It   Describe how drawing files are attached as external references.

Chapter 8

Introducing Printing, Plotting, and Layouts

Getting hard-copy output from AutoCAD is something of an art. You'll need to be intimately familiar with both your output device and the settings available in AutoCAD. You'll probably spend a good deal of time experimenting with AutoCAD's plotter settings and with your printer or plotter to get your equipment set up just the way you want.

With the huge array of output options available, this chapter can provide only a general discussion of plotting and printing. As a rule, the process for using a plotter isn't much different from that for a printer; you just have more media-size options with plotters. Still, every output device is different. It's up to you to work out the details and fine-tune the way you and AutoCAD together work with your particular plotter or printer. This chapter describes the features available in AutoCAD and discusses some general rules and guidelines to follow when setting up your plots.

I'll start with an overview of the plotting features in AutoCAD and then delve into the finer details of setting up your drawing and controlling your plotter or printer.

In this chapter, you'll learn to do the following:

◆ Understand the plotter settings

◆ Use layout views for WYSIWYG plotting

◆ Add an output device

◆ Store a page setup

Plotting the Plan

To see firsthand how the Plot command works, you'll plot the Plan file by using the default settings on your system. You'll start by getting a preview of your plot, before you commit to printing your drawing. As an introduction, you'll plot from the Model view of an AutoCAD drawing, but be aware that typically you should plot from a layout view. Layout views give you a greater degree of control over how your output will look. You'll be introduced to layout views later in this chapter. Now let's get started!

First, try plotting your drawing to no particular scale:

1. Be sure your printer or plotter is connected to your computer and is turned on.

2. Start AutoCAD, and open the Plan.dwg file.

3. Click All from the Zoom flyout in the View tab's Navigate panel or type **Z↵A↵** to display the entire drawing.

4. Click the Plot tool from the Quick Access toolbar to open the Plot dialog box (Figure 8.1).

FIGURE 8.1
The Plot dialog box

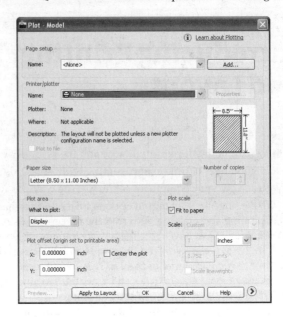

5. If the Name option in the Printer/Plotter group shows None, click the drop-down arrow and select your current Windows system printer.

6. In the Plot Area group, make sure the Display option is selected in the drop-down list (Figure 8.2). This tells AutoCAD to plot the drawing as it looks in the drawing window. You also have the option to plot the limits of the drawing or to select an area to plot with a window. In addition, you can choose to plot the extents of a drawing or a saved view.

FIGURE 8.2
Choose the
Display option.

7. Make sure the Fit To Paper option is selected in the Plot Scale group.

8. Click the Preview button in the lower-left corner of the dialog box. AutoCAD works for a moment and then displays a sample view of how your drawing will appear when printed. Notice that the view also shows the Zoom Realtime cursor. You can use the Zoom/Pan Realtime tools to get a close-up of your print preview.

9. Go ahead and plot the file: Right-click and choose Plot from the shortcut menu. AutoCAD sends the drawing to your printer.

10. Your plotter or printer prints the plan to no particular scale.

You've just plotted your first drawing to see how it looks on paper. You used the minimal settings to ensure that the complete drawing appears on the paper.

You may notice that a message bubble appears in the lower-right corner of the AutoCAD window (Figure 8.3). If you click the text that reads *Click to view plot and publish details,* the Plot And Publish Details dialog box opens to display some detailed information about your plot.

FIGURE 8.3

Click the message text to open the Plot And Publish Details dialog.

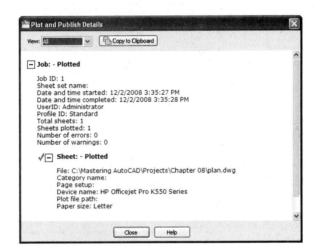

As you become more experienced with AutoCAD and your projects become more demanding, the information presented in the Plot And Publish Details dialog box may be useful to you. For now, make a mental note that this information is available should you need it.

SET THE APPROPRIATE UNITS

It's important to make sure you use the appropriate unit settings in this chapter. If you've been using the metric measurements for previous exercises, make sure you use the metric settings in the exercises of this chapter; otherwise, your results won't coincide.

Next, try plotting your drawing to an exact scale. This time, you'll expand the Plot dialog box to show a few more options:

1. In the status bar, click the Annotation Scale tool and select 1/16′ = 1′-0″ from the flyout.

2. Click Plot from the Quick Access toolbar again to open the Plot dialog box. If the Name option in the Printer/Plotter group shows None, click the drop-down arrow and select your current Windows system printer.

3. Click the More Options button; this is the round button with the > symbol in the lower-right corner of the dialog box. You'll see some additional options appear on the right side of the dialog box (Figure 8.4).

FIGURE 8.4
Open the additional options on the right.

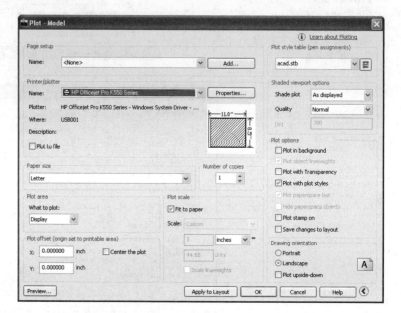

4. If your last printout wasn't oriented on the paper correctly, select the Landscape option in the Drawing Orientation group.

PRINT PREVIEW DEPENDENCIES

The appearance of the print preview depends on the type of output device you chose when you installed AutoCAD or when you last selected a Plotter Device option (described in the section "WYSIWYG Plotting Using Layout Views" later in this chapter). The print preview is also affected by other settings in the Plot dialog box, such as those in the Drawing Orientation, Plot Offset, and Plot Area groups. This example shows a typical preview view using the Windows default system printer in landscape mode.

5. In the Plot Scale group, clear the Fit To Paper check box. Then, select 1⁄16″ = 1′-0″ from the Scale drop-down list. Metric users should select 1:20. As you can see, you have several choices for the scale of your output.

6. In the Paper Size group, select Letter. Metric users should select A4. The options in this drop-down list depend on your Windows system printer or the output device you configured for AutoCAD.

7. In the Plot Area group, select Limits from the drop-down list. This tells AutoCAD to use the limits of your drawing to determine which part of your drawing to plot.

8. Click the Preview button again to get a preview of your plot.

9. Right-click, and choose Plot from the shortcut menu. This time, your printout is to scale.

Here, you were asked to specify a few more settings in the Plot dialog box. Several settings work together to produce a drawing that is to scale and that fits properly on your paper. This is where it pays to understand the relationship between your drawing scale and your paper's size, discussed in Chapter 3. You also saw how you can expand the options in the Plot dialog box.

The following sections are lengthy but don't contain any exercises. If you prefer to continue with the exercises in this chapter, skip to the section "WYSIWYG Plotting Using Layout Views." Be sure to come back and read the following sections while the previous exercises are still fresh in your mind.

Understanding the Plotter Settings

In the following sections, you'll explore all the settings in the Plot dialog box. These settings give you control over the size and orientation of your image on the paper. They also let you control which part of your drawing gets printed. All these settings work together to give you control over how your drawing fits on your printed output.

AUTOCAD REMEMBERS PLOTTER SETTINGS

AutoCAD 2011 relies mainly on the Windows system printer configuration instead of its own plotter drivers. However, It does remember printer settings that are specific to AutoCAD, so you don't have to adjust your printer settings each time you use AutoCAD. This gives you more flexibility and control over your output. Be aware that you'll need to understand the Windows system printer settings in addition to those offered by AutoCAD.

Paper Size

You use the option in this group to select the paper size for your output. You can select a paper size from the Paper Size drop-down list. These sizes are derived from the sizes available from your currently selected system printer. You'll find out how to select a different printer later in this chapter.

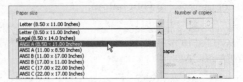

AutoCAD 2011 offers sheet sizes in both Imperial and metric measurements in the Paper Size group. AutoCAD assumes that if you pick a metric sheet size such as A4 or A5, you'll want the sheet dimensions specified in metric measurements, and it adjusts the dialog box settings accordingly.

Drawing Orientation

When you used the Preview button in the first exercise in this chapter, you saw your drawing as it would be placed on the paper. In that example, it was placed in a *landscape orientation*, which places the image on the paper so that the width of the paper is greater than its height. You can rotate the image on the paper 90° into what is called a *portrait orientation* by selecting the Portrait radio button in the Drawing Orientation group. A third option, Plot Upside-Down, lets you change the orientation further by turning the landscape or portrait orientation upside down. These three settings let you print the image in any one of four orientations on the sheet.

In AutoCAD, the preview displays the paper in the orientation it's in when it leaves the printer. For most small-format printers, if you're printing in the portrait orientation, the image appears in the same orientation you see when you're editing the drawing. If you're using the landscape orientation, the preview image is turned sideways. For large-format plotters, the preview may be oriented in the opposite direction. The graphic in the Drawing Orientation group displays a capital *A* on a sheet showing the orientation of your drawing on the paper output.

Remember that you need to click the More Options button in the lower-right corner of the Plot dialog box to access the Drawing Orientation group. The More Options button looks like a circle with a greater-than sign. You can also press Alt+Shift+>.

Plot Area

The What To Plot drop-down list in the Plot Area group lets you specify which part of your drawing you want to plot. You may notice some similarities between these settings and the Zoom command options. Each Plot Area option is described next. Most of these options are used only in a Model view. Typically, when plotting from a layout view, you'll use the Layout option.

Limits The Limits option (available in Model Space only) uses the limits of the drawing to determine the area to print. If you let AutoCAD fit the drawing onto the sheet (by selecting the Fit To Paper check box in the Plot Scale group), the plot displays exactly the same image that you would see on the screen if you selected Zoom All from the Zoom flyout on the navigation bar.

Layout The Layout option (available in layout views only) replaces the Limits option when you plot from a layout view. (See the section "WYSIWYG Plotting Using Layout Views" later in this chapter.) This option plots everything displayed within the paper margins shown in the layout view. Typically, this is the only option you'll use when printing from a layout.

Extents The Extents option uses the extents of the drawing to determine the area to print. If you let AutoCAD fit the drawing onto the sheet (by selecting the Fit To Paper check box in the

Plot Scale group), the plot displays exactly the same image that you would see on the screen if you chose the Zoom Extents tool from the Zoom flyout in the navigation bar.

Display   Display is the default option; it tells AutoCAD to plot what is currently displayed on the screen. If you let AutoCAD fit the drawing onto the sheet (that is, you select the Fit To Paper check box from the Plot Scale group), the plot is exactly the same as what you see on your screen, adjusted for the width and height proportions of your display.

View   The View option is available when you've saved a view in the drawing by using the View command. When you select View from the What To Plot drop-down list, another drop-down list appears, offering a list of views available in the drawing. You can then select the view that you want to plot. If you let AutoCAD fit the drawing onto the sheet (by selecting Fit To Paper from the Plot Scale group), the plot displays exactly the same thing that you would see on the screen if you recalled the view you're plotting. Objects that don't appear in the view are clipped in the plotted view.

GETTING A BLANK PLOT?

Do you get a blank printout even though you selected Extents or Display? Chances are the Fit To Paper check box isn't selected, or the Inches = Units (mm = Units for metric users) setting is inappropriate for the sheet size and scale of your drawing. If you don't care about the scale of the drawing, make sure the Fit To Paper option is selected. Otherwise, make sure the Plot Scale settings are set correctly. The next section describes how to set the scale for your plots.

Window   The Window option enables you to use a window to indicate the area you want to plot. Nothing outside the window prints. To use this option, select it from the drop-down list. The Plot dialog box temporarily closes to allow you to select a window. After you've done this the first time, a Window button appears next to the drop-down list. You can click the Window button and then indicate a window in the drawing area or AutoCAD will use the last indicated window. If you use the Fit To Paper option in the Plot Scale group to let AutoCAD fit the drawing onto the sheet, the plot displays exactly the same thing that you enclose in the window.

Plot Scale

In the previous section, the descriptions of several Plot Area options indicate that the Fit To Paper option can be selected. Bear in mind that when you instead apply a scale factor to your plot, it changes the results of the Plot Area settings and some problems can arise. This is where most new users have difficulty.

For example, the apartment plan drawing fits nicely on the paper when you use Fit To Paper. But if you try to plot the drawing at a scale of 1″ = 1′, you'll probably get a blank piece of paper because, at that scale, hardly any of the drawing fits on your paper. AutoCAD will tell you that it's plotting and then tell you that the plot is finished. You won't have a clue as to why your sheet is blank.

If an image is too large to fit on a sheet of paper because of improper scaling, the plot image is placed on the paper differently, depending on whether the plotter uses the center of the image or the lower-left corner for its origin. Keep this in mind as you specify scale factors in this area of the dialog box.

SCALE

You can select a drawing scale from a set of predefined scales in the Scale drop-down list. These options cover the most common scales you'll need to use.

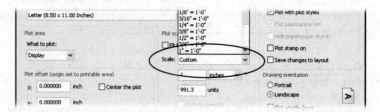

You've already seen how the Fit To Paper option enables you to avoid giving a scale and forces the drawing to fit on the sheet when you're plotting from the Model view. This works fine if you're plotting illustrations that aren't to scale. If you select another option, such as 1/8″ = 1′-0″, the inches and units input boxes change to reflect this scale. The Inches = input box changes to 0.125, and the Units input box changes to 12.

If you're plotting from a layout, you'll use the 1:1 scale option or perhaps a 1:2 scale if you're plotting a half-size drawing. In a layout, the drawing scale is typically set up through the viewport. While you're plotting from a layout, AutoCAD automatically determines the area to plot based on the printer and sheet size you select. For more information, see "WYSIWYG Plotting Using Layout Views" later in this chapter.

CUSTOM SCALE

In some cases, you may need to set up a nonstandard scale (not shown in the drop-down list) to plot your drawing. If you can't find the scale you want in the Scale drop-down list, you can select Custom and then enter custom values in the Inches or mm and Units input boxes.

Through these input boxes, you can indicate how the drawing units in your drawing relate to the final plotted distance in inches or millimeters. For example, if your drawing is of a scale factor of 96, follow these steps:

1. In the Plot Scale group of the Plot dialog box, double-click the Inches = input box, enter **1**, and press the Tab key.

2. Double-click the Units input box, enter **96**, and press the Tab key.

   Metric users who want to plot to a scale of 1:10 should enter **1** in the mm input box and **10** in the Units input box.

If you're more used to the Architectural unit style in the Imperial measurement system, you can enter a scale as a fraction. For example, for a 1/8″ scale drawing, do this:

1. Double-click the Inches = input box, enter **1/8**, and press the Tab key.

2. Double-click the Units input box, enter **12**, and press the Tab key.

If you specify a different scale than the one you chose while setting up your drawing, AutoCAD plots your drawing to that scale. You aren't restricted in any way as to scale, but entering the correct scale is important: If it's too large, AutoCAD will think your drawing is too large to fit on the sheet, although it will attempt to plot your drawing anyway. See Chapter 3 for a discussion of unit styles and scale factors.

DON'T FORGET YOUR ANNOTATION SCALE

You may see a message saying that the "annotation scale is not equal to the plot scale" when you attempt to plot your drawing. You can click Continue at the message and your drawing will still be plotted to the scale you specify. If you are using any text or blocks that use the annotation scale feature, those items will be plotted at the Annotation scale setting for the Model view or layout you are trying to plot. See Chapter 4 for more on Annotation scale.

If you plot to a scale that is different from the scale you originally intended, objects and text appear smaller or larger than is appropriate for your plot. You'll need to edit your text size to match the new scale. You can do so by using the Properties palette. Select the text whose height you want to change, right-click and choose Properties from the shortcut menu, and then change the Height setting in the Properties palette.

ADDING A CUSTOM SCALE TO THE SCALE DROP-DOWN LIST

If you use a custom scale frequently, you may find it annoying to have to input the scale every time you plot. AutoCAD offers the ability to add your custom scale to the Scale drop-down list shown earlier. You can then easily select your custom scale from the list instead of entering it through the text box.

Here are the steps you use to add a custom scale to the Scale drop-down list:

1. Choose Options from the Application menu to open the Options dialog box.

2. Select the User Preferences tab, and then click the Default Scale List button at the bottom of the dialog box.

3. In the Default Scale List dialog box, click the Add button.

4. In the Add Scale dialog box, enter a name for your custom scale in the Name Appearing In Scale List text box, and then enter the appropriate values in the Scale Properties text boxes.

5. Click OK in each dialog box to close it.

There are several options besides Add in the Default Scale List dialog box. Clicking the Edit button lets you edit an existing scale in the list. Clicking the Move Up and Move Down buttons lets you change the location of an item in the list. Clicking Delete deletes an item or a set of items from the list. Clicking the Reset button restores the list to its default condition and removes any custom items you may have added.

SHORTCUT TO THE EDIT SCALE LIST DIALOG BOX

Instead of opening the Options dialog box and clicking Default Scale List on the User Preferences tab, you can enter **Scalelistedit.⌐** at the Command prompt to open the Edit Drawing Scales dialog box directly.

SCALE LINE WEIGHTS

AutoCAD offers the option to assign line weights to objects either through their layer assignments or by directly assigning a line weight to individual objects. The line weight option, however, doesn't have any meaning until you specify a scale for your drawing. After you specify a scale, the Scale Lineweights option is available. Select this check box if you want the line weight assigned to layers and objects to appear correctly in your plots. You'll get a closer look at line weights and plotting later in this chapter.

Shaded Viewport Options

Most of your plotting will probably involve 2D technical line drawings, but occasionally you may need to plot a shaded or rendered 3D view. You may need to include such 3D views combined with 2D or 3D Wireframe views. AutoCAD offers the Shaded Viewport Options group that enables you to plot shaded or rendered 3D views of your AutoCAD drawing. These options give you control over the quality of your rendered output. (LT users don't have the Shaded Viewport Options group.)

Remember that you need to click the More Options button in the lower-right corner of the Plot dialog box to get to the Shaded Viewport Options group. The More Options button looks like a circle with a greater-than sign. You also need to select a printer name in the Printer/Plotter group before these options are made available.

SHADE PLOT

The Shade Plot drop-down list lets you control how a Model Space view or layout is plotted. You can choose from the following options:

As Displayed plots the Model Space view as it appears on your screen.

Legacy Wireframe plots the Model Space view of a 3D object as a Wireframe view.

Legacy Hidden plots your Model Space view with hidden lines removed.

Conceptual/Hidden/Realistic... plots the Model Space using one of several visual styles. These selections override the current Model Space visual style. See Chapter 21 for more on visual styles.

Rendered renders your Model Space view before plotting (see Chapter 23 for more on rendered views).

Draft/Low/Medium/High/Presentation sets the quality of the plot.

The Shade Plot options aren't available if you're plotting from a layout view. You can control the way each layout viewport is plotted through the viewport's Properties settings. You'll learn more about layout viewport properties later in this chapter.

QUALITY AND DPI

The Quality drop-down list determines the dots per inch (dpi) setting for your output. These options aren't available if you select Legacy Wireframe or Legacy Hidden from the Shade Plot drop-down list:

Draft plots 3D views as wireframes.

Preview offers 150dpi resolution.

Normal offers 300dpi resolution.

Presentation offers 600dpi resolution.

Maximum defers dpi resolution to the current output device's settings.

Custom lets you set a custom dpi setting. When Custom is selected, the DPI input box is made available for your input.

If some of the terms discussed for the Shaded Viewport Options group are unfamiliar, don't be alarmed. You'll learn about 3D Shaded and Rendered views in Part 4 of this book. When you start to explore 3D modeling in AutoCAD, come back and review the Shaded Viewport Options group.

Plot Offset

Sometimes, your first plot of a drawing shows the drawing positioned incorrectly on the paper. You can fine-tune the location of the drawing on the paper by using the Plot Offset settings. To adjust the position of your drawing on the paper, enter the location of the view origin in relation to the plotter origin in X and Y coordinates (see Figure 8.5).

FIGURE 8.5
Adjusting the
image location
on a sheet

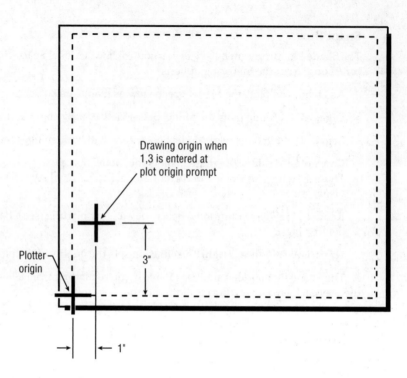

Drawing origin when
1,3 is entered at
plot origin prompt

3"

Plotter
origin

1"

For example, suppose you plot a drawing and then realize that it needs to be moved 1″ to the right and 3″ up on the sheet. You can replot the drawing by making the following changes:

1. Double-click the X input box, type **1**, and press the Tab key.

2. Double-click the Y input box, type **3**, and press the Tab key.

Now proceed with the rest of the plot configuration. With the preceding settings, the image is shifted on the paper exactly 1″ to the right and 3″ up when the plot is done.

You can also tell AutoCAD the location from which the offset is to occur. The Plot And Publish tab of the Options dialog box (choose Options from the Application menu) offers the Specify Plot Offset Relative To button group. This group offers two radio buttons: Printable Area and Edge Of Paper. You can select the option that makes the most sense for you.

Plot Options

The options in the Plot Options group offer a greater amount of control over your output and require some detailed instruction. Here is a brief description of these options. You'll learn more about them in the next section.

PLOT IN BACKGROUND

If you think your plot will take some time to complete, this option plots your drawing in the background so that after you begin a plot you can immediately return to your drawing work. You can also control this option through the Backgroundplot system variable.

PLOT OBJECT LINE WEIGHTS

As mentioned earlier, AutoCAD lets you assign line weights to objects either through their layer assignment or by assigning them directly. If you use this feature in your drawing, this option lets you turn line weights on or off in your output.

PLOT WITH TRANSPARENCY

You can apply a transparency of objects and layers in your drawing. This option lets you control whether transparency is used when your drawing is plotted.

PLOT WITH PLOT STYLES

Plot styles give you a high degree of control over your drawing output. You can control whether your output is in color or black and white, and you can control whether filled areas are drawn in a solid color or a pattern. You can even control the way lines are joined at corners. You'll learn more about these options and how they affect your work in the next chapter.

PLOT PAPERSPACE LAST

When you're using a layout view, otherwise known as Paper Space, this option determines whether objects in Paper Space are plotted before or after objects in Model Space. You'll learn more about Model Space and Paper Space later in this chapter.

HIDE PAPERSPACE OBJECTS

This option pertains to 3D models in AutoCAD. When you draw in 3D, you can view your drawing as a *Wireframe view*. In a Wireframe view, your drawing looks like it's transparent even though it's made up of solid surfaces. Using hidden-line removal, you can view and plot your 3D drawings so that solid surfaces are opaque. To view a 3D drawing in the drawing area with hidden lines removed, use the Hide command or use one of the visual styles other than Wireframe. To plot a 3D drawing with hidden lines removed, choose the Hidden option or a visual style from the Shade Plot drop-down list.

Hide Paperspace Objects doesn't work for views in the Layout viewport described in the next section. Instead, you need to set the viewport's Shade Plot setting to Hidden. (Click the viewport, right-click, and choose Shade Plot ➤ Hidden from the shortcut menu.)

PLOT STAMP ON

The Plot Stamp feature lets you place pertinent data on the drawing in a location you choose. This includes the drawing name, date and time, scale, and other data. When you click the Plot Stamp On check box to turn on this option, an additional button appears.

Click this button to gain access to the Plot Stamp dialog box (Figure 8.6). This dialog box offers many controls over the plot stamp. It is a fairly extensive tool, so rather than fill this chapter with a description of all its features, see Appendix C for a complete rundown of the Plot Stamp options.

SAVE CHANGES TO LAYOUT

When this option is turned on, the changes you make to Plot dialog box settings are saved with the current layout. You'll learn more about layouts in the section "WYSIWYG Plotting Using Layout Views."

FIGURE 8.6
The Plot
Stamp dialog

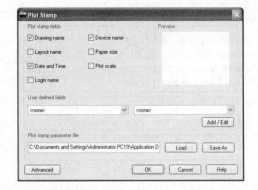

Exit Options

The Plot dialog box has the usual OK, Cancel, and Help buttons at the bottom. You'll also see the Apply To Layout button. This button lets you save the plot settings you make without sending your drawing to the printer or plotter for output. It is convenient for those times when you decide halfway through your plot setup not to plot your drawing.

WYSIWYG Plotting Using Layout Views

So far you've done all your work in the Model view, also known as Model Space. There are other views to your drawing that are specifically geared toward printing and plotting. The *layout* views enable you to control drawing scale, add title blocks, and set up different layer settings from those in the Model view. You can think of the layout views as page-layout spaces that act like a desktop-publishing program.

This section introduces you to layout views as they relate to plotting. You'll also learn more about layout views in Chapter 16.

You can have as many layout views as you like, each set up for a different type of output. You can, for example, have two or three layout views, each set up for a different scale drawing or with different layer configurations for reflected ceiling plans, floor plans, or equipment plans. You can even set up multiple views of your drawing at different scales in a single layout view. In addition, you can draw and add text and dimensions in layout views just as you would in Model Space.

To get familiar with the layout views, try the following exercise:

1. With the Plan file open, click the Quick View Layouts tool in the status bar (Figure 8.7) and then click the Layout1 preview panel.

FIGURE 8.7
Choose the
Layout1 panel.

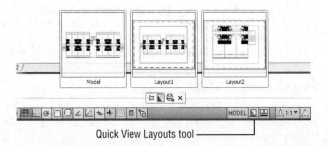

Quick View Layouts tool

OPTIONS IN THE PREVIEW PANEL

When you hover over a Quick View Layouts preview panel, you see two icons along the top of the preview. The icon in the upper-left corner enables you to plot a layout. The icon in the upper-right corner enables you to start the Publish feature. See Chapter 29 for more on the Publish feature.

2. Click in the drawing area. A view of your drawing appears on a gray background, as shown in Figure 8.8. This is a view of your drawing as it will appear when plotted on your current default printer or plotter. The white area represents the printer or plotter paper.

FIGURE 8.8
A view of Layout1

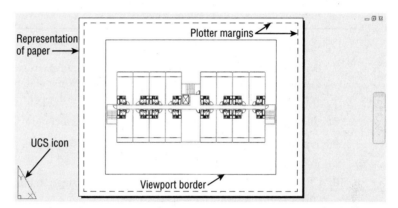

3. Try zooming in and out using the Zoom Realtime tool or the scroll wheel of your mouse. Notice that the entire image zooms in and out, including the area representing the paper.

Layout views give you full control over the appearance of your drawing printouts. You can print a layout view just as you did the view in Model Space.

Let's take a moment to look at the elements in the Layout1 view. As mentioned previously, the white area represents the paper on which your drawing will be printed. The dashed line immediately inside the edge of the white area represents the limits of your plotter's margins. Finally, the solid rectangle that surrounds your drawing is the outline of the viewport border. A *viewport* is an AutoCAD object that works like a window into your drawing from the layout view. Also notice the triangular symbol in the lower-left corner of the view: This is the UCS icon for the layout view. It tells you that you're currently in layout view space. You'll see the significance of this icon in the following exercise:

1. Try using a selection window to select the lobby area of your drawing. Nothing is selected.

2. Click the viewport border, which is the rectangle surrounding the drawing, as shown in Figure 8.8. This is the viewport into Model Space. Notice that you can select it.

3. Right-click, and choose Properties from the shortcut menu. You can see from the Properties palette that the viewport is just like any other AutoCAD object with layer, linetype, and color assignments. You can even hide the viewport outline by turning off its layer.

4. Close the Properties palette.

5. With the viewport still selected, click the Erase tool in the Modify toolbar. The view of your drawing disappears with the erasure of the viewport. Remember that the viewport is like a window into the drawing you created in the Model view. After the viewport is erased, the drawing view goes with it.

6. Type **U↵** or click the Undo button in the Quick Access toolbar to restore the viewport.

CREATING NEW VIEWPORTS

You can create new viewports using the Vports command (the New tool in the View tab's Viewports panel). See the section "Creating New Paper Space Viewports" in Chapter 16 for more information.

---

7. Double-click anywhere within the viewport's boundary. Notice that the UCS icon you're used to seeing appears in the lower-left corner of the viewport. The Layout UCS icon disappears. The Navigation bar and View Cube also appear inside the viewport.

8. Click the lobby in your drawing. You can now select parts of your drawing.

9. Try zooming and panning your view. Changes in your view take place only within the boundary of the viewport.

10. Click Zoom All from the Zoom flyout in the navigation bar or type **Z↵A↵** to display the entire drawing in the viewport.

11. To return to Paper Space, double-click an area outside the viewport. You can also type **PS↵** to return to Paper Space or **MS↵** to access the space within the viewport.

This exercise shows you the unique characteristics of layout views. The objects in the viewport are inaccessible until you double-click the interior of the viewport. You can then move about and edit your drawing in the viewport, just as you would while in the Model view.

Layout views can contain as many viewports as you like, and each viewport can hold a different view of your drawing. You can size and arrange each viewport any way you like, or you can create multiple viewports, giving you the freedom to lay out your drawing as you would a page in a page-layout program. You can also draw in the layout view or import Xrefs and blocks for title blocks and borders.

Setting Plot Scale in the Layout Viewports

In the first part of this chapter, you plotted your drawing from the Model view. You learned that to get the plot to fit on your paper, you had to either use the Fit To Paper option in the Plot dialog box or indicate a specific drawing scale, plot area, and drawing orientation.

The layout view works in a different way: It's designed to enable you to plot your drawing at a 1-to-1 scale. Instead of specifying the drawing scale in the Plot dialog box, as you did when you plotted from the Model view, you let the size of your view in the layout view viewport determine the drawing scale. You can set the viewport view to an exact scale by making changes to the properties of the viewport.

To set the scale of a viewport in a layout view, try the following exercise:

1. Press the Esc key to clear any selections. Then, click the viewport border to select it. You'll see the Viewport Scale tool appear in the status bar.

2. Click the Viewport Scale tool and a list of common drawing scales appears (Figure 8.9).

FIGURE 8.9
Choose a
viewport scale.

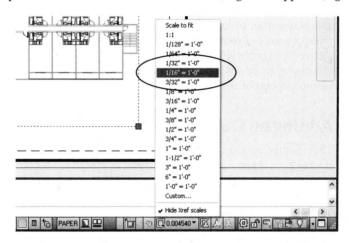

3. Select 1/16″ = 1′ (metric users should select 1:20). The view in the drawing window changes to reflect the new scale for the viewport. Now most of the drawing fits into the viewport, and it's to scale. The scale of 1/16″ = 1′ is similar to the metric 1:200 scale, but because you used centimeters instead of millimeters as the base unit for the metric version of the Plan file, you drop the second 0 in 200. The metric scale becomes 1:20.

4. Use the viewport grips to enlarge the viewport enough to display all of the drawing, as shown in Figure 8.10. As you move a corner grip, notice that the viewport maintains a rectangular shape.

FIGURE 8.10
The enlarged
viewport

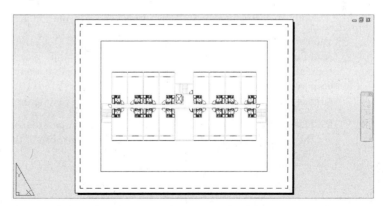

5. Click Plot from the Quick Access toolbar, and in the Plot dialog box, make sure the Scale option is set to 1:1 and your system printer is selected in the Printer/Plotter group; then click OK. Your drawing is plotted as it appears in the Layout tab, and it's plotted to scale.

6. After reviewing your plot, close the drawing without saving it.

In step 2, you saw that you can select a scale for a viewport by selecting it from the Viewport Scale option in the status bar. If you look just below the Standard Scale option, you see the Custom Scale option. Both options work like their counterparts, the options in the Plot Scale group in the Plot dialog box.

Layout views and viewports work in conjunction with your plotter settings to give you a better idea of how your plots will look. There are numerous plotter settings that can dramatically change the appearance of your layout view and your plots. In the next section, you'll learn how some of the plotter settings can enhance the appearance of your drawings. You'll also learn how layout views can display those settings, letting you see on your computer screen exactly what will appear on your paper output.

Adding an Output Device

This chapter mentioned that you can set up AutoCAD for more than one output device. You can do this even if you have only one printer or plotter connected to your computer. You might want multiple printer configurations in AutoCAD for many reasons. You might want to set up your system so that you can print to a remote location over a network or the Internet. Some printer configurations are strictly file oriented, such as the AutoCAD DWF format for Internet web pages or raster file output. (See Chapter 29 for more on DWF files.)

AutoCAD works best with printers and plotters configured as Windows system devices. Although you can add devices through the AutoCAD Plot Manager, Autodesk recommends that you set up your plotters and printers as Windows devices and then use the System Printer option in AutoCAD to select your output device. (In Windows XP, choose Start ➤ Settings ➤ Add A Printer to configure a new printer.) You can use the Add-A-Plotter Wizard to create predefined settings for your system printer so that you can quickly choose a printer or plotter setup.

You can also configure additional printers through the AutoCAD Plot Manager; this method also uses the Add-A-Plotter Wizard. Here's how it's done:

1. Click the Plotter Manager tool on the Output tab's Plot panel to open the Plotters window (Figure 8.11). Your view of the Plotters window may look a little different, depending on your operating system, but the same basic information is there.

You can also open this window by clicking the Add Or Configure Plotters button in the Plot And Publish tab of the Options dialog box. It's just an Explorer window showing you the contents of the `Plotters` folder that is buried in the `Documents and Settings` folder for your Windows user profile (`C:\Documents and Settings\`*User Name*`\Application Data\ Autodesk\AutoCAD 2011\R18.1\enu\Plotters`, where *User Name* is your login name).

2. Double-click the Add-A-Plotter Wizard icon to open the Add Plotter dialog box. You see the Introduction screen, which describes the purpose of the wizard.

FIGURE 8.11

The Plotters window

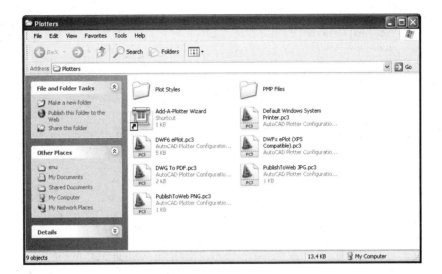

3. Click Next. The next screen of the wizard lets you select the type of setup you want. You're offered three options: My Computer, Network Plotter Server, and System Printer. The My Computer and the Network Plotter Server options offer plotter options based on AutoCAD-specific drivers. The main difference between these two options is that the Network Plotter Server option asks you for a network server name. Otherwise, they both offer the same set of options. The System Printer option uses the existing Windows system printer as the basis for the setup.

4. If you click the My Computer radio button and then click Next, you see a listing of plotter models that are supported by AutoCAD directly through AutoCAD's own drivers. If you use a PostScript device, or if you want to convert drawings to raster formats, this is the place to select those options. You can select the plotter or printer manufacturer name from the Manufacturers list on the left and then select a specific model from the list on the right. If you have a driver for a specific plotter or printer that isn't listed, you can click the Have Disk button to browse to your driver location.

5. After you've made a printer or plotter selection, click Next. You're then asked if you want to use an existing PCP or PC2 configuration file for the selected plotter. PCP and PC2 configurations files are plotter configuration files from earlier releases of AutoCAD.

6. Unless you plan to use one of those files, click Next on the Import PCP Or PC2 screen. If you selected My Computer in step 3, the Ports screen opens (Figure 8.12). With the Plot To A Port option selected, you can use the list to select a port to which your printer or plotter is connected. The Configure Port button lets you set up the port if you have a specific requirement for it. If you intend to plot to a file instead of to a port, you can select the Plot To File radio button at the top as an alternative. An AutoSpool option is also offered if your printer requires this feature.

FIGURE 8.12
The Ports screen of
the Add-A-Plotter
Wizard

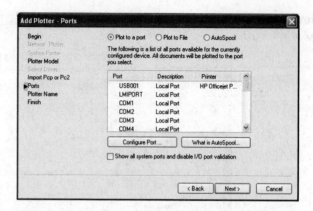

If you selected an option in step 4 that doesn't require a port setup, click the Next button to skip this option; the Plotter Name screen opens. You can enter a descriptive name in the Plotter Name text box. This name will appear in the Printer Name drop-down list of the Plot Or Page Setup dialog box.

7. Enter a name for this configuration in the space provided, then click Next to open the Finish screen.

8. This screen gives you the option to make adjustments to the configuration you've just created by clicking the Edit Plotter Configuration button. Click Finish to exit the Add-A-Plotter Wizard. Your new configuration appears in the Plotters window.

This Edit Plotter Configuration button lets you fine-tune your plotter settings. For example, you can calibrate your plotter for more accurate scaling of your plots, or, if you're creating a raster file output configuration, you can create a custom page setting for extremely high-resolution raster images.

After you've set up a plotter, the plotter information is stored as a file with the .pc3 filename extension in the Plotters folder described earlier.

Editing a Plotter Configuration

In step 8 of the previous exercise, you exited the Add-A-Plotter Wizard without editing the newly created plotter configuration. You can always go back and edit the configuration by opening the Plotters window (choose Plotter Manager on the Output tab's Plot panel) and double-clicking the configuration you want to edit. You can recognize a plotter configuration file by its .pc3 filename extension.

Most users use their Windows system printer or plotter for other applications besides AutoCAD, and frequently the AutoCAD settings for that printer are different from the settings used for other applications. You can set up AutoCAD to use its own settings automatically so you don't have to reconfigure your Windows system printer every time you switch applications. To do so, follow these steps:

1. Click the Page Setup Manager tool on the Output tab's Plot panel to open the Page Setup Manager dialog box.

2. Click the Modify button to open the Page Setup dialog box.

CONTROLLING THE APPEARANCE OF THE LAYOUT VIEWS

The Options dialog box offers a set of controls dedicated to the layout views. If you don't like some of the graphics in the layout views, you can turn them off. Open the Options dialog box and click the Display tab to see a set of options in the Layout Elements group in the lower-left side of the dialog box.

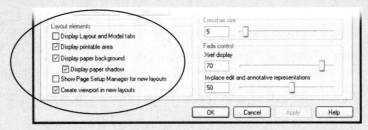

As you can see, you can control the display of the tabs themselves, the margins, the paper background, and the paper shadow. In addition, you can specify whether AutoCAD automatically creates a viewport or opens the Page Setup dialog box when you open a layout view for the first time.

---

3. Select the printer that you want to configure in the Name drop-down list of the Printer/Plotter group.

4. Click the Properties button just to the right of the drop-down list to open the Plotter Configuration Editor dialog box. A list box displays all the properties of the printer or plotter. Not all these properties are editable, however. Each time you click a property in the list box, the lower half of the dialog box displays the options associated with that property.

5. Click the Custom Properties item in the list box. The lower half of the dialog box displays the Custom Properties button (Figure 8.13).

FIGURE 8.13
Click Custom
Properties.

6. Click the Custom Properties button. You'll see the Windows system printer options. These are the same options you see when you edit the properties of your printer by choosing Start ➤ Printers And Faxes or Start ➤ Control Panel ➤ Printers And Other Hardware.

7. Adjust these settings the way you want them when you plot from AutoCAD, and then click OK.

8. Back in the Plotter Configuration Editor dialog box, click the Save As button. A standard Save As dialog box appears.

9. Enter the name of the plot configuration you've set up, or accept the default name, which is usually the name of the Windows printer or plotter, and click Save.

10. Click OK in the Plotter Configuration Editor dialog box, then click OK in the Page Setup dialog box and close the Page Setup Manager.

The Plotter Configuration Editor offers a wide variety of options that are fairly technical in nature. If you want to know more about the Plotter Configuration Editor, see Appendix C.

PLOTTING IMAGE FILES AND CONVERTING 3D TO 2D

If your work involves producing manuals, reports, or similar documents, you may want to add the Raster File Export option to your list of plotter configurations. The Raster File Export option lets you plot your drawings to a wide range of raster file formats, including CALS, JPEG, PCX, Targa, Tiff, and BMP. You can then import your drawings into documents that accept bitmap images. Images can be up to 8,000 × 8,000 pixels (set through the Plotter Configuration Editor) and can contain as many colors as the file format allows. If you need several raster formats, you can use multiple instances of this or any plotter configuration.

To convert your 3D wireframe models into 2D line drawings, use the Flatshot tool described in Chapter 21. You can then include your 2D line drawings with other 2D drawings for plotting and printing.

Storing a Page Setup

Unlike most other programs, AutoCAD offers hundreds of page setup options. It can be quite a chore to keep track of and maintain all these options. But as you settle into using AutoCAD, you'll probably find that you'll set up a few plotter configurations and stick to them. AutoCAD 2011 lets you save a page setup under a name to help you store and manage the settings you use most.

You've already seen the Page Setup Manager dialog box on your way to preparing a page for printing. In this section, you'll take a closer look at this useful tool.

Follow these steps to create a page setup:

1. In AutoCAD, click the Page Setup Manager tool in the Output tab's Plot panel. You can also right-click the Quick View Layouts tool in the status bar and choose Page Setup Manager. The Page Setup Manager dialog box opens (Figure 8.14). So far, you've used only the Modify option in this dialog box to modify an existing page setup. Now you'll try creating a new setup.

FIGURE 8.14
The Page Setup
Manager

2. Click the New button to open the New Page Setup dialog box (Figure 8.15).

FIGURE 8.15
Naming a new
page setup

3. To create a new page setup, first enter a name in the New Page Setup Name input box, and then select a setup from the Start With list box. AutoCAD will use the setup you select as the basis for the new setup. Notice that AutoCAD offers the name Setup1 as a default name for a new setup.

4. Click OK when you're finished. AutoCAD opens the Page Setup dialog box, where you can choose the settings for your new page setup.

5. Click OK to return to the Page Setup Manager, and then close it. Your new page setup is listed in the Current Page Setup list box. From here, you can select a page setup from the list box and then click the Set Current button to make it the current page setup for the layout.

You can also import other user-defined page setups by clicking the Import button. Because page setups are stored in the drawing, the Import button opens a standard file dialog box that displays drawing files. You can then select a file from which you want to import a page setup.

The current page setup applies to the current Layout tab, but after you create a new page setup, it's offered as an option in the Page Setup Manager dialog box for all other Layout tabs. You can also select a page setup directly from the Plot dialog box by using the Name drop-down list in the Page Setup group.

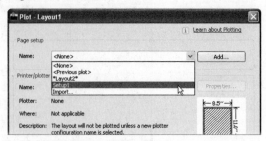

Page setups can be used with the Publish feature described in Chapter 29 to set up batch plots or in the Sheet Set feature to set up sheet layouts quickly. You can also create an entirely new page setup "on the fly" while in the Plot dialog box. To do this, click the Plot tool in the Quick Access toolbar, and then click the Add button in the Page Setup group of the Plot dialog box. This opens a simple dialog box that enables you to enter a name for your new setup. After you enter a new name and click OK, you can proceed to choose your page settings. Then click OK or Apply To Layout and the setup will be saved under the new name.

Plotter and Printer Hardware Considerations

Positioning an AutoCAD drawing on the printer output is something of an art. Before you face a deadline with hundreds of plots to produce, you may want to create some test plots and carefully refine your plotter settings so that you have AutoCAD set up properly for those rush jobs.

As part of the setup process, you'll need to understand how your particular printer or plotter works. Each device has its own special characteristics, so a detailed description of printer hardware setup is beyond the scope of this section. The following sections include a few guidelines.

Understanding Your Plotter's Limits

If you're familiar with a word-processing or page-layout program, you know that you can set the margins of a page, thereby telling the program exactly how far from each edge of the paper you want the text to appear. With AutoCAD, you don't have that luxury. To place a plot on your paper accurately, you must know the plotter's hard clip limits. The *hard clip limits* are like built-in margins, beyond which the plotter won't plot. These limits vary from plotter to plotter (see Figure 8.16).

It's crucial that you know your printer's or plotter's hard clip limits in order to place your drawings accurately on the sheet. Take some time to study your plotter manual and find out exactly what these limits are. Then make a record of them and store it somewhere in case you or someone else needs to format a sheet in a special way.

Hard clip limits for printers often depend on the software that drives them. You may need to consult your printer manual or use the trial-and-error method of plotting several samples to see how they come out.

UNDERSTANDING THE PLOT AND PUBLISH TAB IN THE OPTIONS DIALOG BOX

I mentioned the Plot And Publish tab in the Options dialog box earlier in this chapter. This tab contains several options related to plotting that can be useful. Here's a summary of those options and their purposes.

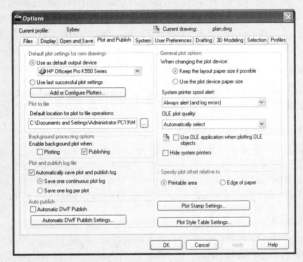

DEFAULT PLOT SETTINGS FOR NEW DRAWINGS

The options in this group let you control the default plot settings for new drawings and for drawings from earlier versions of AutoCAD that are opened for the first time in AutoCAD 2011. The Use As Default Output Device radio button and drop-down list let you select the default plotter or printer to be used with new drawings. When the Use Last Successful Plot Settings radio button is selected, the last successful plotter settings for subsequent plots are used. This is how earlier versions of AutoCAD worked. The Add Or Configure Plotters button opens the Plotters window. This is the same as choosing the Plot Manager tool from the Output tab's Plot panel. From the Plotters window, you can launch the Add-A-Plotter Wizard to add new plotter configurations. You can also edit existing plotter configurations.

GENERAL PLOT OPTIONS

These options control some of the general plotter parameters. The Keep The Layout Paper Size If Possible radio button causes AutoCAD to attempt to plot to the paper size specified in the Plot dialog box, regardless of the paper size in the plotter. If the specified size is larger than the capacity of the plotter, a warning message is displayed. The Use The Plot Device Paper Size option causes AutoCAD to use the paper size specified by the system printer or the PC3 plot configuration file currently in use. Both settings are also controlled by the Paperupdate system variable.

The System Printer Spool Alert drop-down list offers control over printer-spooling alert messages. The OLE Plot Quality drop-down list lets you control the quality of OLE objects embedded in or linked to a drawing. This setting can also be controlled through the Olequality system variable.

When the Use OLE Application When Plotting OLE Objects check box is selected, AutoCAD launches any application that is associated with an OLE object embedded or linked to the AutoCAD drawing that is currently being plotted. This helps improve the plot quality of OLE objects. You can also set this option through the Olestartup system variable.

The Hide System Printers option affects the Printer/Plotter group's Name drop-down list in the Plot and Page Setup dialog boxes. With this option turned on, you see only printers that have a .pc3 filename extension associated with them. These include printers that have been set up using the Add-A-Plotter Wizard discussed earlier in this chapter.

Plot To File

You have the option to plot to a file that can be downloaded to your printer or plotter at a later date. The Plot To File group lets you specify the default destination for the plot files.

Plot And Publish Log File

You can maintain a plot log file that records information about each plot you make. This can be helpful when you must keep records of hard-copy output for billing purposes. The location of the plot and publishing log file can be specified in the Files tab of the Options dialog box under the Plot And Publishing Log File Location listing. The log file has a .csv filename extension.

Background Processing Options

AutoCAD performs background plots so that after you begin a plot, you can immediately return to your drawing work instead of waiting for the plot to be completed. The options in this group let you turn on this feature either for standard plotting or for the Publish feature discussed in Chapter 29. You can also control this option through the Backgroundplot system variable.

Plot Stamp Settings

This button opens the Plot Stamp dialog box, which you saw in the section "Plot Options" earlier in this chapter. The Plot Stamp dialog box lets you determine what information is displayed in a plot stamp, which is a label placed on the print of a drawing to provide information about the source file.

Plot Style Table Settings

When you click this button, the Plot Style Table Settings dialog box opens. This dialog box controls the type of plot styles used in AutoCAD. In the case of named plot styles, you can also select a default plot style for layer 0 and a default plot style for objects. Note that the Use Color Dependent Plot Styles and Use Named Plot Styles radio buttons don't have an effect on the current drawing; they affect only new drawings and pre–AutoCAD 2000 drawings being opened for the first time in AutoCAD 2011. The Default Plot Style Table drop-down list lets you select a default plot style table for new and pre–AutoCAD 2000 drawings. These settings are also controlled by the Pstylepolicy system variable.

The Add Or Edit Plot Style Tables button in the Plot Style Table Settings dialog box opens the Plot Styles dialog box. From there, you can double-click an existing plot style table file or start the Add-A-Plot Style Table Wizard to create a new plot style.

SPECIFY PLOT OFFSET RELATIVE TO

Here you can determine whether the plot offset is set in relation to the printable area of your printer or to the edge of the paper. The printable area is determined by the printer margin.

AUTO PUBLISH

You can set up AutoCAD to automatically publish your file to a DWF, DWFx, or PDF file when you save or close a drawing. Place a checkmark in the Automatic Publish check box to enable this feature. The Automatic Publish Settings button give you control over the location of the published files as well as the file format, password protection, and other file features. Note that this feature will increase the time it takes to save or close a file.

After you've established the limits of your plotter or printer, you'll be better equipped to fit your drawing in those limits. You can then establish some standard drawing limits based on your plotter's limits. You'll also need to know the dimensions of those hard clip limits to define custom sheet sizes. Although AutoCAD offers standard sheet sizes in the Paper Size button group of the Page Setup and Plot dialog boxes, these sizes don't take into account the hard clip limits.

FIGURE 8.16
The hard clip limits of a plotter

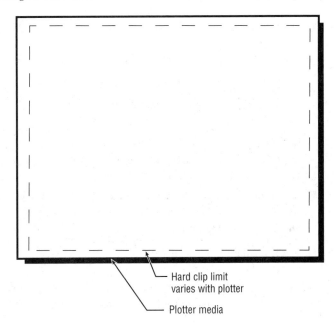

Hard clip limit
varies with plotter

Plotter media

Knowing Your Plotter's Origins

Another important consideration is the location of your plotter's origin. For example, on some plotters, the lower-left corner of the plot area is used as the origin. Other plotters use the center of the plot area as the origin. When you plot a drawing that is too large to fit the sheet on a plotter that uses a corner for the origin, the image is pushed toward the top and to the right of the sheet (see Figure 8.17). When you plot a drawing that is too large to fit on a plotter that uses the center of the paper as the origin, the image is pushed outward in all directions from the center of the sheet.

FIGURE 8.17
Plotting an over-sized image on a plotter that uses the lower-left corner for its origin

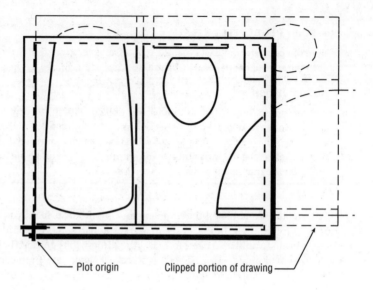

Plot origin   Clipped portion of drawing

In each situation, the origin determines a point of reference from which you can relate your drawing in the computer to the physical output. After you understand this, you're better equipped to place your electronic drawing accurately on the physical medium.

USING BATCH AND ELECTRONIC PLOTS

The focus of this chapter has been printer or plotter hard-copy output. But a major part of your work will involve the transmission of electronic versions of your documents. More than ever, architects and engineers are using the Internet to exchange documents of all types, so AutoCAD offers several tools to make the process easier.

I've mentioned that you can control some of your output settings thorough the Plot And Publish tab of the Options dialog box. The Publish feature includes items that enable you to "print" your drawings as a file that can be emailed to clients and consultants or posted on an FTP site or website. The Publish feature lets you create a single file that contains multiple pages so you can combine several drawing sheets into one file.

The Publish feature also enables you to plot several drawings at once without having to load and print each one individually. This can be helpful when you've finished a set of drawings and want to plot them during a break or overnight. Chapter 29 gives you a detailed look at the Publish feature.

The Bottom Line

Understand the plotter settings. Unlike other types of documents, AutoCAD drawings can end up on nearly any size sheet of paper. To accommodate the range of paper sizes, the AutoCAD plotter settings are fairly extensive and give you a high level of control over your output.

Master It Name a few of the settings available in the Plot dialog box.

Using layout views to control how your plots look. The Layout tabs in AutoCAD offer a way to let you set up how a drawing will be plotted. You can think of the Layout views as a kind of paste-up area for your drawings.

Master It Name some of the items that you see in a layout view.

Add an output device. Typically, AutoCAD will use the Windows system printer as an output device, but often you will find that the printer you use is a dedicated plotter that is not connected to Windows in the usual way. AutoCAD lets you add custom plotters and prints through the Add-A-Plotter Wizard.

Master It How do you start the Add-A-Plotter Wizard?

Store a page setup. Most of the time, you will use the same set of plotter settings for your drawings. You can save plotter settings using the Page Setup feature.

Master It Describe a way to create a page setup. Describe how to retrieve a setup.

Chapter 9

Understanding Plot Styles

To gain full control over the appearance of your output, you'll want to know about plot style tables. By using *plot style tables*, you can control how colors are translated into plotted line weights and how area fills are converted into shades of gray or screened colors in your printer or plotter output. You can also control other aspects of how the plotter draws each object in a drawing.

If you don't use plot style tables, your plotter will produce output as close as possible to what you see in the drawing editor, including colors. With plot style tables, you can force all the colors to print as black, and you can also assign a fill pattern or a screen to a color. This can be useful for charts and maps that require area fills of different gradations. You can create multiple plot style tables to produce plots that fit the exact requirements of your project.

This chapter will show you firsthand how you can use plot style tables to enhance your plotter output. You'll look at how to adjust the line weight of the walls in the Plan file and make color changes to your plotter output.

In this chapter, you'll learn to do the following:

- ◆ Choose between color-dependent and named plot style tables

- ◆ Create a color plot style table

- ◆ Edit and use plot style tables

- ◆ Assign named plot styles directly to layers and objects

Choosing between Color-Dependent and Named Plot Style Tables

You can think of a plot style as a virtual pen that has the attributes of color, width, shape, and screen percentage. A typical drawing may use several different line widths, so you use a different plot style for each line width. Multiple plot styles are collected into *plot style tables* that allow you to control a set of plot styles from one dialog box.

AutoCAD offers two types of plot style tables: color and named. *Color plot style tables* enable you to assign plot styles to the individual AutoCAD colors. For example, you can assign a plot style with a 0.50 mm width to the color red so that anything that is red in your drawing is plotted with a line width of 0.50 mm. You can, in addition, set the plot style's color to black so that everything that is red in your drawing is plotted in black.

Named plot style tables let you assign plot styles directly to objects in your drawing instead of assigning them in a more general way through a color. Named plot style tables also enable you to assign plot styles directly to layers. For example, with named plot styles, you can assign a plot style that is black and has a 0.50 mm width to a single circle or line in a drawing, regardless of its color.

Named plot styles are more flexible than color plot styles, but if you already have a library of AutoCAD drawings set up for a specific set of plotter settings, the color plot styles are a better choice when you're opening files that were created in AutoCAD R14 and earlier. This is because using color plot styles is more similar to the older method of assigning AutoCAD colors to plotter pens. You may also want to use color plot style tables with files that you intend to share with an individual or an office that is still using earlier versions of AutoCAD.

The type of plot style table assigned to the new default Drawing1 depends on the settings in the Plot Style Table Settings dialog box, which you access through the Plot And Publish tab of the Options dialog.

You can change the type of plot style table assigned to a drawing. See the sidebar "Converting a Drawing from Color Plot Styles to Named Plot Styles" later in this chapter for more information on plot style conversions.

Here's how to set up the plot style type for new files:

1. Open the Options dialog box (choose Options from the Application menu), and click the Plot And Publish tab.

2. Click the Plot Style Table Settings button in the lower-right corner of the dialog box to open the Plot Style Table Settings dialog box (Figure 9.1).

FIGURE 9.1
The Plot Style
Table Settings
dialog box

3. In the Default Plot Style Behavior For New Drawings button group, click the Use Color Dependent Plot Styles radio button. In a later exercise, you'll use the Use Named Plot Styles option.

4. Click OK. Then click OK again in the Options dialog box to return to the drawing.

After you've set up AutoCAD for color plot style tables, the default Drawing1 file, which appears when you open AutoCAD, will use only color plot style tables. You can change this setting at any time for new files, but after a file is saved, the type of plot style (named or color dependent) that is current when the file is created is the only plot style available to that file. If you need to change a color plot style for a named plot style drawing, see the sidebar "Converting a Drawing from Color Plot Styles to Named Plot Styles" later in this chapter.

Next you'll set up a custom color plot style table. Plot style tables are stored as files with the `.ctb` or `.stb` filename extension. The tables with filenames that end with `.ctb` are color plot style tables. The table with filenames that end with `.stb` are named plot style tables.

SELECT A PLOT STYLE WHEN STARTING A NEW DRAWING

You can also select between color and named plot styles when selecting a new drawing template. When you choose New from the Quick Access toolbar, you'll see that many of the template files in the Select Template dialog box have *Color Dependent Plot Styles* or *Named Plot Styles* as part of their name. If you have AutoCAD set up to use the Startup dialog box, you'll see the color and named plot style template files when you select the Use A Template option from the Create New Drawing dialog box.

Creating a Color Plot Style Table

You can have several plot style table files on hand to apply plot styles quickly to any given plot or Layout tab. You can set up each plot style table to create a different look for your drawing. These files are stored in the `Plot Styles` folder of the `C:\Documents and Settings\`*User Name*`\Application Data\Autodesk\AutoCAD 2011\R18.1\enu\Plotters\` folder. Follow these steps to create a new plot style table.

You'll use an existing file that was created in Release 14 to learn about the plot style features:

1. Open the sample file called `Plan-color.dwg`, and then click the Layout1 tab below the drawing area. If you don't see the Model and Layout tabs, click the Layout1 tool in the status bar.

2. Click the Page Setup Manager tool in the Output tab's Plot panel. Then click Modify in the Page Setup Manager dialog box.

3. The Page Setup dialog box (Figure 9.2) is similar to the Plot dialog box. The main difference is that the Page Setup dialog box doesn't have the Apply To Layout button at the bottom.

   In the Plot Style Table (Pen Assignments) group at the upper right, open the drop-down list and select New to start the Add Color-Dependent Plot Style Table Wizard.

4. Click the Start From Scratch radio button, and then click Next. The next screen of the wizard asks for a filename.

5. Enter **Mystyle** for the filename, and click Next. The next screen of the wizard lets you edit your plot style and assign the plot style to your current, new, or old drawings. You'll learn about editing plot styles a bit later.

6. Click Finish to return to the Page Setup dialog box.

Creating a new plot
style table

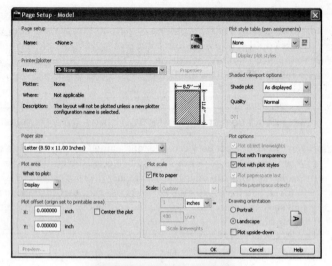

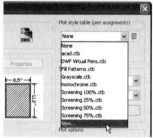

 Plotter Manager   With the Add Color-Dependent Plot Style Table Wizard, you can create a new plot style table from scratch, or you can create one based on an AutoCAD R14 CFG, PCP, or PC2 file. You can also access the Add Color-Dependent Plot Style Table Wizard by clicking the Plotter Manager tool in the Output tab's Plot panel. Open the `Plot Styles` folder and then double-click the Add-A-Plot Style Table Wizard application. You can also choose Print ➢ Manage Plot Styles from the Application menu.

The steps shown here are the same whether your drawing is set up for color plot styles or named plot styles.

Editing and Using Plot Style Tables

You now have your own plot style table. In this exercise, you'll edit the plot style and see first-hand how plot styles affect your drawing:

1. In the Page Setup dialog box, the filename `Mystyle.ctb` should appear in the drop-down list of the Plot Style Table (Pen Assignments) group. If it doesn't, open the drop-down list to select it.

2. Click the Edit button to open the Plot Style Table Editor. The Edit button is the one just to the right of the Plot Style Table drop-down list. Click the Form View tab, which is shown at the top of Figure 9.3.

FIGURE 9.3
The Plot Style
Table Editor dialog
box, open at the
Form View tab

EDITING THE PLOT STYLE TABLES DIRECTLY

You can also open and edit existing plot style tables by clicking the Plotter Manager tool in the Output tab's Plot panel to open the Plotters dialog box. From there, open the Plotter Styles folder; you can then double-click the plot style you want to edit. You can use Windows Explorer to find the plot style tables in `C:\Documents and Settings\`*User Name*`\Application Data\` `Autodesk\AutoCAD 2011\R18.1\enu\Plotters\Plot Styles`.

The Plot Style Table Editor dialog box has three tabs—General, Table View, and Form View—two of which give you control over how each color in AutoCAD is plotted. The Form View tab lets you select a color from a list box and then set the properties of that color by using the options on the right side of the tab.

The Table View tab displays each color as a column of properties. Each column is called a *plot style*. The property names are listed in a column to the far left. Although the layout is different, both the Table View tab and the Form View tab offer the same functions.

Now you'll continue by changing the line width property of the Color 3 (green) plot style. Remember that green is the color assigned to the Wall layer of your Plan drawing.

1. Click Color 3 in the Plot Styles list box.

2. Click the Lineweight drop-down list (Figure 9.4), and select 0.5000 mm. You may have to scroll down the list to find 0.5000 mm.

3. Click Save & Close to return to the Page Setup dialog box.

4. Click the Display Plot Styles check box (Figure 9.5) in the Plot Style Table (Pen Assignments) group. Note that this option is not available in Model Space.

FIGURE 9.4
Set the line weight.

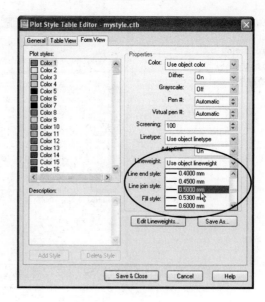

5. Click OK to close the Page Setup dialog box, and click Close to close the Page Setup Manager dialog box.

FIGURE 9.5
Check to display
plot styles.

6. Zoom in to the plan to enlarge the view of a unit bathroom and entrance, as shown in Figure 9.6.

FIGURE 9.6
Adjust your view
to look like this.

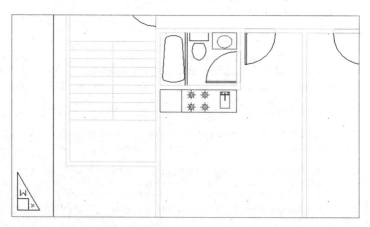

Making Your Plot Styles Visible

You won't see any changes in your drawing yet. You need to make one more change to your drawing options:

1. Type **Lw.** to open the Lineweight Settings dialog box (Figure 9.7). You can also click the User Preferences tab in the Options dialog box and then click the Lineweight Settings button to open the Lineweight Settings dialog box. The Lineweight Settings dialog box lets you control the appearances of line weights in the drawing. If line weights aren't showing up, this is the place to look to make them viewable.

FIGURE 9.7
Check to show the line weights.

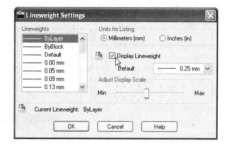

2. Click the Display Lineweight check box to turn on this option.

3. Just below the Display Lineweight option, click the Default drop-down list and select 0.09 mm. This makes any unassigned or default line weight a very fine line.

4. Click OK. The layout displays the drawing with the line weight assignments you set up earlier (see Figure 9.8).

FIGURE 9.8
The drawing with new line weight assignments

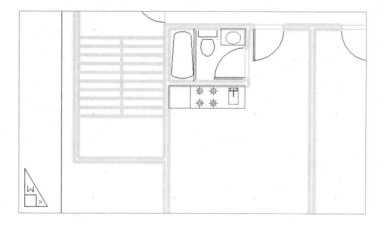

If your view doesn't reflect the Plot Style settings, make sure you have the Display Plot Styles option selected in the Plot Style Table (Pen Assignments) group of the Page Setup dialog box.

Making Changes to Multiple Plot Styles

Chances are you'll want to plot your drawing in black and white for most of your work. You can edit your color plot style table to plot one or all of your AutoCAD colors as black instead of the AutoCAD colors.

You saw how you can open the Plot Style Table Editor from the Page Setup dialog box to edit your color plot style table. In this exercise, you'll try a different route:

1. Click the Plotter Manager tool in the Output tab's Plot panel to open the Plotters folder, and then open the Plot Styles folder.

2. Locate the file Mystyle.ctb, and double-click it to open the Plot Style Table Editor dialog box.

3. Click the Form View tab.

4. Click Color 3 in the Plot Styles list box.

5. Click the Color drop-down list, and select Black (Figure 9.9).

FIGURE 9.9
Select Black from the Color drop-down list.

6. Click Save & Close, and then close the Plot Styles window.

7. Type **Rea**↵ to view your drawing. The green objects appear black in the Layout tab.

8. Click the Model tab in the lower-left portion of the drawing area or the Model tool in the status bar to view your drawing in Model Space. The objects are still their original colors. This shows that you haven't changed the colors of your objects or layers; you've changed only the color of the plotted output.

Next try changing the first 9 output colors to black:

1. Repeat steps 1 and 2 of the previous exercise to open the Mystyle.ctb file and the Plot Style Table Editor dialog box.

2. Click the Form View tab, and then click Color 1 in the Plot Styles list box.

3. Shift+click Color 9 in the Plot Styles list box to select all the plot styles from Color 1 to Color 9 (see Figure 9.10).

4. Click the Color drop-down list and select Black.

FIGURE 9.10

Select the colors from 1 to 9.

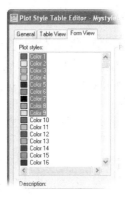

5. Click Save & Close, and close the Plot Styles window.

6. Click the Layout1 tab, and then type **REA↵** to regen the view. All the colors have changed to black.

Now when you plot your drawing, you'll get a plot that is composed entirely of black lines.

These exercises have shown that the Plot Style Table Editor lets you set the color of your printed output to be different from the colors you see in Model Space. In the exercises, you set the plot colors to black, but if you look down the Color drop-down list, you'll see that you can choose from any number of colors. The Select Color option in the Color drop-down list lets you select colors from the Select Color dialog box (see Figure 9.11). To see the view shown in Figure 9.11, make sure the True Color tab is selected and the HSL option is selected in the Color Model drop-down list. LT users won't see a Color Books tab.

FIGURE 9.11

The Select Color dialog box

ACAD only

Chapter 5 introduced you to the Select Color dialog box in the context of selecting colors for layers. Here you can use it to assign colors to plot styles. The same three tabs are available: Index Color, True Color, and Color Books. (LT users won't see the Color Books tab.) The Index Color tab lets you select from the standard AutoCAD 255 index colors. The True Color tab lets you choose virtually any color you want. The Color Books tab lets you use DIC, RAL, and PANTONE colors.

Setting Up Line Corner Styles

You may notice that the corners of the wall lines appear to be rounded instead of crisp and sharp, as shown in Figure 9.12.

FIGURE 9.12
The corners of
thick lines may
appear rounded.

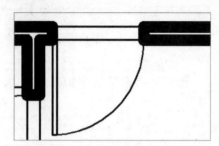

You can adjust the way AutoCAD draws these corners at plot time through the Plot Style Table Editor:

1. Open the `Mystyle.ctb` plot style table as you did in the previous exercise.

2. Click the Form View tab, and then click Color 3 in the Plot Styles list box.

3. Click the Line End Style drop-down list and select Square (Figure 9.13).

4. Click Save & Close, and then close the Plot Styles window.

5. Type **Rea**⏎ to view your changes. Now the corners meet in a sharp angle, as shown in Figure 9.14.

FIGURE 9.13
Choose square
line ends.

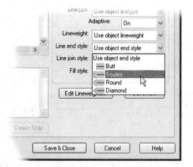

The Square option in the Line End Style drop-down list extends the endpoints of contiguous lines so that endpoints merge in a clean corner instead of a notch. The Line Join Style drop-down list offers a similar settings options for polylines. For example, you can round polyline corners by using the Round option in the Line Join Style drop-down list.

FIGURE 9.14
The Line End Style
setting can alter
the way corners
are drawn.

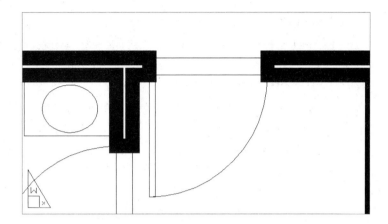

Setting Up Screen Values for Solid Areas

The last option you'll look at is how to change a color into a screened area. Frequently, you'll
want to add a gray or colored background to an area of your drawing to emphasize that area
graphically, as in a focus area in a map or to designate functions in a floor plan. The settings
you're about to use enable you to create shaded backgrounds:

1. Click the Page Setup Manager tool in the Output tab's Plot panel, and click Modify to
   open the Page Setup dialog box again.

2. Click the Edit tool to open the Plot Style Table Editor.

3. Select Color 3 from the Plot Styles list box.

4. In the Screening list box, click the number 100 to select it (see Figure 9.15).

FIGURE 9.15
Select the number
100 in the Screen-
ing list box.

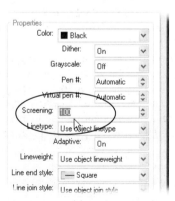

5. Type 50↵.

6. Click Save & Close. Click OK in the Page Setup dialog box, and click Close in the Page Setup Manager dialog box.

7. Type **Rea**↵. The walls are a shade of gray instead of solid black.

In this exercise, you turned a wide black line into a gray one. The Screening option lets you tone down the chosen color from a solid color to one that has 50 percent of its full intensity.

You can use the Screening option in combination with color to obtain a variety of tones. If you need to cover large areas with color, you can use the Solid hatch pattern to fill those areas and then use the Screening option in the Plot Style Table Editor to make fine adjustments to the area's color.

Controlling the Visibility of Overlapping Objects

You should also know about the Draworder command in conjunction with solid filled areas. This command lets you control how objects hide or overlap when displayed or plotted. If your solid hatches are hiding text or other graphics, you need to learn about Draworder. See Chapter 14 for more information. Some output devices offer a Merge Control option that determines how overlapping graphics are plotted. For more information, see Appendix C.

Other Options in the Plot Style Table Editor

You've seen a lot of the plot style options so far, but there are many others that you may want to use in the future. The following sections describe those options that weren't covered in the previous exercises. Be aware that the options in the Plot Style Table Editor are the same regardless of whether you're editing a color plot style table or a named plot style table.

THE GENERAL TAB

You may not have really looked at the General tab of the Plot Style Table Editor in the exercise presented earlier. The General tab offers information regarding the plot style you're currently editing. You can enter a description of the style in the Description box. This can be useful if you plan to include the plot style with a drawing you're sending to someone else for plotting.

The File Information group gives you basic information about the file location and name as well as the number of color styles included in the plot style table.

The Apply Global Scale Factor To Non-ISO Linetypes check box lets you specify whether ISO linetype scale factors are applied to all linetypes. When this item is selected, the Scale Factor input box becomes active, enabling you to enter a scale factor. International Organization for Standardization (ISO) linetypes are special linetypes that conform to ISO standards for technical drawings.

THE TABLE VIEW TAB

The Table View tab offers the same settings as the Form View tab, only in a different format. Each plot style is shown as a column, with the properties of the plot style listed along the left side of the tab. To change a property, click it in the column (see Figure 9.16).

FIGURE 9.16
The plot style
Table View tab

To apply the same setting to all plot styles at once, right-click a setting you want to use from a single plot style and choose Copy from the shortcut menu. Right-click the setting again, and then choose Apply To All Styles from the shortcut menu.

Click the Edit Lineweights button to open the Edit Lineweights dialog box, which lets you adjust the line weight settings for the plot styles.

THE FORM VIEW TAB

You've already seen and worked with the Form View tab, shown in Figure 9.3 earlier in this chapter. This tab contains the same settings as the Table View tab but in a different format. Instead of displaying each color as a column of properties, this tab lists the properties as options along the right side, and the colors are listed in a list box.

To modify the properties of a color, you select the color from the list and then edit the values in the Properties group on the right side of the dialog box. For example, to change the screening value of the Color 3 style, you highlight Color 3 in the Plot Styles list, double-click the Screening input box, and enter a new value.

The names of the properties in the Table View tab are slightly different from those in the Form View tab. The Table View property names are enclosed in brackets in this list.

You've already seen what the Screening, Color, Lineweight, and Line End Style options do. Here's a description of the other style properties:

Description   This option enables you to enter a description for each color.

Dither [Enable Dithering]   *Dithering* is a method that enables your plotter to simulate colors beyond the basic 255 colors available in AutoCAD. Although this option is desirable when you want to create a wider range of colors in your plots, it can also create distortions, including broken, fine lines and false colors. For this reason, dithering is usually turned off. This option isn't available in all plotters.

COLORS AND LINE WEIGHTS IN THE SAN FRANCISCO MAIN LIBRARY

Technical drawings can have a beauty of their own, but they can also be deadly boring. What really sets a good technical drawing apart from a poor one is the control of line weights. Knowing how to vary and control line weights in both manual and CAD drawings can make a huge difference in the readability of the drawing.

In the San Francisco Main Library project, the designers at SMWM Associates were especially concerned with line weights in the reflected ceiling plan. The following graphic shows a portion of the reflected ceiling plan from the library drawings.

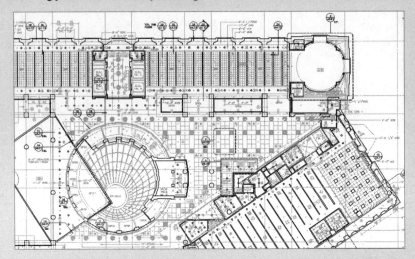

As you can see, it contains a good deal of graphical information, which, without careful line-weight control, could become confusing. (Although you can't see it in the black-and-white print, a multitude of colors were used to vary the line weight.) When the electronic drawings were plotted, colors were converted into lines of varying thickness. Bolder lines were used to create emphasis in components such as walls and ceiling openings, and fine lines were used to indicate ceiling tile patterns.

By emphasizing certain lines over others, you avoid visual monotony and the various components of the drawing can be seen more easily.

Grayscale [Convert To Grayscale]   This option converts colors to grayscale.

Pen # [Use Assigned Pen #]   This option lets you specify which pen number is assigned to each color in your drawing. It applies only to pen plotters.

Virtual Pen #   Many ink-jet and laser plotters offer "virtual pens" to simulate the processes of the old-style pen plotters. Frequently, such plotters offer as many as 255 virtual pens. Plotters with virtual pens often let you assign AutoCAD colors to a virtual pen number. This is significant if the virtual pens of your plotter can be assigned screening, width, end style, and join styles. You can then use the virtual pen settings instead of using the settings in the Plot Style Table Editor. This option is most beneficial for users who already have a library of drawings that are set up for plotters with virtual-pen settings.

You can set up your ink-jet or laser printer for virtual pens under the Vector Graphics listing of the Device And Documents Setting tab of the Plotter Configuration Editor. See Appendix C for more on setting up your printer or plotter configuration.

Linetype   If you prefer, you can use this setting to control linetypes in AutoCAD based on the color of the object. By default, this option is set to Use Object Linetype. I recommend that you leave this option at its default.

Adaptive [Adaptive Adjustment]   This option controls how a noncontinuous linetype begins and ends. It's on by default, which forces a linetype to begin and end with a line segment. With this option turned off, the same linetype is drawn without regard for its ending. In some cases, this can produce a line that appears incomplete.

Line End Style   This option lets you specify the shape of the end of simple lines that have a line weight greater than zero.

Line Join Style   This option lets you determine the shape of the corners of polylines.

Fill Style   This option lets you set up a color to be drawn as a pattern when used in a solid filled area. The patterns appear as shown in the drop-down list.

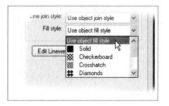

Add Style   Clicking this button lets you add more plot styles or colors. This option isn't available for color plot style tables.

Delete Style   Clicking this button deletes the selected style. This option isn't available for color plot style tables.

Save As   Clicking this button lets you save the current plot style table with a different filename.

LINE JOINT STYLE CAN AFFECT FONTS

The Line Join Style setting can have an adverse affect on AutoCAD fonts. If text appears distorted, check to see whether it's on a layer that uses a line join style other than the default Use Object Join Style setting.

Assigning Named Plot Styles Directly to Layers and Objects

So far, you've learned that you can control how AutoCAD translates drawing colors into plotter output. You've been using a color plot style table, which assigns a plot style to each color in AutoCAD. You can also assign plot styles directly to objects or layers. To do this, you need to employ a named plot style table. As I said earlier, named plot style tables enable you to create plot styles that have names rather than assigning styles directly to colors in AutoCAD. You can then assign a plot style by name to objects or layers in your drawing. In the following sections, you'll learn how to set up AutoCAD with a named plot style table to assign plot styles to objects; then you'll create a new plot style table.

Using Named Plot Style Tables

Out of the box, AutoCAD uses the color-dependent plot style table for all new drawings. You can create a new drawing that uses named plot style tables in two ways. The simpler way is to use any of the named plot style template files when you create a new drawing. You'll see these templates under the Use A Template option in the Create New Drawing dialog box or in the Select Template dialog box (Figure 9.17).

By offering both color and named plot style drawing templates, AutoCAD makes it easy to create and select the type of plot style for your drawing regardless of the current default style.

If you prefer, you can set up AutoCAD to use a named plot style by default when you create a drawing by using the Start From Scratch option in the Create New Drawing dialog box. To set up the default plot style table for new drawings, follow these steps:

1. Choose Options from the Application menu to open the Options dialog box, and click the Plot And Publish tab. This tab offers a variety of settings geared toward your plotter or printer.

2. In the lower-right corner of the dialog box, click the Plot Style Table Settings button.

3. In the Plot Style Table Settings dialog box (Figure 9.18), click the Use Named Plot Styles radio button. Notice that the Default Plot Style For Layer 0 and Default Plot Style For Objects options become available. Click OK.

4. Click OK to close the Options dialog box.

FIGURE 9.17
Templates you can choose from

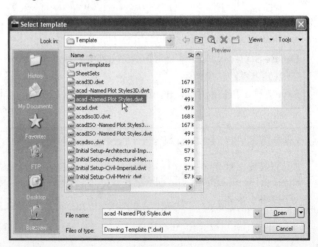

FIGURE 9.18
Check to use
named plot styles.

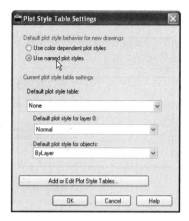

To create and try out a new named plot style, you can open an existing file from an earlier version of AutoCAD. In the next few exercises, you'll use the Plan-named.dwg file. This is a Release 2004 file, to which you'll assign the type of plot style table that is currently the default as determined by the Use Named Plot Styles option you set in the previous exercise. Follow these steps:

1. Open the Plan-named.dwg file.

2. Click the Plotter Manager tool in the Output tab's Plot panel to open a window to the Plotters folder. From there, open the Plot Styles folder.

3. Double-click the Add-A-Plot Style Table Wizard icon to start the Add Plot Style Table Wizard.

4. Click Next to open the Begin screen, choose Start From Scratch, and then click Next to open the Pick Plot Style Table screen.

5. Click the Named Plot Style Table radio button, and then click Next to open the File Name screen.

6. Enter **Mynamedstyle1** in the File Name input box, and click Next to open the Finish screen. Here you can exit, or you can edit the new plot style table. This time, you'll edit the table from the wizard.

7. Click the Plot Style Table Editor button to open the Plot Style Table Editor dialog box (Figure 9.19).

Notice that you have only one style named. Unlike with the color plot style tables, you aren't assigning a style to each AutoCAD color; you don't need a style for each of the 255 colors. Instead, you can create a limited set of styles, giving each style the characteristics you want to apply to objects or layers. Continue by adding some plot styles:

1. Click the Add Style button to display a new Style 1 column (Figure 9.20). If you choose, you can give the style a different name at this point by clicking in the Name box and typing a new name.

2. Click the Form View tab, and then select Style 1 from the Plot Styles list.

3. Click the Lineweight drop-down list, and select 0.5000 mm.

4. Click the Add Style button, and then click OK in the Add Plot Style dialog box.

5. Select Style 2 from the Plot Styles list, and then click the Lineweight drop-down list and select 0.7000 mm.

6. Click Save & Close to return to the Add Plot Style Table dialog box.

7. Click Finish to exit the wizard, and then close the Plot Styles window.

FIGURE 9.19
The Plot Style Table Editor dialog with only one style named

FIGURE 9.20
Adding a style

You may have noticed that the Add-A-Plot Style Table Wizard works in a slightly different way when you start it from the Plot Styles window. It adds an extra option (in step 5 of the exercise before the preceding one) that lets you choose between a color plot style table and a named plot style table.

You've just created a named plot style. Next make `Mynamedstyle1.stb` the default plot style:

1. Open the Options dialog box, and click the Plot And Publish tab.

2. Click the Plot Style Table Settings button. Then, in the Default Plot Style Table drop-down list, select `Mynamedstyle1.stb`, the table you just created.

3. Click OK to exit the Plot Style Table Settings dialog box, and then click OK again to exit the Options dialog box.

Now you're ready to start assigning plot styles to the objects in your drawing.

Assigning Plot Styles to Objects

After you've set up AutoCAD to use named plot styles, you can begin to assign plot styles to objects through the Properties palette. Here are the steps to assign plot styles to objects:

1. Back in the `Plan-named.dwg` file, click the Layout1 tab below the drawing area or the Layout1 tool in the status bar.

2. Click the Page Setup Manager tool in the Plot panel, and then click the Modify button in the Page Setup Manager dialog box.

AutoCAD Wants a Plotter

If your plotter configuration is set up for a nonexistent printer, you'll see a warning message telling you that a driver for the plotter assigned to this drawing can't be found. This often occurs when you receive a file that has been set up to plot on a printer in another location. As the warning message explains, AutoCAD has set your plot device to None. You must then make sure your printer or plotter is selected in the Printer/Plotter group of the Page Setup dialog box.

---

3. In the Page Setup dialog box, select `Mynamedstyle1.stb` from the drop-down list in the Plot Style Table (Pen Assignments) group.

4. Make sure the Display Plot Styles check box is selected, and then click OK.

5. Make sure a printer is selected in the Printer/Plotter group, and then click Close to close the Page Setup Manager dialog box.

You've assigned a named plot style table to Layout1. Note that you can assign different named plot styles to different layouts.

Next, make sure the plot styles will be displayed in the drawing:

1. Type **LW⏎**, make sure that the Display Lineweight check box is selected, and click OK.

2. Set up your view so you see a close-up of the lower-left corner unit.

3. Double-click inside the viewport so that the viewport border becomes a bold outline. This enables you to select objects in the drawing while in a Layout view.

4. Select the line representing the outer wall of the unit in the lower-left portion of the plan, as shown in Figure 9.21; then right-click, and choose Properties from the shortcut menu.

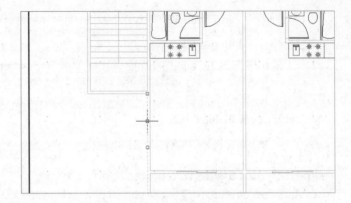

5. In the Properties palette, click the Plot Style option (Figure 9.22). The option turns into a drop-down list with a downward-pointing arrow to the far right.

FIGURE 9.22
Click the Plot Style
option to enable
the drop-down list.

6. Click the downward-pointing arrow, and then select Other from the drop-down list to open the Select Plot Style dialog box (Figure 9.23).

FIGURE 9.23
The Select Plot
Style dialog box

7. Select Style 1, and click OK. Style 1 now appears as the value for the plot style in the Properties palette.

8. Close the Properties palette.

9. Type **Rea↵**. If you have the line weight visibility turned on, you see the results in the drawing editor. (Depending on how your display is set up, you may need to zoom in further.)

Another way to assign plot styles to individual objects is through the Plot Style drop-down list found in the Home tab's Properties panel. You may need to select Other from the drop-down list to view all the plot styles.

This enables you to select a plot style in a manner similar to how you would use the Layer and Linetype drop-down lists. You can assign plot styles to individual objects by selecting the objects and then selecting a plot style from the Plot Style drop-down list. If you're using a color plot style table like the one you created in earlier exercises, the Plot Style drop-down list is unavailable.

Assigning Plot Style Tables to Layers

You can also assign named plot style tables to layers. This has an effect similar to using the color plot style tables. The main difference is that with named plot style tables, you assign the plot style tables directly to the layer instead of assigning a plot style to the color of a layer. Here's how to assign a plot style table to a layer:

1. In the Home tab's Layers panel, click the Layer Properties button to open the Layer Properties Manager dialog box.

2. Select the Wall layer.

3. Click the Normal label in the Plot Style column of the Wall layer listing. You may have to scroll to the right to see the Plot Style column (Figure 9.24). The Select Plot Style dialog box opens.

FIGURE 9.24
Assigning a plot style to a layer

4. Select Style 1 from the Plot Styles list.

5. Click OK. You return to the Layer Properties Manager dialog box. This time, it shows the Plot Style property for the Wall layer listed as Style 1.

6. Close the Layer Properties Manager dialog box, and then type **Rea**↵. Your view of the plan changes to reflect the new plot style assignment to the Wall layer.

CONVERTING A DRAWING FROM COLOR PLOT STYLES TO NAMED PLOT STYLES

If you need to convert a color plot style drawing to a named plot style drawing, you can use the Convertctb and Convertpstyles commands. The conversion is a two-part process. In the first stage, which is needed only the first time you perform the conversion, you convert a color plot style table file into a named plot style table file. Then you convert the drawing file.

Here are the steps for the first part of the process:

1. Start AutoCAD, and at the Command prompt, enter **Convertctb**↵. This command lets you convert a color plot style table file into a named plot style table file. A Select File dialog box opens to enable you to select a color plot style table file; these files have the filename extension .ctb. For this example, choose the acad.ctb file.

2. Click Open to open the Create File dialog box, where you can provide a name for the converted file. If you opened the acad.ctb file in step 1, you may want to give the new file the name AcadConvert so you know it's a converted CTB file. AutoCAD automatically adds the .stb filename extension.

3. After you click Save, AutoCAD creates a new named plot style table file, with the .stb filename extension, from the CTB file you selected in step 1.

4. You see a message box telling you that the STB file was created successfully. Click OK to dismiss the message.

The next part is to convert the drawing file:

1. Open the file you want to convert, and enter **Convertpstyles**↵ at the Command prompt. You'll see a warning message to make sure you've converted a CTB file to an STB file.

2. Click OK to open the Select File dialog box.

3. Select the converted STB file you created using the Convertctb command. The current drawing is converted to use a named plot style table.

In the process shown here, I've suggested converting the acad.ctb file, but if you've saved some custom settings in another CTB file, you may want to convert your custom CTB file instead.

To convert a drawing that uses a named plot style table to one that uses a color plot style table, open the file in question and use the Convertpstyles command. You'll see a warning message telling you that all the named plot styles will be removed from the drawing. Click OK to convert the drawing.

The Bottom Line

Choose between color-dependent and named plot style tables.   Plot styles let you control the way lines are printed on paper. You can control line weights, shading of filled areas, corner treatment of thick lines, and more.

Master It   Describe some of the differences between named plot styles and color-dependent plot styles.

Create a color plot style table.   Both color and named plot styles are stored as files. You can create custom plot styles and apply them to any drawing.

Master It   In what dialog box do you select and edit plot styles?

Edit and use plot style tables.   Plot styles give you a lot of control over the appearance of lines in your plotted output.

Master It   Name some of the settings offered in the Plot Style Table Editor.

Assign named plot styles directly to layers and objects.   Named plot styles offer a bit more control over the way lines are plotted. If you choose, you can assign named plot styles to objects, bypassing layer assignments.

Master It   Describe a method for assigning a plot style to an object.

Chapter 10

Adding Text to Drawings

One of the more tedious drafting tasks is applying notes to your drawing. AutoCAD makes this job faster by enabling you to type your notes, insert text from other sources, and copy notes that repeat throughout a drawing, and it helps you to create more professional-looking notes using a variety of fonts, type sizes, and type styles.

In this chapter, you'll add notes to your apartment building plan. In the process, you'll explore some of AutoCAD's text-creation and text-editing features. You'll learn how to control the size, slant, type style, and orientation of text and how to import text files. You'll start by working through some exercises that show you the process of preparing a drawing for text. You'll then add a few lines of text to the drawing and learn how text size and drawing scale interrelate. The rest of the chapter shows you the tools available for formatting text to fit your application.

In this chapter, you'll learn to do the following:

- Prepare a drawing for text

- Set the annotation scale and add text

- Explore text formatting in AutoCAD

- Add simple single-line text objects

- Use the Check Spelling feature

- Find and replace text

Preparing a Drawing for Text

In these first sections, you'll go through the process of adding text to a drawing that currently has no text. By doing this, you'll gain firsthand experience in using all the tools you'll need for adding text to a drawing. Start by setting up a drawing to prepare it for the addition of text:

1. Start AutoCAD, and open the Unit file. If you haven't created the Unit file, you can use the file called 10a-unit.dwg. Metric users should use 10a-unit-metric.dwg. After the file is open, choose Save As from the Application menu to save the Unit drawing to a file called Unit.dwg.

2. Create a layer called Notes, and make it the current layer. Notes is the layer on which you'll keep all your text information.

3. If it is on, turn off the Flr-pat layer. Otherwise, the floor pattern you added previously will obscure the text you enter during the exercises in this chapter.

4. Set up your view so it looks similar to the top image in Figure 10.1.

FIGURE 10.1
The top image shows the points to pick to place the text boundary window. The bottom image shows the completed text.

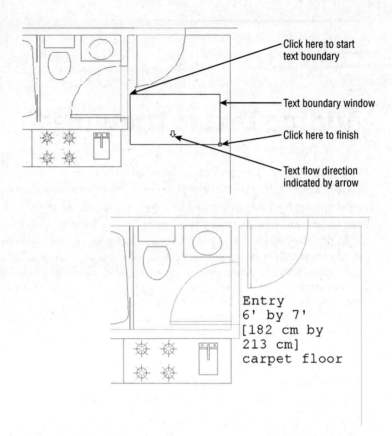

Click here to start text boundary

Text boundary window

Click here to finish

Text flow direction indicated by arrow

Entry
6' by 7'
[182 cm by
213 cm]
carpet floor

ORGANIZE TEXT WITH LAYERS

It's a good idea to keep your notes on a separate layer so you can plot drawings containing only the graphics information or freeze the Notes layer to save redraw/regeneration time.

Organizing Text by Styles

Before you begin to add text to your drawing, you should set up a text style or two. You can think of text styles as a tool to store your most common text formatting. Styles store text height and font information so you don't have to set these options every time you enter text. Generally, you'll need only a few text styles.

Even if you started to add text without creating your own text style, you would still be using a text style. That's because every text object must have a style, so AutoCAD includes the Standard text style in every new drawing. The Standard style uses an AutoCAD font called Txt and includes numerous other settings that you'll learn about in this section. These other settings include width factor, oblique angle, and default height.

SET UP DEFAULT FONTS IN TEMPLATES

If you don't like the way the AutoCAD default style is set up, open the `acad.dwt` template file and change the Standard text style settings to your liking. You can also add other styles that you use frequently. Remember, AutoCAD files that use the `.dwt` filename extension are just AutoCAD DWG files with a slightly different extension to set them apart.

In this next exercise, you'll create a text style called Note1, which you'll use to add notes to the Unit plan you've been working on:

1. Click the Text Style tool from the Home tab's expanded Annotation panel, or type **St↵**. This opens the Text Style dialog box (Figure 10.2).

FIGURE 10.2
The Text Style
dialog box

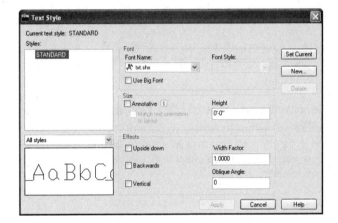

2. Click the New button to the right of the dialog box to open the New Text Style dialog box.

3. Enter **Note1 (Note one)** for the name of your new style, and then click OK.

4. Select a font for your style. In the Text Style dialog box again, click the Font Name drop-down list in the Font group.

5. Locate the Courier New TrueType font and select it. A quick way to locate the font is to click in the list and start typing the font name.

6. Select the Annotative option in the Size group (Figure 10.3).

7. In the Paper Text Height input box, enter **0.1**. You'll see your input change to 1/8″ if you are using the architectural unit style. Metric users should enter **0.15**.

8. Close the dialog box.

The Annotative option you turned on in step 6 is an important feature for keeping your text at the proper size for your drawing scale. You'll see how it works firsthand in the following section's exercises.

FIGURE 10.3
The Annotative
option in the Text
Style dialog box

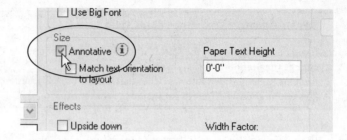

MAKING A STYLE THE DEFAULT

Once you've created a style, you can make it the default current style by selecting it from the Text
Style drop-down list in the Text panel.

Getting Familiar with the Text and Annotation Scale Control Panels

Before you get much further into AutoCAD's text features, take a moment to get familiar with
the Annotate tab's Text and Annotation Scaling panels (see Figure 10.4). You'll be using a few of
these panel tools in this chapter. If you need to, you can refer to this figure as you work through
the exercises.

FIGURE 10.4
The Text panel
(left) and the
Annotation Scaling
panel (right)

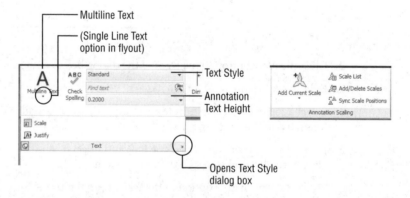

If your Annotation panel doesn't look like the one in this figure, hover over it and the panel
will expand to display the options.

Setting the Annotation Scale and Adding Text

You've got a text style set up and ready to use. Now you'll add some text to your unit plan.
Before you begin, you should determine a drawing scale. This is important because, with the

Annotative feature turned on, AutoCAD needs to know the drawing scale in order to set the size of the text. Follow these steps:

1. In the right side of the status bar, click the arrow next to Annotation Scale.

2. Select ¼″ = 1′-0″. Metric users, select 1:100.

You've just set the drawing scale for the Model view. This isn't a permanent setting; you can change it at any time, as you'll see later. The settings you used for the annotation scale are somewhat arbitrary for the purposes of demonstrating the Annotative Scale feature.

Finally, you can begin to add text:

1. Turn off the Object Snap tool in the status bar.

2. Click the Multiline Text tool in the Annotate tab's Text panel. You can also type **MT↵**. You see a prompt that tells you the current text style and height:

```
Current text style: "Note1" Text height: 4 13/16"
Annotative: Yes
Specify first corner:
```

3. Click the first point indicated in the top image in Figure 10.1 to start the text boundary window. This boundary window indicates the area in which to place the text. Notice the arrow near the bottom of the window: it indicates the direction of the text flow. You don't have to be too precise about where you select the points for the boundary because you can adjust the location and size later.

4. At the `Specify opposite corner or [Height/Justify/Line spacing/Rotation/Style/Width/Columns]:` prompt, click the second point indicated in the top image in Figure 10.1. The Text Editor tab appears, with the text editor superimposed over the area you just selected (Figure 10.5).

5. Click the text editor and type **Entry**. As you type, the word appears in the Text panel just as it will appear in your drawing.

6. Press ↵ to advance one line; then enter **6′ by 7′**.

7. Press ↵ to advance another line, and enter **[182 cm by 213 cm]**.

8. Press ↵ again to advance another line, and enter **carpet floor**.

9. Click Close Text Editor on the Close panel. The text appears in the drawing just as it did in the text editor. (See the bottom image in Figure 10.1.)

After you've added text, if the text doesn't quite fit in the area you've indicated, you can make adjustments to the text boundary. Click the text to expose the text boundary, including the boundary grips. Then click and drag the grips to resize the boundary. AutoCAD's word-wrap feature automatically adjusts the text formatting to fit the text boundary.

FIGURE 10.5
The text editor
floats over the
selected area.

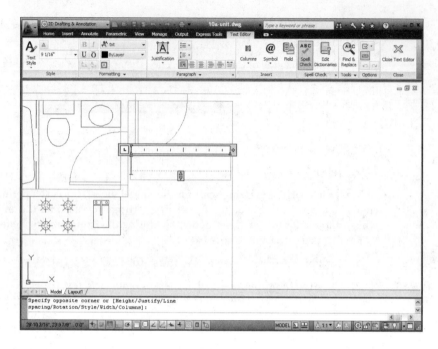

You may have noticed that the Text Editor tab and text editor work like any text editor; if you make a typing error, you can highlight the error and retype the letter or word. You can perform other word-processing functions too, such as using search and replace, importing text, and changing fonts.

You also saw that the text editor shows how your text will appear in the location you selected using the text boundary. If your view of the drawing is such that the text is too small to be legible, the text editor enlarges the text so you can read it clearly. Likewise, if you're zoomed in too closely to see the entire text, the text editor adjusts the text to enable you to see all of it.

MAKING TEXT READABLE OVER HATCH PATTERNS

If text is included in a selection where a hatch pattern is to be placed, AutoCAD automatically avoids hatching over the text. If you add text over a hatched area, you can use the Background Mask tool in the Text Editor tab to make the text more readable. Another option is to use the Add: Select Objects tool in the Hatch Edit dialog box to add text to a hatch selection.

Exploring Text and Scale

Even though your text height is 0.1″, or 0.15 cm, it appears at the appropriately enlarged size for the current scale. If the text were drawn to the size of 0.1″, it would be very small and barely visible. However, the Annotative Scale feature makes the adjustment to your text size based on the Annotation Scale setting.

You can see firsthand how the Annotation Scale setting affects your text:

1. First, make sure the Annotative Visibility tool is turned on in the status bar, or type **Annoallvisible.⏎ 1.⏎**.

2. Click the Annotation Scale setting, and select ½″ = 1′-0″. Metric users should select 1:50. The text changes to the appropriate size for the selected scale.

3. Click the Add/Delete Scales tool in the Annotate tab's Annotation Scaling panel, or enter **Objectscale.⏎**.

4. At the `Select annotative objects:` prompt, select the text, and press ⏎. You see the Annotation Object Scale dialog box (Figure 10.6) listing the two annotation scales you have used for this drawing.

FIGURE 10.6

The Annotation Object Scale dialog box

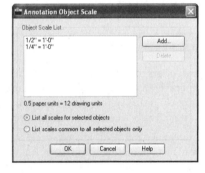

5. You can add additional scales to your text object by clicking the Add button, which opens the Add Scales To Object dialog box (Figure 10.7).

6. Click OK and then click OK again at the Annotation Object Scale dialog box.

FIGURE 10.7

The Add Scales To Object dialog box

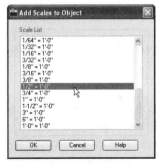

Now test your settings by changing the Annotation Scale value back to the previous setting:

1. In the status bar, click the Annotation Scale setting, and select ¼″ = 1′-0″. Metric users should select 1:100.

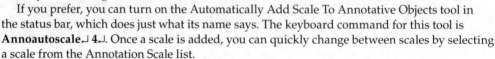

2. The text changes back to its original size.

In steps 2 through 5 of the first exercise in this section, you added a new annotation scale to the text. This is necessary for the text to be aware of the new annotation scale you want to use. Each time you include a new scale for your drawing, you need to add an annotation scale to the text in your drawing.

If you prefer, you can turn on the Automatically Add Scale To Annotative Objects tool in the status bar, which does just what its name says. The keyboard command for this tool is **Annoautoscale.**↵ **4**↵. Once a scale is added, you can quickly change between scales by selecting a scale from the Annotation Scale list.

TEXT AND SCALE IN LEGACY DRAWINGS

AutoCAD 2011 offers the Annotative Scale feature to automate the scaling of text and other objects to their proper size based on the drawing's annotation scale. But there is a good chance that you'll encounter drawings that were created before the Annotative Scale feature was available. For that reason, you should have a basic understanding of scale factors as they apply to text.

As you know by now, AutoCAD lets you draw at full scale; that is, you can represent distances as values equivalent to the actual size of the object. When you later plot the drawing, you tell AutoCAD the scale at which you want to plot and the program reduces the drawing accordingly. This gives you the freedom to enter measurements at full scale and not worry about converting them to various scales every time you enter a distance. Unfortunately, in earlier versions of AutoCAD, this feature created problems when users entered text and dimensions. You had to make the text height very large in order for it to be readable when scaled down.

To illustrate this point, imagine you're drawing the Unit plan at full size on a very large sheet of paper. When you're finished with this drawing, it will be reduced to a scale that enables it to fit on an 8.5″-×-11″ sheet of paper. So you have to make your text large to keep it legible after it's reduced. If you want text to appear 1/8″ high when the drawing is plotted, you must convert it to a considerably larger size when you draw it. To do this, you multiply the desired height of the final plotted text by a scale conversion factor. (See Chapter 3 for more on scale conversion factors.)

For example, if your drawing is at a 1/8″ = 1′-0″ scale, you multiply the desired text height, 1/8″, by the scale conversion factor of 96 to get a height of 12″. This is the height you must make your text to get 1/8″-high text in the final plot.

With AutoCAD 2011, you don't have to work through the math to get the right text size for your drawing. But if you encounter a drawing that was created in an earlier version of AutoCAD and you notice that the text size is very large, you'll know why.

So far, you've only used a single multiline text object. However, if you have many notes distributed throughout a drawing, you'll need to add an annotation scale to all of them before they can automatically adjust themselves to the different scales you'll use with your drawing. If you have the Automatically Add Scale To Annotative Objects tool turned on in the status bar, this happens automatically. Otherwise, you'll have to add the scales to each annotative object. This is easy to do because you have the option to select as many objects as you need when adding annotation scales.

Understanding the Text Style Dialog Box Options

You've just taken nearly all the steps you'll need to know to add text to any drawing. Now let's take a step back and look more closely at some of the finer points of adding text, starting with text styles. The following sections give you more detailed information about the text style settings you saw in the early part of this chapter. They explain those settings and their purposes. Some of them, such as Width Factor, can be quite useful. Others, such as the Backwards and Vertical options, are rarely used. Take a moment to study these settings to become familiar with what is available and make a mental note of these items for future reference.

Style

In the Styles list box you'll see a list showing the current style. This list also contains other styles that may be present in the drawing. The drop-down list below the Styles list box lets you control whether all styles are listed or just those that are being used in the drawing. In addition, there are the Set Current, New, and Delete buttons and options in the Font and Effects groups. You have already seen the Size group.

Set Current/New/Delete

New lets you create a new text style. Set Current makes the selected style the current one. Delete lets you delete the selected style.

The Delete option isn't available for the Standard style.

Font

In the Font group, you have the following options:

Font Name   Lets you select a font from a list of available fonts. The list is derived from the font resources available to Windows 7, Windows Vista, or Windows XP plus the standard AutoCAD fonts.

Font Style   Offers variations of a font, such as italic or bold, when they're available.

Use Big Font   Applicable to Asian fonts. This option is offered only with AutoCAD fonts.

Size

The Size group offers settings relating to text size, scale, and orientation.

Annotative   Causes the text size to automatically adjust to the current annotation scale setting.

Match Text Orientation To Layout Causes the text orientation to match the orientation of a layout view. This option is available only when the Annotative option is on.

Height/Paper Text Height Lets you enter a font size. With the Annotative option turned off, this option is named *Height* and will set the absolute height of the text. With the Annotative option turned on, it shows *Paper Text Height* and will set the height of the text when printed. A 0 height has special meaning when you use the Dtext command to enter text, as described later in this chapter.

EFFECTS

In the Effects group, you have the following options:

Upside Down Displays text upside down.

Backwards Displays text backward.

Vertical Displays text in a vertical column.

Width Factor Adjusts the width and spacing of the characters in the text. A value of 1 keeps the text at its normal width. Values greater than 1 expand the text, and values less than 1 compress the text.

> This is the Simplex font expanded by 1.4
> This is the simplex font using a width factor of 1
> This is the simplex font compressed by .6

Oblique Angle Skews the text at an angle. When this option is set to a value greater than 0, the text appears italicized. A value of less than 0 (–12, for example) causes the text to lean to the left.

> *This is the simplex font*
> *using a 12–degree oblique angle*

You can also set the width factor and oblique angle directly for text using the Width Factor and Oblique Angle tools in the expanded Formatting panel under the Text Editor Ribbon panel. This tab is available when you create new text or double-click existing text.

RENAMING A TEXT STYLE OR OTHER NAMED OBJECT

If you need to rename a text style or other named object in AutoCAD, you can do so using the Rename command. Enter **Ren.⏎** at the Command prompt to open the Rename dialog box. In the Named Objects list box to the left, choose Text Styles. Click the name of the style you want to change from the Items list on the right; the name appears in the Old Name input box below the list. In the input box next to the Rename To button, enter the new name. Click the Rename To button, and click OK.

Exploring Text Formatting in AutoCAD

You've seen how you can set up a style and make scale adjustments. AutoCAD also offers a wide range of text-formatting options that are typical of most word-processing programs. You can control fonts, text height, justification, line spacing, and width. You can even include special characters such as degree symbols or stacked fractions. With these additional formatting tools, you can make adjustments to the text style with which you started.

Adjusting the Text Height and Font

To get some firsthand experience using the text-formatting tools in AutoCAD, try the following exercise. You'll use the Multiline Text tool again, but this time you'll get to try out some of its other features.

In this exercise, you'll see how you can adjust the size and font of text in the editor:

1. Pan your view so the kitchen is just at the top of the drawing, as shown in the first image in Figure 10.8.

FIGURE 10.8
Placing the text-boundary window for the living-room label and the final label

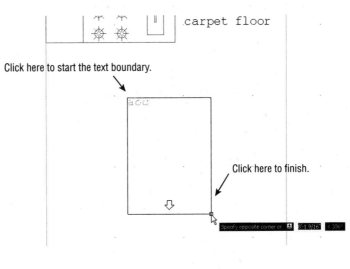

Multiline Text

2. In the status bar, set the Annotation Scale setting back to ¼″ = 1′-0″ (1:100 for metric users).

3. Click the Multiline Text tool on the Annotation tab's Text panel, and then select a text boundary window, as shown in the first image in Figure 10.8.

4. In the text editor, type the following:

```
Living Room
14´-0˝ by 16´-5˝ [427 cm by 500 cm]
```

Make sure you press ⏎ after *Living Room*, but make the rest of the text a continuous string. As you type, the words wrap. AutoCAD uses word wrap to fit the text inside the text boundary area.

5. Highlight the text *14′-0″ by 16′-5″ [427 cm by 500 cm]* as you would in any word processor. For example, you can click the end of the line to place the cursor there and then Shift+click the beginning of the line to highlight the whole line.

6. In the Text Editor tab's Style panel, click in the Text Height text box and enter **1/16**. Metric users, enter **0.08**. The highlighted text changes to a smaller size.

7. Highlight the words *Living Room*.

8. In the Formatting panel, click the Font drop-down list to display a list of font options.

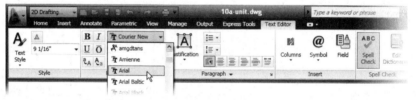

9. Scroll up the list until you find Arial. The text in the text editor changes to reflect the new font.

10. With the words *Living Room* still highlighted, click the Underline button in the Formatting panel.

Close Text Editor

11. Click Close Text Editor in the Close panel. The label appears in the area you indicated in step 3 (see the bottom image in Figure 10.8).

12. To see how you can go back to the Text Editor tab, double-click the text. The Text Editor tab and text editor appear, enabling you to change the text.

13. Click Close Text Editor in the Close panel.

While using the Multiline Text tool, you may have noticed the [Height/Justify/Line spacing/Rotation/Style/Width/Columns]: prompt immediately after you picked the first point of the text boundary. You can use any of these options to make on-the-fly modifications to the height, justification, line spacing, rotation style, or width of the multiline text.

For example, after clicking the first point for the text boundary, you can type **R**↵ and then specify a rotation angle for the text window, either graphically with a rubber-banding line or by entering an angle value. After you've entered a rotation angle, you can resume selecting the text boundary.

Understanding the Text Formatting Toolbar

You've just experimented with a few of the Text Formatting features of the Text Editor tab. A variety of additional formatting tools are available. Figure 10.9 shows where these tools are, and Table 10.1 describes their uses. They're fairly straightforward, and if you've used other word-processing programs, you should find them easy to use. Most are common to the majority of word processors, although a few—such as Symbol, Oblique Angle, and Width Factor—are unique to AutoCAD. Look at Table 10.1 and see if there are any tools you think you'll find useful.

FIGURE 10.9
Additional features of the Text Editor tab

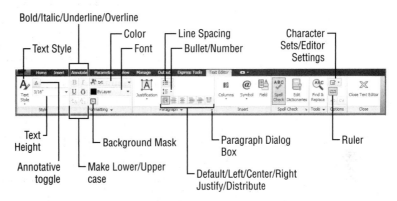

TABLE 10.1: Text formatting tools

TOOL	USE
Text Style	Select a text style.
Annotative	Turn the Annotative feature on or off.
Text Height	Set the "Paper text height" of text currently being entered or edited.
Bold/Italic/Underline/Overline	Select text, and then select one of these options to add bold, italic, underline, or overline to the text.
Color	Select text, and then choose a color from this drop-down list.
Font	Select a font different from the font for the current text style.
Background Mask	This tool gives you control over the background mask feature, which places a background behind text to make it more readable when placed over hatch patterns.
Make Lower/Upper Case	Change the case of text.

TABLE 10.1:   Text formatting tools *(CONTINUED)*

TOOL	USE
Line Spacing	Set the line spacing in paragraphs. You can also set line spacing in the Properties palette for an Mtext object or by using the Paragraph dialog box. (See "Setting Indents and Tabs" later in this chapter.)
Bullet and Numbering	Select a text list, click this tool, and then select Lettered, Numbered, or Bulleted to add letters, numbers, or bullets to the list.
Default/Left/Center/Right / Justify/Distribute	Click the appropriate tool to align the text to the left, center, or right side of the text boundary. Justify adds space between words to force left and right alignment. Distribute adds space between letters to force left and right alignment.
Paragraph	Paragraph opens a dialog box which lets you set up paragraph formatting, including tabs, indents, and paragraph spacing.
Columns	Indicate the number of columns and how the columns are set up.
Symbol	Place the cursor at a location for the symbol, and then click the Symbol tool to find and add a symbol. (See Figure 10.10, later in this chapter, for the available symbols.)
Field	Click to open the Field dialog box where you can add a text field. See "Adding Formulas to Cells," in Chapter 11, for more about fields.
Character Sets/Editor Settings	Character Sets offers foreign language characters such as Cyrillic or Greek, for example. Editor Settings offers settings for the text editor.
Ruler	Click to turn the ruler at the top of the Text panel on or off.

Adding Symbols and Special Characters

The Text Editor tab also offers a tool called Symbol. This tool lets you add special symbols common to technical drawing and drafting. Figure 10.10 shows the symbols that are offered in the Symbol tool in the form of a drop-down list.

At the bottom of the Symbol drop-down list is an option called Other. By clicking the Other option, you open the Windows Character Map dialog box (Figure 10.11). Characters such as the trademark (™) and copyright (©) symbols are often available in the fonts offered in the Character Map. The contents of the Symbol drop-down list depend on the font currently selected.

The Character Map dialog box is a Windows accessory. If it doesn't appear when you choose Other from the Text Formatting Symbol tool menu, you may need to install the Character Map from your Windows installation CD.

Finally, if your application requires music, math, astronomy, Greek, or other symbols, AutoCAD offers a set of fonts with special symbols. Figure 10.17, later in the chapter, shows these fonts and the symbols they contain. You can set up text styles with these fonts or call them up directly from the Formatting Panel's Font option.

FIGURE 10.10

Symbols offered by the Symbol option. (See Symbol in Table 10.1 for information about how to use these symbols.)

Degree	$x°$	Identity	≡
Plus/Minus	±	Initial Length	⌀⟋
Diameter	⌀	Monument Line	ℳℒ
Almost Equal	≈	Not Equal	≠
Angle	∠	Ohm	Ω
Boundary Line	ℬℒ	Omega	Ω
Center Line	℄	Property Line	ℛ
Delta	Δ	Subscript 2	x_2
Electrical Phase	Φ	Squared	x^2
Flow Line	ℱℒ	Cubed	x^3

FIGURE 10.11

The Character Map

Text Justification and Osnaps

You may have noticed that the object-justification list offers three center options: Top Center, Middle Center, and Bottom Center. All three of these options have the same effect on the text's appearance, but they each have a different effect on how osnaps act on the text. Figure 10.12 shows where the osnap point occurs on a text boundary depending on which justification option is selected. A multiline text object has only one insertion point on its boundary, which you can access with the Insert osnap.

The osnap point also appears as an extra grip point on the text boundary when you click the text. If you click the text you just entered, you'll see that a grip point now appears at the top center of the text boundary.

Knowing where the osnap points occur can be helpful when you want to align the text with other objects in your drawing. In most cases, you can use the grips to align your text boundary, but the Top Center and Middle Center justification options enable you to use the center and middle portions of your text to align the text with other objects.

FIGURE 10.12
The location of the
Insert osnap point
on a text boundary,
based on its justifi-
cation setting

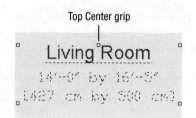

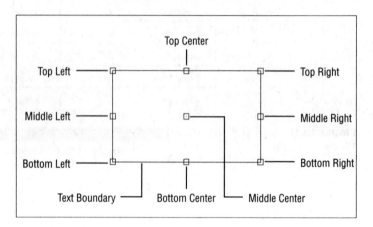

CHANGING JUSTIFICATION OF MULTIPLE TEXT OBJECTS

You've seen how you can change the justification of an individual text object, but you'll often find that you need to change the justification of several text objects at one time. AutoCAD offers the Justifytext command for this purpose. To use it, click the Justify tool in the Annotate tab's expanded Text panel, or type **Justifytext**↵ at the Command prompt. At the Select objects: prompt, select the text you want to change, and then press ↵ to confirm your selection. You'll see the following prompt in the command line (or at the cursor if Dynamic Input is on):

```
[Left/Align/Fit/Center/Middle/Right/TL/TC/TR/ML/MC/MR/BL/BC/BR] <Left>:
```

Enter the letters corresponding to the type of justification you want to use for the text. (See the section "Justifying Single-Line Text Objects" later in this chapter for a description of these options.) After you enter an option, the selected text changes to conform to the selected justification option.

Setting Indents and Tabs

You should also know about the indent and tab features of the text editor. You may have noticed the ruler at the top of the text editor. Figure 10.13 shows that ruler, including tab and indent markers.

The indent markers let you control the indention of the first line and the rest of the paragraph. The tab markers give you control over tab spacing. For new text, the tab markers don't appear until you add them by clicking the ruler. The following exercises will demonstrate the use of these markers more clearly.

FIGURE 10.13

The ruler at the top of the text editor lets you quickly set tabs and indents for text.

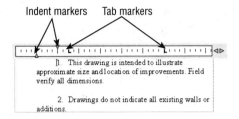

Start by practicing with the indent markers:

1. Save the Unit drawing, and then open the indent.dwg file. This file contains some text you'll experiment with.

2. Double-click the text at the top of the drawing to open the Text Editor tab.

3. Press Ctrl+A to highlight all the text in the text editor. This is necessary to indicate the text group to be affected by your indent settings.

4. Click and drag the top indent marker two spaces to the right. The indent of the first line moves with the marker. A note appears above the ruler showing you how much indent you're applying. Also notice that the text at the first tab remains at its starting location.

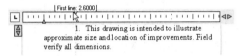

5. Click and drag the bottom indent marker two spaces to the left. The rest of the paragraph moves with the marker. Again, you see a note by the ruler showing how much indent you're applying.

Close
Text Editor

6. Click the Close Text Editor tool in the Text Editor tab to exit.

Here you see how you can control the indents of the selected text with the indent markers. You can set paragraphs of a single Mtext object differently, giving you a wide range of indent-formatting possibilities. Just select the text you want to set, and then adjust the indent markers.

Now try the tab markers. For this exercise, you'll try the text-import feature to import a tab-delimited text file:

Multiline
Text

1. Click the Multiline Text tool on the Annotate tab's Text panel.

2. For the first corner of the text boundary, click the upper-left corner of the large rectangle in the drawing, just below the paragraph.

3. For the opposite corner of the text boundary, click the lower-right corner of the rectangle.

4. Right-click in the text editor, and select Import Text.

5. In the Select File dialog box, locate and select the tabtest.txt file and then click Open. The contents of the tabtest.txt file are displayed in the text editor.

The file you just imported was generated from the Attribute Extraction Wizard in AutoCAD. You'll learn more about this feature in Chapter 13. This file contains tabs to align the columns of information. You can adjust those tabs in the Text Formatting toolbar, as you'll see in the next set of steps.

Now use the tab markers to adjust the tab spacing of the columns of text:

1. Press Ctrl+A to select all the text.

2. Click the ruler at a point that is at the 12th mark from the left (that's three of the taller tick marks in the ruler). An L-shaped marker appears, and the first tab column of text moves to this position.

3. Click the ruler again at the 20th mark. The second tab column aligns to this position.

4. Continue to click the ruler to add more tab markers so the text looks similar to Figure 10.14. Don't worry about being exact; this is just for practice. After you've placed a marker, you can click and drag it to make adjustments.

FIGURE 10.14
Add tab markers so your text looks similar to this figure.

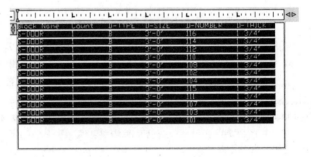

5. Click Close Text Editor in the Text Editor tab's Close panel. The text appears in the drawing as a door schedule.

Here you saw how you can create a table or a schedule from an imported text file. You can also create a schedule from scratch by composing it directly in the text editor of the Multiline Text command. AutoCAD also offers the Table feature, which is specifically designed for creating tables (see Chapter 11). Still, this example offers a way to demonstrate the tab feature in the Multiline Text tool, and you may encounter a file in which a table is formatted in the way described here.

In addition to using the indent and tab markers on the ruler, you can control indents and tabs through the Paragraph dialog box. Do the following to get a firsthand look:

1. Double-click the text at the top of the indent.dwg drawing (the one you edited in the first part of this section), and then press Ctrl+A to select all the text.

2. Right-click the ruler above the text editor, and select Paragraph to open the Paragraph dialog box (Figure 10.15). The Paragraph dialog box also lets you set other paragraph settings, such as alignment, spacing between paragraphs, and line spacing in the paragraph.

FIGURE 10.15

The Paragraph dialog box

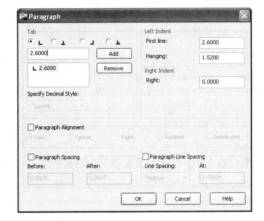

3. Change the value in the First Line input box to **1.5** and the Hanging input box to **2.2**.

4. Double-click the tab position input box in the upper-left corner, just below the row of tab symbols in the Tab group. Enter **2.2,** and click the Add button.

5. Click OK. The text now appears with the text indented from the numbers.

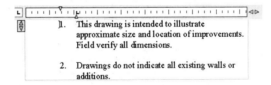

6. Click the Close Text Editor tool in the Close panel. The text in the drawing is now formatted as it appeared in the text editor of the Text Formatting toolbar.

7. Exit but do not save the indent.dwg file.

In this exercise, you used the Paragraph dialog box to set the paragraph indent and the first tab marker to be the same value. This causes the text portion of the list to be aligned at a distance of 2.2 drawing units from the left text boundary, leaving the list number extended farther to the left. This gives the list a more professional appearance.

SETTING EXACT MTEXT WIDTH AND HEIGHT

You may have noticed the Set Mtext Width and Set Mtext Height right-click shortcut menu options in step 2 of the preceding exercise. The Set Mtext Width option opens a dialog box that enables you to enter a width for the text boundary for situations where you need an exact width. You can also click and drag the right inside edge of the ruler to change the text-boundary width.

The Paragraph dialog box gives you fine control over the formatting of your text. It lets you delete tabs by highlighting them in the list and clicking the Remove button. You can also add tabs at specific distances from the left margin of the text boundary by entering new tab locations in the Tab input box and clicking the Add button.

You specify distances in drawing units. If your drawing is set up to use architectural units, for example, you can enter values in feet and inches or just inches. In the First Line and Hanging input boxes, you enter a numeric value for paragraph indents. As you've just seen, you can use the First Line and Hanging input boxes to create a numbered list by setting the Hanging input box value to be the same as the first tab stop position.

What Do the Fonts Look Like?

You've already seen a few of the fonts available in AutoCAD. Chances are you're familiar with the TrueType fonts available in Windows. You have some additional AutoCAD fonts from which to choose. You may want to stick with the AutoCAD fonts for all but your presentation drawings because other fonts can consume more memory.

Figure 10.16 shows the basic AutoCAD text fonts. The Romans font is perhaps the most widely used because it offers a reasonable appearance while consuming little memory. Figure 10.17 lists some of the symbols and Greek fonts.

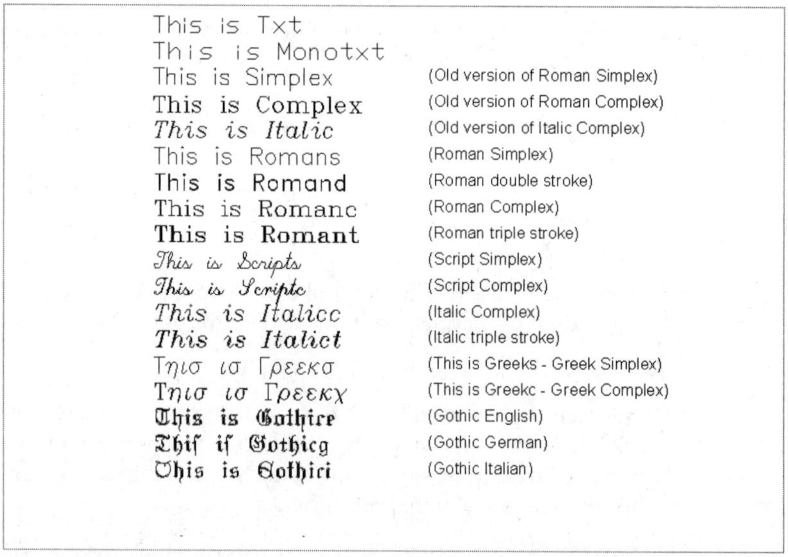

FIGURE 10.16
Some of the standard AutoCAD text fonts

This is Txt	
This is Monotxt	
This is Simplex	(Old version of Roman Simplex)
This is Complex	(Old version of Roman Complex)
This is Italic	(Old version of Italic Complex)
This is Romans	(Roman Simplex)
This is Romand	(Roman double stroke)
This is Romanc	(Roman Complex)
This is Romant	(Roman triple stroke)
This is Scripts	(Script Simplex)
This is Scriptc	(Script Complex)
This is Italicc	(Italic Complex)
This is Italict	(Italic triple stroke)
Τηισ ισ Γρεεκσ	(This is Greeks - Greek Simplex)
Τηισ ισ Γρεεκχ	(This is Greekc - Greek Complex)
This is Gothice	(Gothic English)
Thif if Gothicg	(Gothic German)
This is Gothici	(Gothic Italian)

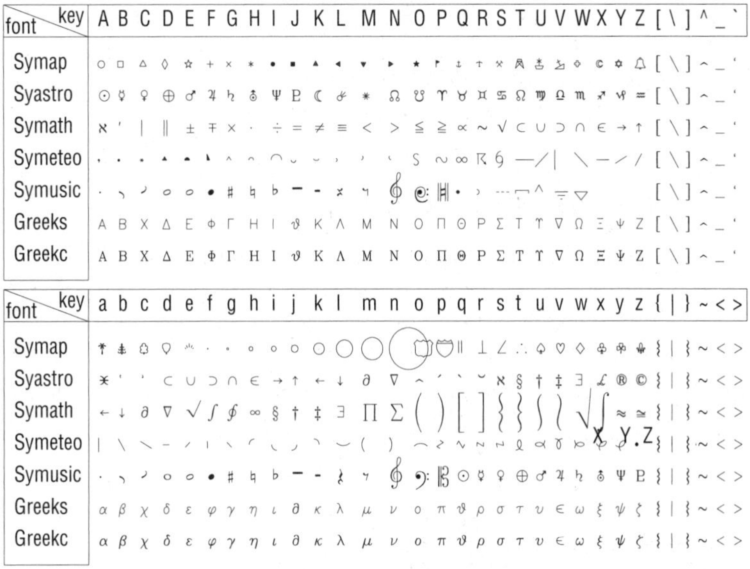

FIGURE 10.17

Some of the Auto-
CAD symbols and
Greek fonts

IMPORTING TEXT FILES

With multiline text objects, AutoCAD enables you to import ASCII text or Rich Text Format (RTF) files. RTF files can be exported from Microsoft Word and most other word-processing programs and retain most of their formatting in AutoCAD. Here's how you import text files:

1. With the Multiline Text Editor open, right-click in the text area, and choose Import Text.

2. In the Select File dialog box, locate a valid text file. It must be a file in either a raw text (ASCII) format, such as a Notepad (.txt) file, or RTF (.rtf). RTF files can store formatting information such as boldface and varying point sizes.

3. After you've highlighted the file you want, double-click it or click Open. The text appears in the Mtext Editor window.

4. Click the Close Text Editor button, and the text appears in your drawing.

In addition, you can use the Windows Clipboard and the Cut and Paste functions to add text to a drawing. To do this, follow these steps:

1. While in a word processor such as Microsoft Word or the Windows WordPad, select some text, and then choose Cut or Copy in any Windows program to place the text on the Windows Clipboard.

2. Open AutoCAD. Right-click in the drawing area and choose Paste from the Home tab's Clipboard panel; the pasted text appears in your drawing. However, it isn't editable in AutoCAD.

If the text is from a text editor like Windows Notepad, the text is inserted as AutoCAD text. If the text contains formatting from a word processor, like Microsoft Word, the text is an OLE object.

Because AutoCAD is an OLE client, you can also attach other types of documents to an AutoCAD drawing file. See Chapter 20 for more on AutoCAD's OLE support.

In the following sections, you'll work with some of the AutoCAD fonts. You can see samples of all the fonts, including TrueType fonts, in the preview window of the Text Style dialog box. If you use a word processor, you're probably familiar with at least some of the TrueType fonts available in Windows and AutoCAD.

THE TEXTFILL SYSTEM VARIABLE

Unlike the standard sticklike AutoCAD fonts, TrueType and PostScript fonts have filled areas. These filled areas take more time to generate, so if you use these fonts for a lot of text, your redraw and regen times will increase. To help reduce redraw and regen times, you can set AutoCAD to display and plot these fonts as outline fonts while still printing them as solid fonts.

To change this setting, type **Textfill**↵, and then type **0**↵. Doing so turns off text fill for PostScript and TrueType fonts. (This is the same as setting the Textfill system variable to 0.)

Adding Simple Single-Line Text Objects

You might find that you're entering a lot of single words or simple labels that don't require all the bells and whistles of the Multiline Text Editor. AutoCAD offers the *single-line text object*, which is simpler to use and can speed text entry if you're adding only small pieces of text.

Continue the tutorial on the Unit.dwg file by trying the following exercise:

1. Adjust your view so you see the part of the drawing shown in Figure 10.18.

FIGURE 10.18
Adding simple labels to the kitchen and bath by using the Dtext command

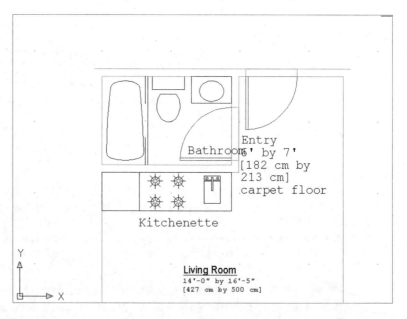

2. Make sure Note1 is the current text style, and then, from the Multiline Text flyout on the Annotate tab's Text panel, click the Single Line tool, or enter **Dt**↵.

3. At the Specify start point of text or [Justify/Style]: prompt, pick the starting point for the text you're about to enter, just below the kitchen at coordinate 17′-2″,22′-5″ (490,664 for metric users). Note that the prompt offers the Justify and Style options.

4. At the Specify rotation angle of text <0>: prompt, press ↵ to accept the default, 0. You can specify any angle you like at this prompt (for example, if you want your text aligned with a rotated object). You see a text I-beam cursor at the point you picked in step 3.

5. Type **Kitchenette**. As you type, the word appears directly in the drawing.

PASTING TEXT FROM OTHER SOURCES

You can cut and paste text from the Clipboard into the cursor location by using the Ctrl+V keyboard shortcut or by right-clicking in the drawing area to access the shortcut menu.

---

6. You can press ↵ to move the cursor down to start a new line below the one you just entered.

7. This time, you want to label the bathroom. Pick a point to the right of the door swing; you can approximate the location since you can always adjust the text location later. The text cursor moves to that point.

8. Type **Bathroom**↵. Figure 10.18 shows how your drawing should look now.

9. Press ↵ again to exit the Dtext command.

CONTINUING WHERE YOU LEFT OFF

If for some reason you need to stop entering single-line text objects to do something else in AutoCAD, you can continue the text where you left off by starting the Dtext command and then pressing ↵ at the Specify start point of text or [Justify/Style]: prompt. The text continues immediately below the last line of text entered.

Here you were able to add two single lines of text in different parts of your drawing fairly quickly. Dtext uses the current default text style settings.

To edit single-line text, you can double-click the text. The text is highlighted, and you can begin typing to replace it all, or you can click a location in the text to make single word or character changes.

This is the end of the tutorial section of this chapter. The rest of this chapter offers additional information about text.

Justifying Single-Line Text Objects

Justifying single-line text objects is slightly different than justifying multiline text. For example, if you change the justification setting to Center, the text moves so the center is placed at the text-insertion point. In other words, the insertion point stays in place while the text location adjusts to the new justification setting. Figure 10.19 shows the relationship between single-line text and the insertion point based on different justification settings.

FIGURE 10.19
Text inserted using the various justification options

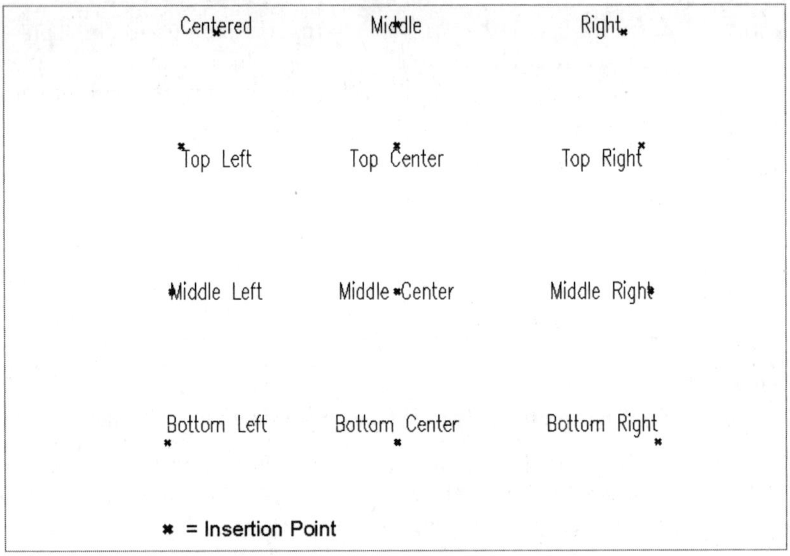

To set the justification of text as you enter it, you must enter **J↵** at the `Specify start point of text or [Justify/Style]:` prompt after issuing the Dtext command. You can also change the current default style by entering **S↵** and then the name of the style at the `Specify start point of text or [Justify/Style]:` prompt.

After you've issued Dtext's Justify option, you get the following prompt:

```
Enter an option
[Align/Fit/Center/Middle/Right/TL/TC/TR/ML/MC/MR/BL/BC/BR]:
```

Here are descriptions of each of these options. (I've left Fit and Align until last because they require more explanation.)

Center   Centers the text on the start point with the baseline on the start point.

Middle   Centers the text on the start point with the baseline slightly below the start point.

Right   Justifies the text to the right of the start point with the baseline on the start point.

TL, TC, and TR   TL, TC, and TR stand for Top Left, Top Center, and Top Right. When you use these justification styles, the text appears entirely below the start point, justified left, center, or right, depending on which option you choose.

ML, MC, and MR   ML, MC, and MR stand for Middle Left, Middle Center, and Middle Right. These styles are similar to TL, TC, and TR except that the start point determines a location midway between the baseline and the top of the lowercase letters of the text.

BL, BC, and BR   BL, BC, and BR stand for Bottom Left, Bottom Center, and Bottom Right. These styles too are similar to TL, TC, and TR, but here the start point determines the bottommost location of the letters of the text (the bottom of letters that have descenders, such as *p*, *q*, and *g*).

Align and Fit   With the Align and Fit justification options, you must specify a dimension in which the text is to fit. For example, suppose you want the word *Refrigerator* to fit in the 26″-wide box representing the refrigerator. You can use either the Fit or the Align option to accomplish this. With Fit, AutoCAD prompts you to select start and end points and then stretches or compresses the letters to fit within the two points you specify. You use this option when the text must be a consistent height throughout the drawing and you don't care about distorting the font. Align works like Fit, but instead of maintaining the current text style height, the Align option adjusts the text height to keep it proportional to the text width without distorting the font. Use this option when it's important to maintain the font's shape and proportion. Figure 10.20 demonstrates how Fit and Align work.

FIGURE 10.20
The word *Refrigerator* as it appears normally and with the Fit and Align options selected

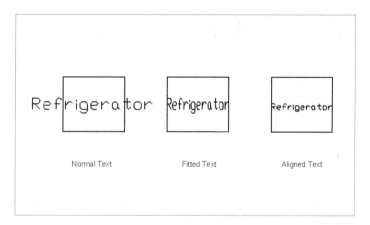

Normal Text   Fitted Text   Aligned Text

[A] Justify

You can change the justification of single-line text by using the Properties palette, but the text moves from its original location while maintaining its insertion point. If you want to change the justification of text without moving the text, you can use the Justifytext command. Click the Justify tool in the Annotate tab's expanded Text panel, or type **Justifytext** at the Command prompt, and then select the text you want to change. Justifytext works on both multiline and single-line text.

KEEPING TEXT FROM MIRRORING

At times, you'll want to mirror a group of objects that contain some text. This operation causes the mirrored text to appear backward. You can change a setting in AutoCAD to make the text read normally even when it's mirrored:

1. At the Command prompt, enter **Mirrtext**↵.

2. At the Enter new value for MIRRTEXT <1>: prompt, enter **0**↵.

Now any mirrored text that isn't in a block will read normally. The text's position, however, will still be mirrored, as shown in the following example. Mirrtext is set to 0 by default.

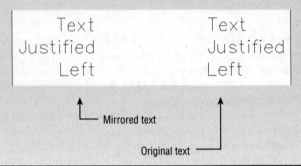

Mirrored text

Original text

Using Special Characters with Single-Line Text Objects

Just as with multiline text, you can add a limited set of special characters to single-line text objects. For example, you can place the degree symbol (°) after a number, or you can *underscore* (underline) text. To accomplish this, you use double percent signs (%%)in conjunction with a special code. For example, to underscore text, you enclose that text with %% followed by the letter *u*, which is the underscore code. So to create this text, "This is underscored text," you enter the following at the prompt:

    This is %%uunderscored%%u text.

Overscoring (putting a line above the text) operates in the same manner. To insert codes for symbols, you place the codes in the correct positions for the symbols they represent. For example, to enter 100.5°, you type **100.5%%d**. Table 10.2 shows some other examples of special character codes.

TABLE 10.2   Special Character Codes

CODE	WHAT IT DOES
%%o	Toggles overscore on and off.
%%u	Toggles underscore on and off.
%%c	Places a diameter symbol where the code occurs.

TABLE 10.2   Special Character Codes *(CONTINUED)*

CODE	WHAT IT DOES
%%d	Places a degree sign (°) where the code occurs.
%%p	Places a plus/minus sign where the code occurs.
%%%	Forces a single percent sign. This is useful when you want a double percent sign to appear or when you want a percent sign in conjunction with another code.
%%*nnn*	Allows the use of extended characters or Unicode characters when these characters are available for a given font. *nnn* is the three-digit value representing the ASCII extended character code.

USING THE CHARACTER MAP DIALOG BOX TO ADD SPECIAL CHARACTERS

You can add special characters to a single line of text in the same way you add special characters to multiline text. You may recall that to access special characters, you use the Character Map dialog box.

To open the Character Map dialog box, choose Start ➤ All Programs ➤ Accessories ➤ System Tools ➤ Character Map. You can then use the procedure discussed in the section "Adding Symbols and Special Characters" earlier in this chapter to cut and paste a character from the Character Map dialog box. If you use the Character Map dialog box often, create a shortcut for it and place the shortcut in your Start menu or on your Desktop.

Using the Check Spelling Feature

Although AutoCAD is primarily a drawing program, you'll find that some of your drawings contain more text than graphics. Autodesk recognizes this fact and has included a spelling checker since AutoCAD Release 14. If you've ever used the spelling checker in a typical word processor, such as Microsoft Word, the AutoCAD spelling checker's operation will be familiar to you. These steps show you how it works:

1. Click the Check Spelling tool in the Annotate tab's Text panel. You can also type **Sp**↵. The Check Spelling dialog box appears (Figure 10.21).

FIGURE 10.21
The Check
Spelling dialog

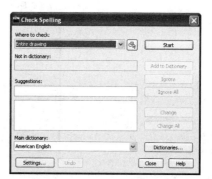

2. You can click the Start button to check the spelling in the entire drawing. Or, if you prefer, you can be more selective of the text you want to check by choosing an option from the Where To Check drop-down list. You can select a mixture of multiline and single-line text as well as dimension text, attributes, and text in Xrefs.

When the spelling checker finds a word it doesn't recognize, the Check Spelling dialog box shows you the word along with a suggested spelling. If the spelling checker finds more than one spelling, a list of suggested alternate words appears below the input box. You can then highlight the desired replacement and click the Change button to change the misspelled word, or you can click Change All to change all occurrences of the word in the selected text. If the suggested word is inappropriate, choose another word from the replacement list (if any) or enter your own spelling in the Suggestions input box. Then click Change or Change All.

Here is a list of the options available in the Check Spelling dialog box:

Add To Dictionary   Adds the word in question to the current dictionary.

Ignore   Skips the word.

Ignore All   Skips all occurrences of the word in the text being checked.

Change   Changes the word in question to the word you've selected from (or entered into) the Suggestions input box.

Change All   Changes all occurrences of the current word when there are multiple instances of the misspelling.

Dictionaries   Lets you use a different dictionary to check spelling. This option opens the Dictionaries dialog box, described in the upcoming section.

The Check Spelling feature includes types of notations that are more likely to be found in technical drawings. It also checks the spelling of text that is included in block definitions.

Choosing a Dictionary

Clicking the Dictionaries button in the Check Spelling dialog box opens the Dictionaries dialog box (Figure 10.22), where you can select a particular main dictionary for foreign languages or create or choose a custom dictionary. The names of main dictionary files have the .dct extension. The main dictionary for the U.S. version of AutoCAD is Enu.dct.

FIGURE 10.22
Choosing a
dictionary

In the Dictionaries dialog box, you can also add or delete words from a custom dictionary. Custom dictionary files are ASCII files with names that end with the .cus extension. Because they're ASCII files, you can edit them outside of AutoCAD. Click the Current Custom Dictionary drop-down list to view a list of existing custom dictionaries.

If you prefer, you can select a main or custom dictionary by using the Dctmain system variable. Click the Help button and search for Dctmain for more on the Dctmain system variable.

You can also select a dictionary from the Files tab of the Options dialog box (Figure 10.23; choose Options from the Application menu). You can find the dictionary list under Text Editor, Dictionary, And Font File Names. Click the plus sign next to this item, and then click the plus sign next to the Main Dictionary item to display the dictionary options. From here, you can double-click the dictionary you prefer.

FIGURE 10.23
Choosing a dictionary via the Options dialog box

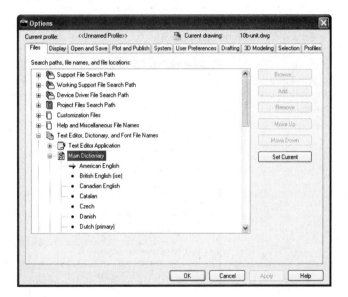

Substituting Fonts

At times, you'll want to change all the fonts in a drawing quickly. For instance, you might want to convert TrueType fonts into a simple Txt.shx font to help shorten redraw times while you're editing. Or you might need to convert the font of a drawing received from another office to a font that conforms to your own office standards. The Fontmap system variable works in conjunction with a font-mapping table, enabling you to substitute fonts in a drawing easily.

The font-mapping table is an ASCII file called Acad.fmp which is located in the C:\Documents and Settings\User Name\Application Data\Autodesk\AutoCAD 2011\R18.1\enu\Support folder. You can also use a file you create yourself. You can give this file any name you choose, as long as it has the .fmp extension.

This font-mapping table contains one line for each font substitution you want AutoCAD to make. A typical line in this file reads as follows:

```
romant; C:\Program Files\Autodesk\AutoCAD 2011\Fonts\txt.shx
```

In this example, AutoCAD is directed to use the txt.shx font in place of the romant.shx font. To execute this substitution, you type **Fontmap**↵ *Fontmap_filename*.

Fontmap_filename is the font-mapping table you created. This tells AutoCAD where to look for the font-mapping information. Then you issue the Regen command to view the font changes. To disable the font-mapping table, type this:

Fontmap↵ .↵

You can also specify a font-mapping file in the Files tab of the Options dialog box. Look for the Text Editor, Dictionary, And Font File Names listing. Click the plus sign next to this listing, and then click the plus sign next to the Font Mapping File listing to display the name and location of the current default font-mapping file. If you hold the cursor over the name, AutoCAD displays the full location of the file (Figure 10.24).

You can double-click this filename to open the Select A File dialog box. From there, you can select a different font-mapping file.

FIGURE 10.24
AutoCAD shows the full path to the font-mapping file.

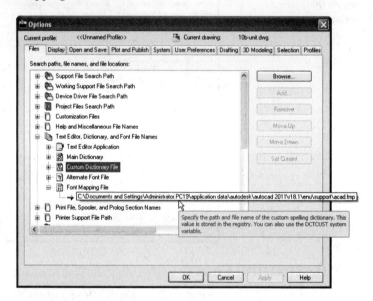

Finding and Replacing Text

One of the most time-consuming tasks in drafting is replacing text that appears repeatedly throughout a drawing. Fortunately, you have a Find And Replace tool to help simplify this task. AutoCAD's Find And Replace works like any other find-and-replace tool in a word-processing program. A few options work specifically with AutoCAD. Here's how it works:

1. Enter the text you want to locate in the Find Text input box located in the middle of the Annotate tab's Text panel (Figure 10.25), and then click the magnifying glass to the right. The Find And Replace dialog box opens and the drawing area displays the part where the text has been found.

2. Enter the replacement text in the Replace With input box.

3. When you've made certain that this is the text you want to change, click Replace. If you want to replace all occurrences of the text in the drawing, click Replace All.

4. If you want to skip over the found text, click Find Next to locate the next instance of the text in your drawing. If text is not found, AutoCAD returns to your original view.

MAKING SUBSTITUTIONS FOR MISSING FONTS

When text styles are created, the associated fonts don't become part of the drawing file. Instead, AutoCAD loads the needed font file at the same time the drawing is loaded. If a text style in a drawing requires a particular font, AutoCAD looks for the font in the AutoCAD search path; if the font is there, it's loaded. Usually this isn't a problem if the drawing file uses the standard fonts that come with AutoCAD or Windows. But occasionally, you'll encounter a file that uses a custom font.

In earlier versions of AutoCAD, you saw an error message when you attempted to open such a file. This missing-font message often sent new AutoCAD users into a panic.

Fortunately, AutoCAD automatically substitutes an existing font for the missing font in a drawing. By default, AutoCAD substitutes the simplex.shx font, but you can specify another font by using the Fontalt system variable. Type **Fontalt**↵ at the Command prompt, and then enter the name of the font you want to use as the substitute.

You can also select an alternate font through the Files tab of the Options dialog box. Locate the Text Editor, Dictionary, And Font File Names listing, and then click the plus sign at the left. Locate the Alternate Font File item, and click the plus sign at the left. The current alternate is listed. You can double-click the font name to select a different font through the Alternate Font dialog box.

Be aware that the text in your drawing will change in appearance, sometimes radically, when you use a substitute font. If the text in the drawing must retain its appearance, substitute a font that is as similar in appearance to the original font as possible.

You can also enter **Find**↵ at the Command prompt to open the Find And Replace dialog box and then enter the text you want in the Find What text box.

FIGURE 10.25
Using Find
And Replace

You can also limit your find-and-replace operation to a specific set of objects in your drawing by choosing Selected Objects from the Find Where drop-down list. Once you've selected this option, click the Select Objects tool in the upper-right corner of the Find And Replace dialog box (Figure 10.26).

FIGURE 10.26
The Select
Objects tool

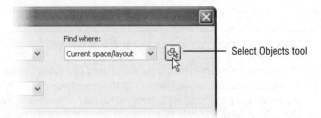

When you click the Select Objects tool, the Find And Replace dialog box closes temporarily to enable you to select a set of objects or a region of your drawing. Find And Replace then limits its search to those objects or the region you select.

You can further control the types of objects that Find And Replace looks for by clicking the More Options tool in the lower-left corner of the Find And Replace dialog box. The dialog box expands to show more options (Figure 10.27).

With this dialog box, you can refine your search by limiting it to blocks, dimension text, standard text, or hyperlink text. You can also specify whether to match the case and find whole words only.

FIGURE 10.27
More extensive
options for Find
And Replace

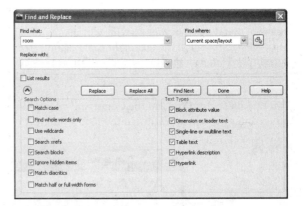

SPEEDING UP AUTOCAD WITH QTEXT

If you need to edit a large drawing that contains a lot of text but you don't need to edit the text, you can use the Qtext command to help accelerate redraws and regenerations when you're working on the drawing. Qtext turns lines of text into rectangular boxes, saving AutoCAD from having to form every letter. This enables you to see the note locations so you don't accidentally draw over them. To use it, enter **qtext**↵ at the Command prompt and enter **On** or select the On option from the dynamic input display.

CREATE PARAGRAPH COLUMNS

You can format Mtext into multiple columns. This can be useful for long lists or to create a newspaper column appearance for your text. Text formatted into columns will automatically flow between columns as you add or remove text.

To format text into columns, do the following:

1. Create the text using the Mtext tool as usual.

2. Click and drag the double-headed arrow at the bottom of the text upward. As you do this, a second column appears.

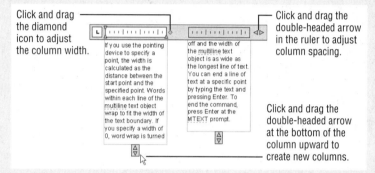

3. If you want to create another column, click and drag the double-headed arrow below the second column upward.

4. To adjust the column width, click and drag the diamond icon that appears just to the right of the first column in the ruler. All the columns will adjust to the width of the first column.

Once you've set up your columns, click the Close Text Editor tool. You can adjust the column width and spacing by using grips that appear when you click on the text.

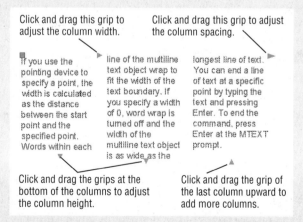

To adjust the column width of existing Mtext, click and drag the arrow grip at the top-right of the first column. To adjust the width between columns, click and drag the arrow grip in the upper-right of the group of columns. The grips at the bottom of each column allow you to adjust the height of the columns.

You can manually set column features through the Column Settings dialog box. To open it, double-click on the Mtext and then choose Column Settings from the Columns flyout in the Text Editor tab's Insert panel.

The Dynamic Columns option is the default for the column type group and it allows you to adjust the column size using grips.

The Bottom Line

Prepare a drawing for text.   AutoCAD offers an extensive set of features for adding text to a drawing, but you need to do a little prep work before you dive in.

> **Master It**   Name two things you need to do to prepare a drawing for text.

Set the annotation scale and add text.   Before you start to add text, you should set the annotation scale for your drawing. Once this is done, you can begin to add text.

> **Master It**   In a sentence or two, briefly describe the purpose of the annotation scale feature. Name the tool you use to add text to a drawing.

Explore text formatting in AutoCAD.   Because text styles contain font and text-size settings, you can usually set up a text style and then begin to add text to your drawing. For those special cases where you need to vary text height and font or other text features, you can use the Formatting panel of the Text Editor tab.

> **Master It**   What text formatting tool can you use to change text to boldface type?

Add simple single-line text objects.   In many situations, you need only a single word or a short string of text. AutoCAD offers the Single Line text object for these instances.

> **Master It**   Describe the methods for starting the single-line text command.

Use the Check Spelling feature.   It isn't uncommon for a drawing to contain the equivalent of several pages of text, and the likelihood of having misspelled words can be high. AutoCAD offers the Check Spelling feature to help you keep your spelling under control.

> **Master It**   What option do you select in the Check Spelling dialog box when it finds a misspelled word and you want to accept the suggestion it offers?

Find and replace text.   A common activity when editing technical drawings is finding and replacing a word throughout a drawing.

> **Master It**   True or false: The Find And Replace feature in AutoCAD works very differently than the find-and-replace feature in other programs.

Chapter 11

Using Fields and Tables

Adding text to a set of drawings can become a large part of your work. You'll find that you're editing notes and labels almost as frequently as you're editing the graphics in your drawings. To make some of those editing tasks easier, AutoCAD provides a few special text objects.

In this chapter, you'll look at fields and tables, two features that can help automate some of the more common tasks in AutoCAD. Fields are a special type of text that can automatically update to reflect changes in the drawing. The Table feature is a tool that helps to automate the process of creating and editing tables and schedules. Tables are a common part of technical drawings and are similar to spreadsheets. In fact, AutoCAD tables behave much like spreadsheets, giving you the ability to add formulas to cells.

You'll start this chapter with an introduction to fields and then go on to learn about tables. Toward the end, you'll revisit fields to see how they can be used to add formulas to tables.

In this chapter, you'll learn to do the following:

◆ Use fields to associate text with drawing properties

◆ Add tables to your drawing

◆ Edit the table line work

◆ Add formulas to cells

◆ Import and export tables

◆ Create table styles

Using Fields to Associate Text with Drawing Properties

The text labels you worked with in Chapter 10 are static and don't change unless you edit them by using the tools described there. Another type of text object, called a *field*, behaves in a more dynamic way than the multiline text. A field can be linked to the properties of other objects and updates itself automatically as the associated properties change. For example, you can create a field that is associated with a block name. If the block name changes, the field text automatically changes as well.

Try the following exercise to see how this works:

1. Open the 11c-unit.dwg file. This file is similar to the drawing you worked on in Chapter 10.

2. Double-click the Kitchen text to highlight it and make it available for editing.

3. Right-click the highlighted Kitchen text, and then choose Insert Field to open the Field dialog box (Figure 11.1). A list to the left shows the types of fields available.

FIGURE 11.1
Choose the field
to insert.

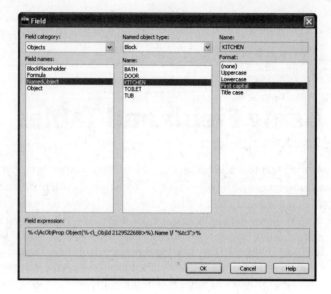

4. In the Field Category drop-down list, select Objects. This limits the display of field types to object fields.

5. In the Field Names list, select NamedObject.

6. Make sure that Block is selected in the Named Object Type drop-down list in the top of the dialog box, and then select Kitchen. This associates the field with the Kitchen block name.

7. In the Format list to the far right, select First Capital. This causes the field text to be lowercase with a capital first letter, regardless of how the block name is actually spelled.

8. Click OK to exit the Field dialog box, and then press ↵ twice to return to the Command prompt.

When you return to the drawing, the text appears in a gray background. This tells you that the text is a field rather than an Mtext or Dtext object. The gray background is just a device to help you keep track of field text; it doesn't plot.

You've converted existing text into a field that is linked to a block name. Now let's see how the field works:

1. Enter **Rename**↵ at the Command prompt to open the Rename dialog box.

2. Make sure Blocks is selected in the Named Objects list, and then select Kitchen from the Items list. The word *KITCHEN* appears in the Old Name input box near the bottom of the dialog box.

3. Enter **Kitchenette** in the input box just below the Old Name box, and then click the Rename To button.

4. Click OK to close the Rename dialog box.

5. Type **Re**↵. The field you created changes to reflect the new block name.

Fields can be associated with a wide variety of properties. You've just seen how a block name can be associated with a field. In this exercise, you'll use a field to display the area of an object:

1. Click Zoom Extents from the Zoom flyout on the navigation bar or type **Z⏎ E⏎** to view the entire plan.

2. Place a rectangle in the living room area so that it fills the area, as in Figure 11.2.

FIGURE 11.2
Place a rectangle that fills the living room.

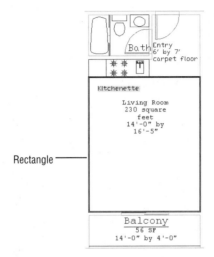

Rectangle ──────

3. Double-click the Living Room text to open the Text Editor tab and the text editor.

4. Highlight the text that reads *230 square feet*. Right-click the selected text, and choose Insert Field from the shortcut menu.

5. In the Field dialog box, select Object from the Field Names list.

6. Click the Select Object button next to the Object Type input box at the top of the Field dialog box (Figure 11.3). The Field dialog box momentarily closes to enable you to select an object.

FIGURE 11.3
Click the Select Object button.

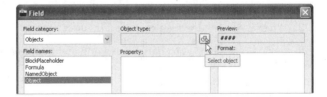

7. Select the rectangle you just added. The Field dialog box returns.

8. In the Property list just below the Object Type input box, select Area.

9. Select Architectural from the Format list to the far right (see Figure 11.4).

FIGURE 11.4
The Architectural
option in the
Format list

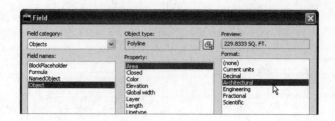

10. Click OK. The field you just added appears in the drawing as the area of the rectangle.

11. Click Close Text Editor in the Text Editor tab's Close panel.

Next you'll alter the rectangle to see how it affects the field:

1. Click the rectangle to expose its grips (Figure 11.5). Then select the top middle grip of the rectangle, and move it upward so the top edge aligns with the bathroom wall.

FIGURE 11.5
Expose the grips.

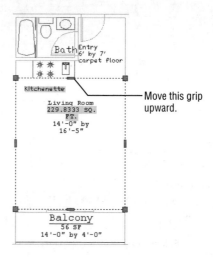

2. Type **Re↵**. The field you just added updates to reflect the new area of the rectangle.

3. After reviewing the results, close `11c-unit.dwg`.

In previous exercises, you changed existing text into fields. You can create new fields in either the Dtext or Mtext command by selecting Insert Field from the shortcut menu whenever you're typing the text content.

In this exercise, you used a rectangle, but you can use any closed polyline to create an area field.

You've touched on just two of the many possible uses for fields. You can associate other types of properties, including the current layer, the drawing name, linetypes, and more. You can include Diesel macros as part of fields. (You'll learn about Diesel macros in Chapter 28.) Fields can also be used in AutoCAD's Table feature, described in the next section, which enables you to create tables and schedules quickly. Fields are used to coordinate sheet labels with reference symbols in the AutoCAD Sheet Set feature described in Chapter 30.

For most of your work, the standard text objects will work just fine, but you may find fields useful when you know a label has to be associated with specific types of data in your drawing. In later chapters, you'll have more opportunities to work with fields.

Adding Tables to Your Drawing

One of the more common text-related tasks you'll do for your drawings is to create schedules, such as door and window schedules or parts schedules. Such schedules are tables used to provide more detailed information regarding the elements in your design.

In the past, AutoCAD users used Mtext or Dtext to create the text for schedules and then used line-drawing tools to create the cells of the schedule. Since AutoCAD 2006, you can use tables to help you generate schedules more quickly. Tables allow you to format the columns and rows of text automatically, similar to formatting in spreadsheet programs.

Creating a Table

The first step in creating a table is to determine the number of rows and columns you want. Don't worry if you aren't certain of the exact number of rows and columns; you can add or subtract them at any time. In this exercise, you'll create a table that contains 11 rows and 9 columns, as shown in Figure 11.6.

FIGURE 11.6
A sample table created with the Table tool

Number	Room	Finish				Ceiling Ht.	Area	Remarks
		Floor	Base	Wall	Ceiling			
110	Lobby	B	1	A	1	10'-0"	200sf	
111	Office	A	1	B	2	8'-0"	96sf	
112	Office	A	1	B	2	8'-0"	96sf	
113	Office	A	1	B	2	8'-0"	96sf	
114	Meeting	C	1	B	2	8'-0"	150sf	
115	Breakout	C	1	B	2	8'-0"	150sf	
116	Womens	D	2	C	3	8'-0"	50sf	
117	Mens	D	2	C	3	8'-0"	50sf	

Room Finish Schedule

Start by creating the basic table layout:

1. Click New from the Quick Access toolbar, and use the standard `acad.dwt` drawing template.

2. Click Table from the Home tab's Annotation panel to open the Insert Table dialog box (Figure 11.7). You can also click the Table tool from the Annotate tab's Tables panel or type **Tb↵**.

3. In the Column & Row Settings group, enter **9** for Columns and **12** for Data Rows.

4. Click OK. The dialog box closes and the outline of a table follows your cursor.

5. Position the table in the center of your drawing area, and click to place it. The table appears with a cursor in the top cell. You also see the Text Editor tab in the Ribbon.

FIGURE 11.7
The Insert
Table dialog

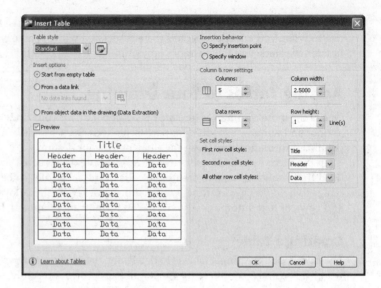

6. Enter **Room Finish Schedule**, and press ↵. The cursor moves to the next cell.

7. Click Close Text Editor in the Text Editor tab's Close panel.

Adding Cell Text

You've just created a table and added a title. Notice that the table actually contains 14 rows, including the title row at the top and an additional row for the headings of each column. You can delete these additional rows if you don't need them, but for now, you'll start to add some text to the table:

1. Adjust your view so the table fills most of the drawing area.

2. Double-click in the first cell at the top left, just below the Room Finish Schedule label (see Figure 11.8). The cell turns gray, and the Text Editor tab appears in the Ribbon. You also see labels across the top and left side showing the row and column addresses.

3. Enter **Number** for the room number column at the far left, and then press the Tab key to advance to the next cell to the right.

FIGURE 11.8
Double-click
the first cell
shown here.

4. Enter **Room**, and press the Tab key again.

5. Enter **Finish**, and press the Tab key four times to advance four columns. You do this because the Finish heading shown in Figure 11.6 has four columns under it: Floor, Base, Wall, and Ceiling. In the next exercise, you'll learn how to format those four columns under the single heading.

6. Enter **Ceiling Ht.**, and press the Tab key again.

7. Enter **Area**, press the Tab key, and enter **Remarks**.

8. Click Close Text Editor in the Text Editor tab's Close panel.

You have the column headings in place. Now you need to do a little extra formatting. In step 5, you left four cells blank because four of the columns will be combined under one heading: the Finish heading covers the Floor, Base, Wall, and Ceiling columns. Next you'll combine the blank cells with the Finish heading:

1. Click in the center of the cell with the Finish label to select it.

2. Shift+click in the third cell to the right of the Finish cell to select all four cells (Figure 11.9).

FIGURE 11.9
Select a group
of four cells.

3. Right-click in the selected cells, and choose Merge ➤ All. The four selected cells merge into a single cell with the word *Finish*.

Now you need to add the subheads under the Finish header:

1. Double-click in the leftmost cell below the Finish cell. The Text Editor tab appears in the Ribbon (Figure 11.10).

FIGURE 11.10
Double-click this
cell and the Text
Editor tab appears.

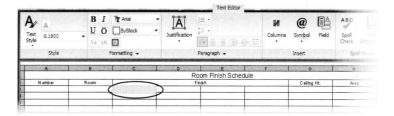

2. Enter **Floor**, and press the Tab key.

3. Enter **Base**, **Wall**, and **Ceiling** in each of the following columns as you've been doing. Remember that the Tab key advances you to the next cell to the right. Your table should look like Figure 11.11.

4. Click Close Text Editor in the Text Editor tab's Close panel.

FIGURE 11.11

The table so far

Adjusting Table Text Orientation and Location

You now have the basic layout of the table, with one difference. The Floor, Base, Wall, and Ceiling labels you just added are oriented horizontally, but you want them oriented vertically, as in Figure 11.6. The following steps will show you how to rotate a set of labels in a table so they appear in the orientation you want:

1. Click in the cell labeled Floor to select it. The Table Cell tab appears in the ribbon.

2. Shift+click in the cell labeled Ceiling to select all four of the cells below the Finish heading. The combined cells have four grips, one on each side of the group.

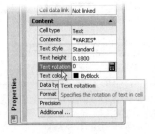

3. Click the grip at the bottom of the selected group, and move it down about four rows. Click to "fix" the row height in place. The entire row becomes taller. This provides room for the text when you rotate it.

4. Right-click in the selected cells, and choose Properties from the shortcut menu to open the Properties palette.

5. In the Properties palette, click the Text Rotation input box under the Content group.

6. Enter **90⏎** for a 90-degree rotation of the text. The text rotates into a vertical orientation.

7. Close the Properties palette.

   With the text in this orientation, the columns are too wide, so you'll change the cell width for the selected cells.

8. Move the right grip to the left to decrease the width of the cells.

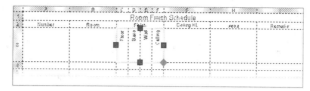

9. For the final touch, you'll center the text in the cells. With the cells still selected, right-click in the selected cells, and choose Alignment ➤ Bottom Center. The text becomes centered in the cells and aligned at the bottom of the cells.

SETTING MARGINS WITH THE PROPERTIES PALETTE

You can also control the margin between the text and the cell border by using the Cell Margin options in the Properties palette. Select a group of cells in the table, right-click, and choose Properties. In the Properties palette, click the Vertical Cell Margin option or the Horizontal Cell Margin option in the Cell group.

In the last exercise, you learned how you can adjust the text orientation through the Properties palette. You can also adjust the width of cells through the Properties palette. Or if you prefer, you can adjust the width of multiple cells by adjusting the grip location of selected cells.

Now continue to add text to the cells and adjust their sizes:

1. Double-click in the cell in the Number column just below the row that contains the Floor, Base, Wall, and Ceiling cells. A text cursor appears in the cell, and the Text Editor tab appears in the Ribbon.

2. Enter **110**, and press ↵. Instead of advancing to the next cell to the right, you advance to the next cell below.

3. Enter **111**, and press ↵ again. Continue to enter each room number in this way until you reach room number 117. When you've finished entering the room numbers, click Close Text Editor in the Text Editor tab's Close panel.

Next you'll reduce the width of the column to fit the text a bit better.

4. Click in the cell with the Number text label. It's the first column heading in the table.

5. Shift+click in the bottom cell of the Number column to select the entire column.

6. Click the grip to the left of the column, and move the grip to the right so the column width is approximately half the width of the Room column. You can zoom in on the column to allow more control over the positioning of the grip.

7. Press Esc to exit the selection and view your table so far (Figure 11.12).

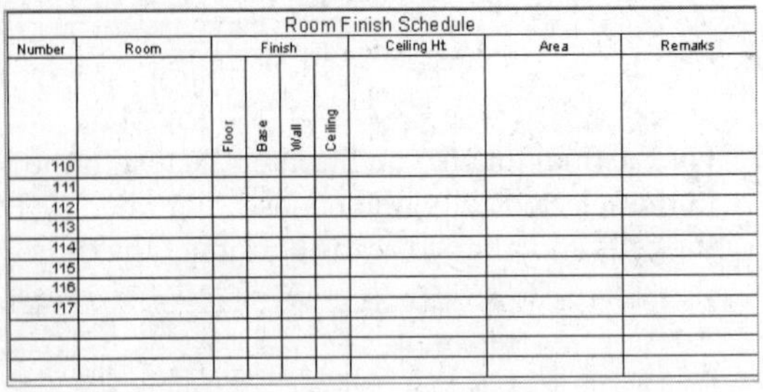

FIGURE 11.12
The table with the columns resized

		Room Finish Schedule							
Number	Room	Finish				Ceiling Ht.	Area	Remarks
		Floor	Base	Wall	Ceiling			
110								
111								
112								
113								
114								
115								
116								
117								

Now, suppose you want to delete one of the extra rows of cells at the bottom of the table or add a new row. Here's what to do:

1. Click the bottom-left cell of the table to select it.

2. Right-click, and choose Rows ➤ Delete from the shortcut menu. The row disappears.

3. To add a row, select a cell, right-click, and choose Rows ➤ Insert Above or Rows ➤ Insert Below, depending on where you want the new row.

You may notice the Delete Columns and Insert Columns options in the shortcut menu that let you add or delete columns. These options function in a way that's similar to how the Delete Rows and Insert Rows options function. You can also use the tools in the Rows and Columns panels of the Table Cell tab to insert and delete rows and columns.

Editing the Table Line Work

So far, you've concentrated on how you can format text and cells in a table, but you'll also want some control over the lines in the table. Typically, heavier lines are used around the border of the table and between the title and the rest of the table.

The Cell Borders shortcut menu option lets you modify the outline of the border. When you select this option, the Cell Border Properties dialog box opens (Figure 11.13).

You can use this dialog box to fine-tune the appearance of the line work of the table. Try the following exercise to see firsthand how this dialog box works:

1. Turn on the display of line weights by typing **LW**↵.

2. In the Lineweight Settings dialog box, turn on the Display Lineweight setting, and then click OK.

3. Click in the title cell at the top of the table to select the cell, and then right-click and choose Borders to open the Cell Border Properties dialog box.

4. Click the Lineweight drop-down list, and select 0.30 mm.

FIGURE 11.13
Setting border
properties

5. Click the Outside Borders button that appears just above the preview panel to tell AutoCAD to change the borders of the cell to the selected line weight (Figure 11.14).

FIGURE 11.14
Click to display
outside borders.

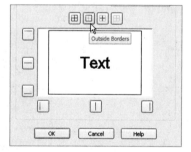

6. Click OK. The title cell is now outlined in a heavier line. To see it clearly, press the Esc key.

You can also adjust the line weights that encircle a group of cells, as in the following exercise:

1. Click the cell in the upper-left corner with the Number label.

2. Shift+click the cell in the lower-right corner of the table so that all the cells from the second-from-the-top row down are selected.

3. Right-click, and choose Borders.

4. Select 0.30 mm from the Lineweight drop-down list. Then click the Outside Borders button as you did in step 5 of the previous exercise.

5. Click OK. The outlines of the selected cells are given the new line weight setting (Figure 11.15).

6. Save this file for future reference.

FIGURE 11.15
The borders
updated

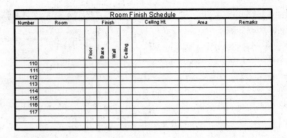

CHANGING THE BACKGROUND COLOR

In addition to the table borders, you can change the background color for the cells of the table through the Table Cell Background Color drop-down list in the Cell Styles panel of the Table Cell tab. You can also use the Background Fill option in the Properties palette to set cell background colors.

The Cell Border Properties dialog box also lets you set the line colors by selecting a color from the Color drop-down list before selecting an Apply To option. In addition, there are several other buttons around the preview panel (Figure 11.16) that let you select the lines that are affected by the Cell Border Properties settings.

You can also use the preview panel to select individual borders by clicking the sample border in the preview panel. The sample changes to show you which border lines are affected.

FIGURE 11.16
Setting which
borders will
be affected

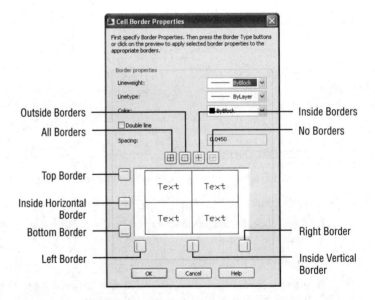

Adding Formulas to Cells

In the beginning of this chapter, I mentioned that you can include formulas in cells of AutoCAD tables. This can be a great timesaver because you can set up a table with quantities that automatically adjust to changes in values in the table. You don't have to calculate the changes manually.

You may recall that formulas are actually a type of field and that a field can be linked with objects in a drawing so that the field displays the linked object's properties. The formula field can be linked to several numeric text values.

Although fields are the tools you use for formulas, you don't have to choose consciously to add a field to a cell every time you want to add a formula. The exercise in the following section will demonstrate how you can add a formula by typing directly in a cell. AutoCAD takes care of converting your input into a field.

Using Formulas Directly in Cells

The simplest way to add a formula to a cell is to double-click the cell and then, when the Text Editor tab appears in the Ribbon, enter the formula directly in the cell with the addition of an = (equal sign) at the beginning. Try the following exercise to see how it works.

1. Open the FieldSample.dwg file.

2. Double-click in the cell, as shown in Figure 11.17, to select the location for your formula.

FIGURE 11.17
Selecting the cell for your formula

Sample Table				
100	200	300	400	
150	250	350	450	
250	350	450	550	

← Double-click this cell.

3. Enter =A2+D4 in the cell to add the values in cell A2 and cell D4.

4. Press ↵ after you enter the formula. The value of A2 plus D4 appears in the cell (Figure 11.18).

FIGURE 11.18
The cell with the sum of two other cells

Sample Table				
100	200	300	400	
150	250	350	450	
250	350	450	550	
				650

In step 3, the equal sign tells AutoCAD to convert the text into a formula field. You may have noticed that when you start to edit a cell in a table, the row and column labels appear along the top and left side of the table. You can use these labels to determine the cell addresses for your formula.

In typical spreadsheet fashion, you can change the formula in a cell any time. Double-click the cell containing the formula, and then edit the formula values and operators.

You can also use the Formula drop-down list from the Table Cell tab's expanded Insert panel to select from a set of predefined math operations (Figure 11.19).

Click in the cell where you want to place the formula; then, in the Table tab, click the Formula flyout from the Insert panel, and select the operation you want to use. Next, place a selection window around the cells you want to include in the formula. Click in the first cell that you want to include in the formula, and then click in the second cell. As you do this, a selection window appears. All the cells that are included in the selection window are included in the formula.

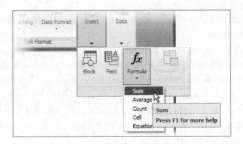

Using Other Math Operations

In the previous exercise, you used the plus sign to add the value of two cells. You can string together several cells' addresses to add multiple cells, as follows:

```
=A2+A3+A4...
```

You can also subtract, multiply, or divide by using the – (subtract or minus), * (multiply or asterisk), or / (divide or hash) sign. To perform multiple operations on several cells, you can group operations within parentheses in a way similar to how you would in a typical spreadsheet formula. For example, if you want to add two cells together and then multiply their sum by another cell, use the following format:

```
=(A2+A3)*A4
```

The Average, Sum, and Count buttons that appear in the Formula flyout on the Table Cell tab's Insert panel give you quick access to these frequently used functions. You can add to a cell the average value of a set of cells, the sum of a set of cells, or the count of the number of cells. When you click one of these options after selecting a cell, you're prompted to select several cells with a selection window. Once you've selected a set of cells, you see the appropriate formula in the current selected cell. Clicking the Average button, for example, produces a formula similar to the following:

```
=Average(A1:B5)
```

Clicking the Sum button produces a formula like the following:

```
=Sum(A1:B5)
```

In both cases, a range of cells is indicated by a colon, as in A1:B5. You can use this format when entering formulas manually. You can also include a single cell with a range by using a comma:

```
=Sum(A1:B5,C6)
```

Importing and Exporting Tables

Frequently, tables are created outside AutoCAD in a spreadsheet program such as Excel. You can import an Excel worksheet as an AutoCAD table by using the AutoCAD Entities option in the Paste Special feature. The ability to import tables lets non-AutoCAD users create the table data while you concentrate on the drawing.

Try the following exercise to see how you can import a table from a worksheet:

1. Open the Excel worksheet called `11a-plan.xls`, and highlight the door data, as shown in Figure 11.20.

FIGURE 11.20
Selecting the
door data in the
`11a-plan.xls`
spreadsheet

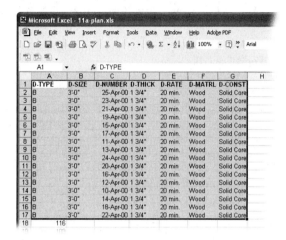

2. Choose Edit ➢ Copy to place a copy of the selected data into the Windows Clipboard, and then switch back to AutoCAD.

3. Click Paste Special from the Paste flyout on the Home tab's Clipboard panel (Figure 11.21) to open the Paste Special dialog box.

FIGURE 11.21
The Paste flyout

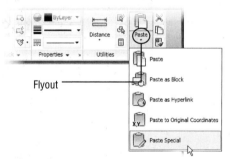

4. With the Paste radio button selected, click AutoCAD Entities in the list, and then click OK.

5. At the `Specify insertion point or [paste as Text]:` prompt, click a point in the lower-right area of the drawing. The worksheet data appears in the drawing as a table.

In this exercise, you imported the worksheet by using the default standard table style. This gives you a simple-looking table using the AutoCAD Txt font. You can set up a custom table style, as described later in this chapter, with the fonts and borders you want and then import the table for a more custom appearance. Make sure your custom table style is the current style before you import the worksheet.

Exporting Tables

Some day, you might want to export your AutoCAD table to a spreadsheet program or database. You can do this through a somewhat hidden option in a shortcut menu. Follow these steps:

1. Select the entire table. You can do so by clicking in a spot above and to the right of the table. With the crossing selection window, completely enclose the table and click.

2. Right-click anywhere in the table, and choose Export from the shortcut menu to open the Export Data dialog box.

3. Specify a name and location for your exported table data, and click Save.

The file is saved with a `.csv` filename extension. This type of file is a comma-delimited file and can be read by most spreadsheet programs, including Microsoft Excel. Unfortunately, the CSV file doesn't retain the AutoCAD table formatting.

To open the exported file from Excel, choose File ➢ Open in the Excel menu bar; then, in the Open dialog box, select Text File (*.prn, *.txt, *.csv) in the Files Of Type drop-down list. You can then locate the exported table and open it.

ADDING GRAPHICS TO TABLE CELLS

One of the more interesting features of the Table tool is its ability to include blocks in a cell. This can be useful if you want to include graphic elements in your table. Adding a block to a cell is a simple process. Here are the steps:

1. Click in a cell to select it.

2. Right-click, and choose Insert ➢ Block from the shortcut menu to open the Insert A Block In A Table Cell dialog box.

3. Select a block name from the Name drop-down list. You can also click the button to the right of the list to open the Select File Name dialog box that enables you to select a drawing file for import to the cell.

4. After you've selected a block and specified the settings in the Properties group of the dialog box, click OK. The block appears in the cell you've selected.

The Properties group in the dialog box enables you to specify the alignment and size of the inserted block. By default, the AutoFit option is turned on. This option adjusts the size of the block to make it fit in the current cell size.

Creating Table Styles

If you find that you're creating the same table layout over and over, you can set up predefined table styles. You can set up the properties of the title, column headings, and data in advance so you don't have to set them up each time you create a table. For example, if you prefer to use Arial bold at 0.25″ for the title and standard Arial at 0.125″ for the column headings, you can create a table style with those settings. The next time you need to create a table, you can select your custom table style and specify the number of columns and rows; then you'll be ready to add the data without having to format the text.

To create a table style, follow these steps:

1. Click Table Style from the Home tab's expanded Annotation panel to open the Table Style dialog box. You can also select the Table Style tool from the Annotate tab's Tables panel title bar. The Table Style tool is the arrowhead at the right end of the Tables panel title bar. You see the Standard table style in the list box (Figure 11.22). This is the one you used in the previous exercises.

FIGURE 11.22
The Table Style dialog box

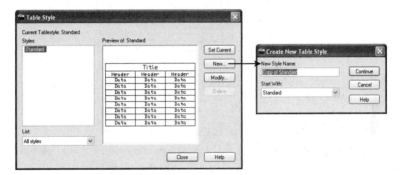

2. Click the New button to open the Create New Table Style dialog box. This is where you give your new table style a name.

3. Enter **My Table Style**, and click Continue to open the New Table Style dialog box (see Figure 11.23).

FIGURE 11.23
The New Table Style dialog box

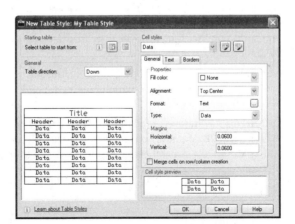

4. You'll learn more about the options in this dialog box next. For now, click OK to close the dialog box.

5. Your new table style now appears in the Styles list of the Table Style dialog box. If you want to edit an existing table style, you can select the style from the list and click the Modify button. The Modify Table Style dialog box will appear, enabling you to edit the existing style. The Modify Table Style dialog box is identical to the New Table Style dialog box shown in Figure 11.23.

6. Click Close to exit the dialog box.

After you've created a style, you can select it from the Table Style group of the Insert Table dialog box that you used to create the sample table (Figure 11.24). To open the Insert Table dialog box, click Table from the Home tab's Annotation panel.

FIGURE 11.24
Select the table style in the Insert Table dialog box.

You can also open the New Table Style dialog box by clicking the Table Style Dialog button just to the right of the Table Style drop-down list in the Insert Table dialog box.

The Table Style Options

Let's take a closer look at the New Table Style dialog box, shown earlier in Figure 11.23. It may seem a bit bewildering at first, but once you take the time to explore the parts of this dialog box, it's fairly straightforward. The following offers a description of the parts of the New Table Style dialog box by group:

Starting Table Typically, you can set up a new table style using the settings in the other groups of this dialog box, but the Starting Table group gives you the ability to use an existing table in the drawing as the basis for your new table style. This can be helpful if you've already done some work formatting a table in your drawing. This group includes two buttons. The one on the left lets you select an existing table in the drawing for your new style. If you click this button, the dialog box closes temporarily to allow you to select a table in your drawing. The button on the right removes your in-drawing table selection and reverts to the settings in the dialog box.

General The General group offers only one setting: the direction for the table. Typically, you'll use the Down option, which means the table reads from top to bottom. If for some reason you need a table with titles at the bottom, choose the Up option.

Cell Styles You have a high degree of control over the appearance of individual cells through the cell styles. By default, your new table style will have three cell styles, called Data, Header, and Title. You can select these cell styles from the drop-down list at the top of the Cell Styles group. You can then edit the selected style using the three tabs below the drop-down list. Here is a brief description of the function of each tab:

- General gives you control over the fill color, alignment, format, and type of information presented in the cell. The Margins options control the margins in the cell. The Merge Cells On Row/Column Creation option at the bottom of the General tab causes the cells to merge into a single cell for the selected cell style.

- Text gives you control over the default text style, the height and color, and the angle of the text in the cell.

- Borders lets you control the line weight for the borders of the cell.

You can also create your own cell style using the two buttons to the right of the Cell Styles drop-down list. The left button lets you create a new cell style. The button on the right lets you create, rename, or delete a cell style through the Manage Cell Styles dialog box.

Cell Style Preview This window gives you a preview of what the cell style will look like with the settings you make in the tabs of the Cell Styles group. This preview changes in real time as you change the settings in the General, Text, or Borders tab.

The Bottom Line

Use fields to associate text with drawing properties. Fields are a special type of text object that can be linked to object properties. They can help to automate certain text-related tasks.

Master It Name two uses for fields that you learned about in the first part of this chapter.

Add tables to your drawing. The Tables feature can help you make quick work of schedules and other tabular data that you want to include in a drawing.

Master It What is the name of the dialog box that appears when you click the Table tool from the Annotate tab's Tables panel?

Edit the table line work. Because tables include line work to delineate their different cells, AutoCAD gives you control over table borders and lines.

Master It How do you get to the Cell Border Properties dialog box?

Add formulas to cells. Tables can also function like a spreadsheet by allowing you to add formulas to cells.

Master It What type of text object lets you add formulas to cells?

Import and export tables. The Table feature allows you to import Microsoft Excel spreadsheets into AutoCAD.

Master It Describe how to import a spreadsheet from Excel into AutoCAD.

Chapter 12

Using Dimensions

Before you determine the dimensions of a project, your design is in flux and many questions may be unanswered. After you begin dimensioning, you'll start to see whether things fit or work together. Dimensioning can be crucial to how well a design works and how quickly it develops. The dimensions answer questions about code conformance if you're an architect; they answer questions about tolerances, fit, and interference if you're involved in mechanical applications. After you and your design team reach a design on a schematic level, communicating even tentative dimensions to others on the team can accelerate design development. Dimensions represent a point from which you can develop your ideas further.

With AutoCAD, you can easily add tentative or final dimensions to any drawing. AutoCAD gives you an accurate dimension without your having to take measurements. You pick the two points to be dimensioned and the dimension line location, and AutoCAD does the rest. AutoCAD's *associative dimensioning* capability automatically updates dimensions whenever the size or shape of the dimensioned object changes. These dimensioning features can save you valuable time and reduce the number of dimensional errors in your drawings.

In this chapter, you'll learn to do the following:

- ◆ Understand the components of a dimension
- ◆ Create a dimension style
- ◆ Draw linear dimensions
- ◆ Edit dimensions
- ◆ Dimension non-orthogonal objects
- ◆ Add a note with a leader arrow
- ◆ Apply ordinate dimensions
- ◆ Add tolerance notation

Understanding the Components of a Dimension

Before you start the exercises in this chapter, it will help to know the names of the parts of a dimension. Figure 12.1 shows a sample of a dimension with the parts labeled. The *dimension line* is the line that represents the distance being dimensioned. It's the horizontal line with the diagonal tick marks on either end. The *extension lines* are the lines that originate from the object being dimensioned. They show you the exact location from which the dimension is taken. The *dimension text* is the dimension value, usually shown inside or above the dimension line.

FIGURE 12.1
The components
of a dimension

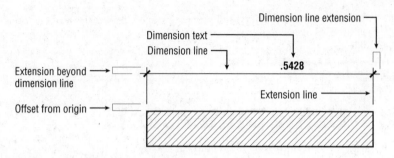

Another component of a dimension line is the *dimension line extension*. This is the part of the dimension line that extends beyond the extension line. Dimension line extensions are usually used only on architectural dimensions. The extension lines usually extend beyond the dimension lines in all types of dimensions. The extension line *offset from origin* is the distance from the beginning of the extension line to the object being dimensioned. The *extension beyond dimension line* is the distance the dimension line extends past the extension line.

You can control each of these components by creating or editing dimension styles. *Dimension styles* are the settings that determine the look of your dimensions. You can store multiple styles in a single drawing. The first exercise in this chapter will show you how to create a dimension style.

DIMENSIONING STANDARDS

In addition to the components of a dimension, you should know about the standards that govern the placement and style of dimensions in a drawing. Each industry has a different set of standards for text size, text style, arrow style, dimension placement, and general dimensioning methods. These issues are beyond the scope of this book; however, I urge you to become familiar with the standards associated with your industry. Many resources are available to you if you want to find out more about dimension standards. Here are a few resources on the subject:

◆ For mechanical drafting in the United States, check the American Society of Mechanical Engineers (ASME) website: http://www.asme.org.

◆ For European standards, see the International Organization for Standardization (ISO) website: http://www.iso.org.

◆ For architectural standards in the United States, see the American Institute of Architects (AIA) website: http://www.aia.org.

Creating a Dimension Style

Dimension styles are similar to text styles. They determine the look of your dimensions as well as the size of dimensioning features, such as the dimension text and arrows. You can set up a dimension style to have special types of arrows, for instance, or to position the dimension text above or in line with the dimension line. Dimension styles also make your work easier by enabling you to store and duplicate your most common dimension settings.

AutoCAD gives you one of two default dimension styles, *ISO-25* or *Standard,* depending on whether you use the metric or Imperial (also called English) measurement system. You'll probably add many other styles to suit the types of drawings you're creating. You can also create variations of a general style for those situations that call for only minor changes in the dimension's appearance.

In this section, you'll learn how to set up your own dimension style based on the Standard dimension style (see Figure 12.2). For metric users, the settings are different, but the overall methods are the same.

FIGURE 12.2
AutoCAD's Standard dimension style compared with an architectural-style dimension

A dimension using the Standard default settings

A dimension set up for architectural drawings

A sample of other arrows

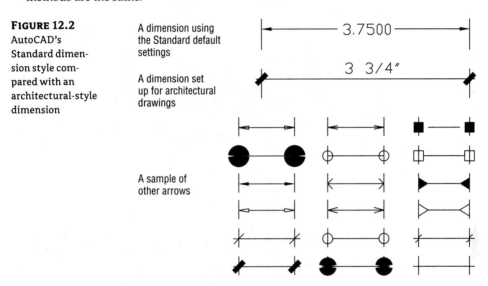

Follow these steps to create a dimension style:

1. Open the 12a-unit.dwg file and rename it Unit.dwg. Metric users should open 12a-unit-metric.dwg and rename it Unit.dwg. These files are the same as the Unit file you used in the previous chapter before the exercises.

2. Choose Zoom All from the Zoom flyout in the navigation bar or type Z↵ A↵ to display the entire floor plan.

3. Click the Dimension Style tool on the Annotate tab's Dimensions panel title bar. You can also click the Dimension Style tool from the Home tab's expanded Annotation panel (it looks like a dimension with a paintbrush) or type D↵ at the Command prompt to open the Dimension Style Manager dialog box.

4. Select Standard from the Styles list box. Metric users should select ISO-25. See Figure 12.3.

5. Click New to open the Create New Dimension Style dialog box (Figure 12.4).

6. With the Copy of Standard or ISO-25 name highlighted in the New Style Name input box, enter **My Architectural**.

7. Click Continue to open the detailed New Dimension Style dialog box (Figure 12.5).

FIGURE 12.3
The Dimension
Style Manager

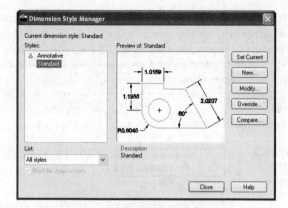

FIGURE 12.4
The Create New
Dimension Style
dialog box

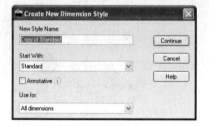

FIGURE 12.5
The New
Dimension Style
dialog box

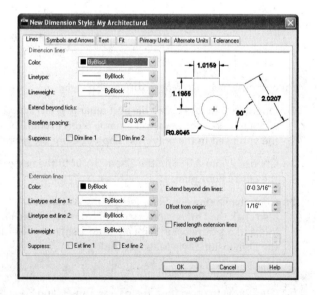

You've just created a dimension style called My Architectural, but at this point it's identical to the Standard style on which it's based. Nothing has happened to the Standard style; it's still available if you need to use it.

Setting Up the Primary Unit Style

Now you need to set up your new dimension style so that it conforms to the U.S. architectural style of dimensioning. Let's start by changing the unit style for the dimension text. Just as you changed the overall unit style of AutoCAD to a feet-and-inches style for your bath drawing in Chapter 3, you must change your dimension styles. Setting the overall unit style doesn't automatically set the dimension unit style. Follow these steps:

1. In the New Dimension Style dialog box, click the Primary Units tab (see Figure 12.6).

FIGURE 12.6
The Primary
Units options

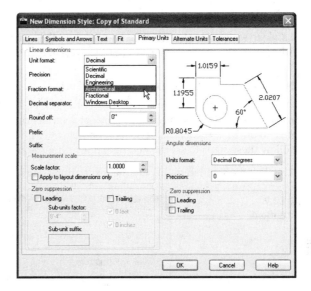

2. In the Linear Dimensions group, open the Unit Format drop-down list and choose Architectural. Notice that this drop-down list contains the same unit styles as the main Drawing Units dialog box (choose Drawing Utilities ➤ Units from the Application menu). Metric users can skip this option.

USING COMMAS OR PERIODS FOR DECIMALS

The Decimal Separator option a few settings below the Unit Format option lets you choose between a period and a comma for decimal points. Metric users often use the comma for a decimal point, and U.S. users use a period. This option doesn't have any meaning for measurements other than decimal, so it's dimmed when the Architectural unit format is selected.

---

3. Select 0′-0 ¼″ from the Precision drop-down list, just below the Unit Format list. Metric users should select 0.00. The Precision option enables you to set the level of precision that is displayed in the dimension text. It doesn't limit the precision of AutoCAD's drawing database. This value is used to limit only the display of dimension text values.

4. Just below the Precision drop-down list, open the Fraction Format drop-down list and select Diagonal. Notice what happens to the graphic: the fractional dimensions change to show how your dimension text will look. Metric users can skip this step because it isn't available when the Decimal unit format is selected.

5. In the Zero Suppression group in the lower-left corner, click 0 Inches to deselect this check box. If you leave it turned on, indications of 0 inches will be omitted from the dimension text. (In architectural drawings, 0 inches are shown as in this dimension: 12′-0″.) Metric users can ignore this option.

If you use the Imperial measurement system, you've set up My Architectural's dimension unit style to show dimensions in feet and inches, the standard method for U.S. construction documents. Metric users have changed the Precision value and kept the Decimal unit system.

Setting the Height for Dimension Text

Along with the unit style, you should adjust the size of the dimension text. The Text tab of the New Dimension Style dialog box lets you set a variety of text options, including text location relative to the dimension line, style, and height.

Follow these steps to set the height of your dimension text:

1. Click the Text tab to display the text options (Figure 12.7).

FIGURE 12.7
The Text options

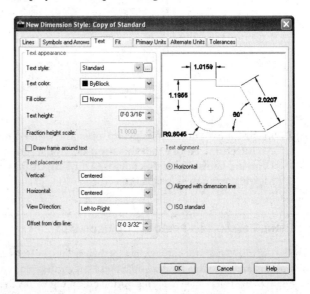

2. Highlight the contents of the Text Height input box.

3. Type **1/8**⏎ to make the text 1/8″ high. Metric users should enter **0.3**⏎ for the text height.

Unlike with the text you created in Chapter 10, you specify the text height by its final plot size. You then specify an overall dimension scale factor that affects the sizing of all dimensioning settings, such as text and arrows.

If you want to use a specific text style for your dimensions, select a text style in the Text Style drop-down list in the Text tab. If the style you select happens to have a height specification greater than 0, that height will override any text height settings you enter in the Text tab.

Setting the Location and Orientation of Dimension Text

AutoCAD's default setting for the placement of dimension text puts the text in line with the dimension line, as shown in the example at the top of Figure 12.2 earlier in this chapter. However, you want the new My Architectural style to put the text above the dimension line, as is done in the center of Figure 12.2. To do that, you'll use the Text Placement and Text Alignment options in the Text tab of the New Dimension Style dialog box:

1. In the Text Alignment group in the lower-right corner of the dialog box, click the Aligned With Dimension Line radio button.

2. In the Text Placement group, open the Vertical drop-down list, and select Above. The appearance of the sample image changes to show how your new settings will look.

3. Again in the Text Placement group, change the Offset From Dim Line value to 1/16″. This setting controls the size of the gap between the dimension line and the dimension text.

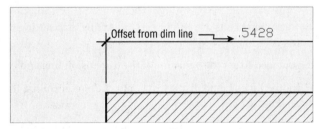

Each time you change a setting, the graphic gives you immediate feedback about how your changes will affect your dimension style.

Choosing an Arrow Style and Setting the Dimension Scale

Next, you'll specify a different type of arrow for your new dimension style. For linear dimensions in architectural drawings, a diagonal line, or *tick* mark, is typically used instead of an arrow.

In addition, you want to set the scale for the graphical components of the dimension, such as the arrows and text. Recall from Chapter 10 that text must be scaled up in size in order to appear at the proper size in the final output of the drawing. Dimensions too must be scaled so they look correct when the drawing is plotted. The arrows are controlled by settings in the Symbols And Arrows tab, and the overall scale of the dimension style is set in the Fit tab.

Here are the steps for specifying the arrow type and scale:

1. Click the Symbols And Arrows tab to display the options for controlling the arrow style and dimension line extensions (Figure 12.8).

2. In the Arrowheads group, open the First drop-down list and choose Architectural Tick. The graphic next to the arrowhead name shows you what the arrowhead looks like. Note that the Second drop-down list automatically changes to Architectural Tick to maintain symmetry on the dimension.

FIGURE 12.8
The Symbols And
Arrows options

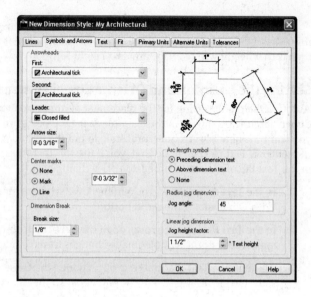

3. In the Arrowheads group, change the Arrow Size setting to **1/8″**. Metric users should enter **.3**.

Next, you need to set the behavior of the dimension line and extension lines:

1. Click the Lines tab to display the options for controlling the dimension and extension lines (Figure 12.9).

FIGURE 12.9
The options for
controlling the
dimension and
extension lines

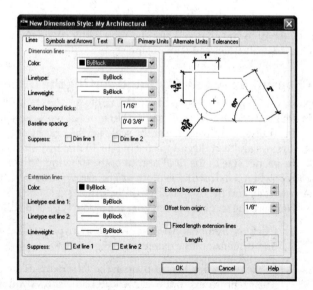

2. In the Dimension Lines group, highlight the value in the Extend Beyond Ticks input box, and enter **1/16**. (Metric users should enter **0.15**.) This causes the dimension lines to extend past the tick arrows. This is a standard graphic practice used for dimensioning linear dimensions in architectural plans.

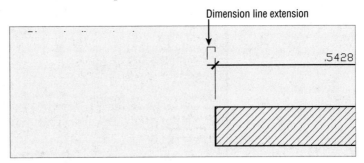

3. In the Extension Lines group, change the Extend Beyond Dim Lines setting to **1/8″**. Metric users should change this to **0.3**. This setting determines the distance the extension line extends past the dimension line.

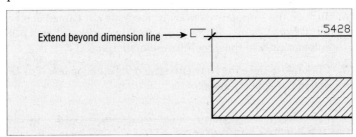

4. Again in the Extension Lines group, change the Offset From Origin setting to **1/8″**. Metric users should change this to **0.3**. This sets the distance from the point being dimensioned to the beginning of the dimension extension line.

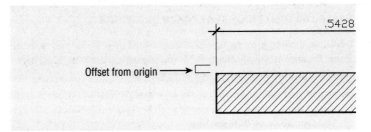

5. Click the Fit tab of the New Dimension Style dialog box to display the options for overall dimension scale and miscellaneous settings (Figure 12.10).

FIGURE 12.10

The Fit options

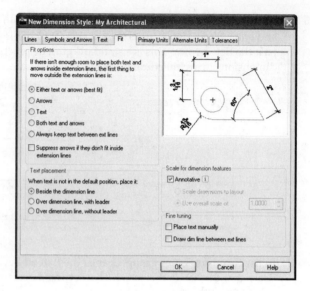

6. Turn on the Annotative option in the Scale For Dimension Features group. You may recall from Chapter 10 that the Annotative option allows AutoCAD to scale an object automatically to the drawing's annotation scale.

7. Click OK to close the New Dimension Style dialog box. The Dimension Style Manager dialog box appears again.

CREATE CUSTOM ARROWHEADS

See Appendix D for details on how you can create your own arrowheads. AutoCAD also lets you set up a separate arrow style for leaders.

SCALE FOR DIMENSIONS IN LEGACY DRAWINGS

Drawings created prior to AutoCAD 2008 relied on scale factors to determine the scaling of dimensions. Because it's likely that you'll run into legacy drawing files, here is some information about the settings used for those earlier dimensions.

Instead of the Annotative option, the Use Overall Scale Of option is used in the Scale For Dimension Features group. You select the Use Overall Scale Of radio button and enter a drawing scale factor in the Use Overall Scale Of input box.

All the values you enter for the options in the New Dimension Style dialog box are multiplied by this Use Overall Scale Of value to obtain the final size of the dimension components. For example, the text height you entered earlier, 1/8″, is multiplied by 48 for a dimension text height of 6″. For metric users, the text height of 0.3 is multiplied by 50 for a text height of 15 cm. For more on the scaling of text and other objects in AutoCAD, see Chapter 3.

USING THE LAYOUT VIEWPORT SCALE FOR DIMENSIONS

If you use the Scale Dimensions To Layout option in the Scale For Dimension Features group of the Fit tab, AutoCAD uses the layout viewport scale to size the dimension components. See Chapter 8 for more information about viewport scale settings. This can be useful if you have a drawing that you want to print at multiple scales.

Setting Up Alternate Units

You can use the Alternate Units tab of the New Dimension Style dialog box to set up AutoCAD to display a second dimension in centimeters or millimeters. Likewise, if you're a metric user, you can set up a second dimension to display feet and inches. The following exercise shows you how to set up alternate dimensions. You don't have to do this exercise now; it's here for your information. If you like, come back later and try it to see how it affects your dimensions. You can pick up the tutorial in the next section, "Setting the Current Dimension Style."

If you decide later that you don't want the alternate units to be displayed, you can turn them off by returning to the New Dimension Style dialog box and removing the checkmark from the Display Alternate Units check box.

Here are the steps for setting up alternate dimensions:

1. In the Dimension Style Manager, select a style and then click Modify. Or, if you want to create a new style, click New.

2. In the Modify Dimension Style dialog box, click the Alternate Units tab (Figure 12.11) This is virtually identical to the New Dimension Style dialog box you've been working with.

3. Click the Display Alternate Units check box. The options in the tab become available for your input.

FIGURE 12.11
The Alternate
Units options

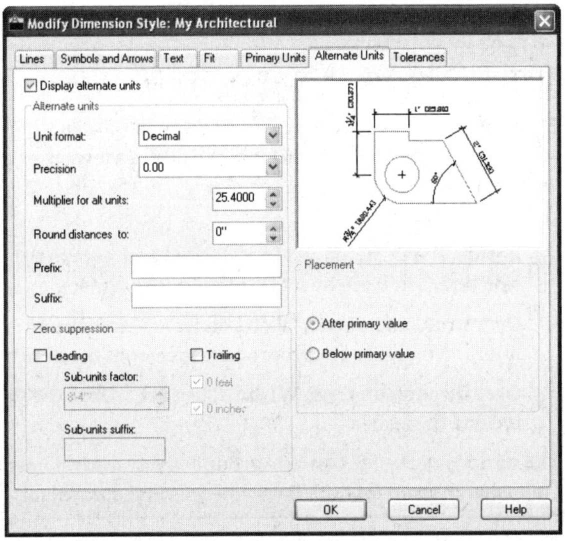

4. Select the appropriate option from the Unit Format drop-down list. U.S. users should select Decimal if you want to show metric alternate units. Metric users should select Architectural.

5. Select an appropriate precision value from the Precision drop-down list.

6. Enter a scale factor for your alternate dimension in the Multiplier For Alt Units input box. For U.S. users, the default value is **25.4**. This value converts feet-and-inch dimensions to millimeters. In our metric examples, you've been using centimeters, so change this setting to 2.54. Metric users should enter **0.3937** to convert centimeters to feet and inches.

7. In the Placement group, select where you want the alternate dimension to appear in relation to the main dimension.

8. You don't really want to display alternate units now, so turn off the Display Alternate Units setting.

9. Click OK to close the Modify Dimension Style dialog box. The Dimension Style Manager dialog box appears again.

Setting the Current Dimension Style

Before you can begin to use your new dimension style, you must make it the current default:

1. Click My Architectural in the Styles list box in the Dimension Style Manager dialog box.

2. Click the Set Current button at the far right in the dialog box.

3. Click Close to exit the Dimension Style Manager dialog box.

You can also select a dimension style from the drop-down list on the Annotate tab's Dimensions panel or the Home tab's expanded Annotation panel. You're now ready to use your new dimension style.

FITTING TEXT AND ARROWS IN TIGHT PLACES

Every now and then, you'll need to dimension a small gap or a small part of an object in which dimension text won't fit. The Fit tab includes a few other settings that control how dimensions act when the extension lines are too close. The Text Placement group contains three options to place the text in tight situations:

Beside The Dimension Line   Places text next to the extension line but close to the dimension line. You'll see how this affects your dimension later.

Over Dimension Line, With Leader   Places the dimension text farther from the dimension line, and includes an arrow or a leader from the dimension line to the text.

Over Dimension Line, Without Leader   Does the same as the previous setting, but doesn't include the leader.

The options in the Fit Options group let you control how text and arrows are placed when there isn't enough room for both between the extension lines.

In the next set of exercises, you'll use the My Architectural style you just created. To switch to another style, open the Dimension Style Manager dialog box again, select the style you want from the Styles list, and click Set Current, as you did in the previous exercise.

Modifying a Dimension Style

To modify an existing dimension style, open the Dimension Style Manager dialog box, highlight the style you want to edit, and then click Modify to open the Modify Dimension Style dialog box. You can then make changes to the different components of the selected dimension style. When you've finished making changes and closed both dialog boxes, all the dimensions associated with the edited style update automatically in your drawing. For example, if you're not using the Annotative scale feature and you decide you need to change the dimension scale of a style, you can open the Modify Dimension Style dialog box and change the Use Overall Scale Of value in the Scale For Dimension Features group of the Fit tab.

So far, you've been introduced to the various settings that let you determine the appearance of a dimension style. I didn't discuss every option; to learn more about the other dimension style options, consult Appendix D. There you'll find descriptions of all the items in the New Dimension Style and Modify Dimension Style dialog boxes, plus reference material covering the system variables associated with each option.

If your application is strictly architectural, you may want to make these same dimension-style changes to the acad.dwt template file or create a set of template files specifically for architectural drawings of different scales.

Drawing Linear Dimensions

The most common type of dimension you'll be using is the *linear dimension*. The linear dimension is an orthogonal dimension measuring the width and length of an object. AutoCAD provides three dimensioning tools for this purpose: Linear (Dimlinear), Continue (Dimcont), and Baseline (Dimbase). These options are readily accessible from the Annotate tab's Dimensions panel.

In the following set of exercises, you'll see figures displaying dimensions in both Imperial and metric units. I've included both measurements so that both Imperial and metric users can more easily follow the tutorial. But in your own drawing, you'll see only one dimension value displayed above the dimension line.

Understanding the Dimensions Panel

Before you apply any dimension, you should study the Annotate tab's Dimensions panel (Figure 12.12). This panel contains nearly all the tools necessary to draw and edit your dimensions.

Many of the dimensioning tools discussed in this chapter can be found in the Home tab's Annotation panel. However, since the focus of this chapter is on dimensioning, unless otherwise noted, use the panels on the Annotate tab.

SELECTING OPTIONS FROM THE DIMENSION FLYOUT

In this chapter, you'll be selecting options from the large flyout on the left side of the Dimensions panel. This flyout starts out showing the Linear tool, but since the flyout name changes depending on the last tool selected, I'll refer to this flyout as the Dimension flyout.

FIGURE 12.12
The Annotate tab's
Dimensions panel.

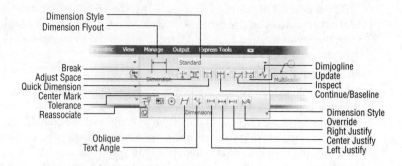

Placing Horizontal and Vertical Dimensions

Let's start by looking at the basic dimensioning tool, Linear. The Linear button (the Dimlinear command) on the Annotate tab's Dimensions panel accommodates both the horizontal and vertical dimensions.

In this exercise, you'll add a vertical dimension to the right side of the Unit plan:

1. Before you start to dimension your drawing, you need to set the scale of your drawing. Select ¼″ = 1′-0″ from the Annotation Scale drop-down list. Metric users should select 1:50.

2. To start either a vertical or horizontal dimension, click Linear from the Dimension flyout on the Annotate tab's Dimensions panel, or enter **Dli↵** at the Command prompt.

3. The `Specify first extension line origin or <select object>:` prompt asks you for the first point of the distance to be dimensioned. An extension line connects the object being dimensioned to the dimension line. Use the Endpoint osnap override, and pick the upper-right corner of the entry, as shown in Figure 12.13.

4. At the `Specify second extension line origin:` prompt, pick the lower-right corner of the living room, as shown in Figure 12.13.

FIGURE 12.13
The dimension line
added to the Unit
drawing

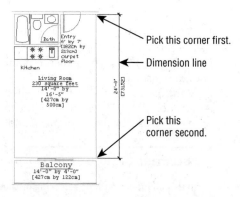

SELECTING OBJECTS TO BE DIMENSIONED

The prompt in step 3 gives you the option of pressing ↵ to select an object. If you do this, you're prompted to pick the object you want to dimension rather than the distance to be dimensioned. This method is discussed later in this chapter.

5. At the next prompt, `Specify dimension line location or [Mtext/Text/Angle/Horizontal/Vertical/Rotated]:`, the dimension line indicates the direction of the dimension and contains the arrows or tick marks. Move your cursor from left to right to display a temporary dimension. This enables you to select a dimension-line location visually.

6. Enter **@4´<0**↵ to tell AutoCAD you want the dimension line to be 4´ to the right of the last point you selected. Metric users should enter **@122<0**↵. (You could pick a point by using your cursor, but this doesn't let you place the dimension line as accurately.) After you've done this, the dimension is placed in the drawing, as shown in Figure 12.13.

Continuing a Dimension

You'll often want to enter a group of dimensions strung together in a line. For example, you may want to continue dimensioning the balcony and align the continued dimension with the dimension you just entered.

To do this, use the Continue option found in the Dimensions panel's Continue/Baseline flyout:

1. Click the Continue tool on the Dimensions panel, or enter **Dco**↵.

2. At the `Specify a second extension line origin or [Undo/Select] <Select>:` prompt, pick the upper-right corner of the balcony. (See the top image in Figure 12.14.)

3. Pick the right end of the rail on the balcony. See the bottom image in Figure 12.14 for the results.

4. Press ↵ twice to exit the command.

If you select the wrong location for a continued dimension, you can click the Undo tool or press **U**↵ to back up your dimension.

The Continue option adds a dimension from where you left off. The last-drawn extension line is used as the first extension line for the continued dimension. AutoCAD keeps adding dimensions as you continue to pick points, until you press ↵.

You probably noticed that the 5˝ dimension is placed away from the dimension line with a leader line pointing to it. This is the result of the 5˝ dimension's text not having enough space to fit between the dimension extension lines. You'll learn about dimension style settings that can remedy this problem. For now, let's continue adding dimensions to the plan.

FIGURE 12.14
The dimension
string, continued
and completed

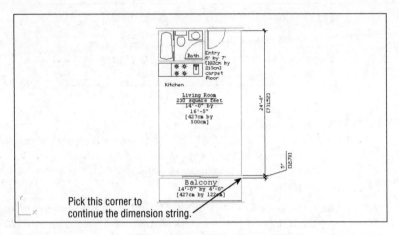

Pick this corner to
continue the dimension string.

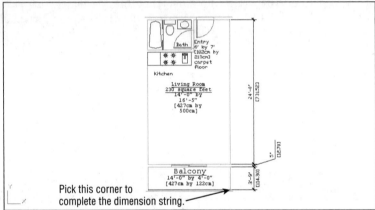

Pick this corner to
complete the dimension string.

CONTINUING A DIMENSION FROM A PREVIOUS DIMENSION

If you need to continue a string of dimensions from an older linear dimension instead of the most recently added one, press ↵ at the Specify a second extension line origin or [Undo/ Select] <Select>: prompt you saw in step 2 of the previous exercise. Then, at the Select continued dimension: prompt, click the extension line from which you want to continue.

Drawing Dimensions from a Common Base Extension Line

Another way to dimension objects is to have several dimensions originate from the same extension line. To accommodate this, AutoCAD provides the Baseline option on the Dimensions control panel and the Dimension drop-down menu.

To see how this works, you'll start another dimension—this time a horizontal one—across the top of the plan:

1. Click the Linear tool in the Dimension flyout on the Dimensions panel. Or, as you did for the vertical dimension, type **Dli**↵ to start the horizontal dimension.

2. At the Specify first extension line origin or <select object>: prompt, use the Endpoint osnap to pick the upper-left corner of the bathroom, as shown in Figure 12.15.

3. At the Specify second extension line origin: prompt, pick the upper-right corner of the bathroom, as shown in Figure 12.15.

FIGURE 12.15
The bathroom with horizontal dimensions

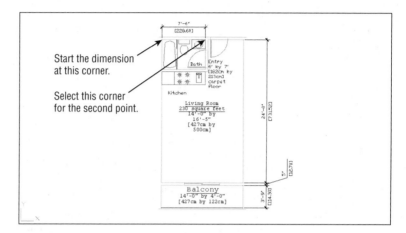

4. At the Specify dimension line location or [Mtext/Text/Angle/ Horizontal/ Vertical/Rotated]: prompt, pick a point above the Unit plan, like the 7′-6″ dimension in Figure 12.15. If you need to, pan your view downward to fit the dimension in.

USE OSNAPS WHILE DIMENSIONING

Because you usually pick exact locations on your drawing as you dimension, you may want to turn on Running Osnaps to avoid the extra step of selecting osnaps from the Osnap shortcut menu.

---

5. You're set to draw another dimension continuing from the first extension line of the dimension you just drew. Click the Baseline tool on the Continue/Baseline flyout of the Dimensions panel. Or, type **Dba**↵ at the Command prompt to start a baseline dimension.

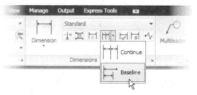

6. At the Specify a second extension line origin or [Undo/Select] <Select>: prompt, click the upper-right corner of the entry, as shown in Figure 12.16.

FIGURE 12.16

The overall width dimension

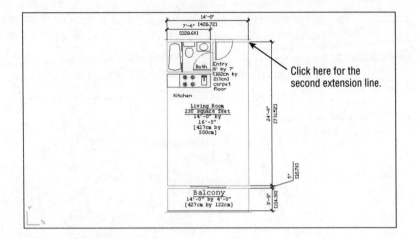

Click here for the second extension line.

7. Press ↵ twice to exit the Baseline command.

8. Pan your view down so it looks similar to Figure 12.16.

In this example, you see that the Baseline option is similar to the Continue option except that the Baseline option enables you to use the first extension line of the previous dimension as the base for a second dimension. The distance between the two horizontal dimension lines is controlled by the Baseline Spacing setting in the Lines tab of the New Dimension Style and Modify Dimension Style dialog boxes.

CONTINUING FROM AN OLDER DIMENSION

You may have noticed in step 7 that you had to press ↵ twice to exit the command. As with Continue, you can draw the baseline dimension from an older dimension by pressing ↵ at the `Specify a second extension line origin [Undo/Select] <Select>:` prompt. You then get the `Select base dimension:` prompt, at which you can either select another dimension or press ↵ again to exit the command.

Adjusting the Distance between Dimensions

As you work toward a deadline, you may find that you cut a few corners, or someone else does, when adding dimensions and a set of parallel dimension lines isn't accurately placed.

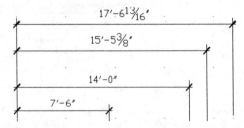

You can quickly adjust the spacing between dimension lines using the Adjust Space tool in the Dimensions panel:

1. Click the Adjust Space tool in the Dimensions panel or type **Dimspace**↵.

2. At the `Select base dimension:` prompt, click the dimension closest to the feature being dimensioned.

3. At the `Select dimensions to space:` prompt, click the next dimension.

4. Continue to select the other parallel dimensions. When you're finished with your selections, press ↵.

5. You see the `Select dimensions to space:` prompt. Enter value or [Auto] <Auto>:

   Enter a value for the distance between the dimension lines. This value should be in full-scale distances. You can also press ↵ and AutoCAD will adjust the distance between dimensions for you.

Editing Dimensions

As you add more dimensions to your drawings, you'll find that AutoCAD occasionally places the dimension text or line in an inappropriate location or that you may need to modify the dimension text. In the following sections, you'll take an in-depth look at how you can modify dimensions to suit those special circumstances that always crop up.

Appending Data to Dimension Text

So far in this chapter, you've been accepting the default dimension text. You can append information to the default dimension value or change it entirely if you need to. At the point when you see the temporary dimension dragging with your cursor, enter **T**↵. Then, using the less-than and greater-than (< and >) symbols, you can add text either before or after the default dimension or replace the symbols entirely to replace the default text. The Properties palette lets you modify the existing dimension text in a similar way (see Chapter 2 for more on the Properties palette). You can open the Properties palette for a dimension by double-clicking on the dimension.

Let's see how this works by changing an existing dimension's text in your drawing:

1. Type **ED**↵. This starts the Ddedit command.

2. Click the last horizontal dimension you added to the drawing at the top of the screen. The Text Editor tab appears in the Ribbon (Figure 12.17).

3. Press the End key to place the cursor at the end of the 14´-0˝ text, and then type **to face of stud** beginning with a space. The space is to ensure that the dimension doesn't run into the text.

4. Click Close Text Editor in the Close panel of the Text Editor tab, and then press ↵ to exit the Ddedit command. The dimension changes to read 14´-0˝ to face of stud.

5. Because you don't need the new appended text for the tutorial, click the Undo button in the Quick Access toolbar to remove the appended text.

FIGURE 12.17
The Text Editor tab

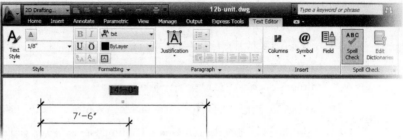

EDITING MULTIPLE DIMENSIONS

In this exercise, you were able to edit only a single dimension. To append text to several dimensions at once, you need to use the Dimension Edit tool. See the sidebar "Making Changes to Multiple Dimensions" later in this chapter for more on this command.

If you need to restore the original dimension text for a dimension whose value has been completely replaced, you can use the steps shown in the previous exercise. However, in step 3, replace the text with the <> bracket symbols.

You can also have AutoCAD automatically add a dimension suffix or prefix to all dimensions instead of just a chosen few by using the Suffix or Prefix option in the Primary Units tab of the New Dimension Style or Modify Dimension Style dialog box. See Appendix D for more on this feature.

AutoCAD provides the associative dimensioning capability to update dimension text automatically when a drawing is edited. Objects called *definition points* determine how edited dimensions are updated.

The definition points are located at the same points you pick when you determine the dimension location. For example, the definition points for linear dimensions are the extension line origins. The definition points for a circle diameter are the points used to pick the circle and the opposite side of the circle. The definition points for a radius are the points used to pick the circle plus the center of the circle.

Definition points are point objects. They're difficult to see because they're usually covered by the feature they define. You can, however, see them indirectly by using grips. The definition points of a dimension are the same as the dimension's grip points. You can see them by clicking a dimension. Try the following:

1. Make sure the Grips feature is turned on. (See Chapter 2 to refresh your memory on the Grips feature.)

2. Click the longest of the three vertical dimensions you drew in the earlier exercise. You'll see the grips of the dimension, as shown in Figure 12.18.

Using Grips to Make Minor Adjustments to Dimensions

The definition points, whose location you can see through their grips, are located on their own unique layer called *Defpoints*. Definition points are displayed regardless of whether the Defpoints layer is on or off.

FIGURE 12.18
The grip points are the same as the definition points on a dimension.

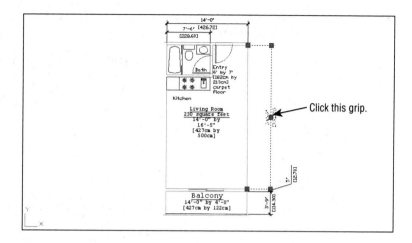

To give you an idea of how these definition points work, try the following exercises that show you how to manipulate the definition points directly.

In this exercise, you'll use coordinates to move a dimension line:

1. With the grips visible, click the grip near the dimension text.

2. Move the cursor around. When you move the cursor vertically, the text moves along the dimension line. When you move the cursor horizontally, the dimension line and text move together, keeping their parallel orientation to the dimensioned floor plan. Here the entire dimension line, including the text, moves. In a later exercise, you'll see how you can move the dimension text independently of the dimension line.

3. Enter @9'<0↵. Metric users should enter @275<0↵. The dimension line, text, and dimension extensions stretch to the new location to the right of the text (see Figure 12.19).

FIGURE 12.19
Moving the dimension line by using its grip

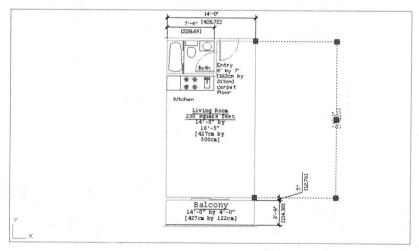

MAKING CHANGES TO MULTIPLE DIMENSIONS

You can use the Dimension Edit tool to edit existing dimensions quickly. This tool gives you the ability to edit more than one dimension's text at one time. One common use for the Dimension Edit tool is to change a string of dimensions to read *Equal* instead of showing the actual dimensioned distance. The following example shows an alternative to using the Properties palette for appending text to a dimension:

1. Type **Ded**↵.

2. At the prompt

   ```
   Enter type of dimension editing [Home/New/Rotate/Oblique]<Home>:
   ```

   type **N**↵ to use the New option. The Text Editor opens, showing 0 in the text box.

3. Use the arrow keys to move the cursor behind or in front of the 0, and then enter the text you want to append to the dimension. You can remove the 0 and replace the dimension with your text as an alternative.

4. Click Close Text Editor in the Close panel of the Text Editor tab.

5. At the Select objects: prompt, pick the dimensions you want to edit. The Select objects: prompt remains, enabling you to select several dimensions.

6. Press ↵ to finish your selection. The dimension changes to include your new text or to replace the existing dimension text.

The Dimension Edit tool is useful in editing dimension text, but you can also use this tool to make graphical changes to the text. Here is a list of the other Dimension Edit tool options:

Home Moves the dimension text to its standard default position and angle.

Rotate Rotates the dimension text to a new angle.

Oblique Skews the dimension extension lines to a new angle. (See the section "Skewing Dimension Lines" later in this chapter.)

MOVING SEVERAL DIMENSION LINES AT ONCE

If you need to move several dimension lines, select them all at the Command prompt, then Shift+click one set of dimension-line grips from each dimension. After you've selected the grips, click one of the hot grips again. You can then move all the dimension lines at once.

In step 3 of the previous exercise, you saw that you can specify an exact distance for the dimension line's new location by entering a relative polar coordinate. Cartesian coordinates work just as well. You can even use object snaps to relocate dimension lines.

Next, try moving the dimension line back by using the Perpendicular osnap:

1. Click the grip at the bottom of the dimension line you just edited.

2. Shift+right-click the right mouse button and choose Perpendicular from the Osnap shortcut menu.

3. Place the cursor on the vertical dimension line that dimensions the balcony and click it.

4. Click Zoom All from the Zoom flyout on the navigation bar and then click Save from the Quick Access toolbar to save this file in its current state.

The selected dimension line moves to align with the other vertical dimension, back to its original location.

Changing Style Settings of Individual Dimensions

In some cases, you have to change an individual dimension's style settings in order to edit it. For example, if you try to move the text of a typical linear dimension, you may find that the text and dimension lines are inseparable. You need to make a change to the dimension style setting that controls how AutoCAD locates dimension text in relation to the dimension line. The following section describes how you can change the style settings of individual dimensions to facilitate changes in the dimension.

Moving Fixed Dimension Text

You've seen how dimension text is attached to the dimension line so that when the text is moved, the dimension line follows. You may encounter situations in which you want to move the text independently of the dimension line. The following steps show how you can separate dimension text from its dimension line. These steps also show how you can change a single dimension's style settings:

1. Click the dimension you want to edit to expose its grips.

2. Right-click and choose Properties from the shortcut menu to open the Properties palette.

3. Scroll down the list of properties until you see the Fit category. If you don't see a list of options under Fit, click the downward-pointing arrow to the right to display a new set of options.

4. Scroll farther down the list until you see the Text Movement option to the right of the Text Movement listing, and then click this option.

5. Click the arrow that appears next to the Keep Dim Line With Text listing to open the drop-down list, then select the Move Text, Add Leader option (Figure 12.20).

6. Close the Properties palette.

Figure 12.20
Select the Move Text, Add Leader option.

In the Properties palette, the Move Text, Add Leader option in the Text Movement listing of the Fit category lets you move the dimension text independently of the dimension line. It also draws a leader from the dimension line to the text. Another option—Move Text, No Leader—does the same thing but doesn't include a leader. You can also set these options for a dimension style by using the Text Placement options in the Fit tab of the New Dimension Style or Modify Dimension Style dialog box.

As you can see from these steps, the Properties palette gives you access to many of the settings you saw for setting up dimension styles. The main difference here is that the Properties palette affects only the dimensions you've selected.

In a previous exercise, you changed the format setting of a single dimension *after* it was placed. These settings can be made a standard part of your Architectural dimension style by using the Modify button in the Dimension Style Manager dialog box.

If you have multiple dimension styles and you want to change an existing dimension to the current dimension style, use the Update tool. Choose Update on the Dimensions panel or type **-Dimstyle**↵ **A**↵. Then select the dimensions you want to change, and press ↵. The selected dimensions will be converted to the current style.

ROTATING AND POSITIONING DIMENSION TEXT

Once in a while, dimension text works better if it's kept in a horizontal orientation, even if the dimension itself isn't horizontal. To rotate dimension text, click the Text Angle tool from the Annotate tab's expanded Dimensions panel, select the dimension text, and then enter an angle or select two points to indicate an angle graphically. You can also enter **0**↵ to return the dimension text to its default angle.

If you need to move the dimension text to the left, center, or right of the dimension line, you can use the Left Justify, Center Justify, or Right Justify tool in the Annotate tab's expanded Dimensions panel.

Editing Dimensions and Other Objects Together

It's helpful to be able to edit a dimension directly by using its grips. But the key feature of AutoCAD's dimensions is their ability to adjust themselves *automatically* to changes in the drawing.

To see how this works, try moving the living room closer to the bathroom wall. You can move a group of lines and vertices by using the Stretch command and the Crossing option:

1. Click the Stretch tool in the Home tab's Modify panel, or type **S**↵ and then **C**↵. You'll see the following prompts:

   ```
   At the Select objects to stretch by crossing-window or crossing-polygon...
   Select objects: C
   Specify first corner:
   ```

2. Pick a crossing window, as illustrated in Figure 12.21, and then press ↵ to confirm your selection.

3. At the Specify base point or [Displacement] <Displacement>: prompt, pick any point on the screen.

FIGURE 12.21

The Stretch crossing window

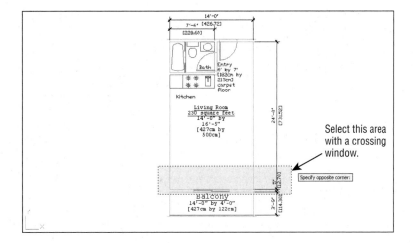

4. At the `Specify second point or <use first point as displacement>:` prompt, enter **@2´<90**↵ to move the wall 2´ in a 90° direction. The wall moves, and the dimension text changes to reflect the new dimensions, as shown in Figure 12.22.

FIGURE 12.22

The moved wall, with the updated dimensions

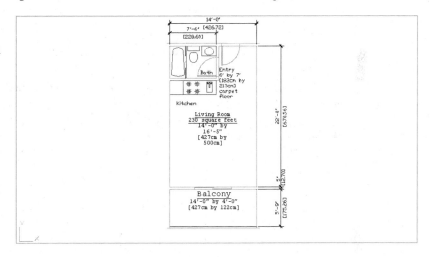

5. After viewing the result of using the Stretch tool, click the Undo tool in the Quick Access toolbar or type **U**↵ to change the drawing back to its previous state.

You can also use the Mirror, Rotate, and Stretch commands with dimensions. The polar arrays also work, and you can use Extend and Trim with linear dimensions.

When you're editing dimensioned objects, be sure to select the dimension associated with the object being edited. As you select objects, using the crossing window (C) or crossing polygon (CP) selection option helps you include the dimensions. For more on these selection options, see Chapter 2.

PLACING DIMENSIONS OVER HATCH PATTERNS

If a hatch pattern or solid fill completely covers a dimension, you can use the Draworder command to have AutoCAD draw the dimension over the hatch or solid fill. See Chapters 7 and 14 for more on various uses of the Draworder command.

MODIFYING THE DIMENSION STYLE SETTINGS BY USING OVERRIDE

In the section "Moving Fixed Dimension Text," you used the Properties palette to facilitate the moving of the dimension text. You can also choose the Override tool in the Annotate tab's expanded Dimensions panel (Dimoverride command) to accomplish the same thing. The Override option enables you to change an individual dimension's style settings. Here's an example that shows how you can use the Override option in place of the Properties palette in the exercise in "Moving Fixed Dimension Text":

1. Press the Esc key twice to make sure you aren't in the middle of a command. Then choose Override from the Annotate tab's expanded Dimensions panel.

2. At the following prompt, type **Dimfit**↵:

   ```
   Enter dimension variable name to override or [Clear overrides]:
   ```

3. At the `Enter new value for dimension variable <3>:` prompt, enter **4**↵. This has the same effect as selecting Move Text, Add Leader from the Fit category of the Properties palette.

4. The `Enter dimension variable name to override:` prompt appears again, enabling you to enter another dimension variable. Press ↵ to move to the next step.

5. At the `Select objects:` prompt, select the dimension you want to change. You can select a group of dimensions if you want to change several dimensions at once. Press ↵ when you've finished with your selection. The dimension settings change for the selected dimensions.

As you can see from this example, the Dimoverride command requires that you know exactly which dimension variable to edit in order to make the desired modification. In this case, setting the Dimfit variable to 4 lets you move the dimension text independently of the dimension line. If you find the Dimoverride command useful, consult Appendix D to determine which system variable corresponds to the Dimension Style dialog box settings.

Associating Dimensions with Objects

You've seen how dimensions and the objects they're associated with can move together so that the dimension remains connected to the object. When you're in the process of editing a drawing, dimensions may lose their association with objects, so you may need to re-create an association between a dimension and an object. The following steps show you how this is done:

1. Choose Reassociate from the Annotate tab's expanded Dimensions panel. You can also type **Dimreassociate**↵ at the Command prompt.

2. At the following prompt, select the dimension that you want to reassociate with an object, and then press ↵:

```
Select dimensions to reassociate
Select Objects:
```

3. At the `Specify first extension line origin or [Select object] <next>:` prompt, an X appears at one of the dimension's definition points.

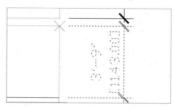

4. Use the Endpoint osnap, and click the end of the object you want to have connected to the definition point indicated in step 3.

5. An X appears at the dimension's other definition point. Use the Endpoint osnap again, and click the other endpoint of the object you want associated with the dimension. You now have the dimension associated with the endpoints of the object. You may have to adjust the location of the dimension line at this point.

In step 3, you see an X at the location of a dimension definition point. If the definition point is already associated with an object, the X appears with a box around it. The box is a reminder that the definition point is already associated with an object and that you'll be changing its association. In this situation, you can press ↵ to switch to the dimension's other definition point.

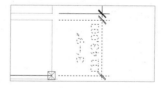

Also in step 3, you have the option to select an object. This option enables you to associate the dimension with an entire object instead of with just one endpoint. If you type **S**↵ at that prompt in step 3, you can then select the object you want to associate with the dimension. The dimension changes so that its definition points coincide with the endpoints of the object. The dimension remains in its original orientation. For example, a vertical dimension remains vertical even if you associate the dimension with a horizontal line. In this situation, the dimension dutifully dimensions the endpoints of the line but shows a distance of zero.

REMOVING DIMENSION ASSOCIATIONS

You can remove a dimension's association with an object by using the Dimdisassociate command. Type **Dimdisassociate**↵ at the Command prompt, select the dimension(s), and then press ↵.

Adding a String of Dimensions with a Single Operation

AutoCAD provides a method for creating a string of dimensions by using a single operation. The Qdim command lets you select a set of objects instead of having to select points. The following exercise demonstrates how the Qdim command works:

1. If you haven't done so already, zoom out so you have an overall view of the Unit floor plan.

2. Click Quick Dimension on the Dimensions panel.

3. At the `Select geometry to dimension:` prompt, place a selection window around the entire left-side wall of the unit.

4. Press ↵ to finish your selection. The following prompt appears:

   ```
   Specify dimension line position, or
   [Continuous/Staggered/Baseline/Ordinate/Radius/Diameter/
   datumPoint/Edit/seTtings] <Continuous>:
   ```

5. Click a point to the left of the wall to place the dimension. A string of dimensions appears, displaying all the dimensions for the wall (Figure 12.23).

FIGURE 12.23
The dimensions for the wall

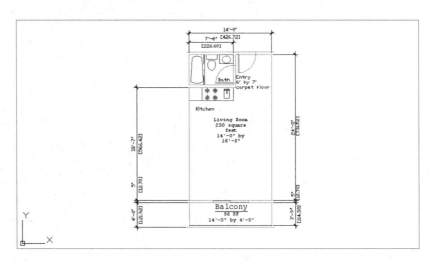

6. When you've finished reviewing the results of this exercise, exit the file without saving it.

The prompt in step 4 indicates several types of dimensions you can choose from. For example, if you want the dimensions to originate from a single baseline, you can enter **B**↵ in step 4 to select the Baseline option.

The Qdim command can be a time-saver when you want to dimension a wall quickly. It may not work in all situations, but if the object you're dimensioning is fairly simple, it can be all you need.

In this exercise, you used a simple window to select the wall. For more complex shapes, try using a crossing polygon selection window. See Chapter 2 for more on crossing polygons.

Adding or Removing the Alternate Dimensions

You may eventually encounter a drawing that contains alternate dimensions, as shown in some of the figures earlier in this chapter. You can remove those alternate dimensions by turning off the alternate dimension features. Here's how it's done:

1. Click the Dimension Style tool in the Annotate tab's Dimensions panel title bar or enter **D**↵ to open the Dimension Style Manager dialog box.

2. Select the style that uses the alternate units. In the Styles list box, choose Modify.

3. Click the Alternate Units tab.

4. Click the Display Alternate Units check box to remove the checkmark.

5. Click OK, and then click Close to close the Dimension Style Manager dialog box.

The dimensions that use the style you just edited change to remove the alternate dimensions. You can also perform the reverse operation and add alternate dimensions to an existing set of dimensions. Follow the steps shown here, but instead of removing the checkmark in step 4, add the checkmark, and make the appropriate setting changes to the rest of the Alternate Units tab.

USING OBJECT SNAP WHILE DIMENSIONING

When you pick intersections and endpoints frequently, as you do during dimensioning, it can be inconvenient to use the Osnap shortcut menu. If you know you'll be using certain osnaps frequently, you can use Running Osnaps. (See the sidebar "The Osnap Options" in Chapter 3 for more on setting up Running Osnaps.)

After you've designated your Running Osnaps, the next time you're prompted to select a point, the selected osnap modes are automatically activated. You can still override the default settings by using the Osnap shortcut menu (Shift+click the right mouse button).

There is a drawback to setting a Running Osnap mode: When your drawing gets crowded, you can end up picking the wrong point by accident. However, you can easily toggle Running Osnap mode off by clicking Object Snap in the status bar or by pressing F3.

Dimensioning Non-orthogonal Objects

So far, you've been reading about how to work with linear dimensions. You can also dimension non-orthogonal objects, such as circles, arcs, triangles, and trapezoids. In the following sections, you'll practice dimensioning a non-orthogonal object.

For the following exercises, you'll use a drawing of a hexagonal-shaped window. Open the 12a-wind.dwg file from the sample files; metric users should open the 12a-wind-metric.dwg file. You can use this file to follow along.

Dimensioning Non-orthogonal Linear Distances

Now you'll dimension the window. The unusual shape of the window prevents you from using the horizontal or vertical dimensions you've used already. However, choosing Aligned from the Dimension flyout in the Dimensions panel enables you to dimension at an angle:

1. Click the Aligned tool in the Dimension flyout on the Dimensions panel. You can also enter **Dal↵** to start the aligned dimension.

2. At the Specify first extension line origin or <select object>: prompt, press ↵. You could pick extension-line origins as you did in earlier examples, but pressing ↵ shows you firsthand how the Select Object option works.

3. At the Select object to dimension: prompt, pick the upper-right face of the hexagon near coordinate 29,22 (75,55 for metric users). As the prompt indicates, you can also pick an arc or a circle for this type of dimension.

4. At the Specify dimension line location or [Mtext/Text/Angle]: prompt, pick a point near coordinate 34,24 (90,60 for metric users). The dimension appears in the drawing as shown in Figure 12.24.

Just as with linear dimensions, you can enter **T↵** in step 4 to enter alternate text for the dimension.

FIGURE 12.24
The aligned dimension of a non-orthogonal line

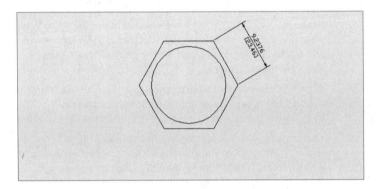

Next, you'll dimension a face of the hexagon. Instead of its actual length, however, you'll dimension a distance at a specified angle—the distance from the center of the face:

1. Click the Linear tool from the Dimension flyout on the Dimensions panel or type **Dli↵**.

2. At the Specify first extension line origin or <select object>: prompt, press ↵.

3. At the Select object to dimension: prompt, pick the lower-right face of the hexagon near coordinate 29,14 (77,33 for metric users).

4. At the Specify dimension line location or [Mtext/Text/Angle/Horizontal/Vertical/Rotated]: prompt, type **R↵** to select the Rotated option.

5. At the Specify angle of dimension line <0>: prompt, enter **30↵**.

6. At the `Specify dimension line location or [Mtext/Text/Angle/Horizontal/Vertical/Rotated]:` prompt, pick a point near coordinate 33,7 (88,12 for metric users). Your drawing will look like Figure 12.25.

FIGURE 12.25
A linear dimension using the Rotated option

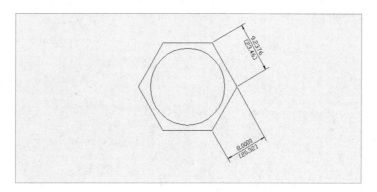

The Dimrotate command accomplishes the same thing with a slight change in the sequence of steps.

Dimensioning Radii, Diameters, and Arcs

To dimension circular objects, you use another set of options from the Dimension menu:

1. Click the Angular tool from the Dimension flyout on the Dimensions panel. Or, enter **Dan**↵.

2. At the `Select arc, circle, line, or <specify vertex>:` prompt, pick the upper-left face of the hexagon near coordinate 15,22 (44,57 for metric users).

3. At the `Select second line:` prompt, pick the top face at coordinate 22,26 (54,62 for metric users).

4. At the `Specify dimension arc line location or [Mtext/Text/Angle]:` prompt, notice that as you move the cursor around the upper-left corner of the hexagon, the dimension changes, as shown in the top images of Figure 12.26.

5. Pick a point near coordinate 21,20 (49,50 for metric users). The dimension is fixed in the drawing. (See the bottom image of Figure 12.26.)

If you need to make subtle adjustments to the dimension line or text location, you can do so using grips after you place the angular dimension.

Now try the Diameter option, which shows the diameter of a circle:

1. Click the Diameter tool in the Dimension flyout on the Dimensions panel, or enter **Ddi**↵ at the Command prompt.

2. At the `Select arc or circle:` prompt, pick the circle.

3. At the `Specify dimension line location or [Mtext/Text/Angle]:` prompt, you see the diameter dimension drag along the circle as you move the cursor. If you move the cursor outside the circle, the dimension line and text also move outside the circle. (See the top image in Figure 12.27.)

FIGURE 12.26
The angular
dimension added
to the window
frame

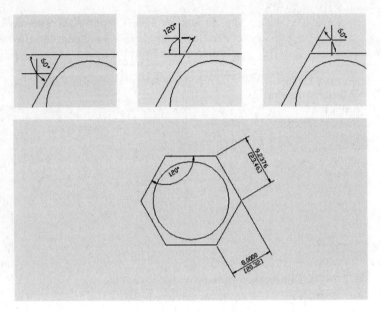

FIGURE 12.27
Dimension show-
ing the diameter
of a circle

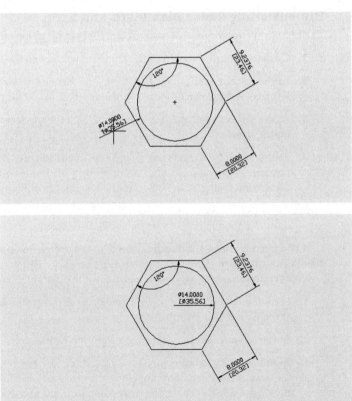

If the dimension text can't fit in the circle, AutoCAD gives you the option to place the dimension text outside the circle as you drag the temporary dimension to a horizontal position.

4. Place the cursor inside the circle so the dimension arrow points in a horizontal direction, as shown in the bottom image of Figure 12.27.

5. With the text centered, click the mouse.

 The Radius tool in the Dimension flyout on the Dimensions panel gives you a radius dimension, just as the Diameter tool provides a circle's diameter.

Figure 12.28 shows a radius dimension on the outside of the circle, but you can place it inside in a manner similar to how you place the diameter dimension. The Center Mark tool on the expanded Dimensions panel places a cross mark in the center of the selected arc or circle.

FIGURE 12.28
A radius dimension shown on the outside of the circle

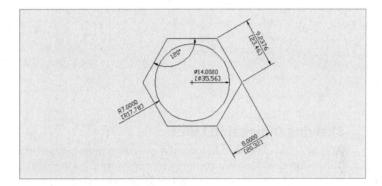

If you need to dimension an arc or a circle whose center isn't in the drawing area, you can use the jogged dimension. Here are the steps:

1. Click the Jogged tool from the Dimension flyout on the Annotate tab's Dimensions panel, or enter **Djo**↵.

2. At the Select arc or circle: prompt, select the object you want to dimension.

3. At the Specify center location override: prompt, select a point that indicates the general direction to the center of the arc or circle. A dimension line appears and follows the movement of your cursor.

4. Position the dimension line where you want it, and then click.

5. Position the dimension line jog where you want it, and then click. The jogged dimension is placed in the drawing (Figure 12.29).

Arc lengths can also be given a dimension using the Arc Length tool. Choose the Arc Length tool from the Dimension flyout on the Dimensions panel, or enter **Dar**↵ at the Command prompt. At the Select Arc or polyline arc segment: prompt, select the arc you want to dimension. It can be either a plain arc or a polyline arc. Once you've selected the arc, the arc dimension appears and moves with the cursor. You can then select the location for the dimension.

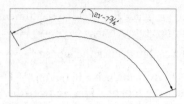

FIGURE 12.29
The jogged dimension in the drawing

Skewing Dimension Lines

At times, you may need to force the extension lines to take on an angle other than 90° to the dimension line. This is a common requirement of isometric drawings, in which most lines are at 30° or 60° angles instead of 90°. To facilitate non-orthogonal dimensions like these, AutoCAD offers the Oblique option:

1. Choose Oblique from the expanded Dimensions panel, or type **Ded.⏎O.⏎**.

2. At the Select objects: prompt, pick the aligned dimension in the upper-right portion of the drawing, and press ⏎ to confirm your selection.

3. At the Enter obliquing angle (Press ENTER for none): prompt, enter **60.⏎** for 60°. The dimension will skew so that the extension lines are at 60° (Figure 12.30).

4. Save the drawing, and exit AutoCAD.

FIGURE 12.30
The extension lines at 60°

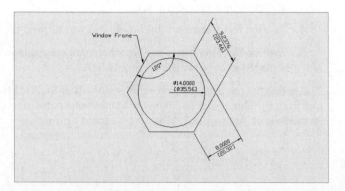

Adding a Note with a Leader Arrow

One type of dimension is something like a text-dimension hybrid. The AutoCAD Multileader tool lets you add a text note combined with an arrow that points to an object in your drawing. Multileaders are easy to use and offer the same text-formatting tools as the Mtext tool. Try the following exercise to get familiar with multileaders:

Multileader

1. Click the Multileader tool in the Annotate tab's Leaders panel (see Figure 12.31), or enter **Mld.⏎**.

FIGURE 12.31
The Leaders panel

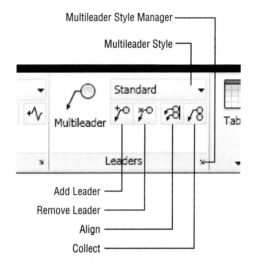

2. At the Specify leader arrowhead location or [leader Landing first/Content first/Options] <Options>: prompt, pick a point near the top-left edge of the hexagon at coordinate 16,24 (45,59 for metric users).

3. At the Specify leader landing location: prompt, enter **@6<110.⏎**. Metric users should enter **@15<110.⏎**. The Text Editor tab appears, along with the text cursor at the note location.

4. Enter **Window Frame** for the note, and then click Close Text Editor in the Text Editor tab's Close panel. Your note appears with the leader arrow similar to the one in Figure 12.32.

FIGURE 12.32
The leader with a note added

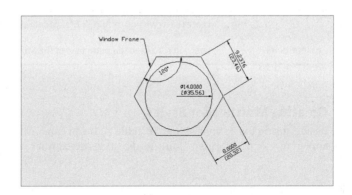

The text in the note is in the current text style unless you specify another style in the Text tab of the New Dimension Style or Modify Dimension Style dialog box. (See the section "The Text Tab" in Appendix D for more information.)

SETTING THE SCALE OF LEADERS

Multileaders have an Annotative option that allows them to automatically adjust to the scale of the drawing. You can find the Annotative option setting in the properties for a specific multileader in the drawing or in the multileader style setting. See the Scale option in Table 12.2, later in this chapter, under Leader Structure Tab.

The Multileader tool offers a lot of options that aren't obvious when you're using it. In step 1 of the previous example, after choosing Multileader, you can press ↵ to modify the behavior of the Multileader tool. You'll see the following prompt:

```
Enter an option [Leader type/leader lAnding/Content
type/Maxpoints/First angle/Second angle/eXit options]
<eXit options>:
```

Table 12.1 gives you a rundown of these options and their functions.

TABLE 12.1:   The Multileader options

OPTION	FUNCTION
Leader type	Allows you to choose between straight-line leaders, curved leaders, or no leaders.
Leader lAnding	Determines whether a leader landing is used. The *leader landing* is the short line that connects the arrow to the note. Also lets you set landing distance.
Content type	Lets you select between mtext or a block for the leader note. You also have the option to choose None.
Maxpoints	Lets you set the number of points you select for the leader. The default is 2.
First angle	Lets you constrain the angle of the leader line to a fixed value.
Second angle	Lets you constrain the angle of the arrow's second line segment if you're using more than two points for the Maxpoints option.
eXit options	Lets you return to the main part of the Multileader command to draw the leader.

Creating Multileader Styles

Besides using the options shown in Table 12.1, you can create multileader styles to control the appearance of multileaders. Multileader styles are similar in concept to text and dimension styles. They allow you to set up the appearance of the leader under a name that you can call up anytime. For example, you may want to have one type of leader that uses a block instead of text for the note and another leader that uses a dot in place of an arrow. Alternatively, you may want to set up a style that uses curved lines instead of straight ones for the leader line. You can create a multileader style for each of these types of leader features and then switch between the leader styles, depending on the requirements of your leader note.

To set up or modify a multileader style, click the Multileader Style Manager tool in the Annotate tab's Leaders panel title bar. You can also enter **mls**↵ at the Command prompt. This opens the Multileader Style Manager dialog box, shown in Figure 12.33. From here, you can select an existing style from the list on the left and click Modify to edit it, or you can click New to create a new one. If you click New, you're asked to select an existing style as a basis for your new style.

FIGURE 12.33
The Multileader Style Manager

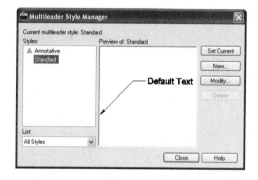

When you click Modify or New, the Modify Multileader Style (Figure 12.34) or New Multileader Style dialog box opens.

Table 12.2 describes the options in each of the tabs of the Modify Multileader Style dialog box. Some of these options are the same as those for the Multileader command.

FIGURE 12.34
The Modify Multileader Style dialog box

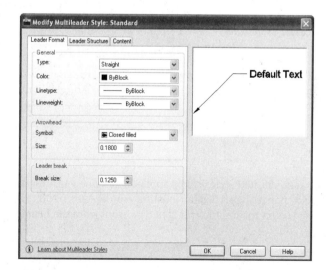

TABLE 12.2: The Modify Multileader Style dialog box options

TAB AND PANEL	FUNCTION
Leader Format tab	
General	Lets you set the leader line to straight or curved. You can also set the color, line weight, and linetype for the leader line.
Arrowhead	Controls the arrowheads.
Leader Break	Controls the size of the gap in a leader line when the Leaderbreak command is applied. Leaderbreak places a break on a leader line where two leader lines cross.
Leader Structure tab	
Constraints	Determines the number of line segments in the leader line. You can also apply angle constraints to the leader-line segments.
Landing Settings	Controls the leader-line landing segment. This is the last line segment that points to the note.
Scale	Lets you control the scale of the leader components. You can either apply a fixed scale or use the Annotative option to have the drawing annotation scale apply to the leader.
Content tab	
Multileader Type	Lets you select the type of object that will be used for the leader note. The options are Mtext, Block, and None.
Text Options	Gives you control over the way the leader note appears. You can control color, text style, size, justification, and orientation.
Leader Connection	Determines the position between the leader line and the note.

Once you've set up a multileader style, you can make it the default style by selecting it from the Multileader Style drop-down list on the Annotate tab's Leaders panel.

The selected style will be applied to any new multileader you add to your drawing. You can also change the style of an existing multileader. To do this, click the multileader to select it, and then select the multileader style you want from the Leaders panel drop-down list.

Editing Multileader Notes

If you need to make changes to the note portion of a multileader, you can do so by double-clicking the note. This brings up the Text Editor tab in the Ribbon, allowing you to make changes as you would in a word processor.

At other times, you may want to change the leader line, arrows, or other graphic features of the multileader. For example, you may want to have all the notes aligned vertically for a neater appearance. As another option, you may want to add more leader arrows so the note points to several objects in the drawing instead of just one.

The Leaders panel offers several tools that let you make these types of changes to your leader notes (refer back to Figure 12.31). The Add Leader and Remove Leader tools let you add or remove leaders from a multileader. The Add Leader tool is a handy tool if you want a single note to point to several objects. The Align tool lets you align the note portion of several multileaders. Finally, the Collect tool lets you collect several multileaders that use blocks for notes into a single note.

Breaking a Dimension Line for a Leader

In a crowded drawing, your multileader arrow may have to cross over a dimension line. In many drafting conventions, when a leader line crosses over a dimension line, the dimension line must be shown with a gap.

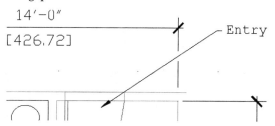

You can apply a gap to a dimension line using the Dimbreak tool. Here's how it works:

1. Choose Break from the Dimensions panel.

2. At the `Select dimension to add/remove break or [Multiple]:` prompt, select a dimension line, or enter **M↵** and select multiple dimension lines.

3. When you're finished with your selection, press ↵. Note that this ↵ is necessary only when using the Multiple option.

4. At the `Select object to break dimension or [Auto/Remove] <Auto>:` prompt, press ↵. A gap appears wherever a leader line or other dimension line crosses over the selected dimension line.

If you prefer to indicate a break manually, enter **M↵** at the prompt in step 4. This allows you to select two points on the dimension, indicating where the gap is to occur. If additional dimension or leader lines are added that cross over the dimension line, repeat your use of the Dimbreak tool. To remove an existing break, use the Remove option in step 4 by entering **R↵**.

Applying Ordinate Dimensions

In mechanical drafting, *ordinate dimensions* are used to maintain the accuracy of machined parts by establishing an origin on the part. All major dimensions are described as X coordinates or Y coordinates of that origin. The origin is usually an easily locatable feature of the part, such as a machined bore or two machined surfaces.

Figure 12.35 shows a typical application of ordinate dimensions. In the lower-right corner, note the two dimensions whose leaders are jogged. Also note the origin location in the center circle.

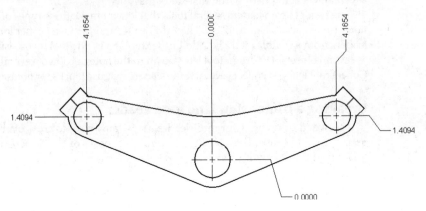

FIGURE 12.35
A drawing
using ordinate
dimensions

To use AutoCAD's Ordinate command, perform the following steps:

1. Click Origin from the View tab's Coordinates panel, or type **UCS.↵Or.↵**.

2. At the Specify new origin point <0,0,0>: prompt, click the exact location of the origin of your part.

3. Toggle Ortho mode on in the status bar.

4. Click the Ordinate tool in the Dimension flyout on the Dimensions panel. You can also enter **Dor.↵** to start the ordinate dimension.

5. At the Specify feature location: prompt, click the item you want to dimension. The direction of the leader determines whether the dimension will be of the Xdatum or the Ydatum.

6. At the Specify leader endpoint or [Xdatum/Ydatum/Mtext/Text/Angle]: prompt, indicate the length and direction of the leader. Do this by positioning the rubber-banding leader perpendicular to the coordinate direction you want to dimension and then clicking that point.

In steps 1 and 2, you used the UCS feature to establish a second origin in the drawing. The Ordinate Dimension tool then uses that origin to determine the ordinate dimensions. You'll get a chance to work with the UCS feature in Chapter 22.

You may have noticed options in the Command window for the Ordinate Dimension tool. The Xdatum and Ydatum options force the dimension to be of the X or Y coordinate no matter what direction the leader takes. The Mtext option opens the Text Editor tab in the Ribbon, enabling you to append or replace the ordinate dimension text. The Text option lets you enter replacement text directly through the Command window.

If you turn off Ortho mode, the dimension leader is drawn with a jog to maintain the orthogonal (look back at Figure 12.35).

Adding Tolerance Notation

In mechanical drafting, *tolerances* are a key part of a drawing's notation. They specify the allowable variation in size and shape that a mechanical part can have. To help facilitate tolerance notation, AutoCAD provides the Tolerance command, which offers common ISO tolerance symbols together with a quick way to build a standard feature-control symbol. *Feature-control symbols* are industry-standard symbols used to specify tolerances. If you're a mechanical engineer or drafter, AutoCAD's tolerance notation options will be a valuable tool. However, a full discussion of tolerances requires a basic understanding of mechanical design and drafting and is beyond the scope of this book.

To use the Tolerance command, choose Tolerance from the expanded Dimensions panel or type **Tol**↵ at the Command prompt to open the Geometric Tolerance dialog box (Figure 12.36).

FIGURE 12.36
The Geometric Tolerance dialog box

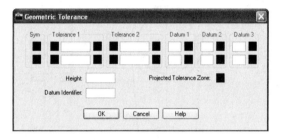

This is where you enter tolerance and datum values for the feature-control symbol. You can enter two tolerance values and three datum values. In addition, you can stack values in a two-tiered fashion.

Click a box in the Sym group to open the Symbol dialog box.

The top image in Figure 12.37 shows what each symbol in the Symbol dialog box represents. The bottom image shows a sample drawing with a feature symbol used on a cylindrical object. The symbols in the sample drawing show that the upper cylinder needs to be parallel within 0.003″ of the lower cylinder. Note that mechanical drawings often use measurements in thousandths, so 0.3 means 0.003.

FIGURE 12.37
The tolerance symbols

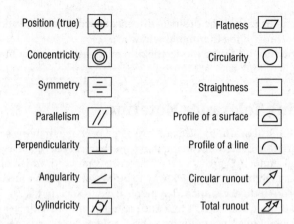

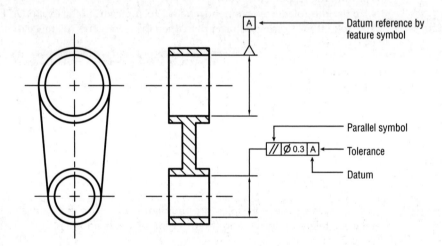

In the Geometric Tolerance dialog box, you can click a box in any of the Datum groups or a box in the right side of the Tolerance groups to open the Material Condition dialog box. This dialog box contains standard symbols relating to the maximum and minimum material conditions of a feature on the part being dimensioned.

Adding Inspection Dimensions

Another type of dimension related to tolerances is the inspection dimension. This is a type of dimension notation that indicates how often the tolerances of a dimension should be checked.

To add an inspection dimension, first add a regular linear dimension as described in the early part of this chapter. Next, follow these steps:

1. Choose Inspect from the Dimensions panel or type **Diminspect**.⏎. The Inspection Dimension dialog box appears (Figure 12.38).

FIGURE 12.38
The Inspection
Dimension
dialog box

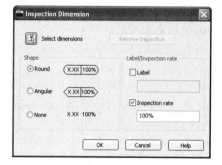

2. Click the Select Dimensions tool. The dialog box temporarily closes to allow you to select a dimension.

3. Select a shape option from the Shape group.

4. Enter a value for the Label and Inspection Rate input boxes, and then click OK.

The dimension appears with the additional changes from the dialog box (Figure 12.39).

FIGURE 12.39
The dimension
with the additional
changes

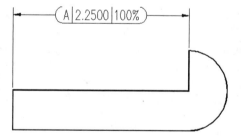

The Bottom Line

Understand the components of a dimension. Before you start to dimension with AutoCAD, it helps to become familiar with the different parts of a dimension. This will help you set up your dimensions to fit the style of dimensions that you need.

  Master It Name a few of the dimension components.

Create a dimension style. As you become more familiar with technical drawing and drafting, you'll learn that there are standard formats for drawing dimensions. Arrows, text size, and even the way dimension lines are drawn are all subject to a standard format. Fortunately,

AutoCAD offers dimension styles that let you set up your dimension format once and then call up that format whenever you need it.

Master It What is the name of the dialog box that lets you manage dimension styles, and how do you open it?

Draw linear dimensions. The most common dimension that you'll use is the linear dimension. Knowing how to place a linear dimension is a big first step in learning how to dimension in AutoCAD.

Master It Name the three locations you're asked for when placing a linear dimension.

Edit dimensions. Dimensions often change in the course of a project, so you should know how to make changes to dimension text or other parts of a dimension.

Master It How do you start the command to edit dimension text?

Dimension non-orthogonal objects. Not everything you dimension will use linear dimensions. AutoCAD offers a set of dimension tools for dimensioning objects that aren't made up of straight lines.

Master It Name some of the types of objects for which a linear dimension isn't appropriate.

Add a note with a leader arrow. In addition to dimensions, you'll probably add lots of notes with arrows pointing to features in a design. AutoCAD offers the multileader for this purpose.

Master It What two types of objects does the multileader combine?

Apply ordinate dimensions. When accuracy counts, ordinate dimensions are often used because they measure distances that are similar to coordinates from a single feature.

Master It What AutoCAD feature do you use for ordinate dimensions that isn't strictly associated with dimensions?

Add tolerance notation. Mechanical drafting often requires the use of special notation to describe tolerances. AutoCAD offers some predefined symbols that address the need to include tolerance notation in a drawing.

Master It How do you open the Geometric Tolerance dialog box?

Part 3

Mastering Advanced Skills

Chapter 13

Using Attributes

Early in this book, you learned how to create blocks, which are assemblies of AutoCAD objects. Blocks enable you to form parts or symbols that can be easily reproduced. Furniture, bolts, doors, and windows are a few common items that you can create with blocks. Whole rooms and appliances can also be made into blocks. There is no limit to a block's size.

AutoCAD also offers a feature called *attributes* that allows you to store text information as a part of a block. For example, you can store the material specifications for a bolt or other mechanical part that you've converted into a block. If your application is architecture, you can store the material, hardware, and dimensional information for a door or window that has been converted into a block. You can then quickly gather information about that block that may not be obvious from the graphics.

Attribute text can be set up to be invisible, or it can be displayed as text in the drawing. If it's invisible, you can easily view the attribute information by double-clicking the block that contains the attribute. The attribute information is displayed in a dialog box. This information can also be extracted to a database or spreadsheet, giving you the ability to keep an inventory of the blocks in your drawing. You can even convert attribute information into tables in an AutoCAD drawing. This can help you make quick work of parts lists or door and window schedules. By using attributes, you can keep track of virtually any object in a drawing or maintain textual information in the drawing that can be queried.

Keeping track of objects is just one way to use attributes. You can also use them in place of text objects when you must keep text and graphic items together. One common example is the reference symbol in an architectural drawing. Reference symbols are used to indicate the location of more detailed information in a drawing set, such as the elevation views of a room or a cross-section of a wall or other part of a building. In this chapter, you'll use attributes for one of their common functions: maintaining lists of parts. In this case, the parts are doors. This chapter also describes how to import these attributes into a database-management program. As you go through the exercises, think about the ways attributes can help you in your particular application.

In this chapter, you'll learn to do the following:

◆ Create attributes

◆ Edit attributes

◆ Extract and export attribute information

Creating Attributes

Attributes depend on blocks. You might think of an attribute as text information attached to a block. The information can be a description of the block or some other pertinent text. For example, you can include an attribute definition with the Door block you created in Chapter 4. Subsequently, every time you insert the Door block, you'll be prompted for a value associated with that door. The value can be a number, a height or width value, a name, or any type of text information you want. After you enter a value, it's stored as part of the Door block in the drawing database. This value can be displayed as text attached to the Door block, or it can be invisible. You can change the value at any time. You can even specify the prompts for the attribute value.

However, suppose you don't have the attribute information when you design the Door block. As an alternative, you can add the attribute to a *symbol* that is later placed by the door when you know enough about the design to specify what type of door goes where. Figure 13.1 shows a sample door symbol and a table to which the symbol refers. The standard door-type symbol suits this purpose nicely because it's an object that you can set up and use as a block independent of the Door block.

FIGURE 13.1
A door symbol tells you what type of door goes in the location shown. Usually, the symbol contains a number or a letter that is keyed to a table that shows more information about the door.

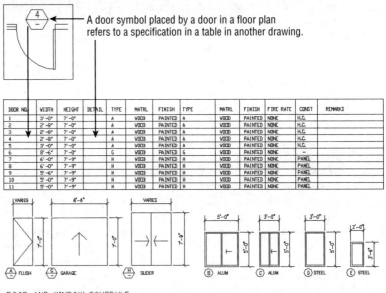

A door symbol placed by a door in a floor plan refers to a specification in a table in another drawing.

DOOR NO.	WIDTH	HEIGHT	DETAIL	TYPE	MATRL	FINISH	TYPE	MATRL	FINISH	FIRE RATE	CONST	REMARKS
1	3'-0"	7'-0"		A	WOOD	PAINTED	A	WOOD	PAINTED	NONE	H.C.	
2	2'-8"	7'-0"		A	WOOD	PAINTED	A	WOOD	PAINTED	NONE	H.C.	
3	2'-8"	7'-0"		A	WOOD	PAINTED	A	WOOD	PAINTED	NONE	H.C.	
4	2'-8"	7'-0"		A	WOOD	PAINTED	A	WOOD	PAINTED	NONE	H.C.	
5	3'-0"	7'-0"		A	WOOD	PAINTED	A	WOOD	PAINTED	NONE	--	
6	8'-6"	7'-0"		G	WOOD	PAINTED	G	WOOD	PAINTED	NONE	--	
7	6'-0"	7'-9"		H	WOOD	PAINTED	H	WOOD	PAINTED	NONE	PANEL	
8	6'-0"	7'-9"		H	WOOD	PAINTED	H	WOOD	PAINTED	NONE	PANEL	
9	5'-6"	7'-9"		H	WOOD	PAINTED	H	WOOD	PAINTED	NONE	PANEL	
10	5'-0"	7'-9"		H	WOOD	PAINTED	H	WOOD	PAINTED	NONE	PANEL	
11	5'-0"	7'-9"		H	WOOD	PAINTED	H	WOOD	PAINTED	NONE	PANEL	

DOOR AND WINDOW SCHEDULE

Adding Attributes to Blocks

In the following exercise, you'll create a door-type symbol, which is commonly used to describe the size, thickness, and other characteristics of any given door in an architectural drawing. The symbol is usually a circle, a hexagon, or a diamond with a number in it. The number is generally cross-referenced to a schedule that lists all the door types and their characteristics.

You'll create a new block containing attribute definitions in the file for which the block is intended: the Plan file. You may also use the 13a-plan file. You'll create the block in the file so you can easily insert it where it belongs in the plan.

First, you open the `Plan` file and set up a view appropriate for creating the block with the attribute:

1. Open the `13a-plan.dwg` file. Metric users can use the file `13a-plan-metric.dwg`. These are similar to the `Plan.dwg` file you've created on your own, with a few additions to facilitate the exercises in this chapter.

2. Click Window from the Zoom flyout on the View tab's Navigate panel. You'll use the Window Zoom option to specify an area in the drawing. You can also use the Zoom Window option on the navigation bar.

3. At the `Specify first corner:` prompt, enter **0,0↵**.

4. At the `Specify opposite corner:` prompt, enter **12,9** (**30.5,22.8** for metric users). This causes your view to zoom in to a location near the origin of the drawing in a 12″-x-9″ area.

You zoom in to this small area because you'll draw the block at its paper size of ¼″ (or 0.6 cm for metric users). Now you're ready to create the block and attribute. You'll start by drawing the graphics of the block, and then you'll add the attribute definition:

1. Draw a circle with its center at coordinate 7,5 (15,11 for metric users) and a diameter of 0.25 (0.6 for metric users). The circle is automatically placed on layer 0, which is the current layer. Remember that objects in a block that are on layer 0 take on the color and linetype assignment of the layer on which the block is inserted.

2. Zoom in to the circle so it's about the same size as that shown in Figure 13.2.

3. If the circle looks like an octagon, type **Re↵** to regenerate your drawing.

FIGURE 13.2
The attribute definition inserted in the circle

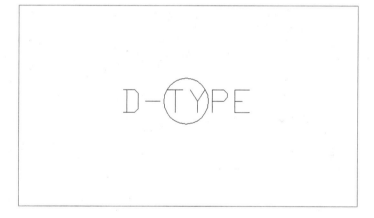

4. Click the Define Attributes tool from the Home tab's expanded Block panel or type **Att↵** to open the Attribute Definition dialog box (Figure 13.3).

5. In the Attribute group, click the Tag input box, and enter **D-TYPE**.

FIGURE 13.3
The Attribute Defi-
nition dialog box

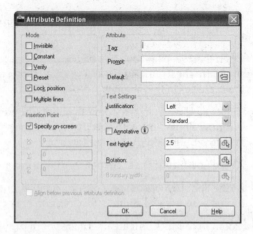

UNDERSTANDING THE ATTRIBUTE TAG

The attribute tag is equivalent to a field name in a database. You can also think of the tag as the attribute's name or ID. It can help to identify the purpose of the attribute. The tag can be a maximum of
255 characters but can't contain spaces. If you plan to use the attribute data in a database program,
check that program's documentation for other restrictions on field names.

---

6. Press the Tab key or click the Prompt input box, and enter **Door type**. This is the text for
the prompt that will appear when you insert the block containing this attribute. Often the
prompt is the same as the tag, but it can be anything you like. Unlike the tag, the prompt
can include spaces and other special characters.

GIVE YOUR PROMPTS MEANINGFUL NAMES

Use a prompt that gives explicit instructions so the user will know exactly what is expected. Consider
including an example in the prompt. (Enclose the example in square brackets to imitate the way
AutoCAD prompts often display defaults.)

---

7. Click the Default input box, and enter a hyphen (-). This is the default value for the door-
type prompt.

MAKE YOUR DEFAULTS USEFUL

If an attribute is to contain a number that will later be used for sorting in a database, use a default
attribute value such as 000 to indicate the number of digits required. The zeros can also serve to
remind the user that values less than 100 must be preceded by a leading zero, as in 099.

---

8. Click the Justification drop-down list, and select Middle center. This enables you to center the attribute on the circle's center. The Text Settings group includes several other options. Because attributes appear as text, you can apply the same settings to them as you would to single-line text.

9. In the Text Height input box, change the value to **0.125**. (Metric users should enter **0.3**.) This makes the attribute text 0.125″ (0.3 cm) high.

10. Select the Annotative option. This allows the attribute to adjust in size automatically according to the annotation scale of the drawing.

11. In the Insertion Point group, make sure the Specify On-Screen check box is selected.

12. Click OK to close the dialog box.

13. Using the Center osnap, pick the center of the circle. You need to place the cursor on the circle's circumference, not in the circle's center, to obtain the center by using the osnap. The attribute definition appears at the center of the circle (see Figure 13.2).

You've just created your first attribute definition. The attribute definition displays its tag in all uppercase letters to help you identify it. When you later insert this file into another drawing, the tag turns into the value you assign to it when it's inserted. If you want only one attribute, you can stop here and save the file. The next section shows how you can quickly add several more attributes to your drawing.

Copying and Editing Attribute Definitions

Next, you'll add a few more attribute definitions, but instead of using the Attribute Definition dialog box, you'll make an arrayed copy of the first attribute and then edit the attribute definition copies. This method can save you time when you want to create several attribute definitions that have similar characteristics. By making copies and editing them, you'll also get a chance to see firsthand how to change an attribute definition.

Follow these steps to make copies of the attribute:

1. Click Array on the Home tab's Modify panel or type **Ar⏎** to open the Array dialog box.

2. Click the Rectangular Array radio button in the upper-left corner.

3. Click the Select Objects button, and select the attribute definition you just created. Press ⏎ to confirm your selection.

4. In the Rows input box, enter **7**; in the Columns input box, enter **1**.

5. Enter **-0.18** in the Row Offset input box (**-0.432** for metric users) and **0** in the Column Offset input box. The Row Offset value is approximately 1.5 times the height of the attribute text height. The minus sign in the Row Offset value causes the array to be drawn downward.

6. Click OK.

7. Click the Zoom Extents tool from the Zoom flyout on the navigation bar or enter **Z**↵ **E**↵ to view all the attributes.

Now you're ready to modify the copies of the attribute definitions:

1. Press Esc twice to clear any selections or commands, and click the attribute definition just below the original.

2. Right-click and choose Properties from the shortcut menu to open the Properties palette.

DOUBLE-CLICK TO EDIT ATTRIBUTE DEFINITIONS

You can double-click an attribute definition to change its Tag, Prompt, or Default value in the Edit Attribute Definition dialog box. However, this dialog box doesn't let you change an attribute definition's visibility mode.

---

3. Scroll down the list of properties until you see the Invisible option in the Misc category.

4. Select Yes from the Invisible option drop-down list.

5. Scroll back up the list of properties and locate the Tag option in the Text category.

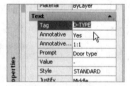

6. Highlight the Tag value to the right, and type **D-SIZE**↵. The attribute changes to reflect the change in the Tag value.

7. While still in the Text category, highlight the Prompt value, and type **Door size**↵.

8. In the Value field, type **3′-0″**↵. Metric users should type **90**↵.

Make sure you press ↵ after entering a new value for the properties in the Properties palette. Pressing ↵ confirms your new entry.

You've just learned how to edit an attribute definition. Now you'll make changes to the other attribute definitions:

1. Press Esc twice so that no attribute is selected, and then click the next attribute down so you can display its properties in the Properties palette.

2. Continue to edit this and the rest of the attribute definition properties by using the attribute settings listed in Table 13.1. To do this, repeat steps 4 through 8 of the preceding exercise for each attribute definition, replacing the Tag, Prompt, and Default values with those shown in Table 13.1. Also, make sure all but the original attributes have the Invisible option set to Yes.

3. When you've finished editing the attribute definition properties, close the Properties palette.

When you later insert a file or a block containing attributes, the attribute prompts will appear in the order that their associated definitions were created. If the order of the prompts at insertion time is important, you can control it by editing the attribute definitions so their creation order corresponds to the desired prompt order. You can also control the order by using the Block Attribute Manager, which you'll look at later in this chapter.

TABLE 13.1:   Attributes for the door-type symbol

TAG	PROMPT	DEFAULT VALUE
D-NUMBER	Door number	-
D-THICK	Door thickness	-
D-RATE	Fire rating	-
D-MATRL	Door material	-
D-CONST	Door construction	-

Make sure the Invisible option is selected for the attributes in this table.

Turning the Attribute Definitions into a Block

You need to perform one more crucial step before these attribute definitions can be of any use. You need to turn the attribute definitions into a block, along with the circle:

1. Click the Create tool in the Home tab's Block panel, or enter **B**↵.

2. In the Block Definition dialog box, enter **S-DOOR** for the name.

3. In the Base Point group, click the Pick Point tool, and then use the Center osnap to select the center of the circle.

4. In the Objects group, click the Select Objects tool, and select the circle and all the attributes. Press ↵ when you've completed your selection.

5. In the Behavior group, select the Annotative option. This ensures that the block is scaled to the appropriate size for the scale of the drawing into which it's inserted.

6. Click OK. When the Edit Attribute dialog box opens, click OK to close it.

7. The attributes and the circle are now a block called S-DOOR. You can delete the S-DOOR block on your screen.

UNDERSTANDING ATTRIBUTE DEFINITION MODES

The Attribute Definition dialog box includes several choices in the Mode group; you've used one of these modes to see what it does. You won't use any of the other modes in this tutorial, but here is a list describing all the modes for your reference:

Invisible   Controls whether the attribute is shown as part of the drawing.

Constant   Creates an attribute that doesn't prompt you to enter a value. Instead, the attribute has a constant, or fixed, value you give it during creation. Constant mode is used when you know you'll assign a fixed value to an object. After constant values are set in a block, you can't change them by using the standard set of attribute-editing commands.

Verify   Causes AutoCAD to review the attribute values you enter at insertion time and to ask you whether they're correct. This option appears only when the Attribute dialog box is turned off (the Attdia system variable is set to 0).

Preset   Causes AutoCAD to assign the default value to an attribute automatically when its block is inserted. This saves time because a preset attribute won't prompt you for a value. Unlike attributes created in Constant mode, a preset attribute can be edited.

Lock Position   Prevents the attribute from being moved from its original location in the block when you're grip editing.

Multiple Lines   Allows the attribute to contain multiple lines of text, similar to Mtext objects. When this option is turned on, you can specify a text boundary width.

With the exception of Invisible mode, none of these modes can be altered after the attribute becomes part of a block. Later in this chapter, I'll show you how to make an invisible attribute visible.

Once you've created the block, you can place it anywhere in the drawing using the Insert command or the Insert tool on the Home tab's Block panel. You'll insert this block in another location in the drawing. If you want to use the block in other drawings, you can use the Wblock command to save the block as a drawing file, or you can use the DesignCenter palette to drag and drop blocks from a drawing file. (See Chapter 29 for more on the DesignCenter.)

Inserting Blocks Containing Attributes

In the preceding section, you created a door-type symbol at the desired size for the plotted symbol. This size is known as the *paper size*. Because you turned on the Annotative option for the attribute and block, you can use the Annotation Scale setting to have the block insert at the appropriate size for the scale of the drawing. The following steps demonstrate the process of inserting a block that contains attributes. First, set up your view and annotation scale in preparation to insert the blocks:

1. Turn on Attribute Dialog mode by entering **Attdia.⏎1.⏎** at the Command prompt. This enables you to enter attribute values through a dialog box in the next exercise. Otherwise, you'd be prompted for the attribute values in the Command window.

2. Select 1/8″=1′-0″ (1:100 for metric users) from the Annotation Scale drop-down list in the lower-right corner of the AutoCAD window. This ensures that the block appears at the proper size for the drawing scale.

Views

3. In the View tab's Views panel, open the Views flyout and select First from the list. This is a view that has been saved in this drawing. (See "Taking Control of the AutoCAD Display" in Chapter 7 for more on saving views.)

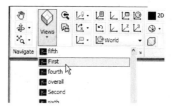

4. Be sure the Ceiling and Flr-pat layers are off. Normally, in a floor plan, the door headers aren't visible anyway and their appearance will interfere with the placement of the door-reference symbol.

5. Finally, you can begin to place the blocks in the drawing. Click the Insert tool on the Home tab's Block panel or type I.⏎ to open the Insert dialog box.

6. Select S-DOOR from the Name drop-down list.

7. In the Insertion Point group, make sure the Specify On-Screen option is turned on.

8. In the Scale group, make sure the Uniform Scale check box is selected.

9. In the Rotation group, make sure the Specify On-Screen option is turned off, then click OK.

   Now you're ready to place the block in your drawing in the appropriate locations and enter the attribute values.

10. AutoCAD is waiting for you to select a location for the symbol. To place the symbol, click in the doorway of the lower-left unit, near coordinate 41′-3″,72′-4″. Metric users should use coordinate 1256,2202. When you click the location, the Edit Attributes dialog box opens (Figure 13.4).

11. In the Door Type input box, enter **A.⏎**. Note that this is the prompt you created. Note also that the default value is the hyphen you specified. Attribute data is case sensitive, so any text you enter in all capital letters is stored in all capital letters.

12. In the Door Number input box, change the hyphen to **116**. Continue to change the values for each input box as shown in Table 13.2.

FIGURE 13.4
The Edit Attributes
dialog box

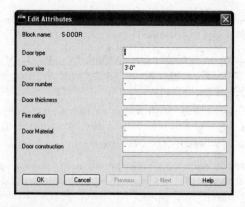

TABLE 13.2: Attribute values for the typical studio entry door

PROMPT	VALUE
Door Type	A
Door Size	3′-0″ (90 cm for metric)
Door Number	(Same as room number; see Figure 13.6)
Door Thickness	1¾″ (4 cm for metric)
Fire Rating	20 min.
Door Material	Wood
Door Construction	Solid core

13. When you're finished changing values, click OK and the symbol appears. The only attribute you can see is the one you selected to be visible: the door type.

14. Add the rest of the door-type symbols for the apartment entry doors by copying or arraying the door symbol you just inserted. You can use the previously saved views found in the 3D Navigation drop-down list in the View tab's Views panel to help you get around the drawing quickly. Don't worry that the attribute values aren't appropriate for each unit; you'll see how to edit the attributes in the next section.

In addition to the S-DOOR block, you'll need another block for the room number. To save some time, I've included a block called S-APART that contains a rectangle and a single attribute definition for the room number (see Figure 13.5).

Do the following to insert the room-number block:

1. Choose Insert from the Home tab's Block panel, and select S-APART from the Name drop-down list.

2. Make sure the Specify On-Screen setting is turned on only for the Insertion point, and then click OK.

FIGURE 13.5
The apartment-
number symbol

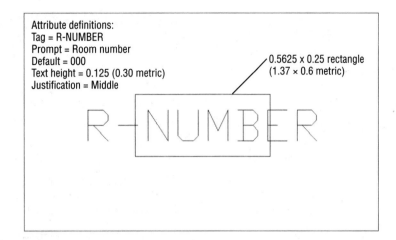

Attribute definitions:
Tag = R-NUMBER
Prompt = Room number
Default = 000
Text height = 0.125 (0.30 metric)
Justification = Middle

0.5625 x 0.25 rectangle
(1.37 × 0.6 metric)

R-NUMBER

3. Insert the S-APART block into the lower-left unit. Give the attribute of this block the value **116**.

4. Copy or array the S-APART block so there is one S-APART block in each unit. You'll learn how to modify the attributes to reflect their proper values in the following section. Figure 13.6 shows what the view should look like after you've entered the door symbols and the apartment numbers.

FIGURE 13.6
An overall view
of the plan with
door symbols
and apartment
numbers added

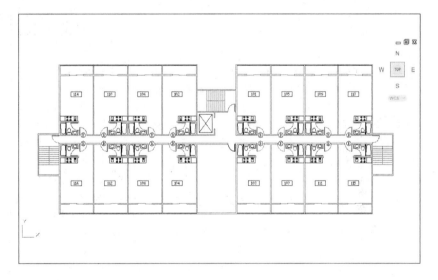

Editing Attributes

Because drawings are usually in flux even after construction or manufacturing begins, you'll eventually have to edit previously entered attributes. In the example of the apartment building, many things can change before the final set of drawings is completed.

Attributes can be edited individually or *globally*—you can edit several occurrences of a particular attribute tag all at one time. In the following sections, you'll use both individual and global editing techniques to make changes to the attributes you've entered so far. You'll also practice editing invisible attributes.

Editing Attribute Values One at a Time

AutoCAD offers an easy way to edit attributes one at a time through a dialog box. The following exercise demonstrates this feature:

1. Restore the First view by selecting First from the Views flyout in the View tab's Views panel.

2. Double-click the apartment number attribute in the unit just to the right of the first unit in the lower-left corner to open the Enhanced Attribute Editor (Figure 13.7). LT users will see the Edit Attributes dialog box, which lists the attributes in a single column.

FIGURE 13.7
The Enhanced Attribute Editor

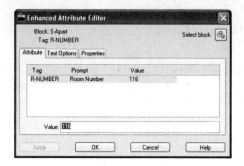

3. Change the value in the Value input box to **112**, and click OK to make the change.

4. Do this for each room, using Figure 13.8 as a reference for assigning room numbers.

FIGURE 13.8
Apartment numbers for one floor of the studio apartment building

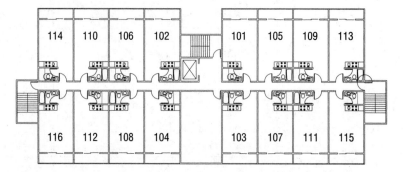

5. Go back and edit the door number attribute for the S-DOOR blocks. Give each door the same number as the room number it's associated with. See Figure 13.8 for the room numbers.

Editing Attribute Text Formats and Properties

You may have noticed that the Enhanced Attribute Editor in the preceding exercise has three tabs: Attribute, Text Options, and Properties. When you double-click a block containing attributes, the Enhanced Attribute Editor dialog box opens at the Attribute tab. You can use the other two tabs to control the size, font, color, and other properties of the selected attribute.

The Text Options tab (Figure 13.9) lets you alter the attribute text style, justification, height, rotation, width factor, and oblique angle. (See Chapter 10 for more on these text options.)

FIGURE 13.9
The Enhanced
Attribute Editor's
Text Options tab

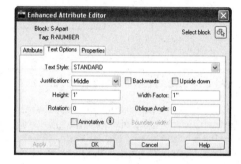

The Properties tab (Figure 13.10) lets you alter the attribute's layer, linetype, color, line weight (effective only on AutoCAD fonts), and plot-style assignments.

FIGURE 13.10
The Enhanced
Attribute Editor's
Properties tab.

In the previous exercise, you edited a block containing a single attribute. Double-clicking a block that contains multiple attributes, such as the S-DOOR block, opens the Enhanced Attribute Editor dialog box at the Attribute tab. This tab displays all the attributes regardless of whether they're visible, as shown in Figure 13.11. You can then edit the value, formats, and properties of the individual attributes by highlighting the attribute in the Attribute tab and using the other tabs to make changes. The changes you make affect only the attribute you've highlighted in the Attribute tab.

The Enhanced Attribute Editor lets you change attribute values, formats, and properties one block at a time, but as you'll see in the next section, you can also make changes to several attributes at once.

FIGURE 13.11

The Enhanced Attribute Editor showing the contents of a block that contains several attributes

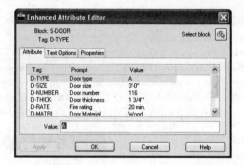

MOVING THE LOCATION OF ATTRIBUTES

If you want to change the location of individual attributes in a block, you can move attributes by using grips. Click the block to expose the grips, and then click the grip connected to the attribute. Or, if you've selected several blocks, Shift+click the attribute grips, and then move the attributes to their new location. They are still attached to their associated blocks. If you don't see grips appear for the attributes, then the attribute definition has its Lock Position property turned on. This is a setting that is available when you create the attribute in the Attribute Definition dialog box.

Making Global Changes to Attribute Values

At times, you'll want to change the value of several attributes in a file so they're all the same value. You can use the Edit Attribute Globally option to make global changes to attribute values.

Suppose you decide you want to change all the entry doors to a type designated as B rather than A. Perhaps door-type A was an input error or type B happens to be better suited for an entry door. The following exercise demonstrates how this is done:

1. Clicked Named Views from the View tab's Views panel or type **V↵** to open the View Manager dialog box, and then restore the view named Fourth. Pan your view down so you can see the eight door-reference symbol for this view.

2. Click Multiple from the Edit Attribute flyout on the Insert tab's Attribute panel, or type **-Attedit↵** at the Command prompt. Make sure you include the hyphen at the beginning of -Attedit.

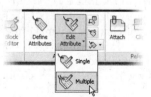

3. At the `Edit Attributes one at a time? [Yes/No] <Y>:` prompt, enter **N↵** for No. You see the message `Performing global editing of attribute values`. This tells you that you're in Global Edit mode.

4. At the `Edit only attributes visible on screen? [Yes/No] <Y>`: prompt, press ↵. As you can see from this prompt, you have the option to edit all attributes, including those out of the view area. You'll get a chance to work with this option later in the chapter.

5. At the `Enter block name specification <*>`: prompt, press ↵. Optionally, you can enter a block name to narrow the selection to specific blocks.

6. At the `Enter attribute tag specification <*>`: prompt, press ↵. Optionally, you can enter an attribute tag name to narrow your selection to specific tags.

7. At the `Enter attribute value specification <*>`: prompt, press ↵. Optionally, you can narrow your selection to attributes containing specific values.

8. At the `Select Attributes`: prompt, select the door-type symbol's attribute value for units 103 to 115. You can use a window to select the attributes if you prefer. Press ↵ when you've finished your selection.

9. At the `Enter string to change`: prompt, enter **A**↵.

10. At the `Enter new string`: prompt, enter **B**↵. The door-type symbols all change to the new value.

In step 8, you were asked to select the attributes to be edited. AutoCAD limits the changes to those attributes you select. If you know you need to change every attribute in your drawing, you can do so by answering the series of prompts in a slightly different way, as in the following exercise:

1. Try the same procedure again, but this time enter **N** for the first prompt and again at the `Edit only attributes visible on screen? [Yes/No] <Y>`: prompt (step 4 in the previous exercise). The message `Drawing must be regenerated afterwards` appears. The AutoCAD Text Window appears.

2. Once again, you're prompted for the block name, the tag, and the value (steps 5, 6, and 7 in the previous exercise). Respond to these prompts as you did earlier.

3. You then get the message `128 attributes selected`. This tells you the number of attributes that fit the specifications you just entered.

4. At the `Enter string to change`: prompt, enter **A**↵ to indicate you want to change the rest of the A attribute values.

5. At the `Enter new string`: prompt, enter **B**↵. A series of *B*s appears, indicating the number of strings that were replaced.

In the previous exercise, AutoCAD skipped the `Select Attribute`: prompt and went directly to the `String to change`: prompt. AutoCAD assumes that you want it to edit every attribute in the drawing, so it doesn't bother asking you to select specific attributes.

Making Invisible Attributes Visible

You can globally edit invisible attributes, such as those in the door-reference symbol, by using the tools just described. You may, however, want to be more selective about which invisible attribute you want to modify. Optionally, you may want to make invisible attributes temporarily visible for other editing purposes.

This exercise shows how you can make invisible attributes visible:

1. On the Insert tab's Attributes panel, click the Retain Display flyout and select Display All. You can also enter **Attdisp⏎ On⏎**. Your drawing looks like Figure 13.12.

FIGURE 13.12
The drawing with all the attributes visible. (Door-type symbols are so close together that they overlap.)

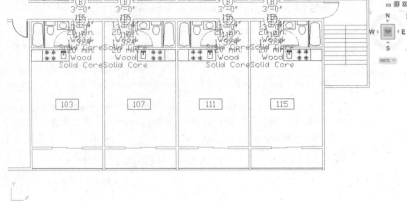

2. At this point, you could edit the invisible attributes individually, as in the first attribute-editing exercise. For now, set the attribute display back to Normal. On the Insert tab's Attributes panel, click the Display All flyout and select Retain Display. You can also enter **Attdisp⏎ N⏎**.

USING SPACES IN ATTRIBUTE VALUES

At times, you may want the default value to begin with a blank space. This enables you to specify text strings more easily when you edit the attribute globally. For example, suppose you have an attribute value that reads 3334333. If you want to change the first 3 in this string of numbers, you have to specify 3334 when prompted for the string to change. Then, for the new string, you enter the same set of numbers again with the first 3 changed to the new number. If you only specify 3 for the string to change, AutoCAD will change all the 3s in the value. If you start with a space, as in _3334333 (I'm using an underscore here only to represent the space; it doesn't mean you type an underscore character), you can isolate the first 3 from the rest by specifying _3 as the string to change (again, type a space instead of the underscore).

You must enter a backslash character (\) before the space in the default value to tell AutoCAD to interpret the space literally rather than as a press of the spacebar (which is equivalent to pressing ⏎).

You've seen the results of the On and Normal options. The Off option makes all attributes invisible regardless of the mode used when they were created.

Because the attributes weren't intended to be visible, they appear to overlap and cover other parts of the drawing when they're made visible. Remember to turn them back off when you're done reviewing them.

Making Global Format and Property Changes to Attributes

While we're on the subject of global editing, you should know how to make global changes to the format and properties of attributes. Earlier you saw how to make format changes to individual attributes by using the Enhanced Attribute Editor dialog box. You can also use the Edit Attribute dialog box to make global changes, as the following exercise demonstrates.

EDITING ATTRIBUTES IN LT

Although LT doesn't support the Edit Attribute dialog box, you can use the command-line version of the Attedit command to edit some of the format and property values of attributes. Enter **-Attedit.⌐** at the command line, and follow the prompts.

Follow these steps to make the global changes:

1. Click Manage Attributes from the Home tab's expanded Block panel to open the Block Attribute Manager dialog box. You can also enter **battman.⌐**.

2. Select S-APART from the Block drop-down list at the top of the dialog box. This list displays all the blocks that contain attributes. The only attribute defined for the selected block is displayed in the list box below it.

3. Click the attribute value in the list, and click the Edit button to open the Edit Attribute dialog box. The Edit Attribute dialog box is nearly identical to the Enhanced Attribute Editor you saw earlier.

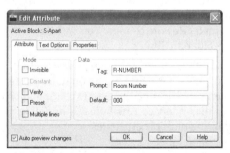

4. Click the Properties tab, select Red from the Color drop-down list, and click OK.

5. Click OK to exit the Block Attribute Manager dialog box.

The Edit Attribute dialog box you saw in this exercise offers a slightly different set of options from those in the Enhanced Attribute Editor dialog box. In the Attribute tab of the Edit Attribute dialog box, you can change some of the mode settings for the attribute, such as visibility and the Verify and Preset modes. You can also change the Tag, Prompt, and Default values. In contrast, the Attribute tab in the Enhanced Attribute Editor dialog box enables you to change the attribute value but none of the other attribute properties.

OTHER BLOCK ATTRIBUTE MANAGER OPTIONS

The Block Attribute Manager dialog box includes a few other options that weren't covered in the exercises. Here's a rundown of the Settings, Move Up, Move Down, Remove, and Sync buttons:

Settings   Click this button to open the Block Attribute Settings dialog box (Figure 13.13), which lets you control which attribute properties are displayed in the list box of the Block Attribute Manager.

FIGURE 13.13
The Block Attribute Settings dialog

The Emphasize Duplicate Tags option highlights duplicate tag names by showing them in red. The Apply Changes To Existing References option forces any changes you make to the attribute properties to be applied to existing attributes. If this setting is turned off, you have to use the Sync button in the Block Attribute Manager dialog box to update existing attributes and the changes you make to attribute properties are applied only to new attributes added after the change. You can also enter **Attsync↵** at the Command prompt to synchronize older attributes.

Move Up and Move Down   Clicking these buttons moves a selected attribute up or down the list of attributes in the list box. If you move an item down the list, the item changes its position when viewed using the Ddatte command or when you're viewing the attribute's properties in the Enhanced Attribute Editor dialog box. Of course, this has an effect only on blocks containing multiple attributes.

Remove   Clicking this button removes the selected attribute from the block, so make sure you mean it before you click.

Sync   This option updates attribute properties such as order, text formatting, mode, and so on. It can also be used to globally update blocks that have had new attribute definitions added or deleted. It doesn't affect the individual attribute values.

Redefining Blocks Containing Attributes

Attributes act differently from other objects when they're included in redefined blocks. Normally, blocks that have been redefined change their configuration to reflect the new block definition. But if a redefined block contains attributes, the attributes maintain their old properties, including their position in relation to other objects in the block. This means the old attribute position, style, and so on don't change even though you may have changed them in the new definition.

Fortunately, AutoCAD offers a tool that's specifically designed to let you update blocks with attributes. The following steps describe how to update attribute blocks:

1. Before you use the command to redefine an attribute block, you must create the objects and attribute definitions that will make up the replacement attribute block. The simplest way to do this is to explode a copy of the attribute block you want to update. This ensures that you have the same attribute definitions in the updated block.

2. Make your changes to the exploded attribute block.

EXPLODE ATTRIBUTE BLOCKS AT A 1-TO-1 SCALE

Before you explode the attribute block copy, be sure it's at a 1-to-1 scale. This is important because if you don't use the original size of the block, you could end up with all your new attribute blocks at the wrong size. Also be sure you use a marker device, such as a line, to locate the insertion point of the attribute block before you explode it. This will help you locate and maintain the original insertion point for the redefined block.

---

3. Type **Attredef**⏎.

4. At the `Enter name of block you wish to redefine:` prompt, enter the appropriate name.

5. At the `Select objects:` prompt, select all the objects, including the attribute definitions, that you want to include in the revised attribute block.

6. At the `Specify insertion base point of new Block:` prompt, pick the same location used for the original block.

After you pick the insertion point, AutoCAD takes a few seconds to update the blocks. The amount of time depends on the complexity of the block and the number of times the block occurs in the drawing. If you include a new attribute definition with your new block, it too is added to all the updated blocks, with its default value. Attribute definitions that are deleted from your new definition are removed from all the updated blocks.

You can also use the Refedit command to modify an attribute definition. Click the Edit Reference tool in the Insert tab's expanded Reference panel to modify attribute definitions. After editing, you must use the Sync option in the Block Attribute Manager to update all instances of the modified block.

Extracting and Exporting Attribute Information

After you enter the attributes in your drawing, you can extract the information contained in the attributes and use it to generate reports or to analyze the attribute data in other programs. You might, for example, want to keep track of the number and type of doors in your drawing through a database manager. This is especially useful if you have a project such as a large hotel that contains thousands of doors.

When you extract attribute data, AutoCAD creates a text file. You can choose to export the file in either comma-delimited or tab-delimited format. If you have Microsoft Excel or Access installed, you can also export the attribute data in a format compatible with these programs.

Performing the Extraction

In the past, extracting the attribute data from a drawing was an error-prone task requiring the creation of a template file. This template file had to contain a series of codes that described the data you wanted to extract. AutoCAD has a greatly improved system for attribute data extraction in the form of the Attribute Extraction Wizard. The following exercises will walk you through a sample extraction.

> **EXTRACTING DATA IN LT**
>
> LT doesn't offer the Attribute Extraction Wizard. Instead, you see the more simplified Attribute Extraction dialog box, which offers the file-format options (comma- or space-delimited or DXF output), the output filename, and template file options. For LT, the template file is used as an option to filter the attributes.

USING THE DATA EXTRACTION WIZARD

In this first exercise, you'll explore the Data Extraction Wizard. You can use the 13c-plan.dwg sample file if you haven't done the tutorials from the beginning of the chapter.

1. Go back to the Plan file, and click Extract Data from the Insert tab's Linking & Extraction panel. In the Begin page (Figure 13.14), you can choose to start an extraction from scratch or use an existing data-extraction setup that you've created from previous extractions.

2. Click Next to open the Save Data Extraction As dialog box. This dialog box lets you save the data-extraction settings you're about to set up in a file with the .dxe filename extension. Enter a name and pick a location for your file and then click Save. The Define Data Source page opens (Figure 13.15).

3. Click Settings to view other options. These options (Figure 13.16) let you further refine the content of your extraction.

FIGURE 13.14
Starting the Data
Extraction Wizard

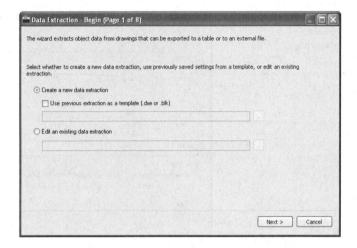

FIGURE 13.15
Defining a
data source

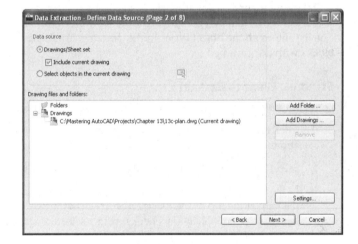

FIGURE 13.16
Additional settings

4. Click Cancel to close the Additional Settings dialog box, and then click Next to open the Select Objects page (Figure 13.17).

FIGURE 13.17
The Select
Objects page

Take a moment to study the Select Objects page. It's the heart of the extraction process. Here you select the blocks that contain attributes as well as the specific attributes you want to extract. The list shows all the object types in the drawing. You'll pare down this list to show only the blocks with attributes.

SELECTING WHAT TO EXTRACT

Let's continue by selecting specific information for the extraction:

1. Click the Display All Object Types option in the lower-left corner of the page to turn it off, and make sure the Display Blocks Only radio button is selected.

2. Select the Display Blocks With Attributes Only option.

3. In the Object list, remove the checkmark next to all but the S-DOOR item. To do this, click the item at the top of the list, then Shift+click the S-APART item so that all but the S-DOOR item is selected. (Click any check box in a selected item to remove the checkmarks.)

4. Click Next to open the Select Properties page (Figure 13.18), which displays a list of the different types of data available for extraction.

5. In the Category Filter panel to the right, deselect all the options except Attribute. Now you see only the attribute data listed in the Properties panel.

6. Make sure that each item in the Properties panel is selected. A checkmark should appear by each item.

7. Click Next. The Refine Data page appears (Figure 13.19). Here you can continue to filter out data. For example, you can deselect the Show Count Column and Show Name Column options because they may be unnecessary for your purpose. You can also get a preview of your extracted data by clicking the Full Preview button.

FIGURE 13.18
The Select Properties screen

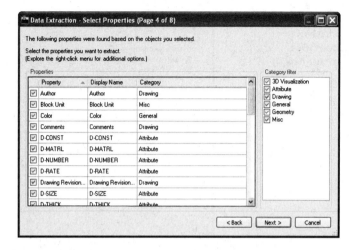

FIGURE 13.19
The Refine Data screen

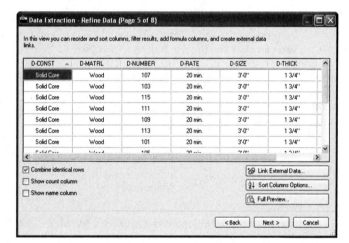

SORTING COLUMNS

If you want to sort your data by column, you can do so by clicking the column title. To change the order of the columns, click and drag the column titles horizontally.

SAVING THE ATTRIBUTE DATA TO A FILE

Now, let's complete the extraction process.

1. Click Next. The Choose Output page appears (Figure 13.20). This window lets you determine whether to convert the data into a table in the drawing, extract the data as an external data file, or do both.

FIGURE 13.20
Decide how to
convert your
attribute data.

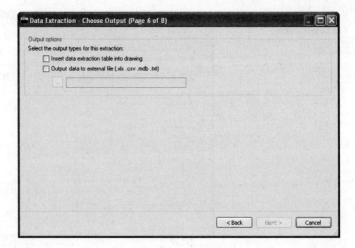

2. Select the Output Data To External File option. The input box just below the option becomes available for input (Figure 13.21). You can type a location for the external file, or you can click the Browse button to browse to a location.

FIGURE 13.21
Enter the location
to which you'll
extract to the data.

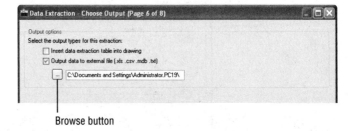

Browse button

3. You have the option to extract an XLS, CSV, MDB, or TXT file. You can select the type of file to use when you click the Browse button to show where you want the file to go. The Browse button opens a Save As dialog box, where you can select the type of file to save from the File Of Type drop-down list. The default filename is the current drawing filename with an .xls extension. Click Save to go to the next step.

4. Click Next to open the Finish screen (Figure 13.22). It gives you a brief message explaining what to do next.

FIGURE 13.22
Completing
the wizard

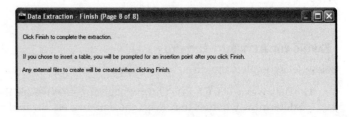

5. Click Finish. A file with the current drawing name and the .xls filename extension is created. By default, the file is placed in the My Documents folder unless you specify a different location in step 3.

You now have a file called Plan.xls (13c-plan.xls if you used the sample file) that contains the data you saw earlier in the Full Preview window of the Attribute Extraction Wizard. You can open this file with Microsoft Excel.

Extracting Attribute Data to an AutoCAD Table

You may have noticed the option to extract the attribute data to an AutoCAD table in the Choose Output screen of the Data Extraction Wizard. This option lets you convert the attribute data directly into a table in the current drawing. Besides making it easy to create parts lists or other types of tables in your drawing, you get the added benefit of having tables update automatically whenever attribute data changes.

If you turn on this option and click Next, you'll see the Table Style screen (Figure 13.23) instead of the Finish screen.

FIGURE 13.23
Styling your table

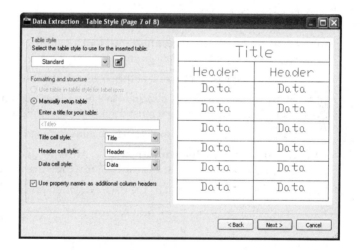

From here, you can follow these steps:

1. Select a table style for the extracted data, enter a title, and click Next. The Finish screen opens.

2. Click Finish. You're prompted to select a point. Click in the drawing to place the table.

The table may appear at a small size depending on the scale of your drawing. Zoom in to the location where you clicked and you'll see the table (Figure 13.24). You'll also see the Data Link icon in the lower-right corner of the AutoCAD window.

With the table in place, you can make changes to the attribute data. When you're ready to update the table, right-click the Data Link icon in the lower-right corner of the AutoCAD window, and select Update All Data Links. The table will be updated to reflect the latest attribute values.

FIGURE 13.24

The table and the
Data Link icon

Quantity	D-CONST	D-MATRL	D-NUMBER	D-RATE	D-SIZE	D-THICK	D-TYPE	Name
1	Solid Core	Wood	103	20 min.	3'-0"	1 3/4"	B	S-DOOR
1	Solid Core	Wood	111	20 min.	3'-0"	1 3/4"	B	S-DOOR
1	Solid Core	Wood	108	20 min.	3'-0"	1 3/4"	B	S-DOOR
1	Solid Core	Wood	107	20 min.	3'-0"	1 3/4"	B	S-DOOR
1	Solid Core	Wood	115	20 min.	3'-0"	1 3/4"	B	S-DOOR
1	Solid Core	Wood	102	20 min.	3'-0"	1 3/4"	B	S-DOOR
1	Solid Core	Wood	101	20 min.	3'-0"	1 3/4"	B	S-DOOR
1	Solid Core	Wood	105	20 min.	3'-0"	1 3/4"	B	S-DOOR
1	Solid Core	Wood	113	20 min.	3'-0"	1 3/4"	B	S-DOOR
1	Solid Core	Wood	109	20 min.	3'-0"	1 3/4"	B	S-DOOR
1	Solid Core	Wood	112	20 min.	3'-0"	1 3/4"	B	S-DOOR
1	Solid Core	Wood	116	20 min.	3'-0"	1 3/4"	B	S-DOOR
1	Solid Core	Wood	106	20 min.	3'-0"	1 3/4"	B	S-DOOR
1	Solid Core	Wood	104	20 min.	3'-0"	1 3/4"	B	S-DOOR
1	Solid Core	Wood	110	20 min.	3'-0"	1 3/4"	B	S-DOOR
1	Solid Core	Wood	114	20 min.	3'-0"	1 3/4"	B	S-DOOR

Data Link

The Bottom Line

Create attributes.   Attributes are a great tool for storing data with drawn objects. You can include as little or as much data as you like in an AutoCAD block.

Master It   What is the name of the object you must include in a block to store data?

Edit attributes.   The data you include in a block is easily changed. You may have several copies of a block, each of which must contain its own unique sets of data.

Master It   What is the simplest way to gain access to a block's attribute data?

Extract and export attribute information.   Attribute data can be extracted in a number of ways so that you can keep track of the data in a drawing.

Master It   How do you start the data-extraction process?

Chapter 14

Copying Existing Drawings into AutoCAD

At times, you'll want to turn an existing drawing into an AutoCAD drawing file. The original drawing may be hand drawn, or it might be a PDF from another source. You may be modifying a design that someone else created or converting your library of older, hand-drafted drawings for AutoCAD use. Perhaps you want to convert a hand-drawn sketch into a formal drawing? This chapter discusses ways to import existing drawings into AutoCAD through tracing, scaling, and scanning. You'll also lean how to incorporate drawings in a PDF format into your AutoCAD work.

In this chapter, you'll learn to do the following:

◆ Convert paper drawings into AutoCAD files

◆ Import a raster image

◆ Work with a raster image

◆ Work with PDF files

Methods for Converting Paper Drawings to AutoCAD Files

Tracing with a digitizing tablet used to be the only way to enter a hand-drafted drawing into AutoCAD. However, a traced drawing usually requires some cleanup and reorganization.

Scaling a drawing is the most flexible method because you don't need a graphics tablet to do it, and generally, you're faced with fewer cleanups afterward. Scaling also facilitates the most accurate input of orthogonal lines because you can read dimensions directly from the drawing and enter them into AutoCAD. The main drawback with scaling is that if the hand-drafted drawing does not contain written dimensions, it would be difficult to produce an accurate copy. In addition, you must constantly look at the hand-drafted drawing and measure distances with a scale, and irregular curves are difficult to scale accurately.

Programs are available that automatically convert an image file into an AutoCAD drawing file consisting of lines and arcs. These programs may offer some help, but they require some editing and checking for errors.

Scanning, much like tracing, is best used for drawings that are difficult to scale, such as complex topographical maps containing more contours than are practical to trace on a digitizer or nontechnical line art, such as letterhead and logos.

The simplest method for converting paper drawings, and the method I show you in this chapter, is to scan your drawings as image files to be used as a background in AutoCAD. You can import your image files into AutoCAD and then trace directly over them. This technique allows you to see the original drawing in the AutoCAD window, preventing you from diverting your attention to other areas of your workstation.

WORKING WITH A DIGITIZER

If you're working with AutoCAD LT, you may find that your only option is to use a digitizing table to trace existing paper drawings. AutoCAD's Help website offers an excellent description of how to use a digitizer.

Use AutoCAD's Help website to find information on the Tablet command. Press the F1 function key, and then, in the AutoCAD Help website, select the Command reference option. Click the Command listing to the right, and then open the T Commands option and select Tablet. If you haven't configured your tablet yet, look at the description of the CFG (configure) option for the Tablet command. Once you've configured your tablet, read the instructions for the CAL (calibration) option.

Importing a Raster Image

If you have a scanner and you'd like to use it to import drawings and other images into AutoCAD, you can take advantage of AutoCAD's ability to import raster images. There are many reasons you may want to import a scanned image. In architectural plans, a vicinity map is frequently used to show the location of a project. With the permission of its creator, you can scan a map into AutoCAD and incorporate it into a cover sheet. That cover sheet can also contain other images, such as photographs of the site, computer renderings and elevations of the project, and company logos. In architectural projects, scans of older drawings can be used as backgrounds for renovation work. This can be especially useful for historical buildings where the building's owner wishes to keep the original architectural detail.

Another reason for importing a scanned image is to use the image as a reference to trace over. You can trace a drawing with greater accuracy by using a scanned image as opposed to a digitizing tablet. Now that the price of a scanner has fallen below $100, it has become a cost-effective tool for tracing a wide variety of graphic material. In this section, you'll learn firsthand how you can import an image as a background for tracing.

Click the External References tool on the Insert tab's Reference panel (Figure 14.1) to open the External References palette, which lets you import a full range of raster image files.

You can also type **XR**↵. This palette should look familiar from Chapter 7. It's the same palette you used to manage external references. Just like external references (Xrefs), raster images are loaded when the current file is open, but they aren't stored as part of the current file when the file is saved. This helps keep file sizes down, but it also means that you need to keep track of inserted raster files. You must make sure they're kept together with the AutoCAD files in which they're inserted. For example, you might want to keep image files in the same folder as the drawing file to which they're attached.

AutoCAD has a utility called eTransmit that collects AutoCAD files and their related support files, such as raster images, external references, and fonts, into any folder or drive you specify. See Chapter 29 for details.

FIGURE 14.1

The External References palette allows you to import raster images.

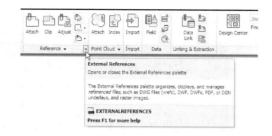

Another similarity between Xrefs and imported raster images is that you can clip a raster image so that only a portion of the image is displayed in your drawing. Portions of a raster file that are clipped aren't stored in memory, so your system won't get bogged down, even if the raster file is huge.

The following exercise gives you step-by-step instructions for importing a raster file. It also lets you see how scanned resolution translates into an image in AutoCAD. This is important if you're interested in scanning drawings for the purpose of tracing over them. Here are the steps:

1. Create a new file called `Rastertrace`.

2. Set up the file as an architectural drawing with a 1/4″=1′ scale on an 8½″-×-11″ sheet (set the Limits settings to 0,0 for the lower-left corner and 528,408 for the upper-right corner). Make sure the drawing units type is set to Architectural. Metric users should set up their drawing at a 1:50 scale on an A4 size sheet. (The Limits settings for metric users should be 0,0 for the lower-left corner and 1480,1050 for the upper-right corner.)

3. Click All from the Zoom flyout on the View tab's Navigate panel or type z↵ a↵ to make sure the entire drawing limits are displayed on the screen.

4. Draw a line across the screen from coordinates 0,20′ to 64′,20′. Metric users should draw the line from 0,600 to 1820,600. You'll use this line in a later exercise.

5. Click the line you just drew, and then select Red from the Object Color drop-down list in the Home tab's Properties panel. This helps make the line more visible. If you have the Quick Properties feature turned on, you can select the color from the Quick Properties panel.

6. Click the External References tool in the title bar of the Insert tab's Reference panel.

7. Choose Attach Image from the Attach flyout on the External References palette's menu bar.

From the Select Reference File dialog box, locate and select the `raster1.jpg` project file. You can see a preview of the file on the right side of the dialog box.

8. Click Open to open the Attach Image dialog box (Figure 14.2). Click OK.

FIGURE 14.2
The Attach Image
dialog box

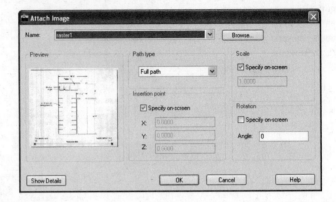

9. Uncheck the Specify On-Screen option in the Insertion Point group to accept the 0,0,0 coordinates.

10. Click OK, and then at the `Specify scale factor <1>:` prompt, use the cursor to scale the image so it fills about half the screen, as shown in Figure 14.3. The `raster1.jpg` filename appears in the External References palette.

FIGURE 14.3
Manually scaling
the raster image

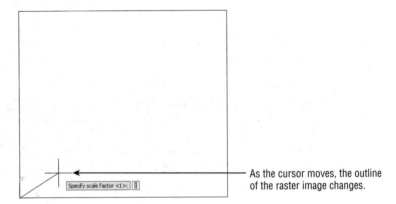

As the cursor moves, the outline of the raster image changes.

Working with a Raster Image

Once you've imported a raster image, you can begin to work with it in a variety of ways. You can resize the image to suit your needs and even adjust its size to a particular scale. Raster images can be made to overlap AutoCAD objects, or you can have raster images appear in the background. There are also rudimentary controls for brightness, contrast, and transparency. In the following sections, you'll continue to use the image you attached to your drawing to explore some of these options.

Real World Scenario

TIPS FOR IMPORTING RASTER IMAGES

When you scan a document into your computer, you get a raster image file. Unlike AutoCAD files, *raster image files* are made up of a matrix of colored pixels that form a picture, which is why raster images are also sometimes called *bitmaps*. *Vector files*, like those produced by AutoCAD, are made up of instructions to draw lines, arcs, curves, and circles. The two formats, raster and vector, are so different that it's difficult to convert one format to the other accurately. It's easier to trace a raster file in AutoCAD than it is to try to use a computer program to make the conversion for you.

But even tracing a raster image file can be difficult if the image is of poor quality. After having worked with scanned images in AutoCAD for a variety of projects, I've discovered that you can make your work a lot easier by following a few simple rules:

- Scan in your drawing using a gray-scale or color scanner, or convert your black-and-white scanned image to gray scale using your image editing software. This will give you more control over the appearance of the image once it's in AutoCAD.

- Use an image editing program such as Photoshop or your scanner software to clean up unwanted gray or spotted areas in the file before importing it into AutoCAD.

- If your scanner software or image editing program has a "de-speckle" or "de-spot" feature, use it. It can help clean up your image and ultimately reduce the raster image's file size.

- Scan at a reasonable resolution. Scanning at 150dpi to 200dpi may be more than adequate.

- If you plan to make heavy use of raster imports, upgrade your computer to the fastest processor and with as much memory as you can afford.

The raster-import commands can incorporate paper maps or plans into 3D AutoCAD drawings for presentations. I know of one architectural firm that produces impressive presentations with little effort by combining 2D scanned images with 3D massing models for urban-design studies. (A *massing model* shows only the rough outline of buildings without giving too much detail, thus showing the general scale of a project without being too fussy.)

Scaling a Raster Image

The `raster1.jpg` file was scanned as a grayscale image at 100dpi. This shows that you can get a reasonable amount of detail at a fairly low scan resolution.

Now suppose you want to trace over this image to start an AutoCAD drawing. The first thing you should do is to scale the image to the appropriate size. You can scale an image file to full size. Try the following steps to see how you can begin the process:

1. Click Zoom Extents from the Zoom flyout on the navigation bar, or type z↵ e↵.

2. Click Scale on the Home tab's Modify panel.

3. Click the edge of the raster image to select it.

4. Press ↵ to finish your selection.

5. At the `Specify base point:` prompt, click the X in the lower-left corner of the image.

6. At the `Specify scale factor or [Copy/Reference]:` prompt, enter **R↵** to use the Reference option.

7. At the `Specify reference length <1>:` prompt, type **@↵**. This tells AutoCAD that you want to use the last point selected as one end of the reference length. After you enter the @ symbol, you'll see a rubber-banding line emanating from the X.

8. At the `Specify second point:` prompt, click the X at the lower-right corner of the image.

9. At the `Specify new length or [Points]:` prompt, enter **44'↵**. Metric users should enter **1341↵**. The image enlarges. Remember that this reference line is 44' or 1341 cm in length.

The image is now scaled properly for the plan it portrays. You can proceed to trace over the image. You can also place the image on its own layer and turn it off from time to time to check your trace work. Even if you don't trace the scanned floor plan line for line, you can read the dimensions of the plan from your computer monitor instead of having to go back and forth between measuring the paper image and drawing the plan on the computer.

Controlling Object Visibility and Overlap with Raster Images

With the introduction of raster-image support, AutoCAD inherited a problem that's fairly common to programs that use such images: raster images obscure other objects that were placed previously. The image you imported in the previous exercise, for example, obscures the line you drew when you first opened the file. In most cases, this overlap isn't a problem, but in some situations you'll want AutoCAD vector objects to overlap an imported raster image. An example is a civil-engineering drawing showing an AutoCAD drawing of a new road super-imposed over an aerial view of the location for the road.

Paint and page-layout programs usually offer a "to front/to back" tool to control the overlap of objects and images. AutoCAD offers the Draworder command. Here's how it works:

1. Click Zoom Extents from the navigation bar or type **z↵ e↵** to get an overall view of the image.

2. Click the Bring Above Objects tool from the Draworder flyout on the Home tab's Modify panel.

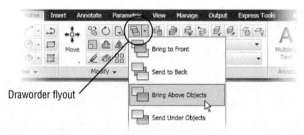

Draworder flyout

3. At the `Select objects:` prompt, select the horizontal line you drew when you first opened the file.

4. You can select other objects if you wish. Press ↵ to finish your selection.

5. At the Select reference objects: prompt, click the edge of the raster image of the utility room, and then press ↵.

The drawing regenerates, and the entire line appears, no longer obscured by the raster image.

MASKING AN AREA OF AN IMAGE

You can mask out areas of an imported raster image by creating a solid hatch area and using the Draworder command to place the solid hatch on top of the raster image. Such masks can be helpful as backgrounds for text that must be placed over a raster image. You can also use the Wipeout command (select Wipeout on the Home tab's expanded Draw panel) to mask areas of a drawing.

The Draworder tool you just used has seven options in the Draworder flyout on the Home tab's Modify panel:

Bring To Front   Places an object or a set of objects at the top of the draw order for the entire drawing. The effect is that the objects are completely visible.

Send To Back   Places an object or a set of objects at the bottom of the draw order for the entire drawing. The effect is that other objects in the drawing may obscure those objects.

Bring Above Objects   Places an object or a set of objects above another object in the draw order. This has the effect of making the first set of objects appear above the second selected object.

Send Under Objects   Places an object or a set of objects below another object in the draw order. This has the effect of making the first set of objects appear underneath the second selected object.

Bring Text To Front   Automatically brings all text in a drawing in front of all objects.

Bring Dimensions To Front   Automatically brings all dimensions in a drawing in front of all objects.

Send Hatch To Back   Automatically sends all hatch patterns in a drawing behind other objects.

You can also use the Dr keyboard shortcut to issue the Draworder command. If you do this, you see these prompts:

```
Select objects:
Enter object ordering option [Above objects/Under objects/Front/Back]<Back>:
```

You must then select the option by typing the capitalized letter of the option.

Although this section discussed the Draworder tools in relation to raster images, they can also be invaluable in controlling visibility of line work in conjunction with hatch patterns and solid fills. See Chapter 7 for a detailed discussion of the Draworder tools and hatch patterns.

Clipping a Raster Image

In Chapter 7, you saw how you can clip an external-reference object so that only a portion of it appears in the drawing. You can clip imported raster images in the same way. Just as with Xrefs, you can create a closed outline of the area you want to clip, or you can specify a simple rectangular area.

> **IMAGES AND THE EXTERNAL REFERENCES PALETTE**
>
> The External References palette you saw in Chapter 7 helps you manage your imported image files. It's especially helpful when you have a large number of images in your drawing. You can control imported images in a way similar to how you control Xrefs; you can temporarily unload images (to help speed up the editing of AutoCAD objects) and reload, detach, and relocate raster image files. See Chapter 7 for a detailed description of these options.

In the following exercise, you'll try the Clip command to control the display of the raster image:

1. Click the Clip tool from the Insert tab's Reference panel, or type **Clip**↵.

2. At the Select object to clip: prompt, click the edge of the raster image.

3. At the Enter image clipping option [ON/OFF/Delete/New boundary]<New>: prompt, press ↵ to create a new boundary.

4. At the [Select polyline/Polygonal/Rectangular/Invert clip] <Rectangular>: prompt, enter **P**↵ to draw a polygonal boundary.

5. Select the points shown in the top image in Figure 14.4 and then press ↵. The raster image is clipped to the boundary you created, as shown in the second image in Figure 14.4.

As the prompt in step 3 indicates, you can turn the clipping off or on, or you can delete an existing clipping boundary through the Clip Image option.

After you clip a raster image, you can adjust the clipping boundary by using its grips:

1. Click the boundary edge of the raster image to expose its grips.

2. Click a grip in the upper-right corner, as shown in the final image in Figure 14.4.

3. Drag the grip up and to the right, and then click a point. The image adjusts to the new boundary.

In addition to hiding portions of a raster image that are unimportant to you, clipping an image file reduces the amount of RAM the raster image uses during your editing session. AutoCAD loads only the visible portion of the image into RAM and ignores the rest.

FIGURE 14.4
Adjusting the boundary of a clipped image

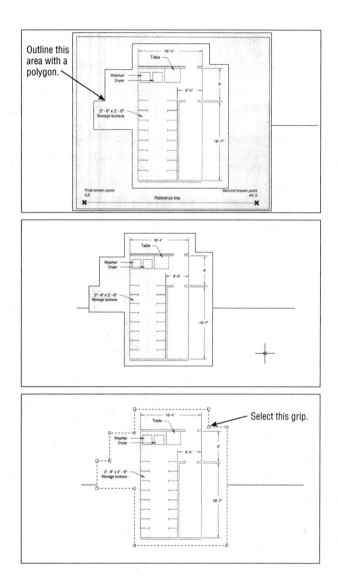

Adjusting Brightness, Contrast, and Fade

AutoCAD offers a tool that enables you to adjust the brightness, contrast, and strength of a raster image. Try making some adjustments to the raster image of the utility room in the following exercise:

1. Click the edge of the raster image. The Image tab appears in the Ribbon (Figure 14.5).

FIGURE 14.5
The Image tab appears when you select a raster image.

2. In the Adjust panel of the Image tab, click and drag the Fade slider to the right so that it's near the middle of the slider scale, or enter **50** in the Fade input box to the right of the slider. The sample image fades to the AutoCAD background color as you move the slider.

3. Press the Esc key to un-select the raster image. The Image tab closes.

4. Save the file as `Rasterimport.dwg`.

You can adjust the brightness and contrast by using the other two sliders in the Adjust panel of the Image tab.

By using the Image tab in conjunction with image clipping, you can create special effects. Figure 14.6 shows an aerial view of downtown San Francisco with labels. This view consists of two copies of the same raster image. One copy serves as a background, which was lightened using the method demonstrated in the previous exercise. The second copy is the darker area of the image with a roughly triangular clip boundary applied. You might use this technique to bring focus to a particular area of a drawing you're preparing for a presentation.

FIGURE 14.6
Two copies of the same image can be combined to emphasize a portion of the drawing.

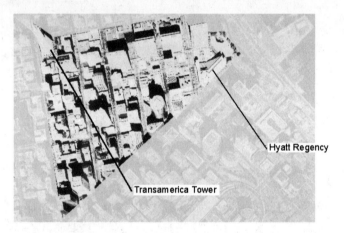

Hyatt Regency

Transamerica Tower

If the draw order of objects is incorrect after you open a file or perform a Pan or Zoom, issue a Regen to recover the correct draw-order view.

In addition to the tools in the Adjust panel, the Image tab offers several other tools that can be used to modify raster images. Table 14.1 gives you rundown of their function.

TABLE 14.1: The tools on the Image tab

TOOL	FUNCTION
Brightness	Adjust the brightness of an image.
Contrast	Adjust the contrast of an image.
Fade	Adjust the fade value of an image.
Create Clipping Boundary	Allows you to create a clipping boundary. This tools works just like the Clip tool.

TABLE 14.1:   The tools on the Image tab *(CONTINUED)*

TOOL	FUNCTION
Remove Clipping	Removes a clipping boundary.
Show Image	Toggles an image on and off.
Transparency	Toggles the transparency of an image on and off.
External References	Opens the External References palette.

Turning Off the Frame, Adjusting Overall Quality, and Controlling Transparency

You can make three other adjustments to your raster image: frame visibility, image quality, and image transparency.

By default, a raster image displays an outline, or a *frame*. In many instances, this frame can detract from your drawing. You can turn off image frames globally by typing **Imageframe↲ 0↲**. This sets the Imageframe setting to 0, which turns off the frame visibility. If it's set to 1, the frame is made visible. You can also set it to 2, which leaves the frame visible but doesn't plot it (Figure 14.7).

Frames can also be controlled through the Frame flyout on the Insert tab's Reference panel. If you turn off a raster image's frame, you can't click the image to select it for editing, though you can still select an image using the All, Previous, or Last selection option (see Chapter 2 for more on selection options). To make a raster image selectable with your mouse, turn on the image frame setting.

If your drawing doesn't require the highest-quality image, you can set the image quality to Draft mode. You may use Draft mode when you're tracing an image or when the image is already of a high quality. To set the image quality, enter **Imagequality↲** and then enter **H** for High mode (high quality) or **D** for Draft mode. In Draft mode, your drawing will regenerate faster.

High mode softens the pixels of the raster image, giving the image a smoother appearance. Draft mode displays the image in a raw, pixilated state. If you look carefully at the regions between the motorcycle and the background in the second image in Figure 14.8, you'll see that the edges of the motorcycle appear a bit jagged. The first image in Figure 14.8 uses the High setting to soften the edges of the motorcycle. You may need to look closely to see the difference.

Finally, you can control the transparency of raster image files that allow transparent pixels. Some file formats, such as the CompuServe GIF 89a format, enable you to set a color in the image to be transparent (usually the background color). Most image-editing programs support this format because it's a popular one used on web pages.

When you turn on the Transparency setting, objects normally obscured by the background of a raster image may show through. Enter **Transparency↲**, and then select the raster image you want to make transparent. Press ↲, and then enter **On** or **Off**, depending on whether you want the image to be transparent. Unlike the Frame and Quality options, Transparency works on individual objects rather than operating globally.

FIGURE 14.7
A raster image
with the frame
on (top) and off
(bottom)

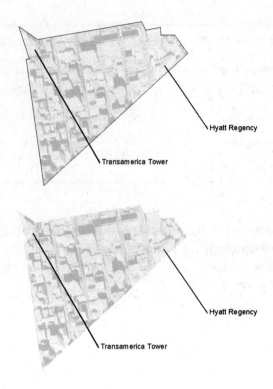

Hyatt Regency

Transamerica Tower

Hyatt Regency

Transamerica Tower

CAN'T GET TRANSPARENCY TO WORK?

The Transparency command does not work on all types of images. As mentioned, it works with GIF files that have the background removed. You can also use a bitonal image, meaning the image must have only two colors, typically black and white. A bitonal image is also referred to as a *bitmap* image in Photoshop. It cannot be grayscale or multicolor. PDF files that have been exported from AutoCAD may also work with the Transparency command.

You can put images that do not work with the Transparency command on a layer with a transparency setting set to a value greater than 0. Transparency can also be set using the Transparency slider in the Home tab's Properties panel. To use the Transparency slider, select the object, such as an image or hatch pattern, then adjust the slider to achieve the level of transparency you want. You can start at 50 and adjust downward or upward.

Note that if you want your image to print or plot with the transparency in effect, you must select the Plot transparency option in the Plot or Page Setup dialog box.

The Properties palette offers many of the same adjustments described in this section, and you can use it for quick access to the Transparency setting and other raster-image settings.

FIGURE 14.8
A close-up of a raster image with quality set to High (top) and Draft (bottom)

Working with PDF Files

If you're using a computer as part of your daily work activity, you will encounter a PDF document. PDFs have become an part of everyday life, so it's no surprise that AutoCAD offers a fair amount of support for PDFs.

In the following sections, you'll learn how to import a PDF document into AutoCAD and how you can control various properties of the document such as fading and the ability to snap to objects in the PDF.

Importing a PDF

To import a PDF, you use a method similar to the one you used earlier to import an image file. In fact, you could perform all of the steps in the exercise in the section "Importing a Raster Image" earlier in this chapter using a PDF file instead of the raster1.jpg file. You just need to know how to set up the Select Reference File dialog box to allow you to locate PDFs.

Try the following to see firsthand how to import a PDF:

1. Open a new file using the acad.dwt file as a template.

2. Use the Save As option in the Application menu and save the drawing as PDFimport.dwg.

3. Click the Attach tool in the Insert tab's Reference panel or type **attach**⏎ to open the Select Reference File dialog box.

4. In the File Of Type drop-down list at the bottom of the dialog box, select PDF Files (*.pdf).

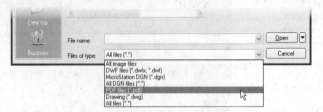

5. Locate and select the SampleImport.pdf file.

6. Click Open to open the Attach PDF Underlay dialog box (Figure 14.9). Notice that you have an option to select a specific page of the PDF document if you are opening a multipage PDF.

FIGURE 14.9
The Attach PDF Underlay dialog box for a PDF file

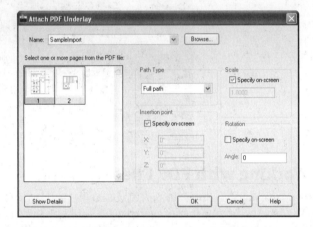

7. Click page 2 of the page preview on the left side of the dialog box.

8. Click OK, and then at the Specify insertion point: prompt, place the outline of the drawing so it is roughly centered in the drawing area and click.

9. At the Specify scale factor <1>: prompt, use the cursor to scale the image so it fills the screen, as shown in Figure 14.10. Page 2 of the SampleImport.pdf file appears in the drawing.

Scaling and Osnaps with PDFs

In an earlier exercise, you were able to scale an image file, though you had to use an existing reference line that was already in the image file to roughly scale the drawing to its proper size in AutoCAD. If you have a PDF that was created from an AutoCAD file or from another vector-based program, you can use osnaps to select exact locations in the PDF.

Try the following exercise to see firsthand how you can use osnaps to select geometry in the PDF. You'll scale the drawing so that the width of the stairs conforms to the known distance for that area.

FIGURE 14.10
Manually scaling
the raster image

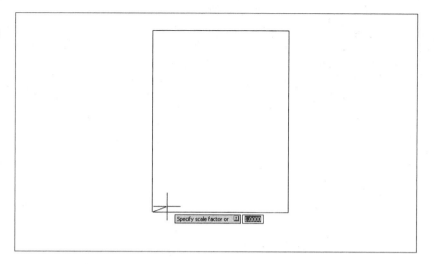

First make sure the Snap To Underlays feature is turned on:

1. In the Insert tab's Reference panel, click the Snap To Underlays tool.

2. Select the Snap To Underlays ON option.

Now you are ready to scale the PDF drawing:

1. Click the Scale tool in the Home tab's Modify panel or type **SC**⏎.

2. Select the imported PDF file and press ⏎.

3. At the `Specify base point:` prompt, turn on the osnaps and select the left endpoint of the horizontal line at the top of the drawing, as shown in Figure 14.11.

4. At the `Specify scale factor or [Copy/Reference]:` prompt, type **R**⏎ to use the Reference option.

5. At the `Specify Reference length:` prompt, click the same endpoint again or type **@**⏎.

6. At the `Specify second point:` prompt, click the endpoint of the line shown in Figure 14.12.

7. At the `Specify new length:` prompt, enter **196**, which is the inch equivalent of 16´-4˝. Metric users should enter **498** to match the dimension of the metric version of the lobby drawing.

8. In the navigation bar, click the Zoom Extents option from the Zoom flyout to center the drawing in the drawing area.

FIGURE 14.11
Selecting the first
endpoint of the
line for the Scale
command

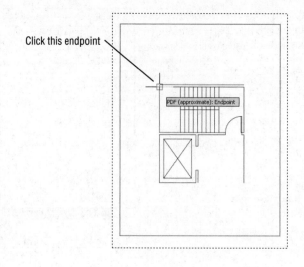

Click this endpoint

PDF (approximate): Endpoint

FIGURE 14.12
Selecting the
second endpoint
of the line for the
Scale command

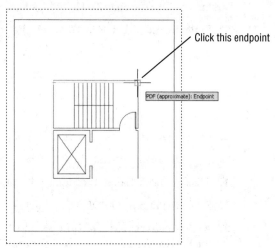

Click this endpoint

PDF (approximate): Endpoint

In this exercise, you were able to use object snaps directly on the imported PDF drawing. You may have noticed that a tool tip appeared with the message "PDF (approximate): Endpoint." The PDF drawing is not an exact representation of the original drawing, so the tool tip reminds you that even though you are using an osnap to select a location in the drawing, it is not an exact location as it would be in an AutoCAD file.

Controlling the PDF Display

You can take advantage of a number of other features of a PDF file. Just as with a typical Xref or image file, you can fade the PDF so it appears as a background image. You can also use the Clip feature you saw earlier in this chapter to clip the PDF to a specific area.

You can gain access to these and other PDF display features through the PDF Underlay Ribbon tab. This tab appears automatically whenever you select an imported PDF drawing. Click the PDF drawing of the lobby and you'll see the PDF Underlay tab appear in the Ribbon (Figure 14.13).

FIGURE 14.13
The PDF Underlay Ribbon tab

Table 14.2 gives a description of the tools in the PDF Underlay Ribbon tab. The tools are fairly self-explanatory. For example, the tools in the Adjust panel let you control the fade and contrast of the PDF drawing. The Display In Monochrome option displays a color PDF in monochrome.

TABLE 14.2: The PDF Underlay tab tools

OPTION	USE
Contrast	Adjusts the contrast setting for the PDF
Fade	Adjusts the amount of fade applied to the PDF image
Display In Monochrome	Displays the PDF image in monochrome
Create Clipping Boundary	Adds a clipping boundary to the PDF
Remove Clipping	Removes a clipping boundary
Show Underlay	Shows or hides the PDF image
Enable Snap	Enables or disables the PDF snap feature
External References	Opens the External References palette
Edit Layers	Opens the Underlay Layers dialog box, allowing you to control layer visibility

One option you'll want to take a closer look at is the Edit Layers tool in the PDF Layers panel. If the source PDF is a drawing that contains layers, you can control the visibility of those layers using this tool. With an imported PDF selected, click the Edit Layers tool to open the Underlay Layers dialog box (Figure 14.14).

You can turn the visibility of a layer on or off by clicking the lightbulb icon to the left of the list. For example, if you turn off the WALL layer in the Underlay Layers dialog box for the SampleImport example, the PDF drawing will change so that the walls will not be shown (Figure 14.15).

FIGURE 14.14
The Underlay
Layers dialog box

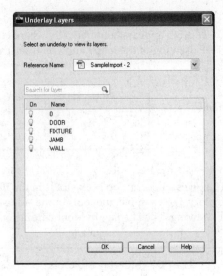

FIGURE 14.15
The imported PDF
with the WALL
layer turned off

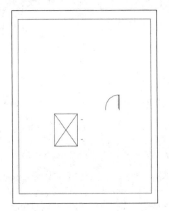

ADDING LAYERS TO YOUR PDF

If you want to create a PDF with layers, you can do so by printing a drawing to a PDF file using the AutoCAD DWG To PDF.pc3 Printer/Plotter option. You can find this option in the Name drop-down list in the Page Setup or Plot dialog box. (See Chapter 8 for more on the Name drop-down list.) You don't have to do anything special. If your drawing contains layers, the DWG to PDF.pc3 plotter will include them in the PDF. The Pro version of Adobe Acrobat 6.0 and later will also include layers when used from AutoCAD.

The Bottom Line

Convert paper drawings into AutoCAD files.   AutoCAD gives you some great tools that let you convert your paper drawings into AutoCAD files. Several options are available. Depending on your needs, you'll find at least one solution that will allow you to convert your drawings quickly.

Master It   Describe the different methods available in AutoCAD for converting paper drawings into CAD files.

Import a raster image.   You can use bitmap raster images as backgrounds for your CAD drawings or as underlay drawings that you can trace over.

Master It   Import a raster image of your choice, and use the AutoCAD drawing tools to trace over your image.

Work with a raster image.   Once imported, raster images can be adjusted for size, brightness, contrast, and transparency.

Master It   Import a raster image of your choice, and fade the image so it appears lighter and with less contrast.

Work with PDF files.   AutoCAD allows you to import and control the display of PDF files. This is significant since the PDF file format is so prevalent in the business world.

Master It   In a PDF that includes layers, how do you gain access to the layer settings?

Chapter 15

Advanced Editing and Organizing

Because you may not know all of a project's requirements when it begins, you usually base the first draft of a design on anticipated needs. As the plan goes forward, you adjust for new requirements as they arise. As more people enter the project, additional design restrictions come into play and the design is further modified. This process continues throughout the project, from the first draft to the end product.

In this chapter, you'll gain experience with some tools that will help you edit your drawings more efficiently. You'll take a closer look at Xrefs and how they may be used to help streamline changes in a drawing project. You'll also be introduced to tools and techniques you can use to minimize duplication of work, such as the Quick Select tool and the QuickCalc feature. AutoCAD can be a powerful time-saving tool if used properly. This chapter examines ways to harness that power.

In this chapter, you'll learn to do the following:

◆ Use external references (Xrefs)

◆ Manage layers

◆ Use advanced tools: Filter and Quick Select

◆ Use the QuickCalc calculator

Using External References (Xrefs)

Chapter 7 mentioned that careful use of blocks, external references (Xrefs), and layers can help improve your productivity. In the following sections, you'll see firsthand how to use these features to help reduce design errors and speed up delivery of an accurate set of drawings. You do this by controlling layers in conjunction with blocks and Xrefs to create a common drawing database for several drawings. You can also use AutoCAD DWF and Acrobat PDF files as Xrefs. See Chapter 14 for more on PDF files and Chapter 29 for more on DWF files.

Later, you'll start to use Xrefs to create different floor plans for the building you worked on earlier in this book. To save some time, I've created a second one-bedroom unit plan called Unit2 that you'll use in these exercises (see Figure 15.1). You can find this new unit plan in the Chapter 15 sample files.

Preparing Existing Drawings for External-Referencing

Chapter 7 discussed how you can use Xrefs to assemble one floor of the apartment. In this section, you'll explore the creation and use of Xrefs to build multiple floors, each containing slightly different sets of drawing information. By doing so, you'll learn how Xrefs enable you to use a single file in multiple drawings to save time and reduce redundancy. You'll see that by sharing common data in multiple files, you can reduce your work and keep the drawing information consistent.

FIGURE 15.1
The one-bedroom unit

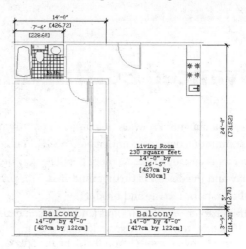

You'll start by creating the files that you'll use later as Xrefs:

1. Open the Plan file. If you didn't create the Plan file, you can use the 15a-plan.dwg or 15a-plan-metric file (see Figure 15.2).

FIGURE 15.2
The overall plan

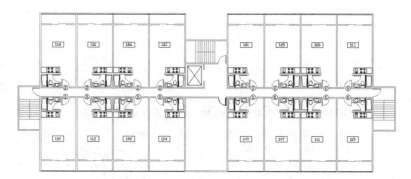

2. Turn off the Ceiling and Flr-pat layers to get a clear, uncluttered view of the individual unit plans.

3. Use the Wblock command (enter **W⏎** at the Command prompt), and write the eight units in the corners of your plan to a file called Floor1.dwg in your My Documents folder (see Figure 15.3). When you select objects for the Wblock, be sure to include the S-DOOR door reference symbols and apartment number symbols for those units. Use 0,0 for the Wblock insertion base point. Also make sure the Delete From Drawing check box is selected in the Write Block dialog box before you click OK.

FIGURE 15.3

Units to be exported to the Floor1 file

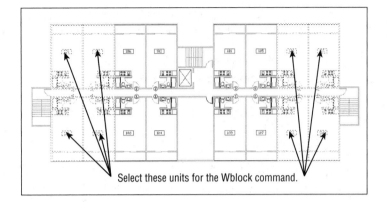

Select these units for the Wblock command.

4. Using Figure 15.4 as a guide, insert the Unit2.dwg file into the corners where the other eight units were previously. Metric users should use Unit2-metric.dwg. These files can be found in the Chapter 15 sample files. If you didn't create the Unit2 file earlier in this chapter, use the 15a-unit2.dwg file.

FIGURE 15.4

Insertion information for Unit2. Metric coordinates are shown in brackets.

Insert Unit2 at coordinate 31'-5", 104'-6" [957,3184]; x-scale factor = 1; y-scale factor = -1 (minus one).

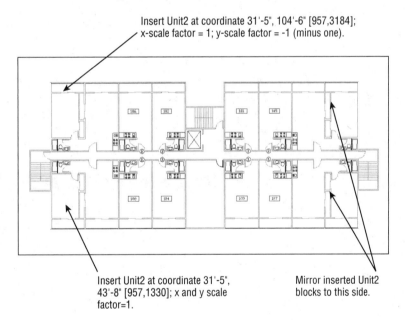

Insert Unit2 at coordinate 31'-5", 43'-8" [957,1330]; x and y scale factor=1.

Mirror inserted Unit2 blocks to this side.

5. After you've accurately placed the corner units, use the Wblock command to write these corner units to a file called Floor2.dwg. Again, use the 0,0 coordinate as the insertion base point for the Wblock, and make sure the Delete From Drawing check box is selected.

6. Choose Save As from the Application menu to turn the remaining set of unit plans into a file called Common.dwg.

You've just created three files: Floor1, Floor2, and Common. Each file contains unique information about the building. Next, you'll use the Xref command to recombine these files for the different floor plans in your building.

Assembling Xrefs to Build a Drawing

You'll now create composite files for each floor using Xrefs of only the files needed for the individual floors. You'll use the Attach option of the Xref command to insert all the files you exported from the Plan file.

Follow these steps to create a file representing the first floor:

1. Close the Common.dwg file, open a new file, and call it Xref-1.

2. Set up this file as an architectural drawing, 8½ ″ × 11″ with a scale of 1/16″ = 1′. The upper-right corner limits for such a drawing are 2112,1632. Metric users should set up a drawing at 1:200 scale on an A4 sheet size. Your drawing area should be 4200 cm × 5940 cm. Click All from the Zoom flyout on the View tab's Navigate panel or type **Z↵ A↵** so your drawing area is adjusted to the window.

3. Set the Ltscale value to 192. Metric users should set it to 200.

4. Click Attach from the Insert tab's Reference panel or type **Xa↵** to open the Select Reference File dialog box.

5. Locate and select the Common.dwg file.

6. In the Attach External Reference dialog box, make sure the Specify On-Screen check box in the Insertion Point group isn't selected. Then make sure the X, Y, and Z values in the Insertion Point group are all 0 (Figure 15.5). Because the insertion points of all the files are the same (0,0), they will fit together perfectly when they're inserted into the new files.

7. Click OK. The Common.dwg file appears in the drawing.

FIGURE 15.5
The Attach
External Reference
dialog box

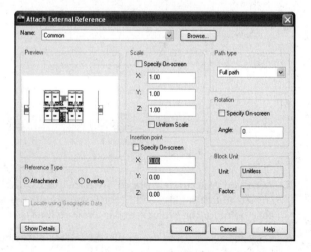

The drawing may appear faded. This is because AutoCAD has a feature that allows you to fade an Xref so that it is easily distinguished from other objects in your current drawing. You can quickly change the reference fade setting by doing the following:

1. In the Insert tab's expanded Reference panel, locate the Xref Fading slider.

2. Click and drag the Xref Fading slider all the way to the left, or you can click in the Xref Fading slider value input box to the right and enter 0↵.

Your Xref should now appear solid. Remember the Xref Fading slider; you may find that you'll need it frequently when working with Xrefs.

Now continue to add some reference files:

1. Click Attach from the Reference panel, and then locate, select, and insert the Floor1 or Floor1-metric file.

2. Repeat step 1 to insert the Col-grid.dwg or Col-grid-metric.dwg file as an Xref. You now have the plan for the first floor.

3. Save this file.

Next, use the current file to create another file representing a different floor:

1. Choose Save As from the Application menu to save this file as Xref-2.dwg.

2. Click the External References tool in the Insert tab's Reference panel title bar, or type **Xr**↵.

3. In the External References palette, select Floor1 in the list of Xrefs. Notice that as you hover over the Floor1 name, a description of the file appears with a thumbnail view (Figure 15.6). This can help you quickly identify Xref files in the list.

4. Right-click and select Detach from the shortcut menu.

5. Right-click in the blank portion of the list in the External References palette, and select Attach DWG from the shortcut menu.

6. Locate and select Floor2.dwg.

7. In the Attach External Reference dialog box, make sure the X, Y, and Z values in the Insertion Point group are all set to 0.

8. Click OK. The Floor2 drawing appears in place of Floor1. Turn off the Notes layer to see the plan clearly.

Now when you need to make changes to Xref-1 or Xref-2, you can edit their individual Xref files. The next time you open Xref-1 or Xref-2, the updated Xrefs will automatically appear in their most recent forms.

FIGURE 15.6
Highlight Floor1 in
the list of Xrefs.

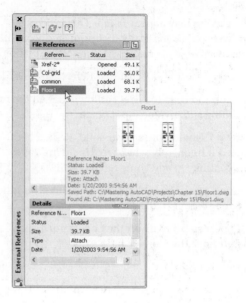

LOCATING XREF FILES

If you move an Xref file after you insert it into a drawing, AutoCAD may not be able to find it later when you attempt to open the drawing. If this happens, you can click the Browse button of the Found At option at the bottom of the External References palette to tell AutoCAD the new location of the Xref file. The Browse button appears at the far right of the Found At text box when you click in the text box.

If you know that you'll be keeping your project files in one place, you can use the Projectname system variable in conjunction with the Options dialog box to direct AutoCAD to look in a specific location for Xref files. Here's what to do:

1. Choose Options from the Application menu or type **OP↵**.

2. Click the Files tab and then locate and select the Project Files Search Path option.

3. Click Add and either enter a name for your project or accept the default name of Project1.

4. Click Browse and locate and select the folder where you plan to keep your Xref files.

5. Close the Options dialog box, and then enter **Projectname↵** at the Command prompt.

6. Enter the project name you used in step 3. Save your file so it remembers this setting.

Xrefs don't need to be permanent. As you saw in the previous exercise, you can attach and detach them easily at any time. This means that if you need to get information from another file— to see how well an elevator core aligns, for example—you can temporarily attach the other file as an Xref to check alignments quickly and then detach it when you're finished.

Think of these composite files as final plot files that are used only for plotting and reviewing. You can then edit the smaller, more manageable Xref files. Figure 15.7 illustrates the relationship of these files.

FIGURE 15.7

A diagram of Xref file relationships

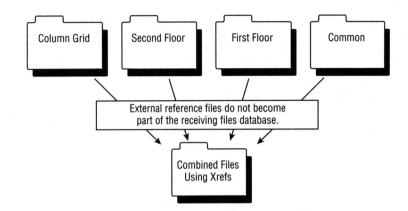

The combinations of Xrefs are limited only by your imagination, but you should avoid multiple Xrefs of the same file in one drawing.

KEEPING TRACK OF XREF LOCATIONS

Because Xref files don't become part of the file they're referenced into, you must take care to keep them in a location where AutoCAD can find them when the referencing file is opened. This can be a minor annoyance when you need to send files to others outside your office. To help keep track of Xrefs, click eTransmit from the Output tab's Send panel. See Chapter 29 for details.

UPDATING BLOCKS IN XREFS

Several advantages are associated with using Xref files. Because the Xrefs don't become part of the drawing file's database, the referencing files remain small. Also, because Xref files are easily updated, work can be split up among several people in a workgroup environment or on a network. For example, for your hypothetical apartment building project, one person can be editing the Common file while another works on Floor1, and so on. The next time the composite Xref-1.dwg or Xref-2.dwg file is opened, it automatically reflects any new changes made in the Xref files. If the Xref is updated while you still have the receiving file open, you receive a balloon message telling you that an Xref requires a reload.

Let's see how to set this up:

Insert

1. Save and close the Xref-2 file, and then open the Common.dwg file.

2. Update the unit plan you edited earlier in this chapter. Click Insert on the Home or Insert tab's Block panel. You can also type **Insert**⏎.

3. In the Insert dialog box, click the Browse button and then locate and select Unit.dwg. If you can't find your Unit.dwg file, you can use 15b-unit.dwg. Click Open, and then click OK in the Insert dialog box.

4. At the warning message, click Redefine Block.

5. At the Insertion point: prompt, press the Esc key.

6. Enter **RE**↵ to regenerate the drawing. You see the new unit plan in place of the old one (see Figure 15.8). You may also see all the dimensions and notes for each unit.

FIGURE 15.8
The Common file with the revised unit plan

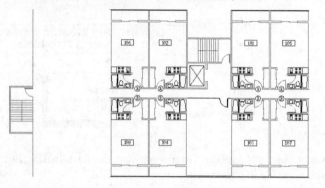
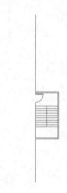

7. If the Notes layer is on, use the Layer drop-down list to turn it off.

Insert

8. Click the Insert tool on the Block panel again, and replace the empty room across the hall from the lobby with the utility room (utility.dwg or utility-metric.dwg) (see Figure 15.9).

9. Save the Common file.

10. Open the Xref-1 file, right-click Common in the External References palette, and select Reload from the shortcut menu. You can also right-click the Manage Xrefs icon in the lower-right corner of the AutoCAD window and select Reload DWG Xrefs. You see the utility room and the typical units in their new form. Your drawing should look like the top image in Figure 15.10.

11. Open Xref-2. You see that the utility room and typical units are updated in this file as well. (See the bottom image in Figure 15.10.)

FIGURE 15.9
The utility room inserted

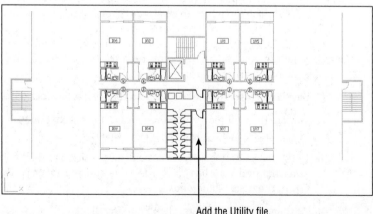

Add the Utility file.

FIGURE 15.10
The Xref-1 and Xref-2 files with the units updated

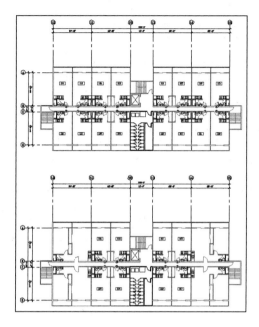

Importing Named Elements from Xrefs

Chapter 5 discussed how layers, blocks, linetypes, and text styles—called *named elements*—are imported along with a file that is inserted into another file. Xref files don't import named elements. You can, however, review their names and use a special command to import the ones you want to use in the current file.

SAVING XREF LAYER SETTINGS

You can set the Visretain system variable to 1 to force AutoCAD to remember layer settings of Xref files. Another choice is to turn on the Retain Changes To Xref Layers option in the Open And Save tab of the Options dialog box. You can also use the Layer States Manager in the Layer Properties Manager dialog box to save layer settings for later recall. The Layer States Manager is described in detail in the section "Saving and Recalling Layer Settings" later in this chapter.

AutoCAD renames named elements from Xref files by giving them the prefix of the filename from which they come. For example, the Wall layer in the Floor1 file is called Floor1|WALL in the Xref-1 file; the Toilet block is called Floor1|TOILET. You can't draw on the layer Floor1|WALL, nor can you insert Floor1|TOILET, but you can view Xref layers in the Layer Properties Manager dialog box, and you can view Xref blocks by using the Insert dialog box.

Next, you'll look at how AutoCAD identifies layers and blocks in Xref files, and you'll get a chance to import a layer from an Xref:

1. With the `Xref-1` file open, open the Layer Properties Manager dialog box. Notice that the names of the layers from the Xref files are all prefixed with the filename and the vertical bar (|) character. Exit the Layer Manager Properties dialog box. You can also open the Layer drop-down list to view the layer names.

2. Enter **Xb↵** to open the Xbind dialog box. You see a listing of the current Xrefs. Each item shows a plus sign to the left. This list box follows the Microsoft Windows format for expandable lists, much like the tree view in Windows Explorer (Figure 15.11).

FIGURE 15.11
The Xbind
dialog box

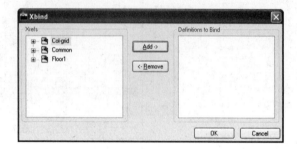

3. Click the plus sign next to the Floor1 Xref item. The list expands to show the types of elements available to bind (Figure 15.12).

FIGURE 15.12
The expanded
Floor1 list

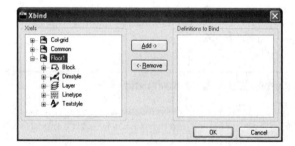

4. Click the plus sign next to the Layer item. The list expands further to show the layers available for binding (Figure 15.13).

FIGURE 15.13
The expanded
Layer list

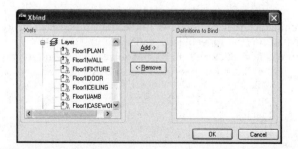

5. Locate Floor1|WALL in the list, click it, and then click the Add button. Floor1|WALL is added to the list to the right, Definitions To Bind.

6. Click OK to bind the Floor1|WALL layer.

7. Open the Layer Properties Manager dialog box.

8. Scroll down the list and look for the Floor1|WALL layer. You won't find it. In its place is a layer called Floor1$0$WALL.

IMPORT DRAWING COMPONENTS WITH DESIGNCENTER

The AutoCAD DesignCenter lets you import settings and other drawing components from any drawing, not just Xref drawings. You'll learn more about the AutoCAD DesignCenter in Chapter 29.

As you can see, when you use Xbind to import a named item, such as the Floor1|WALL layer, the vertical bar (|) is replaced by two dollar signs surrounding a number, which is usually zero. (If for some reason the imported layer name Floor1$0$WALL already exists, the zero in that name is changed to 1, as in Floor1$1$WALL.) Other named items are renamed in the same way, using the 0 replacement for the vertical bar.

You can also use the Xbind dialog box to bind multiple layers as well as other items from Xrefs attached to the current drawing. You can bind an entire Xref to a drawing, converting it to a simple block. By doing so, you have the opportunity to maintain unique layer names of the Xref being bound or to merge the Xref's similarly named layers with those of the current file. See Chapter 7 for details.

NESTING XREFS AND USING OVERLAYS

Xrefs can be nested. For example, if the Common.dwg file created in this chapter used the Unit.dwg file as an Xref rather than as an inserted block, you would still get the same result in the Xref-1.dwg file. That is, you would see the entire floor plan, including the unit plans, when you opened Xref-1.dwg. In this situation, Unit.dwg would be nested in the Common.dwg file, which is in turn externally referenced in the Xref-1.dwg file.

Although nested Xrefs can be helpful, take care in using Xrefs this way. For example, you might create an Xref by using the Common.dwg file in the Floor1.dwg file as a means of referencing walls and other features of the Common.dwg file. You might also reference the Common.dwg file into the Floor2.dwg file for the same reason. After you did this, however, you'd have three versions of the Common plan in the Xref-1.dwg file because each Xref would have Common.dwg attached to it. And because AutoCAD would dutifully load Common.dwg three times, Xref-1.dwg would occupy substantial computer memory, slowing your computer when you edited the Xref-1.dwg file.

To avoid this problem, use the Overlay option in the Attach External Reference dialog box. An overlaid Xref can't be nested. For example, if you use the Overlay option when inserting the Common.dwg file into the Floor1.dwg and Floor2.dwg files, the nested Common.dwg files are ignored when you open the Xref-1.dwg file, thereby eliminating the redundant occurrence of Common.dwg. In another example, if you use the Overlay option to import the Unit.dwg file into the Common.dwg file and then attach the Common.dwg into Xref-1.dwg as an Xref, you don't see the Unit.dwg file in Xref-1.dwg. The nested Unit.dwg drawing is ignored.

Controlling the Xref Search Path

One problem AutoCAD users have encountered in the past is lost or broken links to an Xref. This occurs when an Xref file is moved from its original location or when you receive a set of drawings that includes Xrefs. The Xref links are broken because AutoCAD doesn't know where to look. Since AutoCAD 2005, you have better control over how AutoCAD looks for Xref files.

When you insert an Xref, the Attach External Reference dialog box opens, offering you options for insertion point, scale, and rotation. This dialog box also provides the Path Type option, which enables you to select a method for locating Xrefs. You can choose from three path type options:

Full Path   Lets you specify the exact filename and path for an Xref, including the disk drive or network location. Use this option when you want AutoCAD to look in a specific location for the Xref.

Relative Path   Lets you specify a file location relative to the location of the current or host drawing. For example, if the host drawing is in a folder called C:\mycadfiles and the Xrefs are in a folder called C:\mycadfiles\xrefs, you can specify .\xrefs for the location of the Xref file. This option is useful when you know you'll maintain the folder structure of the host and Xref files when moving or exchanging these files. Note that because this is a relative path, this option is valid only for files that reside on the same local hard disk.

No Path   Perhaps the most flexible option, this tells AutoCAD to use its own search criteria to find Xrefs. When No Path is selected, AutoCAD first looks in the same folder of the host drawing; then it looks in the project search path defined in the Files tab of the Options dialog box. (See Appendix B for more on the Options dialog box.) Last, AutoCAD looks in the Support File Search Path option, also defined in the Files tab of the Options dialog box. If you plan to send your files to a client or a consultant, you may want to use this option.

Managing Layers

In a survey of AutoCAD users, Autodesk discovered that one of the most frequently used features in AutoCAD is the Layer command. You'll find that you turn layers on and off to display and edit the many levels of information contained in your AutoCAD files. As your files become more complex, controlling layer visibility becomes more difficult. Fortunately, AutoCAD offers the Layer States Manager to make your work a little easier.

Saving and Recalling Layer Settings

The Layer States Manager lets you save layer settings. This can be crucial when you're editing a file that serves multiple uses, such as a floor plan and reflected ceiling plan. You can, for example, turn layers on and off to set up the drawing for a reflected ceiling plan view and then save the layer settings. Later, when you need to modify the ceiling information, you can recall the layer settings to view the ceiling data.

The following steps show you how the Layer States Manager works:

1. In AutoCAD, open the 15b-unit.dwg file. Click the Layer Properties tool in the Home tab's Layers panel to open the Layer Properties Manager, and turn on all the layers except Notes and Flr-pat. Your drawing should look similar to the top image in Figure 15.14.

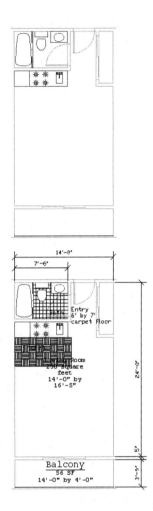

2. Click the Unsaved Layer State drop-down list in the Home tab's Layers panel.

3. Click Manage Layer States to open the Layer States Manager dialog box. Take a moment to look at the options in this dialog box. This is where you can specify which layer settings you want saved with this layer state (Figure 15.15).

FIGURE 15.15

The Layer
States Manager
dialog box

4. You're ready to save the current layer state. Click the New button in the Layer States Manager dialog box. The New Layer State To Save dialog box opens (Figure 15.16).

FIGURE 15.16

The New Layer
State To Save
dialog box

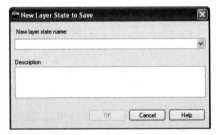

5. Enter **blank floor plan** in the New Layer State Name input box. Note that you can also enter a brief description of your layer state. Click OK to return to the Layer States Manager dialog box.

6. Click the More Restore Options button (Figure 15.17) in the lower-right corner of the Layer States Manager dialog box to expand the list of options.

FIGURE 15.17

The More Restore
Options button

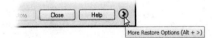

7. Make sure the On/Off check box is selected, and then click Close. Several other options are available, but you can leave them as they are.

8. Back in the Layer Properties Manager dialog box, turn on the Flr-pat and Notes layers and turn off the Ceiling layer.

9. Your drawing looks like the bottom image in Figure 15.14.

You've just saved a layer state and then changed the layer settings to something different from the saved state. The following steps demonstrate how you can restore the saved layer state:

1. In the Home tab's Layers panel, click the Unsaved Layer State drop-down list and select Manage Layer States to open the Layer States Manager dialog box.

2. Select Blank Floor Plan from the list, and click Restore. Your drawing reverts to the previous view with the Notes and Flr-pat layers turned off and the Ceiling layer on.

3. This brings you to the end of the Layer States Manager tutorial. Save the file and close it.

The layer states are saved with the file so you can retrieve them at a later date. As you can see in the Layer States Manager dialog box, you have a few other options, as shown in Table 15.1.

TABLE 15.1:   Layer States Manager dialog box options

OPTION	PURPOSE
New	Creates a new layer state.
Save	Saves the selected layer state after edits.
Edit	Lets you edit the layer settings for the selected layer state.
Rename	Renames a selected layer state.
Delete	Deletes a layer state from the list.
Import	Imports a set of layer states that have been exported using the Export option of this dialog box.
Export	Saves a set of layer states as a file. By default, the file is given the name of the current layer state with the .las filename extension. You can import the layer-state file into other files.
Layer Properties To Restore (in the expanded dialog box)	Lets you select the layer properties to be controlled by the Layer States Manager.

 In addition to saving layer states by name, you can quickly revert to a previous layer setting by clicking the Previous tool on the Home tab's Layers panel. This tool enables you to revert to the previous layer settings without affecting other settings in AutoCAD. Note that Previous mode doesn't restore renamed or deleted layers, nor does it remove new layers.

After you become familiar with these layer-state tools, you'll find yourself using them frequently in your editing sessions.

Other Tools for Managing Layers

The layer controls in AutoCAD have been greatly improved over the years. You now have quite a number of tools that help you quickly set up layers as you work. In the following sections, you'll learn about some of those other tools you've seen in the Layers panel. All the tools discussed in these sections have keyboard command equivalents. Check the tool tip for the keyboard command name when you select one of these tools from the Layers panel.

USING LAYER WALK TO EXPLORE LAYERS

When you work with a file that was produced by someone else, you usually have to spend some time becoming familiar with the way layers are set up in it. This can be a tedious process, but the Layer Walk tool can help.

As the name implies, the Layer Walk tool lets you "walk through" the layers of a file, visually isolating each layer as you select its name from a list. You can use Layer Walk to select the layers that you want visible, or you can turn layers on and off to explore a drawing without affecting the current layer settings. To open the LayerWalk dialog box, do the following:

1. Click the Layer Walk tool on the expanded Layers panel, or enter **Laywalk**⏎.

2. The LayerWalk dialog box appears (Figure 15.18).

FIGURE 15.18
The LayerWalk
dialog box

You can click and drag the bottom edge of the dialog box to expand the list so you can see all the layers in the drawing. When you first open the LayerWalk dialog box, you see the current visible layers selected. Layers that are off aren't selected. Click a single layer and AutoCAD displays just that layer. With a single layer selected, you can "walk" through the layers by pressing the down or up arrow keys.

You can use this dialog box to set up layer settings visually by Ctrl+clicking layer names to make them visible. Turn off Restore On Exit to maintain the layer settings you set up in the LayerWalk dialog box, or turn it on if you want the drawing to revert to the layer settings that were in place before you opened the LayerWalk dialog box. Right-click the list of layers to display a set of other options that let you save the layer state and invert the selection.

CHANGING THE LAYER ASSIGNMENT OF OBJECTS

In addition to the Layer Walk tool, the Layers panel includes two tools that change the layer assignments of objects: the Match tool and the Change To Current Layer tool on the expanded Layers panel.

The Match tool is similar to the Match Properties tool, but it's streamlined to operate only on layer assignments. After clicking this tool on the Layers panel, select the object or objects you want to change, press ⏎, and then select an object whose layer you want to match.

The Change To Current Layer tool on the expanded Layers panel changes an object's layer assignment to the current layer. This tool has long existed as an AutoLISP utility, and you'll find that you'll get a lot of use from it.

CONTROLLING LAYER SETTINGS THROUGH OBJECTS

The remaining Layer tools let you make layer settings by selecting objects in the drawing. These tools are easy to use: click a tool, and then select an object.

The following list describes each tool:

Layer Isolate/Layer Unisolate   Layer Isolate turns off all the layers except for the layer of the selected object. Layer Unisolate restores the layer settings to the way the drawing was set before you used Layer Isolate.

Freeze   Freezes the layer of the selected object.

Off   Turns off the layer of the selected object.

Lock/Unlock   Locks the layer of the selected object. A locked layer is visible but can't be edited.

Layer Walk   Lets you dynamically change layer visibility.

Copy Objects To New Layer   Copies an object or a set of objects to a different layer.

Make Object's Layer Current   Enables you to set the current layer by selecting an object that is on the desired layer.

Turn All Layers On   Turns all layers on.

Thaw All Layers   Thaws all layers.

Isolate To Current Viewport   Enables you to freeze layers in all but the current viewport by selecting objects that are on the layers to be frozen.

Merge   Combines several layers into one layer. First select objects whose layers you want to merge, press ↵, then select an object whose layer you want to merge with.

Delete   Deletes all objects on a layer and then deletes the layer.

Using Advanced Tools: Filter and Quick Select

Two other tools are extremely useful in your day-to-day work with AutoCAD: selection filters and Quick Select. I've saved the discussion of these tools until this part of the chapter because you don't need them until you've become accustomed to the way AutoCAD works. Chances are you've already experimented with some of the AutoCAD menu options not yet discussed in the tutorial. Many of the drop-down menu options and their functions are self-explanatory. Selection filters and QuickCalc, which is discussed later in this chapter, don't appear in any of the menus and require further explanation.

Let's start with selection filters. AutoCAD includes two selection-filtering tools: The *Quick Select tool* offers a quick way to locate objects based on their properties. The *Filter tool* lets you select objects based on a more complex set of criteria.

Filtering Selections

Suppose you need to isolate just the walls of your drawing in a separate file. One way to do this is to turn off all the layers except the Wall layer. You can then use the Wblock command and select the remaining walls, using a window to write the wall information to a file. Filters can simplify this operation by enabling you to select groups of objects based on their properties.

GETTING NOTIFICATION OF NEW LAYERS

AutoCAD can notify you when new layers are added to Xrefs in a drawing or to the current drawing itself. Such new layers are called *unreconciled* layers. This feature can be helpful when you are working with others and need to stay informed about the condition of a drawing. By default, the notification comes in two forms. When new layers are added, a warning icon appears in the right side of the status bar. If you attempt to plot a drawing that contains new layers, the following message appears: `Unreconciled new layers exist in the drawing`. The warning will not prevent you from doing anything. It is just intended as a way to notify you of changes. In addition, the unreconciled layers are grouped into a layer property filter called Unreconciled New Layers, which can be viewed in the Layer Properties Manager.

To "reconcile" unreconciled layers, open the Layer Properties Manager, select the unreconciled layers, right-click, and select Reconcile Layers from the shortcut menu.

New layer notification is turned on by default and is controlled by the Layerevalctl system variable. Type **Layerevalctl** ⏎ **1** ⏎ to turn it on and **Layerevalctl** ⏎ **0** ⏎ to turn it off.

You can also set how you are notified of new layers through the Layereval and Layernotify system variables. Layereval controls when the Unreconciled New Layer filter displays new layers and can be set to 0, 1, or 2. The setting 0 turns Layereval off, 1 sets it to detect new layers in Xrefs, and 2 sets it to detect new layers in Xrefs and the current drawing. Layernotify determines how you are notified of new layers. The setting 0 means no notification; 1 means notify when you start a plot; 2 when the drawing is open; 4 when Xrefs are loaded, reloaded, or attached; 8 when you are restoring a layer state; 16 when you are saving a file; and 32 when you are inserting a drawing.

Follow these steps to select objects based on their layer assignment:

1. Open the `Unit` file.

2. Type **w** ⏎ to start the Wblock command. Then, in the Write Block dialog box, enter **Unitwall** in the File Name And Path input box.

3. Make sure the Objects and Retain radio buttons are selected in the dialog box, and then click the Select Objects button in the Objects group. The dialog box closes so that you can select objects.

4. At the `Select Objects:` prompt, type **'Filter** ⏎ to open the Object Selection Filters dialog box (Figure 15.19).

FIGURE 15.19
The Object
Selection Filters
dialog box

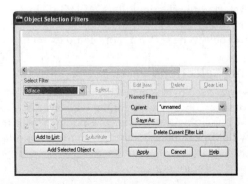

   5. Open the drop-down list in the Select Filter group.

   6. Scroll down the list, and find and highlight the Layer option.

   7. Click the Select button next to the drop-down list to display a list of layers. Highlight Wall, and click OK.

   8. Click the Add To List button toward the bottom of the Select Filter group to add Layer = Wall to the list box.

   9. Click Apply to close the Object Selection Filters dialog box.

  10. Type **all.⏎** to select everything in the drawing. Only the objects assigned to the Wall layer are selected. You see a message in the Command window indicating how many objects were found.

  11. Press ⏎. You see the message `Exiting Filtered selection Resuming WBLOCK command - Select objects: 29 found.`

  12. Press ⏎ again to complete the selection, and then click OK to complete the Wblock command. All the walls are written out to a file called `Unitwall`.

In this exercise, you filtered out a layer by using the Filter command. After you designate a filter, you then select the group of objects you want AutoCAD to filter through. AutoCAD finds the objects that match the filter requirements and passes those objects to the current command.

As you've seen from the previous exercise, you can choose from many options in this utility. Let's take a closer look.

Working with the Object Selection Filters Dialog Box

To use the Object Selection Filters dialog box, first select the criterion for filtering from the drop-down list. If the criterion you select is a named item (layer, linetype, color, or block), you can then click the Select button to choose specific items from a list. If there is only one choice, the Select button is dimmed.

After you've determined what to filter, you must add it to the list by clicking the Add To List button. The filter criterion then appears in the list box at the top of the Object Selection Filters dialog box, and you can apply that criterion to your current command or to a later command. AutoCAD remembers your filter settings, so if you need to reselect a filtered selection set, you don't have to redefine your filter criteria.

Saving Filter Criteria

If you prefer, you can preselect filter criteria. Then, at any `Select objects:` prompt, you can type **'Filter.⏎**, highlight the appropriate filter criteria in the list box, and click Apply. The specifications in the Object Selection Filters dialog box remain in place for the duration of the current editing session.

You can also save a set of criteria by entering a name in the input box next to the Save As button and then clicking the button. The criteria list data is saved in a file called `Filter.nfl` in the `C:\Documents and Settings\`*User Name*`\Application Data\Autodesk\AutoCAD 2011\R18.1\enu\Support`. You can access the criteria list at any time by opening the Current drop-down list and choosing the name of the saved criteria list.

FILTERING OBJECTS BY LOCATION

Notice the X, Y, and Z drop-down lists just below the main Select Filter drop-down list in the Object Selection Filters dialog box. These lists become accessible when you select a criterion that describes a geometric property or a coordinate (such as an arc's radius or center point). You can use these lists to define filter selections even more specifically, using greater than (>), less than (<), equal to or greater than (>=), equal to or less than (<=), equal to (=), or not equal to (!=) comparisons (called *relational operators*).

For example, suppose you want to grab all the circles whose radii are greater than 4.0 units. To do this, choose Circle Radius from the Select Filter drop-down list. Then, in the X list, select >. Enter **4.0** in the input box to the right of the X list, and click Add To List. The items

```
Circle Radius > 4.0000
Object = Circle
```

are added to the list box at the top of the dialog box. You used the > operator to indicate a circle radius greater than 4.0 units.

CREATING COMPLEX SELECTION SETS

At times, you'll want to create a specific filter list. For instance, say you need to filter out all the Door blocks on the layer Floor2 *and* all arcs with a radius equal to 1. To do this, you use the *grouping operators* found at the bottom of the Select Filter drop-down list. You'll need to build a list as follows:

```
** Begin OR
** Begin AND
Block Name = Door
Layer = Floor2
** End AND
** Begin AND
Entity = Arc
Arc Radius = 1.0000
** End AND
** End OR
```

Notice that the Begin and End operators are balanced; that is, for every Begin OR or Begin AND, there is an End OR or End AND.

This list may look simple, but it can get confusing. If criteria are bounded by the AND grouping operators, objects must fulfill *both* criteria before they're selected. If criteria are bounded by the OR grouping operators, objects fulfilling *either* criteria will be selected. If you add the wrong option accidentally, select it from the list and click the Delete button. If you need to insert an option in the middle of the list, select the item that comes after the item you want to insert, and then select and add the item.

Here are the steps to build the previous list:

1. In the Select Filter drop-down list, choose **Begin OR, and then click Add To List. Do the same for **Begin AND.

2. Click Block Name in the Select Filter drop-down list, click the Select button, and select Door from the list that appears. Click Add To List.

3. For the layer, click Layer in the Select Filter drop-down list. Click Select, choose the layer name, and click Add To List.

4. In the Select Filter drop-down list, choose **End AND, and then click Add To List. Do the same for **Begin AND.

5. Select Arc from the Select Filter drop-down list and click Add To List.

6. Select Arc Radius from the Select Filter list, and enter **1.0** in the input box next to the X drop-down list. Be sure the equal sign (=) shows in the X drop-down list, and then click Add To List.

7. Choose **End AND, and click Add To List. Do the same for **End OR.

If you make an error in any step, highlight the item, select an item to replace it, and click the Substitute button instead of the Add To List button. If you need to only change a value, click the Edit Item button near the center of the dialog box.

QUICK ACCESS TO YOUR FAVORITE COMMANDS

As an IT manager, I've discovered that AutoCAD users are very possessive of their keyboard and tool shortcuts, and they are usually the first custom item that a new employee will install. You can collect your favorite commands into a single toolbar or Ribbon panel by using AutoCAD's customization feature. This way, you can have ready access to your most frequently used commands. Chapter 28 gives you all the information you need to create your own custom toolbars and Ribbon panels.

Using Quick Select

The Filter command offers a lot of power in isolating specific types of objects, but in many situations you may not need such an elaborate tool. The Qselect command can filter your selection based on the object properties, which are more common filter criteria. To access the Qselect command, click Quick Select from the Home tab's Utilities panel or right-click the drawing area when no command is active and choose Quick Select from the shortcut menu to open the Quick Select dialog box.

Quick Select is also offered as an option in a few dialog boxes. Try using the Wblock command again, this time using the Quick Select option offered in its dialog box:

1. With the Unit file open, type **W↵** to start the Wblock command. Then, in the Write Block dialog box, enter **Unitwall2** in the File Name And Path input box.

2. Make sure the Objects radio button is selected at the top of the dialog box and the Delete From Drawing option is selected from the Objects group.

3. Click the Quick Select tool to the right of the Select Objects button in the Objects group to open the Quick Select dialog box (Figure 15.20).

4. Select Layer from the Properties list.

5. Select Wall from the Value drop-down list near the bottom of the dialog box.

FIGURE 15.20

The Quick Select dialog box

6. Click the Select Objects button in the upper-right corner of the dialog box. The dialog boxes close so you can select objects.

7. Select the entire drawing by using a window; press ↵ to finish your selection. Both dialog boxes return.

8. Click OK, and then click OK in the Write Block dialog box. The walls disappear, indicating that they have been written to a file.

9. Click the Undo button to undo the deletion.

The Qselect command selects objects based on their properties, as shown in the Properties list box. You can apply the selection criteria based on the entire drawing, or you can use the Select Objects button in the upper-right corner of the dialog box to isolate a set of objects to which you want to apply the selection criteria.

In the previous exercise, you used Quick Select from within another dialog box. As mentioned earlier, you can also use Quick Select by clicking Quick Select from the Home tab's Utilities panel or by right-clicking the drawing area when no command is active and choosing Quick Select from the shortcut menu. Quick Select then uses the Noun/Verb selection method: You select objects using Quick Select first, and then you apply editing commands to the selected objects.

If you want to use Quick Select with a command that doesn't allow the Noun/Verb selection method, you can select objects by using Quick Select, start the command you want to use, and then use the Previous Selection option.

Here is a description of the Quick Select dialog box options:

Apply To Lets you determine the set of objects to which you want to apply the Quick Select filters. The default is the entire drawing, but you can use the Select Objects button to select a set of objects. If you select a set of objects before issuing the Quick Select command, you also see the Current Selection option in the Apply To drop-down list.

Object Type Lets you limit the filter to specific types of objects such as lines, arcs, circles, and so on. The Multiple option lets you filter your selection from all the objects in the drawing regardless of type.

Properties Lets you select the property of the object type you want to filter, after you select an object type. The Properties list changes to reflect the properties that are available to be filtered.

Operator   Offers a set of criteria to apply to the property you select in the Properties list to make your selection. You can select objects that are *equal to* or *not equal to* the criteria you select in the Object Type and Properties lists. Depending on the property you select, you also may have the option to select objects that are *greater than* or *less than* a given property value. For example, you can select all lines whose X coordinate is less than 5 by choosing Line from the Object Type drop-down list and Start X from the Properties list. You then select < Less Than from the Operator drop-down list and enter **5** in the Value input box.

Value   Displays the values of the property you select in the Properties list. For example, if you select Layer from the Properties list, the Value option lists all the layers available.

How To Apply   Lets you specify whether to include or exclude the filtered objects in a new selection set.

Append To Current Selection Set   Lets you append the filtered objects to an existing selection set or create an entirely new selection set.

SELECT SIMILAR OBJECTS OR ISOLATE OBJECT FOR EASIER EDITING

There are a few new features in the right-click menu that can help speed up object selection. If you select an object and right-click, you'll see the Select Similar option.

Just as the name implies, it will select all objects in the drawing that are similar to the one currently selected. For example, if you select a hatch pattern, right-click, and then click Select Similar, all the hatch patterns in the drawing will be selected. Click on a line, right-click, and then click Select Similar and all the lines that are on the selected line's layer will be selected. You can also use the Selectsimilar command to do the same thing.

You can control how the Select Similar feature behaves by entering **Selectsimilar.⏎ SE.⏎**. This opens the Select Similar Settings dialog box, which lets you set the basis for the similar selection such as layer, color, or linetype, to name a few.

Another handy right-click option is Isolate. If you have a set of objects, right-click, and select Isolate ➤ Isolate Objects, all but the selected objects will be made invisible. Or you can right-click and select Isolate ➤ Hide Objects to hide the selected objects. To bring back the objects that were made invisible, right-click and select Isolate ➤ End Object Isolation.

The Isolate feature can also be issued from the Isolate Objects tool in the right side of the status bar. It's the icon that looks like a lightbulb. Click this tool and then select Isolate Object or Hide Object from the menu that appears. You can then select the objects you want to isolate or hide. Or you can use the Isolateobjects command.

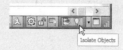

Using the QuickCalc Calculator

You may have noticed a calculator icon in some of the options in the Properties palette or in the right-click shortcut menu. This is the QuickCalc tool. If you click it, you'll see the QuickCalc calculator, shown in Figure 15.21. At first glance, it looks like a typical calculator. It has the standard math as well as the scientific functions that are available when you click the More button. If your view of QuickCalc doesn't look like Figure 15.21, click the More/Less button, and then expand the Number Pad or Scientific section by clicking the arrow in the section title. You'll also see a section for converting units, which comes in handy when you want to find the metric equivalent of an Imperial measurement.

At the bottom is a section for variables. This area lets you store custom formulas and values that you want to refer to frequently.

FIGURE 15.21
QuickCalc and its parts

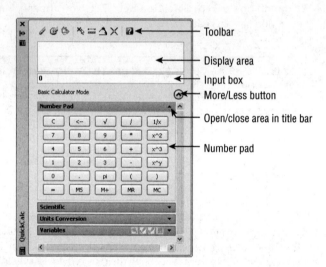

- Toolbar
- Display area
- Input box
- More/Less button
- Open/close area in title bar
- Number pad

Near the top is the display area. This is where QuickCalc keeps a running record of your calculation results. It also allows you to recall both the results and formulas you've used. Just below the display area is the input box. As you type, or as you click the keys of QuickCalc, your input appears in this box. Pressing Enter displays the resulting value both in the input box and in the display area.

Above the display area is a set of tools in a toolbar. These tools let you obtain other types of data from the drawing, such as the coordinate of a point or the intersection of two lines (see Figure 15.22).

FIGURE 15.22
The QuickCalc toolbar

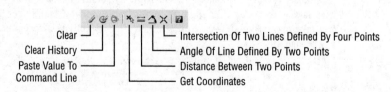

- Clear
- Clear History
- Paste Value To Command Line
- Intersection Of Two Lines Defined By Four Points
- Angle Of Line Defined By Two Points
- Distance Between Two Points
- Get Coordinates

The function of these tools will become clearer as you become familiar with QuickCalc. Table 15.2 describes each tool. Next, you'll get a chance to try out QuickCalc on some typical AutoCAD tasks.

TABLE 15.2:   QuickCalc tools

TOOL	PURPOSE
Clear	Clears the value from the input box.
Clear History	Clears the display area.
Paste Value To Command Line	Pastes data from the input box to the command line.
Get Coordinates	Temporarily closes QuickCalc and prompts you to pick a point or points. Coordinates of the point or the angle value are placed in the input area.
Distance Between Two Points	Temporarily closes QuickCalc and prompts you to enter a point. Select two points; the distance between the points is placed in the input area of QuickCalc.
Angle Of Line Defined By Two Points	Returns the angle of two points.
Intersection Of Two Lines Defined By Four Points	Returns the coordinate of the intersection of four points.

Adding Foot and Inch Lengths and Finding the Sum of Angles

Although QuickCalc may look simple, it provides a powerful aid in your work in AutoCAD. Besides offering the typical calculator functions, QuickCalc also enables you to quickly add and subtract angle values, feet-and-inches lengths, and much more. You can paste the results from calculations into the command line so you can easily include results as part of command-line responses.

To get a full appreciation of what QuickCalc can do for you, try the following exercises.

Imagine that you have a renovation project for which someone has taken dimensions in the field. You may be asked to draw a section of wall for which the overall dimension isn't given, but portions of the wall are dimensioned in a sketch as shown in Figure 15.23.

FIGURE 15.23
A sketch of measurements taken from an existing building

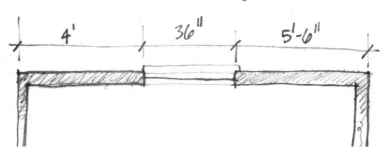

You can use QuickCalc to add a series of feet-and-inches dimensions:

1. Open the `QuickCalc.dwg` sample file, which contains some lines you can work with. It's set up to use architectural units.

2. Right-click and select the QuickCalc tool from the shortcut menu.

3. Double-click in the QuickCalc input box, and then enter **4'+36+5'6**. As you type, your entry appears in the input box (Figure 15.24).

FIGURE 15.24
The QuickCalc input box

4. Press ↵. The sum of the lengths, 12'-6", appears in the input box and in the display area.

Notice that you only had to enter the foot (') sign. QuickCalc assumes that a value is in inches unless you specify otherwise. You can also enter distances in the more traditional way using dashes and zeros, as in 4'-0" or 5'-6". QuickCalc ignores the dashes.

Now, suppose you want to use your newfound length to draw a line. You can quickly add the results from the input box to the command line, as shown in the following exercise.

1. Click the Line tool, and then click a point in the left portion of the drawing area.

2. In the QuickCalc toolbar, click the Paste Value To Command Line tool. Notice that the value in the input box appears in the command line.

3. Make sure the Polar Tracking mode is turned on in the status bar.

4. While pointing the rubber-banding line directly to the right, press ↵. A horizontal line is drawn to the length of 12'-6".

5. Press ↵ to end the Line command.

In this example, you used the Paste Value To Command Line tool in the QuickCalc toolbar. If you want to use a value that has scrolled up in the display area, you can select that value, right-click, and choose Paste To Command Line (Figure 15.25).

This is especially useful when you've used QuickCalc to add several strings of dimensions and you need to recall them individually from the display area. In addition to adding feet and inches, you can perform other math functions, such as dividing a length by two or multiplying a length. If the input value is in feet and inches, the resulting value is returned in feet and inches. For example, if you divide 25' by 6, the result is 4'-2".

FIGURE 15.25
The Paste To
Command Line
option in the
shortcut menu.

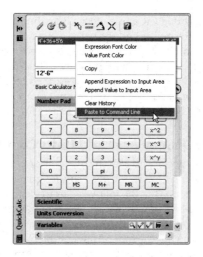

Another useful QuickCalc tool is Angle Of Line Defined By Two Points, which allows you to obtain the angle defined by two points:

1. In QuickCalc, click the Angle Of Line Defined By Two Points tool. QuickCalc temporarily closes to allow you to select points.

2. With osnaps turned on, select the endpoints of the lower line, starting with the bottom endpoint, as shown in Figure 15.26.

3. Back in QuickCalc, click the plus button in the number pad or enter +. Then, click the Angle Of Line Defined By Two Points tool again.

FIGURE 15.26
Select these end-
points using the
Angle Of Line
Defined By Two
Points option.

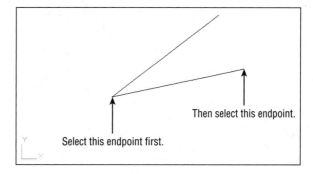

4. Select the endpoints of the upper line, starting with the bottom end of the line.

5. Back in QuickCalc, you see the angle value of the second line added to the input box. Click the equal button in the QuickCalc number pad to get the total angle value.

Here you added the angle of two lines, but you could just as easily have subtracted one angle from another or multiplied the value of a single angle. This can be useful if you need to find a fraction or a multiple of an angle. For example, you might need to find one-quarter of the angle described by a line, or you might want to find the angle that bisects two lines. You can do so by adding the value of two angles, as described in the exercise, and then dividing by 2 using the number pad or including /2 in the input box. Once you've obtained a value, you can paste it into the command line while specifying angles for drawing input.

Using the Display Area and Units Conversion

In addition to performing math functions on distances and angles, you can do some basic unit conversions. QuickCalc performs length, area, volume, and angle conversions in its Units Conversion group. Try the following exercise to learn how to convert a length from centimeters to feet and inches. In the process, you'll also learn how you can move a value from the Units Conversion area to the QuickCalc input box.

Suppose you have a paper drawing that was done in metric and you need to turn it into an AutoCAD drawing in feet and inches. Here's an example of how you can convert centimeters to feet and inches:

1. In QuickCalc, expand the Units Conversion group by clicking the arrow to the right of the Units Conversion title bar (Figure 15.27).

2. Make sure Length appears for the Units Type option. If not, then click in the box to the right of the Units Type option and select Length from the drop-down list that appears.

3. Select Centimeters from the Convert From drop-down list.

FIGURE 15.27
The expanded Units Conversion group

4. Select Feet from the Convert To drop-down list.

5. In the Value To Convert input box, enter **450**↵ for 450 cm. The equivalent value in feet appears in the Converted Value box.

6. Click the Converted Value option, and you also see the QuickCalc icon to the far right. Click this icon to display the value in the input box at the top of QuickCalc.

The value is in feet and decimal feet. You can convert the value to feet and inches by doing the following:

1. Edit the value in the input box to read as follows: **14′ +(.7637795*12)**.

2. Press ↵. The value converts to a feet-and-inches value of 14′-9 3/16″.

One limitation to the unit-conversion feature is that it won't take feet-and-inches input when converting from feet. For example, if you want to convert 12′-4″ to centimeters, you have to enter 12.334. In other words, you have to convert the inches to decimal feet. Because the Unit Conversion area is part of QuickCalc, this just means an extra step. You can quickly calculate the decimal feet equivalent of feet and inch values and then transfer them to the Units Conversion area.

Try the following to see how this works:

1. Click the Clear button in the QuickCalc toolbar (it looks like an eraser), and then double-click in the QuickCalc input box.

2. Enter **12 + (4 / 12)**↵ in QuickCalc's input box. The first 12 is the 12 feet. The 4 / 12 is for the 4 inches converted to decimal feet. Once you press ↵, the value of 12.3333333 appears.

3. Right-click in the QuickCalc input box and then click in the Value To Convert input box in the Units Conversion panel. The 12.3333333 value is pasted into the input box.

4. Select Feet from the Convert From drop-down list, and select Centimeters from the Convert To drop-down list. The centimeter equivalent of 12.3333333 feet appears in the Converted Value input box.

Here you saw how values from the input box automatically transfer to the Units Conversion area. You can also cut and paste values from other sources into either the main calculator input box or the Units Conversion input box.

Using QuickCalc to Find Points

You've seen how QuickCalc will let you add values of distances and angles and how it can perform unit conversions. You can also use it to calculate coordinate locations. To work with coordinates, you need to use a few special functions built into QuickCalc that let you select points and manipulate their value.

Before AutoCAD added the Midpoint Between Two Points osnap, the AutoCAD Cal command was the only way to find the midpoint between two points without drawing a temporary line. In the following example, you'll use QuickCalc to perform the same function as an example of how you can acquire point data and manipulate it to derive other coordinate locations:

1. Click the Clear button on the QuickCalc toolbar; then double-click in the QuickCalc input box.

2. In the QuickCalc input box, enter **(end + end)/2**↵. QuickCalc closes temporarily to allow you to select points.

3. Select the endpoints of the two lines, as shown in Figure 15.28.

4. QuickCalc returns and displays the coordinates of a point exactly between the two end-points you selected in step 3.

In step 2, you used the *end* function that is built into QuickCalc. As you saw, the end function lets you select the endpoint of an object (as you did in step 3). The end + end in the formula tells QuickCalc to add the two coordinates you selected in step 3. The /2 in the formula divides the sum of the coordinates to find their average, which happens to be the midpoint between the two points.

If you were to perform this calculation using pencil and paper, you would add the X, Y, and Z coordinate values of each point separately and then divide each coordinate by 2. Finally, you would combine the resulting X, Y, and Z coordinates back into a single point location.

FIGURE 15.28
The endpoints of
the two lines

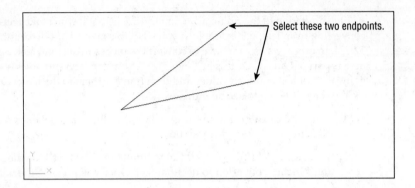

Select these two endpoints.

USING OSNAP MODES IN QUICKCALC EXPRESSIONS

In the previous exercise, you used osnap modes as part of arithmetic formulas (or *expressions*, as they're called in AutoCAD). QuickCalc treats osnap modes as temporary placeholders for point coordinates until you pick the points (at the prompts shown in steps 2 and 3 of the previous exercise).

The expression

```
(end + end)/2
```

finds the average of two values. In this case, the values are coordinates, so the average is the midpoint between the two coordinates. You can take this one step further and find the centroid of a triangle by using this expression:

```
(end + end + end)/3
```

Note that you enter only the first three letters of the osnap mode in calculator expressions. Table 15.3 shows what to enter in an expression for osnap modes. The table includes two items that aren't really osnap modes, although they work similarly when they're used in an expression. The first is Rad. When you include Rad in an expression, you get the following prompt:

```
Select circle, arc or polyline segment for RAD function:
```

You can then select an arc, a polyline arc segment, or a circle to obtain a radius for the expression.

TABLE 15.3: The geometry calculator's osnap modes

CALCULATOR OSNAP	MEANING
End	Endpoint
Ins	Insert
Int	Intersection
Mid	Midpoint
Cen	Center

TABLE 15.3:   The geometry calculator's osnap modes   *(CONTINUED)*

CALCULATOR OSNAP	MEANING
Nea	Nearest
Nod	Node
Qua	Quadrant
Per	Perpendicular
Tan	Tangent
Rad	Radius of object
Cur	Cursor pick

The other item, Cur, prompts you for a point. Instead of looking for specific geometry on an object, it just locates a point. You could have used Cur in the previous exercise in place of the End and Cen modes to create a more general-purpose midpoint locator, as in the following formula:

```
(cur + cur)/2
```

Pasting to the Command Line

Now that you have the coordinate for the midpoint, try the next exercise to apply that coordinate to a command. In this example, you'll use the coordinate found in step 3 as the starting point for a line:

1. Click the Line tool on the Draw panel.

2. In QuickCalc, right-click the (end + end)/2 listing in the display area, and then select Paste To Command Line (Figure 15.29).

3. The coordinate value from the display area is pasted into the command line at the Line command's `Specify first point:` prompt. Press ↵ to accept the input from QuickCalc. You see a rubber-banding line beginning at a point midway between the two endpoints of the lines you selected in the previous exercise (Figure 15.30).

4. Click another point to place the line in the drawing, and then press ↵ to exit the Line command.

Finding Fractional Distances between Two Points

Another common need of AutoCAD users is the ability to find a location that is a fractional distance along a line. For example, users frequently need to find a point that is one-third the distance from the endpoint of a line. Here's how that can be accomplished using QuickCalc:

1. Enter **plt (end, end, 0.333)**↵ in the QuickCalc input box. QuickCalc closes temporarily to allow you to select points.

FIGURE 15.29
Select Paste To
Command Line.

FIGURE 15.30
Starting a line
between two
endpoints

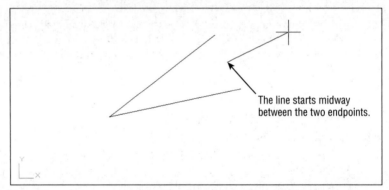

The line starts midway
between the two endpoints.

2. Click the endpoints of the line shown in Figure 15.31, starting with the lower-left endpoint. QuickCalc returns with the coordinates of a point that is 33.33 percent of the length of the line from the first endpoint you selected.

FIGURE 15.31
Select these points
to find a point that
is one-third the
distance from an
endpoint.

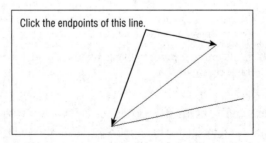

Click the endpoints of this line.

3. Click the Line tool.

4. Click in the QuickCalc display area on the last entry, right-click and choose Paste To Command Line.

5. Press ↵ and you see a line start at a point that is one-third the distance from the endpoint (Figure 15.32).

FIGURE 15.32
A line starting at a point that is one-third the distance from the endpoint.

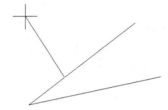

6. Press Esc to exit the Line command. You don't need to draw the line because this exercise is intended to show you only how the formula in step 1 works.

In step 1, you used a formula that contained the plt function. This function finds a point that is a particular percentage between two points. You specify the two points first, using the now-familiar end function, and then you specify the percentage between the two endpoints as a decimal value. The (end, end, 0.333) indicates the two endpoints you selected in step 2 and the percentage as a decimal value of 0.333.

In the formulas you've seen so far, you've used the end function to select endpoints. If you prefer to select your own osnaps during the point-selection process, you can use the cur function. Cur lets you use any osnap you want when selecting points. In the first example, you could use (cur + cur)/2 instead of (end + end)/2.

The plt function is just one of several special functions you can use with QuickCalc. Table 15.4 lists other functions you can use to find points in your drawing and gather other data. In the table, 2D points are represented as pt1, pt2, and so on. 3D points, or points describing a plane are indicated by ptp1, ptp3, and so on. The center of an arc or a circle is indicated with *apex* for a 2D location and *apex1* and *apex2* for a 3D axis.

TABLE 15.4: Functions in QuickCalc and the format for their use

FUNCTION AND FORMAT	DESCRIPTION
Getvar(*system variable name*)	Gets the value of a system variable
Vec(*pt1,pt2*)	Returns the vector described by the distance between the two points
Vec1(*pt1,pt2*)	Returns the vector described by 1 unit length
Abs(*vector*)	Returns the absolute value of the length of a vector
Cur(no arguments required)	Gets a point
@(no arguments required)	Returns the last point

TABLE 15.4: Functions in QuickCalc and the format for their use *(CONTINUED)*

FUNCTION AND FORMAT	DESCRIPTION
w2u(*point*) and u2w(*point*)	Converts world coordinates to current user coordinates (w2u) or user coordinates to world
Pld(*pt1,pt2,distance*)	Returns the point on a line at a specified distance
Plt(*pt1,pt2,percent*)	Returns the point on a line at a percentage (decimal) of the line length
Rot(*pt1,apex,angle*) or Rot(*pt1,apex1,apex2,angle*)	Returns the rotation angle of a point pt1 about an apex
Ill(*pt1,pt2,pt3,pt4*)	Returns the intersection between two lines
Ilp(*pt1,pt2,ptp1,ptp2,ptp3*)	Returns the intersection between a line and a plane; five points required
Dist(*pt1,pt2*)	Returns the distance between two points
Dpl(*point,pt1,pt2*)	Returns the shortest distance between a point and a line
Dpp(*point,ptp1,ptp2,ptp3*)	Returns the shortest distance between a point and a plane
Rad (no arguments required)	Returns a radius
Ang(*vector* or *pt1,pt2* or *apex,pt1,pt2* or *apex1,pt1,pt2,apex2*)	Returns an angle; can use up to four parameters when working in 3D
Nor(*vector* or *pt1,pt2* or *ptp1,ptp2,ptp3*)	Finds the normal of a vector or plane

Using QuickCalc While in the Middle of a Command

In all the previous examples, you've used QuickCalc as a stand-alone calculator. You've also seen how you can insert a calculation into the command line while a command is in progress. A third way to work with QuickCalc is to open it while in the middle of a command.

In a previous exercise, you used the (end + end)/2 formula to find the midpoint between two points, and then you inserted the resulting value into the Line command. Suppose you start the Line command before you open QuickCalc. Try the following to see how you can use QuickCalc once a command has been initiated:

1. Close QuickCalc.

2. Start the Line command.

3. Right-click and select QuickCalc from the shortcut menu.

4. In the QuickCalc input box, enter **(end + end)/2** but don't press ↵. Instead, click the Apply button at the bottom of the QuickCalc window.

5. Select the endpoints of two lines. A line starts at the midpoint between the two points.

6. Click another point to draw the line, and then press ↵ to end the Line command.

In this exercise, you saw that an Apply option appears at the bottom of the QuickCalc window along with Close and Help buttons. These buttons aren't present when you open QuickCalc with no command active. The Apply button executes the formula and then immediately returns the resulting value to the command. Using QuickCalc this way eliminates a few steps.

FINDING A POINT RELATIVE TO ANOTHER POINT

Now, suppose you want to start a line at a relative distance from another line. The following steps describe how to use the calculator to start a line from a point that is 2.5″ in the X axis and 5.0″ in the Y axis from the endpoint of another line:

1. Make sure QuickCalc is closed, start the Line command, and select a point.

2. Right-click, select the QuickCalc tool, and enter **end + [2.5,5.0]** in the input box.

3. Click the Apply button at the bottom of the QuickCalc window.

4. Click the endpoint of the line you just drew. The new line connects to a point that is at a distance of 2.5 in the X axis and 5.0 in the Y axis from the endpoint you selected.

In this example, you used the Endpoint osnap mode to indicate a point of reference. This is added to Cartesian coordinates in square brackets, describing the distance and direction from the reference point. You could enter any coordinate value within the square brackets. You also could enter a polar coordinate in place of the Cartesian coordinate, as in the following: **end + [5.59<63]**.

You can replace the *end* in the expression with the at sign (@) to continue from the last point you selected. Also, it's not necessary to include every coordinate in the square brackets. For example, to indicate a displacement in only one axis, you can leave out a value for the other two coordinates while leaving in the commas, as in the following examples:

```
[4,5] = [4,5,0]
[,1] = [0,1,0]
[,,2] = [0,0,2]
```

COMBINING COORDINATES AND EXPRESSIONS

In the previous two examples, you saw that you can use an expression or enter coordinates, but what if you want to combine an expression within a coordinate? For example, in the beginning of this section, you added feet and inches and then transferred the result to the command line. In that example, you had to switch back and forth between QuickCalc and the command line to create the response for the Command prompt. If you prefer, you can create an expression that supplies the entire command input. Here are the steps to do this:

1. Close QuickCalc, and then start the Line command.

2. Right-click and select QuickCalc from the shortcut menu.

3. Enter the following in the input box:

`End + [(4´+36+5´6)<45]`

4. Click Apply.

5. In the drawing area, click the endpoint of a line. AutoCAD draws a line that begins at 12´-6˝ and at a 45° angle to the endpoint you select.

In this exercise, you used the expression (4´+36+5´6) right in the middle of a coordinate value. As described earlier, the coordinate is within square brackets. By using this method, you can more easily calculate measurements and apply them to commands. The trick is to become familiar with the syntax QuickCalc requires so you can write these expressions without errors.

Storing Expressions and Values

The ability to create expressions to manipulate coordinates can be useful, but you may find it difficult to remember an expression once you've created it. Fortunately, QuickCalc offers the Variables group, which allows you to store frequently used expressions and values.

At the bottom of the QuickCalc window is the Variables group, which has its set of tools in its title bar (see Figure 15.33).

FIGURE 15.33
The Variables group

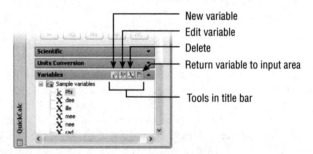

New variable
Edit variable
Delete
Return variable to input area

Tools in title bar

These tools let you add items to the list, edit items, or delete items from the list. A fourth option lets you send a variable to the main calculator input box. You can also right-click in the Variables group list box and select the same options from a shortcut menu. In addition, the shortcut menu lets you create a new category and rename an existing one.

The Variables group also contains a list of currently stored variables. Some sample variables are shown in the list. If you select a variable, you see a description of that variable's function at the bottom of the group. You may need to click the bottom edge of the QuickCalc window and drag downward to see the description.

To use an existing variable, select it from the list and click the Return Variable To Input Area button; it looks like a calculator. To add a variable to the list, click the New Variable button, which opens the Variable Definition dialog box (Figure 15.34).

This dialog box lets you enter the properties of the variable and choose the type. In the Variable Properties group, you enter the name of the variable in the Name text box. In the Group With drop-down list, you select a category under which your formula will appear in the Variables list. You can also create a new category. The Value Or Expression input box is where you put your formula; it can also be a single value, such as a number or a coordinate. At the bottom is a space to enter a description for the variable. This description will appear in the Variables group's detail box at the bottom of QuickCalc.

FIGURE 15.34
The Variable Definition dialog box

At the top, you see two options: Constant and Function. If you choose Function, your variable will behave as it normally does when you enter it in the input box. If you choose Constant and your variable is a formula, your variable will be executed when you close the Variable Definition dialog box. The resulting value will become the value for the variable.

To edit an existing variable, highlight it in the Variables group list, and then click the Edit Variable button to open the Variable Definition dialog box.

Guidelines for Working with QuickCalc

You may notice some patterns in the way expressions are formatted for the calculator. Here are some guidelines to remember:

◆ Coordinates are enclosed in square brackets.

◆ Nested or grouped expressions are enclosed in parentheses.

◆ Operators are placed between values, as in simple math equations.

◆ Object snaps can be used in place of coordinate values.

Table 15.5 lists all the operators and functions available in QuickCalc. You may want to experiment with these functions on your own. You can enter many of these operators using the keys on the number pad or in the scientific group.

TABLE 15.5   The QuickCalc functions

OPERATOR/FUNCTION	WHAT IT DOES	EXAMPLE
+ or −	Adds or subtracts numbers or vectors	$2 - 1 = 1$ [a,b,c] + [x,y,z] = [a+x, b+y, c+z]
* or /	Multiplies or divides numbers or vectors	$2 * 4.2 = 8.4$ a*[x,y,z] = [a*x, a*y, a*z]
^	Returns the exponent of a number	$3^2 = 9$
sin	Returns the sine of an angle	sin (45) = 0.707107
cos	Returns the cosine of an angle	cos (30) = 0.866025
tang	Returns the tangent of an angle	tang (30) = 0.57735
asin	Returns the arcsine of a real number	asin (0.707107) = 45.0
acos	Returns the arccosine of a real number	acos (0.866025) = 30.0
atan	Returns the arctangent of a real number	atan (0.57735) = 30.0
ln	Returns the natural log	ln (2) = 0.693147
log	Returns the base-10 log	log (2) = 0.30103
exp	Returns the natural exponent	exp (2) = 7.38906
exp10	Returns the base-10 exponent	exp10 (2) = 100
sqr	Squares a number	sqr (9) = 81.0
abs	Returns the absolute value	abs (−3.4) = 3.4
rnd	Rounds to the nearest integer	round (3.6) = 4
trunc	Drops the decimal portion of a real number	trunc (3.6) = 3
r2d	Converts radians to degrees	r2d (1.5708) = 90.0002
d2r	Converts degrees to radians	d2r (90) = 1.5708
pi	Provides the constant pi	3.14159

QuickCalc is capable of much more than the typical uses you've seen here. A description of its full capabilities extends beyond the scope of this text. However, the processes described in this section will be helpful as you use AutoCAD. If you want to know more about QuickCalc, consult the AutoCAD Help User Documentation (enter **QuickCalc** in the InfoCenter input box).

SINGLING OUT PROXIMATE OBJECTS

You'll sometimes need to select an object that overlaps or is very close to another object. Often in this situation you end up selecting the wrong object. To select the exact object you want, you can use the Selection Cycling tool and the Draworder command.

Selection Cycling lets you cycle through objects that overlap until you select the one you want. To use this feature, hover over the overlapping objects so one of them is highlighted; then hold down the Shift key and press the spacebar. With each press of the spacebar, a different overlapping object will be highlighted. When the object you want to select is highlighted, click it.

Another way to gain access to an overlapped object is to use the Draworder command. You can select the overlapping object and then choose Send To Back from the Draworder flyout on the Home tab's Modify panel.

The Bottom Line

Use external references (Xrefs).   You've seen how you can use Xrefs to quickly build variations of a floor plan that contain repetitive elements. This isn't necessarily the only way to use Xrefs, but the basic idea of how to use Xrefs is presented in the early exercises.

> **Master It**   Try putting together another floor plan that contains nothing but the Unit2 plan.

Manage layers.   Once you start to edit complex drawings, you'll find that you'll want to save the On/Off or Freeze/Thaw layer states so you can more easily access parts of a drawing. The Layer States Manager offers the ability to save as many layer conditions as you may need in the course of a project.

> **Master It**   What part of the Layer States Manager dialog box lets you control the layer properties that are affected by a saved layer state?

Use advanced tools: Filter and Quick Select.   The Filter and Quick Select tools are great for isolating objects in a crowded drawing. You can select objects by their color or layer assignment. You can select all instances of a specific block.

> **Master It**   True or false: The Quick Select tool lets you select a set of objects to limit your selections.

Use the QuickCalc calculator.   The QuickCalc calculator offers many standard calculator tools plus a few that you may not see in other calculators.

> **Master It**   Name a few of the more unusual features offered by the QuickCalc calculator.

Chapter 16

Laying Out Your Printer Output

Your set of drawings for the studio apartment building would probably include a larger-scale, more detailed drawing of the typical unit plan. You already have the beginnings of this drawing in the form of the Unit file.

As you've seen, the notes and dimensions you entered into the Unit file can be turned off or frozen in the Plan file so they don't interfere with the graphics of the drawing. The Unit file can be part of another drawing file that contains more detailed information about the typical unit plan at a larger scale. To this new drawing, you can add notes, symbols, and dimensions. Whenever the Unit file is altered, you update its occurrence in the large-scale drawing of the typical unit as well as in the Plan file. The units are thus quickly updated, and good coordination is ensured among all the drawings for your project.

Now, suppose you want to combine drawings that have different scales in the same drawing file—for example, the overall plan of one floor plus an enlarged view of one typical unit. You can do so using the layout views and a feature called Paper Space.

In this chapter, you'll learn how to do the following:

◆ Understand Model Space and Paper Space

◆ Work with Paper Space viewports

◆ Create odd-shaped viewports

◆ Understand line weights, linetypes, and dimensions in Paper Space

Understanding Model Space and Paper Space

So far, you've looked at ways to help you get around in your drawing while using a single view. This single-view representation of your AutoCAD drawing is called *Model Space* display mode. You can also set up multiple views of your drawing by using what are called *floating viewports*. You create floating viewports in layout views in what is called *Paper Space* mode.

To get a clear understanding of the Model Space and Paper Space modes, imagine that your drawing is actually a full-size replica or model of the object you're drawing. Your computer screen is your window into a "room" where this model is being constructed, and the keyboard and mouse are your means of access to this room. You can control your window's position in relation to the object through the use of Pan, Zoom, View, and other display-related commands. You can also construct or modify the model by using drawing and editing commands. Think of this room as your Model Space.

You've been working on your drawings by looking through a single window into Model Space. Now, suppose you have the ability to step back and add windows with different views looking into your Model Space. The effect is as if you have several video cameras in your Model Space room, each connected to a different monitor. You can view all your windows at once on your computer screen or enlarge a single window to fill the entire screen. Further, you can control the shape of your windows and easily switch from one window to another. This is what Paper Space is like.

Paper Space lets you create and display multiple views of Model Space. Each view window, called a *viewport*, acts like an individual virtual screen. One viewport can have an overall view of your drawing, while another can be a close-up. You can also control layer visibility individually for each viewport and display different versions of the same area of your drawing. You can move, copy, and stretch viewports and even overlap them. You can set up another type of viewport, called the *tiled viewport*, in Model Space. Chapter 22 discusses this type of viewport.

One of the more powerful features of Paper Space is the ability to plot several views of the same drawing on one sheet of paper. You can also include graphic objects such as borders and notes that appear only in Paper Space. In this function, Paper Space acts much like a page-layout program such as QuarkXPress or Adobe InDesign. You can paste up different views of your drawing and then add borders, title blocks, general notes, and other types of graphic and textual data. Figure 16.1 shows the Plan drawing set up in Paper Space mode to display several views.

FIGURE 16.1
Different views of
the same drawing
in Paper Space

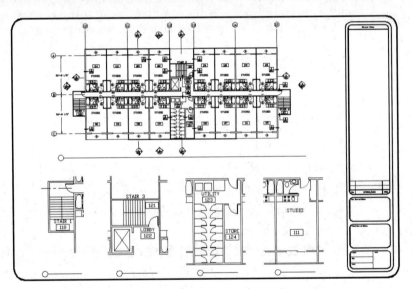

Switching from Model Space to Paper Space

You can get to Paper Space by clicking on any of the Layout tabs below the drawing area. You can also use the Quick View Layouts tool in the status bar.

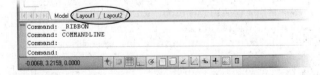

> ## DON'T SEE THE LAYOUT TABS?
>
> If your version of AutoCAD does not show the Layout and Model tabs, you can turn them on by doing the following: Right-click on the Layout1 tool in the status bar and select Display Layout And Model Tabs. To turn the tabs off, right-click on any tab and select Hide Layout And Model Tabs.

If you don't see the Model, Layout1, or Quick View Layouts tool, right-click in a blank area of the status bar and click the name of the missing tool from the shortcut menu.

Let's start with the basics of switching between Model and Paper Space:

1. Open the Xref-1 file you saved from the last chapter, and ensure that your display shows the entire drawing. You can also use 16-xref1.dwg or 16-xref1-metric.dwg.

2. Click the Layout1 tab in the lower-left corner of the drawing area. You see your drawing appear in a kind of page preview view (Figure 16.2).

FIGURE 16.2
Your drawing in a page preview view

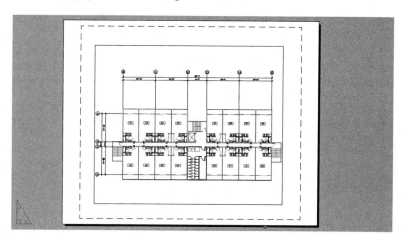

3. Click the Model tab in the lower-left corner of the drawing area to return to Model Space.

This brief exercise shows you how quickly you can shift between Model Space and Paper Space by using the Model and Layout1 tabs. The Quick View Layouts tool lets you do the same thing but offers a little more help. Try the following to see how the Quick View Layouts tool works:

1. Click the Quick View Layouts tool in the status bar. You see two preview panels appear along with a toolbar (Figure 16.3).

2. Click in the preview panel on the right that is labeled Layout1. Notice that the drawing area changes to show the Layout1 Paper Space.

3. Click in the drawing area to confirm your selection of the layout view.

4. Click the Quick View Layouts tool again, but this time click the preview panel to the left labeled Model.

5. Click in the drawing area to go back to the Model Space view.

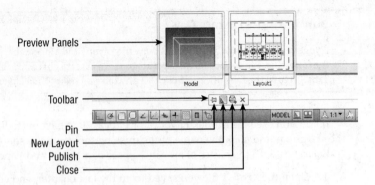

FIGURE 16.3
The Quick View
layouts

If you prefer, you can use keyboard commands to switch between Model and Paper Space. Enter **Tm↵1↵** to go to Model Space. Enter **Tm↵0↵** to go to Paper Space.

Setting the Size of a Paper Space Layout

I mentioned that Paper Space is like a page layout program, and you saw how a Paper Space layout looks like a print preview. You can set up your layout for a specific set of printer settings, including the paper size and printer.

Let's continue our look at Paper Space by seeing how a Paper Space layout can be set up for your printer:

1. Click the Layout1 tab.

2. Right-click the Layout1 tab or the Quick View Layout tool in the status bar, and choose Page Setup Manager to open the Page Setup Manager dialog box. Notice that the name of the current layout is shown in the list of current page setups (Figure 16.4).

3. Click the Modify button to open the Page Setup dialog box.

4. Select the Letter paper-size option from the Paper Size drop-down list. Metric users should select A4 (210 mm × 297 mm). The paper size you select here determines the shape and margin of the Paper Space layout area.

5. Select a printer from the Printer/Plotter name drop-down list.

6. Click OK to close the Page Setup dialog box, and then click Close to close the Page Setup Manager dialog box.

AutoCAD bases the Paper Space layout on the paper size and printer you specify in steps 4 and 5. The area shown in Paper Space reflects the area of the paper size you selected in step 4, and the paper margin shown by a dashed line is determined by the printer. If for some reason you need to change the paper size, repeat steps 2 through 5. You can also store the way you've set up your Paper Space layout using the Page Setup Manager you saw in step 2. See Chapter 8 for more on this feature.

Creating New Paper Space Viewports

As you saw in Chapter 8, the different look of the layout view tells you that you're in Paper Space. You also learned that a viewport is automatically created when you first open a layout view. The layout viewport displays an overall view of your drawing to no particular scale.

FIGURE 16.4
The Page
Setup Manager
dialog box

In this section, you'll work with multiple viewports in Paper Space instead of just the default single viewport you get when you open the layout view.

This first exercise shows you how to create three new viewports at once:

1. Click the viewport border to select it. The viewport border is the solid rectangle surrounding your drawing, just inside the dashed rectangle.

2. Click the Erase tool in the Home tab's Modify panel to erase the viewport. Your drawing disappears. Don't panic; remember that the viewport is like a window to Model Space. The objects in Model Space are still there.

3. Click the New tool in the View tab's Viewports panel to open the Viewports dialog box. You can also type **Vports.↵**. This dialog box contains a set of predefined viewport layouts (Figure 16.5). You'll learn more about the Viewports dialog box and its options in Chapter 22.

FIGURE 16.5
The Viewports
dialog box

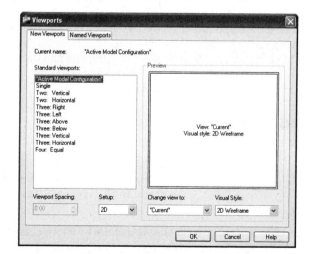

4. Click the Three: Above option in the Standard Viewports list box. The box to the right shows a sample view of the Three: Above layout you selected.

5. Click OK. The Specify first corner or [Fit] <Fit>: prompt appears.

6. Press ↵ to accept the default Fit option. The Fit option fits the viewport layout to the maximum area allowed in your Paper Space view. Three rectangles appear in the formation, as shown in Figure 16.6. Each of these is a viewport to your Model Space. The viewport at the top fills the whole width of the drawing area; the bottom half of the screen is divided into two viewports.

FIGURE 16.6
The newly created viewports

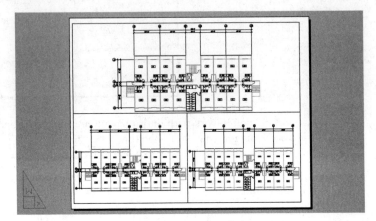

When you create new viewports, AutoCAD automatically fills them with the extents of your Model Space drawing. You can specify an exact scale for each viewport, as you'll see later.

Notice that the dashed line representing your paper margin has disappeared. That's because the viewports are pushed to the margin limits, thereby covering the dashed line.

You could have kept the original viewport that appeared when you first opened the Layout1 view and then added two new viewports. Completely replacing the single viewport is a bit simpler because the Viewports dialog box fits the viewports in the allowed space for you.

After you've set up a Paper Space layout, it remains part of the drawing. You may prefer to use Model Space for doing most of your drawing and then use Paper Space layouts for setting up views for printing. Changes that you make to your drawing in Model Space will automatically appear in your Paper Space layout viewports.

Reaching inside Viewports

Now, suppose you need access to the objects in the viewports in order to adjust their display and edit your drawing. Try these steps:

1. Double-click inside a viewport. This gives you control over Model Space even though you're in Paper Space. (You can also enter **MS**↵ as a keyboard shortcut to enter Model Space mode.)

   The first thing you notice is that the UCS icon changes back to its L-shaped arrow form. It also appears in each viewport, as if you had three AutoCAD windows instead of just one.

2. Move your cursor over each viewport. In one of the viewports, the cursor appears as the AutoCAD crosshair cursor, whereas in the other viewports it appears as an arrow pointer. The viewport that shows the AutoCAD cursor is the active one; you can pan, zoom, and edit objects in the active viewport.

3. Click in the lower-left viewport to activate it.

4. Click Window from the Zoom flyout on the View tab's Navigate panel, and place a window selection around the elevator area.

5. Click the lower-right viewport, and choose Zoom Window from the Zoom flyout on the navigation bar to enlarge your view of a typical unit. You can also use the Pan and Zoom Realtime tools. If you don't see the UCS icon, it has been turned off. Type **UCSicon.↵On.↵** to turn it on. See Chapter 22 for more on the UCS icon.

You can move from viewport to viewport even while you're in the middle of most commands. For example, you can issue the Line command, pick the start point in one viewport, go to a different viewport to pick the next point, and so on. To activate a different viewport, you click inside the viewport (see Figure 16.7).

SWITCHING BETWEEN VIEWPORTS

I've found that users will have a need to overlap viewports from time to time. When they do this, they are often at a loss over how to switch between the overlapping viewports, especially when one is completely surrounded by another or they are exactly the same size and in the same position. In this situation, you can move between viewports by pressing Ctrl+R repeatedly until you get to the viewport you want.

FIGURE 16.7
The three viewports, each with a different view of the plan

Model Space UCS icon

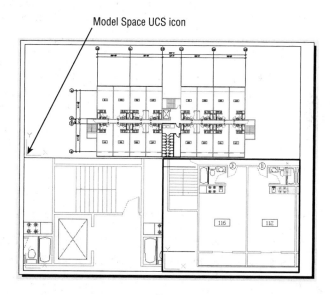

You've seen how you can zoom into a viewport view, but what happens when you use the Zoom command while in Paper Space? Try the following exercise to find out:

1. Double-click an area outside the viewports to get out of Floating Model Space.

2. Click Realtime from the Zoom flyout in the View tab's Navigate panel and then zoom in to the Paper Space view. The entire view enlarges, including the views in the viewports.

3. Right-click, and select Exit. Click All from the Zoom flyout or enter Z↵A↵ to return to the overall view of Paper Space.

This brief exercise showed that you can use the Zoom tool in Paper Space just as you would in Model Space. All the display-related commands are available, including the Pan Realtime command.

Working with Paper Space Viewports

Paper Space is intended as a page-layout or composition tool. You can manipulate viewports' sizes, scale their views independently of one another, and even set layering and linetype scales independently.

Let's try manipulating the shape and location of viewports by using the Home tab's Modify panel options:

1. Make sure Object Snap is turned off in the status bar.

2. Make sure you're in a layout view. Then click the bottom edge of the lower-left viewport to expose its grips (see the top image in Figure 16.8).

3. Click the upper-right grip, and drag it to the location shown in the top image in Figure 16.8.

4. Press the Esc key, and erase the lower-right viewport by selecting it and clicking Erase in the Home tab's Modify panel or by pressing the Delete key.

5. Move the lower-left viewport so it's centered in the bottom half of the window, as shown in the bottom image in Figure 16.8.

In this exercise, you clicked the viewport edge to select it for editing. If, while in Paper Space, you attempt to click the image in the viewport, you won't select anything. Later, you'll see that you can use the osnap modes to snap to parts of the drawing image in a viewport.

Because viewports are recognized as AutoCAD objects, you can manipulate them by using all the editing commands, just as you would manipulate any other object. In the previous exercise, you moved, stretched, and erased viewports.

Next, you'll see how layers affect viewports:

1. Create a new layer called Vport.

2. In the Properties palette, change the viewport borders to the Vport layer.

3. Turn off the Vport layer. The viewport borders disappear.

4. After reviewing the results of step 3, turn the Vport layer back on.

FIGURE 16.8
Stretching,
erasing, and
moving viewports

Stretch the viewport
grip to this location.

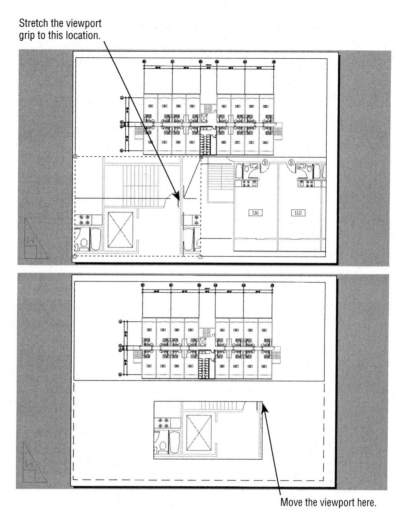

Move the viewport here.

You can assign a layer, a color, a linetype, and even a line weight to a viewport's border. If you put the viewport's border on a layer that has been turned off or frozen, that border becomes invisible, just like any other object on such a layer. Or you can put the viewport border on a nonprinting layer so the border will be visible while you're editing. Making the borders invisible or putting them on a nonprinting layer is helpful when you want to compose a final sheet for printing. Even when turned off, the active viewport has a heavy border around it when you switch to Floating Model Space, and all the viewports still display their views.

Scaling Views in Paper Space

Paper Space has its own unit of measure. You've already seen how you're required to specify a paper size when opening a layout view to a Paper Space view. When you first enter Paper Space, regardless of the area your drawing occupies in Model Space, you're given limits that are set by the paper size you specify in the Page Setup dialog box. If you keep in mind that Paper Space is like a paste-up area that is dependent on the printer you configured for AutoCAD, this difference of scale becomes easier to comprehend. Just as you might paste up photographs and maps representing several square miles onto an 11″-×-17″ board, so can you use Paper Space to paste up views of scale drawings representing city blocks or houses on an 8½″-×- 11″ sheet of paper. But in AutoCAD, you have the freedom to change the scale and size of the objects you're pasting up.

While in Paper Space, you can edit objects in a Model Space viewport, but to do so, you must use Floating Model Space. You can then click a viewport and edit in that viewport. In this mode, objects that were created in Paper Space can't be edited. Double-click outside a viewport to go back to the Paper Space environment.

If you want to be able to print your drawing at a specific scale, you must indicate a scale for each viewport. Viewport scales are set in a way similar to the annotation scale in the Model tab. Let's see how to put together a sheet in Paper Space and still maintain accuracy of scale:

1. Make sure you're in Paper Space. You can tell by the shape and location of the UCS icon. If it looks like a triangle in the lower-left corner of the layout view, then you are in Paper Space.

2. Click the topmost viewport's border to select it.

3. In the lower-right corner of the AutoCAD window, click the Viewport Scale drop-down list, and select 1/32″ = 1′-0″. Metric users should click Custom and add a custom scale of 1:400. Then select the 1:400 scale from the Viewport Scale drop-down list. Notice how the view in the top viewport changes.

4. Press the Esc key twice to clear the selection in the viewport.

5. Click the lower viewport border.

6. Click the VP Scale drop-down list again, and select 3/16″ = 1′-0″ from the list. Metric users should select 1:100. The view in the viewport changes to reflect the new scale (see Figure 16.9).

It's easy to adjust the width, height, and location of the viewports so they display only the parts of the unit you want to see. While in Paper Space, use the Stretch, Move, Scale, or Rotate command to edit any viewport border, or use the viewport's grips to edit its size and shape. The view in the viewport remains at the same scale and location while the viewport changes in size. You can move and stretch viewports with no effect on the size and location of the objects in the view. When you rotate the viewport, the view inside the viewport will also rotate.

FIGURE 16.9
Paper Space view-
port views scaled
to 1/32″ = 1′-0″ and
3/16″ = 1′-0″ (1:400
and 1:100 for
metric users)

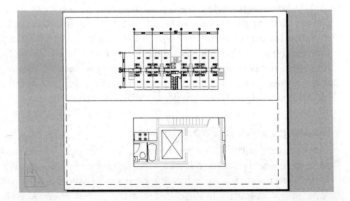

If you need to overlay one drawing on top of another, you can overlap viewports. Use the osnap overrides to select geometry in each viewport, even while in Paper Space. This enables you to align one viewport on top of another at exact locations.

You can also add a title block in Paper Space at a 1:1 scale to frame your viewports and then plot this drawing from Paper Space at a scale of 1:1. Your plot appears just as it does in Paper Space, at the appropriate scale. Paper Space displays a dashed line to show you where the non-printable areas occur near the edge of the paper.

While you're working in Paper Space, pay close attention to whether you're in Paper Space or Floating Model Space mode. It's easy to pan or zoom in a Floating Model Space viewport acciden-tally when you intend to pan or zoom your Paper Space view. This can cause you to lose your view-port scaling or alignment with other parts of the drawing. It's a good idea to save viewport views in case you happen to change a viewport view accidentally. You can do this by choosing Named Views from the View tab's Views panel, and then in the View Manager dialog box, click the New button (see "Saving Views" in Chapter 7 for a description of the View Manager).

Another way to prevent your viewport view from being accidentally altered is to turn on View Lock. To do this, while in Paper Space, click a viewport border. Right-click to open the shortcut menu, and then choose Display Locked ➤ Yes. After the view is locked, you can't pan or zoom within a viewport. This setting is also available in the viewport's Properties palette and in the status bar to the left of the Viewport Scale tool when a viewport is selected.

Setting Layers in Individual Viewports

Another unique feature of Paper Space viewports is their ability to freeze layers independently. You can, for example, display the usual plan information in the overall view of a floor but show only the walls in the enlarged view of one unit.

You control viewport layer visibility through the Layer Properties Manager dialog box. You may have noticed that there are three sun icons for each layer listing.

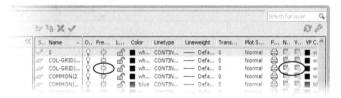

To see all of the layer options, you may need to widen the Layer Properties Manager dialog box to view all the columns. To do so, click and drag the right border of the dialog box to the right.

You're already familiar with the sun icon farthest to the left. This is the Freeze/Thaw icon that controls the freezing and thawing of layers globally. Several columns to the right of that icon are two sun icons with transparent rectangles. These icons control the freezing and thawing of layers in individual viewports. Of this pair, the one on the left controls existing viewports and the one on the right controls settings for newly created viewports.

This exercise shows you firsthand how the sun icon for existing viewports works:

1. Double-click inside a viewport to go to Floating Model Space.

2. Activate the lower viewport.

3. Open the Layer Properties Manager.

4. Locate the COMMON|WALL layer, and then click its name to help you isolate it.

5. Click the column labeled VP Freeze for the selected layer (Figure 16.10). You may need to widen the Layer Properties Manager dialog box to do this; the column title may show only V until you widen the column. The VP Freeze column is the seventh column from the right side of the dialog box. Click the icon, which looks like a transparent rectangle under a sun. The sun changes to a snowflake, telling you that the layer is now frozen for the current viewport.

FIGURE 16.10
Select the VP Freeze option for the COMMON|WALL layer.

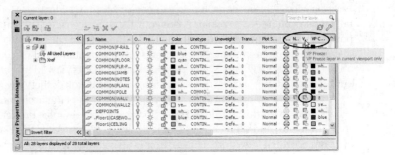

The Wall layer of the Common Xref becomes invisible in the current viewport. However, the walls remain visible in the other viewport (see Figure 16.11).

FIGURE 16.11
The draw-ing with the COMMON|WALL layer turned off in the active viewport

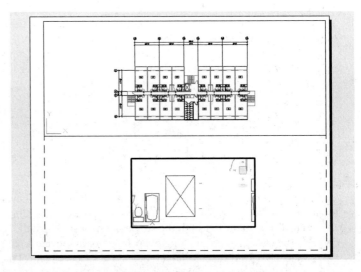

6. After reviewing the effects of the VP Freeze setting, go back to the Layer Properties Manager dialog box and thaw the COMMON|WALL layer by clicking its VP Freeze icon again so it turns back into a sun.

7. Take a moment to study the drawing, and then save the Xref-1 file.

You may have noticed another, identical sun icon next to the one you used in the previous exercise. This icon controls layer visibility in any new viewports you create next, rather than in existing viewports.

If you prefer, you can use the Layer drop-down list in the Layers panel to freeze layers in individual viewports. Double-click in the viewport you want to modify, select the layer from the list, and then click the same sun icon with the small rectangle beneath it.

In addition to setting the visibility of layers, you can set the other layer properties—such as color, linetype, and line weight—for each viewport. First, make sure you're in Floating Model Space for the viewport whose layers you want to set up, and then open the Layer Properties Manager. You can set the properties for the current viewport using the VP Freeze, VP Color, VP Linetype, VP Lineweight, VP Transparency, and VP Plot settings for each layer (Figure 16.12).

FIGURE 16.12
The VP Freeze, VP Color, VP Linetype, VP Lineweight, VP Transparency and VP Plot columns in the Layer Properties Manager palette

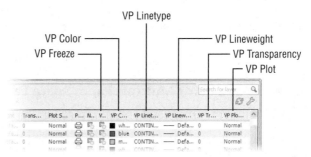

This section concludes the apartment building tutorial. Although you haven't drawn the complete building, you've learned all the commands and techniques you need to do so. Figure 16.13 shows you a completed plan of the first floor. To complete your floor plans and get some practice using AutoCAD, you may want to add the symbols shown in this figure to your Plan file.

FIGURE 16.13
A completed floor of the apartment building

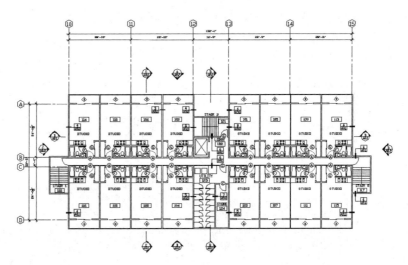

Because buildings like this one often have the same plans for several floors, the plan for the second floor can also represent the third floor. Combined with the first floor, this gives you a three-level apartment building. This project might also have a ground-level garage, which would be a separate file. You can use the Col-grid.dwg file in the garage file as a reference for dimensions. The other symbols can be blocks stored as files that you can retrieve in other files.

MASKING OUT PARTS OF A DRAWING

Chapter 7 described a method for using AutoCAD's Draworder feature to hide floor patterns under equipment or furniture in a floor layout. You can use a similar method to hide irregularly shaped areas in a Paper Space viewport. This is desirable for plotting site plans, civil plans, or floor plans that require portions of the drawing to be masked out. You may also want to mask part of a plan that is overlapped by another to expose dimension or text data.

Creating and Using Multiple Paper Space Layouts

You're not limited to just one or two Paper Space layouts. You can have as many as you want, with each layout set up for a different sheet size containing different views of your drawing. You can use this feature to set up multiple drawing sheets based on a single AutoCAD drawing file. For example, suppose a client requires full sets of plans in both 1⁄8″ = 1′ scale and 1⁄16″ = 1″ scale. You can set up two Layout tabs, each with a different sheet size and viewport scale.

You can also set up different Paper Space layouts for the different types of drawings. A single drawing can contain the data for mechanical layout, equipment and furnishing, floor plans, and reflected ceiling plans. Although a project can require a file for each floor plan, a single file with multiple layout views can serve the same purpose in AutoCAD 2011.

To create new layout views, do the following:

1. Click the Quick View Layouts tool in the status bar.

2. Click the New Layout tool from the toolbar that appears just below the Quick View Layouts preview panels (Figure 16.14). A new preview panel appears, labeled Layout2.

FIGURE 16.14
The New
Layout tool

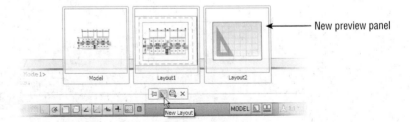

New preview panel

3. Click the new Layout2 preview panel and then click in the drawing area. The new layout appears with a single default viewport.

You've just seen how you can create a new layout using the Quick View Layouts tool. You can also right-click the Quick View Layouts tool to open a shortcut menu that offers a New Layout option (Figure 16.15). This option also creates a new layout, though you won't get any feedback that a new layout has been created.

FIGURE 16.15
The New Layout
right-click option

The Quick View Layouts shortcut menu also includes the From Template option. The From Template option lets you create a Paper Space layout based on an AutoCAD template file. AutoCAD provides several standard layouts that include title blocks based on common sheet sizes.

The Quick View Layouts tool also includes an option that enables you to move or copy tabs and to select all the tabs. Finally, if you want to delete or rename a layout, click the Quick View Layouts tool and then right-click in the preview panel for the layout you want to edit. You can then select Delete or Rename from the shortcut menu that appears. If you select Delete, you'll see a warning message telling you that AutoCAD will permanently delete the layout you have chosen to delete. Click OK to confirm your deletion.

Creating Odd-Shaped Viewports

In many situations, a rectangular viewport doesn't provide a view appropriate for what you want to accomplish. For example, you might want to isolate part of a floor plan that is L shaped or circular. You can create viewports for virtually any shape you need. You can grip edit a typical rectangular viewport to change its shape into a trapezoid or other irregular four-sided polygon. You can also use the Clip tool to create more complex viewport shapes, as the following exercise demonstrates.

Follow these steps to set up a layout view that shows only the lower apartment units and the elevators and stairs:

1. Click the Clip tool in the View tab's Viewports panel. You can also type **Vpclip↵**.

2. At the Select viewport to clip: prompt, click the viewport border.

3. At the Select clipping object or [Polygonal] <Polygonal>: prompt, press ↵.

4. Turn off Running Osnaps, and draw the outline shown in the top portion of Figure 16.16.

5. After you finish selecting points, press ↵. The viewport changes to conform to the new shape.

6. Click the viewport border to expose its grips.

7. Click a grip, and move it to a new location. The viewport view conforms to the new shape.

FIGURE 16.16
Drawing a
polygon outline
for a viewport

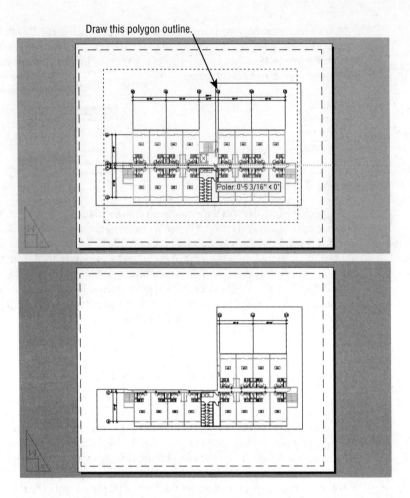

Draw this polygon outline.

The new viewport shape gives you more flexibility in isolating portions of a drawing. This can be especially useful if you have a large project that is divided into smaller sheets. You can set up several layout views, each displaying a different portion of the plan.

What if you want a viewport that isn't rectilinear? This exercise shows you how to create a circular viewport:

1. Erase the viewport you just modified.

2. Draw a circle that roughly fills the Paper Space area.

3. In the View tab's Viewports panel, choose Create From Object from the Create flyout. You can also type **-VPORTS↵O↵**.

4. Click the circle. The plan appears inside the circle, as shown in Figure 16.17.

FIGURE 16.17
A circular
viewpoint

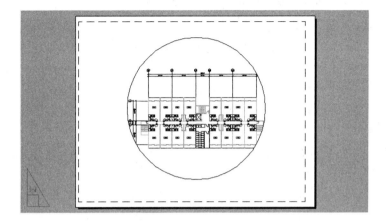

To simplify this exercise, you were asked to draw a circle as the basis for a new viewport. However, you aren't limited to circles; you can use a closed polyline or spline of any shape. (See Chapter 19 for a detailed discussion of polylines and splines.) You can also use the Polygon tool on the Home tab's Draw panel to create a shape and then turn it into a viewport.

If you look carefully at the series of prompts for the previous exercise, you'll notice that the Create From Object tool invokes a command-line version of the Vports command (-vports). This command-line version offers some options that the standard Vports command doesn't. The following options are available with the command-line version of Vports:

```
-vports
[ON/OFF/Fit/Shadeplot/Lock/Object/Polygonal/Restore/Layer/2/3/4] <Fit>:
```

You used two of the options—Polygonal and Object—in the two previous exercises. If you're an experienced AutoCAD user, you may notice that this command-line version of Vports is the same as the Mview command of earlier releases. You can still use the Mview command if you prefer.

Understanding Line Weights, Linetypes, and Dimensions in Paper Space

The behavior of several AutoCAD features depends on whether you're in Paper Space or Model Space. The most visible of these features are line weights, linetypes, and dimensions. In the following sections, you'll take a closer look at these features and see how to use them in conjunction with Paper Space.

Controlling and Viewing Line Weights in Paper Space

Line weights can greatly improve the readability of technical drawings. You can make important features stand out with bold line weights while keeping the noise of smaller details from overpowering a drawing. In architectural floor plans, walls are traditionally drawn with heavier lines so the outline of a plan can be easily read. Other features exist in a drawing for reference only, so they're drawn in a lighter weight than normal.

In Chapter 9, you saw how to control line weights in AutoCAD by using plot style tables. You can apply either a named plot style table or a color plot style table to a drawing. If you already have a library of AutoCAD drawings, you may want to use color plot style tables for backward compatibility. AutoCAD also enables you to assign line weights directly to layers or objects and to view the results of your line weight settings in Paper Space.

Here's an exercise that demonstrates how to set line weights directly:

1. Open the Layer Properties Manager.

2. Right-click the Layer list, and choose Select All.

3. Click the Lineweight column to open the Lineweight dialog box (Figure 16.18).

4. Select 0.13 mm from the list, and click OK. You've just assigned the 0.13 mm line weight to all layers.

5. Right-click the Layer list again, and choose Clear All.

6. Click the Common|WALL layer, and Ctrl+click the Floor1|WALL layer to select these two layers.

7. Click the Lineweight column for either of the two selected layers to open the Lineweight dialog box again.

8. Select 0.40 mm from the dialog box, and click OK. You've just assigned the 0.40 mm line weight to the two selected layers.

9. Click Close in the Layer Properties Manager.

FIGURE 16.18
The Lineweight
dialog box

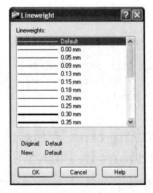

Although you set the line weights for the layers in the drawing, you need to make a few more changes to the file settings before they're visible in Paper Space:

1. Type **LW↵** to open the Lineweight Settings dialog box (Figure 16.19).

2. Select the Display Lineweight check box, and then click OK.

3. Make sure you're in Paper Space, and then zoom in to the drawing.

4. Type **Rea↵**. The lines representing the walls are now thicker, as shown in Figure 16.20.

FIGURE 16.19
The Lineweight
Settings dialog box

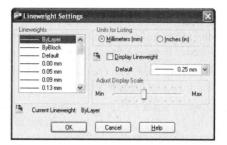

5. After reviewing the results of this exercise, close the file.

FIGURE 16.20
An enlarged
view of the plan
with line weights
displayed

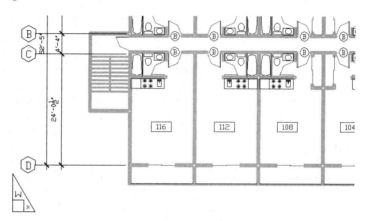

With the ability to display line weights in Paper Space, you have better control over your output. Instead of using a trial-and-error method to print your drawing and then checking your printout to see whether the line weights are correct, in AutoCAD 2011 you can see the line weights on your screen.

This exercise showed you how to set line weights so they appear in Paper Space as they will when you plot your drawing. If you normally plot your drawings in black, you can go one step further and set all your layer colors to black to see how your plots will look. But you'll need to save your layer settings so you can restore the layers to their original colors. Another way to view your drawing in black and white without affecting your layer settings is to use the color plot style table described in Chapter 9.

LINEWEIGHT DISPLAY SHORTCUT

When line weight display is turned on, you see line weights in Model Space as well as in Paper Space. Line weights can be distracting while you work on your drawing in Model Space, but you can quickly turn them off by entering **Lwdisplay.⏎Off.⏎** at the Command prompt. Entering **Lwdisplay.⏎On.⏎** turns the line weight display back on.

The Lineweight Settings Dialog Box

The Lineweight Settings dialog box includes a few other settings that you didn't use in the previous exercise. Here is a description of those settings for your reference:

Units For Listing   You can choose between millimeters and inches for the unit of measure for line weights. The default is millimeters.

Adjust Display Scale   This setting lets you control just how thick line weights appear in the drawing. Move the slider to the right for thicker lines and to the left for thinner lines. This setting affects only the display on your monitor. As you move the slider, you can see a sample of the results in the Lineweights list box.

Default drop-down list   This drop-down list lets you select the default line weight you see in the Layer Properties Manager dialog box. It's set to 0.01″ (0.25 mm) by default. You may want to lower the default line weight to 0.005″ (0.13 mm) as a matter of course because most printers these days can print lines that size and even smaller.

Linetype Scales and Paper Space

As you've seen in previous exercises, you must carefully control drawing scales when creating viewports. Fortunately, this is easily done through the Properties palette. Although Paper Space offers the flexibility of combining images of different scale in one display, it also adds to the complexity of your task in controlling that display. Your drawing's linetype scale in particular needs careful attention.

In Chapter 5, you saw that you had to set the linetype scale to the scale factor of the drawing in order to make the linetype visible. If you intend to plot that same drawing from Paper Space, you have to set the linetype scale back to 1 to get the linetypes to appear correctly. This is because AutoCAD faithfully scales linetypes to the current unit system. Remember that Paper Space units are different from Model Space units. When you scale a Model Space image down to fit in the smaller Paper Space area, the linetypes remain scaled to the increased linetype scale settings. In the Chapter 5 example, linetypes are scaled up by a factor of 24. This causes noncontinuous lines to appear as continuous in Paper Space because you see only a small portion of a greatly enlarged noncontinuous linetype.

The Psltscale system variable enables you to determine how linetype scales are applied to Paper Space views. You can set Psltscale so the linetypes appear the same regardless of whether you view them directly in Model Space or through a viewport in Paper Space. By default, this system variable is set to 1. This causes AutoCAD to scale all the linetypes uniformly across all the viewports in Paper Space. You can set Psltscale to 0 to force the viewports to display linetypes exactly as they appear in Model Space. Psltscale is not a global setting. You must set Psltscale for each layout view that you create, otherwise the default value of 1 will be used.

You can also control this setting in the Linetype Manager dialog box (type **LT↵**). When you click the Show Details button, you see a setting called Use Paper Space Units For Scaling in the lower-left corner. When this check box is selected, Psltscale is set to 1. When it isn't selected, Psltscale is set to 0.

Dimensioning in Paper Space Layouts

At times, you may find it more convenient to add dimensions to your drawing in Paper Space rather than directly on your objects in Model Space. This can be useful if you have a small project with several viewports in a layout and you want to keep dimensions aligned between viewports. You have two basic options when dimensioning Model Space objects in Paper Space.

The Associative Dimensioning feature can make quick work of dimensions for layout views containing drawings of differing scales. Alternatively, if you prefer not to use Associative Dimensioning, you can adjust settings for individual dimension styles.

USING ASSOCIATIVE DIMENSIONING IN PAPER SPACE

Perhaps the simplest way to dimension in Paper Space is to use the Associative Dimensioning feature. With this feature turned on, you can dimension Model Space objects while in a Paper Space layout. Furthermore, Paper Space dimensions of Model Space objects are automatically updated if the Model Space object is edited.

Try the following exercise to see how Associative Dimensioning works:

1. Click New from the Quick Access toolbar, and use the `acad.dwt` template to create a new blank file.

2. Draw a rectangle 12 units wide by 4 units high. If you're using a metric file, make the rectangle 480 units wide by 160 units high.

3. Click the Quick View Layouts tool and select Layout1.

4. Click the Quick View Layouts tool again, and then right-click the Layout1 panel and select Page Setup Manager.

5. In the Page Setup Manager dialog box, click Modify. Then, in the Page Setup dialog box, choose the Letter paper size in the Printer/Plotter section. Metric users can pick ISO A4 (297.00 × 210.00 mm).

6. Click OK, and then close the Page Setup Manager dialog box.

7. Right-click in the drawing area, and choose Options from the shortcut menu.

8. In the Options dialog box, click the User Preferences tab and make sure the Make New Dimensions Associative option in the Associative Dimensioning group is turned on. Click OK to exit the dialog box.

Next, you'll use the rectangle you drew in Model Space to test the Associative Dimensioning feature in the Layout1 view:

1. Click Linear from the Annotate tab's Dimensions panel. Using the Endpoint osnap, dimension the bottom edge of the rectangle you drew in Model Space. The dimension shows 12.0000 (480 for metric drawings), the actual size of the rectangle.

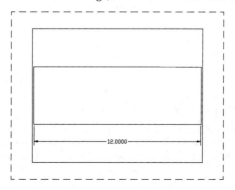

2. Double-click inside the viewport, and use the Zoom Realtime tool to zoom out a bit so the rectangle appears smaller in the viewport. Do not use the scroll wheel of your mouse to do this (see "Updating Associative Dimensions" later in this chapter). After you exit the Zoom Realtime tool, the dimension follows the new view of the rectangle.

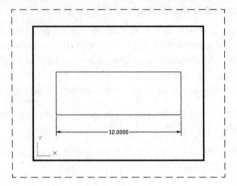

3. While you're in Floating Model Space, click the rectangle, and then click the grip in the lower-left corner and drag it upward and to the right.

4. Click again to place the corner of the rectangle in a new location. The dimension changes to conform to the new shape.

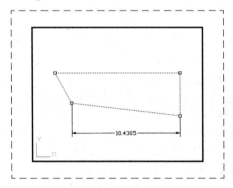

5. Close the rectangle file without saving it. You won't need it in the future.

You've just seen how you can dimension an object in Model Space while in Paper Space. You can also dimension Model Space Xrefs in Paper Space in much the same way. The only difference is that changes to the Xref file don't automatically update dimensions made in Paper Space. You need to employ the Dimregen command to refresh Paper Space dimensions of Xref objects.

Updating Associative Dimensions

If you use a wheel mouse to pan and zoom in a Floating Model Space viewport, you may need to use the Dimregen command to refresh an associative dimension. To do so, type **Dimregen**↵ at the Command prompt. You can also use Dimregen to refresh dimensions from drawings that have been edited in earlier versions of AutoCAD or, as mentioned already, to refresh dimensions of objects contained in external references.

PAPER SPACE DIMENSIONING WITHOUT ASSOCIATIVE DIMENSIONING

In some situations, you may not want to use Associative Dimensioning although you still want to dimension Model Space objects in Paper Space. For example, you might be in an office that has different versions of AutoCAD, or you might be sharing your drawings with other offices that aren't using AutoCAD 2011 and the use of Associative Dimensioning creates confusion.

To dimension Model Space objects in Paper Space without Associative Dimensioning, you need to have AutoCAD adjust the dimension text to the scale of the viewport from which you're dimensioning. You can have AutoCAD scale dimension values in Paper Space so they correspond to a viewport zoom-scale factor. The following steps show you how this setting is made:

1. Open the Dimension Style Manager dialog box by clicking the Dimension Style tool in the Home tab's expanded Annotation panel.

2. Select the dimension style you want to edit, and click Modify.

3. Click the Primary Units tab.

4. In the Measurement Scale group, enter the scale factor of the viewport you intend to dimension in the Scale Factor input box. For example, if the viewport is scaled to a ½″ = 1′-0″ scale, enter **24**.

5. Click the Apply To Layout Dimensions Only check box.

6. Click OK, and then click Close in the Dimension Style Manager dialog box. You're ready to dimension in Paper Space.

Remember that you can snap to objects in a floating viewport so you can add dimensions as you normally would in Model Space. If you're dimensioning objects in viewports of different scales, you need to set up multiple dimension styles, one for each viewport scale.

EXPORTING LAYOUT VIEWS TO MODEL SPACE

You may encounter a situation where you want to export a layout view as a Model Space drawing. You can do this by following these steps:

1. Click the Quick View Layouts tool in the status bar to open the layout preview panels.

2. Right-click in the preview panel of the layout you want to export.

3. Select Export Layout To Model from the shortcut menu. The Export Layout To Model Space Drawing dialog box appears. This is a typical Save dialog box that allows you to select the location and name for your exported layout.

4. Select a folder location, enter a name for your exported layout, and then click Save.

Your layout view will be saved as a separate drawing file with the layout appearing in the Model Space of that file. It will also be in the same scale as the original layout view instead of in full scale. Other drawing elements such as layers, blocks, linetypes, and styles will also be exported, though they may be scaled down to fit the drawing.

Other Uses for Paper Space

The exercises in the preceding sections should give you a sense of how you work in Paper Space and layout views. I've given examples that reflect common uses of Paper Space. Remember that Paper Space is like a page-layout portion of AutoCAD—separate yet connected to Model Space through viewports.

You needn't limit your applications to floor plans. You can take advantage of Paper Space with interior and exterior elevations, 3D models, and detail sheets. When used in conjunction with AutoCAD's raster-import capabilities, Paper Space can be a powerful tool for creating large-format presentations.

The Bottom Line

Understand Model Space and Paper Space.   AutoCAD offers two viewing modes for viewing and printing your drawings. Model Space is where you do most of your work; it's the view you see when you create a new file. Layouts, also called Paper Space, are views that let you arrange the layout of your drawing, similar to how you would in a page-layout program.

Master It   What are the two ways of moving from Model Space to Paper Space?

Work with Paper Space viewports.   While in Paper Space, you can create views into your drawing using viewports. You can have several viewports, each showing a different part of your drawing.

Master It   Name some of the ways you can enlarge a view in a viewport.

Create odd-shaped viewports.   Most of the time, you'll probably use rectangular viewports, but you have the option to create a viewport of any shape.

Master It   Describe the process for creating a circular viewport.

Understand line weights, linetypes, and dimensions in Paper Space.   You can get an accurate view of how your drawing will look on paper by making a few adjustments to AutoCAD. Your layout view will reflect how your drawing will look when plotted.

Master It   Name the two dialog boxes you must use to display line weights in a layout view.

Chapter 17

Making "Smart" Drawings with Parametric Tools

Don't let the term *parametric drawing* scare you. *Parametric* is a word from mathematics, and in the context of AutoCAD drawings, it means that you can define relationships between different objects in a drawing. For example, you can set up a pair of individual lines to stay parallel or set up two concentric circles to maintain an exact distance between each other no matter how they may be edited.

Parametric drawing is also called *constraint-based modeling*, and you'll see the word *constraint* used in the AutoCAD Ribbon to describe sets of tools. The term *constraint* is a bit more descriptive of the tools you'll use to create parametric drawings because when you use them, you are applying a constraint upon the objects in your drawing.

In this chapter, you'll see firsthand how the parametric drawing tools work and how you might apply them to your needs.

In this chapter, you'll learn how to do the following:

- ◆ Use parametric drawing tools
- ◆ Connect objects with geometric constraints
- ◆ Control sizes with dimensional constraints
- ◆ Use formulas to control dimensions
- ◆ Put constraints to use

Why Use Parametric Drawing Tools

If you're not familiar with parametric drawing, you may be wondering what purpose it serves. With careful application of the parametric tools, you can create a drawing that you can quickly modify with just a change of a dimension or two instead of actually editing the lines that make up the drawing. Figure 17.1 shows a drawing that was set up so that the arcs and circles increase in size to an exact proportion when the overall length dimension is increased. This can save a lot of time if you're designing several parts that are similar with only a few dimensional changes.

You can also mimic the behavior of a mechanical assembly to test your ideas. The parametric drawing tools let you create linkages between objects so that if one moves, the others maintain their connection like a link in a chain. For example, you can create 3D AutoCAD models of a crankshaft and piston assembly of a car motor (see Figure 17.2) or the parallel arms of a Luxo lamp. If you move one part of the model, the other parts move in a way consistent with a real motor or lamp.

FIGURE 17.1
The d1 dimension in the top image was edited to change the drawing to look like the one in the lower half.

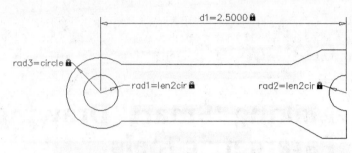

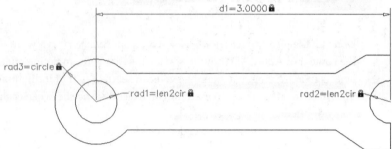

FIGURE 17.2
Move one part of the drawing and the other parts follow.

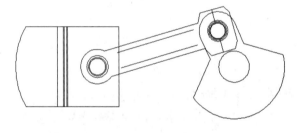

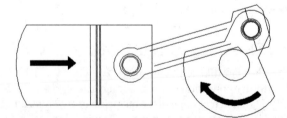

Connecting Objects with Geometric Constraints

You'll start your exploration of parametric drawing by adding geometric constraints to an existing drawing and testing the behavior of the drawing with the constraints in place. Geometric constraints let you assign constrained behaviors to objects to limit their range of motion. Limiting motion to improve editing efficiency may seem counterintuitive, but once you've seen these tools in action, you'll see their benefits.

Using Autoconstrain to Automatically Add Constraints

Start by opening a sample drawing and adding a few geometric constraints. The sample drawing is composed of two parallel lines connected by two arcs, as shown in Figure 17.3. These are just lines and arcs and are not polylines.

1. Open the `Parametric01.dwg` file from the sample files for this chapter (Figure 17.3).

FIGURE 17.3
The Parametric01.dwg file containing simple lines and arcs

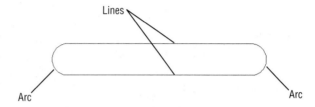

2. Select the Parametric tab, and click the AutoConstrain tool from the Geometric panel, or type **Autoconstrain**↵.

3. Select all of the objects in the drawing, and press ↵.

You've just used the Autoconstrain command to add geometric constraints to all of the objects in the drawing. You can see a set of icons that indicate the constraints that have been applied to the objects (see Figure 17.4). The Autoconstrain command makes a "best guess" at applying constraints.

FIGURE 17.4
The drawing with geometric constraints added

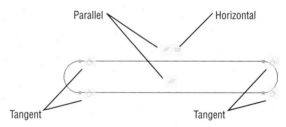

Notice that the constraint icons in the drawing match those you see in the Geometric panel. If you hover your mouse pointer over an icon, you'll see a tool tip that shows the name of the constraint.

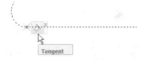

The tangent constraints that you see at the ends of the lines keep the arcs and the lines tangent to each other whenever the arcs are edited. The parallel constraint keeps the two lines parallel, and the horizontal constraint keeps the lines horizontal.

There is one constraint that doesn't show an icon, but you see a clue to its existence by the small blue squares where the arcs join the lines:

1. Place your cursor on one of the blue squares. A new icon appears below the tangent icon.

2. Hover your cursor over the icon that has just appeared. You see a tool tip that says "Coincident."

The coincident constraint makes sure that the endpoints of the lines and arcs stay connected, as you'll see in the next few exercises.

Editing a Drawing Containing Constraints

Now try editing the drawing to see firsthand how these constraints work:

1. Click the arc on the left side of the drawing (top of Figure 17.5).

2. Click the arrowhead grip to the left of the arc and move it to the left to increase the radius of the arc. The objects move in unison to maintain their geometric constraints (bottom of Figure 17.5).

FIGURE 17.5
Changing the radius of one arc causes the other parts of the drawing to follow because of their geometric constraints.

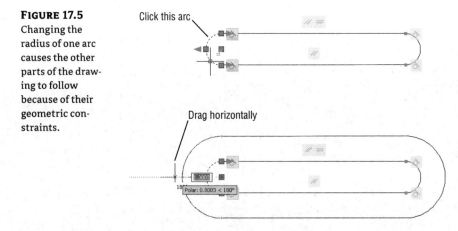

3. Click again to accept the change in the arc radius.

4. Click the Undo tool in the Quick Access toolbar to undo your change.

In this exercise, you saw how the tangent, parallel, horizontal, and coincident constraints worked to keep the objects together while you changed the size of one object. Next, you'll see what happens if you remove a constraint.

REMOVING A CONSTRAINT

The AutoConstrain tool applied quite a few geometric constraints to the drawing. Suppose you want to remove a constraint to allow for more flexibility in the drawing. In the next exercise, you'll remove the parallel constraint and then try editing the drawing to see the results:

1. Click the parallel constraint icon that is just above the lower line.

2. Right-click and select Delete. Notice that the parallel icon disappears from both the top and bottom line.

3. Click the arc at the left end of the drawing.

4. Click the arrowhead grip to the left of the arc, drag it to the left, and then click. This time, only the arc on the left side changes. The lines are no longer parallel but they remain tangent to both arcs and their endpoints remain connected (Figure 17.6).

FIGURE 17.6
Editing the arc with the parallel constraint removed

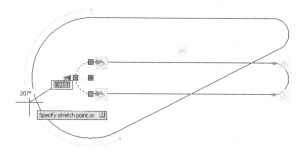

Notice that the top line remains horizontal as you edit the arc. The top line still has the horizontal constraint. Next, try removing the horizontal constraint:

1. Click the Undo tool in the Quick Access toolbar to return to the previous shape.

2. Right-click the horizontal icon above the top line and select Delete.

3. Edit the arc on the left side again as you did in the previous exercises. This time the lines both change their orientation, as shown in Figure 17.7.

FIGURE 17.7
Without the horizontal constraint, both lines change as the arc is edited.

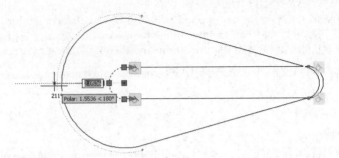

Notice that lines and arcs remain connected and tangent to each other. This is because the coincident and tangent constraints are still in effect.

ADDING A CONSTRAINT

You've seen how the AutoConstrain tool applies a set of constraints to a set of objects. You can also add constraints "manually" to "fine-tune" the way objects behave. In the next exercise, you'll add a circle to the drawing and then add a few specific constraints that you'll select from the Geometric panel:

1. Click the Undo tool in the Quick Access toolbar to change the drawing back to its original shape.

2. From the Home tab, click the Circle tool from the Draw panel.

3. Click a location roughly above and to the left of the drawing as shown in Figure 17.8. You don't need to be exact because you will use a geometric constraint to move the circle into an exact location.

4. Type **0.25**↵ for the radius of the circle.

FIGURE 17.8
Place the circle roughly in the location shown here.

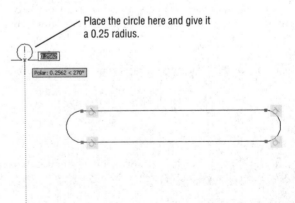

Place the circle here and give it a 0.25 radius.

5. Select the Parametric tab and click the Concentric tool in the Geometric panel.

6. Click the arc at the left side of the drawing, and then click the circle you just added. The circle moves to a location that is concentric to the arc, as shown in Figure 17.9.

FIGURE 17.9
The circle is concentric to the arc on the left side.

In this exercise, you used the geometric constraint as an editing tool to move an object into an exact location. The concentric constraint will also keep the circle inside the arc no matter where the arc moves.

THE ORDER MAKES A DIFFERENCE

When you add constraints, sometimes the order in which you add them makes an important difference. In the concentric constraint example, you selected the arc first, then the circle. Had you selected the circle first, the arcs and lines would have moved to the circle. Instead, as you saw in the exercise, the circle moved to the inside of the arc.

Using Other Geometric Constraints

You've seen firsthand how several of the geometric constraints work. For the most part, each constraint is fairly easy to understand. The tangent constraint keeps objects tangent to each other. The coincident constraint keeps the location of objects together, such as endpoints or midpoints of lines and arcs. The parallel constraint keeps objects parallel.

There are many more geometric constraints you have at your disposal. Table 17.1 gives you a concise listing of the constraints and their purposes. Note that, with the exception of fix and symmetric, all of the constraints affect pairs of objects.

TABLE 17.1: The geometric constraints

NAME	USE
Coincident	Keeps point locations of two objects together, such as the endpoints or midpoints of lines. Allowable points vary between objects and are indicated by a red circle marked with an X while points are being selected.
Collinear	Keeps lines collinear. The lines need not be connected.
Concentric	Keeps circles and arcs concentric.
Fix	Fixes a point on an object to a location in the drawing.
Parallel	Keeps lines parallel.
Perpendicular	Keeps lines or polyline segments perpendicular.

TABLE 17.1: The geometric constraints *(CONTINUED)*

NAME	USE
Horizontal	Keeps lines horizontal.
Vertical	Keeps lines vertical.
Tangent	Keeps curves, or a line and curve, tangent to each other.
Smooth	Maintains a smooth transition between splines and other objects. The first object selected must be a spline. You can think of this constraint as a tangent constraint for splines.
Symmetric	Maintains symmetry between two curves about an axis that is determined by a line. Before using this constraint, draw a line that you will use for the axis of symmetry. You can also use the fix, horizontal, or vertical constraint to fix the axis to a location or orientation.
Equal	Keeps the length of lines or polylines equal or the radius of arcs and circles equal.

The behavior of the geometric constraints might sound simple, but you may find that they can behave in unexpected ways. With the limited space of this book, I can't give exercise examples for every geometric constraint, so I encourage you to experiment with them on your own. And have some fun with them!

Using Constraints in the Drawing Process

Earlier you saw how the concentric constraint allowed you to move a circle into a concentric location to an arc. You can use other geometric constraints in a similar way. For example, you can move a line into a collinear position with another line using the collinear constraint. Or you can move a line into a tangent orientation to a pair of arcs or circles as shown in Figure 17.10. The top image shows the separate line and circles and the bottom shows the objects after applying the tangent constraint. Note that while the line is tangent to the two circles, its length and orientation does not change.

ADDING CONSTRAINTS AS YOU DRAW

In the first part of this chapter, you saw you can add constraints to an existing drawing using the Autoconstrain command. You can also set up AutoCAD to add constraints as you draw. This feature is called Infer Constraints. You can turn Infer Constraints on or off using the Infer Constraints tool in the Status bar.

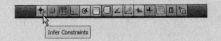

If you use Infer Constraints to draw a series of lines, at the very least it will apply the coincident constraint at the end of each line segment. If you use Osnaps and polar tracking, other constraints like Parallel and Perpendicular may be applied to objects as you draw.

FIGURE 17.10
You can connect two circles so that they are tangent to a line using the tangent constraint.

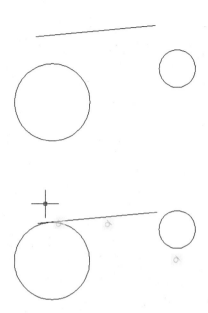

Controlling Sizes with Dimensional Constraints

Perhaps the heart of the AutoCAD parametric tools is the dimensional constraints. These constraints allow you to set and adjust the dimension of an assembly of parts, thereby giving you an easy way to adjust the size and even the shape of a set of objects.

For example, suppose you have a set of parts that you are drafting, each of which is just slightly different in one dimension or another. You can add geometric constraints and then add dimensional constraints, which will let you easily modify your part just by changing the value of a dimension. To see firsthand how this works, try the following exercises.

Adding and Editing a Dimensional Constraint

In this first dimensional constraint exercise, you'll add a horizontal dimension to the drawing you've already been working on. The drawing already has some geometric constraints that you are familiar with, so you can see how the dimensional constraints interact with the geometric constraints.

Start by adding a dimensional constraint between the two arcs:

Aligned

1. In the Parametric tab, click the Aligned tool in the Dimensional panel.

2. Shift+right-click, and select the Center osnap option from the right-click menu.

3. Place the cursor on the arc on the left side of the drawing so that the Center Osnap marker appears for the arc (Figure 17.11). Notice that the arc is highlighted as you select the center.

4. Shift+right-click, and select the Center osnap option as you did in step 2.

5. Click the arc on the right side of the drawing (Figure 17.12).

FIGURE 17.11
Use the Center
osnap to select the
center of the arc.

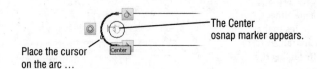

The Center
osnap marker appears.

Place the cursor
on the arc …

Center

FIGURE 17.12
Adding the dimen-
sional constraint

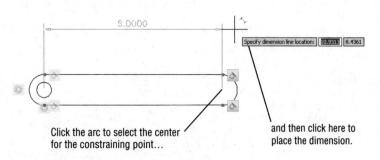

5.0000

Specify dimension line location: 10.9313 8.4361

Click the arc to select the center
for the constraining point…

and then click here to
place the dimension.

6. Click a location above the drawing as shown in Figure 17.12.

7. At the Dimension text = prompt, press ↵ to accept the current value.

The dimension constraint appears above the drawing and shows a value of d1=6.0000. The d1 is the name for that particular dimensional constraint. Each dimensional constraint is assigned a unique name, which is useful later when you want to make changes.

OSNAPS ARE FORCED OFF

In an earlier exercise, you had to select the Center osnap from the Osnap menu. When placing dimensional constraints, you'll need to use the Osnap menu to select Center osnaps. Running Osnaps are automatically turned off when you use the dimensional constraint tools. This is because the dimensional constraint tools use their own method of finding locations on objects.

Now try editing the part by changing the dimension:

1. Double-click the dimension value of the dimension constraint (Figure 17.13).

2. Type **4.5**↵. The part shortens to the dimension you entered.

FIGURE 17.13
Double-click the
dimension value.

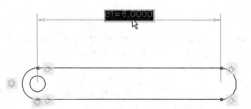

d1 = 6.0000

Next, add a dimension to the arc on the right side:

1. Click the Aligned tool from the Dimensional panel.

2. Select the top endpoint of the arc on the left side (top of Figure 17.14). Do this by first hovering over the arc near the endpoint. When you see the endpoint marker, click the mouse.

3. Select the bottom endpoint of the arc in the same way.

4. Click a point to the left of the arc to place the dimension (bottom of Figure 17.14).

5. At the Dimension text = prompt, press ↵ to accept the current value.

FIGURE 17.14
Adding a dimensional constraint to the arc

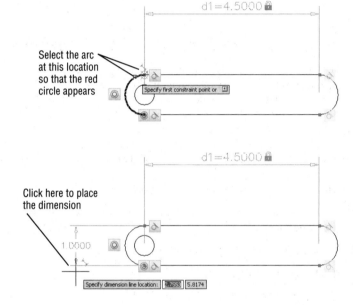

Notice that the new dimensional constraint has been given the name d2. Now try changing the size of the arc using the dimensional constraint:

1. Double-click on the dimension value of the dimensional constraint (Figure 17.15).

2. Enter 2↵. The part adjusts to the new dimension.

As you can see from this example, you can control the dimensions of your drawing by changing the dimensional constraint's value. This is a much faster way of making accurate changes to your drawing. Imagine what you would have to do to make these same changes if you didn't have the geometric and dimensional constraints available.

FIGURE 17.15
Adjusting the arc
dimension

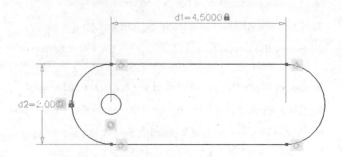

Using Formulas to Control and Link Dimensions

In the last exercise, you saw how the dimensional constraint attached to the arc affected the drawing. But in that example, the circle on the left end of the drawing remained unaffected by the change in the arc size. Now suppose that you want that circle to adjust its size in relation to the size of the arc. To do this, you can employ the Parameters Manager and include a formula that manages the size of the circle.

In the following exercise, you'll add a dimensional constraint to the circle and then apply a formula to that constraint so that the circle will always be one half the diameter of the arc, no matter how the arc is modified.

Start by adding a diameter constraint to the circle:

1. First click the Undo tool in the Quick Access toolbar to change the drawing back to its previous shape.

2. Click the Diameter tool in the Dimensional panel.

3. Click the circle to select it.

4. Click a location inside the drawing to place the constraint, as shown in Figure 17.16.

5. Press ↵ to accept the constraint value.

FIGURE 17.16
Adding a diameter
constraint to
the circle

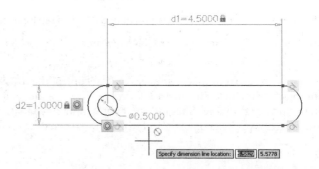

The diameter constraint you just added is given the name dia1. It controls only the diameter of the circle; you could change the value of that constraint, but it would affect only the circle.

Adding a Formula Parameter

Now let's add a formula that will "connect" the value of the circle diameter to the diameter of the arc:

Parameters Manager

1. Click the Parameters Manager tool in the Manage panel. The Parameters Manager appears (Figure 17.17). Notice that the Parameters Manager gives a list of all of the dimensional constraints that exist in the drawing.

FIGURE 17.17
The Parameters Manager

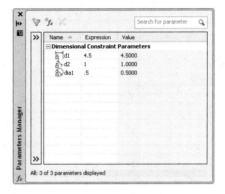

2. Click the Creates A New User Parameter tool at the top of the Parameters Manager. A new category appears in the list called User Parameters, and you see a user1 parameter appear.

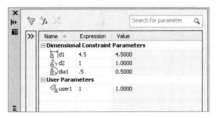

3. Double-click in the Expression column for the user1 parameter (Figure 17.18).

4. With the user1 expression value highlighted, type **d2 * 0.5**↵. You will see your entry replace the expression value (Figure 17.18). This expression is saying, "Give the user1 variable the value of 1/2 the d2 constraint." Remember that the d2 constraint is the one given to the arc.

5. Now double-click the Expression column for the dia1 parameter (Figure 17.19). This is the parameter for the circle's diameter.

6. Type **user1**↵ to change the dia1 expression from .5 to user1. This tells AutoCAD to use the expression in the user1 parameter in place of the fixed 0.5 diameter value.

FIGURE 17.18
Adding an expression to the user1 parameter

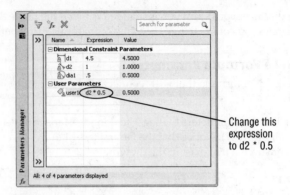

Change this expression to d2 * 0.5

FIGURE 17.19
Applying the user1 parameter to the dia1 parameter

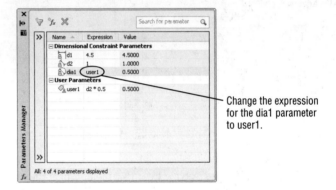

Change the expression for the dia1 parameter to user1.

You've set up your circle to follow any changes to the width of the part. Now any changes to the d2 dimensional constraint will affect the circle.

Testing the Formula

Try the following to see the parameters in action:

1. In the Parameters Manager, double-click the Expression column for the d2 parameter.

2. Change the value from 1 to 2 and observe the effect on the part (Figure 17.20).

FIGURE 17.20
Change the d2 parameter and the part changes in size, including the circle.

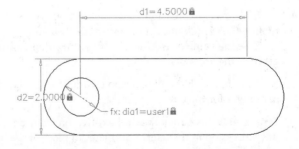

The part changes in width and the circle also enlarges to maintain its proportion to the width of the part. Here you see that you can apply a formula to a constraint so that it is "linked" to another constraint's value. In this case, you set the circle's diameter to follow the width constraint of the part.

In addition, you can adjust the constraint value from the Parameters Manager. You could also have changed the width of the part as before by double-clicking the dimensional constraint for the arc.

Using Other Formulas

In the previous exercise, you used a simple formula that multiplied a parameter, d2, by a fixed value. You used the asterisk to indicate multiplication. You could have used the minus sign in the formula if, for example, you wanted the circle to be an exact distance from the arc. Instead of d2 * 0.5, you could use d2 – 0.125, which would keep the circle 0.125 from the overall width of the part.

You can also choose from a fairly large list of formulas. If you double-click an expression in the Parameters Manager and then right-click, you can select Expressions from the shortcut menu that appears. You can then select from a list of expressions for your parameter (Figure 17.21).

FIGURE 17.21
The expressions offered from the Parameters Manager

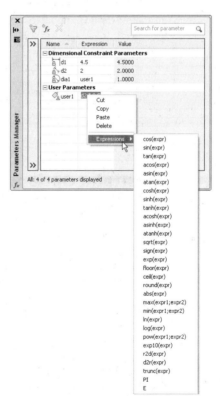

As you can see from the list, you have quite a few expressions to choose from. I won't try to describe each expression, but you should recognize most of them from your high school math training.

ORGANIZING PARAMETERS

If you find that you have a lot of parameters in the Parameters Manager, you can organize them using groups and filters. In the Parameters Manager, click the double arrowhead in the bar to the left of the parameter list.

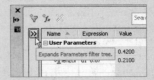

The bar expands to display the Filters list. Click the funnel shaped tool in the upper-left of the Parameters Manager to create a new group filter. Click and drag parameters from the parameters list to the group filter name to add parameters to your group filter.

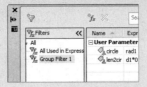

Editing the Constraint Options

AutoCAD offers a number of controls that you can apply to the constraints feature. Like most other features, these controls are accessible through a settings dialog box that is opened from the Ribbon panel title bar. If you click the Constraint Settings tool on the Geometric panel title bar, the Constraint Settings dialog box opens (see Figure 17.22).

You can see that the Constraint Settings dialog box offers three tabs across the top: Geometric, Dimensional, and AutoConstrain. The settings in the Geometric tab let you control the display of the constraint bars, which are the constraint icons you see in the drawing when you add constraints. You can also control the transparency of the constraint bars using the slider near the bottom of the dialog box.

Like the Geometric tab, the Dimensional tab (Figure 17.23) gives you control over the display of dimensional constraints. You can control the format of the text shown in the dimension and whether dynamic constraints are displayed.

Finally, the AutoConstrain tab (Figure 17.24) gives you control over the behavior of the AutoConstrain command. You can control the priority of the constraints applied to a set of objects as well as which geometric constraints are allowed.

FIGURE 17.22
The Constraint Settings dialog box showing the Geometric tab

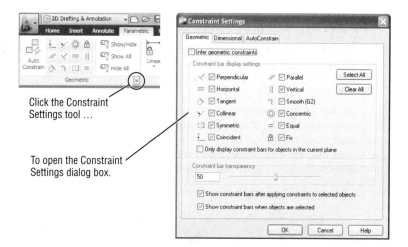

Click the Constraint Settings tool …

To open the Constraint Settings dialog box.

FIGURE 17.23
The Dimensional tab of the Constraint Settings dialog box

FIGURE 17.24
The AutoConstrain tab of the Constraint Settings dialog box

Putting Constraints to Use

So far, you've seen some very simple applications of the parametric tools available in AutoCAD. While the parametric tools may seem simple, you can build some fairly elaborate parametric models using the geometric and dimensional constraints you've learned about here.

Besides having a drawing of a part that adjusts itself to changes in dimensional constraints, you can create assemblies that will allow you to study linkages and motion. For example, you can create a model of a piston and crankshaft from a gas engine and have the piston and crankshaft move together.

In the next exercise, you'll look at a drawing that has been set up to show just how constraints can be set up to mimic the way a mechanical part behaves:

1. Open the piston.dwg file from the sample drawings.

2. Click the arc in the right side of the drawing (Figure 17.25).

3. Click the center grip of the arc, and then right-click and select Rotate.

4. Move the cursor to rotate the arc. Notice that the "piston" that is connected to the arc with a fixed-length line follows the motion of the arc just as a piston would follow the motion of a crankshaft in a gas engine.

FIGURE 17.25
The piston drawing in motion

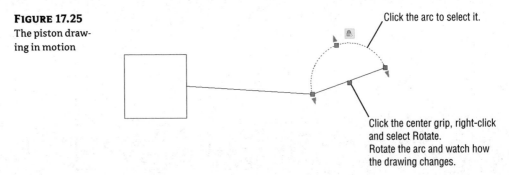

Click the arc to select it.

Click the center grip, right-click and select Rotate.
Rotate the arc and watch how the drawing changes.

As you can see from this example, you can model a mechanical behavior using constraints. The piston in this drawing is a simple rectangle that has been constrained in both its height and width. A horizontal constraint has also been applied so it is only capable of moving in a horizontal direction. The line connecting the piston to the arc is constrained in its length. The coincident constraint connects it to the piston at one end and the arc at the other end. The arc itself, representing the crankshaft, uses a diameter constraint, and a fix constraint is used at its center to keep its center fixed in one location. The net result is that when you rotate the arc, each part moves in unison.

The Bottom Line

Use parametric drawing tools.   Parametric drawing tools enable you to create an assembly of objects that are linked to each other based on geometric or dimensional properties. With the parametric drawing tools, you can create a drawing that automatically adjusts the size of all its components when you change a single dimension.

Master It   Name two examples given in the beginning of the chapter of a mechanical assembly that can be shown using parametric drawing tools.

Connect objects with geometric constraints.   You can link objects together so that they maintain a particular orientation to each other.

Master It   Name at least six of the geometric constraints available in AutoCAD.

Control sizes with dimensional constraints.   Dimensional constraints, in conjunction with geometric constraints, let you apply dimensions to an assembly of objects to control the size of the assembly.

Master It   Name at least four dimensional constraints.

Use formulas to control dimensions.   Dimensional constraints allow you to link dimensions of objects so that if one dimension changes, another dimension follows.

Master It   What example was used to show how formulas can be used with dimensional constraints?

Put constraints to use.   Constraints can be used in a variety of ways to simulate the behavior of real objects.

Master It   Name at least three geometric or dimensional constraints used in the `piston.dwg` sample file to help simulate the motion of a piston and crankshaft.

Chapter 18

Using Dynamic Blocks

Blocks are a great way to create and store ready-made symbols. They can be a real time-saver, especially when you have assemblies that you use often. Earlier in this book, you learned how to create a basic, no-frills block. Once you understand the basics of block creation, you can begin to work with *dynamic blocks*.

Dynamic blocks have properties that you can modify using grips. For example, you can create a dynamic block of a door and then easily grip edit its size and orientation. Or you can use a single block to represent several versions of a similar object. You can have a single block of a bed that can be modified to show a double, queen-, or king-sized shape.

In this chapter, you'll explore the use of dynamic blocks through a series of tutorials. Each tutorial will show you a different way to use dynamic blocks. This will help you become familiar with the methods involved in creating dynamic blocks. You'll start by looking at the Block Editor, which in itself makes editing blocks much easier. Then you'll be introduced to the tools used to create dynamic blocks.

In this chapter, you'll learn to do the following:

◆ Work with the Block Editor

◆ Create a dynamic block

◆ Add scale and stretch actions to a parameter

◆ Add more than one parameter for multiple grip functions

◆ Create multiple shapes in one block

◆ Rotate objects in unison

◆ Fill in a space automatically with objects

Exploring the Block Editor

Before you start to add dynamic block features to blocks, you'll want to get familiar with the Block Editor. The Block Editor offers an easy way to make changes to existing blocks, and as you'll see a bit later, it's also the tool you'll use to give your blocks some additional capabilities.

As an introduction to the Block Editor, you'll make changes to the now-familiar unit plan from earlier tutorials. Start by editing the Kitchen block in the unit:

1. Open the Unit.dwg file you've saved from earlier exercises and freeze the Notes layer. You can also use the 18-unit.dwg file.

2. Double-click the kitchenette in the plan to open the Edit Block Definition dialog box (Figure 18.1). Notice that all the blocks in the drawing are listed in the dialog box and that the Kitchen block is highlighted. You also see a preview of the block in the preview panel.

FIGURE 18.1
The Edit Block Definition dialog box

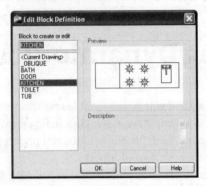

3. With the KITCHEN block name selected, click OK.

4. You see an enlarged view of the kitchenette in the drawing area with a light gray background (see Figure 18.2).

The gray background tells you that you're in the Block Editor. You'll also see the Block Editor tab along the top of the drawing area and the Block Authoring palettes, as shown in Figure 18.2.

FIGURE 18.2
The Block Editor and its components

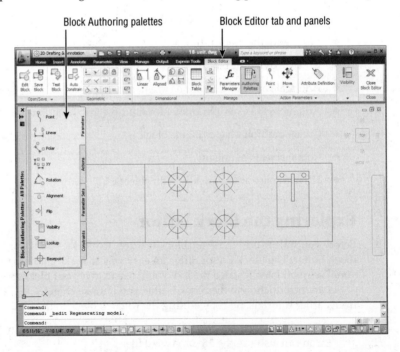

Block Authoring palettes

Block Editor tab and panels

Take a moment to look over the panels and tools on the Block Editor tab. This tab offers several housekeeping tools that let you open, save, and exit the Block Editor. You can point to each tool in the tab's panels to see its description. Figure 18.3 shows the Block Editor tab and tools.

Both the Block Editor tab and the Block Authoring palettes offer tools for adding dynamic block features that you'll explore later in this chapter. You may notice that the Block Editor tab contains the geometric and dimensional constraint panels that you learned about in Chapter 17. Let's continue our look at the basic features of the Block Editor.

Editing a Block and Creating New Blocks

The Block Editor lets you edit a block using all the standard AutoCAD editing tools. In the following exercise, you'll modify the kitchen sink and save your changes to the drawing:

1. Delete the rectangle that represents the sink in the Kitchen block.

2. Click Close Block Editor on the Block Editor tab's Close panel (see the right end of Figure 18.3).

3. A message appears asking if you want to save your changes to the Kitchen block. Click Save The Changes To KITCHEN. Your view returns to the standard AutoCAD drawing area, and you can see the changes you made to the kitchen, as shown in Figure 18.4.

FIGURE 18.4
The unit plan with
the edited Kitchen
block

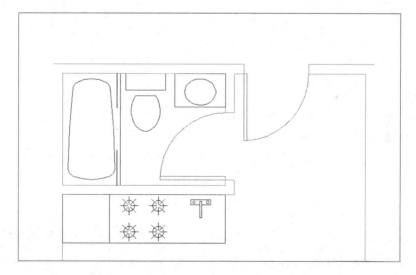

As you can see, editing blocks with the Block Editor is simple and straightforward. In this example, you deleted part of the block, but you can perform any type of drawing or editing to modify the block. The Block Editor tab also offers other block-saving options in its panels. You can save the block as you work by clicking the Save Block Definition button. If you need to create a variation on the block you're currently editing, you can click the Save Block As tool on the Block Editor's expanded Open/Save panel to create a new block or overwrite an existing one with the drawing that is currently in the Block Editor.

If you want to edit a different block after editing the current one, you can click the Save Block tool on the Block Editor's Open/Save panel to save your current block and then click the Edit Block tool.

This tool opens the Edit Block Definition dialog box that you saw earlier. You can then select another block to edit or create a new block by entering a name for your block in the Block To Create Or Edit input box.

Creating a Dynamic Block

Now that you've seen how the Block Editor works, you can begin to explore the creation of dynamic blocks. As an introduction, you'll create a rectangle that you'll use to replace the sink in the kitchen. You'll add a dynamic block feature that will allow you to adjust the width of the sink using grips. In addition, you'll add a control that limits the size to one-unit increments.

Start by creating a block from scratch using the Block Editor:

1. Click the Edit Block tool in the Home tab's Block panel.

2. In the Edit Block Definition dialog box, enter **Sink** in the Block To Create Or Edit input box, and then click OK.

3. Use the Rectangle tool on the Home tab's Draw panel to draw a rectangle that is 12 units in the X axis and 15 units in the Y axis.

4. Zoom in to the rectangle so your view looks similar to Figure 18.5.

You could save this block now and you'd have a simple, nondynamic block. Next, you'll add a couple of features called *parameters* and *actions*. As their names imply, parameters define the parameters, or limits, of what the dynamic block will do, and actions describe the particular action taken when the grips of the dynamic block are edited. For example, in the next section, you'll add a Linear parameter that tells AutoCAD that you want to restrain the grip editing to a linear direction. You'll also add a Stretch action that tells AutoCAD that you want the grip edit to behave like a Stretch command that pulls a set of vertices in one direction or another.

FIGURE 18.5
The rectangle for
the Sink block

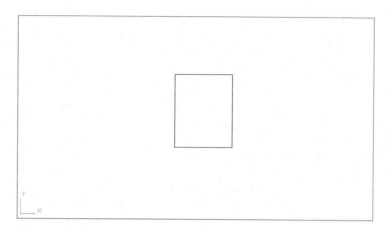

Adding a Parameter

The first parameter you'll add establishes the base point for the block. This will let you determine the point used when inserting the block in your drawing:

1. In the Block Authoring palettes, select the Parameters tab.

2. Click the Basepoint tool, Shift+right-click, select the Endpoint osnap, and then click the lower-left corner of the rectangle. This is how you determine the base point or insertion point of a block while using the Block Editor.

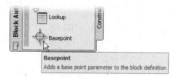

Next, you'll add a parameter that will determine the type of editing you want to add to the block. In this case, you want to be able to grip edit the width of the block. For that you'll use the Linear Parameter tool.

1. Click the Linear tool on the Parameters tab of the Block Authoring palettes, or expand the Parameter tool (Point) on the Block Editor tab's Action Parameters panel and click Linear.

2. At the prompt

    ```
    Specify start point or [Name/Label/Chain/Description/Base/Palette/Value set]:
    ```

    Shift+right-click and select the Midpoint osnap; then select the left side of the rectangle.

3. Shift+right-click again, select Midpoint from the Osnap menu, and select the right side of the rectangle.

4. At the Specify label location: prompt, the parameter name appears with the parameter label at the cursor. Click below the rectangle to place the label as shown in Figure 18.6.

FIGURE 18.6
Placing the Linear parameter

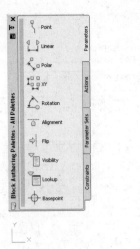

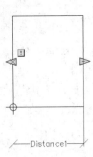

The parameter you just added lets you modify the block in a linear fashion. In this case, it will allow you to change the width of the rectangle. As you'll see, the locations of the parameter's arrows later become the grip locations for the dynamic block.

But just adding the parameter doesn't make the block dynamic. You need to include an action before a parameter can be used. You may have noticed the warning symbol in the parameter you just added. It tells you that you need to take some further steps to make the parameter useful.

Adding an Action

Next, you'll add a Stretch action that will enable you to use the Linear parameter you just added. The Stretch action will let you stretch the block horizontally using grips. As you add the action, notice that it's similar to the Stretch command. The only difference is that you don't stretch the object; you only specify the vertices to stretch and the object you want to stretch.

Follow these steps:

1. Turn off osnaps and then click the Actions tab in the Block Authoring palettes and select Stretch.

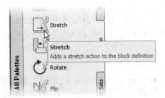

2. At the `Select parameter:` prompt, click the parameter you just created.

3. At the `Specify parameter point to associate with action or enter [sTart point/Second point] <Second>:` prompt, point to the left-pointing arrow. You see

a circle with an X through it showing the location of a parameter point plus an Osnap marker on one of the corners.

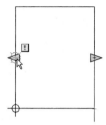

4. Click the circle with the arrow.

5. At the `Specify first corner of stretch frame or [CPolygon]:` prompt, place a selection window around the entire left side of the rectangle. This selects the portion of the rectangle that is to be stretched when you grip edit the block.

6. At the `Specify objects to stretch Select Object:` prompt, select the rectangle and the base point you added earlier, and then press ↵ to complete your selection.

You've just added an action to the Linear parameter you added earlier. You'll see an action icon appear below and to the right of the Distance1 linear parameter. The icon looks like the Stretch tool in the Actions tab to help you identify the action. If you hover over the icon, the parts affected by the action are highlighted.

Notice that the warning symbol is still showing. You need to add another action to the right side of the parameter because the parameter expects that you'll want to be able to grip edit both sides:

1. Repeat the previous set of steps, but instead of clicking the left circle with the arrow of the Linear parameter as you did in step 4 of the preceding exercise, click the right arrow.

2. Place a window selection around the right side of the rectangle (as you did around the left side in step 5 in the preceding exercise).

3. At the `Specify objects to stretch:` prompt, select the rectangle again.

A second action icon appears next to the first one to the lower right of the Distance1 linear parameter. This time the warning symbol disappears, telling you that you've completed the steps you need for the parameter. You're ready to save the block and try it out:

1. Click Close Block Editor on the Block Editor tab's Close panel.

2. At the message asking if you want to save changes to the Sink block, click Save The Changes To Sink.

Next, insert the sink to see how it works:

1. Click the Insert tool on the Home tab's Block panel.

2. In the Insert dialog box, enter **Sink** in the Name input box and then click OK. The sink appears at the cursor.

3. Place the block at the location shown in Figure 18.7.

FIGURE 18.7
The Sink block
in place

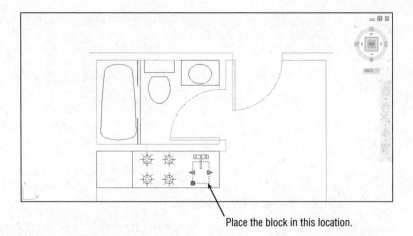

Place the block in this location.

4. Make sure the Dynamic Input feature is turned on by checking the Dynamic Input tool on the status bar, and then click the newly inserted sink. You see two arrows at the vertical midpoints of the block.

5. Turn on Ortho mode, and click and drag the arrow on the right side of the block. The width of the block follows the arrow as you drag it. You also see the dimension of the sink as you drag the arrow.

6. Enter 15↵. The width of the block changes to 15 inches from the original 12.

Although you entered a value in step 6 to change the width of the sink, you could have clicked the mouse to change the width visually. The rectangle is still a block. You didn't have to explode it to change its width. If you hover the cursor over the dynamic block grip, you see the block's width dimension.

Adding an Increment Value

You can grip edit your dynamic Sink block to modify its width, and as you saw in the previous exercise, you can enter a specific value for the width as well. But suppose you'd like to limit grip movement so that the sink changes in only 1″ steps.

You can set parameters to have an increment value so that grip edits are limited to a specific distance. The following steps show how you can set up the Linear parameter of the Sink block so the sink width can be grip edited to 1″ increments:

1. Double-click the Sink block. Then, in the Edit Block Definition dialog box, make sure Sink is selected and click OK.

2. Click the Linear parameter's Distance1 label, right-click, and choose Properties.

3. In the Properties palette, scroll down to the Value Set group and click the Dist Type listing. The Dist Type option changes to a drop-down list.

4. Expand the list and select Increment.

5. Click in the Dist Increment input box just below the Dist Type options, and enter **1** for an increment distance of 1 inch.

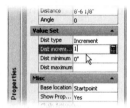

6. Close the Properties palette, and then click Close Block Editor on the Block Editor tab's Close panel.

7. Save the changes.

8. Click the Sink block to expose its grips.

9. Click and drag the right arrow grip to the right. As soon as you click the grip, you see a set of increment marks appear indicating the increment steps for the grip. As you move the grip, the sink width jumps to the increment marks, which are 1 inch apart, as shown in Figure 18.8.

10. Set the width of the sink back to 12 inches.

In addition to an increment distance, you can set a range of movement for the Linear parameter. You may have noticed the minimum and maximum input boxes in the Properties palette in steps 4 and 5. You can enter values for these settings that define the range of movement allowed for the grip edits.

UNDERSTANDING THE CYCLING OPTION

You can turn on the Cycling option in the Misc group of the Properties palette of any parameter grip. Cycling allows you to use the parameter grip as an insertion point. With this option turned on, you can press the Ctrl key to cycle between the standard insertion point and the cycle-enabled grip of a parameter while inserting the block.

FIGURE 18.8
Grip editing the
Sink block with
the Linear param-
eter's increment
value set to 1

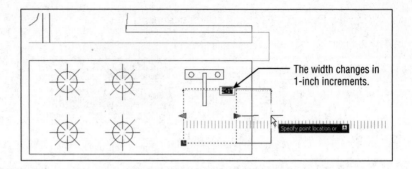

The width changes in
1-inch increments.

The sink exercise is a simple demonstration of how you can create and use dynamic blocks. But as you can see from the Block Authoring palettes, you can add many other parameters and actions to a block.

Editing Parameters and Actions

In the previous exercises, you inserted parameters and actions using the default settings. These settings give you default names and labels for the parameters and actions, but you can always change them later. To change the label that appears for a parameter, double-click the label. The label will then appear in a rectangular box, showing you that you can change its text.

If you want to include additional objects for an action, click the action icon to select it, and then right-click and select Action Selection Set ➤ Modify Selection Set. You can also choose Modify Selection Set ➤ New Selection Set if you want to change the object of the action.

Keeping an Object Centered

Now suppose you want to add a drain to the sink, but to make things a little more complicated, you want to make sure the drain remains centered if the sink is widened or made narrower. You can alter the way the linear parameter behaves so that both sides of the sink move symmetrically. Here's how it works:

1. Double-click the Sink block to open the Edit Block Definition dialog box. Make sure Sink is selected, and click OK.

2. Add a 3˝ diameter circle in the center of the rectangle. This circle will represent the drain (Figure 18.9).

3. Select the Dimension1 linear parameter and then right-click and select Properties.

4. At the Properties palette, scroll down to the bottom and look for the Base Location setting under the Misc group.

5. Click the Base Location option, and then select Midpoint from the drop-down list that appears to the right.

FIGURE 18.9
Adding the
sink drain

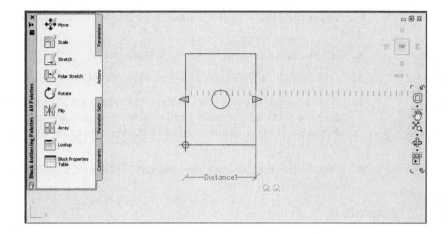

6. Close the Properties palette.

7. Click Close Block Editor in the Close panel, and save the sink block changes.

Now try grip editing the block to see how the Stretch action affects the sink drain:

1. Click the sink to select it.

2. Click and drag the right arrow grip to the right. The drain stays centered in the sink while the two sides expand outward.

In this exercise, you changed the Base Location option for the linear parameter, which causes the block to behave differently when you edit its grips. You can also employ a completely different method to achieve similar results. The Geometric and Dimensional panels of the Block Editor tab offer a set of tools that work in a way that's similar to how the parameters and actions you've already worked with do. You will learn how these tools work next.

Using Constraints in Dynamic Blocks

In the sink example, you added two Stretch actions to a Linear parameter. This enabled the block to be stretched in both the left and right directions. The actions and parameters offer one way of creating dynamic blocks, but you can also use the geometric and dimensional constraints that you were introduced to in the previous chapter.

In this section, you'll turn a simple door block into a dynamic block that will allow you to resize the door to any opening. In the process, you'll learn how to apply geometric and dimensional constraints to create a dynamic block.

At first, you may think that all you need to do to resize a door would be to change the scale. But when you scale the door, all its features, including the door width, are scaled proportionally. To really be accurate, you only want to stretch the door width and scale the door swing, leaving the door thickness at the same dimension. This can be accomplished by adding two aligned dimensional constraints and a few geometric constraints to the door.

Start by opening the Door block in the Block Editor and adding the geometric constraints to the door:

1. Click the Edit tool on the Home tab's Block panel.

2. In the Edit Block Definition dialog box, select DOOR, and then click OK.

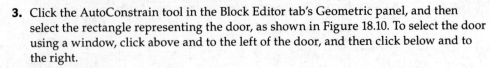

3. Click the AutoConstrain tool in the Block Editor tab's Geometric panel, and then select the rectangle representing the door, as shown in Figure 18.10. To select the door using a window, click above and to the left of the door, and then click below and to the right.

4. Press ↵ when the door has been selected. You'll see the geometric constraint icons appear around the door.

FIGURE 18.10
Select the rectangle representing the door.

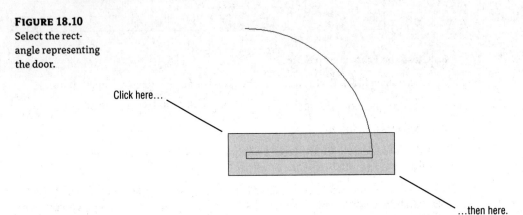

Click here...

...then here.

The geometric constraints will make sure that the door maintains its rectangular shape when you apply changes to the door through the dynamic block feature. The constraints used are parallel, tangent, and horizontal. You'll need to add a constraint to keep the arc connected to the rectangle.

1. Click the Coincident tool in the Geometric panel.

2. Place the cursor near the right end of the bottom horizontal line of the rectangle.

3. When you see the red circle and X marker, click the mouse.

4. Place the cursor near the lower end of the arc where it meets the rectangle.

5. When you see the red circle and X marker, click the mouse.

The coincident constraint you just added will keep the arc and rectangle connected at the bottom-right corner of the rectangle.

Next, add a dimensional constraint. Most likely, you'll need to scale the door based only on the door opening, so place a dimensional constraint between the door hinge and the end of the door swing arc:

Aligned

1. Click the Aligned tool in the Block Editor tab's Dimensional panel.

2. At the `Specify first constraint point or [Object/Point & line/2Lines]` `<Object>:` prompt, point to the line at the bottom of the drawing near the left endpoint, as shown in Figure 18.11.

FIGURE 18.11

Select the locations for the door opening dimensional constraint.

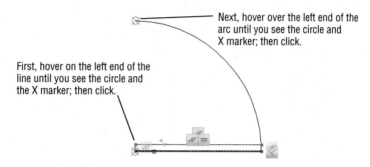

Next, hover over the left end of the arc until you see the circle and X marker; then click.

First, hover on the left end of the line until you see the circle and the X marker; then click.

3. When you see the red circle with the X appear at the left endpoint of the line, click your mouse.

4. At the `Specify second constraint point:` prompt, place the cursor on the top end of the arc so that you see the circle and X marker again at the left end of the arc, as indicated in Figure 18.11.

5. At the `Specify dimension line location:` prompt, place the dimension to the left of the arc (see Figure 18.12).

6. With the dimension highlighted, press ↵. Your drawing will look similar to Figure 18.12.

FIGURE 18.12

The aligned dimensional constraint applied to the door opening

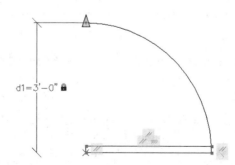

d1=3'-0"

Notice that the constraint you just added is named d1. This will be an important feature in the next two constraints that you add.

Next, add another dimensional constraint to the width of the door rectangle. This time, you want the constraint to follow the door opening constraint, so instead of accepting the default value for the dimension, you'll enter the name of the first dimensional constraint:

Aligned

1. Click the Aligned tool again from the Dimensional panel.

2. Select the left end of the bottom horizontal line again as you did in the previous exercise (see Figure 18.13).

3. Select the right end of the bottom horizontal line as shown in Figure 18.13.

FIGURE 18.13
The door with the opening and door constraints added

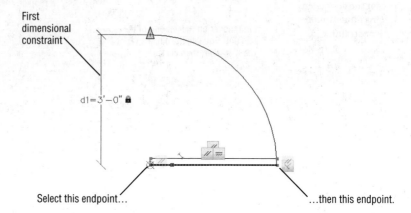

First dimensional constraint

d1=3'−0"

Select this endpoint...   ...then this endpoint.

4. Place the dimension line below the door roughly the same distance away from the door as the first dimensional constraint.

5. With the newly placed dimension highlighted, enter **d1**↵. This will cause the door rectangle to follow the dimension of the d1 door opening dimensional constraint.

Finally, add the dimensional constraint for the arc:

1. Click the Radius tool in the Block Editor tab's Dimensional panel.

2. Click anywhere on the arc.

3. Position the radius dimensional constraint anywhere toward the outside of the arc.

4. With the radius dimension highlighted, enter **d1**↵. This will cause the arc to follow the dimension of the door opening dimensional constraint.

5. You now have all of the constraints in place and are ready to try out your dynamic block. Click Close Block Editor in the Close panel to save the block and return to the drawing.

FIGURE 18.14
The door with all of the constraints added

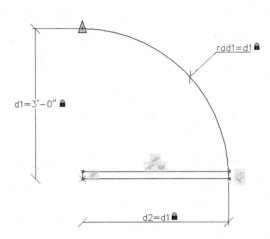

Now try out your new dynamic block by adjusting the door size:

1. Pan your view so you can see the entry door clearly, as shown in Figure 18.15.

2. Click the door to select it. The added aligned constraint arrow appears as a grip on the right end of the Door block.

FIGURE 18.15
The Door block with its grips exposed

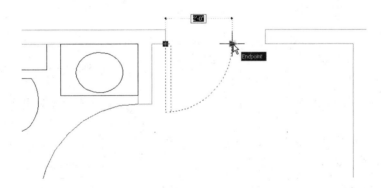

3. Click the arrow grip. The length dimension becomes available for your input, and as you move the mouse, the door changes in size. Note that the thickness of the door doesn't change as you alter its width.

4. Enter 24↵ to change the door width to 24″.

Notice that, although you were able to enter a door dimension directly to the block, you didn't change the door thickness when the door size changed. Only the door swing and width changed to accommodate the new door size. This is most apparent if you scale the door to a small size such as 6″ or 12″.

Adding a List of Predefined Options

Earlier, you saw how you can add an increment value set to make a dynamic block stay in a set range of sizes. You can also set up a dynamic block to offer a range of sizes in a pop-up list. To do this, you need to employ the Block Table feature.

In the following exercise, you'll add a selectable list to the Door block to allow the door size to be selected from a list. Start by adding the block table that will allow you to set up a set of predefined door dimensions:

1. Double-click the door to open the Edit Block Definition dialog box and then click OK.

2. In the Block Editor tab's Dimensional panel, click the Block Table tool.

3. At the `Specify parameter location or [Palette]:` prompt, place the Block Table in the location shown in Figure 18.16.

4. At the `Enter number of grips [0/1] <1>` prompt, press ↵. The Block Properties Table dialog box appears (Figure 18.17).

5. Click the Add Properties tool in the upper-left corner of the Block Properties Table dialog box. The Add Parameter Properties dialog box appears (Figure 18.18).

FIGURE 18.16
Placing the block table

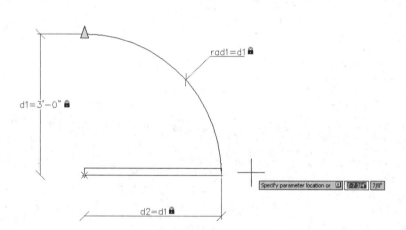

FIGURE 18.17
The Block Properties Table dialog box

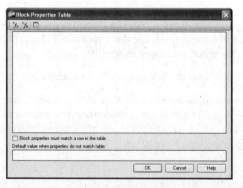

FIGURE 18.18
The Add Parameter
Properties
dialog box

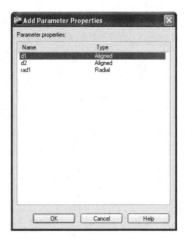

6. Click the d1 listing at the top of the Add Parameter Properties dialog box and click OK. The Block Properties Table returns with a d1 heading in the list box.

7. Click just below the d1 listing, then type **12↵**. You see 1′-0″ added to the list.

8. Type **18↵**. 1′-6″ is added to the list.

9. Type **24↵ 30↵ 36↵**. The values you enter are added to the list in feet and inches format. (Figure 18.19).

FIGURE 18.19
The Block Proper-
ties Table dialog
box with the
values added

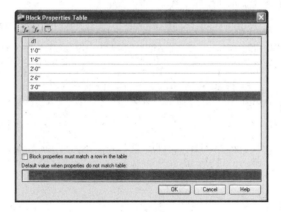

10 Click OK to exit the Block Properties Table dialog box.

11. Click Close Block Editor from the Close panel to return to your drawing.

Now you can select from the door sizes in a pop-up list:

1. Click the door to select it.

2. Click the downward-pointing grip below the door, as shown at the left side of Figure 18.20.

3. Select 3′-0″ door from the list that appears. (See the view to the right in Figure 18.20.) The door changes to a 36″-wide door.

FIGURE 18.20
Selecting a door size from a list

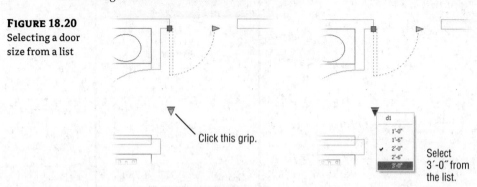

If at a later time you need to make changes to the list or add more dimensions, you can open the block in the Block Editor and then click the Block Table tool. The Block Properties Table dialog box will appear with the data you entered earlier. You can then make changes to the table.

In this example, you saw that you can easily add predefined sizes to the dimensional constraint that appear in a selectable list. You can also give the list a more meaningful name. Right now, when you click on the grip that opens the list, you see d1 as the name. Try the following to change the name from d1 to Width:

1. Double-click the door, and then at the Edit Block Definition dialog box, click OK.

2. Select the d1 dimensional constraint, and then right-click and select Properties.

3. At the Properties palette, select the Name option under the Constraint group and then type **Width**↵. Notice that all of the dimensional constraints that reference the dimension will change to show the name Width instead of d1.

4. Close the Properties palette, and then click the Close Block Editor tool in the Close panel.

5. To see the change, click the downward-pointing grip below the door as you did in the previous exercise. Now you see the word *Width* as the heading in the list of door widths (Figure 18.21).

6. Save and close the file.

As you can see, you have a lot of control over the behavior of various components of the Dynamic Block. In the next section, you'll learn how you can control the visibility of different parts of your block.

Creating Multiple Shapes in One Block

Depending on circumstances, you may need a block to display a completely different form. For example, you might want a single generic bath that can morph into a standard bath, a corner bath, or a large spa-style bath with jets.

FIGURE 18.21
The list with
the word *Width*
appearing as the
column title

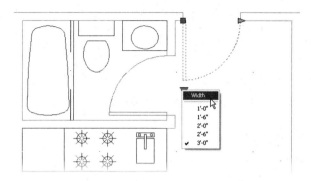

Using dynamic blocks, you can hide or display elements of a block by selecting a *visibility state* from a list. For example, you can draw the three different bath sizes and then set up a visibility state for each size. Each visibility state displays only one bath size. You can then select a visibility state depending on the bath size you want.

Try the following exercise to see how this works firsthand:

1. Open the `visibilitysample.dwg` file, and then click the Edit Block tool on the Home tab's Block panel.

2. In the Edit Block Definition dialog box, select Bathtub from the list, and click OK.

    You see the contents of the Bathtub block (Figure 18.22). It's just the three existing blocks—Standard, Jetted, and Corner—inserted at the same origin.

FIGURE 18.22
The Bathtub block

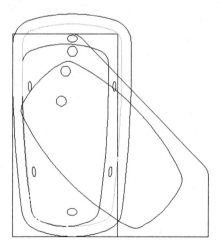

If you were to insert this block in a drawing, it would appear just as you currently see it, with each bathtub type overlaid on another. Next, you'll see how you can add control over the visibility of each bathtub type so that only one is displayed at a time.

The first thing you need to do is add a Visibility parameter:

1. On the Parameters tab of the Block Authoring palettes, click Visibility.

2. Click below the blocks to place the Visibility parameter as shown in Figure 18.23.

FIGURE 18.23
Adding the Visibility parameter

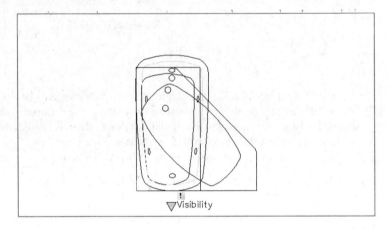

3. Double-click the Visibility parameter you just added to open the Visibility States dialog box (Figure 18.24). One visibility state, VisibilityState0, is already provided.

FIGURE 18.24
The Visibility States dialog

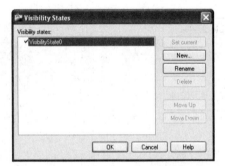

You'll need three visibility states: one for each type of bathtub whose visibility you want to control. You've already got one, but you want a name that is more appropriate to the application:

1. Click the Rename button. The existing visibility state in the list to the left becomes editable.

2. Enter **Standard**↵. This is the visibility state for your standard bathtub.

3. Click the New button to open the New Visibility State dialog box (Figure 18.25).

4. Enter **Jetted** in the Visibility State Name input box.

FIGURE 18.25

Adding a
visibility state

5. Make sure the Leave Visibility Of Existing Objects Unchanged In New State radio button is selected, and then click OK.

6. Click the New button again.

7. In the New Visibility State dialog box, enter **Corner** in the Visibility State Name input box.

8. Make sure Leave Visibility Of Existing Objects Unchanged In New State is selected, and click OK.

You've just created all the visibility states you need.

9. Select Standard from the list, and click the Set Current button. (You can also double-click the Standard item.) A checkmark appears to the left of Standard, showing you that it's now the current state.

10. Click OK to exit the Visibility States dialog box.

You have the visibility states you need, and you have the objects whose visibility you want to control. Now you need to determine which block is visible for each state.

Remember that in step 9 of the previous exercise, you made Standard the current visibility state. You'll want only the standard Bathtub block visible for this state. Do the following to turn off the other two Bathtub blocks for the current state:

1. Select the Jetted and Corner blocks (see Figure 18.26).

FIGURE 18.26

Locating the blocks

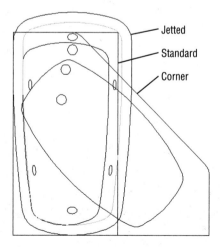

2. Right-click, and choose Object Visibility ➤ Hide For Current State. You can also click the Make Invisible tool on the right side of the Block Editor tab's Visibility panel.

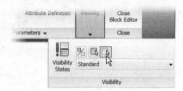

The selected blocks disappear. They didn't go anywhere; they were just made invisible.

3. Click the drop-down list on the Block Editor tab's Visibility panel, and select Jetted. The hidden blocks appear.

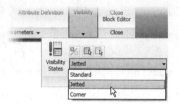

The current visibility state is now Jetted, so you want only the Jetted block to be visible. Select the Standard and Corner blocks, and then right-click and choose Object Visibility ➤ Hide For Current State. You can also click the Make Invisible tool from the Visibility panel. Now only the Jetted block is visible.

4. On the Block Editor tab's Visibility panel, click the drop-down list again and select Corner. All the blocks appear.

5. Select the Standard and Jetted blocks, and click the Make Invisible tool. Now only the Corner block is visible.

You've created visibility states and set up the blocks so they appear only when the appropriate visibility state is current. Next, you'll test the blocks:

1. Click Close Block Editor, and save the changes you've made.

2. Click the Insert tool on the Home tab's Block panel. In the Insert dialog box, select Bathtub from the Name drop-down list.

3. Make sure Specify On-Screen is checked for the Insertion Point group and unchecked for the Scale and Rotation groups.

4. Click OK, and then place the block to the right of the other three blocks.

5. Click the Bathtub block you just inserted, and then click the Visibility grip (see the left image in Figure 18.27).

6. Select Jetted from the list. The Jetted bathtub appears (see the right image in Figure 18.27).

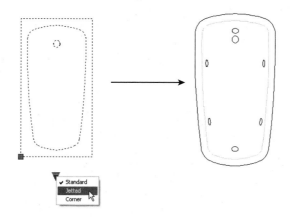

FIGURE 18.27
Using the Visibility grip to change the bathtub

7. Click the Bathtub block again, click the Visibility grip, and select Corner. The Corner tub appears.

8. Save and close the drawing.

CONTROLLING THE VISIBILITY OF INVISIBLE OBJECTS

While you're editing them in the Block Editor, you can set up AutoCAD to display objects whose visibility has been turned off. If you set the bvmode system variable to 1, objects appear gray when their visibility has been turned off. You can also click the Visibility Mode tool in the Block Editor tab's Visibility panel.

In this example, you used a set of bathtubs, but you can use the Visibility parameter for anything that requires a different appearance. As mentioned at the beginning of this chapter, another use might be a block that contains a double-, queen-, and king-sized bed. Going back to the door example, you can create a left- and right-hand door in the same block and then use the Visibility parameter to display a left- or right-hand door in the drawing. Figure 18.28 shows such a door block. The Visibility parameter has been renamed Hand in the block. When the door is inserted in the drawing, you see a list that allows you to select Left or Right.

Rotating Objects in Unison

You've seen how actions and parameters can control the behavior of a single object in a block. You can also apply actions to multiple objects so they move or change in unison. The following example shows how you can apply more than one Angular Constraint parameter to control two objects:

1. Open the gatesample.dwg file. In this sample file, the part that will move are the two non-red objects. The red lines have been added to help facilitate the rotation feature of the block.

2. Double-click the object in the drawing to open the Edit Block Definition dialog box, and then click OK. The Gate block opens for editing.

3. Click the Show All Geometric Constraints tool in the Block Editor tab's Geometric panel to reveal some of the existing constraints.

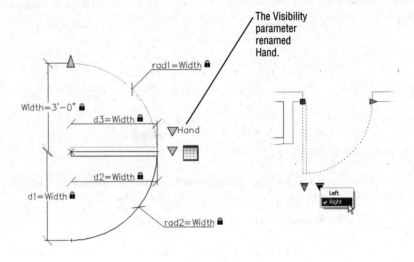

FIGURE 18.28
The Door dynamic block showing a left- and right-hand door (left), and the Door block as it appears in the drawing (right)

You can see how this drawing has been prepared for this exercise. The non-red parts of the drawing, which I'll call gates, are blocks that are constrained to the red lines with coincident constraints. The endpoints of the lines are constrained to the center of the arcs. The horizontal red lines are constrained to the vertical ones, also with coincident constraints, and the vertical lines are constrained at both ends with a fix constraint (Figure 18.29).

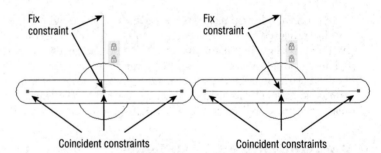

FIGURE 18.29
How the parts of the block are constrained

You'll use the red lines to define the rotation angle of the parts. The vertical line is fixed in place while the rest of the parts are constrained in such a way to allow a rotational motion. Now add some angular constraints to define the rotation.

1. In the Dimensional panel, click the Angular tool.

2. Click the left vertical line toward the top as shown in Figure 18.30.

3. Next, click the left horizontal line toward the right end of the line as shown in Figure 18.30.

4. Place the dimension as shown in Figure 18.30.

FIGURE 18.30
Adding the angular constraint to the gatesample.dwg drawing

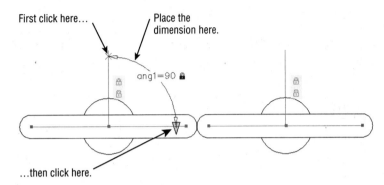

First click here...

Place the dimension here.

ang1=90

...then click here.

5. The dimension text is highlighted. You want to keep the current value, so press ↵ to accept the default.

You have the first angular dimensional constraint in place. Next, add a second one to the gate on the right, but this time, you'll use the name of the first angular constraint as the dimension for the second one:

1. In the Dimensional panel, click the Angular tool.

2. Click the right vertical line near its top as shown in Figure 18.31.

FIGURE 18.31
Adding the angular constraint to the second gate

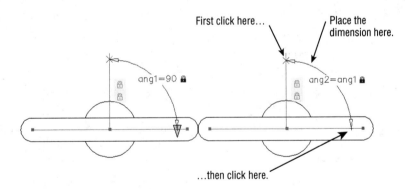

First click here...

Place the dimension here.

ang1=90

ang2=ang1

...then click here.

3. Next, click the right horizontal line near its right end (Figure 18.31).

4. Place the dimension as shown in Figure 18.31.

5. At the highlighted text, type **ang1**↵. This will cause this constraint to follow the first one you added.

Now you're ready to save the block and try it out:

1. Click Close Block Editor on the Block Editor tab's Close panel, and save the block.

2. Click the block to expose its grips.

3. Click the arrow grip on the horizontal line.

4. Type 45↵. Both sides of the block rotate about their own centers to a 45 degree angle (see Figure 18.32).

5. Click the arrow grip again and type 90↵ to set the gate back to its original position.

FIGURE 18.32
The two parts rotate in unison.

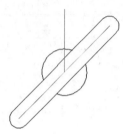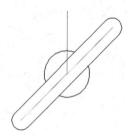

You've got the basic function of the gate working, but you don't want the red lines to appear in the drawing since they are really there to facilitate the action of the gate and not really part of the drawing. Do the following to hide the red lines:

1. Double-click the Gate block to open the Edit Block Definition dialog box, and then click OK. The Gate block opens for editing.

2. Click the Construction Geometry tool in the Manage panel.

3. Select the four red lines and press ↵↵. Notice that the lines change from solid to dashed, indicating that they are now construction geometry.

4. Click the Close Block Editor tool and save the block. The block now appears without the red lines. If you click on the block, the rotation grip still appears, and you can alter the block as before.

Now suppose you want to have the gates rotate in opposite directions instead of in the same direction. You can add a user-defined formula to modify the behavior of the angular constraints:

1. Double-click the Gate block to open the Edit Block Definition dialog box, and then click OK. The Gate block opens for editing.

2. Click the Parameters Manager tool to open the Parameters Manager palette. You may recall that in Chapter 17, you used this palette to control the size of a concentric circle.

3. Double-click in the Expression column of the ang2 option and type **ang1 * -1**↵.

4. Close the Parameters Manager palette, and then save and close the block.

5. Click the gate to select it, and then click the arrow grip.

6. Type **22↵**. Now the two parts rotate in opposite directions (Figure 18.33).

7. Save and Close the file.

FIGURE 18.33
The gates moving
in opposite
directions

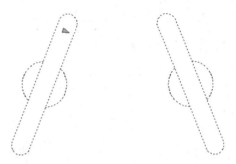

You can go on to add a block table using the Block Table tool to create a predefined set of angles, just as you did for the Door block earlier in this chapter. You can also add incremental values by using the Properties palette to change the angle constraint in a way similar to how you changed constraints in the sink exercise in the first part of this chapter.

Next, take a look at a way to automatically array objects with dynamic blocks.

Filling in a Space Automatically with Objects

Perhaps one of the more tedious tasks you'll face is drawing the vertical bars of a hand railing for an elevation view. You can draw a single bar and then use the Array command to repeat the bar as many times as needed, but when you have to edit the railing, you may find that you're spending more time adding and erasing bars.

In the next example, you'll see how you can create a block that automatically fills in vertical bars as the width of the railing changes. You'll start with an existing drawing of a single vertical bar and an outline of the railing opening around the bar:

1. Open the `railsample.dwg` file.

2. Double-click the object in the drawing to open the Edit Block Definition dialog box, and then click OK. This opens the Railvertical block for editing.

   When the Block Editor opens, notice that the block already has a Linear parameter and a Stretch action added. Recall from the sink example at the beginning of this chapter that the Linear parameter and Stretch action let you vary the width of an object. In this case, the outermost rectangle is being stretched.

3. On the Actions tab of the Block Authoring palettes, click the Array action.

4. At the Select parameter: prompt, click the blue Linear parameter (labeled as Distance), as shown in Figure 18.34.

5. At the Select objects: prompt, select the dark vertical rectangle representing the vertical bar of the railing, as shown in Figure 18.34, and then press ↵.

6. At the Enter the distance between columns (|||): prompt, enter 4↵.

7. Click Close Block Editor on the Block Editor tab's Close panel and save the changes.

8. Click the block to expose its grips.

FIGURE 18.34
Adding the Array action to the Rail-vertical block

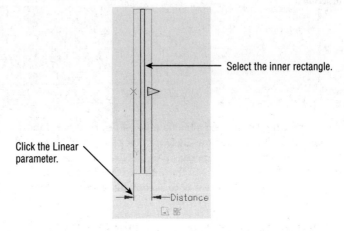

Select the inner rectangle.

Click the Linear parameter.

9. Click and drag the blue arrow grip to the right. As the rail expands, additional vertical bars are added at 4″ intervals (see Figure 18.35).

10. Exit and save the file.

FIGURE 18.35
The Railvertical block adds vertical bars as its width expands.

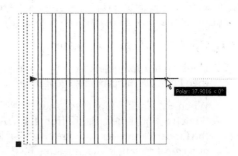

You can now use this block wherever you need to draw a simple railing with vertical bars. Another example of how the Array action might be used is in a side view of a bolt. You could show the threads of the bolt and use the Array action to increase the number of threads as the bolt is lengthened.

USING PARAMETER SETS

You probably noticed the Parameter Sets tab in the Block Authoring palettes. The options in this tab are predefined combinations of parameters and actions that are commonly used together. For example, the Polar Array set inserts a Polar parameter with an Array action. You only need to supply the object. The Polar Array set causes the associated object to rotate about a center point with a grip. You can also array the object by stretching the grip away from the rotation center.

To associate an object with a parameter set, right-click the action icon associated with a parameter (usually appearing below the parameter), and then select Action Selection Set ➤ New Selection Set. At the select objects: prompt, select an object. If a stretch is employed, select a stretch frame and an object to stretch.

Including Block Information with Data Extraction

In Chapter 13, you learned how you can attach data to blocks through attributes and then extract that data to spreadsheets or AutoCAD tables. You can also include dynamic block information that has been included in a property lookup table. This can be extremely useful for generating data for a bill of materials or in other situations if you need to track the numbers and types of items in your drawing.

To see how this works, you'll return to a version of the Door block that has some additions. This enhanced version of the Door block includes a left- and right-hand version of the door that is controlled with the Visibility parameter. Figure 18.36 shows the door inserted into a drawing using different door sizes and left and right variations.

FIGURE 18.36
The door block inserted several times into a drawing with various widths and handedness

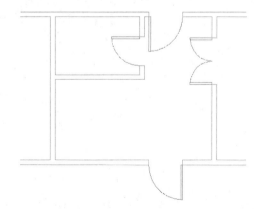

You'll use the Attribute Extraction command to see how the dynamic block data appears as an exported table or a spreadsheet:

1. Open the 18-extractsample.dwg file. This file contains a door dynamic block that is similar to the one you created earlier, with the addition of a left and right Visibility parameter.

2. From the Annotate tab's Tables panel, click the Extract Data tool to start the Data Extraction Wizard.

3. On the Begin screen, click Next.

4. In the Save Data Extraction As dialog box, enter **Test** for the name, and click Save.

5. On the Define Data Source screen, click Next.

6. On the Select Objects screen, remove the checkmark from the Display All Object Types option so that only the Door block appears in the list, and then click Next.

7. On the Select Properties screen, remove the checkmark from all but the Dynamic Block option in the right column, and make sure the Hand and Width options in the left column are the only ones selected (see Figure 18.37).

FIGURE 18.37
Set up the Select Properties screen to look like this.

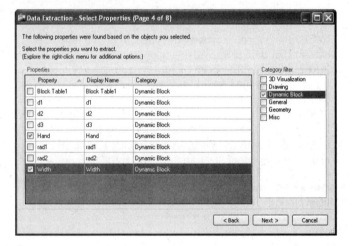

8. Click Next. On the Refine Data page, you see the data that will be exported to a spreadsheet file or table (see Figure 18.38).

9. You don't really want to extract this data, so once you've taken a good look at this screen, click Cancel and then Yes at the Quit Wizard dialog box.

This is the end of the door example, so you can exit this file. Save it for future reference if you like.

As you can see in Figure 18.38, a list is generated that shows each door in the drawing with its size and handedness. You could use this data as part of a door schedule.

TAKE CARE USING THE MIRROR TOOL

If you use the Mirror command to mirror a block that contains a Visibility parameter to control left- and right-hand doors, the Attribute Extraction command will report erroneous results. Therefore, be sure that if you set up a block with a visibility parameter to control mirrored states, you use those actions to edit the door and don't rely on standard editing tools. That way, you'll ensure the accuracy of your extracted data.

FIGURE 18.38
The resulting table to be extracted, as shown on the Refine Data screen of the Data Extraction Wizard

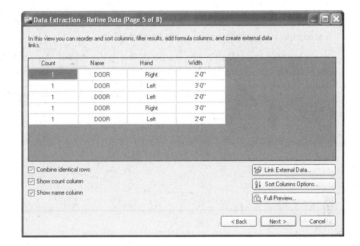

The Bottom Line

Explore the Block Editor.   To create dynamic blocks, you need to become familiar with the Block Editor. You can use the Block Editor to modify existing blocks in your drawing.

Master It   What does the Edit Block Definition dialog box allow you to do?

Create a dynamic block.   Dynamic blocks are blocks to which you add grips that let you modify the block in a number of different ways.

Master It   Name some of the features of the Block Editor that let you add additional grip editing functions to a block.

Add Scale and Stretch actions to a parameter.   You can set up a dynamic block to perform multiple operations with a single grip.

Master It   What do you need to do to have one grip perform two functions?

Add more than one parameter for multiple grip functions.   In addition to having one grip perform multiple operations, you can add as many grips as you need to make your block even more customizable.

Master It   What feature do you use to set up a list of options for a block?

Create multiple shapes in one block. Many of the dynamic-block functions let you adjust the shape of the original block. Another feature lets you choose completely different shapes for the block.

Master It When a block uses the Visibility parameter to set up different shapes, how do you select a different block shape in the drawing?

Rotate objects in unison. Blocks can be set up so the action of one set of objects affects another set. This chapter gives the example of rotating objects in unison.

Master It Name the dimensional constraint that was used in the object rotation example in this chapter.

Fill in a space automatically with objects. A dynamic block can help you automate the addition of repetitive elements to your drawing.

Master It What is the name of the action used to produce an array of an object in a block when the block is stretched?

Chapter 19

Drawing Curves

So far in this book, you've been using basic lines, arcs, and circles to create your drawings. Now it's time to add polylines and spline curves to your repertoire. Polylines offer many options for creating forms, including solid fills and free-form curved lines. Spline curves are perfect for drawing accurate and smooth nonlinear objects.

In this chapter, you'll learn to do the following:

♦ Create and edit polylines

♦ Create a polyline spline curve

♦ Create and edit true spline curves

♦ Mark divisions on curves

Introducing Polylines

Polylines are like composite line segments and arcs. A polyline may look like a series of line segments, but it acts like a single object. This characteristic makes polylines useful for a variety of applications, as you'll see in the upcoming exercises.

Drawing a Polyline

First, to learn about the polyline, you'll begin a drawing of the top view of the joint shown in Figure 19.1.

FIGURE 19.1
A sketch of a
metal joint

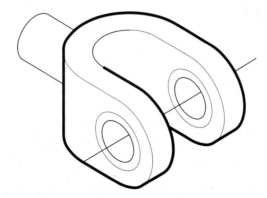

Follow these steps to draw the joint:

1. Open a new file using the `acad.dwt` template, and save it as `Joint2d`. Don't bother to make special setting changes because you'll create this drawing with the default settings.

2. From the navigation bar, choose Zoom All from the flyout or type **Z⏎A⏎**.

3. Click the Polyline tool on the Draw panel, or type **Pl⏎**.

4. At the `Specify start point:` prompt, enter a point at coordinate 3,3 to start your polyline.

5. At the `Specify next point or [Arc/Halfwidth/Length/Undo/Width]:` prompt, enter **@3<0⏎** to draw a horizontal line of the joint.

6. At the `Specify next point or [Arc/Close/Halfwidth/Length/Undo/Width]:` prompt, enter **A⏎** to continue your polyline with an arc.

USING THE ARC OPTION IN THE POLYLINE TOOL

The Arc option enables you to draw an arc that starts from the last point you selected and then select additional options. Select the Arc option; as you move your cursor, an arc follows it in a tangential direction from the first line segment you drew. You can return to drawing line segments by entering **L⏎**.

---

7. At the prompt

   ```
   Specify endpoint of arc or
   [Angle/CEnter/CLose/Direction/Halfwidth/Line/Radius/Second pt/Undo/Width]:
   ```

   enter **@4<90⏎** to draw a 180° arc from the last point you entered. Your drawing should now look similar to Figure 19.2.

8. To continue the polyline with another line segment, enter **L⏎**.

FIGURE 19.2
A polyline line and arc

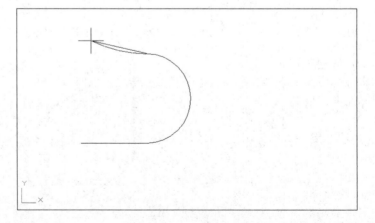

9. At the `Specify next point or [Arc/Close/Halfwidth/Length/Undo/Width]:` prompt, enter **@3<180**↵. Another line segment continues from the end of the arc.

10. Press ↵ to exit the Polyline tool.

You now have a sideways, U-shaped polyline that you'll use in the next exercise to complete the top view of your joint.

Setting Polyline Options

Let's take a break from the tutorial to look at some of the options in the Polyline prompt that you didn't use:

Close Draws a line segment from the last endpoint of a sequence of lines to the first point picked in that sequence. This works exactly like the Close option for the Line command.

Length Enables you to specify the length of a line that will be drawn at the same angle as the last line entered.

Halfwidth Creates a tapered line segment or an arc by specifying half its beginning and ending widths (see Figure 19.3).

FIGURE 19.3
A tapered line segment and an arc created with Halfwidth

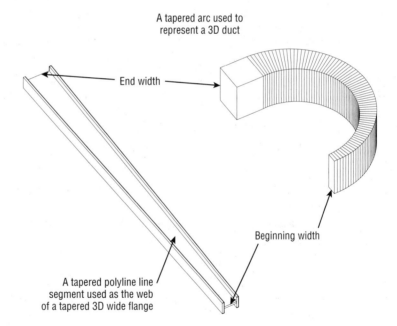

A tapered arc used to represent a 3D duct

End width

Beginning width

A tapered polyline line segment used as the web of a tapered 3D wide flange

Width Creates a tapered line segment or an arc by specifying the full width of the segment's beginning and ending points.

Undo Deletes the last line segment drawn.

Radius/Second pt The Radius and Second pt options appear when you use the arc option to draw polyline segments. Radius lets you specify a radius for the arc and Second pt lets you specify a second point in a three-point arc.

If you want to break a polyline into simple lines and arcs, you can use the Explode option on the Modify panel, just as you would with blocks. After a polyline is exploded, it becomes a set of individual line segments or arcs.

To turn off the filling of solid polylines, open the Options dialog box and click the Display tab. Clear the Apply Solid Fill check box in the Display Performance group.

FILLETING A POLYLINE

You can use the Fillet tool on the Modify panel to fillet all the vertices of a polyline composed of straight-line segments. Click the Fillet tool, set your fillet radius by typing **R↵** and entering a radius value, type **P↵** to select the Polyline option, and then pick the polyline you want to fillet.

Editing Polylines

You can edit polylines with many of the standard editing commands. To change the properties of a polyline, click the polyline to select it, right-click, and select Properties to open the Properties palette. You can use the Stretch command on the Modify panel to move vertices of a polyline. The Trim, Extend, and Break commands on the Modify panel also work with polylines.

In addition, many editing capabilities are offered only for polylines. For instance, later in this section you'll see how to smooth out a polyline by using the Fit option in the Pedit command.

In this exercise, you'll use the Offset command on the Modify panel to add the inside portion of the joint:

1. Click the Offset tool in the Home tab's Modify panel, or type **O↵**.

2. At the `Specify offset distance or [Through/Erase/Layer] <Through>:` prompt, enter **1**.

3. At the `Select object to offset or [Exit/Undo]<Exit>:` prompt, pick the U-shaped polyline you just drew.

4. At the `Specify point on side to offset or [Exit/Multiple/Undo] <Exit>:` prompt, pick a point on the inside of the U shape. You'll see a concentric copy of the polyline appear (see Figure 19.4).

5. Press ↵ to exit the Offset command.

The concentric copy of a polyline made by choosing the Offset tool can be useful when you need to draw complex parallel curves like the ones in Figure 19.5.

Next, complete the top view of the joint. To do this, you'll use the Edit Polyline tool, otherwise known as the Pedit command:

1. Connect the ends of the polylines with two short line segments (see Figure 19.6).

2. Choose Edit Polyline from the expanded Modify panel or type **PE↵**.

3. At the `Select polyline or [Multiple]:` prompt, pick the outermost polyline.

FIGURE 19.4

The offset polyline

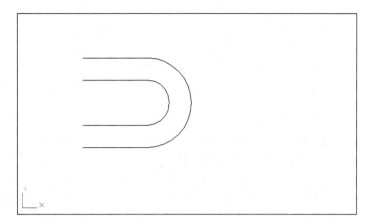

FIGURE 19.5

Sample complex curves drawn by using offset polylines

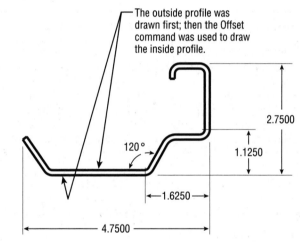

The outside profile was drawn first; then the Offset command was used to draw the inside profile.

2.7500

1.1250

120°

1.6250

4.7500

FIGURE 19.6

The polyline so far

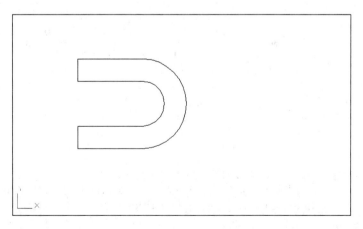

4. At the prompt

```
Enter an option
[Close/Join/Width/Edit vertex/Fit/Spline/Decurve/Ltype gen/Reverse/Undo]:
```

enter **J**↵ for the Join option.

5. At the `Select objects:` prompt, select all the objects you've drawn so far.

6. Press ↵ to join all the objects into one polyline. It appears that nothing has happened.

7. Press ↵ again to exit the Pedit command.

8. Click the drawing to expose its grips. The entire object is highlighted, indicating that all the lines have been joined into a single polyline.

WHAT TO DO IF THE JOIN OPTION DOESN'T WORK

If the objects to be joined don't touch, you can use the *fuzz* join feature. Type **Pe**↵**M**↵ to start the Pedit command with the Multiple option, then select all the objects you want to join and press ↵. If you see a convert message, enter **Y**↵. At the `Enter an option [Close/Open/Join/Width/ Fit/Spline/Decurve/Ltype gen/Undo]:` prompt, enter **J**↵. At the `Enter fuzz distance or [Jointype]:` prompt, enter a distance that approximates the size of the gap between objects. By default, AutoCAD extends the lines so they join end to end. You can use the Jointype option if you want Pedit to join segments with an additional segment.

By using the Width option under Edit Polyline, you can change the width of a polyline. Let's change the width of your polyline to give some width to the outline of the joint. To do this, you'll use the Edit Polyline tool again, but this time you'll use a shortcut:

1. Double-click the polyline.

2. At the `Enter an option [Open/Join/Width/Edit vertex/Fit/Spline/Decurve/ Ltype gen/Reverse/Undo]:` prompt, enter **W**↵ for the Width option.

3. At the `Specify new width for all segments:` prompt, enter **.03**↵ for the new width of the polyline. The line changes to the new width (see Figure 19.7), and you now have a top view of your joint.

4. Press ↵ to exit the Pedit command.

5. Save this file.

In most cases, you can simply double-click on a polyline to start the Pedit command. But if you want to edit multiple polylines or if you want to convert an object or set of objects into a polyline, use the Edit Polyline tool from the Modify panel to start Pedit.

In addition, if you have Dynamic Input turned on in the status bar, you can select the Edit Polyline options from a menu that appears at the cursor (Figure 19.8).

FIGURE 19.7
The polyline with a
new thickness

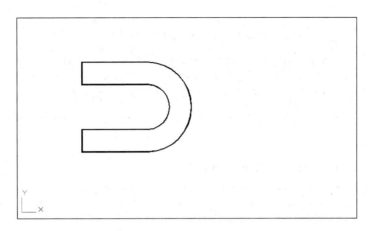

FIGURE 19.8
The Edit Polyline
options that
appear at
the cursor

Setting Pedit Options

Here's a brief look at a few of the Pedit options you didn't try firsthand:

Close   Connects the two endpoints of a polyline with a line segment. If the polyline you selected to be edited is already closed, this option changes to Open.

Open   Removes the last segment added to a closed polyline.

Spline/Decurve   The Spline option smoothes a polyline into a spline curve (discussed in detail later in this chapter). The Decurve option changes a spline polyline back into its original shape before the Spline option was applied.

Edit Vertex   Lets you edit each vertex of a polyline individually (discussed in detail later in this section).

Fit   Turns polyline segments into a series of arcs.

Ltype Gen   Controls the way noncontinuous linetypes pass through the vertices of a polyline. If you have a fitted or spline curve with a noncontinuous linetype, turn on this option.

Reverse   Reverses the orientation of a polyline. The orientation is based on the order in which points are selected to create the polyline. The first point picked is the beginning, or point 1; the next point is point 2, and so on. In some cases, you may want to reverse this order using the Reverse option.

Undo   Removes the last polyline line segment.

USING POLYLINES TO SET LINE WEIGHTS

Typically, you would use the Lineweight feature of AutoCAD to set line weights in your drawing. In cases where the Lineweight feature will not work, you can change the thickness of regular lines and arcs by using Pedit to change them into polylines and then using the Width option to change their width.

Smoothing Polylines

You can create a curve in AutoCAD in many ways. If you don't need the representation of a curve to be accurate, you can use a polyline curve. In the following exercise, you'll draw a polyline curve to represent a contour on a topographical map:

1. Open the `topo.dwg` file. The top image in Figure 19.9 contains the drawing of survey data. Some of the contours have already been drawn in between the data points.

2. Zoom in to the upper-right corner of the drawing so your screen displays the area shown in the bottom image in Figure 19.9.

3. Click the Polyline tool on the Draw panel. Using the Center osnap, draw a polyline that connects the points labeled 254.00. Your drawing should look like the bottom image in Figure 19.9.

4. Press ↵.

5. Next you'll convert the polyline you just drew into a smooth contour line. Double-click the contour line you just drew.

6. At the prompt

   ```
   Enter an option
   [Close/Join/Width/Edit vertex/Fit/Spline/Decurve/Ltype gen/Reverse/Undo]:
   ```

   type **F**↵ to select the Fit option. The polyline smoothes out into a series of connected arcs that pass through the data points.

7. Press ↵ to end the command.

Your contour is now complete. The Fit option under the Pedit command causes AutoCAD to convert the straight-line segments of the polyline into arcs. The endpoints of the arcs pass through the endpoints of the line segments, and the curve of each arc depends on the direction of the adjacent arc. This gives the effect of a smooth curve. Next you'll use this polyline curve to experiment with some of the editing options unique to the Pedit command.

Editing Vertices

One of the Pedit options that I haven't yet discussed, Edit Vertex, is like a command within a command. Edit Vertex has numerous suboptions that enable you to fine-tune your polyline by giving you control over individual vertices.

FIGURE 19.9
The topo.dwg file shows survey data portrayed in an AutoCAD drawing. Notice the dots indicating where elevations were taken. The actual elevation value is shown with a diagonal line from the point.

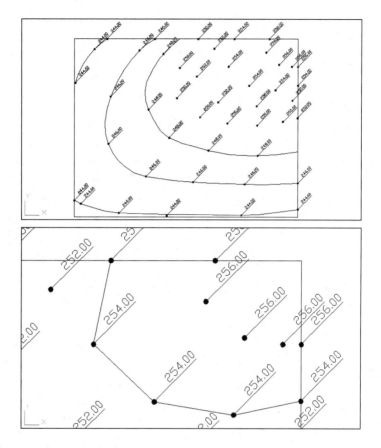

To access the Edit Vertex options, follow these steps:

1. Turn off the Data and Border layers to hide the data points and border.

2. Double-click the polyline you just drew.

3. Type **E↵** to enter Edit Vertex mode. An X appears at the beginning of the polyline, indicating the vertex that will be affected by the Edit Vertex options.

When using Edit Vertex, you must be careful about selecting the correct vertex to be edited. Edit Vertex has 10 options. You often have to exit the Edit Vertex operation and use Pedit's Fit option to see the effect of several Edit Vertex options on a curved polyline.

EDIT VERTEX SUBOPTIONS

After you enter the Edit Vertex mode of the Pedit command, you can perform the following functions:

◆ Break the polyline between two vertices.

◆ Insert a new vertex.

◆ Move an existing vertex.

◆ Regen the drawing to view the current shape of the polyline.

◆ Straighten a polyline between two vertices.

◆ Change the tangential direction of a vertex.

◆ Change the width of the polyline at a vertex.

TURNING OBJECTS INTO POLYLINES AND POLYLINES INTO SPLINES

At times, you'll want to convert regular lines, arcs, or even circles into polylines. You might want to change the width of lines or join lines to form a single object such as a boundary. Here are the steps to convert lines, arcs, and circles into polylines:

1. Click the Edit Polyline tool from the Home tab's expanded Modify panel, or type **Pe↵** at the Command prompt.

2. At the `Select polyline or [Multiple]:` prompt, pick the object you want to convert. If you want to convert a circle to a polyline, first break the circle (using the Break tool on the Modify panel) so it becomes an arc of approximately 359°.

3. At the prompt

   `Object selected is not a polyline. Do you want to turn it into one? <Y>:`

   press ↵. The object is converted into a polyline.

If you want to convert several objects to polylines, type **M↵** at the `Select polyline or [Multiple]:` prompt, then select the objects you want to convert. You will see the `Convert Lines, Arcs and Splines to polylines [Yes/No]? <Y>:` prompt. Type **Y↵**, and all the selected objects are converted to polylines. You can then go on to use other Pedit options on the selected objects.

To turn a polyline into a true spline curve, do the following:

1. Click the Edit Polyline tool from the Home tab's expanded Modify panel, or type **Pe↵**. Select the polyline you want to convert.

2. Type **S↵** to turn it into a polyline spline, then press ↵ to exit the Pedit command.

3. Click the Spline tool on the Home tab's expanded Draw panel or type **Spl↵**.

4. At the `Specify first point or [Method/Knots/Object]:` prompt, type **O↵** for the Object option.

5. At the `Select spline-fit polyline:` prompt, click the polyline spline. Although it may not be apparent at first, the polyline is converted into a true spline.

You can also use the Edit Spline tool on the Home tab's expanded Modify panel (or enter **Spe↵**) to edit a polyline spline. If you do, the polyline spline is automatically converted into a true spline.

If you know you'll always want to convert an object into a polyline when using Pedit, you can turn on the Peditaccept system variable. Enter **peditaccept↵** at the Command prompt, and then enter **1↵**.

These functions are presented in the form of the following prompt:

`[Next/Previous/Break/Insert/Move/Regen/Straighten/Tangent/Width/eXit] <N>:`

The following sections examine each of the options in this prompt, starting with Next and Previous.

The Next and Previous Options

The Next and Previous options let you select a vertex for editing. When you start the Edit Vertex option, an X appears on the selected polyline to designate its beginning. As you select Next or Previous, the X moves from vertex to vertex to show which one is being edited. Let's try this:

1. Press ↵ a couple of times to move the X along the polyline. (Because Next is the default option, you only need to press ↵ to move the X.)

2. Type **P**↵ for Previous. The X moves in the opposite direction. The default option becomes P.

WHY REVERSE A POLYLINE

One of more frequently asked questions I receive from readers is "How can I reverse the direction of a polyline?" It may seem like an odd question to someone new to AutoCAD, but reversing a polyline has quite a few uses. Perhaps the most common use is to turn a polyline that uses a complex linetype, one that includes text, right side up so that the text can be read more easily. (See Chapter 28 for an example of a linetype that includes text.) If for some reason you need to reverse the direction of a polyline or spline, you can do so by using the Reverse option in the Pedit command.

The Break Option

The Break option breaks the polyline between two vertices:

1. Position the X on one end of the segment you want to break.

2. Enter **B**↵ at the Command prompt.

3. At the `Enter an option [Next/Previous/Go/eXit] <N>:` prompt, use Next or Previous to move the X to the other end of the segment to be broken.

4. When the X is in the proper position, enter **G**↵ to break the polyline (see Figure 19.10).

You can also use the Break and Trim options on the Modify panel to break a polyline anywhere, as you did when you drew the toilet seat in Chapter 3.

The Insert Option

Next, try the Insert option, which inserts a new vertex:

1. Type **X**↵ to exit the Edit Vertex option temporarily. Then type **U**↵ to undo the break.

2. Type **E**↵ to return to the Edit Vertex option.

3. Press ↵ to advance the X marker to the next point.

4. Enter I↵ to select the Insert option.

5. When the prompt Specify location for new vertex: appears, along with a rubber-banding line originating from the current X position (see Figure 19.11), pick a point indicating the new vertex location. The polyline is redrawn with the new vertex.

FIGURE 19.10
How the Break
option works

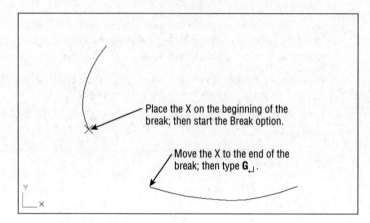

FIGURE 19.11
The new vertex
location

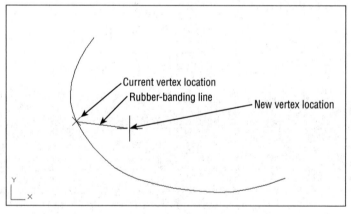

Notice that the inserted vertex appears between the currently marked vertex and the *next* vertex, so the Insert option is sensitive to the direction of the polyline. If the polyline is curved, the new vertex won't immediately be shown as curved. (See the first image in Figure 19.12.) You must smooth it out by exiting the Edit Vertex option and then using the Fit option, as you did to edit the site plan. (See the second image in Figure 19.12.) You can also use the Stretch command (on the Modify panel) to move a polyline vertex.

The Move Option

In this brief exercise, you'll use the Move option to move a vertex:

1. Undo the inserted vertex by exiting the Edit Vertex option (enter X↵) and typing U↵.

2. Restart the Edit Vertex option, and use the Next or Previous option to place the X on the vertex you want to move.

3. Enter **M↵** for the Move option.

4. When the Specify new location for marked vertex: prompt appears, along with a rubber-banding line originating from the X (see the first image in Figure 19.13), pick the new vertex. The polyline is redrawn (see the second image in Figure 19.13). Again, if the line is curved, the new vertex appears as a sharp angle until you use the Fit option (see the final image in Figure 19.13).

FIGURE 19.12
The polyline before and after the curve is fitted

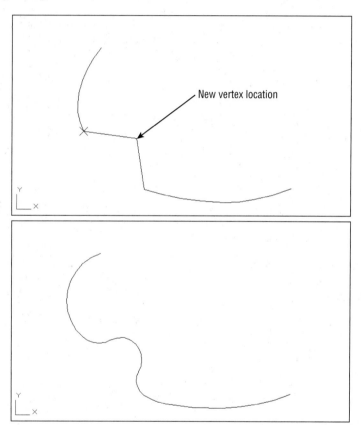

New vertex location

You can also move a polyline vertex by using its grip.

The Regen Option

In some cases, the effect of an option does not appear in the drawing immediately. You can use the Regen option to update the display of the polyline and see any changes you've made up to that point.

FIGURE 19.13
Picking a new loca-
tion for a vertex
with the polyline
before and after
the curve is fitted

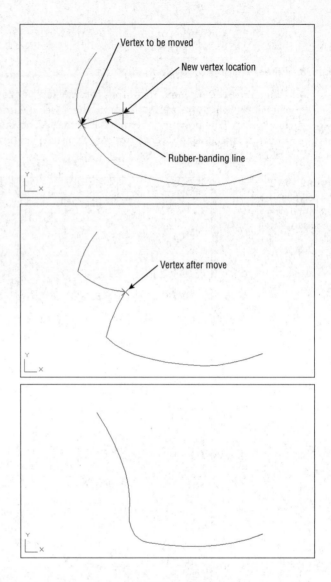

The Straighten Option

The Straighten option straightens all the vertices between two selected vertices. Using the Straighten option is a quick way to delete vertices from a polyline, as shown in the following exercise:

1. Undo the moved vertex (from the previous exercise).

2. Start the Edit Vertex option again, and select the starting vertex for the straight line.

3. Enter **S↵** for the Straighten option.

4. At the `Enter an option [Next/Previous/Go/eXit] <N>:` prompt, move the X to the location for the other end of the straight-line segment.

5. After the X is in the proper position, enter **G↵** for the Go option. The polyline straightens between the two selected vertices (see Figure 19.14).

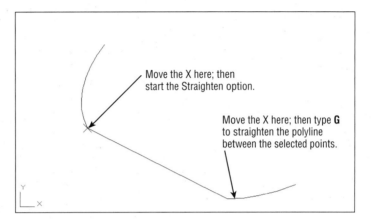

Move the X here; then
start the Straighten option.

Move the X here; then type **G**
to straighten the polyline
between the selected points.

The Tangent Option

The Tangent option alters the direction of a curve on a curve-fitted polyline:

1. Undo the straightened segment from the previous exercise.

2. Restart the Edit Vertex option, and position the X on the vertex you want to alter.

3. Enter **T↵** for the Tangent option. A rubber-banding line appears. (See the top image in Figure 19.15.)

4. Point the rubber-banding line in the direction of the new tangent, and click the mouse. An arrow appears, indicating the new tangent direction. (See the second image in Figure 19.15.)

Don't worry if the polyline shape doesn't change. You must use Fit to see the effect of Tangent. (See the final image in Figure 19.15.)

The Width Option

Finally, you'll try the Width option. Unlike the Pedit command's Width option, the Edit Vertex/ Width option enables you to alter the width of the polyline at any vertex. Thus you can taper or otherwise vary polyline thicknesses. Try these steps:

1. Undo the tangent arc from the previous exercise.

2. Return to the Edit Vertex option, and place the X at the beginning vertex of a polyline segment you want to change.

3. Type **W↵** to issue the Width option.

4. At the `Specify starting width for next segment <0.0000>:` prompt, enter a value—**12↵**, for example—indicating the polyline width desired at this vertex.

5. At the `Specify ending width for next segment <12.0000>:` prompt, enter the width—**24↵**, for example—for the next vertex.

The width of the polyline changes to your specifications (see Figure 19.16).

FIGURE 19.15
Picking a new tangent direction

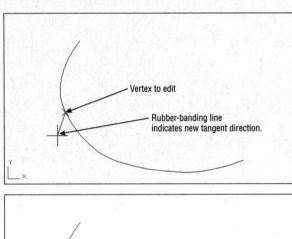

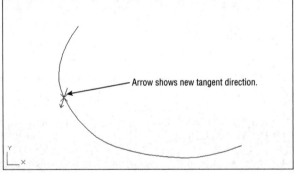

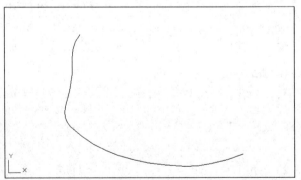

The Width option is useful when you want to create an irregular or curved area in your drawing that is to be filled in solid. This is another option that is sensitive to the polyline direction.

FIGURE 19.16
A polyline with the
width of one seg-
ment increased

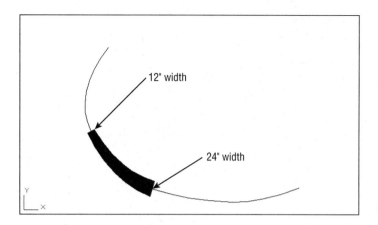

As you've seen throughout these exercises, you can use the Undo option to reverse the last Edit Vertex option used. You can also use the Exit option to leave Edit Vertex at any time. Enter **X**↵ to display the Pedit prompt:

```
Enter an option
[Close/Join/Width/Edit vertex/Fit/Spline/Decurve/Ltype gen/Reverse/Undo]:
```

FILLING IN SOLID AREAS

You've learned how to create a solid area by increasing the width of a polyline segment. But suppose you want to create a solid shape or a thick line. AutoCAD provides the Solid, Trace, and Donut commands to help you draw simple filled areas. The Trace command acts just like the Line command (with the added feature of allowing you to draw wide line segments). Solid lets you create solid filled areas with straight sides, and Donut draws circles with a solid width.

You can create free-form, solid-filled areas by using the Solid hatch pattern. Create an enclosed area by using any set of objects, and then use the Hatch tool to apply a solid hatch pattern to the area. See Chapter 7 for details on using the Hatch tool.

Creating a Polyline Spline Curve

The Pedit command's Spline option (named after the spline tool used in manual drafting) offers you a way to draw smoother and more controllable curves than those produced by the Fit option. A polyline spline doesn't pass through the vertex points as a fitted curve does. Instead, the vertex points act as weights pulling the curve in their direction. These "weighted" vertex points are called *control vertices*. The polyline spline touches only its beginning and end vertices. Figure 19.17 illustrates this concept.

A polyline spline curve doesn't represent a mathematically true curve. See the next section, "Using True Spline Curves," to learn how to draw a more accurate spline curve.

FIGURE 19.17
The polyline
spline curve
pulled toward its
control vertices

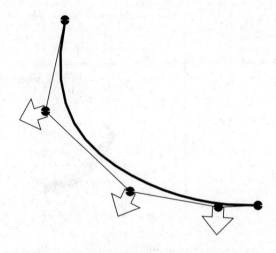

Let's see how using a polyline spline curve may influence the way you edit a curve:

1. Undo the width changes you made in the previous exercise.

2. To change the contour into a polyline spline curve, double-click the polyline to be curved.

3. At the `Enter an option [Close/Join/Width/Edit vertex/Fit/Spline/Decurve/` `Ltype gen/Reverse/Undo]:` prompt, enter **S↵**. Your curve changes to look like Figure 19.18.

4. Press ↵ to exit Edit Polyline.

FIGURE 19.18
A spline curve

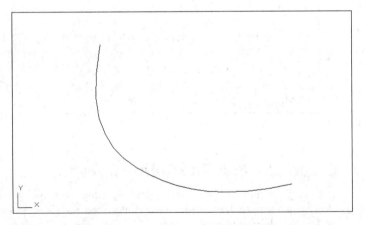

The curve takes on a smoother, more graceful appearance. It no longer passes through the points you used to define it. To see where the points went and to find out how spline curves act, do the following:

1. Click the curve. The original vertices appear as grips. (See the first image in Figure 19.19.)

2. Click the grip that is second from the top of the curve, as shown in the first image in Figure 19.19, and move the grip around. The curve follows your moves, giving you immediate feedback on how it will look.

3. Pick a point as shown in the second image in Figure 19.19. The curve is now fixed in its new position, as shown in the bottom image of Figure 19.19.

FIGURE 19.19
The fitted curve changed to a spline curve, with the location of the second vertex and the new curve

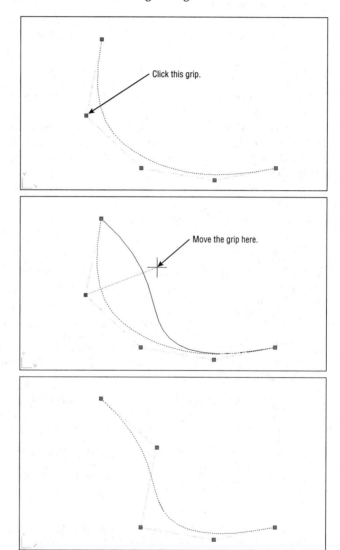

Click this grip.

Move the grip here.

DISPLAYING THE CURVE FRAME

You can set up AutoCAD to display both the curved and the straight segments defining the curve by turning on the Splframe system variable. Enter **splframe.⏎1⏎**, and then issue a Regen command. You'll see a frame that connects the grips of the curve. To turn off the display of the straight segments, enter **splframe.⏎0⏎**.

Using True Spline Curves

So far, you've been working with polylines to generate spline curves. The advantage of using polylines for curves is that they can be enhanced in many ways. You can modify their width, for instance, or join several curves. But at times, you'll need a more exact representation of a curve.

The spline object, created by choosing the Spline tool in the Home tab's expanded Draw panel, produces a more accurate model of a spline curve in addition to giving you more control over its shape.

The spline objects are true *Non-Uniform Rational B-Spline (NURBS)* curves. A full description of NURBS is beyond the scope of this book, but basically, NURBS are standard mathematical forms used to represent shapes.

Drawing a True Spline

The following steps describe the process used to create a spline curve. You don't have to create them now. Make a note of this section, and refer to it when you need to draw and edit a spline. Here are the steps:

1. Choose the Spline tool from the expanded Draw panel, or type **Spl⏎**.

2. At the Specify first point or [Method/Knots/Object]: prompt, select a point to start the curve. (See Figure 19.20.) The prompt changes to Enter next point or [start Tangency/toLerance]:.

3. Continue to select points until you've entered all the points you need. As you pick points, a curve appears, and it bends and flows as you move your cursor. In Figure 19.20, a Center object snap was used to select the donuts that appear as dots in the survey plan.

4. After you've selected the last point, press ⏎ to exit the Spline command.

If you prefer, you can also control the tangency of the spline at its first and last points. The following steps describe how the Tangency option can be used:

1. Start the spline just as before, and select the start point. At the Enter next point or [start Tangency/toLerance]: prompt, type **T⏎**.

2. The prompt changes to Specify start tangent:. Also, a rubber-banding line appears from the first point of the curve to the cursor. Select a point indicating the tangency of the first point.

3. Continue to select the other points of your spline. After you've selected the last point, type **T↵**.

4. Use the cursor to indicate the tangency of the spline at the last point.

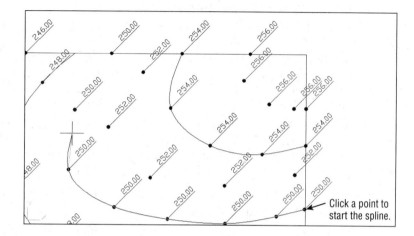

FIGURE 19.20
Start the spline curve at the first data point and then continue to select points.

You now have a smooth curve that passes through the points you selected. These points are called the *fit points*. If you click the curve, you'll see the grips appear at the location of these fit points, and you can adjust the curve by clicking the grip points and moving them. You'll also see an arrowhead grip that appears at the beginning of the spline. If you click this arrowhead grip, you see two options: Show Fit Points and Show Control Vertices (Figure 19.21).

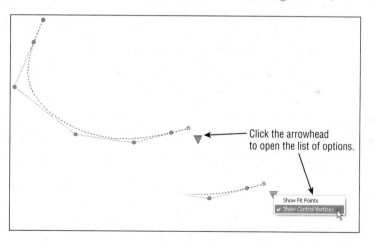

FIGURE 19.21
The Show Fit Points and Show Control Vertices options.

The Show Fit Points option will display the grips at the fit points, which are the points you used to draw the spline in the previous example. By default, these fit points lie on the spline, though you can adjust how close the spline follows the fit points. You can also view the control vertices, or CVs for short, which are points that control the curvature of the spline and do not lie on the spline itself (see Figure 19.17). Along with the control vertices, you see a set of vectors called the control polyline. The control polyline helps you visualize the relationship between the CVs and the spline.

Understanding the Spline Options

You may have noticed a few other options in the first Spline command prompt. When you start the Spline command, you see the Method, Knots, Degree, and Object options:

Method   Method lets you choose between Fit and CV. The Fit option causes the spline to be drawn through the lines you select. The CV, or Control Vertices, option causes the spline to use your selected points as control vertices (see Figure 19.17). Once you've drawn a spline, you can switch between fit and CV views of your polyline (Figure 19.21).

Knots   This option is available only if Fit is chosen in the Method option discussed previously. This option offers three additional options: Chord, Square Root, and Uniform, which affect the shape of the spline as it passes through the fit point.

>   **Chord**   The Chord option numbers the knots with decimal values.

>   **Square Root**   The Square Root option numbers them based on the square root of the chord length between consecutive knots.

>   **Uniform**   The Uniform option numbers the knots in consecutive integers.

Degree   This option is available only if CV is chosen in the Method option discussed previously. The Degree option gives you control over the number of control vectors required to create a bend in the spline. You can use the value 1, 2, or 3. The 1 value will cause the spline to produce straight lines, 2 will generate sharp curves, and 3 will generate less-sharp curves. In simple terms, the Degree value controls how closely the spline follows its control polyline.

Object   Object lets you convert a polyline into a spline. If the Fit option is selected under the Method option, you can convert only a spline-fitted polyline. If the CV option is selected under the Method option, you can select any polyline. With the CV Method option, the polyline will change shape so that the polyline vectors become control vectors.

Once you start to select points for the spline, you see the end Tangency, toLerance, Undo, and Close options. Table 19.1 describes these options.

TABLE 19.1:   The Spline command options for selecting points

OPTION	FUNCTION
end Tangency	Gives you control over the tangency at the beginning and end points of the spline.
toLerance	Lets you control how the curve passes through the fit points. The default value of 0 causes the curve to pass through the fit points. Any value greater than 0 causes the curve to pass close to, but not through, the points.
Undo	Lets you undo a point selection in case you select the wrong point.
Close	Lets you close the curve into a loop. If you choose this option, you're prompted to indicate a tangent direction for the closing point.

JOINING SPLINES TO OTHER OBJECTS

While editing drawings, you may encounter a situation where a spline has been broken into two splines and you need the broken spline to behave as a single spline. The Join command will "mend" a broken spline, or any set of splines for that matter, as long as the splines are contiguous (touching end to end). To use the Join command, click the Join tool from the Home tab's expanded Modify panel or type **Join**↵. Select the first spline, then select the splines you want to join to the first.

Join can be used with other objects as well. You can join lines, polylines, 3D polylines, arcs, elliptical arcs, and Helixes with the following restrictions:

◆ Any of these objects can be joined to a spline, polyline, 3D polyline, or helix.

◆ Lines cannot be joined to arcs or elliptical arcs.

◆ Arcs cannot be joined to elliptical arcs.

◆ Arcs must have the same center point and radius but can have a gap between the segments you wish to join. The same is true for elliptical arcs.

◆ Lines must be collinear but can have gaps between the lines to be joined.

◆ Unless you are joining to a polyline or 3D polyline, objects must be on the same plane.

Fine-Tuning Spline Curves

Spline curves are different from other types of objects, and many of the standard editing commands won't work on splines. AutoCAD offers the Edit Spline option, otherwise known as the Splinedit command, in the Home tab's expanded Modify panel for making changes to splines.

CONTROLLING THE FIT DATA OF A SPLINE

The Fit Data option of the Splinedit command lets you adjust the tangency of the beginning and endpoints, add new control points, and adjust spline tolerance settings. To get to these options, follow these steps:

1. Choose Edit Spline from the expanded Modify panel, or type **Spe**↵ at the Command prompt.

2. At the `Select spline:` prompt, select the last spline you drew in the previous exercise.

3. At the `Enter an option [Close/Join/Fit data/Edit vertex/convert to Polyline/Reverse/Undo/eXit]:` prompt, type **F**↵ to select the Fit Data option.

4. At the `[Add/Close/Delete/Move/Purge/Tangents/toLerance/eXit] <eXit>:` prompt, enter the option you want to use. For example, to change the tangency of the first and last points of your spline, type **t**↵. You're prompted to select the tangent point of the first and last points. Table 19.2 lists the Splinedit Fit Data options and what they're for.

If you prefer, you can double-click on a spline to start the Splinedit command instead of selecting the Edit Spline tool in the Modify panel. If you have the Dynamic Input feature turned on, you can select Splinedit options from a menu that appears at the cursor (Figure 19.22) instead of typing in the option keyboard shortcuts.

TABLE 19.2:   The Fit Data options of the Splinedit command

OPTION	FUNCTION
Add	Lets you add more control points
Close	Lets you close the spline into a loop
Delete	Removes a control point from the spline
Move	Lets you move a control point
Purge	Deletes the fit data of the spline, thereby eliminating the Fit Data option for the purged spline
Tangents	Lets you change the tangency of the first and last points
toLerance	Controls the distance between the spline and a control point
eXit	Exits the Splinedit command

FIGURE 19.22
The Splinedit
options

USING GRIP OPTIONS

The Splinedit command gives you a lot of control when you want to edit a spline. But if you want to make some minor changes, you can use the shortcut menu that appears when you hover over a grip on the spline. First, click on the spline to expose its grips, then hover over a fit point or CV. The list of options appears.

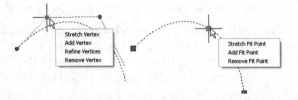

The options are slightly different depending on whether you have the fit points or CVs displayed. The options enable you to quickly add or remove a fit point or CV, and in the case of CVs, you also have the Refine Vertices option. The Refine option lets you control the pull exerted on a spline by a CV.

WHEN CAN'T YOU USE FIT DATA?

The Fit Data option of the Splinedit command offers many ways to edit a spline. However, this option isn't available to all spline curves. When you invoke certain other Splinedit options, a spline curve loses its fit data, thereby disabling the Fit Data option. These operations are as follows:

♦ Fitting a spline to a tolerance (Spline ➢ toLerance) and moving its control vertices.

♦ Fitting a spline to a tolerance (Spline ➢ toLolerance) and opening or closing it.

♦ Refining the spline.

♦ Purging the spline of its fit data by using the Purge option of the Splinedit command. (Choose Edit Spline from the expanded Modify panel, or enter **Splinedit↵**, and then select the spline and enter **F↵P↵**.)

Also note that the Fit Data option isn't available when you edit spline curves that were created from polyline splines. See the sidebar "Turning Objects into Polylines and Polylines into Splines" earlier in this chapter.

If you'd like to learn more about the Splinedit options, check the AutoCAD Help website. It offers a detailed description of how these options work.

CONVERT A SPLINE INTO A POLYLINE

AutoCAD 2011 allows you to convert a spline object into a polyline. This can be very useful when you want to edit a spline using the polyline edit tools instead of the spline editing tools. You will lose some precision in the conversion, but more often than not, this is not an issue.

To convert a spline to a polyline, double-click the spline, and then at the Enter an option prompt, type **P↵**. At the Specify a precision <10>: prompt, enter a value from 0 to 99. Note that a higher precision value may reduce the performance of AutoCAD, so use a reasonable value. You may want to experiment with different values and pick the lowest value that will still give you the results you want.

Marking Divisions on Curves

Perhaps one of the most difficult things to do in manual drafting is to mark regular intervals on a curve. AutoCAD offers the Divide and Measure commands to help you perform this task with speed and accuracy.

You can find the Divide and Measure tools on the expanded Draw Ribbon panel, as shown in Figure 19.23. Click the title bar of the Draw panel, and then click the flyout arrowhead shown next to the Point tool to open the flyout.

The Divide and Measure commands are discussed here in conjunction with polylines, but you can use these commands on any object except blocks and text.

FIGURE 19.23
The Divide and Measure tools are in the expanded Draw Ribbon panel on the Point tool flyout.

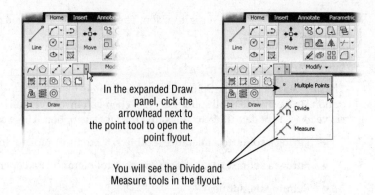

In the expanded Draw panel, cick the arrowhead next to the point tool to open the point flyout.

You will see the Divide and Measure tools in the flyout.

Dividing Objects into Segments of Equal Length

Use the Divide command to divide an object into a specific number of equal segments. For example, suppose you need to mark off the contour you've been working on in this chapter into nine equal segments. One way to do this is to first find the length of the contour by using the List command and then sit down with a pencil and paper to figure out the exact distances between the marks. But there is another, easier way.

The Divide command places a set of point objects on a line, an arc, a circle, or a polyline, marking off exact divisions. The following exercise shows how it works:

1. Open the 19a-divd.dwg file. This file is similar to the one you've been working with in the previous exercises.

2. Click the Point flyout in the expanded Draw panel and select Divide, or type **Div**↵

3. At the Select object to divide: prompt, pick the spline contour line that shows Xs in Figure 19.24.

4. The Enter the number of segments or [Block]: prompt that appears next is asking for the number of divisions you want on the selected object. Enter **9**↵.

The Command prompt returns, and it appears that nothing has happened. But AutoCAD has placed several point objects on the contour that indicate the locations of the nine divisions you requested. To see these points more clearly, continue with the exercise.

FIGURE 19.24
Using the Divide command on a polyline

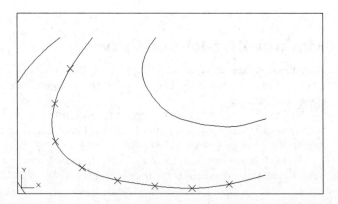

5. Choose Point Style from the Home tab's Utilities panel or type **DDPTYPE**↵ to open the Point Style dialog box (Figure 19.25).

6. Click the X point style at the upper-right corner of the dialog box, click the Set Size Relative To Screen radio button, and then click OK.

7. If the Xs don't appear, enter **Re**↵. A set of Xs appears, showing the nine divisions (shown earlier in Figure 19.24).

You can also change the point style by changing the Pdmode system variable. When Pdmode is set to 3, the point appears as an X.

The Divide command uses *point* objects to indicate the division points. You create point objects by using the Point command. They usually appear as dots. Unfortunately, such points are nearly invisible when placed on top of other objects. But, as you've seen, you can alter their shape by using the Point Style dialog box. You can use these X points to place objects or references to break the object being divided. (The Divide command doesn't cut the object into smaller divisions.)

FINDING HIDDEN NODE POINTS

If you're in a hurry and you don't want to bother changing the shape of the point objects, you can do the following: Set Running Osnaps to Node. Then, when you're in Point Selection mode, move the cursor over the divided curve. When the cursor gets close to a point object, the Node Osnap marker appears.

SKETCHING WITH AUTOCAD

AutoCAD offers the Sketch command, which lets you do freehand drawing. The Sketch command can be set to draw polylines. If you'd like to know more about Sketch, the AutoCAD Help window offers an excellent description of how it works. Click the Help tool (question mark icon) in the InfoCenter, and then on the AutoCAD 2011 Help website, expand the Command Reference listing to Commands ➢ S Commands ➢ Sketch.

FIGURE 19.25
The Point Style
dialog box

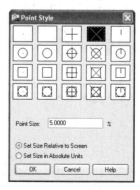

Dividing Objects into Specified Lengths

The Measure command acts just like Divide. However, instead of dividing an object into segments of equal length, the Measure command marks intervals of a specified distance along an object. For example, suppose you need to mark some segments exactly 5″ apart along the contour. Try the following exercise to see how the Measure command is used to accomplish this task:

1. Erase the X-shaped point objects.

2. Click Measure from the Point flyout in the expanded Draw panel, or type **Me**↵.

3. At the `Select object to measure:` prompt, pick the contour at a point closest to its lower endpoint. I'll explain shortly why this is important.

4. At the `Specify length of segment or [Block]:` prompt, enter **60**↵. The X points appear at the specified distance.

5. Exit without saving this file.

Bear in mind that the point you pick on the object to be measured determines where the Measure command begins measuring. In the previous exercise, for example, you picked the contour near its bottom endpoint. If you picked the top of the contour, the results would be different because the measurement would start at the top, not the bottom.

MARKING OFF INTERVALS BY USING BLOCKS INSTEAD OF POINTS

You can also use the Block option under the Divide and Measure commands to place blocks at regular intervals along a line, a polyline, or an arc. Here's how to use blocks as markers:

1. Be sure the block you want to use is part of the current drawing file.

2. Start either the Divide or Measure command.

3. At the `Specify length of segment or [Block]:` prompt, enter **B**↵.

4. At the `Enter name of block to insert:` prompt, enter the name of a block.

5. At the `Align Block with Object? [Yes/No] <Y>:` prompt, press ↵ if you want the blocks to follow the alignment of the selected object. (Entering **N**↵ inserts each block at a 0 angle.)

6. At the `Enter the number of segments:` prompt, or the `Specify length of segment:` prompt, enter the number or length of the segments. The blocks appear at regular intervals on the selected object.

One example of using the Block option of Divide or Measure is to place a row of sinks equally spaced along a wall. Alternatively, you might use this technique to make multiple copies of an object along an irregular path defined by a polyline. In civil-engineering projects, you can indicate a fence line by using Divide or Measure to place Xs along a polyline.

The Bottom Line

Create and edit polylines.   Polylines are extremely versatile. You can use them in just about any situation where you need to draw line work that is continuous. For this reason, you'll want to master polylines early in your AutoCAD training.

Master It   Draw the part shown here.

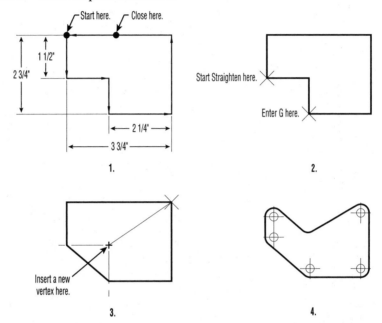

Create a polyline spline curve.   Polylines can be used to draw fairly accurate renditions of spline curves. This feature of polylines make them a very useful AutoCAD object.

Master It   Try drawing the outline of an object that has no or few straight lines in it, as in the file lowerfairing.jpg, which is included in the Chapter 19 sample files. You can use the methods described in Chapter 14 to import a raster image of your object and then trace over the image using polyline splines.

Create and edit true spline curves.   If you need an accurate spline curve, you'll want to use the Spline tool. Spline objects offer many more fine-tuning options that you won't find with polylines.

Master It   Try tracing over the same image from the previous Master It section, but this time use the Spline tool.

Mark divisions on curves.   The Divide and Measure tools offer a quick way to mark off distances on a curved object. This can be a powerful resource in AutoCAD that you may find yourself using often.

Master It   Mark off 12 equal divisions of the spline curves you drew in the previous Master It exercise.

Chapter 20

Getting and Exchanging Data from Drawings

AutoCAD drawings contain a wealth of data—graphic information such as distances and angles between objects as well as precise areas and the properties of objects. However, as you become more experienced with AutoCAD, you'll also need data of a different nature. For example, as you begin to work in groups, the various settings in a drawing become important. You'll need statistics on the amount of time you spend on a drawing when you're billing computer time. As your projects become more complex, file maintenance requires a greater degree of attention. To take full advantage of AutoCAD, you'll want to exchange information about your drawing with other people and other programs.

In this chapter, you'll explore the ways in which all types of data can be extracted from AutoCAD and made available to you, your coworkers, and other programs. First you'll learn how to obtain specific data about your drawings. Then you'll look at ways to exchange data with other programs—such as word processors, desktop-publishing software, and even other CAD programs.

In this chapter, you'll learn to do the following:

- ◆ Find the area of closed boundaries
- ◆ Get general information
- ◆ Use the DXF file format to exchange CAD data with other programs
- ◆ Use AutoCAD drawings in page-layout programs
- ◆ Use OLE to import data

Finding the Area of Closed Boundaries

One of the most frequently sought pieces of data you can extract from an AutoCAD drawing is the area of a closed boundary. In architecture, you want to find the area of a room or the footprint of a building. In civil engineering, you want to determine the area covered by the boundary of a property line or the area of cut for a roadway. In the following sections, you'll learn how to use AutoCAD to obtain exact area information from your drawings.

Finding the Area of an Object

Architects, engineers, and facilities planners often need to know the square footage of a room or a section of a building. A structural engineer might want to find the cross-sectional area of a beam. In this section, you'll practice determining the areas of regular objects.

First you'll determine the square-foot area of the living room and entry of your studio unit plan:

1. Start AutoCAD. Open the Unit file you created earlier, or use the 20a-unit.dwg file.

2. Zoom in to the living room and entry area so you have a view similar to Figure 20.1.

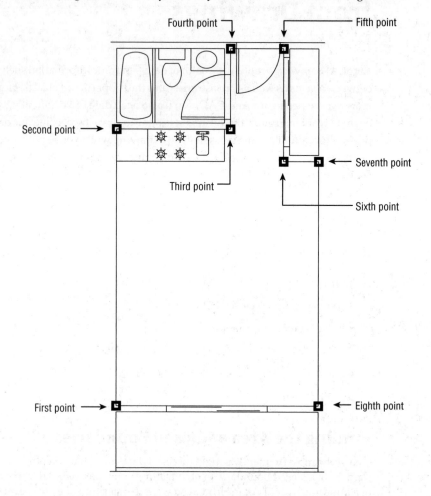

FIGURE 20.1
Selecting the points to determine the area of the living room and entry

Area

3. On the Home tab's Utilities panel, click the Area tool on the Measure flyout, or type **Mea↵Ar↵** at the Command prompt. This starts the Measuregeom command.

4. Using the Endpoint osnap, start with the lower-left corner of the living room and select the points shown in Figure 20.1. You're indicating the boundary. Notice that as you click points, the area being calculated is indicated in green.

5. When you've come full circle to the eighth point shown in Figure 20.1, press ↵. You get the following message:

```
Total area = 39570.00 square in. (274.7917 square ft), Perimeter = 76'-0"
```

6. Type **X**↵ to exit the Measuregeom command.

The number of points you can pick to define an area is limitless, so you can obtain the areas of complex shapes. Use the Blipmode feature to keep track of the points you select so you know when you come to the beginning of the point selections. Blipmode places tiny Xs or blips on the screen each time you click a point. These blips are just visual aids and can be removed with a redraw or regen of the screen.

FIND THE COORDINATE OF A POINT OR A DISTANCE IN A DRAWING

To find absolute coordinates in a drawing, use the ID command. Click the ID Point tool on the Home tab's expanded Utilities panel, or type **ID**↵. At the `Specify point:` prompt, use the Osnap overrides to pick a point; its X, Y, and Z coordinates are displayed on the prompt line.

To find the distance between two points, choose Distance from the Measure flyout on the Home tab's Utilities panel, or type **Dist**↵, and then click two points. AutoCAD will display the distance in the drawing as Delta X, Delta Y, and Delta Z coordinates and as a direct distance between the selected points. The distance is also displayed in the Command prompt.

Using Hatch Patterns to Find Areas

Hatch patterns are used primarily to add graphics to your drawing, but they can also serve as a means for finding areas. You can use any hatch pattern you want because you're interested in only the area it reports back to you. You can also set up a special layer devoted to area calculations and then add the hatch patterns you use to find areas to this layer. That way, you can turn off the hatch patterns so they don't plot, or you can turn off the Plot setting for that layer to ensure that it doesn't appear in your final output.

To practice using hatch patterns to find an area, do the following:

1. Set the current layer to Floor.

2. Turn off the Door and Fixture layers. Also make sure the Ceiling layer is turned on. You want the hatch pattern to follow the interior wall outline, so you need to turn off any objects that will affect the outline, such as the door and kitchen.

3. Click Hatch on the Home tab's Draw panel or type **h**↵ to open the Hatch Creation tab.

MEASURING BOUNDARIES THAT HAVE GAPS

If the area you're trying to measure has gaps, set the Gap Tolerance setting in the Hatch And Gradient dialog box to a value higher than the size of the gaps. If you don't see the Gap Tolerance setting, click the More Options button in the lower-right corner of the Hatch And Gradient dialog box.

---

4. At the `Pick internal point or [Select objects/seTtings]:` prompt, click in the interior of the unit plan. The outline of the interior is highlighted and you see a preview of the pattern. (see Figure 20.2).

FIGURE 20.2
After you click a point on the interior of the plan to place a hatch pattern, an outline of the area is highlighted by a dotted line and a preview of the hatch appears.

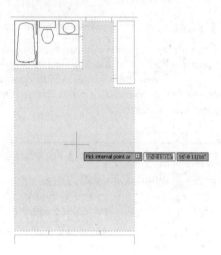

5. Press ↵ to complete the hatch..

6. On the Home tab's Utilities panel, click the Area tool on the Measure flyout and then type **O↵**, or type **Mea↵ Ar↵ O↵** at the Command prompt.

7. Click the hatch pattern you just created. Again, you get the following message:

`Total area = 39570.00 square in. (274.7917 square ft), Perimeter = 76'-0"`

8. Press **X↵** to exit the command.

If you need to recall the last area calculation value you received, enter ´**Setvar↵Area↵**. The area is displayed in the prompt. Enter ´**Perimeter.↵** to get the last perimeter calculated.

The Hatch command creates a hatch pattern that conforms to the boundary of an area. This feature, combined with the ability of the Measuregeom command to find the area of a hatch pattern, makes short work of area calculations. Another advantage of using hatch patterns is that, by default, hatch patterns avoid islands within the boundary of the area you're trying to find.

The area of a hatch pattern is also reported by the Properties palette. Select the hatch pattern whose area you want to find, and then right-click and select Properties. Scroll down to the bottom of the Geometry group and you'll see the Area listing for the hatch pattern you selected. You can select more than one hatch pattern and find the cumulative area of the selected hatch patterns in the Properties palette.

Adding and Subtracting Areas with the Area Command

Hatch patterns work extremely well for finding areas, but if you find that for some reason you can't use hatch patterns, you have another alternative. You can still use a command called Boundary to generate a polyline outline of an enclosed boundary and then obtain the area of the outline using the Measuregeom command (Measure on the Home tab's Utilities panel). If islands are present within the boundary, you have to use the Subtract feature of the Measuregeom command to remove the area of the island from the overall boundary area. In this section, you'll use the example of the flange part, which contains two islands in the form of the two circles at the lower end (see Figure 20.3).

FIGURE 20.3
A flange to a mechanical device

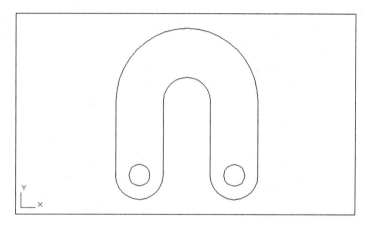

By using the Add and Subtract options of the Measuregeom command, you can maintain a running total of several separate areas being calculated. This gives you flexibility in finding areas of complex shapes. This section guides you through the use of these options.

For the following exercise, you'll use a flange shape that contains circles. This shape is composed of simple arcs, lines, and circles. Use these steps to see how you can keep a running tally of areas:

1. Exit the Unit file, and open the file Flange.dwg (see Figure 20.3). Don't bother to save changes in the Unit file.

2. Click Boundary from the Home tab's expanded Draw panel or type **Bo↵** to open the Boundary Creation dialog box (Figure 20.4).

FIGURE 20.4
The Boundary Creation dialog

3. Click Pick Points.

4. Click in the interior of the flange shape. The entire shape is highlighted, including the circle islands.

5. Press ⏎. You now have a polyline outline of the shape and the circles, although it won't be obvious that polylines have been created because they're drawn over the boundary objects.

6. Continue by using the Measuregeom command's Add and Subtract options. Click Area from the Measure flyout on the Home tab's Utilities panel.

7. Type **A**⏎ to enter Add area mode, and then type **O**⏎ to select an object.

8. Click a vertical edge of the flange outline. You see the selected area highlighted in green, and the following message appears in the Command window:

```
Area = 27.7080, Perimeter = 30.8496
Total area = 27.7080
```

9. Press ⏎ to exit Add area mode.

10. Type **S**⏎ to enter Subtract area mode, and then type **O**⏎ to select an object.

11. Click one of the circles. You see the following message:

```
Total area = 0.6070, Circumference = 2.7618
Total area = 27.1010
```

This shows you the area and perimeter of the selected object and a running count of the total area of the flange outline minus the circle. You also see the area of the subtracted circle change to a different color so you can differentiate between the calculated area and the subtracted area.

12. Click the other circle. You see the following message:

```
Total area = 0.6070, Perimeter = 2.7618
Total area = 26.4940
```

Again, you see a listing of the area and perimeter of the selected object along with a running count of the total area, which now shows a value of 26.4940. This last value is the true area of the flange.

13. Press ⏎ and type **X**⏎ **X**⏎ to exit the Measuregeom command. You can also press the Esc key to exit the command.

In this exercise, you first selected the main object outline and then subtracted the island objects. You don't have to follow this order; you can start by subtracting areas to get negative area values and then add other areas to come up with a total. You can also alternate between Add and Subtract modes, in case you forget to add or subtract areas.

You may have noticed that the Measuregeom Command prompt offered Specify first corner point or [Object/Add area/Subtract area/eXit]: as the default option for both the Add area and Subtract area modes. Instead of using the Object option to pick the circles, you can start selecting points to indicate a rectangular area, as you did in the first exercise in this chapter.

Whenever you press ⏎ while selecting points for an area calculation, AutoCAD automatically connects the first and last points and returns the calculated area. If you're in Add or Subtract mode, you can then continue to select points, but the additional areas are calculated from the *next* point you pick.

As you can see from these exercises, it's simpler to outline an area first with a polyline wherever possible and then use the Object option to add and subtract area values of polylines.

In this example, you obtained the area of a mechanical object. However, the same process works for any type of area you want to calculate. It can be the area of a piece of property on a topographical map or the area of a floor plan. For example, you can use the Object option to find an irregular shape such as the one shown in Figure 20.5, as long as it's a closed polyline.

FIGURE 20.5
The site plan
with an area to
be calculated

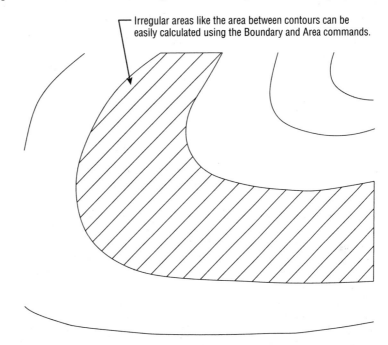

Irregular areas like the area between contours can be easily calculated using the Boundary and Area commands.

When issued through the keyboard as **Mea↵**, the Measuregeom command offers a number of other options for measuring your drawing. The options appear in the Command window as [Distance/Radius/Angle/ARea/Volume/]<Distance> or at the cursor as a Dynamic Input option. These options are automatically selected when you click the related tool from the Measure flyout on the Utilities panel. Remember that to use an option, type the capitalized letter or letters of the option shown in the list. Table 20.1 gives you descriptions of the options and how they are used.

RECORDING AREA DATA IN A DRAWING FILE

In just about every project I've worked on, area calculations were an important part of the drawing process. As an aid in recoding area calculations, I created a block that contains attributes for the room number, the room area, and the date when the room area was last measured. The area and date attributes were made invisible so only the room number appears. The block with the attribute is then inserted into every room. Once the area of the room is discovered, it can be added to the block attribute with the Ddatte command. Such a block can be used with any drawing in which area data needs to be gathered and stored. See Chapter 13 for more on attributes. You can also use the Field object type to automatically display the area of a polyline as a text object. See Chapter 11 for more on fields.

TABLE 20.1:   The Measuregeom command options

OPTION	USE
Distance	Returns the distance between two points. Type **D**↵ and select two points. You can also measure cumulative distances by typing **M**↵ after selecting the first point.
Radius	Returns the radius of an arc or circle. Type **R**↵ and select an arc or circle.
Angle	Returns the angle of an arc or the angle between two lines. Type **A**↵ and select the arc or two nonparallel lines.
ARea	Returns the area of a set of points or boundary. Type **AR**↵ to use this option. See previous exercises for instruction on the use of this option.
Volume	Returns the 3D volume based on an area times height.
eXit	Exits the current option. You can also press the Esc key.

Getting General Information

So far in this book, you've seen how to get data about the geometry of your drawings. AutoCAD also includes a set of tools that you can use to access the general state of your drawings. You can gather information about the status of current settings in a file or the time at which a drawing was created and last edited.

In the following sections, you'll practice extracting this type of information from your drawing, using the tools found in the Tools tab's Inquiry panel.

Determining the Drawing's Status

When you work with a group of people on a large project, keeping track of a drawing's setup becomes crucial. You can use the Status command to obtain general information about the drawing you're working on, such as the base point, current mode settings, and workspace or computer memory use. The Status command is especially helpful when you're editing a drawing someone else has worked on because you may want to identify and change settings for your own style of working. Click Drawing Utilities ➤ Status from the Application menu to display a list like the one shown in Figure 20.6.

USE THE STATUS COMMAND TO GET YOUR BEARINGS

If you have problems editing a file created by someone else, the difficulty can often be attributed to a setting you aren't used to working with. If AutoCAD is acting in an unusual way, use the Status command to get a quick glimpse of the file settings before you start calling for help.

FIGURE 20.6

The Status screen of the AutoCAD Text Window

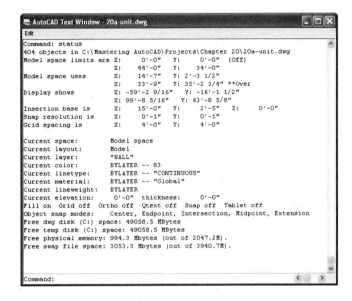

Here is a brief description of each item on the Status screen. Note that some of the items you see on the screen will vary somewhat from what I've shown here, but the information applies to virtually all situations except where noted:

Number **Objects In Drive:\Folder\Subfolder\Name.dwg**   The number of entities or objects in the drawing.

Model Space Limits Are   The coordinates of the Model Space limits. Also indicates whether limits are turned off or on. (See Chapter 3 for more details on limits.)

Model Space Uses   The area the drawing occupies; equivalent to the extents of the drawing.

**Over   If present, means that part of the drawing is outside the limit boundary.

Display Shows   The area covered by the current view.

Insertion Base Is, Snap Resolution Is, and Grid Spacing Is   The current default values for these mode settings.

Current Space   Model Space or Paper Space.

Current Layout   The current tab.

Current Layer   The current layer.

Current Color   The color assigned to new objects.

Current Linetype   The linetype assigned to new objects.

Current Material   The material assigned to new objects.

Current Lineweight   The current default line weight setting.

Current Elevation/Thickness   The current default Z coordinate for new objects, plus the default thickness of objects. These are both 3D-related settings. (See Chapter 21 for details.)

Fill, Grid, Ortho, Qtext, Snap, and Tablet The status of these options.

Object Snap Modes The current active Osnap setting.

Free Dwg Disk (*Drive***:) Space** The amount of space available to store drawing-specific temporary files.

Free Temp Disk (*Drive***:) Space** The amount of space left on your hard drive for AutoCAD's resource temporary files.

Free Physical Memory The amount of free RAM available.

Free Swap File Space The amount of Windows swap-file space available.

When you're in Paper Space, the Status command displays information regarding the Paper Space limits. See Chapter 16 for more on Model Space and Paper Space.

In addition to being useful in understanding a drawing file, the Status command is an invaluable tool for troubleshooting. Frequently, a technical support person can isolate problems by using the information provided by the Status command.

Keeping Track of Time

The Time command enables you to keep track of the time spent on a drawing for billing or analysis purposes. You can also use the Time command to check the current time and find out when the drawing was created and most recently edited. Because the AutoCAD timer uses your computer's time, be sure the time is set correctly in Windows.

To access the Time command, enter **Time↵** at the Command prompt. You get a message like the one in Figure 20.7.

FIGURE 20.7
The Time screen
in the AutoCAD
Text Window

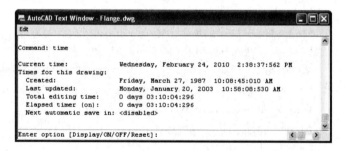

The first four lines of this message tell you the current date and time, the date and time the drawing was created, and the last time the drawing was saved.

The fifth line shows the total time spent on the drawing from the point at which the file was opened. This elapsed timer lets you time a particular activity, such as changing the width of all the walls in a floor plan or redesigning a piece of machinery. The last line tells you when the next automatic save will be.

You can turn the elapsed timer on or off or reset it by entering **ON**, **OFF**, or **Reset** at the prompt shown at the bottom of the message. Or press ↵ to exit the Time command.

Getting Information from System Variables

If you've been working through this book's ongoing studio apartment building tutorial, you'll have noticed that I've occasionally mentioned a *system variable* in conjunction with a command.

You can check the status or change the setting of any system variable while you're in the middle of another command. To do this, you type an apostrophe (´) followed by the name of the system variable at the Command prompt.

For example, if you start to draw a line and suddenly decide you need to restrict your cursor movement to 45°, you can do the following:

1. At the `Specify next point or [Undo]:` prompt, enter ´snapang.

2. At the `>>Enter new value for SNAPANG <0>:` prompt, enter a new cursor angle. You're returned to the Line command with the cursor in its new orientation.

You can also recall information such as the last area or distance calculated by AutoCAD. Type **Setvar↵Area↵** to read the last area calculation. The Setvar command also lets you list all the system variables and their status as well as access each system variable individually by entering ´**Setvar↵?↵**. You can then indicate which variables to list using wildcard characters such as the asterisk or question mark. For example, you can enter **g*** to list all the system variables that start with the letter *G*.

Many system variables give you direct access to detailed information about your drawing. They also let you fine-tune your drawing and editing activities. In Appendix D, you'll find all the information you need to familiarize yourself with the system variables. Don't feel that you have to memorize them all at once; just be aware that they're available.

Keeping a Log of Your Activity

At times, you may find it helpful to keep a log of your activity in an AutoCAD session. A *log* is a text file containing a record of your activities. It can also contain notes to yourself or others about how a drawing is set up. Such a log can help you determine how frequently you use a particular command, or it can help you construct a macro for a commonly used sequence of commands.

The following exercise demonstrates how to save and view a detailed record of an AutoCAD session by using the Log feature:

1. Choose Options from the Application menu to open the Options dialog box. Click the Open And Save tab. A new set of options appears.

2. In the File Safety Precautions group, click the Maintain A Log File check box and then click OK.

3. Type **Status↵** at the Command prompt.

4. Return to the Open And Save tab of the Options dialog box, and turn off the Maintain A Log File option.

5. Click OK to exit the dialog box.

6. Switch to Windows, and start the Notepad application or any text editor.

7. With the text editor, open the log file whose name starts with `Flange` in the folder listed here:

   `C:\Documents and Settings\`*User Name*`\Local Settings\Application Data\Autodesk\AutoCAD 2011\R18.1\enu\`

This file stores the text data from the Command prompt whenever the Log File option is turned on. You must turn off the Log File option before you can view this file. When you're attempting to view the log file using Windows Notepad, make sure you set File Of Type in the Notepad Open dialog box to All Files. Note that this location is usually a hidden one. See "Finding Hidden Folders That Contain AutoCAD Files" in Appendix B for more information.

As a shortcut, you can quickly turn the Maintain A Log File feature on and off by typing **Logfileon.**↵ and **Logfileoff.**↵, respectively, at the Command prompt. As you can see in step 7, the log file is given the name of the drawing file from which the log is derived, with some additional numeric values. Because the F1ange log file is a standard text file, you can easily send it to other members of your workgroup or print it for a permanent record.

FINDING THE LOG FILE

If you can't find the log file for the current drawing, you can enter **logfilename.**↵ at the Command prompt and AutoCAD will display the filename, including the full path. If you want to change the default location for the log file, open the Options dialog box and click the Files tab. Click the plus sign to the left of the Log File Location option in the list box. A listing appears showing you where the drawing log file is stored. You can then modify this setting to indicate a new location. LT users, enter **Modemacro.**↵ and then **$(getvar, logfilepath)**.

Capturing and Saving Text Data from the AutoCAD Text Window

If you're working in groups, it's often helpful to have a record of the status, editing time, and system variables for particular files readily available to other group members. It's also convenient to keep records of block and layer information so you can see whether a specific block is included in a drawing or what layers are normally on or off.

You can use the Windows Clipboard to capture and save such data from the AutoCAD Text Window. The following steps show you how it's done:

1. Move the arrow cursor to the Command prompt at the bottom of the AutoCAD Text Window.

2. Right-click and choose Copy History from the shortcut menu to copy the contents of the AutoCAD Text Window to the Clipboard.

If you want to copy only a portion of the AutoCAD Text Window to the Clipboard, perform the following steps:

1. Press the F2 function key to open the AutoCAD Text Window.

2. Using the I-beam text cursor, highlight the text you want to copy to the Clipboard.

3. Right-click and choose Copy from the shortcut menu. Or you can type Ctrl+C. The highlighted text is copied to the Clipboard.

4. Open Notepad or another text-editing application, and paste the information.

Although you used the AutoCAD Text Window to copy text in this exercise, you can also copy from the docked command line at the bottom of the AutoCAD window.

You may notice four other options on the shortcut menu: Recent Commands, Paste, Paste To CmdLine, and Options. Choosing Recent Commands displays a list of the most recent commands. For most activities, you'll use a handful of commands repeatedly; the Recent Commands option can save you time by giving you a shortcut to those commands you use the most. The Paste options paste the first line of the contents of the Clipboard into the command line or input box of a dialog box. This can be useful for entering repetitive text or for storing and retrieving a frequently used command. Choosing Options opens the Options dialog box.

Items copied to the Clipboard from the AutoCAD Text Window can be pasted into dialog box input boxes. This can be a quick way to transfer layers, linetypes, or other named items from the AutoCAD Text Window into dialog boxes. You can even paste text into the drawing area.

Storing Searchable Information in AutoCAD Files

As you start to build a library of AutoCAD files, you'll have to start thinking about how to manage them. Keeping track of AutoCAD files can be a daunting task. Most AutoCAD users start to name files by their job number to keep things organized. But even the best organization schemes don't help if you need to find that one special file among thousands of files in your library. In this section, you'll learn how to include information in an AutoCAD file that you can use later to locate the file by using the Windows Search utility.

AutoCAD includes the DesignCenter, a tool that can help you locate a file more easily based on a keyword or description. Chapter 29 contains a complete discussion of the DesignCenter.

To add general, searchable information about your drawing file, use the drawing's Properties dialog box (Figure 20.8; choose Drawing Utilities ➢ Drawing Properties from the Application menu).

FIGURE 20.8
A drawing's
properties

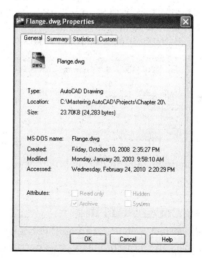

Here are descriptions of the four tabs in this dialog box:

General   The General tab gives you general information about the file. This information is similar to what you see if you use the Properties options in Windows Explorer to view the properties of a file.

Summary   In the Summary tab, enter any text in the Title, Subject, Author, and Keywords fields that is appropriate to the drawing. The information you enter here is stored with the drawing and can be used to locate the file through the AutoCAD DesignCenter or the Windows Search utility.

In addition, you can enter a base location for hyperlinks that are applied to objects in your drawing. This base location can be a folder on your computer or network or an Internet web address. See Chapter 29 for more information on hyperlinks.

Statistics   The Statistics tab contains the Windows username of the person who last saved the drawing as well as the time spent on the file. The username is the name used to log in at the beginning of the Windows session.

Custom   The Custom tab contains two columns of input boxes. This tab lets you store with the drawing additional custom data that is also searchable. For example, you might enter **Job Number** in the Name column and then enter **9901** in the Value column. You might also include information such as project manager names, consultants, or revision numbers. You can then locate the file by using the AutoCAD DesignCenter or the Windows Search utility and doing a search for those keywords from the Name and Value columns.

Searching for AutoCAD Files

After you've included information in a file's Properties dialog box, you can use the AutoCAD DesignCenter, the File dialog box, or the Windows Search function to locate your file.

A Find option is also located in the Tools menu in the upper-right corner of the AutoCAD Select File dialog box. To access it, click the Open tool from the Quick Access toolbar; then, in the Select File dialog box, choose Tools ➢ Find.

This option opens a Find dialog box that works just like the Windows XP Search Results window.

Recovering Corrupted Files

No system is perfect. Eventually, you'll encounter a file that is corrupted in some way. Two AutoCAD tools can frequently salvage a corrupted file:

Audit   Enables you to check a file that you can open but suspect has some problem. Audit checks the currently opened file for errors and displays the results in the AutoCAD Text Window.

Recover Enables you to open a file that is so badly corrupted that AutoCAD is unable to open it in a normal way. A Select File dialog box appears in which you select a file for recovery. After you select a file, it's opened and checked for errors.

You can access these tools from the Drawing Utilities option on the Application menu. More often than not, these tools will do the job, although they aren't a panacea for all file-corruption problems. In the event that you can't recover a file even with these tools, make sure your computer is running smoothly and that other systems aren't faulty.

If for some reason your computer shuts down while you're in the middle of editing a file, you'll see the Drawing Recovery Manager the next time you start AutoCAD. The Drawing Recovery Manager lets you recover the file you were working on when AutoCAD unexpectedly shut down. This feature works just like the file-recovery feature in Microsoft Office: A panel appears to the left of the AutoCAD Text Window showing you a list of recoverable files. You can then select the filename from the panel to open the file. You can find the Drawing Recovery Manager in the Application menu under Drawing Utilities ➢ Open The Drawing Recovery Manager.

Using the DXF File Format to Exchange CAD Data with Other Programs

AutoCAD offers many ways to share data with other programs. Perhaps the most common type of data exchange is to share drawing data with other CAD programs. In the following sections, you'll see how to export and import CAD drawings using the DXF file format.

A *Drawing Interchange Format (DXF) file* is a plain-text file that contains all the information needed to reconstruct a drawing. It's often used to exchange drawings created with other programs. Many CAD and technical drawing programs, including some 3D perspective programs, can generate or read files in DXF format. You might want to use a 3D program to view your drawing in a perspective view, or you might have a consultant who uses a different CAD program that accepts DXF files.

Be aware that not all programs that read DXF files accept all the data stored therein. Many programs that claim to read DXF files throw away much of the DXF files' information. Attributes are perhaps the most commonly ignored objects, followed by many of the 3D objects, such as meshes and 3D faces.

Exporting DXF Files

To export your current drawing as a DXF file, follow these steps:

1. Choose Save As from the Application menu to open the Save Drawing As dialog box.

2. Click the Files Of Type drop-down list. You can export your drawing under a number of formats, including five DXF formats.

3. Select the appropriate DXF format, and then enter a name for your file. You don't have to include the `.dxf` filename extension.

4. Select a folder for the file and click Save.

In step 3, you can select from the following DXF file formats:

◆ AutoCAD 2010 DXF

◆ AutoCAD 2007/LT 2007 DXF (AutoCAD 2007, 2008, and 2009 share file formats.)

◆ AutoCAD 2004/LT 2004 DXF

◆ AutoCAD 2000/LT 2000 DXF

◆ AutoCAD R12/LT2 DXF

Choose the format appropriate to the program you're exporting to. In most cases, the safest choice is AutoCAD R12/LT2 DXF if you're exporting to another CAD program, although AutoCAD won't maintain the complete functionality of AutoCAD 2011 for such files.

After you've selected a DXF format from the Files Of Type drop-down list, you can set more detailed specifications by choosing Tools ➤ Options in the upper-right corner of the Save Drawing As dialog box. Doing so opens the Saveas Options dialog box. For DXF files, select the DXF Options tab (Figure 20.9).

FIGURE 20.9
The DXF save-as options

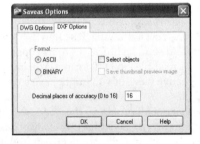

The DXF Options tab contains the following options:

Format   Lets you choose between ASCII (plain-text) and binary file formats. Most other programs accept ASCII, so it's the safest choice. Some programs accept binary DXF files, which have the advantage of being more compact than the ASCII format files.

Select Objects   Lets you select specific objects in the drawing for export. You can select objects after you close the Saveas Options dialog box and choose Save from the Save Drawing As dialog box.

Decimal Places Of Accuracy (0 To 16)   Enables you to determine the accuracy of the exported file. Keeping this value low helps reduce the size of the exported file, particularly if it's to be in ASCII format. Some CAD programs don't support AutoCAD's high accuracy, so using a high value here may have no significance.

In addition to using the Save Drawing As dialog box, you can type **Dxfout**↵ at the Command prompt to open the Save Drawing As dialog box. This is a standard Windows file dialog box that includes the Options button described in the next section.

Opening or Importing DXF Files

Some offices have made the DXF file format their standard for CAD drawings. This is most commonly seen in offices that use a variety of CAD software besides AutoCAD.

AutoCAD can be set up to read and write DXF files instead of the standard DWG file format by default. Here's how it's done:

1. Choose Options from the Application menu to open the Options dialog box.

2. Select the Open And Save tab.

3. In the File Save group, select any of the DXF formats from the Save As drop-down list.

4. Click OK.

After you do this, all your drawings are automatically saved in the DXF format of your choice.

You can also set the default AutoCAD file type by clicking the Tools button in the Save Drawing As dialog box and clicking Options. As you saw in the preceding section, the Saveas Options dialog box includes the DWG Options tab (Figure 20.10). You can select a default file type from the Save All Drawings As drop-down list.

FIGURE 20.10
The DWG
save-as options

If you need to open a DXF file only once in a while, you can do so by selecting DXF from the Files Of Type drop-down list in the Select File dialog box. This is the dialog box you see when you click Open from the Quick Access toolbar. You can also use the Dxfin command:

1. Type **Dxfin**↵ at the Command prompt to open the Select File dialog box.

2. Locate and select the DXF file you want to import.

3. Double-click the filename. If the drawing is large, the imported file may take several minutes to open.

If you want to import a DXF file into the current drawing, you can use the Insert dialog box. (Click Insert on the Home tab's Block panel.) Click the Browse button to locate and select a file. Make sure the Files Of Type option is set to DXF.

Using AutoCAD Drawings in Page-Layout Programs

As you probably know, AutoCAD is a natural for creating line art, and because of its popularity, most page-layout programs are designed to import AutoCAD drawings in one form or another.

Those of you who employ page-layout software to generate user manuals or other technical documents will probably want to use AutoCAD drawings in your work. In this section, you'll examine ways to output AutoCAD drawings to formats that most page-layout programs can accept.

You can export AutoCAD files to page-layout software formats in two ways: by using raster export and by using vector file export.

Exporting Raster Files

In some cases, you may need only a rough image of your AutoCAD drawing. You can export your drawing as a raster file that can be read in virtually any page-layout and word-processing program. To do this, you need to use the PublishToWebJPG.pc3 or PublishToWebPNG.pc3 printer option that comes with AutoCAD. To use it, do the following.

1. Click the Plot tool in the Quick Access toolbar.

2. In the Printer/Plotter group of the Plot dialog box, select PublishToWebJPG.pc3 or PublishToWebPNG.pc3 from the Name drop-down list.

3. The first time you use this printer option, you'll see the Plot – Paper Size Not Found dialog box. Select from the options presented in the dialog box.

4. Back in the Plot dialog box, you can select a size in pixels for your image file from the Paper Size drop-down list.

5. Click OK to create the image file.

6. In the Browse For Plot File dialog box, select a location for your file and click Save.

If you don't see a "paper size" you want to use, you can create a custom size using the Properties button in the Plot dialog box:

1. Follow the steps in the previous exercise, but at step 5, instead of clicking OK, click the Properties button to the right of the Printer/Plotter group's Name drop-down list. The Plotter Configuration Editor dialog box appears (see Figure 20.11).

2. Click Custom Paper Sizes in the large list box at the top of the dialog box. The options change in the lower half of the dialog box.

3. Click the Add button to start the Custom Paper Size Wizard.

4. Click the Start From Scratch radio button, and then click Next to open the Media Bounds screen.

5. Enter a height and width in pixels for your image file, and then click Next to open the Paper Size Name screen. Enter a name that best describes the size of the image file, and click Next to open the File Name screen.

6. Enter a name for the Plotter Model Parameters file. This file stores specific setting information about the plotter. Click Next when you're finished.

7. On the Finish screen, click Finish. The Plotter Configuration Editor dialog box reappears. Click OK.

FIGURE 20.11
Editing the plotter
configuration

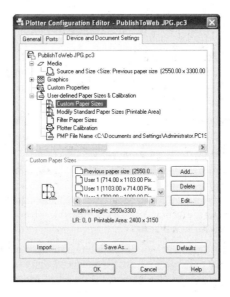

You can edit these settings at any time by opening the PC3 file in the `Application Data\` `Autodesk\AutoCAD 2011\R18.1\enu\Plotters` subfolder of your profile folder. You can access this file through Windows Explorer or from AutoCAD by clicking Plotter Manager from the Output tab's Plot panel.

FINDING THE *APPLICATION DATA* FOLDER

The `Application Data` folder is typically a hidden folder. To get to it, you have to turn off the "hide hidden folders" feature of Windows Explorer. See "Finding Hidden Folders That Contain AutoCAD Files" in Appendix B for more information.

To create a raster file version of your drawing, click Plot from the Quick Access toolbar. Then, in the Plot dialog box, select your raster file plotter configuration from the Name drop-down list of the Printer/Plotter group. You can then proceed to plot your drawing, but instead of paper output, you'll get a raster file. You can specify the filename and location when you click the OK button to plot the file.

If you need to make changes to your raster file configuration, click Plotter Manager from the Output tab's Plot panel. Then, in the Plotters window, double-click your raster file configuration file. You'll see the same Plotter Configuration Editor you used to set up the raster plotter configuration.

You can set up a different plotter configuration for each type of raster file you use. You can also set up plotter configurations for different resolutions if you choose. To learn more about plotting in general, see Chapter 8. Appendix C provides detailed information on the Plotter Configuration Editor.

EXCHANGING FILES WITH EARLIER RELEASES

One persistent dilemma that has plagued AutoCAD users is how to exchange files between earlier versions of the program. In the past, if you upgraded AutoCAD, you were locked out from exchanging your drawings with people using earlier versions. Release 12 alleviated this difficulty by making Release 12 files compatible with Release 11 files.

With Release 13, the file structure was radically different from the file structure in earlier versions of AutoCAD. Then, AutoCAD 14 made it possible to exchange files freely between Release 13 and 14.

AutoCAD 2002 uses the AutoCAD 2000 file format, which has some features, such as multiple layouts and searchable properties, that don't translate to earlier versions. AutoCAD 2006 and AutoCAD 2004 share the same file format, but AutoCAD 2006 has new features that make it incompatible with AutoCAD 2000 and 2002. AutoCAD 2007, 2008, and 2009 share the same file format, which is a unique file format that isn't compatible with earlier versions. AutoCAD 2011 uses the same file format as AutoCAD 2010.

If compatibility with earlier versions is more important than the new features of AutoCAD 2011, you can set up AutoCAD 2011 to read and write to AutoCAD 2007 or earlier. Or, if you're willing to work with DXF files, you can set up AutoCAD 2011 to automatically save drawings as AutoCAD 2007 DXF files.

To set up AutoCAD to save drawings in the format used by an earlier version automatically, use the Options dialog box to set the default file type, as described earlier in the section "Opening or Importing DXF Files." However, instead of selecting a DXF file type, select the DWG file type you want to use.

Another option is to use a separate program to "downgrade" drawings to earlier versions. Autodesk offers its DWG TrueView software as a free download. DWG TrueView will batch-convert 2011 files to earlier versions.

Exporting Vector Files

If you need to preserve the accuracy of your drawing, or if you want to take advantage of TrueType or PostScript fonts, you can use the DXF, Windows Metafile (WMF), or PostScript vector format. You can also export to DGN and SAT file formats. Intergraph's DGN format is popular in civil engineering, mapping, and other CAD applications. The SAT format is associated with ACIS and is a 3D modeling format.

For vector-format files, DXF is the easiest to work with, and with TrueType support, DXF can preserve font information between AutoCAD and page-layout programs that support the DXF format. The WMF format is also a commonly accepted file format for vector information, and it preserves TrueType fonts and line weights used in your drawings.

PostScript is a raster/vector hybrid file format that AutoCAD supports. Unfortunately, AutoCAD dropped direct PostScript font support with Release 14. However, you can still use substitute fonts to stand in for PostScript fonts. These substitute fonts are converted to true PostScript fonts when AutoCAD exports the drawing. You don't see the true results of your PostScript output until you print your drawing on a PostScript printer.

The DXF file export was covered in a previous section of this chapter, so the following sections will concentrate on the WMF and PostScript file formats.

WMF OUTPUT

The WMF file type is one of the more popular vector file formats in Windows. It can be opened and edited by most illustration programs, including CorelDRAW and Adobe Illustrator. Most word-processing, database, and worksheet programs can also import WMF files. It's a great option for AutoCAD file export because it preserves TrueType fonts and line-weight settings. You can export WMF files that preserve line weights as well.

To export WMF files, do the following:

1. Click Export ➢ Other Formats from the Application menu to open the Export Data dialog box.

2. Enter a name and location for your WMF file, select Metafile (*.wmf) from the File Of Type drop-down list, and then click Save. The dialog box closes, and you're prompted to select objects.

3. Select the objects you want to export to the WMF file and press ↵. The objects are saved to your WMF file.

POSTSCRIPT OUTPUT

AutoCAD can export to the Encapsulated PostScript (EPS) file format. If you're using AutoCAD 2011, you can obtain PostScript output in two ways: You can choose Export ➢ Other Formats from the Application menu, or you can enter **Psout**↵ at the Command prompt. If you choose Export ➢ Other Formats, you can use the Files Of Type drop-down list in the Export Data dialog box to select Encapsulated PS. Another method is to install a PostScript printer driver and plot your drawing to an EPS file. If you're an LT user, you can't export to EPS by clicking Export; you must set up a PostScript plotter and use it to plot to a file.

To set up AutoCAD to plot your drawing to an EPS file, follow these steps:

1. Choose Print ➢ Manage Plotters, and then in the Plotters dialog box, double-click the Add-A-Plotter Wizard.

2. Choose Next on the Introduction screen.

3. On the Begin screen of the Add-A-Plotter Wizard, choose My Computer.

4. On the Plotter Model screen, select Adobe from the Manufacturers list, and then select the appropriate PostScript level from the Models list.

5. Skip the Import PCP Or PC2 screen and the Ports screen.

6. Enter a name for your EPS output settings on the Plotter Name screen.

7. On the Finish screen, click the Finish button.

AutoCAD doesn't preserve font information when creating EPS files from the printer option. It also produces larger files, especially if your drawing contains a lot of area fills and filled fonts. As an alternative to EPS, you can "plot" to an Adobe PDF file. EPS files can often be substituted with PDF files. When you get to the Plotter Model screen, select the Autodesk ePlot (PDF) option from the Manufacturers list. You can also use the full version of Adobe Acrobat or Acrobat Pro to produce PDF files from AutoCAD.

The HPGL plot-file format is another vector format you can use to export your AutoCAD drawings. Use the method described earlier in the section "Exporting Raster Files" to add the HPGL plotter driver to your printer/plotter configuration.

USING AUTOCAD DWF FILES

The Autodesk DWF file format is another format you can use to exchange drawing data with others. It offers features that are geared toward AutoCAD users. You can import DWF files as external references, and, using a free DWF viewer, you can gather information about a drawing such as block information, attribute data, and distance measurements. See Chapter 29 for more on DWF.

Using OLE to Import Data

To import data from other applications, you use the Cut and Paste features found in virtually all Windows programs. You cut the data from the source document and then paste it into AutoCAD. Typically, you'll want to paste data into AutoCAD in AutoCAD's native object format, but if you prefer, you can use a Windows feature called Object Linking and Embedding (OLE) to import files.

FINDING THE COPY AND PASTE TOOLS

There are several variations of the Copy and Paste tools in AutoCAD, so they have been combined into tools and flyouts on the Home tab's Clipboard panel. The Paste flyout is in the large icon to the left and the Copy Clip tool is the middle icon on the right.

When you paste data into your AutoCAD file using OLE, you can link it to the source file or you can embed it. If you *link* it to the source file, the pasted data is updated whenever the source file is modified. This is similar to an AutoCAD Xref file. (See Chapter 15 for more on Xref files.) If you *embed* data, you're pasting it into AutoCAD without linking it. You can still open the application associated with the data by double-clicking it, but the data is no longer associated with the source file. Importing files using OLE is similar to other cut-and-paste operations. First, cut the data from the source application. This could be Microsoft Excel or Word. In AutoCAD, click Paste Special from the Paste flyout on the Home tab's Utilities panel to open the Paste Special dialog box (Figure 20.12).

Click the Paste Link radio button to tell AutoCAD that you want this paste to be a link. Notice that the list of source types changes to show only one option: Microsoft Office Excel Worksheet. Click OK. You're prompted to select an insertion point. Place the cursor in the location for the paste, and click. The imported data appears within a bounding box. You can adjust the size of the bounding box to fit the scale of the drawing.

FIGURE 20.12
Use Paste Special
to link your data.

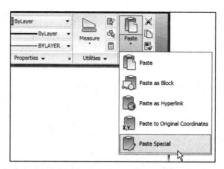

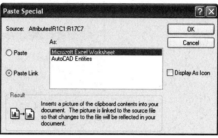

 In addition to using the Paste Special tool, you can import an OLE object by clicking OLE Object on the Insert tab's Data panel to open the Insert Object dialog box (Figure 20.13).

FIGURE 20.13
Inserting a
new object

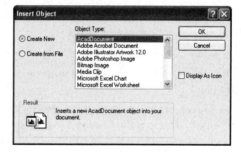

You can then select the type of object you want to import from the Object Type list box. Two radio buttons to the left of the list box let you import an existing object or create a new object of the type listed in the list box. If you choose the Create New radio button, the application associated with the object type will start and open a new file. If you choose the Create From File radio button (Figure 20.14), the dialog box changes to show a filename and a Browse button.

You can then browse for an existing file to import. The Link check box lets you specify whether the imported file is to be linked and needs to be selected in order to use the Olelinks command described in the next section.

Editing OLE Links

After you've pasted an object with links, you can control the links by typing **Olelinks**↵ at the Command prompt. If there are no linked objects in the drawing, this option is grayed out; otherwise it opens the Links dialog box (Figure 20.15).

FIGURE 20.14
Inserting an
existing object

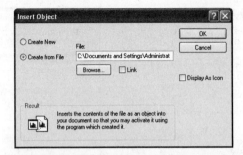

FIGURE 20.15
Editing links

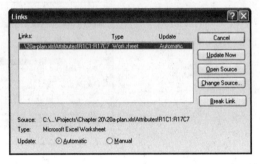

The options available in the Links dialog box are as follows:

Cancel Cancels the link between a pasted object and its source file. After you use this option, changes in the source file have no effect on the pasted object. This is similar to using the Bind option in the Xref command.

Update Now Updates an object's link when the Manual option is selected.

Open Source Opens the linked file in the application associated with the object and lets you edit it.

Change Source Lets you change the object's link to a different file. When you select this option, AutoCAD opens the Change Link dialog box, where you can select another file of the same type. For example, if you're editing the link to a sound file, the Change Link dialog box displays files with the .wav filename extension.

Break Link Disconnects the link between the inserted data and the source document. The inserted data then becomes embedded rather than linked.

Automatic and Manual Radio buttons that control whether linked objects are updated automatically or manually.

Importing Worksheets as AutoCAD Tables

Although it can be beneficial to import worksheets as linked OLE objects, you may prefer to import worksheets as AutoCAD entities. You may not need the direct link to the source material that OLE linking offers. The ability to edit the imported worksheet directly in AutoCAD may have a higher priority for you.

In Chapter 11, you saw how you could create tables in AutoCAD by using the Table tool. You can import an Excel worksheet as an AutoCAD table by using the AutoCAD Entities option in the Paste Special dialog box. By importing worksheets as tables, you have more control over the layout and appearance of the worksheet data.

Try the following exercise to see how you can create a table from a worksheet:

1. Open the Excel worksheet called 20a-plan.xls, and highlight the door data, as shown in Figure 20.16.

FIGURE 20.16

The Excel worksheet

	A	B	C	D	E	F	G	H	I	J	K
1	D-TYPE	D-SIZE	D-NUMBER	D-THICK	D-RATE	D-MATRL	D-CONST				
2	B	3'-0"	116	1 3/4"	20 min.	Wood	Solid Core				
3	B	3'-0"	114	1 3/4"	20 min.	Wood	Solid Core				
4	B	3'-0"	112	1 3/4"	20 min.	Wood	Solid Core				
5	B	3'-0"	110	1 3/4"	20 min.	Wood	Solid Core				
6	B	3'-0"	106	1 3/4"	20 min.	Wood	Solid Core				
7	B	3'-0"	108	1 3/4"	20 min.	Wood	Solid Core				
8	B	3'-0"	102	1 3/4"	20 min.	Wood	Solid Core				
9	B	3'-0"	104	1 3/4"	20 min.	Wood	Solid Core				
10	B	3'-0"	115	1 3/4"	20 min.	Wood	Solid Core				
11	B	3'-0"	111	1 3/4"	20 min.	Wood	Solid Core				
12	B	3'-0"	107	1 3/4"	20 min.	Wood	Solid Core				
13	B	3'-0"	103	1 3/4"	20 min.	Wood	Solid Core				
14	B	3'-0"	101	1 3/4"	20 min.	Wood	Solid Core				
15	B	3'-0"	105	1 3/4"	20 min.	Wood	Solid Core				
16	B	3'-0"	109	1 3/4"	20 min.	Wood	Solid Core				
17	B	3'-0"	113	1 3/4"	20 min.	Wood	Solid Core				
18		116									
19		108									
20		112									
21		104									
22		115									
23		107									

2. Press Ctrl+C to place a copy of the selected data into the Windows Clipboard, and then switch back to AutoCAD.

3. Click Paste Special from the Paste flyout on the Home tab's Clipboard panel (Figure 20.17) to open the Paste Special dialog box.

4. With the Paste radio button selected, select AutoCAD Entities from the list and click OK.

FIGURE 20.17

The Paste Special tool

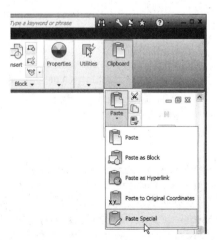

5. At the Specify insertion point or [paste as Text]: prompt, click a point in the lower-right area of the drawing. The worksheet data appears in the drawing as a table object (see Chapter 11 for more on tables).

6. Use the Scale tool to enlarge the table to a readable size (Figure 20.18), and use the corner grips to adjust the width.

FIGURE 20.18
Scale and size the table.

D-TYPE	D-SIZE	D-NUMBER	D-THICK	D-RATE	D-MATRL	D-CONST
B	3'-0"	116	1 3/4"	no rating	Wood	Solid Core
B	3'-0"	114	1 3/4"	20 min	Wood	Solid Core
B	3'-0"	112	1 3/4"	20 min	Wood	Solid Core
B	3'-0"	110	1 3/4"	20 min	Wood	Solid Core
B	3'-0"	106	1 3/4"	20 min	Wood	Solid Core
B	3'-0"	108	1 3/4"	20 min	Wood	Solid Core
B	3'-0"	102	1 3/4"	20 min	Wood	Solid Core
B	3'-0"	104	1 3/4"	20 min	Wood	Solid Core
B	3'-0"	115	1 3/4"	20 min	Wood	Solid Core
B	3'-0"	111	1 3/4"	20 min	Wood	Solid Core
B	3'-0"	107	1 3/4"	20 min	Wood	Solid Core
B	3'-0"	103	1 3/4"	20 min	Wood	Solid Core
B	3'-0"	101	1 3/4"	20 min	Wood	Solid Core
B	3'-0"	105	1 3/4"	20 min	Wood	Solid Core
B	3'-0"	109	1 3/4"	20 min	Wood	Solid Core
B	3'-0"	113	1 3/4"	20 min	Wood	Solid Core

7. Close the Excel file.

You can edit this imported worksheet using the editing methods for AutoCAD tables described in Chapter 11. In that chapter, you learned that you can edit the text format, the border line weight and color, and the background of cells. You can add rows and columns and rotate text so that it fits more uniformly in a vertical column.

In this exercise, the worksheet was imported using the default standard table style. This gives you a simple-looking table using the AutoCAD Txt font. You can set up a custom table style with the fonts and borders you want and then import the table for a more custom appearance. Make sure your custom table style is the current style before you import the worksheet.

Understanding Options for Embedding Data

The Paste Special dialog box offers several other options that may better suit your needs. Here is a brief description of each format that is available:

Microsoft Document   Imports data from Microsoft Office documents. This option may show Word or Excel in the title, depending on the source. The pasted object will inherit the appearance of the source document.

Picture (Metafile)   Imports the data as vector or bitmap graphics, whichever is appropriate. If applicable, text is also maintained as text, although you can't edit it in AutoCAD.

Bitmap   Imports the data as a bitmap image, closely reflecting the appearance of the data as it appears on your computer screen in the source application.

Picture (Enhanced Metafile)   Similar to the Picture (Metafile) option, with support for more features.

AutoCAD Entities   Converts the data into AutoCAD objects such as lines, arcs, and circles. Text is converted into AutoCAD single-line text objects. Worksheets are converted into AutoCAD tables.

Image Entity   Converts the data into an AutoCAD raster image. You can then edit it by using the raster image–related tools such as Adobe Photoshop or the Microsoft Windows Paint program. See Chapter 14 for more on how to use raster images.

Unicode Text Imports text data in the Unicode format. Unicode is an international standard for encoding text. If the Text option doesn't work, try Unicode Text.

Text Converts the data into AutoCAD multiline text objects. Formatting isn't imported with text.

The options you see in the Paste Special dialog box depend on the type of data being imported. You saw how the Microsoft Excel Worksheet option maintains the imported data as an Excel worksheet. If the contents of the Clipboard come from another program, you're offered that program as a choice in place of Excel.

Using the Clipboard to Export AutoCAD Drawings

Just as you can cut and paste data into AutoCAD from applications that support OLE, you can cut and paste AutoCAD images to other applications. This can be useful as a way of including AutoCAD images in word-processing documents, worksheets, or page-layout program documents. It can also be useful in creating background images for visualization programs such as Autodesk's 3ds Max and 3ds Max Design and for paint programs such as Corel Painter.

If you cut and paste an AutoCAD drawing to another file by using OLE and then send the file to someone using another computer, they must also have AutoCAD installed before they can edit the pasted AutoCAD drawing.

The receiving application doesn't need to support OLE, but if it does, the exported drawing can be edited with AutoCAD and will maintain its accuracy as a CAD drawing. Otherwise, the AutoCAD image will be converted to a bitmap graphic.

To use the Clipboard to export an object or a set of objects from an AutoCAD drawing, click Copy Clip from the Home tab's Clipboard panel. You're then prompted to select the objects you want to export. If you want to export and erase objects simultaneously from AutoCAD, click Cut from the Home tab's Clipboard panel.

In the receiving application, choose Edit ➢ Paste Special. You'll see a dialog box similar to AutoCAD's Paste Special dialog box. Select the method for pasting your AutoCAD image, and then click OK. If the receiving application doesn't have a Paste Special option, choose Edit ➢ Paste. The receiving application converts the image into a format it can accept.

The Bottom Line

Find the area of closed boundaries. There are a number of ways to find the area of a closed boundary. The easiest way is also perhaps the least obvious.

Master It What AutoCAD feature would you use to quickly find the area of an irregular shape like a pond or lake?

Get general information. A lot of information that is stored in AutoCAD drawings can tell you about the files. You can find out how much memory a file uses as well as the amount of time that has been spent editing the file.

Master It What feature lets you store your own searchable information about a drawing file, and how do you get to this feature?

Use the DXF file format to exchange CAD data with other programs. Autodesk created the DXF file format as a means of sharing vector drawings with other programs.

Master It Name some of the versions of AutoCAD you can export to using the Save As option.

Use AutoCAD drawings in page-layout programs. AutoCAD drawings find their way into all types of documents, including brochures and technical manuals. Users are often asked to convert their CAD drawings into formats that can be read by page-layout software.

Master It Name some file formats, by filename extension or type, which page-layout programs can accept.

Use OLE to import data. You can import data into AutoCAD from a variety of sources. Most sources, such as bitmap images and text, can be imported as native AutoCAD objects. Other sources may need to be imported as OLE objects.

Master It To link imported data to a source program through OLE, what dialog box would you use?

Part 4

3D Modeling and Imaging

Chapter 21

Creating 3D Drawings

Viewing an object in three dimensions gives you a sense of its true shape and form. It also helps you conceptualize your design, which results in better design decisions. In addition, using three-dimensional objects helps you communicate your ideas to those who may not be familiar with the plans, sections, and side views of your design.

A further advantage to drawing in three dimensions is that you can derive 2D drawings from your 3D models, which may take considerably more time with standard 2D drawing methods. For example, you can model a mechanical part in 3D and then quickly derive its 2D top, front, and right-side views by using the techniques discussed in this chapter.

In this chapter, you'll learn to do the following:

- ◆ Know the 3D modeling workspace
- ◆ Draw in 3D using solids
- ◆ Create 3D forms from 2D shapes
- ◆ Isolate coordinates with point filters
- ◆ Move around your model
- ◆ Get a visual effect
- ◆ Turn a 3D view into a 2D AutoCAD drawing
- ◆ Import point cloud data

Getting to Know the 3D Modeling Workspace

Most of this book is devoted to showing you how to work in the 2D Drafting & Annotation workspace. This workspace is basically a 2D drawing environment, although you can certainly work in 3D as well.

AutoCAD offers something called the *3D Modeling* workspace, which gives you a set of tools to help ease your way into 3D modeling. This 3D Modeling workspace gives AutoCAD a different set of Ribbon panels, but don't worry. AutoCAD behaves in the same basic way, and the AutoCAD files produced are the same regardless of whether they're 2D or 3D drawings.

To get to the 3D Modeling workspace, you need to click the Workspace tool in the Quick Access toolbar and then select 3D Modeling (see Figure 21.1).

FIGURE 21.1
The Workspace tool

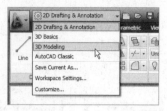

If you're starting a new 3D model, you'll also want to create a new file using a 3D template. Try the following to get started with 3D modeling:

1. Start AutoCAD, and then click on the Workspace tool in the Quick Access toolbar and select 3D Modeling. You'll see a new set of panels appear as well as the Tool Palettes window.

2. Next, to create a new 3D modeling file, click New in the Quick Access toolbar to open the Select Template dialog box. Select the acad3D.dwt template file and click Open. Your screen will look similar to Figure 21.2.

FIGURE 21.2
The AutoCAD
3D Modeling
workspace

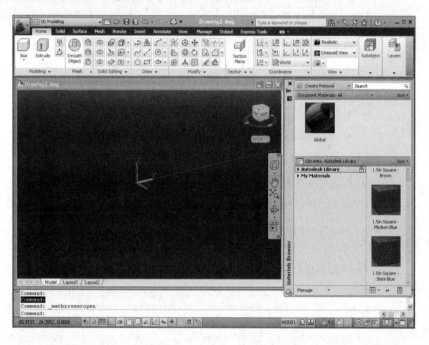

The drawing area displays the workspace as a perspective view with a dark gray background and a grid. This is really just a typical AutoCAD drawing file with a couple of setting changes. The view has been set up to be a perspective view by default, and a feature called *Visual Styles* has been set to show 3D objects as solid objects. You'll learn more about the tools you can use to adjust the appearance of your workspace later in this chapter. For now, let's look at the tool palette and Ribbon that appear in the AutoCAD window.

To the far right is the AutoCAD Materials Browser. It shows a graphical list of surface materials that you can easily assign to 3D objects in your model. You'll learn more about materials in Chapter 23.

The Ribbon along the top of the AutoCAD window offers all the tools you'll need to create 3D models. The 3D Modeling workspace Ribbon offers a few of the tabs and panels you're already familiar with, but many of the tabs will be new to you (see Figure 21.3). You see the familiar Draw and Modify panels in the Home tab, but there are several other panels devoted to 3D modeling: Modeling, Mesh, Solid Editing, View, and Subobject.

FIGURE 21.3
Some of the Ribbon tabs and panels of the 3D Modeling workspace

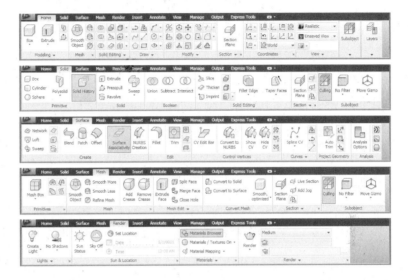

In addition, other Ribbon tabs offer more sets of tools designed for 3D modeling. For example, the Render tab contains tools that control the way the model looks. You can set up lighting and shadows and apply materials to objects such as brick or glass. You can also control the way AutoCAD displays the model through the Visual Styles, Edge Effects, Lights, Sun & Location, and Materials panels. In the next section, you'll gain firsthand experience creating and editing some 3D shapes using the Home tab's Modeling and View panels and the View tab's Visual Styles panel. This way, you'll get a feel for how things work in the 3D Modeling workspace.

Drawing in 3D Using Solids

You can work with two types of 3D objects in AutoCAD: solids and surfaces. You can treat solid objects as if they're solid material. For example, you can create a box and then remove shapes from the box as if you're carving it, as shown in Figure 21.4.

With surfaces, you create complex surface shapes by building on lines, arcs, or polylines. For example, you can quickly turn a series of curved polylines, arcs, or lines into a warped surface, as shown in Figure 21.5.

Next, you'll learn how to create a solid box and then make simple changes to it as an introduction to 3D modeling.

FIGURE 21.4
Solid modeling lets you remove or add shapes.

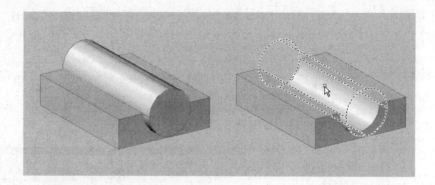

FIGURE 21.5
Using the Loft tool, you can use a set of 2D objects (left) to define a complex surface (right).

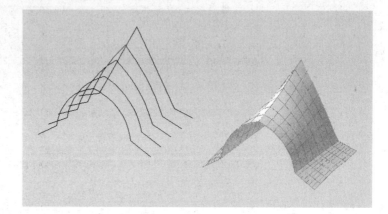

CONVERTING OLD-STYLE SURFACE OBJECTS

If you have some experience with AutoCAD 3D, note that the new surface-modeling features aren't the same as the surface objects you may have created in the older version of AutoCAD. The new surface objects can interact with solid primitive objects and can be converted into 3D solids. You can still create the old-style 3D surface objects, but be aware that they aren't the same type of object as the 3D surfaces in AutoCAD 2009 and 2010. You can convert the old-style surfaces into the new 3D surfaces using the Convtosurface command described in the sidebar "Converting Objects with Thickness into 3D Solids" later in this chapter.

Adjusting Appearances

Before you start to work on the exercise, you'll want to change the visual style to one that will make your work a little easier to visualize in the creation phase. Visual Styles offers a way to let you see your model in different styles from sketchlike to realistic. You'll learn more about Visual Styles in "Getting a Visual Effect" later in this chapter, but for now, you'll get a brief introduction by changing the style for the exercises that follow:

1. In the Home tab's View panel, click the Visual Styles drop-down list to view the options.

2. Select the Shades Of Gray option. This will give the solid objects in your model a uniform gray color and will also "highlight" the edges of the solids with a dark line so you can see them clearly.

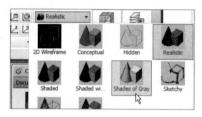

Creating a 3D Box

Start by creating a box using the Box tool in the Home tab's Modeling panel:

1. Close the Materials Browser by clicking on the X in the upper-right corner of its title bar. You won't need it for this chapter. If you feel you need to have it back later, you can go to the Materials panel in the Render tab and click the Materials Browser tool.

2. Click the Box tool from the Solids flyout on the Home tab's Modeling panel.

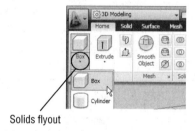

Solids flyout

3. Click a point near the origin of the drawing shown in Figure 21.6. You can use the coordinate readout to select a point near 0,0. Once you click, you see a rectangle follow the cursor.

4. Click another point near coordinate 20,15, as shown in Figure 21.6. As you move the cursor, the rectangle is fixed and the height of the 3D box appears.

5. Enter 4↵ for a height of 4 units for the box. You can also click to fix the height of the box.

FIGURE 21.6
Drawing a 3D
solid box

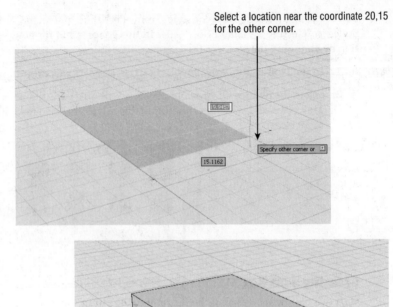

Select a location near the coordinate 20,15
for the other corner.

WHY THE SCREEN LOOKS DIFFERENT

I'd like to point out that I have set up my display with a lighter background than the default background in AutoCAD. This is intended to help you see the various parts of the display more easily on the printed page.

In addition, when you start a 3D model using the acad3D.dwt template, the default layer 0 is set to a color that is a light blue instead of the white or black that is used in the standard acad.dwt template. The blue color is used so you can see the 3D shapes clearly when the model is displayed using a shaded visual style. If you happen to start a 3D model using the acad.dwt template, you may want to change the default color to something other than white or black.

You used three basic steps in creating the box. First, you clicked one corner to establish a location for the box. Then, you clicked another corner to establish the base size. Finally, you selected a height. You use a similar set of steps to create any of the other 3D solid primitives found in the Solids flyout of the Home tab's Modeling panel. For example, for a cylinder, you select the center, then the radius, and finally the height. For a wedge, you select two corners as you did with the box, and then you select the height. You'll learn more about these 3D solid primitives in Chapter 24.

Editing 3D Solids with Grips

Once you've created a solid, you can fine-tune its shape by using grips:

1. Adjust your view so it looks similar to Figure 21.7, and then click the solid to select it. Grips appear on the 3D solid, as shown in the figure.

FIGURE 21.7

Grips appear on 3D solid.

Click this arrow grip to adjust the length of the box.

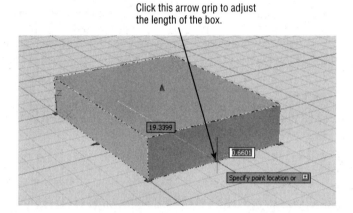

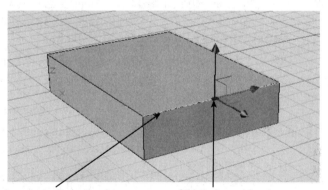

Ctrl-click the top edge to display the gizmo.   Click the base of the gizmo.

You can adjust the location of the square grips at the base of the solid in a way that is similar to adjusting the grips on 2D objects. The arrow grips let you adjust the length of the site to which the arrows are attached. If you click an arrow grip and you have Dynamic Input turned on, a dimension appears at the cursor, as shown in Figure 21.7. You can enter a new dimension for the length associated with the selected grip, or you can drag and click the arrow to adjust the length. Remember that you can press the Tab key to shift between dimensions shown in the Dynamic Input display.

2. Click the arrow grip toward the front of the box, as shown at upper left in Figure 21.7. Now, as you move the cursor, the box changes in length.

3. Press Esc twice to clear the grip selection and the box selection.

You can also move individual edges by using a Ctrl+click:

1. Hold down the Ctrl key and move the cursor over the different surfaces and edges of the box. Notice that surfaces and edges are highlighted as you do so.

2. While still holding the Ctrl key, hover over the top-front edge. When it is highlighted, click it. A graphic tool called a gizmo appears at the midpoint of the edge, as shown at the lower-right image in Figure 21.7. The gizmo has three legs pointing in the X, Y, and Z axes. It also has a grip at the base of the three legs. If your Ctrl+click doesn't work as described, you may need to change the setting for the Legacyctrlpick system variable. At the Command prompt, enter **legacyctrlpick**⏎, and then enter **0**⏎.

3. Click the grip at the base of the gizmo, and move the cursor. The edge follows the grip.

4. Hold down the Shift key, and pull the grip forward, away from the box's center. The Shift key constrains the motion in the X, Y, or Z axis.

5. Click a point to fix the edge's new position.

6. Click the Undo button to return the box to its original shape.

As you can see, you have a great deal of flexibility in controlling the shape of the box. Using the Shift key lets you constrain the motion of the grip.

Constraining Motion with the Gizmo

You were introduced to the gizmo in the last exercise. This is an icon that looks like the UCS icon and appears whenever you select a 3D solid or any part of a 3D solid. Try the next exercise to see how the gizmo works:

1. Ctrl+click the top-front edge of the box again to expose the edge's grip.

2. Place the cursor on the blue Z axis of the gizmo, but don't click. A blue line appears that extends across the drawing area, and the Z axis of the gizmo changes color, as shown in Figure 21.8.

3. Click the Z axis. Now as you move the cursor, the grip motion is constrained in the Z axis.

4. Click again to fix the location of the grip.

5. Press the Esc key to clear your grip selection.

6. Click the Undo tool to undo the grip edit.

Here you used the gizmo to change the Z location of a grip easily. You can use the gizmo to modify the location of a single grip or the entire object.

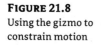

FIGURE 21.8

Using the gizmo to constrain motion

Hover over the Z axis of the gizmo and a blue line appears.

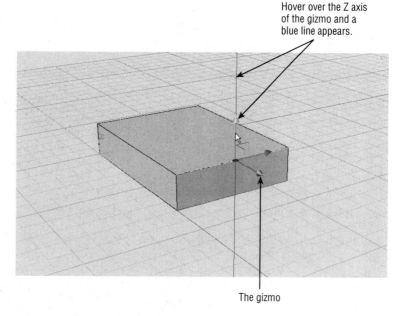

The gizmo

Rotating Objects in 3D Using Dynamic UCS

Typically, you work in what is known as the *World Coordinate System (WCS)*. This is the default coordinate system that AutoCAD uses in new drawings, but you can also create your own coordinate systems that are subsets of the WCS. A coordinate system that you create is known as a *User Coordinate System (UCS)*.

UCSs are significant in 3D modeling because they can help you orient your work in 3D space. For example, you could set up a UCS on a vertical face of the 3D box you created earlier. You could then draw on that vertical face just as you would on the drawing's WCS. Figure 21.9 shows a cylinder drawn on the side of a box. If you click on the Cylinder tool, for example, and place the cursor on the side of the box, the side will be highlighted to indicate the surface to which the cylinder will be applied. In addition, if you could see the cursor in color, you would see that the blue Z axis is pointing sideways to the left and is perpendicular to the side of the box.

The UCS has always been an important tool for 3D modeling in AutoCAD. The example just described demonstrates the Dynamic UCS, which automatically changes the orientation of the X, Y, and Z axes to conform to the flat surface of a 3D object.

You may have noticed that when you created the new 3D file using the acad3D.dwt template, the cursor looked different. Instead of the usual cross, you saw three intersecting lines. If you look carefully, you'll see that each line of the cursor is a different color. In its default configuration, AutoCAD shows a red line for the X axis, a green line for the Y axis, and a blue line for the Z axis. This mimics the color scheme of the UCS icon, as shown in Figure 21.10.

FIGURE 21.9
Drawing on the side of a box

The face is highlighted.

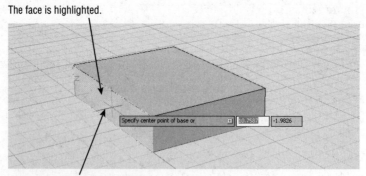

The cursor's Z axis is perpendicular to the side of the box.

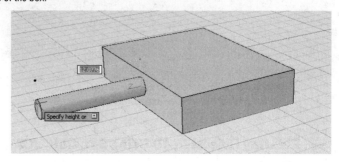

FIGURE 21.10
The UCS icon at the left and the cursor in 3D to the right are color matched.

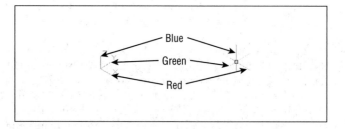

As you work with the Dynamic UCS, you'll see that the orientation of these lines changes when you point at a surface on a 3D object. The following exercise shows you how to use the Dynamic UCS to help you rotate the box about the X axis:

1. Be sure the Object Snap and Allow/Disallow Dynamic UCS features are turned on.

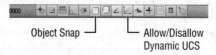

Object Snap ⎯⎯⎯ ⎿ Allow/Disallow Dynamic UCS

2. Click Rotate from the Home tab's Modify panel or enter **Ro↵**.

3. At the Select objects: prompt, click the box, and then press ↵ to finish your selection.

4. At the Specify base point: prompt, don't click anything, but move the cursor from one surface of the box to a side of the box. As you do this, notice that the surface you point to becomes highlighted. The orientation of the cursor also changes depending on which surface you're pointing to.

5. Place the cursor on the left side, as shown in the top image of Figure 21.11; then Shift+right-click your mouse and select Endpoint from the Osnap shortcut menu.

FIGURE 21.11
Selecting a base point, and the resulting box orientation

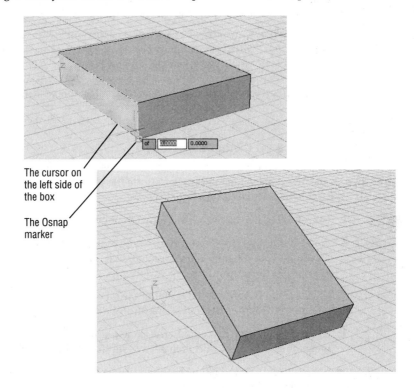

The cursor on the left side of the box

The Osnap marker

6. While keeping the side highlighted, place the Osnap marker on the lower-front corner of the box, as shown in the top image in Figure 21.11. Click this corner. As you move the cursor, the box rotates about the Y axis.

7. Enter **–30** for the rotation angle. Your box should look like the image at the bottom in Figure 21.11.

Here you saw that you can hover over a surface to indicate the plane about which the rotation is to occur. Now, suppose you want to add an object to one of the sides of the rotated box. The next section will show you another essential tool, one you can use to do just that.

USING OBJECT SNAPS AND OSNAP TRACKING IN 3D SPACE

If you need to place objects in precise locations in 3D, such as at endpoints or midpoints of other objects, you can do so using object snaps, just as you would in 2D. But you must take care when using osnaps where the Dynamic UCS is concerned.

In the exercise in the section "Rotating Objects in 3D Using Dynamic UCS," you were asked to make sure you placed the cursor on the side of the box that coincided with the rotational plane *before* you selected the Endpoint osnap. This ensures that the Dynamic UCS feature has selected the proper rotational plane; otherwise, the box may rotate in the wrong direction.

In some operations, you can't use osnaps in perspective mode. Osnap Tracking also doesn't work in perspective mode. Switch to a parallel projection view if you know you'll want to use osnaps. (See the section "Changing from Perspective to Parallel Projection" later in this chapter.) If you need to snap to points that are in the back of an object, switch to 2D or 3D wireframe visual style. See the section "Getting a Visual Effect" later in this chapter for more on visual styles.

Drawing on a 3D Object's Surface

In the rotation exercise, you saw that you can hover over a surface to indicate the plane of rotation. You can use the same method to indicate the plane on which you want to place an object. Try the following exercise to see how it's done:

1. Click Center, Radius from the Circle flyout on the Home tab's Draw panel or enter **C**↵.

2. Place the cursor on the top surface of the rectangle, as indicated in the top image of Figure 21.12, and hold it there for a moment. The surface is highlighted and the cursor aligns with the angle of the top surface.

3. Click a point roughly at the center of the box. The circle appears on the surface, and as you move the cursor, the circle's radius follows.

4. Adjust the circle so it's roughly the same 6-unit radius as the one shown on the lower image in Figure 21.12, and then click to set the radius. You can also enter **6**↵.

5. Click Offset from the Home tab's Modify panel, and offset the circle 2 units inward, as shown in the lower image of Figure 21.12. You can use the Center osnap to indicate a direction toward the center of the circle.

USING A FIXED UCS

If you're working in a crowded area of a drawing, or if you know you need to do a lot of work on one particular surface of an object, you can create a UCS that remains in a fixed orientation until you change it instead of relying on the Dynamic UCS feature. Click Face from the View flyout on the View tab's Coordinates panel, and then click the surface that defines the plane on which you want to work. The UCS aligns with the selected surface. Press ↵ to accept the face that the Face option has found, or you can use one of the options [Next/Xflip/Yflip] to move to another surface or flip the UCS. Once you've set the UCS, you won't have to worry about accidentally drawing in the wrong orientation. To return to the WCS, click World from the View tab's UCS panel. You'll learn more about the UCS in Chapter 22.

This demonstrates that you can use Dynamic UCS to align objects with the surface of an object. Note that Dynamic UCS works only on flat surfaces. For example, you can't use it to place an object on the curved side of a cylinder.

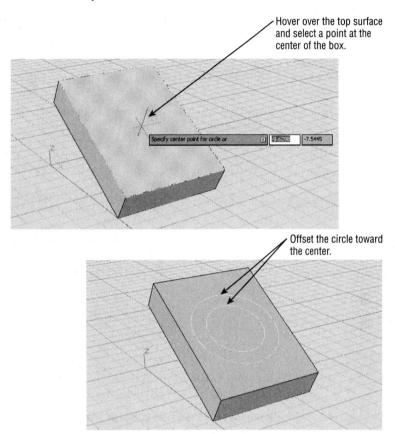

FIGURE 21.12
Drawing circles on the surface of a 3D solid

Hover over the top surface and select a point at the center of the box.

Offset the circle toward the center.

Pushing and Pulling Shapes from a Solid

You've just added a 2D circle to the top surface of the 3D box. AutoCAD offers a tool that lets you use that 2D circle or any closed 2D shape to modify the shape of your 3D object. The Presspull tool in the Home tab's Modeling panel lets you "press" or "pull" a 3D shape to or from the surface of a 3D object. The following exercise shows how this works:

1. Make sure the Polar Tracking tool in the status bar is turned on, and then click the Presspull tool in the Home tab's Modeling panel. You can also enter **Presspull↵** at the Command prompt.

2. Move the cursor to the top surface of the box between both circles. (See the lower-right panel of Figure 21.13.)

FIGURE 21.13
Move the cursor over different areas of the box and notice how the areas are highlighted.

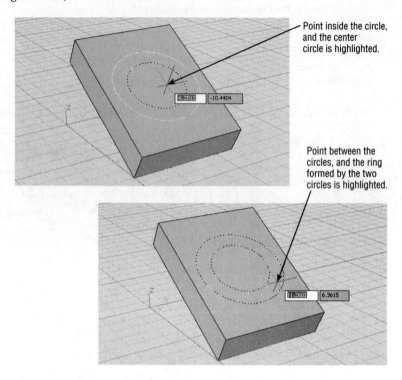

Point inside the circle, and the center circle is highlighted.

Point between the circles, and the ring formed by the two circles is highlighted.

3. With the cursor between the two circles, click the mouse. As you move the mouse, the circular area defined by the two circles moves.

4. Adjust the cursor location so the cursor is positioned below the center of the circle, as shown in the top-left panel of Figure 21.14. Enter 3↵ to create a 3-unit indentation, as shown in the second panel of Figure 21.14.

You've created a circular indentation in the box by pressing the circular area defined by the two circles. You could have pulled the area upward to form a circular ridge on the box. Pressing the circle into the solid is essentially the same as subtracting one solid from another. When you press the shape into the solid, AutoCAD assumes you want to subtract the shape.

Presspull works with any closed 2D shape, such as a circle, closed polyline, or other completely enclosed area. An existing 3D solid isn't needed. For example, you can draw two concentric circles without the 3D box and then use Presspull to convert the circles into a 3D solid ring. In the previous exercise, the solid box showed that you can use Presspull to subtract a shape from an existing solid.

As you saw in this exercise, the Presspull tool can help you quickly subtract a shape from an existing 3D solid. Figure 21.15 shows some other examples of how you can use Presspull. For example, you can draw a line from one edge to another and then use Presspull to extrude the resulting triangular shape. You can also draw concentric shapes and extrude them; you can even use offset spline curves to add a trough to a solid.

FIGURE 21.14
Creating an indentation in the box using Presspull

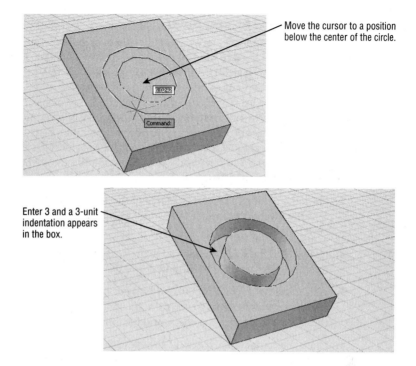

Move the cursor to a position below the center of the circle.

Enter 3 and a 3-unit indentation appears in the box.

DRAWING OUTSIDE THE SURFACE

If you use an open 2D object such as a curved spline or line on a 3D surface, the endpoints must touch exactly on the edge of the surface before Presspull will work.

FIGURE 21.15
Adding complex shapes using the Presspull tool

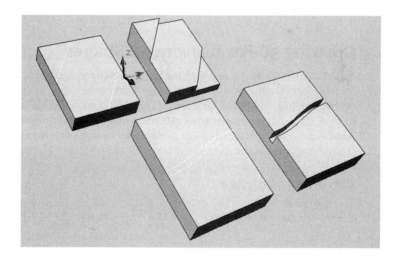

Making Changes to Your Solid

When you're creating a 3D model, you'll hardly ever get the shape right the first time. Suppose you decide that you need to modify the shape you've created so far by moving the hole from the center of the box to a corner. The next exercise will show you how you can gain access to the individual components of a 3D solid to make changes.

The model you've been working with is composed of two objects: a box and a cylinder formed from two circles. These two components of the solid are referred to as *subobjects* of the main solid object. Faces and edges of 3D solids are also considered subobjects. When you use the Union, Subtract, and Intersect tools later on in this book, objects merge into a single solid—or at least that is how it seems at first. You can gain access to and modify the shape of the subobjects from which the shape is constructed by using the Ctrl key while clicking the solid. Try the following:

1. Place the cursor on the components of the solid you've made so far. They are highlighted as if they were one object. If you were to click it (don't do it yet), the entire object would be selected.

2. Hold down the Ctrl key, and move the cursor over the circular indentation. As you do this, the indentation is highlighted (see the left image in Figure 21.16).

3. While still holding down the Ctrl key, click the indentation. The grips for the indentation appear, as shown in the lower-right image in Figure 21.16. As you may guess, you can use these grips to change the shape and location of a feature of the selected solid.

4. Click the center square grip of the indentation, and move your cursor around. If you find it a bit uncontrollable, turn off Polar Tracking mode. As you move the cursor, the indentation moves with it.

5. Place the indentation in the location shown in Figure 21.17 and click. You've just moved the indentation from the center to the edge of the cylinder.

6. Press the Esc key to clear the selection. Exit the file and save it.

This example showed that the Ctrl key can be an extremely useful tool when you have to edit a solid; it allows you to select the subobjects that form your model. Once the subobjects are selected, you can move them, or you can use the arrow grips to change their size.

Creating 3D Forms from 2D Shapes

3D solid primitives are great for creating basic shapes, but in many situations, you'll want to create a 3D form from a more complex shape. Fortunately, you can extrude 2D objects into a variety of shapes using additional tools found in the Home tab's Modeling panel. For example, you can draw a shape like a star and then extrude it into a third dimension, as shown in Figure 21.18. Alternatively, you can use several strategically placed 2D objects to form a flowing surface like the wing of an airplane.

Extruding a Polyline

You can create a 3D solid by extruding a 2D closed polyline. This is a more flexible way to create shapes because you can create a polyline of any shape and extrude it to a fairly complex form.

Hold down the Ctrl key and hover over the
circular indentation. Click the mouse when
the indentation is highlighted.

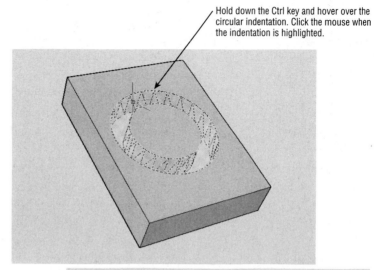

Click the center square grip.
The indentation will move
with the mouse.

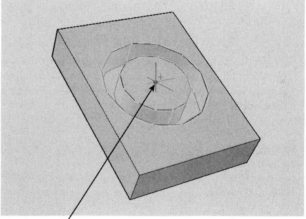

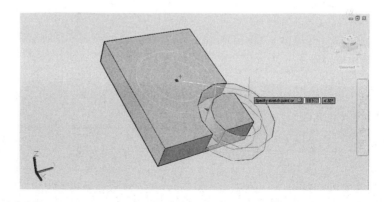

FIGURE 21.18
The closed polyline on the left can be used to construct the 3D shape on the right.

In the following set of exercises, you'll turn the apartment room from previous chapters into a 3D model. I've created a version of the apartment floor plan that has a few additions to make things a little easier for you. Figure 21.19 shows the file you'll use in the exercise. It's the same floor plan you've been working with in earlier chapters but with the addition of closed polylines outlining the walls.

FIGURE 21.19
The unit plan with closed polylines outlining the walls

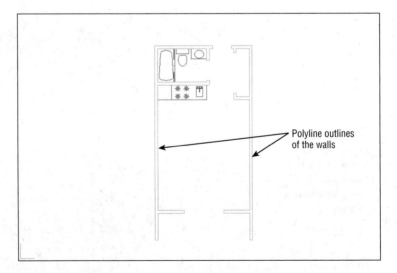

Polyline outlines of the walls

The plan isn't shaded as in the previous examples in this chapter. You can work in 3D in this display mode just as easily as in a shaded mode:

1. Open the 21-unit.dwg file. Metric users should open 21-unit-metric.dwg.

2. Choose SW Isometric from 3D Navigation drop-down list in the Home tab's View panel (Figure 21.20). You can also type **-View↵ Swiso↵**.

FIGURE 21.20
Selecting a
view from the
3D Navigation
drop-down list

Your view now looks as if you're standing above and to the left of your drawing rather than directly above it (see Figure 21.21). The UCS icon helps you get a sense of your new orientation.

FIGURE 21.21
A 3D view of the
unit plan

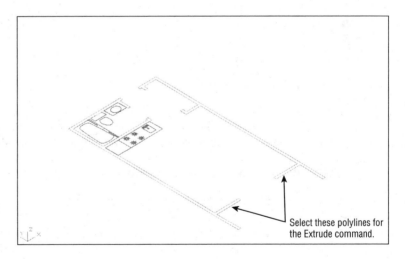

Select these polylines for
the Extrude command.

3. Click the Extrude tool in the Home tab's Modeling panel (see Figure 21.22).

FIGURE 21.22
Selecting the
Extrude tool from
the Modeling panel

You can also enter **Extrude**↵ at the Command prompt. You see the message Current wire frame density: ISOLINES=4, Closed profiles creation mode = Solid in the Command window, followed by the Select objects to extrude or [Mode]: prompt.

4. Select the wall outlines shown in Figure 21.21, and then press ↵.

5. At the Specify height of extrusion or [Direction/Path/Taper angle/Expression] <-0´-3″>: prompt, place the cursor near the top of the drawing area and enter **8´**↵. Metric users should enter **224**↵. The walls extrude to the height you entered, as shown in Figure 21.23.

FIGURE 21.23
The extruded walls

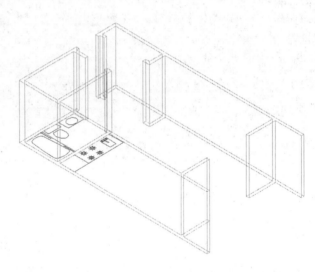

Unlike in the earlier exercise with the box, you can see through the walls because this is a Wireframe view. A *Wireframe view* shows the volume of a 3D object by displaying the lines representing the edges of surfaces. Later in this chapter, I'll discuss how to make an object's surfaces appear opaque as they do on the box earlier in this chapter.

Next you'll add door headers to define the wall openings:

1. Adjust your view so you get a close look at the door shown in Figure 21.24. You can use the Pan and Zoom tools in this 3D view as you would in a 2D view.

2. Turn off Dynamic UCS mode by clicking the Allow/Disallow Dynamic UCS tool in the status bar so it's grayed out. This helps you avoid accidentally orienting your cursor to the wall behind the door header (Figure 21.25).

3. Click the Box tool in the Solids flyout of the Modeling panel.

4. Use the Endpoint osnaps, and click the two points shown in Figure 21.26.

5. At the Specify height or [2Point] <8´-0″>: prompt, point the cursor downward from the points you just selected, and enter **12**↵. Metric users should enter **30**↵. The door header appears.

6. Repeat steps 4 and 5 to draw the other door headers shown in Figure 21.26.

FIGURE 21.24
Adding the door
header to the open-
ing at the balcony
of the unit plan

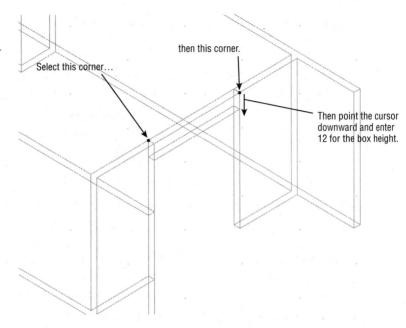

Select this corner…

then this corner.

Then point the cursor
downward and enter
12 for the box height.

FIGURE 21.25
Turn off
Dynamic UCS

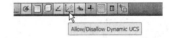

Allow/Disallow Dynamic UCS

FIGURE 21.26
Adding the
remaining door
headers

Add these three door headers.

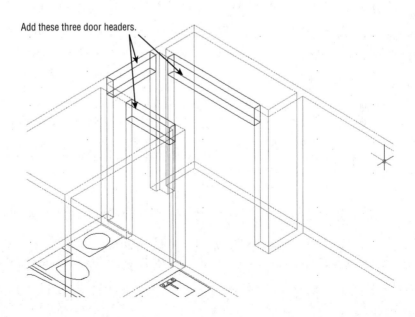

The walls and door headers give you a better sense of the space in the unit plan. To enhance the appearance of the 3D model further, you can join the walls and door headers so they appear as seamless walls and openings:

1. Zoom out so you can see the entire unit, and then click the Union tool in the Solid Editing panel (Figure 21.27). You can also enter **Uni↵**.

2. At the Select objects: prompt, select all the walls and headers, and then press ↵.

Now the walls and headers appear as one seamless surface without any distracting joint lines. You can really get a sense of the space of the unit plan. You'll want to explore ways of viewing the unit in 3D, but before you do that, you need to know about one more 3D modeling feature: *point filters*.

Isolating Coordinates with Point Filters

AutoCAD offers a method for 3D point selection that can help you isolate the X, Y, or Z coordinate of a location in 3D. Using *point filters*, you can enter an X, Y, or Z value by picking a point on the screen and telling AutoCAD to use only the X, Y, or Z value of that point or any combination of those values. For example, suppose you want to start the corner of a 3D box at the X and Y coordinates of the corner of the unit plan but you want the Z location at 3′ instead of at ground level. You can use point filters to select only the X and Y coordinates of a point and then specify the Z coordinate as a separate value. The following exercise demonstrates how this works:

1. Zoom in to the balcony door, and turn on the F-RAIL layer.

2. Click the Box tool from the Solids flyout on the Modeling panel.

3. At the Specify first corner or [Center]: prompt, Shift+right-click to display the Osnap menu, and then choose Point Filters ➤ .XY. As an alternative, you can enter **.xy↵**. By doing this, you are telling AutoCAD that first you're going to specify the X and Y coordinates for this beginning point and then later indicate the Z coordinate.

   You may have noticed the .X, .Y, and .Z options on the Object Snap menu (Shift+right-click) in step 3. These are the 3D point filters. By choosing one of these options as you select points in a 3D command, you can filter an X, Y, or Z value, or any combination of values, from that selected point. You can also enter filters through the keyboard.

4. At the Specify first corner or [Center]: .XY of: prompt, pick the corner of the unit plan, as shown in Figure 21.28.

5. At the (need Z): prompt, enter **36↵** (the Z coordinate). Metric users enter **92↵**. The outline of the box appears at the 36″ (or 92 cm) elevation and at the corner you selected in step 4.

6. At the Specify other corner or [Cube/Length]: prompt, Shift+right-click to display the Osnap menu again, and choose Point Filters ➤ .XY. Select the other endpoint indicated in Figure 21.28.

7. At the (need Z): prompt, a temporary outline of the box appears at the 36″ height. Click the mouse to fix the base outline of the box.

8. Enter 4↵ (10↵ for metric users) for the height of the box. The box appears as the balcony rail.

CONVERTING OBJECTS WITH THICKNESS INTO 3D SOLIDS

If you've worked with 3D in AutoCAD before, you probably know that you can give an object a thickness property greater than 0 to make it a 3D object. For example, a line with a thickness property greater than 0 looks like a vertical surface.

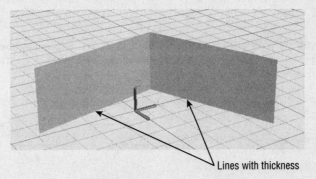

Lines with thickness

In the unit plan exercise, you can do the same for the polylines used to draw the walls. Click the wall polylines, and then right-click and choose Properties. In the Properties palette, change the Thickness value to 8′ or 224 cm.

Close the Properties palette. The walls appear in three dimensions. But be aware that these walls aren't 3D solids. If you zoom in to a detail of the walls, they appear hollow.

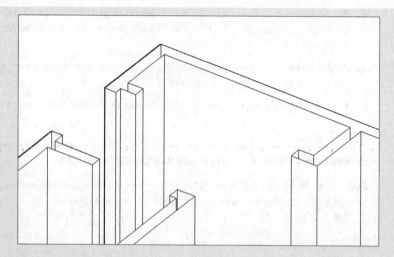

Fortunately, AutoCAD supplies a tool that converts a closed polyline with thickness into a solid. Expand the Home tab's Solid Editing panel, and then click the Convert To Solid tool. You can also enter **convtosolid**⏎.

Select the polyline walls; press ⏎ when you've finished your selection. Once you do this, the walls become 3D solids. This operation works with any closed polyline, providing an alternate way of creating a 3D solid. If you have existing 3D models that have been produced using the Thickness property, you can use the Convert To Solid tool to bring your 3D models up-to-date. The Convert To Solid tool can also convert open polylines that have a width and thickness greater than 0. (See Chapter 19 for more on polylines.)

Another tool, called Convert To Surface, converts objects with thickness into 3D surface objects. You can use 3D surfaces to slice or thicken 3D solids into full 3D solids. You'll learn more about 3D surfaces in Chapter 25.

GET TO KNOW POINT FILTERS

In my own work in 3D, point filters are a real lifesaver. They can help you locate a position in 3D when the drawing becomes crowded with objects. And since a lot of architectural models start from floor plans, you can easily "project" locations into 3D using point filters. Understanding this tool will greatly improve your ability to work in 3D.

In step 4, you selected the corner of the unit, but the box didn't appear right away. You had to enter a Z value in step 5 before the outline of the box appeared. Then, in step 6, you saw the box begin at the 36″ elevation. Using point filters allowed you to place the box accurately in the drawing even though there were no features that you could snap to directly.

Now that you've gotten most of the unit modeled in 3D, you'll want to be able to look at it from different angles. Next you'll see some of the tools available to control your views in 3D.

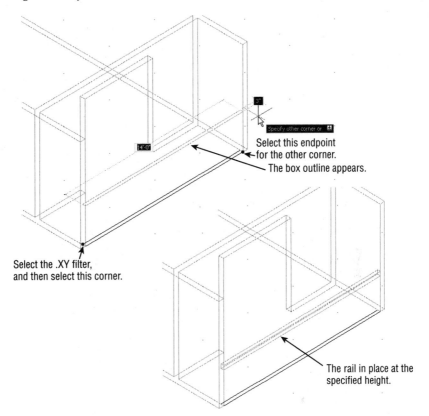

FIGURE 21.28
Constructing the rail using point filters

Select this endpoint for the other corner.
The box outline appears.

Select the .XY filter, and then select this corner.

The rail in place at the specified height.

Moving around Your Model

AutoCAD offers a number of tools to help you view your 3D model. You've already used one to get the current 3D view. Choosing Southwest Isometric from the View panel's drop-down list displays an isometric view from a southwest direction. You may have noticed several other isometric view options in that list. The following sections introduce you to some of the ways you can move around in your 3D model.

Finding Isometric and Orthogonal Views

Figure 21.29 illustrates the isometric view options you saw earlier in the Home tab's View panel drop-down list: Southeast Isometric, Southwest Isometric, Northeast Isometric, and Northwest Isometric. The cameras represent the different viewpoint locations. You can get an idea of their location in reference to the grid and UCS icon.

FIGURE 21.29
The isometric viewpoints for the four isometric views available from the Home tab's View panel drop-down list

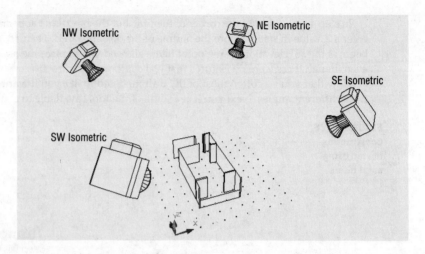

The Home tab's View panel's 3D Navigation drop-down list also offers another set of options: Top, Bottom, Left, Right, Front, and Back. These are orthogonal views that show the sides, top, and bottom of the model, as illustrated in Figure 21.30. In this figure, the cameras once again show the points of view.

FIGURE 21.30
This diagram shows the six viewpoints of the orthogonal view options on the View panel's 3D Navigation drop-down list.

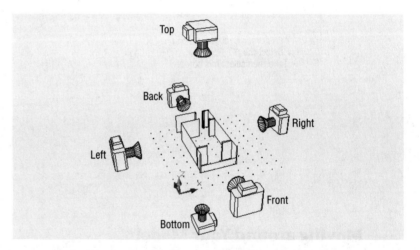

When you use any of the view options described here, AutoCAD attempts to display the extents of the drawing. You can then use the Pan and Zoom tools to adjust your view.

Rotating Freely around Your Model

You may find the isometric and orthogonal views a bit restrictive. The Orbit tool lets you move around your model in real time. You can fine-tune your view by clicking and dragging the mouse using this tool. Try the following to see how it works:

1. Zoom out so you see an overall view of your model.

2. Click the Orbit tool in the Orbit flyout on the View tab's Navigate panel.

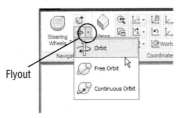

Flyout

You can also enter **3dorbit**↵ and then right-click and select Other Navigation Modes ➢ Constrained Orbit.

3. Click and drag in the drawing area. As you drag the mouse, the view revolves around your model. The cursor changes to an orbit icon to let you know you're in the middle of using the Constrained Orbit tool.

If you have several objects in your model, you can select an object that you want to revolve around and then click the Orbit tool. It also helps to pan your view so the object you select is in the center of the view.

When you've reached the view you want, right-click and choose Exit. You're then ready to make more changes or use another tool.

Changing Your View Direction

One of the first tasks you'll want to do with a model is to look at it from all angles. The ViewCube is the perfect tool for this purpose. The ViewCube is a device that lets you select a view by using a sample cube. You have already seen the ViewCube in the early part of this chapter. If it is not visible in your drawing, do the following:

1. First make sure Visual Styles is set to something other than 2D Wireframe by selecting an option from the Visual Styles drop-down list in the Home tab's View panel.

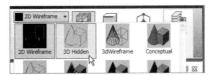

2. If you don't already see the ViewCube in the upper-right corner of the drawing area, then go to the View tab's Windows panel and turn on the ViewCube option in the User Interface flyout.

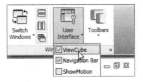

CONSTRAINED ORBIT SHORTCUT

If you have a mouse with a scroll wheel, you can hold down the Shift key while clicking and dragging the wheel to get the same effect as using the Constrained Orbit tool.

The following list explains what you can do with the ViewCube (see Figure 21.31):

♦ Click the Home icon to bring your view to the "home" position. This is helpful if you lose sight of your model.

♦ You can get a top, front, right-side, or other orthogonal view just by clicking the word *Top*, *Front*, or *Right* on the ViewCube.

♦ Click a corner of the cube to get an isometric-style view, or click an edge to get an "edge-on" view.

♦ Click and drag the N, S, E, or W label to rotate the model in the XY plane.

♦ To rotate your view of the object in 3D freely, click and drag the cube.

♦ From the icon at the bottom, select an existing UCS or create a new one from the UCS list.

FIGURE 21.31
The ViewCube and its options

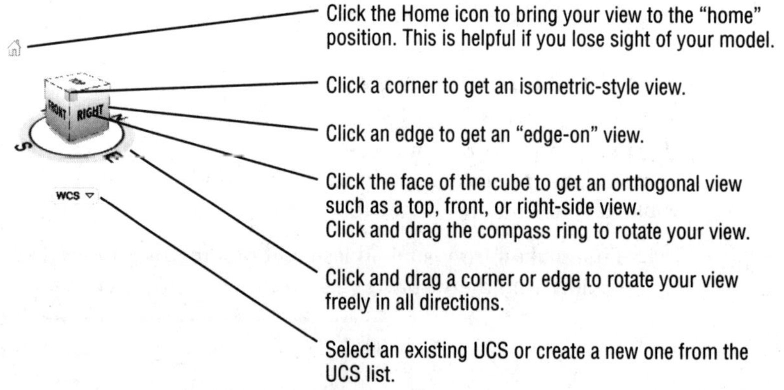

Click the Home icon to bring your view to the "home" position. This is helpful if you lose sight of your model.

Click a corner to get an isometric-style view.

Click an edge to get an "edge-on" view.

Click the face of the cube to get an orthogonal view such as a top, front, or right-side view.
Click and drag the compass ring to rotate your view.

Click and drag a corner or edge to rotate your view freely in all directions.

Select an existing UCS or create a new one from the UCS list.

You can also change from a perspective view to a parallel projection view by right-clicking the cube and selecting Parallel Projection. To go from parallel projection to perspective, right-click and select Perspective or Perspective With Ortho Faces. The Perspective With Ortho Faces option works like the Perspective option except it will force a parallel projection view when you use the ViewCube to select a top, bottom or side orthographic view.

When you are in a plan or top view, the ViewCube will look like a square, and when you hover your cursor over the cube, you'll see two curved arrows to the upper right of the cube (Figure 21.32).

You can click on any of the visible corners to go to an isometric view or click the double curved arrows to rotate the view 90 degrees. The four arrowheads that you see pointing toward the cube allow you to change to an orthographic view of any of the four sides.

FIGURE 21.32
The ViewCube
top view

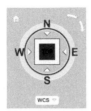

SETTING THE HOME VIEW

In a new file, the ViewCube's home view is similar to the SW Isometric view. To set your own home view, right-click the ViewCube and select Set Current View As Home.

Using SteeringWheels

The ViewCube is great for looking at your model from different angles. But if your application requires you to be inside your model, you'll want to know how to use the *SteeringWheels* feature. The SteeringWheels feature collects a number of viewing tools in one interface. You can open SteeringWheels by clicking the SteeringWheels tool in the View tab's Navigate panel (Figure 21.33) or from the navigation bar.

FIGURE 21.33
The Steering-
Wheels tool

You can also type **Navswheel↵** or click the SteeringWheels tool from the navigation bar. When you do this, the SteeringWheels tool appears in the drawing area and moves with the cursor.

The SteeringWheels options are fairly self-explanatory. Just be aware that you need to use a click-and-drag motion to use them.

Pan   To pan your view, click and drag the Pan option.

Zoom   To zoom, click and drag the Zoom option.

Orbit   The Orbit option lets you revolve your view about your model.

Look   The Look option swivels your point of view around your model as if you were standing still and moving your "camera" around.

Center   The Center option is a bit less obvious, but it is an important tool for the SteeringWheels feature. Click and hold the Center option and then drag the circular cursor that appears onto a 3D object. In any visual style other than 2D Wireframe, you will see a green sphere that indicates the center of your view for the Orbit option. Place this green sphere on the object at the desired center of your orbit. For example, if you want to use the Orbit option to look at all sides of a cube, click and drag the Center option so that the green sphere is at the center of the cube. Release the mouse button when you've placed the sphere where you want it (Figure 21.34).

If you are in a 2D Wireframe view, you will have to place the cursor on the edge of the object before you'll see the green sphere.

Walk The Walk option is similar to the Walk tool in the Render tab's Animations panel (see "Changing Where You Are Looking" later in this chapter for more on the Walk tool). Click and drag the Walk option and you'll see a blue square and a cursor arrow that points in a direction away from the square (Figure 21.35). Your view moves smoothly in the direction of the arrow as if to follow it.

FIGURE 21.35
Using the
Walk option

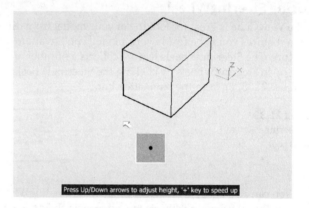

Rewind The Rewind option literally rewinds the views you've seen while using the SteeringWheels feature. Click and drag the Rewind option and you see a series of panels like movie frames in a video editing program (Figure 21.36).

FIGURE 21.36
The frames of the
Rewind option

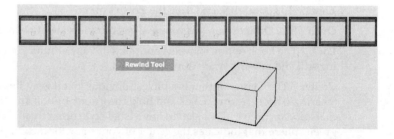

As you move the mouse from right to left, the views in the AutoCAD drawing area are played back smoothly in reverse order. Move left to right to move forward in time through the views. This is especially helpful if your model has accidentally shifted out of view. You can roll back your views to one before the model flew out of view.

SteeringWheels offers a number of options in a right-click menu. This menu can also be opened by clicking the arrowhead in the lower-right corner of the wheel. Most of these right-click menu options are self-explanatory, but a few of them are worth a brief description.

If you click the Basic Wheels option in the SteeringWheels right-click menu, you'll see Tour Building and View Object (Figure 21.37). These are variations on the basic SteeringWheels wheel and offer a pared-down set of options for the two types of viewing options indicated by the name of the wheels.

FIGURE 21.37

Variations of the Steering-Wheels wheel

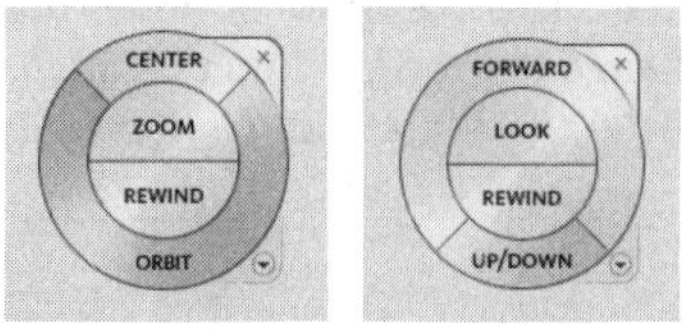

View Object   Tour Building

You'll also see mini versions available for the wheels from the SteeringWheels menu. The mini versions are much smaller, and they do not have labels indicating the options. Instead, you see segmented circles. Each segment of the circle is an option. Tool tips appear when you point at a segment, telling you what option that segment represents. Other than that, the mini versions work the same as the full-size wheels.

The SteeringWheels feature takes a little practice, but once you've become familiar with it, you may find that you use it frequently when studying a 3D model. Just remember that a click-and-drag motion is required to use the tools effectively.

Changing Where You Are Looking

AutoCAD uses a camera analogy to help you set up views in your 3D model. With a camera, you have a camera location and a target, and you can fine-tune both in AutoCAD. AutoCAD also offers the Swivel tool to let you adjust your view orientation. Using the Swivel tool is like keeping the camera stationary while pointing in a different direction. While viewing your drawing in perspective mode, click Pan on the View tab's navigation bar, right-click in the drawing area, and select Other Navigation Modes ➢ Swivel. (Remember that you need to right-click on the ViewCube and select Perspective for the perspective mode.)

At first, the Swivel tool might seem just like the Pan tool. But in the 3D world, Pan actually moves both the camera and the target in unison. Using Pan is a bit like pointing a camera out the side of a moving car. If you don't keep the view in the camera fixed on an object, you are panning across the scenery. Using the Swivel tool is like standing on the side of the road and turning the camera to take in a panoramic view.

To use the Swivel tool, do the following:

1. While in a perspective view, click Pan on the View tab's Navigate panel or from the navigation bar.

2. Right-click in the drawing area, and choose Other Navigation Modes ➢ Swivel. You can also type **3dswivel.↵** at the Command prompt.

3. Click and drag in the drawing to swivel your point of view.

4. When you have the view you want, right-click and select Exit.

If you happen to lose your view entirely, you can use the Undo tool in the Quick Access tool-bar to return to your previous view and start over.

Flying through Your View

Another way to get around in your model is to use the Walk or Fly view options. If you're famil-iar with computer games, this tool is for you. To get to these options, start the Pan tool as you did in the last exercise, and then right-click and select Other Navigation Modes ➢ Walk or Fly. If you don't see the Other Navigation Modes menu option, make sure that you are in a perspective view. Click Change to proceed. You may then see a message under the Communication Center telling you how to use Walk and Fly (Figure 21.38).

FIGURE 21.38
Walk and Fly tip shown on the Com-munication Center

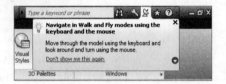

This message tells you all you need to know about the Walk and Fly tools. You can use the arrow keys to move through your model. Click and drag the mouse to change the direction in which you're looking.

If you press the F key, Walk changes to Fly mode. The main difference between Walk and Fly is that in Walk, both your position in the model and the point at which you're looking move with the Up and Down arrow keys. Walk is a bit like Pan. When you're in Fly mode, the arrow keys move you toward the center of your view, which is indicated by a crosshair.

In addition to the crosshair, you'll see a palette that shows your position in the model from a top-down view (Figure 21.39).

You can use the palette to control your view by clicking and dragging the camera or the view target graphic. If you prefer, you can close the palette and continue to "walk" through your model. When you're finished using Walk, right-click and choose Exit.

Changing from Perspective to Parallel Projection

When you create a new drawing using the `acad3D.dwt` template, you're automatically given a perspective view of the file. If you need a more schematic parallel projection style of view, you can get one from the ViewCube's right-click shortcut menu (see Figure 21.40). You can return to a perspective view by using the same shortcut menu shown in the figure.

WHERE TO FIND WALK

The Walk tool is part of a flyout on the Animations panel. Typically, the Animations panel is not dis-played. To display it, select the Render tab, right-click in the Ribbon, and select Panels ➢ Animations. The Walk tool is in the upper-right corner of the panel. The Fly tool is in the flyout of the Walk tool.

FIGURE 21.39
The Position Locator palette uses a top-down view.

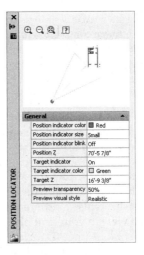

General	
Position indicator color	■ Red
Position indicator size	Small
Position indicator blink	Off
Position Z	70'-5 7/8"
Target indicator	On
Target indicator color	□ Green
Target Z	16'-9 3/8"
Preview transparency	50%
Preview visual style	Realistic

FIGURE 21.40
The Perspective Projection and Parallel Projection tools

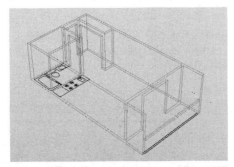

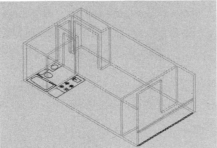

Getting a Visual Effect

3D models are extremely useful in communicating your ideas to others, but sometimes you find that the default appearance of your model isn't exactly what you want. If you're only in a schematic design stage, you may want your model to look more like a sketch instead of a finished product. Conversely, if you're trying to sell someone on a concept, you may want a realistic look that includes materials and even special lighting.

AutoCAD provides a variety of tools to help you get a visual style, from a simple wireframe to a fully rendered image complete with chrome and wood. In the following sections, you'll get a preview of what is available to control the appearance of your model. Later, in Chapter 23, you'll get an in-depth look at rendering and camera tools that allow you to produce views from hand-sketched "napkin" designs to finished renderings.

Using Visual Styles

In the earlier tutorials in this chapter, you drew a box that appeared to be solid. When you then opened an existing file to extrude the unit plan into the third dimension, you worked in a Wireframe view. These views are known as *visual styles* in AutoCAD. You used the default 3D visual style called Realistic when you drew the box. The unit plan used the default 2D Wireframe view that is used in the AutoCAD Classic style of drawing.

Sometimes, it helps to use a different visual style, depending on your task. For example, the 2D Wireframe view in your unit plan model can help you visualize and select things that are behind a solid. AutoCAD includes several shaded view options that can bring out various features of your model. Try the following exercises to explore some of the other visual styles:

1. Click the Visual Styles drop-down list in the Home tab's View panel. You can also find the list in the View tab's Visual Styles panel. A set of graphic images appear that give you an idea of what each visual style shows you (Figure 21.41).

FIGURE 21.41
The Visual Styles flyout

The Visual Styles drop-down list

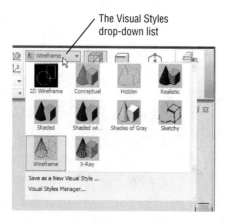

2. Select Wireframe. You can also enter **Vscurrent.⏎ wireframe.⏎**. Your model appears as a transparent wireframe object with a gray background.

3. To get to the shaded view of your model, choose Realistic from the Visual Styles drop-down list or enter **Vscurrent.⏎ Realistic.⏎**.

You may have noticed a few other Visual Styles options. Figure 21.42 shows a few of those options as they're applied to a sphere. 2D Wireframe and Wireframe may appear the same, but Wireframe uses a perspective view and a background color, whereas 2D Wireframe uses a parallel projection view and no background color.

FIGURE 21.42
Visual styles
applied to a sphere

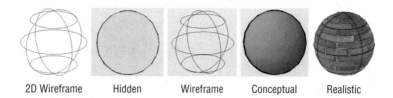

2D Wireframe   Hidden   Wireframe   Conceptual   Realistic

Creating a Sketched Look with Visual Styles

You may notice blanks in the visual styles options in the View tab's Visual Styles drop-down list. These spaces allow you to create custom visual styles. For practice, you'll create a visual style similar to the existing Sketchy style so you can learn how the rough look of that style was created. The following exercise will step you through the process:

1. Click the Visual Styles Manager tool in the View tab's Palettes panel. The Visual Styles Manager palette appears (Figure 21.43). You can also enter Visualstyles ↵. This palette looks similar to the Properties palette, with the addition of thumbnail examples of the visual styles at the top of the palette.

FIGURE 21.43
The Visual
Styles Manager

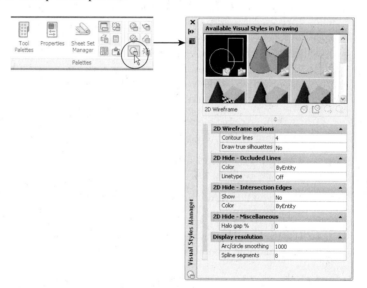

2. Click the Create New Visual Style tool in the Visual Styles Manager palette toolbar (Figure 21.44). The Create New Visual Style dialog box opens.

3. Enter **Sketch**↵ in the Name input box.

4. Enter **Hand Drawn Appearance** in the Description input box, and then click OK. You see a new thumbnail in the bottom-left corner of the samples at the top of the palette.

FIGURE 21.44
Open the
Create New Visual
Style dialog.

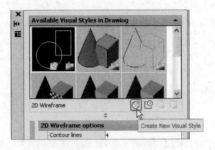

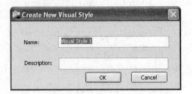

You've just created a new visual style. This new style uses the default settings that are similar to the Realistic visual style but without the Material Display option turned on. The material setting causes objects in your drawing to display any material assignments that have been given to objects. You'll learn more about materials in Chapter 23.

Now that you have a new visual style, you can begin to customize it. But before you start your customization, make your new visual style the current one so you can see the effects of your changes as you make them:

1. Click the Apply Selected Visual Style To Current Viewport tool in the Visual Styles Manager toolbar (Figure 21.45).

   The display changes slightly, and you see the name Sketch appear in the Visual Styles panel drop-down list.

   Next, you'll turn on the two features that will give your new visual style a sketchlike appearance.

2. Use the scroll bar to the left of the Visual Styles Manager toolbar to scroll down to the bottom of the list of options.

FIGURE 21.45
Apply the selected
visual style.

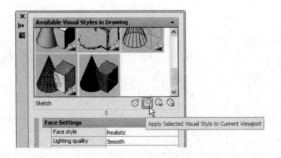

3. Locate the Edge Modifiers option group, and click the Line Extensions Edges tool in the Edge Modifiers title bar (Figure 21.46).

FIGURE 21.46
Use the Line Extensions Edges tool.

Edges of your model now appear to be drawn with lines extending beyond the corners.

4. Click the Jitter Edges tool (Figure 21.47) in the Edge Modifiers title bar.

FIGURE 21.47
Applying the Jitter Edges tool

5. The edges take on a sketched look, as shown in Figure 21.48.

FIGURE 21.48
The 3D unit plan with the Sketch visual style

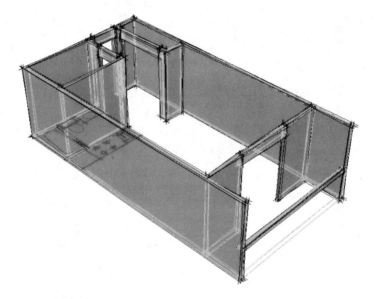

6. Close the Visual Styles Manager palette.

7. Save the unit plan file.

The 3D view has taken on a hand-drawn appearance. Notice that the lines overhang the corners in a typical architectural sketch style. This is the effect of the Line Extensions Edges option you used in step 3. The lines are made rough and broken by the Jitter Edges setting. You can control the amount of overhang and jitter in the Edge Modifiers group of the Visual Styles Manager to exaggerate or soften these effects.

With your newly created Sketch visual style, the model looks like it's transparent. You can make it appear opaque by turning off the Show option under the Occluded Edges group in the Visual Styles Manager (Figure 21.49).

FIGURE 21.49
The Show option in the Occluded Edges group in the Visual Style Manager

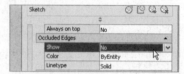

Finally, you can control some of the more commonly used visual style properties using options in the View tab's Visual Styles panel. This panel offers control over isolines, color, face style, shadows, and textures for the current visual style (Figure 21.50).

FIGURE 21.50
Visual Styles options in the Visual Styles panel

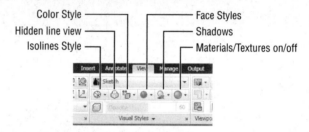

Turning a 3D View into a 2D AutoCAD Drawing

Many architectural firms use AutoCAD 3D models to study their designs. After a specific part of a design is modeled and approved, they convert the model into 2D elevations, ready to plug in to their elevation drawing.

If you need to convert your 3D models into 2D line drawings, you can use the Flatshot tool in the Home tab's expanded Section panel.

Set up your drawing view, and then click the Flatshot tool or enter **Flatshot.⏎** at the Command prompt to open the Flatshot dialog box (Figure 21.51).

FIGURE 21.51

The Flatshot dialog

PRINTING YOUR MODEL USING VISUAL STYLES

You can print a drawing that uses visual styles either from the Model tab or from a Layout tab. If you're printing from the Model view, click Plot from the Quick Access toolbar. Then, in the Plot dialog box, select the visual style from the Shade Plot drop-down list in the Shaded Viewport Options group. If you're plotting from a Layout tab, select the layout viewport border, right-click, and choose Shade Plot from the shortcut menu. You can select from a list of visual styles on a cascading menu. Once you've done this, plot your layout as you normally would.

Select the options you want to use for the 2D line drawing, and then click Create. Depending on the options you select, you'll be prompted to select an insertion point or indicate a location for an exported drawing file. The 2D line drawing will be placed on the plane of the current UCS, so if you are viewing your model in a 3D view but you are in the world UCS, the 2D line drawing will appear to be projected onto the XY plane.

Flatshot offers the ability to place the 2D version of your model in the current drawing as a block, to replace an existing block in the current drawing, or to save the 2D version as a DWG file. Table 21.1 describes the Flatshot options in more detail.

TABLE 21.1 Flatshot options

OPTION	WHAT IT DOES
Destination	
Insert As New Block	Inserts the 2D view in the current drawing as a block. You're prompted for an insertion point, a scale, and a rotation.

TABLE 21.1 Flatshot options *(CONTINUED)*

OPTION	WHAT IT DOES
Replace Existing Block	Replaces an existing block with a block of the 2D view. You're prompted to select an existing block.
Select Block	If Replace Existing Block is selected, lets you select a block to be replaced. A warning is shown if no block is selected.
Export To A File	Exports the 2D view as a drawing file.
Filename And Path	Displays the location for the export file. Click the Browse button to specify a location.
Foreground Lines	
Color	Sets the overall color for the 2D view.
Linetype	Sets the overall linetype for the 2D view.
Obscured Lines	
Show	Displays hidden lines.
Color	If Show is turned on, sets the color for hidden lines.
Linetype	If Show is turned on, sets the linetype for hidden lines. The Current Linetype Scale setting is used for linetypes other than continuous.
Include Tangential Edges	Displays edges for curved surfaces.

THINGS TO WATCH OUT FOR WHEN EDITING 3D OBJECTS

You can use the Move and Stretch commands on 3D objects to modify their Z coordinate values—but you have to be careful with these commands when editing in 3D. Here are a few tips that I've picked up while working on various 3D projects:

◆ If you want to move a 3D solid using grips, you need to select the square grip at the bottom center of the solid. The other grips move only the feature associated with the grip, like a corner or an edge. Once that bottom grip is selected, you can switch to another grip as the base point for the move by doing the following: After selecting the base grip, right-click, select Base Point from the shortcut menu, and click the grip you want to use.

◆ The Scale command will scale an object's Z coordinate value as well as the standard X coordinate and Y coordinate. Suppose you have an object with an elevation of 2 units. If you use the Scale command to enlarge that object by a factor of 4, the object will have a new elevation of 2 units times 4, or 8 units. If, on the other hand, that object has an elevation of 0, its elevation won't change because 0 times 4 is still 0. You can use the 3dscale command to restrict the scaling of an object to a single plane.

- You can also use Array, Mirror, and Rotate (on the Modify panel) on 3D solid objects, but these commands don't affect their Z coordinate values. Z coordinates can be specified for base and insertion points, so take care when using these commands with 3D models.

- Using the Move, Stretch, and Copy commands (on the Modify panel) with osnaps can produce unpredictable and unwanted results. As a rule, it's best to use point filters when selecting points with osnap overrides. For example, to move an object from the endpoint of one object to the endpoint of another on the same Z coordinate, invoke the .XY point filter at the Specify base point: and Specify second point: prompts before you issue the Endpoint override. Proceed to pick the endpoint of the object you want; then, enter the Z coordinate or pick any point to use the current default Z coordinate.

- When you create a block, it uses the currently active UCS to determine its own local coordinate system. When that block is later inserted, it orients its own coordinate system with the current UCS. (The UCS is discussed in more detail in Chapter 22.)

One very useful feature of Flatshot is that it can create a 2D drawing that displays the hidden lines of a 3D mechanical drawing. Turn on the Show option, and then select a line type such as Hidden for obscured lines to produce a 2D drawing like the one shown in Figure 21.52.

FIGURE 21.52
A sample of a 2D drawing generated from a 3D model using Flatshot. Note the dashed lines showing the hidden lines of the view.

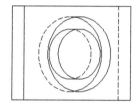
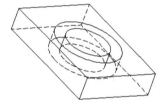
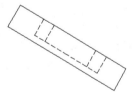

Using the Point Cloud Feature

As you might guess from the name, a point cloud is a set of data points in a 3D coordinate system. They are often the product of 3D scanners which are devices that can analyze and record the shape of real-world objects or environments. Point cloud data can be used to reproduce an object or environment as a digital model which can then be used for a video game or movie production.

AutoCAD enables you to import point cloud data through a set of tools that can be found in the Insert tab's Point Cloud panel.

FIGURE 21.53
The Point Cloud
panel in the
Insert tab.

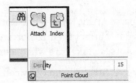

AutoCAD can import point cloud data from four file types: FLS, FWS, LAS and XYB. To import a file, it must first be indexed using the Index tool in the Point Cloud panel. The Index tool can take some time to process a file, so indexing is performed in the background. This enables you to continue to work while a file is being indexed.

The Indexing icon appears in the status bar to remind you that a point cloud is being indexed. If for some reason, you need to cancel the indexing, you can right-click on the point cloud icon and select Cancel Indexing.

AutoCAD produces an ISD or PCG file from the indexed data. These files can then be attached to a drawing file using the Attach tool in the Point Cloud panel. Since point clouds can consume a great deal of memory, you can use the Density slider in the expanded Point Cloud panel to control the density of the point cloud. The lower the density, the less impact the point cloud will have on AutoCAD's performance.

Once you have the point cloud attached to a drawing, you can use the points to help guide you in building a 3D model. You can use the Node osnap to snap to the individual points in the point cloud.

The Bottom Line

Know the 3D modeling workspace. When you work in 3D, you need a different set of tools from those for 2D drafting. AutoCAD offers the 3D Modeling workspace, which provides the tools you need to create 3D models.

Master It Name some of the Ribbon panels that are unique to the 3D Modeling workspace.

Draw in 3D using solids. AutoCAD offers a type of object called a 3D solid that lets you quickly create and edit shapes.

Master It What does the Presspull command do?

Create 3D forms from 2D shapes. The Modeling panel offers a set of basic 3D shapes, but other tools enable you to create virtually any shape you want from 2D drawings.

Master It Name the command that lets you change a closed 2D polyline into a 3D solid.

Isolate coordinates with point filters. When you're working in 3D, selecting points can be a complicated task. AutoCAD offers point filters to let you specify the individual X, Y, and Z coordinates of a location in space.

Master It What does the .XY point filter do?

Move around your model. Getting the view you want in a 3D model can be tricky.

Master It Where is the drop-down list that lets you select a view from a list of predefined 3D views?

Get a visual effect.   At certain points in your model making, you'll want to view your 3D model with surface colors and even material assignments. AutoCAD offers several ways to do this.

   Master It   What are the steps to take to change the view from Wireframe to Conceptual?

Turn a 3D view into a 2D AutoCAD drawing.   Sometimes, it's helpful to convert a 3D model view into a 2D AutoCAD drawing. AutoCAD offers the Flatshot tool, which quickly converts a 3D view into a 2D line drawing.

   Master It   What type of object does Flatshot create?

Chapter 22

Using Advanced 3D Features

AutoCAD 2011's extended set of tools for working with 3D drawings lets you create 3D objects with few limitations on shape and orientation. This chapter focuses on the use of these tools, which help you easily generate 3D forms and view them in both perspective and orthogonal modes.

AutoCAD LT doesn't support any of the features described in this chapter.

In this chapter, you'll learn to do the following:

◆ Master the User Coordinate System

◆ Understand the UCS options

◆ Use viewports to aid in 3D drawing

◆ Create complex 3D surfaces

◆ Create spiral forms

◆ Create surface models

◆ Move objects in 3D space

Setting Up AutoCAD for This Chapter

Before you start, I'd like you to set up AutoCAD in a way that will make your work a little easier. You'll use the 3D Modeling workspace you were introduced to in Chapter 21. To do so, follow these steps:

1. Start AutoCAD, and then click the Workspace tool in the Quick Access toolbar and select 3D Modeling. You'll see a new set of panels appear as well as the Materials Browser window.

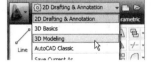

2. Close the Materials Browser window to get a clear view of the drawing area. Your screen should look similar to Figure 22.1.

In Chapter 21, you started a new 3D model using a template set up for 3D modeling. Here you'll start to work with the default 2D drawing. Now you're ready to get to work.

FIGURE 22.1
The AutoCAD
window set up for
this chapter

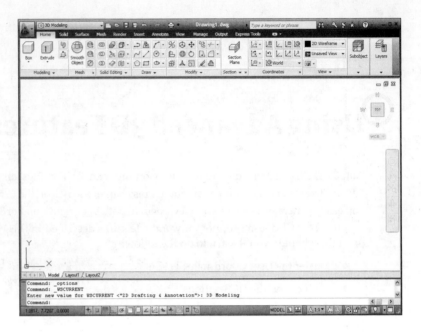

Mastering the User Coordinate System

The User Coordinate System (UCS) enables you to define a custom coordinate system in 2D and 3D space. You've been using a default UCS, called the *World Coordinate System (WCS)*, all along. By now, you're familiar with the L-shaped icon in the lower-left corner of the AutoCAD screen, containing a small square and the letters X and Y. The square indicates that you're currently in the WCS; the X and Y indicate the positive directions of the X and Y axes. WCS is a global system of reference from which you can define other UCSs.

It may help to think of these AutoCAD UCSs as different drawing surfaces, or two-dimensional planes. You can have several UCSs at any given time. By setting up these different UCSs, you can draw as you would in the WCS in 2D yet draw a 3D image.

Suppose you want to draw a house in 3D with doors and windows on each of its sides. You can set up a UCS for each of the sides, and then you can move from UCS to UCS to add your doors and windows (see Figure 22.2). In each UCS, you draw your doors and windows as you would in a typical 2D drawing. You can even insert elevation views of doors and windows that you created in other drawings.

In this chapter, you'll experiment with several views and UCSs. All the commands you'll use are available both at the command line and via the View tab's Coordinates panel.

Defining a UCS

In the first set of exercises, you'll draw a chair that you can later add to your 3D unit drawing. In drawing this chair, you'll be exposed to the UCS as well as to some of the other 3D capabilities available in AutoCAD:

1. Open the barcelona1.dwg file. Metric users should open barcelona1_metric.dwg. This file contains two rectangles that you'll use to create a chair.

2. Select Southwest Isometric from the View drop-down list on the Home tab's View panel. You can also type **-V⏎SWISO⏎**. This gives you a 3D view from the lower left of the rectangles, as shown in the bottom image in Figure 22.3. Zoom out a bit to give yourself some room to work.

3. Select the two rectangles and then right-click and select Properties.

FIGURE 22.2
Different UCSs in a
3D drawing

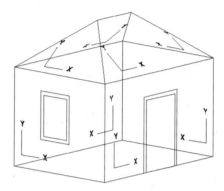

FIGURE 22.3
The chair seat and
back in the Plan
(top) and Isometric
(bottom) views

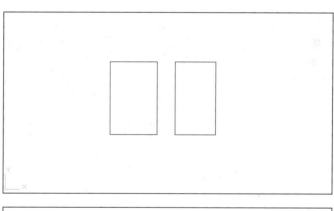

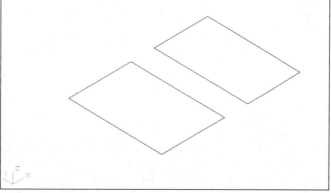

4. In the Properties palette, enter **3** in the Thickness setting and press ⏎. This gives the seat and back a thickness of 3″. Metric users should make the thickness 7.6 cm.

5. Press the Esc key, and close the Properties palette. Click the Convert To Solid tool in the Home tab's expanded Solid Editing panel.

6. Select the two rectangles, and then press ⏎.

Notice that the UCS icon appears in the same plane as the current coordinate system. The icon will help you keep track of which coordinate system you're in. Now you can see the chair components as 3D objects.

Next, you'll define a UCS that is aligned with one side of the seat:

1. Click Named UCS from the View tab's Coordinates panel or type **Ucsman**⏎ to open the UCS dialog box.

2. Select the Orthographic UCSs tab to view a set of predefined UCSs.

3. Select Front in the list box. Figure 22.4 shows the orientation of the Front UCS.

FIGURE 22.4
The six predefined
UCS orientations

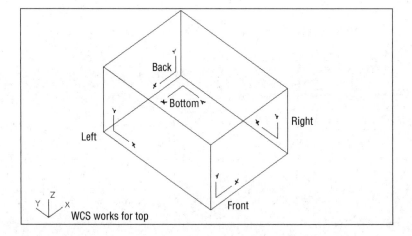

4. Click the Set Current button to make the Front UCS current.

5. Click OK to close the dialog box.

The Orthographic UCSs tab offers a set of predefined UCSs for each of the six standard orthographic projection planes. Figure 22.4 shows these UCSs in relation to the WCS.

Because a good part of 3D work involves drawing in these orthographic planes, AutoCAD supplies the ready-made UCS orientations for quick access. But you aren't limited to these six orientations. If you're familiar with mechanical drafting, you'll see that the orthographic UCSs correspond to the typical orthographic projections used in mechanical drafting. If you're an architect, the Front, Left, Back, and Right UCSs correspond to the south, west, north, and east elevations of a building.

Before you continue building the chair model, you'll move the UCS to the surface on which you'll be working. Right now, the UCS has its origin located in the same place as the WCS origin.

You can move a UCS so that its origin is anywhere in the drawing where it's needed:

1. Click the Origin tool from the View tab's Coordinate panel or type **UCS⏎O⏎**.

2. Use the Endpoint osnap and click the bottom-front corner of the chair seat, as shown in Figure 22.5. The UCS icon moves to indicate its new origin's location.

FIGURE 22.5
Setting up a UCS

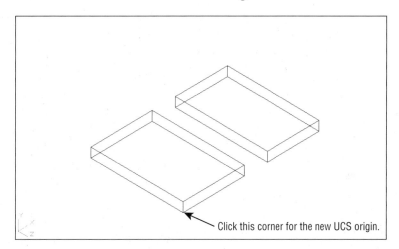

Click this corner for the new UCS origin.

You just created a new UCS based on the Front UCS you selected from the UCS dialog box. Now, as you move your cursor, the origin of the UCS icon corresponds to a 0,0 coordinate. Although you have a new UCS, the WCS still exists; you can always return to it when you need to.

Saving a UCS

After you've gone through the work of creating a UCS, you may want to save it, especially if you think you'll come back to it later. Here's how to save a UCS:

1. Choose Named from the Coordinates panel or type **Ucsman⏎** to open the UCS dialog box.

2. Make sure the Named UCSs tab is selected, and then highlight the Unnamed option in the Current UCS list box.

3. Click on the word *Unnamed*. The item changes to allow editing.

4. Type **3DSW⏎** for the name of your new UCS.

5. Click OK to exit the dialog box.

Your UCS is now saved with the name 3DSW. You can recall it from the UCS dialog box or by using other methods that you'll learn about later in this chapter.

Working in a UCS

Next, you'll arrange the seat and back and draw the legs of the chair. Your UCS is oriented so that you can easily adjust the orientation of the chair components. As you work through the next exercise, notice that although you're manipulating 3D objects, you're really using the same tools you've used to edit 2D objects.

Follow these steps to adjust the seat and back and to draw legs:

1. Click the seat back to expose its grips. The seat back is the box to the right.

2. Click the bottom grip, as shown in the first image in Figure 22.6.

3. Right-click the mouse to open the Grip Edit shortcut menu.

4. Choose Rotate from the menu. The seat back now rotates with the movement of the cursor. It rotates in the plane of the new UCS you created earlier.

5. Type **80**↵ to rotate the seat back 80°. Your view looks like the second image in Figure 22.6.

FIGURE 22.6
Moving the components of the chair into place

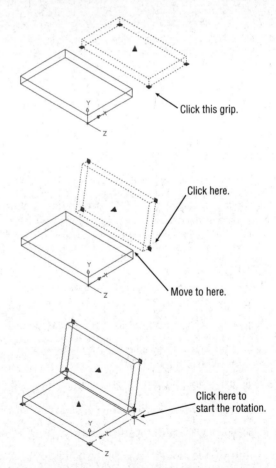

Click this grip.

Click here.

Move to here.

Click here to start the rotation.

6. Click the bottom grip, as shown in the second image in Figure 22.6.

7. Right-click the mouse again and choose Move.

8. Using the Endpoint osnap, click the top corner of the chair seat to join the chair back to the seat, as shown in the second image in Figure 22.6.

9. Click the chair seat; then click the bottom-corner grip of the seat, as shown in the third image in Figure 22.6.

10. Right-click and choose Rotate from the Grip Edit shortcut menu.

11. Enter –10↵ to rotate both the seat and back minus 10°. Press the Esc key to clear the grips. Your chair looks like Figure 22.7.

FIGURE 22.7
The chair after rotating and moving the components

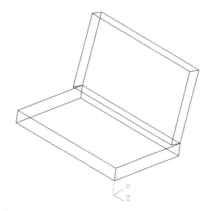

The new UCS orientation enabled you to use the grips to adjust the chair seat and back. All the grip rotation in the previous exercise was confined to the plane of the new UCS. Mirroring and scaling will also occur in relation to the current UCS.

Building 3D Parts in Separate Files

As you work in 3D, your models will become fairly complex. When your model becomes too crowded for you to see things clearly, it helps to build parts of the model and then import them instead of building everything in one file. In the next set of exercises, you'll draw the legs of the chair and then import them to the main chair file to give you some practice in the procedure.

I've prepared a drawing called legs.dwg, which consists of two polylines that describe the shape of the legs. I did this to save you some tedious work that isn't related to 3D modeling. You'll use this file as a starting point for the legs, and then you'll import the legs into the barcelona1.dwg file:

1. Open the legs.dwg file. Metric users should open the legs_metric.dwg file. The file consists of two polyline splines that are in the shape of one set of legs. You'll turn these simple lines into 3D solids.

2. Click the Edit Polyline tool in the Home tab's expanded Modify panel.

3. At the `Select polyline or [Multiple]:` prompt, enter **M**↵ to select multiple polylines. Then select the two polylines, and press ↵.

4. At the `Enter an option [Close/Open/Join/Width/Fit/Spline/Decurve/Ltype gen/ Undo]:` prompt, enter **W**↵.

5. At the `Specify new width for all segments:` prompt, enter **0.5**↵ to give the polylines a width of 0.5″. Metric users should enter **1.27**↵.

6. Press ↵ to exit the Pedit command.

Next, you need to change the Thickness property of the two polylines to make them 2″ or 5 cm wide:

1. With the two polylines selected, open the Properties palette, and set their thickness to 2. Metric users should set their thickness to 5.

2. Close the Properties palette.

3. Click the Convert To Solid tool in the Home tab's expanded Solid Editing panel, or enter **convtosolid**↵ at the Command prompt.

4. Select the two polylines, and then press ↵. The lines become 3D solids.

5. Click the Union tool in the Home tab's Solid Editing panel, select the two legs, and press ↵. The two legs are now a single 3D solid, as shown in Figure 22.8.

FIGURE 22.8
The polylines con-
verted to 3D solids

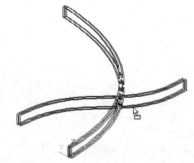

As you've just seen, you can convert polylines that have both a width and a thickness into 3D solids. Now you're ready to add the legs to the rest of the chair.

1. Click the Tile Vertically tool in the View tab's Windows panel. You see the legs drawing on the left and the rest of the chair on the right.

2. Adjust the views so your screen looks similar to Figure 22.9. If you see a third `Drawing1. dwg` panel, close it and click the Tile Vertically tool again.

3. Click in the barcelona1 drawing, and click Extents from the Zoom flyout on the View tab's Navigate panel to get an overall view of the chair so far.

4. Click in the legs drawing, and then click the legs 3D solid to select it.

5. Click and hold the cursor on the legs until you see the arrow cursor with a small rectangle (Figure 22.8).

FIGURE 22.9
Click and drag the leg from the left window to the right window and align the leg with the chair seat and back.

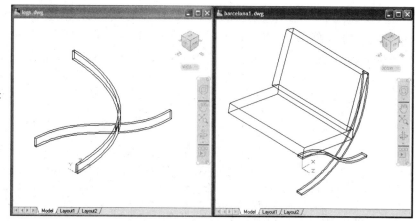

6. When you see the rectangle, drag the mouse into the barcelona1 drawing. The legs appear in the proper orientation.

7. Release the mouse button to place the legs in the barcelona1 drawing. You don't need to be precise about placing the legs; you can move them into position next.

8. Use the Move tool to move the legs so the endpoint of the horizontal leg joins the chair seat, as shown in the image in the right panel of Figure 22.9.

9. Save and close the legs.dwg file, and expand the barcelona1.dwg file to fill the AutoCAD window.

USE COPY AND PASTE

You can also use a "copy and paste" to copy the legs to the barcelona1 drawing. In step 4, right-click and select Copy from the shortcut menu. Skip steps 5 through 7 and instead click in the barcelona1 drawing, right-click, and select Paste.

In these last few exercises, you worked on the legs of the chair in a separate file and then imported them into the main chair file with a click-and-drag motion. By working on parts in separate files, you can keep your model organized and more manageable. You may have also noticed that although the legs were drawn in the WCS, they were inserted in the 3DSW UCS that you created earlier. This shows you that imported objects are placed in the current UCS. The same would have happened if you inserted an Xref or another file.

Understanding the UCS Options

You've seen how to select a UCS from a set of predefined UCSs. You can frequently use these preset UCSs and make minor adjustments to them to get the exact UCS you want.

CONTROLLING THE UCS ICON

If the UCS icon isn't behaving as described in this chapter's exercises, chances are that its settings have been altered. You can control the behavior of the UCS icon through the UCS dialog box. To open the UCS dialog box, click Named from the View tab's Coordinates panel or type **Ucsman**↵; then click the Settings tab.

The settings in the UCS Icon Settings group affect the way the UCS icon behaves. Normally, the On and Display At UCS Origin Point check boxes are selected. If On isn't selected, you won't see the UCS icon. If the Display At UCS Origin Point check box isn't selected, the UCS icon remains in the lower-left corner of the drawing window no matter where its origin is placed in the drawing.

If you have multiple viewports set up in a drawing, you can set these two options independently for each viewport. The third option, Apply To All Active Viewports, forces the first two settings to apply in all viewports.

Two more options appear in the UCS Settings group. If you have multiple viewports open, the Save UCS With Viewport option enables AutoCAD to maintain a separate UCS for each viewport. The Update View To Plan When UCS Is Changed option forces the display to show a plan view of the current UCS. This means that if you change a UCS orientation, AutoCAD automatically shows a plan view of the new UCS orientation. This option also forces viewport views to show the extents of plan views. If you find that your views are automatically zooming to extents when you don't want them to, turn off this setting.

Another tool for controlling the UCS icon is the UCS Icon dialog box. To open it, click the UCS Icon tool in the View tab's Coordinates panel or enter **Ucsicon**↵ **P**↵.

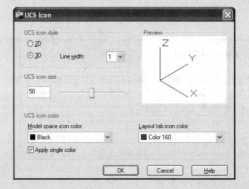

Using this dialog box, you can fine-tune the appearance of the UCS icon, including its size and color. The 2D radio button in the UCS Icon Style group changes the UCS icon to the old-style UCS icon used in earlier versions of AutoCAD.

You can define a UCS in other ways. You can, for example, use the surface of your chair seat to define the orientation of a UCS. In the following sections, you'll be shown the different ways you can set up a UCS. Learning how to move effortlessly between UCSs is crucial to mastering the creation of 3D models, so you'll want to pay special attention to the command options shown in these examples.

Note that these examples are for your reference. You can try them out on your own model. These options are accessible from the View tab's Coordinates panel.

UCS Based on Object Orientation

You can define a UCS based on the orientation of an object. This is helpful when you want to work on a predefined object to fill in details on its surface plane. The following steps are for information only and aren't part of the tutorial. You can try this at another time when you aren't working through an exercise.

Follow these steps to define a UCS this way:

1. Type **UCS↵OB↵**.

2. At the `Select object to align UCS:` prompt, pick the object that you want to use to define the UCS. For example, you could click a 3D solid that you want to edit. The UCS icon shifts to reflect the new coordinate system's orientation. Figure 22.10 shows an example of using the OB option to select the edge of the chair back.

When you create a UCS using the Object option, the location of the UCS origin and its orientation depend on how the selected object was created. Table 22.1 describes how an object can determine the orientation of a UCS.

TABLE 22.1:   Effects of objects on the orientation of a UCS

OBJECT TYPE	UCS ORIENTATION
Arc	The center of the arc establishes the UCS origin. The X axis of the UCS passes through the pick point on the arc.
Circle	The center of the circle establishes the UCS origin. The X axis of the UCS passes through the pick point on the circle.
Dimension	The midpoint of the dimension text establishes the UCS origin. The X axis of the UCS is parallel to the X axis that was active when the dimension was drawn.
Face (of a 3D solid)	The origin of the UCS is placed on a quadrant of a circular surface or on the corner of a polygonal surface.
Line	The endpoint nearest the pick point establishes the origin of the UCS, and the XZ plane of the UCS contains the line.
Point	The point location establishes the UCS origin. The UCS orientation is arbitrary.
2D polyline	The starting point of the polyline establishes the UCS origin. The X axis is determined by the direction from the first point to the next vertex.

TABLE 22.1: Effects of objects on the orientation of a UCS *(CONTINUED)*

OBJECT TYPE	UCS ORIENTATION
3D polyline	Returns the message This object does not define a coordinate system.
Spline	The UCS is created with its XY plane parallel to the XY plane of the UCS that was current when the spline was created.
Solid	The first point of the solid establishes the origin of the UCS. The second point of the solid establishes the X axis.
Trace	The direction of the trace establishes the X axis of the UCS, and the beginning point sets the origin.
3D Face	The first point of the 3D Face establishes the origin. The first and second points establish the X axis. The plane defined by the 3D Face determines the orientation of the UCS.
Shapes, text, blocks, attributes, and attribute definitions	The insertion point establishes the origin of the UCS. The object's rotation angle establishes the X axis.

FIGURE 22.10
Using the Object
option of the
UCS command to
locate a UCS

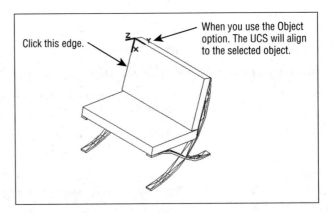

UCS Based on Offset Orientation

At times, you may want to work in a UCS that has the same orientation as the current UCS but is offset. For example, you might be drawing a building that has several parallel walls offset with a sawtooth effect (see Figure 22.11).

You can easily hop from one UCS to a new, parallel UCS by using the Origin option. Click the Origin tool on the Coordinates panel, or type **UCS↵O↵**. At the Specify new origin point <0,0,0>: prompt, pick the new origin for your UCS.

Another UCS option, called Move, will move an existing, named UCS to a new location and keep its original orientation. You won't find the UCS Move option on any panel or toolbar, but you can use it by entering **UCS↵ M↵** at the Command prompt.

FIGURE 22.11
Using the Origin option to shift the UCS

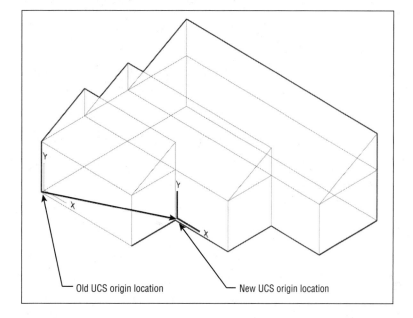

Old UCS origin location   New UCS origin location

The steps in the following section are for information only and aren't part of the tutorial. You can try this at another time when you aren't working through an exercise.

UCS Rotated around an Axis

Suppose you want to change the orientation of the X, Y, or Z axis of a UCS. You can do so by using the X, Y, or Z flyout on the View tab's Coordinates panel. These are perhaps among the most frequently used UCS options:

1. Click the X tool flyout arrowhead on the View tab's Coordinates panel and select Z from the flyout. You can also type **UCS↵Z↵**. This enables you to rotate the current UCS around the Z axis.

2. At the Specify rotation angle about Z axis <90>: prompt, press ↵ to accept the default of 90°. The UCS icon rotates about the Z axis to reflect the new orientation of the current UCS (see Figure 22.12).

Similarly, the X and Y options enable you to rotate the UCS about the current X and Y axis, respectively, just as you did for the Z axis earlier. The X and Y tools are helpful in orienting a UCS to an inclined plane. For example, if you want to work on the plane of a sloped roof of a building, you can first use the Origin UCS tool to align the UCS to the edge of a roof and then use the X tool to rotate the UCS to the angle of the roof slope, as shown in Figure 22.13. Note that the default is 90°, so you only have to press ↵ to rotate the UCS 90°, but you can also enter a rotation angle.

FIGURE 22.12
Rotating the UCS
about the Z axis

FIGURE 22.12
Rotating the UCS
about the Z axis

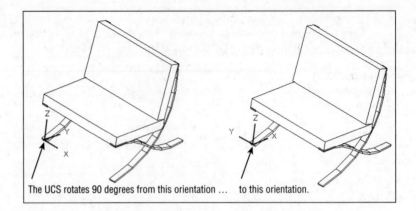

The UCS rotates 90 degrees from this orientation …   to this orientation.

FIGURE 22.13
Moving a UCS
to the plane of a
sloping roof

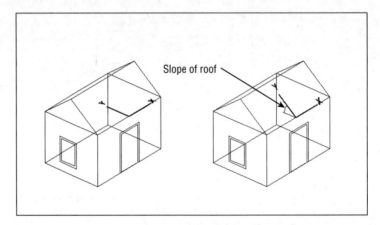

Slope of roof

Finally, you align the Z axis between two points using the Z-Axis Vector option. This is useful when you have objects in the drawing that you can use to align the Z axis. Here are the steps:

1. Click the Z-Axis Vector tool on the Coordinates panel, or type **UCS↵ZA↵**.

2. At the `Specify new origin point or [Object]<0,0,0>:` prompt, press ↵ to accept the default, which is the current UCS origin, or you can select a new origin.

3. At the prompt

   `Specify point on positive portion of Z-axis <0'-0", 0'-0", 0'-1">:`

   select another point to indicate the Z axis orientation. Figure 22.14 shows the resulting UCS if you use the bottom of the barcelona1 chair leg to define the Z axis.

Because your cursor location is in the plane of the current UCS, it's best to pick a point on an object by using either the Osnap overrides or the coordinate filters.

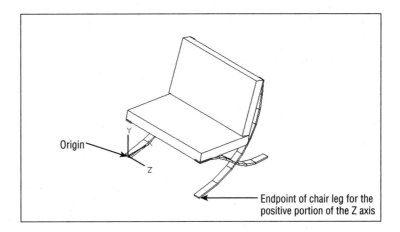

FIGURE 22.14
Picking points
for the Z-Axis
Vector tool

Orienting a UCS in the View Plane

Finally, you can define a UCS in the current view plane. This points the Z axis toward the user. This is useful if you want to switch quickly to the current view plane for editing or for adding text to a 3D view.

Click the View tool on the Coordinates panel, or type **UCS↵V↵**. Note that the View tool also has a flyout arrowhead that contains the Object and Face tools. If you accidentally click the flyout arrowhead, make sure to click the View tool in the flyout. The UCS icon changes to show that the UCS is aligned with the current view.

AutoCAD uses the current UCS origin point for the origin of the new UCS. By defining a view as a UCS, you can enter text to label your drawing, just as you would in a technical illustration. Text entered in a plane created this way appears normal.

You've finished your tour of the UCS command. Set the UCS back to the WCS by clicking the UCS, World tool in the View tab's Coordinates panel, and save the barcelona1.dwg file.

You've explored nearly every option in creating a UCS except one. Later in this chapter, you'll learn about the 3 Point option for creating a UCS. This is the most versatile method for creating a UCS, but it's more involved than some of the other UCS options.

Saving a UCS with a View

AutoCAD has the ability to save a UCS with a view. Click the View Manager option, found at the bottom of the 3D Navigation drop-down list in the Home tab's View panel (Figure 22.15). At the View Manager dialog box, click the New button. This opens the New View/Shot Properties dialog box. Enter a name for your new view in the View Name input box, and then choose a UCS to save with a new view by using the UCS drop-down list located in the Settings group of the dialog box.

Using Viewports to Aid in 3D Drawing

In Chapter 16, you worked extensively with AutoCAD's floating viewports in Paper Space. In this section, you'll use *tiled* viewports to see your 3D model from several sides at the same time. This is helpful in both creating and editing 3D drawings because it enables you to refer to different portions of the drawing without having to change views.

FIGURE 22.15
Select the View
Manager option in
the 3D Navigation
drop-down list.

Tiled viewports are created directly in Model Space, as you'll see in the following exercise:

1. Click the New tool on the View tab's Viewports panel to open the Viewports dialog box (Figure 22.16).

2. Make sure the New Viewports tab is selected, and then select Three: Right from the Standard Viewports list on the left. The window on the right changes to display a sample of the viewport configuration. It shows three rectangles, which represent the viewports, arranged with two on the left and one larger one to the right. Each rectangle is labeled as Current; this tells you that the current view will be placed in each viewport.

FIGURE 22.16
The Viewports
dialog

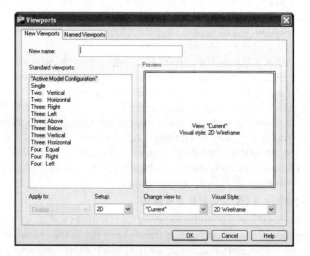

3. Open the Setup drop-down list at the bottom of the dialog box, and select 3D. The labels in the viewport sample change to indicate Top, Front, and SE Isometric. This is close to the arrangement you want, but you need to make one more adjustment. The viewport to the right, SE Isometric, shows the back side of the chair. You want an SW Isometric view in this window.

4. Click the SE Isometric viewport sample. The sample viewport border changes to a double border to indicate that it's selected.

5. Open the Change View To drop-down list just below the sample viewports, and select SW Isometric. The label in the selected viewport changes to let you know that the view will now contain the SW Isometric view. The Change View To list contains the standard four isometric views and the six orthogonal views. By clicking a sample viewport and selecting an option from the Change View To drop-down list, you can arrange your viewport views nearly any way you want.

6. To name this viewport arrangement, enter **My Viewport Setup** in the New Name input box.

7. Click OK. Your display changes to show three viewports arranged as they were indicated in the Viewports dialog box (see Figure 22.17).

You've set up your viewports. Let's check to see that your viewport arrangement was saved:

1. Click the Named tool in the View tab's Viewports panel to open the Viewports dialog box again.

2. Click the Named Viewports tab. My Viewport Setup is listed in the Named Viewports list box. If you click it, a sample view of your viewport arrangement appears on the right.

3. After you've reviewed the addition to the Named Viewports list, close the dialog box.

FIGURE 22.17
Three viewports, each displaying a different view

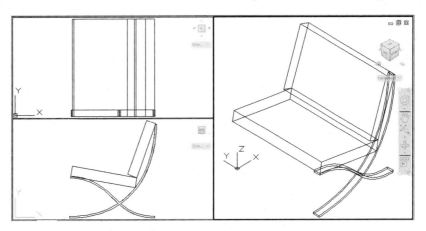

Now, take a close look at your viewport setup. The UCS icon in the orthogonal views in the two left viewports is oriented to the plane of the view. AutoCAD enables you to set up a different UCS for each viewport. The top view uses the WCS because it's in the same plane as the WCS. The side view has its own UCS, which is parallel to its view. The isometric view to the right retains the current UCS.

Another Viewports dialog box option you haven't tried yet is the Apply To drop-down list in the New Viewports tab (Figure 22.18).

FIGURE 22.18
The Apply To drop-down list

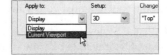

This list shows two options: Display and Current Viewport. When Display is selected, the option you choose from the Standard Viewports list applies to the overall display. When Current Viewport is selected, the option you select applies to the selected viewport in the sample view in the right side of the dialog box. You can use the Current Viewport option to build multiple viewports in custom arrangements.

You have the legs for one side. The next step is to mirror those legs for the other side:

1. Click the top view of the chair in the upper-left viewport.

2. Turn on Polar Tracking in the status bar, and then click the Mirror tool on the Home tab's expanded Modify panel.

3. In the upper-left viewport, click the 3D solid representing the chair legs, and then press ↵.

4. At the Specify first point of mirror line: prompt, use the Midpoint osnap and select the midpoint of the chair seat, as shown in Figure 22.19.

FIGURE 22.19
Mirroring the legs from one side to another

Click the midpoint of this edge.

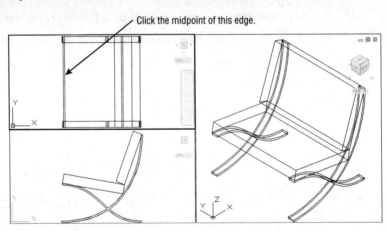

5. At the Specify second point of mirror line: prompt, pick any location to the right of the point you selected so the rubber-banding line is exactly horizontal.

6. Press ↵ at the Erase source objects? [Yes/No] <N>: prompt. The legs are mirrored to the opposite side of the chair. Your screen should look similar to Figure 22.19.

Your chair is complete. Let's finish by getting a better look at it:

1. Click the viewport to the right, showing the Isometric view.

2. Click Single from the Viewport Configurations drop-down list in the View tab's Viewports panel (Figure 22.20), or enter **-Viewports**↵ (with a minus sign) **Si**↵.

3. Use the Zoom tool to adjust your view so that it looks similar to Figure 22.21.

4. Click the Visual Styles drop-down list on the Home tab's View panel (Figure 22.22), and select Shades Of Gray to get a view similar to Figure 22.21. Note that your background may appear much darker.

FIGURE 22.20
Click Single in
the Viewport
Configurations
drop-down list.

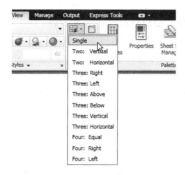

FIGURE 22.21
The chair in
3D with hidden
lines removed

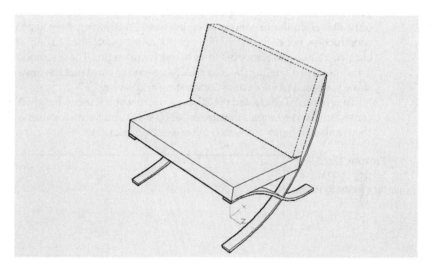

5. Exit the file. You can save if you like or close without saving in case you want to do the exercise again.

FIGURE 22.22
The Visual Styles
drop-down list.

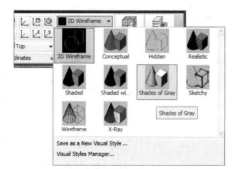

Creating Complex 3D Surfaces

In the previous example, you drew a chair composed of objects that were mostly straight lines or curves with a thickness. All the forms in that chair were defined in planes perpendicular to one another. For a 3D model such as this, you can get by using the orthographic UCSs. At times, however, you'll want to draw objects that don't fit so easily into perpendicular or parallel planes. In the following sections, you'll create more-complex forms by using some of AutoCAD's other 3D commands.

Laying Out a 3D Form

In this next group of exercises, you'll draw a butterfly chair. This chair has no perpendicular or parallel planes to work with, so you'll start by setting up some points that you'll use for reference only. This is similar in concept to laying out a 2D drawing. As you progress through the drawing construction, notice how the reference points are established to help create the chair. You'll also construct some temporary 3D lines to use for reference. These temporary lines will be your layout. These points will define the major UCSs needed to construct the drawing. The main point is to show you some of the options for creating and saving UCSs.

To save time, I've created the 2D drawing that you'll use to build your 3D layout. This drawing consists of two rectangles that are offset by 4″ (10 mm for metric users). To make it more interesting, they're also off center from each other (see Figure 22.23).

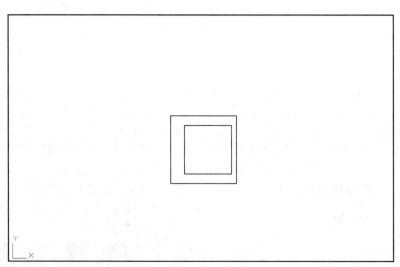

FIGURE 22.23
Setting up a layout for a butterfly chair

The first thing you'll need to do is set up the drawing for the layout:

1. Open the butterfly1.dwg file.

2. Click SW Isometric in the 3D Navigation drop-down list in the Home tab's View panel (Figure 22.24) or type –V↵ **SWISO**↵. This gives you a view from the lower-left side of the rectangles.

3. Zoom out so the rectangles occupy about a third of the drawing area window.

FIGURE 22.24
Click SW
Isometric in the
3D Navigation
drop-down list.

Now you need to move the outer rectangle in the Z axis so its elevation is 30″ (76 cm for metric users):

1. Click the outer rectangle, and then click one of its grips.

2. Right-click to open the Grip Edit shortcut menu.

3. Choose Move, and then enter **@0,0,30↵**; metric users should enter **@0,0,76↵**. This tells AutoCAD to move the rectangle a 0 distance in both the X and Y axes and 30″ (or 76 cm) in the Z axis.

4. Pan your view downward so it looks similar to Figure 22.25.

FIGURE 22.25
The finished
chair layout

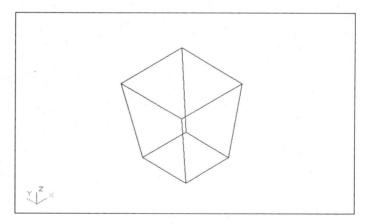

5. Use the Line tool to draw lines from the corners of the outer square to the corners of the inner square. Use the Endpoint osnap to select the exact corners of the squares. This is the layout for your chair—not the finished product.

As an alternate method in step 3, after choosing Move from the Grip Edit shortcut menu, you can turn on Ortho mode and point the cursor vertically so it shows –Z in the coordinate readout. Then enter **30↵**, or **76↵** for metric users.

Spherical and Cylindrical Coordinate Formats

In the previous exercise, you used relative Cartesian coordinates to locate the second point for the Move command. For commands that accept 3D input, you can also specify displacements by using the Spherical and Cylindrical Coordinate formats.

The *Spherical Coordinate format* lets you specify a distance in 3D space while specifying the angle in terms of degrees from the X axis of the current UCS and degrees from the XY plane of the current UCS (see the top image in Figure 22.26). For example, to specify a distance of 4.5″ (11.43 cm) at a 30° angle from the X axis and 45° from the XY plane, enter @4.5<30<45 (or @11.43<30<45 for metric users). This refers to the direct distance followed by a < symbol, then the angle from the X axis of the current UCS followed by another < symbol, and then the angle from the XY plane of the current UCS. To use the Spherical Coordinate format to move the rectangle in the exercise, enter @30<0<90 at the Second point: prompt, or @76<0<90 for metric users.

FIGURE 22.26
The Spherical and Cylindrical Coordinate formats

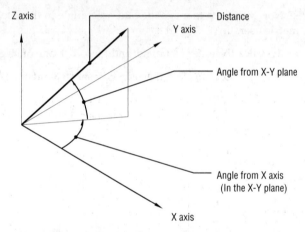

[Distance] < [Angle from X axis] < [Angle from X-Y plane]

The Spherical Coordinate Format

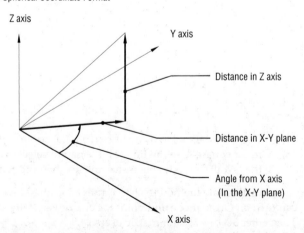

[Distance in X-Y plane] < [Angle from X axis] , [Distance in Z axis]
The Cylindrical Coordinate Format

The *Cylindrical Coordinate format,* on the other hand, lets you specify a location in terms of a distance in the plane of the current UCS and a distance in the Z axis. You also specify an angle from the X axis of the current UCS (see the bottom image in Figure 22.26). For example, to locate a point that is a distance of 4.5″ (11.43 cm) in the plane of the current UCS at an angle of 30° from the X axis and a distance of 3.3″ (8.38 cm) in the Z axis, enter **@4.5<30,3.3** (or **@11.43<30,8.38** for metric users). This refers to the distance of the displacement from the plane of the current UCS followed by the < symbol, then the angle from the X axis followed by a comma, and then the distance in the Z axis. Using the Cylindrical Coordinate format to move the rectangle, you enter **@0<0,30** at the Second point: prompt, or **@0<0,76** for metric users.

Using a 3D Polyline

Now you'll draw the legs for the butterfly chair by using a 3D polyline. This is a polyline that can be drawn in 3D space. Here are the steps:

1. Click 3D Polyline from the Home tab's Draw panel, or type **3p**↵.

2. At the Specify start point of polyline: prompt, pick a series of points, as shown in Figure 22.27 (top), by using the Endpoint and Midpoint osnaps. Use the Close option to close the series of lines.

FIGURE 22.27
Using 3D polylines to draw the legs of the butterfly chair

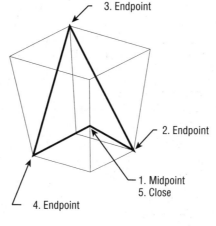

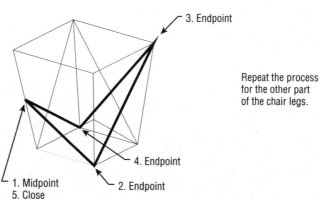

3. Draw another 3D polyline in the mirror image of the first (see the lower image in Figure 22.27).

4. Erase the connecting vertical lines that make up the frame, but keep the rectangles. You'll use them later.

All objects, with the exception of lines and 3D polylines, are restricted to the plane of your current UCS. Two other legacy 3D objects, 3D faces and 3D meshes, are also restricted. You can use the Pline command to draw polylines in only one plane, but you can use the 3DPoly command to create a polyline in three dimensions. 3DPoly objects can't, however, be given thickness or width.

Creating a Curved 3D Surface

Next, you'll draw the seat of the chair. The seat of a butterfly chair is usually made of canvas, and it drapes from the four corners of the chair legs. You'll first define the perimeter of the seat by using arcs, and then you'll use the Edge Surface tool on the Hometab's Modeling panel to form the shape of the draped canvas. The Edge Surface tool creates a surface based on four objects defining the edges of that surface. In this example, you'll use arcs to define the edges of the seat.

To draw the arcs defining the seat edges, you must first establish the UCSs in the planes of those edges. In the previous example, you created a UCS for the side of the chair before you could draw the legs. In the same way, you must create a UCS defining the planes that contain the edges of the seat.

Because the UCS you want to define isn't orthogonal, you'll need to use the three-point method. This lets you define the plane of the UCS based on three points:

1. Click the 3 Point tool on the View tab's Coordinates panel, or type **UCS⏎3⏎**. This option enables you to define a UCS based on three points that you select. Remember, it helps to think of a UCS as a drawing surface situated on the surface of the object you want to draw or edit.

2. At the Specify new origin point <0,0,0>: prompt, use the Endpoint osnap to pick the bottom of the chair leg to the far left, as shown in the left image of Figure 22.28. This is the origin point of your new UCS.

3. At the Specify point on positive portion of X-axis: prompt, use the Endpoint osnap to pick the bottom of the next leg to the right of the first one, as shown in the left image in Figure 22.28.

FIGURE 22.28
Defining and saving three UCSs

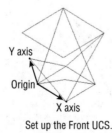

Set up the Front UCS.

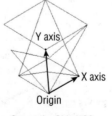

Set up the Side UCS.

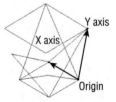

Set up the Back UCS.

4. At the `Specify point on positive-Y portion of the UCS XY plane:` prompt, pick the top corner of the butterfly chair seat, as shown in the left image in Figure 22.28. The UCS icon changes to indicate your new UCS.

5. Now that you've defined a UCS, you need to save it so that you can return to it later. Click Named from the View tab's Coordinates panel, or type UC↵ to open the UCS dialog box.

6. With the Named UCSs tab selected, right-click the Unnamed item in the list box, and choose Rename from the shortcut menu.

7. Enter **Front**↵.

8. Click OK to exit the UCS dialog box.

You've defined and saved a UCS for the front side of the chair. As you can see from the UCS icon, this UCS is at a non-orthogonal angle to the WCS. Continue by creating UCSs for two more sides of the butterfly chair:

1. Define a UCS for the side of the chair, as shown in the middle image in Figure 22.28. Use the UCS dialog box to rename this UCS Side, just as you did for Front in steps 5 through 8 in the previous exercise. Remember that you renamed the unnamed UCS.

2. Repeat these steps for a UCS for the back of the chair, named Back. Use the right image in Figure 22.28 for reference.

3. Open the UCS dialog box again; in the Named UCSs tab, highlight Front.

4. Click the Set Current button, and then click OK. This activates Front as the current UCS.

5. Click the Start, End, Direction tool from the Arc flyout on the Home tab's Draw panel.

6. Draw the arc defining the front edge of the chair (see Figure 22.29). Use the Endpoint Osnap override to pick the top endpoints of the chair legs as the endpoints of the arc. (If you need help with the Arc command, refer to "Choosing Command Options" in Chapter 3.)

7. Repeat steps 3 through 6 for the UCS named Back—each time using the top endpoints of the legs for the endpoints of the arc.

8. Restore the UCS for the side, but instead of drawing an arc, use the Polyline tool and draw a polyline spline similar to the one in Figure 22.29. If you need help with polyline splines, see Chapter 19.

FIGURE 22.29
Drawing the front and back seat edge using arcs and a polyline spline

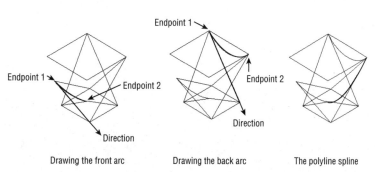

Drawing the front arc   Drawing the back arc   The polyline spline

Next, you'll mirror the side-edge spline to the opposite side. This will save you from having to define a UCS for that side:

1. Click the World UCS tool on the View tab's Coordinates panel to restore the WCS. You do this because you want to mirror the arc along an axis that is parallel to the plane of the WCS. Remember that you must use the coordinate system that defines the plane in which you want to work.

2. Click the polyline you drew for the side of the chair (the one drawn on the Side UCS).

3. Click the midpoint grip of the arc in the Side UCS; then right-click and choose Mirror from the shortcut menu.

4. Enter **C**↵ to select the Copy option.

5. Enter **B**↵ to select a new base point for the mirror axis.

6. At the `Specify base point:` prompt, use the Midpoint override to pick the midpoints of the rectangle at the bottom of the model. Refer to Figure 22.30 for help. The polyline should mirror to the opposite side, and your chair should look like Figure 22.31.

7. Press the Esc key twice to clear the grips.

FIGURE 22.30
Set your UCS to World, and then mirror the arc that defines the side of the chair seat.

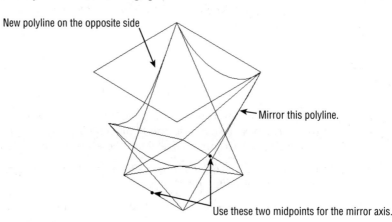

New polyline on the opposite side

Mirror this polyline.

Use these two midpoints for the mirror axis.

FIGURE 22.31
Your butterfly chair so far

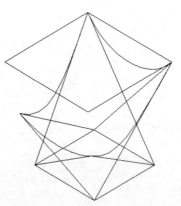

QUICK HOPS TO YOUR UCSs

If you find you're jumping from one saved UCS to another, you'll want to know about the Named UCS Combo Control drop-down list. This list is located in the View tab's Coordinates panel and it contains the World and other standard UCS options as well as all the saved UCSs in a drawing. You can use this list as a quick way to move between UCSs that you've set up or between the predefined orthogonal UCSs.

Another great way to jump quickly between UCSs is to use the UCS Face option. The Face option requires a 3D solid, but once you have one in place, you can choose Face from the View flyout on the View tab's Coordinates panel and then click on the face of the solid to which you want to align your UCS. For example, you can use the Loft command (see the section "Shaping the Solid" later in this chapter) to create a solid similar to the solid shown later in Figure 22.34 that connects the top and bottom rectangles of the butterfly chair. You can then use the UCS Face option to align to the sides of that solid to draw the arcs and polylines for the seat outline. This way, you're using the 3D solid as a layout tool.

Finally, let's finish this chair by adding the mesh representing the chair seat:

1. Click the Loft tool from the Extrude flyout in the Home tab's Modeling panel, or enter **Loft⏎** at the Command prompt.

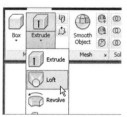

2. At the Select cross-sections in lofting order or [POint/Join multiple edges/MOde]: prompt, click the arc at the front of the layout.

3. At the Select cross-sections in lofting order or [POint/Join multiple edges/MOde]: prompt, click the arc at the back of the layout, and then press ⏎ to finish your selection of cross sections.

4. At the Enter an option [Guides/Path/Cross sections only/settings] <Cross sections only>: prompt, enter **G⏎** for the Guides option. You'll use the two polylines as guides.

5. At the Select guide profiles or [Join multiple edges]: prompt, select the two polylines on the sides of the layout, and then press ↵ to complete your selection. Your chair begins to take form, as shown in Figure 22.32.

6. Click Save from the Quick Access toolbar to save the chair so far.

FIGURE 22.32
The butterfly
chair so far

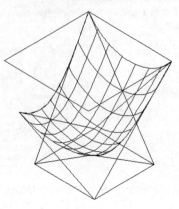

You've got the beginnings of a butterfly chair with the legs drawn in schematically and the seat as a 3D surface. You can add some detail by using a few other tools, as you'll see in the next set of exercises.

Converting the Surface into a Solid

In the previous example, you used the Loft tool to create a 3D surface. Once you have a surface, you can convert it to a solid to perform other modifications.

You'll want to round the corners of the seat surface to simulate the way a butterfly chair hangs off its frame. You'll also round the corners of the frame and turn the frame into a tubular form. Start by rounding the seat surface. This will involve turning the surface into a solid so you can use solid editing tools to get the shape you want:

1. Click the Thicken tool in the Home tab's Solid Editing panel.

You can also enter **Thicken**↵ at the Command prompt.

2. Select the seat surface, and press ↵ to finish your selection.

3. At the Specify thickness <0'-0">: prompt, enter **0.01**↵, or **0.025**↵ for metric users.

The seat surface appears to lose its webbing, but it has just been converted to a very thin 3D solid.

Shaping the Solid

The butterfly chair is in a fairly schematic state. The corners of the chair are sharply pointed, whereas a real butterfly chair would have rounded corners. In this section, you'll round the corners of the seat with a little help from the original rectangles you used to form the layout frame.

First, you'll use the Fillet command to round the corners of the rectangles. Then, you'll use the rounded rectangles to create a solid from which you'll form a new seat:

1. Choose the Fillet tool from the Home tab's Modify panel, or enter **F↵** at the Command prompt.

2. At the `Select first object or [Undo/Polyline/Radius/Trim/Multiple]:` prompt, enter **R↵**.

3. At the `Specify fillet radius <0'-0">:` prompt, enter **3↵**. Metric users enter **7.5↵**.

4. At the `Select first object or [Undo/Polyline/Radius/Trim/Multiple]:` prompt, enter **P↵** for the Polyline option.

5. At the `Select 2D polyline:` prompt, select the top rectangle, as shown in Figure 22.33. The polyline corners become rounded.

FIGURE 22.33
Round the corners of the rectangles with the Fillet command.

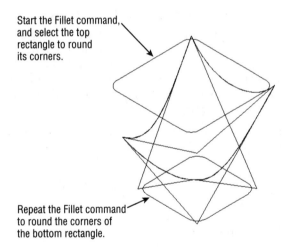

Start the Fillet command, and select the top rectangle to round its corners.

Repeat the Fillet command to round the corners of the bottom rectangle.

6. Press ↵ to repeat the Fillet command.

7. Enter **P↵** to use the Polyline option, and then click the bottom rectangle as shown in Figure 22.33. Now both polylines have rounded corners.

Next, create a 3D solid from the two rectangles using the Loft tool:

1. Click the Loft tool in the Home tab's Modeling panel, or enter **Loft↵**.

2. At the `Select cross-sections in lofting order or [POint/Join multiple edges/MOde]:` prompt, select the two rectangles and press ↵ to finish your selection.

3. At the Enter an option [Guides/Path/Cross sections only/Settings] <Cross sections only>: prompt, press ↵. The rectangles join to form a 3D solid (see Figure 22.34).

FIGURE 22.34
The lofted rectangles form a 3D solid.

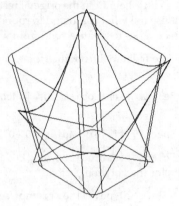

Finding the Interference between Two Solids

In this next exercise, you'll use a tool that is intended to find the interference between two solids. This is useful if you're working with crowded 3D models and you need to check whether objects may be interfering with each other. For example, a mechanical designer might want to check to make sure duct locations aren't passing through a structural beam.

You'll use Interfere as a modeling tool to obtain a shape that is a combination of two solids: the seat and the rectangular solid you just created. Here are the steps:

1. Click the Interfere tool in the Home tab's Solid Editing panel.

You can also enter **interfere**↵ at the Command prompt.

2. At the Select first set of objects or [Nested selection/Settings]: prompt, select the chair seat solid, and then press ↵.

3. At the Select second set of objects or [Nested selection/checK first set] <checK>: prompt, click the rectangular solid you created in the previous exercise and press ↵. The Interference Checking dialog box appears (Figure 22.35), and the drawing temporarily changes to a view similar to the Realistic visual style.

The view shows the interference of the two solids in red. Notice that the corners are rounded on the red interference.

4. In the Interference Checking dialog box, turn off the Delete Interference Objects Created On Close option and click Close. The display returns to the Wireframe view. If you look carefully at the seat corners, you see a new solid overlaid on the seat (see Figure 22.36).

FIGURE 22.35
Checking for
interference

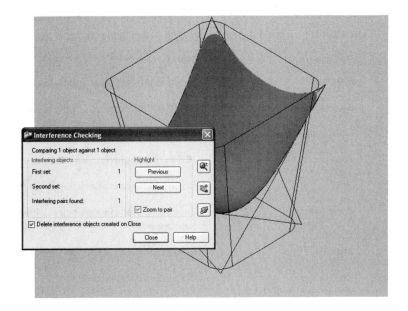

5. Delete the rectangular solid and the original seat, as shown in Figure 22.36.

As mentioned earlier, the Interference Checking tool is intended to help you find out whether objects are colliding in a 3D model; as you've just seen, though, it can be an excellent modeling tool that can help you derive a form that you may not otherwise have the ability to create.

A number of other options are available when you're using the Interference Checking tool. Table 22.2 lists the options in the Interference Checking dialog box.

FIGURE 22.36
The interference
solid appears
on top of the
original seat.

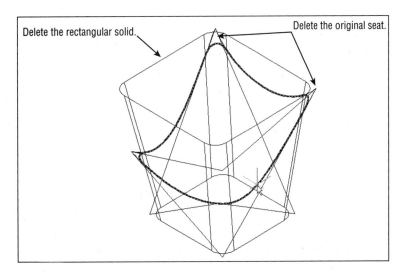

TABLE 22.2:   Interference Checking dialog box options

OPTION	WHAT IT DOES
First Set	Specifies the number of objects in the first set of selected objects
Second Set	Specifies the number of objects in the second set of selected objects
Interfering Pairs Found	Indicates the number of interferences found
Previous	Highlights the previous interference object
Next	Highlights the next interference object if multiple objects are present
Zoom To Pair	Zooms to the interference object while you're using the Previous and Next options
Zoom Realtime	Closes the dialog box to allow you to use Zoom Realtime
Pan Realtime	Closes the dialog box to allow you to use Pan
3D Orbit	Closes the dialog box to allow you to use 3D Orbit
Delete Interference Objects Created On Close	Deletes the interference object after the dialog box is closed

The prompt for the Interference Checking command also showed some options. The prompt in step 2 shows Nested selection/Settings. The Nested selection option lets you select objects that are nested in a block or an Xref. The Settings option opens the Interference Settings dialog box (Figure 22.37).

FIGURE 22.37
Settings for
interference

This dialog box offers settings for the temporary display of interference objects while you're using the Interference command. Table 22.3 lists the options for this dialog box.

TABLE 22.3:   Interference Settings dialog box options

OPTION	WHAT IT DOES
Visual Style	Controls the visual style for interference objects
Color	Controls the color for interference objects
Highlight Interfering Pair	Highlights the interfering objects
Highlight Interference	Highlights the resulting interference objects
Visual Style	Controls the visual style for the drawing while displaying the interference objects

Creating Tubes with the Sweep Tool

One more element needs to be taken care of before your chair is complete. The legs are currently simple lines with sharp corners. In this section, you'll learn how you can convert lines into 3D tubes. To make it more interesting, you'll add rounded corners to the legs.

Start by rounding the corners on the lines you've created for the legs:

1. Use the Explode tool to explode the 3D polyline legs into simple lines.

2. Choose the Fillet tool from the Home tab's Modify panel, or enter **F↵** at the Command prompt.

3. At the `Select first object or [Undo/Polyline/Radius/Trim/Multiple]:` prompt, enter **R↵**.

4. At the `Specify fillet radius <0´-0˝>:` prompt, enter **2↵**. Metric users should enter **5↵**

5. At the `Select first object or [Undo/Polyline/Radius/Trim/Multiple]:` prompt, enter **M↵**, and then select pairs of lines to fillet their corners.

6. When all the corners are rounded, press ↵ to exit the Fillet command.

7. Delete the two polyline splines you used to form the sides of the seat. Your drawing should look like Figure 22.38.

The chair is almost complete, but the legs are just wireframes. Next you'll give them some thickness by turning them into tubes. Start by creating a set of circles. You'll use the circles to define the diameter of the tubes:

1. Draw a 3⁄8˝ (19 mm) radius circle in the location shown in Figure 22.38. Don't worry if your location is a little off; the placement of the circle isn't important.

2. Use the Array command to make 15 copies of the circle. In Figure 22.38, a 4-×-4 array is used with the default 1˝ spacing. Metric users should use a spacing of about 30 mm.

FIGURE 22.38
Drawing the circles
for the tubes

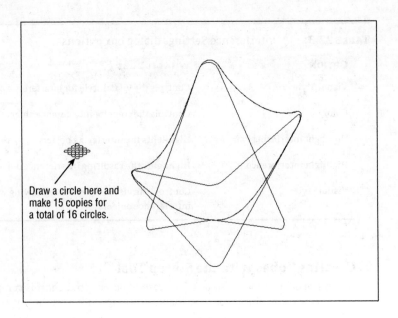

Draw a circle here and
make 15 copies for
a total of 16 circles.

Now you're ready to form the tubes:

1. Click the Sweep tool from the Extrude flyout in the Home tab's Modeling panel. You can also enter **sweep**↵ at the Command prompt.

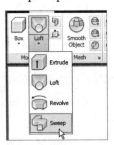

2. At the `Select objects to sweep or [MOde]:` prompt, click one of the circles you just created. It doesn't matter which circle you use because they're identical. Press ↵ when you're finished.

3. At the `Select sweep path or [Alignment/Base point/Scale/Twist]:` prompt, select one of the lines or fillet arcs that make up the legs.

4. Press ↵ to repeat the Sweep command, and then repeat steps 2 and 3 for each part of the leg segments, including the fillet arcs.

5. Continue with step 4 until all the lines in the legs have been converted into tubes.

6. Change the color of the solid representing the seat to cyan, and then select the Realistic visual style from the Visual Styles flyout on the Home tab's View panel. Your drawing will look similar to the image on the left of Figure 22.39, which shows a perspective view. The image on the right is the chair with some materials assigned to its parts and a slight adjustment to the seat location.

7. Close the file. You can save it or, if you intend to repeat the exercise, close and do not save.

FIGURE 22.39
A perspective view of the butterfly chair with tubes for legs

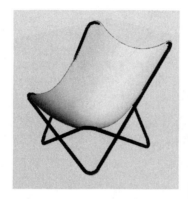

Using Sweep to Create Complex Forms

Although you used circles with the Sweep command to create tubes, you can use any closed polyline shape. Figure 22.40 gives some examples of other shapes you can use with the Sweep command.

FIGURE 22.40
You can use any closed shape with the Sweep command.

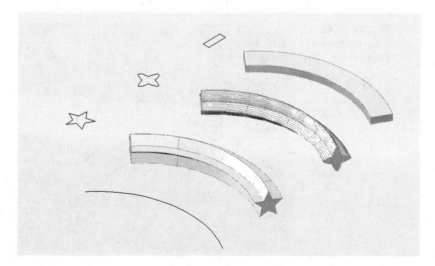

In step 3 of the previous exercise, you may have noticed some command-line options. These options offer additional control over the way Sweep works. Here is a rundown on how they work:

Alignment This option lets you determine whether the object to sweep is automatically set perpendicular to the sweep path. By default, this option is set to Yes, which means the object to sweep is set perpendicular to the path. If set to No, Sweep assumes the current angle of the object, as shown in Figure 22.41.

FIGURE 22.41
Alignment lets you set the angle between the object to sweep and the sweep path.

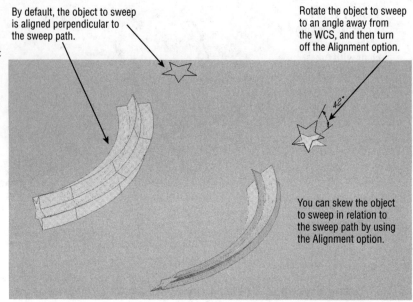

By default, the object to sweep is aligned perpendicular to the sweep path.

Rotate the object to sweep to an angle away from the WCS, and then turn off the Alignment option.

You can skew the object to sweep in relation to the sweep path by using the Alignment option.

Base Point By default, Sweep uses the center of the object to sweep as the location to align with the path, as shown in Figure 22.42. Base Point lets you set a specific location on the object.

FIGURE 22.42
Using the Base Point option

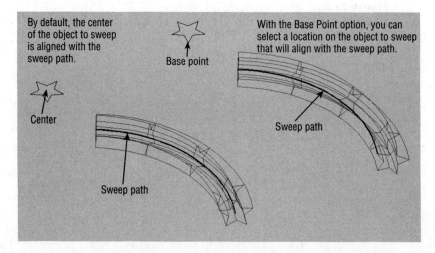

By default, the center of the object to sweep is aligned with the sweep path.

Base point

With the Base Point option, you can select a location on the object to sweep that will align with the sweep path.

Center

Sweep path

Sweep path

Sweep path

Scale   You can have Sweep scale the sweep object from one end of the path to the other to create a tapered shape, as shown in Figure 22.43. This option requires a numeric scale value.

FIGURE 22.43
Scale lets you scale the object to sweep as it's swept along the path.

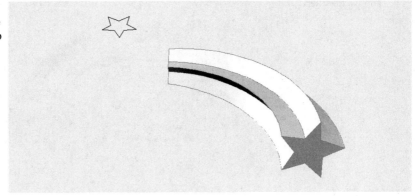

Twist   You can have the object to sweep twist along the path to form a spiral shape, as shown in Figure 22.44. This option requires a numeric value in the form of degrees of rotation.

FIGURE 22.44
You can have the object to sweep twist along the path to create a spiral effect.

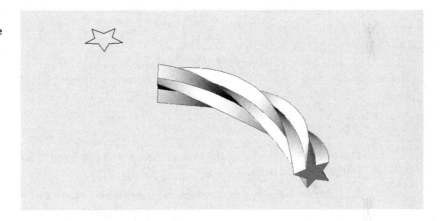

These options are available as soon as you select the sweep object and before you select the path object. You can use any combination of options you need. For example, you can apply the Twist and Scale options together, as shown in Figure 22.45.

Creating Spiral Forms

You can use the Sweep tool in conjunction with the Helix tool to create a spiral form, such as a spring or the threads of a screw. You've already seen how the Sweep tool works. Try the following to learn how the Helix tool works firsthand.

FIGURE 22.45
The Scale and
Twist options
applied together

In this exercise, you'll draw a helicoil thread insert. This is a device used to repair stripped threads; it's basically a coiled steel strip that forms internal and external threads. Here are the steps:

1. Open the Helicoil.dwg file. This is a standard AutoCAD drawing containing a closed polyline in a stretched octagon shape.

This is the cross section of the helicoil thread, and you'll use it as an object to sweep after you've created a helix.

2. Click the Helix tool in the Home tab's expanded Draw panel, or type **Helix**↵.

You see the following prompt:

```
Number of turns = 3.0000     Twist=CCW
Specify center point of base:
```

3. Pick a point roughly in the center of the view. A rubber-banding line appears along with a circle.

4. At the `Specify base radius or [Diameter] <1.0000>:` prompt, enter **0.375**↵.

5. At the `Specify top radius or [Diameter] <0.3750>:` prompt, press ↵ to accept the default, which is the same as the value you entered in step 4.

6. At the `Specify helix height or [Axis endpoint/Turns/turn Height/tWist] <1.0000>:` prompt, enter **T**↵ to use the Turns option.

7. At the `Enter number of turns <3.0000>:` prompt, enter **15**↵ to create a helix with 15 turns total.

8. At the `Specify helix height or [Axis endpoint/Turns/turn Height/tWist] <1.0000>:` prompt, press ↵ to accept the default height of 1. The helix appears as a spiral drawn to the dimensions you've just specified for diameter, turns, and height (see Figure 22.46).

FIGURE 22.46
The helix and the helicoil after using Sweep

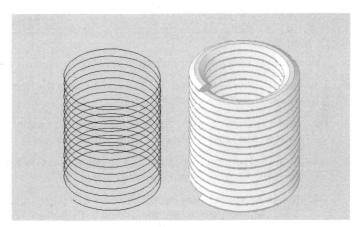

In step 6, you used the Turns option to specify the total number of turns in the helix. You also have other options that give you control over the shape of the helix. Figure 22.47 shows you the effects of the Helix command options. You may want to experiment with them on your own to get familiar with Helix.

EDIT A HELIX WITH THE PROPERTIES PALETTE

If you find that you've created a helix with the wrong settings, you don't have to erase and re-create it. You can use the Properties palette to make adjustments to any of the helix options presented in Figure 22.47, even after a helix has been created. Select the helix, right-click, and choose Properties. Look in the Geometry section of the Properties palette for the helix settings.

FIGURE 22.47
The Helix command options

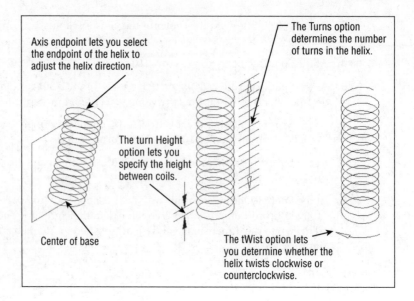

Now, use the Sweep tool to complete the helicoil:

1. Click the Sweep tool from the Extrude flyout in the Home tab's Modeling panel, or enter **Sweep** at the Command prompt.

2. At the `Select objects to sweep or [MOde]:` prompt, select the thread cross section in the lower-left corner of the drawing, and then press ↵.

3. At the `Select sweep path or [Alignment/Base point/Scale/Twist]:` prompt, select the helix. After a moment, the helicoil appears.

4. To see the helicoil more clearly, choose the Realistic option from the Visual Styles drop-down list, and then change the helicoil to the helicoil layer.

5. Close and save the file. If you intend to repeat this exercise, close but don't save.

If the space between the coils is too small for the cross section, you may get an error message. If you get an error message at step 3, make sure you created the helix exactly as specified in the previous exercise. You may also try increasing the helix height.

In step 3, instead of selecting the sweep path, you can select an option to apply to the object to sweep. For example, by default, Sweep aligns the object to sweep at an angle that is perpendicular to the path and centers the object to sweep. See "Using Sweep to Create Complex Forms" earlier in this chapter.

Creating Surface Models

In an earlier exercise, you used the Loft command to create the seat of a butterfly chair. In this section, you'll return to the Loft command to explore some of its other uses. This time, you'll use it to create a 3D model of a hillside based on a set of site-contour lines. You'll also see how you can use a surface created from the Loft command to slice a solid into two pieces, imprinting the solid with the surface shape.

🌐 Real World Scenario

ARCHITECTURAL APPLICATIONS FOR THE HELIX TOOL

The helix example given here is a device often used to repair spark plug threads that have been stripped, but the helix can be used in other applications besides mechanical modeling. I've used a helix to draw a circular ramp for a parking garage. Instead of multiple turns, I would use a single rotation or a half rotation. The radius of the helix was much larger, to accommodate the width of a car.

OLD VERSUS NEW SURFACES

If you've used earlier versions of AutoCAD to create 3D models, you've probably used surface modeling to create some of your 3D objects. If you open an old drawing file that contains those 3D surfaces, you'll see that they are called polygon meshes. You can convert those older mesh objects into new surface objects using the Convert To Surface tool, which is next to the Convert To Solid tool in the Home tab's expanded Solid Editing panel. If you prefer to use the older 3D surface modeling tools like Revsurf and Rulesurf, they are still available, though they now create mesh surfaces. You will learn more about mesh modeling in Chapter 25.

Start by creating a 3D surface using the Loft command:

1. Open the contour.dwg file.

2. Click the Loft tool from the Extrude flyout on the Home tab's Modeling panel.

3. Select each brown contour in consecutive order from right to left or left to right. It doesn't matter whether you start at the left end or the right end, but you must select the contours in order.

4. When you're finished selecting all the contours, press ↵ and wait a moment. AutoCAD requires a bit of time to calculate the surface. Once it does, you see the surface applied over the contour lines (Figure 22.48).

5. At the `Enter an option [Guides/Path/Cross sections only/Settings] <Cross sections only>:` prompt, press ↵ to exit the Loft command.

FIGURE 22.48
Creating a 3D
surface from
contour lines

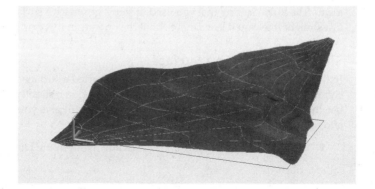

Once the loft surface has been placed, you can make adjustments to the way the loft is generated by using the arrow grip that appears when you select the surface:

1. Click the surface to select it.

2. Click the arrowhead that appears by the surface. This is known as a multifunction grip.

Multifunction Grip

3. Select the Ruled option from the menu. The surface changes slightly to conform to the new Ruled surface option (Figure 22.49).

FIGURE 22.49
The surface
with the Ruled
option selected

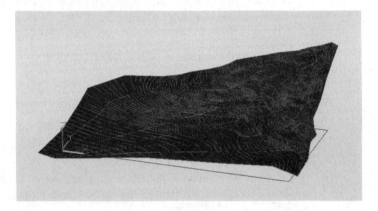

In the butterfly chair exercise, you used the Guides option in the Loft Command prompt. This allowed you to use the polyline curves to guide the loft shape from the front arc to the back arc. In this exercise, you didn't use the command options and went straight to the multifunction grip menu. The Ruled setting that you used in step 3 generates a surface that connects the cross sections in a straight line. You'll learn more about the options in this grip menu later in this chapter.

Slicing a Solid with a Surface

In the barcelona1.dwg chair example, you converted a surface into a solid using the Thicken command. Next, you'll use a surface to create a solid in a slightly different way. This time, you'll use the surface to slice a solid into two pieces. This will give you a form that is more easily read and understood as a terrain model:

1. Click the Extrude tool from the Extrude flyout in the Home tab's Modeling panel.

2. At the `Select objects to extrude or [MOde]:` prompt, select the large rectangle below the contours, and press ↵. The rectangle turns into a box whose height follows your cursor.

3. At the `Specify height of extrusion or [Direction/Path/Taper angle/Expression]:` prompt, move the cursor upward so the box looks similar to the one in Figure 22.50. Then click the mouse to fix the box's height.

FIGURE 22.50
The box extruded through the contours

You may have noticed that as you raised the box height, you could see how it intersected the contour surface. Next you'll slice the box into two pieces:

1. Click the Slice tool in the Home tab's Solid Editing panel (Figure 22.51).

2. At the `Select objects to slice:` prompt, select the box and press ↵.

FIGURE 22.51
The Slice tool

3. At the `Specify start point of slicing plane or [planar Object/Surface/Zaxis/View/XY/YZ/ZX/3points] <3points>:` prompt, enter **S**↵ to use the Surface option.

4. At the `Select a surface:` prompt, select the contour surface.

5. At the `Select solid to keep or [keep Both sides] <Both>:` prompt, click the part of the box that is below the surface. The top part of the box disappears, and you see the surface once again.

6. Delete the contour surface and the contour lines. The box remains with an imprint of the surface, as shown in Figure 22.52.

FIGURE 22.52
The box with the
contour surface
imprinted

FIGURE 22.52
The box with the
contour surface
imprinted

In step 3, you saw a prompt that offered a variety of methods for slicing the box. The Surface option allowed you to slice the box using an irregular shape, but most of the other options let you slice a solid by defining a plane or a series of planar objects.

Finding the Volume of a Cut

A question I hear frequently from civil engineers is "How can I find the volume of earth from an excavated area?" This is often referred to as a *cut* from a *cut and fill* operation. To do this, you first have to create the cut shape. Next, you use the Interfere command to find the intersection between the cut shape and the contour surface. You can then find the volume of the cut shape using one of AutoCAD's inquiry commands. The following exercise demonstrates how this is done.

Suppose that the contour model you've just created represents a site where you'll excavate a rectangular area for a structure. You want to find the amount of earth involved in the excavation. A rectangle has been placed in the contour drawing representing such an area:

1. Select 3dWireframe from the Visual Styles flyout on the Home tab's View panel (Figure 22.53). This allows you to see the excavation rectangle more clearly.

2. Turn on the Selection Cycling tool in the status bar. This will help you select the rectangle in step 3.

3. Click the Extrude tool in the Home tab's Modeling panel.

FIGURE 22.53
Select
3dWireframe
from the Visual
Styles flyout.

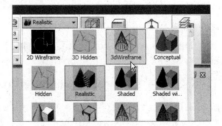

4. Select the rectangle shown in Figure 22.54.

5. At the Selection dialog box, select Polyline and then press ↵.

6. Extrude the rectangle to the height of 10´.

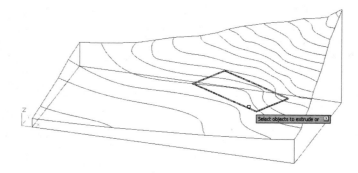

Figure 22.54
Selecting the rectangle representing the excavation area

Here you used the Selection Cycling tool to help you select the rectangle, which is overlapped by the contour solid. The Selection Cycling tool presents the Selection dialog box, which let you determine the type of object you want to select, thereby filtering out other objects nearby that might be selected accidentally.

With the excavation rectangle in place, you can use the Interfere command to find the volume of the excavation:

1. Click the Interfere tool in the Home tab's Solid Editing panel.

2. At the `Select first set of objects or [Nested selection/Settings]:` prompt, click the contour and press ↵.

3. At the `Select second set of objects or [Nested selection/checK first set]` `<checK>:` prompt, select the box and press ↵. The Interference Checking dialog box appears.

4. In the Interference Checking dialog box, turn off the Delete Interference Objects Created On Close option, and click Close.

5. Delete the box you used to represent the excavation area. The remaining shape contains the volume of the excavation.

6. Type **Massprop**↵.

7. At the `Select objects:` prompt, select the excavation solid, as shown in Figure 22.55, and then press ↵. The AutoCAD Text Window appears, and it displays the properties of the excavation area. At the top, you see the volume of the selected solid in cubic inches (Figure 22.56).

8. Press ↵↵, and then at the `Write analysis to a file? [Yes/No] <N>:` prompt, you can press ↵ to exit the command or enter **Y**↵ to save the information to a text file.

Understanding the Loft Command

As you've seen from the exercises in this chapter, the Loft command lets you create just about any shape you can imagine, from a simple sling to the complex curves of a contour map. If your loft cross sections are a set of closed objects like circles or closed polygons, the resulting object is a 3D solid instead of a surface.

FIGURE 22.55
The 3D solid representing the excavation

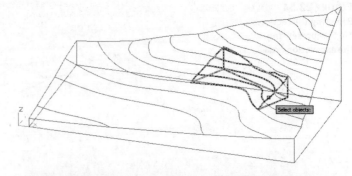

FIGURE 22.56
The mass and volume information from the Region/Mass Properties tool

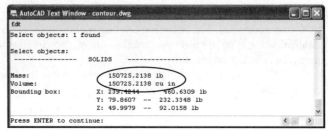

The order in which you select the cross sections is important because Loft will follow your selection order to create the surface or solid. For example, Figure 22.57 shows a series of circles used for a lofted solid. The circles are identical in size and placement, but the order of selection is different. The solid on the left was created by selecting the circles in consecutive order from bottom to top, creating an hourglass shape. The solid on the right was created by selecting the two larger circles first from bottom to top; the smaller, intermediate circle was selected last. This selection order created a hollowed-out shape with more vertical sides.

In addition to the selection order, several other settings affect the shape of a solid created by the Loft command. In the contour-map example, you selected the Ruled setting from a multifunction grip after you had completed the Loft command. You can also set Loft command options through the Loft Settings dialog box (Figure 22.58). This dialog box appears during the Loft command when you select the Settings option after you've selected a set of cross sections.

FIGURE 22.57
The order in which you select the cross sections affects the result of the Loft command.

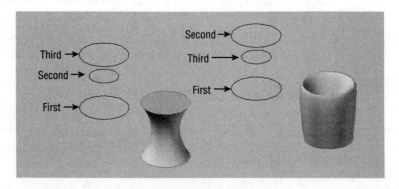

FIGURE 22.58
Loft Settings:
Smooth Fit

You can radically affect the way the Loft command forms a surface or a solid through the options in this dialog box, so it pays to understand what those settings do. Take a moment to study the following sections, which describe the Loft Settings dialog box options.

RULED AND SMOOTH FIT

The Ruled option connects the cross sections with straight surfaces, as shown in the sample to the left in Figure 22.59.

FIGURE 22.59
Samples of a Ruled
loft at left and a
Smooth Fit loft on
the right

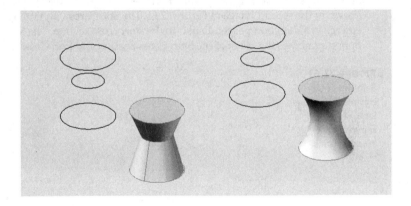

The Smooth Fit option connects the cross sections with a smooth surface. It attempts to make the best smooth transitions between the cross sections, as shown in the right image in Figure 22.59.

NORMAL TO

Normal To is a set of four options presented in a drop-down list. To understand what this option does, you need to know that *normal* is a mathematical term referring to a direction that is perpendicular to a plane, as shown in Figure 22.60. In these options, Normal refers to the direction the surface takes as it emerges from a cross section.

FIGURE 22.60
A normal is a direction perpendicular to a plane.

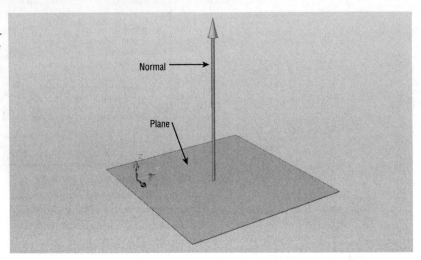

If you use the All Cross Sections option, the surfaces emerge in a perpendicular direction from all the cross sections, as shown in the first image in Figure 22.61. If you use the End Cross Section option, the surface emerges in a direction that is perpendicular to just the end cross section, as shown in the second image in Figure 22.61. The Start Cross Section option causes the surface to emerge in a direction perpendicular to the start cross section. The Start And End Cross Sections option combines the effect of the Start Cross Section and End Cross Section options.

FIGURE 22.61
Samples of the Normal To options applied to the same set of cross sections

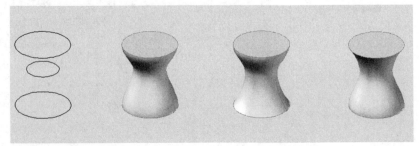

DRAFT ANGLES

The Draft Angles option affects only the first and last cross sections. This option generates a smooth surface with added control over the start and end angle. Unlike the Normal To option, which forces a perpendicular direction to the cross sections, Draft Angles allows you to set an angle for the surface direction. For example, if you set Start Angle to a value of 0, the surface will bulge outward from the start cross section, as shown in the first image of Figure 22.62.

FIGURE 22.62
The Draft
Angles options

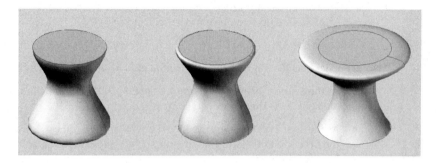

Likewise, an End Angle setting of 0 will cause the surface to bulge at the end cross section (see the second image in Figure 22.62).

The Start and End Magnitude settings let you determine a relative strength of the bulge. The right image in Figure 22.62 shows a draft angle of 0 and magnitude of 50 for the last cross section.

CLOSE SURFACE OR SOLID AND PREVIEW CHANGES

The Close Surface Or Solid option is available only when the Smooth Fit option is selected. It causes the first and last cross section objects to be connected so the surface or solid loops back from the last to the first cross section. Figure 22.63 shows the cross sections at the left, a smooth version in the middle, and a smooth version with the Close Surface Or Solid option turned on. The Close Surface Or Solid option causes the solid to become a tube.

FIGURE 22.63
The Close Surface
Or Solid option
connects the end
and the beginning
cross sections.

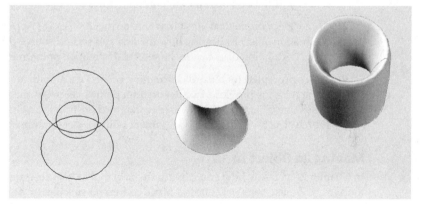

Moving Objects in 3D Space

AutoCAD provides three tools specifically designed for moving objects in 3D space: Align, 3D Move, and 3D Rotate. You can find all three commands in the Home tab's Modify panel. These tools help you perform some of the more common moves associated with 3D editing.

Aligning Objects in 3D Space

In mechanical drawing, you often create the parts in 3D and then show an assembly of the parts. The Align command can greatly simplify the assembly process. The following steps show how to use Align to line up two objects at specific points:

1. Open the Align.dwg file from the Chapter 22 folder of the sample files.

2. Click the 3D Align tool on the Home tab's Modify panel or type **3dalign**↵.

3. At the Select objects: prompt, select the 3D wedge-shaped object and press ↵. (The *source object* is the object you want to move.)

4. At the Specify base point or [Copy]: prompt, pick a point on the source object that is the first point of an alignment axis, such as the center of a hole or the corner of a surface. For the Align drawing, use the upper-left corner of the wedge.

5. At the Specify second point or [Continue] <C>: prompt, pick a point on the source object that is the second point of an alignment axis, such as another center point or other corner of a surface. For this example, select the other top corner of the wedge.

6. At the Specify third source point or [Continue] <C>: prompt, you can press ↵ if two points are adequate to describe the alignment. Otherwise, pick a third point on the source object that, along with the first two points, best describes the surface plane you want aligned with the destination object. Pick the lower-right corner of the wedge shown in Figure 22.64.

7. At the Specify first destination point: prompt, pick a point on the destination object to which you want the first source point to move. (The *destination object* is the object with which you want the source object to align.) This is the top corner of the rectangular shape. (See the first destination point in Figure 22.64.)

8. At the Specify second destination point or [eXit]: prompt, pick a point on the destination object indicating how the first and second source points are to align in relation to the destination object. (See the second destination point in Figure 22.64.)

9. You're prompted for a third destination point. Pick a point on the destination object that, along with the previous two destination points, describes the plane with which you want the source object to be aligned. (See the third destination point in Figure 22.64.) The source object will move into alignment with the destination object.

Moving an Object in 3D

In Chapter 21, you saw how you can use the grip tool to help restrain the motion of an object in the X, Y, or Z axis. AutoCAD offers a Move command specifically designed for 3D editing that includes a grip tool to restrain motion.

You don't need to perform these steps as an exercise. You can try the command on your own when you need to use it.

Here's how it works:

1. Click the 3D Move tool in the Home tab's Modify panel, as shown in Figure 22.65. You can also enter **3dmove**↵.

FIGURE 22.64
Aligning two
3D objects

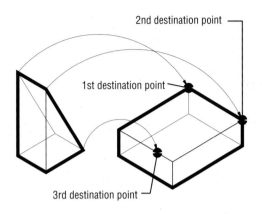

2nd destination point

1st destination point

3rd destination point

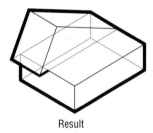

Result

FIGURE 22.65
The 3D Move tool

2. Select the object or set of objects you want to move, and press ↵. The Move gizmo appears on the object (Figure 22.66).

FIGURE 22.66
The Move gizmo

The Move gizmo

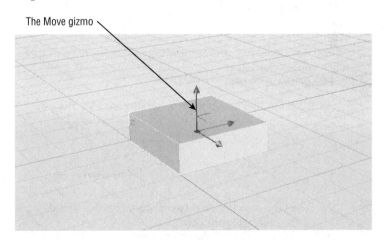

3. Point to the X, Y, or Z axis of the Move gizmo but don't click it. As you hover over an axis, a motion axis vector appears indicating the direction your object will move if you click the axis, as shown in Figure 22.67.

FIGURE 22.67
An axis vector appears when you hover over an axis of the gizmo

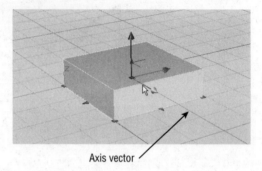

Axis vector

4. Click on an axis while the vector appears and then enter a distance along the axis, or click a point to complete the move.

Alternately, in step 3, you can hover over and click on a plane indicator on the gizmo to restrain the motion along one of the planes defined by two of the axes (Figure 22.68).

FIGURE 22.68
Hover over the plane indicator to restrain the motion along a plane.

Plane indicator

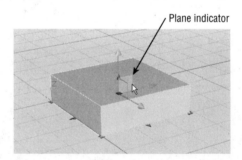

Rotating an Object in 3D

The 3D Rotate command is another command that is like an extension of its 2D counterpart. With 3D Rotate, a rotate gizmo appears that restrains the rotation about the X, Y, or Z axis.

You don't need to perform these steps as an exercise. You can try the command on your own when you need to use it.

Here's how it works:

1. Click the 3D Rotate tool in the Home tab's Modify panel. You can also enter **3drotate**↵.

2. Select the object or objects you want to rotate and then press ↵. The Rotate gizmo appears on the object (Figure 22.69).

FIGURE 22.69
The Rotate gizmo

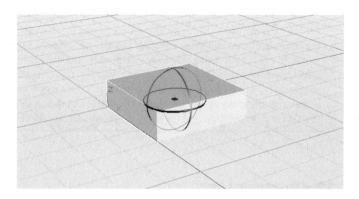

3. At the `Specify a base point:` prompt, you can select a point about which the selected objects are to be rotated. The gizmo will move to the point you select.

4. Point to the colored circle that represents the axis of rotation for your objects. A vector appears, representing the axis of rotation. When you're happy with the selected axis, click the mouse.

5. At the `Specify angle start point or type an angle:` prompt, you can enter an angle value or click a point. You can use the Shift key or Ortho mode to restrain the direction to 90°.

6. If you click a point in step 5, you will see the `Specify angle end point:` prompt. Enter an angle value or click another point for the rotation angle.

You can also just select one of the circles in step 3 instead of selecting a base point. If you do this, then the selected object begins to rotate. You don't have to select a start and end angle.

USING 3DMIRROR AND 3DARRAY

Two other tools, 3D Mirror and 3D Array, are available in the Home tab's Modify panel. These are 3D versions of the Mirror and Array tools. They work in a way that's similar to how the standard Mirror and Array tools work, with a slight difference.

3D Mirror begins by asking you to select objects. Then you're asked to specify a mirror plane instead of a mirror axis. You can define a plane using the default three points, or you can use one of the seven other options: `Object/Last/Zaxis/View/XY/YZ/ZX`. By using a plane instead of an axis, you can mirror an object or set of objects anywhere in 3D space. One way to visualize this is to imagine holding a mirror up to your 3D model. The mirror is your 3D plane, and the reflected image is the mirrored version of the object. Imagine tilting the mirror to various angles to get a different mirror image. In the same way, you can tilt the plane in the 3D Mirror tool to mirror an object in any number of ways.

3D Array works like the command-line version of the Array command and offers the same prompts with a couple of additions. If you choose to do a rectangular array, you're prompted for the usual row and column numbers, along with the number of levels for the third dimension. You're also prompted for the distance between rows, columns, and levels.

For the Polar option of 3D Array, you are prompted for the number of items to array, the direction, the angle to fill, and whether to rotate the arrayed objects, just as with the standard Array command. In addition to being asked for a point to indicate the center of the array, you're prompted to select two points to indicate an axis of rotation. The axis can be defined in any direction in 3D space, so your array can be tilted from the current UCS. One way to visualize this is to think of a bicycle wheel with the array axis as the axle of the wheel and the array objects as the spokes. You can align the axle in any direction and the array of spokes will be perpendicular to the axle.

The Bottom Line

Master the User Coordinate System.   The User Coordinate System (UCS) is a vital key to editing in 3D space. If you want to master 3D modeling, you should become familiar with this tool.

Master It   Name some of the predefined UCS planes.

Understand the UCS options.   You can set up the UCS orientation for any situation. It isn't limited to the predefined settings.

Master It   Give a brief description of some of the ways you can set up a UCS.

Use viewports to aid in 3D drawing.   In some 3D modeling operations, it helps to have several different views of the model through the Viewports feature.

Master It   Name some of the predefined standard viewports offered in the Viewports dialog box.

Create complex 3D surfaces.   You aren't limited to straight, flat surfaces in AutoCAD. You can create just about any shape you want, including curved surfaces.

Master It   What tool did you use in this chapter's chair exercise to convert a surface into a solid?

Create spiral forms.   Spiral forms frequently occur in nature, so it's no wonder that we often use spirals in our own designs. Spirals are seen in screws, stairs, and ramps as well as in other manmade forms.

Master It   Name the commands used in the example in the section "Creating Spiral Forms," and name two elements that are needed to create a spiral.

Create surface models.   You can create a 3D surface by connecting a series of lines that define a surface contour. You can create anything from a 3D landscape to a car fender using this method.

Master It   What is the tool used to convert a series of lines into a 3D surface?

Move objects in 3D space.   You can move objects in 3D space using tools that are similar to those for 2D drafting. But when it comes to editing objects, 3D modeling is much more complex than 2D drafting.

Master It   What does the Rotate gizmo do?

Chapter 23

Rendering 3D Drawings

In this chapter, you'll learn how to use rendering tools in AutoCAD to produce rendered still images of your 3D models. With these tools, you can add materials, control lighting, and even add landscaping and people to your models. You also have control over the reflectance and transparency of objects, and you can add bitmap backgrounds to help set the mood.

AutoCAD LT 2011 doesn't support any of the features described in this chapter.

In this chapter, you'll learn to do the following:

- ◆ Simulate the sun
- ◆ Use materials
- ◆ Create effects using materials and lights
- ◆ Apply and adjust texture maps
- ◆ Understand the rendering options
- ◆ Add cameras for better view control
- ◆ Print your renderings
- ◆ Simulate natural light

Testing the Waters

Before we get into the main tutorial in this chapter, let's first take a peek at what's possible with AutoCAD's rendering tools. This first exercise will give you a chance to see how you can quickly see a rendered view of a 3D model and how you can easily add materials to objects.

The first file you'll work with in this section is simply a collection of primitive shapes in a random arrangement. First, you'll use the Render command to view the file without any materials, and then you'll add a few materials to get familiar with the Materials Browser and see how it can be used to create a more lifelike rendering. Start by opening a sample file and render it as is.

1. First turn on the Selection Cycling tool in the status bar. You'll need it in some of the later exercises.

2. Make sure 3D Modeling is selected in the Workspace drop-down list in the upper-left corner of the AutoCAD window.

3. Next, if you don't see the Materials Browser to the right of the AutoCAD window, open it by selecting the Materials Browser tool from the Render tab's Materials panel (Figure 23.1).

4. Open the Rendering_example_raw.dwg file.

5. Choose the Render tool in the Render tab's Render panel (Figure 23.1).

FIGURE 23.1
The Materials Browser tool and the Render tool

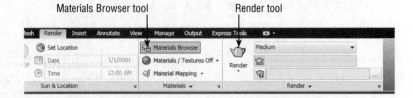

6. The Render window opens and takes a moment to produce the rendered view (Figure 23.2).

FIGURE 23.2
The Render window with the rendered view

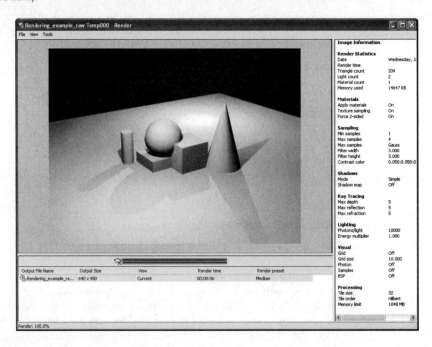

All of the objects in the view are rendered using the default Global material. You can see a sample of this material at the top of the Materials Browser (Figure 23.3).

Now try adding a material to the sphere:

1. Take a look at the Materials Browser in Figure 23.3. If you don't see the Autodesk Library and My Materials listed, click the Display Libraries tool just below the three sample images at the top. This opens a list of material categories in the left side of the Materials Browser.

FIGURE 23.3
The Materials
Browser

2. Click the arrowhead next to the Autodesk Library heading, and then scroll down the list and select Metal. A set of materials is displayed in the panel to the right of the list.

3. From the list on the right, locate Brass – Polished.

4. Click and drag Brass – Polished from the list to the sphere in the drawing area. You'll notice that the sphere changes color to indicate its new material. Brass – Polished also appears at the top of the Materials Browser.

5. Click the Render tool again to see the result.

You now see that the sphere appears to be made of polished brass in the rendered view. In this exercise, you applied a material by clicking and dragging it to an object.

Now add a few more materials using a slightly different method:

1. Click the cylinder to the far left of the drawing area to select it. If you have Selection Cycling turned on and the Selection dialog box appears, select 3D Solid from the Selection dialog box. Make sure that nothing else is selected.

2. In the Materials Browser, scroll down the list of materials on the right-side panel to locate Chrome – Polished.

3. Click Chrome – Polished to apply it to the cylinder.

4. Press the Esc key to clear your selection.

5. Next, click the foreground of the 3D model to select the rectangle that defines the "ground," as shown in Figure 23.4.

FIGURE 23.4
Click the fore-
ground surface
to select it.

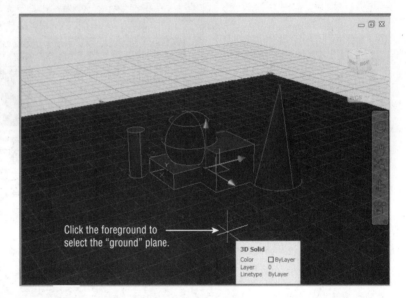

Click the foreground to
select the "ground" plane.

3D Solid
Color ☐ ByLayer
Layer 0
Linetype ByLayer

6. Back in the Materials Browser, scroll up the list on the left-hand side to locate and select Fabric.

7. In the panel to the right, locate and select Plaid 1. This applies the Plaid 1 material to the "ground."

8. Click the Render tool again.

9. Once you've had a chance to look at the rendering, close the Rendering_example_raw .dwg file without saving it.

After rendering the view in step 8, you could see the Plaid 1 material of the foreground reflected in the brass sphere and chrome cylinder (Figure 23.5). The added materials give the rendered view a more realistic appearance.

This brief introduction to materials and rendering shows you some of the potential of these tools. In the rest of the chapter, you'll get an in-depth view of the many ways you can control the appearance of rendered views from your 3D models.

FIGURE 23.5
The rendered view
with additional
materials

USING SELECTION CYCLING

In this chapter, you'll use the Selection Cycling tool to help you select the right object in a 3D environment. It enables you to filter through objects that AutoCAD might otherwise accidentally select. For example, if you are working in a wireframe visual style and you want to select a polyline that is clearly visible but behind a 3D solid, Selection Cycling will bring up the Selection dialog box, which will allow you to choose the object from a list of objects that AutoCAD detects. Without Selection Cycling, AutoCAD will pick the first object it encounters, like the solid that is in front of the polyline.

Creating a Quick-Study Rendering

Throughout the rest of this chapter, you'll work with a 3D model that was created using AutoCAD's 3D modeling tools. The model is of two buildings on a street corner. You'll start by using the default rendering settings to get a quick view of what you have to start with:

1. Open the facade.dwg file.

2. Click the Render tool in the Render tab's Render panel.

3. The Render window appears, and you see the rendering generated in the Render window display (see Figure 23.6).

FIGURE 23.6
The Render window with your first rendered view

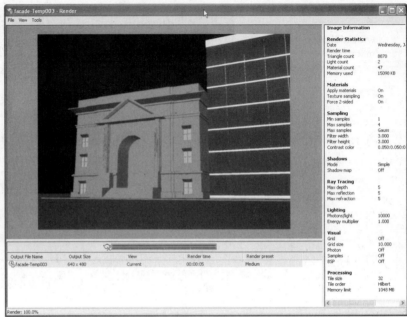

The Render window displays the render settings in a column to the right. At the bottom of the window, you see the name that AutoCAD gives to the rendering as well as the rendering resolution in pixels, the time it took, and the preset that was used for the rendering. You'll learn more about these options later in this chapter.

Simulating the Sun

AutoCAD allows you to create several types of light sources. If you don't add a light source, AutoCAD uses a default lighting source that has no particular direction or characteristic. The rendering you just did uses the default lighting to show your model.

You can add a point light that behaves like a lightbulb, a spotlight, or a directed light that behaves like a distant light source such as the sun. AutoCAD also offers a sunlight option that can be set for the time of the year and the hour of the day. This sunlight option is especially important for shadow studies in architectural models.

Setting Up the Sun

Let's add the sun to the model to give a better sense of the building's form and relationship to its site. Start by making sure the sun is set for your location:

1. Click the Sun Status tool in the Render tab's Sun & Location panel (see Figure 23.7).

   You may see a message box warning you that the default lighting must be turned off when other lights are used. Click Turn Off The Default Lighting.

2. Click the Set Location tool in the Render tab's Sun & Location panel (Figure 23.8).

FIGURE 23.7

The tools available on the Render tab

Sun Status tool

FIGURE 23.8

Click the Set Location tool in the Sun & Location panel.

3. You'll see a message asking you how you want to define the location. Select the Enter The Location Values option. The Geographic Location dialog box appears (Figure 23.9).

4. Click the Use Map button in the upper-right corner of the dialog box. The Location Picker appears.

FIGURE 23.9

Choose your location.

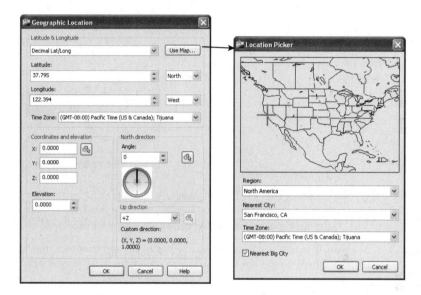

5. For the sake of this tutorial, suppose the Facade model is a building in San Francisco, California, USA. Select North America from the Region drop-down list below the map.

6. Locate and select San Francisco, CA in the Nearest City drop-down list and then click OK. The Latitude and Longitude input boxes at upper left in the Geographic Location dialog box change to reflect the location of San Francisco. For locations not listed, you can enter values manually in those input boxes.

7. Click OK in the Geographic Location dialog box. Next, you need to set the date and time of day for the rendering.

Once you've set the location, you can enter information about the sun's location in the sky. The sun's location is dependent upon the time of year and the time of day you wish to simulate. Follow these steps:

1. Click the Sun Properties tool in the Render tab's Sun & Location panel title bar. It looks like an arrow at the far right side of the title bar.

2. In the Date input box of the Sun Properties palette, enter **9/21/2010**.

3. Click in the Time input box of the Sun Properties palette, and select 2:00 p.m. from the drop-down list (Figure 23.10).

FIGURE 23.10
Select the time from the drop-down list.

4. Close the Sun Properties palette, and then click the Render tool in the Render tab's Render panel. The Render window appears and begins to create a new rendering with the sunlight option turned on, as shown in Figure 23.11.

Now that you've added the sun, you can see the shadows that the sunlight casts. You can turn off the shadows for the sun if you prefer, but they're on by default.

Setting Polar North

If you're including the sun as a light source in a drawing in order to run shade studies, it's essential to orient your drawing accurately. To set the direction of polar north in your drawing, you use the North Direction setting in the Geographic Location dialog box (see Figure 23.12).

By using this setting, you can set polar north in one of the following ways:

◆ Click and drag the north arrow in the graphic to point to the north direction.

◆ Directly in the input box, enter a value that indicates an angle away from vertical. A positive value moves the north arrow clockwise, while a negative value moves it counterclockwise.

◆ Click the Select tool to indicate true north visually, using your cursor.

FIGURE 23.11
The rendering with
the sun turned on

FIGURE 23.12
The North Direc-
tion setting in the
Geographic Loca-
tion dialog box

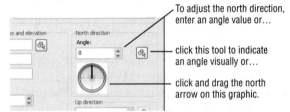

To adjust the north direction,
enter an angle value or…

click this tool to indicate
an angle visually or…

click and drag the north
arrow on this graphic.

Real World Scenario

IMPROVING THE SMOOTHNESS OF CIRCLES AND ARCS

Here is an issue that readers are constantly asking me about. You may notice that at times, when you're using the Render, Hide, or Shade tool, the edge of solids or region arcs appears segmented rather than curved. This may be fine for producing layouts or backgrounds for hand-rendered drawings, but for final plots, you want arcs and circles to appear as smooth curves. You can adjust the accuracy of arcs in your hidden, rendered, or shaded views through a setting in the Options dialog box.

You can modify the Rendered Object Smoothness setting in the Display tab of the Options dialog box to improve the smoothness of arcs. Its default value is 0.5, but you can increase this to as high as 10 to smooth out faceted curves. In the facade.dwg model, you can set Rendered Object Smoothness to 1.5 to render the arch in the entry as a smooth arc instead of a series of flat segments. You can also adjust this setting by using the Facetres system variable.

Adding a Distant Light

The rendering gives you a fairly accurate idea of how the shadows will fall. This may be all you need if you're doing a shadow study. For example, you can render a plan view of a 3D model to see where the shadow will fall on a street or a neighboring building, as shown in Figure 23.13.

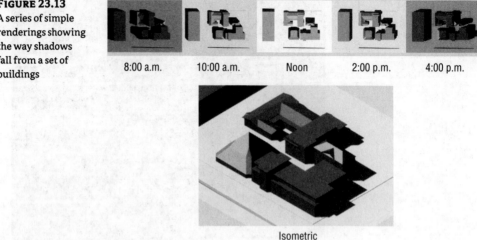

8:00 a.m.   10:00 a.m.   Noon   2:00 p.m.   4:00 p.m.

Isometric

But the current rendering needs more attention in order to show the building detail. One problem is that the shadows are too dark and hide some of the building's features. To bring out those features, you'll add ambient light.

In the real world, a good deal of light is reflected from the ground. You can simulate that reflected light by adding a distant light that shines from below the model. A distant light is like a cross between a point light and a spotlight. The sun is a point source of light, but it's so far away that its rays are essentially parallel (see Figure 23.14). A distant light behaves in a similar way. It has a point location, yet its light rays are parallel.

FIGURE 23.14
A distant light is a
source whose light
rays are parallel,
much like the
sun's rays.

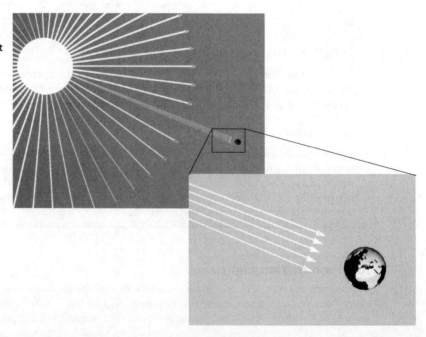

A distant light pointing up and toward the buildings can simulate reflected light from the ground; in the following set of exercises, you'll add a directed light to do just that. In the process, you'll see how you can quickly switch from a single view to a multi-viewport view using tools in the View tab's Viewports panel.

First, change your single view to a four-viewport view:

1. In the View tab's View panel, click the Views flyout and select Left (Figure 23.15).

FIGURE 23.15
The Left option on
the Views flyout

2. Go back to the Render tab and click Distant from the Create Light flyout on the Render tab's Lights panel (Figure 23.16) or enter **Distantlight**↵.

FIGURE 23.16
Select Distant
from the Create
Light flyout.

3. At the `Specify light direction FROM <0,0,0> or [Vector]:` prompt, click below the model, as shown in Figure 23.17.

4. At the `Specify light direction TO <1,1,1>:` prompt, click a point to indicate an upward direction that is leaning toward the buildings, as shown in Figure 23.17.

5. At the `Enter an option to change [Name/Intensity/Status/shadoW/Color/eXit] <eXit>:` prompt, press ↵ to exit the distant light command.

I'd like to point out that in step 1, you were directed to select Left from the Views flyout. You could also arrive at the left-side view by using the ViewCube. The difference is that the Views flyout option also changes the UCS to the plane of the left view, allowing you to place the distant light in the appropriate orientation. In fact, all the orthogonal view options on the Views flyout will change the UCS to the plane of the view. The ViewCube does not affect the UCS.

FIGURE 23.17
Add the distant light as shown in the lower-left viewport.

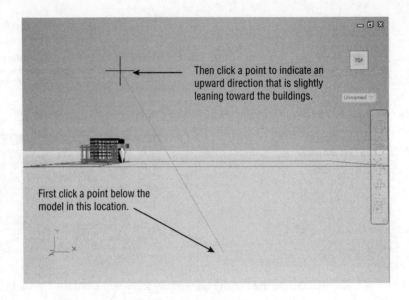

Then click a point to indicate an upward direction that is slightly leaning toward the buildings.

First click a point below the model in this location.

Now that you've added the distant light, go back to the view you want to render. To do so, follow these steps:

1. Click the Views flyout arrowhead in the View tab's Views panel.

2. Select the Temp option in the flyout list.

You've just added a distant light, and even though it isn't visible, you can access it through the Lights In Model tool. In the next exercise, you'll see how you can control the intensity of the distant light through the Lights In Model tool:

1. Click the Lights In Model tool in the Render tab's Lights panel. It is the small arrow at the far right side of the Lights panel title bar (Figure 23.18). Or you can also enter **Lightlist**↵. The Lights In Model palette appears.

FIGURE 23.18
Click the Lights In Model tool to open the Lights In Model palette.

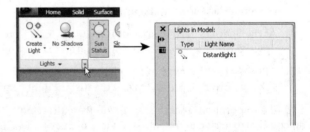

2. Double-click Distantlight1 in the list. The Properties palette appears, displaying the properties of the distant light you just added.

3. Locate the Intensity Factor setting in the General group of the Properties palette, and change the value to **0.5**.

4. Locate the Shadows setting, and turn it off.

5. Close the Properties palette and the Lights In Model palette.

6. Click the Render tool in the Render tab's Render panel. Your rendering now shows more natural-looking shadows on the building to the left, as shown in Figure 23.19.

FIGURE 23.19
The model rendered with the distant light added

Using Materials

The rendering methods you've learned so far can be of enormous help in your design effort. Simply being able to see how the sun affects your design can help sell your ideas or move plans through a tough planning-board review. But the look of the building is still somewhat cartoonish. You can further enhance the rendering by adding materials to the objects in your model.

Adjusting the Global Material

AutoCAD uses a default material, called *global*, for objects in a drawing that don't have a specific material assigned to them. The global material is just like other materials you could use in your drawing, but it's set up in a way that is as generic as possible to produce simple renderings. For example, the global material uses the object's color to determine the rendered color.

As an introduction to materials, try the following exercise. You'll change the global material so that it applies a specific color to objects when they're rendered rather than rely on the object's color:

1. If you don't see the Materials Browser on the right side of the AutoCAD window, click the Materials Browser tool in the Render tab's Materials panel.

2. Double-click the Global sample swatch that is displayed at the top of the Materials Browser (Figure 23.20).

The Materials Editor appears (shown in Figure 23.21). At the top, you see a sample image of the current default material, which is the global material. This is a default material that is applied to everything in the drawing that doesn't already have a material assignment.

FIGURE 23.20
Double-click the
Global material
sample swatch.

FIGURE 23.21
The Materials
Editor

3. Click the flyout icon to the far right of the Color option and then select Color (Figure 23.22). The Color option changes to show the RGB value for the color.

FIGURE 23.22
Click the fly-
out icon.

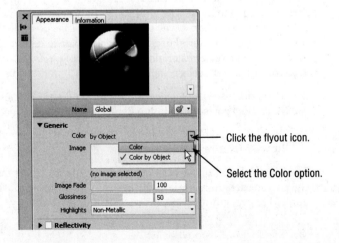

4. Click the RGB 0 0 0 option that now appears in the Color option. The Select Color dialog box appears.

5. Select the True Color tab if it isn't already selected, then move the Luminance slider up until the Luminance value is set to 93.

6. Click OK to close the Select Color dialog box (Figure 23.23).

FIGURE 23.23
Set the Luminance slider to 93.

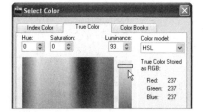

7. Click the Render tool in the Render tab's Render panel. This time, you see a monochrome image in the Render window (Figure 23.24).

FIGURE 23.24
Rendering your image in grays

You've just changed the color of the global material to off-white. Everything in the model now appears in shades of gray because so far, the only material in the model is the global one.

Creating a New Material and Changing Its Properties

Two of the most glaring problems in the rendering are the black background and the white glass in the building. You'll learn how to add a background later, but first you'll tackle the glass.

AutoCAD comes with several glass and glazing materials that you could use for this model, but to get a closer look at how materials work, you're now going to create a glass material from scratch. This will give you a chance to become familiar with the Materials Editor:

1. In the Materials Editor, click the Creates Or Duplicates A Material flyout (Figure 23.25).

2. Select Generic from the list that appears.

FIGURE 23.25
The Creates Or
Duplicates A
Material tool

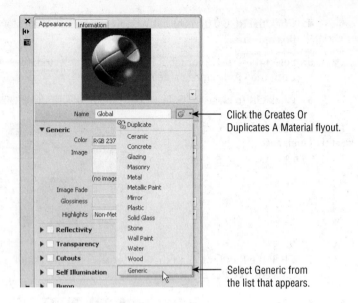

Click the Creates Or
Duplicates A Material flyout.

Select Generic from
the list that appears.

3. In the Name input box, replace the Default Generic name with Glass1.

You've just created a new material and given it a name. To make this new Glass1 material appear as glass, you need to make some adjustments. You can make a material translucent or transparent, give it color, and even have it glow with self-illumination. You'll start by giving your new material a set of predefined values that will provide the basis for your glass:

1. In the Generic panel of the Materials Editor, click the Color value (RGB 80 80 80) to open the Select Color dialog box.

2. Move the Luminance slider upward to set the Luminance value to 60, and then click OK.

3. Back in the Generic panel of the Materials Editor, change the Glossiness value to 100. This gives the glass a perfectly smooth appearance. A lower value will cause the glass to appear frosted (Figure 23.26).

4. Click the arrowhead to the left of the Transparency option in the lower part of the editor (Figure 23.26).

5. Click the box next to the word *Transparency* to activate this feature.

6. Change the Amount value from 30 to 75. This makes the material more transparent.

7. To get a preview of your material, click the Swatch Shape And Render Quality flyout icon and select Glass Curtain Wall.

You've set up your material. The next step is to apply it to the glass in the model. You might have noticed that when you created the Glass1 material, its sample image appeared in the Materials Browser. You can now add this material to objects in your model just as you did in the very first exercise in this chapter.

FIGURE 23.26
The settings for
your new Glass1
material

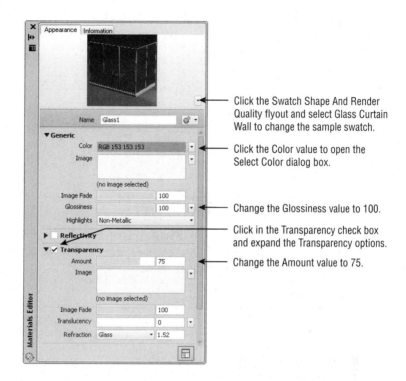

Click the Swatch Shape And Render
Quality flyout and select Glass Curtain
Wall to change the sample swatch.

Click the Color value to open the
Select Color dialog box.

Change the Glossiness value to 100.

Click in the Transparency check box
and expand the Transparency options.

Change the Amount value to 75.

To add the Glass1 material to the glass curtain wall of the building, do the following:

1. Click on the glass in the model to select it. It's the blue object in the square building (Figure 23.27).

FIGURE 23.27
Selecting the glass

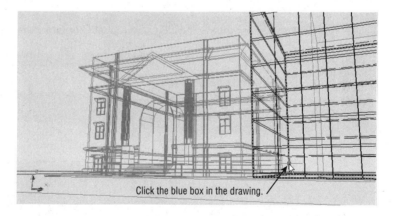

Click the blue box in the drawing.

2. If you see the Selection dialog box, click the Surface (Extrusion) option (Figure 23.28).

FIGURE 23.28
The Selection
dialog box

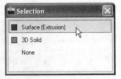

3. Click the Glass1 swatch in the Materials Browser to assign Glass1 to the selected object.

Render

4. Click the Render tool in the Render tab's Render panel. The building on the right now has the glass exterior.

USING READY-MADE MATERIAL TYPES

When you first started to make your glazing material, you may have noticed an option called Glazing in the Creates Or Duplicates A Material list (Figure 23.25). The Glazing option is set up with most of the glazing features already built in. With the Glazing option, you only need to set the color and reflectance. AutoCAD offers a wide range of predefined "base" materials on which you can build your own materials.

Adding a Background

You may have noticed the Reflectivity option in the Materials Editor and guessed that this option lets you set how much of the surrounding scene a material will reflect. In this next exercise, you'll add a background to the model and turn on the Reflectivity option for the glass to add a bit more realism to the rendered view:

1. Open the 3D Navigation drop-down list on the View tab's Views panel, and then select View Manager. The View Manager dialog box appears (Figure 23.29).

2. Click the New button. The New View/Shot Properties dialog box appears (Figure 23.30).

FIGURE 23.29
Select View Manager from the 3D Navigation drop-down list.

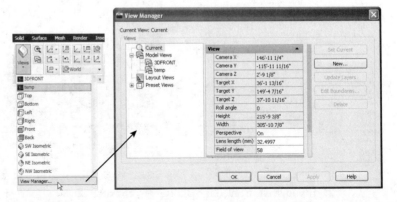

FIGURE 23.30
The New View/
Shot Properties
dialog box

3. Enter **My 3D View** in the View Name input box.

4. In the Background group toward the bottom of the dialog box, select Image from the drop-down list. The Background dialog box appears (Figure 23.31).

FIGURE 23.31
Choose your back-
ground image.

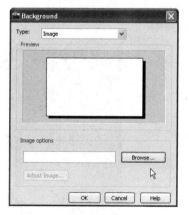

5. In the Image Options group, click the Browse button.

6. Make sure Files Of Type is set to JFIF (*.jpg, *.jpeg), browse to the Chapter 23 sample file folder, and select and open the sky.jpg file.

7. Click the Adjust Image button to open the Adjust Background Image dialog box (Figure 23.32).

FIGURE 23.32
Size and position
your background.

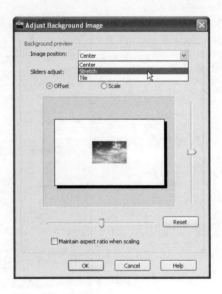

8. The sky.jpg file appears in the sample panel. Select Stretch from the Image Position drop-down list. The image expands to fill the sample panel area.

9. Click OK in all the dialog boxes until you get to the View Manager dialog box.

10. In the View Manager dialog box, select My 3D View from the list to the left, and then click the Set Current button.

11. Click OK to exit the View Manager dialog box. The background appears in the drawing area.

12. Render the view to see the results. You should have something that looks similar to Figure 23.33.

FIGURE 23.33
The rendered
model with a back-
ground added

Next, turn on the Reflectivity option for your Glass1 material to have the glass reflect the background that you have just added:

1. If the Materials Editor is not open, double-click on the Glass1 swatch in the Materials Browser.

2. Click the check box next to the Reflectivity option to turn it on and display its options, as shown in Figure 23.34.

FIGURE 23.34
The Reflectivity option

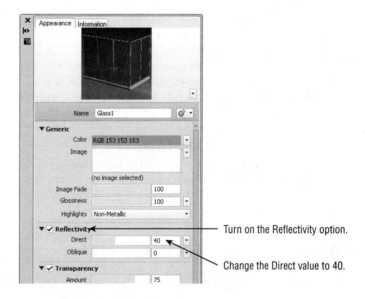

Turn on the Reflectivity option.

Change the Direct value to 40.

3. Double-click the Direct input box that shows 50 and change the value to 40.

4. Render the view to see the result. You should have something that looks similar to Figure 23.35.

FIGURE 23.35
The model rendered with the Glass1 Reflectivity setting turned on

As you can see, the glass now reflects the sky background, giving the glass a more realistic appearance. The Direct setting adjusts how much of the surrounding scene the glass reflects when your view is directly in front of the surface. The Oblique setting lets you control the reflection when your view is at a steeper angle to the surface.

Creating Effects Using Materials and Lights

Up to now, you've used only two light sources: a distant light and the sun. Two other light sources are available to help simulate light: point-light sources and spotlights. The following sections will show you some examples of how to use these types of light sources, along with some imagination, to perform any number of visual tricks.

The office building on the right half of the rendering is still a bit cold looking. It's missing a sense of activity. You may notice that when you look at glass office buildings, you can frequently see the ceiling lights from the exterior of the building—provided the glass isn't too dark. In a subtle way, those lights lend a sense of life to a building.

Adding a Self-Illuminated Material

To help improve the image, you'll add some ceiling lights to the office building. I've already supplied the lights in the form of square 3D Faces arrayed just at the ceiling level of each floor, as shown in Figure 23.36. In this section, you'll learn how to make the ceiling lights appear illuminated.

FIGURE 23.36
The 3D Face squares representing ceiling light fixtures

The ceiling lights appear as squares.

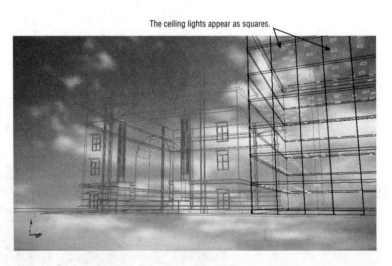

Follow these steps to assign a reflective white material to the ceiling fixtures:

1. Click the Creates Or Duplicates A Material tool in the Materials Editor and select Generic.

2. Enter **Ceiling Light** in the Name input box.

3. Click the Self Illumination check box to turn on this feature and expand its panel.

4. Click the Luminance list that shows Dim Glow and select Custom (Figure 23.37). As you can see, you have a set of predefined illumination options.

5. Set the Luminance value to 1. You want only the slightest glow from fixtures to make them visible.

FIGURE 23.37
Select Custom from the Luminance list.

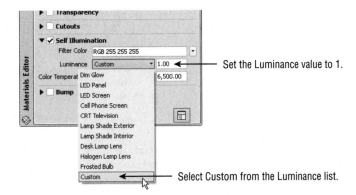

Set the Luminance value to 1.

Select Custom from the Luminance list.

USING PROCEDURAL MAPS

Procedural maps are texture maps that are derived mathematically rather than from a bitmap image. The advantage of a procedural map is that it gives a more natural representation of a material. For example, if you cut a notch out of a box that uses a wood procedural map, the notch appears correctly with the appropriate wood grain. Do the same for a box that uses a bitmap texture map and the grain doesn't appear correctly. With a bitmap texture map, the same image is placed on all four sides of the box, so cuts don't show the grain properly.

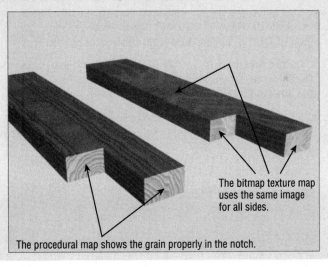

The bitmap texture map uses the same image for all sides.

The procedural map shows the grain properly in the notch.

AutoCAD offers several types of procedural maps. You can select them from the Image flyout of the Materials Editor for generic materials or the Color flyout for some of the other types of materials, such as ceramic, concrete, masonry, plastic, stone, or wood.

If you select a procedural map, the Texture Editor palette opens and offers options that let you control the map's properties. You can set the color and grain thickness of wood or the vein spacing and width of marble. These options let you customize a texture to your specifications. You may want to experiment with these settings on your own to see how they affect the appearance of an object.

Procedural maps aren't affected by the material map of an object. (See "Applying and Adjusting Texture Maps" later in this chapter.) Also, they don't appear in the Realistic visual style like other texture maps. You must render your view to see the results of a procedural map.

Assigning Materials by Layer

You've just created a self-illuminated material. The next step is to assign the material to the ceiling lights in the model. So far, you've applied materials to objects one at a time, but it would be too time-consuming to have to select each light individually. You can assign materials to layers, which can save time as long as you've organized your model into layers that represent materials.

In the Facade drawing, I've already set up some layers for you. The ceiling lights are on a layer called CLGLITE. The next exercise shows you how to apply a material to a layer:

1. Click the Attach By Layer tool in the Render tab's expanded Materials panel (Figure 23.38). The Material Attachment Options dialog box appears. You see a list of materials on the left and a list of layers on the right.

2. Click and drag Ceiling Light from the left panel to the CLGLITE item in the right panel. The name Ceiling Light appears next to the CLGLITE layer name along with an X.

3. While you're here, click and drag Glass1 from the left panel to the DKGLASS and GLASS layers in the right panel.

4. Click OK to exit the dialog box.

5. Render your view. The lights appear in the ceiling of each of the floors (see Figure 23.39).

In the previous exercise, you created a self-illuminated material that, when assigned to an object, appears to glow. You then added this material to the ceiling lights in the model. This self-illuminated material doesn't actually produce light in the model, however. To do that, you'll have to add light objects such as a distant lights or spotlights.

FIGURE 23.38
Clicking the
Attach By Layer
tool allows you to
assign materials
to layers.

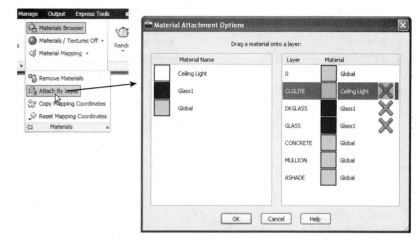

FIGURE 23.39
The lights appear
in the ceilings
of the building to
the right.

Simulating a Night Scene with Spotlights

Spotlights are lights that can be directed and focused on a specific area. They're frequently used to provide emphasis and are usually used for interior views or product presentations. In this exercise, you'll set up a night view of the Facade model by using spotlights to illuminate the facade.

You'll start by setting up a view to help place the spotlights. You'll save this view because you'll be going back to it several times:

1. Select Temp from the 3d Navigation drop-down list on the Home tab's View panel, and then select SE Isometric from the 3D Navigation drop-down list. By selecting the Temp option, you switch to a view that doesn't have the sky background. This helps to keep your view less cluttered.

2. If it isn't already on the screen, open the ViewCube; right-click the ViewCube and select Parallel (see Figure 23.40).

FIGURE 23.40
Select Parallel from the ViewCube's shortcut menu.

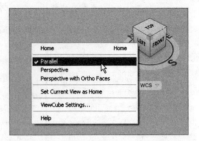

3. Adjust your view so it looks similar to Figure 23.41.

FIGURE 23.41
Set up your view to look similar to this, and then add the spotlight.

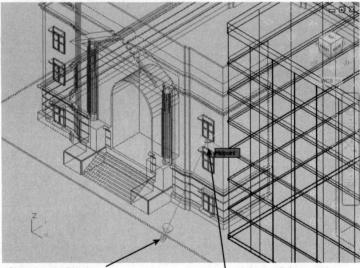

Place the spotlight here...   and the spotlight target here.

4. Select View Manager from the bottom of the 3D Navigation drop-down list on the Home tab's View panel.

5. In the View Manager dialog box, click the New button.

6. In the New View/Shot Properties dialog box (Figure 23.42), enter **SE Isometric Wireframe** for the name and click OK.

7. Click OK at the View Manager dialog box.

8. Select SE Isometric Wireframe from the 3D Navigation drop-down list on the Home tab's View panel. If you can't see the full name of the view, hover over the names in the list and the full name will appear.

FIGURE 23.42

Enter a view name.

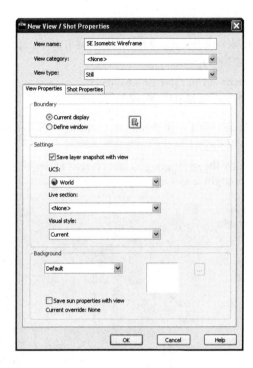

Now you're ready to add the lights:

1. Click the Spot tool from the Create Light flyout on the Render tab's Lights panel (Figure 23.43), or enter **spotlight.⏎** at the Command prompt.

FIGURE 23.43

Click Spot from the Create Light flyout.

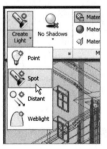

2. At the Specify source location <0,0,0>: prompt, click the point shown in Figure 23.41. Don't use osnaps because you don't want the light to be placed accidentally below the ground plane. You don't have to be exact, but the idea is to place the spotlight in front of the windows on the right side of the entrance to the building.

3. At the `Specify target location <0,0,-10>`: prompt, use the Midpoint osnap, and select the bottom of the window sill of the upper window, as shown in Figure 23.41. You see the prompt

```
Enter an option to change
[Name/Intensity/Status/Hotspot/Falloff/shadoW/Attenuation/Color/eXit] <eXit>:
```

4. Press ↵ to accept the default settings. You can always change the optional settings for the light through the Properties palette.

5. Copy the spotlight you just created to the location shown in Figure 23.44. You can use the spotlight target to copy from the midpoint of one window sill to the other.

FIGURE 23.44
Copy the spotlight to this location.

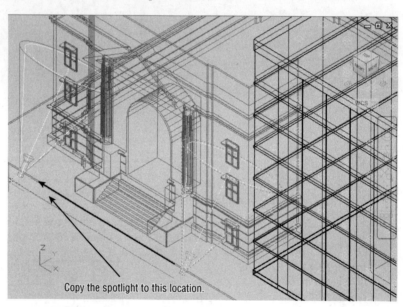

Copy the spotlight to this location.

6. You're trying to produce a nighttime rendering, so turn off the sun by clicking the Sun Status tool in the Render tab's Sun & Location panel.

7. Return to the original view by choosing My 3D View from the 3D Navigation drop-down list on the View tab's Views panel (Figure 23.45).

8. Click the Render tool in the Render tab's Render panel to see the results of your spotlight addition. Your rendering will look similar to Figure 23.46.

FIGURE 23.45
Select My 3D View from the 3D Navigation drop-down list.

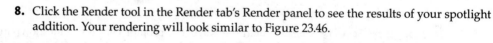

FIGURE 23.46
The rendered view
of the model with
the spotlights

Adding a Point Light

A few things still need to be added to improve this rendering. You can adjust the spotlight so it casts light over a wider area. You can also add a light in the entrance so it isn't quite so dark. The next section will show you how to make adjustments to your spotlight. First, you'll add a point light to obtain a different lighting effect:

1. Return to the view you used to add the spotlights by choosing SE Isometric Wireframe from the 3D Navigation drop-down list on the Home tab's View panel.

2. Click the Point tool from the Light flyout on the Render tab's Lights panel (Figure 23.47) or enter **Pointlight**↵.

FIGURE 23.47
Click the Point tool
from the Create
Light flyout.

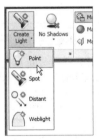

3. At the Specify source location <0,0,0>: prompt, Shift+right-click and select Center. Then select the arch over the entrance, as shown in Figure 23.48, to place the point light.

4. At the prompt

   Enter an option to change [Name/Intensity/Status/shadoW/
   Attenuation/Color/eXit] <eXit>:

   press ↵ to accept the default settings for the point light.

5. The point light appears as a spherical glyph in the archway of the building.

FIGURE 23.48
Select the center of the arch.

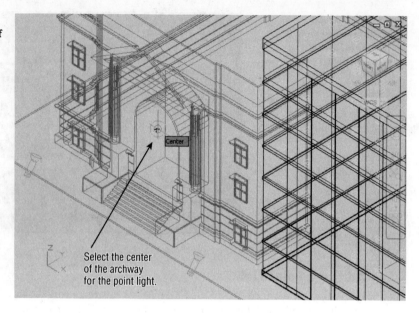

Select the center
of the archway
for the point light.

Editing Lights

You've added the point light. Before you see the results in a rendering, you'll also change the spread of the spotlights. In this exercise, you'll edit the properties of the spotlight. Not all lights have the same properties, but the basic process for editing all lights is the same:

1. Click the two spotlights, and then right-click and choose Properties. The Properties palette appears. If you see the Selection dialog box, select Light from the list.

> **EASY ACCESS TO ALL OF THE LIGHTS**
>
> You can also access the properties of lights by clicking the Lights In Model tool in the Render tab's Lights panel title bar (Lightlist command) and then, from the Lights In Model palette, selecting the lights whose properties you want to adjust. Right-click and select Properties. This method is useful if your light glyphs are turned off.

2. Look for the Falloff Angle setting in the General section of the palette, and change the value from 50 to 90. Notice how the falloff cone changes in the drawing (see Figure 23.49).

3. Close the Properties palette.

4. Return to the original view by choosing My 3D View from the 3D Navigation drop-down list on the Home tab's View panel.

5. Click the Render tool in the Render tab's Render panel to see the results of your spotlight addition. Your rendering will look similar to Figure 23.50.

Render

FIGURE 23.49
Adjust the falloff of the spotlight.

The falloff cones enlarge in the drawing when the Falloff Angle value is increased to 90.

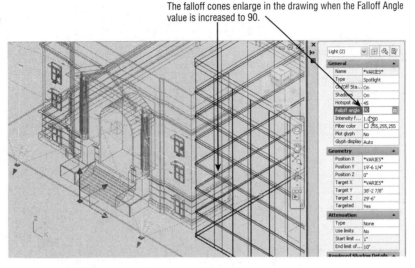

FIGURE 23.50
The rendered view of the model with the spotlights modified and the point light added

In step 2, you saw a list of options for the spotlight. Many of these options are available when you first insert the light; they appear as command-line options. Often, it's easier to place the light first and then play with the settings.

In this example, you adjusted the spotlight's falloff. By increasing the falloff angle, you broadened the spread of the light cast by the spotlight and also made the transition from light to dark appear smoother, as shown in Figure 23.51. The hotspot can also be adjusted to a narrow beam or a wide swath.

Many other light properties are available to you in the Properties dialog box. Table 23.1 describes them.

FIGURE 23.51
The hotspot and falloff of a spotlight at the top produce the lighting shown at the bottom.

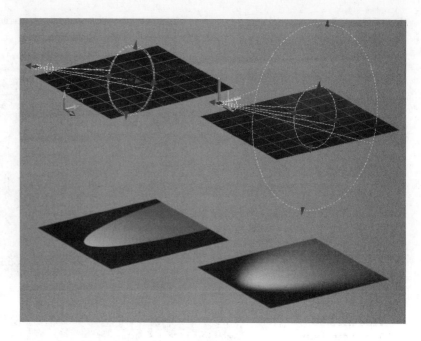

TABLE 23.1: Properties available for lights

GENERAL	
Name	Shows the name of the light
Type	Sets the type of light
On/Off Status	Shows whether light is on or off
Hotspot Angle	Sets the spotlight hotspot angle
Falloff Angle	Sets the spotlight falloff angle
Intensity Factor	Sets the light intensity
Filter Color	Sets the secondary light color simulating a color filter over a lamp
Plot Glyph	Allows the light glyph to be plotted
Glyph Display	Controls the display of the light glyph
Attenuation	
Type	Type of attenuation: Inverse Linear, Inverse Square, or None
Use Limits	Lets you turn on attenuation limits

TABLE 23.1: Properties available for lights *(CONTINUED)*

GENERAL	
Start Limit Offset	If Use Limits is on, sets the distance to the beginning of attenuation
End Limit Offset	If Use Limits is on, sets the distance to the end of attenuation
Render Shadow Details	
Type	Lets you select between Sharp and Soft shadow edges
Map Size	When shadow maps are used, lets you determine the size of the shadow map in pixels
Softness	When shadow maps are used, determines the softness of shadows

Applying and Adjusting Texture Maps

You've already seen how to assign a material to an object by adding the glass material to the building in the `facade.dwg` file. You can create other surface textures by using bitmaps in other ways to help enhance your rendering. For example, you can include a photograph of existing buildings that may be in the scene you're rendering.

Creating a Building from a Box

Figure 23.52 shows a bitmap image that was scanned into the computer and edited using a popular paint program.

FIGURE 23.52
A bitmap image of a building you'll use in the model

I've added some blank white space to the bitmap image of the building so you can get some practice fitting an image to an object. Imagine that this building is across the street from the Facade model and you want to include it in the scene to show its relationship to your building. The following exercise will show you how it's done:

1. Return to the view you used to add the spotlights by choosing SE Isometric Wireframe from the 3D Navigation drop-down list on the Home tab's View panel.

2. Adjust your view so it looks similar to Figure 23.53, and then draw a box that is approximately 130′ square by 80′ tall.

FIGURE 23.53
The box representing the building on the next block

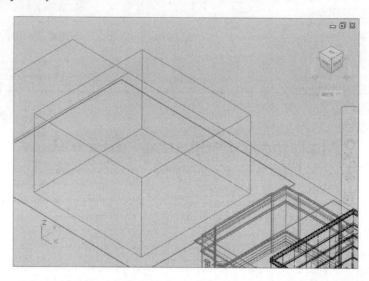

The box you just added represents the building on the next block. Now create the material that you'll use to give this building some detail:

1. In the upper-left corner of the Materials Browser, click the Create Material tool and select Generic.

2. In the Materials Editor, enter **Building1** for the material name.

3. Click the flyout icon to the far right of the Generic panel's Image option and select Image (Figure 23.54).

4. Locate and select the MARKET1.tif file in the Chapter 23 sample files.

5. Click Open to exit this dialog box.

6. In the Materials Editor, double-click in the Image sample box to open the Texture Editor.

7. In the Texture Editor, expand the Transforms option (Figure 23.55).

8. Expand the Scale option and then change the Sample Size value from 1 foot (12 inches) to 130 feet. After you enter the value, it may change to 1560 inches.

FIGURE 23.54
The Image flyout

FIGURE 23.55
The Texture Editor

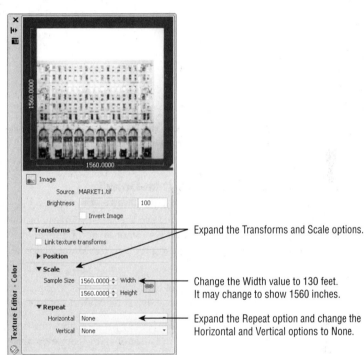

Expand the Transforms and Scale options.

Change the Width value to 130 feet.
It may change to show 1560 inches.

Expand the Repeat option and change the
Horizontal and Vertical options to None.

9. Expand the Repeat option and change the Horizontal and Vertical options from Tile
   to None.

10. Close the Texture Editor.

You've just set up a material that will apply the MARKET1.tif image to any object in your
model. You gave it a size of 130 feet because that is the size of the box representing the building
on the next block.

Now continue by adding the material to the box and applying the appropriate mapping style:

1. Click the recently created box to select it, and then click Building1 from the Materials Browser. If you don't see the Building1 material, select Show All from the Document Materials drop-down list at the top of the Materials Browser.

2. To see how the bitmap fits on the box, choose Realistic from the Visual Styles drop-down list on the View tab's Visual Styles panel (Figure 23.56).

FIGURE 23.56
Select Realistic from the Visual Styles drop-down list.

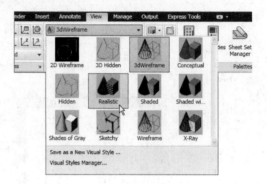

3. If it isn't on already, click the Sun Status tool in the Render tab's Sun & Location panel so you can see the model in a brighter light.

Adjusting a Material to Fit an Object

The entire image, including the blank white space, is placed on the box. You even see the image on the rooftop, although you won't see the rooftop in any of the renderings. (You can hide it with another box or 3D surface if you want an aerial view.) You can adjust the position and scale of the bitmap by using the mapping tools in the Materials panel. The mapping tools make the mapping gizmo visible:

1. Click the Box Mapping tool from the Materials Mapping flyout in the Render tab's Materials panel (Figure 23.57). You can also enter **Materialmap**↵ and then enter **B**↵ for the Box option.

2. At the Select faces or objects: prompt, click the box you just created, and press ↵. The box is outlined in yellow and a set of arrows appears around it, as shown in Figure 23.58. This yellow outline is the mapping gizmo.

FIGURE 23.57
Click the Box tool.

FIGURE 23.58
The material mapping appears as a yellow outline around the selected box.

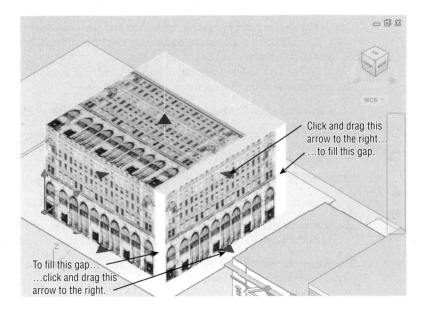

3. Hover on the arrow at the lower right of the box (see Figure 23.58); when it turns green, click it. Now as you move the cursor, the arrow follows and the image stretches or compresses.

4. Stretch the image downward and to the right until the entire building image fills the upper portion of the box. When you're satisfied, click the mouse.

5. Hover over the arrow pointing to the north (see Figure 23.58); when it turns green, click it.

6. Drag the arrow to the right until the white space toward the right of the image is gone and the image of the building fills the box. Your box should look similar to Figure 23.59.

7. Press ↵ to exit the Materialmap command.

FIGURE 23.59
The box after adjusting the map

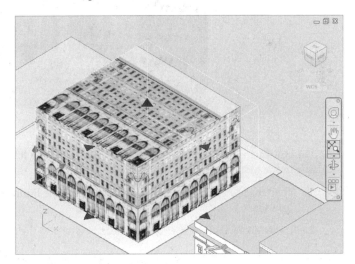

You just added a mapping gizmo to the box and then adjusted the gizmo so the material fits the box. If you need to make further adjustments to the gizmo, click the Box Mapping tool again and click the object you need to adjust.

Now look at the rendered version. First you'll turn off the spotlights and point light, and then make sure the sun is on to return to a daylight setting:

1. Click the Lights In Model tool in the title bar of the Render tab's Lights panel.

2. Select the two spotlights and the point light from the list box of the Lights In Model palette.

3. Right-click and select Properties.

4. Select Off in the On/Off Status setting of the Properties palette.

5. Close the Properties palette and the Lights In Model palette.

6. If you haven't done so already, click the Sun Status tool in the Sun & Location panel to turn the sun back on. The Sun Status tool should turn blue, indicating that it is on.

You've set the lighting for a daylight rendering. Notice that you were able to select several lights to turn them off all at once.

Next, render your view:

1. Choose My 3D View from the 3D Navigation drop-down list in the Home tab's View panel.

Render

2. Click the Render tool in the Render tab's Render panel. The building appears on the left side of the image (see Figure 23.60).

FIGURE 23.60
The rendering with the new building

The building is too dark in the shadow. You can lighten it by increasing the Self Illumination setting in the Materials Editor:

1. Open the Materials Editor by double-clicking the Building1 material in the Materials Browser.

2. In the Materials Editor, click the check box next to the Self Illumination option.

3. Set the Luminance value to 0.10.

4. Render the view again. This time, the building on the next block shows up more clearly.

Another option is to use a paint program to refine the bitmap image before you use it in AutoCAD. AutoCAD attempts to place the bitmap accurately on a surface, so if the bitmap is fairly clean and doesn't have any extra blank space around the edges, you can usually place it on an object without having to make any adjustments other than its orientation. I purposely made the spaces in the image so you can practice using the Materialmap feature.

You briefly encountered the Template drop-down list in the Materials palette when you created a material. The settings of these templates depend on the kind of material you're trying to model.

Exploring Your Other Material-Mapping Options

You may have noticed several material-mapping options in the previous exercise. You used the Box option because it was a natural fit for the box you created. But options are offered for a planar surface, a cylinder, and a sphere. Figure 23.61 shows how these other options may be applied to the shapes for which they're intended.

FIGURE 23.61
The planar, box, cylinder, and sphere material maps

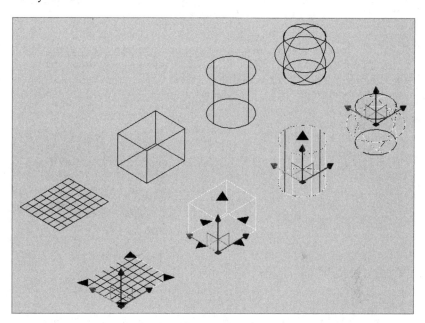

You don't have to apply the maps to the shapes they describe. Later, you'll see how you can apply a planar map to a box. You can apply a cylinder map to a thin box to achieve an interesting effect. Also, a spherical map can be applied to a cube (see Figure 23.62).

Specifying the Size of a Bitmap

As you've just seen, the Materialmap feature gives you a quick and intuitive way to set the location of a material map onto an object. There are several other ways to control the appearance of a material on an object. If you have a surface pattern that repeats over the surface, such as a tile pattern, you can set the frequency and size of the pattern. For example, you might have a brick pattern that repeats over a 12′ square area and you want that pattern reproduced accurately on a surface.

FIGURE 23.62
A material map applied to a different shape

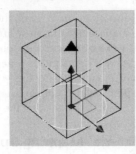

Imagine that you need to apply a brick pattern to a wall that is 8′ wide by 4′ tall. The blocks are the standard 8″ × 16″ split-face concrete masonry units, and you have an image that shows four courses of blocks two blocks wide, as shown in Figure 23.63. This is the `Masonry.Unit Masonry.CMU.Split-Face.Running.jpg` file in the `Textures` folder that is installed with AutoCAD 2011.

FIGURE 23.63
The bitmap image of a set of blocks

The following exercise shows you how you can control the size of a material map:

1. Open the `CMUwall.dwg` sample file. This file contains a simple box representing the 4′ × 8′ wall.

2. Click the Create Materials tool in the upper-left corner of the Materials Browser and select Masonry. A new material called Default Masonry appears in the Materials Browser.

3. Give your new material the name CMU by entering **CMU** in the Name input box just below the image at the top.

4. Click the Select Color flyout in the Masonry panel and select Image.

5. Locate and select `CMU.Split-Face.Running.jpg` in the sample project files for Chapter 23. The Texture Editor – Masonry palette opens.

6. Close the Texture Editor, and then click the wall object to select it.

7. Click the CMU material in the Materials Browser. The wall displays the material you just created, as shown in the left panel of Figure 23.64.

The wall has a concrete block texture. You see the results of a material with the default settings. Although it looks OK, the blocks are too small for the scale of the wall. You need to adjust the bitmap options so the texture appears to the proper scale on the wall object:

1. In the Materials Editor, within the Masonry panel, double-click the image of the CMU `.Split-Face.Running.jpg` file. This opens the Texture Editor.

2. In the Texture Editor, expand the Transforms panel by clicking the arrowhead to the left of the Transforms title.

3. Expand the Scale panel under the Transforms panel to reveal the Scale options.

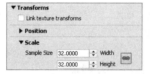

4. Change the Sample Size Width and Height values to 32″. You use 32″ because that is the actual width and height of the set of blocks shown in the bitmap image used for the CMU (see Figure 23.63). As you enter these values, the block wall changes to reveal the blocks at the proper size, as shown in the image at right in Figure 23.64.

5. Close the Texture Editor and the Materials Editor, and then close and save the `CMUwall.dwg` file.

FIGURE 23.64
The wall with the material applied

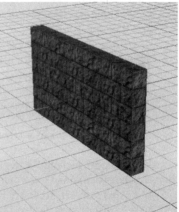

Now, suppose you want the blocks to appear 4″ high instead of 8″ high. You can go back to the Texture Editor and change the Sample Size Height setting to 16 (half the height you specified originally).

Note that to change the width to a value different from the height, you need to click the link icon to the right of the Width and Height input boxes to turn off the link between the height and width values.

The block wall changes to show a 4″ high block, as shown in Figure 23.65.

FIGURE 23.65
Change the Height
setting in the
Texture Editor
and the wall
also changes.

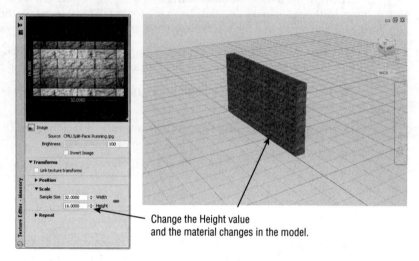

Change the Height value
and the material changes in the model.

You can use many other settings in the Adjust Bitmap dialog box to fine-tune the appearance of a material over an object. You've used the major settings in these exercises.

Simulating Trees and People with Opacity Maps

There's nothing like adding landscaping and people to a rendering to add a sense of life and scale. Computer images in particular need landscape props because they tend to appear cold and lifeless.

In the following set of exercises, you'll create a tree material and apply it to a 3D solid to simulate a tree. In doing so, you'll get a chance to explore some of the other features of the Materials palette. To create a tree, you'll use the same image option of the Materials Editor you've been using so far, but you'll also add something called an *opacity map*, or *cutouts* as they are called in AutoCAD. A cutout lets you "cut out" areas of a texture map through a black-and-white image file. For example, in the tree you'll be creating, you'll apply a tree material to a simple rectangular region. Since the tree is an irregular shape, you'll want the area around the tree to be removed, or "cut out," from the material, creating an illusion of a complex, tree-shaped outline without showing the entire rectangular region.

The opacity map lets you determine which areas are cut out through black-and-white areas of an image. Black areas are cut out, and white areas are opaque. You can use shades of gray to vary transparency. Figure 23.66 shows an example of how an opacity map works.

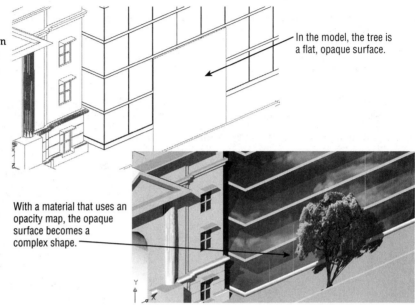

FIGURE 23.66
A material using an opacity map can be applied to a 3D solid to create the illusion of a complex outline such as a tree.

In the model, the tree is a flat, opaque surface.

With a material that uses an opacity map, the opaque surface becomes a complex shape.

In the following exercise, you'll go back to the Facade model and experiment with opacity maps. To start your tree, create a new material in the Materials palette:

1. Click the Create Material tool in the Materials Browser and select Generic.

2. In the Materials Editor, give the new material the name **Tree1**.

Next, add a texture map of a tree:

1. In the Generic group, click the flyout arrowhead to the far right of the Image option and select Image.

2. In the Chapter 23 project folder, locate and open the file CamphorAM.tif.

3. In the Texture Editor, expand the Transforms panel and then expand the Scale panel.

4. Change the Width and Height values to 30 feet.

Finally, add an opacity map for the tree. The process is basically the same as adding a texture map:

1. In the Materials Editor, expand the Cutouts group and click the check box next to the Cutouts group title to turn it on.

2. Click the flyout arrowhead to the far right of the Image option and select Image.

3. Use the Materials Editor Open File dialog box to browse to the Chapter 23 project folder and locate and open the file CamphorOP.tif.

4. In the Texture Editor, expand the Transforms and Scale panels and set the Width and Height values to 30 feet.

Next, create an object representing a tree in the drawing, and then apply the Tree1 material to the object:

1. Go to the SE Isometric Wireframe view and adjust your view so it looks similar to Figure 23.67.

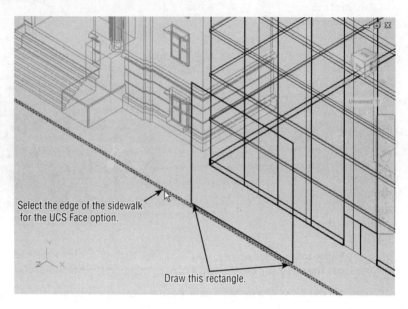

Select the edge of the sidewalk for the UCS Face option.

Draw this rectangle.

2. Set up a UCS that is vertical to the ground plane. Click Face from the View/Object/Face flyout on the View tab's Coordinates panel, and then click the location shown in Figure 23.67.

3. Click 3D Solid from the Selection dialog box. Press ↵ to accept the new UCS.

4. Click the Rectangle tool on the Home tab's Draw panel.

5. Make sure that Dynamic UCS and osnaps are off, and then draw a rectangle that is 30′ by 30′ (see Figure 23.67). The 30′ square dimension is intended to match the Tree1 Texture Editor settings.

6. Click Region from the expanded Draw panel and select the rectangle you just drew. At the Selection dialog box, select Polyline and press ↵. This converts your rectangle into a region.

7. Click the region you just created to select it.

8. Click the Tree1 material from the Materials Browser.

9. Select My 3D View from the 3D Navigation drop-down list in the Home tab's View panel, and then click Render in the Render tab's Render panel to see the results of your work (see Figure 23.68).

FIGURE 23.68
The tree added to
your rendering

The process of adding people is just the same. You create a material that includes a texture map and an opacity map and then apply the material to a flat box. Make sure you turn on the Fit To Object option in the Adjust Bitmap dialog box for both the texture and the opacity map. Figure 23.69 shows a rendering that includes some additional trees and people.

FIGURE 23.69
A rendering
with more trees
and people

Understanding the Rendering Options

Quite a few settings are available to control the quality of your renderings. Take a look at the tools available in the Render tab's Render panel, shown in Figure 23.70.

FIGURE 23.70

The expanded Render panel

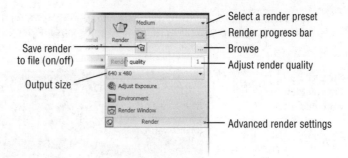

Select a render preset
Render progress bar
Save render to file (on/off)
Browse
Adjust render quality
Output size
Advanced render settings

The Save Rendering To File option lets you set up a file to which the renderings will be saved. If you turn on this option, then each time you render your model, the rendering will be saved automatically to the file you designate.

WHAT IS A BUMP MAP?

You may have noticed the Bump option in the Materials Editor. You'll see the Bump option at the bottom of the list of panels. The Bump option lets you insert another image to add texture to a surface. For example, you can include a series of dots on a material to simulate a bumpy surface.

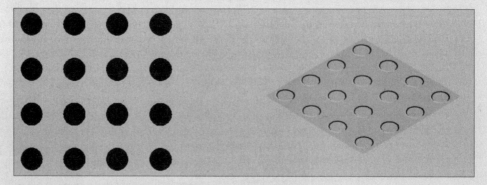

You can adjust the height of the bump using the Amount slider in the expanded Bump panel. Move the slider to the right for a higher bump. Note that the Bump option does not actually deform the object it is attached to. The bump is applied when the model is rendered.

As with other Materials Editor panels, you can use an image for the bump map and control the size of the bump map in the Texture Editor.

The Output Size option lets you set the vertical and horizontal resolution of the rendering in pixels. The default is 640 × 480. You can choose from a set of predetermined standard sizes or set a custom size.

The Environment option lets you add a fog effect to your rendering (see Figure 23.71). Click this option to open the Render Environment dialog box. This dialog box offers a set of options to control how the fog appears in the rendering. For example, Enable Fog lets you turn the fog effect on or off. Color lets you select a color for the fog. You can experiment with the Render Environment dialog box on your own.

FIGURE 23.71
The Render Environment option lets you add fog to a rendering.

Select Render Preset is a drop-down list that gives you a set of options you can use to select the quality of the rendering. The default is Medium, which is the setting you've been using. This offers a decent-quality rendering without taking a lot of time. When you want to produce a final, high-quality rendering, select Presentation from this list. The rendering will take longer, but more detail will be brought out.

Clicking Advanced Render Settings opens the Advanced Render Settings palette. These settings are for the advanced user, and most users won't need to work with them. Rendering presets are predetermined sets of the advanced render settings. You can make adjustments to these settings if you need to (see "Rendering Interior Views" later in this chapter for more on the advanced render settings).

The Adjust Exposure tool opens the Adjust Rendering Exposure dialog box. Note that a system variable called Lightingunits must be set to 1 or 2 before this option works. The Adjust Rendering Exposure dialog box lets you set the brightness, contrast, and midtones of renderings that use photometric lighting. You'll see how this works later in this chapter.

Checking and Saving Renderings in the Render Window

All your renderings appear in the Render window, which has a few options you'll want to know about. At the bottom of the window is a list of all the renderings you've done in the current AutoCAD session. If you've done several renderings, you can go back to an earlier rendering by clicking it in the list. Right-click an item in the list to display a list of options that you can apply to the selected item. Table 23.2 describes these options.

TABLE 23.2: Right-click options for image filenames in the render Window

OPTION	WHAT IT DOES
Render Again	Renders the selected image again.
Save	Saves the selected image to a file. AutoCAD offers a choice of monochrome, 8-bit grayscale, 8-bit color, and 24-bit color. You can save your image as a BMP, PCX, TGA, TIFF, JPEG, or PNG file.
Save Copy	If you've already saved a file once, lets you save it again under a different name.
Make Render Settings Current	If you've rendered several views and you want to return to the setting of a previous rendering, select the view whose settings you want to restore and select this option.
Remove From the List	Removes the selected rendering from the list.
Delete Output File	If you've saved a rendered view as a file, deletes the file.

Perhaps the most important of these options are Save and Save Copy. They enable you to keep copies of your rendered views as bitmap images.

If you want to check a detail in the rendering, you can use the Tools menu to zoom in or zoom out of the image. When you zoom in, horizontal and vertical scroll bars are displayed to allow you to pan over the image.

To the right of the window is a listing of the rendering's statistics. You can make adjustments to many of these settings through system variables and the Advanced Render Settings palette.

USING THE RENDER REGION TOOL FOR A QUICK CHECK

At times, you may want to just check a part of your model to see if it will render correctly without having to do a full-blown rendering. You can use the Render Region tool in the Render flyout of the Render panel to do just that.

Click the Render Region tool, and then place a selection window around the area you want to check. AutoCAD renders just the selected area directly in the drawing area. Type **R.⏎** to clear the screen of the rendered region.

Adding Cameras for Better View Control

Throughout this chapter, you've seen how you can save and recall views. Views can be real time-savers, especially if you have several views that you save and recall. Views will also save background and visual styles. Typically, you set up a view using the tools you've learned about so far, but there's another tool that can give you that extra level of control you may need for special circumstances: the Camera tool.

What isn't obvious is that your views are also represented as cameras. Right now, you can't see the cameras because a setting called *Camera Glyph* is turned off. Try the following to visualize your My 3D View as a camera:

1. Return to the SE Isometric Wireframe view from the 3D Navigation drop-down list in the Home tab's View panel.

2. Adjust your view so it looks similar to Figure 23.72.

FIGURE 23.72
Adding a new camera

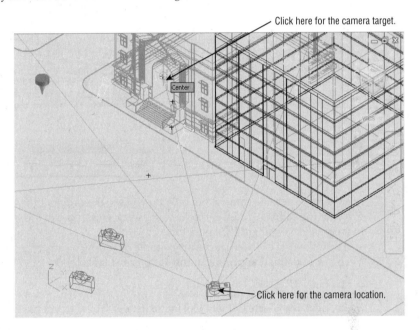

Click here for the camera target.

Click here for the camera location.

3. Open the Render tab, and then right-click anywhere in the Ribbon and select Panels ➢ Camera.

4. Click the Show Cameras tool in the Render tab's Camera panel that you just opened. You can also type **Cameradisplay↵1↵**. You see three cameras in the lower half of the drawing (Figure 23.73).

5. Click one of the cameras, and then at the Selection dialog box, select Camera. A window appears that shows you what the camera sees (Figure 23.74).

6. Press the Esc key, and then click the other camera. The camera preview changes to show you a sample of the other view.

FIGURE 23.73
Displaying
cameras

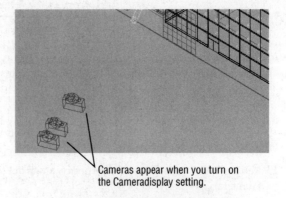

Cameras appear when you turn on
the Cameradisplay setting.

FIGURE 23.74
Viewing the
camera preview

When you select a camera, not only do you see the camera preview, but you also see a set of grips for the camera. You'll get a chance to work with some of those grips a little later. Next, try to create a view using the Camera tool.

The following exercise shows an example of adding a camera to the Facade model. You'll add a camera, and you'll apply one of the options available for it:

1. Enter **UCS↵ W↵** to go to the WCS.

2. Click the Create Camera tool in the Render tab's Camera panel. You can also type **Camera↵**.

You see this prompt:

```
Current camera settings: Height=0˝ Lens Length=50.0000 mm
Specify camera location:
```

3. Click the point shown in Figure 23.72 to set the camera location.

4. At the `Specify target location:` prompt, use the Center osnap and select the center of the arch. You see this prompt:

```
Enter an option [?/Name/LOcation/Height/Target/LEns/Clipping/View/eXit]<eXit>:
```

5. To set the height of the camera at eye level, type **H↵** for the Height option.

6. At the Specify camera height <0″>: prompt, enter 5↵. The options prompt returns to allow you to enter more options.

7. Press ↵ to complete the camera insertion. The camera appears at the location you selected in step 3.

AutoCAD gives your camera the default name Camera1. You can rename it at any time in the Properties palette or in the View Manager dialog box.

You were able to set the height of the camera independent of the location you selected in step 3 by using one of the options in the prompt. Table 23.3 describes the other options that are available.

TABLE 23.3: Camera prompt options

OPTION	WHAT IT DOES
?	Displays a list of cameras in the current drawing
Name	Lets you provide a name for your camera (no spaces allowed)
LOcation	Lets you change the location of the camera
Height	Lets you specify the height of the camera
Target	Lets you select a target location
LEns	Lets you specify a lens focal length in mm
Clipping	Lets you include front and back clipping planes
View	Lets you go to the camera's view
eXit	Exits the command

Making Adjustments to Your Camera

Now that you've got the camera in place, you can see what the view looks like. You can use the 3D Navigation drop-down list to display the view from your new camera, or you can click the camera to open the Camera Preview window. Before you do any of that, try making some adjustments to the camera:

1. Click the camera you just created, and then click Camera from the Selection dialog box. The Camera Preview dialog box shows a sample of the view from your camera (see Figure 23.75). You also see the camera view frame and target.

2. Click the camera grip, and move the camera around. You can see the changes you make in real time in the Camera Preview dialog box.

3. Press the escape key twice to exit the grip edit mode. The camera moves back to its original location so your preview looks similar to the one in Figure 23.75.

FIGURE 23.75

The Camera Preview dialog box

Now turn on the clipping planes to see how they work:

1. Select the camera again, and then right-click and select Properties.

2. At the bottom of the Properties palette, click the Clipping option and select Front And Back On (Figure 23.76). The sample view changes.

FIGURE 23.76

Select the Front And Back On option in the Properties palette.

3. Change the Front Plane value to 20´ and the Back Plane value to –20´ (minus 20 feet). The Camera Preview view now shows the view of just the entry.

The clipping planes hide objects either behind or in front of the target location. As you've just seen, you can indicate the clipping-plane distance from the target in the Properties palette. You can also make adjustments to the clipping plane directly in the drawing using the camera's grips:

1. Hover over the Front Clip Plane arrowhead grip shown in Figure 23.77 so you can see the tool tip describing the grip.

2. Click the grip, drag it back and forth, and watch the camera preview. You can see how the clipping plane hides more or less of the foreground as you move the grip.

3. Click the original location of the grip (the red grip) to keep it at 20´.

You can adjust the back grip the same way so you can get direct feedback on how much of your view is being clipped.

Next try adjusting one of the other grips:

1. Click the Lens Length/FOV grip on the left side, as shown in Figure 23.77, and drag it to the left. This has the effect of shortening the lens length. The shorter the lens length, the more of the view the camera is able to take in. But past a certain point, the view begins to distort.

2. Click a point to the left to fix the view at a lower lens length. The Lens Length and Field Of View values change in the Properties palette.

3. In the Properties palette, change the Field Of View value back to the default of 54.

FIGURE 23.77
Selecting the camera grips

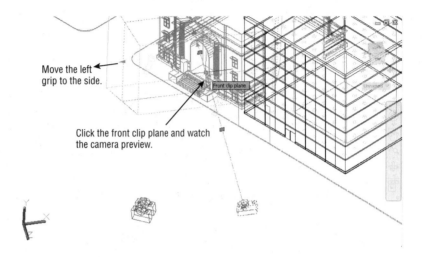

Move the left grip to the side.

Click the front clip plane and watch the camera preview.

As you can see in the Properties palette for the camera, you have a number of controls to affect the view. Because cameras and user-created views are basically the same thing, the properties you see for cameras are the same as those you would see for views in the View Manager. (Open the 3D Navigation drop-down list and select Manage Views at the bottom of the list.) Obviously, the options presented here apply to other views as well.

Let's see the results of your work: Select Camera1 from the 3D Navigation drop-down list in the Home tab's View panel. You see the camera view you just set up (Figure 23.78).

FIGURE 23.78
The Camera1 view

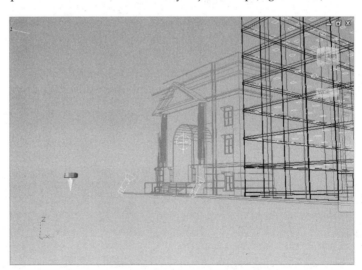

Creating an Animated Walk-Through

Another feature that is related to the camera is *motion path animation*. This is a feature that allows you to create an animated walk-through of your design. Such animations can be a great aid in helping others to visualize your ideas more clearly. Try this exercise:

1. Choose SE Isometric Wireframe from the 3D Navigation drop-down list in the Home tab's View panel, and then adjust your view so it looks similar to Figure 23.79.

FIGURE 23.79
Draw the polyline for the motion path and select the arch center.

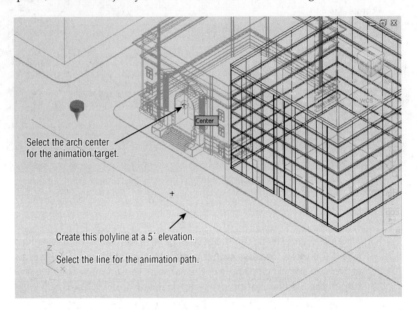

Select the arch center for the animation target.

Center

Create this polyline at a 5′ elevation.

Select the line for the animation path.

2. Draw the polyline shown in Figure 23.79, and then move the polyline in the Z axis so it's at the 5′ level.

3. Open the Animations panel. While in the Render tab, right-click anywhere in the Ribbon and select Panel ➤ Animations.

Animation
Motion Path

4. Click the Animation Motion Path tool on the Render tab's Animations panel. You can also type **Anipath.**↵. The Motion Path Animation dialog box appears (Figure 23.80).

FIGURE 23.80
The Motion Path
Animation dialog

5. In the Camera group, select the Path option and then click the Select Path tool (Figure 23.81).

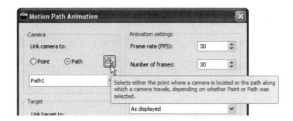

6. Select the polyline you just drew, and then click OK to accept the default path name.

7. Back in the Motion Path Animation dialog box, select Point in the Target group, and then click the Pick Point tool (Figure 23.82).

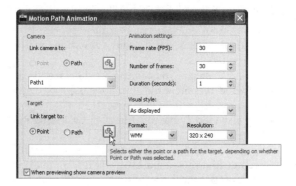

8. Pick the center of the arch in the building entrance, as shown in Figure 23.79, and then click OK in the Point Name dialog box to accept the default name.

9. Make sure As Displayed is selected in the Visual Styles drop-down list, and then click the Preview button. A preview window appears, and you see a sample of your animation. The animation is a bit fast, but you can make adjustments later.

10. Close the Animation Preview window, and then click OK.

11. In the Save As dialog box, save your animation with the default filename and place it in the My Documents folder. AutoCAD takes a moment to generate the animation, and then you see a camera at the end of your animation path.

You were asked to save the animation even though it was in a fairly crude state and was too fast. The advantage of saving the animation right away is that you then have access to the animation camera.

AutoCAD creates a new camera with default settings when an animation is created. You can then make adjustments to the camera and other animation settings to refine your animation.

Fine-Tuning the Animation

Once you've created and saved an animation, no matter how crude, you can edit its camera settings as well as its speed, resolution, and visual style. To get a feel for how to edit an animation, try the following:

1. Click the camera at the end of the animation path, right-click, and select Properties.

2. In the Properties palette, make sure Lens Length (mm) is set to 35 to get a wide field of view. Close the Properties palette.

Animation
Motion Path

3. With the animation camera still selected, click the Animation Motion Path tool on the Render tab's Animations panel.

4. Change the Duration (seconds) setting to 8.

5. Change the visual style to 3D Hidden.

6. Click OK, and save the animation again. You can save it under a different name if you like so you have a record of the original animation.

This time, AutoCAD takes more time to process the animation because you've increased the duration. When it's done, locate your animation file using Windows Explorer, and double-click it to view the results.

As you saw in step 5, you can use any visual style that is in the drawing. You can even create a fully rendered version of the animation—but be aware that the more complex the animation, the longer AutoCAD will take to process it.

You can also modify the polyline path by adding more segments or changing the location of the path's vertices.

You've seen how a few of the options in the Motion Path Animation dialog box work. If you think you may find this tool useful, you'll want to experiment with some of the other settings. Table 23.4 describes these options.

TABLE 23.4:   Motion path animation, camera, and target options

OPTION	WHAT IT DOES
Camera and Target Options	
Point/Path	Selects between a point or a path for the camera or target.
Select Path/Pick Point	Temporarily closes the dialog box to allow you to select a path or a point.
Drop-down list	Lets you choose from a point or a path that has already been selected.
Animation Settings Options	
Frame Rate (FPS)	Sets the frame rate in frames per second. The lowest you can go for a smooth animation is 16. TV is usually around 30 fps.
Number Of Frames	Sets the total number of frames in the animation. The lower the number, the faster the animation. This setting is dependent on the Duration and Frame Rate settings.

TABLE 23.4: Motion path animation, camera, and target options *(CONTINUED)*

OPTION	WHAT IT DOES
Duration (seconds)	Sets the duration of the animation. A typical duration is 10 seconds.
Visual Style	Sets the visual style for the animation. You can also select Rendered for a fully rendered animation.
Format	Lets you choose an animation file format. If you plan to use the Windows Movie Maker application to edit your animation, use WMV. Other options are AVI (Windows), MOV (QuickTime), and MPG (Mpeg 1 or 2).
Resolution	Sets the resolution of the animation. 320×240 is typical for computer video and VCD. 640×480 is typical for DVD quality.
Other Options	
Corner Deceleration	Automatically decelerates the animation motion at corners for smoother transitions.
Reverse	Reverses the animation.
When Previewing Show Camera Preview	Displays the preview in a window; otherwise, the camera motion is shown along the animation path.
Preview	Shows a preview of your animation.

Printing Your Renderings

When you've decided that your rendering is perfect, you can print a copy directly from AutoCAD. Through a layout view, you can also put together presentations that include 2D floor plans and elevations with your rendering on a single sheet. Alternatively, you can have several renderings on one sheet.

Try the following to set up a layout view to render the 3D model in both a rendered view and a hidden-line view:

1. Click the Layout1 tab or the Layout1 tool in the status bar.

2. Click the viewport border to expose its grips, and then use a grip to make the viewport smaller so it's about half the height of the Paper Space layout. Keep the height-to-width proportions of the viewport as close to the original as possible.

3. Double-click inside the viewport, and enter **V↵** to open the View Manager dialog box.

4. Select My 3D View from the Views list, and then click Set Current. Click OK to exit the View Manager dialog box.

5. Make sure the Sun Status tool in the Render tab's Sun & Location panel is on.

6. Double-click outside the viewport, and then copy the viewport so you have an identical viewport near the original (Figure 23.83).

Now you're ready to set up the viewport to render the views in specific ways. For example, you can set one viewport to render as a fully rendered view while rendering another viewport as a hidden-line view:

1. Click the border of the top viewport, right-click, and choose Shade Plot ➤ Rendered.

2. Click the border of the lower viewport, right-click, and choose Shade Plot ➤ Hidden.

3. Click Plot from the Quick Access toolbar.

4. Choose a printer name for the Printer/Plotter group, and then click Preview. After a moment, you see a preview of your plot showing a fully rendered view in the top viewport and a hidden-line view in the lower viewport (Figure 23.84).

FIGURE 23.83
The preview with duplicate views

FIGURE 23.84
The final comparison rendering

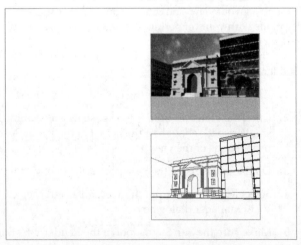

You can add viewports to include floor plans and elevations if needed. Another option is to add isometric views with labels that point out drawing features.

You also have control over the quality of the rendered viewport. If you go to the layout view, right-click the Quick View Layout tool in the status bar and choose Page Setup Manager, the Page Setup Manager dialog box opens. Click the Modify button to open the Page Setup dialog box. You can use the Shaded Viewport Options group to select from a set of viewport-quality settings (Figure 23.85).

FIGURE 23.85
Select a quality setting from the Quality drop-down list.

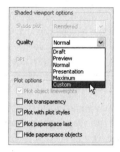

You can choose from Draft, Preview, Normal, Presentation, Maximum, and Custom. These options are described in detail in Chapter 8, so I won't go into detail here. Just remember that the options are available to help you get the most from your rendered printer output.

Simulating Natural Light

Most of the rendering you've done so far relies on fairly simple lighting methods. These methods can give you a decent rendering in a short amount of time, and you'll probably do 90 percent of your rendering work using these methods. But you may eventually want to see the way your model looks under more realistic lighting conditions.

 Real World Scenario

GETTING A SKETCH PRESENTATION WITH VISUAL STYLES

One of the more interesting issues I've encountered while creating 3D presentations of buildings is that quite often architects do not want a realistic rendering of their design. The reason is that a realistic rendering gives the impression that the design is already "set in stone" or has progressed to a more advanced level than it actually has.

So although this chapter has focused on getting a realistic rendering of your model, frequently you'll want to show your model in a less-realistic view. This is especially true in the early stages when you don't want to give the impression that you've created a finished design.

In Chapter 21, you saw how you can create a custom visual style. You may find that for most of your work, a custom visual style is all you need to get your ideas across. You can plot visual styles from either the Model view or a layout view. If you choose a layout view to plot a visual style, select the viewport border, right-click, and select the Shadeplot option. You'll see a cascading menu that contains a list of the visual styles available. Select the visual style you want to use for your plot.

In addition, if you need to get a bitmap version of your plot file for use in Photoshop or another image-editing program, you can add a raster plotter to AutoCAD. Use the Add-A-Plotter Wizard as described in Chapter 8; when you get to the part that asks for the plotter model, select Raster File Format and continue with the wizard. Once you've installed the raster plotter, you can select it as a plot device in the Plot Or Page Setup dialog box. The raster plotter will produce a bitmap image file. See Chapter 8 for more on plotting your drawing.

AutoCAD offers advanced lighting tools that can add impressive realism to your renderings. These tools simulate the way light behaves in the real world by taking into account the effects of light bouncing off nearby surfaces. In the following sections, you'll get a glimpse of some of the AutoCAD tools that will give your renderings an added level of realism.

Rendering Interior Views

If you're more interested in rendering interior architectural views, you should know about some of the advanced rendering settings that are available in AutoCAD 2011. Two groups of settings are particularly important to understand when you're rendering interior views.

Figure 23.86 is a rendering of a simple model using the material techniques described in this chapter. It also includes a sunlight source. As you can see, the rendering is fairly dark and not interesting.

FIGURE 23.86
An interior rendering using just the sun

Figure 23.87 is the same model rendered using two advanced rendering features: Global Illumination and Final Gather. Global Illumination simulates the way light bounces off objects

in a scene. When you turn on this option, AutoCAD calculates the reflection of light off the various surfaces in the model and applies that reflected light to neighboring objects. For example, the orange hue from the floor is reflected on the walls. The Final Gather feature has the effect of refining the rendering by increasing the amount of detail that Global Illumination produces.

FIGURE 23.87
The interior rendering shown in Figure 23.86 but with Global Illumination and Final Gather turned on

In Figure 23.87, a background image was used to simulate a view out the window. After you've rendered your view using Global Illumination, go back to the image you used for a background and adjust its brightness to match the rendering's brightness.

You can turn on and edit these two features using the Advanced Render Settings tool in the title bar of the Render tab's Render panel. This tool opens the Advanced Render Settings palette, shown in Figure 23.88.

FIGURE 23.88
The Advanced Render Settings palette

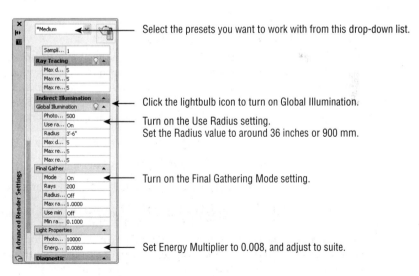

Select the presets you want to work with from this drop-down list.

Click the lightbulb icon to turn on Global Illumination.

Turn on the Use Radius setting.
Set the Radius value to around 36 inches or 900 mm.

Turn on the Final Gathering Mode setting.

Set Energy Multiplier to 0.008, and adjust to suite.

Select the Render preset you want to use from the Select Render Preset drop-down list at the top. You can then turn on the Global Illumination feature by clicking the lightbulb icon in the Global Illumination title bar. To turn on the Final Gather feature, go to the Final Gather Mode option and select On.

Just turning on these features won't give you great results right away, however. You'll need to make some careful setting adjustments. First, you must set up your drawing units using the Drawing Units dialog box (choose Drawing Utilities ➤ Units from the Application menu). Once you've done this, you must stick to that unit style. If you choose Architectural, for example, you don't want to change to decimal.

After you've set your units, turn on the Use Radius setting in the Global Illumination group, and then set Radius to 36˝. If you're working in metrics, set Radius to a value similar to 36˝. If this value is too small, the rendering will appear splotchy.

Next, scroll down to the Light Properties group, and change the Energy Multiplier setting to a value around 0.008.

Once you've made these settings, you can render your interior view and see the results. If the direct sunlight is too bright, reduce the sun's intensity factor by clicking the Sun Properties tool in the title bar of the Render tab's Sun & Location panel and adjusting the intensity factor in the Sun Properties palette. If the interior appears too dark or too light, adjust the Energy Multiplier value in the Light Properties group of the Advanced Render Settings palette.

You can adjust the sun angle by setting the date and time in the Sun Properties palette. To do quick study renderings, you can turn off Final Gather and increase the Global Lighting Radius setting to 100 inches or 2000 mm. You can also reduce the Global Illumination Photons/Sample setting and the Light Properties Photons/Light setting while making your study rendering. You'll probably end up making several renderings before you arrive at one that you like.

Although it isn't perfect, Global Illumination can greatly improve your interior views. You can save time by getting a rendering close to what you want and then using an image-editing program to fine-tune the image.

If you'd like to see how the file used in Figure 23.87 is set up, you can find it as `23-settings .dwg` in the projects folder for this chapter. Use the saved view named Scene1 when you render the model.

Using the Sun and Sky Simulation

Just as with the interior view discussed in the last section, you can set up AutoCAD to simulate realistic lighting effects in exterior views. Earlier in this chapter, you added a distant light to approximate the light bouncing off the ground. AutoCAD's Sun and Sky Simulation feature offers a more accurate rendition of reflected light that takes into account the light bouncing off neighboring buildings and surfaces. To see how this feature works, try the following exercise:

1. Go back to the `facade.dwg` file and restore the My 3D View view.

2. At the Command prompt, enter **Lightingunits**↵.

3. At the `Enter new value for LIGHTINGUNITS <0>:` prompt, enter **2**.

If you have a drawing that uses distant lights, you will see a warning message asking if you want to disable distant lights. Leave them enabled by selecting Allow Distant Lights.

By changing the Lightingunits setting, you turn on the Photometric Lighting feature in AutoCAD. The Photometric Lighting feature gives you finer control over the intensity of the lights you add to your model. The Lightingunits system variable can be set to 0 (off), 1 (international units), or 2 (American units). When you are in a perspective view and Lightingunits is set to 1 or 2, you can turn on the Sun and Sky Simulation feature.

MAKING YOUR OWN RENDERING PRESETS

If you want to create your own custom rendering presets so you have the default ones available, follow these steps:

1. In the Advanced Render Settings palette (shown in Figure 23.88), select Manage Render Presets from the drop-down list at the top of the palette. The Render Presets Manager dialog box opens.

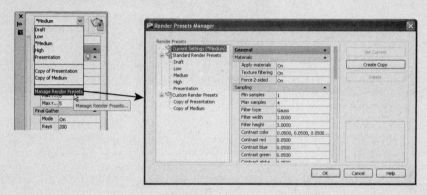

2. Select a preset that you'd like as your prototype from the list to the left, and then click the Create Copy button.

3. In the Copy Render Preset dialog box, enter a name for your presets and a description if you like. Click OK.

4. Your copy appears at the bottom of the list to the right, under Custom Render Presets.

You can also edit the render presets from the Render Presets Manager using the settings in the middle column. Once you've created a set of custom render presets, you can select it from the Render tab's Render panel drop-down list.

This next exercise demonstrates how the Sun and Sky Simulation feature works:

1. Click the Sky Background flyout in the Render tab's Sun & Location panel and select the Sky Background And Illumination option.

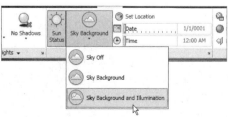

2. The background of your main view changes. This sky background replaces the bitmap image of the sky.

Render

3. Click the Render tool. After a minute or two, you get a finished rendering. Your model renders using the current Sun setting. The shadows on the center building are more realistic and show more detail of the building (see Figure 23.89).

FIGURE 23.89
The rendering with the Sky Background And Illumination feature turned on

You can further refine your image by adjusting the brightness and contrast. To do this, you use the Adjust Rendered Exposure dialog box:

1. Click the Adjust Exposure tool in the expanded Render tab's Render panel, or type **Renderexposure.⏎**.

2. The Adjust Rendered Exposure dialog box appears (Figure 23.90) and generates a thumbnail rendering.

FIGURE 23.90
Adjusting exposure in your render

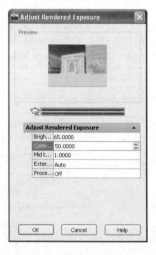

3. Click in the Brightness input box. A pair of arrows appears to the right.

4. Click and drag the arrows upward. The value in the input box changes and the image brightens. Make sure the Brightness value is set to 65 using the click-and-drag motion on the arrows.

5. Click in the Contrast input box, and click and drag the input-box arrows to adjust the value upward to 80.

6. Click OK, and render the view again.

This time, the rendering is brighter and has more contrast. If you prefer, you can also set the brightness, contrast, and midtone settings in the Render tab's expanded Lights panel (Figure 23.91).

FIGURE 23.91

The brightness, contrast, and midtone settings

The Sun and Sky Simulation feature causes AutoCAD to take more time to render a view, so you should use it only when you really need the lighting effects it offers.

As mentioned earlier, when the Lightingunits system variable is set to 1 or 2, the Photometric Lighting feature is turned on. Photometric lighting offers additional settings for the sun in the Sun Properties palette. For example, you can set the appearance of the sun disk, the horizon, and the ground color through the Sun Properties palette. You can open the Sun Properties palette by clicking the Sun Properties tool in the title bar of the Sun & Location panel.

With photometric lighting turned on, you see additional settings in the Properties palette for other types of lights as well. You have finer control over lighting intensity through the Photometric Properties panel (see Figure 23.92). If you change the Type setting in the General panel to Web, you can import IES web files that control the way a fixture spreads its light. Once a web file is selected, its Goniometric diagram is displayed in the Properties palette, as shown in the figure. A *Goniometric diagram* is a graphic that shows the distribution of light intensity from a light fixture.

AutoCAD offers some sample IES web files in the `C:\Documents and Settings\All Users\ Application Data\Autodesk\AutoCAD 2011\R18.1\enu\WebFiles` folder. To use these web files, you'll need to add this location to the Web File Search Path setting in the Files tab of the Options dialog box. See Appendix B for more on the Options dialog box.

This brings us to the end of the chapter. I've just scratched the surface of AutoCAD's rendering capabilities. You'll want to explore many more features once you get the basics down. To find out more about the Photometric Lighting feature, look up *Photometric and Sky* in the index of the AutoCAD 2011 Help website.

FIGURE 23.92

Photometric lighting offers additional options in the Properties palette for lights.

Change the Type setting to Web to import IES web files.

Click the dialog box icon in the Lamp Intensity input to to open the Lamp Intensity dialog box.

Use the Web File input box to import IES web files.

Once a web file is imported, the Goniometric diagram of the file appears.

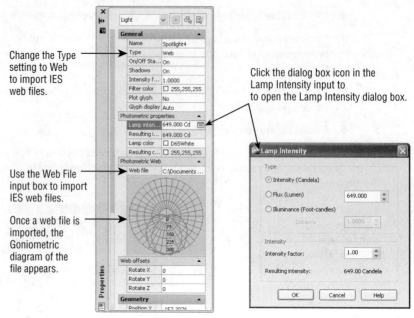

The Bottom Line

Simulate the sun.   One of the more practical uses of AutoCAD's rendering feature is to simulate the sun's location and resulting shadows. You can generate shadow studies for any time of the year in any location on the earth.

Master It   Name three items that can be set to position the sun in relation to your model.

Use materials.   AutoCAD lets you create materials that you can apply to the objects in your model to simulate a realistic appearance.

Master It   Name the parts of AutoCAD that can be used to create materials, and describe some of their features.

Create effects using materials and lights.   You can use materials and lights together to control the appearance of your model.

Master It   Name the part of the example model in this chapter that was used to show how a material can appear to glow.

Apply and adjust texture maps.   Texture maps can be used to create a number of effects in your model. You can use a brick texture map that repeats over a surface to simulate a brick wall, or you can use a photograph of a building to turn a box into a building.

Master It   What is the name of the feature that lets you graphically adjust a texture map on an object?

Understand the rendering options. In addition to adjusting the materials and lighting to control the look of your rendering, you can make other adjustments to your rendering through the Render panel and the Render window.

Master It Name some of the right-click menu options that appear for image filenames in the Render window.

Add cameras for better view control. When you create a view using the View Manager dialog box, you're actually creating a camera. Cameras are objects that let you control the orientation and view target for a view, among other things.

Master It Name some of the options you can set to control a camera.

Print your renderings. You can save your rendered views as bitmap files using the Render window. If you prefer, you can also have AutoCAD include a rendering in a layout. You can include different renderings of the same file in a single layout.

Master It Give a general description of the process for setting up a rendered viewport in a layout.

Simulate natural light. When you want to get a more accurate rendition of the lighting effects on your model, you can use some of the advanced rendering features that simulate natural light.

Master It Name the two setting groups you need to use to render an interior view accurately.

Chapter 24

Editing and Visualizing 3D Solids

In the previous 3D chapters, you spent some time becoming familiar with the AutoCAD 3D modeling features. In this chapter, you'll focus on 3D solids and how they're created and edited. You'll also learn how you can use some special visualization tools to show your 3D solid in a variety of ways.

You'll create a fictitious mechanical part to explore some of the ways you can shape 3D solids. This will also give you a chance to see how you can turn your 3D model into a standard 2D mechanical drawing. In addition, you'll learn about the 3D solid editing tools that are available through the Solid Editing Ribbon panel.

In this chapter, you'll learn to do the following:

- ◆ Understand solid modeling
- ◆ Create solid forms
- ◆ Create complex solids
- ◆ Edit solids
- ◆ Streamline the 2D drawing process
- ◆ Visualize solids

Understanding Solid Modeling

Solid modeling is a way of defining 3D objects as solid forms. When you create a 3D model by using solid modeling, you start with the basic forms of your model—cubes, cones, and cylinders, for example. These basic solids are called *primitives*. Then, using more of these primitives, you begin to add to or subtract from your basic forms.

3D Solids Are Not Available in LT

LT users don't have solid-modeling capabilities. However, you can take advantage of the region objects and their related editing commands described in the sidebar "Using 3D Solid Operations on 2D Drawings" later in this chapter.

For example, to create a model of a tube, you first create two solid cylinders, one smaller in diameter than the other. You then align the two cylinders so that they're concentric and tell AutoCAD to subtract the smaller cylinder from the larger one. The larger of the two cylinders becomes a tube whose inside diameter is that of the smaller cylinder, as shown in Figure 24.1. Several primitives are available for modeling solids in AutoCAD (see Figure 24.2).

FIGURE 24.1
Creating a tube by using solid modeling

Create two cylinder primitives, one for the outside diameter and one for the inside diameter.

Cylinder for inside diameter

Cylinder for outside diameter

Superimpose the cylinder for the inside diameter onto the cylinder for the outside diameter.

Use the Subtract command to subtract the inside diameter cylinder from the outside diameter cylinder.

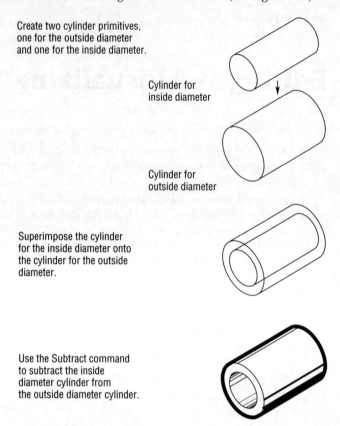

FIGURE 24.2
The solid primitives

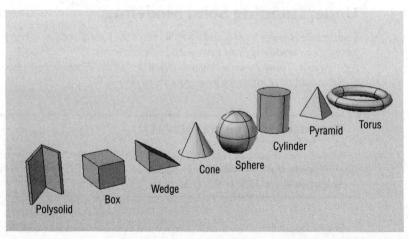

You can join these shapes—polysolid, box, wedge, cone, sphere, cylinder, pyramid, and donut (or *torus*)—in one of four ways to produce secondary shapes. The first three, demonstrated in Figure 24.3 using a cube and a cylinder as examples, are called *Boolean operations*. (The name comes from the nineteenth-century mathematician George Boole.)

FIGURE 24.3

The intersection, subtraction, and union of a cube and a cylinder

A solid box and a solid cylinder are superimposed.

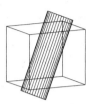

The intersection of the primitives creates a solid cylinder with the ends skewed.

The cylinder subtracted from the box creates a hole in the box.

The union of the two primitives creates a box with two round pegs.

The three Boolean operations are as follows:

Intersection   Uses only the intersecting region of two objects to define a solid shape.

Subtraction   Uses one object to cut out a shape in another.

Union   Joins two primitives so they act as one object.

The fourth option, *interference*, lets you find exactly where two or more solids coincide in space—similar to the results of a union. The main difference between interference and union is that interference enables you to keep the original solid shapes, whereas union discards the original solids, leaving only their combined form. With interference, you can have AutoCAD either show you the shape of the coincident space or create a solid based on the shape of the coincident space.

Joined primitives are called *composite solids*. You can join primitives to primitives, composite solids to primitives, and composite solids to other composite solids.

Now let's look at how you can use these concepts to create models in AutoCAD.

EXERCISE EXAMPLES ARE "UNITLESS"

To simplify the exercises in this chapter, the instructions don't specify inches or centimeters. This way, users of both the metric and Imperial measurement systems can use the exercises without having to read through duplicate information.

Creating Solid Forms

In the following sections, you'll begin to draw the object shown later in the chapter in Figure 24.19. In the process, you'll explore the creation of solid models by creating primitives and then setting up special relationships between them.

Primitives are the basic building blocks of solid modeling. At first, it may seem limiting to have only eight primitives to work with, but consider the varied forms you can create with just a few two-dimensional objects. Let's begin by creating the basic mass of your steel bracket.

First, prepare your drawing for the exercise:

1. Open the file called Bracket.dwg. This file contains some objects that you'll use in the first half of this chapter to build a 3D solid shape.

2. If you aren't already in the 3D Modeling workspace, select 3D Modeling from the Workspace Switching tool or the Workspace drop-down list in the Quick Access toolbar.

3. Close the Materials Browser if it opens with the 3D Modeling workspace.

Joining Primitives

In this section, you'll merge the two box objects. First, you'll move the new box into place. Then you'll join the two boxes to form a single solid:

1. Start the Move command, pick the smaller of the two boxes, and then press ↵.

2. At the Specify base point or [Displacement] <Displacement>: prompt, use the Midpoint Osnap override, and pick the middle of the front edge of the smaller box, as shown in the top image in Figure 24.4.

3. At the Specify second point or <use first point as displacement>: prompt, use the Midpoint osnap to pick the middle of the bottom edge of the larger box, as shown in the bottom image in Figure 24.4.

4. Click the Union tool in the Home tab's Solid Editing panel, or type **Uni**↵.

5. At the Select objects: prompt, pick both boxes and press ↵. Your drawing now looks like Figure 24.5.

FIGURE 24.4
Moving the
smaller box

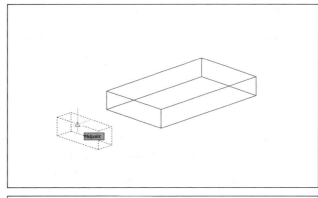

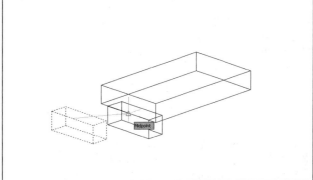

FIGURE 24.5
The two
boxes joined

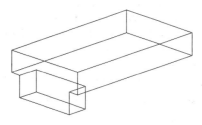

As you can see in Figure 24.5, the form has joined to appear as one object. It also acts like one object when you select it. You now have a composite solid made up of two box primitives.

Now let's place some holes in the bracket. In this next exercise, you'll discover how to create negative forms to cut portions out of a solid:

1. Turn on the layer called Cylinder. Two cylinder solids appear in the model, as shown in Figure 24.6. These cylinders are 1.5 units tall.

2. Click the Subtract tool from the Solid Editing panel, or type **Su**↵.

3. At the `Select solids, surfaces and regions to subtract from...` `Select objects:` prompt, pick the composite solid of the two boxes and press ↵.

FIGURE 24.6
The cylinders appear when the Cylinder layer is turned on.

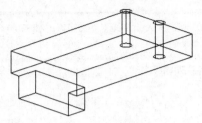

4. At the Select solids, surfaces and regions to subtract… Select objects: prompt, pick the two cylinders and press ↵. The cylinders are subtracted from the bracket.

5. To view the solid, choose 3D Hidden from the Visual Styles flyout of the View panel. You see a hidden-line view of the solid, as shown in Figure 24.7.

FIGURE 24.7
The bracket so far, with hidden lines removed

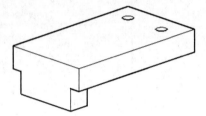

As you learned in the earlier chapters in Part 4, Wireframe views, such as the one in the previous exercise, are somewhat difficult to decipher. Until you use the 3D Hidden visual style (step 5) or the Hide command, you can't be sure that the subtracted cylinders are in fact holes. Using the Hide command frequently will help you keep track of what's going on with your solid model.

You may also have noticed in step 4 that even though the cylinders were taller than the opening they created, they worked fine to remove part of the rectangular solid. The cylinders were 1.5 units tall, not 1 unit, which is the thickness of the bracket. Having drawn the cylinders taller than needed, you saw that when AutoCAD performed the subtraction, it ignored the portion of the cylinders that didn't affect the bracket. AutoCAD always discards the portion of a primitive that isn't used in a subtract operation.

FIGURE 24.8
You can use the regional model to create complex 2D surfaces for use in 3D surface modeling.

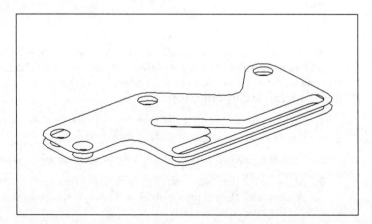

USING 3D SOLID OPERATIONS ON 2D DRAWINGS

You can apply some of the features described in this chapter to 2D drafting by taking advantage of AutoCAD's region object. *Regions* are two-dimensional objects to which you can apply Boolean operations.

The following illustration shows how a set of closed polyline shapes can be quickly turned into a drawing of a wrench using regions. The shapes at the top of the figure are first converted into regions using the Region tool on the Draw panel. Next, the shapes are aligned, as shown in the middle of the image. Finally, the circles and rectangle are joined with the Union command (type **Uni.↵**); then, the hexagonal shapes are subtracted from the combined shape (type **Su.↵**). You can use the Region . dwg sample file if you'd like to experiment.

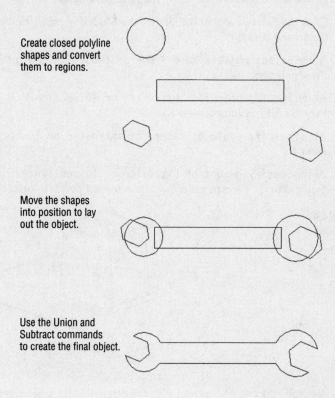

Create closed polyline shapes and convert them to regions.

Move the shapes into position to lay out the object.

Use the Union and Subtract commands to create the final object.

You can use regions to generate complex surfaces that may include holes or unusual bends (see Figure 24.8). Keep in mind the following:

◆ Regions act like surfaces; when you remove hidden lines, objects behind the regions are hidden.

◆ You can explode regions to edit them. However, exploding a region causes the region to lose its surfacelike quality, and objects no longer hide behind its surface(s).

◆ You can Ctrl+click the edge of a region to edit a region's shape.

Creating Complex Solids

As you learned earlier, you can convert a polyline into a solid by using the Extrude tool in the Modeling panel. This process lets you create more-complex shapes than the built-in primitives. In addition to the simple straight extrusion you've already tried, you can extrude shapes into curved paths or you can taper an extrusion.

Tapering an Extrusion

Let's look at how you can taper an extrusion to create a fairly complex solid with little effort:

1. Turn on the Taper layer. A rectangular polyline appears. This rectangle has its corners rounded to a radius of 0.5 using the Fillet command.

2. Click the Extrude tool in the Home tab's Modeling panel, or enter **Ext**↵ at the Command prompt.

3. At the Select objects to extrude or [MOde]: prompt, pick the polyline you just drew and press ↵.

4. At the Specify height of extrusion or [Direction/Path/Taper angle/ Expression]: prompt, enter **t**↵.

5. At the Specify angle of taper for extrusion or [Expression] <0>: prompt, enter **4**↵.

6. At the Specify height of extrusion or [Direction/Path/Taper angle/ Expression]: prompt, enter **3**↵. The extruded polyline looks like Figure 24.9.

FIGURE 24.9
The extruded polyline

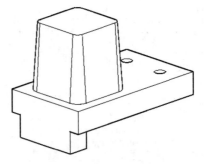

7. Join the part you just created with the original solid. Click the Union tool from the Home tab's Solid Editing panel or type **Uni**↵.

8. Select the extruded part and the composite solid just below it. Press ↵ to complete your selection.

In step 5, you can indicate a taper for the extrusion. Specify a taper in terms of degrees from the Z axis, or enter a negative value to taper the extrusion outward. You can also press ↵ to accept the default of 0° to extrude the polyline without a taper.

WHAT ARE ISOLINES?

You may have noticed the message that reads as follows:

```
Current wire frame density: ISOLINES=4
```

This message tells you the current setting for the Isolines system variable. This variable controls the way curved objects, such as cylinders and holes, are displayed. A setting of 4 causes a cylinder to be represented by four lines with a circle at each end. You can see this in the holes that you created for the Bracket model in the previous exercise. You can change the Isolines setting by entering **Isolines.⏎** at the Command prompt. You then enter a value for the number of lines to use to represent surfaces. This setting is also controlled by the Contour Lines Per Surface option in the Display tab of the Options dialog box.

Sweeping a Shape on a Curved Path

As you'll see in the following exercise, the Sweep command lets you extrude virtually any polyline shape along a path defined by a polyline, an arc, or a 3D polyline. At this point, you've created the components needed to do the extrusion. Next, you'll finish the extruded shape:

1. Turn on the Path layer. This layer contains the circle you'll extrude and the polyline path, which looks like an *S*, as shown in Figure 24.10.

FIGURE 24.10
Hidden-line view showing parts of the drawing you'll use to create a curved extrusion

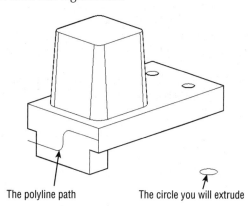

The polyline path   The circle you will extrude

2. Click the Sweep tool from the Extrude flyout in the Home tab's Modeling panel, or type **Sweep.⏎**. Click the circle, and then press ⏎.

3. At the `Select sweep path or [Alignment/Base point/Scale/Twist]:` prompt, click the polyline curve.

4. AutoCAD generates a solid tube that follows the path. The tube may not look like a tube because AutoCAD draws extruded solids such as this with four lines showing their profile.

5. Click the Subtract tool in the Home tab's Solid Editing panel or type **SU⏎**, and then select the composite solid.

6. Press ↵. At the Select objects: prompt, click the curved solid and press ↵. The curved solid is subtracted from the square solid. Your drawing looks like Figure 24.11.

FIGURE 24.11
The solid after subtracting the curve

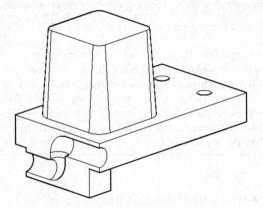

In this exercise, you used a curved polyline for the extrusion path, but you can use any type of 2D or 3D polyline, as well as a line or arc, for an extrusion path.

Revolving a Polyline

When your goal is to draw a circular object, you can use the Revolve command on the Modeling panel to create a solid that is *revolved*, or swept in a circular path. Think of Revolve's action as similar to a lathe that lets you carve a shape from an object on a spinning shaft. In this case, the object is a polyline, and rather than carve it, you define the profile and then revolve the profile around an axis.

In the following exercise, you'll draw a solid that will form a slot in the tapered solid. I've already created a 2D polyline that is the profile of the slot. You'll simply use cut and paste to bring the polyline into the bracket drawing:

1. In the View tab's Visual Styles panel, open the Visual Styles drop-down list and select 2D Wireframe.

2. Zoom in to the top of the tapered box so you have a view similar to Figure 24.12.

FIGURE 24.12
An enlarged view of the top of the tapered box and pasted polyline

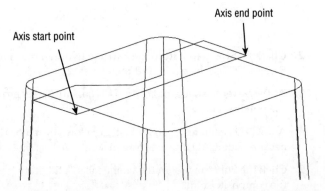

Axis start point

Axis end point

3. Turn on the Revolve layer. This layer contains a closed polyline that you'll use to create a cylindrical shape.

4. Click the Revolve tool from the Sweep flyout in the Home tab's Modeling panel, or type **Rev**↵ at the Command prompt.

5. At the `Select objects to revolve or [MOde]:` prompt, pick the polyline on the top of the tapered surface and press ↵.

6. When you see the prompt

   `Specify axis start point or define axis by [Object/X/Y/Z] <Object>:`

   use the Endpoint Osnap override and pick the beginning corner endpoint of the polyline you just added, as shown in Figure 24.12.

7. At the `Specify axis endpoint:` prompt, pick the axis endpoint indicated in Figure 24.12.

8. At the `Specify angle of revolution or [STart angle/Reverse/eXpression]` `<360>:` prompt, press ↵ to sweep the polyline a full 360°. The revolved form appears, as shown in Figure 24.13.

FIGURE 24.13
The revolved
polyline

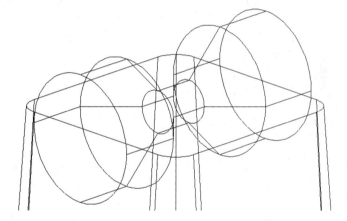

You just created a revolved solid that will be subtracted from the tapered box to form a slot in the bracket. However, before you subtract it, you need to make a slight change in the orientation of the revolved solid:

1. Click the 3D Rotate tool in the Modify panel, or type **3drotate**↵. You see the following prompt:

   `Current positive angle in UCS:  ANGDIR=counterclockwise  ANGBASE=0`
   `Select objects:`

2. Select the revolved solid and press ↵.

3. At the `Specify base point:` prompt, use the Midpoint osnap and click the right side edge of the top surface, as shown in Figure 24.14.

FIGURE 24.14
Selecting the
points to rotate
the revolved solid
in 3D space

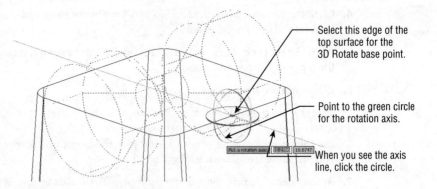

Select this edge of the
top surface for the
3D Rotate base point.

Point to the green circle
for the rotation axis.

When you see the axis
line, click the circle.

4. At the `Pick a rotation axis:` prompt, point to the green rotation grip tool. When you see a green line appear along the Y axis, click the mouse.

5. At the `Specify angle start point or type an angle:` prompt, enter **–5↵** for a minus 5 degrees rotation. The solid rotates 5° about the Y axis.

6. Click the Subtract tool in the Solid Editing panel, or type **Su↵**. Click the tapered box, and then press ↵.

7. At the `Select objects:` prompt, click the revolved solid and press ↵. Your drawing looks like Figure 24.15.

FIGURE 24.15
The composite solid

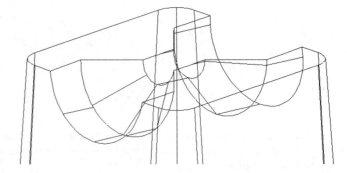

Editing Solids

Basic solid forms are fairly easy to create. Refining those forms requires some special tools. In the following sections, you'll learn how to use familiar 2D editing tools, as well as some new tools, to edit a solid. You'll also be introduced to the Slice tool, which lets you cut a solid into two pieces.

Splitting a Solid into Two Pieces

One of the more common solid-editing tools you'll use is the Slice tool. As you may guess from its name, Slice enables you to cut a solid into two pieces. The following exercise demonstrates how it works:

1. Click the Zoom All option to get an overall view of your work so far.

2. Click the Slice tool in the Home tab's Solid Editing panel, or type **Slice**↵.

3. At the `Select objects to slice:` prompt, click the part you've been working on and press ↵. You could select more than one solid. The Slice command would then slice all the solids through the plane indicated in steps 4 and 5.

4. At the prompt

   ```
   Specify start point of slicing plane or
   [planar Object/Surface/Zaxis/View/XY/YZ/ZX/
   3points] <3points>:
   ```

   type **XY**↵. This lets you indicate a slice plane parallel to the XY plane.

5. At the `Specify a point on the XY-plane <0,0,0>:` prompt, type **0,0,0.5**↵. This places the slice plane at the Z coordinate of 0.5 units. You can also use the Midpoint osnap and pick any vertical edge of the rectangular base of the solid. If you want to delete one side of the sliced solid, you can indicate the side you want to keep by clicking it in step 6 instead of entering **B**↵.

6. At the `Specify a point on desired side or [keep Both sides]:` prompt, type **B**↵ to keep both sides of the solid. AutoCAD divides the solid horizontally, one-half unit above the base of the part as shown in Figure 24.16.

FIGURE 24.16
The solid sliced through the base

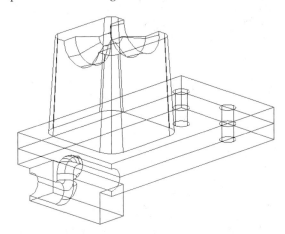

In step 4, you saw a number of options for the Slice command. You may want to make note of those options for future reference. Table 24.1 provides a list of the options and their purposes.

TABLE 24.1:   Slice command options

OPTION	PURPOSE
planar Object	Lets you select an object to define the slice plane.
Surface	Lets you select a surface object to define the shape of a slice (see Chapter 21).
Zaxis	Lets you select two points defining the Z axis of the slice plane. The two points you pick are perpendicular to the slice plane.
View	Generates a slice plane that is perpendicular to your current view. You're prompted for the coordinate through which the slice plane must pass—usually a point on the object.
XY/YZ/ZX	Pick one of these to determine the slice plane based on the X, Y, or Z axis. You're prompted to pick a point through which the slice plane must pass.
3points	The default setting; lets you select three points defining the slice plane. Normally, you pick points on the solid.

Rounding Corners with the Fillet Tool

Your bracket has a few sharp corners that you may want to round in order to give it a more realistic appearance. You can use the Modify panel's Fillet and Chamfer tools to add these rounded corners to your solid model:

1. Click the Fillet tool on the Home tab's Modify panel or type **F**↵.

2. At the Select first object or [Undo/Polyline/Radius/Trim/Multiple]: prompt, pick the edge indicated in the first image in Figure 24.17.

3. At the Enter fillet radius or [eXpression] <0.5000>: prompt, type **0.2**↵.

4. At the Select an edge or [Chain/Radius]: prompt, type **C**↵ for the Chain option. Chain lets you select a series of solid edges to be filleted.

5. Select one of the other seven edges at the base of the tapered form and press ↵.

6. Type **Hide**↵ to get a quick look at your model in a hidden line view, as shown in the second image in Figure 24.17.

As you saw in step 4, Fillet acts a bit differently when you use it on solids. The Chain option lets you select a set of edges instead of just two adjoining objects.

Chamfering Corners with the Chamfer Tool

Now let's try chamfering a corner. To practice using Chamfer, you'll add a countersink to the cylindrical hole you created in the first solid:

1. Type **Regen**↵ to return to a Wireframe view of your model.

FIGURE 24.17
Filleting solids

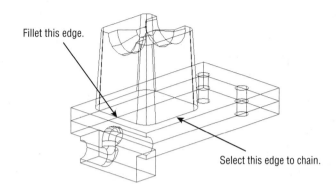

Fillet this edge.

Select this edge to chain.

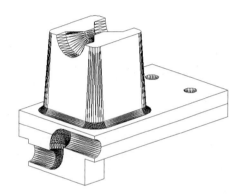

2. Click the Chamfer tool on the Modify panel (click the Fillet flyout if you don't see Chamfer; see Figure 24.18) or type **Cha⤶**.

FIGURE 24.18
Click the
Chamfer tool.

Flyout arrowhead

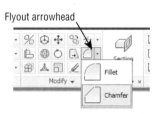

3. At the prompt

```
Select first line or [Undo/Polyline/Distance/Angle/Trim/mEthod/Multiple]:
```

pick the edge of the hole, as shown in Figure 24.19. Notice that the top surface of the solid is highlighted and that the prompt changes to `Enter surface selection option [Next/OK (current)] <OK>:`. The highlighting indicates the base surface, which will be used as a reference in step 5. (You could also type **N⤶** to choose the other adjoining surface, the inside of the hole, as the base surface.)

4. Press ↵ to accept the current highlighted face.

5. At the `Specify base surface chamfer distance or [Expression] <0.1250>:` prompt, type **0.125**↵. This indicates that you want the chamfer to have a width of 0.125 across the highlighted surface.

FIGURE 24.19
Picking the edge
to chamfer

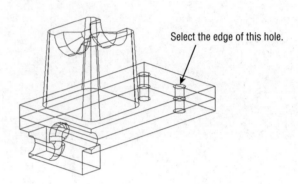

Select the edge of this hole.

6. At the `Specify other surface chamfer distance <0.2000>:` prompt, type **0.2**↵.

7. At the `Select an edge or [Loop]:` prompt, click the top edges of both holes, and then press ↵. When the Chamfer command has completed its work, your drawing looks like Figure 24.20.

8. After reviewing the work you've done here, save the `Bracket.dwg` file.

FIGURE 24.20
The chamfered edges

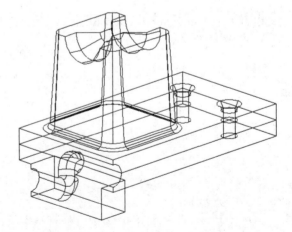

The Loop option in step 7 lets you chamfer the entire circumference of an object. You don't need to use it here because the edge forms a circle. The Loop option is used when you have a rectangular or other polygonal edge you want to chamfer.

Using the Solid Editing Tools

You've added some refinements to the Bracket model by using standard AutoCAD editing tools. There is a set of tools that is specifically geared toward editing solids. You already used the Union and Subtract tools found in the Solid Editing panel. In the following sections, you'll explore some of the other tools in that panel.

You don't have to perform the exercises, but reviewing them will show you what's available. When you're more comfortable working in 3D, you may want to come back and experiment with the file called solidedit.dwg shown in the figures in the following sections.

PARALLEL-PROJECTION NEEDED FOR SOME FEATURES

Many of the features discussed in these sections work only in a parallel-projection view. You can switch to a parallel-projection view by choosing the 2D Wireframe visual style, or, if you have the ViewCube turned on, right-click the ViewCube and select Parallel.

FINDING TOOLS IN THE SOLID EDITING PANEL

Many of the tools in the Solid Editing panel are in flyouts. This makes it a bit difficult to describe their location since the default tool changes depending on the last flyout tool that was selected. To help you easily find the tools described in these sections, Figure 24.21 shows the flyouts in their open position with each tool labeled. You can use this figure for reference when you are ready to use a tool.

FIGURE 24.21
The flyouts in the Home tab's Solid Editing panel

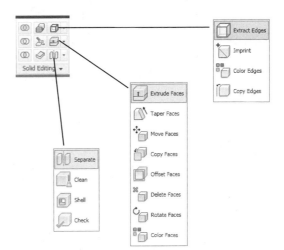

MOVING A SURFACE

You can move any flat surface of a 3D solid using the Move Faces tool from the Faces flyout on the Solid Editing panel. When you click this tool, you're prompted to select faces. Because you can select only the edge of two joining faces, you must select an edge and then use the Remove option to remove one of the two selected faces from the selection set (see Figure 24.22). Once you've made your selection, press ↵. You can then specify a distance for the move.

FIGURE 24.22

To select the vertical surface to the far right of the model, click the edge and then use the Remove option to remove the top surface from the selection.

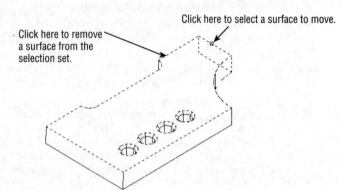

After you've selected the surface you want to move, the Move Faces tool acts just like the Move command: You select a base point and a displacement. Notice how the curved side of the model extends its curve to meet the new location of the surface. This shows you that AutoCAD attempts to maintain the geometry of the model when you make changes to the faces.

Move Faces also lets you move entire features, such as the hole in the model. In Figure 24.23, one of the holes has been moved so that it's no longer in line with the other three. This was done by selecting the countersink and the hole while using the Move Faces tool.

If a solid's History setting is set to record, you can Ctrl+click on its surface to expose the surface's grip. You can then use the grip at the center of the surface to move the surface.

FIGURE 24.23

Selecting a surface to offset

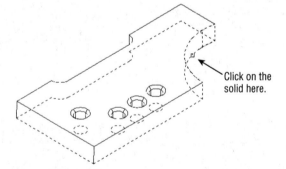

OFFSETTING A SURFACE

Suppose you want to decrease the radius of the arc in the right corner of the model and you also want to thicken the model by the same amount as the decrease in the arc radius. To do this, you can use the Offset Faces tool. The Offset Faces tool and the Offset command you used earlier in this book perform similar functions. The difference is that the Offset Faces tool in the Faces flyout on the Solid Editing panel affects 3D solids.

When you click the Offset Faces tool from the Faces flyout on the Solid Editing panel, you're prompted to select faces. As with the Move tool, you must select an edge that will select two faces. If you want to offset only one face, you must use the Remove option to remove one of the faces. In Figure 24.23, an edge is selected. Figure 24.24 shows the effect of the Offset Faces tool when both faces are offset.

FIGURE 24.24
The model after offsetting the curved and bottom surfaces

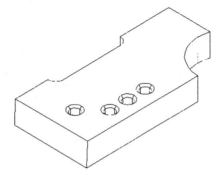

DELETING A SURFACE

Now suppose you've decided to eliminate the curved part of the model. You can delete a surface by using the Delete Faces tool. Once again, you're prompted to select faces. Typically, you'll want to delete only one face, such as the curved surface in the example model. You use the Remove option to remove the adjoining face that you don't want to delete before finishing your selection of faces to remove.

When you attempt to delete surfaces, keep in mind that the surface you delete must be recoverable by other surfaces in the model. For example, you can't remove the top surface of a cube, expecting it to turn into a pyramid. That would require the sides to change their orientation, which isn't allowed in this operation. You can, on the other hand, remove the top of a box with tapered sides. Then, when you remove the top, the sides converge to form a pyramid.

ROTATING A SURFACE

All the surfaces of the model are parallel or perpendicular to each other. Imagine that your design requires two sides to be at an angle. You can change the angle of a surface by using the Rotate Faces tool.

As with the prior solid-editing tools, you're prompted to select faces. You must then specify an axis of rotation. You can either select a point or use the default of selecting two points to define an axis of rotation, as shown in Figure 24.25. Once the axis is determined, you can specify a rotation angle. Figure 24.26 shows the result of rotating the two front-facing surfaces 4°.

TAPERING A SURFACE

In an earlier exercise, you saw how to create a new tapered solid by using the Extrude command. But what if you want to taper an existing solid? Here's what you can do.

The Taper Faces tool from the Faces flyout on the Solid Editing panel prompts you to select faces. You can select faces, as described for the previously discussed solid-editing tools, using the Remove or Add option (see Figure 24.27). Press ↵ when you finish your selection, and then indicate the axis from which the taper is to occur. In the model example in Figure 24.27, select two corners defining a vertical axis. Finally, enter the taper angle. Figure 24.28 shows the model tapered at a 4° angle.

FIGURE 24.25
Defining the axis of rotation

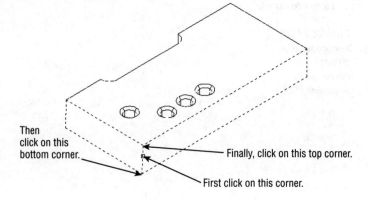

Then click on this bottom corner.

Finally, click on this top corner.

First click on this corner.

FIGURE 24.26
The model after rotating two surfaces

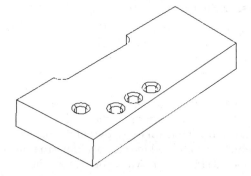

FIGURE 24.27
Selecting the surfaces to taper and indicating the direction of the taper

Select these corners first.

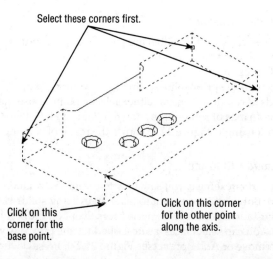

Click on this corner for the base point.

Click on this corner for the other point along the axis.

Figure 24.28
The model after tapering the sides

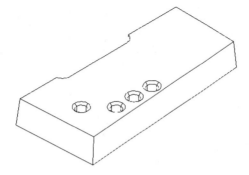

EXTRUDING A SURFACE

You've used the Extrude tool to create two of the solids in the Bracket model. The Extrude tool requires a closed polyline as a basis for the extrusion. As an alternative, the Solid Editing panel offers the Extrude Faces tool, which extrudes a surface of an existing solid.

When you click the Extrude Faces tool from the Faces flyout on the Solid Editing panel or type **Solidedit**↵ **F**↵ **E**↵, you see the Select faces or [Undo/Remove]: prompt. Select an edge or a set of edges or use the Remove or Add option to select the faces you want to extrude. Press ↵ when you've finished your selection, and then specify a height and taper angle. Figure 24.29 shows the sample model with the front surface extruded and tapered at a 45° angle. You can extrude multiple surfaces simultaneously if you need to by selecting them.

Figure 24.29
The model with a surface extruded and tapered

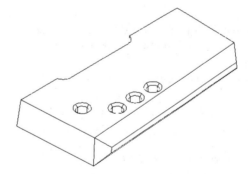

Aside from those features, the Extrude Faces tool works just like the Extrude command.

TURNING A SOLID INTO A SHELL

In many situations, you'll want your 3D model to be a hollow mass rather than a solid mass. The Shell tool lets you convert a solid into a shell.

When you click the Shell tool from the Separate/Clean/Shell/Check flyout on the Solid Editing panel, or type **Solidedit**↵ **B**↵ **S**↵, you're prompted to select a 3D solid. You're then prompted to remove faces. At this point, you can select an edge of the solid to indicate the surface you want removed. The surface you select is completely removed from the model, exposing the interior of the shell. For example, if you select the front edge of the sample model shown in Figure 24.30, the top and front surfaces are removed from the model, revealing the interior of the solid, as shown in Figure 24.31. After selecting the surfaces to remove, you can enter a shell offset distance.

FIGURE 24.30
Selecting the edge
to be removed

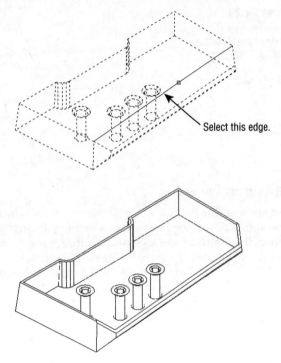

Select this edge.

FIGURE 24.31
The solid model
after using the
Shell tool

The shell thickness is added to the outside surface of the solid. When you're constructing your solid with the intention of creating a shell, you need to take this into account.

COPYING FACES AND EDGES

At times, you may want to create a copy of a surface of a solid to analyze its area or to produce another part that mates to that surface. The Copy Faces tool creates a copy of any surface on your model. The copy it produces is a type of object called a *region*.

The copies of the surfaces are opaque and can hide objects behind them when you perform a hidden-line removal (type **Hide↵**).

Another tool that is similar to Copy Faces is Copy Edges. Instead of selecting surfaces as in the Copy Faces tool, you select all the edges you want to copy. The result is a series of simple lines representing the edges of your model. This tool can be useful if you want to convert a solid into a set of 3D Faces. The Copy Edges tool creates a framework onto which you can add 3D Faces.

ADDING SURFACE FEATURES

If you need to add a feature to a flat surface, you can do so with the Imprint tool. An added surface feature can then be colored using the Color Faces tool or extruded using the Presspull tool. This feature is a little more complicated than some of the other solid-editing tools, so you may want to try the following exercise to see firsthand how it works.

You'll start by inserting an object that will be the source of the imprint. You'll then imprint the main solid model with the object's profile:

Insert

1. Click the Insert tool in the Insert tab's Block panel to open the Insert dialog box, or type **I**↵.

2. Click Browse, and then locate the `imprint.dwg` sample file and select it.

3. In the Insert dialog box, make sure the Explode check box is selected and remove the checkmark from the Specify On-Screen check box in the Insertion Point group.

4. Click OK. The block appears in the middle of the solid.

5. Click the Imprint tool from the Edges flyout on the Home tab's Solid Editing panel or type **Imprint**↵.

6. Click the main solid model.

7. Click the inserted solid.

8. At the `Delete the source object [Yes/No]<N>:` prompt, enter **Y**↵↵.

You now have an outline of the intersection between the two solids imprinted on the top surface of your model. The imprint is really a set of edges that have been added to the surface of the solid. To help the imprint stand out, try the following steps to change its color:

1. Click the Color Faces tool from the Edges flyout on the Solid Editing panel, or type **Solidedit**↵ **F**↵ **L**↵.

2. Click the imprint from the previous exercise. The imprint and the entire top surface are highlighted.

3. At the `Select faces or [Undo/Remove/ALL]:` prompt, type **R**↵; then click the outer edge of the top surface to remove it from the selection set.

4. Press ↵ to open the Select Color dialog box.

5. Click the red color sample in the dialog box, and then click OK. The imprint is now red.

6. Press ↵ twice to exit the command.

7. To see the full effect of the Color Faces tool, choose the Conceptual or Realistic visual style from the Visual Styles flyout in the View panel.

If you want to remove an imprint from a surface, Ctrl+click the imprint and press the Delete key.

SEPARATING A DIVIDED SOLID

While editing solids, you can end up with two separate solid forms that were created from one solid, as shown in Figure 24.32. Even though the two solids appear separated, they act like a single object. In these situations, AutoCAD offers the Separate tool from the Separate/Clean/Shell/Check flyout on the Solid Editing panel. To use it, click the Separate tool or type **Solidedit**↵ **B**↵ **P**↵ and select the solid that has been separated into two forms.

USING THE COMMAND LINE FOR SOLID EDITING

The solid-editing tools are options of a single AutoCAD command called Solidedit. If you prefer to use the keyboard, here are some tips on using the Solidedit command. When you first enter **Solidedit.⏎** at the Command prompt, you see the following prompt:

```
Enter a solids editing option [Face/Edge/Body/Undo/eXit] <eXit>:
```

You can select the Face, Edge, or Body option to edit the various parts of a solid. If you select Face, you see the following prompt:

```
[Extrude/Move/Rotate/Offset/Taper/Delete/Copy/coLor/mAterial/Undo/eXit] <eXit>:
```

The options from this prompt produce the same results as their counterparts on the Solid Editing panel.

If you select Edge at the first prompt, you see the following prompt:

```
Enter an edge editing option [Copy/coLor/Undo/eXit] <eXit>:
```

The Copy option lets you copy a surface, and the coLor option lets you add color to a surface.

If you select Body from the first prompt, you see the following prompt:

```
[Imprint/seParate solids/Shell/cLean/Check/Undo/eXit] <eXit>:
```

These options also perform the same functions as their counterparts on the Solid Editing panel. As you work with this command, you can use the Undo option to undo the last Solidedit option you used without exiting the command.

FIGURE 24.32
When the tall, thin solid is subtracted from the larger solid, the result is two separate forms, yet they still behave as a single object.

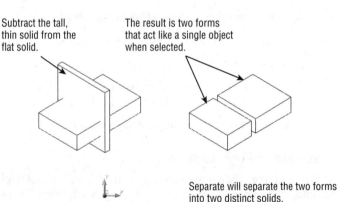

Subtract the tall, thin solid from the flat solid.

The result is two forms that act like a single object when selected.

Separate will separate the two forms into two distinct solids.

Figure 24.32 is included in the sample figures under the name `Separate example.dwg`. You can try the Separate tool in this file on your own.

Through some simple examples, you've seen how each of the solid-editing tools works. You aren't limited to using these tools in the way they were demonstrated in this chapter, and this book can't anticipate every situation you might encounter as you create solid models. These examples are intended as an introduction to these tools, so feel free to experiment with them. You can always use the Undo option to backtrack in case you don't get the results you expect.

This concludes your tour of the Solid Editing panel. Next you'll learn how to use 3D solid models to generate 2D working drawings quickly.

FINDING THE PROPERTIES OF A SOLID

All this effort to create a solid model isn't designed just to create a pretty picture. After your model is drawn and built, you can obtain information about its physical properties.

You can find the volume, the moment of inertia, and other physical properties of your model by using the Massprop command. These properties can also be recorded as a file on disk, so you can modify your model without worrying about losing track of its original properties.

To find the mass properties of a solid, enter **Massprop**↵, and then follow the prompts. LT users can use the Massprop command described here to find the properties of solids that are part of an existing drawing.

Streamlining the 2D Drawing Process

Using solids to model a part—such as with the bracket and Solidedit examples in this chapter—may seem a bit exotic, but there are definite advantages to modeling in 3D, even if you only want to draw the part in 2D as a page in a set of manufacturing specs.

The exercises in the following sections show you how to generate a typical mechanical drawing from your 3D model quickly by using Paper Space and the Solid Editing panel. You'll also examine techniques for dimensioning and including hidden lines.

 **Real World Scenario**

ARCHITECTURAL ELEVATIONS FROM 3D SOLIDS

If your application is architecture and you've created a 3D model of a building by using solids, you can use the tools described in the following sections to generate 2D elevation drawings from your 3D solid model.

I've used solid models in the past to generate 2D line drawings of elevations. Such line drawings can be "rendered" in a 2D drawing program like Adobe Photoshop or Illustrator. Be aware that such drawings will not be as accurate as those drawn from scratch, but they are fine for the early stages of a design project.

Drawing Standard Top, Front, and Right-Side Views

One of the more common types of mechanical drawings is the *orthogonal projection*. This style of drawing shows separate top, front, and right-side views of an object. Sometimes a 3D image is added for clarity. You can derive such a drawing in a few minutes using the Flatshot tool described in Chapter 21 (see "Turning a 3D View into a 2D AutoCAD Drawing" in Chapter 21).

With Flatshot, you can generate the standard top, front, and right-side orthogonal projection views, which you can further enhance with dimensions, hatch patterns, and other 2D drawing features. Follow these steps:

1. In the Bracket.dwg file, open the 3D Navigation drop-down list in the Home tab's View panel, and then click on an orthogonal projection view from the list, such as Top, Left, or Right (Figure 24.33). You can also use the 3D Navigation flyout in the View tab's Views panel or use the ViewCube to select an orthogonal view. See Chapter 21 for more on the ViewCube.

2. Click the Flatshot tool on the Home tab's expanded Section panel or type **Flatshot↵**.

3. In the Flatshot dialog box, select the options you want and click Create (Figure 24.34). See Table 21.1 in Chapter 21 for the Flatshot options.

FIGURE 24.33
The 3D Navigation drop-down list and 3D Navigation flyout

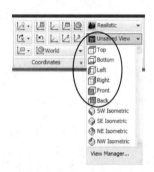 

If you select Insert As New Block in the Flatshot dialog box, you're prompted to select an insertion point to insert the block that is the 2D orthogonal view of your model. By default, the view is placed in the same plane as your current view, as shown in Figure 24.35. Once you've created all your views, you can move them to a different location in your drawing so you can create a set of layout views to your 2D orthogonal views, as shown in Figure 24.36. You can also place the orthogonal view blocks on a separate layer and then, for each layout viewport, freeze the layer of the 3D model so that only the 2D views are displayed.

If your model changes and you need to update the orthogonal views, you can repeat the steps listed here. However, instead of selecting Insert As New Block in the Flatshot dialog box, select Replace Existing Block to update the original orthogonal view blocks. If you want, you can include an isometric view to help communicate your design more clearly.

FIGURE 24.34
The Flatshot
dialog box

FIGURE 24.35
The 2D orthogonal
views shown
in relation to the
3D model

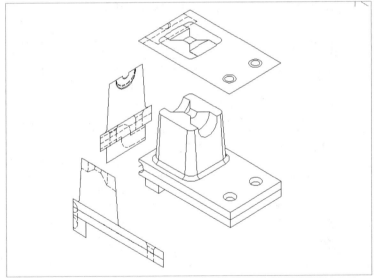

SET UP STANDARD VIEWS IN A LAYOUT VIEWPORT

To set up a layout viewport to display a view, like a top or right-side view of a 3D model, select a view from the 3D Navigation drop-down list in the Home tab's View panel, and then click on the viewport border. To set the scale of a viewport, click the viewport border and then select a scale from the VP Scale drop-down list on the status bar. If you'd like to refresh your memory on layouts in general, refer to Chapter 16.

FIGURE 24.36
You can use a layout to arrange a set of views created by Flatshot. Dimensions, notes, and a title block can be added to complete the layout.

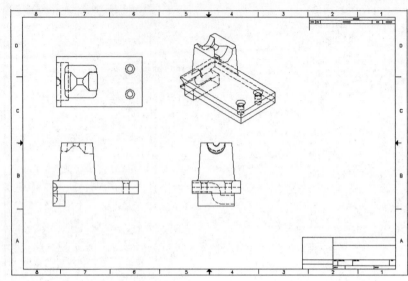

Adding Dimensions and Notes in a Layout

Although I don't recommend adding dimensions in Paper Space for architectural drawings, it may be a good idea for mechanical drawings such as the one in this chapter. By maintaining the dimensions and notes separate from the actual model, you keep these elements from getting in the way of your work on the solid model. You also avoid the confusion of having to scale the text and dimension features properly to ensure that they will plot at the correct size. See Chapters 10 and 12 for a more detailed discussion of notes and dimensions.

As long as you set up your Paper Space work area to be equivalent to the final plot size, you can set dimension and text to the sizes you want at plot time. If you want text 1⁄4″ high, you set your text styles to be 1⁄4″ high.

To include dimensions, make sure you're in a layout view, and then use the dimension commands in the normal way. However, you need to make sure full associative dimensioning is turned on. Choose Options from the Application menu to open the Options dialog box, and then click the User Preferences tab. In the Associative Dimensioning group, make sure the Make New Dimensions Associative check box is selected. With associative dimensioning turned on, dimensions in a layout view display the true dimension of the object being dimensioned regardless of the scale setting of the viewport.

If you don't have the associative dimensioning option turned on and your viewports are set to a scale other than 1 to 1, you have another option: You can set the Annotation Units option in the Dimension Style dialog box to a proper value. The following steps show you how:

1. Select the Model tool in the status bar, and then click the Dimension Style tool from the Annotate tab's Dimensions panel title bar to open the Dimension Style Manager dialog box.

2. Make sure you've selected the style you want to use, and then click Modify to open the Modify Dimension Style dialog box.

3. Click the Primary Units tab.

4. In the Scale Factor input box in the Measurement Scale group, enter the value by which you want your Paper Space dimensions multiplied. For example, if your Paper Space views are scaled at one-half the actual size of your model, enter **2** in this box to multiply your dimensions' values by two.

5. Click the Apply To Layout Dimensions Only check box. This ensures that your dimension is scaled only while you're adding dimensions in Paper Space. Dimensions added in Model Space aren't affected.

6. Click OK to close the Modify Dimension Style dialog box, and then click Close in the Dimension Style Manager dialog box.

You've had to complete a lot of steps to get the final drawing, but compared with drawing these views by hand, you undoubtedly saved a great deal of time. In addition, as you'll see later in this chapter, what you have is more than just a 2D drafted image. With what you created, further refinements are now easy.

Using Visual Styles with a Viewport

In Chapter 21, you saw how you can view your 3D model using visual styles. A visual style can give you a more realistic representation of your 3D model, and it can show off more of the details, especially on rounded surfaces. You can also view and plot a visual style in a layout view. To do this, you make a viewport active and then turn on the visual style you want to use for that viewport. The following exercise gives you a firsthand look at how this is done:

1. Back in the `Bracket.dwg` drawing, click the Quick View Layouts tool in the status bar and select the Layout1 panel that appears just over the Command window.

2. Double-click inside the viewport with the isometric view of the model to switch to Floating Model Space.

3. Select Conceptual from the Visual Styles drop-down list on the View tab's Visual Styles panel or the Home tab's View panel (Figure 24.37).

The view may appear a bit dark because of the black color setting for the object. You can change the color to a lighter one such as cyan or blue to get a better look.

4. Double-click outside the isometric viewport to return to Paper Space.

If you have multiple viewports in a layout, you changed the visual style of one viewport without affecting the other viewports. This can help others visualize your 3D model more clearly.

You'll also want to know how to control the hard-copy output of a shaded view. For this, you use the shortcut menu:

1. Click the isometric view's viewport border to select it.

2. Right-click to open the shortcut menu, and select the Shade Plot option to display a set of Shade Plot options (Figure 24.38).

3. Take a moment to study the menu, and then click As Displayed.

FIGURE 24.37
The Visual Styles
panel and the
View panel

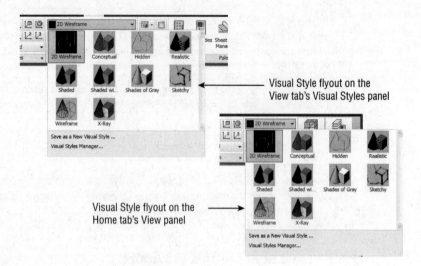

Visual Style flyout on the
View tab's Visual Styles panel

Visual Style flyout on the
Home tab's View panel

FIGURE 24.38
The Shade
Plot option

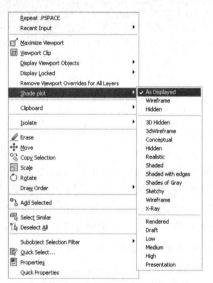

The As Displayed option plots the viewport as it appears in the AutoCAD window. You use this option to plot the currently displayed visual style. Wireframe plots the viewport as a Wireframe view. Hidden plots the viewport as a hidden-line view similar to the view you see when you use the Hide command. Below the Hidden option in the shortcut menu is a list of the available visual styles. At the bottom of the menu is the Rendered option, which plots the view by using AutoCAD's Render feature, described in Chapter 23. You can use the Rendered option to plot ray-traced renderings of your 3D models.

Remember these options on the shortcut menu as you work on your drawings and when you plot. They can be helpful in communicating your ideas, but they can also get lost in the array of tools that AutoCAD offers.

Visualizing Solids

If you're designing a complex object, sometimes it helps to be able to see it in ways that you couldn't in the real world. AutoCAD offers two visualization tools that can help others understand your design ideas.

If you want to show off the internal workings of a part or an assembly, you can use X-Ray effect, which can be found in the View tab's Visual Styles panel.

Figure 24.39 shows an isometric view of the bracket using the Realistic visual style and with the X-Ray effect turned on. The color of the bracket has also been changed to a light gray to help visibility. You can see the internal elements as if the object were semitransparent. The X-Ray effect works with any visual style, although it works best with a style that shows some of the surface features (such as the Conceptual or Realistic visual style).

FIGURE 24.39
The bracket displayed using a Realistic visual style and the X-Ray effect

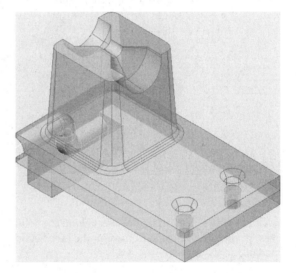

Another tool to help you visualize the internal workings of a design is the Sectionplane command. This command creates a plane that defines the location of a cross section. A section plane can also do more than just show a cross section. Try the following exercise to see how it works:

1. In the Bracket file, click the Model tab at the bottom of the drawing area, and then change the color of layer 0 to a light gray so you can see the bracket more clearly when using the Realistic visual style.

2. Select Realistic from the Home tab's Visual Styles flyout in the View panel.

Realistic

3. Make sure that the Object Snap and Object Snap Tracking tools are turned off in the status bar. This will allow you to point to surfaces on the model while using the Sectionplane command.

4. Adjust your view so it looks similar to Figure 24.40.

5. In the Home tab's Section panel, click the Section Plane tool. You can also enter **sectionplane.⏎** at the Command prompt. You'll see the following prompt:

```
Select face or any point to locate
section line or [Draw section/Orthographic]:
```

6. Click the front plane of the bracket, as shown in Figure 24.40. A plane appears on that surface.

FIGURE 24.40
Adding the section plane to your bracket

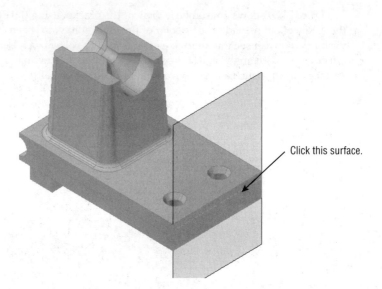

Click this surface.

You can move the section plane object along the solid to get a real-time view of the section it traverses. To do this, you need to turn on the Live Section feature. To check whether Live Section is turned on, do the following:

1. Click the section plane, and then right-click. If you see a checkmark by the Activate Live Sectioning option, then you know it's on. If you don't see a checkmark, then choose Activate Live Sectioning to turn it on.

2. Click the red axis on the Move gizmo, as shown in Figure 24.41. The axis turns yellow to indicate that it is active and you see a red vector appear.

3. Move the cursor slowly toward the back of the bracket. As you do this, the bracket becomes lighter in the foreground.

4. When the section plane is roughly in the middle of the tapered portion of the bracket, click the mouse to fix the plane in place. You should have a view similar to Figure 24.42.

FIGURE 24.41
Moving the surface plane across the bracket

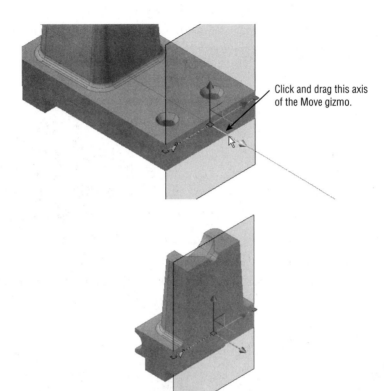

Click and drag this axis of the Move gizmo.

FIGURE 24.42
The surface plane fixed at a location

Now you see only a portion of the bracket behind the section plane plus the cross section of the plane, as shown in Figure 24.42. You can have the section plane display the front portion as a ghosted image by doing the following:

1. With the section plane selected (you should still see its Move gizmo), right-click and choose Show Cut-Away Geometry. The front portion of the bracket appears in red (see Figure 24.43).

2. Press the Esc key to remove the section plane from the current selection. The cut-away geometry remains in view.

You can double-click on the section plane to toggle between a solid view and a cut-away view of the geometry. This toggles the Active Live Sectioning option.

You can also add a jog in the section plane to create a more complex section cut. Here's how it's done:

1. Select the section plane, right-click, and select Show Cut-Away Geometry to turn this feature off. There should be no checkmark by this feature name in the menu. This is necessary in order to gain access to the section plane Jog features.

2. Right-click, and choose Add Jog To Section.

FIGURE 24.43
The front portion
of the bracket is
displayed with the
Show Cut-Away
Geometry option
turned on.

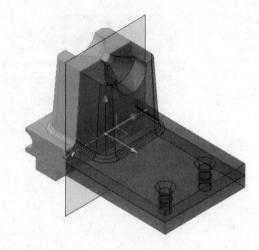

3. At the Specify a point on the section line to add jog: prompt, use the Nearest object snap to select a point on the section plane line (see Figure 24.44).

FIGURE 24.44
Moving the jog in
the section plane

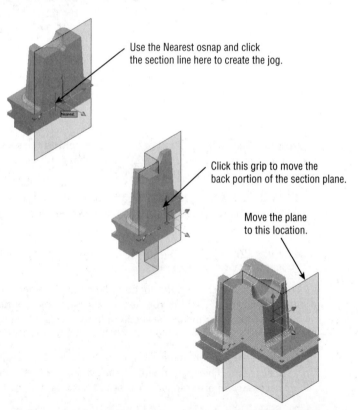

Use the Nearest osnap and click
the section line here to create the jog.

Click this grip to move the
back portion of the section plane.

Move the plane
to this location.

4. Click the grip on the back portion of the section plane, as shown in Figure 24.44, and drag it toward the right so the jog looks similar to the third panel in the figure.

5. Press the Esc key to get a clear view of the new section.

As you can see from this example, you can adjust the section using the grips on the section plane line. You can use the Nearest osnap to select a point anywhere along the section line to a jog. Click and drag the endpoint grips to rotate the section plane to an angle.

You may have also noticed another arrow in the section plane. (see Figure 24.45).

FIGURE 24.45
The arrow presents additional options for the section plane.

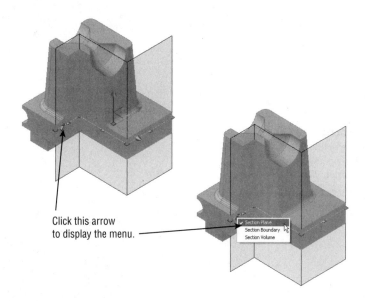

Click this arrow
to display the menu.

When you click the downward-pointing arrow, you see three options for visualizing the section boundary: Section Plane, Section Boundary, and Section Volume.

By using these other settings, you can start to include sections through the sides, back, top, or bottom of the solid. For example, if you click the Section Boundary option, another boundary line appears with grips (see Figure 24.46). To see it clearly, you may have to press Esc and then select the section plane again.

You can then manipulate these grips to show section cuts along those boundaries.

The Section Volume option displays the boundary of a volume along with grips at the top and bottom of the volume (see Figure 24.47). These grips allow you to create a cut plane from the top or bottom of the solid.

Finally, you can get a copy of the solid that is behind or in front of the section plane. Right-click the section plane, and choose Generate 2D/3D Section to open the Generate Section/Elevation dialog box. Click the Show Details button to expand the dialog box and display more options (Figure 24.48).

FIGURE 24.46
Another boundary
line appears with
grips when you
click the Section
Boundary option.

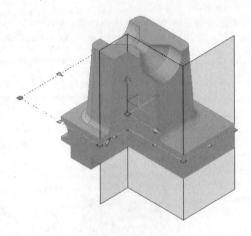

FIGURE 24.47
The boundaries
shown using the
Section Volume
option

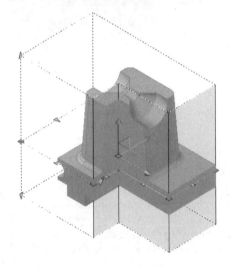

If you select 2D Section/Elevation, a 2D image of the section plane is inserted in the drawing in a manner similar to the insertion of a block. You're asked for an insertion point, an X and Y scale, and a rotation angle.

The 3D Section option creates a copy of the portion of the solid that is bounded by the section plane or planes, as shown in Figure 24.49.

USING A SECTION PLANE IN AN ARCHITECTURAL MODEL

If your application is architectural, you can use a section plane and the 2D Section/Elevation option to get an accurate elevation drawing. Instead of placing the section plane inside the solid, move it away from the solid model and use the 2D Section/Elevation shortcut menu option.

FIGURE 24.48

The Generate Section/Elevation dialog box

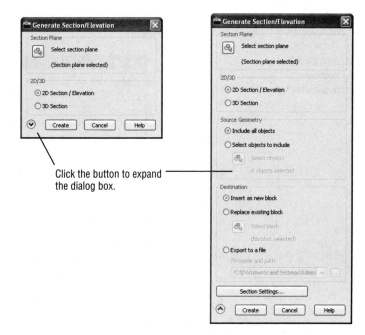

Click the button to expand the dialog box.

FIGURE 24.49

A copy of the solid minus the section area is created using the 3D Section option of the Generate Section/Elevation dialog box.

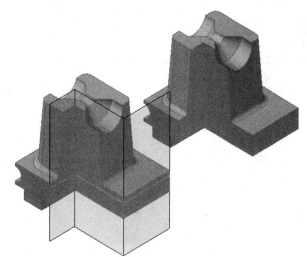

You can access more detailed settings for the 2D Section/Elevation, 3D Section, and Live Section Settings options by clicking the Section Settings button at the bottom of the Generate Section/Elevation dialog box. This button opens the Section Settings dialog box (Figure 24.50), which lists the settings for the section feature.

If you create a set of orthogonal views in a layout, the work you do to find a section is also reflected in the layout views (Figure 24.51).

FIGURE 24.50
The Section
Settings dialog box

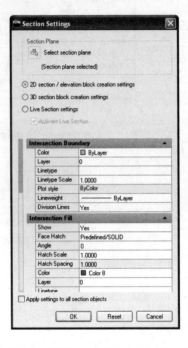

FIGURE 24.51
A set of orthogonal
views in a layout

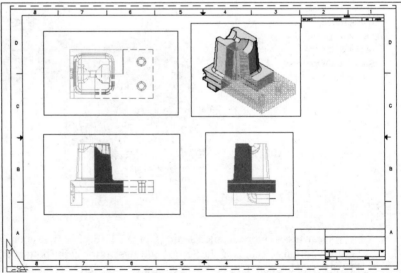

TAKING ADVANTAGE OF STEREOLITHOGRAPHY

A discussion of solid modeling wouldn't be complete without mentioning stereolithography. This is one of the more interesting technological wonders that has appeared as a by-product of 3D computer modeling. *Stereolithography* is a process that generates physical reproductions of 3D computer solid models. Special equipment converts your AutoCAD-generated files into a physical model.

This process offers the mechanical designer a method for rapidly prototyping designs directly from AutoCAD drawings, though applications don't have to be limited to mechanical design. Architects can take advantage of this process too. My own interest in Tibetan art led me to create a 3D AutoCAD model of a type of statue called a Zola, shown here. I sent this model to a service to have it reproduced in resin.

AutoCAD supports stereolithography through the 3dprint and Stlout commands. These commands generate an STL file, which can be used with a *Stereolithograph Apparatus (SLA)* to generate a model. You must first create a 3D solid model in AutoCAD. Then you can use the Export Data dialog box to export your drawing in the STL format. Choose Export ➤ Other Formats from the Application menu, and make sure the Files Of Type drop-down list shows Lithography (*.stl) before you click the Save button. You can also choose Send To 3D Print Service from the Output tab's 3D Print panel.

The AutoCAD 3D solids are translated into a set of triangular-faceted meshes in the STL file. You can use the Rendered Object Smoothness setting in the Display tab of the Options dialog box to control the fineness of these meshes. See Chapter 23 for more information on this setting.

When you use the Send To 3D Print Service tool in the 3D Print panel, you will see a message box asking if you want to learn more about preparing a 3D model for printing. If you are unfamiliar with stereolithography and 3D printing, it is a good idea to select the Learn About Preparing A 3D Model For Printing option so you don't make some of the more common mistakes.

The Bottom Line

Understand solid modeling.   Solid modeling lets you build 3D models by creating and joining 3D shapes called solids. There are several built-in solid shapes called primitives, and you can create others using the Extrude tool.

Master It   Name some of the built-in solid primitives available in AutoCAD.

Create solid forms.   You can use Boolean operations to sculpt 3D solids into the shape you want. Two solids can be joined to form a more complex one, or you can remove one solid from another.

Master It   Name the three Boolean operations you can use on solids.

Create complex solids.   Besides the primitives, you can create your own shapes based on 2D polylines.

Master It   Name three tools that let you convert closed polylines and circles into 3D solids.

Edit solids.   Once you've created a solid, you can make changes to it using the solid-editing tools offered on the Solid Editing panel.

Master It   Name at least four of the tools found on the Solid Editing panel.

Streamline the 2D drawing process.   You can create 3D orthogonal views of your 3D model to create standard 2D mechanical drawings.

Master It   What is the name of the tool in the Solid Editing panel that lets you create a 2D drawing of a 3D model?

Visualize solids.   In addition to viewing your 3D model in a number of different orientations, you can view it as if it were transparent or cut in half.

Master It   What is the name of the command that lets you create a cut view of your 3D model?

Chapter 25

Exploring 3D Mesh and Surface Modeling

AutoCAD has always offered tools that allowed users to construct fairly complex 3D models. With the introduction of the latest solid modeling tools, you can even model some very organic forms. But there are some types of forms that require a type of modeling known as *mesh modeling*. Mesh modeling enables you to create smooth, curved volumes by manipulating faces that make up an object's surface.

With mesh modeling, you can quickly create curved shapes that are difficult or even impossible to create by other means. AutoCAD also offers the ability to convert a mesh model into a 3D solid so that you can perform Boolean operations.

AutoCAD 2011 introduces a set of 3D surface modeling tools that extend its ability to produce and edit curved, organic forms. In this chapter, you'll get a chance to explore many of the current features of mesh modeling through a series of exercises, and you'll be introduced to the new surface modeling tools. You'll also learn how you can convert a mesh or 3D surface into a solid. You'll start by creating a simple shape as an introduction, and then you'll move on to a more complex form.

In this chapter you'll learn to do the following:

- ◆ Create a simple 3D mesh
- ◆ Edit faces and edges
- ◆ Create mesh surfaces
- ◆ Convert meshes to solids
- ◆ Understand 3D surfaces
- ◆ Edit 3D surfaces

Creating a Simple 3D Mesh

As an introduction to the mesh modeling features in AutoCAD, you'll draw a simple box and then smooth the box. This first exercise will show you some of the basic mesh modeling tools and what types of control you can exert on a model.

First make sure you are in the 3D Modeling workspace and that you have a blank drawing set up for the mesh. Then follow these steps:

1. Click the Workspace drop-down list in the Quick Access toolbar and select 3D Modeling.

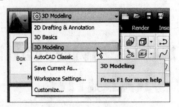

2. Next, open a new file using the acad3D.dwt template. Click the New tool from the Quick Access toolbar.

3. At the Select Template dialog box, select the acad3D.dwt template and then click Open.

4. Choose the Shaded With Edges visual style from the Visual Styles drop-down list in the Home tab's View panel. This will give you a close approximation of the appearance of meshes you'll see in the figures shown in this book.

Creating a Mesh Primitive

Meshes are similar to solids in that they start from what is called a *primitive*. You may recall that 3D solid primitives are predetermined shapes from which you can form more complex shapes. The mesh primitives are very similar to the 3D solid primitives you learned about in Chapters 21 and 24. You can see the different mesh primitives that are available by clicking the Mesh fly-out in the Primitives panel (Figure 25.1).

FIGURE 25.1
The primitives in the Mesh flyout of the Primitives panel

In the next exercise, you'll use the Mesh Box primitive to start your cushion.

1. In the Mesh tab's Primitives panel, click the Mesh Box tool, or type **Mesh↵ B↵**.

2. At the `Specify first corner or [Center]:` prompt, enter **0,0↵** to start the mesh at the drawing origin.

3. You'll want a mesh that is 21 units in the X axis by 32 units in the Y axis, so at the `Specify other corner or [Cube/Length]:` prompt, enter **21,32↵**.

4. At the `Specify height or [2Point]:` prompt, place your cursor anywhere above the base of the mesh and enter **4↵** for a 4-inch height. You now have a basic shape for your mesh (Figure 25.2).

FIGURE 25.2
The Mesh Box
primitive

You've just created a mesh box, but you have several other mesh primitives at your disposal. If you click the Mesh flyout on the Modeling panel, you'll see the cylinder, cone, sphere, pyramid, wedge, and torus primitives. When creating your model, consider which of these primitives will best suit your needs.

Understanding the Parts of a Mesh

Before you go any further, you'll want to understand the structure of a mesh. Notice that each side is divided into nine panels, or *faces*, as they are called in AutoCAD. You can edit these faces to change the shape and contour of your mesh. You can control the number of faces of a mesh through an options dialog box that you'll learn about later.

Figure 25.3 shows the names of the different parts of a simple mesh: the vertex, the edge, and the face. These three parts are called subobjects of the mesh, and you can move their position in the mesh to modify a mesh's shape.

To help you select different subobjects on a mesh, the Subobject panel offers the Filter flyout, which shows the No Filter tool by default. You'll get to use this flyout in many of the exercises in this chapter.

Smoothing a Mesh

One of the main features of a mesh is its ability to become a smooth, curved object. Right now your cushion has sharp edges, but you can round the corners using the Smooth tools.

Try modifying the mesh to smooth its corners:

1. Click the rectangular mesh to select it.

2. Click the Smooth More tool in the Mesh panel or type **Meshsmoothmore↵**. The edges of the mesh become faceted and smoother in appearance.

3. Click Smooth More again. The mesh becomes smoother still (Figure 25.4).

4. Now click Smooth Less (just below the Smooth More tool) or type **Meshsmoothless**↵. The mesh becomes less smooth.

5. Press Esc to clear the selection.

FIGURE 25.3
The subobjects of a mesh

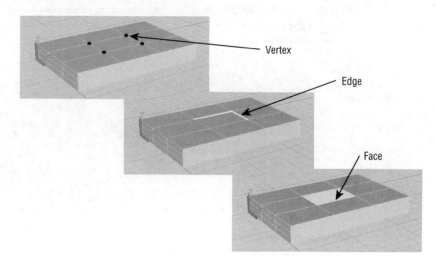

FIGURE 25.4
The mesh after applying the Smooth More tool twice

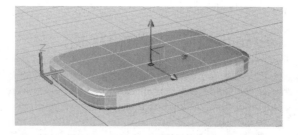

As you can see from this exercise, you can smooth a mesh using the Smooth More tool. The more times you apply it to a mesh, the smoother your mesh becomes. The number of faces of the mesh determines how the Smooth More tool affects the mesh. The fewer the faces, the broader the application of smoothness.

When you apply the Smooth More tool to a mesh, the faces of the mesh become faceted. This simulates the smooth appearance. If you look closely at a mesh that has only one or two levels of smoothing applied, you can see the facets.

Editing Faces and Edges

The shape you created earlier demonstrates one of the main features of meshes. In this section, you'll create a model of a surfboard to see how you can push and pull the subobjects of a mesh to create a form.

You'll start with the same form, a box shape, but this time you'll modify some of the parameters that define the box's structure. You can control the number of faces that a mesh primitive will have before it is created. The following exercise introduces you to the tools and methods used to edit meshes.

Start by creating a new drawing and setting up the parameters for the mesh.

1. Click the New tool in the Quick Access toolbar, select `acad3D.dwt`, and then click Open.

2. In the Mesh tab, click the Mesh Primitive Option tool in the Primitives panel title bar. The Mesh Primitive Options dialog box appears (Figure 25.5).

FIGURE 25.5
The Mesh Primitive Options dialog box

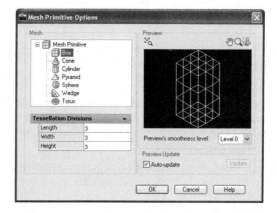

3. In the Tessellation Divisions group, change the Length and Width values to 4 and the Height value to 1. Click OK when you've finished making the changes.

4. In the Home tab's View panel, choose the Shaded visual style from the Visual Styles drop-down list.

The parameters you change alter the number of faces on mesh primitives that you create, including the box primitive in the next exercise. You'll see the results in the next set of steps:

1. Click the Mesh Box tool in the Primitives panel.

2. At the `Specify first corner or [Center]:` prompt, type **0,0**↵ to start the corner at the origin of the drawing.

3. At the `Specify other corner or [Cube/Length]:` prompt, enter **50,30**↵ to create a 50″ × 30″ base for the box.

4. At the `Specify height or [2Point]` prompt, point the cursor in the positive Z direction and then enter **3.5↵** for a 3.5″ thickness.

5. Center the box in your view. Your model should look similar to Figure 25.6.

FIGURE 25.6
The mesh box

6. Click the box to select it. Then, in the Mesh panel, click the Smooth More tool twice. The edges of the mesh become more rounded.

WHAT DOES THE SMOOTH OBJECT TOOL DO?

It's hard not to notice the very large Smooth Object tool in the Mesh panel. My first reaction was to try to use this tool on a mesh, but it is not intended to work on meshes. Instead, it converts 3D objects other than meshes into mesh objects. You can convert a solid into a mesh, for example, using this tool. 3D surfaces can also be converted, and it even works on region objects that are technically not 3D objects.

You might be tempted to convert a mesh to a solid, edit it, and then turn it back into a mesh. Although this can be done, I wouldn't recommend it. You'll find that your model becomes too unwieldy to work with.

Stretching Faces

You now have the basis for the surfboard, though it might seem like an odd shape for a surfboard. Next you'll start to form the surfboard by manipulating the faces and edges of the mesh. Start by pulling two sides of the mesh to give it a shape more like a surfboard:

1. Use the ViewCube and Pan tools to adjust your view so it looks similar to Figure 25.8. This view will allow you to easily select and "pull" some of the faces that will become the front and back of the surfboard.

2. In the Subobject panel, select Face from the Filter flyout (see Figure 25.7).

3. Click on the box mesh to expose its mesh lines. This will help you see where to place the selection window in the next step.

4. Hold down the Ctrl key and then click and drag a crossing selection window over the middle faces at the front edge of the box, as shown in Figure 25.8. The faces are highlighted, and you see the XYZ gizmo.

FIGURE 25.7
Select the
Face filter.

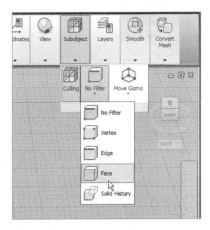

5. Place your cursor on the red X axis of the gizmo.

6. When the red axis extension line appears, click and drag the gizmo downward in a positive X direction. The mesh begins to elongate.

7. When your mesh looks similar to Figure 25.9, release your mouse.

8. Press Esc to remove the faces from the current selection.

FIGURE 25.8
Hold down the
Ctrl key and place
a crossing selec-
tion window as
shown here.

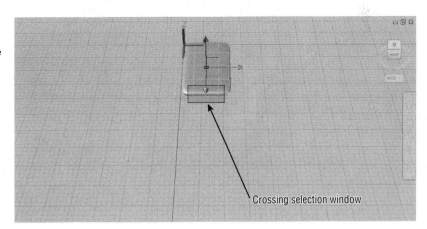

Crossing selection window

The portion of the mesh you "pull" out will become the front. Next, do the same for the back of the surfboard:

1. Use the Pan tool to adjust your view so it looks similar to Figure 25.10. This view will allow you to easily select and "pull" some of the faces that will become the back of the surfboard.

2. Click on the box mesh to expose its mesh lines again.

3. Hold down the Ctrl key and then place a crossing selection window over the middle faces at the back edge of the box as shown in Figure 25.10. The faces are highlighted, and you see the XYZ gizmo.

FIGURE 25.9
Click and drag the gizmo when you see the red axis extension.

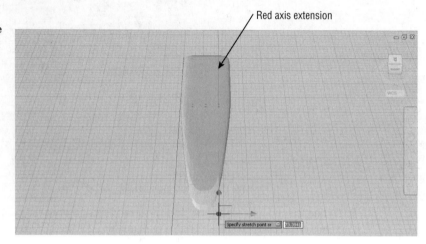

FIGURE 25.10
Hold down the Ctrl key and place a crossing selection window as shown here.

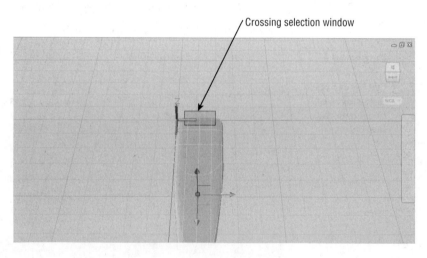

4. Place your cursor on the red X axis of the gizmo, and when the red axis extension line appears, click and drag the gizmo upward in a negative X direction.

5. When your mesh looks similar to Figure 25.11, release your mouse.

6. Press Esc to remove the faces from the current selection.

7. Click the Home tool on the ViewCube (it looks like a house and is in the upper-left side of the ViewCube) to get a better view of your mesh so far (Figure 25.12).

FIGURE 25.11
Adjust the mesh to look similar to this one.

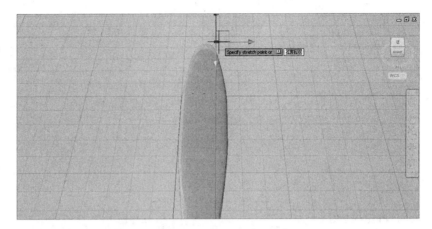

FIGURE 25.12
The mesh so far

Moving an Edge

The surfboard needs a sharper point at the front. Instead of moving the faces as you've already done, you can move an edge to give the front a more pointed shape. The next set of steps will show you how to do this:

1. Using the ViewCube, adjust your view so you have a close-up of the front tip of the surfboard, as shown in Figure 25.13.

2. In the Subobject panel, select Edge from the Filter flyout.

3. Hover over the front edge until you see the edge line, and then click the edge, as shown in Figure 25.13. The XYZ gizmo appears.

4. Hover over the X axis of the gizmo, and when the red extension line appears, click and drag the X axis downward along the positive X direction.

5. When it looks similar to Figure 25.14, release the mouse.

FIGURE 25.13
Click the front-
center edge
shown here.

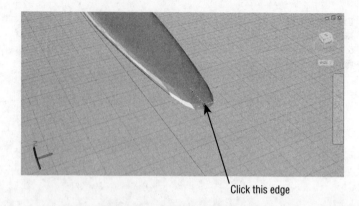

Click this edge

FIGURE 25.14
Pull the front edge
so that the mesh
looks similar to
this image.

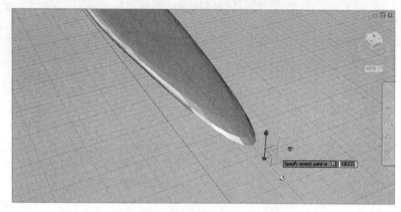

Next, give the front of the mesh a slight curve by adjusting the Z axis of the front edge:

1. Hover over the Z axis of the gizmo, and when the blue axis extension line appears, click and drag the Z axis downward in the negative Z direction.

2. When it looks similar to Figure 25.15, release the mouse.

FIGURE 25.15
Move the front
edge downward
in the Z axis.

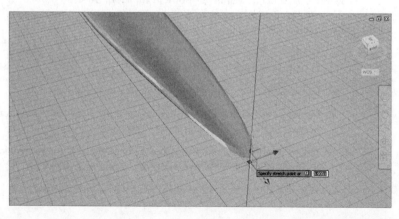

3. Press the Esc key twice to clear your edge selection.

4. Click the Home tool in the ViewCube to return to the home view.

I asked you to adjust the edge downward because you'll want to have a bottom view of your surfboard. This will enable you to add fins to the board without having to flip the mesh over.

FINE-TUNE THE MESH

You might notice that the surfboard has a slight trough down the middle after you move the front edge downward. You can remove that trough and add some additional curvature to the board by moving the two edges on the side of the mesh toward the front.

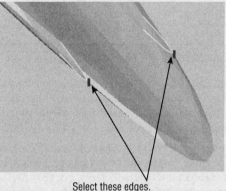

Select these edges.

You can Ctrl+click these edges with the Edge subobject filter selected. Once you have these edges selected, use the Z axis on the gizmo to move them down to eliminate the trough.

Adding More Faces

The surfboard is still missing some fins. You could model some fins as separate meshes and then later join them to the surfboard. You can also use the Refine Mesh tool to add more edges and then use those edges as the basis for your fins. The following exercise will show how this is done:

1. Adjust your view so it looks similar to the top image in Figure 25.16.

2. From the View tab's Visual Styles panel, open the Visual Styles drop-down list and select Shaded With Edges. This will allow you to see the edge lines of the mesh as you work through the following steps.

3. Click the mesh and then, from the Mesh tab's Mesh panel, click Smooth More. This will increase the number of edges that are generated in the next step.

4. Press the Esc key to clear your selection.

5. On the Subobject panel, select Face from the Filter flyout.

6. Click the two faces shown in the top image of Figure 25.16.

7. Click the Refine Mesh tool on the Mesh panel or type **Meshrefine**↵. The selected faces will be subdivided into smaller faces and edges, as shown in the bottom image of Figure 25.16.

UNDERSTANDING HOW REFINE MESH WORKS

You have some control over the number of faces that Refine Mesh creates through the level of smoothness applied to a mesh. If you reduce the smoothness of a mesh, the Refine Mesh tool will produce fewer faces. If you increase the smoothness, Refine Mesh will produce more faces—four more per facet to be precise.

To understand how this works, you have to take a closer look at how the Smooth More tool works. Each time you apply the Smooth More tool to a mesh, every face of the mesh is divided into four facets. These facets aren't actually faces, but they divide a face in such a way as to simulate a rounded surface. The Refine Mesh tool further divides each of these facets into four faces. You can see this division clearly if you apply Refine Mesh to a face in a mesh that has only one level of smoothness applied.

The next step in creating the fins is to edit some of the newly created edges:

1. Zoom into the surfboard so your view looks similar to Figure 25.17.

2. On the Subobject panel, select Edge from the Filter flyout.

3. Click the edges shown in Figure 25.17.

4. Hover over the Z axis on the gizmo so that the axis extension appears, and then click and drag the Z axis upward in the positive Z direction. If you run out of room at the top of the window, you can move the Z axis as far as you can with one click and drag, and then repeat the Z axis move.

5. Adjust the edges so they look similar to those in Figure 25.18, and then release the mouse.

6. Adjust the X axis of the gizmo toward the back of the surfboard so the fins look similar to how they look in Figure 25.19.

7. Press the Esc key to clear your selection of mesh edges.

FIGURE 25.16
Select the faces
to refine.

Ctrl+click these two faces

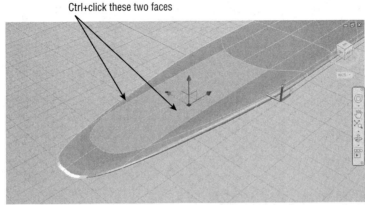

FIGURE 25.17
Select the edges
for the fins.

Ctrl+click these two edges

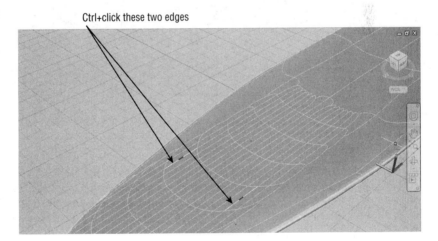

Rotating an Edge

The fins aren't quite the right shape. They are a bit too broad at the base. The next exercise shows you how to rotate an edge to further adjust the shape of the fins:

1. With the Edge subobject filter still selected, click the back edge of the fins as shown in Figure 25.20.

FIGURE 25.18
Adjust the edges
to create the fins.

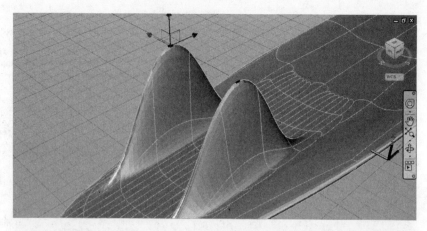

FIGURE 25.19
Adjust the fins
toward the back of
the surfboard.

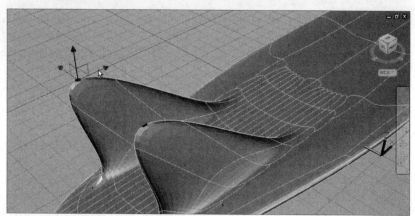

2. In the Subobject panel, select the Rotate Gizmo tool from the Gizmo flyout (see Figure 25.21).

3. Hover over the green circle of the Rotate gizmo in the location shown in the top panel of Figure 25.20 until you see the green axis extension, and then click and drag the mouse to rotate the edge. Adjust the rotation of the edge so that the fins look similar to those in the lower panel of Figure 25.20, and then release the mouse button.

4. Press the Esc key to clear your selection.

5. Use the Home tool on the ViewCube to get an overall view of the surfboard (Figure 25.22).

In this exercise, you switched from the Move gizmo to the Rotate gizmo. You can also use the Scale gizmo to scale a face or edge.

This may not be the most accurate rendition of a surfboard (my apologies if you are a surfer), but the general shape of the surfboard has given you a chance to explore many of the features of the Mesh toolset.

FIGURE 25.20
Click and drag the
green circle on the
Rotate gizmo.

Hover over this circle.

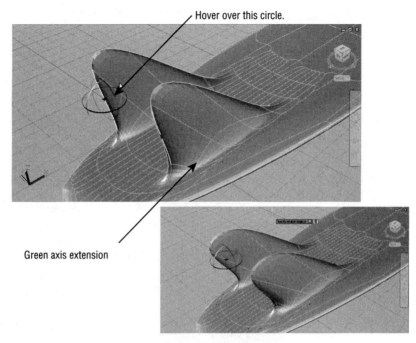

Green axis extension

FIGURE 25.21
Select the Rotate
Gizmo tool.

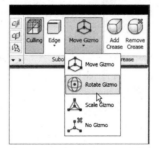

FIGURE 25.22
The finished
surfboard

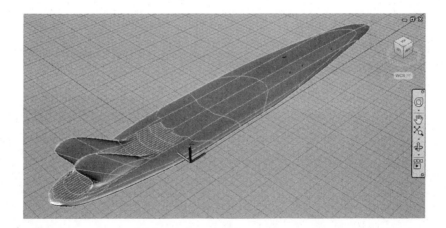

CHANGING THE GIZMO ON THE FLY

Instead of using the Gizmo flyout on the Subobject panel, you can right-click the gizmo to change it. You can also set the orientation of the gizmo through the shortcut menu, which will allow you to move subobjects in directions other than perpendicular to the face or edge. You can orient the gizmo to the WCS, the current UCS, or a face on a mesh through the Align Gizmo With right-click option.

Adding a Crease

There is one more tool that you'll want to know about that can help you fine-tune your mesh shapes. The Add Crease tool on the Mesh panel does exactly what it says. It can introduce a crease in your otherwise smooth mesh shape. The Add Crease tool does this in two ways: it can flatten a face or remove the smoothing around an edge.

In the following exercises, you'll use the surfboard one more time to experiment with the Add Crease tool. First you'll see how you can add a sharp point to the surfboard:

1. Adjust your view of the surfboard so you can see the front point, as shown in Figure 25.23. Turn off the grid so you can see the shape clearly.

FIGURE 25.23
Set up your view. Select the front edge of the surfboard.

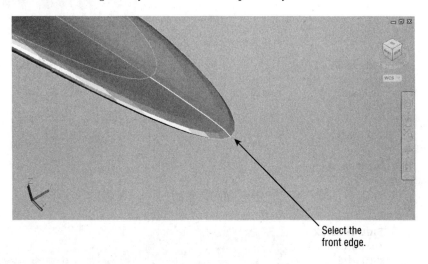

Select the front edge.

2. From the Mesh tab's Subobject panel, select the Move Gizmo tool from the Gizmo flyout.

3. Click the Add Crease tool in the Mesh panel.

4. Click the front edge of the surfboard, as shown in Figure 25.23.

5. Press ↵. The point of the surfboard becomes much more sharp.

You can see from this exercise that the front edge of the surfboard is now quite sharp since it no longer has any smoothness.

Now try applying the Add Crease tool to a face:

1. From the Subobject panel, select Face from the Filter flyout.

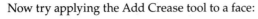

2. Click the two faces on either side of the front edge, as shown in Figure 25.24.

3. Click the Add Crease tool in the Mesh panel.

4. Press ↵. The faces are flattened and the point of the surfboard becomes even more sharp, as shown in Figure 25.25.

The surfboard is grossly deformed, but you can see how the side faces have now become flat and the edges of the face form a crease. You could use the Add Crease tool to sharpen the edge of the fins. This would also have the effect of making the fins thinner. I didn't use that example for this exercise because the effects would have been too subtle to see clearly.

FIGURE 25.24
Click these faces to flatten them.

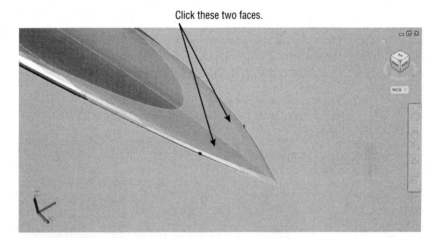

Click these two faces.

FIGURE 25.25
The surfboard after applying Add Crease to the side faces on the front

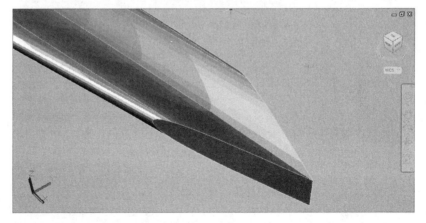

Splitting and Extruding a Mesh Face

Before we move on to the next topic, there are two more tools that can be a great aid in editing your meshes. The Split Face tool does just what its name says. It will split a face into two faces. The Extrude Face tool behaves like the Extrude Face tool you have seen for 3D solids. Both of these tools are a bit tricky to use, so they bear a closer look.

To use the Split Face tool, you first select a mesh face, then select two points, one on each side of the face. The following exercise shows how it works:

1. Open the SplitMesh.dwg sample file from the Chapter 25 folder. This file contains a simple mesh box that has been smoothed.

2. In the Mesh tab's Mesh Edit panel, click the Split Face tool or type **Meshsplit**⏎.

3. Make sure the Face filter tool is selected on the Subobject panel.

4. Click the face shown in the top panel of Figure 25.26.

5. Move the cursor to the left edge of the face until you see a knife icon appear next to the cursor.

6. Click roughly in the middle of the edge.

7. Move the cursor along the right edge of the face. You'll see some temporary lines giving you a preview of the location of the split (Figure 25.26).

FIGURE 25.26
Selecting the points for the split

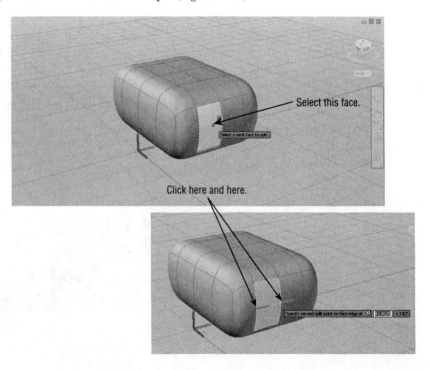

8. Move the cursor roughly in the middle of the right edge. The face changes temporarily to show you how it will look when it is divided into two faces.

9. Click the mouse. The shape of the mesh changes to accommodate the new face.

As you can see, the Split Face is not a precision tool, but if you don't like the location of the split, you can move the newly created edge using one of the gizmos.

Next, let's look at the Extrude Face tool. At first, you might think that the Extrude Face tool is redundant since you can use the Move gizmo to move a face in a direction away from the mesh, as you saw in an earlier exercise. Using the Extrude Face tool is different from moving a face because it isolates the movement to the selected face as much as possible. To see how this works, try the following:

1. With the Face filter selected in the Subobject panel, Ctrl+click the face indicated in Figure 25.27.

2. Click and drag the X axis in the positive direction. When the mesh looks similar to the upper-left panel of Figure 25.28, click to finish the move. The smoothness of the side is maintained as you pull the face.

 FIGURE 25.27
Select this face.

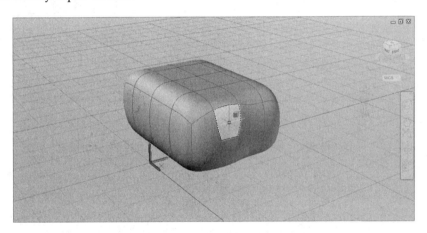

3. Press the Esc key and click Undo to revert back to the mesh as it was before you moved the face.

4. Click the Extrude Face tool in the Mesh Edit panel.

5. Click the same face you selected before, and then press ↵.

6. Move the cursor along the Z axis in the positive direction. The face is extruded, leaving the faces around it unmoved except for a slight curvature at the base (the lower right panel of Figure 25.28).

You can see from this example that the Extrude Face tool confines the deformation of the mesh to only the face you select. Note that you can select multiple faces for the extrusion.

FIGURE 25.28
A moved face and
an extruded face

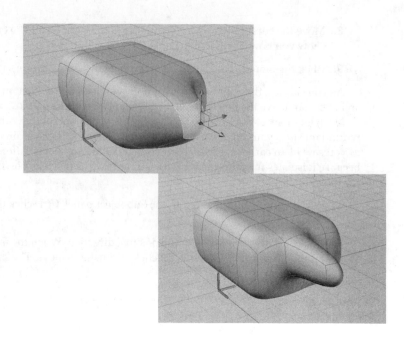

 Real World Scenario

USING SPLIT MESH FACE AND ADD CREASE TOGETHER

In a "usability study" conducted by Autodesk, the product designers gave an example of how to add a crease to the top surface of a computer mouse model. In the example, the Add Crease tool and the Split Face were used together. First, a new edge was created using the Split Face tool, and then the Add Crease tool was applied to the newly created edge to form the crease. Using these two tools together in this way, you can add a crease just about anywhere on a mesh.

Creating Mesh Surfaces

So far, you've been working with mesh volumes, but the Primitives panel of the Mesh tab offers four tools that let you create a variety of surface meshes. These are the *revolved*, *edge*, *ruled*, and *tabulated surfaces*. If you're an old hand at using AutoCAD 3D, then these tools should be familiar. They are the latest incarnation of some of the earliest 3D tools offered by AutoCAD, and they work exactly like the old features they replace. But just like the mesh volumes you've been working with, the mesh surfaces can be quickly smoothed and their subobjects can be edited using the gizmos you learned about in this and earlier chapters. The following sections give a little more detail about these tools and how they are used. The figures used in these sections are taken directly from the cue cards for each tool.

TRY OUT THESE TOOLS ON A SAMPLE FILE

The following instructions are for your reference only and you are not required to do them as exercises. But if you like, you can try them out on the SurfaceMeshSamples.dwg file provided with the sample drawings for this chapter.

Revolved Surface

To create a revolved surface, you need a profile to revolve and a line that acts as an axis of revolution (Figure 25.29). The profile can be any object, but a polyline or spline is usually used. To create a revolved surface, follow these steps:

1. Click the Revolved Surface tool in the Primitives panel or type **Revsurf**↵.

2. Select the profile object, then select the axis object.

3. At the Specify start angle <0>: prompt, enter a start angle, or just press ↵ to accept the default angle of zero.

4. At the Specify included angle (+=ccw, -=cw) <360>: prompt, enter the angle of rotation for the surface, or just press ↵ to accept the default angle of 360 degrees. As you might infer from the prompt, you can create a revolved surface that is not completely closed.

GETTING SMOOTHER SURFACES

The mesh surfaces will appear faceted when you first create them. Typically, the revolved, ruled, and tabulated surfaces will have 6 faces. The edge surface will have an array of 36 faces. You can increase the number of faces that are generated by these tools by changing the Surftab1 and Surftab2 settings. Surftab1 will increase the faces generated by the revolved, ruled, and tabulated surface tools. Surftab1 and surftab2 can be used to increase the faces of an edge surface.

To use the Surftab settings, type **Surftab1**↵ or **Surftab2**↵ and enter a numeric value. The value you enter will be the number of faces generated by these surface mesh tools. Don't get carried away as an increase in the number of faces will also increase the size of your file. Besides, you can always use the Smooth More tool to smooth out the appearance of these surface objects.

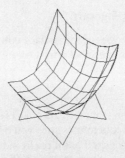

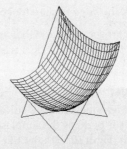

Surftab1 and Surftab2 are set to 6.

Surftab1 is set to 12 and Surftab2 is set to 24.

FIGURE 25.29
The Revolved
Surface tool's
cue card

Edge Mesh

In Chapter 22 you learned how to draw a butterfly chair that has the shape of a draped fabric seat. Before the newer 3D modeling tools were introduced, the Edge Surface tool (Figure 25.30) was used in that butterfly chair example. This tool is a bit trickier to use only because the objects defining the surface must be selected in sequential order. In other words, you can't randomly select the objects.

FIGURE 25.30
The Edge Surface
cue card

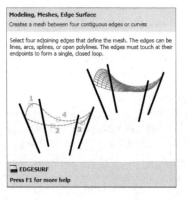

Here's how it works:

1. Click the Edge Surface tool or type **Edgesurf.**↵.

2. Select the four objects that are the edges of the surface you want to create. Make sure you select the objects in clockwise or counterclockwise order. Don't select them "crosswise."

Ruled Mesh

The Ruled Mesh tool creates a surface mesh from two 2D objects such as lines, arc, polylines, or splines. This is perhaps the simplest mesh tool to use since you only have to click two objects to form a mesh (Figure 25.31). But like Edge Mesh, it has a tricky side. The location where you click will affect the way the mesh is generated. You'll want to click the same side of each object unless you want the surface to twist as shown in Figure 25.32.

FIGURE 25.31
The Ruled Surface
cue card

FIGURE 25.32
Where you click an
object affects the
outcome.

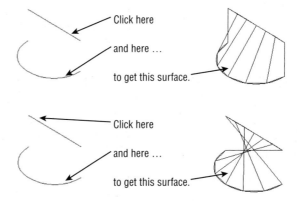

To create a ruled mesh, take the following steps:

1. Click the Ruled Surface tool or type **Rulesurf**↵.

2. Click two objects that are not on the same XY plane. The mesh is created between the objects.

Tabulated Mesh

The Tabulated Mesh tool is like an extrude tool for surfaces (Figure 25.33). Chapter 21 showed you how you can use the Extrude tool to create a 3D solid from a closed polygon. The Extrude tool will also work on open polygons, lines, and arcs, but it will extrude the object in only a perpendicular direction. The Tabulated Surface tool lets you "extrude" an object in a direction you control with a line. The line can point in any direction in space.

Here's how to use it:

1. Click the Tabulated Surface tool in the Primitives panel or enter **Tabsurf**↵.

2. Select the object that defines the profile of your mesh.

3. Click the object that defines the direction for the surface.

FIGURE 25.33
The Tabulated
Surface cue card

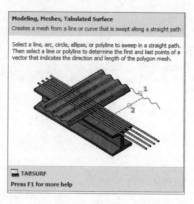

As with the other surface mesh tools, the point at which you select objects will affect the way the object is generated. For the tabulated mesh, the direction of the mesh depends on where you click the line that defines the surface direction.

Converting Meshes to Solids

I mentioned earlier that you can convert a mesh to a solid. In doing so, you can take advantage of the many solid editing tools available in AutoCAD. The Boolean tools can be especially useful in editing meshes that have been turned into solids.

The conversion process is a fairly simple process using the tools in the Convert Mesh panel of the Mesh tab. Just click the Convert To Solid tool, or type **Convtosolid**↵, and then select the mesh or meshes you want to convert. Press ↵ to complete the process. The Convert To Surface tool (**Convtosurface**↵) works in much the same way, but it creates a surface object instead of a solid.

When you convert a mesh to a solid, you have the option to apply more or less smoothing to the conversion process. The Smoothed, Optimized flyout in the Convert Mesh panel gives you four options. You can select one of these options before you use the Convert To Solid or Convert To Surface tool to get a different smoothing effect during the conversion. Table 25.1 describes these options and how they affect the conversion of meshes.

TABLE 25.1:   Options on the Convert Mesh panel's flyout

OPTION	EFFECT ON MESH
Smoothed, Optimized	The mesh is smoothed and the faces are merged.
Smoothed, Not Optimized	The mesh is smoothed but maintains the same number of faces as the original.
Faceted, Optimized	The facets are maintained, and the smoothing remains the same, but planar faces are merged.
Faceted, Not Optimized	The facets are maintained, the smoothing remains the same, and the number of faces also remains the same.

WHY CONTROL FACES IN THE CONVERSION?

The mesh-to-solid conversion options shown in Table 25.1 may seem like overkill, but there is a good reason for offering these settings. Many of the solid editing tools in the Home tab's Solid Editing panel are designed to work on solid faces. You can apply many of these tools to the faces of a converted mesh. Having control over the way faces are converted from a mesh to a solid will give you some control over how you are able to edit the solid later on. See Chapter 24 for more on the solid editing tools.

Understanding 3D Surfaces

So far in this book, you've worked with 3D solids and meshes. A third type of 3D object called a surface completes AutoCAD's set of 3D modeling tools to make AutoCAD 2011 a complete 3D modeling application in its own right.

Click the Surface tab and you'll see the Surface panels that offer the tools you'll need to work with surface modeling (Figure 25.34).

FIGURE 25.34
The Surface tab and ribbon panels

In the Create tab, you see quite a few new tools, but a handful should look familiar. The Loft, Sweep, Extrude, and Revolve tools at the far left of the Create panel are tools you've seen in previous chapters. These surface creation tools work in the same way as the tools of the same name in the Solid tab. In fact, they are the essentially the same tools. They just use a different command option to create a surface instead of a solid. The big difference is that to create a solid, you need to start with a closed polyline. With the surface version of the Loft, Sweep, Extrude, and Revolve tools, you can start with an open spline, polyline, or other object. And even if you do use a closed object, such as a circle or closed polyline, you will still get a 3D surface instead of a solid (see Figure 25.35).

DRAWING 2D CURVES WITH THE CURVES PANEL

Since 3D surfaces are derived from 2D objects, the Surface tab has the convenient Curves panel, which offers most of the 2D drawing tools you'll need to build your surfaces from scratch. The Spline flyout even features the Spline Freehand tool, which will let you draw a curve "freehand" with a click and drag of your mouse. Experienced AutoCAD users will recognize this Spline Freehand tool as an updated version of the Sketch command.

FIGURE 25.35
A circle extruded
using the solid
Extrude and the
surface Extrude

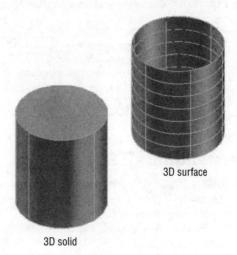

3D surface

3D solid

Two other surface creation tools that are unique to the Surface ribbon are the Network and
Planar Surface tools. Here's a brief description of each:

Network tool The Network tool lets you create a surface from several curves. The cue card
for the Network tool gives you a good idea of how this tool works (see Figure 25.36).

Planar Surface tool The Planar Surface tool creates a flat surface either by selecting two
points to indicate a rectangular surface or by selecting a closed 2D object to create a flat
surface with an irregular boundary (see Figure 25.37).

FIGURE 25.36
The cue card
description of
the Network
Surface tool

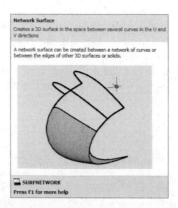

LEARNING FROM ANIMATED CUE CARDS

Animated cue cards show you how many of the tools on the Surface Ribbon tab work. These animated cue cards can help get you up and running with surface modeling. Just hover over a tool for a
moment after the tool tip appears. For tools that have animated cue cards, you will see the message
"Video is loading" in the lower-right corner of the tool tip.

FIGURE 25.37
Creating a
planar surface

Click the Planar Surface tool and
click two points to create a rectangular surface.

Click the Planar Surface tool
and press ↵, and then select a
closed 2D shape like a circle or polyline.

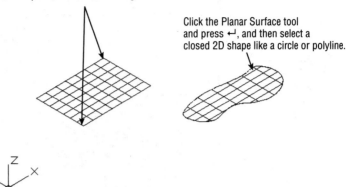

Editing Surfaces

Once created, surface objects have a unique set of editing tools that allow you to create fairly detailed models. Some tools, like Surface Fillet and Surface Trim, offer the same function as their 2D drawing counterparts. The following list includes a description of each tool:

Surface Fillet   With the Surface Fillet tool, you can join one surface to another with an intermediate rounded surface (see Figure 25.38).

FIGURE 25.38
Using Surface Fillet and Surface Trim tools

Trim these sides on the surfaces.

Fillet these surfaces.

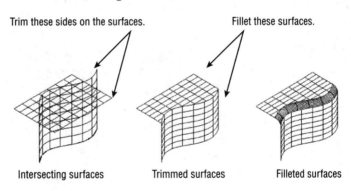

Intersecting surfaces   Trimmed surfaces   Filleted surfaces

Surface Trim   The Trim tool lets you trim one or several surfaces to other surfaces.

Surface Untrim   Untrim does exactly what it says. It reverses a trim operation.

Surface Extend   The Extend tool simply enables you to extend the edge of a surface beyond its current location. Unlike its 2D equivalent, it does not extend a surface to another surface object, though you could extend beyond a surface and then use the Trim tool.

Surface Sculpt The Sculpt tool is like a super trim. You can align several surfaces to completely enclose a volume (left image in Figure 25.39), then use the Sculpt tool to trim all of the surfaces at once into a completely closed 3D shape (right image in Figure 25.39). By default, the new object is a solid.

FIGURE 25.39
The Sculpt tool creates a container-like shape from several surfaces.

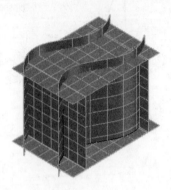 

The Create panel also offers three other tools that could be considered editing tools. Blend, Patch and Offset need existing surfaces to do their job, so they may seem a bit like editing tools. Here's a description of each:

Blend Blend will connect two surfaces with an intermediate surface.

Patch The Patch tool will close an open surface like the end of a tube. Patch also lets you control whether the closing "patch" is flat or curved, as shown in Figure 25.40.

FIGURE 25.40
The Patch tool can create a flat or rounded patch over a open surface.

Open surface   Flat patch   Curved patch

Offset Offset, like the surface Trim tool, mimics its 2D counterpart. It will create a new surface that is parallel to the original. When you start the Offset tool from the Create panel and select a surface, you'll see arrows indicating the direction of the offset. You can type **F↵** to flip the direction of the offset. Enter a distance for the offset and press ↵ to create the offset surface (see Figure 25.41).

Using Extrude, Trim, and Fillet

Now that you have an overview of the basic surface modeling tools, try the following set of exercises to see firsthand how they work.

FIGURE 25.41
Using the Create
panel's Offset tool

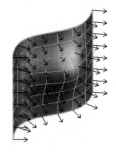

Select the surface.　　Determine the direction　　Enter a distance
　　　　　　　　　　　of the offset.　　　　　for the offset.

USING THE EXTRUDE TOOL

Start with the Extrude tool on two basic shapes:

1. Open the Surfaces1.dwg file from the sample folder.

2. Choose Extrude from the Surface tab's Create panel.

3. Click the circle in the drawing, and then press ↵. A surface appears and its length changes as you move the cursor.

4. Adjust the surface height to 5 units so it looks similar to Figure 25.42.

5. Click Extrude again and extrude the arc horizontally 5 units so it looks similar to the extrusion in Figure 25.42.

FIGURE 25.42
Extrude the circle
and arc (left image)
5 units to look
like the image on
the right.

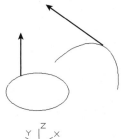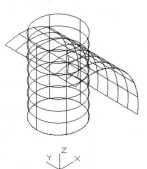

As you can see, the Extrude tool works in a way similar to the Extrude tool in the Solid tab, but the objects created are surfaces.

Using the Trim Tool

Next try out the Trim tool:

1. Click Surface Trim from the Surface tab's Edit panel.

2. Click both the cylinder and the extruded arc surface, and then press ↵. This first step selects the objects to trim.

3. Click both objects again and then press ↵. This time you're selecting the objects to trim to. You want to trim the top of the cylinder to the arc and the arc to the cylinder.

4. Finally, click the cylinder near the top edge to indicate what part you want to trim. Also click the extruded arc surface anywhere outside of the cylinder. Your surfaces should look like the right-side image in Figure 25.43.

Using the Surface Tool

The Surface Trim tool is similar to the 2D Trim tool except there is the additional step at the beginning where you have to select the object you intend to trim. At first it seems redundant, but after using this tool for a while, it begins to make more sense. Also notice that the original arc you used to extrude the arc surface is still there. You'll use that a little later in this chapter.

FIGURE 25.43
Trimming the surfaces

Click the top edge of the cylinder.

Click the extruded arc anywhere outside the cylinder.

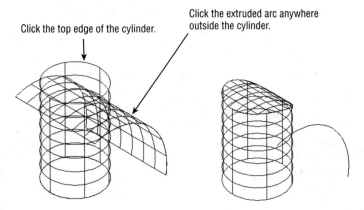

Now try out the Fillet tool:

1. Click the Surface Fillet tool in the Surface tab's Edit panel.

2. Click the top surface and then click the cylinder. The two surfaces are "filleted," as shown in Figure 25.44.

3. The following prompt appears: `Press Enter to accept the fillet surface or [Radius/Trim surface]`. Type **R**↵ to enter a different radius.

4. Type **0.5**↵. The radius changes. You still have the opportunity to change the radius again.

5. Type **R**↵ and then type **0.2**↵. The radius changes again.

6. Press ↵ to finish the fillet.

FIGURE 25.44
Using the Surface
Fillet tool

FIGURE 25.44
Using the Surface
Fillet tool

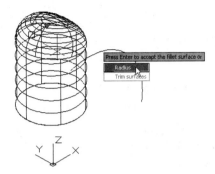

Using Surface Blend, Patch and Offset

As mentioned earlier, a few of the tools on the Create panel are a bit like editing tools. Surface Blend, Surface Patch, and Surface Offset create new surfaces that use existing surfaces as their basis. Surface Blend is a bit like the Surface Fillet tool in that it will join two surfaces with an intermediate surface. Surface Offset creates a new surface that is parallel to an existing one and is similar to the 2D offset command. Surface Patch will create a surface that closes an open-ended surface.

To get a better idea of how these three tools work, try the following set of exercises. Start by creating a parallel copy of an existing surface using the Offset tool:

1. Open the `Patch1.dwg` sample file from the Chapter 25 sample folder.

2. Click the Surface Offset tool from the Surface tab's Create panel.

3. Click the surface in the drawing and then press ↵. You see a set of arrows appear as shown in the left image of Figure 25.45.

4. Type **F↵**. The arrows now point in the opposite direction.

5. Type **F↵** again to return the arrows to their previous direction facing outward.

6. Enter **0.5↵** for the offset distance. The offset surface appears around the original surface as shown in the right-side image of Figure 25.45.

FIGURE 25.45
Using the Surface
Offset tool

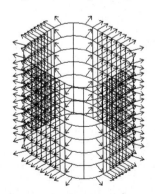
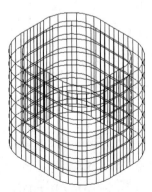

Here you see how the Surface Offset tool differs from the 2D Offset tool that you've seen in Chapter 19 of this book. The arrows play an important role in helping you visualize the result of your offset, so instead of picking a direction, you adjust the direction of the arrows.

Using the Surface Blend Tool

Now try the SurfaceBlend tool:

1. Use the Move command to move the outer surface vertically in the Z axis roughly 5 units. Remember that you can hold down the Shift key to restrain the cursor to the Z axis. If you see the Surface Associativity message, click Continue. You'll learn more about associativity later in this chapter.

2. Adjust your view so you can see both surfaces, and then click the Surface Blend tool on the Surface tab's Create panel.

3. Select the eight edges along the top of the lower surface as shown in left-side image in Figure 25.46. When you're sure you've selected all of the edges, press ⏎.

4. Select the eight edges along the bottom of the upper surface as shown in the left-side image in Figure 25.46. When you're sure you've selected all of the edges, press ⏎. A new, preview, surface appears that joins the upper and lower surfaces.

FIGURE 25.46
Selecting the edges
for the Surface
Blend tool

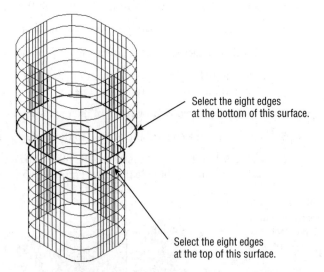

Select the eight edges
at the bottom of this surface.

Select the eight edges
at the top of this surface.

5. You might notice a couple of grip arrowheads that appear along the top and bottom edge of the new blend surface. Click one of them and a menu appears offering three options: Position, Tangent, and Curvature (see Figure 25.47).

6. Click Curvature, and then press ⏎ to place the blend surface.

The Surface Blend tool offers a number of options that control the shape of the blend surface. You saw three options available from the grip arrowhead. The options are available even after you have placed the surface. You can click on the surface to expose the grip arrowheads.

FIGURE 25.47
Using the grip
arrowhead to
adjust the
blend surface

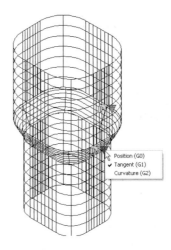

In addition, the Surface Blend tool offered two command options: CONtinuity and Bulge magnitude. Table 25.2 describes these features and their functions.

USING THE SURFACE PATCH TOOL

Now let's take a look at the Surface Patch tool. The Surface Patch tool lets you close the end of a surface with another surface. You can add a flat or curved surface as you'll see in the next exercise.

Try adding a patch surface to the top of the upper surface in the `Patch1.dwg` model:

1. Pan your view so you can clearly see the top of the surface model as shown in the left-side image in Figure 25.48.

2. Click the Surface Patch tool in the Surface tab's Create panel.

3. Select the edges of the surface as shown in Figure 25.48.

4. Press ↵ when you are sure you've selected all of the edges. The patch surface appears.

5. Click the grip arrowhead that appears along the edge of the patch and select Tangent. The surface is now curved.

FIGURE 25.48
Adding the patch
surface to the end
of the model

Select the top edges.

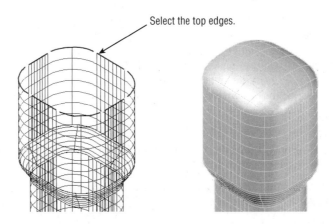

6. Press ↵ to finish the patch surface.

7. To get a better view of the surface, select the Shaded With Edges option from the Visual Styles drop-down list in the View tab's Visual Styles panel.

You may have noticed that the grip arrowhead options in step 5 were similar to the grip options you saw for the Surface Blend tool. The Surface Patch tool offers an additional command option called CONStrain geometry. Table 25.2 describes these options.

TABLE 25.2:   The Blend and Patch options

FEATURE OPTION	FUNCTION
Position (G0)	Causes the surface to connect without any blending curvature
Tangent (G1)	Causes the surface to blend with direction
Curvature (G2)	Causes the surface to blend with direction and similar curvature or rate of change in surface direction
COMMAND OPTION	**FUNCTION**
CONtinuity	Controls how smoothly the surfaces flow into each other
Bulge magnitude	Allows you to adjust the amount of bulge or curvature in the blend surface. Values can be between 0 and 1
CONStrain geometry (Surfpatch command)	Offers additional guide curves to control the patch surface

Understanding Associativity

You may have noticed the Surface Associativity icon in the Create panel. This is a feature that is on by default, and its function is similar to the Associative feature of hatches (see Chapter 7 for more on hatches). You may recall that when you create a 2D hatch pattern with the hatch associative feature turned on, the hatch's shape will conform to any changes made to the boundary used to enclose the hatch pattern.

The Associativity feature in surface modeling works in a similar way, only instead of a hatch pattern conforming to changes in a boundary, the surface conforms to changes in the shapes that are used to create them. For example, if you were to make changes to the arc that you used to extrude the arc surface, the arc surface and the trimmed cylinder would also follow the changes.

USING ASSOCIATIVITY TO EDIT A SURFACE MODEL

This concept is a bit tricky to explain in words. Try the following exercise to see how associativity works firsthand:

1. Return to the Surfaces1.dwg file and click the arc to expose its grips.

2. Click the square grip at the arc's left endpoint and drag it downward along the Z axis. When it is roughly in the position shown in Figure 25.49, click again to fix the grip's location. The shape of the surface model changes to conform to the new shape of the arc.

3. Zoom into the top of the surface model so you have a view similar to Figure 25.50.

4. Click the filleted portion of the surface. An arrowhead grip appears.

5. Click the arrowhead grip. Another arrowhead grip appears.

6. Click this arrowhead grip and slowly drag it toward the center of the cylinder. Notice that the radius of the fillet changes as you move the grip.

7. Click to fix the fillet radius to its new size.

8. Press the Esc key to clear your selection.

FIGURE 25.49
Adjusting the shape of the arc

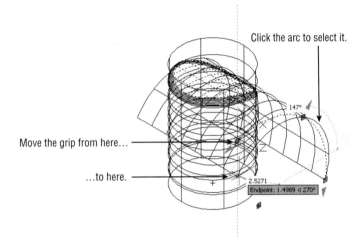

Click the arc to select it.

Move the grip from here...

...to here.

FIGURE 25.50
Adjusting the fillet radius

Click and drag this arrowhead grip toward the center of the cylinder.

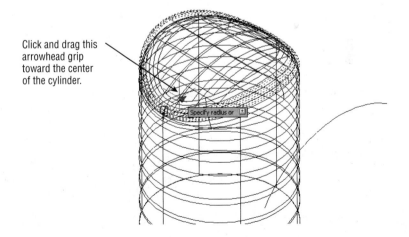

Using Arrowhead Grips to Edit a Surface

You've just seen the Associativity feature in action. You can also change the shape of the circle used to extrude the cylinder to modify the surface model's diameter. There are additional hidden grips that allow you to adjust the shape of the surfaces directly. For example, you can modify the taper of the cylinder using an arrowhead grip that you can turn on through the Properties palette, as shown in these steps:

1. Click the cylindrical part of the surface model.

2. Right-click and select Properties.

3. Scroll down to the bottom of the Properties palette to the Surface Associativity panel.

4. Click the Show Associativity option and select Yes.

5. Close the Properties palette. You now see the circle at the base of the cylinder in a bold outline.

6. At the top of the cylinder, click and drag the right-pointing arrowhead grip to the right. As you do this, you see the dynamic display showing you an angle (see the left-side image in Figure 25.51).

7. Position the arrowhead grip so that the angle shows 6°, and then click to fix the grip in place. The cylinder is now tapered and the top surface conforms to the new shape as shown in the right-side image in Figure 25.51.

FIGURE 25.51
Changing the taper of the cylinder

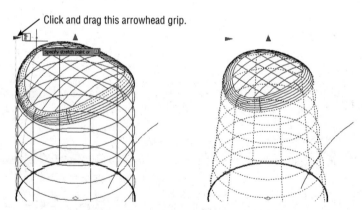

Click and drag this arrowhead grip.

Surface Associativity can be very useful, but in order to take full advantage of this feature, you will want to plan your model construction carefully. In addition, the Associativity feature can limit some editing and creation functions. For example, the Surface Fillet tool may not work on a complex surface model with associativity turned on but will when the associativity is turned off for the objects involved.

TURNING OFF OR REMOVING ASSOCIATIVITY

You can turn off or remove associativity for an object through the Properties palette. Select the object, then right-click and select Properties. In the Properties palette, scroll down the panels to the Surface Associativity panel (see Figure 25.52). This group offers two options: Maintain Associativity and Show Associativity. The Maintain Associativity option offers Yes, Remove, and None.

FIGURE 25.52

The Surface Associativity panel in the Properties Palette

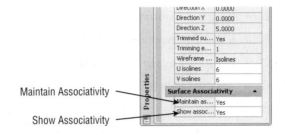

Maintain Associativity

Show Associativity

You can select Remove to remove associativity altogether or None to limit the associativity to the set of objects currently associated with the surface model. Once you change this setting, you can't return to a previous setting except with an Undo.

CONSTRAINTS, SURFACES, AND ASSOCIATIVITY

In Chapter 17, you learned that you can add constraints to objects to control their behavior. With Surface Associativity turned on, you can extrude constrained objects and the resulting surface will also follow the constraints of the source 2D objects. But remember that if you use constraints with 3D surfaces in this way, you need to carefully plan the way you build your model to make efficient use of constraints.

Editing with Control Vertices

So far you've been creating what are called *procedural surfaces,* which are surfaces that allow you to take advantage of associativity. AutoCAD also allows you to create NURBS surfaces. You may recall that splines are also NURBS, so you might think of a NURBS surface as a kind of 3D surface spline. Splines allow you to move, add, or subtract control vertices or CVs, and you can control the way the CVs "pull" on the curve of the spline. Likewise, NURBS surfaces allow you to add or remove VCs and adjust the direction and force of the CVs.

There are two ways to create a NURBS surface. You can turn on the NURBS Creation option in the Surface tab's Create panel and then go about creating your 3D surfaces. Any 3D surface you create with this option turned on will be a NURBS surface. Or you can convert an existing surface to a NURBS surface.

CONVERTING A SURFACE TO A NURBS SURFACE

You can convert an existing surface to a NURBS surface by using the Convert To NURBS tool on the Surface tab's Control Vertices panel. This tool also converts 3D solids and meshes. To use it, follow these steps:

1. Open the CVedit1.dwg sample file.

2. Turn off Surface Associativity in the Surface tab's Create panel.

3. Turn on NURBS Creation in the Surface tab's Create panel.

4. Click the Extrude tool in the Surface tab's Create panel.

5. Click the spline and press ↵.

6. Point the cursor upward and type 6↵ to make the extruded surface 6 units in the Z axis.

EXPOSING CVs TO EDIT A NURBS SURFACE

You've just created a NURBS surface. You can expose the CVs for the surface using the Show CV tool. Try the following to view and edit the CVs.

1. Click the Show CV tool in the Control Vertices panel.

2. Click the surface you just created and press ↵. The CVs appear for the surface.

3. Click the surface to select it and then click the CV as shown in Figure 25.53.

FIGURE 25.53
Exposing the CVs

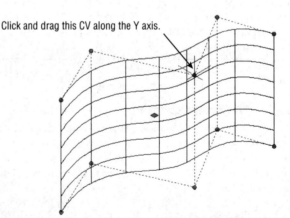

Click and drag this CV along the Y axis.

4. Move the CV in the Y axis and notice how the surface deforms. The top edge moves with the CV, while the bottom edge maintains its shape.

5. Press the Esc key twice to clear your selection.

In this exercise, you saw how you can gain access to the CVs of a NURBS surface to make changes to the shape. Right now, the CVs are located only at the top and bottom of the surface, but you can add more CVs to give you more control over the shape of the surface.

ADDING CVS TO A NURBS SURFACE

The next exercise shows you how you can add additional CVs through the Rebuild option:

1. Click the Surface Rebuild tool in the Control Vertices panel and then click the surface. Or you can click the surface to select it and then right-click and select NURBS Editing ➤ Rebuild. The Rebuild Surface dialog box appears (Figure 25.54).

2. In the Control Vertices Count group of the Rebuild Surface dialog box, make sure the In U Direction option is set to 8 and the In V Direction option is set to 7. You'll see what these settings do in a moment.

3. Click OK. Now you see that many more CVs are available.

FIGURE 25.54
The Rebuild Surface dialog box

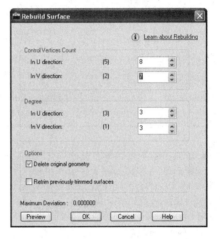

In step 2 you specified the number of CVs you want in the U and V directions. The U direction is along the horizontal curve, while the V direction is along the straight, vertical direction. If you count the CVs in each row or column, you'll see that they match the values you entered in step 2.

Now if you were to move a CV, the surface is able to deform along the Z axis, where it remained a straight line before.

WHAT ARE THE U AND V DIRECTIONS?

While working in 3D, you'll see references to the U and V directions. You can think of these as the X and Y axes of a 3D surface. There is also a W direction, which corresponds to the Z axis, or the normal direction to a surface.

The Rebuild Surfaces dialog box offers a number of other options you'll want to know about. Table 25.3 gives you a rundown.

TABLE 25.3: The Rebuild Surfaces dialog box

CONTROL VERTICES COUNT	
In U Direction	Sets the number of CVs in the U direction
In V Direction	Sets the number of CVs in the V direction
DEGREE	
In U Direction	Sets the number of CVs available per span in the U direction
In V Direction	Sets the number of CVs available per span in the V direction
OPTIONS	
Delete Original Geometry	Determines whether the original geometry is retained or not
Retrim Previously Trimmed Surfaces	Determines whether trimmed surfaces are retained from the original surface
Maximum Deviation	Displays the maximum deviation between the original and rebuilt surface

Two other tools just below the Surface Rebuild tool allow you to either add or remove a set of CVs. The Surface CV – Add tool lets you place a row of CVs. The Surface CV – Remove tool will remove a row of CVs. Both options allow you to toggle between the U and V directions for the row addition or removal by typing **D↵**.

The Surface CV Add and Remove tools can be useful when you want to fine-tune the curvature of a surface. Where you want a "tighter" curve, you can add more CVs to an area of the surface. You can then move the CVs in the selected area to increase the curvature. To smooth out the curvature of an area, remove the CVs.

Editing with the CV Edit Bar

You've seen how a NURBS surface can be set up to add additional CVs, which in turn allow you to adjust the shape of the surface. But the CVs by themselves allow you to adjust their pull on the surface only by moving the CVs closer or farther away from the surface.

The CV Edit bar gives you more control over the behavior of individual CVs. With the CV Edit bar, you can change the strength and direction of the "pull" exerted by a CV.

Try the following exercise to see firsthand how the CV Edit bar works:

CV Edit Bar

1. Click the CV Edit Bar tool in the Control Vertices panel.

2. Select the surface. Now as you move the cursor across the surface, you see two red lines that follow the U and V directions of the surface (see Figure 25.55).

FIGURE 25.55
The CV Edit bar's
U and V directions
are shown by two
red lines.

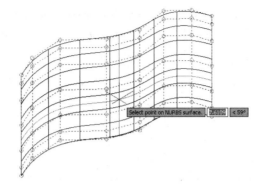

3. Click the point shown in Figure 25.55. A Move gizmo appears along with two other features called the magnitude handle and the expansion grip (see Figure 25.56).

FIGURE 25.56
The magnitude
handle and expansion grip

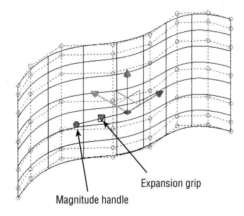

Expansion grip

Magnitude handle

The Move gizmo gives you a bit more control over the location of the CV since it allows you to isolate movement in the X, Y, or Z direction. The expansion grip lets you change the tangency of the CV, while the magnitude grip lets you control the strength of the CV.

Try the following steps to see how these two features work:

1. Click the expansion grip. Notice that the Move gizmo switches to the location of the expansion grip.

2. Hover over the green Y axis of the gizmo, and when you see the green Y axis vector, click and drag the mouse. Notice how the surface warps as you move the mouse. If you look carefully at the CV Edit bar, you see that it pivots around the new location of the expansion grip, the CV location.

3. Press the Esc key to release the Y axis, and then click the expansion grip. The Move gizmo returns to its original location at the CV.

4. Now click the magnitude handle and move it horizontally. You see that the surface is "pulled" in both directions of the U axis of the surface.

5. Press the Esc key to release the magnitude handle.

6. Right-click on the CV Edit bar and select V Tangent Direction. Notice that the magnitude handle changes its orientation so that it is aligned to the V direction of the surface.

7. Click and drag the magnitude handle to see how it affects the surface.

8. Press the Esc key twice to exit the CV Edit bar.

As you can see from this exercise, the CV Edit bar gives you much more control over a CV than you would have otherwise. You also saw the shortcut menu for the CV Edit bar in step 6 (see Figure 25.57). As you've seen, the shortcut menu allows you to change the direction of the magnitude grip, but it also lets you switch the position of the Move gizmo and the expansion grip with the Move Point Location and Move Tangent Direction options. The Relocate option enables you to move to a different CV location. Table 25.4 includes descriptions of these options.

FIGURE 25.57
The CV Edit bar's shortcut menu

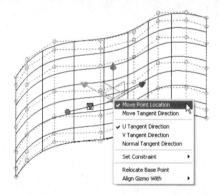

TABLE 25.4: The CV Edit bar's right-click options

OPTION	PURPOSE
Move Point Location	Places the Move gizmo at the CV location
Move Tangent Direction	Places the Move gizmo at the expansion grip location to allow adjustment to the tangent direction of the CV
U Tangent Direction	Aligns the magnitude grip to the surface's U direction
V Tangent Direction	Aligns the magnitude grip to the surface's V direction
Normal Tangent Direction	Aligns the magnitude grip to a direction that is normal (perpendicular) to the surface
Set Constraint	Constrains changes to the tangency in a specific direction such as X, Y, or Z or in a plane defined by a pair of axes

TABLE 25.4: The CV Edit bar's right-click options *(CONTINUED)*

OPTION	PURPOSE
Relocate Base Point	Moves the CV Edit bar to a different location on the surface
Align Gizmo With	Aligns the gizmo with the world or current UCS or with a face on the surface

Making Holes in a Surface with the Project Geometry Panel

Eventually, you'll need to place an opening in a surface, so AutoCAD offers the Project Geometry panel. This panel contains several tools that allow you to project a closed 2D object's shape onto a 3D surface. For example, if you want to place a circular hole in the surface you edited in the previous exercise, you would draw a circle parallel to that surface and then use the Surface Projection UCS tool.

Try the following exercise to see how the Project Geometry feature works:

1. Click the Layer Properties tool from the Layers panel of the Home tab.

2. Turn on the Circle layer. A circle appears in the drawing.

3. Type **UCS.↵** and then type **OB↵**. This lets you align the UCS to an object.

4. Click the circle to align the UCS to the circle.

5. In the Surface tab's Project Geometry panel, click the Auto Trim tool to turn it on.

6. Click the Surface Projection UCS tool in the Project Geometry panel.

7. Click the circle and press ↵.

8. Click the surface. The circle is projected onto the surface and the area inside the projected circle is trimmed (Figure 25.58).

FIGURE 25.58
The circle projected onto the surface

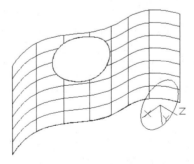

In this exercise, you aligned the UCS to the circle. The Surface Projection UCS tool you used in step 6 projected the circle in the Z axis of this new UCS that is aligned with the circle.

The other two Project Geometry tools use different criteria to project geometry. The Surface Projection View will project geometry along the line of sight. If you had used this tool in the previous exercise, the projected circle and opening would appear directly behind the circle from your current view. The Surface Projection Vector projects geometry along a vector that you indicate with two points. You can use the 3D object snaps to select points on the geometry and the surface.

Visualizing Curvature: Understanding the Analysis Panel

In addition to the surface editing tools, AutoCAD offers several surface analysis options. These options offer some visual aids to help you see the curvature of your surfaces models more clearly. They can be found in the Analysis panel of the Surface tab and are called Analysis Zebra, Analysis Curvature, and Analysis Draft.

Analysis Zebra displays stripes that allow you to better visualize how the curvature of surfaces blend (Figure 25.59). The smoother the stripes, the better the transition between surfaces.

USING THE 3D OBJECT SNAPS

You may have noticed the 3D Object Snap tool in the status bar.

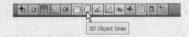

This tool works in a way that is similar to how the Object Snap tool you've used in earlier chapters works. When the 3D Object Snap tool is on, you can snap to geometry on 3D objects. If you right-click on this tool, you'll see the list of locations you can snap to.

You can think of the 3D Object Snap tool as an extension of the standard set of object snaps that allow you to pick locations on 3D solids, meshes, and surfaces. Right-click on the 3D Object Snap tool and select Settings and you will see the Drafting Settings dialog box open to the 3D Object Snap tab. There you can choose which 3D object snap you want to appear as the default when this tool is turned on.

Analysis Curvature displays colors to indicate the direction and amount of curvature in a surface (Figure 25.60). As the cue card describes, a negative curvature is a saddle shape and displays a blue color. A positive curvature or bowl shape displays in red.

FIGURE 25.59
The cue card
description for
Analysis Zebra

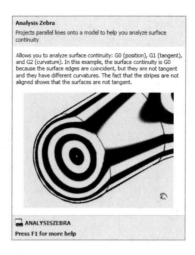

Analysis Zebra

Projects parallel lines onto a model to help you analyze surface continuity

Allows you to analyze surface continuity: G0 (position), G1 (tangent), and G2 (curvature). In this example, the surface continuity is G0 because the surface edges are coincident, but they are not tangent and they have different curvatures. The fact that the stripes are not aligned shows that the surfaces are not tangent.

ANALYSISZEBRA
Press F1 for more help

FIGURE 25.60
The cue card
description for
Analysis Curvature

Analysis Curvature

Displays a color gradient onto surface parts so that you can evaluate the high and low areas of curvature

Allows you to visualize Gaussian, minimum, maximum, and mean U and V surface curvature. Maximum curvature and a positive Gaussian value display as red; minimum curvature and a negative Gaussian value display as blue. Positive Gaussian curvature means that the surface is shaped like a bowl. Negative Gaussian curvature means the surface is shaped like a saddle (as shown below). Mean curvature and a zero Gaussian value means that the surface is flat in at least one direction (planes, cylinders, and cones have zero Gaussian curvature).

ANALYSISCURVATURE
Press F1 for more help

Analysis Draft displays colors to help you determine draft angles (Figure 25.61). Draft angles are often used in the design of objects that are to be cast from a mold and are important in allowing the cast object to be easily removed from the mold.

The Analysis Options tool opens the Analysis Options dialog box, which enables you to control the way the different analysis tools are displayed. Note that the graphics hardware acceleration must be turned on before you can use these tools. You must also use a visual style other than wireframe.

To turn on graphics hardware acceleration, right-click the Hardware Acceleration tool in the right portion of the status bar and select Hardware Acceleration.

FIGURE 25.61
The cue card
description for
Analysis Draft

The Bottom Line

Create a simple 3D mesh. Mesh modeling allows you to create more organic 3D forms by giving you unique smoothing and editing tools. You can start your mesh model by creating a basic shape using the mesh primitives.

Master It Name at least six mesh primitives available on the Primitives panel of the Mesh Modeling tab.

Edit faces and edges. The ability to edit faces and edges is essential to creating complex shapes with mesh objects.

Master It Name the tool that is used to divide a face into multiple faces.

Create mesh surfaces. The Mesh primitives let you create shapes that enclose a volume. If you just want to model a smooth, curved surface in 3D, you might find the surface mesh tools helpful.

Master It How many objects are needed to use the Edge Surface tool?

Convert meshes to solids. You can convert a mesh into a 3D solid to take advantage of many of the solid editing tools available in AutoCAD.

Master It Name at least two tools you can use on a solid that you cannot use on a mesh.

Understand 3D surfaces. 3D surfaces can be created using some of the same tools you use to create 3D solids.

Master It Name at least two tools you can use to create both 3D solids and 3D surfaces.

Edit 3D surfaces. AutoCAD offers a wide range of tools that are unique to 3D surfaces.

Master It Name at least four tools devoted to CV editing.

Part 5

Customization and Integration

Chapter 26

Using the Express Tools

You can use a wealth of AutoCAD features to improve your productivity. But even with these aids to efficiency, you can always further automate in certain situations. In Part 5 of this book, you'll learn how to use AutoCAD's customization features to adapt it to fit your particular needs. I'll introduce you to some ways you can enhance AutoCAD with add-on utilities. You'll explore ways to create custom toolbars and panels and discover how you can create custom linetypes and hatch patterns.

In this beginning chapter of Part 5, you'll be introduced to customization through the AutoCAD Express tools that are supplied on the AutoCAD distribution CD. You'll also be introduced to AutoLISP, AutoCAD's macro language.

In this chapter, you'll learn to do the following:

◆ Use enhancements straight from the source

◆ Put AutoLISP to work

BEFORE YOU WORK IN THIS CHAPTER

Before you go any further, make sure that you are in the 2D Drafting & Annotation workspace. Click the Workspace Switching tool in the status bar, or the Workspace drop-down menu on the Quick access toolbar, and select 2D Drafting & Annotation.

If you're using LT, you can skip this chapter.

Using Enhancements Straight from the Source

If you've followed the tutorials in this book, you've already used a few add-on programs that come with AutoCAD, perhaps without even being aware that they were not part of the core AutoCAD program. In this section, I'll introduce you to the AutoCAD Express tools: a set of AutoLISP and ARX tools that showcase these powerful customization environments. The best part about the Express tools is that you don't have to know a thing about programming to take advantage of them.

There are so many Express tools that I can't provide step-by-step instructions for all of them. Instead, I'll give you details about some of the more complicated tools and provide shorter descriptions of others. You can find the Express tools in the Express Tools Ribbon tab (Figure 26.1).

FIGURE 26.1

The Express Tools tab on the Ribbon

LOADING THE EXPRESS TOOLS

If for some reason, you do not see the Express Tools tab on the Ribbon, you can install the Express tools separately without having to reinstall the entire program. Open the Windows Control Panel and double-click the Add Or Remove Programs option. Click the Change/Remove button for AutoCAD 2011 in the Add Or Remove Programs dialog box. Click the Add Or Remove Features option in the AutoCAD Installation Wizard. Locate Express Tools under the Select Features To Install list box, and click Next. Click Next at the next page of the wizard to confirm your changes.

You may need to place the AutoCAD 2011 installation CD in your CD drive.

Blocks Panel Tools

Every now and then, you'll want to use objects in a block to trim or extend to, or perhaps you'll want to copy a part of a block to another part of your drawing. In these situations, you can use the following tools. They're fairly simple to use, so the descriptions in this section should be enough to get you started.

You'll find these tools on the Blocks panel of the Express Tools tab:

Explode Attributes Explodes blocks containing attributes so that the attribute values are converted into plain single-line text.

Replace Block Replaces one set of block references with another. For example, you can replace the Tub block in the apartment plan with the Door block, turning all the bathtubs into doors. This tool is similar to the Convert Block To Xref tool.

List Properties Displays basic information about an Xref or a block.

Import Attributes Enables you to import changes to the attribute information that has been exported using the Export Attribute Information tool.

Export Attributes Offers a quick way to extract attribute information from a block to a simple text file. You're prompted to select a file location and name and then select the attributes you want to export. The text file is formatted as a tab-delimited file. You can then edit the exported text file and use the Import Attributes tool (described previously) to update the drawing with the modifications you made to the text file.

Convert Block To Xref Lets you replace block references in your drawing with Xrefs. For example, you can replace the Tub blocks in the apartment plan from earlier tutorials with an Xref of a different tub. When you select this option, the BLOCKTOXREF dialog box opens (Figure 26.2).

From here, you can select the block you want to replace. You're then asked to select a file that will be the replacing Xref.

Copy Nested Objects   Lets you copy single objects within a block. You're allowed to select objects only individually—one click at a time.

Extend To Nested Objects   Extends to objects in a block. This tool also works like its standard counterpart with the exception that you must select the boundary-edge objects you want to extend to individually.

Trim To Nested Objects   Trims to objects in a block. This tool works just like the standard Trim command with the exception that you must select the cutting-edge objects individually.

FIGURE 26.2

The BLOCKTOXREF dialog box

Text Panel Tools

It seems that we can never have enough text-editing features. Even in the realm of word processors, numerous tools let you configure fonts, paragraphs, tabs, and tables. Some programs even check your grammar. Although you may not be trying to write the great American novel in AutoCAD, you're interested in getting your text in the right location, at the right size, and with some degree of style. This often means using a mixture of text- and graphics-editing tools. The following describes some additional tools that will help ease your way through otherwise difficult editing tasks.

MASKING TEXT BACKGROUNDS

One problem AutoCAD users frequently face is how to get text to read clearly when it's placed over a hatch pattern or other graphic. The Hatch command hatches around existing text, leaving a clear space behind it. But what about those situations in which you need to mask behind text that is placed over a non-hatch object, such as a dimension leader or raster image?

The Text Mask tool addresses this problem by masking the area behind text with a special masking object called a Wipeout.

If you want to remove the effects of the Text Mask tool, choose Unmask Text from the expanded Text panel of the Express Tools tab. This option prompts you to select an object. Select the masked text, and press ⏎ to delete the mask background.

USING THE MTEXT COMMAND TO MASK TEXT

The AutoCAD Mtext command offers a Background Mask option that performs a function similar to that of the Text Mask tool. While editing text with the text editor, select the text, right-click, and select Background Mask. You can also turn on Background Mask through the Properties palette of an Mtext object.

ADDING LINKED TEXT DOCUMENTS

One of the more frustrating and time-consuming aspects of drafting is editing lengthy notes. General notes and specifications change frequently in the life of a project, so editing notes can be a large part of what you do in AutoCAD. Frequently, notes are written by someone else, perhaps a specifications writer who doesn't work directly with the drawings.

To help make note-editing easier, AutoCAD supplies the Remote Text object. This special object is linked to an external text document. Remote Text objects automatically update their contents when the source document changes.

Using Remote Text is fairly straightforward. Click the Remote Text tool from the expanded Text panel of the Express Tools tab, or type **Rtext.⌐** at the Command prompt. Press ⌐ when you see the Enter an option[Style/Height/Rotation/File/Diesel] <File>: prompt, and then locate and select a text file to import.

OTHER TEXT TOOLS

Besides the text tools already described, several others can help to simplify some common text-related operations. Table 26.1 offers a description of these other tools.

TABLE 26.1: Tools on the Text panel

TOOL NAME	FUNCTION
Arc Aligned	Draws text along an arc
Modify Text	A flyout that offers tools to explode, change case, rotate, fit, or justify text
Convert To Mtext	Converts single-line text created with Text or Dtext into multiline text
Auto Number	Adds numbers to a text list
Enclose In Object	Encloses text in a circle, slot, or rectangle

Modify Panel Tools

The Express Tools Modify panel seems to be the answer to most AutoCAD users' wish lists. As with many of the Express tools discussed so far, these tools have been floating around in the AutoCAD user community as AutoLISP utilities. Stretch Multiple lets you use the crossing polygon selection option to select endpoints and vertexes for stretching. The Move/Copy/Rotate tool combines these three functions into one command. Delete Duplicates removes duplicate objects that may be hidden by overlapping objects.

INTERACTING WITH BLOCKS

In the earlier part of this chapter, you saw the tools on the Block panel. There are two more block-related tools that have a more general use, so they've been placed in the Modify panel.

Extended Clip   In Chapter 7, you saw how to limit the display of an Xref to an L-shaped, rectilinear area. Extended Clip adds the ability to use arcs, circles, and polylines to clip the view of an Xref.

Convert Shape To Block   Converts a shape object into a block. You can then explode the block to its component objects if needed.

USING EXTENDED CLIP TO CLIP A RASTER IMAGE TO A CURVED SHAPE

In Chapter 7, you saw how you can clip an Xref or a raster image so that only a portion is visible. One limitation to the Raster Clip option is that you can clip only areas defined by straight lines. You can't, for example, clip an area defined by a circle or an ellipse.

Extended Clip is designed for those instances when you absolutely need to clip a raster image to a curved area. The following steps show you how it works:

1. Create a clip boundary by using a curved polyline or circle.

2. Choose Extended Clip from the expanded Modify panel of the Express Tools tab.

3. Click the boundary.

4. Click the Xref, block, or image you want to clip.

5. At the following prompt, press ↵:

   ```
   Enter maximum allowable error distance for
   resolution of arc segments <7–16″>:
   ```

   The Xref, block, or image clips to the selected boundary.

6. You can erase the boundary you created in step 1 or keep it for future reference.

Extended Clip doesn't really clip to the boundary you created but instead approximates that boundary by creating a true clip boundary with a series of very short line segments. The prompt in step 5 lets you specify the maximum allowable distance between the straight-line segments it generates and the curve of the boundary you create (see Figure 26.3).

FIGURE 26.3
Extended Clip enables you to set the maximum distance from your clip boundary and the one it generates.

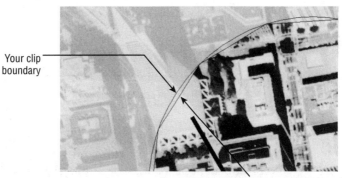

Your clip boundary

The clip boundary produced by Extended Clip

Layout Panel Tools

AutoCAD includes some Express tools that will help make your work with layouts a lot easier. These tools, found in the Layout panel of the Express Tools tab, address some of the more common operations you'll encounter as you work with layouts.

ALIGNING MODEL SPACE OBJECTS WITH LAYOUT OBJECTS

If you've ever tried to align an object in a layout with objects in a Model Space viewport, you know how difficult it can be. This situation often arises when you accidentally pan or zoom a Model Space viewport and objects drawn in Paper Space (such as break lines or dimensional notations) become misaligned with the underlying view.

The Align Space tool helps you quickly align objects in a Model Space viewport with objects in the layout Paper Space. Align Space can even rotate a viewport view to align objects that are at an angle. To see how it works, try the following exercise. You'll align a plan view of a set of survey data points to a north arrow in Paper Space:

1. Open the `alignspace.dwg` sample file.

2. Choose Align Space from the Layout panel. The viewport automatically becomes active.

3. At the FIRST alignment point in MODEL space: prompt, click the upper endpoint of the north arrow in the viewport, as shown in Figure 26.4.

FIGURE 26.4
Select these points to align the Model Space north arrow with a Paper Space north arrow.

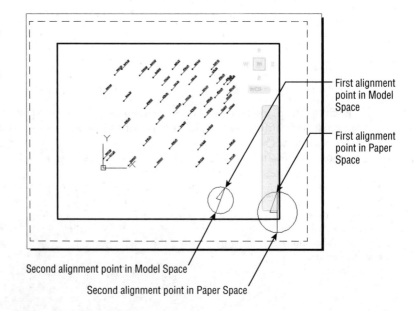

First alignment point in Model Space

First alignment point in Paper Space

Second alignment point in Model Space

Second alignment point in Paper Space

4. At the SECOND point in MODEL space or <Return> for none: prompt, click the endpoint of the bottom end of the north arrow, as shown in Figure 26.4.

5. At the FIRST alignment point in PAPER space: prompt, AutoCAD automatically switches to Paper Space to allow for your next input. Click the upper endpoint of the layout Paper Space north arrow.

6. At the SECOND alignment point in PAPER space: prompt, click the lower end of the Paper Space arrow. The two arrows align, and a message tells you the scale of the viewport.

In this exercise, the two north arrows were aligned in both scale and direction. The object you're aligning to in Paper Space doesn't have to be in the area of the viewport, either.

If you prefer, you can align a single point without changing the scale or rotation of the viewport by pressing ↵ in step 4 when you see the SECOND point in MODEL space or <Return> for none: prompt.

ALIGNING MULTIPLE VIEWPORTS TO A SINGLE VIEWPORT

The Align Space tool lets you align a Model Space object to a Paper Space object—but what if you want to align two Model Space views? For example, suppose you want to overlap two viewports of the same view, with one viewport displaying graphics while the other displays just the power and signal symbols for a small region of the plan.

The Synchronize Viewports tool lets you do just that. It aligns one or more viewports to another *master* viewport. The Synchronize Viewports tool aligns the coordinates in one viewport with the coordinates and scale of another so the views are matched like pieces of a jigsaw puzzle. To get a better idea of what this means, try the following exercise. Suppose you have an enlarged plan showing a portion of a building. You want to include the grid lines in your plan, but you don't want to have to include other portions of the plan or redraw the grids. Synchronize Viewports makes easy work of this project:

1. Open the synchronize.dwg file, and then choose Synchronize Viewports from the Layout panel.

2. Click the border of the viewport in the lower-right corner.

3. At the Select viewports to be aligned to master viewport. Select objects: prompt, click the other two viewports, and press ↵. The two viewports change to show the adjacent areas of the first viewport.

The three views of the layout combine to show a contiguous Plan view instead of three random views (Figure 26.5).

FIGURE 26.5
Synchronizing
three viewports

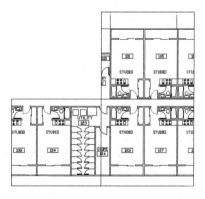

You could use Synchronize Viewports this way to piece together parts of a floor plan in a nonrectangular shape.

To finish adding the grid lines, do the following:

1. Double-click in the top viewport, and then click the Pan tool in the Home tab's Navigate panel.

2. Shift+click and drag the view downward to bring the grid lines into view. Then, Shift+click and drag and keep the pan motion in an exact vertical direction. Pan downward until you see only the grids and dimensions.

3. Press Esc to exit the Pan tool; then double-click the left viewport and use the Pan tool to Shift+click and drag the view toward the right. Keep panning until just the grid lines show (Figure 26.6).

FIGURE 26.6
Pan to see the grid lines.

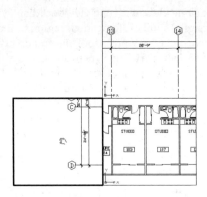

If you've ever tried to do this operation without the aid of the Synchronize Viewports tool, you can see how helpful a tool it is.

FINDING VIEWPORT SCALES AND MERGING LAYOUTS

The Layout panel includes two more fairly simple tools: List Viewport Scale and Merge Layout. List Viewport Scale does just what its name says. Choose List Viewport Scale from the expanded Layout panel, and then click a viewport border to display the viewport scale. Merge Layout combines the contents of one layout with another. This tool is handy if you're exporting files to earlier versions of AutoCAD in which only one layout is possible. Choosing Merge Layouts from the Layout panel opens the LAYOUTMERGE dialog box. This dialog box is a list showing the layouts in the current drawing.

You can select the layout that you want merged with the current layout. After you make your selection and click OK, another dialog box appears that looks identical to the first LAYOUTMERGE dialog box. This time, you select the destination layout for the merged layouts.

That covers the Express layout tools. As with many of the other Express tools, you may find yourself using these tools more than the other standard AutoCAD commands; keep them in mind as you work on the layout of your next set of drawings.

Draw Panel Tools

Two tools offer functions not found in the rest of the AutoCAD program: Break-Line Symbol and Super Hatch. The Break-Line Symbol tool is a very easy-to-use tool that just draws a break line. It is a command-line tool that offers options to use a custom block for the break symbol, adjust the size of the break symbol, or set the extension distance for the break line.

The Super Hatch tool is quite powerful because it allows you to create a custom hatch pattern from just about anything, including image files. This tool is a bit more complicated, so it requires a bit more information to master.

CREATING CUSTOM HATCH PATTERNS WITH SUPER HATCH

You can access a number of hatch patterns from AutoCAD's Hatch And Gradient dialog box, but at times none of those patterns will fulfill your needs. This is where the Super Hatch tool comes in. With Super Hatch, you can create virtually any hatch pattern you want. You can use objects in your drawing as a basis for a hatch pattern, or you can import bitmap images and use them to form a hatch pattern, such as tiled wallpaper in the Windows Desktop background.

The following exercise shows you how to use Super Hatch:

1. Open the superhatch.dwg file. You see a block of an arrow on the left side of the screen and a rectangular area to the right. In this exercise, you'll turn the arrow into a hatch pattern.

2. Click the Super Hatch tool to open the SuperHatch dialog box (Figure 26.7).

3. Click the Select Existing button to close the SuperHatch dialog box.

4. Click the arrow. It becomes highlighted, and a magenta rectangle encircles it.

At this point, you can indicate the area you want repeated in your pattern. The default is the extents of the selected item, as indicated by the magenta rectangle.

5. Click the two points shown in Figure 26.8 to indicate the area that you want repeated. The rectangle changes to reflect the new area. You can repeat the area selection as many times as you need until you get exactly the area you want.

6. Press ↵ to move to the next step.

FIGURE 26.7
The SuperHatch dialog box

FIGURE 26.8
Selecting the area
to be repeated

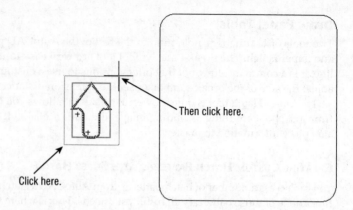

Then click here.

Click here.

7. Click the interior of the rectangle to indicate the area you want to hatch. If you have multiple hatch areas, you can continue to select them at this step.

8. Press ↵ to finish your selection of hatch areas. The arrow appears repeated as a pattern in the rectangle, as shown in Figure 26.9.

FIGURE 26.9
The custom
hatch pattern

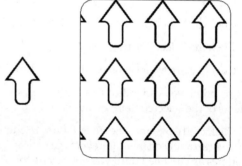

The object you select by using the Select Existing option in the SuperHatch dialog box must be a block. You can modify that block by using the techniques described in Chapter 7 and the changes will appear in the hatch pattern, as shown in Figure 26.10.

FIGURE 26.10
The custom hatch
pattern after the
arrow block has
been modified to
include the diago-
nal hatch pattern

As you can see from the SuperHatch dialog box, you can incorporate Xrefs, blocks, and even image files into your custom hatch pattern. Each of these options prompts you to insert the object before you convert it into a hatch pattern. You use the usual insertion method for the type of object you select. For example, if you choose the Block option, you're prompted for an insertion point, the X and Y scale factors, and a rotation angle. For image files, you see the same dialog box that you see when you insert an image file, offering the options for insertion point, scale, and rotation. Figure 26.11 shows a sample hatch pattern with an image file used instead of an AutoCAD block.

FIGURE 26.11
A custom hatch pattern using a bitmap image

Dimension Panel Tools

Early in AutoCAD's history, the dimension feature was almost like its own program within AutoCAD. A user would have to enter the dimension command, add whatever dimensions were needed, and then exit the dimension command. Dimensioning is much easier now, but it is still a complex feature that can require some additional help from outside the standard dimensioning feature set.

The Dimension panel offers several tools that simplify some of the more common editing tasks for dimensions. The Annotation Attachment flyout offers tools that let you add or remove leaders to annotation. The Reset Dim Text Value tool lets you reset the text of a dimension that has been overridden or otherwise modified.

Perhaps the most frequently used dimension-related tools are the Dimstyle Export and Import tools. Dimstyles can take a fair amount of time to set up, and they contain a lot of settings that would be difficult to remember. If you're moving from one computer to another or from one office to another, the dimstyle tools can save a lot of time and effort.

Using Dimstyle Export and Dimstyle Import

Most AutoCAD users need to set up their dimension styles only once and then make minor alterations for drawing scale. You can set up your dimension styles in a template file and then use that template whenever you create new drawings. That way, your dimension styles will already be set up the way you want them.

But frequently, you'll receive files created by someone else, and they may not have the same ideas about dimension styles as you do. Normally, this would mean you'd have to re-create your favorite settings in a new dimension style. With the Express tools Dimstyle Export and Dimstyle Import options, you can export and import dimension styles at any time, saving you the effort of re-creating them.

Tools Panel Tools

Besides the tools you've seen so far, there are several that don't fit into a neat category. The Tools panel of the Express Tools tab contains a mix of tools that let you do everything from creating and editing your command aliases to creating new line types.

CONTROLLING SHORTCUTS WITH THE COMMAND ALIAS EDITOR

Throughout this book, I've been showing you the keyboard shortcuts to the AutoCAD commands. In Windows, all these shortcuts are stored in a file called acad.pgp in the C:\Documents and Settings*Username*\Application Data\Autodesk\AutoCAD 2011\R18.1\enu\Support folder. (Check the Working Support File Search Path option in the Files tab in the Options dialog box to find the exact location for the support files on your system.) In the past, you had to edit this file with a text editor to modify these command shortcuts (otherwise known as command *aliases*). But to make our lives simpler, Autodesk has supplied the Command Alias Editor, which automates the process of editing, adding, or removing command aliases in AutoCAD.

In addition, the Command Alias Editor lets you store your own alias definitions in a separate file. You can then recall your file to load your own command aliases. Here's how the Command Alias Editor works:

1. Choose Command Aliases from the Tools panel to open the AutoCAD Alias Editor dialog box (Figure 26.12).

FIGURE 26.12
The AutoCAD Alias
Editor dialog box

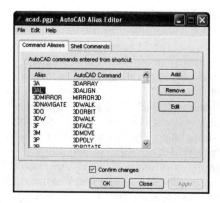

2. As you can see from the button options, you can add, delete, or edit an alias. Click the Add button to open the New Command Alias dialog box (Figure 26.13).

FIGURE 26.13
The New
Command Alias
dialog box

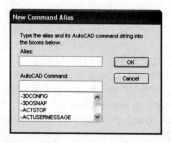

In this dialog box, you enter the desired alias in the Alias input box and then select the command from the AutoCAD Command list box. You can also enter a command or macro name, such as Wipeout, in the input box. When you click the Edit option in the AutoCAD Alias Editor dialog box, you see a dialog box identical to this one with the input boxes already filled in.

3. After you create or edit an alias, click OK to return to the AutoCAD Alias Editor dialog box.

4. Click OK to exit the dialog box. A message tells you that your aliases have been saved and the current AutoCAD session has been updated.

5. Click OK.

If you're a veteran AutoCAD user, you may be accustomed to your own set of command aliases. If so, you may want to create your own PGP file containing just your custom aliases. Then, whenever you use AutoCAD, you can open the AutoCAD Alias Editor, choose File ➤ Import, and load your personal PGP file. From then on, the aliases in your file will be included with those of the standard acad.pgp file.

USING MAKE LINETYPE TO CREATE A CUSTOM LINETYPE

Most of the time, the linetypes provided by AutoCAD are adequate. But if you're looking for that perfect linetype, you can use the Make Linetype tool to create your own. Here's how it works:

1. Open the customltype_completed.dwg sample file. The sample drawing is made up of simple lines with no polylines, arcs, or circles. When you create your own linetype prototype, make sure the lines are all aligned. Draw a single line, and break it to form the segments of the linetype (see Figure 26.14). Also make sure it's drawn to the actual plotted size.

FIGURE 26.14
Creating a custom linetype by using Make Linetype

Click here for the start point.   Click here for the endpoint.

2. Choose Make Linetype from the expanded Tools panel to open the MKLTYPE dialog box. This is a typical save dialog box allowing you to create a new linetype file.

3. Enter **myltype** for the filename, select a location for the file, and then click Save.

4. At the Enter linetype name: prompt, enter **MyLinetype** or any name you want to use for the linetype. The name must be a single word.

5. At the Enter linetype description: prompt, enter a description for your linetype. This can be a sentence that best describes your linetype.

6. At the Specify starting point for line definition: prompt, pick one endpoint of the sample linetype.

7. At the `Specify ending point for line definition:` prompt, pick a point just past the opposite end of the sample linetype. Pick a point past the endpoint of the sample to indicate the gap between the end of the first segment of the linetype and the beginning of the repeating portion, as shown in Figure 26.14.

8. At the `Select objects:` prompt, select the sample linetype lines. When you're done, press ↵. You now have a custom linetype.

If you send your file to someone else, you need to make sure you include your custom linetype files with the drawing file. Otherwise, anything drawn using your custom linetype will appear as a continuous line, and your recipient will get an error message saying that AutoCAD can't find a linetype resource.

The Make Linetype tool creates a single linetype file for each linetype you create. The linetype file is a simple ASCII text file. If you end up making several linetypes, you can combine your linetype files into one file by using a simple text editor such as Windows Notepad. Don't use WordPad or Word because these programs will introduce special codes to the linetype file.

CREATING CUSTOM SHAPES AS AN ALTERNATIVE TO BLOCKS

Shapes are special types of AutoCAD objects that are similar to blocks. They're usually simple symbols made up of lines and arcs. Shapes take up less memory and can be displayed faster, but they're much less flexible than blocks, and they aren't very accurate. You can't use object snaps to snap to specific parts of a shape, nor can you explode shapes. They're best suited for symbols or as components in complex linetypes.

Shapes have always been difficult to create. In the past, you couldn't create a shape by drawing it. You had to create something called a *shape definition* by using a special code. A shape definition is an ASCII file that contains a description of the geometry of the shape. Creating such a file was a tedious, arcane process and few users bothered to do it.

With the introduction of complex linetypes in recent versions of AutoCAD, interest in shapes has revived. To make it easier for users to create shapes, AutoCAD 2011 provides a tool that creates a shape definition file for you based on a line drawing. Try this simple exercise to learn how to create and use a shape:

1. Open the `makeshape.dwg` sample file from the Chapter 26 folder of the sample project files. This file contains a simple drawing of an upward-pointing arrow. It contains lines and arcs.

2. Choose Make Shape from the expanded Tools panel to open the MKSHAPE dialog box. This is a typical save dialog box that enables you to specify a name and location for your shape definition file.

3. In the File Name input box, enter **Arrow**; then, locate the My Documents folder and place your new file there.

4. Click Save to create your file.

5. At the `Enter the name of the shape:` prompt, enter **Arrow**↵.

6. At the `Enter resolution <128>:` prompt, enter **512**↵. Shapes are defined with a square matrix of points. All the endpoints of lines and arcs must be on a point in that matrix. At this prompt, you can define the density of that matrix. A higher density will give you a better-looking shape, but you don't want to get carried away with this setting.

7. At the `Specify insertion base point:` prompt, select the tip of the arrow, as shown in Figure 26.15. This will be the insertion point of your shape, which is similar to the insertion point of a block.

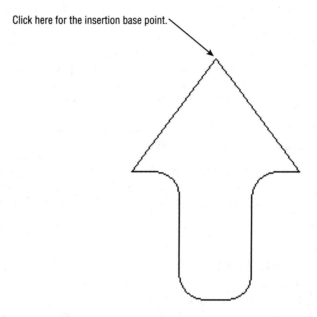

FIGURE 26.15
Creating a shape from an existing drawing

Click here for the insertion base point.

8. At the `Select objects:` prompt, select the entire arrow, and then press ↵.

9. A series of messages tells you what AutoCAD is doing. The next to last message tells you whether AutoCAD was successful in creating the shape file, and it tells you the location and name of the new shape file:

```
Compilation successful.  Output file C:\Documents and Settings\User Name\My
    Documents\Arrow.shx contains 309 bytes.
Shape "ARROW" created.
Use the SHAPE command to place shapes in your drawing.
```

To see how your shape came out, try the following. Here you'll learn how to load and insert a shape:

1. At the Command prompt, type **Load**↵ to open the Select Shape File dialog box. This is a typical file open dialog box.

2. In the `My Documents` folder, locate the file `Arrow.shx`, and click Open to load it.

3. Type **Shape**↵.

4. At the `Enter shape name or [?]:` prompt, type **Arrow**↵. If you've forgotten the name of a shape you're loading, you can enter a question mark (?) to see a listing of available shapes. Now the arrow follows the cursor as you move it across the drawing area.

5. At the `Specify insertion point:` prompt, click to the right of the original arrow.

6. At the Specify height <1.0000>: prompt, press ↵ to accept the default of 1.

7. At the Specify rotation angle: prompt, enter **45**↵. The arrow appears at a 45° angle.

In many ways, a shape acts like a block, but you can't snap to any of its points. It's also less accurate than a block in its representation, although for some applications this may not be a great concern. Finally, you can't use complex shapes such as 3D objects for your shape; you can use only lines and arcs.

Still, you may find shapes useful in your application. As mentioned earlier, you can include shapes in linetype definitions. See "Creating Complex Linetypes" in Chapter 28 for a description of how to create a linetype that includes shapes as part of the line.

CONVERT A SHAPE TO A BLOCK

You may also notice a tool that converts shapes into AutoCAD blocks. Choose Convert Shape To Block from the expanded Modify panel, and then select a shape. A prompt asks for a name for the block. You can accept the default name, which is the same name as the shape you're converting.

ATTACHING DATA TO OBJECTS

This set of options is less likely to get as much use as the others you've looked at so far, so I've included a brief description of them here without going into too much detail. They're fairly easy to use, and you shouldn't have any trouble trying them. You can access both tools from the Tools panel:

Attach Xdata   Lets you attach extended data to objects. Extended data is usually used only by AutoLISP or ARX applications. You're asked to select the object that will receive the data, and then you're asked for an application name that serves as a tag to tell others the name of the person to whom the data belongs. You can then select a data type. After this is done, you can enter your data.

List Object Xdata   Displays extended data that has been attached to an object.

Web Panel Tools

AutoCAD enables you to add URL links to objects. This is a great feature that can help you link drawings to other types of data. The Express Web tools on the Web panel add some enhancements to the URL linking features of AutoCAD:

Show URLs   Displays the URL link attached to an AutoCAD object.

Change URLs   Lets you quickly edit an object's existing URL. You must still choose Insert ➢ Hyperlink to attach a new URL to an object.

Find And Replace URLs   Replaces a set of existing URLs with a URL of your specification.

Tools You Won't Find on the Ribbon

In previous versions of AutoCAD, many of the Express tools could only be found in the menu bar under the Express menu. In AutoCAD 2011, many of those tools do not appear in the Ribbon, but you can still use them by entering their keyboard command names. You can also find these tools in the Express Tools menu if you enable the menu bar (click the Customize The Quick Access Toolbar flyout and select Show Menu Bar). The following section describes these tools along with the keyboard commands you'll need to use them.

USING FILE MANAGEMENT TOOLS

AutoCAD has always made extensive use of external files for its operation. Everything from fonts to keyboard shortcuts depends on external files. The Express File tools offer options to simplify a few file-related operations. You may find some of these tools, such as Save All Drawings and Close All Drawings, helpful on a daily basis. Others may be useful to know about, such as Edit Image when you need to edit an image. The following is a list of these tools:

Move Backup Files (Moveback) Lets you specify a location for AutoCAD BAK files for the current drawing session.

Convert PLT To DWG (Plt2dwg) Converts HPGL plot files to drawing files. You must first set up AutoCAD or Windows for an HPGL plotter and then specify that HPGL plotter in the Plot Or Page Setup dialog box. You must also indicate that you want to plot to a file at the time you produce the plot (select the Plot To File check box in the Printer/Plotter group of the Plot dialog box).

Edit Image (Imageedit) Offers a quick way to open and edit an image file that has been inserted into an AutoCAD drawing. Type **Imageedit↵**, and then select the image you want to edit. A File dialog box opens, showing the file in a list box. Click Open, and the program associated with the image file type will open the image file.

Redefine Path (Redir) Lets you redefine the path to external files that are referenced from the current drawing. This includes Xrefs, images, shapes, styles, and Rtext. You can strip a path from a referenced file by using the asterisk option (*) when you see the Enter old directory (use '*' for all), or ? <options>: prompt. When you see the Replace "*" with: prompt, press ↵. If you strip the path in this way, AutoCAD will use the support file search path specified in the Files tab of the Options dialog box. You can specify the type of external file you want to redefine by pressing ↵ at the first prompt to open the REDIRMODE dialog box. This dialog box contains a simple check box list of the types of support files whose path you want to redefine.

Update Drawing Property Data (Propulate) Drawing property data can be a handy feature of AutoCAD, but using it requires some discipline. (See Chapter 20 for more on drawing property data.) For one thing, the amount of data you must enter can be a bit daunting. The Update Drawing Property Data Express tool offers a way to let you quickly add drawing property data by utilizing property data templates. Drawing property data is often the same for a set of drawings, so you can create a template and apply it to similar drawings in a set by using the Update Drawing Property Data tool.

To create a drawing property data template, type Propulate.↵. At the `Enter an option [Active template/Edit template/List/Remove/Update] <Update>:` prompt, enter E.↵ to open the Edit Propulate Template dialog box (Figure 26.16).

FIGURE 26.16

The Edit Propulate
Template dialog box

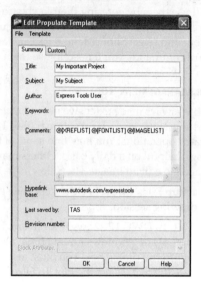

Fill in the data, click OK, and then choose Save As from the Application menu. Use the Update option in the Update Drawing Property Data Command prompt to apply the template to a drawing or to a set of drawings in a folder.

Save All Drawings (Saveall)   Saves all currently open files. The files remain open for additional editing.

Close All Drawings (Closeall)   Closes all currently open drawings. AutoCAD remains open.

Quick Exit (Qquit)   Closes all currently open drawings, and exits AutoCAD. You're asked whether you want to save changes to each file before it's closed.

Revert To Original (Revert)   Causes a drawing to revert to its last saved state. AutoCAD does this by closing the file without saving any changes (since the last Save) and then reopening the file.

USING SELECTION TOOLS

Sometimes it seems that there aren't enough selection tools available in AutoCAD. In Chapter 2, you learned about the various methods you can use to select groups of objects (thereby building a *selection set*, which is a set of objects selected for an operation such as a move or copy). The Express tools offer a few more ways to select objects.

The Get Selection Set tool (Getsel) sets up a selection set based on layers or types of objects. When you type **Getsel**.↵, you're prompted to select an object whose layer contains all the objects you want to select. You can press ↵ to create a selection set of all the objects in the drawing. Next, you're prompted to select an object of the type you want. If you press ↵ at the first prompt and then select a line at the second prompt, all the lines in the drawing will be included in a new selection set. You won't see anything happen on the screen, but the next time you use a command that asks you to select objects, you can enter **P↵** to select the lines.

Another selection tool is Fast Select (Fastsel). When you type **Fastsel↵** in the Command prompt, you're prompted to select an object. After you do so, the object you select plus any object touching it will be selected.

CONTROLLING AND SAVING SYSTEM VARIABLE SETTINGS

With the menu bar open, you can choose Express ➤ Tools ➤ System Variable Editor or enter **Sysvdlg↵** to open the System Variables dialog box. This dialog box gives you control over system variables, which are settings that control nearly all of the options you find in AutoCAD.

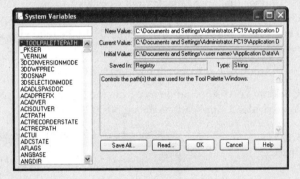

The System Variables dialog box can help you understand what a system variable does by giving you a description in a text panel. You can change the value of system variables, and perhaps more important, you can save settings to an external file using the Save All button. This opens a Save As dialog box that allows you to determine the location and name of your file. AutoCAD adds the .svf filename extension. You can later retrieve system variable settings using the Read button. This can be helpful if you are switching from one PC to another and you want to make sure your AutoCAD settings are the same on the next PC you use.

In addition, you can use the System Variables dialog box to restore all of the default system variable settings. To do this, open the System Variables dialog box and click Read. Using the Open dialog box, navigate to the Express folder, typically found in the C:\Program Files\Autodesk\AutoCAD 2011\ folder, and select the default.svf file. This contains the default system variable settings. AutoCAD may take a few seconds to load the file. When finished, click OK.

Putting AutoLISP to Work

Most high-end CAD packages offer a macro or programming language to help users customize their systems. AutoCAD has *AutoLISP*, which is a pared-down version of the popular LISP artificial intelligence language.

Don't let AutoLISP scare you. In many ways, an AutoLISP program is just a set of AutoCAD commands that help you build your own features. The only difference is that you have to follow a different set of rules when using AutoLISP. But this isn't so unusual. After all, you had to learn some basic rules about using AutoCAD commands too—how to start commands, for instance, and how to use command options.

If the thought of using AutoLISP is a little intimidating, bear in mind that you don't need substantial computer knowledge to use this tool. In the following sections, you'll see how to get AutoLISP to help out in your everyday editing tasks, without having to learn the entire programming language.

Loading and Running an AutoLISP Program

Many AutoCAD users have discovered the usefulness of AutoLISP through the thousands of free AutoLISP utilities that are available from websites and online services. It's common for users to maintain a toolbox of their favorite utilities on a disk. But before you can use these utilities, you need to know how to load them into AutoCAD. In the following exercise, you'll load and use a sample AutoLISP utility:

1. Start AutoCAD, and open the 26-unit.dwg file.

2. Click the Load Application tool from the Manage tab's Applications panel to open the Load/Unload Applications dialog box (Figure 26.17).

FIGURE 26.17
The Load/Unload Applications dialog box

3. Locate and select the GETAREA.LSP file that is included with the Chapter 26 sample files.

4. Click the Load button. The message GETAREA.LSP successfully loaded appears in the message box at the bottom of the dialog box. If you scroll down the list in the Loaded Applications tab, you also see GETAREA.lsp listed there, which tells you that it's loaded.

5. Click Close to close the Load/Unload Applications dialog box.

6. Enter **getarea**⏎.

7. At the Pick point inside area to be calculated: prompt, click inside the unit plan.

8. At the Select location for area note: prompt, pick a point just above the door to the balcony.

9. At the Select location for area note: prompt, click to place the area note. A label appears, displaying the area of the room in square feet.

You've just loaded and used an AutoLISP utility. As you saw in the Load/Unload Applications dialog box, you can load and try several other utilities. Next, you'll look more closely at the Load/Unload Applications dialog box.

Managing Your AutoLISP Library

The Load/Unload Applications dialog box gives you plenty of flexibility in managing your favorite AutoLISP utilities. You can also manage your ARX applications. As you saw in the previous exercise, you can easily find and select utilities by using this dialog box. If you often use a custom application, you can include it in the History List tab of the Load/Unload Applications dialog box, as you'll see in the following steps:

1. Click the Load Application tool from the Manage tab's Applications panel to open the Load/Unload Applications dialog box.

2. Select the Add To History check box.

3. Click the History List tab.

4. Select GETAREA.LSP from the list of applications at the top of the dialog box.

5. Click Load. GETAREA.LSP now appears in the History List tab (Figure 26.18).

6. Click Close to close the Load/Unload Applications dialog box.

FIGURE 26.18
The utility
now shows up
in the list.

Now when you exit AutoCAD, the dialog box retains the name of the GETAREA.LSP utility in the History List tab. When you want to load GETAREA.LSP in a future session, you won't have to hunt it down. You can highlight it in the History List tab and then load it from there. You can add as many items as you want to your History List tab or remove items by highlighting them and clicking the Remove button. The History List tab works with all types of applications that AutoCAD supports.

WHAT HAPPENED TO VBA?

Microsoft no longer supports Visual Basic for Applications (VBA) in its newest operating systems, so Autodesk will be fazing out VBA support in AutoCAD. If you have VBA applications that you use with AutoCAD, you'll need to port them over to .NET.

Loading AutoLISP Programs Automatically

As you start to build a library of AutoLISP applications, you may find that you use some of them all the time. You can set up AutoCAD to load your favorite applications automatically. To do this, you use the Startup Suite in the Load/Unload Applications dialog box:

1. Choose Load Application from the Manage tab's Applications panel to open the Load/Unload Applications dialog box.

2. Click the Contents button or the suitcase icon in the Startup Suite group to open the Startup Suite dialog box. This dialog box contains a list box that shows any applications that are to be started whenever AutoCAD starts. You add applications with the Add button at the bottom. If there are applications in the list, you can use the Remove button to remove them.

3. Click the Add button to open the Add File To Startup Suite dialog box. This is a typical file open dialog box that enables you to search for and select a file.

4. Locate and select the GETAREA.LSP file in the Chapter 26 folder and click Add. The Startup Suite dialog box reappears and GETAREA.LSP is listed.

5. Click Close, and then click Close again in the Load/Unload Applications dialog box.

From now on, GETAREA.LSP will be loaded automatically whenever you start AutoCAD. You can add several files to the Startup Suite list.

Creating Keyboard Macros with AutoLISP

You can write simple AutoLISP programs of your own that create what are called keyboard macros. *Macros*—like script files—are strings of predefined keyboard entries. They're invaluable for shortcuts to commands and options you use frequently. For example, you might often use the Break command to break an object at a single point while editing a particular drawing. Here's a way you can turn this operation into a macro:

1. Close the 26-unit.dwg file without saving it, and then open it again and enter the following text at the Command prompt. Be sure you enter the line exactly as shown here. If you make

a mistake while entering this line, you can use the I-beam cursor or arrow keys to go to the location of your error to fix it:

```
(defun C:breakat () (command "break" pause "f" pause "@")).⎦
```

2. Enter **breakat**.⎦ at the Command prompt. The Break command starts, and you're prompted to select an object.

3. Click the wall on the right side of the unit.

4. At the Specify first break point: prompt, click a point on the wall where you want to create a break, and make sure osnaps are turned off.

5. To see the result of the break, click the wall again. It's been split into two lines, as shown in Figure 26.19.

FIGURE 26.19
With the grips exposed, you can see that the wall is split into two lines.

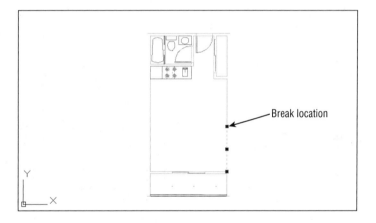

Break location

You've just written and run your first AutoLISP macro! Let's take a closer look at this simple program (see Figure 26.20). It starts with an opening parenthesis, as do all AutoLISP programs, followed by the word defun. Defun is an AutoLISP function that lets you create commands; it's followed by the name you want to give the command (Breakat, in this case). The command name is preceded by C:, telling defun to make this command accessible from the Command prompt. If the C: were omitted, you would have to start Breakat by using parentheses, as in (Breakat).

After the command name is a set of opening and closing parentheses. This set encloses what is called the *argument list*. The details aren't important; just be aware that these parentheses must follow the command name.

Finally, a list of words follows enclosed by another set of parentheses. This list starts with the word command. Command is an AutoLISP function that tells AutoLISP that whatever follows should be entered just like regular keyboard input. Only one item in the Breakat macro—the word pause—isn't part of the keyboard input series. Pause is an AutoLISP function that tells AutoLISP to pause for input. In this particular macro, AutoLISP pauses to let you pick an object to break and the location for the break.

Most of the items in the macro are enclosed in quotation marks. Literal keyboard input must be enclosed in quotation marks this way. The pause function, on the other hand, doesn't require quotation marks because it's a proper function, one that AutoLISP can recognize.

FIGURE 26.20
Breakdown of the
Breakat macro

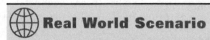

(DEFUN c:breakat ( ) (command "break" pause "f" pause "@"))

AutoLISP function
to define a command.

Name of command.

Argument list.

AutoLISP function
to issue standard
AutoCAD commands.

AutoCAD Break command.

AutoLISP function to pause
for user input.

F is entered to allow the
selection of a break point.

Keyboard input.

Another pause so the user
can select a break point.

The @ sign is entered
to select the last point
again for the break.

The program ends with a closing parenthesis. All parentheses in an AutoLISP program must be in balanced pairs, so these final two parentheses close the opening parenthesis at the start of the command function as well as the opening parenthesis back at the beginning of the defun function.

🌐 Real World Scenario

YOUR PORTABLE TOOLKIT

I've mentioned in earlier chapters that AutoCAD users tend to be quite attached to their keyboard shortcuts. One of the more popular methods I've seen for transporting keyboard shortcuts is to store them in an AutoLISP file that can be easily installed on a PC. An AutoLISP file is compact and easily stored in a USB flash drive or media player. If you use this method, just make sure your IT manager is OK with it.

Storing AutoLISP Macros as Files

When you create a program at the Command prompt, as you did with the Breakat macro, AutoCAD remembers it only until you exit the current file. Unless you want to re-create this macro the next time you use AutoCAD, save it by copying it into an ASCII text file with an .lsp filename extension using the Windows Notepad application. Figure 26.21 shows a file named Keycad.lsp, which contains the saved Breakat macro along with some other macros I use often.

FIGURE 26.21
The contents of Keycad.lsp

```
Keycad.lsp - Notepad
File  Edit  Format  View  Help
(defun c:bpt   () (COMMAND "break" PAUSE "f" PAUSE "@"))
(defun c:ard   () (COMMAND "arc" pause "e" pause "d"))
(defun c:fzr   () (COMMAND "fillet" "r" "0" "fillet"))
(defun c:ptx   () (COMMAND "pdmode" "3"))
```

The other macros are commands that include optional responses. For example, the third item, defun c:fzr, causes AutoCAD to start the Fillet command, enter an **R.** to issue the Radius option, and finally enter a **0** for the fillet radius. Use the Windows Notepad application and enter the macros listed in Figure 26.21. Give this file the name Keycad.lsp, and be sure you save it as an ASCII file. Then, whenever you want to use these macros, you don't have to load each one individually. Instead, you load the Keycad.lsp file the first time you want to use one of the macros, and they're all available for the rest of the session.

After the file is loaded, you can use any of the macros in it by entering the macro name. For example, entering **ptx.** sets the point style to the shape of an X.

Macros loaded in this manner are available to you until you exit AutoCAD. Of course, you can have these macros loaded automatically every time you start AutoCAD by including the Keycad.lsp file in the Startup Suite of the Load/Unload Applications dialog box. That way, you don't have to remember to load it in order to use the macros.

Now that you have some firsthand experience with AutoLISP, I hope these examples will encourage you to try learning more about this powerful tool.

Record and Play Back Actions

If AutoLISP seems a bit too intimidating but you still need a way to automate certain tasks, the Action Recorder is a feature you'll want to explore. The Action Recorder enables you to record a series of actions in AutoCAD and store them as *action macros*. You can play back your action macros at any time. This is a great time-saver when you are performing repetitive tasks, something that you may find yourself doing frequently in AutoCAD.

An entire panel is devoted to the Action Recorder in the Manage tab.

To use the Action Recorder, click the Record button. The Record button changes to a Stop button, and a red dot appears next to the cursor to remind you that you are recording your activity. You'll also see the Action Tree appear just below the recorder.

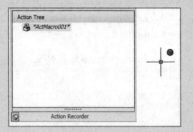

Proceed to work as you normally would in AutoCAD. As you work, your activity is displayed in the Action Tree. When you've completed the activity that you want to record, press the Stop button. The Action Macro dialog box appears, enabling you to give the recorded activity a name and description.

Once you've closed the Action Macro dialog box, you can play back your recorded action macro at any time. From the Action Recorder panel, select the macro name from the Available Action Macro drop-down list and then click Play.

The Action Tree enables you to include some interactivity in your macro. You can right-click on an individual action in the Action Tree to modify its behavior to allow user input. Perhaps the most common modification you'll want to make is to allow different selections or to change coordinate input and point selections. To do this, right-click on an action and select Pause For User Input.

Upon selecting this option, you will be prompted for input when this particular action comes up in the macro. You can also use the Insert User Message option to have a message display while the macro is running. Messages can be helpful for users who are unfamiliar with your macro.

The Bottom Line

Use enhancements straight from the source.   The Express tools have been around for a while and were originally intended to show what could be done with customization. Many users have come to rely on some of these tools.

Master It   In which panel will you find the Align Space tool?

Put AutoLISP to work.   AutoLISP is a macro language that gives you the ability to create your own commands.

Master It   Name the filename extension for AutoLISP programs.

Chapter 27

Exploring AutoLISP

In the previous chapter, you were introduced to AutoLISP, AutoCAD's macro and programming language. You learned that you can take advantage of this powerful tool without having to know anything about its internal workings. In this chapter, you'll see how you can take more control of AutoLISP and have it do the things you want to do for your own AutoCAD environment. You'll learn how to store information such as text and point coordinates, how to create smart macros, and how to optimize AutoLISP's operation on your computer system.

A word of advice as you begin this chapter: Be prepared to spend lots of time with your computer—not because programming in AutoLISP is all that difficult, but because it's so addicting! You've already seen how easy it is to use AutoLISP programs. I won't pretend that learning to program in AutoLISP is just as easy as using it, but it isn't as hard as you may think. Once you've created your first program, you'll be hooked. Note that AutoLISP is not available in AutoCAD LT.

In this chapter you'll learn to do the following:

- ◆ Understand the interpreter
- ◆ Use arguments and expressions
- ◆ Create a simple program
- ◆ Select objects with AutoLISP
- ◆ Control the flow of an AutoLISP program
- ◆ Convert data types
- ◆ Store your programs as files

Understanding the Interpreter

You access AutoLISP through the AutoLISP *interpreter*, which is a little like a handheld calculator. When you enter information at the Command prompt, the interpreter *evaluates* it and then returns an answer. *Evaluating* means performing the instructions described by the information you provide. You could say that evaluation means "find the value of." The information you give the interpreter is like a formula, called an *expression* in AutoLISP.

Let's examine the interpreter's workings in more detail:

1. Start AutoCAD, open a new file, and save it as Temp27a. You'll use this file just to experiment with AutoLISP.

2. At the Command prompt, enter **(+ 2 2)**↵ and make sure you include a space between the characters in the parentheses. The answer, 4, appears in the Command window. AutoLISP has *evaluated* the formula (+ 2 2) and returned the answer, 4.

By entering information this way, you can perform calculations or even write short programs on the fly.

The plus sign you used in step 2 represents a *function*, an instruction telling the AutoLISP interpreter what to do. In many ways, it's like an AutoCAD command. A simple example of a function is the math function Add, represented by the plus sign. AutoLISP has many built-in functions, and you can create many of your own.

Defining Variables with *Setq*

Another calculator-like capability of the interpreter is its ability to remember values. You probably have a calculator that has some memory. This capability allows you to store the value of an equation for future use. In a similar way, the AutoLISP interpreter lets you store values using variables.

A *variable* is like a container that holds a value. That value can change many times in the course of a program's operation. You assign values to variables by using the Setq function. For example, let's assign the numeric value 1.618 to a variable named Golden. This value, often referred to as the *golden section*, is the ratio of a rectangular area's height to its width. Aside from having some interesting mathematical properties, the golden section is said to represent a ratio that occurs frequently in nature. Follow these steps:

1. At the Command prompt, enter **(setq Golden 1.618)**↵. The value 1.618 appears just below the line you enter. The value of the Golden variable is now set to 1.618. Let's check it to make sure.

2. Enter **!Golden**↵ at the Command prompt. As expected, the value 1.618 appears at the prompt.

The exclamation point (!) acts as a special character that extracts the value of an AutoLISP variable at the prompt. From now until you close the drawing, you can access the value of Golden at any time by preceding the variable name with an exclamation point.

In addition to using math formulas as responses to prompts, you can use values stored as variables. Let's see how you can use the variable Golden as the radius for a circle:

1. Click the Circle button on the Draw toolbar.

2. At the Specify center point: prompt, pick a point in the center of your screen.

3. At the **Specify radius of circle or [Diameter]:** prompt, enter !Golden↵. A circle appears with the radius 1.618. Check this using the Properties palette (see Figure 27.1).

Numbers aren't the only things that you can store using Setq. Let's look at the variety of other data types that variables can represent.

Understanding Data Types

Understanding the various data types and how they differ is important because they can be a source of confusion if not carefully used. Remember that you can't mix data types in most operations, and quotes and parentheses must always be used in opening and closing pairs.

FIGURE 27.1

The circle, using the Golden variable as the radius

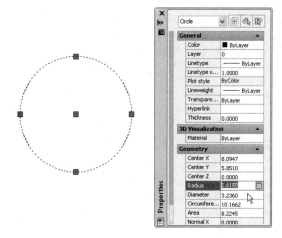

Variables are divided into several categories called *data types*. Categorizing data into types lets AutoLISP determine precisely how to evaluate the data and keep programs running quickly. Your computer has different ways of storing various types of data, so the use of data types helps AutoLISP communicate with the computer more efficiently. Also, data types aid your programming efforts by forcing you to think of data as having certain characteristics. The following list describes each of the available data types:

Integers   Integers are whole numbers. When a mathematical expression contains only integers, only an integer is returned. For example, the expression

```
(/ 2 3)
```

means two divided by three. (The forward slash is the symbol for the division function.) This expression returns the value 0 because the answer is less than 1. Integers are best suited for counting and numbering. The numbers 1, −12, and 144 are all integers.

Real numbers   Real numbers, often referred to as *reals*, are numbers that include decimals. When a mathematical expression contains a real number, a real number is returned. For example, the expression

```
(/ 2.0 3)
```

returns the value 0.66667. Real numbers are best suited in situations that require accuracy. Examples of real numbers are 0.1, 3.14159, and −2.2.

Strings   Strings are text values. They're always enclosed in double quotes. Here are some examples of strings: `"1"`, `"George"`, and `"Enter a value"`.

Lists   Lists are groups of values enclosed in parentheses. Lists provide a convenient way to store whole sets of values in one variable. There are two classes of lists: those meant to be evaluated and those intended as repositories for data. In the strictest sense, AutoLISP programs are lists because they're enclosed in parentheses. Here are some examples of lists: `(6.0 1.0 0.0)`, `(A B C D)`, and (setq golden 1.618).

Elements There are two basic elements in AutoLISP: *atoms* and *lists*. I've already described lists. An atom is an element that can't be taken apart. Atoms are further grouped into two categories: *numbers* and *symbols*. A number can be a real number or an integer. A symbol, on the other hand, is often a name given to a variable, such as `point1` or `dx2`. A number can be used as part of a symbol's name; however, its name must always start with a letter. Think of a symbol as a name given to a variable or function as a means of identifying it.

Using Arguments and Functions

In the previous exercise, you used the `Setq` function to store variables. The way you used `Setq` is typical of all functions.

Functions act on *arguments* to accomplish a task. An argument can be a symbol, a number, or a list. A simple example of a function acting on numbers is the addition of 0.618 and 2. In AutoLISP, this function is entered as

```
(+ 0.618 2)
```

and returns the value 2.618.

This formula—the function followed by the arguments—is called an *expression*. It starts with the left (opening) parenthesis, then the function, then the arguments, and finally the right (closing) parenthesis.

Arguments can also be *expressions*. An expression is a list that contains a function and arguments for that function. You can *nest* expressions. For example, here is how to assign the value returned by 0.618 + 2 to the variable `Golden`:

```
(setq Golden (+ 0.618 2))
```

This is called a *nested expression*. Whenever expressions are nested, the deepest nest is evaluated first, then the next deepest, and so on. In this example, the expression adding 0.618 to 2 is evaluated first. On the next level out, `setq` assigns the result of the expression (+ 0.168 2) to the variable `Golden`.

Arguments to functions can also be variables. For example, suppose you use `setq` to assign the value 25.4 to a variable called `Mill`. You can then find the result of dividing `Mill` by `Golden`, as follows:

1. Enter **(setq Mill 25.4)**⏎ to create a new variable called `Mill`.

2. Enter **(/ Mill Golden)**⏎. (As mentioned earlier, the forward slash is the symbol for the division function.) This returns the value 15.6984. You can assign this value to yet another variable.

3. Enter **(setq B (/ Mill Golden))**⏎ to create a new variable, B. Now you have three variables, `Golden`, `Mill`, and B, which are all assigned values that you can later retrieve, either in an AutoCAD command (by entering an ! followed by the variable) or as arguments in an expression.

Using Text Variables with AutoLISP

The examples so far have shown only numbers being manipulated, but you can manipulate text in a similar way. Variables can be assigned text strings that can later be used to enter values in commands requiring text input. For text variables, you must enclose text in quotation marks, as in the following example:

```
(setq text1 "This is how text looks in AutoLISP")
```

This example shows a sentence being assigned to the variable `text1`.

Strings can also be *concatenated*, or joined together, to form new strings. Here is an example of how two pieces of text can be added together:

```
(setq text2 (strcat "This is the first part and " "this is the second part"))
```

Here, the AutoLISP function `strcat` is used to join the two strings. The result is as follows:

```
"This is the first part and this is the second part"
```

Strings and numeric values can't be evaluated together, however. This may seem like a simple rule, but if not carefully considered, it can lead to confusion. For example, it's possible to assign the number 1 to a variable as a text string, by entering this:

```
(setq foo "1")
```

Later, you may accidentally try to add this string variable to an integer or real number and AutoCAD will return an error message.

The `Setq` and the addition and division functions are but three of many functions available to you. AutoLISP offers all the usual math functions, plus many others used to test and manipulate variables. Table 27.1 shows some commonly used math functions.

WATCHING PARENTHESES AND QUOTES

You must remember to close all sets of parentheses when using nested expressions. Take the same care to enter the second quote in each pair of quotes used to enclose a string.

If you get the prompt showing a parenthesis or set of parentheses followed by the > symbol, such as

```
(_>
```

then you know you have an incomplete AutoLISP expression. This is the AutoLISP prompt. The number of parentheses in the prompt indicates how many parentheses are missing in your expression. If you see this prompt, you must type the closing parenthesis the number of times indicated by the number. AutoCAD won't evaluate an AutoLISP program that has the wrong number of parentheses or quotes.

TABLE 27.1:   Math functions available in AutoLISP

OPERATION	EXAMPLE
Add	(+ *number number*)
Subtract	(- *number number*)

TABLE 27.1: Math functions available in AutoLISP *(CONTINUED)*

OPERATION	EXAMPLE
Multiply	(* number number)
Divide	(/ number number)
Find largest number in list	(Max number number)
Find smallest number in list	(Min number number)
Find the remainder of a division	(Rem number number)
Add 1 to *number*	(1+ number)
Subtract 1 from *number*	(1- number)
Find the absolute value of *number*	(Abs number)
Arc tangent of *angle*	(Atan angle in radians)
Cosine of *angle*	(Cos angle in radians)
e raised to the nth power	(Exp n)
Number raised to the *n*th power	(Expt number n)
Greatest common denominator	(Gcd integer integer)
Natural log of *number*	(Log number)
Sine of *angle*	(Sin angle in radians)
Square root of *number*	(Sqrt number)

Storing Points as Variables

Like numeric values, point coordinates can also be stored and retrieved. But because coordinates are sets of two or three numeric values, they have to be handled differently. AutoLISP provides the Getpoint function to handle the acquisition of points. Try the following to see how it works:

1. At the Command prompt, enter **(getpoint)**↵. The Command prompt goes blank momentarily.

2. Pick a point near the middle of the screen. In the prompt area, you see the coordinate of the point you picked.

Here, Getpoint pauses AutoCAD and waits for you to pick a point. Once you do, it returns the coordinate of the point you pick in the form of a list. The list shows the X, Y, and Z axes enclosed by parentheses.

You can store the coordinates obtained from `Getpoint` using the `Setq` function. Try the following:

1. Enter **(setq point1 (getpoint))**↵.

2. Pick a point on the screen.

3. Enter **!point1**↵.

Here you stored a coordinate list in a variable called `point1`. You then recalled the contents of `point1` using the `!`. The value of the coordinate is in the form of a list with the X, Y, and Z values appearing as real numbers separated by spaces instead of the commas you've been used to.

Creating a Simple Program

So far, you've learned how to use AutoLISP to do simple math and to store values as variables. Certainly, AutoLISP has enormous value with these capabilities alone, but you can do a good deal more. In this section, you'll examine how to combine these three capabilities—math calculations, variables, and lists—to write a program for drawing a rectangle:

1. Press F2 to flip to a text display.

2. At the Command prompt, enter **(defun c:rec ()**↵. You get a new prompt that looks like this:

   ```
   (_>
   ```

   This is the AutoLISP prompt. It tells you, among other things, that you're in the AutoLISP interpreter. While you see this prompt, you can enter instructions to AutoLISP. You'll automatically exit the interpreter when you have finished entering the program. A program is considered complete when you've entered the last parenthesis, thereby balancing all the parentheses in your program.

3. Very carefully enter the following several lines. If you make a mistake while typing a line, use the arrow keys to navigate to the location of the error, and then highlight and correct the error. Each time you enter a line and press ↵, you'll see the AutoLISP prompt appear. Once you've entered the final closing parenthesis, you can't go back to fix a line:

   ```
   (setq Pt1 (getpoint "Pick first corner point:" ))↵
   (setq Pt3 (getpoint "Pick opposite corner:" ))↵
   (setq Pt2 (list (nth 0 Pt3) (nth 1 Pt1)))↵
   (setq Pt4 (list (nth 0 Pt1) (nth 1 Pt3)))↵
   (command "Pline" Pt1 Pt2 Pt3 Pt4 "C")↵
   ) ↵
   ```

AUTOLISP ISN'T CASE SENSITIVE

It doesn't matter if you type entries in uppercase or lowercase letters; AutoLISP will work either way. The only time you must be careful with uppercase and lowercase is when you use string data types.

Once you enter the last parenthesis, you return to the standard AutoCAD Command prompt.

4. Check the lines you entered against the listing in step 3, and make sure you entered everything correctly. If you find a mistake, start over from the beginning and reenter the program.

USE AUTOLISP WHILE PERFORMING OTHER FUNCTIONS

You can use AutoLISP programs transparently, as long as the program doesn't contain an embedded AutoCAD command.

When you're done, you get the message C:REC. This confirms that the rectangle-drawing program is stored in memory. Let's see it in action:

1. Enter **Rec⏎** at the Command prompt.

2. At the Pick first corner point: prompt, pick a point at coordinate 1,1.

3. At the Pick opposite corner: prompt, pick a point at 6,4. A box appears between the two points you picked (see Figure 27.2).

FIGURE 27.2
Using the rectangle-drawing program

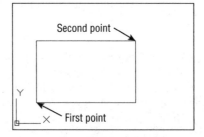

Dissecting the Rectangle Program

The rectangle-drawing program incorporates all the things you've learned so far. Let's see how it works. First, it finds the two corner coordinates of a rectangle, which it gets from you as input; then, it extracts parts of those coordinates to derive the coordinates for the other two corners of the rectangle. Once it knows all four coordinates, the program can draw the lines connecting them. Figure 27.3 illustrates what the rec program does. Next, we'll look at the program in more detail.

GETTING INPUT FROM THE USER

In the previous exercise, you started with the following line:

```
(defun c:rec ()
```

You may recall from Chapter 26 that the defun function lets you create commands. The name that follows the defun function is the name of the command as you enter it through the keyboard. The c: tells AutoLISP to make this program act like a command. If the c: was omitted, you'd have to enter (rec) to view the program. The set of empty parentheses is for an argument list, which I'll discuss later.

In the next line, the variable `Pt1` is assigned a value for a point you enter using your cursor. `Getpoint` is the AutoLISP function that pauses the AutoLISP program and allows you to pick a point using your cursor or to enter a coordinate. Once a point is entered, `Getpoint` returns the coordinate of that point as a list.

Immediately following `Getpoint` is a line that reads as follows:

```
"Pick first corner point:"
```

`Getpoint` allows you to add a prompt in the form of text. You may recall that when you first used `Getpoint`, it caused the prompt to go blank. Instead of a blank, you can use text as an argument to the `Getpoint` function to display a prompt describing what action to take.

The third line is similar to the second. It uses `Getpoint` to get the location of another point and then assigns that point to the variable `Pt3`:

```
(setq Pt3 (getpoint "Pick opposite corner:" ))
```

Once AutoLISP has the two corners, it has all the information it needs to find the other two corners of the rectangle.

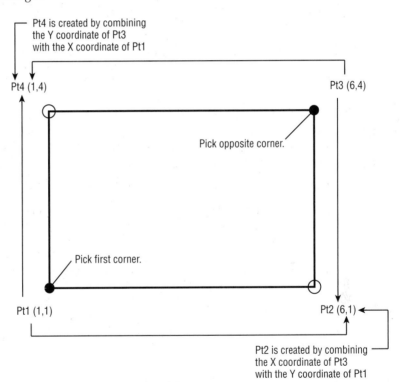

FIGURE 27.3

The rec program draws a rectangle by getting two corner points of the rectangle from you and then recombining coordinates from those two points to find the other two points of the rectangle.

Pt4 is created by combining the Y coordinate of Pt3 with the X coordinate of Pt1

Pt4 (1,4)   Pt3 (6,4)

Pick opposite corner.

Pick first corner.

Pt1 (1,1)   Pt2 (6,1)

Pt2 is created by combining the X coordinate of Pt3 with the Y coordinate of Pt1

TAKING LISTS APART

The next thing AutoLISP must do is take apart `Pt1` and `Pt3` to extract their X and Y coordinates and then reassemble those coordinates to get the other corner coordinates. AutoLISP must take the

X coordinate from Pt3 and the Y coordinate from Pt1 to get the coordinate for the lower-right corner of the rectangle (see Figure 27.3). To do this, you use two new functions: Nth and List.

The nth function extracts a single element from a list. Because coordinates are lists, nth can be used to extract an X, Y, or Z component from a coordinate list. In the fourth line of the program, you see this:

```
(nth 0 Pt3)
```

Here the zero immediately following the Nth function tells Nth to take element number 0 from the coordinate stored as Pt3. Nth starts counting from 0 rather than 1, so the first element of Pt3 is considered item number 0. This is the X component of the coordinate stored as Pt3.

To see how Nth works, try the following:

1. Enter **!point1**↵. You see the coordinate list you created earlier using Getpoint.

2. Enter **(nth 0 point1)**↵. You get the first element of the coordinate represented by point1.

Immediately following the first Nth expression is another Nth expression similar to the previous one:

```
(nth 1 Pt1)
```

Here, Nth extracts element number 1, the second element, from the coordinate stored as Pt1. This is the Y component of the coordinate stored as Pt1. If you like, try the previous exercise again, but this time, enter **(nth 1 point1)** and see what value you get.

COMBINING ELEMENTS INTO A LIST

AutoLISP has extracted the X component from Pt3 and the Y component of Pt1. They must now be joined together into a new list. This is where the List function comes in. The List expression looks like this:

```
(list (nth 0 pt3) (nth 1 pt1))
```

You know that the first Nth expression extracts an X component and that the second extracts a Y component, so the expression can be simplified to look like this:

```
(list X Y)
```

Here X is the value derived from the first Nth expression, and Y is the value derived from the second Nth expression. The List function recombines its arguments into another list, in this case another coordinate list.

Finally, the outermost function of the expression uses Setq to create a new variable called Pt2, which is the new coordinate list derived from the List function. The following is a schematic version of the fourth line of the rec program so you can see what is going on more clearly:

```
(setq pt2 (list X Y))
```

Pt2 is a coordinate list derived from combining the X component from Pt3 and the Y component from Pt1.

Try the following exercise to see how List works:

1. Enter **(list 5 6)**↵. The list (5 6) appears in the prompt.

2. Enter **(list (nth 0 point1) (nth 1 point1))**↵. The X and Y coordinates of point1 appear in a list, excluding the Z coordinate.

The fifth line is similar to the fourth. It creates a new coordinate list using the X value from Pt1 and the Y value from Pt2:

```
(setq Pt4 (list (nth 0 Pt1) (nth 1 Pt3)))
```

The next to last line tells AutoCAD to draw a polyline through the four points to create a box:

```
(command "Pline" Pt1 Pt2 Pt3 Pt4 "C")
```

The Command function issues the Pline command and then inputs the variables Pt1 through Pt4. Finally, it enters C to close the polyline. Note that in this expression, keystroke entries, such as "Pline" and "C", are enclosed in quotes.

At the very end, the single parenthesis balances the very first parenthesis in the first line. Remember that the parentheses have to be balanced.

GETTING OTHER INPUT FROM THE USER

In your rec program, you prompted the user to pick some points by using the Getpoint function. Several other functions allow you to pause for input and tell the user what to do. Nearly all these functions begin with the Get prefix.

Table 27.2 shows a list of these Get functions. They accept single values or, in the case of points, a list of two values.

In Getstring, string values are case sensitive. This means that if you enter a lowercase letter in response to Getstring, it's saved as a lowercase letter; uppercase letters are saved as uppercase letters. You can enter numbers in response to the Getstring function, but they're saved as strings and can't be used in mathematical operations. Also, AutoLISP automatically adds quotes to string values it returns, so you don't have to enter any.

TABLE 27.2: Functions that pause to allow input

FUNCTION	DESCRIPTION
Getint	Allows entry of integer values.
Getreal	Allows entry of real values.
Getstring	Allows entry of string or text values.
Getkword	Allows filtering of string entries through a list of keywords.
Getangle	Allows keyboard or mouse entry of angles based on the standard AutoCAD compass points (returns values in radians).

TABLE 27.2: Functions that pause to allow input *(CONTINUED)*

FUNCTION	DESCRIPTION
Getorient	Allows keyboard or mouse entry of angles based on the Units command setting for angles (returns values in radians).
Getdist	Allows keyboard or mouse entry of distances (always returns values as real numbers, regardless of the unit format used).
Getpoint	Allows keyboard or mouse entry of point values (returns values as coordinate lists).
Getcorner	Allows selection of a point by using a window.*
Initget	Allows definition of a set of keywords for the Getkword function; keywords are strings, as in (initget " Yes No ").

This function requires a base point value as a first argument. This base point defines the first corner of the window. A window appears, allowing you to select the opposite corner.

Just as with Getpoint, all these Get functions allow you to create a prompt by following the function with the prompt enclosed by quotation marks, as in the following expression:

```
(getpoint "Pick the next point:" )
```

This expression displays the prompt Pick the next point: while AutoCAD waits for your input.

The functions Getangle, Getorient, Getdist, Getcorner, and Getpoint let you specify a point from which the angle, distance, or point is to be measured, as in the following expression:

```
(getangle Pt1 "Pick the next point:" )
```

Here, Pt1 is a previously defined point variable. A rubber-banding line appears from the coordinate defined by Pt1 (see Figure 27.4).

Once you pick a point, the angle defined by Pt1 and the point you pick are returned in radians. You can also enter a relative coordinate through the keyboard in the unit system currently being used in your drawing. Getangle and Getdist prompt you for two points if a point variable isn't provided. Getcorner always requires a point argument and generates a window rather than a rubber-banding line (see Figure 27.5).

FIGURE 27.4
Using Getangle

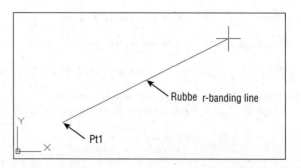

Rubbe r-banding line

Pt1

FIGURE 27.5
Using Getcorner

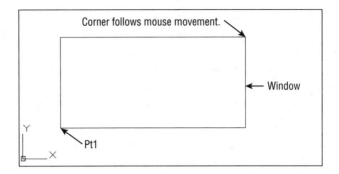

Selecting Objects with AutoLISP

You can easily create an AutoLISP expression that lets you select a single object and perform an operation on it. Here is an example of a macro that rotates an object 90°:

```
(defun c:r90 () (command "rotate" pause "" pause "90"))
```

In this example, the `pause` after `"rotate"` allows you to make a selection. The double quotes that follow act like an ↲, and then another pause lets you select a rotation point. Finally, 90 is supplied to tell the Rotate command to rotate your selection 90°.

If you load this macro into AutoCAD and run it, you're prompted to select an object. You're then immediately prompted to pick a point for the rotation center. You won't be allowed to continue to select other objects the way you can with most AutoCAD commands.

But what if you want that macro to let you make several selections instead of just one? At this point, you almost know enough to create a program to do that. The only part missing is `Ssget`.

The *Ssget* Function

So far, you know you can assign numbers, text, and coordinates to variables. `Ssget` is a function that assigns a set of objects to a variable, as demonstrated in the following exercise:

1. Draw a few random lines on the screen.

2. Enter **(setq ss1 (ssget))**↲.

3. At the `Select objects:` prompt, select the lines using any standard selection method. You can select objects just as you would at any object-selection prompt.

4. When you're done selecting objects, press ↲. You get the message <`Selection set:` *n*>, in which *n* is an alphanumeric value that identifies the selection set.

5. Start the Move command, and at the object-selection prompt, enter **!ss1**↲. The lines you selected previously are highlighted.

6. Press ↲, and then pick two points to finish the Move command.

In this exercise, you stored a selection set as the variable ss1. You can recall this selection set from the Command prompt using the !, just as you did with other variables.

USING *SSGET* IN AN EXPRESSION

You can also use the ss1 variable in an AutoLISP expression. For example, the r90 macro in the next exercise lets you select several objects to be rotated 90°:

1. Enter (defun c:r90 (/ ss1)↵. The AutoLISP prompt appears.

2. To complete the macro, enter **(setq ss1 (ssget))(command "rotate" ss1 "" pause "90"))** and press ↵.

3. Enter **r90**↵ to start the macro.

4. At the Select objects: prompt, select a few of the random lines you drew earlier.

5. Press ↵ to confirm your selection, and then pick a point near the center of the screen. The lines you selected rotate 90°.

The defun function tells AutoLISP this is to be a command called r90. A list follows the name of the macro; it's called an *argument list*. We'll look at argument lists a bit later in this chapter.

Following the argument list is the (setq ss1 (ssget)) expression you used in the previous exercise. This is where the new macro stops and asks you to select a set of objects to later be applied to the Rotate command.

The next expression uses the Command function. Command lets you include standard AutoCAD command-line input in an AutoLISP program. In this case, the input starts by issuing the Rotate command. It then applies the selection set stored by ss1 to the Rotate command's object-selection prompt. Next, the two " " marks indicate an ↵. The pause lets the user select a base point for the rotation. Finally, the value 90 is applied to the Rotate command's angle prompt. The entire expression when entered at the Command prompt would look like the following:

```
Command: Rotate↵
Select objects:!ss1↵
Select objects:↵
Specify base point: (pause for input)
Specify rotation angle or [Copy/Reference] <0>: 90↵
```

In this macro, the Ssget function adds flexibility by allowing the user to select as many objects as desired. (You could use the Pause function in place of the variable ss1, but with Pause, you can't anticipate whether the user will use a window, pick points, or select a previous selection set.)

CONTROLLING MEMORY CONSUMPTION WITH LOCAL VARIABLES

Selection sets are memory hogs in AutoLISP. If you create too many of them, you'll end up draining AutoLISP's memory reserves. To limit the memory used by selection sets, you can turn them into *local variables*. Local variables are variables that exist only while the program is executing its instructions. Once the program is finished, local variables are discarded.

The vehicle for making variables local is the *argument list*. Let's look again at the set of empty parentheses that immediately follow the program name in the rec program:

```
(defun c:rec () ...)
```

If you include a list of variables between those parentheses, those variables become local. In the new r90 macro you just looked at, the ss1 selection-set variable is a local variable:

```
(defun c:r90 (/ ss1)...)
```

WATCH THOSE SPACES

The space after the / in the argument list is very important. Your macro won't work properly without it.

The argument list starts with a forward slash and then a space followed by the list of variables. Once the r90 macro is done with its work, any memory assigned to ss1 can be recovered.

Sometimes, you'll want a variable to be accessible at all times by all AutoLISP programs. Such variables are known as *global variables*. You can use global variables to store information in the current editing session. You could even store a few selection sets as global variables. To control memory consumption, however, use global variables sparingly.

Controlling the Flow of an AutoLISP Program

A typical task for a program is to execute one function or another depending on an existing condition. This type of operation is often called an *if-then-else conditional statement*: "If a condition is met, then perform computation A; else perform computation B." AutoLISP offers the If function to facilitate this type of operation.

Using the *If* Function

The If function requires two arguments. The first argument must be a value that returns true or false—in the case of AutoLISP, T for true or *nil* for false. The second argument is the action to take if the value returned is true. It's like saying, "If true then do A," where "true" is the first argument and "A" is the second. Optionally, you can supply a third argument, which is the action to take if the value returned is nil ("If true then do A; else do B").

WHY USE THE *IF* FUNCTION

A common use for the if-then-else statement is to direct the flow of a program in response to a user's yes or no reply to a prompt. If the user responds with a yes to the prompt Do you want to continue?, for example, that response can be used in the if-then-else statement to direct the program to go ahead and perform some function, such as erasing objects or drawing a box.

Here is an example of an If expression:

```
(if Exst (+ a b) (* a b))
```

Here the value of the Exst variable determines which of the two following expressions is evaluated. If Exst has a value, it returns T for true; that is, when AutoLISP evaluates Exst, the value returned is T. The expression then evaluates the second argument, (+ a b), which is itself an expression. If Exst doesn't have a value or is nil, the expression evaluates the third argument, (* a b).

Several special AutoLISP functions test variables for specific conditions. For example, you can test a number to see if it's equal to, less than, or greater than another number. In this expression, if A is equal to B, the second argument is evaluated:

```
(if (= A B) (+ A B) (* A B))
```

In this expression, if A is greater than B, the second argument is evaluated:

```
(if (> A B) (+ A B) (* A B))
```

The functions that test for T or nil are called *predicates* and *logical operators*. Table 27.3 shows a list of these functions.

TABLE 27.3:   Predicates and logical operators

FUNCTION	RETURNS T (TRUE) IF...
<	One numeric value is less than another.
>	One numeric value is greater than another.
<=	One numeric value is less than or equal to another.
>=	One numeric value is greater than or equal to another.
=	Two numeric or string values are equal.
/=	Two numeric or string values aren't equal.
eq	Two values are exactly the same.
equal	Two values are the same (approximate).
atom	A symbol represents an atom (as opposed to a list).
listp	A symbol represents a list.
minusp	A numeric value is negative.
numberp	A symbol is a number, real or integer.
zerop	A symbol evaluates to zero.
and	All of several expressions or atoms return non-nil.
not	A symbol is nil.
null	A list is nil.
or	One of several expressions or atoms returns non-nil.

Let's see how conditional statements, predicates, and logical operators work together. Suppose you want to write a program that either multiplies two numbers or adds the numbers together. You want the program to ask the user which action to take depending on which of the two values is greater. Follow these steps:

1. Enter the following program at the Command prompt, just as you did for the rec program:

```
(defun c:mul-add ()↵
(setq A (getreal "Enter first number:" ))↵
(setq B (getreal "Enter second number:" ))↵
(if (< A B) (+ a b) (* a b))↵
)↵
```

2. Run the program by entering **Mul-add**↵.

3. At the Enter first number: prompt, enter **3**↵.

4. At the Enter second number: prompt, enter **4**↵. The value 7.0 is returned.

5. Run the program again, but this time enter **4** at the first prompt and **3** at the second prompt. This time, you get the returned value 12.0.

In this program, the first two Setq expressions get two numbers from you. The conditional statement that follows, (< A B), tests to see if the first number you entered is less than the second. If this predicate function returns T for true, (+ a b) is evaluated. If it returns nil for false, (* a b) is evaluated.

You'll often find that you need to perform not just one but several steps, depending on some condition. Here is a more complex If expression that evaluates several expressions at once:

```
(if (= A B) (progn (* A B)(+ A B)(- A B) ))
```

In this example, the function Progn tells the If function that several expressions are to be evaluated if (= A B) returns true.

Repeating an Expression

Sometimes, you'll want your program to evaluate a set of expressions repeatedly until a particular condition is met. If you're familiar with BASIC, you know this function as a *loop*.

You can repeat steps in an AutoLISP program by using the While function in conjunction with predicates and logical operators. Like the If function, While's first argument must be one that returns a T or nil. You can have as many other arguments to the While function as you like as long as the first argument is a predicate function:

```
(while test (expression 1) (expression 2) (expression 3)...)
```

The While function isn't the only one that will repeat a set of instructions. The Repeat function causes a set of instructions to be executed several times, but unlike While, Repeat requires an integer value for its first argument, as in the following:

```
(Repeat 14 (expression 1) (expression 2) (expression 3)...)
```

In this example, Repeat will evaluate each expression 14 times.

A third function, Foreach, evaluates an expression for each element of a list. The arguments to Foreach are first a variable, then a list whose elements are to be evaluated, and then the expression used to evaluate each element of the list:

```
(foreach var1 ( list1 ) (expression var1))
```

Foreach is a bit more difficult to understand at first because it involves a variable, a list, and an expression, all working together.

Using Other Built-in Functions

At this point, you've seen several useful programs created with just a handful of AutoLISP functions. Although I can't give a tutorial showing you how to use every available AutoLISP function, in these final sections I'll demonstrate a few more. This is far from a complete list, but it should be enough to get you well on your way to making AutoLISP work for you. Experiment with the functions at your leisure, but remember, using AutoLISP can be addicting!

KEEPING TRACK OF DATA TYPES

In many of the examples in the following sections, you'll see numeric values or lists as arguments. As in all AutoLISP functions, you can use a variable as an argument as long as the variable's value is of the proper data type.

GEOMETRIC OPERATIONS

These functions are useful for manipulating geometric data. (And don't forget the Get functions listed earlier, in Table 27.2.)

AN APOSTROPHE MEANS DON'T EVALUATE

In some examples, an apostrophe (') precedes a list. This apostrophe tells AutoLISP not to evaluate the list but to treat it as a repository of data.

Angle   Finds the angle between two points, and returns a value in radians. For example,

```
(angle '(6.0 4.0 0.0) '(6.0 5.0 0.0))
```

returns 1.5708. This example uses two coordinate lists for arguments, but point variables can also be used.

Distance   Finds the distance between two points. The value returned is in base units. Just like Angle, Distance requires two coordinates as arguments. The expression

```
(distance '(6.0 4.0 0.0) '(6.0 5.0 0.0))
```

returns 1.0.

Polar   Returns a point in the form of a coordinate list based on the location of a point, an angle, and a distance. The expression

```
(polar '(1.0 1.0 0.0) 1.5708 1.0)
```

returns (0.999996 2.0 0.0). The first argument is a coordinate list, the second is an angle in radians, and the third is a distance in base units. The point must be a coordinate list.

Inters   Returns the intersection point of two vectors, with each vector described by two points. The points must be in this order: the first two points define the first vector, and the second two points define the second vector. The expression

```
(inters
'(1.0 4.0 0.0)'(8.0 4.0 0.0)'(5.0 2.0 0.0)'(5.0 9.0 0.0)
)
```

returns (5.0 4.0 0.0). If the intersection point doesn't lie between either of the two vectors, you can still obtain a point, provided you include a non-nil fifth argument.

STRING OPERATIONS

These functions allow you to manipulate strings. Although you can't supply strings for the text input of the text command, you can use the Command function with string variables to enter text, as in the following:

```
(Setq note "Hello World")
(command "text" (getpoint) "2.0" "0" note)
```

In this example, note is first assigned a string value. Then, the Command function is used to issue the Text command and place the text in the drawing. Notice the (getpoint) function, which is included to obtain a point location.

Two other string functions, Substr and Strcat, let you manipulate text.

Substr   Returns a portion of a string, called a substring, beginning at a specified location. The expression

```
(substr "string" 3 4)
```

returns *ring*. The first argument is the string containing the substring to be extracted. The second argument, 3, tells Substr where to begin the new string; this value must be an integer. The third argument, 4, is optional and tells Substr how long the new string should be in characters. The length must also be an integer.

Strcat   Combines several strings, and the result is a string. The expression

```
(strcat string1  string2  etc. )
```

returns *string1 string2 etc.* In this example, the

```
etc.
```

indicates that you can have as many string values as you want.

Converting Data Types

While using AutoLISP, you'll often have to convert values from one data type to another. For example, because most angles in AutoLISP must be represented in radians, you must convert them to degrees before you can use them in commands. You can do so using the `Angtos` function. `Angtos` converts a real number representing an angle in radians into a string in the degree format you desire. The following example converts an angle of 1.57 radians into surveyor's units with a precision of four decimal places:

```
(angtos 1.57 4 4)
```

This expression returns N 0d2´44˝ E. The first argument is the angle in radians, the second argument is a code that tells AutoLISP which format to convert the angle to, and the third argument tells AutoLISP the degree of precision desired. (The third argument is optional.) The conversion codes for `Angtos` are as follows:

0 = Degrees

1 = Degrees/minutes/seconds

2 = Grads

3 = Radians

4 = Surveyor's units

CONVERTING RADIANS

The `Angtos` and `Rtos` functions are especially useful for converting radians to any of the standard angle formats available in AutoCAD. For example, using `Angtos`, you can convert 0.785398 radians to 45d0´ 0˝, or N 45d0´0˝ E. Using `Rtos`, you can convert the distance value of 42 to 42.00 or 3´-6˝ (three feet six inches). Be aware that `Angtos` and `Rtos` also convert numeric data into strings.

Now that you've seen an example of what the `Angtos` data-type conversion can do, let's briefly look at similar functions:

Atof and Atoi `Atof` converts a string to a real number. The expression

```
(atof "33.334")
```

returns 33.334.

`Atoi` converts a string to an integer. The expression

```
(atoi "33.334")
```

returns 33.

Itoa and Rtos `Itoa` converts an integer to a string. The argument must be an integer. The expression

```
(itoa 24)
```

returns "24".

Rtos converts a real number to a string. As with Angtos, a format code and precision value are specified. The expression

```
(rtos 32.3 4 2)
```

returns "2'-8 1/4\"".

WHY THE \ SIGN?

You may notice the \ just after the 1/4 in the returned value. This is an AutoLISP symbol indicating that the following " symbol is part of the string text and not the closing " that indicates the end of the string.

The first argument is the value to be converted, the second argument is the conversion code, and the third argument is the precision value. The codes are as follows:

1 = Scientific

2 = Decimal

3 = Engineering

4 = Architectural

5 = Fractional

Fix and Float   Fix converts a real number into an integer. The expression

```
(fix 3.3334)
```

returns 3.

Float converts an integer into a real number. The expression

```
(float 3)
```

returns 3.0.

Storing Your Programs as Files

When you exit AutoCAD, the rec program will vanish. But just as you were able to save keyboard shortcuts in Chapter 26, you can create a text file on a disk containing the rec program. That way, you'll have ready access to it at all times.

To save your programs, open a text editor and enter them through the keyboard just as you entered the rec program, including the first line that contains the defun function. Be sure you save the file with the .lsp filename extension. You can recall your program by choosing Load Application from the Manage tab's Applications panel, which opens the Load/ Unload Applications dialog box.

If you prefer, you can use the manual method for loading AutoLISP programs. This involves the Load AutoLISP function. Just as with all other functions, it's enclosed by parentheses. In Chapter 26, you loaded the GETAREA.LSP file using the Load/Unload Applications dialog box. To use the Load function instead to load GETAREA.LSP, enter the following:

```
(Load "getarea")
```

Load is one of the simpler AutoLISP functions because it requires only one argument: the name of the AutoLISP file you want to load. Notice that you don't have to include the .lsp filename extension.

If the AutoLISP file resides in a folder that isn't in the current path, you need to include the path in the filename, as in the following example:

```
(Load "C:/Mastering AutoCAD/Projects/Chapter 26/getarea")
```

Instead of the usual Windows \, / is used to indicate folders. The forward slash is used because the backslash has special meaning to AutoLISP in a string value: It tells AutoLISP that a special character follows. If you attempted to use \ in the previous example, you'd get an error message.

As you may guess, the Load function can be a part of an AutoLISP program. It can also be included as part of a menu to load specific programs whenever you select a menu item. You'll learn more about customizing the menu in the next chapter.

USING SCRIPTS

Before AutoLISP, scripts were used to automate tasks in AutoCAD, and many users still use scripts for simple tasks. Scripts are simply a list of instructions to AutoCAD to perform a set of operations. You store scripts in text files using the Windows Notepad application.

To write a script, open a text file and type in your AutoCAD instructions as if you were entering them at the AutoCAD Command prompt. If a command requires point input or object selections, you can supply coordinate locations. You have to be very careful to make sure your text file contains the exact keystrokes that would be used if you were entering them in AutoCAD.

Once you have entered your script, make sure the very last line has a return at the end (press the Enter key). Then you can save your script file with the .scr filename extension.

To run the script in AutoCAD, type **Script⏎**, and then use the Select Script File dialog box that appears to select and run your script. You'll probably have to test your script and make adjustments before it works perfectly.

Scripts are very inflexible, and one missing keystroke or misplaced space can render your script useless. Today, you have AutoLISP and the Action Recorder to handle most automation projects. But if you have a simple operation that is repetitive, a script can be a useful tool.

Getting More Help with AutoLISP

I hope you'll be enticed into trying some programming on your own and learning more about AutoLISP. You can find a wealth of information in the AutoCAD 2011 Help website:

1. Choose Additional Resources ➤ Developer Help from the Help flyout on the Communication Center. The AutoCAD 2011 Help website opens.

2. In the panel on the left, select one of the two options: the AutoLISP Developers Guide and the AutoLISP Reference Guide. Additional options are displayed in the main body of the page.

The AutoLISP Developers Guide offers instructions on the Visual LISP programming environment and also provides some online tutorials. This guide can be helpful to new users. The AutoLISP Reference Guide is intended for users with basic knowledge of AutoLISP and provides detailed information on the AutoLISP functions.

As you work with AutoLISP material in the AutoCAD 2011 Help website, you'll also see references to Visual LISP. This is a self-contained programming environment for AutoLISP. Visual LISP is an excellent tool if you intend to make extensive use of AutoLISP in your work. Once you understand the basics of AutoLISP, you may want to explore Visual LISP through the tutorial in the AutoCAD Help system. You can find the Visual LISP tutorial by choosing Help ➤ Additional Resources ➤ Developer Help. In the AutoCAD 2011 Help: Developer Documentation window, look under the AutoLISP Tutorial section.

The Bottom Line

Understand the interpreter.   One of the simplest ways to start using AutoLISP is to enter an AutoLISP expression directly into the command line.

Master It   Give an example of an AutoLISP formula that performs a simple math function.

Use arguments and functions.   AutoLISP needs two elements, an argument and an expression, to do any work.

Master It   Which is the function in the following AutoLISP expression?

```
(+ 45 33)
```

Create a simple program.   You can input a simple program directly into AutoCAD by entering it through the command line.

Master It   Name a function that pauses an AutoLISP program for user input.

Select objects with AutoLISP.   AutoLISP offers an expression that lets you select objects and then perform some operation on the set of objects.

Master It   What function lets you select objects, and what AutoLISP feature do you use to store your selection?

Control the flow of an AutoLISP program.   You can set up an AutoLISP program to test for conditions and perform different operations depending on the result.

Master It   Name some functions that test for a condition.

Convert data types.   The functions in AutoLISP are designed to work with their own types of data. For example, math functions work only with numbers, and string operations work only with text. If you need to use the result of a math function in text, you can convert the number into text.

Master It   What is the name of the function that converts an angle in radians to text?

Store your programs as files.   You can save your AutoLISP program in a text editor like Windows Notepad and then later have AutoCAD retrieve your program for use.

Master It   What is the filename extension for AutoLISP programs?

Chapter 28

Customizing Toolbars, Menus, Linetypes, and Hatch Patterns

AutoCAD offers a high degree of flexibility and customization, enabling you to tailor the software's look and feel to your requirements. In this chapter, you'll see how to customize AutoCAD so that it integrates more smoothly into your workgroup and office environment.

The first part of the chapter shows how to adapt AutoCAD to fit your particular needs. You'll learn how to customize AutoCAD by modifying its menus, and you'll learn how to create custom macros for commands that your workgroup uses frequently.

You'll then look at some general issues that arise when you use AutoCAD in an office. In this discussion, you may find help with problems you've encountered when using AutoCAD in your particular work environment. I'll also discuss how to manage AutoCAD projects.

In this chapter you'll learn to do the following:

◆ Use workspaces

◆ Customize the user interface

◆ Create macros in tools and menus

◆ Edit keyboard shortcuts

◆ Save, load, and unload your customizations

◆ Understand the Diesel macro language

◆ Create custom linetypes

◆ Create hatch patterns

Using Workspaces

Once you're comfortable with AutoCAD, you may find that you like a certain arrangement of Ribbon panels, toolbars, and palettes or that you have several sets of panels and toolbars that you like to use depending on your type of work. You've already worked with two of the workspaces AutoCAD offers out of the box: 2D Drafting & Annotation and 3D Modeling. You can also set up your own custom panel and toolbar arrangements and then save those arrangements for later retrieval using the Workspace feature. Let's take a closer look at how you can create a custom workspace.

The Workspace Switching tool and its menu are shown in Figure 28.1. In Chapter 1, you saw how you can use this tool to save your AutoCAD window layout. You can save multiple arrangements of panels, toolbars, and palettes and then recall them easily by selecting them from the Workspace Switching tool in the status bar or Workspace drop-down list in the Quick Access toolbar.

FIGURE 28.1
The Workspace
Switching tool

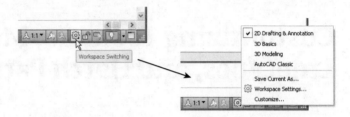

Click the Workspace Switching tool on the status bar and select Workspace Settings to open the Workspace Settings dialog box, shown in Figure 28.2. You can also select Workspace Settings from the Workspace drop-down list in the Quick Access toolbar or type **Wssettings.⏎**.

FIGURE 28.2
The Workspace
Settings dialog box

With the Workspace Settings dialog box open, you can see the 2D Drafting & Annotation, 3D Basics, 3D Modeling, and AutoCAD Classic options. If you've used the Initial Setup Wizard to create an industry-specific workspace, you'll see the Initial Setup Workspace option here as well. From here, you can control the behavior of the settings.

The check box next to each setting lets you control whether the item appears in the Workspace Switching tool menu. For example, if you remove the checkmark from the AutoCAD Classic setting, you'll see only 2D Drafting & Annotation, 3D Basics, and 3D Modeling in the Workspace Switching tool menu.

The My Workspace = drop-down list lets you select which workspace setting is activated when you click the My Workspace tool on the Workspace toolbar (you'll see the Workspace toolbar when you switch to the AutoCAD Classic workspace). You can use this option for your most-frequently used workspace settings.

The options in the When Switching Workspaces group at the bottom of the Workspace Settings dialog box let you determine whether workspace changes are saved automatically. For example, if you select Automatically Save Workspace Changes, then the next time you switch to a different workspace setting, AutoCAD will save any changes you've made to the current workspace.

The Workspace Switching tool is the easiest customization feature you'll find in AutoCAD, and it can go a long way toward helping you stay organized. But workspaces are just the tip of the iceberg when it comes to customizing AutoCAD. In the next section, you'll delve into the Customize User Interface (CUI) feature to see how you can customize the AutoCAD menus, panels, and toolbars directly.

ARE YOU IN THE RIGHT WORKSPACE?

The exercises in this chapter assume that you are in the 2D Drafting & Annotation workspace.

Customizing the User Interface

Out of the box, AutoCAD offers a generic arrangement of Ribbon panels, tools, and palettes that works fine for most applications. But the more you use AutoCAD, the more you may find that you tend to use tools that are scattered over several Ribbon panels. You'll probably feel that your work would go more easily if you could create a custom set of panels and menus to consolidate those tools. If you're to the point of creating custom macros, you may want a way to have easy access to them.

The *Customize User Interface (CUI)* is a one-stop location that gives you nearly total control over the menus, panels, and toolbars in AutoCAD. With the CUI feature, you can mold the AutoCAD interface to your liking. The main entry point to the CUI is the Customize User Interface dialog box.

The following section introduces you to the CUI by showing you how to add a tool to the Draw Ribbon panel. You'll also get a chance to see how to create an entirely new panel and custom tools.

Taking a Quick Customization Tour

The most direct way to adapt AutoCAD to your way of working is to customize the Ribbon. AutoCAD offers new users an easy route to customization through the Customize User Interface dialog box. With this dialog box, you can create new Ribbon panels and toolbars, customize tools, and even create new icons. You can also create keyboard shortcuts.

To get your feet wet, try adding a tool to the Draw panel:

1. If it's still open, close the Workspace Settings dialog box.

2. Click the User Interface tool in the Manage tab's Customization panel to open the Customize User Interface dialog box, shown in Figure 28.3. You can also type **Cui**↵. You see three groups in this dialog box: Customizations In All Files, Command List, and Properties.

3. In the Customizations In All Files group, expand the Ribbon option, and then expand the Panels option that appears just below. Scroll down the list and expand the Home 2D – Draw option. You see a set of options labeled Row 1, Row 2, and so on.

4. Click the Home 2D – Draw option. A view of the Draw Ribbon panel appears in the Panel Preview group (Figure 28.4).

5. Expand the Row 4 item under the Home 2D – Draw option. You'll see the names of the three tools that appear at the very bottom of the Draw panel. These tools are 3D Polyline, Helix, and Donut.

6. In the Command List group, select Dimension from the Filter The Command List By Category drop-down list (Figure 28.5).

FIGURE 28.3
The Customize User Interface dialog box

FIGURE 28.4
The Draw Ribbon panel appears.

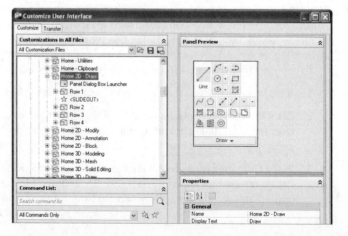

FIGURE 28.5
Choose the Dimen-
sion command.

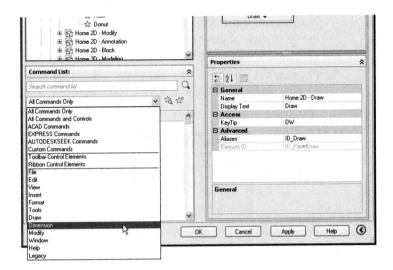

FIGURE 28.5
Choose the Dimen-
sion command.

7. In the bottom panel of the Command List group, scroll down the list and then locate
and select Dimension, Linear. This is the Linear Dimension command. When you select
Linear, the Properties group displays the properties of the Linear command. The Preview
group changes to show the Button Image group, and you see the Linear Dimension icon,
as shown in Figure 28.6.

FIGURE 28.6
The Panel Preview
groups change
when you select
an element from
the Command List
group or the Cus-
tomizations In All
Files group.

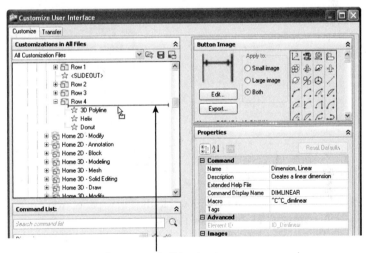

The bar tells you where the command will be placed.

8. Carefully click and drag the Dimension, Linear item from the Command List group into
the Customizations In All Files group, but don't release the mouse button yet. As you
drag the item over the tool names in the Customizations In All Files group, a bar tells you
where your dragged item will appear (see Figure 28.6). If you pause over an option, you'll
see an arrowhead appear next to the option. The arrowhead also indicates where the

dragged command will be placed. The list may automatically scroll up or down depending on where you place the bar. This is to allow you to place the bar in an area of the list that isn't currently displayed.

9. Place the bar just above 3D Polyline, and release the mouse button. Dimension, Linear appears above 3D Polyline in the list (Figure 28.7), and you see its icon in the Panel Preview area.

FIGURE 28.7
After positioning
the Dimension icon

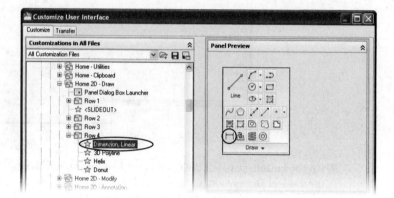

10. Click OK. The next time you check, you'll see the Dimension, Linear tool appear in the expanded Draw panel just to the left of the 3D Polyline tool (Figure 28.8).

FIGURE 28.8
The tool is in place.

You've just added a command to the Draw panel. You can follow the previous steps to add any command to any Ribbon panel, toolbar, or menu bar menu. Now, suppose you change your mind and you decide to remove Dimension, Linear from the Draw panel. Here's how it's done:

1. Click User Interface in the Manage tab's Customization panel or type **Cui↵**.

2. In the Customizations In All Files group of the Customize User Interface dialog box, expand the Ribbon option and Panels option and then continue to expand options as you did before to get to the Dimension, Linear command you added earlier.

3. Click Dimension, Linear and then right-click and choose Remove from the shortcut menu. You'll see a warning message asking if you "really want to delete this element."

4. Click Yes. The Dimension, Linear command is removed.

5. Click OK to close the dialog box.

Dimension, Linear has been removed from the Draw panel. As you've just seen, adding tools to a panel is a matter of clicking and dragging the appropriate item from one list to another. To remove tools, right-click the tool and select Remove.

Before you go too much further, you may want to know a little more about the Customize User Interface dialog box and how it works. You saw briefly how each group displayed different elements of AutoCAD's interface, from a listing of panel tools to an individual tool's icon. Let's look at each group independently to see how it's organized.

Understanding the Customizations In All Files Panel

In the previous exercise, where you placed the Dimension, Linear command in the Draw panel, you saw an arrowhead appear when you hovered over an option. The arrowhead indicates the location where the command will be placed when you release the mouse button. If the arrowhead points to a command, the new command will be placed after the item indicated by the arrowhead. If the item is a folder icon, then the new command will be placed inside that folder.

You may see items called *Sub-Panel* options. These allow you to mix single tools and rows like the Line tool and the three rows you see to the right of the Line tool at the top of the Draw panel. Finally, the <SLIDEOUT> item you see in the list indicates the division between the main part of the panel and the expanded panel. Figure 28.9 shows how the list in the Customizations In All Files group relates to the Ribbon panel components.

FIGURE 28.9

The Customizations In All Files list compared to the Ribbon panel

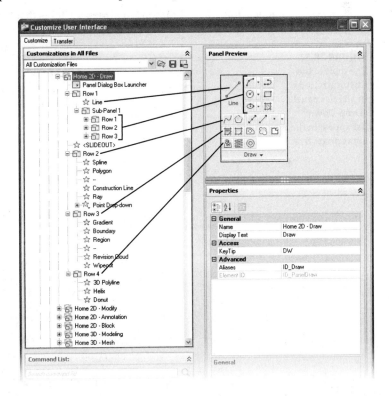

Notice that the Line tool straddles the top three rows in the Draw panel. This is done by placing the Line command at the same level as the Sub-Panel option. The Sub-Panel option is further divided into rows. Figure 28.10 shows how the rows appear when they are expanded. Flyouts on the Ribbon panel appear as "Drop-Down" options in the Customizations In All Files group.

FIGURE 28.10
The Sub-Panel1 option contains the rows that in turn contain flyouts labeled as "Drop-Down" options.

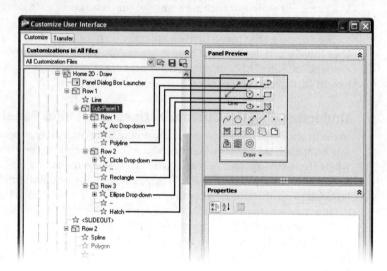

If you expand a "Drop-Down" option, you'll see the tools that appear in the flyouts of the tool in the panel (Figure 28.11).

FIGURE 28.11
The tools in the Customizations In all Files panel's "Drop-Down" list appear in the appropriate flyout.

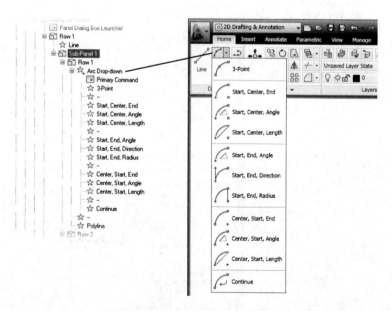

You can add new panels, rows, sub-panels, and drop-downs (flyouts) by right-clicking an item in the list and selecting the appropriate option from the shortcut menu (Figure 28.12).

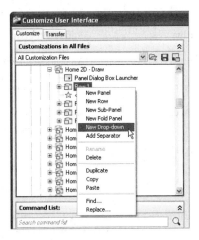

If you understand the structure of these lists, you'll find that it is quite easy to customize the Ribbon panels to your liking.

Getting the Overall View

When you first opened the Customize User Interface dialog box by right-clicking the Ribbon, you saw a listing of the AutoCAD interface elements in the Customizations In All Files group. Just as you saw with the Ribbon panels, each of the other interface elements in the list can be expanded to get to its individual commands. If you expand the Toolbars list, for example, all the AutoCAD toolbars are available. Expand a toolbar and the commands contained in the toolbar are displayed. As you saw earlier, you can expand the Ribbon Panels list to gain access to the Ribbon panels. Table 28.1 lists all the interface elements in the Customizations In All Files group with a brief explanation of their contents.

TABLE 28.1 Main headings in the Customizations In All Files group

ITEM	WHAT IT CONTAINS
Workspaces	Workspaces that are currently available
Quick Access Toolbars	Quick Access toolbars
Ribbon	The Ribbon tabs, panels and contextual tab states
Toolbars	Toolbars
Menus	Menu bar menus
Quick Properties	Options on the Quick Properties palette

TABLE 28.1 Main headings in the Customizations In All Files group *(CONTINUED)*

ITEM	WHAT IT CONTAINS
Rollover Tooltips	Rollover tool tip settings
Shortcut Menus	Menus shown with right-clicks
Keyboard Shortcuts	Current keyboard shortcuts, such as Ctrl+C and Ctrl+V
Double Click Actions	Object-dependent double-click actions
Mouse Buttons	Mouse button options, such as Shift+click and Ctrl+click
LISP Files	Any custom LISP files that are used with your CUI
Legacy	Any legacy custom items you use, such as table or screen menus
Partial Customization Files	Custom CUI files that have been included in the main CUI file

You can customize any of the interface elements. For example, if you want to create new keyboard shortcuts, you can expand the Keyboard Shortcuts listing and add new shortcuts or edit existing ones. Right-click any item to add or delete options. If you click an item, its properties appear in the Properties group, where you can modify the item's function. Just as you added the Dimension, Linear dimension command to the Draw panel, you can click and drag a command into one of the menus under the Menus listing to add a command there.

You also see some options in the Customizations In All Files title bar. These options give you control over what is displayed in this group. You can also load and save CUI files from here.

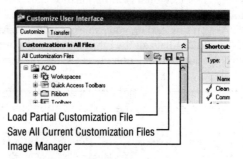

Load Partial Customization File
Save All Current Customization Files
Image Manager

You'll learn more about these options later in this chapter.

Finding Commands in the Command List

You've already seen how the Command List group contains all the commands in AutoCAD. You also saw that you can click and drag these items into options in the Customizations In All Files group. This list also contains predefined macros, icons used for tools, and *Control Elements* (called combo boxes in the Ribbon panels), which are the drop-down lists you see in panels and toolbars. The Layer drop-down list in the Layers panel is an example of a Control Element. The drop-down lists in the Home tab's Properties panel are also examples of Control Elements. When you select an item in the Command List group, you see either its properties in the Properties group or its icon in the Button Image group or both. The exception to this is the Control Elements, which have no editable features.

Opening Preview, Button Image, and Shortcuts

You've already seen how you can get a preview of a Ribbon panel by selecting the panel from the Customizations In All Files group. If you click a Ribbon panel from the list, you'll see the Panel Preview group, which shows you how the selected panel will appear. Previews aren't editable and are there for your reference.

If you click a tool listing, or *element* in AutoCAD nomenclature, in the Customizations In All Files group, you see the Button Image group. You can open this group by clicking the double-arrow head to the right of the Button Image group title bar. This group lets you select an icon for that tool by clicking a list of icons (see Figure 28.13), or you can edit an existing icon or create an entirely new icon. You'll get a chance to see this firsthand later in this chapter.

FIGURE 28.13
The Button Image group

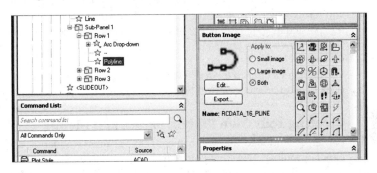

The Keyboard Shortcuts area in the Customizations In All Files group shows the Shortcuts group, which lists the existing keyboard shortcuts.

Getting to the Core of Customization in the Properties Group

Finally, when you're ready to do some serious customizing, you'll work with the Properties group. You see the Properties group in the lower half of the right side of the Customize User Interface dialog box when you select a command from the left side of the dialog box.

The Properties group is set up just like the Properties palette, and it works the same way. On the left side, you see a listing of options, and to the right of each option is a description or a text input box where you can make changes (see Figure 28.14).

If you go to the Customizations In All Files group and select the Line tool under the Home 2D – Draw option that you worked on earlier (Ribbon ➢ Panels ➢ Home 2D – Draw ➢ Row 1 ➢ Line), you see the properties for that tool in the Properties group, as shown in Figure 28.14. You'll have to close the Button Image group to get a complete view of the Properties group. You can close any group by clicking the double arrow on the right side of the group's title bar.

In the Command category, you see the Line tool's name in the Command Name listing. You also see the description that is displayed in the tool tip for the Line tool. You can change this description here in the Properties group and the description will change in the status bar.

FIGURE 28.14
The Properties group showing the properties for the Line tool

In the Macro listing, you see the command as it would be entered through the keyboard. The ^C^C that precedes the actual line command input is equivalent to pressing the Esc key twice. If you scroll down, you'll see the Advanced category, which offers information regarding the ID of this particular tool. Finally, the Images category lists the name of the image files used for the Line tool icon. Two icons are listed: one for the large icon version and one for the small icon version of the tool.

You'll get a chance to work with the Properties group later in this chapter. Next, you'll try your hand at creating your own custom toolbar.

Creating Your Own Ribbon Panels and Menus

Earlier, I mentioned that you can collect your most frequently used tools into a custom Ribbon panel or toolbar. Now that you've had a chance to become familiar with the Customize User Interface dialog box, you can try the following exercise to create your own Ribbon panel:

1. If the Customize User Interface dialog box isn't open, click User Interface from the Manage tab's Customization panel.

2. In the Customizations In All Files group, expand the Ribbon option and then right-click Panels and choose New Panel. The list expands and you see a new panel called Panel1 at the bottom of the Panels list. The name *Panel1* is highlighted and ready to be edited.

3. Replace *Panel1* by typing **My Panel** to give your panel a distinct name (Figure 28.15). As you type, the name changes. If you decide to change a panel name later, right-click a panel listing and then choose Rename.

You now have a custom Ribbon panel. You'll want to start to populate your panel with some commands. You've already seen how this works, but for review, try adding a few commands:

1. Select Draw from the Filter The Command List By Category drop-down list.

2. In the Command List group, locate the command you want to add. In this instance, locate the Line tool.

3. Click and drag the Line command to your new panel so that you see an arrowhead pointing to the Row 1 option (Figure 28.16).

FIGURE 28.15

The new Panel1 option changed to My Panel

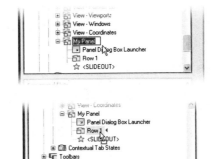

FIGURE 28.16

Point to the Row 1 option and you'll see the arrowhead appear.

4. Release the mouse button. The Line tool appears below Row 1.

5. Repeat steps 2, 3, and 4 to add more commands to your panel.

6. To add another row, right-click on My Panel and select New Row. You can add more tools to your second row.

You can add several more rows to your panel, but after the first row, additional rows will be placed below the <SLIDEOUT>, thereby placed in the expanded portion of the panel.

DELETING A CUSTOM TOOL OR PANEL

You can delete any tool from your custom panel by right-clicking the tool and choosing Remove while in the Customizations In All Files group of the Customize User Interface dialog box. You can also delete your entire panel using this method. Take care not to delete any of the existing panels you want to keep.

Customizing Ribbon Panel Tools

Let's move on to more serious customization. Suppose you want to create an entirely new button with its own functions. For example, you might want to create a set of buttons that insert your favorite symbols. Or you might want to create a Ribbon panel containing a set of tools that open some of the other toolbars that are normally put away.

CREATING A CUSTOM TOOL

Follow these steps to create a custom tool:

1. Open the Customize User Interface dialog box, expand the Ribbon Panels list, and then expand the My Panel list.

2. In the Command List panel title bar, click the Create A New Command button. A new command called Command1 appears in the list of commands (Figure 28.17).

FIGURE 28.17
Click the Create
A New Command
tool and a new
command appears
in the list.

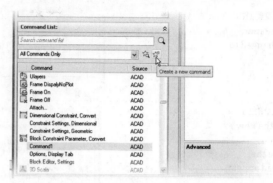

3. Right-click the Command1 item, select Rename from the shortcut menu, and change the name to **Door**.

4. In the Properties group to the right, change Description to **Insert a 36″ door**.

5. Change the Macro option to the following:

```
^C^C-insert door;\36;;
```

6. Click and drag the Door element from the Command List panel into Row 1 of your My Panel item in the Customizations In All Files group. If you look at the Panel Preview group, you see that the Door tool you just added appears as a blank tool. This happens when no icon has been assigned to the tool.

The series of keystrokes you entered for the macro in step 5 are the same as those you would use to insert the door, with the addition of a few special characters. The semicolons are equivalent to a ⏎, and the backward slash (\) is a special macro code that tells AutoCAD to pause the macro for user input. In this case, the pause allows you to select the insertion point for the door. The Properties group should look like Figure 28.18.

FIGURE 28.18
The Properties
group for your new
custom tool that
inserts a door block

You've created your panel, but it will not appear anywhere in the AutoCAD interface until you add it to a Ribbon Tab group. Here's how this is done:

1. Under your My Panel listing in the Customizations In All Files group, click the My Panel panel option you just created, and then right-click and select Copy.

2. In the Customizations In All Files group, scroll up to top of the list and expand the Tabs option.

3. Right-click Home – 2D just below Ribbon Tabs, and then select Paste from the shortcut menu. Your My Panel panel appears at the bottom of the Home – 2D list.

4. Click OK in the Customize User Interface dialog box to close it. Your panel appears in the Home tab of the Ribbon.

 Real World Scenario

LOCATE FILES SO AUTOCAD CAN FIND THEM

A misplaced file is one of the more common problems I have to troubleshoot in my job supporting an office full of AutoCAD users. AutoCAD likes to place files in a lot of different places. When it can't find a file it needs, it will give you an error message, or worse, it just won't work. It helps to know where AutoCAD looks for files so you can place the resources for your custom tools in the right places.

In the Door example, the door drawing used in your macro must be in the default folder, My Documents, or in the acad search path before the door will be inserted. For easy access, copy the Door.dwg file from the Chapter 4 project folder to the My Documents folder.

Next, try the custom tool to make sure it works:

1. Put a copy of the Door.dwg file in your My Documents folder.

2. Point to the Door tool in your My Panel panel in the Home tab. You see the Door tool tip.

3. Click the Door tool. The door appears in the drawing area at the cursor. It may appear very small because initially, it's being inserted at its default size of 1 unit.

4. Click a location to place the door, and then click a point to set the door rotation. The door appears in the drawing.

In this example, you created a custom tool that inserts the door block. Later in this chapter, you'll learn more about creating macros for menus and tools. Next, you'll learn how to add a custom icon for your custom tool.

CREATING A CUSTOM ICON

You have all the essential parts of the button defined. Now you just need to create a custom icon to go with your Door button:

1. Open the Customize User Interface dialog box.

2. Expand the Customizations In All Files Ribbon list to your My Panel option (Ribbon ➤ Panels ➤ My Panel).

3. Expand the Row1 list, and select Door.

4. Open the Button Image group and click any icon image. The icon appears in the Panel Preview group, replacing the blank image for your Door tool.

5. In the Button Image group, click the Edit button to open the Button Editor dialog box. The Button Editor is like a simple drawing program. Across the top are the tools to draw lines, circles, and points as well as an eraser. Along the left side is a color toolbar from which you can choose colors for your icon. At upper right, you see a preview of your button.

YOU CAN USE THE EXISTING ICONS

If you prefer, you can use any of the predefined icons in the scroll box to the right of the Button Image group in the Customize User Interface dialog box. Click the icon you want to use, and then click Apply.

---

6. Before you do anything else, click the Clear button. This clears the current image.

7. Draw the door icon shown in Figure 28.19. Don't worry if it's not perfect; you can always go back and fix it.

FIGURE 28.19
Draw this door icon.

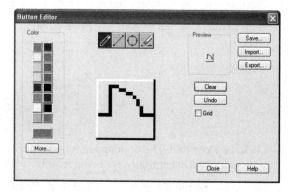

8. Click Save, and then at the Save Image dialog box, enter **Door36** for the name. The door icon is saved in the AutoCAD CUI file that stores all of the interface data.

9. Click OK, and then click Close at the Button Editor dialog box.

10. Click OK to close the Customize User Interface dialog box. You see your custom icon for the Door tool.

The Button Editor behaves like a simplified image editing tool and is fairly straightforward to use. The only part that may be confusing is that you have to clear the image and save any new image under a new name.

You can continue to add more buttons to build a panel of symbols. Of course, you're not limited to a symbols library. You can also incorporate your favorite macros or even AutoLISP routines that you accumulate as you work with AutoCAD. The possibilities are endless.

Creating Macros in Tools and Menus

Combining existing commands into new panels or toolbars can be useful, but you'll get even more benefit from the CUI by creating your own macros. *Macros* are predefined sets of responses to commands that can help automate your most frequently used processes.

Early on, you saw how a macro was included in a tool to insert a door. You added a special set of instructions in the Macro option of the Properties group to perform the door insertion and scale. You also saw how the Line command was formatted as part of a tool.

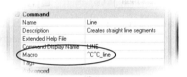

Let's take a closer look at how macros are built. Start by looking at the existing Line tool and how it's formatted.

The Macro option for the Line tool starts with two ^C elements, which are equivalent to pressing the Esc key twice. This cancels any command that is currently operative. The Line command follows, written just as it would be entered through the keyboard. Two Cancels are issued in case you're in a command that has two levels, such as the Edit Vertex option of the Pedit command.

The underscore character (_) that precedes the Line command tells AutoCAD that you're using the English-language version of this command. This feature lets you program non-English versions of AutoCAD by using the English-language command names.

WHAT IS THE HYPHEN FOR?

In the previous door macro example, you used a hyphen in front of the Insert command. The hyphen causes the Insert command to run in the command line instead of using a dialog box, where the macro keyboard input will not work. Many commands will run in the command line when preceded with a hyphen.

You may also notice that there is no space between the second ^C and the Line command. A space in the line would be the same as ↵. If there were a space between these two elements, ↵ would be entered between the last ^C and the Line command, causing the command sequence to misstep. Another way to indicate ↵ is by using the semicolon, as in the following example:

```
^C^C_Line;;
```

HELP MAKE YOUR MACRO READABLE

If a menu macro contains multiple instances of ↵, using semicolons instead of spaces can help make your macro more readable.

In this sample menu option, the Line command is issued, and then an additional ↵ is added. The effect of choosing this option is a line that continues from the last line entered into your drawing. The two semicolons following `Line` tell AutoCAD to start the Line command and then issue ↵ twice; the first ↵ starts the Line command, and then the second ↵ tells AutoCAD to begin a line from the endpoint of the last line entered. (AutoCAD automatically issues a single ↵ at the end of a menu line. In this case, however, you want two instances of ↵, so they must be represented as semicolons.)

Pausing for User Input

Another symbol used in the Macro option is the backslash (\); it's used when a pause is required for user input. For example, the following sample macro starts the Arc command and then pauses for your input:

```
^C^C_arc \_e \_d
```

The space between `^c^c_arc` and the backslash (\) represents pressing the spacebar. The backslash indicates a pause to enable you to select the starting endpoint for the arc. The _e represents the selection of the Endpoint option under the Arc command after you've picked a point. A second backslash allows another point selection. Finally, the _d represents the selection of the Direction option. Figure 28.20 illustrates this. If you want the last character in a menu item to be a backslash, you must follow the backslash with a semicolon.

FIGURE 28.20
The execution of
the Arc menu item

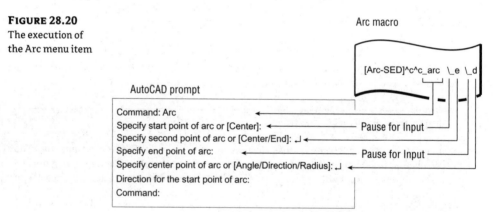

Opening an Expanded Text Box for the Macro Option

As you become more expert at creating macros, you may find the line provided in the Macro option too small for your needs. Fortunately, you can open an expanded text box in which to write longer macros. For example, suppose you want to include the following macro in a tool:

```
(defun c:breakat ()
(command "break" pause "f" pause "@")
)
breakat
```

This example shows the `Breakat` AutoLISP macro. Everything in this segment is entered just as it would be from the keyboard at the Command prompt. You may find it a bit cumbersome to try to enter this macro in the text box provided by the Macro option in the Properties group of the Customize User Interface dialog box, but if you click the Macro text box, a Browse button appears to the right (Figure 28.21).

FIGURE 28.21
The Browse
button in the
Macro option

Click the Browse button to open the Long String Editor.

You can then enter the macro and see it clearly. The following shows how it would be entered:

```
^c^c(defun c:breakat ()+
(command "break" pause "f" pause "@")+
);breakat
```

It starts with the usual `^c^c` to clear any current commands. The plus sign at the end of lines 1 and 2 tells AutoCAD that the macro continues in the next line without actually breaking it. The break is there to help make the macro easier to read as you enter it. It's okay to break an AutoLISP program into smaller lines. Doing so can help you read and understand the program more easily.

LOADING AUTOLISP MACROS

As you become a more advanced AutoCAD user, you may want many of your own AutoLISP macros to load with your custom interface. You can make them do that by combining all your AutoLISP macros into a single file. Give this file the same name as your menu file but with the `.mnl` filename extension. Such a file automatically loads with its menu counterpart. For example, say you have a file called `Mymenu.mnl` containing the `Breakat` AutoLISP macro. Whenever you load `Mymenu.cui`, `Mymenu.mnl` is automatically loaded along with it, giving you access to the `Breakat` macro. This is a good way to manage and organize any AutoLISP program code you want to include with a menu.

Editing Keyboard Shortcuts

Another area of customization that can be useful is the keyboard shortcut. You probably already know about the standard Ctrl+C and Ctrl+V, which are shortcuts to the Windows Copy and Paste functions. In AutoCAD, Shift+Ctrl+A toggles groups on and off, and Ctrl+1 opens the Properties palette.

You can edit existing keyboard shortcuts or create new ones by opening the Keyboard Shortcuts list in the Customizations In All Files group of the Customize User Interface dialog box. If you expand this list, you see Shortcut Keys and Temporary Override Keys. These can be expanded to reveal their elements. Select an element to display its properties in the Properties group.

You can click and drag a command from the Command List group into the Shortcut Keys group and then edit its properties to set the shortcut keys you want to use for the command. For example, if you click and drag the 3D Free Orbit command from the Command List group into the Shortcut Keys list and then select it from that list, you see its properties in the Properties group (Figure 28.22).

FIGURE 28.22
The Properties group

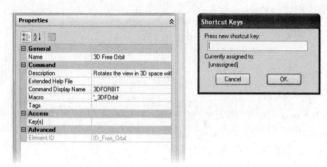

Click the Key(s) option in the Properties group and then click the Browse button that appears to the far right of the Keys option to open the Shortcut Keys dialog box.

Click in the Press The New Shortcut Key input box, and then press the shortcut key you want to use for this command. For example, if you press Shift+Ctrl+Z, that sequence appears in the input box. If the shortcut you selected is already assigned to another command, you see a message that says so just below the input box. Click OK when you're done.

Saving, Loading, and Unloading Your Customizations

You may want to save the custom menus, panels, and toolbars you create with the Customize User Interface dialog box so that you can carry them with you to other computers and load them for ready access. To save your customization work, you need to use the Transfer tab of the Customize User Interface dialog box. Here's how it works:

1. Open the Customize User Interface dialog box.

2. Click the Transfer tab. This tab contains two panels: the left panel shows the Customizations In Main File group, and the right panel shows a similar group called Customizations In New File.

3. In the left panel, locate your custom component, such as a menu, a Ribbon panel, or a toolbar.

4. Click and drag it to the appropriate item in the right panel. For example, click and drag a custom panel from the Ribbon panel list of the left group to the Ribbon panel section in the right group.

5. Repeat step 4 for each custom component you've created.

6. When you've copied everything from the left group to the right, click the drop-down list in the Customizations In New File title bar, and select Save As.

7. In the Save As dialog box, enter a name for your customization file, and select a location.

8. Click Save to complete the process.

Your customization is saved with the `.cuix` filename extension. Once it's saved as a file, you can load it into another copy of AutoCAD by doing the following:

1. Open the Customize User Interface dialog box.

2. Click the Load Partial Customization File tool in the Customizations In All Files group title bar.

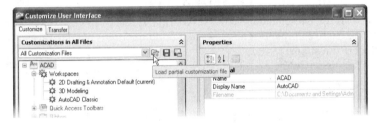

3. In the Open dialog box, locate and select your CUI file, and then click Open.

4. Back in the Customize User Interface dialog box, click OK.

5. If your CUI file contains menus, enter **Workspace↵↵↵** at the Command prompt. Or select a workspace from the Workspace Switching tool in the status bar. If it contains toolbars, right-click in a blank area next to an existing docked toolbar, and then select the name of your CUI file and the toolbar.

As an alternative to using the Customize User Interface dialog box, you can use the CUIload command. Enter **Cuiload↵** at the Command prompt to open the Load/Unload Customizations dialog box.

Click the Browse button to locate and select your CUI file. Once you've done this, the name of your file appears in the File Name input box. You can then click the Load button to import it into your AutoCAD session.

Finally, if you want to unload a CUI file, do the following:

1. Open the Customize User Interface dialog box.

2. Scroll down to the bottom of the list in the Customizations In All Files group, and expand the Partial Customization Files item.

3. Right-click the partial CUI file you want to unload, and select Unload *name*.cuix.

4. Close the dialog box by clicking OK.

Understanding the Diesel Macro Language

Diesel is one of many macro languages AutoCAD supports, and you can use it to perform simple operations and add some automation to menus. As with AutoLISP, parentheses are used to enclose program code.

In the following sections, you'll look at the different ways to use the Diesel macro language. You'll start by using Diesel directly from the command line. This will show you how a Diesel macro is formatted and will give you a chance to see Diesel in action. Then you'll go on to see how Diesel can be used as part of a menu option to test AutoCAD's current state. In the third section, you'll see how Diesel can be used as part of the menu label to control what is shown in the menu. Finally, you'll learn how to use Diesel with field objects to control text in your drawing.

Using Diesel at the Command Line

You can use Diesel at the AutoCAD command line by using a command called Modemacro. The Modemacro command sends information to the status bar. Diesel can be used with Modemacro to perform simple tasks.

Try the following exercise to experiment with Diesel:

1. At the Command prompt, type **Modemacro**↵.

2. At the Enter new value for MODEMACRO, or . for none <" ">: prompt, enter **$(/,25,2)**↵. The answer to the equation appears at far left in the status bar.

The answer to the equation appears here.

3. To clear the status bar, enter **Modemacro**↵.↵.

The equation you entered in step 2 is referred to as an *expression*. The structure of Diesel expressions is similar to that of AutoLISP expressions. The dollar sign tells AutoCAD that the information that follows is a Diesel expression.

A Diesel expression must include an operator of some sort, followed by the items to be operated on. An *operator* is an instruction to take a specific action, such as adding two numbers or dividing one number by another. Examples of mathematical operators include the plus sign (+) for addition and the forward slash (/) for division.

The operator is often referred to as a *function* and the items to be operated on as the *arguments* to the function, or simply the arguments. In the expression (/,25,2), the / is the function and 25 and 2 are the arguments. All Diesel expressions, no matter what size, follow this structure and are enclosed by parentheses.

Parentheses are important elements of an expression. All parentheses must be balanced; for each left parenthesis, there must be a right parenthesis.

You can do other things with Diesel besides performing calculations. The Getvar function is an AutoLISP function that you can use to obtain the drawing prefix and name. Try the following to see how Diesel uses Getvar:

1. Type **Modemacro.⏎** again.

2. Type **$(getvar,dwgprefix).⏎**. The location of the current drawing appears in the status bar.

3. Press ⏎ to reissue the Modemacro command; then type **$(getvar,dwgname).⏎**. The name of the drawing appears in the status bar.

In this example, the Getvar function extracts the drawing prefix and name and displays it in the status bar. You can use Getvar to extract any system variable you want. If you've been working through the tutorials in this book, you've seen that virtually all AutoCAD settings are also controlled through system variables. (The AutoCAD Help window contains a list of all the system variables.) This can be a great tool when you're creating custom menus because with Getvar, you can poll AutoCAD to determine its state. For example, you can find out what command is currently being used. Try the following exercise to see how this works:

1. Click the Line tool on the Draw panel.

2. Type **'Modemacro.⏎**. The apostrophe at the beginning of Modemacro lets you use the command while in another command.

3. Type **$(getvar,cmdnames).⏎**. The word *LINE* appears in the status bar, indicating that the current command is the Line command.

Diesel can be useful in a menu when you want an option to perform a specific task depending on which command is currently active.

LT USERS CAN USE DIESEL

LT users can't use AutoLISP to find the location of AutoCAD resource files. However, you can use the Diesel macro language. For example, to find the log file path, enter **Modemacro** and then **$(getvar,logfilepath)**. The path is displayed in the status bar. To get the status bar tools back, enter **Modemacro** and then enter a period.

Using Diesel in a Custom Menu Macro

So far, you've been experimenting with Diesel through the Modemacro command. Using Diesel in a menu macro requires a slightly different format. You still use the same Diesel format of a dollar sign followed by the expression, but you don't use the Modemacro command to access Diesel. Instead, you use $M=. You can think of $M= as an abbreviation for Modemacro.

Here's a Diesel expression that you can use in a menu macro:

```
^C^C_Blipmode;$M=$(-,1,$(getvar,Blipmode))
```

This menu option turns Blipmode on or off depending on Blipmode's current state. As you may recall, Blipmode is a feature that displays point selections in the drawing area as tiny crosses.

These tiny crosses, or *blips*, don't print and can be cleared from the screen with a redraw. They can be helpful when you need to track your point selections.

In this example, the Blipmode command is invoked, and then the $M= tells AutoCAD that a Diesel expression follows. The expression

```
$(-,1,$(getvar,Blipmode))
```

returns either 1 or a 0, which is applied to the Blipmode command to turn it either on or off. This expression shows that you can nest expressions. The most deeply nested expression is evaluated first, so AutoCAD begins by evaluating

```
$(getvar,Blipmode)
```

This returns either 1 or a 0, depending on whether Blipmode is on or off. Next, AutoCAD evaluates the next level in the expression

```
$(-,1,getvar_result)
```

in which *getvar_result* is either 1 or a 0. If *getvar_result* is 1, the expression looks like

```
$(-,1,1)
```

which returns 0. If *getvar_result* is 0, the expression looks like

```
$(-,1,0)
```

which returns 1. In either case, the end result is that the Blipmode command is assigned a value that is opposite of the current Blipmode setting.

Using Diesel as a Menu Bar Option Label

In the previous example, you saw how to use Diesel in a menu macro to read the status of a command and then return a numeric value to alter that status. You can also use Diesel as part of the menu bar option name so the text it displays depends on certain conditions. The following expression shows how to write a menu option name to display the current setting for Blipmode. It includes Diesel code as the menu option label:

```
$(eval,Blipmode = $(getvar,blipmode))
```

Normally, you would just have a menu name, but here you see some Diesel instructions. These instructions tell AutoCAD to display the message Blipmode = 1 or Blipmode = 0 in the menu, depending on the current Blipmode setting. You would place this code in the Properties group for the Blipmode custom command in the Customize User Interface dialog box. It goes in the Display/Name input box.

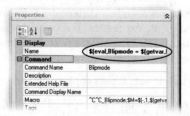

Here's how it works. You see the familiar `$(getvar,blipmode)` expression, this time embedded in a different expression. You know that `$(getvar,blipmode)` returns either 1 or a 0, depending on whether Blipmode is on or off. The outer expression

`$(eval,Blipmode = getvar_result)`

displays `Blipmode` = and then combines this with *getvar_result*, which, as you've learned, will be either 1 or 0. The `eval` function evaluates any text that follows it and returns its contents. The end result is the appearance of Blipmode = 1 or Blipmode = 0 in the menu, depending on the status of Blipmode. Here's how the properties looks as a menu bar option under the Tools list of the Menus option in the Customizations In All Files panel.

You can get even fancier and set up the menu option label to read Blipmode On or Blipmode Off by using the `if` Diesel function. Here's that same menu listing with additional Diesel code to accomplish this:

`$(eval,Blipmode = $(if,$(getvar,blipmode),Off,On))`

In this example, the simple `$(getvar,blipmode)` expression is expanded to include the `if` function. The `if` function reads the result of `$(getvar,blipmode)` and then returns the Off or On value depending on whether `$(getvar,blipmode)` returns 0 or a 1. Here's a simpler look at the expression:

`$(if, getvar_result, Off, On)`

If *getvar_result* returns 1, the `if` function returns the first of the two options listed after *getvar_result*, which is Off. If *getvar_result* returns 0, the `if` function returns On. The second of the two options is optional. Here's how the fancier Blipmode option appears in a menu.

You've just skimmed the surface of what Diesel can do. To get a more detailed description of how Diesel works, press the F1 function key to open the AutoCAD 2011 Help website. Click the Contents tab, expand the Customization Guide listing, and click the DIESEL listing that appears.

Table 28.2 shows some of the commonly used Diesel functions. Check the AutoCAD Help dialog box for a more detailed list.

TABLE 28.2:   Sample of Diesel functions

CODE	FUNCTION	EXAMPLE	RESULT	COMMENTS
+	Add	$(+,202,144)	346	
−	Subtract	$(-,202,144)	58	

TABLE 28.2:   Sample of Diesel functions   *(CONTINUED)*

CODE	FUNCTION	EXAMPLE	RESULT	COMMENTS
*	Multiply	$(*,202,144)	29,088	
/	Divide	$(/,202,144)	1.4028	
=	Equal to	$(=,202,144)	0	If numbers are equal, 1 is returned.
<	Less than	$(<,202,144)	0	If the first number is less than the second, 1 is returned.
>	Greater than	$(>,202,144)	1	If the first number is greater than the second, 1 is returned; otherwise 0 is returned.
!	Not equal to	$(!,202,144)	1	If the numbers are equal, 0 is returned.
<=	Less than or equal to	$(<=,202,144)	0	If the first number is less than or equal to the second, 1 is returned.
>=	Greater than or equal to	$(>=,202,144)	1	If the first number is greater than or equal to the second, 1 is returned; otherwise 0 is returned.
eq	Equal string	$(eq,Yes, No)	0	If both text strings are the same, 1 is returned.
eval	Evaluate text	$(eval,Here I Am)	Here I Am	Returns the text that follows.
getvar	Get system variable value	$(getvar,ltscale)	Current linetype scale	Returns the value of the system variable.
if	If/Then	$(if,1,Yes,No)	Yes	The second argument is returned if the first argument evaluates to 1. Otherwise, the third argument is returned. The third argument is optional.

Note: To indicate true or false, Diesel uses 1 or 0.

Using Diesel and Fields to Generate Text

Using Diesel expressions in the status bar or in a menu can be helpful to gather information or to create a more interactive interface, but what if you want the results of a Diesel expression to become part of the drawing? You can employ field objects to do just that.

For example, suppose you want to create a note that shows the scale of a drawing based on the dimension scale. Further, you want the scale in the note to be updated automatically whenever the dimension scale changes. You can add a field object and associate it with a Diesel expression that displays the dimension scale as it relates to the drawing scale. Try the following steps to see how it's done:

1. In the Annotate tab, click the Multiline Text tool and select two points to indicate the text location. The Text Editor Ribbon tab and text editor appear.

2. Right-click in the text editor, and select Insert Field to open the Field dialog box.

3. In the Field Category drop-down list, select Other; then, in the Field Names list box, select DieselExpression.

4. Add the following text in the Diesel Expression box to the right. If you need to expand the width of the dialog box, click and drag its right edge:

   ```
   $(eval,Dimension Scale: 1/)$(/,$(getvar, dimscale),12)$(eval, inch = 1 foot)
   ```

5. Click OK in the Field dialog box, and then click Close Text Editor in the Text Editor Ribbon tab. The following text is displayed in the drawing:

   ```
   Dimension Scale: 1/0.08333333 inch = 1 foot
   ```

The resulting text may not make sense until you change the dimension scale to a value that represents a scale other than 1-to-1. Here's how to do that:

1. Enter **Dimscale↵** at the Command prompt.

2. At the `Enter new value for DIMSCALE <1.0000>:` prompt, enter **96**. This is the value for a 1/8″ scale drawing.

3. Type **Re↵**. The text changes to read

   ```
   Dimension Scale: 1/8 inch = 1 foot
   ```

In this example, several Diesel operations were used. The beginning of the expression uses the eval operation to tell AutoCAD to display a string of text:

```
$(eval Dimension Scale: 1/)
```

The next part tells AutoCAD to get the current value of the Dimscale system variable and divide it by 12:

```
$(/,$(getvar, dimscale),12)
```

Notice that this is a nested expression: $(getvar,dimscale) obtains the value of the Dimscale system variable, which is then divided by 12. The end of the expression adds the final part to the text:

```
$(eval, inch = 1 foot)
```

When it's all put together, you get the text that shows the dimension scale as an architectural scale. Because it's an AutoCAD text object, this text is part of the drawing.

Creating Custom Linetypes

As your drawing needs expand, the standard linetypes may not be adequate for your application. Fortunately, you can create your own. The following sections explain how to do so.

You'll get an in-depth view of the process of creating linetypes. You'll also learn how to create complex linetypes that can't be created by using the Make Linetype Express tool.

Viewing Available Linetypes

Although AutoCAD provides the linetypes most commonly used in drafting (see Figure 28.23), the dashes and dots may not be spaced the way you would like, or you may want an entirely new linetype.

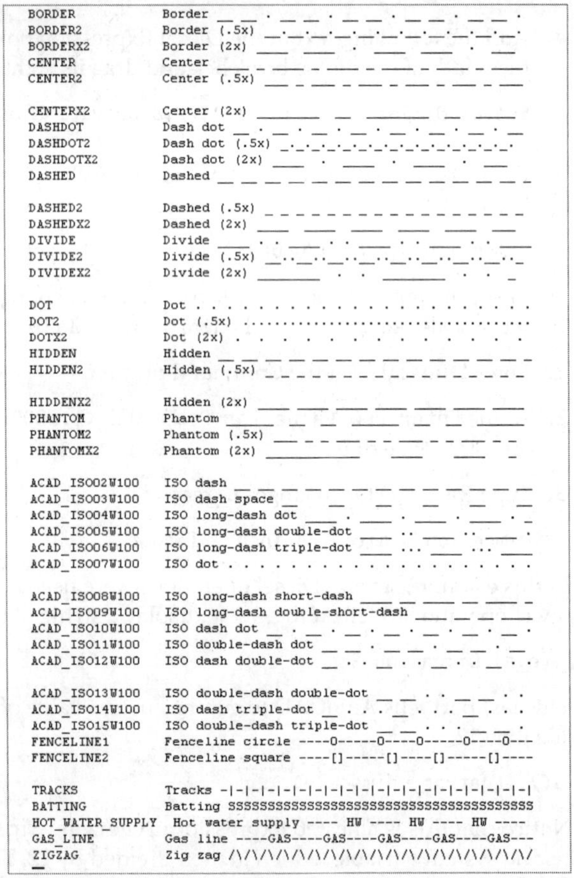

FIGURE 28.23
The lines in this list of standard linetypes were generated with the underscore key (_) and the period (.) and are only rough representations of the actual lines.

```
BORDER            Border     ___ ___ . ___ ___ . ___ ___ . ___ .
BORDER2           Border (.5x) _._._._._._._._._._._._._._._.
BORDERX2          Border (2x)  ___    ___  .  ___    ___  .
CENTER            Center     ____ _ ____ _ ____ _ ____ _ ____
CENTER2           Center (.5x) ___ _ ___ _ ___ _ ___ _ ___ _

CENTERX2          Center (2x)  _____ __ _____ __ _____
DASHDOT           Dash dot   __ . __ . __ . __ . __ . __ . __ .
DASHDOT2          Dash dot (.5x) _._._._._._._._._._._._._._.
DASHDOTX2         Dash dot (2x)  ___  .  ___  .  ___  .  ___
DASHED            Dashed     __ __ __ __ __ __ __ __ __ __ __

DASHED2           Dashed (.5x) _ _ _ _ _ _ _ _ _ _ _ _ _ _ _ _
DASHEDX2          Dashed (2x)  ___  ___  ___  ___  ___  ___
DIVIDE            Divide     __ . . __ . . __ . . __ . . __
DIVIDE2           Divide (.5x) _.._.._.._.._.._.._.._.._.._.
DIVIDEX2          Divide (2x)  _____  . .  _____  . .

DOT               Dot        . . . . . . . . . . . . . . . . .
DOT2              Dot (.5x)  ...............................
DOTX2             Dot (2x)   .  .  .  .  .  .  .  .  .  .  .
HIDDEN            Hidden     __ __ __ __ __ __ __ __ __ __ __
HIDDEN2           Hidden (.5x) _ _ _ _ _ _ _ _ _ _ _ _ _ _ _

HIDDENX2          Hidden (2x)  ___  ___  ___  ___  ___  ___
PHANTOM           Phantom    _____ __ __ _____ __ __ _____
PHANTOM2          Phantom (.5x) ___ _ _ ___ _ _ ___ _ _ ___
PHANTOMX2         Phantom (2x)  _____    __    ____

ACAD_ISO02W100    ISO dash   __ __ __ __ __ __ __ __ __ __ __
ACAD_ISO03W100    ISO dash space __    __    __    __    __
ACAD_ISO04W100    ISO long-dash dot  ____ . ____ . ____ . ___
ACAD_ISO05W100    ISO long-dash double-dot ____ .. ____ .. ___ .
ACAD_ISO06W100    ISO long-dash triple-dot ____ ... ____ ... ___
ACAD_ISO07W100    ISO dot    . . . . . . . . . . . . . . . .

ACAD_ISO08W100    ISO long-dash short-dash ____ __ ____ __ ___
ACAD_ISO09W100    ISO long-dash double-short-dash ____ __ __ ____
ACAD_ISO10W100    ISO dash dot  __ . __ . __ . __ . __ . __
ACAD_ISO11W100    ISO double-dash dot __ __ . __ __ . __ __ .
ACAD_ISO12W100    ISO dash double-dot __ . . __ . . __ . . __ .

ACAD_ISO13W100    ISO double-dash double-dot __ __ . . __ __ . .
ACAD_ISO14W100    ISO dash triple-dot __ . . . __ . . . __ . . .
ACAD_ISO15W100    ISO double-dash triple-dot __ __ . . . __ __ .
FENCELINE1        Fenceline circle ----O-----O----O-----O----O---
FENCELINE2        Fenceline square ----[]-----[]----[]-----[]----

TRACKS            Tracks -|-|-|-|-|-|-|-|-|-|-|-|-|-|-|-|-|-|-|
BATTING           Batting SSSSSSSSSSSSSSSSSSSSSSSSSSSSSSSSSSSSSS
HOT_WATER_SUPPLY  Hot water supply ---- HW ---- HW ---- HW ----
GAS_LINE          Gas line ----GAS----GAS----GAS----GAS----GAS---
ZIGZAG            Zig zag /\/\/\/\/\/\/\/\/\/\/\/\/\/\/\/\/
```

WHERE ARE THE LINETYPES STORED?

AutoCAD stores the linetypes in a file called acad.lin, which is in ASCII format. When you create a new linetype, you add information to this file. Or, if you create a new file containing your own linetype definitions, it too will have the extension .lin at the end of its name. You can edit linetypes as described here, or you can edit them directly in these files.

To create a custom linetype, use the Linetype command. Let's see how this handy command works by first listing the available linetypes:

1. Open a new AutoCAD file.

2. At the Command prompt, enter **–Linetype**↵. (Don't forget the minus sign at the beginning.)

3. At the Enter an option [?/Create/Load/Set]: prompt, enter **?**↵.

4. In the dialog box, locate and double-click acad.lin in the listing of available linetype files. You get a list that shows the linetypes available in the acad.lin file along with a simple description of each line.

5. A message at the bottom says Press ENTER to continue:. Do so until you see the Command prompt.

Creating a New Linetype

Next, let's try creating a new linetype:

1. Enter **–Linetype**↵ again.

2. At the [?/Create/Load/Set]: prompt, enter **C**↵.

3. At the Enter name of linetype to create: prompt, enter **Custom**↵ as the name of your new linetype.

4. The dialog box you see next is named Create Or Append Linetype File. You need to enter the name of the linetype file you want to create or add to. If you select the default linetype file, acad, your new linetype is added to the acad.lin file. If you choose to create a new linetype file, AutoCAD opens a file containing the linetype you create and adds .lin to the filename you supply.

5. Let's assume you want to start a new linetype file. Enter **Newline**↵ in the File Name input box.

NEW OR EXISTING LINETYPE FILE

If you accept the default linetype file, acad, the prompt in step 4 is Wait, checking if linetype already defined. … This protects you from inadvertently overwriting an existing linetype you want to keep.

---

6. At the `Descriptive text:` prompt, enter a text description of your linetype. You can use any keyboard character as part of your description, but the actual linetype can be composed of only a series of lines, points, and blank spaces. For this exercise, enter the following, using the underscore key (_) to simulate the appearance of your line:

```
Custom - My own center line _____ _ _____    ↵
```

7. At the `Enter linetype pattern (on next line):` prompt, enter the following numbers, known as the *linetype code* (after the `A,` that appears automatically):

```
1.0,-.125,.25,-.125↵
```

YOU CAN SET THE DEFAULT LINETYPE

If you use the Set option of the -Linetype command to set a new default linetype, you'll get that linetype no matter what layer you're on.

---

8. At the `New linetype definition saved to file. Enter an option [?/Create/Load/Set]:` prompt, press ↵ to exit the -Linetype command.

Remember, after you've created a linetype, you must load it in order to use it, as discussed in Chapter 5.

ADD LINETYPES DIRECTLY TO THE ACAD.LIN FILE

You can also open the acad.lin or other LIN file in Windows Notepad and add the descriptive text and linetype code directly to the end of the file.

Understanding the Linetype Code

In step 6 of the previous exercise, you entered a series of numbers separated by commas. This is the linetype code, representing the lengths of the components that make up the linetype. The separate elements of the linetype code are as follows:

◆ The 1.0 following the A is the length of the first part of the line. (The A that begins the linetype definition is a code that is applied to all linetypes.)

◆ The first -.125 is the blank or broken part of the line. The minus sign tells AutoCAD that the line is *not* to be drawn for the specified length, which is 0.125 units in this example.

◆ Next comes the positive value 0.25. This tells AutoCAD to draw a line segment 0.25 units long after the blank part of the line.

◆ The last negative value, -.125, again tells AutoCAD to skip drawing the line for the distance of 0.125 units.

This series of numbers represents the one segment that is repeated to form the line (see Figure 28.24). You can also create a complex linetype that looks like a random broken line, as in Figure 28.25.

FIGURE 28.24

Linetype description with plotted line

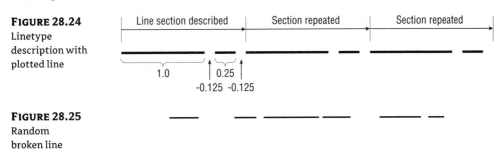

FIGURE 28.25

Random broken line

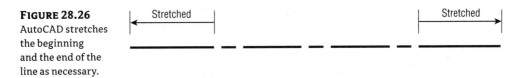

You may be wondering what purpose the A serves at the beginning of the linetype code. A linetype is composed of a series of line segments and points. The A, which is supplied by AutoCAD automatically, is a code that forces the linetype to start and end on a line segment rather than on a blank space in the series of lines. At times, AutoCAD stretches the last line segment to force this condition, as shown in Figure 28.26.

FIGURE 28.26

AutoCAD stretches the beginning and the end of the line as necessary.

LINE-SEGMENT LENGTHS AND SCALE

The values you enter for the line-segment lengths are multiplied by the Ltscale factor, so be sure to enter values for the plotted lengths.

As mentioned earlier, you can also create linetypes outside of AutoCAD by using a word processor or text editor such as Windows Notepad. The standard acad.lin file looks like Figure 28.23 with the addition of the code used by AutoCAD to determine the line-segment lengths.

Normally, to use a linetype you've created, you have to load it through either the Layer Properties Manager or the Linetype Manager dialog box (choose Other from the Linetype drop-down list in the Home tab's Properties panel). If you use one of your own linetypes frequently, you may want to create a button macro so it will be available as an option on a menu.

Creating Complex Linetypes

A *complex linetype* is one that incorporates text or special graphics. For example, if you want to show an underground gas line in a site plan, you normally show a line with the intermittent word *GAS*, as in Figure 28.27. Fences are often shown with an intermittent circle, square, or X.

For the graphics needed to compose complex linetypes, use any of the symbols in the AutoCAD font files discussed in Chapter 10. Create a text style by using these symbol fonts, and then specify the appropriate symbol by using its corresponding letter in the linetype description.

FIGURE 28.27

Samples of complex linetypes

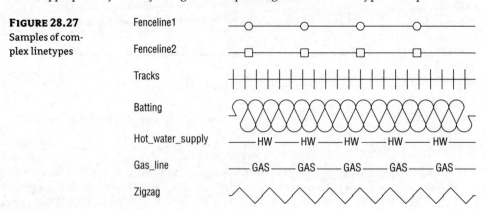

To create a linetype that includes text, use the same linetype code described earlier, with the addition of the necessary font file information in brackets. For example, say you want to create the linetype for the underground gas line mentioned previously by using just the letter *G*. You add the following to your `acad.lin` file:

```
*Gas_line, -G-G-G-
A,1.0,-0.25,["G",STANDARD,S=.2,R=0,X=-.1,Y=-.1],-0.25
```

The first line serves as a description for anyone looking at this linetype code. The next line is the code itself. Note that the code should not contain spaces—spaces are used here for clarity.

The information in the square brackets describes the characteristics of the text. The actual text that you want to appear in the line is surrounded by quotation marks. Next are the text style, scale, rotation angle, X displacement, and Y displacement.

EDIT THE *ACAD.LIN* FILE TO CREATE COMPLEX LINETYPES

You can't use the -Linetype command to define complex linetypes. Instead, you must open the `acad.lin` file by using a text editor, such as Windows Notepad, and add the linetype information to the end of the file. Make sure you don't duplicate the name of an existing linetype.

You can substitute A for the rotation angle (the R value), as in the following example:

```
A,1.0,-0.25,["G",standard,S=.2,A=0,X=-.1,Y=-.1],-0.25
```

This has the effect of keeping the text at the same angle regardless of the line's direction. Notice that in this sample, the X and Y values are -.1; this will center the *G*s on the line. The scale value of .2 will cause the text to be 0.2 units high, so .1 is half the height.

In addition to fonts, you can specify shapes for linetype definitions. Instead of letters, shapes display symbols. Shapes are stored not as drawings but as definition files, similar to text font files. Shape files have the same `.shx` filename extension as font files and are also defined similarly.

Figure 28.28 shows some symbols from sample shape files. The names of the files are shown at the top of each column.

To use a shape in a linetype code, you use the same format as shown previously for text. However, instead of using a letter and style name, you use the shape name and the shape file-name, as in the following example:

```
*Capline, ====
a,1.0,-0.25,[CAP,ES.SHX,S=.5,R=0,X=-.1,Y=-.1],-0.25
```

FIGURE 28.28

Samples of shapes

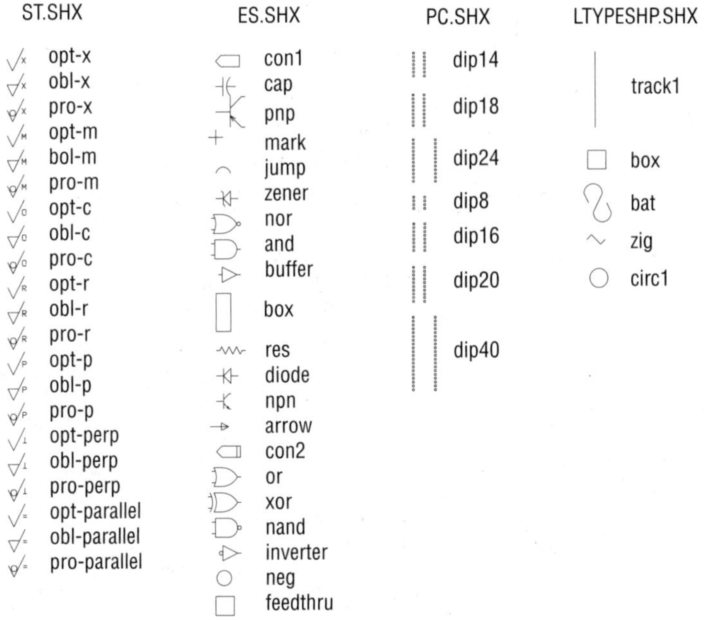

ST.SHX	ES.SHX	PC.SHX	LTYPESHP.SHX
opt-x	con1	dip14	track1
obl-x	cap	dip18	
pro-x	pnp		
opt-m	mark	dip24	box
bol-m	jump		bat
pro-m	zener	dip8	zig
opt-c	nor	dip16	circ1
obl-c	and		
pro-c	buffer	dip20	
opt-r			
obl-r	box		
pro-r			
opt-p	res	dip40	
obl-p	diode		
pro-p	npn		
opt-perp	arrow		
obl-perp	con2		
pro-perp	or		
opt-parallel	xor		
obl-parallel	nand		
pro-parallel	inverter		
	neg		
	feedthru		

This example uses the CAP symbol from the Es.shx shape file. The symbol is scaled to 0.5 units with 0 rotation and an X and Y displacement of -0.1.

Here is another example that uses the arrow shape:

```
*Arrowline, -|-|-|->
a,1.0,-0.25,[ARROW,ES.SHX,S=.5,R=90,X=-.1,Y=-.1],-0.25
```

Just as with the Capline example, the ARROW symbol in this example is scaled to 0.5 units with 0 rotation and an X and Y displacement of -0.1. Figure 28.29 shows what the Arrowline linetype looks like when used with a spline.

In this example, the Ltype generation option is turned on for the polyline. Note that the arrow from the Es.shx sample shape file is used for the arrow in this linetype.

FIGURE 28.29

The Arrowline linetype used with a spline

Creating Hatch Patterns

AutoCAD provides several predefined hatch patterns you can choose from, but you can also create your own. This section demonstrates the basic elements of pattern definition.

Unlike linetypes, hatch patterns can't be created while you're in an AutoCAD file. The pattern definitions are contained in an external file named `acad.pat`. You can open and edit this file with a text editor that can handle ASCII files, such as Windows Notepad. Here is one hatch pattern definition from that file:

```
*SQUARE,Small aligned squares
0, 0,0, 0,.125, .125,-.125
90, 0,0, 0,.125, .125,-.125
```

You can see some similarities between pattern descriptions and linetype descriptions. They both start with a line of descriptive text and then give numeric values defining the pattern. However, the numbers in pattern descriptions have a different meaning. This example shows two lines of information. Each line represents a line in the pattern. The first line determines the horizontal line component of the pattern, and the second line represents the vertical component (see the image to the far right in Figure 28.30). A pattern is made up of line groups. A *line group* is like a linetype that is arrayed a specified distance to fill the area to be hatched. A line group is defined by a line of code, much as a linetype is defined. In the square pattern, for instance, two lines—one horizontal and one vertical—are used. Each of these lines is duplicated in a fashion that makes the lines appear as boxes when they're combined. Figure 28.30 illustrates this point.

FIGURE 28.30
The individual
and combined
line groups

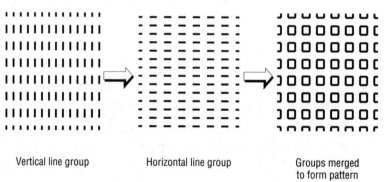

Vertical line group   Horizontal line group   Groups merged
to form pattern

Look at the first line in the definition:

```
0, 0,0, 0,.125, .125,-.125
```

This example shows a series of numbers separated by commas. It represents one line group. It contains four sets of information, separated by blank spaces:

♦ The first component is the 0 at the beginning. This value indicates the angle of the line group, as determined by the line's orientation. In this case, it's 0 for a horizontal line that runs from left to right.

◆ The next component is the origin of the line group, 0 , 0. This doesn't mean the line begins at the drawing origin (see Figure 28.31). It gives you a reference point to determine the location of other line groups involved in generating the pattern.

FIGURE 28.31
The origin of
the patterns

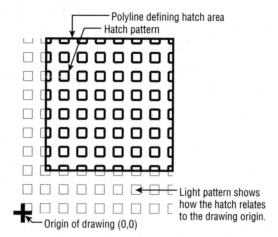

◆ The next component is 0 , .125. This determines the distance and direction for arraying the line, as illustrated in Figure 28.32. This value is like a relative coordinate indicating X and Y distances for a rectangular array. It isn't based on the drawing coordinates, but on a coordinate system relative to the orientation of the line. For a line oriented at a 0° angle, the code 0 , .125 indicates a precisely vertical direction. For a line oriented at a 45° angle, the code 0 , .125 represents a 135° direction. In this example, the duplication occurs 90° in relation to the line group, because the X value is 0. Figure 28.33 illustrates this point.

◆ The last component is the description of the line pattern. This value is equivalent to the value given when you create a linetype. Positive values are line segments, and negative values are blank segments. This part of the line group definition works exactly as in the linetype definitions you studied in the previous section.

This system of defining hatch patterns may seem somewhat limiting, but you can do a lot with it. Autodesk managed to come up with 69 patterns—and that was only scratching the surface.

ADDING THICK LINES TO LINETYPES

If you want to include thick lines in your hatch patterns, you have to build up line widths with multiple linetype definitions.

FIGURE 28.32

The distance and direction of duplication

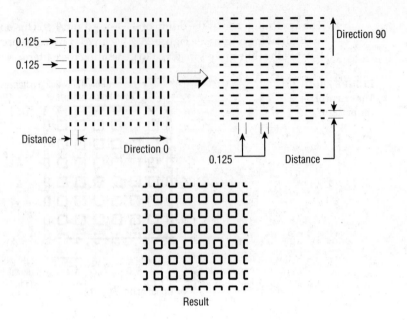

0.125

0.125

Direction 90

Distance

Direction 0

0.125

Distance

Result

FIGURE 28.33

How the direction of the line group copy is determined

The X and Y coordinate values given for the array distance are based on the orientation of the line group.

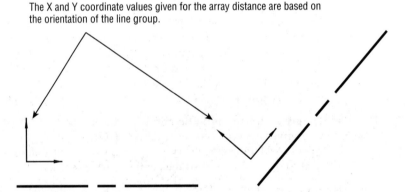

The Bottom Line

Use workspaces.   Often with AutoCAD, you find that you have different sets of panels or toolbars open to perform specific tasks. You might have one set of Ribbon panels for editing text and dimensions, whereas another set is more useful for design. Using workspaces is a great way to organize your different editing modes.

Master It   Where do you find the Customize option for workspaces?

Customize the user interface.   In addition to using workspaces to organize tools and Ribbon panels, you can customize the AutoCAD interface to make it fit the way you like to work. You can add tools to Ribbon panels or even create your own tools for operations you perform frequently.

Master It   What does the Customizations In All Files group display?

Create macros in tools and menus. A macro is a set of instructions that performs more complex operations than single commands. Macros are often built on commands with additional predefined responses to help speed data input.

Master It What does the ^C do in a macro?

Edit keyboard shortcuts. Keyboard shortcuts can help improve your speed when drawing in AutoCAD. They can reduce several clicks of the mouse to a simple keystroke. AutoCAD lets you create custom shortcuts for your favorite commands.

Master It What is the keyboard shortcut for Copy?

Save, load, and unload your customizations. To keep your customizations organized, you can save new toolbars, menus, and Ribbons as files that you can load on demand. When you save your custom elements as a file, you can move them to other computers.

Master It Name the tab that contains the group you use to save your custom elements.

Understand the Diesel macro language. If you're adventurous, you may want to try your hand at creating more-complex macros. The Diesel macro language is an easy introduction to AutoCAD macro customization and is most useful in controlling the behavior in menu options.

Master It What does the expression $(getvar, blipmode) do?

Create custom linetypes. AutoCAD offers a number of noncontinuous linetypes, and you may find them adequate for most of your work. But every now and then, you may need a specific linetype that isn't available. Creating custom linetypes is easy once you understand the process.

Master It What is the purpose of a negative value in the linetype code?

Create hatch patterns. Like linetypes, the hatch patterns provided by AutoCAD will probably fill most of your needs. But every now and then, you may need to produce a specific pattern.

Master It How are a hatch pattern code and a linetype code similar?

Chapter 29

Managing and Sharing Your Drawings

Whether you're a one-person operation working out of your home or one of several hundred AutoCAD users in a large company, file sharing and file maintenance can become the focus of much of your time. In our interconnected world, the volume of messages and files crossing our paths seems to be on the rise constantly. In addition, the Internet has enabled us to be more mobile, adding yet more complexity to file-management tasks.

In this chapter, you'll learn about some of the tools AutoCAD offers to help you manage your files and the files you share with others. You'll also examine some general issues that arise while using AutoCAD in a workgroup environment. You may find help with problems you've encountered when using AutoCAD in your particular work environment in the discussion throughout the chapter.

In this chapter you'll learn to do the following:

◆ Share drawings over the Internet

◆ ePublish your drawings

◆ Manage your drawings with DesignCenter and the tool palettes

◆ Establish office standards

◆ Convert multiple layer settings

Sharing Drawings over the Internet

The Internet has become a major part of our daily working lives. It provides AutoCAD users with some real, practical benefits by giving them the ability to publish drawings and other documents online. AutoCAD gives you tools that enable you to post drawings on the Internet that others can view and download. In the architecture, engineering, and civil (AEC) industry in particular, this can mean easier access to documents needed by contractors, engineers, cost estimators, and others involved in the design, bidding, and construction of architectural projects. Suppliers of products can post symbol libraries of their products or even 3D solid models.

In the following sections, you'll learn about the tools AutoCAD provides for publishing and accessing drawings over the Internet (and on any local or wide area network). You'll start by looking at one of the most common uses of the Internet: file transmission.

Sharing Project Files with eTransmit

Perhaps the most common use of the Internet is sending and receiving files. Whether you're a 1-person office or a member of a 50-person firm, you'll eventually have to share your work with others outside your building. Before eTransmit existed as a feature in AutoCAD, you had to examine what you were sending carefully to make sure you included all the ancillary files needed to view or work on your drawings. Xref, font, and custom linetype files all had to be included with the drawings that you sent to consultants or partners in a project, and often one of these items was omitted from the transmission.

By using eTransmit, you can quickly collect all your project drawings into a single archive file, or you can store the files in a separate folder for later processing. This collection of files is included with a report file as a transmittal. Try the following to see how eTransmit works:

1. In AutoCAD, open a file you intend to send to someone and then choose Send ➤ eTransmit from the Application menu to open the Create Transmittal dialog box (Figure 29.1). If you've edited the file before choosing eTransmit, you will see a message telling you that you must save the drawing before continuing.

FIGURE 29.1
Creating a transmittal

2. In the dialog box, a tree structure lists the files that are included in the transmittal. If you need to add more files to the transmittal than are shown in the list, you can click the Add File button to open a file dialog box. To remove files, expand the listed item and remove the checkmark that appears next to the file you want to exclude. You can also use the Files Table tab to view the files as a simple list.

3. Click in the Enter Notes To Include With This Transmittal Package input box, and enter a description or other note.

4. In the Select A Transmittal Setup group, click the Transmittal Setups button to open the Transmittal Setups dialog box (Figure 29.2). From here, you can create a new transmittal or rename or modify an existing one.

FIGURE 29.2
Choose whether to
create from scratch
or edit an existing
transmittal.

FIGURE 29.2
Choose whether to
create from scratch
or edit an existing
transmittal.

5. Click the Modify button to open the Modify Transmittal Setup dialog box (Figure 29.3).

FIGURE 29.3
Set your transmit-
tal options.

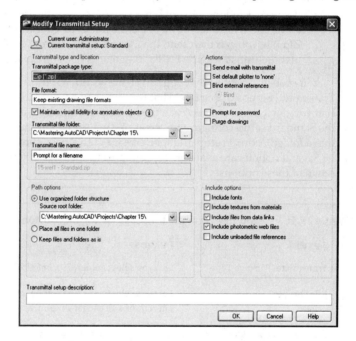

6. In the Transmittal Package Type drop-down list, select the format for your collection of files. You can create a Zip or self-extracting executable archive, or you can save the files in a folder. If you choose the Zip or executable option, you can also add a password by selecting the Prompt For Password check box in the Actions group of the dialog box. The person receiving the transmittal file must then enter a password to extract the files. If you choose the Folder option, you can tell AutoCAD where to place the files by using the Browse button to the right of the Transmittal File Folder drop-down list. For this exercise, choose the Folder option in the Transmittal Package Type list.

7. Click the Browse button to open the Specify Location Folder dialog box. This is a typical AutoCAD file dialog box that you can use to select a location for your files. You can use the Create New Folder tool to create a new folder for your files. You'll want to keep your transmittal files separate from other files. After you select a location, click Open to return to the Modify Transmittal Setup dialog box.

8. After you've set up your transmittal, click OK. Then click Close in the Transmittal Setups dialog box.

9. Preview the report file by clicking the View Report button in the Create Transmittal dialog box. This report gives you a detailed description of the types of files included in the transmittal. It also alerts you to files that AutoCAD was unable to find but that are required for the drawing.

10. Close the report. After you've set up the eTransmit options, click OK in the Create Transmittal dialog box.

11. If you selected the Zip option in step 6, you see the Specify Zip File dialog box. Enter a name and a location for the file and AutoCAD collects the files into an archive folder or a Zip file. You can then send the files over the Internet or put them on a removable disk for manual transport. The EXE option works in a similar way.

You probably noticed that you can create additional transmittal setup options in the Transmittal Setups dialog box. That way, you can have multiple transmittal options on hand that you don't have to set up each time a different situation arises. For example, you might have the Standard setup configured to create a Zip file and another setup configured to copy the files into a folder. A third setup might be created with a password.

Several options are available for configuring the transmittal setup. Table 29.1 gives a rundown of those options.

TABLE 29.1:   Modify Transmittal Setup dialog box options

OPTION	PURPOSE
Transmittal Package Type	Lets you select Folder, Zip, or Self-Extracting Executable.
File Format	Lets you select 2010, 2007, 2004, or 2000 file formats in case your recipient requires an earlier version.
Maintain Visual Fidelity For Annotative Objects	Maintains visual fidelity for annotative objects when drawings are viewed in AutoCAD 2007 and earlier.
Transmittal File Folder	Lets you determine the location for your transmittal package.
Transmittal File Name	Not available if you select Folder as the transmittal package type. Options are Prompt For A File Name, Overwrite If Necessary, and Increment File Name If Necessary.
Use Organized Folder Structure	Preserves the folder structure for the files in the transmittal. This can be important when Xref and other files are located across several folder locations.
Place All Files In One Folder	Self-explanatory.

TABLE 29.1:   Modify Transmittal Setup dialog box options *(CONTINUED)*

OPTION	PURPOSE
Keep Files And Folders As Is	Preserves the entire folder structure for the files in the transmittal.
Include Fonts	Tells AutoCAD to include the font files in the transmittal.
Include Textures From Materials	Lets you include bitmap files that are part of a file's material settings.
Include Files From Data Links	Lets you include external data-link files for tables.
Include Photometric Web Files	Lets you include photometric web files for 3D lighting models.
Include Unloaded File References	Include references for unloaded Xref files.
Send E-Mail With Transmittal	Lets you send an e-mail with the files included as an attachment.
Set Default Plotter To 'None'	Removes any reference to printers or plotters that you've set up for the drawing. (The type of printer you've set up for your files is stored with the drawing file.)
Bind External References	Lets you bind external references to the drawings that contain them if it isn't important for the recipient to maintain the external references as separate drawings.
Prompt For Password	Gives you the option to password-protect the transmittal file.
Purge Drawings	Purge drawings of unused elements.

eTransmit gives you a quick way to package a set of files to be sent to others working on the same project. But you may need to offer a wider distribution of your files. You might want to let others view and plot your drawings from a website without exposing your drawing database to anyone who might visit your site. If this sounds like something you're interested in, you'll want to know about the AutoCAD DWF file format, which lets anyone view AutoCAD files whether they own the program or not. You'll learn more about the DWF file format in the section "ePublishing Your Drawings" later in this chapter.

Protecting AutoCAD Drawing Files

Because AutoCAD drawings specify the methods and materials used to produce an object or a building, they are frequently treated like legal documents. After an AutoCAD drawing is issued, it's often archived and guarded as a legal record of a design. For this reason, many AutoCAD users are concerned about possible tampering with drawings that are sent to third parties. Even minor, unauthorized changes to a drawing can have major repercussions to the integrity of a design.

AutoCAD 2011 offers tools that can help minimize file tampering. The eTransmit feature offers a password-protection option to reduce the possibility of unauthorized tampering with transmittal files. AutoCAD also offers password protection for individual files as well as a digital-signature feature that helps protect both the author of a drawing and the recipient in the event of file tampering.

ADDING PASSWORD PROTECTION TO FILES

The basic type of file protection is password protection of individual files. AutoCAD offers password protection through the Save Drawing As dialog box and the Options dialog box.

To add a password to a drawing when you save it, do the following:

1. Choose Save As from the Application menu to open the Save Drawing As dialog box.

2. Choose Tools ➤ Security Options from the menu in the upper-right corner of the dialog box.

3. In the Security Options dialog box, enter a password or phrase in the input box.

4. Click OK. You're prompted to enter the password again.

5. Enter the password again, and click OK to return to the Save Drawing As dialog box.

6. Enter the name and location of your file, and then click Save.

In addition to the Save Drawing As dialog box, you can add password protection through the Options dialog box:

1. Choose Options from the Application menu to open the Options dialog box, and then click the Open And Save tab.

2. Click the Security Options button in the File Safety Precautions group to open the Security Options dialog box.

3. Enter your password, select other options as necessary, and then click OK. You may have to enter your password a second time to confirm.

As a third option, you can enter **Securityoptions↵** at the Command prompt to go directly to the Security Options dialog box.

After you've added a password, anyone attempting to open the file will be asked to provide the password before the file can be opened. This includes any attempt to use the file as an Xref or a file insertion.

AUTOCAD REMEMBERS THAT YOU'VE OPENED A FILE

After you open a password-protected file and give the password, you can open and close the file repeatedly during that AutoCAD session without having to reenter the password. If you close and reopen AutoCAD, AutoCAD will prompt you for a password the next time you attempt to open the password-protected file.

USING A DIGITAL SIGNATURE

In addition to password protection, you can use a digital signature to authenticate files. A digital signature can't prevent someone from tampering with a file, but it offers a way to validate whether a file has been modified after it has been saved. This protects you in the event that your file is unofficially altered. It also protects the recipient of your file by verifying the file's authenticity and by verifying that it was not altered from the time it left your computer.

The first time you attempt to use the digital signature feature, you see a message telling you that you need a digital ID.

As the message explains, a digital ID is required to use the digital signature feature. AutoCAD uses a digital ID issued by any certificate authority, such as, for example, VeriSign, a company that specializes in Internet security. The VeriSign digital ID service is fee based, with prices ranging from about $15 for a basic one-year enrollment to nearly $700 for a professional-level ID. A free 60-day trial is also offered. The following steps show how to acquire a digital ID:

1. Make sure you have a connection to the Internet.

2. From the Windows Taskbar, choose Start ➢ (All) Programs ➢ Autodesk ➢ AutoCAD 2011 ➢ Attach Digital Signatures. Or, from AutoCAD, enter **Securityoptions**↵ to open the Security Options dialog box and then click the Digital Signature tab. The No Valid Digital ID Is Available warning dialog box appears.

3. Click the Obtain ID button. Your web browser opens at the VeriSign page.

4. Select the security services you want, and follow the rest of the instructions.

After you've obtained a digital ID, the signature resides in the Registry on your computer. You can then access the digital ID from AutoCAD by using the Digital Signature tab of the Security Options dialog box. Here are the steps:

1. Open the drawing to which you want to attach the digital signature, and then open the Security Options dialog box by entering **Securityoptions**↵ at the Command prompt.

2. Click the Digital Signature tab (Figure 29.4).

3. Select the Attach Digital Signature After Saving Drawing option. The Signature Information options become available. You can add a date stamp and a brief description.

4. Click OK to exit the dialog box.

FIGURE 29.4
Attach a signature.

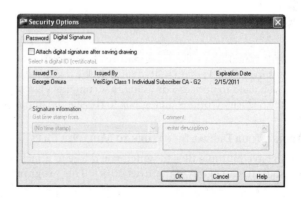

The next time you save the file, depending on the level of security you choose during the digital ID setup, you may be prompted for a password. After you enter the password, the file is saved.

The next time the file is opened, you'll see the Digital Signature Contents dialog box (Figure 29.5), which verifies that no one has tampered with the drawing.

FIGURE 29.5
The signature is verified when the file opens.

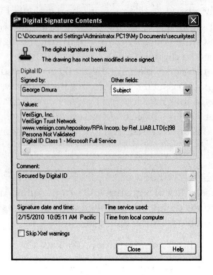

You'll also see a stamp icon in the lower-right corner of the AutoCAD window. You can click this icon at any time to view the file's digital signature status. You can also issue the Sigvalidate command to view the status. If the file is modified in any way and then saved, a warning message (Figure 29.6) will appear at the top of the Digital Signature Content dialog box the next time the file is opened.

FIGURE 29.6
Checking signature status

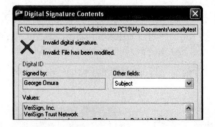

A file containing a digital signature also displays a warning when it's being modified, stating that saving a new version will invalidate the digital signature.

If you need to update a drawing that contains your digital signature, you can do so and then use the Security Options dialog box to reissue the digital signature.

ADDING YOUR DIGITAL SIGNATURE TO MULTIPLE FILES

If you have multiple files to which you'd like to attach your digital signature, you should use the Attach Digital Signatures utility. This program runs outside AutoCAD, and it provides a convenient way to attach your digital signature to a set of drawings. Here's how it works:

1. From the Windows Taskbar, choose Start ➤ Programs ➤ Autodesk ➤ AutoCAD 2011 ➤ Attach Digital Signatures to open the Attach Digital Signatures dialog box (Figure 29.7).

FIGURE 29.7
Signing
multiple files

A DIGITAL ID IS REQUIRED

If you haven't obtained a digital ID, you see a message telling you that no valid digital ID is available on your system. To proceed, you'll have to obtain a digital ID from a certificate authority such as VeriSign, as described earlier in "Using a Digital Signature."

---

2. Click the Add Files button to locate and select files. You can also search for files in a particular folder by clicking the Search Folders button. The files you add appear in the Files To Be Signed list box.

3. If you decide to remove a file from the list box, highlight it and then click Remove. You can also remove all the files from the list by clicking Clear List.

4. The rest of the dialog box is the same as the Digital Signature tab of the Security Options dialog box. You can enter the date and time and a comment for the files you've selected.

5. Click Sign Files when you're sure you've selected the correct files and entered an appropriate comment.

If you exchange AutoCAD drawings regularly with clients and consultants, you'll want to obtain a digital ID and use AutoCAD's digital signature feature. Be aware, however, that because this feature was new in AutoCAD 2004, it works only if you exchange files with others using AutoCAD 2004 or later. In fact, a quick way to remove a digital signature from a file is to save the file in the AutoCAD 2002 or earlier file format.

If you intend to use the password feature in conjunction with your digital signature, you must add the signature first before adding the password.

 **Real World Scenario**

DIGITAL IDS AND PDFS

In the office where I work, PDFs are being used more often for submittals, which are common documents used during the construction phase of a project. In the past, paper submittals were stamped to validate their review by an architect. PDF submittals can be "stamped" using digital IDs that are unique to the individual who is reviewing the submittal. If you've obtained a digital ID from VeriSign and you have the full version of Adobe Acrobat, you can use the Acrobat Advanced Security and stamp feature to apply an ID to any PDF document. Acrobat will also generate its own digital ID. Unfortunately, the ID from Acrobat cannot be used with AutoCAD.

---

ePublishing Your Drawings

The features discussed so far are intended mostly for exchanging files with others who need to work directly with your AutoCAD files. However, there are always associates and clients who need to see only your final drawings and don't care whether they get AutoCAD files. Alternatively, you might be working with people who don't have AutoCAD but still need to view and print your drawings. For those non-AutoCAD end users, AutoCAD offers the DWF file format.

You can think of the DWF file format as a kind of Adobe Acrobat file for AutoCAD drawings. DWF offers a way to get your plans and design ideas in the hands of more people more easily. With the help of the free Autodesk DWF Viewer—equivalent to the Adobe Reader for Acrobat documents—DWF files can be viewed using the same types of pan and zoom tools available in AutoCAD, which allows greater detail to be presented in your drawings. In addition, you can embed URL links that can open other documents with a single mouse click. These links can be attached to objects or areas in the drawing.

You can also print DWF files using your Windows system printer or plotter, all without having AutoCAD installed. A single DWF file can contain multiple drawing sheets, so you can combine a complete set of drawings into one DWF file. By default, AutoCAD saves DWF files in a new DWFx format that is compatible with the Windows Vista XPS format.

Exchanging Drawing Sets

Imagine that you're working on a skylight addition to a house and you need to send your drawings to your client for review. In addition to the skylight plans, you want to include some alternate floor plans that your client has asked you to generate. In this exercise, you'll put together a set of drawings that will become a single DWF file that you'll send as an e-mail attachment to your client:

1. Open the Sample house.dwg file, which can be found in the Chapter 29 folder of the sample files. The file has several layout views, each representing a separate drawing sheet.

2. Click the Save tool in the Quick Access toolbar. If you don't do this, the Publish tool you use later will ask you to do it.

3. Choose Publish from the Application menu to open the Publish dialog box (Figure 29.8). You can also type **Publish**↵. The dialog box lists all the layouts in its main list box, including Model, which is equivalent to the Model Space tab. (See Chapter 8 for more on layouts.)

FIGURE 29.8
Choosing the layouts to publish

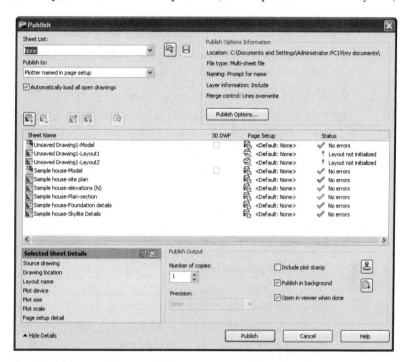

4. In the list box, Ctrl+click Sample House-Model, Sample House-Foundation Details, and Sample House-Skylite Details to select them. Also Ctrl+click the three Unsaved Drawing items in the list. You don't want to include these layouts in your DWF file.

5. Right-click and choose Remove, or click the Remove Sheets button just above the list of sheets. The items you selected are removed from the list.

At this point, you could go ahead and create a DWF file. However, suppose you want to include layouts from a file that isn't currently open? The following steps show you how to accomplish this:

1. Right-click and choose Add Sheets or click the Add Sheets button to open the Select Drawings dialog box.

2. Locate and select the `sample house alt.dwg` file, which can be found in the `Chapter 29` folder of the sample files. You see two new items, Sample House Alt-Model and Sample House Alt-Alternate Plan, in the list box. These are the layout and Model views that are in the `sample house alt.dwg` file.

> **AUTOMATICALLY EXCLUDING LAYOUTS**
>
> In step 2 of the previous exercise, the Model tab was imported. You can prevent Model tabs from being included in the sheets list by turning off the Include Model When Adding Sheets option. This option is located in the shortcut menu when you right-click in the Sheets list.

All the sheets your client needs are listed in the list box. You're ready to create the DWF file:

1. Save the current list in case you want to reproduce it later. Click the Save Sheet List button. The Save List As dialog box, which is a standard file dialog box, appears.

2. Select a location and name for the sheet list and click Save.

3. Back in the Publish dialog box, in the Publish To drop-down list near the top of the dialog box, make sure the DWF option is selected. Notice that you can also select Plotter Named In Page Setup, DWFx, and PDF.

4. Turn off the Publish In Background option. By turning this feature off, you'll get your results faster.

5. Click the Publish button. The Specify DWF File dialog box appears. This is a standard file dialog box in which you can find a location for your DWF file and also name it. Select a name and location for the DWF file. By default, AutoCAD uses the same name as the current file and the folder location of the current file. You can also set up a default location in the Publish Setup dialog box.

6. Once AutoCAD is finished publishing your drawings, you can view the DWF file using the Autodesk Design Review program.

7. Go back to AutoCAD and click the Plot And Publish Details Report icon in the right side of the status bar. The Plot And Publish Details dialog box appears, offering detailed information about the sheets you published. You can then click the Copy To Clipboard button to export the list to a file as a record. If you want to recall this dialog box later, you can do so by choosing Print ➢ View Plot And Publish Details from the Application menu.

You may notice that when you click the Publish button in the previous exercise, AutoCAD behaves as if it's printing the layouts in your list—and that is exactly what it's doing. AutoCAD uses its own DWF printer driver to "print" your drawings to a DWF file. AutoCAD uses the layout settings from the Plot dialog box for each layout to produce the DWF pages.

Exploring Other Publish Options

A few more options are available when you use the Publish feature. Let's take a moment to review some of the options in the Publish dialog box toolbar:

◆ The Preview tool lets you preview a sheet based on the current settings.

◆ The Add Sheets tool lets you add sheets to the list. The Remove Sheets tool removes a selected item from the list.

♦ The Move Sheet Up and Move Sheet Down tools let you move an item in the list up or down. These are important options because the order of drawings in the list determines the order that the drawings will appear in the Autodesk DWF Viewer. The item at the top of the list appears first, the next one down the list is second, and so on.

♦ The Load Sheet List and Save Sheet List tools let you load and save the list you've compiled, respectively. It's a good idea to save your list in case you need to reproduce the DWF file at some future date.

♦ You can use the Plot Stamp Settings tool to specify the data you want to include in the plot stamp. This tool opens the Plot Stamp dialog box. (See Appendix C for more on the Plot Stamp dialog box.)

Shortcut Menu Options

If you right-click an item or a set of items in the Publish dialog box list box, you see a menu with the standard options mentioned earlier plus some additional options. You'll want to know about a few of these options.

Viewing DWF files

The Autodesk Design Review program offers a fast and simple way to view DWF files, and as I mentioned earlier, it's free. It's installed automatically when you install AutoCAD. Choose Start ➤ All Programs ➤ Autodesk ➤ Autodesk Design Review 2011 to get it started.

If the person receiving your DWF file doesn't have a copy of the Autodesk DWF Viewer, send them to the Products page of the Autodesk website (www.autodesk.com) to download their own copy. The download file is relatively small, and it is easily downloaded. If they are using Windows Vista, they won't need the viewer since the default DWF file format (DWFx) is XPS compatible. If you're using Windows Vista or Windows 7, DWF files may be viewed directly without the aid of a viewer program.

By default, AutoCAD applies the existing layout settings for each layout when it produces the DWF file. These are the settings found in the Plot Or Page Setup dialog box and include settings such as the sheet size, scale, and page orientation. The Change Page Setup option lets you use a different set of layout settings for a selected layout in the list. To use this option, you must have saved a page setup in the file's Page Setup or Plot dialog box. (See Chapter 8 for more on the Page Setup dialog box and its options.) You can import a page setup from a different AutoCAD file, or you can assign a page setup to a sheet. Do this by clicking the sheet name and selecting a page setup from the list box that appears in the Page Setup column.

To change the page setup for multiple sheets, select the sheets from the list first and then select the setup from the list box.

If you happen to have two layouts with the same name, right-click a layout name, and then select the Rename Sheet option on the shortcut menu to rename a layout. The Copy Selected Sheets option adds copies of selected layouts to the list. The copies have the word *copy* appended to their names. The last two items in the shortcut menu let you control what is displayed in the list box. Include Layouts When Adding Sheets controls whether layouts are automatically imported from a drawing into the list box. Include Model When Adding Sheets controls whether Model Space views are automatically imported from a drawing into the list box.

THE PUBLISH OPTIONS DIALOG BOX

You can set up additional options by clicking the Publish Options button in the Publish dialog box. You'll then see the Publish Options dialog box (Figure 29.9).

This dialog box offers options for the location and type of output. The Default Output Location group lets you select the location for DWF files. The General DWF/PDF Options group lets you choose between a multi-sheet DWF file, which combines multiple sheets into one file, or single-sheet DWF files, which creates a file for each sheet. If you choose the multi-sheet file option, you have the added option to specify a default name for your DWF files or to have AutoCAD prompt you for a name each time you create a DWF file. The DWF Data Options group lets you add password protection to the DWF file by using the Password option. If your drawing contains 3D information, you can use the 3D DWF options, which control Xref hierarchy and materials.

FIGURE 29.9
Publish options

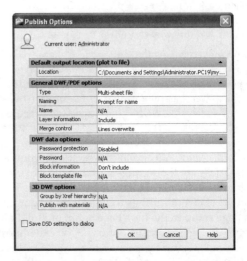

Creating a DWF File by Using the Plot Dialog Box

Another way to create DWF files is through the Plot dialog box. If you need to create a DWF file of only a single sheet, you may want to use the Plot dialog box because it's a simple and familiar procedure.

Open the file that you want to convert to DWF, and then proceed as if you're going to plot the drawing. In the Plot dialog box, select DWF6 ePlot.PC3 or DWFx ePlot (XPS Compatible).pc3 from the Name drop-down list in the Printer/Plotter area. The DWFx ePlot (XPS Compatible).pc3 option creates a file that is readable in Windows Vista without the need of any special viewing program.

Proceed with the plot the normal way. When AutoCAD would normally send the drawing to the printer, you'll see a dialog box asking you to enter a name for your plot file and finish with the rest of the plot. You can control the DWF plot as you would any plot.

In addition to using the settings available in the Plot dialog box, you can make some special configuration adjustments to the DWF plotter configuration file. Here is where to find those configuration settings:

1. Right-click the Quick View Layouts tool in the status bar and select Page Setup Manager to open the Page Setup Manager dialog box, select a setup from the Page Setups list, and then click Modify to open the Page Setup dialog box.

2. Make sure the DWF6 ePlot.pc3 configuration file is listed in the Name list box of the Printer/Plotter group.

3. Click the Properties button to the right of the Name drop-down list to open the Plotter Configuration Editor dialog box.

4. Make sure the Device And Document Settings tab is selected, and then click Custom Properties in the list box (Figure 29.10).

FIGURE 29.10
Controlling the plotter configuration file

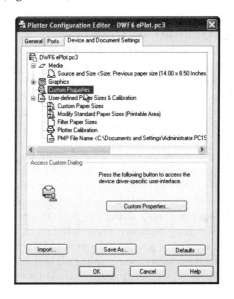

5. Click the Custom Properties button that appears in the lower half of the dialog box to open the DWF6 ePlot Properties dialog box. Here you can set the resolution, format, background color, and paper boundary for your DWF file. You can also specify whether to include layer and font information.

6. Click OK after selecting your settings. The Plotter Configuration Editor dialog box reappears. After you've set the custom properties, you can save any new settings in

the DWF6 ePlot.pc3 file, or you can create a new DWF6 PC3 plot-configuration file. To save any setting changes, click the Save As button and select the PC3 file in which you want to save the settings. For more information about PC3 plot configuration files, see "Fine-Tuning the Appearance of Output" in Appendix C.

7. Click OK in the Plotter Configuration Editor dialog box to return to the Page Setup dialog box.

8. Click OK to exit the Page Setup dialog box, and then close the Page Setup Manager.

After you select your custom configuration settings in step 5, you needn't open the Plotter Configuration Editor dialog box again the next time you plot a DWF file. If you save your new settings as a new PC3 file, you can select it from the File drop-down list in the Plotter Configuration group. You needn't reenter the custom settings.

You can either use the Publish feature described in the previous section to create single or multiple DWF files or create DWF files directly through the Plot dialog box. You can post the output from either method to a website to offer a wide distribution of your drawings. Just create a link to the DWF file from your web page. Be aware that the person attempting to view your DWF file from a web browser will need a copy of the free Autodesk DWF Viewer program that lets you view AutoCAD DWF files. The Autodesk DWF Viewer is automatically installed with AutoCAD 2011.

Adding Hyperlinks to Drawings

The Internet gave the world a tool that is so simple yet so powerful that it has permanently altered the way we look at information. Virtually every web page we view contains a hypertext link—a word, a sentence, or an image that takes us to another web page. Such links enable the viewer to explore the content of a website or gather more information on a particular topic.

AutoCAD offers a similar tool that you can apply to your AutoCAD drawings; it's called a *hyperlink*. With AutoCAD hyperlinks, you can link any document to an AutoCAD object. Then, with a few clicks of your mouse, you can follow the links to view other drawings, text files, spreadsheets, or web pages. After you create a hyperlink in an AutoCAD drawing, you can export the drawing to a DWF file and that DWF file will also contain the same links. You can then post that DWF file on a web page where others can gain access to those links.

The inclusion of hyperlinks in drawings and DWF files opens a world of new possibilities in the way you work with drawings. You can link product specifications directly to the objects in the drawing that represent the product. You can also link to extended data beyond the simple symbol or graphic in a drawing, such as to a database table or a spreadsheet.

You don't have to limit your links to HTML files containing AutoCAD drawings. You can link to all sorts of web documents, to drawings on your computer or your company network, and even to documents on other sites.

CREATING HYPERLINKS

The following shows you how to add links to a sample floor plan:

1. In AutoCAD, open the file houseplan.dwg.

2. In the Insert tab's Data panel, click the Hyperlink tool.

3. At the `Select objects:` prompt, click on the hexagonal door symbol, as shown in Figure 29.11.

FIGURE 29.11
The door symbol in the houseplan .dwg file

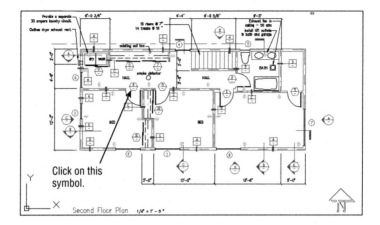

FIGURE 29.11
The door symbol in the houseplan .dwg file

Click on this symbol.

4. When you're done, press ↲. The Insert Hyperlink dialog box opens (see Figure 29.12).

FIGURE 29.12
The Insert Hyperlink dialog box

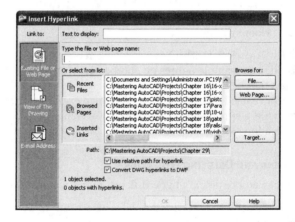

5. Click the File button on the right side of the dialog box to open the Browse The Web – Select Hyperlink dialog box. It's a typical file dialog box.

6. Locate the `doorsch.dwf` file and select it.

7. Click Open. The Insert Hyperlink dialog box reappears. Notice that `doorsch.dwf` appears in the list box at the top of the dialog box.

8. Make sure the Use Relative Path For Hyperlink option isn't selected, and then click OK.

The link you just created is stored with the drawing file. You can create a DWF file from this drawing and the link will be preserved in the DWF file.

Now let's see how you can use the link from within the AutoCAD file:

1. Move your cursor over the hexagonal door symbol. Notice that the cursor changes to the hyperlink icon when it's placed on the symbol. It also shows the name of the file to which the object is linked. This tells you that the object is linked to another document somewhere on your system, on your network, or on the World Wide Web (Figure 29.13).

FIGURE 29.13
The hyperlink icon and tool tip

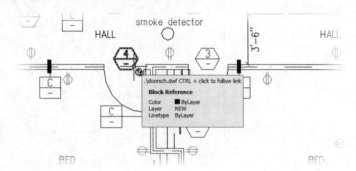

2. Click the hexagonal door symbol to select it.

3. Right-click a blank area of the drawing. In the shortcut menu, choose Hyperlink ➢ Open ".\doorsch.dwf" to choose the link to the `doorsch.dwf` file. You can also Ctrl+click the door symbol.

The Autodesk Design Review program opens and displays the file `doorsch.dwf` file. If you installed the sample figures on another drive or folder location, the Hyperlink menu option will reflect that location.

You've used the `doorsch.dwf` file as an example in these exercises, but this could have been a text file, a spreadsheet, a database, or even another AutoCAD file. AutoCAD will start the application associated with the linked file and open the file.

EDITING AND DELETING HYPERLINKS

You can edit or delete a hyperlink by doing the following:

1. Select and right-click the object whose link you want to edit, and then choose Hyperlink ➢ Edit Hyperlink from the shortcut menu to open the Edit Hyperlink dialog box, which offers the same options as the Insert Hyperlink dialog box (see Figure 29.12, earlier in this chapter) with the addition of the Remove Link button.

2. You can now change the link, or you can click the Remove Link button in the lower-left corner of the dialog box to delete the link.

TAKING A CLOSER LOOK AT THE HYPERLINK OPTIONS

You were introduced to the Insert Hyperlink dialog box, shown in Figure 29.12, in the previous exercises. Let's take a moment to study this dialog box in a little more detail.

To specify a file or a website to link to, you can enter either a filename or a website URL in the Type The File Or Web Page Name input box or use the Or Select From List area, which offers a list box and three button options. When you select one of the buttons, the list box changes to offer additional related options:

Recent Files Displays a list of recently edited AutoCAD files, as illustrated in Figure 29.12. You can then link the object to a file in the list by clicking the filename.

Browsed Pages Displays a list of websites that you recently visited using your web browser.

Inserted Links Displays a list of recently inserted links, including files or websites.

You can also use the three buttons to the right of the list box to locate specific files (the File button), websites (the Web Page button), or saved views (the Target button) in the current drawing.

As you saw in the exercise, the File button opens the Browse The Web dialog box, which lets you locate and select a file from your computer, from your local area network, or even from an FTP site. This is a typical AutoCAD file dialog box with some additional features.

The Web Page button on the right opens a simplified web browser that lets you locate a web page for linking. In this dialog box, you can use the standard methods for accessing web pages, such as using the Look In drop-down list to select recently visited pages or entering a URL in the Name Or URL input box. The page is then displayed in the main window of the dialog box.

If the selected hyperlink file is an AutoCAD DWG file, the Target button in the Insert Hyperlink dialog box opens the Select Place In Document dialog box, which lists the saved views in the drawing.

Views are subdivided by layout tabs. At the top is the Model Space tab listing, and below that are other layout tab listings. If the current drawing contains saved views, you see a plus sign next to the layout tab name. Click the plus sign to display a listing of the views in that layout.

At the top of the Insert Hyperlink and Edit Hyperlink dialog boxes is an input box labeled Text To Display. When a hyperlink is added to an object in AutoCAD, AutoCAD will display a hyperlink icon whenever the cursor passes over the object. You can also include descriptive text that will display along with the icon by entering a description in the Text To Display input box.

By default, the text is the name of the hyperlinked item that you select. You can change the text to provide a better description of the link.

There is a column of options at the far left in the Insert Hyperlink dialog box, labeled Link To. The top button, Existing File Or Web Page, displays the options discussed so far in this section. The other two buttons change the appearance of the Insert Hyperlink dialog box to offer different but familiar options:

View Of This Drawing This button changes the display to show just the views that are available in the current drawing. This option performs the same function as the Target button described earlier.

E-Mail Address This button changes the Insert Hyperlink dialog box to enable you to link an e-mail address to an object. Clicking the object will then open your default e-mail application, enabling you to send a message to the address.

Managing Your Drawings with DesignCenter and the Tool Palettes

As you start to build a library of drawings, you'll find that you reuse many components of existing drawing files. Most of the time, you'll probably be producing similar types of drawings with some variation, so you'll reuse drawing components such as layer settings, dimension styles, and layouts. It can be a major task to keep track of all the projects you've worked on. It's especially frustrating when you remember setting up a past drawing in a way that you know would be useful in a current project but you can't remember that file's name or location.

AutoCAD offers DesignCenter to help you keep track of the documents you use in your projects. You can think of DesignCenter as a kind of super Windows Explorer that is focused on AutoCAD files. DesignCenter lets you keep track of your favorite files and helps you locate files, blocks, and other drawing components. In addition, you can import blocks and other drawing components from one drawing to another by using a simple click and drag. If you've been diligent about setting a unit format for each of your drawings, you can use DesignCenter to import symbols and drawings of different unit formats into a drawing, and the symbols will maintain their proper size. For example, a 90 cm door symbol from a metric drawing can be imported into a drawing in Imperial units and the DesignCenter will translate the 90 cm metric door size to a 35.43″ door.

Getting Familiar with DesignCenter

At first glance, DesignCenter looks a bit mysterious. But it takes only a few mouse clicks to reveal a tool that looks much like Windows Explorer. Try the following steps to get familiar with DesignCenter:

1. Open AutoCAD to a new file, and then click the DesignCenter tool from the View tab's Palettes panel.

   DesignCenter opens as a floating palette (see Figure 29.14).

2. Click the Favorites tool on the DesignCenter toolbar.

   DesignCenter displays a listing of the Favorites folder. You're actually looking at a view into the C:\Documents and Settings*Username*\Favorites\Autodesk folder, where *Username* is your login name. Unless you've already added items to the \Favorites\ Autodesk folder, you see a blank view in the right panel. You can add shortcuts to this folder as you work with DesignCenter. You may also see a view showing the tree structure of the files you have open in AutoCAD.

OPENING THE TREE VIEW

If your DesignCenter view doesn't look like this, with the DesignCenter window divided into two parts, click the Tree View Toggle tool on the DesignCenter toolbar. The Tree view opens on the left side of the DesignCenter window. Click the Home tool to display the contents of the \Sample\ DesignCenter folder.

FIGURE 29.14
DesignCenter
opens as a
floating palette.

FIGURE 29.14
DesignCenter
opens as a
floating palette.

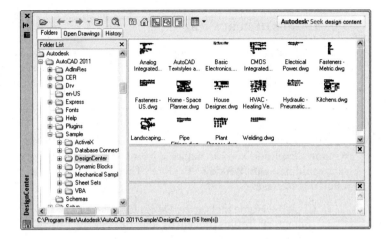

3. Place your cursor in the lower-right corner of the DesignCenter window so that a double-headed diagonal arrow shows. Then click and drag the corner out so you have an enlarged DesignCenter window that looks similar to Figure 29.15. The view on the right, containing the Favorites folder, is called the Palette view. The view on the left is called the Tree view.

FIGURE 29.15
The components of
the DesignCenter
palette

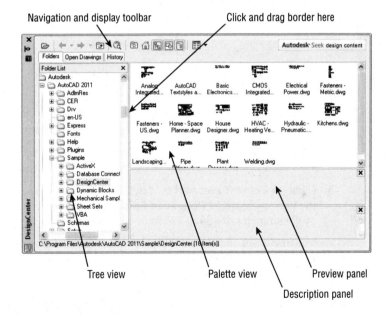

Navigation and display toolbar

Click and drag border here

Tree view

Palette view

Preview panel

Description panel

4. Place your cursor on the border between the Tree view and the Palette view until you see a double-headed cursor. Then click and drag the border to the right to enlarge the Tree view until it covers about one-third of the window.

5. Use the scroll bar at the bottom to adjust your view of the Tree view so you can easily read its contents.

AUTO-HIDE DESIGNCENTER

Like the tool palettes and the Properties palette, DesignCenter has an Auto-hide feature. To use it, click the double-headed arrow icon near the bottom of the DesignCenter title bar. DesignCenter will disappear except for the title bar. You can quickly open DesignCenter by placing the cursor on the title bar.

After you have it set up like this, you can see the similarities between DesignCenter and Windows Explorer. You can navigate your computer or network by using the Tree view, just as you would navigate Windows Explorer. There are a few differences, however, as you'll see in the following exercise:

1. Click the Home tool on the DesignCenter toolbar. The Palette view changes to display the contents of the `DesignCenter` folder under the `\AutoCAD 2011\Sample\DesignCenter` folder (Figure 29.16).

FIGURE 29.16
The DesignCenter display

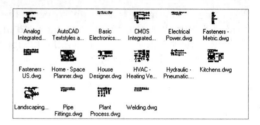

2. Instead of the usual list of files, you see a sample image of each file. These are called *preview icons*.

3. Click the Views tool on the DesignCenter toolbar, and choose Details from the menu. The Palette view changes to show a detailed list of the files in the `DesignCenter` folder.

4. Click the Views tool again, and choose Large Icons to return to the previous view. The Views tool is similar to the various View options in Windows Explorer.

5. Click the `Basic Electronics.dwg` file to select it. You see a preview of the selected file in the Preview panel of DesignCenter. You can adjust the vertical size of the Preview panel by clicking and dragging its top or bottom border.

You can also open and close the Preview panel by clicking the Preview tool in the DesignCenter toolbar. The preview can be helpful if you prefer viewing files and drawing components as a list in the main part of the Palette view.

Below the Preview panel is the Description panel. This panel displays any text information included with the drawing or drawing element selected in the Palette view. To add a description to a drawing that will be visible here, choose Drawing Utilities ➤ Drawing Properties from the Application menu; to add a description to a block, use the Summary tab in the Block Definition dialog box.

You can open and close this panel by clicking the Description tool on the DesignCenter toolbar. Because the `Basic Electronics.dwg` file doesn't have a description attached, the description panel shows the message `Last saved by: Autodesk`.

Both the Preview and the Description panels can offer help in identifying files that you may be looking for. After you find a file, you can click and drag it into a folder in the Tree view to organize your files into separate folders.

You can also add files to the Favorites folder by right-clicking and then choosing Add To Favorites. The file itself isn't moved to the Favorites folder; instead, a shortcut to the file is created in the Favorites folder. If you want to work on organizing your Favorites folder, you can open a window to the Favorites folder by right-clicking a file in the Palette view and choosing Organize Favorites. A window to the Favorites folder appears.

Because you'll be working with the sample drawings, go ahead and add the Projects folder to the Favorites folder:

1. Locate the Projects folder (the one created when you installed the sample files) in the left panel Tree view, and right-click it.

2. Choose Add To Favorites from the shortcut menu.

3. To go directly to the Favorites folder, click the Favorites tool on the DesignCenter toolbar. The Projects folder appears in the right panel in Palette view.

4. Double-click the Projects shortcut in the Palette view. You see the contents of the Projects folder.

You can go beyond just looking at file listings. You can look inside files to view their components:

1. In the Palette view, locate the file named 16-unit.dwg in the Chapter 16 folder, and double-click it. You see a listing of its components in the Palette view. The Tree view also shows the file highlighted.

2. Double-click the Blocks listing in the Palette view. Now you see a listing of all the blocks in 16-unit.dwg.

WHAT IS AUTODESK SEEK?

You might notice the Autodesk Seek banner in the upper-right corner of the DesignCenter palette. If you click this banner, your web browser opens to the Autodesk Seek home page where you will find a rich resource for drawings and models from manufacturers and users. 2D and 3D files are available in a number of formats, including DWG, DWF, and PDF. You can even share your own drawings with other users using the Output tab's Autodesk Seek panel. There are numerous other ways to share your own content. For example, you can find type **Sharewithseek.⏎** to upload content or **Seek.⏎** to search the Autodesk Seek site for downloads.

From here, you can import any of the drawing components from the DesignCenter palette into an open drawing in AutoCAD. But before you try that, try a few other features of the DesignCenter.

Opening and Inserting Files with DesignCenter

By using DesignCenter, you can more easily locate the files you're looking for because you can view thumbnail preview icons. But often that isn't enough. For example, you might want to locate all the files that contain the name of a particular manufacturer in an attribute of a drawing.

After you've found the file you're looking for, you can load it into AutoCAD by right-clicking the filename in the Palette view and then choosing Open In Window. Try it with the following exercise:

1. Click the Up tool in the DesignCenter toolbar twice. This takes you up two levels in the Palette view, from the view of the drawing blocks to the list of filenames.

2. In the Tree view, select the Chapter 12 folder. Then, in the Palette view of DesignCenter, locate the 12c-unit.dwg sample.

3. Right-click the 12c-unit.dwg file and select Open In Application Window. The drawing appears in the AutoCAD window.

If you want to insert a file into another drawing as a block, you can do so by clicking and dragging the file from the DesignCenter Palette view into an open drawing window. You can also right-click and select Insert As Block. You're then prompted for the insertion point, scale, and rotation angle. If you prefer to use the Insert dialog box to insert a drawing from DesignCenter, right-click the filename in the Palette view and then choose Insert As Block. The Insert dialog box opens, offering you the full set of Insert options, as described in Chapter 4.

Finally, you can attach a drawing as an Xref by right-clicking a file in the Palette view of DesignCenter and choosing Attach As Xref. The Attach External Reference dialog box opens, offering the insertion point, scale, and rotation options similar to the options in the Insert dialog box. This is the same dialog box described in Chapter 7.

Finding and Extracting the Contents of a Drawing

Aside from the convenience of being able to see thumbnail views of your drawing, DesignCenter may not seem like much of an improvement over Windows Explorer. But DesignCenter goes beyond Windows Explorer in many ways. One of the main features of DesignCenter is that it enables you to locate and extract components of a drawing.

Imagine that you want to find a specific block in a drawing. You remember the name of the block, but you don't remember the drawing you put it in. You can search the contents of drawings by using DesignCenter's Search dialog box. In the following exercise, you'll search for a block named Kitchen2-metric among a set of files:

1. In the DesignCenter toolbar, click the Search tool to open the Search dialog box. It looks similar to the Search tool that comes with Windows.

2. Select the drive that contains your Projects folder from the In drop-down list. Make sure the Search Subfolders option is checked.

3. Select Blocks from the Look For drop-down list. As you can see from the list, you can look for a variety of drawing component types (Figure 29.17).

FIGURE 29.17
Select Blocks
from the Look For
drop-down list.

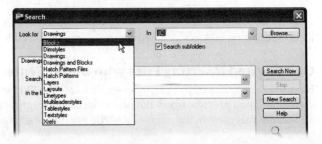

4. Enter **Kitchen2-metric.**⏎ in the Search For The Name input box, and then click the Search Now button to start the search. The magnifying glass icon in the lower-right corner moves back and forth, telling you that the Search function is working. After a minute or two, the name of the block appears in the window at the bottom of the dialog box.

5. Double-click the block name. DesignCenter displays the block in the Palette view and the file that contains the block in the Tree view.

EXPLORING THE SEARCH OPTIONS

As you saw from the previous example, the Search dialog box can be helpful in finding items that are buried in a set of drawings. In the exercise, you searched for a block, but you can search for any named drawing component, including attribute data and text. For example, if you want to find all attributes that contain the name *ABC Manufacturing Company* in your drawings, you can do so with the DesignCenter Search dialog box. Table 29.2 shows a summary of its features. When you select Drawings from the Look For drop-down list, you see a set of additional tabs in the Search dialog box, as described in Table 29.3.

TABLE 29.2:   DesignCenter Search dialog box options

OPTION	PURPOSE
In	Lets you select the drive you want to search.
Look For options	Lets you select the type of item to search for. The options are Blocks, Dimstyles, Drawings, Drawings And Blocks, Hatch Pattern Files, Hatch Patterns, Layers, Layouts, Linetypes, Multileaderstyles, Tablestyles, Textstyles, and Xrefs.
Browse	Lets you locate a specific folder to search.
Search Subfolders	Lets you determine whether Search searches subfolders in the drive and folder you specify.
Search Now	Starts the search process.
Stop	Cancels the current search.
New Search	Clears all the settings for the current search so you can start fresh on a new search.
Help	Opens the AutoCAD help system to the Search topic.

TABLE 29.3: DesignCenter Search dialog box tab options when Drawings is selected from the Look For drop-down list

DRAWINGS TAB	
Search For The Word(s)	Lets you specify the text to search for in the Drawing Properties fields.
In The Field(s)	Lets you specify the field of the Drawing Properties dialog box to search through, including Filename, Title, Subject, Author, and Keywords. These are the fields you see in the Summary tab of the Drawing Properties dialog box, which can be opened by choosing Drawing Utilities ➢ Drawing Properties from the Application menu.
Date Modified Tab	
Radio buttons	Lets you limit search criteria based on dates.
Advanced Tab	
Containing	Lets you select from a list of data to search for, including block name, block and drawing description, attribute tag, and attribute value.
Containing Text	Lets you specify the text to search for in the types of data you select from the Containing option.
Size Is	Lets you restrict the search to files larger than or smaller than the size you specify.

AUTOMATICALLY SCALING BLOCKS AT INSERTION

After you've found a block by using DesignCenter, you can click and drag the block into your open drawing. In the following exercise, you'll do that, but with a slight twist. The block you've found is drawn in centimeters, but you'll insert the Kitchen2-metric block into a drawing named 12c-unit.dwg, which was created in the Imperial measurement system. If you were to insert the Kitchen2-metric block into 12c-unit.dwg, the kitchen would be exactly 2.54 times larger than it should be for 12c-unit.dwg. But as you'll see, DesignCenter takes care of scaling for you. Follow these steps:

1. If you haven't done so already, load the 12c-unit.dwg sample drawing in AutoCAD. You can temporarily close DesignCenter to do this.

2. Back in DesignCenter, click and drag the Kitchen2-metric block from the Palette view into the 12c-unit.dwg window in AutoCAD. The kitchen appears at the appropriate scale.

3. To see that DesignCenter did indeed adjust the scale of the Kitchen2-metric block, click it in the 12c-unit window, and then right-click and choose Properties.

4. Check the Scale X, Scale Y, and Scale Z settings in the Geometry category. Notice that they show 0.3937 as the scale factor instead of 1.

5. After reviewing the Properties palette, close it.

You may recall from Chapter 3 that you have the opportunity to specify the type of units the drawing is set up for in the Drawing Units dialog box under the Insertion Scale group. DesignCenter uses this information when you drag and drop blocks from DesignCenter into an open drawing. This is how DesignCenter is able to scale a block drawn in metric to a drawing that is drawn in the Imperial format correctly. The same option is offered in the Block Definition dialog box.

Blocks aren't the only type of drawing component you can click and drag from the Palette view. Linetypes, layouts, dimension styles, and text styles can all be imported from files on your computer or network through DesignCenter's Palette view.

Exchanging Data between Open Files

You've seen how you can extract a block from a file stored on your hard disk and place it into an open drawing, but what if you want to copy a block from one open drawing to another open drawing? You change the way the Tree view displays data so that it shows only the files that are loaded in AutoCAD. The following exercise demonstrates how this works:

1. In AutoCAD, make sure that `12c-unit.dwg` is still open, and then open the `12b-unit-metric.dwg` file.

2. In DesignCenter, click the Open Drawings tab above the Tree view. The Tree view changes to display only the drawings that are open.

3. Click the plus sign (+) to the left of the `12c-unit.dwg` filename in the Tree view. The list expands to show the components in `12c-unit.dwg`.

4. Click Blocks in the Tree view. The Palette view changes to show a list of blocks available in `12c-unit.dwg`.

5. Locate the Kitchen block in the Palette view.

6. Click and drag Kitchen from the Palette view into the open `12b-unit-metric.dwg` drawing in AutoCAD. The block moves with the cursor. Once again, DesignCenter has automatically scaled the block to the appropriate size, this time from Imperial to metric.

7. Release the mouse anywhere in the drawing to place the Kitchen block.

In this example, you inserted a block from one open drawing into another drawing. If you prefer to use the Insert dialog box, you can right-click the block name in step 6 and choose Insert Block. The Insert dialog box opens, enabling you to set the insertion point, scale, and rotation options.

Just as with drawings, you can see a preview and descriptive text for blocks below the Palette view. In Chapter 4, you had the option to save a preview image with the block when you first created a block. This is where that preview icon can be really helpful. The preview icon gives you a chance to see what the block looks like when you use DesignCenter to browse through your drawing files. If you don't save a preview icon, you'll see the same block icon that was displayed in the previous Palette view.

You can also add the text description at the time you create the block. Before saving the block, enter a description in the Description input box of the Block Definition dialog box.

If you're updating older drawing files to be used with DesignCenter, you can add text descriptions to blocks by using the Create tool in the Home tab's Block panel or the Create tool in the Blocks & References tab's Block panel. Click the Create tool and then, in the Block

Definition dialog box, select the name of a block from the Name drop-down list. Enter the description you want for this block in the Description input box toward the bottom of the Block Definition dialog box. When you're finished, click OK.

Loading Specific Files into DesignCenter

You've seen how you can locate files through the Tree view and Palette view. If you already know the name and location of the file you want to work with, you can use a file dialog box to open files in DesignCenter. Instead of choosing the Open tool on the Quick Access toolbar, you use the Load tool on the DesignCenter toolbar to open the Load dialog box. This is a standard file dialog box that lets you search for files on your computer or network.

If you want to open a file in DesignCenter that you've recently opened, you can use the History tab just above the Tree view. The Tree view closes and you see a list of the files you've worked on most recently.

Downloading Symbols from DesignCenter Online

In addition to obtaining files and blocks from your computer or network, you can download symbols directly from Autodesk's DesignCenter Online website. This option offers thousands of ready-to-use symbols for a variety of disciplines. But before you can use DesignCenter Online, you'll need to enable it. The following describes how to do this:

1. Make sure AutoCAD is not open, and then use your AutoCAD 2011 installation DVD to start the installation process.

2. At the AutoCAD 2011 window, select the Install Tools And Utilities option.

3. At the Select The Products To Install window, select a language from the drop-down list, and then make sure you only check the Autodesk CAD Manager Tools option.

4. Click Next, and at the License Agreement window, click the I Accept option.

5. At the Begin Installation window, make sure only the Autodesk CAD Manager Tools Settings appear in the Current Settings panel. Click Install.

Once the CAD Manager Tools have been installed, you will need to enable DesignCenter Online. Here's how:

1. From the Windows Desktop, choose Start ➢ Programs ➢ Autodesk ➢ CAD Manager Tools ➢ CAD Manager Control Utility.

2. At the CAD Manager Control Utility, select the DesignCenter Online tab and click the Enable the DC Online tab in DesignCenter.

3. Click Apply and OK.

Now, you're ready to use the DesignCenter Online feature. Follow these steps:

1. Make sure you're connected to the Internet.

2. In AutoCAD, open the DesignCenter and click the DC Online tab that appears above the Tree view. The DesignCenter Online symbol categories appear in the Tree view, and the Palette view shows the same categories in a text view.

3. Expand the 2D Architectural listing in the panel to the left to display a set of subcategories.

4. Expand the Bathrooms category, and then click Bath Tubs. The Palette view displays a set of bathtubs.

5. Click one of the bathtubs. The i-drop icon appears.

6. Click a tub to display an enlarged preview of it in the display panel along with a description of the symbol.

7. Click and drag a symbol into the current open drawing. The i-drop cursor appears in the drawing. When you release the mouse button, the symbol appears at the cursor, waiting for you to select an insertion point.

8. Click a location to place the symbol.

9. To return to the opening page of DesignCenter Online, click the DesignCenter Online item at the top of the Tree view.

Because DesignCenter Online is a website, AutoCAD uses the i-drop feature to bring the symbols into your drawing. As you can see, the list of symbols is fairly extensive. Many of the symbols are samples from third-party vendors that offer expanded symbols libraries.

Customizing the Tool Palettes with DesignCenter

Many AutoCAD users have built their own custom library of symbols and are accustomed to using them in conjunction with custom menus. But creating and editing menus is a bit cumbersome and can become difficult to manage. In Chapter 1, you saw how easy it is to drag and drop a symbol, known as a tool, from the tool palettes. At first glance, there is no obvious way to add your own tools to the palettes. Adding tools and additional palettes to the tool palettes is fairly simple once you're familiar with DesignCenter. The following exercise shows you how it's done:

1. If tool palettes aren't open already, click the Tool Palettes tool in the View tab's Palettes panel.

2. Right-click in the tool palettes, and then choose New Palette from the shortcut menu.

3. Enter **My Tool Palette**↵. A new, blank tab is added to the tool palettes.

4. Go back to DesignCenter, make sure the Folders tab is selected, and click the Home tool.

5. In the Palette view to the right, double-click the Landscaping.dwg file, and then double-click the Blocks icon that appears in the Palette view.

6. Make sure the tool palettes are visible behind DesignCenter, and then Ctrl+click Clump Of Trees Or Bushes – Plan and North Arrow.

7. Click and drag the selection to the tool palettes.

BE CAREFUL CLICKING IN THE TOOL PALETTE

If you click a tool in a tool palette, it's inserted in the current drawing, so take care when clicking around in the tool palettes.

You've just created a tool palette and added two symbols. You can continue to add symbols from other drawings to your custom tool palette. Or, if you have a drawing that contains all the blocks you need for a tool palette, you can quickly create a tool palette directly from a file. Here's how that's done:

1. In DesignCenter, go up two folder levels so you can select the Landscaping.dwg file.

2. Right-click Landscaping.dwg, and then choose Create Tool Palette. After a few moments, a new tool palette called Landscaping appears in the tool palettes. This new palette contains all the blocks found in the Landscaping.dwg file.

This exercise showed that you can quickly create a palette of all the blocks from a file. You can do the same thing with entire folders of drawings, although you may want to make sure such folders don't contain too many files.

But what if you don't want some of the items in your custom palette? You can remove items easily by using a shortcut menu:

1. In the Landscaping palette, select the top three symbols by right-clicking the tool that is third from the top and then Shift+clicking the top tool. This is a little different from the typical Windows method for selecting items from a list.

2. Right-click and choose Delete from the shortcut menu. Click OK to confirm the deletion.

You may have noticed the Cut and Copy options in the shortcut menu in step 2. You can use these options to move symbols from one palette to another. For example, instead of deleting the three symbols in step 2, you can choose Cut from the shortcut menu, open another palette, right-click, and choose Paste. The symbols move to the new palette location. In the next section, you'll see how you can use the Copy and Paste shortcut menu options to make a copy of a tool in the same palette.

CUSTOMIZING A TOOL

Other shortcut menu options let you delete entire palettes or rename tools or palettes. You can also edit the properties of symbols in a palette. The following exercise shows how to use the shortcut menu options to create two scale versions of the same tool:

1. In the Landscaping tab of the tool palettes, right-click the North Arrow tool and choose Copy from the shortcut menu.

2. Right-click a blank area of the palette and choose Paste. A copy of the North Arrow tool appears in the palette.

3. Right-click the copy of the North Arrow tool, choose Rename from the shortcut menu, and then enter **North Arrow Copy**.

4. Right-click the North Arrow Copy tool and choose Properties to open the Tool Properties dialog box (Figure 29.18).

5. Click 1 to the right of the Scale listing, and change the value to **4**.

6. Click OK, and then click and drag the North Arrow Copy tool into the drawing.

7. Click and drag the original North Arrow tool into the drawing. Notice that the original North Arrow is smaller than the North Arrow Copy, whose scale you changed to 4.

FIGURE 29.18

The Tool Properties dialog box

This exercise demonstrated that you can have multiple versions of a tool at different scales. You can then use the tool that's appropriate to the scale of your drawing. As you can see from the Tool Properties dialog box, you can modify other tool properties, such as color and layer assignments. You can use this feature to create sets of tools for different scale drawings. For example, you can create a palette of architectural reference symbols for 1/4″-scale drawings, and you can create another palette for 1/8″-scale drawings.

ADDING HATCH PATTERNS AND SOLID FILLS

You've seen how you can turn blocks into tool palette tools, but what about solid fills? In Chapter 1, you saw that sample hatch patterns and solid fills are available in the tool palettes. Here's how you can add your own:

1. In DesignCenter, use the Tree view to locate the AutoCAD 2011 Support folder. In Windows XP or Vista, it's typically in C:\Documents and Settings*Username*\Application Data\ Autodesk\ AutoCAD 2011\R18.1\enu\Support (*Username* is your Windows login name).

LOCATING SUPPORT FILES

To find out exactly where support files are located, choose Options from the Application menu to open the Options dialog box. Click the Files tab. Expand the Support File Search Path item at the top of the list, and then place the cursor on the item just below Support File Search Path. You see the path to the Support folder. You can also enter **(findfile 'acad.pat')** at the Command prompt as a shortcut to find the support file search path. If you use this shortcut, note that the directory names are separated with double hash marks (\\). This is an artifact of AutoLISP.

---

2. Double-click the acad.pat file shown in the Palette view. AutoCAD builds a list of the patterns and displays the list in the Palette view.

3. You can now click and drag a pattern into any tool palette. You can also click and drag an entire PAT file into the tool palette to create a palette of all the patterns in a hatch pattern file.

In this exercise, you used the standard hatch patterns that come with AutoCAD. You can also create your own custom hatch patterns and import them to the tool palettes by using the method described here. See Chapter 26 for more information on creating custom hatch patterns.

If you want to set up a set of solid fill colors, you can do the following:

1. Click and drag the SOLID pattern from the `acad.pat` file into the tool palette.

2. Right-click the new solid fill tool, choose Properties from the shortcut menu, and select a color from the Color drop-down list in the Tool Properties dialog box.

You can select any color, including colors from the True Color or Color Books tab in the Select Color dialog box that you learned about in Chapter 5. You can also cut and paste an existing solid fill tool to make copies. You can then modify the color property for each copy to get a set of custom solid fill colors.

MANAGING THE TOOL PALETTES

You can perform other types of tool palette maintenance operations by using the Customize dialog box. For example, you can change the order of the tool palette tabs, or you can group tabs into categories that can be turned on or off. The following steps offer a glimpse of what you can do by showing you how to group palettes:

1. To open the Customize dialog box (Figure 29.19), right-click the tool palettes, and choose Customize Palettes from the shortcut menu.

FIGURE 29.19
Customize dialog box for tool palettes

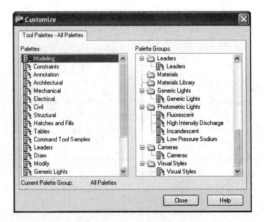

2. Right-click in a blank area of the Palette Groups panel, and choose New Group.

3. Enter **My Group** for the new group name.

4. Click and drag My Group to a position just above another group so that it's its own group instead of a subgroup.

5. Click and drag Landscaping from the left panel to the right panel just below My Group. A black bar appears below My Group. Release the mouse button.

6. Click and drag My Tool Palette from the left panel to the right, just below Landscaping.

You've just created a new palette group and moved the two new palettes. You can view the palettes separately or all together:

1. Click Close to close the Customize dialog box. The tool palette still displays all the tabs.

2. To display only the new tabs, click the Properties button at the top of the palette.

3. Select My Group. Now the tool palette shows only the two tabs you just created.

You may have noticed that in the Properties menu, you also have the option to show just the new groups or all the palettes. This feature lets you keep the tabs in the tool palettes organized.

The list on the left side of the Customize dialog box also lets you change the order of the tabs by clicking and dragging the tab names up or down in the left panel. If you select a palette in the left panel and right-click, you can rename, delete, import, or export a palette.

DON'T FORGET THE SOURCE FILES WHEN EXPORTING

If you use the Export or Import option to move a palette from one computer to another, be aware that you must also import or export the drawings that are the source files for the palette tools.

DesignCenter and tool palettes offer great features that will prove invaluable to AutoCAD users. Although these examples show you how to use DesignCenter on a stand-alone computer, you can just as easily perform the same functions across a network or even across the Internet.

This ends our exploration of DesignCenter and tool palettes. In the next part of this chapter, you'll look at AutoCAD's tools for maintaining layer naming and other standards throughout an organization and for converting between your own layering system and those of clients or partners.

Establishing Office Standards

Communication is especially important when you're one of many people working on the same project on separate computers. A well-developed set of standards and procedures helps to minimize problems that may be caused by miscommunication. In this section, you'll find some suggestions for setting up these standards.

Establishing Layering and Text Conventions

The issue of CAD standards has always been difficult to resolve. Standardizing layers, dimensions, and text can go a long way toward making file exchange more seamless between different trades, and standards can also make files easier to understand. When everyone follows a standard, the structure of a drawing is more easily understood, and those who have to edit or interpret your work can do so without having to ask a lot of questions.

You've seen how layers can be a useful tool. But they can easily get out of hand when you have free rein over their creation and naming. With an appropriate layer-naming convention, you can minimize this type of problem (although you may not eliminate it entirely). A too-rigid naming convention can cause as many problems as no convention at all, so it's best to give general guidelines rather than force everyone to stay within narrow limits. As mentioned in Chapter 5, you can create layer names in a way that enables you to group them by using wildcards. AutoCAD allows up to 31 characters in a layer name, so you can use descriptive names.

Line weights should be standardized in conjunction with colors. If you intend to use a service bureau for your plotting, check with them first; they may require that you conform to their color and line-weight standards.

KNOW THE STANDARDS

If you're an architect, an engineer, or in the construction business, check out some of the CAD layering standards set forth by the American Institute of Architects (AIA) and the Construction Specifications Institute (CSI). The AIA has a website at www.aia.org, and the CSI has a website at www.csinet.org.

NOT AVAILABLE IN LT

The Standards command discussed in the following sections isn't available in AutoCAD LT.

Checking Office Standards

AutoCAD offers an open-ended environment that lends itself to easy customization, but this also leaves the door wide open for on-the-fly creation of layer names, dimension styles, and other drawing format options. It's easy to stray from standards, especially when you're under pressure to get a project out on a deadline. To help you and your office maintain a level of conformity to office or industry standards, AutoCAD includes the Standards command.

The Standards command lets you quickly compare a drawing against a set of standard layer names, dimension style settings, linetypes, and text styles. A dialog box displays any item that doesn't conform to the standards you selected. You can then adjust the file to make it conform to your standards.

You can create several sets of standards for different types of files, and you can assign the standards directly to a file so that anyone editing that file can make periodic checks against your office standards while the drawing is being edited.

SETTING UP STANDARDS FILES

The first step in using the Standards command is to set up a file to which other drawing files can be compared. Standards uses an AutoCAD drawing file with a .dws filename extension. Here are the steps to create a new DWS standards file:

1. Open AutoCAD, and click New from the Quick Access toolbar to create a new file.

2. Set up the file with the layers, linetypes, dimension styles, and text styles you want as your standards.

3. Choose Save As from the Application menu.

4. In the Save Drawing As dialog box, choose AutoCAD Drawing Standards (*.dws) from the Files Of Type drop-down list.

5. Choose a convenient folder for the location of your standards file, and click Save.

As an alternative to creating a new file, you can open an existing file that contains all the typical settings you'll want to use on your projects. You can then delete all the graphics in the file and purge all its blocks and shapes. After you've done this, you can begin at step 3 of the previous exercise to save the file as a DWS standards file.

You can set up as many DWS files as you need for your office. Often, a single set of standards is too limiting if your office is involved in a diverse range of projects, so you may want to set up DWS files on a project basis, drawing on a core of generic DWS files.

Using the Standards Command to Associate Standards

After you've created your DWS standards files, you can begin to check other files for conformity. The next task is to assign your DWS file to the drawing file that you want to check:

1. In AutoCAD, open the file you want to check for standards conformity.

2. Click Configure on the Manage tab's CAD Standards panel to open the Configure Standards dialog box. This dialog box contains a list box and a description area. A row of buttons appears vertically between the list box and description.

3. Click the Add Standards File (F3) button in the middle column of the dialog box.

4. The Select Standards File dialog box opens. This is a typical AutoCAD file dialog box. Notice that the Files Of Type drop-down list shows the Standards (*.dws) file type.

5. Locate and select the standards file that you want to use to check the current file. After a moment, the name of the file you select appears in the list box of the Configure Standards dialog box (Figure 29.20). On the right side of the dialog box, you see a description of the standards file.

FIGURE 29.20
Associating a
set of standards
with a file

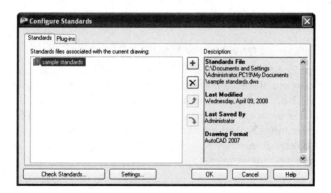

6. Check the current file against the DWS standards file. Click the Check Standards button in the lower-left corner of the Configure Standards dialog box. AutoCAD pauses while it checks the current file, and then you see the Check Standards dialog box.

If AutoCAD finds a discrepancy between the standards file and the current file, a description of the problem appears at the top of the dialog box. For example, if the name of a dimension style appears in the current file that isn't in the standards file, a message appears indicating that a nonstandard dimension style exists in the current drawing. If this happens, take the following steps:

1. Below the problem statement is the Replace With list box, which contains options related to the nonstandard item. You can replace the nonstandard item in your file with an option in the Replace With list box by selecting the option and clicking the Fix button in the lower half of the dialog box. Or you can leave the problem alone for now.

2. Click the Next button in the lower-right corner of the Check Standards dialog box to move to the next problem.

3. Repeat steps 1 and 2 until you see the statement `Checking is complete` in the Problem list box and the Checking Complete dialog box opens to display a summary of the checking results.

You can check Mark This Problem As Ignored if you want the Check Standards dialog box to ignore the problem in future standards checking sessions.

In this example, you entered the Check Standards dialog box directly from the Configure Standards dialog box. After you've used the Check Standards dialog box on a file, the DWS standards file is associated with the checked file. You can go directly to the Check Standards dialog box by choosing Tools ➤ CAD Standards ➤ Check during any subsequent editing session.

DON'T LOSE THE DWS

After you've assigned a DWS standards file to a drawing, you'll need to save the drawing or its association with the DWS file will be lost.

CHECKING STANDARDS FOR MULTIPLE DRAWINGS

The Standards and Check Standards commands are great for checking individual files, but eventually you'll want a method to batch-check a set of files. AutoCAD 2011 provides a utility that does just that. The Batch Standards Checker is a stand-alone utility that audits a set of drawing files and checks them against their associated DWS files. The Batch Standards Checker can also check a set of drawings against a single DWS file of your choice. It then generates an audit report showing any problems it encounters.

Here's how it works:

1. From the Windows Desktop, choose Start ➤ All Programs ➤ Autodesk ➤ AutoCAD 2011 ➤ Batch Standards Checker to open the Batch Standards Checker dialog box (see Figure 29.21).

2. Click the plus button in the middle of the dialog box to open the Batch Standards Checker – File Open dialog box. This is a typical AutoCAD file dialog box.

3. Locate and select the drawings you want to check. You return to the Batch Standards Checker dialog box, and after a moment, a list of the drawings you selected appears in the Drawings To Check list box.

4. Click the Standards tab (Figure 29.22). This is where you can select the standards file against which your selection will be checked.

FIGURE 29.21
The Batch Standards Checker dialog box

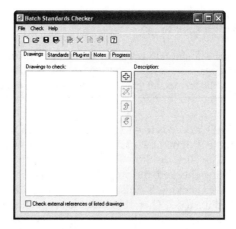

FIGURE 29.21
The Batch Standards Checker dialog box

If the drawings you selected in step 3 already have a standards file associated with them, you can use the Check Each Drawing Using Its Associated Standards Files option to check each file. You can then skip to step 7.

FIGURE 29.22
Choose the files to check.

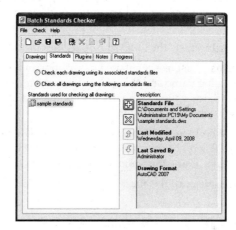

5. If you select the Check All Drawings Using The Following Standards Files option, click the plus sign in the middle of the dialog box to open the file dialog box.

6. Locate and select a DWS standards file. The file then appears in the Standards Used For Checking All Drawings list box on the left of the Standards tab in the Batch Standards Checker dialog box.

7. Click the Save button at the top of the Batch Standards Checker dialog box.

    The Batch Standards Checker file save dialog box opens to enable you to specify a standards check filename and location. This file has a .chx filename extension.

8. After you've specified the location and name of a check file, click the Start Check button.

WHAT IS A CHX FILE?

The Batch Standards Checker file is an audit file that stores the drawing list and the list of standards files in the current session. It also stores the results of the audit. The CHX file is an XML-based file. XML is a file format designed to allow data exchange over the Internet.

AutoCAD proceeds to check each file listed in the Drawings tab list box. The progress is shown in the Progress tab of the Batch Standards Checker dialog box. If you decide to cancel the audit, you can click the Stop Check button, which cancels the current audit in progress. When files are being checked, the Stop Check button turns red.

When the checking is finished, the data from the audit is automatically saved in the check file you created in step 7. Then the audit file is opened in your web browser and you see the results of the audit.

The audit report file displays a number of options in a set of radio buttons:

Overview   Displays a simplified view of the problems encountered by the audit. It lists the drawings audited and the number of problems encountered.

Plug-Ins   Shows the standard plug-ins used to audit the drawings. Autodesk supplies these standard plug-ins, which test for layers, dimension styles, linetypes, and text styles. Third-party developers can create other plug-ins to check for additional problems.

Standards   Lists the DWS standards files used for the audit.

Problems   Displays a detailed description of the problems encountered in the audit. It gives the drawing name and the name of the specific item that is a problem. For example, if the audit discovers a nonstandard layer name, the layer name is listed under the drawing name as a nonstandard layer name.

Ignored Problems   Displays problems that have previously been flagged as problems to ignore. You can flag problems to be ignored by using the Check Standards command in AutoCAD. (See the section "Using the Standards Command to Associate Standards" earlier in this chapter.)

All   Displays all the audit information.

REVIEWING PREVIOUSLY SAVED STANDARDS AUDITS

After you've created a check file and completed a standards audit, you can always return to the audit by opening the Batch Standards Checker utility and clicking the Open tool in the toolbar.

This opens the Batch Standards Checker file open dialog box, where you can locate and open a previously saved standards check file with the .chx filename extension. In this file, you see a list of the files that were checked in the Drawings tab and the DWS standards file used in the Standards tab.

You can then view the results of the audit by clicking the View Report tool in the toolbar. This opens a web browser and displays the audit results contained in the standards check file.

Converting Multiple Layer Settings

As AutoCAD files flow in and out of your office, you're likely to find yourself working with layering standards from another system. You might, for example, receive files from an architect who uses the CSI standard for layer names, whereas your office prefers the AIA standard. If your job involves extensive reworking of such files, you'll want to change the layering system to one you're most familiar with. But converting layer settings is a painstaking and time-consuming process, especially if several files need conversion.

Fortunately, AutoCAD offers a tool that can make layer conversion from one standard to another much easier. The Layer Translator lets you map nonstandard layers (that is, those using a system different from your own) to your own set of standard layers. It can then convert those layers to match your office standards. After you've mapped a set of layers between two files, you can save the map settings in a drawing file. Then any other files you receive that contain the same nonstandard layer settings can be converted to your own layer standards quickly. Let's take a closer look at how the Layer Translator works.

When using the Layer Translator, you must initially match the layers of your incoming file with those of a file whose layers are set up the way you want. Here are the steps to do this:

1. Open the file whose layers you want to convert in AutoCAD. Click the Layer Translator tool from the Manage tab's CAD Standards panel to open the Layer Translator dialog box, which lists the layers from the current file in the Translate From list box.

2. Click the Load button in the Translate To group to open the Select Drawing File dialog box. Locate and select a file that contains the layer settings you want to use for this project. The file can be a standard DWG file, or it can be a DWS standards file or a DWT template file. After you've opened a file, its layer names appear in the Translate To list box.

3. Select a layer name in the Translate From list, and then select the layer you want to convert it to from the Translate To list box. After you've made your two selections, click the Map button in the middle of the dialog box. An item in the Layer Translation Mappings group shows you the old and new layer names and the layer settings for the conversion (see Figure 29.23).

FIGURE 29.23

The Layer Translator dialog box

4. Repeat step 3 for all the layers you want to convert. You can map several layers from the Translate From list to a single layer in the Translate To list if you need to.

5. If there are matching layers in the Translate From and Translate To list boxes, the Map Same button in the middle of the dialog box becomes active. You can then click this button to automatically map layers that have the same names in both the Translate From and the Translate To lists.

After you've completed your layer mapping, you can save the mapping for future use:

1. While still in the Layer Translator dialog box, click the Save button in the Layer Translation Mappings group to open the Save Layer Mappings dialog box. This is a typical AutoCAD file dialog box.

2. Enter a name for your saved settings and click Save. You can save the layer-map settings as either a DWS standards file or a DWG file.

3. Click the Translate button and AutoCAD will proceed to translate the mapped layers.

After you've saved the layer mapping in step 2, you can load the saved layer-map settings into the Layer Translator dialog box in future layer translations. This saves you the effort of mapping each layer individually each time you want to perform a translation. This will work for incoming files that use the same layer settings, but you'll have to create another layer-map settings file for each different layer system you encounter.

To use a saved layer map, click the Load button in the Translate To group of the Layer Translator dialog box, and then select the layer-map file you saved in step 2. You can have several layer-map files for each project involving files with nonstandard layer settings.

Exploring Other Layer Translator Options

You'll often come across situations in which the layers in the Translate From list don't correspond directly to those in the Translate To list. For these situations, the Layer Translator offers a few additional options.

If you have difficulty finding a match for layers in the Translate From list, you can create a new layer by clicking the New button in the Translate To group. This opens the New Layer dialog box (Figure 29.24), in which you can enter the properties for your new layer.

After you create a new layer with this dialog box, it appears in the Translate To list box, enabling you to map Translate From layers to your new layer.

FIGURE 29.24
Creating a
new layer

Another option you'll find useful is the Edit button in the Layer Translation Mappings group. You may find that after you've mapped a Translate From layer to a Translate To layer, the Translate To layer isn't exactly what you want. You can highlight the mapped layer in the Layer Translation Mappings group list box and then click Edit to open the Edit Layer dialog box (Figure 29.25). From here, you can modify the new layer's settings from their original values.

FIGURE 29.25
Changing a layer's properties

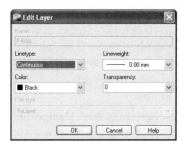

Finally, the Layer Translator offers a set of options that give you some control over the way translations are performed. For example, you can control whether layer colors and linetypes are forced to the ByLayer setting or whether layer assignments for objects in blocks are translated. You can access these options by clicking the Settings button in the lower-left corner of the Layer Translator dialog box. Figure 29.26 shows the Settings dialog box. The options are self-explanatory.

FIGURE 29.26
The Layer Translator and its Settings dialog box

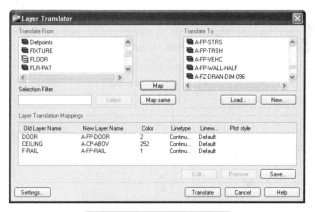

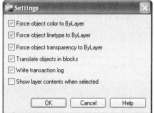

The Bottom Line

Share drawings over the Internet.   As a drafter or designer, it's very likely that you'll be involved in collaborative efforts, which means you'll have to share your work with others. The Internet has made it much easier to do this.

Master It   Why is eTransmit important for sending AutoCAD drawings over the Internet?

ePublish your drawings.   Autodesk offers the DWF drawing format, which lets non-CAD users view and add comments to simplified versions of your drawings. You can use the Publish feature to create a single DWF file from several drawings.

Master It   True or false: The Publish feature can be used to plot multiple drawings in the background.

Manage your drawings with DesignCenter and the tool palettes.   The DesignCenter is a great tool for managing your drawings' resources, like blocks, custom linetypes, and other elements.

Master It   True or false: The DesignCenter has the capacity to scale a block automatically to the correct size when moving from metric to Imperial drawings.

Establish office standards.   AutoCAD allows for a wide range of settings in a drawing. For this reason, it's a good idea to create standards for the way drawings are set up.

Master It   Name the filename extension for an AutoCAD drawing standards file.

Convert multiple layer settings.   If you exchange files with another office, you may find that their layer scheme is different from yours. AutoCAD offers the Layer Translator to help you translate layer names from an unfamiliar drawing to names you're more comfortable with.

Master It   Name the filename extensions of the types of files that you can use as a template for layer-name translations.

Chapter 30

Keeping a Project Organized with Sheet Sets

It's rare to have a drawing project fit on one sheet. Most CAD projects require multiple sheets, sometimes numbering in the hundreds. With multiple sheets in a project, you often spend a fair amount of time checking cross-references between the drawings and making sure that information like sheet titles is correct.

Even the smallest project requires some coordination of cross-references between drawings in a set and checking for consistency across sheets. For example, a floor plan of a house will have callout symbols that direct you to a sheet with building elevations, construction details, or door and window schedules. As a CAD user, you eventually spend a lot of time just making sure that you have your set of drawings in the proper order and labeled correctly. Checking a set of drawings for continuity and correctness is a time-consuming job, and errors can easily creep in.

To help make your sheet coordination efforts easier, AutoCAD 2011 offers the Sheet Set Manager. (If you're an LT user, you may be interested in the information presented here, but the Sheet Set Manager isn't available in AutoCAD LT 2011.)

In this chapter you'll learn to do the following:

- ◆ Understand sheet sets
- ◆ Create a sheet set from an existing project
- ◆ Manage title blocks and cross-references
- ◆ Customize sheet sets
- ◆ Archive, publish, and eTransmit sheet sets

Understanding Sheet Sets

The Sheet Set Manager is a tool that keeps track of all the drawings in a project. It also helps maintain the integrity of cross-references between sheets in a set of drawings by automatically updating sheet numbers throughout a set as sheets are added or moved. The Sheet Set Manager won't replace a careful check of a set of drawings before they're released for consumption, but it will reduce the amount of time you spend on coordinating and checking the drawings.

Sheet sets and the Sheet Set Manager can be a bit difficult to understand clearly, so in the following sections, you can take a moment to get a better idea of what sheet sets are all about.

Organizing by Reference Files and Sheet Files

To better understand how sheet sets work, it helps to consider the methods used to organize AutoCAD files. One common method for organizing files is to separate drawings into two categories: reference files and sheet files. You can think of *reference files* as the data sources. These are the drawing files that contain the core drawing geometry of a project. For example, they might be the floor plan drawings that contain the paving, finish, ceiling, and power information, all drawn in Model Space.

Sheet files are files that represent the actual printed sheets or pages in the drawing set. Sheet files include title block information as well as the different views of the reference files needed for the sheet. They also include view titles and scale information.

You use one layout view in the sheet file for each physical sheet that eventually gets printed. The reference files are included as Xrefs in the sheet files with the appropriate views and layers set up for each sheet.

For example, you might have one sheet file called A1 Floor Plan.dwg that has a title block in its layout view. That layout view has a viewport containing a view of an Xref floor plan file. Another sheet file called A2 Enlarged Plan.dwg might contain the same Xref but with a layout view including multiple viewports to show a more detailed set of views of the plan.

The Sheet Set Manager can take this reference/sheet system of file organization and automate it. Without the Sheet Set Manager, you must create the sheet file, import the reference file, and then add a title block, viewport, and labels to produce a finished sheet. The Sheet Set Manager automates many of the fussy details of creating and maintaining the sheet files.

DON'T LIMIT YOUR USE OF SHEET SETS

The example given here illustrates one way that sheet sets can be used. You don't have to organize your drawings in this way to take advantage of sheet sets when you're working on projects in the real world. You can use sheet sets to organize any project that uses multiple drawings. For example, I've seen sheet sets used to help trainers keep track of tutorial files. Others have used it to keep track of their AutoCAD presentations.

Managing Your Files with Sheet Sets

Sheet sets also serve as a way to gain an overview of your drawing set in a way similar to using the table of contents of a book. When you use the Sheet Set Manager, you can view a list of all the drawings in your project and quickly find and open the drawing you need to work on.

You can think of the Sheet Set Manager as a database that contains information about the drawings in the set. It uses a file with the .dst filename extension to store this information. Like a database, this file is updated automatically whenever you make changes to the sheet set. It doesn't wait for you to save the sheet set data manually. In fact, you won't see a Save option in the Sheet Set Manager.

The Sheet Set Manager can change multiple drawing files whenever a change affects the entire set. For example, if there is a change in the project information in the title block, you can update all the title blocks in the set by making a single change in the Sheet Set Manager. The Sheet Set Manager can keep track of title-block data such as submission dates, drawing titles, people who have worked on the individual drawings, and related information.

Finally, the Sheet Set Manager can help simplify the printing of whole sets of drawings by automatically setting up AutoCAD's Publish feature. It can help automate your archiving tasks and help collect all the necessary files to send your set to a different location for editing.

Creating a Sheet Set from an Existing Project

As an introduction to sheet sets, you'll first create a sheet set from an existing set of drawings. You'll then see how your sheet set can be used as a way to keep track of the files in a project.

This example is a small house remodel with some basic drawings. Although the project is small, it will show you the main elements of the Sheet Set Manager.

Using the Create Sheet Set Wizard

The Create Sheet Set Wizard is the main tool you'll use when creating a sheet set. It offers a step-by-step method for setting up new sheet sets, and, as with all wizards, you can back up and make changes along the way. Here's how to use it:

Sheet Set Manager

1. In AutoCAD, click the Sheet Set Manager tool on the View tab's Palettes panel to open the Sheet Set Manager palette (Figure 30.1). (You may see the title bar and tabs reversed from the example shown here, depending on whether the palette is located on the left or right side of the AutoCAD window.)

FIGURE 30.1
The Sheet Set
Manager palette

2. Click the drop-down list at the top of the palette, and select New Sheet Set to start the Create Sheet Set Wizard.

YOU'LL NEED AT LEAST ONE FILE OPEN

The Sheet Set Manager won't allow you to create a new sheet set unless a drawing is currently open.

---

3. Click the Existing Drawings radio button, and then click Next. The Sheet Set Details screen of the wizard appears (Figure 30.2).

FIGURE 30.2
Naming a new
sheet set

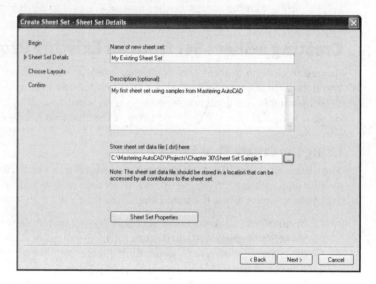

4. Enter **My Existing Sheet Set** for the name of the sheet set.

5. Enter **My first sheet set using samples from Mastering** AutoCAD in the Description text box.

6. Click the Browse button to the right of the Store Sheet Set Data File (.dst) Here text box.

7. Browse to and open the location of the `Sheet Set Sample 1` folder, which is in the `\Projects\Chapter 30\` folder. This is a folder created when you installed the *Mastering AutoCAD* sample files.

8. Click Next. The Choose Layouts screen of the wizard appears.

9. Click the Import Options button to open the Import Options dialog box (Figure 30.3).

FIGURE 30.3
Options for
importing layouts

10. Make sure all three options are selected, and then click OK. You'll learn more about the options in this dialog box in the next section.

11. Click the Browse button, and then locate and select the `Sheet Set Sample 1` folder you selected earlier. After you've selected the folder, click OK to see the list of subfolders in that folder.

SETTING A DEFAULT LOCATION

You can set a default location for your sheet sets by using the Files tab of the Options dialog box. See Appendix B for more on the Options dialog box.

---

12. Click the plus signs to expand the listings for `Architectural` and `Structural` (Figure 30.4). You see the drawings in those folders. Expand the list for each drawing to see the layouts available in each drawing. You can select and deselect the layouts and drawings to include in the sheet set. Your list may not be in the same order as shown here, but the contents will be basically the same.

FIGURE 30.4
Browse to the drawings.

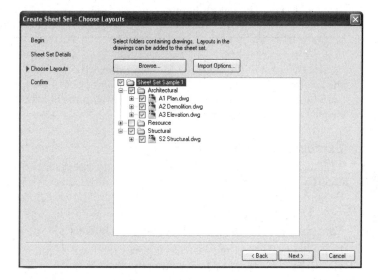

13. Remove the checkmark next to the `Resource` folder shown in the list. You don't want to include the `Resource` folder because that contains the files used as Xrefs in the Paper Space files. For this exercise, you want to select only the drawings and layouts that represent the sheets in your set.

14. Click Next. You see the last screen of the wizard, which shows you the statistics of your new sheet set. It shows only the layouts from the selected drawings because the layouts are the focus of the Sheet Set Manager. Click Finish to exit the wizard. AutoCAD creates a new sheet set.

15. Select the Sheet List tab in the Sheet Set Manager to view its contents. The Sheet Set Manager now shows a list of the drawings in the `Sheet Set Sample 1` folder (Figure 30.5). It didn't display the main folder called `Sheet Set Sample 1` because the Ignore Top Level Folder option is on (see "Formatting Sheet Sets with the Import Options" under "Exploring the Sheet Set Manager," which is the next section).

FIGURE 30.5
The list of
drawings

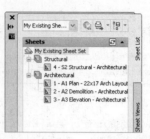

THE SHEET SET MANAGER CAN CHANGE

Your Sheet Set Manager may look slightly taller or narrower than the one shown here because it can be resized by stretching its borders. The order of the drawings may also be different, but the same drawings will be shown. You can click and drag items in the list to change their order.

The sheet list in the Sheet Set Manager shows the name of each existing drawing files with the layout name appended. This helps you identify both the filename and the layout associated with the sheet. As you become more familiar with the Sheet Set Manager, you can choose to display only the layout name.

Exploring the Sheet Set Manager

Although you have more work to do before the sheet set becomes a useful tool, it's complete enough that you can explore some features of the Sheet Set Manager before you add the resource drawings.

FORMATTING SHEET SETS WITH THE IMPORT OPTIONS

In step 9 of the preceding exercise, you saw the Import Options dialog box. This dialog box lets you control how files and folders are organized in the Sheet Set Manager and how the sheets are assigned names. Here is a list of these options:

Prefix Sheet Titles With File Name   The Sheet Set Manager displays only the layout names in its sheet list. With this option selected, the Sheet Set Manager adds the name of the file containing the layout as a prefix to the sheet name. If you want only the layout name to appear in the sheet list, turn off this option.

Create Subsets Based On Folder Structure   If you set up your file structure to separate your project folder into subfolders (such as architectural, mechanical, structural, and civil), you can retain that structure in the Sheet Set Manager by selecting this option. Turn off this option if you want the Sheet Set Manager to display all the sheets in your project in a single column with no subfolders.

Ignore Top Level Folder   When you select a project folder containing your drawings for the sheet set and subfolders are used to keep separate categories of drawings organized, this option causes the Sheet Set Manager to ignore the top-level folder and display only the sub-folders. This is useful if you have one main folder that contains subfolders of your drawings.

The sample folders you used for the previous exercise were set up to demonstrate how these options work. All the options were turned on. As a result, the Sheet Set Manager displayed the sheets with two main categories, Architectural and Structural, reflecting the folder structure of the sample project files. The sheet names showed the layout names appended to the drawing filenames because the Prefix Sheet Titles With File Name option was turned on.

SETTING THE SHEET SET PROPERTIES

In the Sheet Set Details screen of the Create Sheet Set Wizard is a button labeled Sheet Set Properties. If you click this button, the Sheet Set Properties dialog box opens, showing you some of the settings that are part of your new sheet set.

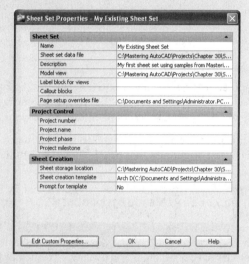

Much of this information describes the location that the Sheet Set Manager will use as you work with sheet sets. Also note the Edit Custom Properties button at the bottom of the dialog box. This enables you to add or edit some of the properties of the sheet set. This information can be edited in the Sheet Set Manager, as you'll see later.

PREVIEWING AND OPENING DRAWINGS IN THE SHEET SET MANAGER

You can view quite a bit of information about the drawings in your list. You can also open a file by double-clicking its name in the sheet list. Here's how:

1. Select 1 – A1 Plan – 22x17 Arch Layout – Plan from the sheet list. A panel appears (Figure 30.6) and displays a description of the sheet, including a thumbnail view and the name, location, and size of the file that contains the sheet.

2. Double-click the 1 – A1 Plan – 22x17 Arch Layout – Plan listing. AutoCAD opens the drawing.

FIGURE 30.6
The flyout information panel

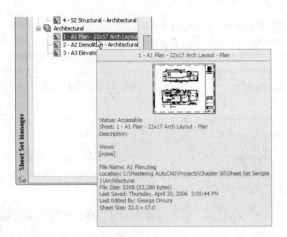

ADDING THE RESOURCE DRAWINGS

Now you'll add the resource drawings to the Sheet Set Manager's sheet list. Remember that the resource drawings are the source Xref files for the sheet drawings. By adding them to the Sheet Set Manager, you'll have ready access to all the files in your project:

1. Select the Model Views tab in the Sheet Set Manager. The palette changes to show the Locations list. Right now, nothing is shown except the Add New Location listing.

WHY NOT INCLUDE THE RESOURCES FOLDER?

You may recall that earlier, in the section "Using the Create Sheet Set Wizard," I asked you not to include the Resource folder. That's because the Create Sheet Set Wizard attempts to create a sheet from all the files in your selection. You don't want to include your resource files as sheets, but you do want to include them as resources.

---

2. Double-click the Add New Location item. A standard file dialog box opens.

3. Locate and select the Resource subfolder under the Sheet Set Sample 1 folder that you've been using, then click Open. The Sheet Set Manager palette displays the list of drawings in that folder.

4. Double-click plans.dwg. You'll see an AutoCAD alert message telling you that the file is currently in use. Click Yes. The plans file opens, showing you the source drawing for the 1 – A1 Plan drawing.

Your sheet set now contains a list of all the files in the project. You can use the Sheet Set Manager to keep track of your AutoCAD files as the project progresses. If you need to plot all your sheets, archive them, or move them, you can do so with relative ease by using options described toward the end of this chapter.

Adding New Sheets to Your Sheet Set

Now that you've created a sheet set from an existing project, as the project continues you'll want to use the Sheet Set Manager to create any new sheets that you want to add to your set. Doing so ensures that the Sheet Set Manager knows about all the files in the project at all times.

But before you start to add new sheets, you need to do a bit of setup. You'll need to make sure the Sheet Set Manager knows which template file to use for any new sheet drawings you add to the set.

POINTING TO A SHEET TEMPLATE

The following exercise will show you how to tell the Sheet Set Manager which template file to use for new sheets:

1. Select the Sheet List tab of the Sheet Set Manager.

2. Right-click My Existing Sheet Set at the top of the Sheet List, and then select Properties. The Sheet Set Properties dialog box opens. (See the sidebar "Setting the Sheet Set Properties" earlier in this chapter.) You see three groups of listings: Sheet Set, Project Control, and Sheet Creation. The Sheet Set group offers information about the current sheets and sheet set. The Project Control group lets you add information regarding the sheet set, such as the project name, number, and milestones. The Sheet Creation group lists information about new sheets.

3. Click the Sheet Creation Template option in the Sheet Creation group. If you can't read the names of the options, hover your cursor over a name and the full option name will appear as a tool tip. A Browse button appears to the right of the option.

4. Click the Browse button to open the Select Layout As Sheet Template dialog box.

The Drawing Template File Name text box shows the location of the current default file from which a new sheet will be derived. That default location is as follows:

```
C:\Documents and Settings\User Name\Local Settings
\Application Data\Autodesk\AutoCAD 2011\R18.1\enu
\Template\SheetSets\Architectural Imperial.dwt
```

CHANGING THE TEMPLATE LOCATION

You can change the default location for sheet set templates in the Files tab of the Options dialog box (choose Options from the Application menu). In the Files tab, expand the list for Template Settings, select Sheet Set Template File Location, click Browse, and then locate and select your sheet set template file location.

Also note that a layout name is listed in the Select A Layout To Create New Sheets list box.

5. Continue to select a template file. Click the Browse button to the far right of the Drawing Template File Name text box to open the Select Drawing dialog box. This is a standard file dialog box.

6. Browse to the \Chapter 30\Sheet Set Sample 1\Resource folder, select the 22x17 Arch.dwt file, and then click Open. This is the template file used for the sheet drawings of the set you've been working with.

7. Back in the Select Layout As Sheet Template dialog box, select Architectural Title Block from the Select A Layout To Create New Sheets list, then click OK. Click OK in the Sheet Set Properties dialog box.

8. A confirmation window asks whether you want to apply the change you made to all nested subsets. Click Apply Changes To Nested Subsets.

You've just set up your sheet set to point to a custom template that contains the title block for any new sheet files you may create. The last step points out a feature of which you'll want to be aware.

In this exercise, you set the 22x17 Arch.dwt template file to be the file the Sheet Set Manager uses for all new drawings. If you prefer, you can set up the Sheet Set Manager to use different template files for new sheets in the sheet subsets. For example, you can have one template for the Architectural subset and a different one for the Structural subset, if they require different title blocks.

To set up the template for the subsets, follow the steps in the previous exercise, but instead of right-clicking My Existing Sheet Set, select the subset name. In the Sheet Set Sample 1 sheet set, the name would be Architectural or Structural.

Another option is to select the Prompt For Template option near the bottom of the Sheet Set Properties dialog box. As the option name indicates, it prompts you for a template file whenever you create a new sheet.

ADDING A NEW SHEET

You're ready to create new sheets that are based on the same title block as the existing sheets in the set:

1. In the Sheet Set Manager palette, right-click the Architectural subset listing, and select New Sheet to add a sheet under this heading. The New Sheet dialog box opens.

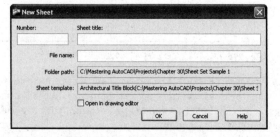

2. In the Number text box, enter **A4**, and in the Sheet Title text box, enter **Details**. As you type, the File Name text box is automatically filled in. You can enter a different sheet title if you like.

3. Click OK to finish creating your new sheet. Your new sheet appears in the sheet list of the Sheet Set Manager palette.

4. Double-click the A4 – Details listing in the sheet list. The A4 Details drawing opens to the layout view. The layout view has been given the name A4 Details, which you can check by clicking the Quick View Layouts tool in the status bar or by just looking at the layout tab.

5. After reviewing these steps, you can close all the drawings (except for Drawing1) and the Sheet Set Manager.

Before you added the new A4 Details sheet, the Sheet Set Manager was only collecting data about your sheet set and displaying that data in the palette. It hadn't created any new files. In the preceding exercise, the Sheet Set Manager created the A4 Details file, although it didn't open it until you double-clicked it in step 4.

Now that the A4 sheet has been created, you can edit it as you would any other drawing to include Xref files, blocks, or other drawing data. You can then create a viewport in the layout to arrange the sheet the way you want.

SHEET SETS ARE VERSATILE

In addition to keeping track of existing and new drawing files in a project, the Sheet Set Manager can help you with plotting, archiving, and publishing your set. See the section "Archiving, Publishing, and eTransmitting Sheet Sets" later in this chapter.

In a large project with many sheets, managing title-block information can be a lot of work. In the next section, you'll look at some other sheet set features that can automate much of the work of maintaining title-block information. You'll also learn how the Sheet Set Manager can simplify the creation of callout bubbles and cross-references between drawings.

Managing Title Blocks and Cross-References

You've just seen that at a basic level, you can use the Sheet Set Manager to keep track of files in a set of drawings. But other features can help reduce the time it takes to create and maintain sheets. In the next section, you'll look at some of the more advanced sheet set features by creating a sheet set based on an existing one.

The Sheet Set Manager can use specially designed template files to automate the creation and management of your sheets. You can include fields (see Chapter 11 for more on fields) that are *sheet set aware*, enabling the Sheet Set Manager to update text automatically whenever there is a change in the sheet set. In addition, the Sheet Set Manager can use blocks with field attributes to automate the process of adding drawing titles and reference symbols, called *callout blocks*, in the Sheet Set Manager. You can customize these templates and callout blocks to fit your particular style of drawing and method of organization.

Creating a New Sheet Set Based on an Existing One

To see firsthand how the Sheet Set Manager can help you manage title blocks and cross-references, you'll create a new sheet set based on an existing sample sheet set created by Autodesk. You'll use a sample sheet set found in the user template folder for new AutoCAD 2011 installations. This sample sheet set uses a template file that has the title block and callout blocks already set up and available for use.

Sheet Set
Manager

Just as before, you'll start by opening the Create Sheet Set Wizard. Follow these steps:

1. If the Sheet Set Manager isn't already open, click the Sheet Set Manager tool in the View tab's Palettes panel.

2. Open a new, blank file. Click the drop-down list at the top of the palette, and select New Sheet Set to start the Create Sheet Set Wizard.

3. Make sure the An Example Sheet Set radio button is selected and click Next. The Sheet Set Example screen appears. Here you can select from the standard sheet set examples provided by Autodesk. Or, if you have a custom sheet set or sheet sets from a third party, you can use the Browse To Another Sheet Set To Use As An Example option.

4. Make sure the Select A Sheet Set To Use As An Example radio button is selected. Then select Architectural Imperial Sheet Set from the list box and click Next. The Sheet Set Details screen appears.

5. Enter **My Sheet Set** in the Name Of New Sheet Set input box. You also have the opportunity to add a description of the sheet set in the Description box. The Store Sheet Set Data File (`.dst`) Here option lets you determine where the sheet set data file is stored. You can see the current location by placing the cursor over the input box. A tool tip displays the path to the location. This tool tip is useful if the path is too long to read from the input box.

6. Click the Browse button to the right of the Store Sheet Set Data File input box, and browse to the location of the sample files for this chapter. Typically, this location is `\Chapter 30\Sheet Set Sample 2`. Click Open.

7. Back in the Sheet Set Details screen of the Create Sheet Set Wizard, click Next. The Confirm screen appears. This screen lets you review the settings before you confirm the creation of your sheet set. You've seen this information in the Sheet Set Properties dialog box.

8. Click the Finish button to create your new sheet set. A list of predefined sheet categories appears in the Sheet List tab of the Sheet Set Manager.

Now, if you check your sample file folder, `\Chapter 30\Sheet Set Sample 2`, you'll find the `My Sheet Set.dst` file that you've just created. As you've seen in prior steps, this file holds the information regarding the location of the files and custom settings for your sheet set.

The first sheet set you created was from drawings that already had Xrefs and views set up for the sheets. The next section shows you how to use the Sheet Set Manager to create a sheet from scratch, including views and Xrefs.

Building a Set of Drawings

The sheet set you just created is like the framework of your set of plans. It isn't the actual set of drawings but rather a structure onto which you can start to build your set of drawings. The Sheet Set Manager manages the coordination and continuity of the set as you add sheets to the set.

To see how these drawing components are managed by the Sheet Set Manager, you'll create some sheets from existing Model Space files. You'll start by adding a couple of floor plans to the sheet set.

You'll use the resource drawings that you saw in the first set of exercises in this chapter as the basis for the new sheets.

SETTING UP SOME VIEWS

The Sheet Set Manager uses drawing views to help simplify the creation of viewports in a sheet, so you'll start by creating some views in a plan drawing. These views will define the areas and layer settings that will be needed later when you create the plan sheets. Follow these steps:

1. Open the `plans.dwg` file from the `Chapter 30\Sheet Set Sample 2\Resource` folder. You see two plans of the house. The top plan is a floor plan, and the lower plan is a combination of a floor plan and a site plan.

2. Click Plan_site from the Layer State drop-down list in the Home tab's Layers panel.

You've just restored a layer state that shows all the appropriate layers for the site plan. Next you'll save a view of just the site plan, which you'll use a bit later when you create the site plan sheet:

1. Click Named Views from the View tab's Views panel or type **V**↵ to open the View Manager dialog box.

2. Make sure Current is selected in the list to the left. Then click the New button.

3. In the New View/Shot Properties dialog box, enter **Site Plan** for the view name.

4. Click the Define View Window button. The dialog box temporarily closes to enable you to select a window to define the view area.

5. Place a selection window around the area shown in Figure 30.7. Don't worry if you don't get it right the first time. You can use a selection window repeatedly until you have the view you want.

FIGURE 30.7
Selecting the
view area

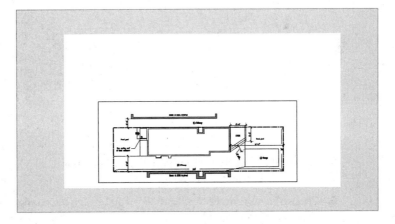

6. Press ↵ when you're satisfied with the boundary selection.

7. Back in the New View/Shot Properties dialog box, make sure the Save Layer Snapshot With View option is selected, and click OK.

8. Click OK in the View Manager dialog box to close it.

READJUSTING YOUR VIEWS

If you need to adjust the view area, open the View Manager dialog box again, select the view name from the list box, and click the Edit Boundaries button. The dialog box closes temporarily, and the drawing displays with the view area highlighted. You can then reselect the view area with a selection window.

You've just created a view for the site plan. Now create another view for the floor plan:

1. Go to the Home tab's Layers panel and select Plan_finish from the Layer State drop-down list.

2. Choose Named Views from the View tab's Views panel or type **V**↵ to open the View Manager dialog box.

3. Make sure Current is selected in the left panel. Then click New.

4. In the New View/Shot Properties dialog box, enter **Floor Plan** for the view name. Click the Define View Window button. Then place a selection window around the area shown in Figure 30.8. Press ↵ when you're satisfied with the area you've selected.

FIGURE 30.8
Selecting the
view area

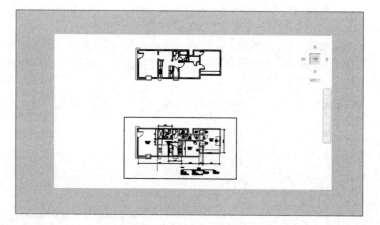

5. Back in the New View/Shot Properties dialog box, click OK. Then click OK in the View Manager dialog box to close it.

6. Choose Save from the Application menu to save the changes you've just made, and then close the plans.dwg file.

If you know that you want to use other views for your sheets, you can continue to define more views. But for this exercise, let's move on to creating a sheet from the views you just created.

CREATING A SHEET

Now that you have some views defined, you're ready to create a sheet for those views:

Sheet Set
Manager

1. If the Sheet Set Manager isn't already open, click the Sheet Set Manager tool on the View tab's Palettes panel.

2. Select Architectural from the list, right-click, and select New Sheet to open the New Sheet dialog box.

3. Enter **A1** in the Number input box. This defines the sheet number that will appear in the lower-right corner of the sheet. As you type, your entry appears in both the Number input box and the File Name input box.

4. Enter **Site Plan And Floor Plan** in the Sheet Title input box. Again, as you type, your entry appears in both the Sheet Title input box and the File Name input box.

5. Click OK. AutoCAD creates a new file called A1 – Site Plan and Floor Plan, and the new drawing name appears as a subhead below Architectural in the Sheet Set Manager.

6. Double-click the A1 – Site Plan And Floor Plan listing. The sheet appears in AutoCAD.

If you look closely, you'll notice that the sheet number is already in place in the lower-right corner of the drawing. The Sheet Set Manager was able to apply the sheet number you entered in step 3 to the new sheet because the template uses a field for the sheet-number text. You'll learn how to add such a field to your own title block later in this chapter. For now, you'll add the views you created in the plans.dwg file to this new sheet.

ADDING YOUR VIEWS TO THE NEW SHEET

You've created views in your plans.dwg resource drawing, and you've created a new sheet for the plan views. The next step is to insert those saved views into the sheet.

Start by adding the resource drawings to the sheet set:

1. Click the Model Views tab in the Sheet Set Manager, and then double-click Add New Location in the Location list.

2. Browse to and open the \Chapter30\Sheet Set Sample 2\Resource folder and click Open. The files in the Resource folder appear in the list of resource drawings.

With the resource files added to the Sheet Set Manager, you can add a view to the A1 sheet from the plans.dwg file you worked on earlier:

1. Click the plus sign next to the plans.dwg item. The list expands to show the Site Plan and Floor Plan views you created earlier in this chapter.

2. Select Site Plan from the list, right-click, and choose Place On Sheet. Don't click your mouse yet, but as you move the cursor over the A1 – Site Plan And Floor Plan layout, a rectangle appears at the cursor and covers most of the drawing.

3. Right-click in the layout view to display a list of drawing scales.

4. Select 1/8″ = 1′ from the list. You see the Site Plan view of `plans.dwg` along with a title bubble, all following the cursor (Figure 30.9). You can also click and drag the Site Plan view from the list into the sheet to get the same result.

FIGURE 30.9
Adding and positioning a view

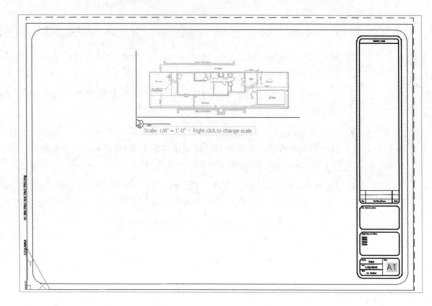

5. Place the view in the top half of the layout and click. The Site Plan view is placed in the layout along with a title bubble, drawing scale, and view title.

6. Back in the Sheet Set Manager, select Floor Plan from the list. Right-click and select Place On Sheet.

7. Right-click in the Layout view, and select 1/4″ = 1″ from the list.

8. Place the view in the lower half of the layout and click. The Floor Plan view is placed in the layout along with a title bubble, drawing scale, and view title.

9. Zoom in to the title bubble for the Site Plan view. It already has the proper view name and scale.

In the preceding exercise, the Sheet Set Manager performed several steps that you could have done manually with much more effort. It imported the `plans.dwg` file as an Xref into the A1 – Site Plan And Floor Plan layout. It then created a viewport in the layout, it scaled the layout view according to your selections in steps 4 and 7, and finally, it added a title bubble and the title and scale for each view.

EDITING THE VIEW NUMBERS

You need to take care of one more item for this sheet. Although the view names and scales have been provided by the Sheet Set Manager, you still need the view numbers. Right now they're just three dashes. Follow these steps:

1. In the Sheet Set Manager, select the Sheet Views tab.

2. Expand the A1 Site Plan And Floor Plan list, and select Site Plan; then right-click and select Rename & Renumber to open the Rename & Renumber View dialog box (Figure 30.10).

FIGURE 30.10
The Rename & Renumber View dialog box

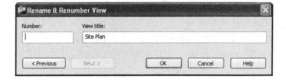

3. Enter **1** in the Number input box. The name of the view is available for editing as well.

4. Click the Next or Previous button, whichever is available for selection. This advances the data in the dialog box to the next view, which is the Floor Plan view. Enter **2** in the Number input box. Once again, you see the name of the view.

5. Click OK to close the Rename & Renumber View dialog box.

6. Type **Re↵**. The title bubbles change to show the numbers 1 and 2 for the two views.

The final task is to hide the viewport borders. You can do this by creating a layer just for the viewports and then turning off that layer:

1. Use the Layer Properties Manager to create a layer called Viewport.

2. Turn off the Viewport layer, and close the Layer Properties Manager.

3. Select the two viewports. Select Viewport from the Layer drop-down list in the Home tab's Layers panel. The viewports disappear.

Adding the view numbers is important for two reasons. The obvious one is so that you have a number you can refer to when referencing this plan sheet in the future. But the Sheet Set Manager also keeps track of this view number so that later, when you start to add callout blocks to your drawing set, the Sheet Set Manager knows which view goes with the callout block you're adding. The next section will show you how this works.

Adding Callout Blocks as Cross-Reference Symbols

As mentioned earlier, in the process of building a set of drawings, you'll have to add cross-reference symbols. One common type of cross-reference indicates an elevation view of a building from a floor plan.

In a typical set of architectural drawings, you'll have a sheet or several sheets that show the sides of a building. The most common views are the north, south, east, and west sides of a building. Elevation drawings are used to indicate window locations, wall finishes, building heights, floor levels, and other key elements in the design. Reference symbols, called *callout blocks* in AutoCAD, are placed in the floor plan and tell the viewer which sheet contains these elevation drawings and show where the view is taken from in relation to the plan.

In this section, you'll learn how to set up an elevation view and place callout blocks in the floor plan that show which sheet contains the elevation. You'll see how callout blocks are tied to sheet numbers so that even if a sheet number changes, the callout block always indicates the right sheet number.

You'll use a sheet set similar to the one you just started, but with a few additions to save some work for you. The My Sheet Set 1.dst sheet set has the A1 Site Plan And Floor Plan sheet already created and an additional sheet called A2 Elevation Plan. This additional sheet contains two elevation views. They were created in the same way as the plan views in the previous exercise, so no method was used to create them that you haven't already been shown.

In the following steps, you'll add a callout block to the A1 sheet that references the A2 sheet. Along the way, you'll become familiar with some of the other features of the Sheet Set Manager.

Start by closing the current sheet set and the files associated with it:

1. In the Sheet Set Manager, select the Sheet List tab.

2. Right-click My Sheet Set in the list, and choose Close Sheet Set.

3. Close and save any drawing that may be open except the blank default drawing file.

Next, open the sample sheet set:

1. Click Open from the Sheet Set Manager drop-down list. Then, in the Open Sheet Set dialog box, locate and select My Sheet 1.dst in the Chapter 30\Sheet Set Sample 3 folder. Click Open in the Open Sheet Set dialog box.

2. Make sure the Sheet List tab is selected, then double-click A1-Site Plan And Floor Plan and A2 Elevations to open these two files.

Next you'll add the callout symbol to the A1 sheet. In the next few steps, you will be adding callout symbols based on preexisting views from the A2 Elevations drawing:

1. In the Sheet List tab of the Sheet Set Manager, double-click the A1 sheet again. Because it's already open, double-clicking the A1 sheet makes it the current drawing file.

2. Enlarge your view of the floor plan so it looks similar to Figure 30.11.

3. Click the Sheet Views tab in the Sheet Set Manager, then select and right-click 1 – South Elevation.

4. Choose Place Callout Block ➤ Elev Indicator Ext – Up from the shortcut menu. As you move the cursor into the drawing area, a symbol appears at the cursor. This is the callout block for the exterior elevation.

5. Position the callout block as shown in Figure 30.11 for the south elevation and click. The callout block already shows the appropriate drawing number and sheet number.

6. Right-click 2 – West Elevation, and choose Place Callout Block ➤ Elev Indicator Ext – Right from the shortcut menu.

7. Place this callout block to the left of the floor plan, as shown in Figure 30.11.

When you inserted the callout blocks in steps 4 through 7, the Sheet Set Manager automatically added the appropriate sheet and view number to the block. This action saves you the effort of checking which drawing contains the elevation view and of making sure the numbers between the callout block and view match.

FIGURE 30.11
Enlarge your view, and place the callout blocks as shown.

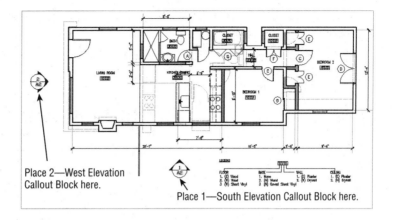

Place 2—West Elevation
Callout Block here.

Place 1—South Elevation Callout Block here.

ADDING HYPERLINKS

Later, when you learn how to create your own custom callout blocks, you'll learn about the hyperlink feature. The callout blocks you just added have this feature turned on. If you Ctrl+click the text of either of the callout blocks, AutoCAD will open the drawing containing the view that the callout block references—namely, the A2 Elevation drawing.

Editing Sheet Numbers and Title Block Information

Suppose you need to change the sheet number of the elevation sheet from A2 to A3 to make room for a demolition plan. The following exercise demonstrates how the Sheet Set Manager can make quick work of such a change:

1. In the Sheet Set Manager, select the Sheet List tab.

2. Right-click the A2 Elevations sheet item, and choose Rename & Renumber.

3. In the Rename & Renumber Sheet dialog box, change the number from A2 to A3 and click OK.

4. Type **Re↵**. The elevation callout blocks you just added now show the new sheet number for the elevation sheet.

5. Double-click A3 Elevations from the Sheet List tab, and type **Re↵**. The sheet number in the lower-right corner of the drawing changes to A3.

As you saw from this exercise, the drawing numbers are coordinated through settings in the Sheet Set Manager as long as you use the callout symbols from the Sheet Set Manager.

Drawing numbers aren't the only part that can be managed through the Sheet Set Manager. You have two sheets in the set now, but they were created without regard for the client name and address in the title block. You'll need to go back and add this information to the sheets. Here's a quick way to do it:

1. In the Sheet List tab of the Sheet Set Manager, right-click My Sheet Set 1 at the top of the list box, and then choose Properties to open the Sheet Set Properties dialog box (Figure 30.12).

FIGURE 30.12
Sheet set properties

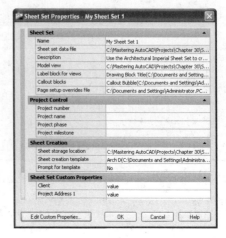

2. Scroll down to the lower half of the Sheet Set Properties dialog box, where you see a set of options labeled Sheet Set Custom Properties. Click the Project Address 1 label, and enter **444 Ramona Way** for the first line of the address. (Or you can add any street address you like.) You may need to widen the first column to read the label or hover over the label to see a tool tip showing the full label.

3. In the next option, Project Address 2, enter **Big Bear, CA.**

4. Enter **Smith Residence** for the project name.

5. Leave the Client, Project Number, and Project Address 3 options as Value. Click OK.

6. Zoom in to the lower-right corner of the sheet so you can clearly see the title-block information, and then type **Re.↵** to display the changes in the current sheet.

The changes you made in this exercise affect all the existing sheets in the set. If you add new sheets, they will also display the new address and project name.

Closing a Sheet Set

By now, you have two sheet sets open: the one you created from an existing set of drawings and the one you opened for the latest set of exercises. In the next sections, you'll look at customizing sheet sets. You won't need both sheet sets open. Close the one you've been working on by following these steps:

1. Click the drop-down list at the top of the Sheet Set Manager.

2. Right-click My Sheet Set 1, and select Close Sheet Set.

CLOSE ALL OF THE FILES

In preparation for the next sections, close all the drawings that are open in AutoCAD. Closing a sheet set doesn't automatically close the drawings associated with it.

As you can see, you can have multiple sheet sets open at any one time. This feature can facilitate the movement of drawing data from one project to another. For example, you may want to borrow construction details from one set to add to a new set. You can use the Sheet Set Manager to locate the detail sheet from the prior project and then cut and paste drawing data from that drawing into a drawing in your most current project.

Customizing Sheet Sets

In the preceding sections, you created and used a sheet set that was based on a canned sheet set from Autodesk. That sheet set included a title block with many of the field text objects already embedded so you could take advantage of the Sheet Set Manager's ability to control the text in the title block. The view title bubbles and callout blocks were also supplied, and they contained the field text objects to automate the insertion of view names and coordination of callout cross-reference numbers.

But not everyone will want to use the title blocks and symbols offered in the Autodesk samples. You aren't limited to using the canned sheet set from Autodesk. In the following sections, you'll look at how to customize your own title block to work with the Sheet Set Manager. You'll also learn how to create custom view titles and callout blocks.

Customizing a Title Block

To begin your exploration of sheet set customization, you'll add field objects to the sample title block you used at the beginning of this chapter. Remember that the first project included an existing set of drawings that wasn't set up to take full advantage of all the sheet set features you saw in the latest set of exercises. The title block in that early exercise contained some attributes that could be used to include text information, but the title block was not *sheet set aware*. To prepare a title block for use with the Sheet Set Manager, you'll need to convert those attribute values into field objects. This entails editing the title block and saving it as the template file for the sheet set.

DEFINING TITLE BLOCKS

In the following sections, I use the terms *title block* and *AutoCAD block*, which may cause confusion. *Title block* is a standard drafting term meaning the drawing border and drawing title information, including a business logo and other textual information about the drawing. *AutoCAD block* refers to the type of AutoCAD object known as a *block* that is a collection of objects combined into one object. See Chapter 4 for more on AutoCAD blocks.

SETTING UP SHEET NUMBERS AND TITLES

The first thing you'll do is set up the title block to create a sheet-set-aware number and title. This will enable the Sheet Set Manager to control the number and title that appears in the title block, as you saw in earlier exercises.

You could open the template file and start editing the title block without involving the Sheet Set Manager in any way. But now, in the following set of exercises, you'll edit the template file with a little help from the Sheet Set Manager. By using the Sheet Set Manager while editing your template file, you'll be able to get instant feedback on your edits.

Start by creating a new sheet in the sheet set you created in the beginning of this chapter. You'll use this new sheet to edit the title block. Follow these steps:

1. Start a new, blank drawing, and then, if the Sheet Set Manager is closed, open it by clicking the Sheet Set Manager tool in the View tab's Palettes panel.

2. Open the sheet set named My Existing Sheet Set. Remember that this was the first sheet set in the \Chapter 30\Sheet Set Sample 1 folder. You can open it by selecting Recent ➢ *project file location*\Chapter 30\Sheet Set Sample 1\My Sheet Set.dst, where *project file location* is the location for your Mastering AutoCAD sample files.

3 In the Sheet List tab, right-click the sheet set name at the top of the list and choose New Sheet.

4. In the New Sheet dialog box, enter **000** for the sheet number and **Template Edit** for the sheet title. Click OK. The sheet number and title can be anything because this isn't a sheet you'll save.

5. In the Sheet Set Manager, double-click 000 – Template Edit. The sheet you just created appears in the AutoCAD window.

Remember that a new file based on a template is really just a copy of the template. As I mentioned earlier, the title block is an AutoCAD block that contains attribute definitions. To edit those definitions, you'll need to explode the block:

1. Click the title block to select it.

2. Click the Explode tool on the Home tab's Modify panel.

Now you're ready to edit the attribute definitions. Start by editing the definition for the sheet number in the lower-right corner of the title block:

1. Locate the attribute definition that is in the lower-right corner of the title block and shows a large *No.* and double-click it. This is the attribute definition for the sheet number. The Edit Attribute Definition dialog box opens (Figure 30.13).

2. Double-click in the Default text box. Right-click it and choose Insert Field to open the Field dialog box (Figure 30.13).

3. Select SheetSet from the Field Category drop-down list.

4. In the Field Names list box, select CurrentSheetNumber.

5. In the Format list box, select Uppercase. Then click OK.

FIGURE 30.13

Inserting a field in
the attributes

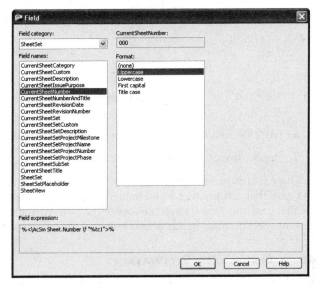

6. Back in the Edit Attribute Definition dialog box, the Default text box now shows 000, the number you assigned to this drawing. This tells you that your field attribute is working properly because the default value shows the current sheet number. The gray background of the text tells you that the text is a field.

7. Click OK to exit the Edit Attribute Definition dialog box.

8. Press ↵ to exit attribute-editing mode.

In step 6, you received instant feedback when you assigned the CurrentSheetNumber attribute field to the attribute definition. The default value changed to the sheet number of the current drawing.

Next you'll make a similar change to add the project name to the title block:

1. Zoom in to the area of the title block that shows the project information (Figure 30.14).

2. Double-click the DRAWING_TITLE attribute definition just below the OWNER3 attribute definition.

3. As in the preceding exercise, select the Default value, right-click, and choose Insert Field.

4. Select CurrentSheetTitle from the Field Names list, and select Title Case from the Format list.

5. Click OK. Now the Default value is the current sheet title, Template Edit.

FIGURE 30.14
Zoom in to the
project info.

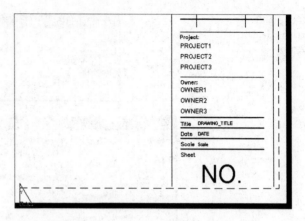

6. Click OK to accept the changes in the Edit Attribute Definition dialog box.

7. Press ↵ to exit attribute-editing mode.

These two exercises demonstrated how you can add a field object to an attribute definition and have that definition give you immediate feedback about its association to the sheet set. In the first case, the default sheet number in the Edit Attribute Definition dialog box reflected the current sheet number. In the second exercise, you saw that the sheet title appeared.

ADDING CUSTOM SHEET SET PROPERTIES

You've added two of the standard sheet set fields to the title block. The standard fields are the ones that appear in the Field Names list in the Field dialog box. But what if you want to add custom sheet set fields that aren't on the list? You can create your own field categories in the Sheet Set Manager. In the following set of exercises, you'll create some custom fields in the Sheet Set Manager properties dialog box and then add those fields to your title block.

First, set up some new custom fields:

1. In the Sheet Set Manager, right-click My Existing Sheet Set at the top of the sheet list and choose Properties.

2. At the bottom of the Sheet Set Properties dialog box, click the Edit Custom Properties button to open the Custom Properties dialog box.

3. Click the Add button to open the Add Custom Property dialog box.

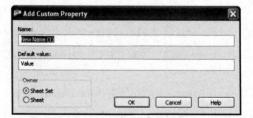

4. In the Name text box, enter **Project 1**. This will be the first line for the project information area in the title block.

5. In the Default Value text box, enter **Project Line 1**.

6. In the Owner group at the bottom of the dialog box, make sure Sheet Set is selected. This tells the Sheet Set Manager that this value applies to all the sheets in the set, not just the individual sheets.

7. Click OK to return to the Custom Properties dialog box.

8. Repeat steps 3 through 7 to add two more custom properties called Project 2 and Project 3, with the values Project Line 2 and Project Line 3.

9. Click OK to close the Custom Properties dialog box, and then click OK in the Sheet Set Properties dialog box.

You've created some custom properties. Now include those properties in your title block:

1. Pan up to the area in the title block that shows the project information.

2. Double-click the Project 1 attribute definition. In the Edit Attribute Definition dialog box, highlight the Default text box, right-click, and choose Insert Field.

3. In the Field Names list box (Figure 30.15), select CurrentSheetSetCustom.

4. Open the Custom Property Name drop-down list near the bottom of the dialog box, and select Project 1. All the custom properties you created are listed here.

FIGURE 30.15
Choose from the
list of field names.

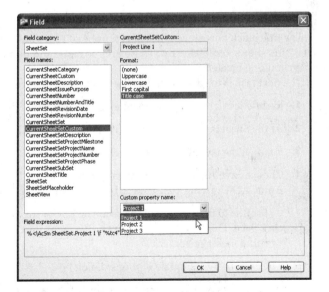

5. Click OK to return to the Edit Attribute Definition dialog box. The default field value shows Project Line 1, which is the default value you gave for the custom properties in the previous exercise.

6. Click OK, and then repeat steps 2 through 5 for the Project 2 and Project 3 attribute definitions.

7. Press ⏎ to exit attribute-editing mode.

SAVING YOUR NEW TITLE BLOCK AS A TEMPLATE

You've just seen how to include custom sheet set properties in your title block. Now you're ready to convert your newly edited title block back into the template file you're using for this sheet set. First you need to turn your exploded title block back into an AutoCAD block object:

1. Zoom out so you can see all of the title block.

2. Click the Create tool on the Home tab's Block panel.

3. In the Block Definition dialog box, select 22x17ArchBlock from the Name drop-down list.

4. In the Objects group, click the Select Objects button, and select the entire title block.

5. Make sure the Convert To Block radio button is selected in the Objects group.

6. Click OK. A warning message tells you that you're about to redefine the 22x17ArchBlock block. Click Redefine.

7. The Edit Attributes dialog box opens. You don't need to change anything here, so click OK.

The title block now shows the sheet number 000. If you look closely, you'll also see that the sheet title shows Template Edit. These are the name and number you assigned to this sheet when you first created it.

The next task is to save the file as the template file for the current sheet set:

1. Right-click in the Layout tab labeled 000 Template Edit, and choose Rename.

2. At the Sheet Set – Rename Layout dialog box, click Rename Layout Only.

3. Rename the layout **My Title Block**.

4. Choose Save As from the Application menu. In the Save Drawing As dialog box, select AutoCAD Drawing Template (*.dwt) from the File Of Type drop-down list.

Browse to the location of the template file for this sheet set, select 22x17 Arch.dwt, and click Save. This location is \Chapter 30\Sheet Set Sample 1\Resource. Click Yes in the warning message box.

5. Click OK in the Template Options dialog box.

Normally, at this point you could close the newly saved template file and remove the 000 – Template Edit sheet from the sheet list. However, you'll use this file again when you create other components of the sheet set.

TESTING THE NEW TEMPLATE

Now you can test the new template to make sure it's working. You'll start by creating a new sheet to check whether the sheet number and title appear correctly:

1. Right-click My Existing Sheet Set, and choose New Sheet.

2. Enter **A5** for the number and **Schedules** for the title, and then click OK.

3. Double-click A5 – Schedules from the sheet list of the Sheet Set Manager to open it. The sheet shows A5 for the number and Schedules for the title.

TAKING ADVANTAGE OF OTHER FIELD OPTIONS

As you learned in Chapter 11, you can add field objects directly to a drawing if you want drawing data to appear as text. For example, you can add field text directly in a drawing layout to provide information about the author of a drawing, the date the drawing was printed, or the scale to which the layout is set to plot.

This information can be included in small print on the border of the drawing to aid others when they need to know more about the drawing's origin. You can either add the field directly to the drawing by using the Field command or include it in Mtext or Dtext as part of a paragraph or sentence. Here is a list of field options from the Field Category list in the Field dialog box to help you get an idea of what you can include as text in a sheet:

Date & Time   Lets you add a date and time stamp to your drawing. You can select from a variety of date and time styles or show only a date or only a time.

Document   Lets you add data from the drawing properties that are stored in AutoCAD by using the Dwgprops command (choose File ➤ Drawing Properties). This includes information such as the author, filename and size, comments, title, and subject.

Linked   Lets you add a hyperlink to another file.

Objects   Lets you include the name or property of an object. For example, you can add a block name as a field text label, or you can add an object's layer.

Other   Lets you add Diesel expressions or system-variable values as field text.

Plot   Lets you display plot settings as text in your drawing. This can be useful to help others determine how a drawing was plotted.

SheetSet   Offers options to help automate many of the labeling chores you normally do when creating sheets.

You also added some custom sheet set properties. Do the following to see if they're working properly:

1. Right-click My Existing Sheet Set at the top of the sheet list in the Sheet Set Manager and choose Properties.

2. Toward the bottom of the Sheet Set Properties dialog box, change the value for Project 1 to **John Smith Residence**.

3. Change the value for Project 2 to **123 Anystreet**. Change the value for Project 3 to **Roseville, California**.

4. Click OK.

5. Type **Re.⏎**. The title block now shows the new project information you just edited.

You've customized the title block with custom properties and a sheet-set-aware number and title. Armed with this information, you can customize any title block to take full advantage of the sheet set features.

You can include a lot of information in the title block through the Sheet Set field option. Table 30.1 gives you a rundown of the sheet set options to help you decide what you may want to include.

TABLE 30.1: Field options available for sheet sets

FIELD NAME	PURPOSE
CurrentSheetCustom	Displays custom sheet data. Custom sheet data can be added and edited through the Sheet Set Properties dialog box.
CurrentSheetDescription	Displays the description for the current sheet found in the properties for the sheet. Select the sheet name from the Sheet Set Manager's Sheet List tab, right-click, and choose Properties.
CurrentSheetNumber	Displays the current sheet number.
CurrentSheetNumberAndTitle	Displays the sheet number and title combined into one line of text.
CurrentSheetSet	Displays the name of the current sheet set.
CurrentSheetSetCustom	Displays a custom value for the current sheet set.
CurrentSheetSetDescription	Displays the sheet set description, which can be found in the Sheet Set Properties dialog box.
CurrentSheetSetSubSet	Displays the name of a subset of the current sheet set.
CurrentSheetTitle	Displays the current sheet title.
SheetSet	Displays any standard sheet set value (such as sheet number and title, sheet title, sheet number, or sheet description) from any sheet in the sheet set.
SheetSetPlaceholder	Displays standard sheet set values from within callout blocks.
SheetView	Displays sheet set view data such as view title, view number, and view scale.
CurrentSheetCategory	Displays a category field.

TABLE 30.1: Field options available for sheet sets *(CONTINUED)*

FIELD NAME	PURPOSE
CurrentSheetIssuePurpose	Displays an Issue Purpose field.
CurrentSheetRevisionDate	Displays a Revision Date field.
CurrentSheetRevisionNumber	Displays a Revision Number field.
CurrentSheetProjectMilestone	Displays a Project Milestone field.
CurrentSheetProjectName	Displays a Project Name field.
CurrentSheetProjectNumber	Displays a Project Number field.
CurrentSheetProjectPhase	Displays a Project Phase field.

Creating Custom View Labels and Callout Blocks

In the section "Managing Title Blocks and Cross-References" earlier in this chapter, you learned how to create a new sheet set from an existing one. You saw that the Sheet Set Manager was able to create a viewport and add a view label automatically, including a view number bubble, a view title, and the scale for the view. Just like the title block, the view label you used in the section "Adding Your Views to the New Sheet" was a block with field attribute values. You can create your own view label block or edit an existing one by using the methods you've already seen for the title block. Callout blocks are also created and edited in the same way.

CREATING THE COMPONENTS OF YOUR VIEW LABEL

In this section, you'll create a custom view label. This will help you to understand which field attributes are used for the view label. You'll also learn how to set up the Sheet Set Manager to use your custom block.

Just as with the title block, you could create the view label block in AutoCAD without using the Sheet Set Manager, but using the Sheet Set Manager simplifies your work and also helps verify that you're on the right track. You'll start by going back to the template file you edited earlier, and then you'll create the graphics and attribute definitions for your custom view label. Follow these steps:

1. Close the A5 Schedules.dwg file and return to the 22x17 Arch.dwt file that you updated in the earlier exercise. You can use the Application menu to return to the file. You'll add the view label block to this drawing.

2. Make sure the current layer is set to 0; then draw a circle with a 0.25″ diameter.

3. Add a line to the right of the circle that is 1″ long, as shown in Figure 30.16.

4. Click the Define Attributes tool in the Home tab's expanded Block panel to open the Attribute Definition dialog box (Figure 30.17).

FIGURE 30.16
Beginning to
create the view
label block

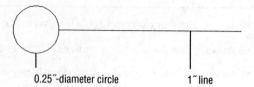

0.25˝-diameter circle   1˝ line

5. Enter **ViewNumber** in the Tag text box and **View Number** in the Prompt text box.

6. Click the Insert Field button to the right of the Default text box to open the Field dialog box.

7. Select SheetSet in the Field Category drop-down list, and then select SheetSetPlaceholder from the Field Names list.

8. Select ViewNumber from the Placeholder Type list and Uppercase from the Format list (Figure 30.18).

FIGURE 30.17
Defining an
attribute

FIGURE 30.18
Defining the field
to insert

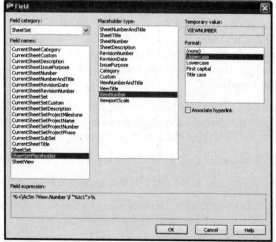

You've just added the field that this block will need for the view number. Next, you need to make sure the text is formatted correctly.

9. Click OK to return to the Attribute Definition dialog box. Set the Justification value in the Text Settings group to Middle, and set the Text Height value to 0.15.

10. Turn on the Preset option in the Mode group. If you don't turn on the Preset option, you'll be prompted for the attribute value when the view is inserted even though the Sheet Set Manager supplies these values automatically.

11. Click OK. Then use the Center osnap to place the attribute definition in the center of the circle. *VIEWNUMBER* appears in large letters, centered on the circle.

If you forgot a setting in the previous steps, you can always go back and use the Properties palette to modify the attribute definition settings. Select the attribute definition, right-click, and choose Properties.

Next you need to add the view title and scale. The steps to add these parts of the view label are the same as for the view number you just added. You first create an attribute definition by using the Insert Field option for the attribute value. The only difference is the location and text options for the attribute definition. Here are the steps:

1. Click the Define Attributes tool in the Home tab's expanded Block panel to open the Attribute Definition dialog box again. Enter **ViewTitle** in the Tag text box and **View Title** in the Prompt text box.

2. Click the Insert Field button to the right of the Default text box to open the Field dialog box. Select SheetSet in the Field Category drop-down list, and select SheetSetPlaceholder from the Field Names list.

3. Select ViewTitle from the Placeholder Type list and Title Case from the Format list.

4. Click OK. Then, in the Attribute Definition dialog box, set Justification to Left and Text Height to 0.15. Also make sure the Preset option in the Mode group is selected.

5. Click OK, and place the attribute definition approximately as shown in Figure 30.19.

FIGURE 30.19
The parts of the view label block

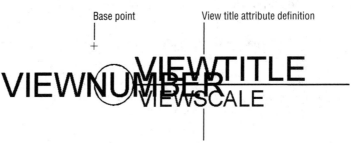

Finally, you need to add the scale information to the view title:

1. Click the Define Attributes tool in the Home tab's expanded Block panel to open the Attribute Definition dialog box a third time. Enter **ViewScale** in the Tag text box and **View Scale** in the Prompt text box.

2. Click the Insert Field button to open the Field dialog box. Make sure SheetSet is selected in the Field Category drop-down list and SheetSetPlaceholder is selected in the Field Names list.

3. Select ViewportScale from the Placeholder Type list, and select #″ = 1′-0″ from the Format list.

4. Click OK to exit the Field dialog box.

5. Set the Justification value in the Text Settings group to Left, set the Text Height value to 0.1, and select the Preset option.

6. Click OK. Then place the View Scale attribute definition approximately as shown in Figure 30.19.

TURNING THE COMPONENTS INTO A BLOCK

You have all the attribute definitions you'll need. The next task is to turn the whole thing into a block:

1. Choose Create from the Home tab's Block panel.

2. In the Block Definition dialog box, enter **ViewTitle** for the block name.

3. Click the Select Objects button. Select all the objects you created in this set of exercises, including the circle and line you started with. Press ↵ when you've made your selection.

4. Click the Pick Point button in the Base Point group, and select the point indicated in Figure 30.19. This is important because the insertion point of the block will coincide with the lower-left corner of the viewport that the Sheet Set Manager creates when adding views to a sheet.

5. Click OK to finish the block. The block is now a part of your template file. All you need to do is save it to have the block available to the Sheet Set Manager.

6. If the ViewTitle block remains in the drawing, erase it. Then zoom out so you see the entire layout.

7. Click Save on the Quick Access toolbar to save the template file, which now includes your ViewTitle block.

You may notice that in step 5, the text in the block obscured the circle and line graphic. Fields always show a gray background to distinguish them from other types of text. The gray background doesn't print, so even though it appears to cover the line and circle, the fields won't interfere with the printing of those objects.

INCLUDING YOUR VIEW LABEL IN THE SHEET SET

You must complete one more task to let the Sheet Set Manager know that your ViewTitle block is available. To do this, you need to open the Sheet Set Manager Preferences dialog box and point to the ViewTitle block. Here's how that's done:

1. Right-click My Existing Sheet Set in the sheet list and choose Properties.

2. In the Sheet Set Properties dialog box, click Label Block For Views in the Sheet Set group (Figure 30.20).

FIGURE 30.20
Choose to label
the block.

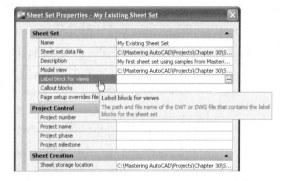

3. Click the Browse button to the far right of Label Block For Views.

4. In the Select Block dialog box, click the Browse button to the far right of the Enter The Drawing File Name text box.

5. Choose AutoCAD Drawing Template (*.dwt) in the Files Of Type drop-down list at the bottom of the Select Drawing dialog box. Then locate and select the `22x17 Arch.dwt` template file you've been working with for this sheet set.

6. Back in the Select Block dialog box (Figure 30.21), click the Choose Blocks In The Drawing File radio button. Select ViewTitle from the list box just below the option. Click OK after you've made the selection, and then click OK in the Sheet Set Properties dialog box.

Remember that you created the ViewTitle block inside the `22x17 Arch.dwt` template file, so when you saved that file, the block became a part of that template file. In steps 4 and 5, you selected the template file and then selected the block in that file. If you prefer, you can save your view title blocks as individual files. If you choose this route, make sure you select the Select The Drawing File As A Block option in step 4.

FIGURE 30.21
Set the Select
Block options.

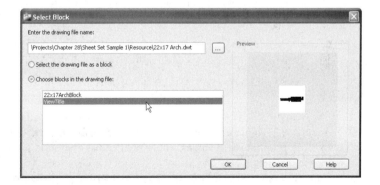

Now you're ready to test the block by adding a sheet and inserting a view. Remember that the Sheet Set Manager uses views to determine the contents of new viewports. Follow these steps:

1. Right-click My Existing Sheet Set in the sheet list, and choose New Sheet.

2. Enter **001** for the number and **View Test** for the sheet title, and click OK.

3. Double-click 001 View Test in the sheet list to open the file.

4. Click the Model Views tab of the Sheet Set Manager, expand the list for the `\Projects\ Chapter 30\Sheet Set Sample 1\Resources` listing, and then expand the `elevations .dwg` listing.

5. Right-click South Elevation in the list, and choose Place On Sheet.

6. Right-click the layout drawing area, and choose 1/8″ = 1′-0″. Click in the layout to place the view. The view appears along with the ViewTitle block you created in the beginning of this section.

You've seen how to create a custom view label block. The process for creating a callout block is basically the same.

CREATING A CALLOUT BLOCK

You may recall that you were able to insert a callout block in a Plan view that was linked to an elevation drawing on another sheet. You can create a custom callout block by using the same steps you used to create the view title block in the preceding section. The only difference is that you select a different set of field values for the block's attribute definitions.

A callout block typically shows a circle with a view number on top and a sheet number on the bottom, as shown in Figure 30.22.

FIGURE 30.22
A typical callout block inserted in a drawing

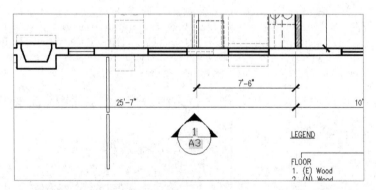

Figure 30.23 shows an exploded version of the callout block with the attribute definitions labeled with the appropriate field values. Those field values are found under the SheetSetPlaceholder field names in the Field dialog box.

In addition, you'll want to select the Associate Hyperlink option in the Field dialog box (Figure 30.24).

FIGURE 30.23
The attribute definitions of a callout block and their associated field values

ViewNumber field

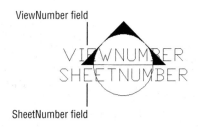

SheetNumber field

FIGURE 30.24
Choose to create a hyperlink.

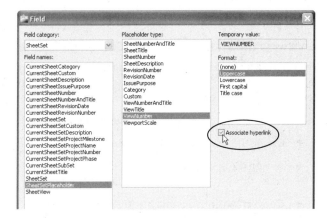

With this option selected, a hyperlink is created between the callout block and the view associated with it. This hyperlink will enable you to go directly to the sheet and the view being referenced by the callout block by Ctrl+clicking the field value in the callout block.

Just as with the view-title block, you can include the callout block inside the template file, or you can create individual files for each of your callout blocks. You can also have several callout blocks for different purposes.

For example, in the My Sample Sheet Set you created toward the beginning of this chapter, several callout blocks were available in the View List shortcut menu (Figure 30.25).

In that example, there was a callout block for the arrow directions. You can create a similar set of callout blocks for your drawings. You can also include callout blocks for details and finishes. You can even invent some uses on your own.

FIGURE 30.25
Choose a callout format.

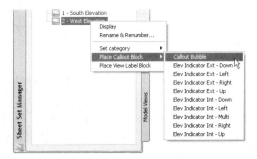

> **USE AUTOCAD'S CALLOUT BLOCKS**
>
> If you like the callout blocks and label blocks that are already available in the My Sample Sheet Set exercise, you can find them as blocks in the template file used for that project. The location of that template file is C:\Documents and Settings*UserName*\Local Settings\ Application Data\ Autodesk\AutoCAD 2011\R18.1\enu\Template\ SheetSets\Architectural Imperial.dwt. You can customize the graphics for that template file and use them for your own projects.

REVIEWING THE STEPS FOR CREATING CUSTOM CALLOUT AND VIEW LABEL BLOCKS

The callout block and view label feature will save you a lot of time when you're building your set of drawings, but you must go through a lot of steps when creating them. To help you get a better overall grasp of the process, here is a checklist of the general steps you need to take:

◆ Create the graphics for the callout blocks.

◆ Create the attribute definitions for the text in the callout blocks.

◆ Assign the appropriate fields for the attribute definition values. For callout blocks and view titles, this is usually a SheetSetPlaceholder field.

◆ Convert the graphics and attribute definitions into a block. Place the insertion point of view title blocks in the upper-left corner of the block to coincide with the location of the lower-left corner of the viewport with which it will be associated.

◆ Use the Sheet Set Properties dialog box to indicate the file location of your callout and view title blocks. These can be blocks in a file or individual files.

Also remember to turn on the Associate Hyperlink option when selecting the fields for your callout blocks.

Archiving, Publishing, and eTransmitting Sheet Sets

The sheet set feature is a great way to keep your project files organized while you're creating your drawings. You can also use the Sheet Set Manager to turn your set into a package that can be easily sent to others who may need to work on the drawings or view them. And, you can use the Sheet Set Manager to create an archive of your set for safekeeping at the end of the project.

You may have noticed that the Sheet Set shortcut menu contains several options. Right-click the main title of your sheet set in the Sheet Set Manager's sheet list and you see the Archive, Publish, and eTransmit options:

◆ The Archive option lets you collect your sheet set files into a Zip archive file.

◆ The Publish option offers a convenient way to convert your set into a format that can be easily read by others who don't have AutoCAD.

◆ The eTransmit option offers a way to transport your sheet set easily to others who may need to work on the set.

In the following sections, you'll take a closer look at these three sets of features for sharing your sheet set.

Archiving Your Sheet Set

One of the more important housekeeping jobs you'll do is archiving completed projects. If you organize your projects by folders, you could archive the entire folder for a project, but in so doing, you might archive many files that weren't part of the set.

The sheet set Archive option lets you be more selective about the files you archive. You can exclude files in the sheet set or include other files that aren't necessarily AutoCAD drawings.

When you're ready to archive your sheet set, save all the files in your archive, and then open the Archive dialog box. To do this, right-click the name of your sheet set in the Sheet List tab of the Sheet Set Manager and choose Archive from the shortcut menu to open the Archive A Sheet Set dialog box (Figure 30.26).

FIGURE 30.26

Archiving a
sheet set

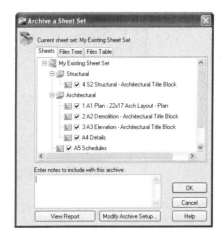

The Archive A Sheet Set dialog box has three tabs. On the Sheets tab, the check boxes by the sheet names indicate the sheets that will be archived. If you decide that you want to leave a sheet out of the archive, you can remove the checkmark. The unchecked file and its associated Xref aren't archived.

The Files Tree tab offers a slightly different view of the archive. Instead of just showing you the sheet names, the Files Tree tab shows you the names of the files that will be archived. These include support files such as the sheet set data file and the template file associated with the sheet set.

The Files Table tab shows you even more detail about the files that will be archived, such as the path, the AutoCAD version, and similar information. It also includes information about the resource files that are Xrefs in the sheet files.

In both the Files Tree and Files Table tabs, the Add A File button enables you to include other files with the archive that aren't necessarily AutoCAD related but are part of the overall project. You can use this option to include Excel or Word documents that represent correspondence or worksheets.

MODIFYING THE ARCHIVE SETUP

By default, the sheet set Archive feature saves files in the Zip archive format (.zip filename extension). You can change the way the archives are saved as well as the location of the archive, the archive name, and several other settings through the Modify Archive Setup dialog box.

Click the Modify Archive Setup button in the Archive A Sheet Set dialog box to open the Modify Archive Setup dialog box (Figure 30.27).

FIGURE 30.27
Editing the archive setup

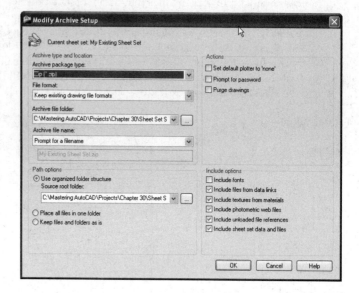

Here you can make adjustments to the properties of the archive file, including the type of file to create and whether to preserve the file structure.

SAVING THE VITAL STATISTICS OF YOUR ARCHIVE

You can also view and save pertinent information about your archived sheet set by clicking the View Report button in the Archive A Sheet Set dialog box. Clicking this button opens the View Archive Report dialog box.

You can view the vital statistics regarding your sheet set archive. You also have the option to save the information in a file by clicking the Save As button. This opens a standard save file dialog box where you can assign a name and location for the information file. It's stored as a plain-text file with the .txt filename extension.

Batch-Plotting and Publishing Your Sheet Set

Another advantage of using sheet sets is that you can print all the sheets in a set at once and in the background. The Publish option in the Sheet Set shortcut menu enables you to turn the Sheet Set Manager into a batch-plot utility.

When you right-click the sheet set title in the sheet list of the Sheet Set Manager, you see the Publish option. Click Publish and another set of options appears (Figure 30.28), offering several plotting and publishing options.

FIGURE 30.28
Options for
publishing

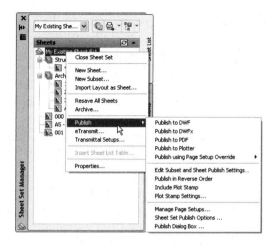

The following list gives a rundown of these options. More detailed descriptions are offered in Chapters 8 and 29. See Appendix C for more on plot stamps.

Publish To DWF   Publishes your sheet set to a DWF file. This option uses the Publish command's current default settings and the Sheet Set Publish Options. Before you use this option, make sure your settings are correct by using the Sheet Set Publish Options command in the Sheet Set shortcut menu.

Publish To DWFx   Publishes your sheet set to a DWFx file. This file format is similar to the DWF format with the added ability that it can be viewed in Windows Vista without any special viewing program.

Publish To PDF   Publishes your sheet set to a PDF file. This file format is so prevalent in the business world that it's often the format of choice when exchanging CAD drawings.

Publish To Plotter   Sends your sheet set to a printer or plotter. This option uses the Publish command's current default settings and the Sheet Set Publish Options. Before you use this option, make sure your settings are correct by choosing Publish ➢ Sheet Set Publish in this shortcut menu.

Publish Using Page Setup Override   Enables you to override the default layout settings in your sheets with a named page setup. See Chapter 8 for more on page setups. This can help to unify the plotter settings for all the sheets in your sheet set.

Edit Subset And Sheet Publish Settings   Enables you to select specific sheets to be published from the sheet set. Use this feature if you want to publish only a subset of the entire sheet set.

Publish In Reverse Order   Sends the drawing sheets to the printer or plotter starting with the last sheet and adding subsequent sheets from back to front.

Include Plot Stamp   Turns on the plot stamp feature in AutoCAD. A checkmark appears next to this option when it is turned on. See Appendix C for more on plot stamps.

Plot Stamp Settings   Opens the Plot Stamp dialog box. You can then make setting changes to your plot stamps. See Appendix C for more on plot stamps.

Manage Page Setups Lets you edit or create a page setup that you want to apply to your sheets as they're published. When you click this option, the Page Setup Manager dialog box opens, which is the same dialog box you see when you right-click a layout preview panel and choose Page Setup Manager. See Chapter 8 for more on page setups.

Sheet Set Publish Options Opens the Sheet Set Publish Options dialog box, which is essentially the same as the Publish Options dialog box described in Chapter 29. This dialog box lets you set the type of DWF file to create, the file location, and security options.

Publish Dialog Box Opens the Publish dialog box, and populates the Sheets To Publish list with the sheets in the sheet set. See Chapter 29 for more on the Publish dialog box.

Packaging Sheet Sets with eTransmit

In Chapter 29, you learned that you can use the eTransmit feature to package a set of AutoCAD files into a Zip file in order to send the files to someone else who may need to edit them. eTransmit is similar to the sheet set Archive feature, but it also makes sure all the supporting files, including fonts, font maps, and plotter configuration files, are included in the Zip file.

When you select eTransmit from the Sheet Set shortcut menu, the list of files to include in the eTransmit file is automatically populated with the files from the current sheet set. This means that you don't have to build the list of drawings manually for the eTransmit file.

If you need to make setting changes for the eTransmit feature, you can do so by selecting the Transmittal Setups option in the sheet set shortcut menu.

Preparing Your Project Files

Now that you've seen how sheet sets work, you can start to use them on your own projects. Sheet sets work best when your project files are organized and you have some additional files prepared and on hand. Here's a checklist of things to keep in mind when you start to use sheet sets:

◆ Organize your files so that when you import your project into a sheet set, the files will be automatically organized by discipline or sheet number.

◆ Use only one layout per sheet set drawing file. The Sheet Set Manager uses only one drawing per sheet and one layout per drawing.

◆ Create a template file containing the title block that you want to use for your project. Make sure to include any sheet set fields you want to use in the title block attribute definitions. You can also include your callout blocks in the template file for convenience.

◆ Because all the sheets in your project will most likely be printed on the same size sheet with the same plot specifications, it helps to create a sheet setup that you can apply to all your sheets. You can store the sheet setup in any drawing file and then use the Sheet Set Properties option to locate that file to assign the page setup to the entire sheet set.

RESTORE THE BACKUP EXAMPLE FILES

If you want to repeat the exercises in this chapter, you can reset the sheet set sample folders to their original state by copying them from the \Chapter 30\backup folder into the \Chapter 30 folder.

The Bottom Line

Understand sheet sets. The sheet set feature is like a database that automatically keeps track of drawings and drawing resources for your projects. To use sheets sets successfully, you need to make sure the Sheet Set Manager is aware of all the drawings and resources used in a project.

Master It Name the two main categories of files that sheets sets use and that were mentioned at the beginning of this chapter.

Create a sheet set from an existing project. If you have existing project files, you can set up a sheet set to work with them.

Master It Name the option on the first page of the Create Sheet Set Wizard that lets you set up a sheet set for an existing project.

Manage title blocks and cross-references. When the Sheet Set Manager is aware of a drawing or drawing resource, you can automate the creation of sheets such as elevations and sections. You can also control the naming and numbering of drawings in a set through the Sheet Set Manager.

Master It What is the name of the right-click option that lets you change the name and number of a drawing?

Customize sheet sets. To use sheets sets to their full potential, you should create title blocks and callout blocks that are sheet set aware so they can communicate with the Sheet Set Manager.

Master It What is the name of the object you must include in a block to store data?

Archive, publish, and eTransmit sheet sets. As a project starts to grow, you'll have to keep track of sheet and reference drawings as well as other drawing resources. Because the Sheet Set Manager is already aware of all the files needed for a project, you can use it to help keep track of project files.

Master It Name the three AutoCAD features that help you manage your files.

Appendices

In this section you will find:

Appendix A

The Bottom Line

Each of The Bottom Line sections in the chapters suggest exercises to deepen skills and understanding. Sometimes there is only one possible solution, but often you are encouraged to use your skills and creativity to create something that builds on what you know and lets you explore one of many possible solutions.

Chapter 1: Exploring the AutoCAD and AutoCAD LT Interface

Use the AutoCAD window.   AutoCAD is a typical Windows graphics program that makes use of menus, toolbars, Ribbon panels, and palettes. If you've used other graphics programs, you'll see at least a few familiar tools.

Master It   Name the components of the AutoCAD window you can use to select a function.

Solution   AutoCAD offers the Quick Access toolbar, the Application menu, Ribbon panels, the navigation bar, and the status bar to give you access to the most common functions.

Get a closer look with the Zoom command.   One of the first things you'll want to learn is how to manipulate your views. The Zoom command is a common tool in graphics programs.

Master It   Name at least two ways of zooming into a view.

Solution   Choose options from the Zoom flyout in the View tab's Navigate panel. You can also right-click and select Zoom from the shortcut menu and select Zoom options from the navigation bar's Zoom flyout.

Save a file as you work.   Nothing is more frustrating than having a power failure cause you to lose hours of work. It's a good idea to save your work frequently. AutoCAD offers an Automatic Save feature that can be a lifesaver if you happen to forget to save your files.

Master It   How often does the AutoCAD Automatic Save feature save your drawing?

Solution   Automatic Save saves a copy of a drawing every 10 minutes by default. This interval can be modified by the user.

Make changes and open multiple files.   As with other Windows programs, you can have multiple files open and exchange data between them.

Master It   With two drawings open, how can you copy parts of one drawing into the other?

Solution   Use Windows Copy and Paste. Select the parts you want to copy, right-click, and select Clipboard and then Copy. Go to the other drawing and then right-click in the drawing area and select Clipboard and then Paste.

Chapter 2: Creating Your First Drawing

Specify distances with coordinates.   One of the most basic skills you need to learn is how to indicate exact distances through the keyboard. AutoCAD uses a simple annotation system to indicate distance and direction.

Master It   What would you type to indicate a relative distance of 14 units at a 45 ° angle?

Solution   @14<45.

Interpret the cursor modes and understand prompts.   AutoCAD's cursor changes its shape depending on the command that is currently active. These different cursor modes can give you a clue regarding what you should be doing.

Master It   Describe the Point Selection cursor and the Pickbox cursor.

Solution   The Point Selection cursor is a simple crosshair. The Pickbox cursor is a small square or pickbox.

Select objects and edit with grips.   Grips are small squares or arrowheads that appear at key points on the object when they're selected. They offer a powerful way to edit objects.

Master It   How do you select multiple grips?

Solution   Hold down the Shift key while clicking the grips.

Use Dynamic Input.   Besides grips, objects display their dimensional properties when selected. These dimensional properties can be edited to change an object's shape.

Master It   How do you turn on Dynamic Input? And once it's on, what key lets you shift between the different dimensions of an object?

Solution   The Dynamic Input button on the AutoCAD status bar turns Dynamic Input on and off. When an object is selected, you can move between the dimensional properties by pressing the Tab key.

Get help.   AutoCAD's Help window is thorough in its coverage of AutoCAD's features. New and experienced users alike can often find answers to their questions thorough the Help window, so it pays to become familiar with it.

Master It   What keyboard key do you press for context-sensitive help?

Solution   F1.

Display data in a text window.   AutoCAD offers the AutoCAD Text Window, which keeps a running account of the commands you use. This can be helpful in retrieving input that you've entered when constructing your drawing.

Master It   Name a command that displays its results in the AutoCAD Text Window.

Solution   The List command.

Display the properties of an object.   The Properties palette is one of the most useful sources for drawing information. Not only does it list the properties of an object, it lets you change the shape, color, and other properties of objects.

Master It   How do you open the Properties palette for a particular object?

Solution   Select the object whose properties you want to view. Right-click the object and select Properties.

Chapter 3: Setting Up and Using AutoCAD's Drafting Tools

Set up a work area.   A blank AutoCAD drawing offers few clues about the size of the area you're working with, but you can get a rough idea of the area shown in the AutoCAD window.

Master It   Name two ways to set up the area of your work.

Solution   You can use the Limits command to define the work area, otherwise known as the limits of the drawing. You can also draw a rectangle that is the size of your work area.

Explore the drawing process.   To use AutoCAD effectively, you'll want to know how the different tools work together to achieve an effect. The drawing process often involves many cycles of adding objects and then editing them.

Master It   Name the tool that causes the cursor to point in an exact horizontal or vertical direction.

Solution   Polar Tracking. Ortho mode can also perform this function.

Plan and lay out a drawing.   If you've ever had to draw a precise sketch with just a pencil and pad, you've probably used a set of lightly drawn guidelines to lay out your drawing first. You do the same thing in AutoCAD, but instead of lightly drawn guidelines, you can use any object you want. In AutoCAD, objects are easily modified or deleted, so you don't have to be as careful when adding guidelines.

Master It   What is the name of the feature that lets you select exact locations on objects?

Solution   Object Snap, or Osnap.

Use the AutoCAD modes as drafting tools.   The main reason for using AutoCAD is to produce precision technical drawings. AutoCAD offers many tools to help you produce a drawing with the precision you need.

Master It   What dialog box lets you set both the grid and snap spacing?

Solution   The Drafting Settings dialog box.

Chapter 4: Organizing Objects with Blocks and Groups

Create and insert a symbol.   If you have a symbol that you use often in a drawing, you can draw it once and then turn it into an AutoCAD block. A block can be placed in a drawing multiple times in any location, like a rubber stamp. A block is stored in a drawing as a block definition, which can be called up at any time.

Master It   Name the dialog box used to create a block from objects in a drawing, and also name the tool to open this dialog box.

Solution   The Block Definition dialog box can be opened using the Create tool.

Modify a block.   Once you've created a block, it isn't set in stone. One of the features of a block is that you can change the block definition and all the copies of the block are updated to the new definition.

Master It   What is the name of the tool used to "unblock" a block?

Solution   You can use the Explode tool to break a block down to its component objects. Once this is done, you can modify the objects and then redefine the block.

Understand the annotation scale. In some cases, you'll want to create a block that is dependent on the drawing scale. You can create a block that adjusts itself to the scale of your drawing through the annotation scale feature. When the annotation scale feature is turned on for a block, the block can be set to appear at the correct size depending on the scale of your drawing.

Master It What setting in the Block Definition dialog box turns on the annotation scale feature, and how do you set the annotation scale of a block?

Solution The Annotative option in the Block Definition dialog box turns on the annotation scale feature. You can set the scales for a block by selecting the block, right-clicking, and selecting Object Scale ➤ Add/Delete Scales.

Group objects. Blocks can be used as a tool to group objects together, but blocks can be too rigid for some grouping applications. AutoCAD offers groups, which are collections of objects that are similar to blocks but aren't as rigidly defined.

Master It How are groups different from blocks?

Solution Objects in a group can be easily edited by turning groups off with a Shift+Ctrl+A keystroke. Also, unlike blocks, groups don't have a single definition that's stored in the drawing and defines the group's appearance. You can copy a group, but each copy is independent of the other groups.

Chapter 5: Keeping Track of Layers and Blocks

Organize information with layers. Layers are perhaps the most powerful feature in AutoCAD. They help to keep drawings well organized and they give you control over the visibility of objects. They also let you control the appearance of your drawing by setting colors, lineweights, and linetypes.

Master It Describe the process of creating a layer.

Solution First, click the Layer Properties Manager tool in the Home tab's Layers panel. Second, click the New Layer button at the top of the palette. Finally, type the name for your new layer.

Control layer visibility. When a drawing becomes dense with information, it can be difficult to edit. If you've organized your drawing using layers, you can reduce its complexity by turning off layers that aren't important to your current session.

Master It Describe two methods for hiding a layer.

Solution Open the Layer Properties Manager, select a layer, and click the Freeze icon for the layer. You can also open the Layer drop-down list in the Home tab's Layers panel and click the Freeze icon for the layer you want to hide.

Keep track of blocks and layers.   At times, you may want a record of the layers or blocks in your drawing. You can create a list of layers using the log-file feature in AutoCAD.

Master It   Where do you go to turn on the log-file feature?

Solution   You can open the Options dialog box or use the Logfilemode system variable.

Chapter 6: Editing and Reusing Data to Work Efficiently

Create and use templates.   If you find that you're using the same settings when you create a new drawing file, you can set up an existing file the way you like and save it as a template. You can then use your saved template for any new drawings you create.

Master It   Describe the method for saving a file as a template.

Solution   After setting up a blank drawing with the settings you use most frequently, choose Save As from the Application menu. In the Save Drawing As dialog box, choose AutoCAD Drawing Template from the Files Of Type drop-down list, give it a name and click Save. In the Template Options dialog box, enter a descriptive name, and click OK to save the template.

Copy an object multiple times.   Many tools in AutoCAD allow you to create multiple copies. The Array command offers a way to create circular copies or row and column copies.

Master It   What names are given to the two types of arrays in the Array dialog box?

Solution   Rectangular and polar.

Develop your drawing.   When laying down simple line work, you'll use a few tools frequently. The exercises in the early part of this book showed you some of these commonly used tools.

Master It   What tool can you use to join two lines end to end?

Solution   Fillet.

Find an exact distance along a curve.   AutoCAD offers some tools that allow you to find an exact distance along a curve.

Master It   Name the two tools you can use to mark off exact distances along a curve.

Solution   Measure and Divide.

Change the length of objects.   You can accurately adjust the length of a line or arc in AutoCAD using a single command.

Master It   What is the keyboard alias for the command that changes the length of objects.

Solution   The command is len.

Create a new drawing by using parts from another drawing.   You can save a lot of time by reusing parts of drawings. The Export command can help.

Master It   True or false: The Export command saves only blocks as drawing files.

Solution   False. You can use Export any type of object or set of objects in a drawing.

Chapter 7: Mastering Viewing Tools, Hatches, and External References

Assemble the parts.   Technical drawings are often made up of repetitive parts that are drawn over and over. AutoCAD makes quick work of repetitive elements in a drawing, as shown in the first part of this chapter.

Master It   What is the object used as the basic building block for the unit plan drawing in the beginning of this chapter?

Solution   Blocks of a typical unit plan are used to build a floor plan of an apartment building.

Take control of the AutoCAD display.   Understanding the way the AutoCAD display works can save you time, especially in a complex drawing.

Master It   Name the dialog box used to save views in AutoCAD. Describe how to recall a saved view.

Solution   The View Manager dialog box allows you to save views. You can recall views by selecting them from the Views flyout on the View tab's Views panel.

Use hatch patterns in your drawings.   Patterns can convey a lot of information at a glance. You can show the material of an object, or you can indicate a type of view, like a cross section, by applying hatch patterns.

Master It   How do you open the Hatch And Gradient dialog box?

Solution   Choose Hatch from the Home tab's Draw panel and then click the Hatch Settings tool in the Hatch Creation tab's Options panel title bar.

Understand the hatch options.   The hatch options give you control over the way hatch patterns fill an enclosed area.

Master It   Describe an island as it relates to boundary hatch patterns.

Solution   An island is an enclosed object that is found in an area to be hatched.

Use external references.   External references are drawing files that you've attached to the current drawing to include as part of the drawing. Because external references aren't part of the current file, they can be worked on at the same time as the referencing file.

Master It   Describe how drawing files are attached as external references.

Solution   Open the External References palette, click the Attach DWG tool at the upper left, and then locate and select the file you want to attach. You can also click the Attach DWG tool in the External References palette.

Chapter 8: Introducing Printing, Plotting, and Layouts

Understand the plotter settings.   Unlike other types of documents, AutoCAD drawings can end up on nearly any size sheet of paper. To accommodate the range of paper sizes, the AutoCAD plotter settings are fairly extensive and give you a high level of control over your output.

Master It   Name a few of the settings available in the Plot dialog box.

Solution   Paper Size, Plot Area, Plot Scale, and Printer/Plotter Name are a few of the settings available in the Plot dialog box.

Using layout views to control how your plots look.   The Layout tabs in AutoCAD offer a way to let you set up how a drawing will be plotted. You can think of the Layout views as a kind of paste-up area for your drawings.

Master It   Name some of the items that you see in a layout view.

Solution   The layout view shows the paper orientation, plotter margins, and the location of your drawing on the final plotted output.

Add an output device.   Typically, AutoCAD will use the Windows system printer as an output device, but often you will find that the printer you use is a dedicated plotter that is not connected to Windows in the usual way. AutoCAD lets you add custom plotters and prints through the Add-A-Plotter Wizard.

Master It   How do you start the Add-A-Plotter Wizard?

Solution   Click the Plotter Manager tool on the Output tab's Plot panel, and double-click the Add-A-Plotter Wizard application in the Plotters window.

Store a page setup.   Most of the time, you will use the same set of plotter settings for your drawings. You can save plotter settings using the Page Setup feature.

Master It   Describe a way to create a page setup. Describe how to retrieve a setup.

Solution   Click the Page Setup Manager tool in the Output tab's Plot panel; then click New in the Page Setup Manager dialog box. Enter a name for your page setup in the New Page Setup dialog box, and then click OK. When you plot your drawing, you can retrieve a page setup by selecting it from the Page Setup drop-down list in the Plot dialog box.

Chapter 9: Understanding Plot Styles

Choose between color-dependent and named plot style tables.   Plot styles let you control the way lines are printed on paper. You can control line weights, shading of filled areas, corner treatment of thick lines, and more.

Master It   Describe some of the differences between named plot styles and color-dependent plot styles.

Solution   Color-dependent plot styles use the color of objects to control line weights and other printed features. Named plot styles can be used to assign printed features to individual objects.

Create a color plot style table.   Both color and named plot styles are stored as files. You can create custom plot styles and apply them to any drawing.

Master It   In what dialog box do you select and edit plot styles?

Solution   Click the Plotter Manager tool in the Output tab's Plot panel and then open the Plot Styles folder. In the Plot Styles window, locate and double-click the plot style you want to edit.

Edit and use plot style tables. Plot styles give you a lot of control over the appearance of lines in your plotted output.

Master It Name some of the settings offered in the Plot Style Table Editor.

Solution Color, Screening, Lineweight, Line End Style, and Line Join Style are a few of the available options.

Assign named plot styles directly to layers and objects. Named plot styles offer a bit more control over the way lines are plotted. If you choose, you can assign named plot styles to objects, bypassing layer assignments.

Master It Describe a method for assigning a plot style to an object.

Solution You can assign a plot style to an object through the Plot Style setting in the Properties palette. You can also use the Plot Style drop-down list in the Home tab's Properties panel.

Chapter 10: Adding Text to Drawings

Prepare a drawing for text. AutoCAD offers an extensive set of features for adding text to a drawing, but you need to do a little prep work before you dive in.

Master It Name two things you need to do to prepare a drawing for text.

Solution Set up a layer for your text. Create a text style for your drawing.

Set the annotation scale and add text. Before you start to add text, you should set the annotation scale for your drawing. Once this is done, you can begin to add text.

Master It In a sentence or two, briefly describe the purpose of the annotation scale feature. Name the tool you use to add text to a drawing.

Solution The annotation scale feature converts your text size to the proper height for the scale of your drawing. To add text to a drawing, use the Mtext tool.

Explore text formatting in AutoCAD. Because text styles contain font and text-size settings, you can usually set up a text style and then begin to add text to your drawing. For those special cases where you need to vary text height and font or other text features, you can use the Formatting panel of the Text Editor tab.

Master It What text formatting tool can you use to change text to boldface type?

Solution The Bold button.

Add simple single-line text objects. In many situations, you need only a single word or a short string of text. AutoCAD offers the Single Line text object for these instances.

Master It Describe the methods for starting the single-line text command.

Solution Click the Single Line text tool in the Text panel. Enter **DT**↵ at the command prompt.

Use the Check Spelling feature. It isn't uncommon for a drawing to contain the equivalent of several pages of text, and the likelihood of having misspelled words can be high. AutoCAD offers the Check Spelling feature to help you keep your spelling under control.

> **Master It** What option do you select in the Check Spelling dialog box when it finds a misspelled word and you want to accept the suggestion it offers?
>
> **Solution** Change.

Find and replace text. A common activity when editing technical drawings is finding and replacing a word throughout a drawing.

> **Master It** True or false: The Find And Replace feature in AutoCAD works very differently than the find-and-replace feature in other programs.
>
> **Solution** False.

Chapter 11: Using Fields and Tables

Use fields to associate text with drawing properties. Fields are a special type of text object that can be linked to object properties. They can help to automate certain text-related tasks.

> **Master It** Name two uses for fields that you learned about in the first part of this chapter.
>
> **Solution** Fields can be used to update text that labels a block. They can also be used to update text and report the area enclosed by a polyline.

Add tables to your drawing. The Tables feature can help you make quick work of schedules and other tabular data that you want to include in a drawing.

> **Master It** What is the name of the dialog box that appears when you click the Table tool from the Annotate tab's Tables panel?
>
> **Solution** Insert Table.

Edit the table line work. Because tables include line work to delineate their different cells, AutoCAD gives you control over table borders and lines.

> **Master It** How do you get to the Cell Border Properties dialog box?
>
> **Solution** Select the cell or cells in the table, right-click, and choose Borders.

Add formulas to cells. Tables can also function like a spreadsheet by allowing you to add formulas to cells.

> **Master It** What type of text object lets you add formulas to cells?
>
> **Solution** Field.

Import and export tables. The Table feature allows you to import Microsoft Excel spreadsheets into AutoCAD.

> **Master It** Describe how to import a spreadsheet from Excel into AutoCAD.
>
> **Solution** Open the spreadsheet and select the cells you want to import. Choose Edit ➤ Copy to copy the spreadsheet data into the Clipboard. In AutoCAD, choose Paste Special from the Paste flyout of the Home tab's Clipboard panel. In the Paste Special dialog box, select AutoCAD Entities, and click OK.

Chapter 12: Using Dimensions

Understand the components of a dimension. Before you start to dimension with AutoCAD, it helps to become familiar with the different parts of a dimension. This will help you set up your dimensions to fit the style of dimensions that you need.

Master It Name a few of the dimension components.

Solution Dimension line, dimension text, extension line, and arrow.

Create a dimension style. As you become more familiar with technical drawing and drafting, you'll learn that there are standard formats for drawing dimensions. Arrows, text size, and even the way dimension lines are drawn are all subject to a standard format. Fortunately, AutoCAD offers dimension styles that let you set up your dimension format once and then call up that format whenever you need it.

Master It What is the name of the dialog box that lets you manage dimension styles, and how do you open it?

Solution The Dimension Style Manager is the name of the dialog box. You can open it by clicking the Dimension Style tool in the Annotate tab's Dimensions panel title bar.

Draw linear dimensions. The most common dimension that you'll use is the linear dimension. Knowing how to place a linear dimension is a big first step in learning how to dimension in AutoCAD.

Master It Name the three locations you're asked for when placing a linear dimension.

Solution First extension line origin, second extension line origin, and dimension line location.

Edit dimensions. Dimensions often change in the course of a project, so you should know how to make changes to dimension text or other parts of a dimension.

Master It How do you start the command to edit dimension text?

Solution Enter **ed**↵ at the Command prompt.

Dimension non-orthogonal objects. Not everything you dimension will use linear dimensions. AutoCAD offers a set of dimension tools for dimensioning objects that aren't made up of straight lines.

Master It Name some of the types of objects for which a linear dimension isn't appropriate.

Solution Arc and angle between two lines. Linear dimensions can be used for circles in certain situations.

Add a note with a leader arrow. In addition to dimensions, you'll probably add lots of notes with arrows pointing to features in a design. AutoCAD offers the multileader for this purpose.

Master It What two types of objects does the multileader combine?

Solution Leader lines (arrowhead and line) and text.

Apply ordinate dimensions. When accuracy counts, ordinate dimensions are often used because they measure distances that are similar to coordinates from a single feature.

Master It What AutoCAD feature do you use for ordinate dimensions that isn't strictly associated with dimensions?

Solution UCS.

Add tolerance notation. Mechanical drafting often requires the use of special notation to describe tolerances. AutoCAD offers some predefined symbols that address the need to include tolerance notation in a drawing.

Master It How do you open the Geometric Tolerance dialog box?

Solution Click the Tolerance tool in the Dimensions panel.

Chapter 13: Using Attributes

Create attributes. Attributes are a great tool for storing data with drawn objects. You can include as little or as much data as you like in an AutoCAD block.

Master It What is the name of the object you must include in a block to store data?

Solution Attribute definition.

Edit attributes. The data you include in a block is easily changed. You may have several copies of a block, each of which must contain its own unique sets of data.

Master It What is the simplest way to gain access to a block's attribute data?

Solution Double-click the block to open the Enhanced Attribute Editor.

Extract and export attribute information. Attribute data can be extracted in a number of ways so that you can keep track of the data in a drawing.

Master It How do you start the data-extraction process?

Solution Click the Extract Data tool in the Insert tab's Linking & Extraction panel to open the Data Extraction Wizard.

Chapter 14: Copying Existing Drawings into AutoCAD

Convert paper drawings into AutoCAD files. AutoCAD gives you some great tools that let you convert your paper drawings into AutoCAD files. Several options are available. Depending on your needs, you'll find at least one solution that will allow you to convert your drawings quickly.

Master It Describe the different methods available in AutoCAD for converting paper drawings into CAD files.

Solution The methods are tracing with a digitizer, scaling directly from a drawing, scanning and converting with a third-party program, and scanning to a raster file that can then be imported into AutoCAD to be traced over.

Import a raster image. You can use bitmap raster images as backgrounds for your CAD drawings or as underlay drawings that you can trace over.

Master It Import a raster image of your choice, and use the AutoCAD drawing tools to trace over your image.

Solution Click Attach from the Insert tab's Reference panel or type **Attach↵** to open the Select Reference File dialog box. Locate and select the raster image file you want to import. Click Open to open the Attach Image dialog box, and then click OK. Specify an insertion point and scale factor.

Work with a raster image.   Once imported, raster images can be adjusted for size, brightness, contrast, and transparency.

   Master It   Import a raster image of your choice, and fade the image so it appears lighter and with less contrast.

   Solution   Click a raster image's border to expose the Image tab. Click and drag the Fade slider to the right so that it's near the middle of the slider scale, or enter **50** in the Fade input box to the right of the slider. Click OK. The raster image appears faded.

Work with PDF files.   AutoCAD allows you to import and control the display of PDF files. This is significant since the PDF file format is so prevalent in the business world.

   Master It   In a PDF that includes layers, how do you gain access to the layer settings?

   Solution   Click the imported PDF drawing, and then click the Edit Layers tool that appears in the PDF Underlay tab. You can then control layer visibility through the Underlay Layers dialog box.

Chapter 15: Advanced Editing and Organizing

Use external references (Xrefs).   You've seen how you can use Xrefs to quickly build variations of a floor plan that contain repetitive elements. This isn't necessarily the only way to use Xrefs, but the basic idea of how to use Xrefs is presented in the early exercises.

   Master It   Try putting together another floor plan that contains nothing but the Unit2 plan.

   Solution   Replace the eight studio units in the Common.dwg file with four of the Unit2 plans.

Manage layers.   Once you start to edit complex drawings, you'll find that you'll want to save the On/Off or Freeze/Thaw layer states so you can more easily access parts of a drawing. The Layer States Manager offers the ability to save as many layer conditions as you may need in the course of a project.

   Master It   What part of the Layer States Manager dialog box lets you control the layer properties that are affected by a saved layer state?

   Solution   The Layer Properties To Restore group in the expanded view of the Layer States Manager.

Use advanced tools: Filter and Quick Select.   The Filter and Quick Select tools are great for isolating objects in a crowded drawing. You can select objects by their color or layer assignment. You can select all instances of a specific block.

   Master It   True or false: The Quick Select tool lets you select a set of objects to limit your selections.

   Solution   True.

Use the QuickCalc calculator.   The QuickCalc calculator offers many standard calculator tools plus a few that you may not see in other calculators.

   Master It   Name a few of the more unusual features offered by the QuickCalc calculator.

   Solution   Add feet and inch lengths; find percentages of lengths; obtain coordinates, lengths, and angles graphically from a drawing.

Chapter 16: Laying Out Your Printer Output

Understand Model Space and Paper Space.   AutoCAD offers two viewing modes for viewing and printing your drawings. Model Space is where you do most of your work; it's the view you see when you create a new file. Layouts, also called Paper Space, are views that let you arrange the layout of your drawing, similar to how you would in a page-layout program.

Master It   What are the two ways of moving from Model Space to Paper Space?

Solution   You can use the Quick View Layouts tool in the status bar to display the Model and Layout preview panels, or you can use the Model and Layout tabs in the lower-left corner of the drawing area.

Work with Paper Space viewports.   While in Paper Space, you can create views into your drawing using viewports. You can have several viewports, each showing a different part of your drawing.

Master It   Name some of the ways you can enlarge a view in a viewport.

Solution   You can double-click inside a viewport and then use the Zoom tool to enlarge the view. You can also use the Viewport Scale setting in the status bar to set the scale of the view.

Create odd-shaped viewports.   Most of the time, you'll probably use rectangular viewports, but you have the option to create a viewport of any shape.

Master It   Describe the process for creating a circular viewport.

Solution   In Paper Space, draw a circle. Next, click Create From Object from the View tab's Viewports panel, and then follow the prompts.

Understand line weights, linetypes, and dimensions in Paper Space.   You can get an accurate view of how your drawing will look on paper by making a few adjustments to AutoCAD. Your layout view will reflect how your drawing will look when plotted.

Master It   Name the two dialog boxes you must use to display line weights in a layout view.

Solution   The Layer Properties Manager to set up line weights and the Lineweight Settings dialog box.

Chapter 17: Making "Smart" Drawings with Parametric Tools

Use parametric drawing tools.   Parametric drawing tools enable you to create an assembly of objects that are linked to each other based on geometric or dimensional properties. With the parametric drawing tools, you can create a drawing that automatically adjusts the size of all its components when you change a single dimension.

Master It   Name two examples given in the beginning of the chapter of a mechanical assembly that can be shown using parametric drawing tools.

Solution   The examples are a crankshaft and piston and a Luxo lamp.

Connect objects with geometric constraints. You can link objects together so that they maintain a particular orientation to each other.

Master It Name at least six of the geometric constraints available in AutoCAD.

Solution The constraints are coincident, collinear, concentric, fix, parallel, perpendicular, horizontal, vertical, tangent, smooth, symmetric, and equal.

Control sizes with dimensional constraints. Dimensional constraints, in conjunction with geometric constraints, let you apply dimensions to an assembly of objects to control the size of the assembly.

Master It Name at least four dimensional constraints.

Solution The dimensional constraints are linear, horizontal, vertical, aligned, radius, diameter, and angular. In addition, a tool allows you to convert a normal dimension into a dimensional constraint.

Use formulas to control dimensions. Dimensional constraints allow you to link dimensions of objects so that if one dimension changes, another dimension follows.

Master It What example was used to show how formulas can be used with dimensional constraints?

Solution A circle's diameter was linked to the width dimension of a drawing of a simple part.

Put constraints to use. Constraints can be used in a variety of ways to simulate the behavior of real objects.

Master It Name at least three geometric or dimensional constraints used in the `piston.dwg` sample file to help simulate the motion of a piston and crankshaft.

Solution The geometric constraints used were horizontal, parallel, fix, and coincident. The dimensional constraints used were horizontal, vertical, aligned, and diameter.

Chapter 18: Using Dynamic Blocks

Explore the Block Editor. To create dynamic blocks, you need to become familiar with the Block Editor. You can use the Block Editor to modify existing blocks in your drawing.

Master It What does the Edit Block Definition dialog box allow you to do?

Solution The Edit Block Definition dialog box lets you select the block you want to edit from a list of blocks in the drawing.

Create a dynamic block. Dynamic blocks are blocks to which you add grips that let you modify the block in a number of different ways.

Master It Name some of the features of the Block Editor that let you add additional grip editing functions to a block.

Solution Geometric constraints, dimensional constraints, parameters, and actions.

Add Scale and Stretch actions to a parameter. You can set up a dynamic block to perform multiple operations with a single grip.

    Master It What do you need to do to have one grip perform two functions?

    Solution Use a single parameter to control two actions.

Add more than one parameter for multiple grip functions. In addition to having one grip perform multiple operations, you can add as many grips as you need to make your block even more customizable.

    Master It What feature do you use to set up a list of options for a block?

    Solution The Block Table.

Create multiple shapes in one block. Many of the dynamic-block functions let you adjust the shape of the original block. Another feature lets you choose completely different shapes for the block.

    Master It When a block uses the Visibility parameter to set up different shapes, how do you select a different block shape in the drawing?

    Solution Click the block, and then click the Visibility grip. A list appears showing the different shapes that are available.

Rotate objects in unison. Blocks can be set up so the action of one set of objects affects another set. This chapter gives the example of rotating objects in unison.

    Master It Name the dimensional constraint that was used in the object rotation example in this chapter.

    Solution Angular.

Fill in a space automatically with objects. A dynamic block can help you automate the addition of repetitive elements to your drawing.

    Master It What is the name of the action used to produce an array of an object in a block when the block is stretched?

    Solution The Array action.

Chapter 19: Drawing Curves

Create and edit polylines. Polylines are extremely versatile. You can use them in just about any situation where you need to draw line work that is continuous. For this reason, you'll want to master polylines early in your AutoCAD training.

Master It   Draw the part shown here.

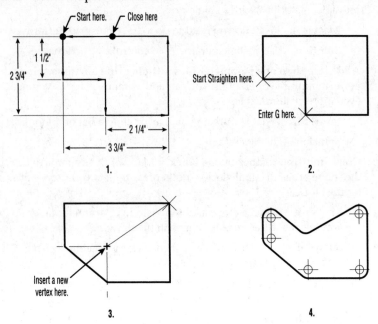

1.

2.

3.

4.

Solution   There are many ways to create this drawing. Use these instructions as guidelines and not the only way to create the drawing:

1.   Open a new file called PART14 using the acad.dwt template. Set the Snap spacing to
0.25, and be sure Snap mode is on. Use the Pline command to draw the object shown in
step 1 of the drawing shown previously. Start at the upper-left corner, and draw in the
direction indicated by the arrows. Use the Close option to add the last line segment.

2.   Start the Pedit command, select the polyline, and then type **E↵** to issue the Edit Vertex
option. Press ↵ until the X mark moves to the first corner, shown here. Enter **S↵** for the
Straighten option.

3.   At the Enter an option prompt, press ↵ twice to move the X to the other corner, shown
in step 2 of the drawing. Press **G↵** for Go to straighten the polyline between the two
selected corners.

4.   Press ↵ three times to move the X to the upper-right corner, and then enter **I↵** for Insert.
Pick a point as shown in step 3 of the drawing. The polyline changes to reflect the new vertex. Enter **X↵** to exit the Edit Vertex option, and then press ↵ to exit the Pedit command.

5.   Start the Fillet command, use the Radius option to set the fillet radius to 0.30, and then
use the Polyline option and pick the polyline you just edited. All the corners become
rounded to the 0.30 radius. Add the 0.15 radius circles as shown in step 4 of the drawing,
and exit and save the file.

Create a polyline spline curve. Polylines can be used to draw fairly accurate renditions of spline curves. This feature of polylines make them a very useful AutoCAD object.

Master It Try drawing the outline of an object that has no or few straight lines in it, as in the file `lowerfairing.jpg`, which is included in the Chapter 19 sample files. You can use the methods described in Chapter 14 to import a raster image of your object and then trace over the image using polyline splines.

Solution Import a raster image by using the Attach tool in the Insert tab's Reference panel. Use the Polyline tool to trace over the image. Use short, straight polyline segments while you trace. After you place each polyline, double-click it and select the Spline option. Once you change the line to a spline curve, it may shift away from the original line you traced over. Click the polyline, and then adjust the grips so the line fits over the raster image.

Create and edit true spline curves. If you need an accurate spline curve, you'll want to use the Spline tool. Spline objects offer many more fine-tuning options that you won't fine with polylines.

Master It Try tracing over the same image from the previous Master It section, but this time use the Spline tool.

Solution Import a raster image by using the Attach tool in the Insert tab's Reference panel. Use the Spline tool to trace over the image. As you draw the spline, select control points that are closer together for tighter curves. The closer the control points are, the tighter you can make the curve. Notice that, unlike with a polyline spline, you don't have to readjust the curve after it's been placed.

Mark divisions on curves. The Divide and Measure tools offer a quick way to mark off distances on a curved object. This can be a powerful resource in AutoCAD that you may find yourself using often.

Master It Mark off 12 equal divisions of the spline curves you drew in the previous Master It exercise.

Solution Choose Divide from the Point flyout in the expanded Draw panel, click the spline, and then enter **12.↵**. If you don't see the points that mark off the divisions, type **DDPTYPE↵**, select the X point style, and click OK.

Chapter 20: Getting and Exchanging Data from Drawings

Find the area of closed boundaries. There are a number of ways to find the area of a closed boundary. The easiest way is also perhaps the least obvious.

Master It Which AutoCAD feature would you use to quickly find the area of an irregular shape like a pond or lake?

Solution Hatch.

Get general information. A lot of information that is stored in AutoCAD drawings can tell you about the files. You can find out how much memory a file uses as well as the amount of time that has been spent editing the file.

Master It What feature lets you store your own searchable information about a drawing file, and how do you get to this feature?

Solution You can open the Properties dialog box by choosing Drawing Utilities ➢ Drawing Properties from the Application menu.

Use the DXF file format to exchange CAD data with other programs. Autodesk created the DXF file format as a means of sharing vector drawings with other programs.

Master It Name some of the versions of AutoCAD you can export to using the Save As option.

Solution 2010, 2007, 2004, 2002, and R12.

Use AutoCAD drawings in page-layout programs. AutoCAD drawings find their way into all types of documents, including brochures and technical manuals. Users are often asked to convert their CAD drawings into formats that can be read by page-layout software.

Master It Name some file formats, by filename extension or type, which page-layout programs can accept.

Solution PDF (.pdf), WMF (.wmf), EPS (.eps), and a wide variety of bitmap image files.

Use OLE to import data. You can import data into AutoCAD from a variety of sources. Most sources, such as bitmap images and text, can be imported as native AutoCAD objects. Other sources may need to be imported as OLE objects.

Master It To link imported data to a source program through OLE, what dialog box would you use?

Solution Paste Special.

Chapter 21: Creating 3D Drawings

Know the 3D modeling workspace. When you work in 3D, you need a different set of tools from those for 2D drafting. AutoCAD offers the 3D Modeling workspace, which provides the tools you need to create 3D models.

Master It Name some of the Ribbon panels that are unique to the 3D Modeling workspace.

Solution Modeling, Solid Editing, Visual Styles, Edge Effects, Lights, Sun & Location, Materials, Palettes, Animations, and Render.

Draw in 3D using solids. AutoCAD offers a type of object called a 3D solid that lets you quickly create and edit shapes.

Master It What does the Presspull command do?

Solution Presspull lets you press or pull a 3D solid shape from another 3D solid. It can also be used to press or pull a closed 2D object drawn on the surface of a solid.

Create 3D forms from 2D shapes. The Modeling panel offers a set of basic 3D shapes, but other tools enable you to create virtually any shape you want from 2D drawings.

Master It Name the command that lets you change a closed 2D polyline into a 3D solid.

Solution Extrude.

Isolate coordinates with point filters.   When you're working in 3D, selecting points can be a complicated task. AutoCAD offers point filters to let you specify the individual X, Y, and Z coordinates of a location in space.

Master It   What does the .XY point filter do?

Solution   The .XY point filter lets you select an X,Y coordinate, after which you can specify a Z coordinate as a separate value.

Move around your model.   Getting the view you want in a 3D model can be tricky.

Master It   Where is the drop-down list that lets you select a view from a list of pre-defined 3D views?

Solution   The Home tab's View panel contains a drop-down list that offers predefined 3D views.

Get a visual effect.   At certain points in your model making, you'll want to view your 3D model with surface colors and even material assignments. AutoCAD offers several ways to do this.

Master It   What are the steps to take to change the view from Wireframe to Conceptual?

Solution   Click the Visual Styles drop-down list, and select Conceptual.

Turn a 3D view into a 2D AutoCAD drawing.   Sometimes, it's helpful to convert a 3D model view into a 2D AutoCAD drawing. AutoCAD offers the Flatshot tool, which quickly converts a 3D view into a 2D line drawing.

Master It   What type of object does Flatshot create?

Solution   A block or drawing file.

Chapter 22: Using Advanced 3D Features

Master the User Coordinate System.   The User Coordinate System (UCS) is a vital key to editing in 3D space. If you want to master 3D modeling, you should become familiar with this tool.

Master It   Name some of the predefined UCS planes.

Solution   Front, Back, Left, Right, Top, Bottom.

Understand the UCS options.   You can set up the UCS orientation for any situation. It isn't limited to the predefined settings.

Master It   Give a brief description of some of the ways you can set up a UCS.

Solution   Object orientation, selection of three points, rotation about an axis, selection of a Z axis direction, and selection of the view plane.

Use viewports to aid in 3D drawing.   In some 3D modeling operations, it helps to have several different views of the model through the Viewports feature.

Master It   Name some of the predefined standard viewports offered in the Viewports dialog box.

Solution   Two: Vertical, Two: Horizontal, Three: Right, Three: Left, Three: Above, Three: Below, Three: Vertical, Three: Horizontal, Four: Equal, Four: Right, and Four: Left.

Create complex 3D surfaces. You aren't limited to straight, flat surfaces in AutoCAD. You can create just about any shape you want, including curved surfaces.

Master It What tool did you use in this chapter's chair exercise to convert a surface into a solid?

Solution The Thicken tool.

Create spiral forms. Spiral forms frequently occur in nature, so it's no wonder that we often use spirals in our own designs. Spirals are seen in screws, stairs, and ramps as well as in other manmade forms.

Master It Name the commands used in the example in the section "Creating Spiral Forms," and name two elements that are needed to create a spiral.

Solution The commands are Helix and Sweep. A helix and a profile are needed.

Create surface models. You can create a 3D surface by connecting a series of lines that define a surface contour. You can create anything from a 3D landscape to a car fender using this method.

Master It What is the tool used to convert a series of lines into a 3D surface?

Solution Loft.

Move objects in 3D space. You can move objects in 3D space using tools that are similar to those for 2D drafting. But when it comes to editing objects, 3D modeling is much more complex than 2D drafting.

Master It What does the Rotate gizmo do?

Solution It lets you graphically determine the axis of rotation for an object being rotated.

Chapter 23: Rendering 3D Drawings

Simulate the sun. One of the more practical uses of AutoCAD's rendering feature is to simulate the sun's location and resulting shadows. You can generate shadow studies for any time of the year in any location on the earth.

Master It Name three items that can be set to position the sun in relation to your model.

Solution Date, time, and geographic location.

Use materials. AutoCAD lets you create materials that you can apply to the objects in your model to simulate a realistic appearance.

Master It Name the parts of AutoCAD that can be used to create materials, and describe some of their features.

Solution The Materials Browser and Materials Editor let you create materials that you can then apply to objects in your model. You use a bitmap image to simulate a texture. You can also control a material's transparency. Other features allow you to set the size of the material over the surface of an object.

Create effects using materials and lights. You can use materials and lights together to control the appearance of your model.

Master It Name the part of the example model in this chapter that was used to show how a material can appear to glow.

Solution Ceiling lights.

Apply and adjust texture maps. Texture maps can be used to create a number of effects in your model. You can use a brick texture map that repeats over a surface to simulate a brick wall, or you can use a photograph of a building to turn a box into a building.

Master It What is the name of the feature that lets you graphically adjust a texture map on an object?

Solution Mapping Gizmo.

Understand the rendering options. In addition to adjusting the materials and lighting to control the look of your rendering, you can make other adjustments to your rendering through the Render panel and the Render window.

Master It Name some of the right-click menu options that appear for image filenames in the Render window.

Solution Render Again, Save, Save Copy, Make Render Settings Current, Remove From The List, and Delete Output File.

Add cameras for better view control. When you create a view using the View Manager dialog box, you're actually creating a camera. Cameras are objects that let you control the orientation and view target for a view, among other things.

Master It Name some of the options you can set to control a camera.

Solution Name, camera location, height, target location, focal length, and front and back clipping.

Print your renderings. You can save your rendered views as bitmap files using the Render window. If you prefer, you can also have AutoCAD include a rendering in a layout. You can include different renderings of the same file in a single layout.

Master It Give a general description of the process for setting up a rendered viewport in a layout.

Solution Create a viewport, and then set up the view you want for the viewport using the View Manager dialog box. Select the viewport's border, right-click, and select a Shade Plot menu option.

Simulate natural light. When you want to get a more accurate rendition of the lighting effects on your model, you can use some of the advanced rendering features that simulate natural light.

Master It Name the two setting groups you need to use to render an interior view accurately.

Solution The Global Illumination and Final Gather groups of the Advanced Render Settings palette.

Chapter 24: Editing and Visualizing 3D Solids

Understand solid modeling.   Solid modeling lets you build 3D models by creating and joining 3D shapes called solids. There are several built-in solid shapes called primitives, and you can create others using the Extrude tool.

Master It   Name some of the built-in solid primitives available in AutoCAD.

Solution   Box, wedge, cone, sphere, cylinder, pyramid, torus, and polysolid.

Create solid forms.   You can use Boolean operations to sculpt 3D solids into the shape you want. Two solids can be joined to form a more complex one, or you can remove one solid from another.

Master It   Name the three Boolean operations you can use on solids.

Solution   Intersection, subtraction, and union.

Create complex solids.   Besides the primitives, you can create your own shapes based on 2D polylines.

Master It   Name three tools that let you convert closed polylines and circles into 3D solids.

Solution   Extrude, Revolve, and Sweep.

Edit solids.   Once you've created a solid, you can make changes to it using the solid-editing tools offered on the Solid Editing panel.

Master It   Name at least four of the tools found on the Solid Editing panel.

Solution   The tools found on the Solid Editing panel are Union, Subtract, Intersect, Interfere, Slice, Thicken, tools on the Edges flyout, tools on the Faces flyout, tools on the Separate flyout, Convert To Solid, and Convert To Surface.

Streamline the 2D drawing process.   You can create 3D orthogonal views of your 3D model to create standard 2D mechanical drawings.

Master It   What is the name of the tool in the Solid Editing panel that lets you create a 2D drawing of a 3D model?

Solution   Flatshot.

Visualize solids.   In addition to viewing your 3D model in a number of different orientations, you can view it as if it were transparent or cut in half.

Master It   What is the name of the command that lets you create a cut view of your 3D model?

Solution   Sectionplane.

Chapter 25: Exploring 3D Mesh and Surface Modeling

Create a simple 3D mesh.   Mesh modeling allows you to create more organic 3D forms by giving you unique smoothing and editing tools. You can start your mesh model by creating a basic shape using the mesh primitives.

Master It Name at least six mesh primitives available on the Primitives panel of the Mesh Modeling tab.

Solution The mesh primitives are box, cylinder, cone, sphere, pyramid, wedge, and torus.

Edit faces and edges. The ability to edit faces and edges is essential to creating complex shapes with mesh objects.

Master It Name the tool that is used to divide a face into multiple faces.

Solution The Refine Mesh tool.

Create mesh surfaces. The Mesh primitives let you create shapes that enclose a volume. If you just want to model a smooth, curved surface in 3D, you might find the surface mesh tools helpful.

Master It How many objects are needed to use the Edge Surface tool?

Solution Four.

Convert meshes to solids. You can convert a mesh into a 3D solid to take advantage of many of the solid editing tools available in AutoCAD.

Master It Name at least two tools you can use on a solid that you cannot use on a mesh.

Solution Union, Subtract, Intersect, Interfere, any of the edge or face editing tools on the Solid Editing panel of the Home tab.

Understand 3D surfaces. 3D surfaces can be created using some of the same tools you use to create 3D solids.

Master It Name at least two tools you can use to create both 3D solids and 3D surfaces.

Solution Any of the following: Loft, Sweep, Extrude, and Revolve.

Edit 3D surfaces. AutoCAD offers a wide range of tools that are unique to 3D surfaces.

Master It Name at least four tools devoted to CV editing.

Solution Any of the following: CV Edit bar, Convert To NURBS, Show CV, Hide CV, Surface Rebuild (Rebuild), Surface CV – Add (or just CV Add), and Surface CV – Remove (or just CV Remove).

Chapter 26: Using the Express Tools

Use enhancements straight from the source. The Express tools have been around for a while and were originally intended to show what could be done with customization. Many users have come to rely on some of these tools.

Master It In which panel will you find the Align Space tool?

Solution Layout.

Put AutoLISP to work. AutoLISP is a macro language that gives you the ability to create your own commands.

Master It Name the filename extension for AutoLISP programs.

Solution The filename extension is .lsp.

Chapter 27: Exploring AutoLISP

Understand the interpreter.   One of the simplest ways to start using AutoLISP is to enter an AutoLISP expression directly into the command line.

Master It   Give an example of an AutoLISP formula that performs a simple math function.

Solution   (+ 2 2)

Use arguments and functions.   AutoLISP needs two elements, an argument and an expression, to do any work.

Master It   Which is the function in the following AutoLISP expression?

(+ 45 33)

Solution   +

Create a simple program.   You can input a simple program directly into AutoCAD by entering it through the command line.

Master It   Name a function that pauses an AutoLISP program for user input.

Solution   Getpoint or any of the Get functions.

Select objects with AutoLISP.   AutoLISP offers an expression that lets you select objects and then perform some operation on the set of objects.

Master It   What function lets you select objects, and what AutoLISP feature do you use to store your selection?

Solution   Ssget, variable.

Control the flow of an AutoLISP program.   You can set up an AutoLISP program to test for conditions and perform different operations depending on the result.

Master It   Name some functions that test for a condition.

Solution   If, While, Foreach.

Convert data types.   The functions in AutoLISP are designed to work with their own types of data. For example, math functions work only with numbers, and string operations work only with text. If you need to use the result of a math function in text, you can convert the number into text.

Master It   What is the name of the function that converts an angle in radians to text?

Solution   Angtos.

Store your programs as files.   You can save your AutoLISP program in a text editor like Windows Notepad and then later have AutoCAD retrieve your program for use.

Master It   What is the filename extension for AutoLISP programs?

Solution   .lsp

Chapter 28: Customizing Toolbars, Menus, Linetypes, and Hatch Patterns

Use workspaces. Often with AutoCAD, you find that you have different sets of panels or toolbars open to perform specific tasks. You might have one set of Ribbon panels for editing text and dimensions, whereas another set is more useful for design. Using workspaces is a great way to organize your different editing modes.

Master It Where do you find the Customize option for workspaces?

Solution The Workspace drop-down menu or the Workspace Switching tool.

Customize the user interface. In addition to using workspaces to organize tools and Ribbon panels, you can customize the AutoCAD interface to make it fit the way you like to work. You can add tools to Ribbon panels or even create your own tools for operations you perform frequently.

Master It What does the Customizations In All Files group display?

Solution Interface elements like toolbars, menus, ribbons, and so on.

Create macros in tools and menus. A macro is a set of instructions that performs more complex operations than single commands. Macros are often built on commands with additional predefined responses to help speed data input.

Master It What does the ^C do in a macro?

Solution The ^C is equivalent to pressing the Esc key.

Edit keyboard shortcuts. Keyboard shortcuts can help improve your speed when drawing in AutoCAD. They can reduce several clicks of the mouse to a simple keystroke. AutoCAD lets you create custom shortcuts for your favorite commands.

Master It What is the keyboard shortcut for Copy?

Solution Co↵.

Save, load, and unload your customizations. To keep your customizations organized, you can save new toolbars, menus, and Ribbons as files that you can load on demand. When you save your custom elements as a file, you can move them to other computers.

Master It Name the tab that contains the group you use to save your custom elements.

Solution Transfer tab.

Understand the Diesel macro language. If you're adventurous, you may want to try your hand at creating more-complex macros. The Diesel macro language is an easy introduction to AutoCAD macro customization and is most useful in controlling the behavior in menu options.

Master It What does the expression $(getvar, blipmode) do?

Solution It returns 1 or 0 depending on the current state of the Blipmode system variable.

Create custom linetypes. AutoCAD offers a number of noncontinuous linetypes, and you may find them adequate for most of your work. But every now and then, you may need a specific linetype that isn't available. Creating custom linetypes is easy once you understand the process.

Master It What is the purpose of a negative value in the linetype code?

Solution A blank or break in the line.

Create hatch patterns. Like linetypes, the hatch patterns provided by AutoCAD will probably fill most of your needs. But every now and then, you may need to produce a specific pattern.

Master It How are a hatch pattern code and a linetype code similar?

Solution They both use numeric values to describe lines.

Chapter 29: Managing and Sharing Your Drawings

Share drawings over the Internet. As a drafter or designer, it's very likely that you'll be involved in collaborative efforts, which means you'll have to share your work with others. The Internet has made it much easier to do this.

Master It Why is eTransmit important for sending AutoCAD drawings over the Internet?

Solution An AutoCAD drawing can have many different external files associated with it, such as fonts, Xrefs, and image files. eTransmit offers a quick way to gather these files into one place or into a single archive file.

ePublish your drawings. Autodesk offers the DWF drawing format, which lets non-CAD users view and add comments to simplified versions of your drawings. You can use the Publish feature to create a single DWF file from several drawings.

Master It True or false: The Publish feature can be used to plot multiple drawings in the background.

Solution True.

Manage your drawings with DesignCenter and the tool palettes. The DesignCenter is a great tool for managing your drawings' resources, like blocks, custom linetypes, and other elements.

Master It True or false: The DesignCenter has the capacity to scale a block automatically to the correct size when moving from metric to Imperial drawings.

Solution True.

Establish office standards. AutoCAD allows for a wide range of settings in a drawing. For this reason, it's a good idea to create standards for the way drawings are set up.

Master It Name the filename extension for an AutoCAD drawing standards file.

Solution .dws.

Convert multiple layer settings. If you exchange files with another office, you may find that their layer scheme is different from yours. AutoCAD offers the Layer Translator to help you translate layer names from an unfamiliar drawing to names you're more comfortable with.

Master It Name the filename extensions of the types of files that you can use as a template for layer-name translations.

Solution .dwg, .dws, and .dwt.

Chapter 30: Keeping a Project Organized with Sheet Sets

Understand sheet sets. The sheet set feature is like a database that automatically keeps track of drawings and drawing resources for your projects. To use sheets sets successfully, you need to make sure the Sheet Set Manager is aware of all the drawings and resources used in a project.

> **Master It** Name the two main categories of files that sheets sets use and that were mentioned at the beginning of this chapter.
>
> **Solution** Reference files and sheet files.

Create a sheet set from an existing project. If you have existing project files, you can set up a sheet set to work with them.

> **Master It** Name the option on the first page of the Create Sheet Set Wizard that lets you set up a sheet set for an existing project.
>
> **Solution** The Existing Drawings radio button.

Manage title blocks and cross-references. When the Sheet Set Manager is aware of a drawing or drawing resource, you can automate the creation of sheets such as elevations and sections. You can also control the naming and numbering of drawings in a set through the Sheet Set Manager.

> **Master It** What is the name of the right-click option that lets you change the name and number of a drawing?
>
> **Solution** Rename & Renumber.

Customize sheet sets. To use sheets sets to their full potential, you should create title blocks and callout blocks that are sheet set aware so they can communicate with the Sheet Set Manager.

> **Master It** What is the name of the object you must include in a block to store data?
>
> **Solution** Attribute definition.

Archive, publish, and eTransmit sheet sets. As a project starts to grow, you'll have to keep track of sheet and reference drawings as well as other drawing resources. Because the Sheet Set Manager is already aware of all the files needed for a project, you can use it to help keep track of project files.

> **Master It** Name the three AutoCAD features that help you manage your files.
>
> **Solution** Archive, Publish, and eTransmit.

Appendix B

Installing and Setting Up AutoCAD

This appendix gives you information about installing AutoCAD 2011 on your system and describes the system parameters you should set to configure AutoCAD to meet the needs of your operating environment. Throughout this appendix, the system variable associated with a setting, when available, is included at the end of an option description, enclosed in brackets. System variables are settings that enable you to control AutoCAD's behavior when you're using commands and features. You'll find a detailed description of the AutoCAD system variables in the AutoCAD 2011 Help website.

Before Installing AutoCAD

Before you begin the installation process, be sure you have at least 1 GB of free disk space for the 32-bit version and 1.5 GB of free disk space for the 64-bit version. You should also have at least an additional 100 MB of free disk space for AutoCAD temporary files and swap files, plus another 20 MB for the tutorial files you'll create. AutoCAD will work with Microsoft Windows 7, Windows Vista or Windows XP (Home, Professional, or Tablet edition) with service pack 3. AutoCAD also works with Internet Explorer 7.

For 2D work, you'll also need a Pentium IV CPU or better with at least 2 GB of RAM and a video card that supports at least 1024×768 resolution and True Color.

For serious 3D work, Autodesk recommends 2 GB of RAM, 2 GB of free disk space (not including the AutoCAD installation), and a 128 MB or greater OpenGL/Direct3D-capable workstation-class graphics card. Autodesk has a list of certified graphics cards for 3D modeling. This list is always being updated, so check the Autodesk website for the latest information.

Finally, have your AutoCAD vendor's name and phone number ready. You'll be asked to enter this information during the installation. Single-user systems have a 30-day grace period, so you can install and use AutoCAD without entering your authorization code right away. You can obtain an authorization code by fax, by phone, or over the Internet as indicated when you first start AutoCAD. The trial software that comes with this book can't be authorized, so be sure that you have a good block of free time to study AutoCAD before you install it.

Proceeding with the Installation

AutoCAD 2011 installs like most other Windows programs, but you should know a few things before you start. The following sections provide some information that can be helpful as you begin your installation.

Installing the AutoCAD Software

Installing AutoCAD is simple and straightforward. AutoCAD uses an installation wizard like most other Windows programs. Here are some guidelines to follow during the installation process:

◆ Before you start, make sure you have enough disk space, and also make sure no other programs are running. You'll need your AutoCAD serial number, which is usually on the package label. If you're installing the trial version from the companion CD, select the "I want to try this product for 30 days" option on the User and Product Information page of the installation wizard.

◆ Typically, the AutoCAD installation program starts automatically when you insert the AutoCAD 2011 DVD into your computer. In the event that it doesn't, do the following:

 1. In Windows, choose Start ➢ Run to open the Run dialog box.

 2. In the Open box, enter **D:\setup**. Enter the letter of your DVD drive in place of the D in this example. Click OK when you're ready. The AutoCAD 2011 Master Setup dialog box opens.

 3. After the installation starts, follow the directions in the installation wizard.

 4. You're asked to select the location for your AutoCAD files. The tutorials in this book assume that you have AutoCAD on drive C and in a folder called `\Program Files\Autodesk\AutoCAD 2011\`—these are the defaults during the installation.

 5. You're given the choice of including the Autodesk Design Review 2011 program and the Autodesk Material Library 2011 Medium Image library. Include the Autodesk Material Library in the installation.

 6. You may also be asked if you want to install the Express tools and sample files. Go ahead and install them.

 7. If you don't have enough disk space, the installation wizard lets you know exactly how much room you need on each drive involved in the installation. You can take steps to make more room by using Windows Explorer or the Windows Disk Cleanup utility. If you do this, make sure you close those programs when you've finished making room and before you return to the AutoCAD setup.

After the installation is complete, you see the AutoCAD 2011 Setup dialog box, which may ask whether you want to restart your computer. It's usually better to restart your computer immediately after installing AutoCAD if it requests that you do so.

Configuring AutoCAD

In the following sections, you'll learn how to configure AutoCAD to work the way you want it to. You can configure AutoCAD at any time during an AutoCAD session by using the Options dialog box.

The tutorials in this book assume that you're using the default Options settings. As you become more familiar with the workings of AutoCAD, you may want to adjust the way AutoCAD works by using the Options dialog box. You can also set many of the options in the Options dialog box through system variables.

Choose Options from the Application menu or type **options.⏎** at the Command prompt to open the Options dialog box, which has the tabs and settings described in the following sections.

Many of the options in the Options dialog box show an AutoCAD file icon. This icon indicates that the option's setting is saved with the file as opposed to being saved as part of AutoCAD's default settings.

The Files Tab

You use the options on the Files tab (Figure B.1) to tell AutoCAD where to place or find files it needs to operate. It uses a hierarchical list, similar to the one presented by Windows Explorer. You first see the general topics in the Search Paths, File Names, And File Locations list box. You can expand any item in the list by clicking its plus sign.

FIGURE B.1

The Files tab

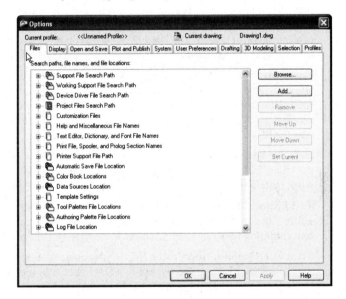

Following are descriptions of each item in the list box. Chances are you won't have to use most of them, but you may change others occasionally.

When available, the related system variable is shown in brackets at the end of the description.

Support File Search Path   AutoCAD relies on external files for many of its functions. Menus, text fonts, linetypes, and hatch patterns are a few examples of features that rely on external files. The Support File Search Path item tells AutoCAD where to look for these files. You can add folder paths to this listing by selecting it and clicking the Add button and entering a new path, or you can select it and use the Browse button. It's probably not a good idea to delete any of the existing items under this heading unless you really know what you're doing.

If you're familiar with using environment variables, you can include them in the search paths.

Working Support File Search Path   The Working Support File Search Path item contains a read-only list of the support-file search paths for the current session, including any special settings that may be included with command switches and environment settings.

Device Driver File Search Path   The Device Driver File Search Path item locates the device drivers for AutoCAD. *Device drivers* are applications that enable AutoCAD to communicate directly with printers, plotters, and input devices. In most cases, you don't have to do anything with this setting.

Project Files Search Path   Eventually, a consultant or other AutoCAD user will provide you with files that rely on Xrefs or raster images. Often, such files expect the Xref or raster image to be in a particular folder. When they are moved to another location with a different folder system, Xref-dependent files won't be able to find their Xrefs. The Project Files Search Path item enables you to specify a folder where Xrefs or other dependent files are stored. If AutoCAD is unable to find an Xref or other file, it will look in the folder you specify in this listing.

To specify this folder, highlight Project Files Search Path and then click the Add button. AutoCAD suggests `Project1` as the folder name. You can change the name if you prefer. Click the plus sign next to `Project1`, and then click Browse to select a location for your project-file search path. The project-file search path is stored in a system variable called Projectname [Projectname].

Customization Files   If you're customizing AutoCAD with your own menu files and icons, you can use this setting to locate your files. This option makes it convenient to keep your customization files in a place that is separate from the built-in AutoCAD files. You can specify a location for the main customization files like your CUI menu files, enterprise customization files for files you want to share, and your custom icons.

Help And Miscellaneous File Names   This item lets you set the location of a variety of support files, including menu, help, automatic save, log, and configuration files. If you have a network installation, you can also set the License Manager location on your network.

Text Editor, Dictionary, And Font File Names   Use this item to set the location of the text editor [Mtexted], custom and main dictionaries [Dctmain, Dctust], and the alternate font and font-mapping files [Fontalt]. Chapter 10 describes these tools in more detail.

Print File, Spooler, And Prolog Section Names   You can specify a print filename other than the default that is supplied by AutoCAD whenever you plot to a file. The Spooler option lets you specify an application intended to read and plot a plot file. The Prolog option is intended for PostScript export. It lets you specify the Prolog section from the `acad.psf` file that you want AutoCAD to include with exported Encapsulated PostScript files [Psprolog].

Printer Support File Path   Several support files are associated with the AutoCAD printing and plotting system. This item enables you to indicate where you want AutoCAD to look for these files.

Automatic Save File Location   You can indicate the location for AutoCAD's Automatic Save file by using this item [Savefilepath].

Color Book Locations   This item lets you specify the locations for the PANTONE color books. This is an optional installation item, so if the PANTONE color books aren't installed, you can install them through your AutoCAD 2011 Installation DVD.

Data Sources Location   This item lets you specify the location for Open Database Connectivity (ODBC) data-link files for linking AutoCAD drawings to database files.

Template Settings   When you select the Use A Template option in the Create New Drawing dialog box, AutoCAD looks at this setting for the location of template files. You can modify this setting, but chances are you won't need to.

Tool Palettes File Locations   This item lets you specify a location for your custom tool palettes resource files. When you create custom palettes, AutoCAD stores its data regarding those palettes in this location.

Authoring Palette File Locations   If you're creating custom dynamic blocks, you can designate a folder location where you keep your custom block settings and files.

Log File Location   With this item, you can indicate where log files are to be placed [Logfilepath].

Action Recorder Settings   The Action Recorder saves action macros as files on your computer. You can specify the location of those saved macros in this option.

Plot And Publish Log File Location   With this item, you can indicate where plot and publish log files are to be placed [Logfilepath].

Temporary Drawing File Location   AutoCAD creates temporary files to store portions of your drawings as you work on them. You usually don't have to think about these temporary files unless they start crowding your hard disk or unless you're working on a particularly large file on a system with little memory. This item lets you set the location for temporary files. The default location is the `C:\Documents and Settings\`*Username*`\local settings\ temp\` folder. *Username* is your login name. If you have a hard disk that has lots of room and is very fast, you may want to change this setting to a location on that drive to improve performance [Tempprefix, read-only].

Temporary External Reference File Location   If you're on a network and you foresee a situation in which another user will want to open an Xref of a file you're working on, you can set the Demand Load Xrefs setting in the Open And Save tab to Enabled With Copy. This causes AutoCAD to make and use a copy of any Xref that is currently loaded. This way, others can open the original file. The Temporary External Reference File Location item lets you specify the folder where AutoCAD stores this copy of an Xref [Xloadpath].

Texture Maps Search Path   This item specifies the location for AutoCAD Render texture maps. In most cases, you won't have to change this setting. You can, however, add a folder name to this item for your own texture maps as you acquire or create them.

Web File Search Path   Although you may think this is for Internet files, it's really for photometric web files that are used to control the way lights behave in 3D models. These files have an `.ies` filename extension.

i-drop Associated File Location   This is where you specify the location of files imported to your computer through the i-drop function in AutoCAD. By default, no location is specified, so the i-drop imported DWG file is placed in the same folder location as the current drawing.

DGN Mapping Setup Locations   You can specify the location for the `DGNsetup.ini` file, which is a file used for DGN commands. These commands enable you to import or export DGN files. They also enable you to control the translation of layers, linetypes, line weights, and color between the AutoCAD DWG file format and the DGN file format.

While in AutoCAD, you may want to quickly find the location of a resource file such as a log file or the Automatic Save file. You can do so by using the system variable associated with the resource. For example, to find the location of the log-file path quickly, enter **logfilepath**↵ at the Command prompt. For the Automatic Save file, enter **savefilepath**↵. LT users can employ the Modemacro command as in **Modemacro↵$(getvar,logfilepath)**↵ or **Modemacro↵$(getvar,savefilepath)**↵. See Chapter 28 for more on Modemacro.

The Display Tab

The settings on this tab (Figure B.2) let you control AutoCAD's appearance. You can make AutoCAD look completely different with these settings if you choose. Scroll bars, fonts, and colors are all up for grabs.

FIGURE B.2
The Display tab

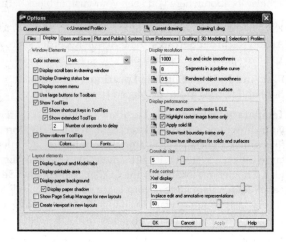

THE WINDOW ELEMENTS GROUP

These options control the general settings for AutoCAD windows:

Color Scheme   Lets you select between a dark or light color scheme for the AutoCAD interface, including toolbars, Ribbon panels, and dialog boxes.

Display Scroll Bars In Drawing Window   Lets you turn the scroll bars on and off. If you have a small monitor with low resolution, you may want to turn off the scroll bars for a larger drawing area.

Display Drawing Status Bar   When turned on, displays the Annotation Scale settings at the bottom of the drawing area instead of at the bottom of the AutoCAD window.

Display Screen Menu   Turns on the old AutoCAD Format Screen menu that once appeared on the right side of the screen. If you must have it displayed, this is where you can turn it back on.

Use Large Buttons For Toolbars   Controls whether large icon buttons are used in toolbars.

Show ToolTips   Controls whether tool tips are shown when you hover the mouse over tools [Tooltips].

Show Shortcut Keys In ToolTips   Controls whether shortcut keys are displayed in tool tips.

Show Extended ToolTips   Controls whether extended tool tips are displayed.

Show Rollover ToolTips   Controls whether rollover tool tips are displayed [Rollovertips].

Colors   Opens a dialog box that lets you set the color for the various components of the AutoCAD window. This is where you can change the background color of the drawing area if you find that black doesn't work for you.

Fonts   Opens a dialog box that lets you set the fonts of the AutoCAD window. You can select from the standard set of Windows fonts available in your system.

THE DISPLAY RESOLUTION GROUP

These options control the way objects are displayed in AutoCAD. You can choose between display accuracy and speed:

Arc And Circle Smoothness   Controls the appearance of arcs and circles, particularly when you zoom in on them. In some instances, arcs and circles appear to be octagons even though they plot as smooth arcs and circles. If you want arcs and circles to appear smoother, you can increase this setting. An increase also increases memory use [Viewres].

Segments In A Polyline Curve   Controls the smoothness of polyline curves. Increase the value to make curved polylines appear smoother and less segmented. Decrease the value for improved display performance [Splinesegs].

Rendered Object Smoothness   Controls the smoothness of curved solids when they're rendered or shaded. Values can range from 0.01 to 10 [Facetres].

Contour Lines Per Surface   Lets you set the number of contour lines used to represent solid, curved surfaces. Values can range from 0 to 2047 [Isolines].

THE LAYOUT ELEMENTS GROUP

These options control the display of elements in the Paper Space Layout tabs. See Chapters 8 and 16 for more information. Most of these options are self-explanatory. The Show Page Setup Manager For New Layouts option opens the Page Setup Manager dialog box whenever a layout is first opened. The Create Viewport In New Layouts option automatically creates a viewport in a layout when it's first opened.

THE DISPLAY PERFORMANCE GROUP

You can adjust a variety of display-related settings from this group:

Pan And Zoom With Raster & OLE   Controls the way raster images react to real-time pans and zooms. If this option is selected, raster images move with the cursor. Turn off this option for better performance [Rtdisplay].

Highlight Raster Image Frame Only   Determines how raster images appear when selected. Turn on this option for better performance [Imagehlt].

Apply Solid Fill   Controls the display of filled objects such as wide polylines and areas filled with the solid hatch pattern. This option is also controlled by the Fillmode system variable. Turn off this option for better performance [Fillmode].

Show Text Boundary Frame Only   Controls the way text is displayed. Turn on this option to display text as rectangular boundaries [Qtextmode].

Draw True Silhouettes For Solids And Surfaces   Controls whether surface meshes for solid models are displayed. Turn off this option for better performance [Dispsilh].

THE CROSSHAIR SIZE SLIDER

This slider controls the size of the crosshair cursor. You can set this to 100 percent to simulate the full-screen crosshair cursor of earlier versions of AutoCAD [Cursorsize].

FADE CONTROL

These two sliders control the fade effect on external references. The Xref display option sets the overall fade effect [Xdwgfadectl]. The In-Place Edit And Annotative Representations option controls the display of nonselected objects during in-place reference editing. See Chapter 7 for more information on in-place reference editing [Xfadectl].

The Open and Save Tab

The Open And Save tab (Figure B.3) offers general file-related options such as the frequency of the automatic save and the default file version for the Save and Save As options.

THE FILE SAVE GROUP

You can control how AutoCAD saves files by using the options in this group:

Save As   Lets you set the default file type for the Save and the Save As Application menu options. If you're working in an environment that requires Release 14 files as the standard file type, for example, you can use this option to select Release 14 as the default file type. You can also set up AutoCAD to save DXF files by default.

Maintain Visual Fidelity For Annotative Objects   Ensures that annotative scale is preserved in layouts when you save drawings to earlier versions of AutoCAD. If you work primarily in Model Space, leave this setting off.

Maintain Drawing Size Compatibility   AutoCAD 2011 has removed restrictions on object size. This option ensures that those restrictions are still in place in case you want to save your file to an earlier version.

Thumbnail Preview Settings   Lets you determine whether a preview image is saved with a drawing. Preview images are used in the AutoCAD file dialog box and in DesignCenter to let you preview a file before opening it [Rasterpreview]. You can also control the display of the sheet set preview [Updatethumbnail].

Incremental Save Percentage   Controls the degree to which the Incremental Save feature is applied when a file is saved. An incremental save improves the time required to save a file to disk, but it also makes the file size larger. If you have limited disk space, you can set this value to 25. A value of 0 turns off Incremental Save altogether but reduces AutoCAD performance [Isavepercent].

THE FILE SAFETY PRECAUTIONS GROUP

These options control AutoCAD's automatic backup features:

Automatic Save   Offers control over the Automatic Save features. You can turn it on or off by using the check box or set the frequency at which files are saved by using the Minutes Between Saves input box. You can set the location for the Automatic Save files by using the Automatic Save File Location item in the Files tab of the Options dialog box. You can also set the frequency of automatic saves through the Savetime system variable [Savefilepath, Savefile].

FIGURE B.3
The Open And
Save tab

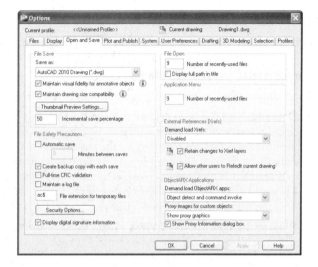

Create Backup Copy With Each Save   Lets you determine whether a BAK file is saved along with every save you perform. You can turn off this option to conserve disk space [Isavebak, Tempprefix].

Full-Time CRC Validation   Controls the cyclic redundancy check feature, which checks for file errors whenever AutoCAD reads a file. This feature is helpful in troubleshooting hardware problems in your system.

Maintain A Log File   Lets you record the data in the AutoCAD Text Window. See Chapter 20 for more on this feature. You can set the location for log files in the Files tab of the Options dialog box [Logfilemode, Logfilename].

File Extension For Temporary Files   Lets you set the filename extension for AutoCAD temporary files. These are files AutoCAD uses to store drawing data temporarily as you work on a file. If you're working on a network where temporary files from multiple users may be stored in the same folder, you may want to change this setting to identify your temporary files.

Security Options   Opens the Security Options dialog box, in which you can either password-protect a file or add a digital signature. See Chapter 29 for more on these features.

Display Digital Signature Information   When a file containing a digital signature is opened, this option will display a warning message alerting you to the presence of the signature [Sigwarn]. See Chapter 29 for more on the digital signature feature.

THE FILE OPEN GROUP

You can control how AutoCAD displays filenames in the File menu or the drawing title bar:

Number Of Recently-Used Files   Lets you specify the number of files listed in the File menu history list. The default is 9, but you can enter a value from 0 to 9.

Display Full Path In Title   Controls whether the full path is included in the title bar with a drawing's name.

THE APPLICATION MENU GROUP

This option controls the number of recently used files that are displayed in the Application menu.

THE EXTERNAL REFERENCES (XREFS) GROUP

These options let you control memory and layer features of Xrefs:

Demand Load Xrefs Lets you turn on the Demand Load feature of Xrefs. Demand Load helps to improve the performance of files that use Xrefs by loading only those portions of an Xref drawing that are required for the current open drawing. This option is a drop-down list with three choices: Disabled turns off demand loading, Enabled turns on demand loading, and Enabled With Copy turns on demand loading by using a copy of the Xref source file. This last option enables others on a network to edit the Xref source file while you're working on a file that also uses it [Xloadctl].

Retain Changes To Xref Layers Lets you save layer settings of Xref files in the current drawing. This doesn't affect the source Xref file. With this setting turned off, the current file imports the layer settings of the Xref file when it loads that file [Visretain].

Allow Other Users To Refedit Current Drawing Lets you specify whether others can simultaneously edit a file that you're editing. This option is intended to enable others to use the Xref And Block Editing option (the Refedit command or the Edit Reference tool found on the Insert tab's expanded Reference panel) on files you currently have loaded in AutoCAD [Xedit].

THE OBJECTARX APPLICATIONS GROUP

AutoCAD allows users and third-party developers to create a custom object that usually requires the presence of a custom ObjectARX application to support it. These options control the way AutoCAD treats custom objects and their related ObjectARX applications:

Demand Load ObjectARX Apps Controls when a supporting third-party application is loaded if a custom object is present in a file. This option offers several settings that you can select from a drop-down list. The available settings are Disable Load On Demand, Custom Object Detect, Command Invoke, and Object Detect And Command Invoke. Disable Load On Demand prevents AutoCAD from loading third-party applications when a custom object is present. Some standard AutoCAD commands won't work if you select Disable Load On Demand because AutoCAD itself uses ObjectARX applications. Custom Object Detect causes AutoCAD to automatically load an ARX application if a custom object is present. Command Invoke loads a custom application when you invoke a command from that application. The Object Detect And Command Invoke option loads an ARX application when either a custom object is present or you invoke a command from that application [Demandload].

Proxy Images For Custom Objects Offers a drop-down list with three settings that control the display of custom objects when the objects supporting ARX applications aren't present on your system. Do Not Show Proxy Graphics turns off the display of custom objects. Show Proxy Graphics displays the custom objects. Show Proxy Bounding Box shows a bounding box in place of a custom object [Proxyshow].

Show Proxy Information Dialog Box Lets you determine whether the Show Proxy Information warning dialog box is used. When this option is selected, the Show Proxy Information warning appears when a drawing with custom objects is opened but AutoCAD can't find the objects' associated ARX application [Proxynotice].

The Plot and Publish Tab

The Plot And Publish tab in the Options dialog box offers settings related to printing and plotting. See Chapter 8 and Appendix C for a description of these options.

The System Tab

The options in the System tab (Figure B.4) offer control over some of AutoCAD's general interface settings, such as settings for display drivers and pointing devices.

FIGURE B.4

The System tab

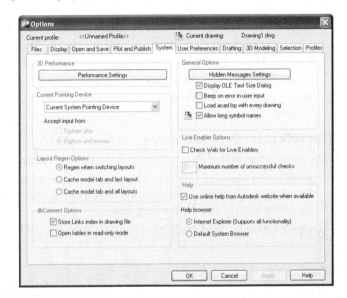

THE 3D PERFORMANCE GROUP

Clicking the Performance Settings button in this group displays a variety of settings to help you fine-tune the performance of your 3D graphics. When you click this option, the Adaptive Degradation And Performance Tuning dialog box opens. *Adaptive degradation* refers to the way AutoCAD's display behaves as you change views such as camera or orbital. AutoCAD degrades the view to keep up with real-time changes in a view (thus the term *adaptive degradation*). You can control how the view degrades using these options. The Hardware And Performance Tuning section gives you information about your current graphic system and allows you to make setting changes. See the section "Adjusting AutoCAD's 3D Graphics System" later in this appendix.

THE CURRENT POINTING DEVICE GROUP

You can choose the type of pointing device you want to use with AutoCAD through the options in this group. The drop-down list offers Current System Pointing Device and Wintab Compatible Digitizer ADI 4.2 – By Autodesk. If you want to use the default Windows pointing device, choose Current System Pointing Device. If you have a digitizer that uses the Wintab driver, you can select Wintab Compatible Digitizer.

You can further limit AutoCAD's use to the Wintab Compatible Digitizer by selecting the Digitizer Only radio button. If you select the Digitizer And Mouse radio button, AutoCAD will accept input from both devices.

THE LAYOUT REGEN OPTIONS GROUP

This set of radio buttons enables you to specify how regens are applied when working with layout tabs:

Regen When Switching Layouts   Causes AutoCAD to force a regen when you select a layout tab or the Model tab. Use this option when your computer is limited in RAM.

Cache Model Tab And Last Layout   Causes AutoCAD to suppress regens when you switch to the Model tab or the most recently opened layout tab. Other layouts will regen when selected.

Cache Model Tab And All Layouts   Causes AutoCAD to suppress regens when you select any layout tab or the Model tab.

THE dbCONNECT OPTIONS GROUP

The check boxes in this group offer controls over the dbConnect feature:

Store Links Index In Drawing File   Lets you specify where database link data is stored. If this check box is selected, link data is stored in the drawing that is linked to a database. This increases file size and file-loading time.

Open Tables In Read-Only Mode   Lets you limit access to database files.

THE GENERAL OPTIONS GROUP

This set of check boxes enables you to set options related to the general operation of AutoCAD:

Hidden Messages Settings   A number of dialog boxes offer the "Do not show me again" option. If you select it and later find that you would like to see the message or dialog box again, you can use this button to view the message.

Display OLE Text Size Dialog   Lets you control the display of the OLE Text Size dialog box, which normally appears when you insert OLE text objects into an AutoCAD drawing by choosing Paste from the Paste flyout on the Home tab's Clipboard panel.

Beep On Error In User Input   Turns on an alarm beep that sounds whenever there is an input error.

Load Acad.lsp With Every Drawing   Lets you determine whether an Acad.lsp file is loaded with every drawing. If you're used to using an Acad.lsp file with your AutoCAD system, you can select this option. Otherwise, AutoCAD will load only the Acaddoc.lsp file [Acadlspasdoc].

Allow Long Symbol Names   Enables you to use long names for items such as layers, blocks, linetypes, and text-styles. With this option turned on, you can enter as many as 255 characters for names [Extnames].

THE LIVE ENABLER OPTIONS GROUP

Since AutoCAD 14, third-party developers have had the ability to create custom objects, also known as *proxy objects*, through a programming tool known as ObjectARX. When this feature was first introduced, you had to have the third-party application installed on your computer in order to view or edit such custom objects. *Object enablers* are small programs, like plug-ins to AutoCAD, that enable you to view and edit custom third-party objects without having the full third-party application present. These object enablers may be available on the Web for free download if the third-party producer has posted them.

Check Web For Live Enablers Causes AutoCAD to look for enablers over the Internet. For example, if you receive a file created in AutoCAD Architecture that contains a custom object, AutoCAD can automatically go to the Autodesk website and download the AutoCAD Architecture Object Enabler so you can edit and view the file. The Live Enabler options let you control how the Object Enabler feature is engaged when AutoCAD encounters custom objects [Proxywebsearch].

Maximum Number Of Unsuccessful Checks Lets you specify the number of times AutoCAD checks the Internet for object enablers after an attempt to make a connection has failed.

THE HELP GROUP

This set of options lets you control AutoCAD's Web-based help feature:

Use Online Help From Autodesk Website When Available Controls whether AutoCAD's help feature uses the Autodesk website or help documents installed on your computer.

Internet Explorer (Supports All Functionality) Causes AutoCAD to use Internet Explorer to open the AutoCAD 2011 Help website.

Default System Browser Causes AutoCAD to use your default browser to open the AutoCAD 2011 Help website.

The User Preferences Tab

The options in the User Preferences tab (Figure B.5) enable you to adjust the way AutoCAD reacts to user input.

THE WINDOWS STANDARD BEHAVIOR GROUP

These settings enable you to control how AutoCAD reacts to keyboard accelerators and mouse right-clicks:

Double Click Editing Controls whether a double-click on an object automatically starts an editing command for the object. If this option is turned off, double-clicking objects has no effect [Dblclkedit].

Shortcut Menus In Drawing Area Lets you see the shortcut menu when you right-click. When this check box isn't selected, AutoCAD responds to a right-click with a ⏎ [Shortcutmenu].

FIGURE B.5
The User Preferences tab

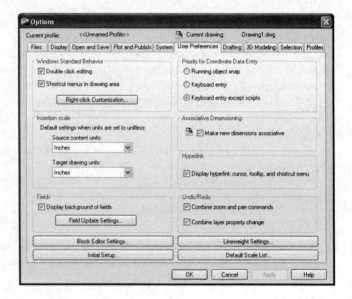

Right-Click Customization Opens the Right-Click Customization dialog box (Figure B.6), which offers further options for the behavior of the right-click in AutoCAD. The Turn On Time-Sensitive Right-Click option causes AutoCAD to respond differently depending on whether you right-click quickly or hold the right mouse button down momentarily. With this option, a rapid right-click issues a ↵, as if you pressed the Enter key. If you hold down the right mouse button, the shortcut menu appears. You can further adjust the time required to hold down the mouse button by adjusting this setting.

FIGURE B.6
The Right-Click Customization dialog

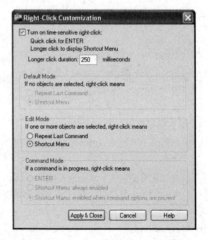

THE INSERTION SCALE GROUP

These settings control how the DesignCenter or i-drop feature determines the scale of blocks when blocks are given a unitless setting for their DesignCenter unit type. Each drop-down list offers the standard set of unit types that are available in the Block Definition dialog box under the Insert Units drop-down list. See Chapter 4 for more information on blocks and Chapter 29 for information on DesignCenter [Insunits].

THE FIELDS GROUP

These settings offer control over the display of fields and how they refresh. Display Background Of Fields lets you control the display of the gray background on fields. This background lets you see at a glance which text object in a drawing is a field. The background doesn't print. Clicking the Field Update Settings button opens a dialog box that lets you select the action that updates fields [Fielddisplay, Fieldeval].

THE PRIORITY FOR COORDINATE DATA ENTRY GROUP

These options control the way AutoCAD responds to coordinate input:

Running Object Snap   Forces AutoCAD to use Running Osnaps at all times [Osnapcoord].

Keyboard Entry   Enables you to use keyboard entry for coordinate input [Osnapcoord].

Keyboard Entry Except Scripts   Enables you to use keyboard entry for coordinate input for everything but scripts [Osnapcoord].

THE ASSOCIATIVE DIMENSIONING GROUP

This area has one option, Make New Dimensions Associative, which you can toggle on or off. This option lets you control whether AutoCAD uses the true associative dimensioning feature. With true associative dimensioning, a dimension follows changes to an object whenever the object is edited. In the old method, you have to include a dimension definition point during the editing process to have the dimension follow changes in an object [Dimassoc].

THE HYPERLINK GROUP

The one option in this group turns on or off the display of the hyperlink cursor, tool tip, and shortcut menu [Hyperlinkoptions].

THE UNDO/REDO GROUP

These options control how Undo and Redo react with the Zoom and Pan commands.

BLOCK EDITOR SETTINGS

Click the Block Editor Settings button to open the Block Editor Settings dialog box. The Block Editor Settings dialog box allows you to control the appearance of objects and features in the Block Editor.

INITIAL SETUP

This option allows you to create industry-specific workspaces using the Initial Setup Wizard. This is the same wizard that appears when you first start AutoCAD in a new installation. You can create a workspace for architectural, civil, electrical, manufacturing, mechanical, structural, or other types of work.

LINEWEIGHT SETTINGS

Click the Lineweight Settings button to open the Lineweight Settings dialog box. See Chapters 9 and 16 for more information about the Lineweight Settings dialog box.

DEFAULT SCALE LIST

Click the Default Scale List button to open the Default Scale List dialog box. You can add your own custom scales, which appear in the Plot dialog box.

The Drafting Tab

The Drafting tab (Figure B.7) offers settings that relate to the drawing cursor, including the AutoSnap and AutoTrack features.

FIGURE B.7
The Drafting tab

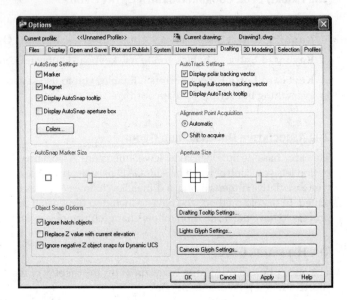

THE AUTOSNAP SETTINGS GROUP

The options in this group control the AutoSnap features that are engaged when you use osnaps:

Marker   Turns on the small, square graphic that appears on the osnap location. If you prefer not to see this marker, clear this check box [Autosnap].

Magnet   Causes the Osnap cursor to jump to an osnap location as it moves close to that location [Autosnap].

Display AutoSnap Tooltip   Controls the display of the osnap tool tip [Autosnap].

Display AutoSnap Aperture Box   Displays a square over the cursor whenever osnaps are active. If you're familiar with earlier versions of AutoCAD, you'll recognize the aperture box as the graphic used to indicate osnaps before the AutoSnap feature was introduced [Apbox].

Colors   Lets you determine the color for the AutoSnap marker. Opens the Drawing Window Colors dialog box.

THE AUTOSNAP MARKER SIZE SLIDER

Move the slider to control the size of the AutoSnap marker.

THE OBJECT SNAP OPTIONS GROUP

This group offers the Ignore Hatch Objects and Replace Z Value With Current Elevation options. When Ignore Hatch Objects is turned off, osnaps attempt to snap to geometry in hatch patterns. When turned on, Replace Z Value With Current Elevation causes AutoCAD to use the current UCS default Z value instead of the Z value of the selected point. Ignore Negative Z Object Snaps For Dynamic UCS causes osnaps to ignore locations with negative Z values while you're using the Dynamic UCS feature.

THE AUTOTRACK SETTINGS GROUP

These options offer control over the tracking vector used for Polar Tracking and Osnap Tracking:

Display Polar Tracking Vector   Turns the Polar Tracking vector on or off [Trackpath].

Display Full-Screen Tracking Vector   Lets you control whether the tracking vector appears across the full width of the drawing window or stops at the cursor location or the intersection of two tracking vectors [Trackpath].

Display AutoTrack Tooltip   Turns the Osnap Tracking tool tip on or off [Autosnap].

THE ALIGNMENT POINT ACQUISITION GROUP

These options let you determine the method for acquiring Osnap Tracking alignment points.

THE APERTURE SIZE SLIDER

Move the slider to set the size of the osnap aperture pickbox [Aperture].

THE DRAFTING TOOLTIP SETTINGS BUTTON

Click the Drafting Tooltip Settings button to control the color, size, and transparency of tool tips.

THE LIGHTS GLYPH SETTINGS BUTTON

Click the Lights Glyph Settings button to control the color and size of the spot and point light glyphs.

THE CAMERAS GLYPH SETTINGS BUTTON

Click the Cameras Glyph Settings button to control the color and size of the cameras glyph.

The 3D Modeling Tab

The options on this tab control the behavior and display of your drawing when you're working in 3D modes. You can adjust the appearance of the crosshair and the UCS icon. You can specify the default method for displaying 3D objects, and you can specify the default settings for Walk And Fly and Animation features.

3D Crosshairs

These settings control the behavior and appearance of the crosshair cursor when you're viewing your drawing in 3D:

Show Z Axis In Crosshairs   Displays the Z axis in the crosshair.

Label Axes In Standard Crosshairs   Displays the X, Y, and Z axis labels on the crosshair.

Show Labels For Dynamic UCS   Displays the axis labels during the use of Dynamic UCS regardless of the Label Axes In Standard Crosshairs setting.

Crosshair Labels   Lets you select from three label styles: Use X, Y, Z; Use N, E, Z; or Use Custom Labels. If you select Use Custom Labels, you can enter the labels you want to display for the X, Y, and Z axes in the boxes provided.

Display ViewCube or UCS Icon

These three options pretty much explain themselves. Each option determines when the ViewCube or UCS icon is displayed. By default, they're all turned on, so the ViewCube and UCS icon are always displayed.

3D Objects

These settings affect the display of 3D objects. Visual Style While Creating 3D Objects is self-explanatory. Deletion Control While Creating 3D Objects lets you determine whether objects AutoCAD uses to create 3D objects are saved or deleted.

The U and V isoline settings let you set the number of isolines on 3D solids and surface meshes. Isolines are the lines you see on a mesh or solid that help you visualize their shape. You see them in wireframe and realistic visual styles.

3D Navigation

If you want to adjust the way AutoCAD behaves when you're navigating a 3D view, these settings will help. Reverse Mouse Wheel Zoom is self-explanatory. The remaining two buttons give you control over the behavior of the Walk And Fly feature and the Animation settings:

Walk And Fly   Click this button to open the Walk And Fly Settings dialog box (Figure B.8). When you first start the 3DWalk or 3DFly feature, you see an instructional window that tells you how to use the feature. You use the options in the Settings group of the Walk And Fly Settings dialog box to specify when that instructional window appears. After using these features a few times, you may find the instructional window annoying and turn it off. You can turn it back on in this dialog box. You can also set the Position Locator window to automatically appear or not appear.

The Current Drawing Settings group lets you set the step size and steps per second when you're "walking" or "flying" through your model. These are the same settings you see in the Navigate control panel for Step Size and Steps Per Second.

FIGURE B.8
The Walk And Fly
Settings dialog

ViewCube   Click this button to open the ViewCube Settings dialog box (Figure B.9). These settings allow you to control the behavior and appearance of the ViewCube.

FIGURE B.9
The ViewCube
Settings dialog

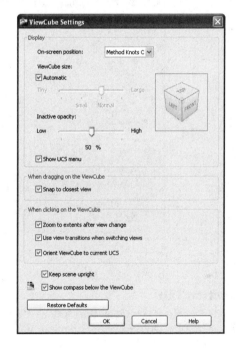

Animation   Click this button to open the Animation Settings dialog box (Figure B.10). Here you can control the default visual style, resolution, frame rate, and animation file format when using the Motion Path Animation (Anipath) feature.

SteeringWheels   Click this button to open the SteeringWheels Settings dialog box (Figure B.11). Here you can set the appearance and behavior of the SteeringWheels feature.

FIGURE B.10
The Animation
Settings dialog

DYNAMIC INPUT

When turned on, the Show Z Field For Pointer Input option offers a Z coordinate for input when Dynamic Input mode is used.

FIGURE B.11
The Steering-
Wheels Settings
dialog

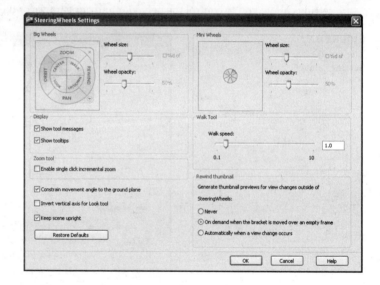

The Selection Tab

The options in the Selection tab of the Options dialog box (Figure B.12) control the way you select objects in AutoCAD. You can also make adjustments to the Grips feature.

THE PICKBOX SIZE SLIDER

This control lets you adjust the size of the pickbox [Pickbox].

THE SELECTION PREVIEW GROUP

These options let you control the behavior of the selection preview when you hover over objects. Click the Visual Effect Settings button to fine-tune the visual effects of the object selection, including the color and pattern of Autoselect windows.

FIGURE B.12

The Selection tab

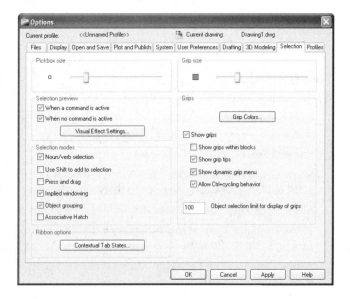

THE SELECTION MODES GROUP

These options let you control the degree to which AutoCAD conforms to standard graphical user interface (GUI) methods of operation:

Noun/Verb Selection   Makes AutoCAD work more like other Windows programs by letting you select objects before you choose an action or command [Pickfirst].

Use Shift To Add To Selection   Lets you use the standard GUI method of holding down the Shift key to select multiple objects. When the Shift key isn't held down, only the single object picked or the group of objects indicated with a window will be selected. Previously selected objects are deselected unless the Shift key is held down during selection. To turn on this feature by using system variables, set Pickadd to 0 [Pickadd].

Press And Drag   Lets you use the standard GUI method for placing window selections. When this option is selected, you click and hold down the Pick button on the first corner of the window. Then, while holding down the Pick button, drag the other corner of the window into position. When the other corner is in place, you let go of the Pick button to finish the window. This setting applies to both Verb/Noun and Noun/Verb operations. In the system variables, set Pickdrag to 1 for this option [Pickdrag].

Implied Windowing   Causes a window or crossing window to start automatically if no object is picked at the `Select objects:` prompt. This setting has no effect on the Noun/Verb setting. In the system variables, set Pickauto to 1 for this option [Pickauto].

Object Grouping   Lets you select groups as single objects [Pickstyle].

Associative Hatch   Lets you select both a hatch pattern and its associated boundary by using a single pick [Pickstyle].

THE GRIP SIZE SLIDER

This control lets you adjust the size of grips [Gripsize].

THE GRIPS GROUP

These options control the Grips feature:

Grip Colors   Lets you select a color for grips in their various states, such as unselected, selected, hovered, and contour [Gripcolor].

Show Grips   Controls the display of grips [Grips].

Show Grips Within Blocks   Turns on the display of grips in blocks. Although you can't edit grips in blocks, you can use grips in blocks as selection points [Gripblock].

Show Grip Tips   Controls the display of grip tool tips [Griptips].

Show Dynamic Grip Menu   Displays a dynamic menu when you're hovering over a multi-function grip [Gripmultifunctional].

Allow Ctrl+Cycling Behavior   Turns on Ctrl+cycling behavior for multifunction grips [Gripmultifunctional].

Object Selection Limit For Display Of Grips   Controls the display of grips based on the number of objects selected. If this is set to 1, grips aren't displayed if more than one object is selected. You can select a range from 1 to 32,767. The default is 100 [Gripobjlimit].

THE RIBBON OPTIONS GROUP

The Contextual Tab States button in the Ribbon Options group opens the Ribbon Contextual Tab State Options dialog box. This dialog box lets you set the conditions under which the ribbon contextual tabs are displayed. Contextual tabs are Ribbon tabs that offer tools that are designed to edit certain types of objects such as Xrefs or 3D meshes.

The Profiles Tab

In Windows, a user profile is saved for each login name. Depending on the login name you use, you can have a different Windows setup. The Profiles tab (Figure B.13) offers a similar function for AutoCAD users. You can store different settings from the Options dialog box in a profile and recall them at any time. You can also save them to a file with the `.arg` filename extension and then take that file to another system. It's a bit like being able to take your Options settings with you wherever you go.

The main part of the Profiles tab displays a list of available profiles. The default profile is shown as `<<Unnamed Profile>>`. As you add more profiles, they appear in the list.

To create a new profile, highlight a profile name from the list, and then click Add To List. The Add Profile dialog box opens, enabling you to enter a profile name and a description of the profile. The description appears in the box below the list on the Profiles tab whenever that profile is selected.

FIGURE B.13

The Profiles tab

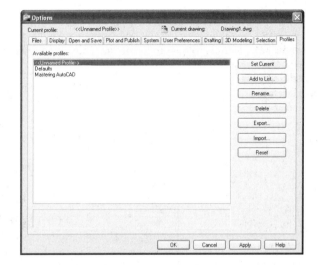

After you've created a new profile, you can modify the settings on the other tabs of the Options dialog box, and the new settings will be associated with the new profile. Profiles store the way menus are set up, so you can use them as an aid to managing both your own custom schemes and third-party software. Here is a brief description of the options on the Profiles tab:

Set Current Installs the settings from the selected profile.

Add To List Creates a new profile.

Rename Enables you to rename a profile and change its description.

Delete Removes the selected profile from the list.

Export Lets you save a profile to a file.

Import Imports a profile that has been saved to a file.

Reset Resets the values for a selected profile to its default settings.

Configuring the Tablet Menu Area

If you own a digitizing tablet and you would like to use it with a tablet menu template, you must configure your tablet menu. Install your table menu into AutoCAD using the Loadmenu command, then do the following:

1. Securely fasten your tablet menu template to the tablet. Be sure the area covered by the template is completely within the tablet's active drawing area.

2. Type **Tablet.⌐Cfg.⌐. The following prompt appears:**

   ```
   Enter number of tablet menus desired (0-4) <0>:
   ```

Enter the number of table areas your menu uses and the press ↵. For the next series of prompts, you'll be locating the tablet menu areas, starting with menu area 1. Figure B.14 shows an example of how to locate the table menu areas for the legacy AutoCAD tablet menu.

FIGURE B.14
How to locate the tablet menu areas

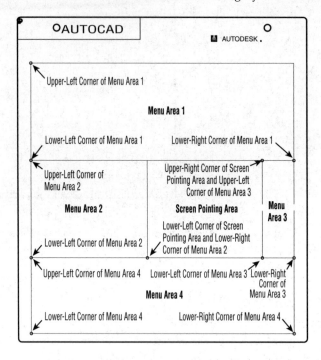

3. Follow the instructions provided by the Command prompt.

4. When you're asked if you want to respecify the fixed screen-pointing area, enter **Y↵**, and then select the corners of the pointing area as indicated by the prompts.

Turning On the Noun/Verb Selection Method

If for some reason the Noun/Verb Selection method isn't available, follow these steps to turn it on:

1. Choose Options from the Application menu. Then, in the Options dialog box, click the Selection tab.

2. In the Selection Modes group, click the Noun/Verb Selection check box.

3. Click OK.

You should now see a small square at the intersection of the crosshair cursor. This square is actually a pickbox superimposed on the cursor. It tells you that you can select objects, even while the Command prompt appears at the bottom of the screen and no command is currently active. As you saw earlier, the square momentarily disappears when you're in a command that asks you to select points.

You can also turn on Noun/Verb Selection by entering '**Pickfirst**↵ at the Command prompt. At the `Enter new value for PICKFIRST <0>:` prompt, enter **1**↵. (Entering 0 turns off the Pickfirst function.) The Pickfirst system variable is stored in the AutoCAD configuration file. See Appendix D for more on system variables.

Turning On the Grips Feature

If for some reason the Grips feature isn't available, follow these steps to turn it on:

1. Choose Options from the Application menu. Then, in the Options dialog box, click the Selection tab.

2. In the Grips group, click the Show Grips check box.

3. Click OK and you're ready to proceed.

The Selection tab of the Options dialog box also lets you specify whether grips appear on objects that compose a block (see Chapter 4 for more on blocks) as well as set the grip color and size. You can also set these options by using the system variables.

You can also turn the Grips feature on and off by entering '**Grips**↵. At the `Enter new value for GRIPS <0>:` prompt, enter **1** or **2** to turn grips on or **0** to turn grips off. The 2 option turns on grips and displays additional midpoint grips on polyline line segments. Grips is a system variable that is stored in the AutoCAD configuration file.

Setting Up the Tracking Vector Feature

If AutoCAD doesn't display a tracking vector as described in the early chapters of this book, or if the tracking vector doesn't behave as described, chances are this feature has been turned off or altered. Take the following steps to configure the tracking vector so it behaves as described in this book:

1. Open the Options dialog box by choosing Options from the Application menu.

2. Click the Drafting tab.

3. Click all three options in the AutoTrack Settings group.

4. Make sure the Marker, Magnet, and Display AutoSnap Tooltip check boxes are selected in the AutoSnap Settings group.

5. Make sure the Automatic radio button in the Alignment Point Acquisition group is selected.

6. Click OK to exit the dialog box.

Adjusting AutoCAD's 3D Graphics System

You can adjust the performance of AutoCAD's 3D graphics system through the Adaptive Degradation And Performance Tuning dialog box (Figure B.15). To open this dialog box, click the System tab in the Options dialog box and then click the Performance Settings button in the 3D Performance group.

FIGURE B.15

Tuning graphics performance

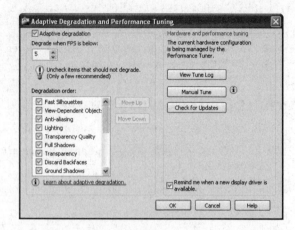

This dialog box offers control over the way AutoCAD displays 3D models when you use the 3D Orbit tool or when you're using a visual style. The following sections describe the options for the Adaptive Degradation And Performance Tuning dialog box.

The Adaptive Degradation Group

The 3D navigation tools enable you to adjust your view in real time, which places high demands on your display system. To maintain the smoothness of the real-time update of your 3D views, AutoCAD degrades the display while performing the view transformations.

The options in the Adaptive Degradation group let you set the level to which the view is degraded while you're navigating your model in real time. You can turn off this feature completely by deselecting the Adaptive Degradation check box. If you prefer, you can determine the specific feature to be degraded on an individual basis by unchecking the check box next to an item name in the Degradation Order list box. The Degrade When FPS Is Below setting lets you set when, in frames per second, the degradation takes effect.

The Hardware and Performance Tuning Group

The Hardware And Performance Tuning group lets you view and adjust your display system's performance. The View Tune Log button displays the vital statistics for your display system. The Manual Tune button opens the Manual Performance Tuning dialog box. The Check For Updates button takes you to the Autodesk website to allow you to see if new drivers are available for your graphics display card.

The Manual Performance Tuning Dialog Box

When you click the Manual Tune button in the Adaptive Degradation And Performance Tuning dialog box, the Manual Performance Tuning dialog box opens (Figure B.16).

The Hardware Settings group lets you determine whether to use hardware acceleration. If you turn on Enable Hardware Acceleration, the Driver Name option becomes available, and the available features for the selected type of acceleration are displayed in the list box.

FIGURE B.16
Manually tuning
performance

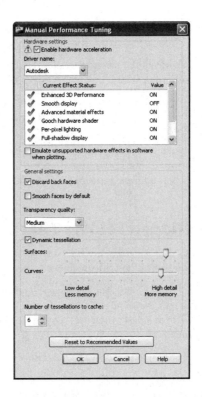

The General Settings group offers three options:

Discard Back Faces   In most 3D rendering systems, surfaces have just one visible side. The back sides of surfaces are invisible. This doesn't matter for objects such as cubes and spheres because you see only one side of a surface at any given time, but in some situations, you can see both sides of a surface, such as a single surface used as a wall.

If your drawing is composed of mostly closed objects such as cubes and spheres and you'll see only one surface, you can select the Discard Back Faces check box to improve system performance. If you have many single surfaces that will be viewed from both sides, you should leave this option turned off.

Smooth Faces By Default   If you are importing objects from 3D Studio Max using the 3DSin command, this option is helpful in displaying PFACE objects smoothly.

Transparency Quality   This option lets you control the visual quality of transparent objects in your model when you're viewing your model in a realistic visual style. You can set transparency to a high-, medium-, or low-quality level. Low-quality levels show transparent objects with a screen-door effect, whereas medium and high options give transparent objects a smoother appearance. The low-quality level allows faster view changes.

The options in the Dynamic Tessellation group determine the smoothness of 3D objects when you use a visual style other than a wireframe or hidden view. To simulate smoothness, the graphics system divides curved surfaces into triangles called *tessellations*. You can turn all these features on or off by using the check box next to the group title:

Surfaces Controls the amount of detail shown for surfaces. Greater detail requires more surface tessellation, which in turn requires more system memory.

Curves Controls the amount of detail shown for curved surfaces. Greater detail requires more surface tessellation, which in turn requires more system memory.

Number Of Tessellations To Cache Controls the number of tessellations that are cached. A *cache* is a part of memory reserved to store frequently used data. AutoCAD always caches one tessellation. Caching two tessellations improves the appearance and performance of 3D objects when you use multiple viewports.

Finding Hidden Folders That Contain AutoCAD Files

Many of AutoCAD's features rely on external files to store settings and other resources. Many of these files reside in hidden folders. These folders are as follows:

```
C:\Documents and Settings\Username\Application
  Data\Autodesk\AutoCAD 2011\R18.1\enu
C:\Documents and Settings\All Users\Application
  Data\Autodesk\AutoCAD 2011\R18.1\enu
```

If you attempt to use Windows Explorer to browse to these locations, you may not find the `Application Data` folder. You can unhide this folder by doing the following:

1. Right-click the Start button in the lower-left corner of your screen, and then choose Explore to open Windows Explorer.

2. Choose Tools ➢ Folder Options from the menu bar.

3. In the Folder Options dialog box, select the View tab.

4. In the Advanced Settings list, look for the Hidden Files And Folders option. You see two radio buttons just below this option.

5. Select the Show Hidden Files And Folders radio button.

6. Click OK to close the Folder Options dialog box.

After you've done this, the `Application Data` folder will be visible and you'll be able to browse to AutoCAD folders that are found there. Once you're able to explore these folders, you may want to create a shortcut to them (right-click the folder and choose Create Shortcut). Place the shortcut on your desktop or other convenient location. That way, you can get to them without having to navigate through several layers of folders.

Appendix C

Hardware and Software Tips

Because some of the items that make up an AutoCAD system aren't found on the typical desktop system, I have provided this appendix to help you understand them. This appendix also discusses ways you can improve AutoCAD's performance through software and hardware.

The Graphics Display

There are two issues to consider concerning the graphics display: *resolution* and *performance.* Fortunately, nearly all computers sold today have display systems that are more than adequate for AutoCAD, thanks to the popularity of 3D games. You do need to make sure that your resolution is set to at least 1024 × 768, preferably higher. The higher your resolution, the more detail you'll be able to see in your drawings.

If you have an older system that needs a graphics display upgrade, you should consider the following factors in choosing a new display.

Contemporary motherboards use high-speed PCI Express (PCIe) slots that offer the fastest video throughput available. Check that your system is of this type. If you're doing only 2D work, you can get by with an older Accelerated Graphics Port (AGP) graphics card. Windows 7, Windows Vista, and Windows XP also provide options for using multiple monitors, an approach that has been popular among AutoCAD users. Multiple monitors enable AutoCAD users to view multiple or large documents more easily.

If you want to take full advantage of AutoCAD's new 3D features, you'll want one of the Autodesk-certified graphics cards in your system. To get the most up-to-date information on the latest graphics-card support, check the Autodesk Service and Support website by doing the following:

1. Enter **3dconfig** at the Command prompt.

2. In the Adaptive Degradation And Performance Tuning dialog box, click the Check For Updates button. Your default browser opens to the Autodesk Service and Support page, where you'll find a description of general hardware issues.

3. Click the Graphics Hardware List option in the left column of the page to go to the page that gives you more detailed information about available graphics hardware drivers.

Even if you already have one of these cards, make sure you have the latest drivers. You can go to the Autodesk web page and download the appropriate driver by doing the following:

1. Choose Options from the Application menu, and select the System tab.

2. Click the Performance Settings button. Then, in the Adaptive Degradation And Performance Tuning dialog box, click the Check For Updates button.

The Autodesk AutoCAD Certified Hardware XML Database page opens. You can locate driver updates on this page.

Pointing Devices

The basic means of communicating with a computer is through its keyboard and pointing device. Most likely you'll use a mouse, but if you're still in the market for a pointing device, choose an input device that generates smooth cursor movement. Some of the lesser-quality input devices cause erratic movement. Because AutoCAD relies on precise input, you may want to upgrade to an optical mouse, which is less likely to wear out or accumulate dirt in its mechanism.

If you need to trace large drawings, you may want to consider a digitizing tablet. It's usually a rectangular object with a penlike *stylus* or a device called a *puck*, which resembles a mouse. It has a smooth surface on which to draw. The most common size is 4″ by 5″, but digitizing tablets are available in sizes up to 60″ by 70″. The tablet gives a natural feel to drawing with the computer because the movement of the stylus or puck is directly translated into cursor movement.

AutoCAD supports Wintab-compatible digitizers. If your digitizer has a Wintab driver, you can use your digitizer as both a tracing device (to trace drawings on a tablet) and a general pointing device for Windows to choose program menu items.

Your Wintab digitizer must be installed and configured under Windows. Make sure it's working in Windows before enabling it in AutoCAD or you won't be able to use the digitizer as a pointing device (mouse). To enable the digitizer in AutoCAD, choose Options from the Application menu to open the Options dialog box, and click the System tab. Open the Current Pointing Device drop-down list, and select Wintab Compatible Digitizer ADI 4.2 – by Autodesk.

Output Devices

Output options vary greatly in quality and price. Quality and paper size are the major considerations for printers. Nearly all printers give accurate drawings, but some produce better line quality than others. Some plotters give merely acceptable results, whereas others are impressive in their speed, color, and accuracy.

AutoCAD can use the Windows 7, Windows Vista, or XP system printer, so any device that Windows supports is also supported by AutoCAD. You can also plot directly to an output device, although Autodesk recommends that you set up your plotter or printer through Windows and then select the device from the Plot Configuration group in the Plot Device tab of the Plot dialog box or the Page Setup dialog box.

Fine-Tuning the Appearance of Output

In Chapter 8, you were introduced to AutoCAD's printing and plotting features. You learned about the AutoCAD features you can use to control the appearance of your output, including layouts and line weights. The following sections cover some of the finer points of printer and plotter setup. You'll find information about controlling how lines overlap, how to include more media sizes, adding plot stamps, adjusting the aspect ratio of your printer, and more.

Making Detailed Adjustments with the Printer/Plotter Configuration Options

If you open the Plot dialog box or the Page Setup dialog box, you see the option groups that offer control over how your plotter or printer works. These groups seem innocent enough, but behind two of them lies a vast set of options that can be quite intimidating. You've already seen in Chapter 8 how the Plot Style Table options work. This section covers the options available when you click the Properties button in the Printer/Plotter group.

The Printer/Plotter Configuration options enable you to adjust those printer or plotter settings that you may want to change only occasionally. These settings are fairly technical and include such items as the port your printer is connected to, the quality of bitmap-image printing, custom paper sizes, and printer calibration, which lets you adjust your plotter for any size discrepancies in output. You won't use most of these settings often, but you should know that they exist just in case you encounter a situation in which you need to make some subtle change to your printer's configuration. You can also use these options to create multiple configurations of the same plotter for quick access to custom settings.

All the settings in this group are stored in a file with the `.pc3` filename extension. You can store and recall any number of configuration files for situations that call for different plotter settings. PC3 files are normally stored in the `Plotters` folder under the following folder:

```
C:\Documents and Settings\Username\
Application Data\Autodesk\AutoCAD 2011\R18.1\enu\
```

Username is your login name. You can access this folder by choosing Print ➢ Manage Plotters from the Application menu.

The Printer/Plotter group in the Plot and Page Setup dialog boxes offers a drop-down list from which you can select a printer or file output configuration. If a PC3 file exists for a plotter configuration, the drop-down list displays it, and the list displays any Windows system printer. After you've selected an output device from the list, you can click the Properties button to access the Plotter Configuration Editor dialog box.

You can configure AutoCAD to create bitmap files in the most common file formats (such as PDF, TIFF, Targa, and PCX) or to create files in Autodesk's DWF file format for the Internet. After you've configured AutoCAD for these types of output, the Plotter Configuration Editor dialog box is where you select the file output type.

The Plotter Configuration Editor dialog box has three tabs: General, Ports, and Device And Document Settings. The General tab displays a list of Windows drivers that this configuration uses, if any, and there is a space for your own comments.

You can access and edit the plotter configuration settings without opening AutoCAD. To do this, locate the PC3 file in the `Plotters` subfolder under the

```
C:\Documents and Settings\Username\Application Data\Autodesk\AutoCAD 2011\
R18.1\enu\
```

folder (*Username* is your login name), and double-click it.

The Ports tab lets you specify where your plotter data is sent. This is where you should look if you're sending your plots to a network plotter or if you decide to create plot files. You can also select the AutoSpool feature, which enables you to direct your plot to an intermediate location for distribution to the appropriate output device.

The Device And Document Settings tab (Figure C.1) is the main part of this dialog box. It offers a set of options ranging from OLE output control to custom paper sizes. The main list box offers options in a hierarchical list, similar to a listing in Windows Explorer. Toward the bottom of the dialog box are the Import, Save As, and Defaults buttons. These buttons let you import configuration settings from earlier versions of AutoCAD, save the current settings as a file, or return the settings to their default values.

FIGURE C.1

The Plotter Configuration Editor's Device And Document Settings tab

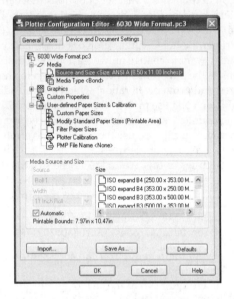

The list has four main categories: Media, Graphics, Custom Properties, and User-Defined Paper Sizes & Calibration. Not all the options under these categories are available for all plotters. When you select an item from this list, the area just below the list displays the options associated with that item. The following sections describe each category and its options, using the Xerox Engineering Systems XES6050 as an example.

THE MEDIA CATEGORY

Some plotters, such as the Xerox Engineering Systems 6050 series, offer options for the source and size of printer media and for the media type. If the Source And Size option is available, the dialog box offers a listing of the sources, such as sheet feed or roll, and the sheet sizes. The Media Type option lets you choose from bond, vellum, or glossy paper or any other medium that is specifically controlled by the plotter. Duplex Printing, when available, controls options for double-sided printing in printers that support this feature. Media Destination, when available, lets you select a destination for output such as collating or stapling in printers that support such features.

THE PHYSICAL PEN CONFIGURATION CATEGORY (SHOWN ONLY FOR PEN PLOTTERS)

Pen plotters have features that diverge from the typical laser or ink-jet printers or plotters. When these options are present, they let you control some of the ways that AutoCAD generates data for pen plotters. Here is a listing of those pen-plotter feature settings:

Prompt For Pen Swapping   Stops the plotter to enable you to switch pens. This feature is designed primarily for single-pen plotters.

Area Fill Correction   Tells AutoCAD to compensate for pen width around the edges of a solid-filled area in order to maintain dimensional accuracy of the plot.

Pen Optimization Level   Sets how AutoCAD sorts pen movement for optimum speed. AutoCAD does a lot of preparation before sending your drawing to the plotter. If you're using a pen plotter, one of the things it does is optimize the way it sends vectors to your plotter so your plotter doesn't waste time making frequent pen changes and moving from one end of the plot to another just to draw a single line.

Physical Pen Characteristics   Lets you assign plotter pen numbers to AutoCAD colors, adjust the speed of individual pens, and assign pen widths.

THE GRAPHICS CATEGORY

These settings give you control over both vector and raster output from your plotter. The Vector Graphics settings let you control resolution and color depth as well as the method for creating shading. If you want to configure your printer for virtual pens, select 255 Virtual Pens under the Color Depth option.

The Raster And Shaded/Rendered Viewports slider gives you control over the quality of any bitmap images. If this slider is placed all the way to the left, raster images aren't plotted. As you move the slider to the right, the raster image quality increases, the speed of printing decreases, and memory requirements increase. The OLE slider controls the quality of OLE linked or embedded files. With the slider all the way to the left, OLE objects aren't printed. As you move the slider farther to the right, OLE image quality and memory requirements increase while speed is reduced.

The Trade-Off slider (Figure C.2) lets you choose how the Raster and OLE sliders improve speed. You can choose between lower resolution and fewer colors.

FIGURE C.2
Use the Trade-Off slider to adjust resolution against the number of colors.

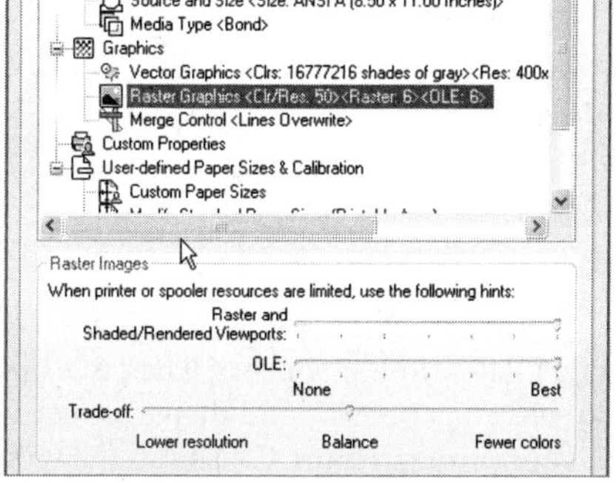

For printers and plotters that support TrueType fonts, the TrueType Text options enable you to select between plotting text as graphics or as TrueType text.

THE CUSTOM PROPERTIES CATEGORY

Select Custom Properties from the Device And Document Settings tab and the Custom Properties button appears in the lower part of the dialog box. This button gives you access to the same printer or plotter settings that are available from the Windows system printer settings. You can also access these settings by choosing Start ➤ Printers And Faxes, right-clicking the desired printer, and choosing Properties from the shortcut menu.

The options offered through the Custom Properties button often duplicate many of the items in the Device and Documents Settings tab. If an option isn't accessible from the Device And Documents tab, select the options under Custom Properties.

THE INITIALIZATION STRING

Some plotters require preinitialization and postinitialization codes in the form of ASCII text strings to get the plotter's attention. If you have such a plotter, this option lets you enter those strings.

USER-DEFINED PAPER SIZES & CALIBRATION

The User-Defined Paper Sizes & Calibration category offers some of the more valuable options in this dialog box. In particular, the Plotter Calibration option can be useful in ensuring the accuracy of your plots.

Plotter Calibration

If your printer or plotter isn't producing an accurate plot, focus on the Plotter Calibration option. If your plotter stretches or shrinks your image in one direction or another, this option lets you adjust the width and height of your plotter's output. To use it, click Plotter Calibration (Figure C.3).

FIGURE C.3
Click the Plotter Calibration node to access the wizard.

A Calibrate Plotter button appears. Click this button to start the Calibrate Plotter Wizard. You're asked first to select a paper size and then to select a width and height for a rectangle that will be plotted with your printer. Figure C.4 shows the wizard screen that asks for the rectangle size.

FIGURE C.4

The Calibrate Plotter Wizard lets you adjust the width and height scaling of your plotter output in order to fine-tune the accuracy of your plots.

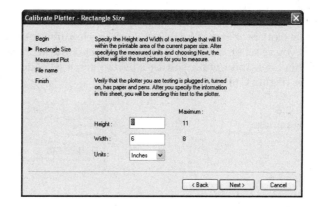

You can use the Calibrate Plotter Wizard to plot a sample rectangle of a specific size. You then measure the rectangle and check its actual dimensions against the dimensions that you entered. If there are any discrepancies between the plotted dimensions and the dimensions you specified, you can enter the actual plotted size and print another test rectangle. You can repeat this process until your plotted rectangle exactly matches the dimensions entered into the wizard.

Toward the end of the Calibrate Plotter Wizard's steps, you're asked to give a name for a Plot Model Parameter (PMP) file that will store your calibration data. The PMP file also stores any custom paper-size information that you input from other parts of the User-Defined Paper Sizes & Calibration options. This file is then associated with the PC3 file that stores your plotter configuration data.

If you have more than one PC3 file for your plotter, you can associate the PMP file with your other PC3 files by using the PMP File Name option (Figure C.5) in the Device And Document Settings tab. You need only one calibration file for each plotter or printer you're using. This option appears under the User-Defined Paper Sizes & Calibration category.

To associate a PMP file with a PC3 plotter configuration file, select the PC3 file from the Name drop-down list in the Printer/Plotter section of the Plot dialog box. Click the Properties button, and then, in the Device And Document Settings tab, click the PMP File Name listing. The PMP options appear in the bottom of the dialog box. Click the Attach button, and then select the PMP file from the Open dialog box. Click OK. You'll see that the PMP file has been added to the PMP filename listing.

FIGURE C.5

Click the PMP File Name node to see PMP options.

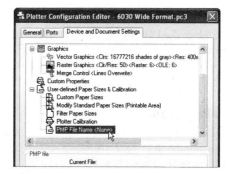

Custom Paper Sizes

Some plotters offer custom paper sizes. This feature is usually available for printers and plotters that you've set up to use the AutoCAD drivers instead of the Windows system drivers. If your plotter offers this option, you see a list box and a set of buttons when you select Custom Paper Sizes (Figure C.6).

FIGURE C.6
Creating a custom paper size

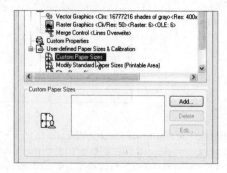

Clicking the Add button starts the Custom Paper Size Wizard, which lets you set the sheet size and margin as well as the paper source. This information is then saved in a PMP file. You're asked to provide a specific name for the custom paper size, which will be listed in the Custom Paper Size list box.

After you've created a custom paper size, you can edit or delete it by clicking the Edit or Delete button in the Custom Paper Sizes options.

Modify Standard Paper Sizes

The last item in the Device And Document Settings tab is the Modify Standard Paper Sizes option. If this option is available, you can adjust the margins of a standard paper size.

If you're using an older pen plotter, you'll see the Physical Pen Configuration options in the Device And Document Settings tab. These additional options give you control over pen speed, pen optimization, and area fill correction.

IMPORT, SAVE AS, AND DEFAULTS

The Import, Save As, and Defaults buttons at the bottom of the Plotter Configuration Editor let you import or save your plotter settings as PC3 files, which you can then load from the Plot Device tab of the Plot dialog box and the Page Setup dialog box, as described earlier in this appendix. The Import button lets you import PCP and PC2 files from earlier versions of AutoCAD. Save As lets you save your current settings under an existing or a new PC3 filename. The Defaults button restores the default settings, if any, for the current plotter configuration.

Adding a Plot Stamp

To help cross-reference your printer or plotter output to AutoCAD drawing files, it's a good idea to add a *plot stamp* to your drawings so you can identify the date, time, and filename of the drawing that generated your plot. To accomplish this, the Plot Stamp feature lets you imprint data onto your plotted drawings, usually in the lower-left corner. In addition, Plot Stamp lets you keep a record of your plots in a log file.

To use Plot Stamp, type **Plotstamp.↵** at the AutoCAD Command prompt. You can also turn on the Plot Stamp On option in the Plot dialog box and then click the Plot Stamp Settings button that appears to the right of the option. The Plot Stamp dialog box opens (see Figure C.7).

FIGURE C.7
The Plot Stamp
dialog box

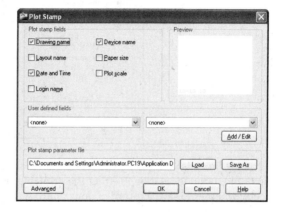

The Plot Stamp dialog box offers several options that let you determine what to include in the stamp.

If the options are grayed out, click the Save As button to save Plot Stamp settings in a new file.

The Plot Stamp Fields group lets you include seven predefined options in your stamp, including drawing, layout, and output device name. The User Defined Fields group lets you add custom text to the stamp. To use this feature, click the Add/Edit button in the User Defined Fields group. The User Defined Fields dialog box opens (Figure C.8).

FIGURE C.8
The User Defined
Fields dialog box

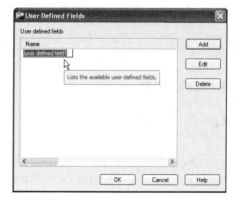

You can use the Add, Edit, or Delete button to add or make changes to the user-defined fields. After you add a field, it appears in both the list boxes in the User Defined Fields group of the Plot Stamp dialog box.

To control the location, orientation, font, and font size of the plot stamp, click the Advanced button in the lower-left corner of the Plot Stamp dialog box to open the Advanced Options dialog box, shown in Figure C.9.

FIGURE C.9
The Advanced
Options dialog box

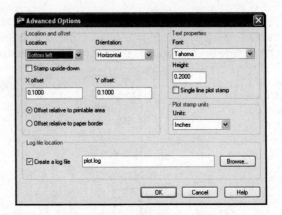

This dialog box lets you specify the orientation of the stamp on the page as well as the exact location of the stamp in relation to either the printable area or the paper border. In addition, you can specify whether to save a record of your plotting activities in a log file by using the options in the Log File Location group.

Controlling How Lines Overlap

Some output devices let you control how overlapping lines and shaded areas affect one another, a feature known as *merge control*. In versions of AutoCAD prior to 2000, merge control was handled through additional commands such as Hpconfig and OCEconfig. AutoCAD 2011 includes merge control as part of the Plotter Configuration Editor dialog box.

You can gain access to merge control by opening the Plotter Configuration Editor and, in the Graphics area of the Device And Document Settings tab, clicking the plus sign next to Graphics to expand the list of Graphics options.

If your device supports merge control, you'll see it listed under Graphics, as shown in Figure C.10.

Filtering Paper Sizes

AutoCAD displays all the available paper sizes for a selected output device in the Page Setup dialog box and the Plot dialog box. For some plotters, the list can be a bit overwhelming. You can filter out paper sizes that you don't need by using the Filter Paper Sizes option in the Plotter Configuration Editor.

Open the Plotter Configuration Editor, and click the plus sign next to the User-Defined Paper Sizes & Calibration item. You see Filter Paper Sizes as an option. After you select this option, you see the Filter Paper Sizes area in the lower half of the Plotter Configuration Editor. Remove the check mark in the box next to any size you won't need.

Filtering Printers

In some instances, you may want to hide the Windows system printer from the list of printers shown in the AutoCAD Plot dialog box. For example, there may be several shared system printers on a network that aren't intended for AutoCAD use, so you wouldn't want those printers to appear in your list of available printers. You can hide a printer by turning on the Hide System

Printers option at the bottom of the General Plot Options group in the Plot And Publish tab of the Options dialog box (choose Options from the Application menu). This limits the selection of printers and plotters to those that have a PC3 plotter configuration. You can further limit the plotter selections by moving any unneeded PC3 files out of the AutoCAD Plotters folder and into another folder for storage.

FIGURE C.10

The location of the Merge Control setting in the Plotter Configuration Editor

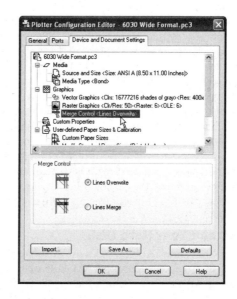

Controlling the Plot-Preview Background Color

If you prefer to use a color other than white for the plot-preview background, you can set the plot-preview background color by using the Color Options dialog box:

1. Choose Options from the Application menu to open the Options dialog box.

2. Select the Display tab.

3. In the Window Elements group, click the Colors button to open the Drawing Window Colors dialog box.

4. Select Plot Preview from the Context list.

5. Select a color from the Color drop-down list.

6. Click the Apply & Close button.

Controlling the Windows Metafile Background Color

If you prefer using the Windows metafile file type to export AutoCAD drawings to other programs, you can control the background color of your exported file. The AutoCAD Wmfbkgnd system variable lets you control the background color of exported Windows metafiles. Wmfbkgnd offers two settings: off generates a transparent background, and on generates the background color of the current view. The initial value is off.

Memory and AutoCAD Performance

Next to your computer's CPU, memory has the greatest impact on AutoCAD's speed. How much you have, and how you use it, can make a big difference in whether you finish that rush job on schedule or work late nights trying. The following sections will clarify some basic points about memory and how AutoCAD uses it.

AutoCAD is a virtual memory system. This means that when your RAM resources reach their limit, part of the data stored in RAM is temporarily moved to your hard disk to make more room in RAM. This temporary storage of RAM to your hard disk is called *virtual memory paging*. Through memory paging, AutoCAD continues to run, even though your work may exceed the capacity of your RAM. The Windows operating system manages this virtual memory paging. If you have several programs open at once, Windows determines how much memory to allocate to each program. AutoCAD always attempts to store as much of your drawing in RAM as possible. When the amount of RAM required for a drawing exceeds the amount of physical RAM in your system, Windows pages parts of the data stored in RAM to the hard disk. Your drawing size, the number of files you have open in AutoCAD, and the number of programs you have open under Windows affect how much RAM you have available. For this reason, if your AutoCAD editing session is slowing down, try closing other applications you may have open or closing files that you're no longer using. This will free up more memory for AutoCAD and the drawing file.

AutoCAD and Your Hard Disk

You'll notice that AutoCAD slows down when paging occurs. If this happens frequently, the best thing you can do is add more RAM. But you can also improve the performance of AutoCAD under these conditions by ensuring that you have adequate hard-disk space and that free hard-disk space has been *defragmented* or *optimized*. A defragmented disk offers faster access, thereby improving paging speed.

Windows dynamically allocates swap-file space. However, make sure there is enough free space on your hard disk to allow Windows to set up the space. A good guideline is to allow enough space for a swap file that is twice the size of your RAM capacity. If you have the minimum 1 GB of RAM, you need to allow space for a 1024 MB swap file (at a minimum). This will give your system 1024 MB of virtual memory. Also consider setting the minimum and maximum swap file space to be equal.

Fast, high-capacity hard disks are fairly inexpensive, so even if you aren't running out of space, you may want to consider adding another hard disk with as much capacity as you can afford. You can greatly improve your system speed by upgrading from an old hard drive to a new one. Consider upgrading to an SATA or SATA2 hard-drive controller and drive. You may also consider a Raid-0 hard-drive setup if your system supports it. Raid-0 can greatly improve the speed of your system by dividing hard-drive access between two drives. Such a system can nearly double access speeds.

Keep Your Hard Disk Clean

If you aren't in the habit of emptying your Recycle Bin, you'll want to get into the habit of doing so. Every file that you "delete" using Windows Explorer is actually passed to the Recycle Bin. You need to clear this out frequently. If you're a regular Internet user, check your Internet cache folder for unnecessary files. You can employ one of the many hard-disk cleaning utilities to do this. Finally, it's a good idea to perform regular maintenance on your hard disk to keep it clear of fragmentation and unused files. The Tools tab of the Properties dialog box for your hard disk offers error-checking and defragmenting options.

AutoCAD Tools to Improve Memory Use

AutoCAD offers some tools to help make your use of system memory more efficient. Partial Open and the Spatial and Layer indexes let you manage the memory use of large drawings and multiple open files by reducing the amount of a file that is loaded into memory. Using these tools, you can have AutoCAD open only those portions of a file that you want to work on.

Using Partial Open to Conserve Memory and Improve Speed

Use the Partial Open option in the File dialog box when you know you're going to work on only a small portion or a particular set of layers of a large drawing. Choose Open from the Application menu, and then locate and select the file you want to open. At the bottom-right corner of the dialog box, click the down arrow next to the Open button and select Partial Open to open the Partial Open dialog box (Figure C.11). Note that this option is available only for files created and edited in AutoCAD 2000 and later.

You can use this dialog box to open specific views of your drawing by selecting the view name from the View Geometry To Load list box. Only the geometry displayed in the selected view is loaded into memory. This doesn't limit you to only that view as you edit the drawing. Subsequent views cause AutoCAD to load their geometry as needed.

You can further limit the amount of a drawing that is loaded into memory by selecting only those layers you want to work with. Place a check mark next to the layers you want in the Layer Geometry To Load list box.

FIGURE C.11
Choosing to open only certain layers

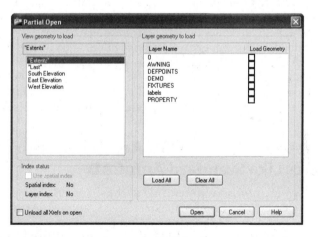

After you open a file by using the Partial Open option, you can always make further adjustments by typing **Partialload**↵ This opens the Partial Load dialog box, which offers the same options as the Partial Open dialog box. The Partial Load dialog box isn't available for files that are opened normally without using the Partial Open option.

Using Spatial and Layer Indexes to Conserve Memory

The Spatial and Layer indexes are lists that keep a record of geometry in a drawing. A *Spatial index* lists a drawing's geometry according to the geometry's location in space. A *Layer index* lists the drawing's geometry according to layer assignments. These indexes offer more-efficient memory use and faster loading times for drawings that are being used as Xrefs. They take effect only when Demand Load is turned on. (See Chapter 7 for more on Demand Load.) The Layer index enables AutoCAD to load only those layers of an Xref that aren't frozen. AutoCAD uses the Spatial index to load only objects in an Xref that are within the boundary of a clipped Xref.

You can turn on the Spatial and Layer indexes for a file through the Indexctl system variable. Indexctl has four settings:

♦ 0 is the default. This turns off Spatial and Layer indexing.

♦ 1 turns on Layer indexing.

♦ 2 turns on Spatial indexing.

♦ 3 turns on both Layer and Spatial indexing.

To use the Indexctl system variable, type **Indexctl**↵. Then, at the `Enter new value for INDEXCTL <0>:` prompt, enter the number of the setting option you want to use.

The Partial Open option in the Select File dialog box includes the Index Status button group, which offers information on the index status of a drawing. If the drawing you're opening has Spatial or Layer indexing turned on, you can use it by selecting the Spatial Index check box.

Using the Incremental Save Percentage to Conserve Disk Space

If your disk is getting crowded and you need to squeeze as many files as you can onto it, you can reduce the amount of wasted space in a file by adjusting the Incremental Save value in the Open And Save tab of the Options dialog box. By setting Incremental Save Percentage to a lower value, you can reduce the size of files to some degree. The trade-off is slower performance when saving files. See Appendix B for more information on this setting.

Another related option is to turn off the BAK file option, also located in the Open And Save tab of the Options dialog box. Each time you save a file, AutoCAD creates a backup copy of your file with the `.bak` filename extension. When you turn off the Create Backup Copy With Each Save option, BAK files aren't created, thereby saving disk space.

Setting Up AutoCAD Architecture to Act Like Standard AutoCAD

Many users who have AutoCAD Architecture 2011 would like to use this book to learn AutoCAD 2011. However, the interface to AutoCAD Architecture is quite different from the standard AutoCAD interface. Still, underneath the AutoCAD Architecture menus and palettes lies the basic AutoCAD program discussed in this book. If you have AutoCAD Architecture 2011, the following instructions show you how to set up a shortcut on your Windows Desktop to launch standard AutoCAD 2011:

1. To make a copy of the AutoCAD Architecture Windows Desktop shortcut, right-click the AutoCAD Architecture 2011 shortcut, and choose Copy.

2. Right-click a blank spot on the Desktop, and choose Paste.

3. Right-click the copy of the AutoCAD Architecture shortcut, and choose Properties.

4. In the Target text box, change the value to read as follows:

```
"C:\Program Files\ AutoCAD Architecture 2011\
acad.exe" /t "acad.dwt" /p "Standard AutoCAD"
```

Note that this example is broken into two lines so it can fit on the page. You should enter it as a single line. The /t is a command switch that tells AutoCAD to use a specific template file, which in this case is acad.dwt. The /p is a command switch that tells AutoCAD to use the Standard AutoCAD profile when starting AutoCAD. Note that the Standard AutoCAD profile doesn't exist. AutoCAD creates it when you attempt to start AutoCAD from the shortcut. Click Apply after you've made the change to the Target text box.

5. Click the Change Icon button, and then click the Browse button in the Change Icon dialog box. From here, you can select a different icon from the Change Icon dialog box.

6. Click OK to exit the Shortcut Properties dialog box. Then, right-click the shortcut copy again and choose Rename.

7. Rename the shortcut to **AutoCAD 2011**.

Double-click your new AutoCAD 2011 Desktop shortcut to start AutoCAD 2011. You'll see a warning message that the Standard AutoCAD profile doesn't exist and that AutoCAD will create it using the default AutoCAD settings. Once AutoCAD has started, the title bar will still show AutoCAD Architecture 2011, but the program will behave like standard AutoCAD 2011. You can still start the full version of AutoCAD Architecture by using the AutoCAD Architecture 2011 shortcut or if you launch AutoCAD by double-clicking an AutoCAD file.

When Things Go Wrong

AutoCAD is a complex program and at times doesn't behave the way you expect. If you run into problems, chances are they won't be insurmountable. Here are a few tips on what to do when AutoCAD doesn't work the way you expect.

Starting Up or Opening a File

The most common reason you'll have difficulty opening a file is a lack of free disk space. If you encounter errors attempting to open files, check whether you have adequate free disk space on all your drives.

If you've recently installed AutoCAD but you can't start it, you may have a configuration problem. Before you panic, try reinstalling AutoCAD from scratch. Particularly if you're installing the DVD version, this doesn't take long. (See Appendix B for installation instructions.) Before you reinstall AutoCAD, use the Uninstall program to remove the current version of AutoCAD. After you've uninstalled AutoCAD, delete the AutoCAD 2011 folder from the Program Files folder and also delete the AutoCAD 2011 folders under the following two locations:

```
C:\Documents and Settings\Username\Application Data\Autodesk
C:\Documents and Settings\Username\Local Settings\Application Data\Autodesk
```

Make sure you have your authorization code, serial number, and CD key handy. Make sure you've closed all other programs when you run the AutoCAD installation. As a final measure, restart your computer when you've completed the installation.

Restoring Corrupted Files

Hardware failures can result in data files becoming corrupted. When this happens, AutoCAD is unable to open the drawing file. Fortunately, there is hope for damaged files. In most cases, AutoCAD runs through a file-recovery routine automatically the next time you open it after a crash. You'll see a panel on the left side of the AutoCAD window listing files that are available for recovery, including BAK files. You can double-click the file you want to recover and then save it.

If you have a file you know is corrupted but it doesn't appear in the panel described in the previous paragraph, you can start the file-recovery utility by choosing Drawing Utilities ➤ Recover from the Application menu. This opens the Select File dialog box, enabling you to select the file you want to recover. After you enter the name, AutoCAD goes to work. You'll see a series of messages, most of which have little meaning to the average user. Then the recovered file is opened. You may lose some data, but a partial file is better than no file at all, especially when the file represents several days of work.

Another possibility is to attempt to recover your drawing from the BAK file—the last saved version before your drawing was corrupted. Rename the BAK file as a DWG file with a different name, and then open it. The drawing will contain only what was in your drawing when it was previously saved.

If you want to restore a file that you've just been working on, you can check the file with the alphanumeric name and the `.sv$` filename extension. This is the file AutoCAD uses to store your drawing during automatic saves. Change the `.sv$` filename extension to `.dwg`, and then open the file.

In some situations, a file is so badly corrupted it can't be restored. By backing up frequently, you can minimize the inconvenience of such an occurrence. You may also want to consider a third-party utility that performs regular disk maintenance.

Troubleshooting Other Common Problems

AutoCAD is a large and complex program, so you're bound to encounter difficulties from time to time. This section covers a few of the more common problems experienced while using AutoCAD.

You cannot open a file that others in your group are able to open. This may be happening because you have a corrupted temporary file. You can usually correct this problem by doing the following: Open the AutoCAD temporary drawing file location. This is usually `C:\Documents and Settings\`*Username*`\local settings\temp\`, where *Username* is your Windows username. Delete the SV$ and AC$ files from this folder. Note that the SV$ files are the automatic save files and you can restore them to regular AutoCAD files by changing the `.sv$` filename extension to `.dwg`.

You can see but can't select objects in a drawing someone else has worked on. This may be happening because you have a Paper Space view instead of a Model Space view. To make sure you're in Model Space, type **Tilemode**↵ and then type **1**↵. Alternatively, you can turn on the UCS icon (by typing **Ucsicon**↵**On**↵). If you see the triangular UCS icon in the lower-left corner, you're in Paper Space. You must go to Model Space before you can edit the drawing. Another item to check is the layer lock setting. If a layer is locked, you can't edit objects on that layer.

Grips don't appear when objects are selected.   Make sure the Grips feature is enabled. See Appendix B for details.

Selecting objects doesn't work as described in this book.   Check the Selection settings to make sure they're set the same way as the exercise specifies. See "Selecting Objects" in Chapter 2 for details. Also check the Selection tab in the Options dialog box (choose Options from the Application menu). See Appendix B for more on the Selection tab of the Options dialog box.

Text appears in the wrong font style or an error message says AutoCAD can't find font files. When you're working on files from another company, it's not uncommon that you'll encounter a file that uses special third-party fonts you don't have. You can usually substitute standard AutoCAD fonts for any fonts you don't have without adverse effects. AutoCAD automatically displays a dialog box that lets you select font files for the substitution. You can either choose a font file or press the Esc key to ignore the message. (See Chapter 10 for more on font files.) If you choose to ignore the error message, you may not see some of the text that would normally appear in the drawing.

You can't import DXF files.   Various problems can occur during the DXF import, the most common of which is that you're trying to import a DXF file into an existing drawing rather than a new drawing. Under some conditions, you can import a DXF file into an existing drawing by using the Dxfin command, but AutoCAD may not import the entire file.

To ensure that your entire DXF file is safely imported, choose Open from the Application menu, and select *.DXF from the File Type drop-down list. Then import your DXF file.

If you know that the DXF file you're trying to import is in the ASCII format and not a binary DXF, look at the file with a text editor. If it contains odd-looking lines of characters, chances are the file is damaged or contains extra data that AutoCAD can't understand. Try deleting the odd-looking lines of characters, and then import the file again. (Make a backup copy of the file before you attempt this.)

A file can't be saved to disk.   Frequently, a hard disk will fill up quickly during an editing session. AutoCAD can generate temporary and swap files many times larger than the file you're editing. This may leave you with no room to save your file. If this happens, you can empty the Recycle Bin to clear some space on your hard disk or delete old AutoCAD BAK files you don't need. *Don't delete temporary AutoCAD files.*

The keyboard shortcuts for commands aren't working.   If you're working on an unfamiliar computer, chances are the keyboard shortcuts (or command aliases) have been altered. The command aliases are stored in the `Acad.pgp` file. Use the Windows Search utility to locate this file, and make sure the `Acad.pgp` file is in the `C:\Documents and Settings\`*Username*`\ Application Data\Autodesk\AutoCAD 2011\R18.1\enu\Support` folder.

Plots come out blank.   Check the scale factor you're using for your plot. Often, a blank plot means your scale factor is making the plot too large to fit on the sheet. Try plotting with the Scale To Fit option. If you get a plot, you know your scale factor is incorrect. See Chapter 8 for more on plotting options. Check your output before you plot by using the Full Preview option in the Plot Configuration dialog box. In addition, if only parts of a drawing are not showing up in a plot, try running the Audit command.

Dimensions appear as objects or lines and text and don't act as described in this book. The Dimassoc system variable has been set to 0 or was 0 when the dimension was created. Another possibility is that the dimension was reduced to its component objects via the Explode command. Make sure Dimassoc is on by typing **Dimassoc↵2↵**. Unfortunately, an exploded dimension or one that was created with Dimassoc turned off can't be converted to a true dimension object. You must redraw the dimension.

A file containing an Xref appears to be blank, or parts are missing. AutoCAD can't find the Xref file. Use the External References palette (click the External References tool on the Insert tab's Reference panel title bar) to reestablish a connection with the Xref file. After the External References palette is open, select the missing Xref from the list, and then click the Found At option in the Details panel of the palette. Click the Browse button in the input box to the right of the Found At option and locate and select the file by using the Browse dialog box.

You may also want to run the Audit tool to make sure your current and Xref files are not corrupted. Choose Drawing Utilities ➢ Audit from the Application menu.

As you draw, little marks appear on your screen where you have selected points. The Blipmode system variable is on. Turn it off by typing **Blipmode↵off↵**.

A file you want to open is read-only, even though you know no one else on the network is using it. Every now and then, you may receive a file that you can't edit because it's read-only. This frequently happens with files that have been archived to a CD. If you have a file that is read-only, try the following:

1. Locate the read-only file with Windows Explorer, and right-click its filename.

2. Choose Properties from the shortcut menu to open the Properties dialog box.

3. Click the General tab.

4. Click the Read-Only check box to remove the check mark.

Tracking vectors don't appear in the drawing as described in this book. Make sure that the AutoTrack features are turned on. See the discussion of the Drafting tab in the Options dialog box in Appendix B.

The hyperlink icon doesn't appear as described in Chapter 29. Make sure the hyperlink options are turned on in the User Preferences tab in the Options dialog box.

When you open new files, the drawing area isn't the same as described in this book. Make sure you're using the correct default unit style for new drawings. In the Create New Drawing dialog box, click the Start From Scratch button and select the appropriate unit style from the Default Settings button group. If you're using feet and inches, select Imperial (feet and inches). If you're using metric measurements, select Metric. AutoCAD uses the `acad.dwt` file template for new Imperial measurement drawings and the `acadiso.dwt` template for metric measurement drawings. You can also use the Measureinit system variable to set the default unit style.

When you offset polylines, such as rectangles or polygons, the offset object has extra line segments or rounded corners. Set the Offsetgaptype system variable to 0. Offsetgaptype controls the behavior of the line segments of offset polylines. When Offsetgaptype is set to 0, the individual line segments of a polyline are extended to join end to end. When Offsetgaptype is set to 1, the line segments retain their original length and are joined with an arc. If Offsetgaptype is set to 2, the line segments retain their original length and are joined by a straight-line segment.

Your older AutoCAD file contains filled areas that were once transparent, but in AutoCAD 2011 the text and line work are obscured by solid fills.   Earlier versions of AutoCAD let you adjust the Merge Control feature of your plotter, which in turn allowed solid filled areas to appear transparent. The Merge Control feature is still available, but it has been moved to the Plotter Configuration Editor. See the section "Controlling How Lines Overlap" earlier in this appendix.

Another option is to use the Draworder command to move the solid filled area behind other objects in the drawing. See Chapter 14 for more on the Draworder command.

Filled, non-TrueType fonts appear to have extraneous lines around the edges.   If your font looks distorted and lines appear around the edges, it may be due to a setting in the plot style table. Open the plot style table for your drawing (see Chapter 9), and make sure the Line End Style setting for the text's layer or plot style is set to Use Object End Style.

Appendix D

System Variables and Dimension Styles

AutoCAD is a complex program with a vast set of options and settings. You don't need to know everything about AutoCAD to be a productive user, but it does help to be aware of some of the inner workings that let you fine-tune the program.

This appendix covers a few of the details that can help you get tighter control over the way AutoCAD works. You'll find a brief discussion of system variables that give you direct control over options and features. That discussion is followed by a detailed look at dimension styles settings.

System Variables

System variables let you fine-tune your AutoCAD environment. Most of the system variables control the same options you find in AutoCAD's dialog boxes and palettes. The main advantage of system variables is that you can set them without having to dig through a series of dialog boxes.

To set a system variable, you enter the variable name at the Command prompt. Or, if you're in the middle of another command, you can set a system variable by entering the variable name preceded by an apostrophe. For example, if you're drawing a series of line segments, you can enter ´Snapang.⌐ at the `Specify next point or [Undo}:` prompt to change the Snapang system variable on the fly.

Because system variables are command-line driven and don't require access to a dialog box, you can use them in your custom macros to control settings. You can also access system variables through AutoLISP by using the Getvar and Setvar functions as well as through ActiveX automation. LT users can use the Modemacro command and the Diesel macro language to obtain information from the system variables. (See Chapter 28 for more on Modemacro and Diesel.)

A list of the system variables and their functions could take up a full chapter. A detailed look at system variables is beyond the scope of this book, but you have an excellent resource for information about system variables in the AutoCAD 2011 Help website. Click the Help tool (the question mark icon) in the InfoCenter to open the AutoCAD 2011 Help website, or you can press the F1 key. Select the Command Reference option in the left panel and then select System Variables just to the right of the list. You see the system variables listed in alphabetical order.

You can also find system variables through the features and commands they control. For example, if you search for *Grip* in the AutoCAD 2011 Help website (Figure D.1), you'll see Use Grip Mode at the top of a list. Select this option and a page describing the grip modes is displayed. Toward the bottom of this page, you'll find the system variables for the grip mode.

FIGURE D.1
Getting help
with the system
variables

Taking a Closer Look at the Dimension Style Dialog Boxes

As you saw in Chapter 12, you can control the appearance and format of dimensions through dimension styles. You can create new dimension styles or edit existing ones. The following sections describe all the components of the dialog boxes you use to create and maintain dimension styles.

The Dimension Style Manager Dialog Box

The Dimension Style Manager dialog box is the gateway to dimension styles. With this dialog box, you can create a new dimension style, edit existing dimension styles, or make an existing dimension style current. To open the Dimension Style Manager dialog box (Figure D.2), click the Dimension Style tool on the Annotate tab's Dimensions panel or type **Dimstyle**⏎.

FIGURE D.2
The Dimension
Style Manager

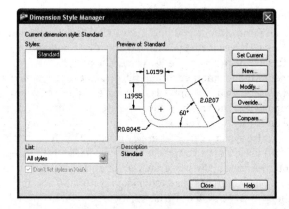

You can use the DesignCenter to import dimension styles from one drawing into another. The following sections describe the options in the Dimension Style Manager dialog box.

PREVIEW OF

The image in the right half of the Dimension Style Manager dialog box gives you a preview of your dimension style. It shows a sample of most of the types of dimensions you'll use, formatted the way you specified when you created or modified your dimension style.

THE STYLES LIST BOX

The Styles list box displays the available dimension styles. You can highlight the dimension style names in the Styles list box to indicate a style to be used with the Set Current, New, Modify, and Override options. You can also right-click a style name and then rename or delete the selected style.

THE LIST DROP-DOWN LIST

The List drop-down list lets you control what is listed in the Styles list box. You can display either all the styles available or only the styles in use in the drawing.

DON'T LIST STYLES IN XREFS

The Don't List Styles In Xrefs check box lets you specify whether dimension styles in Xrefs are listed in the Styles list box. This option is grayed out if no Xrefs are present in the current drawing.

THE SET CURRENT BUTTON

The Set Current button lets you set the dimension style highlighted in the Styles list box to be current.

THE NEW BUTTON

The New button lets you create a new dimension style. It uses the dimension style that is highlighted in the Styles list box as the basis for the new style. Clicking New opens the Create New Dimension Style dialog box.

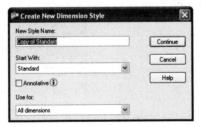

In the Create New Dimension Style dialog box, you can enter the name for your new dimension style. You can also select the source dimension style on which your new dimension style will be based.

New Style Name   Lets you specify the name for your new dimension style.

Start With   Lets you select an existing style on which to base your new dimension style.

Annotative   Lets you turn on the Annotation Scale feature for the style you are creating. See Chapter 10 for more on the Annotation Scale feature.

Use For   Lets you choose a dimension type for your new dimension style. For a completely new dimension style, use the All Dimensions option in the Use For drop-down list. If you want to modify the specifications for a particular dimension type of an existing dimension style, select a dimension type from this list. Your modified dimension type will appear in the

Styles list box under the main style you specify in the Start With drop-down list. After you've modified a dimension type, the new type will be applied to any new dimensions.

After you've entered your options in the Create New Dimension Style dialog box, click Continue. You see the New Dimension Style dialog box described later. When you're finished setting up your new style, it's listed in the Styles list box.

THE MODIFY BUTTON

The Modify button lets you modify the dimension style that is selected in the Styles list box. Clicking this option opens the Modify Dimension Style dialog box. See the section 'New/ Modify/Override Dimension Style Dialog Box' described later in this appendix.

THE OVERRIDE BUTTON

The Override button lets you create a temporary dimension style based on an existing style. You may want to use this option if you need to create a dimension that differs only slightly from an existing style.

To use the Override option, select a style from the Styles list box, and then click Override. You'll see the Override Current Style dialog box described later. After you create an override, it's listed as <style overrides> in the Styles list box, right under the style you used to create the override.

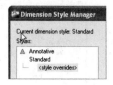

The override then becomes the default dimension style until you select another one from the Styles list. When you select a different style to be current, a message tells you that the unsaved style will be discarded. To save an override style, select the override from the Styles list box and click New. Then click Continue in the Create New Dimension Style dialog box, and click OK in the New Dimension Style dialog box. You can also merge the override style with its source style by right-clicking <style overrides> and selecting Save To Current Style.

THE COMPARE BUTTON

The Compare button lets you compare the differences between two dimension styles. When you click the Compare button, the Compare Dimension Styles dialog box opens (Figure D.3).

You can select the two styles you want to compare from the Compare and With drop-down lists. The differences appear in the list box. Just above the upper-right corner of the list box is a Copy button; this copies the contents of the list box to the Windows Clipboard, enabling you to save the comparison to a word-processing document.

FIGURE D.3
Comparing two
dimension styles

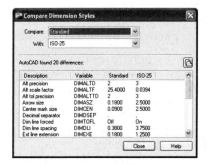

The New/Modify/Override Dimension Style Dialog Box

When you click the New button in the Dimension Style Manager dialog box and then click Continue in the Create New Dimension Style dialog box, the New Dimension Style dialog box opens.

You'll also see this same dialog box under a different name when you click the Modify or Override button in the Dimension Style Manager dialog box. Clicking Modify brings up the Modify Dimension Style dialog box and clicking Override brings up the Override Current Style dialog box. The options in these dialog boxes let you determine all the characteristics of your dimension style. The following sections provide detailed descriptions of each available option.

The equivalent dimension style variables are shown in brackets at the end of the description of each option.

THE LINES TAB

The options in this tab (Figure D.4) give you control over the appearance of dimension and extension lines. Figure D.5 shows an example of some of the dimension components that are affected by these options. The values you enter here for distances should be in final plot sizes and will be multiplied by the dimension scale value in the Fit tab to derive the actual extension distance in the drawing.

FIGURE D.4
The Lines tab

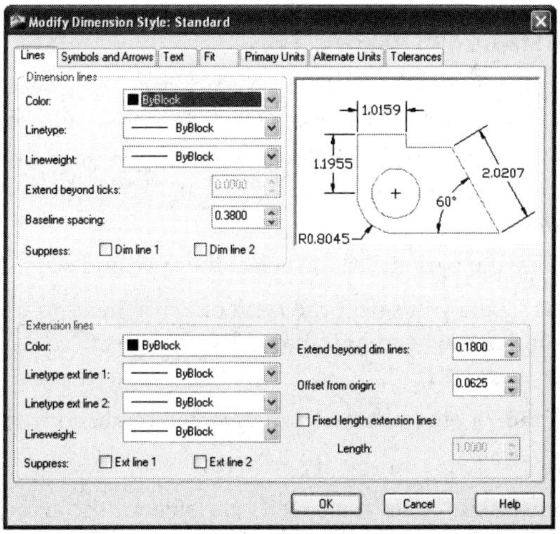

The Dimension Lines Group

The following options let you control the general behavior and characteristics of the dimension lines:

Color   Lets you set the color of the dimension line [Dimclrd].

Linetype   Lets you set the linetype for dimension lines.

Lineweight   Lets you set the line weight for dimension lines [Dimlwd].

Extend Beyond Ticks   Lets you set the distance that the dimension line extends beyond the extension lines. [Dimdle].

Baseline Spacing   Lets you specify the distance between stacked dimensions [Dimdli].

Suppress   Check boxes let you suppress the dimension line on either side of the dimension text [Dim Line1, Dim Line 2].

The Extension Lines Group

The following options let you control the general behavior and characteristics of the extension lines:

Color   Lets you set the color for extension lines [Dimclre].

Linetype Ext Line 1   Controls the linetype for the first extension line.

Linetype Ext Line 2   Controls the linetype for the second extension line.

Lineweight   Lets you set the line weight for extension lines [Dimlwe].

Extend Beyond Dim Lines   Lets you set the distance that extension lines extend beyond dimension lines [Dimexe].

Offset From Origin   Lets you set the distance from the extension line to the object being dimensioned [Dimexo].

Fixed Length Extension Lines   Lets you set the extension lines to a fixed length. The Length input box provides a space to enter the length you want.

Suppress   Check boxes let you suppress one or both extension lines [Ext Line 1, Ext Line 2].

THE SYMBOLS AND ARROWS TAB

The options in this tab give you control over the appearance of arrowheads and center marks. The values you enter in this tab for distances should be in final plot sizes and will be multiplied by the dimension scale value in the Fit tab to derive the actual extension distance in the drawing.

Arrowheads

The following options let you select the type and sizes of arrowheads for dimensions and leaders:

First   Lets you select the type of arrowhead to use on dimension lines. By default, the second arrowhead automatically changes to match the arrowhead you specify for this setting [Dimblk1].

Second   Lets you select a different arrowhead from the one you select for First [Dimblk2].

Leader   Lets you specify an arrowhead for leader notes [Dimldrblk].

Arrow Size   Lets you specify the size for the arrowheads [Dimasz].

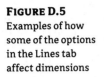

FIGURE D.5

Examples of how
some of the options
in the Lines tab
affect dimensions

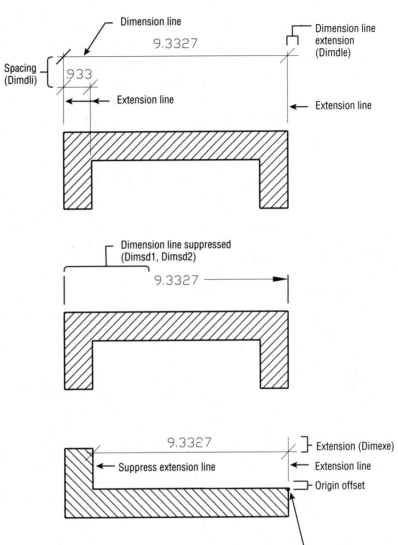

The Center Marks Group

The following options let you set the center mark for radius and diameter dimensions:

None/Mark/Line   Lets you select the type of center mark used in radius and diameter
dimensions. The Mark option draws a small cross mark, Line draws a cross mark and center
lines, and None draws nothing [Dimcen].

Size input box   Lets you specify the size of the center mark [Dimcen].

The Arc Length Symbol Group

This set of radio buttons controls the display of the arc-length symbol in arc-length dimensions:

Preceding Dimension Text   Places the symbol before the dimension text.

Above Dimension Text   Places the symbol above the dimension text.

None   No symbol.

The Radius Jog Dimension Group

You can set the angle of the radius-dimension jog with this setting. The radius-dimension jog is the short line in the radius dimension that indicates that the dimension is measured to a point out of view.

The Linear Jog Dimension Group

You can set the size of the linear-dimension jog with this setting. The linear-dimension jog is the zigzag line that indicates a break in the dimension line.

THE TEXT TAB

The options in the Text tab (Figure D.6) give you control over the appearance of the dimension text. You can set the text style and default location of text in relation to the dimension line. If the text style you select for your dimension text has a height value of 0, you can set the text height from this tab.

FIGURE D.6

The Text tab

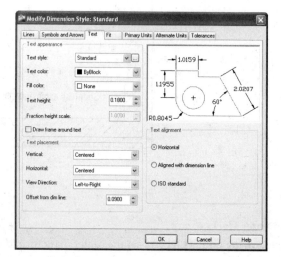

The Text Appearance Group

The following options give you control over the appearance of text:

Text Style   Lets you select an existing text style for your dimension text. You can also create a new style for your dimension text by clicking the Browse button [Dimtxsty].

Text Color Lets you select a color for your dimension text [Dimclrt].

Fill Color Lets you select a color for your dimension background.

Text Height Lets you specify a text height for dimension text. This option is valid only for text styles with 0 height [Dimtxt].

Fraction Height Scale Lets you specify a scale factor for the height of fractional text. This option is available only when Architectural or Fractional is selected in the Primary Units tab [Dimtfac].

Draw Frame Around Text When this option is selected, it draws a rectangle around the dimension text [Dimgap].

The Text Placement Group

The following options give you control over the placement of text, including the ability to specify the distance of text from the dimension line:

Vertical Lets you set the vertical position of the text in relation to the dimension line. The options are Centered, Above, Outside, and JIS. Centered places the text in line with the dimension line; the dimension line is broken to accommodate the text. Above places the text above the dimension line, leaving the dimension line unbroken. Outside places the text away from the dimension line at a location farthest from the object being dimensioned. JIS places the text in conformance with the Japanese Industrial Standards [Dimtad].

Horizontal Lets you set the location of the text in relation to the extension lines. The options are Centered, At Ext Line 1, At Ext Line 2, Over Ext Line 1, and Over Ext Line 2. Centered places the text between the two extension lines. At Ext Line 1 places the text next to the first extension line but still between the two extension lines. At Ext Line 2 places the text next to the second extension line but still between the two extension lines. Over Ext Line 1 places the text above and aligned with the first extension line. Over Ext Line 2 places the text above and aligned with the second extension line the second extension line [Dimjust].

View Direction Lets you set the direction of dimension text. The default is Left-to-Right, but you can also set it to Right-to-Left [Dtxtdirection].

Offset From Dim Line Lets you determine the distance from the baseline of text to the dimension line when text is placed above the dimension line. It also lets you set the size of the gap between the dimension text and the endpoint of the dimension line when the text is in line with the dimension line. You can use this option to set the margin around the text when the dimension text is in a centered position that breaks the dimension line into two segments [Dimgap].

The Text Alignment Group

The following options give you control over the alignment of text in relation to the dimension line:

Horizontal Keeps the text in a horizontal orientation regardless of the dimension line orientation.

Aligned With Dimension Line Aligns the text with the dimension line.

ISO Standard Aligns the text with the dimension line when it's between the extension lines; otherwise the text is oriented horizontally [Dimtih, Dimtoh].

THE FIT TAB

The options in the Fit tab (Figure D.7) let you fine-tune the behavior of the dimension text and arrows under special conditions. For example, you can select an optional placement for text and arrows when there isn't enough room for them between the extension lines.

FIGURE D.7

The Fit tab

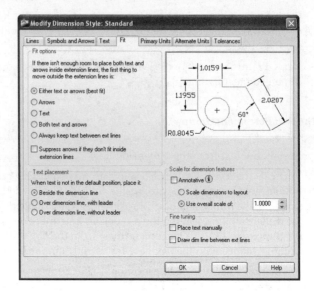

The Fit Options Group

The Fit Options radio buttons let you determine which dimension component is moved when there isn't enough room between the extension lines for either the text or the arrows or both:

Either Text Or Arrows (Best Fit)   Automatically determines whether only text, only arrows, or both text and arrows will fit between the extension lines, and then places them accordingly. For example, if there isn't enough room for both text and arrows and the text is wider than the two arrows combined, the text is placed outside the extension lines. If the width of the arrows is greater than the width of the text, the arrows are moved outside the extension lines. If the gap between the extension lines is too narrow for either the text or arrows, both the arrows and the text are moved outside the extension lines [Dimatfit].

Arrows   Moves the arrows outside the extension lines when there isn't enough room for both arrows and text between the extension lines. If the gap between the extension lines is too narrow for either the text or the arrows, both the arrows and the text are moved outside the extension lines [Dimatfit].

Text   Moves the text outside the extension lines when there isn't enough room for both arrows and text between the extension lines. If the gap between the extension lines is too narrow for either the text or the arrows, both the arrows and the text are moved outside the extension lines [Dimatfit].

Both Text And Arrows   Moves both the text and the arrows outside the extension lines when there isn't enough room for both arrows and text between the extension lines [Dimatfit].

Always Keep Text Between Ext Lines   Places the text between the extension lines regardless of whether the text fits there [Dimtix].

Suppress Arrows If They Don't Fit Inside Extension Lines   Removes the arrows entirely if they don't fit between the extension lines [Dimsoxd].

The Text Placement Group

The Text Placement radio buttons determine how the dimension text behaves when it's moved from its default location:

Beside The Dimension Line   Keeps the text in its normal location relative to the dimension line [Dimtmove].

Over Dimension Line, With Leader   Lets you move the dimension text independent of the dimension line. A leader is added between the dimension line and the text [Dimtmove].

Over Dimension Line, Without Leader   Lets you move the dimension text independent of the dimension line. No leader is added [Dimtmove].

The Scale for Dimension Features Group

These options offer control over the scale of the dimension components. You can set a fixed scale, or you can allow the dimension components to be scaled depending on the Paper Space viewport in which they're displayed:

Annotative   Turns on the Annotative Scale feature, which lets you quickly set the size of text to correspond with your drawing's annotation or viewport scale setting [Annotativedwg].

Scale Dimensions To Layout   Scales all the dimension components to the scale factor assigned to the Paper Space viewport in which the drawing appears [Dimscale].

Use Overall Scale Of   Lets you determine the scale of the dimension components. All the settings in the Dimension Style dialog box are scaled to the value you set in the input box if this radio button is selected [Dimscale].

The Fine Tuning Group

The following two check boxes offer miscellaneous settings for dimension text and dimension lines:

Place Text Manually   Enables you to manually place the dimension text horizontally along the dimension line when you're inserting dimensions in your drawing [Dimupt].

Draw Dim Line Between Ext Lines   Forces AutoCAD to draw a dimension line between the extension lines no matter how narrow the distance is between the extension lines [Dimtofl].

THE PRIMARY UNITS TAB

The options in the Primary Units tab (Figure D.8) let you set the format and content of the dimension text, including the unit style for linear and angular dimensions.

FIGURE D.8

The Primary
Units tab

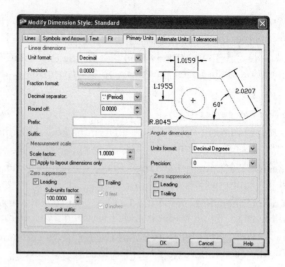

The Linear Dimensions Group

The following options give you control over the unit style and the formatting of dimension text for linear dimensions:

Unit Format   Lets you determine the unit style of the dimension text. The options are Scientific, Decimal, Engineering, Architectural, Fractional, and Windows Desktop. You must set this option independent of the overall drawing units setting (choose Drawing Utilities ➢ Units from the Application menu) if you want the dimension text to appear in the appropriate style [Dimunit].

Precision   Lets you set the precision of the dimension text. This option rounds off the dimension text to the nearest precision value you set. It doesn't affect the actual precision of the drawing [Dimdec].

Fraction Format   Available only for Architectural and Fractional unit formats. This option lets you select between vertically stacked, diagonally stacked, and horizontal fractions [Dimfrac].

Decimal Separator   Lets you select a decimal separator for dimension unit formats that display decimals. You can choose a period, a comma, or a space. If you want to use a dimension separator not included in the list, you can use the Dimsep system variable to specify a custom dimension separator [Dimsep].

Round Off   Lets you determine the degree of rounding applied to dimensions. For example, you can set this option to 0.25 to round off dimensions to the nearest 0.25, or 1/4, of a unit [Dimrnd].

Prefix   Lets you include a prefix for all linear-dimension text. For example, if you want all your linear dimension text to be preceded by the word *Approximately,* you can enter **Approximately** in this input box. Control codes can be used for special characters. See Chapter 10 for more information on character codes [Dimpost].

Suffix   Lets you include a suffix for all linear-dimension text. Control codes can be used for special characters. See Chapter 10 for more information on character codes [Dimpost].

The Measurement Scale Group

This group offers options that can convert dimension values to different scale factors. For example, dimensions in Imperial units can be scaled to metric and vice versa. The options are as follows:

Scale Factor   Lets you set a scale factor for the dimension text. This option scales the value of the dimension text to the value you enter. For example, if you want your dimensions to display distances in centimeters, even though the drawing was created in inches, you can enter **2.54** for this option. Your dimension text will then display dimensions in centimeters. Conversely, if you want your dimension text to show dimensions in inches, even though you've created your drawing using centimeters, you enter **0.3937** (the inverse of 2.54) for this option [Dimlfac].

Apply To Layout Dimensions Only   Causes AutoCAD to apply the measurement scale factor to Paper Space layouts only. With this check box selected, the Dimlfac dimension variable gives a negative value [Dimlfac].

The Zero Suppression Group

Lets you suppress zeros so they don't appear in the dimension text. For dimensions other than architectural, you can suppress leading and trailing zeros. For example, 0.500 becomes .500 if you suppress leading zeros. It becomes 0.5 if you suppress trailing zeros. For architectural dimensions, you can suppress zero feet or zero inches, although typically you wouldn't suppress zero inches [Dimzin].

Sub-Units Factor lets you control the number of places for numbers to the right of the decimal point. This is helpful if you are working in metric measurements. Sub-Unit Suffix allows you to add a suffix to a dimension. For example, you can enter *cm* here to display centimeter abbreviation after a sub-unit value.

The Angular Dimensions Group

The following options enable you to format angle dimensions:

Units Format   Lets you select a format for angular dimensions. The options are Decimal Degrees, Degrees Minutes Seconds, Gradians, and Radians [Dimaunit].

Precision   Lets you set the precision for the angular dimension text [Dimadec].

Zero Suppression   The check boxes in this group let you suppress leading or trailing zeros in angular dimensions. For example, 0.500 becomes .500 if you suppress leading zeros. It becomes 0.5 if you suppress trailing zeros. [Dimazin].

THE ALTERNATE UNITS TAB

The Alternate Units tab (Figure D.9) lets you apply a second set of dimension text labels for dimensions. This second set of text labels can be used for alternate dimension styles or units. Typically, alternate units are used to display dimensions in metric if your main dimensions are in feet and inches.

Select the Display Alternate Units check box to turn on alternate units. This causes AutoCAD to include additional dimension text in the format you specify in the Alternate Units tab [Dimalt].

FIGURE D.9
The Alternate
Units tab

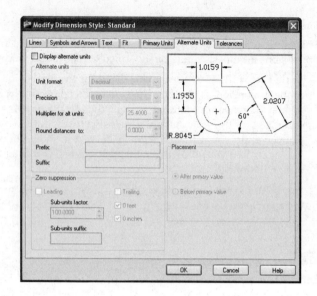

The Alternate Units Group

The following options offer control over the unit style and the formatting of dimension text for linear dimensions:

Unit Format   Lets you determine the unit style of the dimension text. The options are Scientific, Decimal, Engineering, Architectural Stacked, Fractional Stacked, Architectural, Fractional, and Windows Desktop. You must set this option independent of the overall drawing units setting (choose Drawing Utilities ➢ Units from the Application menu) if you want the dimension text to appear in the appropriate style [Dimaltu]. You can adjust the size of fractions relative to the main dimension text by using the Dimfac dimension variable.

Precision   Lets you set the precision of the dimension text. This option rounds off the dimension text to the nearest precision value you set. It doesn't affect the actual precision of the drawing [Dimaltd].

Multiplier For Alt Units   Lets you set a multiplier value for the dimension text. This option multiplies the value of the dimension text by the value you enter. For example, if you want your alternate dimensions to display distances in centimeters even though the drawing was created in inches, you can enter **2.54** for this option. Your alternate dimension text will then display dimensions in centimeters. Conversely, if you want to have your alternate dimension text show dimensions in inches, even though you've created your drawing by using centimeters, you enter **0.3937** (the inverse of 2.54) for this option [Dimaltf].

Round Distances To   Lets you determine the degree of rounding applied to alternate dimensions. For example, you can set this option to 0.25 to round off dimensions to the nearest 0.25, or 1/4″, of a unit [Dimaltrnd].

Prefix   Lets you include a prefix for all linear alternate dimension text. For example, if you want all linear-dimension text to be preceded by the word *Approximately,* you can enter

Approximately in the Prefix input box. Control codes can be used for special characters. See Chapter 10 for more information on character codes [Dimpost].

Suffix   Lets you include a suffix for all linear alternate dimension text. Control codes can be used for special characters. See Chapter 10 for more information on character codes [Dimapost].

The Zero Suppression Group

The check boxes in this group let you suppress zeros so they don't appear in the alternate dimension text. For dimensions other than architectural, you can suppress leading and trailing zeros. For example, 0.500 becomes .500 if you suppress leading zeros. It becomes 0.5 if you suppress trailing zeros. For architectural dimensions, you can suppress zero feet or zero inches, although typically you wouldn't suppress zero inches. The 0 feet and 0 inches options are grayed out until you select the Leading or Trailing options. [Dimaltz].

Sub-Units Factor lets you control the number of places for numbers to the right of the decimal point. This is helpful if you are working in metric measurements. Sub-Units Suffix allows you to add a suffix to a dimension. For example, you can enter *cm* here to display the centimeter abbreviation after a sub-unit value.

The Placement Group

The following options let you determine the location for the alternate units:

After Primary Value   Places the alternate dimension text behind and aligned with the primary dimension text [Dimapost].

Below Primary Value   Places the alternate dimension text below the primary dimension text and above the dimension line [Dimapost].

THE TOLERANCES TAB

The options in the Tolerances tab (Figure D.10) offer the inclusion and formatting of tolerance dimension text.

FIGURE D.10

The Tolerances tab

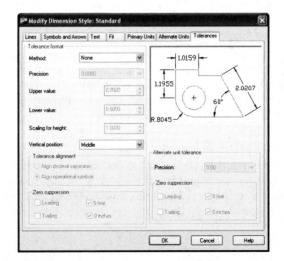

The Tolerance Format Group

The following options offer control over the format of tolerance dimension text:

Method   Lets you turn on and set the format for the tolerance dimension text. The options are None, Symmetrical, Deviation, Limits, and Basic. None turns off the tolerance dimension text. Symmetrical adds a plus/minus tolerance dimension; this is a single dimension preceded by a plus/minus sign. Deviation adds a stacked tolerance dimension showing separate upper and lower tolerance values. The Limits option replaces the primary dimension with a stacked dimension showing maximum and minimum dimension values. The Basic option draws a box around the primary dimension value. If an alternate dimension is used, the box encloses both primary and alternate dimension text [Dimtol, Dimlim, (minus) Dimgap].

Precision   Lets you set the precision of the tolerance dimension text. This option rounds off the dimension text to the nearest precision value you set. It doesn't affect the actual precision of the drawing [Dimtdec].

Upper Value   Lets you set the upper tolerance value for the Symmetrical, Deviation, and Limits tolerance methods [Dimtp].

Lower Value   Lets you set the lower tolerance value for the Deviation and Limits tolerance methods [Dimtm].

Scaling For Height   Lets you adjust the size for the tolerance dimension text as a proportion of the primary dimension text height [Dimtfac].

Vertical Position   Lets you determine the vertical position of the tolerance text. The options are Top, Middle, and Bottom. The Top option aligns the top tolerance value of a stacked pair of values with the primary dimension text. Middle aligns the gap between stacked tolerance values with the primary dimension text. Bottom aligns the bottom value of two stacked tolerance values with the primary dimension text [Dimtolj].

Tolerance Alignment Group

These radio buttons set the alignment of stacked tolerance values. The two options, Align Decimal Separators and Align Operational Symbols, are self-explanatory.

The Zero Suppression Groups

These options let you suppress zeros so they don't appear in the tolerance dimension text. For dimensions other than architectural, you can suppress leading and trailing zeros. For example, 0.500 becomes .500 if you suppress leading zeros. It becomes 0.5 if you suppress trailing zeros. For architectural dimensions, you can suppress zero feet or zero inches, although typically you wouldn't suppress zero inches [Dimtzin].

The Alternate Unit Tolerance Group

The Precision drop-down list lets you set the precision of the alternate tolerance dimension text. This option rounds the dimension text to the nearest precision value you set. It doesn't affect the actual precision of the drawing [Dimalttd]. You can also control zero suppression (see the preceding section, "The Zero Suppression Groups").

Notes on Metric Dimensioning

The AutoCAD user community is worldwide, and many of you may be using the metric system in your work. As long as you aren't mixing Imperial (feet and inches) and metric measurements, using the metric version of AutoCAD is fairly easy. In the Drawing Units dialog box (choose Drawing Utilities ➤ Units from the Application menu), set your measurement system to decimal, set the Units To Scale Inserted Content option to the appropriate metric option, and then draw distances in millimeters or centimeters. At plot time, select the MM radio button (millimeters) under Paper Size and Paper Units in the Plot dialog box.

If your drawings are to be in both Imperial and metric measurements, you'll be concerned with several settings, as follows:

Dimlfac Sets the scale factor for dimension values. The dimension value will be the measured distance in AutoCAD units times this scale factor. Set Dimlfac to 25.4 if you've drawn in inches but want to dimension in millimeters. The default is 1.0000. If you want to scale dimension values from millimeters to inches, use a value of 0.03937.

Dimalt Turns the display of alternate dimensions on or off. Alternate dimensions are made up of dimension text added to your drawing in addition to the standard dimension text.

Dimaltf Sets the scale factor for alternate dimensions (that is, to metric from Imperial). The default is 25.4, which is the millimeter equivalent of 1˝. If you're using metric ISO units, the default is 0.03937, which is the inch equivalent of 1 mm.

Dimaltd Sets the number of decimal places displayed in the alternate dimensions.

Dimapost Adds a suffix to alternate dimensions, as in 4.5 mm.

USING THE AUTOCAD METRIC TEMPLATE

If you prefer, you can use the metric template drawing supplied by AutoCAD:

1. Choose New from the Quick Access toolbar. If you see the Select Template dialog box, go to step 2; otherwise, skip to step 3.

2. Select the acadiso.dwt file and click Open. You can also select acadISO - Named Plot Styles.dwt if you want to use a named plot style. Your new drawing based on the selected template appears.

3. If you use the Select Template dialog box, click the Template button in the Create New Drawing dialog box. Then select the filename acadiso.dwt and click OK to open a new drawing based on the template. You can also select acadISO - Named Plot Styles.dwt if you want to use a named plot style.

These templates are set up for metric/ISO standard drawings.

You can also click the Metric radio button in the Start From Scratch option of the Create New Drawing dialog box. When you do so, subsequent new files will be set to metric by default.

If the AutoCAD 2011 Startup dialog box doesn't appear when you open AutoCAD, or if you don't see the Create New Drawing dialog box when you choose New from the Application menu, you can turn on these dialog boxes by using the Startup option in the System tab of the Options dialog box. Choose Options from the Application menu, and then click the System tab in the Options dialog box. In the General Options group, select Show Startup Dialog Box from the Startup drop-down list.

Drawing Blocks for Your Own Dimension Arrows and Tick Marks

If you don't want to use the arrowheads supplied by AutoCAD for your dimension lines, you can create a block of the arrowheads or tick marks you want, to be used in the Arrowheads group of the Dimension Styles/Geometry dialog box.

To access the Arrowhead options, open the Symbols And Arrows tab of the New Dimension Style, Modify Dimension Style, or Override Current Style dialog box.

For example, suppose you want a tick mark that is thicker than the dimension lines and extensions. You can create a block of the tick mark on a layer you assign to a thick pen weight and then assign that block to the Arrowhead setting. To do so, type **Dimstyle.⏎** to open the Dimension Styles dialog box; then select a style from the Styles list, and click the Modify button. In the Symbols And Arrows tab, select User Arrow from the First drop-down list in the Arrowheads group. In the User Arrow dialog box, enter the name of your arrow block.

When you draw the arrow block, make it 1 unit long. The block's insertion point will be used to determine the point of the arrow that meets the extension line, so make sure you place the insertion point at the tip of the arrow. Because the arrow on the right side of the dimension line will be inserted with a zero rotation value, create the arrow block so that it's pointing to the right (see Figure D.11). The arrow block is rotated 180° for the left side of the dimension line.

FIGURE D.11
The orientation and size of a block used in place of the default arrow

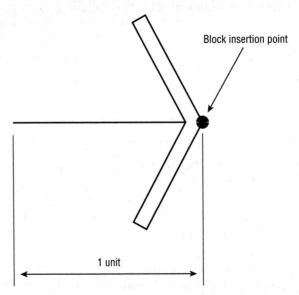

Block insertion point

1 unit

If you want a different type of arrow at both ends of the dimension line, create a block for each arrow. In the Symbols And Arrows tab of the Dimension Styles dialog box, choose User Arrow in the drop-down list for the first arrowhead and enter the name of one block. Then choose User Arrow in the drop-down list for the second arrowhead and enter the name of the other block.

Appendix E

About the Companion DVD

In this appendix:

◆ What you'll find on the DVD

◆ System requirements

◆ Using the DVD

◆ Troubleshooting

What You'll Find on the DVD

The following sections are arranged by category and provide a summary of the software and other goodies you'll find on the DVD. If you need help with installing the items provided on the DVD, refer to the installation instructions in the section "Using the DVD" later in this appendix.

Some programs on the DVD might fall into one of these categories:

Shareware programs are fully functional, free, trial versions of copyrighted programs. If you like particular programs, register with their authors for a nominal fee and receive licenses, enhanced versions, and technical support.

Freeware programs are free, copyrighted games, applications, and utilities. You can copy them to as many computers as you like—for free—but they offer no technical support.

GNU software is governed by its own license, which is included inside the folder of the GNU software. There are no restrictions on distribution of GNU software. See the GNU license at the root of the DVD for more details.

Trial, demo, or *evaluation* versions of software are usually limited either by time or by functionality (such as not letting you save a project after you create it).

PDF of the Book

For Windows

We have included an electronic version of the text in PDF format. You can view the electronic version of the book with Adobe Reader.

Adobe Reader

For Windows

We've also included a copy of Adobe Reader so you can view PDF files that accompany the book's content. For more information on Adobe Reader or to check for a newer version, visit Adobe's website at www.adobe.com/products/reader/.

Tutorial Files

For Windows

All the files needed for the tutorials in this book are located in the Chapter Files directory on the DVD and work with Windows XP and later computers. The structure of the examples directory is Mastering AutoCAD/Projects/Chapter 01.

AutoCAD 2011 Video Tutorials

For Windows

Learn the fundamentals of AutoCAD from this set of video tutorials. These 20 tutorials walk you through the basics of AutoCAD so you'll be up and running in no time.

For more information and updates of AutoCAD 2011, visit the Link It All Net website: www.omura.com.

AutoCAD 2011

30-day trial version; for Windows

Design and shape the world around you with AutoCAD design and documentation software, one of the world's leading CAD programs. Speed documentation, share ideas seamlessly, explore ideas more intuitively in 3D, and customize it for your specific needs. It's time to take design further.

For more information and updates of AutoCAD 2011, visit www.autodesk.com/autocad.

AutoCAD 2011 Video Demos

For Windows

These Autodesk-created videos provide a great overview of new AutoCAD features that let you create parametric drawings and free-form models as well as highlight PDF features and other new AutoCAD enhancements.

For more information and updates of AutoCAD 2011 video demos, visit the Link It All Net website: http://resources.autodesk.com/autocad.

Autodesk Design Review

For Windows

Accelerate your reviews with Autodesk Design Review software, which is installed with AutoCAD 2011 and is an integrated, all-digital way to view, print, mark up, and compare versions of 2D and 3D drawings, maps, and models—without the original design-creation software. For everyone in the review chain, sharing and collaborating on designs has never been this easy.

For more information and updates of Autodesk Design Review, visit the Link It All Net website: http://usa.autodesk.com/adsk/servlet/index?siteID=123112&id=4086277.

Autodesk Impression

30-day trial version; for Windows

Impress your colleagues and clients with compelling presentation-ready graphics created directly from your DWG and DWF files. Autodesk Impression design presentation software is easy to use, saves you time, and recognizes data from your CAD files.

For more information and updates of Autodesk Impression, visit `http://usa.autodesk.com/adsk/servlet/pc/index?id=9246650&siteID=123112`

Autodesk DWG TrueView

For Windows

Use DWG TrueView CAD file conversion software to accurately view, plot, and publish authentic DWG and DWF files.

For more information and updates of Autodesk DWG TrueView, visit the Link It All Net website: `http://usa.autodesk.com/adsk/servlet/index?id=6703438&siteID=123112`.

ShapeBook 2009

30-day trial version; for Windows

South Fork Technologies, Inc.'s ShapeBook 2009 is a versatile productivity tool for commercial and industrial steel design, engineering, estimating, detailing, fabrication, and erection. ShapeBook is based on the *AISC Steel Construction Manual, Thirteenth Edition* and also includes information on large pipe sizes, small bar size materials, plates, flat bars, round bars, and square bars. ShapeBook is a powerful structural steel estimating and quick reference tool for steel industry professionals.

For more information and updates of ShapeBook 2009, visit `www.southforktech.com/shapebook.htm`.

System Requirements

Make sure your computer meets the minimum system requirements shown in the following list. If it doesn't match up to most of these requirements, you may have problems using the software and files on the companion DVD. For the latest and greatest information, please refer to the Readme file located at the root of the DVD-ROM.

- A PC running Microsoft Windows 7, Windows XP, or Windows Vista
- An Internet connection
- A DVD-ROM drive
- Hard drive and RAM requirements to run AutoCAD (See the section "Before Installing AutoCAD" in Appendix B.)

Using the DVD

To install the items from the DVD to your hard drive, follow these steps.

1. Insert the DVD into your computer's DVD-ROM drive. The license agreement appears.

FOR WINDOWS USERS

The interface won't launch if you have autorun disabled. In that case, click Start ➤ Run (for Windows Vista, Start ➤ All Programs ➤ Accessories ➤ Run). In the dialog box that appears, type **D:\Start .exe**. (Replace *D* with the proper letter if your DVD drive uses a different letter. If you don't know the letter, see how your DVD drive is listed under My Computer.) Click OK.

---

2. Read through the license agreement, and then click the Accept button if you want to use the DVD.

The DVD interface appears. The interface allows you to access the content with just one or two clicks.

Troubleshooting

Wiley has attempted to provide programs that work on most computers with the minimum system requirements. Alas, your computer may differ, and some programs may not work properly for some reason.

The two likeliest problems are that you don't have enough memory (RAM) for the programs you want to use or you have other programs running that are affecting installation or how a program is running. If you get an error message such as "Not enough memory" or "Setup cannot continue," try one or more of the following suggestions and then try using the software again:

Turn off any antivirus software running on your computer. Installation programs sometimes mimic virus activity and may make your computer incorrectly believe that it's being infected by a virus.

Close all running programs. The more programs you have running, the less memory is available to other programs. Installation programs typically update files and programs, so if you keep other programs running, installation may not work properly.

Have your local computer store add more RAM to your computer. This is, admittedly, a drastic and somewhat expensive step. However, adding more memory can really help the speed of your computer and allow more programs to run at the same time.

Customer Care

If you have trouble with the book's companion DVD-ROM, please call the Wiley Product Technical Support phone number at (800) 762-2974. Outside the United States, call +1(317) 572-3994. You can also contact Wiley Product Technical Support at http://sybex.custhelp.com. John Wiley & Sons will provide technical support only for installation and other general quality control items. For technical support on the applications themselves, consult the program's vendor or author.

To place additional orders or to request information about other Wiley products, please call (877) 762-2974.

Appendix F

The AutoCAD 2011 Certification Exams

The AutoCAD 2011 Certifications are a great way to prove to the world that you know your stuff! Autodesk offers both Associate and Certified Professional level exams, and they kindly provided the following exam preparation roadmap. To further help you focus your studies on the skills you'll need for these exams, I've augmented Autodesk's Section and Exam Objectives tables with information directing you to the chapters in this book that will help you master the objectives for each exam. Please note the objectives are subject to change; visit www.autodesk.com/certification and this book's site, www.sybex.com/go/masteringautocad2011 for updates.

AutoCAD 2011 Exam Preparation Roadmap

Autodesk certifications are industry-recognized credentials that can help you succeed in your design career—providing benefits to both you and your employer. The certifications provide reliable validation of skills and knowledge, and they can lead to accelerated professional development, improved productivity, and enhanced credibility.

Autodesk highly recommends that you structure your examination preparation for success. This means scheduling regular time to prepare, reviewing this exam preparation roadmap, using the Autodesk Official Training Guide, taking an Assessment test, and using a variety of resources to prepare for your certification. Equally as important, actual hands-on experience is recommended.

The AutoCAD 2011 Certified Associate exam consists of 30 questions that assess your knowledge of the tools, features, and common tasks of AutoCAD 2011. Question types include multiple choice, matching, and point-and-click (hotspot). The exam has a 1-hour time limit. In some countries the time limit may be extended.

The AutoCAD 2011 Certified Professional exam is a performance-based test. The exam is comprised of 20 questions. Each question requires you to use AutoCAD 2011 to create or modify a data file, and then type your answer into an input box. The answer you enter will either be a text entry or a numeric value. The exam has a 90-minute time limit (in some countries the time limit may be extended).

To earn the credential of AutoCAD 2011 Certified Professional, you must also pass the AutoCAD 2011 Certified Associate exam. You can pass the exams in any order.

To recertify from AutoCAD 2010 Professional to AutoCAD 2011 Professional, you need only pass the AutoCAD 2011 Certified Associate exam.

Assessment Tests

Autodesk assessment tests will help identify areas of knowledge that you should develop in order to prepare for the certification exam. At the completion, you will be able to review the items you missed and their correct answers. Contact an Autodesk Certification Center for more information at http://autodesk.starttest.com.

ATC® INSTRUCTOR-LED COURSES

The Autodesk Authorized Training Center (ATC®) program is a global network of professional training providers offering a broad range of learning resources. Visit the online ATC locator at http://www.autodesk.com/atc.

RECOMMENDED EXPERIENCE LEVELS FOR AUTOCAD 2010 CERTIFICATION EXAMS

Actual hands-on experience is a critical component in preparing for the exam. You must spend time using the product and applying the skills you have learned.

2011 Certified Associate Exam

Mastering AutoCAD 2011 course (or equivalent) plus 100 hours of hands-on application

2011 Certified Professional Exam

Mastering AutoCAD 2011 course (or equivalent) plus 400 hours of hands-on application

TABLE F.1:   AutoCAD 2011 Certified Associate Examination Objectives

TOPIC	OBJECTIVE	CHAPTER
Creating Basic Drawings	• Use Object snaps	Chapter 2
	• Use Polar and Object snap tracking	Chapter 3
Manipulating Objects	• Use appropriate selection set methods	Chapter 2, 15
	• Apply mirror techniques to mirror copies of objects	Chapter 3, 22
	• Use Rectangular arrays	Chapter 6
	• Use polar arrays	Chapter 6
	• Use rotation reference angles to rotate an object	Chapter 2, 22, 24, 25
Drawing Organization and Inquiry Commands	• Analyze a closed object to find the area	Chapter 20
	• Apply changes to an object's property	Chapter 2, 7, 13
	• Apply layer transparency to select layers	Chapter 5

TABLE F.1:   AutoCAD 2011 Certified Associate Examination Objectives *(CONTINUED)*

TOPIC	OBJECTIVE	CHAPTER
Altering Objects	• Identify methods for creating a radius between two objects	Chapter 3, 24, 25
	• Join two objects to create one object	Chapter 19
	• Apply modify techniques to change an object's shape by stretching	Chapter 2, 6, 12
Working with Layouts	• Demonstrate how to create or manipulate viewports	Chapter 8, 16
Annotating the Drawing	• Demonstrate the methods for editing Multi-line text	Chapter 10
	• Identify text justification locations	
	• Describe a paragraph of text with multiple columns	
Dimensioning	• Describe dimension styles	Chapter 12, 16
	• Apply methods for editing dimensions	
	• Apply linear dimensions to a drawing	
Hatching Objects	• Describe hatch editing	Chapter 7
Working with Reusable Content	• Apply the uses for Tool Palettes	Chapter 1, 29
	• Create, insert, and edit blocks in a drawing	Chapter 4, 18
Creating Additional Drawing Objects	• Identify table cell data contents	Chapter 11
	• Describe how to create a polyline	Chapter 19
Parametric Design	• Apply geometrical or dimensional constraints	Chapter 17
Working with Annotative Objects	• Use annotative text and dimensions in a drawing at various viewport or annotation scales	Chapter 4, 10, 12
Isolate or Hide Displayed Objects	• Use hide or isolate techniques to objects	Chapter 15
Grip Editing	• Explain how to modify a drawing using grips	Chapter 2, 6, 12
Viewing Drawings in 3D	• Use the ViewCube to view drawings in 3D	Chapter 21, Appendix B

TABLE F.2: Certified Professional Exam Sections and Objectives

TOPIC	OBJECTIVE	CHAPTER
Manipulating Objects	• Apply mirror techniques to mirror copies of objects	Chapter 3, 22
	• Apply rotation techniques to rotate objects	Chapter 2, 22, 24, 25
	• Create rectangular and polar arrays	Chapter 6
	• Create copies of objects	Chapter 1, 2, 6
	• Apply move techniques to move objects to new positions	
Drawing Organization and Inquiry Commands	• Analyze a closed object to find the area	Chapter 20
	• Apply changes to an object's property	Chapter 2, 7, 13
Altering Objects	• Create parallel geometry by offsetting an object	Chapter 2, 6, 12
	• Apply modify techniques to change an object's shape by stretching	
Working with Layouts	• Create a new layout and viewports with page setups	Chapter 8, 16
Dimensioning	• Edit multileaders using proper alignment or collection techniques	Chapter 12, 16
	• Edit linear and aligned dimensions in a drawing	
	• Edit dimension text and text placement in a drawing	
Hatching Objects	• Create and edit hatch objects	Chapter 7
Working with Reusable Content	• Create, insert, and edit blocks in a drawing	Chapter 4, 18
Creating Additional Drawing Objects	• Edit polyline features	Chapter 19
Parametric Design	• Apply geometrical and dimensional constraints	Chapter 17
Working with Annotative Objects	• Use annotative text and dimensions in a drawing at various viewport or annotation scales	Chapter 4, 10, 12

TABLE F.2: Certified Professional Exam Sections and Objectives *(CONTINUED)*

TOPIC	OBJECTIVE	CHAPTER
Insert and Manage External References	• Apply External References	Chapter 7
Isolate or Hide Displayed Objects	• Apply hide and isolate techniques to objects	Chapter 15

Index

Note to the Reader: Throughout this index **boldfaced** page numbers indicate primary discussions of a topic. *Italicized* page numbers indicate illustrations.

WILEY PUBLISHING, INC. END-USER LICENSE AGREEMENT